T Volume 19

The World Book Encyclopedia

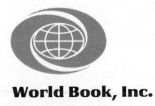

World Book, Inc.

a Scott Fetzer company

Chicago London Sydney Toronto

The World Book Encyclopedia

Copyright © 1989, U.S.A.
by
World Book, Inc.

Tt

T is the 20th letter of our alphabet. It was also a letter in the alphabet of the Semites, who once lived in Syria and Palestine. They called the letter *taw,* their word for *mark.* They used a cross-shaped mark they may have borrowed from an Egyptian *hieroglyphic,* or picture symbol, used as a check mark. The Greeks borrowed the letter from the Phoenicians. However, when they adopted the letter, they moved the crossbar to the top of the vertical stroke. The Greeks called their letter *tau.* See **Alphabet.**

Uses. *T* or *t* is about the second most frequently used letter in books, newspapers, and other printed material in English. As an abbreviation in geographic names, it may stand for *territory* or *township.* As a musical abbreviation, *t* may indicate *tenor, tempo,* or *time.* In grammars and dictionaries, it means *tense* or *transitive.* It may also stand for *ton, temperature,* or *Testament,* as in *O.T.,* or *Old Testament.*

Pronunciation. A person pronounces *t* by placing the point of the tongue on the upper teethridge, with the lips and vocal cords open, and expelling the breath between the teeth and tongue. In such words as *fasten* or *castle,* the *t* is silent. In the combination *tion, t* may be pronounced *sh* as in *nation,* or *ch* as in *question.* In the combination *th,* as in *thin,* a person pronounces *t* by placing the tongue blade below the points of the upper teeth and expelling the breath between the tongue and teeth, with the vocal cords relaxed. In words like *thine,* the process is the same, but the vocal cords vibrate. See **Pronunciation.**   Marianne Cooley

Development of the letter T

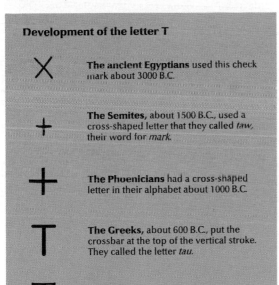

The **ancient Egyptians** used this check mark about 3000 B.C.

The **Semites,** about 1500 B.C., used a cross-shaped letter that they called *taw,* their word for *mark.*

The **Phoenicians** had a cross-shaped letter in their alphabet about 1000 B.C.

The **Greeks,** about 600 B.C., put the crossbar at the top of the vertical stroke. They called the letter *tau.*

The **Romans** gave the letter T its capital form about A.D. 114.

The **small letter t** developed during the A.D. 500's from Roman writing. The letter changed slightly in the 800's. By the 1500's, it had the form we use today.

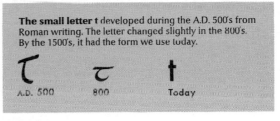

A.D. 500   800   Today

Special ways of expressing the letter T

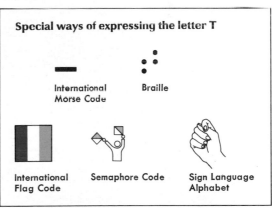

International Morse Code

Braille

International Flag Code

Semaphore Code

Sign Language Alphabet

Common forms of the letter T

Handwritten letters vary from person to person. *Manuscript* (printed) letters, *left,* have simple curves and straight lines. Cursive letters, *right,* have flowing lines.

Roman letters have small finishing strokes called *serifs* that extend from the main strokes. The type face shown above is Baskerville. The italic form appears at the right.

Sans-serif letters are also called *gothic letters.* They have no serifs. The type face shown above is called Futura. The italic form of Futura appears at the right.

Computer letters have special shapes. Computers can "read" these letters either optically or by means of the magnetic ink with which the letters may be printed.

T cell. See Thymus.

Tabasco, *tuh BAS koh* or *tah VAHS koh,* is a state of southeastern Mexico along the Bay of Campeche (see **Mexico** [political map]). Tabasco has 1,149,756 people, and covers an area of 9,756 square miles (25,267 square kilometers). It lies on a low, tropical plain, much of which is marshy. Tabasco is the largest source of petroleum in Mexico. Its chief farm products include bananas, coconuts, cacao, and sugar cane. The large forests produce hardwoods, rubber, chicle, resins, and dyes. Tabasco was crossed by Hernando Cortés in 1524. It is one of the original states of Mexico. Villahermosa is its capital. See also **Olmec Indians.**　　Charles C. Cumberland

Tabby. See **Cat** (Coat; picture).

Tabernacle, also called the Tent of Meeting, was the center of worship of the Israelites during early Biblical times. According to the Book of Exodus, the Hebrews built the Tabernacle during their wanderings in the desert. Its purpose was to provide a symbolic dwelling place for God in the midst of the Israelite camp or settlement. Other places of worship are sometimes called tabernacles.

While on Mount Sinai, Moses received instructions for building the Tabernacle. The materials were provided by the free offerings of the people. The Tabernacle was dedicated on the first day of the second year after the Israelites fled from Egypt on their way to the Promised Land (modern Israel).

According to the Bible, the place of worship was 45 feet (14 meters) long and had a height and width of 15 feet (4.6 meters). Its framework of acacia wood was overlaid with fine gold. The ceiling was of white linen with figures of blue, purple, and scarlet angels woven into it. The structure was covered with a curtain of goat's hair and a layer of skins. A veil of linen divided the inside into two sections, the Holy of Holies and the Holy Place. The Holy of Holies contained the Ark of the Covenant, which held the Tables of the Law—the Ten Commandments.

The Ark was called the Ark of the Covenant because it was a symbol of the Jews' *covenant* (agreement) with God. Above the Ark was a cover of gold with a figure called a cherub at each end. In the Holy Place were the table of the *shewbread* (bread made without yeast), the altar of incense, and a candlestick, all made of gold.

The Tabernacle stood within a court, enclosed by rich curtains and brass pillars. It opened toward the east and faced the altar where the people brought their sacrifices to be offered by the priests. The court also contained a *laver* (basin), where the priests washed their hands and feet before entering the Holy Place.

The Tabernacle could be carried from place to place. The Bible reports that it was moved from the desert to Gilgal, then to Shiloh after the Israelites conquered Canaan. Later, it was moved to Jerusalem, where its relics were preserved in Solomon's Temple.　　B. Barry Levy

See also **Ark of the Covenant; Mormons** (picture: The Mormon Tabernacle); **Temple.**

Tabernacles, Feast of. See Sukkot.

Tabes, *TAY beez,* means a wasting away of the body. It once was used to describe any condition that caused such wasting. But its modern usage is almost exclusively to describe the wasting caused by syphilis, one of the venereal diseases (see **Venereal disease**). In this condition it is called *tabes dorsalis,* meaning a wasting away of the *dorsal* (back) part of the spinal cord. Persons with tabes dorsalis have difficulty coordinating their movements. They may lose all feeling in their arms and legs, and their leg muscles deteriorate. The *optic nerve,* an eye nerve, may be affected.　　Louis D. Boshes

Illustration from the *First Leningrad Bible;* Leningrad Public Library

The Tabernacle was an ornate portable place of worship that the Israelites built during their wanderings in the desert. This fragment from a Bible dating from A.D. 929 shows the Tabernacle and its implements. A fence with a triple gate encloses the Tabernacle. In the center, a sacred candlestick called a *menorah* appears in the court, beneath the Ark of the Covenant.

David R. Frazier

Table tennis, also called *ping-pong,* provides indoor recreation for people of all ages. Many schools and youth clubs have table tennis tables, which can be used by two or four players.

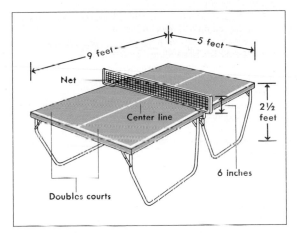

A table tennis table is divided into halves by a low net. A white center line further divides the surface of the table into four courts, which are used when playing doubles.

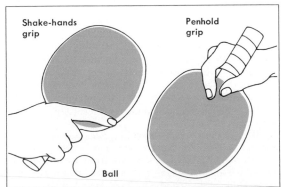

WORLD BOOK illustrations by Richard Fickle

Two ways to hold a table tennis racket are shown above. The *shake-hands grip* is used by most players in the United States and other Western countries.

Table tennis, or ping-pong, is a lively indoor game that resembles a miniature version of tennis. The players use rackets, which are often called *paddles,* to hit a ball back and forth over a net that stretches across a table. They score points by hitting the ball so their opponent or opponents cannot return it. Table tennis may be played by two or four persons. If two persons play, the game is called *singles.* If four play, the game is called *doubles.*

Table tennis developed in England during the late 1800's. Today, it is a popular form of recreation and an international sport. Players from more than 100 countries belong to the International Table Tennis Federation (ITTF). The ITTF holds a world championship tournament every two years. The United States Table Tennis Association sponsors national tournaments, including the National Team Championships and the U.S. National Open.

Equipment for table tennis consists of a table, net, rackets, and ball. The table measures 9 feet (274 centimeters) long, 5 feet (152.5 centimeters) wide, and 30 inches (76 centimeters) high. Most tables are dark green with a white line along the edges. A white center line runs the length of the table. The center line divides the table into *courts* that are used for doubles. The net, which is suspended between two posts, extends across the width of the table at its center. The net measures 6 inches (15.25 centimeters) high.

The rackets may be any shape, size, or weight. All are made of wood and are covered with pimpled or smooth sponge. Each side must be of a uniform dark color, though the sides may be different colors. The covering material cannot be more than $\frac{1}{6}$ inch (4 millimeters) thick on either side of the racket.

The ball is round and hollow and made of celluloid. It measures from 1.4 to 1.5 inches (37.2 to 38.2 millimeters) in diameter and weighs from $\frac{1}{12}$ ounce (2.4 grams) to $\frac{1}{11}$ ounce (2.53 grams).

How the game is played. Table tennis players toss a coin to determine who serves first. The server places the ball on the palm of the hand, throws it up vertically, and hits it with the racket. When throwing the ball, the server must keep the fingers straight and together, and the thumb extended. The hand must be behind the end of the table when the server hits the ball. The ball must bounce on the server's side of the net, clear the net, and bounce on the opponent's side.

For a good return, a player must hit the ball after one bounce so that it clears the net and bounces on the opponent's court. *Volleying* (hitting the ball before it bounces) is not allowed. Play continues until one person misses the ball, hits it off the table, or hits it into the net. When a player fails to make a good serve or a good return, the opponent scores a point. After every five points, the other player serves.

The player who first scores 21 points wins the game. However, the winner must have at least a two-point lead. If both players score 20 points, they alternate serving after each point until one person leads by 2 points. A match consists of either two out of three games or three out of five games.

When playing doubles, the server must serve from his or her right-hand court into the opponents' right-hand court. The teammates must alternate in hitting the ball on the returns.   Leah Neuberger

Tabloid. See Newspaper (Kinds of newspapers).

Taboo is an action, object, person, or place forbidden by law or culture. The word *taboo* comes from the Polynesian word *tapu,* or *tabu,* which means *something sacred, special, dangerous,* or *unclean.* Many societies believe that people who go to a taboo place or touch a taboo object will suffer serious injury. Society may also punish the offenders or may consider them to be taboo.

Sacred objects or people are taboo because they supposedly have a mysterious force that enables them to injure or kill a person. Unclean objects are taboo because they supposedly bring evil to a person or group.

People in many parts of the world avoid taboos. Until the 1900's, for example, Fiji Islanders could not touch any article that belonged to the tribal chief or priest. Australian Aborigines must not say the name of a dead person aloud. Muslims and Orthodox Jews must not eat pork or shellfish. Societies in many parts of the world consider *incest* taboo. These societies forbid marriage or sexual relations between closely related people, such as a brother and sister.   Alan Dundes

See also **Magic** (The magician; Homeopathic magic); **Mythology** (Mythology of the Pacific Islands).

Tabriz, *tuh BREEZ* (pop. 852,296), is the fourth largest city in Iran. It is the capital of East Azerbaijan province, in the northwestern corner of Iran. It lies about 35 miles (56 kilometers) from Lake Urmia, and is almost surrounded by mountains. For location, see **Iran** (map). Earthquakes have nearly destroyed the city several times.

Tabriz is famous for its fine Persian rugs, and has a large trade in dried fruits and leather goods. It also produces matches, flour, and textiles.

Historians do not know exactly when the city was founded, but it was probably before the A.D. 300's. It served as Iran's capital for a short time in the early 1500's. Russian troops occupied Tabriz in 1827, and again during World Wars I and II.   Richard Nelson Frye

Tabularium, *TAB yoo LAIR ee uhm,* was a magnificent library in which the ancient Romans stored their records. It stood on Capitoline Hill. The Romans built it in 73 B.C. See also **Forum, Roman.**

Taché, *ta SHAY,* **Sir Étienne-Paschal,** *ay TYEN PAS kuhl* (1795-1865), was a Canadian statesman. He served twice as prime minister of the Province of Canada, and presided over the Quebec Conference of 1864 that paved the way for the federation of the British North American colonies.

Taché was born in St. Thomas, Quebec. He was graduated from the Quebec Seminary. After serving in the British militia during the War of 1812, he practiced medicine. In 1841, Taché entered the Legislative Assembly of Canada. He later served as commissioner of public works, member of the legislative council, and receiver-general. He was knighted in 1858.

Taché formed a cabinet with John A. Macdonald in 1856, and became prime minister. In 1864, the two men again formed a cabinet with Taché as prime minister. But Macdonald was the real head of the government in both ministries.   William R. Willoughby

See also **Macdonald, Sir John A.**

Tachistoscope. See Audio-visual materials (Programmed instruction).

Tachometer, *ta KAHM uh tuhr* or *tuh KAHM uh tuhr,* is a device that is used for measuring the speed of rotation of a spinning shaft or wheel, usually in terms of revolutions per minute (rpm). Tachometers often are used to measure engine rpm in cars, ships, and aircraft. Tachometers indicate an engine's power and its efficiency in converting energy into mechanical force.

The *drag-type tachometer* is widely used in automobiles. It consists of a permanent magnet connected to the automobile's crankshaft and an aluminum disk attached to a spring near the magnet. As the crankshaft turns, it causes the magnet to rotate, thus producing a rotating magnetic field. This field creates small electric currents that cause the disk to turn. As the engine's speed increases, the rotation of the disk increases proportionally. A pointer attached to the disk indicates the engine's rpm on a dial on the dashboard.

A *digital tachometer* measures rpm by means of a pulse accompanying each rotation of the crankshaft. A meter counts the number of pulses per minute, which equals rpm.

For some moderately high-speed machines, a tachometer consisting of a set of vibrating reeds may be used. The reeds resemble teeth of a comb. Each reed vibrates at just one frequency. By noting which reed is shaking, a person can tell how fast the machine is vibrating and, thus, how fast it is turning. *Reed tachometers* are used on steam turbines and engines.

An *electric tachometer* is commonly used in airplanes. It consists of a voltage generator turned by the engine and connected by wires to a voltmeter. The voltmeter shows engine rpm.   Don R. Kozlowski

Tachycardia, *tak uh KAHR dee uh,* is an unusually fast heartbeat sometimes referred to as *palpitations.* The disorder is usually organic. There are several types of tachycardia, depending upon the chamber of the heart from which the palpitations originate and how often they occur. For example, *paroxysmal atrial tachycardia (PAT)* is a rapid heart action that originates in the heart's atria (upper chambers) and occurs at intervals.

Bruce A. Reitz

Tachyon, *TAK ee ahn,* is a hypothetical elementary particle. An elementary particle is a subatomic particle that has no known smaller parts. If tachyons exist in nature, they never stand still but always move at speeds greater than the speed of light. Light travels 186,282 miles (299,792 kilometers) per second. The faster a tachyon travels, the lower its energy. The name *tachyon* comes from a Greek word meaning *swift.*

According to the special theory of relativity, ordinary matter can move only at speeds less than the speed of light. The German-American physicist Albert Einstein published the special theory of relativity in 1905. But in 1962, several physicists realized that the existence of particles that travel faster than light is not necessarily incompatible with Einstein's theory. No convincing experimental evidence has been found for the existence of tachyons.   Joel R. Primack

Tacitus, *TAS ih tuhs,* **Cornelius,** *kawr NEE lee uhs* (about A.D. 55-about 120), was one of the world's greatest historians. His most important works were the *Histories,* which tell of the short reigns of the emperors Galba, Otho, and Vitellius; and the *Annals,* which describe Roman history from Augustus to Nero. Tacitus favored the republican form of government, and his *Histories* and *Annals* were extremely critical of the Roman emperors. He condemned them in sharp, unforgettable phrases, and overlooked any merits of the imperial system. The *Histories* and *Annals* cover periods for which our other sources are scanty. Another work, *Germania,* is important because it contains one of the first written accounts of the customs and habits of the Germanic peoples, who later spread over most of western Europe. He also wrote *Life of Agricola* and *Dialogue on Orators.*

Little is known of Tacitus' life except for a few references in his own works and letters written to him by his friend, Pliny the Younger. Tacitus rose to be a praetor (see **Praetor**).   Thomas A. Brady

Tack. See Horse (Riding equipment).

Tackle. See Block and tackle.

Tacloban, *tah KLOH bahn* (pop. 102,523), is the chief city of Leyte Island in the Philippines. It overlooks the San Juanico Strait that separates the northeast corner of Leyte from Samar Island. For location, see **Philippines** (map). The city is the trading center and chief port for an area that produces abacá, rice, coconuts, and tobacco.

David J. Steinberg

Taco. See Mexico (Food).

Tacoma, *tuh KOH muh* (pop. 158,501; met. area pop. 485,667), is one of the largest cities in Washington. This seaport is also an industrial and commercial center, and the heart of a major military complex. The city lies on Commencement Bay, an inlet of Puget Sound, between Seattle and Olympia (see **Washington** [political map]).

Tacoma is located between the Olympic Mountains on the west and the Cascade Mountains on the east. The city rises steeply from the bay to more than 300 feet (91 meters) above sea level. The Puyallup River flows

Aperture PhotoBank

Tacoma lies on an inlet of Puget Sound between the Olympic Mountains and the Cascade Range. Mount Rainier, *background,* rises about 55 miles (89 kilometers) southeast of the city.

through the city from Mount Rainier, which lies 40 miles (65 kilometers) to the southeast. The name *Tacoma* is the Indian word for Mount Rainier, which is the state's highest peak at 14,410 feet (4,392 meters).

Seattle-Tacoma International Airport, along with several smaller airports, railroads, and steamship lines, serves the Tacoma area. The Tacoma Narrows Bridge, one of the world's longest suspension bridges, crosses Puget Sound and connects Tacoma with the Kitsap Peninsula.

Tacoma is one of the nation's chief gateways of trade. Major imports include automobiles, rubber, and ore. Exports include grain, logs, and wood products. Tacoma was a shipbuilding center for many years, but that industry had declined greatly by the 1980's. The city is a center for chemical processing, oil refining, and metal processing. Tacoma is also the home of a large forest products industry, including milling, woodworking, furniture making, and pulp and paper making. The city operates hydroelectric dams on rivers draining the Cascade and Olympic mountains.

Several military bases and military medical facilities operate in the Tacoma area. Near the outskirts of the city are Fort Lewis, McChord Air Force Base, and Madigan Army Medical Center. Tacoma is the home of the University of Puget Sound and Pacific Lutheran University. The Tacoma Dome, a large domed arena, hosts many concerts, conventions, and sporting events.

Puyallup Indians occupied what is now Tacoma before the first white settlers arrived. The Puyallup now have a reservation in the city and an adjoining area. White people settled the region when a sawmill was built near the bay in 1852. In 1868, two settlements developed, called Tacoma and Tacoma City. In 1873, the Northern Pacific Railroad located the western end of its transcontinental railroad at a site called New Tacoma. The villages merged into a single city in 1884. Tacoma has a council manager form of government. It is the seat of Pierce County.   David L. Workman

Taconite, *TAK uh nyt,* is a hard rock that contains about 30 per cent iron in the form of fine specks of iron oxide. The rest of the rock consists of a mineral called *chert.* Taconite is named for the Taconic Mountains of western Massachusetts and Vermont.

Taconite is found in large quantities in the Mesabi Range of Minnesota. It is the mother rock from which the great Mesabi iron-ore deposits were formed. These important iron-ore deposits lie like raisins in a great cake of taconite, 100 miles (160 kilometers) long and 1 to 2 miles (1.6 to 3.2 kilometers) wide. The iron in taconite occurs principally as the black oxide *magnetite,* or *loadstone,* and the red oxide *hematite.*

Taconite is so hard that ordinary drilling and blasting methods cannot be used to obtain it. In one method of processing taconite, miners use a jet piercing machine, which shoots alternate streams of burning kerosene and cold water. The kerosene heats the taconite to about 4700° F. (2590° C), making it white hot. The cold water jet then cracks the rock by suddenly changing its temperature. The taconite can then be blasted into chunks.

Taconite next goes through several stages of crushing, until the pieces are less than $\frac{3}{4}$ inch (19 millimeters) in size. Cylinders grind it down into even smaller pieces, and magnets separate the useful taconite from the sand.

E. R. Degginger

Taconite, *above,* is a hard rock that contains iron. It is mined at the Mesabi iron range of Minnesota, *left.* The rock is shipped to steel mills on the southern shores of the Great Lakes, where mills process the taconite into iron.

Cameramann International, Ltd.

After the taconite has been ground almost to a powder and purified, it is fed into a steel barrel. The particles of taconite, when mixed with clay and then heated, form marble-sized balls. When the clay burns away, the taconite marbles are strong enough to be shipped to the blast furnaces where they are used to make iron.

In 1955, the first large-scale taconite processing plant was opened by Reserve Mining Company in Silver Bay, Minn., near Lake Superior. In 1976, a federal court ordered the company to end water pollution and reduce air pollution caused by the way the plant disposed of taconite waste materials. In 1980, the company stopped emptying such waste into Lake Superior, and began putting it in a land-disposal basin.   Robert W. Charles

See also **Hematite; Iron and steel** (Kinds of iron ore; Processing); **Loadstone.**

Tactile sense. See Touch.

Tadpole, also called *polliwog,* is an immature frog or toad. A tadpole is a *larva,* which is an early stage of an animal. Tadpoles live in water. When a tadpole hatches from its egg, it looks like a small fish. As the tadpole grows, it gradually develops the physical characteristics of the mature animal. The process of changing from a larva to an adult is called *metamorphosis.* The tadpole stage may last from 10 days to more than 2 years, depending on the species of frog or toad.

Tadpoles live in shallow waters wherever frogs and toads are found. Most tadpoles inhabit ponds, lakes, or slow-moving rivers. The greatest variety of tadpoles are found in the tropics. Tadpoles hatch from a jellylike mass of eggs laid in the water. A tadpole has a large, rounded head and a long, flat tail. The animal uses the tail to propel itself through the water. Tadpoles breathe by means of gills. Most tadpoles eat plants.

Most tadpoles are dark-colored, varying from solid black in common toads to olive-green in some frogs. Tadpoles of most species are less than 1 inch (2.5 centimeters) long. Bullfrog tadpoles are over 4 inches (10 centimeters) long. Tadpoles of the paradoxical frog of South America grow to lengths of over 10 inches (25 centimeters).

A tadpole has no legs when it hatches, but it begins to grow hind legs during the first stages of metamorphosis. Gradually, the tadpole's head flattens and the tail becomes shorter. The digestive system changes, enabling the animal that develops to eat insects and other animals. During the final stages of metamorphosis, the

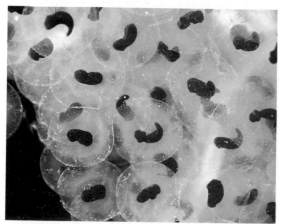

Jane Burton, Bruce Coleman Inc.

Eggs of the common European frog are jellylike and transparent. Inside each egg is an unborn tadpole. The rounded head and long tail of some of them have already formed.

Richard Lewington, The Garden Studio, London

A newly hatched tadpole resembles a small fish. Gradually, the animal develops the physical traits of a mature frog or toad. The tadpole stage may last only 10 days or as long as 2 years.

front legs of the tadpole appear. The gills disappear as lungs develop, forcing the tadpole to gulp air at the water's surface. The animal absorbs the remaining part of the tail after emerging from the water to become a land-living adult.   J. Whitfield Gibbons

See also **Frog** (with pictures); **Toad.**

Tadzhikistan. See Tajikistan.

Taegu, *ty goo* (pop. 2,030,672), is the third largest city in South Korea. Only Seoul and Pusan have more people. Taegu lies in southern South Korea (see **Korea** [map]). The city is a commercial and educational center.

Taegu stands on a fertile plain and is surrounded by huge mountains on the north and south. Its landmarks include the Talsong fortress, constructed during the Iron Age (1500-1000 B.C.), and many Confucian shrines. The city has two universities, a women's college, and several technical schools. Buddhist monasteries lie in the mountains around Taegu. The city ranks as South Korea's largest producer of textiles, and it is a market for farm products and minerals of its area.

Korean people had established a settlement on the site of what is now Taegu by A.D. 366. Taegu became a major commercial center in the 1400's.   Chong-Sik Lee

Tael, *tayl,* was a Chinese weight indicating a unit of value in silver. Although its worth often varied, the tael was the basis of value for Chinese money until 1935.

Tafari, Ras. See Haile Selassie I.

Taffeta, *TAF uh tuh,* is a smooth, rather stiff cloth of rayon, nylon, or silk. The name *taffeta* comes from the Persian word *taftah,* meaning *twisted* or *woven.* Taffeta has a plain, close weave. It comes in broad widths for making clothing, bedspreads, and draperies, and in narrow widths for making ribbons.   Christine W. Jarvis

Taft, Lorado (1860-1936), was an American sculptor, teacher, and writer. He is best remembered for *The History of American Sculpture* (1903), the first book on the subject. Taft's most famous sculptures are large, symbolic outdoor groups. They include *Fountain of Columbus* (1912) in Washington, D.C., *Fountain of the Great Lakes* (1913) and *Fountain of Time* (1922) in Chicago, and *Thatcher Memorial Fountain* (1917) in Denver. In 1911,

Taft completed a giant outdoor statue of the Indian chief Black Hawk near Oregon, Ill.

Taft was born in Elmwood, Ill., and studied art in France. He established a studio in Chicago and taught at the Art Institute of Chicago and the University of Illinois from 1886 to 1929.   Bess L. Hormats

Taft, Robert Alphonso (1889-1953), was an American statesman. He was called Mr. Republican because of his influence as a policymaker in his party.

Taft was born in Cincinnati, Ohio, the son of William Howard Taft, the 27th President of the United States. He attended Yale University and Harvard Law School. Taft practiced law in Cincinnati, and served in the Ohio legislature.

Taft was elected to the United States Senate in 1938, and was reelected in 1944 and 1950. In the Senate, he argued for a balanced budget, and opposed most of President Franklin D. Roosevelt's proposals for domestic spending. He was coauthor of the Taft-Hartley Act of 1947, which set up controls over labor unions. Taft also supported federal aid for housing and education.

Before World War II (1939-1945), Taft objected to major U.S. involvement in foreign affairs. Later, however, he accepted U.S. policies aimed at blocking attempts by the Soviet Union and China to spread Communism to other lands. Taft expressed his views on foreign affairs in his book *A Foreign Policy for Americans* (1951).

Taft was a candidate for the Republican nomination for President in 1940, 1948, and 1952. He was the leading opponent of Dwight D. Eisenhower for the presidential nomination in 1952. After Eisenhower's election to the presidency, Taft became Senate majority leader and one of the President's most trusted advisers. From 1971 to 1977, his son Robert A. Taft, Jr., served as a U.S. senator from Ohio.   James T. Patterson

Additional resources

Kirk, Russell A., and McClellan, J. P. *The Political Principles of Robert A. Taft.* Fleet, 1967.
Patterson, James T. *Mr. Republican: A Biography of Robert A. Taft.* Houghton, 1972.

Artstreet

United Press Int.

Lorado Taft, *above,* was a popular American sculptor in the early 1900's. He became known for his large outdoor sculpture groups. His *Fountain of the Great Lakes* (1913), *left,* stands outside the Art Institute of Chicago.

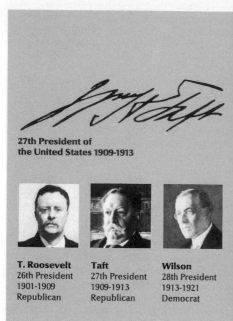

**27th President of
the United States 1909-1913**

T. Roosevelt
26th President
1901-1909
Republican

Taft
27th President
1909-1913
Republican

Wilson
28th President
1913-1921
Democrat

**James S.
Sherman**
Vice President
1909-1913

Oil painting by Anders L. Zorn (1911), © White House Historical Association (National Geographic Society)

Taft, William Howard (1857-1930), was the only man in the history of the United States who served first as President, then as chief justice. Taft did not want to be President. At heart, he was a judge and had little taste for politics. Above all, he wanted to be a justice of the Supreme Court of the United States.

Taft, a Republican, spent most of the first 20 years of his career as a lawyer and judge. His mother recognized his distaste for politics. "I do not want my son to be President," she said. "His is a judicial mind and he loves the law." But Taft's wife opposed his career as a judge because she felt it was a "fixed groove."

In the end, Taft's mother proved to be right. Hardly any other President has been so unhappy in office. When Taft left the White House in 1913, he told incoming President Woodrow Wilson: "I'm glad to be going. This is the lonesomest place in the world." When he was appointed chief justice of the United States eight years later, Taft said it was the highest honor he ever received. He wrote: "The truth is that in my present life I don't remember that I ever was President."

Taft was the largest person ever to serve as President. He stood 6 feet (183 centimeters) tall and weighed more than 300 pounds (136 kilograms). A newspaperman wrote that he looked "like an American bison—a gentle, kind one." He had a mild, pleasant personality, but he clung firmly to what he considered the rugged virtues. He did not smoke or drink. He was honest by nature, plain of speech, and straightforward in action. He was completely, and sometimes blindly, loyal to his friends and to his political party.

The modest Taft felt he was not fully qualified for the presidency. He had no gift of showmanship like his predecessor, Theodore Roosevelt. Taft gave the public an adequate Administration, but a poor show. Partly because of this, he failed to capture popular imagination, and many people called him a failure as President.

During Taft's Administration, most of the world was at peace. In Europe, the leading nations lined up in a balance of power that later led to World War I. In China, a revolution overthrew the imperial government and set up a republic. Explorers reached both the North Pole and the South Pole.

In the United States, the pace of life was speeding up. A majority of the people still lived on farms, but more and more were moving to cities. Women had won the right to vote in 12 states. Amendment 16 to the Constitution allowed Congress to pass a federal income tax, although it did not do so until Wilson's Administration. The United States grew to 48 states with the admission of Arizona and New Mexico.

Early life

William Howard Taft was born in Cincinnati, Ohio, on Sept. 15, 1857. He was the second son of Alphonso Taft and his second wife, Louise Maria Torrey Taft. Alphonso Taft's ancestors had lived in Massachusetts and Vermont since emigrating from England in the 1600's. His wife was descended from an English family that helped settle Weymouth, Mass., in 1640. The elder Taft, whose father was a Vermont judge, moved to Cincinnati about 1838. He became a successful lawyer and a nationally prominent figure in the Republican Party.

Will Taft was a large, fair, and attractive youth. He was brought up in the Unitarian faith. Two older half brothers, two younger brothers, and a younger sister were his playmates. They called Taft "Big Lub" because of his size. During the summers, the five Taft boys visited their

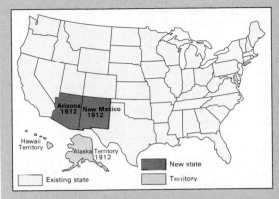

New Mexico and Arizona joined the Union during Taft's term. They became the 47th and 48th states in 1912. Congress established Alaska as a U.S. territory in 1912.

The United States flag had 46 stars when Taft took office. Two more stars—for New Mexico and Arizona—were added during his presidency.

The world of President Taft

The National Association for the Advancement of Colored People (NAACP) was founded in 1909 to promote racial equality.

The invention of Bakelite, the first completely synthetic resin, was a milestone in the plastics industry. New York chemist Leo Baekeland invented the substance in 1909.

Polar explorers gained world attention. In 1909, Admiral Robert Peary of the United States became the first person to reach the North Pole. Norwegian explorer Roald Amundsen led the first successful expedition to the South Pole in 1911.

Revolution erupted in Mexico in 1910 and led to the overthrow of dictator Porfirio Díaz.

Youth organizations developed in the United States. Boy Scouts and Camp Fire Girls were founded in 1910. Girl Scouts was established in 1912.

Hollywood became the nation's movie capital after the first motion-picture studio was built there in 1911.

Ragtime piano music became popular and led to such new dance crazes as the "turkey trot."

The Republic of China was founded in 1912, with Sun Yat-sen as provisional president.

The electric starter, a major improvement in automobiles, was introduced by General Motors in its 1912 Cadillac.

The passenger ship *Titanic* sank after hitting an iceberg in the Atlantic Ocean on the night of April 14-15, 1912. About 1,500 passengers drowned, and about 700 were rescued.

Amendment 16 to the Constitution took effect in 1913, giving Congress authority to levy a national income tax.

WORLD BOOK map

Grandfather Torrey in Millbury, Mass. He made them cut wood in his wood lot to pay for their vacations, and also to teach them the value of money.

When Taft was 13 years old, he entered Woodward High School in Cincinnati. At 17, he enrolled in Yale College. In 1878, Taft graduated second in his class. He then studied law at the Cincinnati Law School. He received a law degree in 1880 and was admitted to the Ohio bar.

Political and public career

First offices. During 1881 and 1882, Taft served as assistant prosecuting attorney of Hamilton County, Ohio. In March 1882, President Chester A. Arthur appointed him collector of internal revenue for the first district, with headquarters at Cincinnati. Taft resigned a year later because he did not want to discharge good workers just to make jobs for deserving Republicans. He then formed a successful law partnership.

Taft's family. On June 19, 1886, Taft married Helen "Nellie" Herron (Jan. 2, 1861-May 22, 1943), the daughter of John W. Herron of Cincinnati. Herron had been a law partner of President Rutherford B. Hayes. Taft wrote that his wife was "a woman who is willing to take me as I am,

for better or for worse." Mrs. Taft was both intelligent and ambitious. Throughout her husband's career, she encouraged him to seek public office.

The Tafts had three children. Robert Alphonso Taft (1889-1953) became a famous U.S. senator from Ohio and a leader of the Republican Party (see **Taft, Robert Alphonso**). Helen Herron Taft Manning (1891-1987) served as professor of history and dean of Bryn Mawr College in Bryn Mawr, Pa. Charles Phelps Taft II (1897-1983), a lawyer, was mayor of Cincinnati from 1955 to 1957.

State judge. Taft was happy as a lawyer, but his father's importance in the Republican Party kept pushing

Important dates in Taft's life

1857 (Sept. 15) Born in Cincinnati, Ohio.
1886 (June 19) Married Helen Herron.
1892 Appointed judge of U.S. Circuit Court of Appeals.
1901 Appointed governor of the Philippines.
1904 Appointed secretary of war.
1908 Elected President of the United States.
1912 Defeated for reelection by Woodrow Wilson.
1921 Appointed chief justice of the United States.
1930 (March 8) Died in Washington, D.C.

William Howard Taft National Historic Site

Taft's birthplace was this comfortable house in the Mt. Auburn section of Cincinnati, Ohio. Taft spent his entire boyhood there, with two half brothers, two brothers, and a sister.

Helen Herron Taft was an intelligent and ambitious woman who urged her husband to seek the presidency. She was known as a gracious hostess, as well as a trusted presidential adviser.

him toward political life. Early in 1885, Taft was named assistant county solicitor for Hamilton County. In March 1887, Governor J. B. Foraker of Ohio appointed him to a vacancy on the Cincinnati Superior Court. The next year, the voters elected Taft to the court for a five-year term. This was the only office except the presidency that Taft won by popular vote.

Solicitor general. Taft resigned from the Cincinnati Superior Court in 1890 to accept an appointment by President Benjamin Harrison as solicitor general of the United States. During his first year, he won 15 of the 18 government cases that he argued before the Supreme Court.

Federal judge. In March 1892, President Harrison appointed Taft a judge of the sixth circuit of the newly established United States Circuit Court of Appeals (now the United States Court of Appeals). Taft spent the next eight years as a circuit judge. From 1896 to 1900, he also was dean of the University of Cincinnati Law School.

Governor of the Philippines. In 1900, President William McKinley appointed Taft chairman of a civil commission to govern the newly acquired Philippines. The next year Taft was named the first civil governor of the islands.

Taft's career in the Philippines was an example of the best in colonial government. He established new systems of courts, land records, vital and social statistics, and sanitary regulations. He built roads and harbors, worked toward the establishment of limited self-government, and led a movement for land reform. Taft also established schools in many areas and worked steadily to improve the economic status of the people.

Taft ardently desired to be a justice of the Supreme Court. But in 1902, he turned down his first chance for appointment to the court because he felt he had not finished his work in the Philippines.

Secretary of war. Secretary of War Elihu Root resigned in January 1904, and Taft returned to Washington

to assume this post in President Theodore Roosevelt's Cabinet. Taft's appointment was good politics. The 1904 presidential campaign was approaching, and Taft had won great popularity for his work in the Philippines.

The President soon began using Taft as his unofficial troubleshooter, both at home and abroad. Taft's department supervised the construction of the Panama Canal and set up the government in the Canal Zone. Taft himself advanced Roosevelt's tariff policy and assisted the President in negotiating the Treaty of Portsmouth, which ended the Russo-Japanese War. Everything was all right in Washington, the President said, because Taft was "sitting on the lid."

Election of 1908. Roosevelt announced he would not seek reelection in 1908, and recommended Taft as the man who would follow his policies. At first, Taft objected, preferring to wait for possible appointment to the Supreme Court. But Mrs. Taft and his brothers helped change his mind.

With Roosevelt's support, Taft won the nomination on the first ballot at the Republican National Convention. Representative James S. Sherman of New York received the vice presidential nomination. The voters gave Taft a plurality of more than a million votes over William Jennings Bryan, who suffered his third loss as Democratic nominee for President. Bryan shared the Democratic ticket with John W. Kern, a Democratic Party leader of Indiana.

Taft's Administration (1909-1913)

"Even the elements do protest," said Taft unhappily when a blizzard swept Washington on the morning of his inauguration in March 1909. From the start, Taft was filled with doubt about being President. He knew he could not be another Roosevelt. "There is no use trying to be William Howard Taft with Roosevelt's ways," he remarked. "Our ways are different." Taft decided to "complete and perfect the machinery" with which Roosevelt had tried to solve the problems of the United States.

Legislative defeats. Taft began his term with a divided party, although the Republicans controlled both

As governor of the Philippines, Taft earned a reputation for fair and effective leadership. Appointed by President William McKinley, Taft served as governor from 1901 to 1904.

Collection of Edmund Sullivan

An election plate for the 1908 election featured Taft and his running mate, Representative James S. Sherman of New York.

Taft's election

Place of nominating convention	Chicago
Ballot on which nominated	1st
Democratic opponent	William Jennings Bryan
Electoral vote*	321 (Taft) to 162 (Bryan)
Popular vote	7,676,258 (Taft) to 6,406,801 (Bryan)
Age at inauguration	51

*For votes by states, see Electoral College (table).

houses of Congress. On the advice of Roosevelt, Taft refused to support the liberal Republicans in their fight to curb the almost unrestricted powers of the Speaker of the House, Joseph "Uncle Joe" Cannon of Illinois. But these Republicans, led by Representative George W. Norris of Nebraska, overthrew "Cannonism" (see **Norris, George William**). Because of his political inexperience in this and other matters, Taft soon lost the support of most liberal Republicans.

Like many other Americans, Taft believed in tariff protection. But he also felt that somewhat lower tariffs would help control trusts. He called Congress into special session to pass a tariff-reduction law but was reluctant to impose his ideas on Congress. The House passed a bill with big reductions. But in the Senate, Nelson W. Aldrich of Rhode Island, one of Taft's chief advisers, led the campaign to keep high tariffs. The resulting law, the Payne-Aldrich Tariff, lowered some tariff rates slightly but left the general level of rates as high as they had been. Taft said he knew he "could make a lot of cheap popularity by vetoing the bill." Instead, he accepted it as better than nothing, defended it in public, and suffered from the great unpopularity that the bill received.

Taft further antagonized the liberal Republicans by his stand in the Pinchot case. In late 1909, Chief Forester Gifford Pinchot made sensational charges that the De-

Vice President and Cabinet

Vice President	* James S. Sherman
Secretary of state	* Philander C. Knox
Secretary of the treasury	Franklin MacVeagh
Secretary of war	Jacob M. Dickinson
	* Henry L. Stimson (1911)
Attorney general	George W. Wickersham
Postmaster general	Frank H. Hitchcock
Secretary of the navy	George von Lengerke Meyer
Secretary of the interior	Richard A. Ballinger
	Walter L. Fisher (1911)
Secretary of agriculture	James Wilson
Secretary of commerce and labor	Charles Nagel

*Has a separate biography in WORLD BOOK.

partment of the Interior, and especially Secretary of the Interior Richard A. Ballinger, had abandoned the conservation policies of Theodore Roosevelt. Pinchot also accused the department of selling land concessions to water and power companies too cheaply, and of illegal transactions in the sale of Alaska coal lands. Taft upheld Ballinger, who was later cleared by a congressional investigating committee. Taft then dismissed Pinchot. Liberal Republicans became convinced that some of Pinchot's charges were true and began turning to Roosevelt as their true leader.

Legislative achievements of the Taft Administration included the first scientific investigation of tariff rates, for which the President established the Tariff Board. Taft took the first steps toward establishing a federal budget by asking his Cabinet members and their staffs to submit detailed reports of their financial needs. Congress created the Postal Savings System in 1910 and parcel post in 1913. At Taft's request, Congress also organized a commerce court and enlarged the powers of the Interstate Commerce Commission. The President pushed a bill through Congress requiring that campaign expenses in federal elections be made public. During Taft's Administration, Alaska received full territorial government, and the Federal Children's Bureau was established. The President took action against many trusts. Nearly twice as many "trust-busting" prosecutions for violation of the Sherman Antitrust Act took place during Taft's four years in office as had occurred during Roosevelt's Administration of almost eight years.

Foreign affairs. The Taft Administration had an uneven record in international relations. During the late 1800's, nations customarily used diplomacy to expand their commercial interests. "Dollar diplomacy," as promoted by Secretary of State Philander C. Knox, had just the opposite purpose. To Knox, it meant the use of trade and commerce to increase a nation's diplomatic influence (see **Dollar diplomacy**). The United States made loans to China, Nicaragua, Honduras, and other countries in order to encourage investments by bankers in loans to these nations. Taft ended the second American occupation of Cuba in 1909 and negotiated treaties of arbitration with Great Britain and France. These treaties ranked as landmarks in the effort of nations to settle their differences peacefully, but the Senate rejected them.

Life in the White House. Mrs. Taft, a skillful hostess, enjoyed presiding at state functions and entertaining

Bettmann Archive

A presidential tradition began when President Taft threw out the first ball to open the 1910 major league baseball season.

friends at small teas. She hired a woman to replace the traditional male steward because she thought the service would be improved. At Mrs. Taft's request, the mayor of Tokyo presented about 3,000 cherry trees to the American people. The trees were planted along the banks of the Potomac River. Mrs. Taft suffered a stroke in the winter of 1909. Thereafter, her daughter, Helen, or her sister, Mrs. Louis More, often acted as Taft's official hostess.

Mrs. Taft had a better head for politics than did her husband. He relied on his wife's judgment and missed her help after she became ill. Mrs. Taft might have controlled the President's fellow Republicans better than he did.

On summer evenings, the Tafts often sat on the south portico of the White House and listened to favorite phonograph recordings. Taft, although a large man, was an excellent dancer, and Mrs. Taft organized a small dancing class for his diversion. He played tennis and golf well and often rode horseback.

Election of 1912. Theodore Roosevelt had returned in 1910 from an African hunting trip. He denied an interest in running for the presidency again but began making speeches advocating a "New Nationalism." Under this slogan, Roosevelt included his old policies of honest government, checks on big business, and conservation, as well as demands for social justice, including old-age and unemployment insurance. Conservative Republicans lined up with Taft against Roosevelt.

Although Roosevelt won most of the primary elections, a majority of the delegates to the nominating convention were pledged to Taft. The President was renominated on the first ballot, and James S. Sherman was renominated as Vice President. Roosevelt and the progressive Republicans accused Taft of "stealing" the convention by recognizing the votes of pro-Taft delegations. They organized the Progressive Party with Roosevelt as their nominee, and chose Senator Hiram W. Johnson of California as his running mate. The Democrats nominated Governor Woodrow Wilson of New Jersey for President and Governor Thomas R. Marshall of Indiana for Vice President. Taft faced inevitable defeat. He re-

ceived only 8 electoral votes, against 88 for Roosevelt and 435 for Wilson.

Later years

Law professor. After Taft left the White House in March 1913, he became professor of constitutional law at Yale University. That same year, he was elected president of the American Bar Association. During World War I (1914-1918), President Wilson appointed Taft joint chairman of the National War Labor Board.

Chief justice. In 1921, President Warren G. Harding appointed Taft chief justice of the United States. Taft regarded this appointment as the greatest honor of his life. His accomplishments as administrator of the nation's highest court were more important than his decisions. The Supreme Court had fallen far behind in its work. In 1925, Taft achieved passage of the Judiciary Act. This law gave the court greater control over the number and kinds of cases it would consider and made it possible for the court to function effectively and get its work done. Taft was also instrumental in obtaining congressional approval for a new court building. See **Supreme Court of the United States.**

Taft performed more than his share of the court's great workload and often advised President Calvin Coolidge. He watched his health and held his weight to about 300 pounds (136 kilograms). Taft became a familiar figure in Washington as he walked the 3 miles (5 kilometers) between his home and the court almost every morning and evening. But finally the strain of overwork became too great. Bad health, chiefly due to heart trouble, forced his retirement on Feb. 3, 1930. Taft died on March 8 and was buried in Arlington National Cemetery. Taft and President John F. Kennedy are the only Presidents buried there.   John M. Blum

Critically reviewed by Robert Taft, Jr.

Related articles in *World Book* include:
Dollar diplomacy	Tariff
President of the United States	Wilson, Woodrow
Roosevelt, Theodore	

Outline

I. Early life
II. Political and public career

A. First offices	E. Federal judge
B. Taft's family	F. Governor of the Philippines
C. State judge	G. Secretary of war
D. Solicitor general	H. Election of 1908

III. Taft's Administration (1909-1913)

A. Legislative defeats	C. Foreign affairs
B. Legislative achievements	D. Life in the White House
	E. Election of 1912

IV. Later years
A. Law professor
B. Chief justice

Questions

What were Taft's chief personal virtues?
What were the main legislative achievements of his Administration?
What was Taft's lifelong ambition? Did he achieve it?
What was the Pinchot case? The Payne-Aldrich Tariff?
How did Taft lose the confidence of liberal Republicans during his term?
What was the only public office except the presidency to which Taft was elected?
What were Taft's main achievements as governor of the Philippines?
What were some of Taft's accomplishments as secretary of war?

Additional resources

Anderson, Donald F. *William Howard Taft: A Conservative's Conception of the Presidency.* Cornell Univ. Press, 1973.
Anderson, Judith I. *William Howard Taft: An Intimate History.* Norton, 1981.
Manners, William. *TR and Will: A Friendship That Split the Republican Party.* Harcourt, 1969.
Pringle, Henry F. *The Life and Times of William Howard Taft.* 2 vols. Farrar, 1939. The standard biography.
Scholes, Walter V. and M. V. *The Foreign Policies of the Taft Administration.* Univ. of Missouri Press, 1970.
Severn, Bill. *William Howard Taft: The President Who Became Chief Justice.* McKay, 1970.

Taft-Hartley Act is the popular name for the federal *Labor-Management Relations Act of 1947.* The act was named for its main sponsors, Senator Robert A. Taft and Representative Fred Hartley. It was an amendment to the Wagner Act (National Labor Relations Act of 1935). It continued the Wagner Act's basic guarantees of workers' rights, and outlawed certain union practices. The Taft-Hartley Act provided that the start of strikes which might cause a national emergency can be delayed for 80 days.

The act forbids unions to use force or discrimination against individuals during organizing campaigns. It also prohibits union political contributions in national elections. The act prohibits use of the *secondary boycott, sympathy strike,* and *jurisdictional strike.* A secondary boycott occurs when striking employees bring pressure on a party not involved in the dispute in hopes that the party will stop doing business with their employer. A sympathy strike is called by one union in support of another union striking against its employer. A jurisdictional strike is called by rival unions over which union has the right to work on a job.

The act outlaws the *closed shop,* the practice of hiring only union members, and gives the states power to restrict the *union shop,* in which employees have to join the union after being hired. It requires unions to file such information as constitutions and financial statements with the federal government.

Taft-Hartley supporters said the act equalized power between union and management. Unions called it a "slave labor law," and tried to repeal or amend it. The Landrum-Griffin Act of 1959, the first major amendment to Taft-Hartley, strengthened federal regulation of internal union affairs. Gerald G. Somers

See also **Closed shop; Open shop; Union shop.**

Additional resources

Bornstein, Jerry. *Unions in Transition.* Messner, 1981.
Lee, R. Alton. *Truman and Taft-Hartley: A Question of Mandate.* Greenwood, 1980. First published in 1966.
Millis, Harry A., and Brown, E. C. *From the Wagner Act to Taft-Hartley: A Study of National Labor Policy and Labor Relations.* Univ. of Chicago Press, 1950.

Taglioni, *tah LYOH nee,* **Marie** (1804-1884), was one of the most famous ballerinas of the early 1800's. She was the first ballerina to make toe-dancing beautiful. Her leaps are described as slow flights through the air. To audiences, the effortless grace of her movements made her appear weightless. Her dancing and her acting looked effortless and cool.

Taglioni was born in Stockholm, Sweden. She was rigorously trained by her father, Filippo Taglioni, an Italian dancer and *choreographer* (dance composer). Her dancing in his ballets, particularly in *La Sylphide* (1832), brought about the romantic period in ballet which lasted until the mid-1840's. Audiences all over Europe idolized her. She retired in 1848. P. W. Manchester

See also **Ballet** (Romantic ballet; picture).

Tagore, *tuh GAWR,* **Sir Rabindranath,** *ruh BEEN druh NAHT* (1861-1941), was an Indian poet, philosopher, and supporter of freedom for India. In his many poems and songs, he stirred pride among his fellow Hindus. He also had a strong influence on the West. Tagore was influenced by European models in his writings. He was a mystical and religious poet, and saw God in all beauties of nature. He wrote prose and poetry in the Bengali language. Tagore received the 1913 Nobel Prize in literature.

Tagore was born in Calcutta, and went to England to study law. He returned to Bengal, a province of British India and the center of the Hindu cultural and spiritual revival in the 1800's. In 1901, he set up a school at Shantiniketan which tried to blend the best in Hindu and Western culture. T. Walter Wallbank

Tagus River, *TAY guhs,* also called *Tajo,* is the longest river of the Iberian Peninsula of southwest Europe. It rises in central Spain and flows west across Portugal to the Atlantic Ocean. The river is 626 miles (1,007 kilometers) long and drains an area of about 31,000 square miles (80,300 square kilometers). The mouth of the Tagus gives Lisbon, Portugal, one of the finest harbors in Europe. George Kish

Tahiti, *tuh HEE tee,* an island in the South Pacific Ocean, is famous for its exotic beauty and tropical climate. It is the largest island in French Polynesia, a French overseas territory made up of several island groups. Tahiti is one of the 14 Society Islands. For location, see **Pacific Islands** (map). Papeete is the largest city and chief port of Tahiti. The city is also the capital of French Polynesia.

Tahiti gained worldwide fame as a tropical paradise through the works of many artists and writers who visited the island or lived there. The French artist Paul Gauguin portrayed Tahiti's lush beauty and peaceful atmosphere in many paintings. Many authors, including Herman Melville and James Michener of the United States and Robert Louis Stevenson of Scotland, wrote glowing descriptions of the island. Such works have helped make Tahiti popular with tourists.

Tahiti covers 402 square miles (1,041 square kilometers). A broken coral reef surrounds the island. A strip of flat, fertile land lies along the coast, where most of the people live. The interior of the island is mountainous, and the land is so steep that it is almost entirely uninhabited. Heavy rainfall helps create many fast-flowing streams and spectacular waterfalls there. The island has much lush vegetation, including coconut palms and banana, orange, and papaya trees.

About 85,000 people live on Tahiti. Most of them are Polynesians or have mixed Polynesian and European ancestry. The population also includes a few thousand Chinese and a few hundred Europeans.

Many Tahitians live in or near Papeete and work in the tourist industry, which is the base of the island's economy. Tahiti's Chinese population controls much of the retail and shipping trade on the island. People in rural areas farm the land or work in the fishing in-

Tahiti is an island in the South Pacific Ocean. The island is famous as a tropical paradise. Papenoo Beach, *left,* lies on the northern coast of Tahiti.

© Bruce Berg

dustry. The farmers grow breadfruit, taro, and yams for their own use and produce small quantities of copra and vanilla for export.

The earliest inhabitants of Tahiti were Polynesians who came there from Asia hundreds of years ago. The first European to visit the island was the British sea captain Samuel Wallis in 1767. He claimed Tahiti for Great Britain. The next year, a French navigator named Louis Antoine de Bougainville landed on Tahiti and claimed it for France. Tahiti became a French protectorate in 1842 and a colony of France in 1880. In 1946, France declared Tahiti and the other islands of French Polynesia to be a French overseas territory. Several independence movements began in French Polynesia during the mid-1900's, but most of the people want to remain under French rule.   Phillip Bacon

See also **Gauguin, Paul; Society Islands.**

Tahoe, Lake. See Lake Tahoe.

Taiga. See Forest (Kinds of forests).

Taika reform. See Japan (History).

Tail is the part of the body of a vertebrate animal that extends backward beyond the pelvis. In animals without limbs, the tail is the part of the body that extends beyond the anus. The term *tail* includes both the fleshy portion and the outgrowths it may have, such as fins and feathers.

Animals use their tails in many ways. The tails of most water animals serve to move them and to steer them. Squirrels use their tails to keep their balance when they are leaping and climbing. Woodpeckers and kangaroos prop themselves up with their tails. Spider monkeys and opossums grasp things with their tails.

Tailorbird is a songbird found in tropical regions of China, India, Malaya, and the Philippines. Its name comes from the way it builds its nest in a large folded leaf. It sews the edges of the leaf together with strips of silk or wool thread, or vegetable fiber, using its bill as a needle. The nest inside the leaves is made from plant down, fine grass, and hair. The female lays three or four eggs. They vary in color from reddish-white to bluish-green and are marked with brownish-red. Tailorbirds are 4 to 5$\frac{1}{2}$ inches (10 to 14 centimeters) long. There are nine species.

Scientific classification. Tailorbirds belong to the subfamily Sylviinae of the family Muscicapidae. They are classified as genus *Orthotomus.*   Fred J. Alsop, III

See also **Bird** (picture: Kinds of bird nests).

Taine, *tayn* or *tehn,* **Hippolyte Adolphe,** *ee paw LEET a DAWLF* (1828-1893), was a French intellectual and critic. His application of the philosophy of *determinism* to art and literature did much to shape French intellectual attitudes in the 1800's.

To understand the origin and development of an art-

WORLD BOOK illustration by Trevor Boyer, Linden Artists Ltd.

The tailorbird uses its long bill as a needle.

ist's or writer's work, Taine said we must discover all the significant facts about the person's *race* (heredity), *milieu* (environment), and *moment* (state of the artistic tradition in which the person worked). Through this theory and through his emphasis on documentation, Taine greatly influenced the naturalist movement in literature (see **Naturalism**). Taine's *History of English Literature* (1863) and *Philosophy of Art* (1865-1869) illustrate his deterministic philosophy. His *Origins of Contemporary France* (1875-1893) blames the French Revolution for the decline he saw in France's greatness.

Taine was born in Vouziers. He was a professor at the École des Beaux-Arts in Paris almost continuously from 1864 to 1883.　　Thomas H. Goetz

Taipei, *ty pay* or *ty bay* (pop. 2,220,427), is the capital and largest city of the island country of Taiwan. It lies on the Hsintien, Keelung, and Tanshui rivers at the north end of the island of Taiwan. For location, see **Taiwan** (map). The name *Taipei* means *north Taiwan*.

Taipei and its surrounding area make up the commercial, cultural, and tourist center of Taiwan. Taipei's landmarks include Chiang Kai-shek Memorial Hall; the Lungshan Temple, which is believed to be the oldest Buddhist temple in the city; and the Grand Hotel, which resembles an ancient Chinese palace. The city's National Palace Museum houses an outstanding collection of Chinese art. Taipei has large department stores and exotic bazaars. It is the home of several universities, including National Taiwan University, National Taiwan Normal University, and National Chengchi University.

In 1967, Taipei annexed the towns of Chingmei, Mucha, Nankang, Neihu, Shihlin, and Peitou. As a result, the city grew from 26 to 105 square miles (67 to 272 square kilometers).

Taipei is one of the most densely populated cities in the world. Overcrowded housing is a problem in the city. Many high-rise buildings have been erected in Taipei, with little concern for zoning laws. Heavy traffic is another problem. Air pollution has resulted from motor vehicles and the factories in and near the city.

Products made in Taipei include textiles, electrical machinery and appliances, wires and cables, refrigerators, motorcycles, rubber goods, and various handicrafts. More than a dozen airlines serve the nearby Chiang Kai-shek International Airport. Railways and buslines connect the city to all parts of Taiwan.

The Chinese began making large settlements in Taiwan during the 1600's. The Chinese founded Taipei in 1708. Japan took control of Taipei and the rest of Taiwan from China in 1895. The Japanese made Taipei the administrative and economic center of the island and greatly expanded the city's area.

After World War II ended in 1945, Japan returned Taiwan to China. In 1949, the army of the Chinese Communist Party overthrew the Nationalist government of China. The Nationalist Chinese, led by Chiang Kai-shek, retreated from the mainland to Taiwan and established their own government in Taipei. Since then, Taipei and its suburbs have expanded greatly.　　Parris H. Chang

Taira, *tah ee rah* or *TY rah,* was the name of a family that ruled Japan from about 1160 to 1185. The family is also known by its Chinese name, Heike (pronounced *hay keh*). After the emperor lost his political influence in the late 700's, powerful families fought for control of the

government. The Taira family became a leader of this new warrior class that ruled the country until 1867.

Taira Kiyomori, the head of the family, seized control of the government about 1160. Through arranged marriages, Kiyomori's grandson became heir to the throne as Emperor Antoku. After Kiyomori died in 1181, the family's power declined. Taira rule ended in 1185, when the family was defeated in a sea battle by its main rival, the Minamoto family. The young Emperor Antoku drowned in the battle.　　Tetsuo Najita

Taiwan, *ty wahn,* is a mountainous island in the South China Sea, about 90 miles (140 kilometers) off the Chinese coast. The Chinese call the island *Taiwan,* meaning *terraced bay.* The wild, forested beauty of the island led Portuguese sailors in 1590 to name it *Ilha Formosa,* meaning *beautiful island.*

After the Chinese Communists conquered mainland China in 1949, the Chinese Nationalist government moved to Taiwan. Generalissimo Chiang Kai-shek, the Nationalist president, made Taipei the capital of the Republic of China. The Nationalist government also controls several islands in the Formosa Strait, including the Matsu, Pescadores, and Quemoy groups.

Government. The Chinese Nationalist government is based on a Constitution adopted in 1946 on the mainland. It provides for five branches of government—executive, legislative, judicial, control, and examination. Each branch is headed by a *yuan* (council).

The president, who heads the executive yuan, is Taiwan's most powerful government official. The president is elected by the National Assembly, a body whose chief functions are to elect the president and to amend the Constitution. The National Assembly has about 1,000

Dallas and John Heaton, Click/Chicago

Taipei is Taiwan's capital. Downtown Taipei includes a pleasant park and an art museum. A hotel tower, *background,* rises above modern office buildings.

Taiwan

- ▬▬ International boundary
- ━━ Road
- ┄┄┄ Railroad
- ⊛ National capital
- • Other city or town
- + Elevation above sea level

WORLD BOOK map

Guangdong (Kwangtung) provinces on the mainland. Over 1½ million more people fled to Taiwan from the mainland after the Communist take-over in 1949. About 2 per cent of the population are non-Chinese native peoples related to Indonesians and Filipinos. Most of the native peoples, sometimes called *aborigines,* live on reservations in the mountains.

About a fifth of the people of Taiwan farm the land. Farms on the island average only 2 or 3 acres (0.8 to 1.2 hectares) in size, but Taiwanese farmers live well by Asian standards. Power tillers are gradually replacing water buffaloes in the fields. Many farmers can afford bicycles, motorcycles, refrigerators, radios, and television sets. Most of the farmhouses are made of brick, with tile roofs and central courtyards of packed earth or cement. A typical Taiwanese meal includes rice, served with vegetables and chopped meat or fish. Farmers and other people who work in the hot sun wear cone-shaped straw hats. Most city people in Taiwan wear Western-style clothing.

The Taiwanese speak various Chinese dialects. But almost all the people also use Northern Chinese (Mandarin), the official Chinese dialect. About half of the Taiwanese people practice a local traditional religion that blends Buddhism, Confucianism, and Taoism. About 42 per cent of the country's people are Buddhists, and about 8 per cent are Christians.

About 90 per cent of the people can read and write. The law requires children to have six years of elementary school and three years of high school.

Land and climate. Taiwan, including the Pescadores islands, covers 13,900 square miles (36,000 square kilometers). This area does not include the Matsu and Quemoy island groups, which are part of Fujian province on the mainland.

Thickly forested mountains run from north to south and cover about half of Taiwan. The highest peak, Yü Shan (Mount Morrison), rises 13,113 feet (3,997 meters) above sea level. At many places along the eastern coast,

members, most of whom are "life-term" members elected in 1947 on the mainland. Most lawmaking is done by the legislative yuan, which has about 320 members. Most of the legislative yuan's members are also "life-term" members elected in 1947 on the mainland. When a "life-term" member of one of these bodies dies, the seat generally remains vacant. Some members of the National Assembly and the legislative yuan are elected by the people of Taiwan.

The judicial yuan is Taiwan's highest court. The control yuan reviews the activities of government officials and has the power of impeachment. The examination yuan gives tests that are used to hire and promote government workers.

Although Taiwan is the seat of the Chinese Nationalist government, it is administered as a province of China. The president appoints a provincial governor who serves an indefinite term. The people elect the members of a provincial Assembly to four-year terms. The people also elect county and city government officials.

People. Almost all the people of Taiwan live on the coastal plain that makes up the western third of the island. Most Taiwanese are Chinese whose ancestors came to the island from Fujian (also spelled Fukien) and

Facts in brief

Capital: Taipei.

Official language: Northern Chinese (Mandarin, or putonghua).

Area: 13,900 sq. mi. (36,000 km²), including the Pescadores islands, but excluding Matsu and Quemoy. *Greatest distances*— north-south, 235 mi. (378 km); eastwest, 90 mi. (145 km). *Coastline*—555 mi. (893 km).

Elevation: *Highest*—Yü Shan (Mount Morrison), 13,113 ft. (3,997 m) above sea level. *Lowest*—sea level.

Population: *Estimated 1989 population*—20,289,000; density, 1,460 persons per sq. mi. (564 per km²); distribution, 71 per cent urban, 29 per cent rural. *1980 census*—17,968,797. *Estimated 1994 population*—21,315,000.

Chief products: *Agriculture*—asparagus, bananas, chickens and ducks, citrus fruits, hogs, mushrooms, pineapples, rice, sugar cane, sweet potatoes, tea, vegetables. *Fishing*—shrimp, snapper, tuna. *Forestry*—cedar, hemlock, oak. *Manufacturing* —calculators, clothing and textiles, iron and steel, paper, plastics, plywood, processed foods, radios, ships, sporting goods, sugar, television sets, toys.

Flag: The flag has a red field. A white sun appears on a blue canton in the upper left-hand corner. Red stands for liberty and sacrifice, and white for fraternity and honesty. Adopted in 1928. See **Flag** (picture: Flags of Asia and the Pacific).

Money: *Basic unit*—New Taiwan dollar or yuan. See **Money** (table: Exchange rates). See also **Yuan.**

A fertile valley near Taipei is the home of a farming community. About a fifth of the people of Taiwan farm the land. Most of the country is too mountainous for farming.

the mountains drop sharply to the sea. Short, swift rivers have cut gorges through the mountains. In the western part of Taiwan, the mountains slope to gently rolling hills and level land.

Taiwan has a subtropical climate, with hot, humid summers and an average annual rainfall of more than 100 inches (250 centimeters). Temperatures average about 80° F. (27° C) in summer and 65° F. (18° C) in winter. Summer monsoons bring strong winds and rain to Taiwan. In winter, monsoons bring rain and cooler weather to the north. Typhoons occur almost every year, with damaging rains and strong winds.

Economy. Taiwan has few natural resources except its mountain forests. Cedars, hemlocks, and oaks are the most valuable timber trees. Other forest products include bamboo, camphor, paper, and plywood. Taiwan's economy depends heavily on manufacturing and foreign trade. Taiwanese factories produce calculators, cement, clothing and textiles, furniture, iron and steel, plastic goods, processed foods, ships, shoes, sporting equipment, sugar, televisions and radios, and toys. Many of these manufactured goods are exported, especially televisions, radios, calculators, clothing and textiles, plastic goods, plywood, and toys. Taiwan's chief trading partners include the United States, Japan, Hong Kong, and West Germany.

Only about a fourth of Taiwan's land can be farmed. The farmers have terraced many hills to provide more fields for growing rice. The farmers use much fertilizer and harvest two or three crops a year from the same field. The chief crops include asparagus, bananas, citrus fruits, corn, mushrooms, peanuts, pineapples, rice, sugar, sweet potatoes, tea, and vegetables. The farmers raise hogs, chickens, and ducks. Workers in the fishing industry catch such ocean fish as shrimp, snapper, and

tuna. Carp, eels, and other fish are caught in inland ponds.

Coal is Taiwan's most important mineral, though the island has only small deposits. Copper, gold, limestone, natural gas, petroleum, salt, and sulfur are also mined.

Taiwan has a good network of roads, including an expressway that connects Taipei and Kaohsiung. The country has an average of about 1 automobile for every 30

Manufacturing plays a major role in Taiwan's economy. The worker above is assembling a television set. Taiwan exports TV sets, radios, and many other manufactured products.

people. Bus service is excellent. The government operates several railroad lines. Kaohsiung and Chilung are the chief seaports. Taipei has a major international airport.

About 30 daily newspapers are published in Taiwan. Most Taiwanese families own a television set and one or more radios.

History. Aborigines were the first inhabitants of Taiwan. Some Chinese came to the island from the mainland as early as the 500's, but large settlements did not begin until the 1600's. Dutch traders occupied a Taiwanese port from 1624 until 1661. Koxinga, a Chinese Ming dynasty official, drove them out. Manchu conquerors had overthrown the Ming dynasty in mainland China, and Koxinga hoped to restore the dynasty to power. He wanted to use Taiwan as a base from which to attack the Manchus. But the Manchus conquered Taiwan in 1683 and administered it as part of China.

In 1895, Japan gained control of Taiwan as a result of the first Chinese-Japanese War. The Japanese developed Taiwan's agriculture and industry and expanded its transportation networks. China regained Taiwan after World War II ended in 1945.

In 1949, the Chinese Communists defeated Chiang Kai-shek's Nationalist forces and took control of the mainland. Chiang moved his government to Taiwan on Dec. 8, 1949. Both governments consider Taiwan a province of China. Each claims to be the legal ruler of all China, and each has declared its determination to take over the other's territory.

After the Korean War began in 1950, the United States said it would protect Taiwan against possible attack from mainland China. The U.S. and Chinese Nationalist governments signed a mutual defense treaty in 1954. The Chinese Communists repeatedly shelled Matsu and Quemoy during the 1950's. The shelling of Quemoy in 1958 led U.S. air and naval forces to patrol the Formosa Strait. Taiwan received about $1½ billion in U.S. economic and technical aid up to 1965. That year, Taiwan said its economy could stand on its own. But it continued to receive U.S. military aid.

In the early 1970's, Taiwan expressed concern over improved relations between the United States and Communist China. In 1971, the United States announced it favored United Nations (UN) membership for Communist China. But the United States also said that Nationalist China—a charter member of the UN—should retain its UN seat. In October 1971, the UN expelled the Nationalists and admitted Communist China. In 1972, President Richard M. Nixon visited Communist China and agreed to gradually withdraw U.S. military forces from Taiwan.

During the 1970's, a number of nations ended their diplomatic relations with Taiwan and established ties with Communist China. The United States ended its diplomatic relations with Taiwan at the end of 1978, and established diplomatic relations with Communist China at the start of 1979. The mutual defense treaty between the two countries was ended on Dec. 31, 1979. But the U.S. agreed to continue to supply Taiwan with some military aid. Also, the two countries agreed to carry on unofficial relations through nongovernmental agencies. Trade between Taiwan and the United States continues to thrive.

President Chiang Kai-shek died in 1975. Chiang's son Chiang Ching-kuo had become prime minister in 1972.

He became the country's most powerful leader after his father died. He was elected president of Taiwan in 1978 and was reelected in 1984. Chiang died in 1988. Vice President Lee Teng-hui succeeded him as president.

Parris H. Chang

See also **Chiang Kai-shek; Chiang Soong Mei-ling; Pescadores; Quemoy; Taipei; Chiang Ching-kuo.**

Additional resources

The Anthropology of Taiwanese Society. Ed. by Emily M. Ahern and Hill Gates. Stanford, 1981. Reports on aspects of Taiwan, such as family, economics, and religion.
China's Island Frontier: Studies in the Historical Geography of Taiwan. Ed. by Ronald G. Knapp. Univ. of Hawaii Press, 1980.
Clough, Ralph N. *Island China.* Harvard, 1978.
Kuo, Shirley W. Y. *The Taiwan Economy in Transition.* Westview, 1983.

Taj Mahal, *TAHJ muh HAHL,* is one of the most beautiful and costly tombs in the world. The Indian ruler Shah Jahan ordered it built in memory of his favorite wife, Mumtaz Mahal, who died in 1629. The tomb stands at Agra in northern India. About 20,000 workers built it between about 1630 and 1650.

According to tradition, the Taj Mahal was designed by a Turkish architect. It is made of white marble and rests on a platform of red sandstone. At each corner of the platform stands a slender *minaret* (prayer tower). Each tower is 133 feet (40.5 meters) high. The building itself is 186 feet (56.7 meters) square. A dome covers the center of the building. It is 70 feet (21.3 meters) in diameter and 120 feet (36.6 meters) high. Passages from the Muslim holy book, the *Koran,* decorate the outside along with inlaid floral patterns. A central room contains two *cenotaphs* (monuments). Visitors can see the monuments through a carved alabaster screen. The bodies of Shah Jahan and his wife lie in a vault below. The tomb stands in a garden.   William J. Hennessey

See also **Asia** (picture); **India** (picture).

Tajikistan, *tah ЛНК ih STAN,* is a region that makes up the Tajik Soviet Socialist Republic, one of the 15 republics of the Soviet Union. It is also spelled *Tadzhikistan.* Tajikistan borders Afghanistan and China in a mountainous area of Central Asia (see **Union of Soviet Socialist Republics** [political map]). It covers 55,251 square miles (143,100 square kilometers), and has about 4,365,000 people. Most of the people are Tajiks. Their language is much like Farsi, the chief language of Iran. Dushanbe (formerly Stalinabad) is the capital and largest city of Tajikistan. Cotton is the chief crop. Other crops grown in the region include barley, millet, rice, and wheat. Tajikistan's huge Nurek Dam provides hydroelectric power for a large aluminum plant. The mines of the region produce antimony, fluorite, lead, molybdenum, tungsten, uranium, and zinc.   Theodore Shabad

Tajo River. See Tagus River.

Takakkaw Falls, *TAK uh kaw,* consist of a series of waterfalls in the Canadian Rockies. The main falls drop 1,200 feet (366 meters). The Takakkaw Falls are near the eastern border of British Columbia, near the village of Field. They are on the Yoho River in Canada's Yoho National Park. See also **Waterfall** (chart).

Takin, *TAH kihn,* is a large hoofed mammal closely related to goats, sheep, and musk oxen. Takins live in central, western, and southwestern China, in Burma, and in the Himalaya. They inhabit dense bamboo forests and thickets of rhododendrons on steep, rugged slopes.

Takins resemble musk oxen, with stout forelegs, a large head, and a thick neck. They have shaggy fur that varies from blackish-brown to golden or yellowish-white. A stripe runs along the middle of the back. Both males and females grow horns, but the females' horns are smaller. Takins measure up to $3\frac{1}{2}$ feet (107 centimeters) tall at the shoulder and weigh up to 770 pounds (350 kilograms). Males are heavier than females.

Takins are active mostly at dusk and dawn, but they may be active throughout the day in foggy or cloudy weather. Normally, they spend the daylight hours hidden in dense vegetation. During the warm months, takins feed primarily on young trees, grass, and tender herbs. In winter, they eat mostly the tips of bamboo stems and willow branches.

During the summer, takins gather in large herds led by an old *bull* (male). In winter, the herds are smaller and move to valleys at lower elevations. Takins mate in July or August. The *cow* (female) gives birth to a single young, called a *kid,* in March or April.

Scientific classification. Takins belong to the bovid family, Bovidae. They are *Budorcas taxicolor.*   Duane A. Schlitter

Zoological Society of San Diego

The takin is a large hoofed mammal that resembles a musk ox. The animal lives in Burma, the Himalaya, and parts of China.

Taklimakan Desert, *tahk lee mah kahn,* lies in northwestern China between the Tian Shan and Kunlun mountains. Its small hills and shifting sand dunes cover about 125,000 square miles (323,700 square kilometers) in the Xinjiang region. For location, see **China** (physical map).   Theodore H. E. Chen

Talbotype, *TAWL buh typ,* is a picture made by an early photographic process. The name honors its inventor, W. H. Fox Talbot, an English scientist. He first described the process in 1839. He made a sheet of paper sensitive to light by putting it in a series of baths of

International Museum of Photography at George Eastman House

A talbotype is a picture made by an early photographic process. The process was named after its inventor, W. H. Fox Talbot, who made this talbotype, called *Wood Sawers,* around 1845.

sodium-chloride and silver-nitrate solutions. Then he exposed the paper to light in a camera or to sunlight. The silver salts formed a negative image by turning dark where light fell upon them. After Fox Talbot treated this master negative with salt solution, he could print an endless number of paper positives.

In 1841, Fox Talbot increased the sensitivity of the paper by developing it in gallo-nitrate of silver and treating it in sodium thiosulfate. He called the new process *calotype.* Later, he called it *talbotype.* Fox Talbot's work, however, did not make such a clear picture as the daguerreotype (see **Daguerreotype**). The talbotype process was the first negative-positive process. After 1851, the wet-collodion technique, which used glass for negative material, replaced the talbotype process.
Beaumont Newhall

Talc (chemical formula, $Mg_3Si_4O_{10}(OH)_2$) is a soft mineral found in flat, smooth layers of rock, and in compact masses. It is so soft that it can be scratched with the fingernail, and it feels soapy or greasy. Talc is translucent, which means that it will allow light to go through, yet is not transparent. Talc is white, greenish, or dark gray. *Steatite* (soapstone) is a compact talc.

Talc has many commercial uses. It is sold in slabs or in powdered form. Slabs are used to line furnaces and heating stoves, and for electric insulation, because talc is a poor conductor of heat and electricity. It is ground up to make talcum powder. Powdered talc is also used in crayons, paint, paper, and soap.

The leading talc-producing nations include Finland, Japan, the Soviet Union, and the United States. Montana, New York, Texas, and Vermont are important talc-producing states.   John C. Butler

See also **Hardness; Soapstone; Mineral** (picture: Common minerals with nonmetallic luster).

Talent is a famous old unit of weight and value. The Hebrews, Babylonians, Greeks, and Romans used it. No coin of this denomination was ever *struck* (made), because such a coin would be too large. Instead, a certain number of other coins equaled a talent. The Hebrew silver talent equaled 3,000 shekels in silver. The gold talent had different weights and values in different places. The present use of the word *talent,* meaning *special ability,* may come symbolically from a Bible story (Matthew 25: 14-30). Burton H. Hobson

Talipes. See Clubfoot.

Talking book. See Handicapped (Special education); Library (Services for special·groups).

Tallahassee, *TAL uh HAS ee* (pop. 81,548; met. area pop. 190,220), is the capital of Florida. It lies in the northwest part of the state, near the Georgia border. For location, see **Florida** (political map). The name Tallahassee comes from an Indian word meaning *old town.*

The economy of Tallahassee is based on government activities. The city's industries include printing, publishing, seafood processing, and the production of computers and wood products. Tallahassee is the home of Florida Agricultural and Mechanical University, Florida State University, and Tallahassee Community College.

Tallahassee has been the capital since 1824, two years after Florida became a U.S. territory. A new, high-rise State Capitol opened in Tallahassee in 1977. Other new state government office buildings have been built since then. Tallahassee has a commission-manager government and is the seat of Leon County. Bob Stiff

See also **Florida** (pictures; Climate).

Tallchief, Maria (1925-   ), became the first American-trained ballerina of international importance. She was known especially for her technical brilliance. Tallchief danced with the Ballet Russe de Monte Carlo from 1942 to 1947, but her career was chiefly associated with the New York City Ballet. She danced with this company from 1947 to 1965.

Tallchief was born in Fairfax, Okla., the daughter of an Osage Indian father and a Scottish-Irish-Dutch mother. She was married to New York City Ballet director George Balanchine from 1946 to 1951. She created roles in many of his ballets, including *Orpheus* (1948) and *Scotch Symphony* (1952). Her dancing in Balanchine's

© Martha Swope
Maria Tallchief danced the title role in *The Firebird, above,* with American ballet dancer Francisco Moncion.

version of *Firebird* (1949) established her international reputation. Tallchief founded the Chicago City Ballet in 1980 and served as its artistic director from 1980 to 1987.
Dianne L. Woodruff

Talleyrand, *TAL ih rand* (1754-1838), was a French statesman famous for his diplomatic achievements under Napoleon I and at the Congress of Vienna. His full name was Charles Maurice de Talleyrand-Périgord, Prince de Bénévent. He was born in Paris. A childhood accident made him lame, and he was educated for a religious career. He became a priest in 1775. In 1789, he was named bishop of Autun, a high post in the church.

Supports state above church. Talleyrand was elected in 1789 to the States-General, the French parliament. He became a moderate leader of the French Revolution. He favored constitutional monarchy and signed the Declaration of the Rights of Man and of the Citizen. He was elected president of the National Assembly in 1790. Talleyrand won popularity for proposing that the government take church property to pay its debts. The Pope excommunicated him in 1791 for his part in giving control of the French Catholic Church to the state, and for taking an oath to the constitution.

Talleyrand was in England on a diplomatic mission when the Revolution took a radical turn in 1792, and he was exiled as a royalist sympathizer. After two years in England, he fled to America.

Joins Napoleon. Talleyrand was allowed to return to France in 1796. Through the influence of Madame de Staël, one of his friends, Talleyrand was made Minister of Foreign Affairs. While serving his nation, he decided to rebuild his fortune. In the famous XYZ Affair in 1797, he was accused of demanding bribes of the United States representatives (see **XYZ Affair**).

Talleyrand also decided to build his political future by attaching himself to Napoleon. He helped Napoleon replace the Directory, first with the Consulate in 1799, and then with the Empire in 1804. As Napoleon's adviser and foreign minister, he conducted delicate negotiations such as those that produced the Peace of Tilsit with Russia in 1807. See **Napoleon I.**

Deserts Napoleon. Napoleon depended on Talleyrand, but distrusted him. Talleyrand came to oppose Napoleon's conquests as injurious to France and to European peace. After 1807, Talleyrand resigned from office and became the center of the growing opposition to the emperor. His leadership was decisive in securing Napoleon's abdication and the restoration of the Bourbon kings in 1814. His diplomatic skill at the Congress of Vienna of 1814 and 1815 gave defeated France a powerful voice there (see **Vienna, Congress of**).

His last years. After 1815, the Bourbon court excluded Talleyrand from public affairs. But in 1830, when the Bourbons lost public confidence, Talleyrand helped steer a revolution toward constitutional monarchy under Louis Philippe. He became ambassador to Great Britain, where he guided negotiations that made Belgium independent, and brought France and Britain into alliance. Raymond O. Rockwood

See also **French Revolution.**

Additional resources

Bernard, Jack F. *Talleyrand: A Biography.* Putnam, 1973.
Orieux, Jean. *Talleyrand: The Art of Survival.* Knopf, 1974.

Tallinn, *TAHL lihn* (pop. 458,000), is the capital and largest city of Estonia, one of the 15 republics of the Soviet Union. It lies on the northern coast of Estonia, along the Gulf of Finland. For the location of Tallinn, see **Estonia** (map).

Tallinn is an important industrial and cultural center and seaport. Its products include industrial machinery, paper, and textiles. The city is best known for its many beautiful churches, castles, and other buildings that were erected from the 1200's to the 1500's.

Tallinn existed before the mid-1100's, but its founding date is unknown. It was the capital of the independent nation of Estonia from 1918 to 1940. In 1940, the Soviets seized Estonia and forced it to become part of the Soviet Union.   V. Stanley Vardys

Tallis, *TAL ihs,* **Thomas** (1505?-1585), was an English composer of religious vocal music during the Renaissance period. Tallis' earlier music was written for the Roman Catholic Church. It was complicated, with many interweaving voices known as *counterpoint,* and used Latin words. Later, under the Protestant Queen Elizabeth I, Tallis composed *anthems* (choral pieces with English words). His late music is less elaborate and more expressive. *Spem in alium,* a spectacular unaccompanied choral work called a *motet,* is often performed by choruses today.

With his younger colleague William Byrd, Tallis shared the post of organist at the Chapel Royal, the queen's private chapel. Elizabeth gave Tallis and Byrd a monopoly of music publishing. In 1575, the two composers published a famous collection called *Cantiones sacrae (Sacred Music).* Tallis' birthplace is unknown.

Joscelyn Godwin

Tallow is a fatty substance used in many products. It is obtained by *rendering* (melting) the fat of cattle, goats, or sheep. Tallow is classified as either *edible* or *inedible.* Edible tallow is used primarily as an ingredient in shortening for cooking and baking. Most inedible tallow produced in the United States is used to make animal feed, such as cattle feed and pet food. In addition, inedible tallow is treated with chemicals to make bar soap, soap flakes, and detergents (see **Detergent and soap** [How detergents are made]). Edible tallow is white and almost tasteless. Inedible tallow may be white, yellow, or brown.

Tallow is an important source of certain fatty acids that are used to make hundreds of everyday products. These products include automobile tires, cosmetics, detergents, lubricants, and plastics. Fatty acids obtained from tallow can do the job of many of the chemicals that are ordinarily manufactured from petroleum. Thus, tallow can help conserve the world's limited supply of petroleum.   Gerhard Maerker

Tallowtree is the name of several trees that produce a waxy substance that can be used like tallow for making candles. Today, mineral waxes usually are used instead of tallow in candle making. In the past, the tree most often used for its tallow was the *Chinese tallowtree.* The seeds of this tree hang on waxlike threads among the leaves. Workers crushed and boiled the capsules and seeds and skimmed off the tallow as it rose to the surface. The tallow was then melted and refined.

The Chinese tallowtree has been planted as a shade tree and along streets in the Southeastern United States

for more than 100 years. It now grows wild in areas along the Atlantic and Gulf coasts. Its leaves flutter in the slightest breeze and give it the appearance of a poplar. The leaves turn brilliant red in autumn.

Scientific classification. Tallowtrees belong to the spurge family, Euphorbiaceae. The Chinese tallowtree is *Sapium sebiferum.*   Harrison L. Flint

Talmud, *TAL muhd,* is a collection of Jewish religious and civil laws, together with scholarly interpretations of their meaning. The Talmud ranks second to the Bible as the most sacred and influential written work of the Jewish religion. Judaism considers the full-time study of the Talmud to be one of the most honorable occupations.

The Talmud consists of two parts, the *Mishnah* and the *Gemara.* The Mishnah is the written version of traditional Jewish oral law. Short passages of the Mishnah are followed by extremely thorough explanations, which make up the Gemara. The scholars who wrote the Gemara did not always agree in their interpretations of the Mishnah. As a result, the Gemara includes many debates on small details of Jewish law. It also discusses history and Jewish customs and includes Jewish folk tales.

The Talmud consists of 63 sections called *tractates,* which are divided into six *orders.* Each order deals with a different subject. For example, the order *Nashim* (Women) discusses marriage, divorce, and other matters that concern relationships between a man and a woman. Other orders cover such subjects as cleanliness, religious feasts, and civil and criminal law.

According to Jewish tradition, the Mishnah originated in the time of Moses during the 1200's B.C. and was memorized and handed down from generation to generation. Its contents were collected and written down from about A.D. 70 to 200. The Gemara, which has two versions, was written between about 200 and 500. The *Palestinian Gemara* was completed about 425 and the *Babylonian Gemara* about 500.   Jacob Neusner

See also **Akiva Baer ben Joseph.**

Additional resources

Adler, Morris. *The World of the Talmud.* 2nd ed. Schocken, 1963.
Neusner, Jacob. *Invitation to the Talmud: A Teaching Book.* Rev. ed. Harper, 1984.
Steinsaltz, Adin. *The Essential Talmud.* Basic Books, 1976.

Talon, *tah LOHN,* **Jean Baptiste,** *zhahn bah TEEST* (1625-1694), a French official, served from 1665 to 1672 as Intendant of Justice and Finance in Canada, which was then called New France. He put the Canadian colony on a sound economic basis. Talon established a royal shipyard in Quebec. In addition, he encouraged the search for iron, copper, and other minerals, and he urged the colonists to grow flax and weave their own linen and cloth. Talon was born in Châlons-sur-Marne, France.

Edward R. Adair

Tamales. See Mexico (Food).
Tamarack. See Larch.
Tamarin, *TAM uhr ihn,* is a type of small monkey that lives in tropical rain forests in Central and South America. It is closely related to, but slightly larger than, the marmoset (see **Marmoset**). Tamarins grow up to 12 inches (31 centimeters) long, not including the tail, which may be up to 17 inches (44 centimeters) long. The animals weigh up to 2 pounds.

There are 14 species of tamarins. Most are multicol-

San Diego Zoo

Lion tamarins have long, golden-orange hair. These small monkeys are found in tropical rain forests of eastern Brazil.

ored, with red, white, and brown the most common color patterns. Some species have long hair on the top of the head and showy mustaches. The *lion tamarins* of eastern Brazil have a mane of long, silky hair on the head and a bright golden-orange coloring. Lion tamarins are in danger of extinction. The growth of urban areas has destroyed much of their habitat.

Tamarins eat fruit, insects, frogs, and tree gums. They live in groups of up to 40 members and communicate with each other by using a wide variety of high-pitched calls. Infant tamarins cling to the backs of their parents or other family members.

Scientific classification. Tamarins belong to the tamarin and marmoset family, Callitrichidae. Lion tamarins are genus *Leontopithecus.* Other tamarins are genus *Saguinus.*

Roderic B. Mast

Tamarind, *TAM uhr ihnd,* is an attractive evergreen tree that grows in the tropics. It may grow 75 feet (23 meters) high. The tamarind develops small pale green leaves and tiny yellow flowers. Pods about 3 to 4 inches (8 to 10 centimeters) long contain the seeds of the tree. These pods contain an acid brown pulp used to prepare refreshing drinks. In India and Arabia, the pulp is

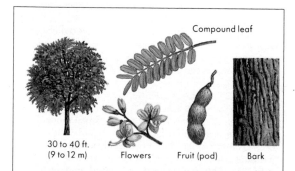

Compound leaf

30 to 40 ft.
(9 to 12 m)   Flowers   Fruit (pod)   Bark

WORLD BOOK illustration by John D. Dawson

The tamarind has compound leaves and tiny flowers. The pods contain an acid pulp used to make cakes and tart drinks.

pressed into cakes and sold as a delicacy. Ornamental tamarinds are grown in warm regions of the United States.

Scientific classification. The tamarind belongs to the pea family, Leguminosae. It is classified as *Tamarindus indica.*

Julian C. Crane

Tamayo, *tah MAH yoh,* **Rufino,** *roo FEE noh* (1899-   ), is an important Mexican painter. He is noted for his bold, brightly colored paintings of human figures, animals, and still lifes. Tamayo paints in a semiabstract style, in which he distorts forms to make them more expressive. His paintings reflect the influence of the folklore, history, and landscape of Mexico. But unlike other major Mexican artists of his day, Tamayo seldom emphasized nationalism or political ideology.

Tamayo was born in Oaxaca. In the early 1920's, he worked sketching ancient Indian sculpture for the National Museum of Anthropology in Mexico City. In the 1930's and early 1940's, his style was affected by his exposure to the works of the modern European painters Georges Braque, Joan Miró, and Pablo Picasso. Beginning about 1970, Tamayo's paintings became more abstract and philosophical, often exploring the individual's relation to the universe.   Judith Berg Sobré

Tambourine, *TAM buh REEN,* is a percussion instrument that consists of a narrow wooden or metal hoop

WORLD BOOK photo   WORLD BOOK illustration by Zorica Dabich

The tambourine is a hoop that has metal disks on the rim and a thin membrane stretched across one side. It can be played by shaking or striking.

with a thin sheet of plastic or animal skin stretched across one side. All tambourines have small metal disks attached to the hoop. Performers hold the tambourine in one hand. They play it by striking it with the other hand, by hitting it against the knee or upper leg, and by shaking it. The tambourine was made popular by Turkish soldiers called Janissaries, who played the instrument in military bands from the 1400's to the early 1800's. Western musicians began using the tambourine during the 1700's.   John H. Beck

See also **Music** (Percussion instruments).

Tamerlane, *TAM uhr LAYN* (1336?-1405), was an Asian conqueror who created by the sword a vast but short-lived empire. Tamerlane was also referred to as Timur the Lame.

Tamerlane was a Tartar, a Mongol Turk descended from Genghis Khan, another Asian conqueror. He was born of a chief's family near Samarkand in Turkestan. He was a well-educated, devout Muslim. As a youth, Tamerlane became noted for his athletic prowess. After 1358 he engaged in numerous wars. Tamerlane mounted the throne at Samarkand in 1369, and ruled an extensive central Asian kingdom. After 1369, his armies struck west and south into Afghanistan, Persia, India, and Asia Minor.

Tamerlane invaded India in 1398, sacked Delhi, and massacred most of its inhabitants. In 1401, he turned to Syria. He captured Baghdad, and in 1402 he completely destroyed the Turkish army that had been sent against him. He then captured Damascus and defeated Egyptian armies. Tamerlane was now the ruler of a vast empire with its heart in Turkestan. He next moved to conquer China. But before he could reach his objective, he died of fever in his camp. His empire soon fell apart.

T. Walter Wallbank

Tamm, Igor Yevgenevich (1895-1971), a Soviet physicist, shared the 1958 Nobel Prize for physics with Pavel A. Cherenkov and Ilya M. Frank. Tamm and Frank explained theoretically the origin of the blue light, or radiation, which Cherenkov discovered and which is now named for him.   R. T. Ellickson

Tammany, Society of, also called the Columbian Order, was founded in New York City in 1789 by William Mooney. The organization took its name from the Sons of Saint Tammany. This colonial society was named after an early Delaware Indian chief known for his wisdom. Tammany began as a "fraternity of patriots solemnly consecrated to the independence, the popular liberty, and the federal union of the country."

But Tammany soon came to have a political purpose. For many years, it wielded vast powers as a Democratic political machine in New York and New York City. Its popular name, Tammany Hall, came from the name of its headquarters building, located at 331 Madison Avenue, New York City. Many scandals have darkened the organization's history. The most famous one was exposed in 1871, when Tammany boss William M. Tweed and others were arrested and charged with defrauding New York City of several million dollars. The organization soon regained its power and dominated much of the city's politics until 1933.   Donald R. McCoy

See also **Bucktails; Nast, Thomas; Tweed, William M.; Cleveland, Grover** (Governor of New York).

Tampa, Fla. (pop. 271,523), is a major United States seaport and an important commercial and industrial center of the state. It ranks as Florida's third largest city. Only Jacksonville and Miami have more people. Tampa lies on the northeast shore of Tampa Bay (see **Florida** [political map]). St. Petersburg, Tampa's "twin city," lies about 15 miles (25 kilometers) southwest across the bay from Tampa. The metropolitan area of Tampa, St. Petersburg, and Clearwater has a population of 1,613,603. The area has grown rapidly since the mid-1900's.

In 1823, Robert J. Hackley, a pioneer from New York City, became the first United States citizen to settle in the area that is now Tampa. The U.S. Army built Fort Brooke there the next year. White settlers soon established a village near the fort. They named the village Tampa for the bay. The bay was named for an Indian village that once stood in the area.

Description. Tampa, the county seat of Hillsborough County, covers about 150 square miles (388 square kilo-

meters). This area includes about 65 square miles (168 square kilometers) of inland water. Part of the city lies on islands and peninsulas. Tampa's downtown area lies at the mouth of the Hillsborough River, near the point where the river empties into Hillsborough Bay. Hillsborough Bay is the northeast arm of Tampa Bay.

Latinos make up 13 per cent of Tampa's population. Most of the city's Latinos live in a neighborhood known as Ybor City that is located just northeast of downtown. Blacks make up 24 per cent of Tampa's population. Most blacks live in neighborhoods west and north of Ybor City.

Tampa is the home of the University of Tampa. The University of South Florida is just north of the city. The city's public schools form part of the Hillsborough County school system. The Tampa Public Library operates about 15 branch libraries.

Cultural attractions in Tampa include the Tampa Museum, the Hillsborough County Museum of Science and Industry, and the Henry B. Plant Museum on the campus of the University of Tampa. The Florida Symphony, Tampa Ballet, and San Carlo Opera Company perform in the Tampa Bay Performing Arts Center. The three-theater complex was completed in 1987. The Dark Continent/Busch Gardens, a famous theme park and zoo, attracts millions of visitors annually. Every February, the Gasparilla Festival is held in Tampa. The festival features a "pirate attack" on the city. The Florida State Fair is also held in Tampa every February. The Tampa Bay Buccaneers of the National Football League play in Tampa Stadium.

Economy of Tampa is based mainly on service industries. The most important service industries include banking, wholesale trade, and tourism. The tourist-related activities include the operation of hotels, motels, car rental agencies, and cruise ship lines. Data

William Koplitz, Southern Stock Photos

Tampa, a major seaport and an important commercial and industrial center, is one of Florida's largest cities.

processing and health care are also important service industries in Tampa. Food processing is the city's most important manufacturing activity. Tampa's leading food products are fish and soft drinks.

The Port of Tampa handles more cargo than any other Florida port—about 50 million short tons (45 million metric tons) yearly. The port's annual exports include about 10 million short tons (9 million metric tons) of phosphate ore from nearby mines. Fishing fleets based in Tampa catch large amounts of shrimp and other seafood. Nearby MacDill Air Force Base employs many residents of the Tampa area. Major airlines use Tampa International Airport. Passenger trains also serve Tampa.

Government. Tampa has a mayor-council form of government. The voters elect the mayor and the seven council members, all to four-year terms.

History. Calusa and Timucuan Indians lived near what is now Tampa Bay when white people first arrived. Several groups of Spanish explorers visited the area during the 1500's. One of these expeditions, led by Hernando de Soto, landed near the bay in 1539.

Robert J. Hackley, a pioneer from New York City, came to the area in 1823 and built a plantation. In 1824, the United States government moved many Seminole Indians to a reservation near Tampa Bay. The Indians had fought to keep their hunting grounds in northern Florida, but had been defeated by the Army. The Army built Fort Brooke on Tampa Bay to supervise the Seminole. Tampa grew up around the fort. The city was incorporated in 1855 and had a population of 885 in 1860. Union troops occupied Tampa during the Civil War (1861-1865).

Henry B. Plant, an Atlanta, Ga., industrialist, spent millions of dollars during the 1880's and early 1890's to develop Tampa. He built a railroad that linked Tampa with the North and established the city's tourist industry. In 1886, a Florida tobacco processor named Vicente Martinez Ybor founded a cigar industry in what is now Ybor City. Phosphate mining began near Tampa in 1888. The city served as a military base during the Spanish-American War (1898) and as a shipbuilding center during World War I (1914-1918). By 1920, 51,608 people lived in Tampa.

Real estate speculation in Florida attracted thousands of people to Tampa during the 1920's. The city had 101,161 people by 1930. For an account of the real estate boom, see **Florida** (History [The early 1900's]). Shipbuilding thrived in Tampa during World War II (1939-1945), and the Army Air Forces operated three bases nearby. The 1950's brought industrial growth to the city. By 1960, Tampa had 274,970 people.

In the 1960's and 1970's, Tampa undertook several urban renewal projects. One project eliminated some slums near the Hillsborough River. New construction on the site included apartment buildings, a convention hall, a new city library, and office towers.

Tampa has grown at a rapid rate since the late 1970's. The growth included a boom in the construction of new buildings. More than a dozen new office towers were constructed in downtown Tampa in the late 1970's and early 1980's. A major new office complex was completed near Tampa International Airport in the mid-1980's. The airport itself was expanded in the late 1980's to accommodate more passengers and freight. The Tampa Bay Performing Arts Center opened in 1987.

Tampa's rapid growth has caused problems. Some public services and facilities have been unable to keep pace with the growth. For example, roads and highways have become overcrowded.   Peter O. Muller

Tampere, *TAHM puh* RAY (pop. 167,344; met. area pop. 249,606), is Finland's second largest city and industrial center. Only Helsinki has more people and industry. Tampere lies in southern Finland between Lakes Näsijärvi and Pyhäjärvi. For location, see **Finland** (political map).

Tampere's chief industries are food and metal processing and paper and textile production. The Tammerkoski River and waterfalls run through the city. Tampere has abundant parks and other recreational areas. It is the home of the University of Tampere. Most of the city's people live in apartments. Some of its suburbs stand on beautiful ridges overlooking the lakes.

During the Middle Ages, the site of what is now Tampere was an important market and milling center. King Gustavus III of Sweden and Finland established Tampere as a city in 1779. The city began its industrial growth in the mid-1800's.   Pekka Kalevi Hamalainen

Tampico, *tam PEE koh* (pop. 239,970; met. area pop. 375,029), is the second most important port in Mexico, after Veracruz. It stands 7 miles (11 kilometers) west of the Gulf of Mexico on the Pánuco River (see **Mexico** [political map]). Tampico serves as a refining center for Mexico's petroleum industry and is the chief outlet for oil exports. A mild winter climate and good hunting and fishing make it a favorite resort center. Spaniards settled the city in the 1500's.   James D. Riley

Tana, Lake. See Lake Tana.

Tanager, *TAN uh juhr,* is the common name given a subfamily of American birds, many of which have brilliant red, blue, or green feathers. Tanagers are from 6 to 8 inches (15 to 20 centimeters) long, and are usually found in the forests, where they feed on insects, fruits,

Ron Austing

The summer tanager nests in the Southern United States. The male, *above,* is also called the *summer redbird.*

and flowers. There are more than 200 species of tanagers, most of which live in Central and South America. Only a few species of tanagers live in the United States.

The well-known *scarlet tanager* has a loud, cheery song somewhat like that of the robin. Scarlet tanagers nest in the eastern United States and as far north as Eastern Canada. They are sometimes called *firebirds.* The male has bright red feathers, with velvety black wings and tail. The female is dull yellow below and olive green above, with darker wings and tail. The tanager builds its frail, saucer-shaped nest near the end of a horizontal limb. The female lays three to five bluish-green eggs with reddish-brown markings.

In the Southern States, the *summer tanager* is a familiar bird. It has rosy-red feathers. Its nesting habits are much like those of the scarlet tanager. The *western tanager,* or *Louisiana tanager,* lives in summer from the Rockies to the Pacific Coast. The male has a black back, tail, and wings, red head, and yellow underparts.

The tanagers eat many types of insects, including some insect pests. The western tanager has a great fondness for cherries and may harm cherry orchards.

Scientific classification. The tanagers make up the tanager subfamily, Thraupinae. The scarlet tanager is *Piranga olivacea;* the summer tanager is *P. rubra;* the western tanager is *P. ludoviciana.* Bertin W. Anderson

See also **Bird** (picture: Birds' eggs).

Tananarive. See Antananarivo.

Taney, *TAW nee,* **Roger Brooke** (1777-1864), was one of the great chief justices of the United States. But the merit of his work is clouded by his decision in the Dred Scott case, which helped bring on the Civil War. Taney held that Congress had no power to abolish slavery in the territories.

Taney was born in Calvert County, Maryland, and attended Dickinson College. He began practicing law in Annapolis, Md., in 1799. He entered politics, and served several years in the state Senate. He also gained a high reputation as a lawyer. In 1831, President Andrew Jackson appointed him U.S. attorney general and made him a trusted adviser.

Brown Bros.

Roger B. Tanoy

Jackson was opposed to the United States Bank and decided to end its influence by withdrawing the government deposits over the opposition of Congress (see **Bank of the United States**). In 1833, he appointed Taney secretary of the treasury to have him withdraw the funds. The Senate was so angered that it refused to confirm Taney's appointment, and he retired to private life.

In 1835, Jackson appointed Taney an associate justice of the Supreme Court, but the Senate refused to confirm the appointment. In 1836, the Senate majority changed. Jackson named Taney as chief justice, and the Senate approved. Taney favored states' rights but not at the expense of basic national powers. He kept most of John Marshall's broad interpretation of the Constitution.

Jerre S. Williams

See also **Dred Scott decision.**

Tang dynasty, *tahng,* was a series of rulers who governed China from A.D. 618 to 907. Many historians consider the Tang period the golden age of Chinese civilization. The dynasty's capital city, Chang'an (now Xian), became one of the great cultural centers of the world. Artists, poets, scholars, and government and religious leaders from many countries visited Chang'an and the Chinese coastal trading centers.

The Tang rulers united China and established a strong central government. They carefully hand-picked their chief officials. The Tang emperors also set up a council of ministers to act as advisers. In addition, the emperors sent inspectors into the provinces of China to check on the activities of local governors.

The Tang rulers also promoted trade, which became the basis of the empire's great prosperity. Jade, porcelain, rice, silks, spices, tea, and other Chinese products flowed to India, the Middle East, and Europe along trade routes opened by the Tang emperors.

During the Tang period, the Chinese invented block printing, which soon replaced the handwritten scriptures of the Chinese Buddhists. In 868, the Chinese produced the *Diamond Sutra,* the world's first block-printed book.

The rise of the dynasty. The Tang dynasty followed the Sui dynasty, which had ruled China from A.D. 589 to 618. Li Yuan, an aristocrat, overthrew the Sui emperor and became the first Tang ruler (see **Li Yuan**). He set up his capital at Chang'an in northwestern China. *Chang'an* meant *long peace,* but China was soon torn by civil war. In addition, a struggle for power developed among the nobility. In 627, Li Yuan turned the control of China over to his son, Li Shimin, who took the name Tang Taizong (also spelled *Tang Tai-tsung*). Taizong ruled for 22 years and became one of the greatest emperors in Chinese history.

Taizong was a powerful leader. He destroyed his competitors for the throne, began an alliance with the Korean state of Silla, and forced Turkish nomads out of Northern China. His armies conquered parts of Tibet and Turkestan, opening overland trade routes from China to India and central Asia. The trade routes not only brought great wealth to the empire, but they also promoted religious and cultural exchange. The routes gave Christian and other foreign missionaries an over land entrance into China and allowed Chinese Buddhist pilgrims to visit India.

Taizong reorganized the administration of the empire. He built colleges to help select and train officials for government work. Although Buddhism was the country's main religion, Taizong knew that many Chinese who could help him carry out his programs followed Confucianism. As a result, he named many Confucians to high government posts.

In 649, Tang Gaozong (also spelled *Tang Gao-tsung*) became emperor. But his wife, Empress Wu, soon took control of the government. Gaozong died in 683, and his son became emperor—but in name only. Empress Wu continued to control the government, and she became the second great leader of the Tang dynasty.

Empress Wu governed China with a great amount of skill. She appointed able ministers to major government posts and had the complete loyalty of her advisers and officials. Empress Wu maintained the high reputation of the Tang dynasty abroad because of her political brilliance. The empress also showed great favoritism to Buddhism and promoted art and literature. During the late 600's, Tibet forced the Chinese out of Turkestan. To protect China's trade routes there, Empress Wu sent her armies into the region and recovered the Tang territory.

The middle years. Tang Xuanzong, the grandson of Empress Wu, became emperor in 712. Xuanzong, also known as Ming Huang, was the last of the three great

The Tang Empire about A.D. 750

This map shows the land ruled by the Tang emperors from their capital at Chang'an. The Tang Empire reached its greatest size under Emperor Xuanzong. It controlled territory from eastern China to Persia. Arabs defeated Chinese armies at Athlach in A.D. 751. This battle marked the end of Tang power in Turkestan and the closing of overland trade routes to the west.

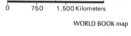

- Tang Empire
- Area of Islamic influence
- Trade route
- • Major city
- China boundary today
- ∿∿∿ Great Wall

| 0 | 750 | 1,500 Miles |
| 0 | 750 | 1,500 Kilometers |

WORLD BOOK map

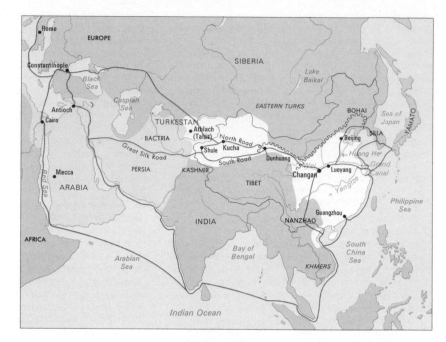

Tang rulers. During his reign, China produced some of its best artists and such great poets as Li Bo (also spelled *Li Po*) and Du Fu (also spelled *Tu Fu*). Xuanzong's economic programs, including the development of new farming regions in the Yangtze Valley, greatly increased China's wealth.

In 747, China reached its peak of influence in western Asia. Tang armies invaded Bactria and Kashmir and defeated an Arab-Tibetan alliance that had been formed against China's allies in central Asia. But in 751, a revolt in Turkestan closed China's trade routes to the Middle East.

When Xuanzong was more than 60 years old, he fell in love with his son's wife and took her as his mistress. She soon gained control over the emperor and made him appoint a cunning Manchurian military governor, An Lushan, to the royal court. In 755, An Lushan organized a rebellion against Xuanzong and captured and briefly occupied the capital of Chang'an. In 756, Xuanzong turned the throne over to his son, Suzong. In 766, a combination of Chinese and foreign troops defeated the rebel armies of An Lushan. But during the rebellion, army generals and military governors in the provinces had increased their power, weakening the central government.

In addition, Tibet had been united into a powerful kingdom while Suzong was fighting An Lushan. In 763, Tibetan forces invaded China. Forces of the Tang rulers battled the Tibetans in northwestern China for about 80 years. This long conflict further weakened the Tang dynasty.

The fall of the dynasty. Border wars and rebellions in the provinces troubled China between 766 and 868. Yet the Tang dynasty remained prosperous, largely because of a new tax system. The Chinese had been required to pay their taxes with labor and goods. Under the new system, they could also pay with cash. This new system was more efficient than the older one and provided increased income.

In 868, a second long and powerful military revolt broke out against the Tang dynasty. In 881, peasant rebels led by Huang Chao captured the capital of Chang'an. One by one, the governors of the provinces declared their independence from the central government of the Tang dynasty.

In 907, the Tang dynasty finally came to an end. Until the Song dynasty gained control of China in 960, the country was governed by a series of short-lived military dynasties.   Eugene Boardman

See also **China** (The Tang dynasty; picture: Multicolor ceramics).

The Snite Museum of Art, University of Notre Dame, Gift of Mr. and Mrs. Lester Wolfe

Figures of four female musicians illustrate the simple charm of pottery figures of the Tang dynasty. The figures were created to be placed in a tomb when a person was buried.

Additional resources

The Cambridge History of China, Vol. 3, Part 1: Sui and Tang China, 589-906. Ed. by Denis Twitchett. Cambridge, 1979.
Reischauer, Edwin O. *Ennin's Travels in Tang China.* Ronald, 1955. A Japanese monk tells of his visit to China during the 800's.

Tanganyika. See Tanzania.

Tanganyika, Lake. See Lake Tanganyika.

Tangelo, *TAN juh loh,* is a mandarin citrus fruit that results from cross-pollination between a tangerine and a grapefruit. The word tangelo comes from *tang*erine and pom*elo,* another name for grapefruit. Tangelos have thin peels and a delicious flavor. Important American varieties include the Minneola and the Orlando. The Ugli is a Jamaican tangelo that is widely grown in the West Indies.   Wilfred F. Wardowski

See also **Tangerine; Tangor.**

Tangerine, *TAN juh REEN,* is the popular name for a citrus fruit of the mandarin group. These fruits look like oranges, but are smaller and flatter, peel more easily, and the sections separate more readily. The tangerine is an orange-red mandarin fruit which originated in South-

WORLD BOOK illustration by Kate Lloyd Jones Linden Artists Ltd.

The tangerine is a popular citrus fruit. Tangerines are smaller than oranges, peel more easily, and have a delicate taste.

east Asia. It has a thin, fragrant peel. The fruit is delicate, but the tree is more resistant to cold than is the orange tree. Varieties of tangerines include Clementine, Dancy, Ponkan, and hybrid varieties such as Kinnow, Robinson, Sunburst, and Wilking. In the United States, tangerines are grown in Arizona, California, and Florida. They are also grown in Brazil, China, Italy, Japan, and Spain.

Scientific classification. The tangerine belongs to the rue family, Rutaceae. It is *Citrus reticulata.*   Wilfred F. Wardowski

See also **Tangelo; Tangor.**

Tangier, *tan JEER,* also spelled *Tanger,* is a region on the Atlantic coast of Morocco (see **Morocco** [map]). It covers 144 square miles (365 square kilometers) between the sea and the Rif Mountains. It includes the city of Tangier (pop. 187,894).

Location and description. The city of Tangier lies opposite Gibraltar at the western opening to the Mediterranean Sea. Tangier ranks second to Casablanca among Morocco's seaports. From the sea, the city looks like an amphitheater, with rows of white houses lining the hills.

Most of the people of the Tangier region are Muslim Berbers or Arabs. Spanish, French, and Arabic are the

official languages. The city of Tangier has few industries, but it ranks as an important shipping center.

History. Portugal, Spain, and England held Tangier at different times from the 1400's until the late 1600's, when the Moors gained control. The Moors held the city until 1924, but granted special privileges to several European countries. In 1925, an international zone was established in Tangier, under the control of leading world powers. Spanish forces occupied Tangier in World War II. In 1945, Tangier regained its international status. It became a part of Morocco after Morocco gained its independence from France and Spain in 1956. That same year, the sultan of Morocco called a conference of the nine nations that formerly controlled Tangier. They voted to end Tangier's international status, and to give up most of their former rights in the area.   Hibberd V. B. Kline, Jr.

Tango, *TANG goh,* was the first Latin American dance to gain great international popularity. The tango is a ballroom dance in slow $\frac{2}{4}$ time with an irregularly accented beat. The dancing couple glide smoothly through a variety of step patterns. They alternate long, slow steps with short, quick steps, and strike elaborate poses. The music for this dance is also called *tango,* and is very dramatic.

Today's tango probably began as an Argentine dance called the *milonga* and includes elements of the Andalusian tango from Spain and the Cuban *habanera.* At first, the tango was considered indecent. But people liked the steps and rhythm so much that they modified the dance into a more acceptable form. The tango was popularized in the United States about 1912 by Vernon and Irene Castle, a famous ballroom dance team. It also became popular in Paris and London.   Dianne L. Woodruff

Tangor, *TAN jawr,* is a citrus fruit that belongs to the mandarin family (see **Mandarin**). It is produced by cross-pollination between a tangerine and an orange. The parents of tangors are seldom known for certain, except when the fruits result from carefully controlled plant breeding programs. The *Temple* and the *Honey Tangerine* are among the most important tangors cultivated today.   Wilfred F. Wardowski

Tank is an armored combat vehicle. Most tanks travel on continuous tracks. They carry such weapons as cannons, machine guns, and missile launchers. In most tanks, these weapons are mounted in a revolving structure called a *turret.* A tank has a crew of three to five members.

Tanks are used to attack other armored vehicles, infantry, and ground targets; and to fire on aircraft. Armies throughout the world have a total of more than 150,000 tanks. The Soviet Union has over 50,000, and the United States has more than 10,000. Tanks are classified as *main battle tanks* or as *armored reconnaissance vehicles.* Main battle tanks weigh from 35 to 60 short tons (32 to 54 metric tons). Armored reconnaissance vehicles weigh from 10 to 25 short tons (9 to 23 metric tons).

Performance. Tanks travel as fast as 50 miles (80 kilometers) per hour on level ground. They average only 10 to 20 miles (16 to 32 kilometers) per hour on rough terrain. Tanks can climb and descend slopes as steep as 30 degrees, and can turn around within their own length.

The newest tanks have 100- to 125-millimeter guns, which can be combined with computer fire control systems. These guns can hit small targets 1 mile (1.6 kilometers) away, even if the tank is moving. The new tanks also

The crew and basic parts of a tank

This diagram of a U.S. Army M60A1 main battle tank shows the position of the crew members, plus some parts of the vehicle. The crew consists of a commander and three other people. One crew member drives the tank, one loads the guns, and the other two fire the guns. The tank has a 105-mm gun and two machine guns.

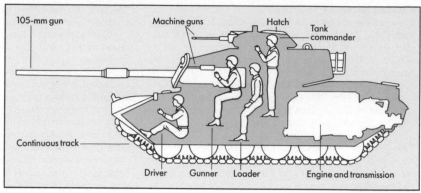

WORLD BOOK illustration by Richard B. Fickle

U.S. Army

A main battle tank, such as the U.S. Army's M60A1 shown above, is used to attack other armored vehicles, infantry, and various ground targets; and for defense against aircraft.

have heavy armor that can withstand attack by conventional and nuclear weapons.

History. Tanks got their name from the British, who developed them during World War I (1914-1918). While they were being built, the British called them water tanks to conceal their purpose. The British first used tanks against the Germans in the Battle of the Somme in 1916. The early tanks were slow and clumsy, but they were used successfully in the Battle of Cambrai in 1917.

During World War II (1939-1945), all the warring nations used tanks. German tank units won important victories over Poland, France, and the Soviet Union. In 1943, the Soviets defeated the Germans at Kursk, in the Soviet Union, in the greatest tank battle in history. Thousands of tanks fought in this battle. In 1944, Allied tanks swept into Germany, helping to assure victory in Europe.

Since World War II, tanks have taken part in many regional wars, especially in the Middle East. More than 6,000 tanks were used in the Arab-Israeli war of 1973. Nearly half the tanks were destroyed in only 18 days of combat. During this war, precision-guided weapons were used against tanks for the first time. Despite the high tank losses, the vehicles were effective when given infantry and artillery support.   Kenneth S. Brower

See also **Army, U.S.** (Armor); **Periscope; World War I** (picture); **World War II** (picture).

Tanka. See **Japanese literature.**

Tanker is a ship designed to carry liquid cargo. Most tankers transport oil, but some carry such products as molasses, wine, and even coal, grain, and iron ore.

A tanker consists basically of a series of as many as 25 tanks, the walls of which are formed in part by the hull. It has a crew of 25 to 40 people. They live in the deckhouse, which forms part of an enclosed area called the *superstructure.* The superstructure is on the main deck, above the engines. It has five or six stories, with the bridge on top. Some larger tankers have a second superstructure for the bridge halfway between the bow and stern. Cargo pumps and piping line the main deck.

Kinds of tankers. There are three chief kinds of tankers: (1) oil tankers, (2) ore-bulk-oil carriers, and (3) liquefied natural gas carriers.

Oil tankers carry crude oil and refined petroleum products. The hull forms the outside of the tanks. *Bulkheads* (walls) run the length and width of the ship and divide the tanks into compartments. This type of construction strengthens the hull. It also enables an oil tanker to carry several products, such as diesel fuel, gasoline, and kerosene, at the same time.

An extra large type of oil tanker, called a *supertanker* or *very large crude carrier (VLCC),* was developed during the 1960's. The largest supertanker measures more than 1,300 feet (396 meters) long and 200 feet (61 meters) wide. It can hold over 500,000 short tons (450,000 metric tons) of oil. When filled, a supertanker's hull extends as much as 92 feet (28 meters) under the water line. Supertankers cruise at speeds of about 15 knots (nautical miles per hour) and are extremely difficult to maneuver. A VLCC with its engines off may travel over 3 miles (5 kilometers) before stopping completely.

Supertankers sail from Africa and the Middle East to Canada, the Caribbean, Europe, and Japan. In Europe, Japan, and the Persian Gulf, VLCC's load and unload their cargo through underwater pipelines provided by offshore ports. The Deepwater Port Act of 1974 authorized the construction of offshore ports for VLCC's in the United States. The first of these ports, located off the coast of Louisiana, opened in 1981. It has a capacity of 1.4 million barrels of oil a day.

Ore-bulk-oil carriers (O/B/O's) carry such cargoes as bauxite, coal, grain, and iron, as well as oil. They have tanks and pumps for storing and unloading liquids. They also have large hatches on the main deck for loading and unloading dry cargo. Such ships can carry oil in one direction and dry bulk cargo on the return voyage.

E. R. Degginger

Tankers transport chiefly liquid cargo, but some carry such dry cargoes as coal, grain, and iron ore. Oil tankers, such as the one shown above, are divided into compartments. This enables the ship to carry more than one product at the same time.

Liquefied natural gas (LNG) carriers were developed in the 1960's. When natural gas is chilled to −260° F (−162° C), it shrinks to about $\frac{1}{600}$ of its volume and becomes liquid. Plants on shore liquefy natural gas and pump it into spherical insulated tanks on the tankers. These tanks rise high above the decks.

Water pollution by tankers ranks as one of the chief problems of the oil industry. Tankers spill more than 2 million short tons (1.8 million metric tons) of oil into the world's oceans annually. This pollution results from accidents and from normal ship operations.

The oil industry has taken various steps to reduce pollution. Some tankers have double hulls to minimize the loss of oil in accidents. Methods have been developed to keep spilled oil from spreading over the water and to remove spills from its surface.   Joseph E. Kasputys

See also Ship (Tankers; pictures); Petroleum (diagram: How oil is transported).

Tanner, Henry Ossawa, *AHS uh wuh* (1859-1937), was an American painter. During the early 1880's, he studied under the noted artist Thomas Eakins at the Pennsylvania Academy of the Fine Arts in Philadelphia. Eakins encouraged Tanner to paint professionally.

Tanner's early works reflect the influence of Eakins' realistic style. Tanner, a black, first gained recognition for his pictures of black life on plantations. Perhaps his best-known early work is *The Banjo Lesson*.

In 1891, Tanner moved to Europe to continue his studies and to escape the racial prejudice he had experienced in the United States. He settled in Paris and began to paint pictures with religious themes. These works show the influence of the Dutch artist Rembrandt in their glowing, warm colors and dramatic contrasts between light and dark areas. Tanner was born in Pittsburgh and died in Paris.   Sarah Burns

Tannhäuser, *TAHN hoy zuhr* or *TAN hoy zuhr,* was a German *minnesinger* (minstrel) of the 1200's. He led a restless life and even went to the Holy Land on a crusade. A ballad of the 1500's tells the story that one evening, as he was riding by the Hörselberg in Thuringia, a beautiful woman appeared before him. He recognized her as the goddess Venus. He followed her to a palace inside the mountain and spent seven years there.

Finally, Tannhäuser left Venus and went on a pilgrimage to Rome to seek forgiveness for his sins. The pope said that just as the staff he held in his hand could never blossom, so would Tannhäuser's sins never be forgiven. Tannhäuser went sorrowfully back to Germany. Three days later, the pope's staff miraculously bore flowers. Messengers hurried to seek out Tannhäuser, but he had gone back to Venus. Richard Wagner's opera *Tannhäuser* is based on this legend.   James F. Poag

Tannic acid, also called tannin, is an organic compound obtained chiefly from the *galls* (unnatural growths) of oak tree leaves. Most other trees also contain some tannin. The word tannin comes from the early French word *tan,* which meant *bark of an oak.*

Tannins are used to tan animal hides. Hides contain

Oil painting on canvas; Collis P. Huntington
Memorial Library, Hampton Institute, Hampton, Va.

Tanner's *The Banjo Lesson* shows the painter's sympathetic treatment of life among Southern blacks during the late 1800's.

gelatin that combines with the tannin, converting the hides to leather. Tannins are also used as *mordants* (dye-fixatives), and in manufacturing inks.

Tannins from different kinds of trees have various chemical formulas. The most important difference is the color produced in the tanned leather. Tannic acid is a bulky powder, ranging from light yellow to brown in color. It is soluble in water.   John E. Leffler

See also **Gall; Leather** (Tanning).

Tanning. See **Leather; Tannic acid.**

Tansy, *TAN zee,* is a plant related to the thistle. The tansy first grew in Europe, but is now found throughout North America. It is usually grown in gardens, but also grows wild. The leaves and flowers of the tansy have a bitter taste and a strong odor. The leaves were once used in flavoring. These dark green leaves give off an oil which is known as *oil of tansy.* This oil is poisonous, but is used to some extent in medicines. The flowers of the tansy are yellow.

Scientific classification. Tansies make up the genus *Tanacetum* in the family Compositae.   Margaret R. Bolick

Tantalum, *TAN tuh luhm,* is a rare metallic element. At normal temperatures, a film of tantalum oxide forms on the surface of tantalum and protects the metal from corrosion. The electronics industry uses tantalum in the manufacture of capacitors because the tantalum oxide film serves as an efficient insulator. The metal is also widely used in building nuclear reactors, and in certain aircraft and missile parts. Tantalum oxide is an important component of camera lenses because it increases the *refracting* (light bending) properties of glass. In addition, tantalum does not react with bodily fluids, and it is therefore ideal for such surgical applications as bone repair and internal stitching.

Tantalum occurs in nature with the element niobium in the minerals columbite and tantalite. Tantalum is difficult to separate from niobium because of the chemical similarity of the two elements. Commercially, tantalum is obtained as a by-product in the extraction of tin from mineral deposits in Malaysia and Nigeria.

The chemical symbol for tantalum is Ta. The element's atomic number is 73, and its atomic weight is 180.948. The metal has high melting and boiling points. It melts at 2996° C and boils at 5425° C ($\pm$100° C). Tantalum was discovered in 1802 by the Swedish chemist Anders Ekeberg.   R. Craig Taylor

See also **Element, Chemical** (table).

Tantalus, *TAN tuh luhs,* was a king of Lydia in Greek mythology. He was the son of Zeus and the nymph Pluto. Tantalus was punished because he killed his son Pelops and served him to the gods as food. Later, Pelops was restored to life. In Hades, the land of the dead, Tantalus was forced to stand under threat of a hanging rock and up to his chin in water. When he tried to drink, the water always vanished. Fruit hung above him. When he tried to eat the fruit, the winds whirled the branches out of reach. The word *tantalize,* which means to tease or torment by keeping something out of reach, is taken from his name.   Justin M. Glenn

Tanzania, *TAN zuh NEE uh* or *tan ZAN ee uh,* is a large country in eastern Africa. It consists of Tanganyika, a large area on the African mainland; and Zanzibar, a group of several islands in the Indian Ocean. The largest island is also called Zanzibar. The second largest is

called Pemba. Both Tanganyika and Zanzibar were British possessions until the early 1960's, when they became independent. In 1964, Tanganyika and Zanzibar united to form one nation, officially called the United Republic of Tanzania. Dar es Salaam is Tanzania's capital and largest city (see **Dar es Salaam**).

Tanzania has much wildlife and beautiful scenery. The country is noted for its buffaloes, elephants, giraffes, leopards, lions, zebras, and many varieties of antelope. Such animals thrive in such protected areas as Serengeti National Park on the Serengeti Plain, Ngorongoro Crater, Lake Manyara National Park, and the Selous Game Reserve. Africa's highest mountain, Kilimanjaro, rises 19,340 feet (5,895 meters) in the north. Lake Victoria, Africa's largest lake, extends into northern Tanzania. Lake Tanganyika, the world's longest freshwater lake, forms part of the western border.

Government

A president heads Tanzania's government. The president is nominated by the country's only legal political party—the Chama Cha Mapinduzi (CCM), or the Revolutionary Party of Tanzania. The CCM's choice for president must be approved in an election by the people of Tanzania. The country's legislature—the National Assembly—has 244 members. Most of the members are elected by the people, from candidates nominated by the CCM. All of the Assembly members and the president of Tanzania serve five-year terms. For purposes of local government, the mainland is divided into 20 regions, and the islands into 5 regions.

People

Tanzania has a population of about 25 million. About 95 per cent of the people live on the mainland, and about 5 per cent live on the islands. Almost all of the people are black Africans. The blacks are divided into about 120 ethnic groups. The largest group, the Sukuma, live just south of Lake Victoria and make up about 13 per cent of the country's population. Other important black ethnic groups include the Chagga, the Makonde, and the Nyamwezi. Tanzania's population also includes Arabs and people of Asian descent. English and Swahili are the official languages (see **Swahili**).

About a third of all Tanzanians follow traditional Afri-

Facts in brief

Capital: Dar es Salaam.
Official languages: English and Swahili.
Area: 364,900 sq. mi. (945,087 km²).
Population: *Estimated 1989 population*—25,079,000; density, 69 persons per sq. mi. (27 persons per km²); distribution, 82 per cent rural, 18 per cent urban. *1978 census*—17,512,611. *Estimated 1994 population*—29,499,000.
Chief products: *Agriculture*—bananas, beef, cashews, cassava, cloves, coconuts, coffee, corn, milk, rice sisal, sugar cane. *Manufacturing*—food processing, textiles.
National anthem: "Mungo Ibariki Africa" ("God the Almighty Bless Africa").
Flag: The flag combines the old Tanganyika and Zanzibar flag colors in diagonal stripes. Green symbolizes the land, yellow represents mineral wealth, black stands for the people, and blue symbolizes the sea. See **Flag** (picture: Flags of Africa).
Money: *Basic unit*—shilling. See **Money** (table).

Tanzania

Legend:

- National park (N.P.) or reserve
- International boundary
- Road
- Railroad
- ⊛ National capital
- • Other city or town
- + Elevation above sea level

WORLD BOOK map

can religions. Christians and Muslims also make up about a third of the population.

About two-thirds of all Tanzanian adults can read and write. The government provides free education at the elementary school, high school, and university levels. More than 90 per cent of Tanzania's children attend elementary school. But only about 5 per cent of them go to high school. The University of Dar es Salaam is Tanzania's largest university. The university has about 4,000 students.

Land

The mainland's 500-mile (800-kilometer) coastal strip is covered with mangrove swamps and coconut palm groves. Temperatures on the coastal strip are always high. The mainland of Tanzania rises from the coast to plateaus that reach about 4,000 feet (1,200 meters) above sea level. The plateaus are hot, dry grasslands that have patches of thorn trees and open woodlands.

Several mountains and mountain ranges rise above the plateaus region. They include Kilimanjaro and the Usambara Mountains in northeastern Tanzania. Near the country's western border, the plateaus region drops in a steep, rugged slope to the basins of Lake Nyasa and Lake Tanganyika. These two basins are part of the Great Rift Valley that runs north and south through eastern Africa.

The Zanzibar Channel, 22 miles (35 kilometers) wide, separates Zanzibar Island from the mainland. Pemba lies 25 miles (40 kilometers) northeast of Zanzibar Island. Zanzibar Island, the largest coral island off the African coast, covers 640 square miles (1,658 square kilometers).

Pemba covers 380 square miles (984 square kilometers). The islands have a hot, tropical climate.

Economy

Tanzania is chiefly an agricultural country and most of the people are farmers. They raise crops on the coastal plain, along the lake shores, and in the highlands. Their

Odyssey Productions

A market in Dar es Salaam, the capital and largest city of Tanzania, attracts shoppers seeking food and other goods. This building has replaced many of the city's open-air markets.

Zebras and gnus graze on the Serengeti Plain in northern Tanzania. Abundant wildlife live in the country on land set aside by the government as game reserves.

M. Philip Kahl, Jr., Photo Researchers

most important food crops are bananas, cassava, and corn. They also raise beans, beef and dairy cattle, mangoes, rice, sugar cane, and tobacco. Cooperative farms and plantations produce cashews, coffee, cotton, tea, and *sisal* (a plant used to make rope).

Zanzibar Island and Pemba are noted for their cloves and coconuts. Tanzanians catch fish in lakes Tanganyika and Victoria and in the Indian Ocean. Important exports are cashews, cloves, coffee, cotton, and sisal fibers. Factories process foods and manufacture textiles.

Dar es Salaam, Tanga, and Mtwara are important seaports. Tanzania's main international airports are in Dar es Salaam and near Arusha.

Tanzania has three daily newspapers and six radio stations. Zanzibar has two television stations, but there is no television service on the mainland.

History

Archaeologists have discovered the fossils of several types of humanlike creatures called *australopithecines* (southern apes) in the Olduvai Gorge in northern Tanzania. Scientists believe some of these creatures lived more than 4 million years ago (see **Australopithecus**).

Historians believe that Greek explorers traveled down the east African coast in the first hundred years A.D. The Portuguese established settlements in the area in the 1500's, but were later forced out.

The slave trade. In 1832, the town of Zanzibar, on Zanzibar Island, became the capital of a large Arab sultanate. It became the main town in eastern Africa. Many Africans from Tanganyika were sold in the Zanzibar slave market. The Arabs closed the market in 1873, and slavery was abolished on the mainland in 1876.

German and British rule. The German Colonization Society made treaties in 1884 with African chiefs for their lands. Germany gained the coastal area of the mainland from the Sultan of Zanzibar in 1890. At the same time, Zanzibar became a British protectorate. In 1891, Germany declared the mainland territory the Pro-

tectorate of German East Africa. After World War I, Britain received a League of Nations mandate over most of German East Africa and renamed it Tanganyika.

Independence. Tanganyika became a United Nations trust territory under British rule in 1946. Julius K. Nyerere, a nationalist leader, and his political party, the Tanganyika African National Union (TANU), won the country's first general election in 1958. Tanganyika became an independent country on Dec. 9, 1961. Nyerere became the first president, and a one-party system of government was adopted.

Great Britain granted Zanzibar internal self-government in early 1963. Sheik Muhammed Shamte Hamadi, leader of the Zanzibar and Pemba People's Party, became the first prime minister. Zanzibar achieved full independence on Dec. 10, 1963.

The united republic. In January 1964, the Afro-Shirazi Party, representing the African majority in Zanzibar, ousted the Arab government. Abeid Karume became president, and the sultan fled the country.

On April 23, 1964, Tanganyika and Zanzibar signed an Act of Union that made them one nation. Nyerere became the first president of the united republic. Karume became the vice president. Nyerere was elected president in 1965 and reelected in 1970, 1975, and 1980. Karume was assassinated in 1972. As president, Nyerere adopted a number of socialist policies. They included establishing government control of Tanzania's banks and most of its industry. Nyerere also moved thousands of rural people to *ujamaa* (familyhood) villages set up by the government. He believed that moving people to the villages would improve farm efficiency and enable the people to be closer to schools and to medical and social services. In 1977, TANU and the Afro-Shirazi Party combined to form the Chama Cha Mapinduzi (CCM), or Revolutionary Party of Tanzania. President Nyerere became chairman of the new party.

In 1978, a border dispute led to fighting between Tanzania and Uganda, which was ruled by Idi Amin Dada. In

1979, Tanzanian troops, aided by Ugandans who opposed Amin, defeated Uganda's army and overthrew Amin's government. The Ugandans who opposed Amin then took control of the government.

In 1973, Tanzanians voted to move the capital from the coastal city of Dar es Salaam to Dodoma, near the country's center. The move was scheduled for completion by the 1990's. In 1985, Nyerere retired and was succeeded as president of Tanzania by Ali Hassan Mwinyi.

Michael F. Lofchie

Related articles in *World Book* include:

Dodoma	Lake Victoria	Races, Human
Kilimanjaro	Leakey family	(picture: African)
Lake Tanganyika	Nyerere, Julius K.	Zanzibar

Tanzanite, *TAN zuh nyt,* is a semiprecious gemstone. It is a variety of a mineral called *zoisite.* Tanzanite crystals are *trichroic* (three-colored). As the gemstone is turned, its color changes from deep blue to purple to yellowish-green.

When heat is applied to tanzanite crystals, they become uniformly blue. The blue color is most popular, so the majority of tanzanite is heat-treated. Tanzanite is cut into gemstones with numerous *facets* (flat, polished surfaces), which emphasize its light-reflecting quality. The gemstones are used in such jewelry as rings, earrings, and pendants.

Tanzanite was discovered in 1967 in Tanzania, for which it was named. Tanzania is the only known source of tanzanite. Because the supply is limited, the gemstones are expensive. Pansy D. Kraus

Tao Te Ching. See Taoism; Laozi.

Taoism, *TOW ihz uhm* or *DOW ihz uhm,* is a philosophy that began in China, probably during the 300's B.C. Taoism is also the name of a religion that began in about the 100's B.C. Through the centuries, the philosophy has influenced artists and writers in the East and West. The word *tao* (also spelled *dao*) originally meant *road* or *way.* The Tao (Way) represents the characteristics or behavior that makes each thing in the universe what it is. The word is also used to mean reality as a whole, which consists of all the individual "ways."

Taoism as a philosophy. The beliefs of Taoism as a philosophy appear in two books, the *Lao-tzu* (later renamed the *Tao Te Ching, The Classic of the Way and the Virtue*) and the *Chuang-tzu.* The *Lao-tzu* is a collection from several sources and its authors and editors are unknown. The ideas were partly a reaction against *Confucianism,* a philosophy that developed in China beginning in about 500 B.C.

According to Confucianism, people can live a good life only in a well-disciplined society that stresses attention to ceremony, duty, and public service. The Taoist ideal, on the other hand, is a person who avoids conventional social obligations and leads a simple, spontaneous, and meditative life close to nature.

Taoist philosophy had a great influence on Chinese literature and art. For example, the poetry of Tao Qian (T'ao Ch'ien) (A.D. 365?-472?) expresses a distaste for worldly affairs and a yearning for a life in harmony with nature. During the early 1200's, Xia Gui (Hsia Kuei) painted landscapes that reflect the Taoist sensitivity to nature (see **Painting** [Oriental painting]).

Taoism as a religion was influenced by Chinese folk religion. In folk religion, most of the gods are human beings who displayed exceptional powers during their lifetimes. For example, Guan Di, who is the protector of business people, lived as a general during the A.D. 200's.

Taoism has a hereditary priesthood. The priests conduct public rituals, during which they submit the people's prayers to the gods of folk religion. The chief priest, who is in a trance, prays to other divinities on behalf of the worshipers. These divinities are not former human beings but represent aspects of the Tao.

The symbol of Taoism stands for what Taoists believe are the two basic forces in the universe—*yin* (female) and *yang* (male). The black shape in the center and the broken lines represent yin. The center red shape and the solid lines symbolize yang.

The members of some Taoist groups have sought to attain immortality through magic, meditation, special diets, breath control, or the recitation of scriptures. The Taoist search for knowledge of nature has led many believers to pursue various sciences, such as alchemy, astronomy, and medicine. N. Sivin

See also **Confucianism; Laozi; Religion** (Taoism; picture: Taoist deities); **Zhuangzi.**

Additional resources

The Tao: The Sacred Way. Ed. by Tolbert McCarroll. Crossroad, 1982. Translation of the *Tao Te Ching.*

Welch, Holmes. *Taoism: The Parting of the Way.* Beacon Press, 1966. First published in 1957 under the title *Parting of the Way: Lao Tzu and the Taoist Movement.*

Taos, *tows,* N. Mex. (pop. 3,369), is three communities in one. Taos proper, which was originally founded as Don Fernando de Taos during the 1790's, serves as a center of trade for the nearby farm and ranch region. The ancient Pueblo Indian village of San Geronimo de Taos is located north of the town. To the south is the old

Shostal

Taos includes San Geronimo de Taos, a Pueblo Indian village. The village has adobe buildings that stand several stories high. Indians have lived there for more than 1,000 years.

Panasonic   WORLD BOOK photo by Dan Miller   WORLD BOOK photo by Dan Miller

Audio tape recorders include three basic models—reel-to-reel, *left,* cassette, *center,* and cartridge, *right.* Reel-to-reel recorders generally produce better-quality sound than do cassette or
cartridge recorders. But cassette and cartridge models are more compact and easier to operate.

Spanish farming center, Ranchos de Taos, which was established by Spaniards in the early 1700's. All three communities lie at an elevation of about 7,000 feet (2,100 meters) at the base of the Sangre de Cristo Mountains in
the Southern Rockies. Taos lies in north-central New
Mexico, 75 miles (121 kilometers) north of Santa Fe (see
New Mexico [political map]).

The well-known Taos "art colony" started in 1898.
Sights of interest to tourists include the Plaza, the center
of community life during the 1800's; the "Kit" Carson
House, a home of the famous frontiersman; the Charles
Bent House, where Governor Bent was murdered during a revolt against American rule in 1847; and the Milli-
cent Rogers Museum, which displays American and His-
panic art.

The Pueblo Indian village has adobe houses, several
stories high, in which Indians have lived for more than
1,000 years. White people first saw these when a group
led by Francisco Vásquez de Coronado visited the region in 1540.

Taos has a mayor-council form of government and it
is the seat of Taos County.   Robin McKinney Martin

Tap. See Plumbing.

Tap-dancing. See Dancing (The rise of romanticism).

Tape recorder is a device for recording sound, pictures, and various kinds of information on magnetic
tape. It can also play back tape recordings. Tape recorders are widely used by the recording industry and in
radio and television broadcasting. Millions of people
enjoy listening to music on tape recorders in their
homes and automobiles. Portable tape recorders are
also popular. Tape recordings can help students learn to
speak a foreign language or to play a musical instrument. Tape recordings of books, called *talking books,*
are made especially for the blind. Tape recorders can
also be used to record computer data, dictation, readings from scientific instruments, and signals that activate
automated equipment.

Recording tape is a thin plastic ribbon coated on one
side with particles of iron oxide or a similar substance
that is easily magnetized. Before sounds, pictures, or information are recorded on the tape, they are first converted into a series of electric signals. During the re-

cording process, these signals magnetize the particles
on the tape into varying patterns. When the tape is
played back, the magnetic patterns reproduce the electric signals, which are then changed back into their original form.

Tape recordings have several advantages over phonograph records. They can be played back immediately
after being made, and the same tape can be used to record many times by erasing the previous recording. Tape
recordings can easily be edited by cutting out the unwanted sections and then joining the ends of the tape.
Tapes are also more durable than records.

Tape recorders are commonly used to record sound,
and this article deals with audio tape recorders. For information on tape recorders that record visual images
and sound, see the article on **Videotape recorder.**

How tape recorders work

All audio tape recorders operate on the same basic
principles. Most recorders have two reels—a full *supply
reel* of magnetic tape and an empty *take-up reel.* One
end of the tape from the supply reel is attached to the
take-up reel. Between the two reels, a soft rubber *pinch*

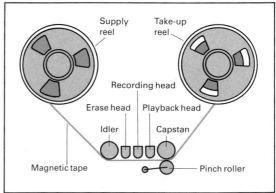

WORLD BOOK diagram

The tape transport system. The capstan, aided by the pinch
roller, pulls the tape from the supply reel, around an idler, and
past the various heads. The tape winds onto the take-up reel.

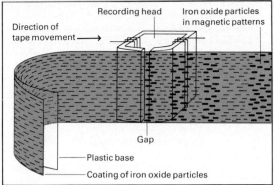

WORLD BOOK diagram

The recording process. Recording tape consists of a plastic base coated with iron oxide particles or a similar substance that is easily magnetized. In recording, electric signals from a microphone create a magnetic field around a gap in the recording head. The field magnetizes the particles on the tape into a pattern like that of the sound waves entering the microphone.

roller presses the tape tightly against a metal rod called a *capstan*. When the tape recorder is switched on, a motor turns the capstan. As the capstan turns, it pulls tape from the supply reel. At the same time, the take-up reel pulls gently on the tape to wind it up.

Before the tape reaches the capstan, it passes the *heads* of the tape recorder. The heads are small electromagnets that perform three functions—erasing, recording, and playing back. The speed at which the tape moves past the heads depends on the type of tape recorder. The speeds are measured in *inches per second* (*ips*). The most commonly used speeds are $1\frac{7}{8}$, $3\frac{3}{4}$, $7\frac{1}{2}$, and 15 ips (4.8, 9.5, 19, and 38 centimeters per second). The higher speeds produce recordings of the best qual

ity, but recording at slower speeds adds to the playing time of the tape.

Erasing and recording. When a tape recording is being made, the tape first comes into contact with the *erase head*. The erase head, which is automatically activated during recording, produces a strong magnetic field that removes any previous recording from the tape. The blank tape then moves past the *recording head*.

The sounds to be recorded on the tape are converted into an electric current by a microphone (see **Microphone**). An *amplifier* strengthens the current, which is then fed into the recording head. As the current flows through the head, it sets up a changing magnetic field around a small gap in the electromagnet. When the tape passes the gap, the magnetic field magnetizes the iron oxide particles on the tape into a pattern like that of the sound waves entering the microphone.

Different kinds of tape recorders use different widths of magnetic tape. The most common tape widths are 0.15 inch (3.8 millimeters), $\frac{1}{4}$ inch (6.4 millimeters), and 2 inches (51 millimeters). The wider the tape is, the more *tracks* (separate recordings) it can hold. Most tape recorders can record more than one track on a tape. A tape recorder must be able to record two tracks from two separate channels at the same time in order to produce stereophonic sound (see **High-fidelity system** [The tape recorder]).

Playing back. Before a tape recording can be played, it must be rewound on the supply reel. The tape is then sent through the recorder again. This time, the *playback head* is switched on, and neither the erase head nor the recording head is activated. As the tape passes the playback head, the magnetic patterns on the tape generate a weak electric current in the electromagnet. The pattern of the electric current corresponds to the pattern of the recorded sound waves. Another amplifier strengthens

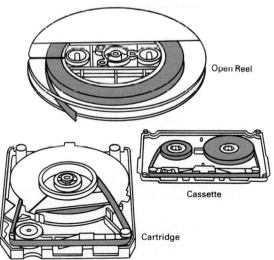

Open Reel

Cassette

Cartridge

WORLD BOOK diagram

Kinds of tape holders. Tape used in reel-to-reel recorders is wound on open reels. It must be threaded by hand past the heads of the recorder and through the capstan and pinch roller. Cassette and cartridge tapes come in small plastic cases. They are simply snapped into the recorder and are ready to use.

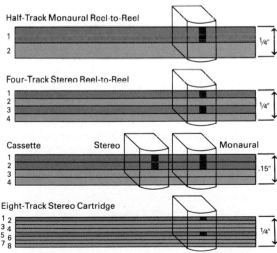

Half-Track Monaural Reel-to-Reel
1
2
¼"

Four-Track Stereo Reel-to-Reel
1
2
3
4
¼"

Cassette   Stereo   Monaural
1
2
3
4
.15"

Eight-Track Stereo Cartridge
1 2
3 4
5 6
7 8
¼"

WORLD BOOK diagram

Four tape track systems are shown above. The darker color indicates the placement of one of the tracks on monaural tapes and of one pair of stereo tracks on stereo tapes. The lighter color represents additional tracks. In most recorders, the tape must be turned over to play additional tracks.

the current before it reaches a speaker, which reproduces the recorded sounds.

Kinds of tape recorders

There are three main kinds of audio tape recorders: (1) reel-to-reel, (2) cassette, and (3) cartridge.

Reel-to-reel tape recorders are used by recording studios and in many homes. In general, they produce better-quality sound than do cassette or cartridge recorders. To use a reel-to-reel recorder, the operator places a supply reel and a take-up reel on spindles on the outside of the recorder. The tape is threaded by hand past the heads of the recorder and through the capstan and pinch roller.

Reel-to-reel recorders for home use run at $3\frac{3}{4}$ and $7\frac{1}{2}$ ips. Most home models record one, two, or four tracks on $\frac{1}{4}$-inch tape. Recording studios operate their recorders at 15 ips or 30 ips (38 or 76 centimeters per second). Many professional recorders use $\frac{1}{2}$-inch tape, which can carry as many as 24 tracks.

Cassette tape recorders are in most ways small copies of reel-to-reel recorders. But they are easier to operate because the tape does not have to be threaded through them. A cassette recorder uses a small plastic case called a *cassette,* which encloses a miniature supply reel and take-up reel. The cassette is simply snapped into the recorder and is ready to use. Part of one edge of the cassette is cut out to enable the tape to come into contact with the heads and capstan.

Cassette tape is only .15-inch wide, but it can carry four tracks. Cassette tape recorders operate at $1\frac{7}{8}$ ips. These recorders are widely used in homes and in automobiles. Portable cassette recorders are also extremely popular.

Cartridge tape recorders, like cassette recorders, are smaller and easier to operate than reel-to-reel models. The tape comes in a small plastic case called a *cartridge,* which is inserted into the recorder. A single reel inside the cartridge acts as the supply reel and the take-up reel. The tape unwinds from the center of the reel and rewinds around the outside. Most cartridge recorders are designed for use in automobiles. They run at $3\frac{3}{4}$ ips. They use $\frac{1}{4}$-inch tape, which carries eight tracks.

History

In 1898, Valdemar Poulsen, a Danish engineer, invented the first machine for recording sound magnetically. He called his invention the *telegraphone.* It used an electromagnet to make a magnetic recording on steel wire. However, phonograph recordings were more popular at that time, and little use was made of magnetic recording for a number of years.

A small number of audio recorders began to be produced commercially in the early 1930's. Initially, steel wire and steel ribbon were the only recording materials used. But they were awkward to handle and store and nearly impossible to edit. During World War II (1939-1945), German engineers perfected the *magnetophon,* the first recorder to use plastic magnetic tape.

By 1950, tape recorders were being widely used in the radio and recording industries. Manufacturers began to produce stereo tape recorders for use in the home in the mid-1950's. Cartridge tape systems were introduced in 1958, and, in the mid-1960's, cassettes revolutionized the tape recorder market.

Since the late 1960's, the sound quality of audio recorders has been steadily improving. Many recorders are now equipped with electronic noise reduction systems that considerably reduce the faint hissing sound made by tape. Chromium dioxide and other new tape coatings have improved the recording capability of cassette tapes. A recording technique called *digital recording,* developed in the late 1970's, results in sound reproduction of extremely high quality. Digital recorders store sound on tape in the form of a numerical code.

Stanley R. Alten

See also **Electromagnet; Headphones; High-fidelity system; Phonograph; Speaker; Videotape recorder.**

Additional resources

Dolan, Edward F. *It Sounds Like Fun: How to Use and Enjoy Your Tape Recorder and Stereo.* Simon & Schuster, 1981. For younger readers.
Jorgensen, Finn. *The Complete Handbook of Magnetic Recording.* TAB, 1980.

Tapestry is a woven fabric made from threads of different colors to form a picture or design. Most tapestries serve as indoor wallhangings.

How tapestries are made. Tapestries are woven on a loom. Like other woven fabrics, tapestries consist of vertical threads, which make up the *warp,* and horizontal threads, which form the *weft.* A tapestry weaver winds the threads of the weft over and under the threads of the warp, which are attached to the loom. In ordinary woven cloth, the warp and the weft can both be seen. But in the tapestry technique, the weft completely covers the warp. The weaver achieves this effect

Tapestry from the series *Acts of the Apostles;* Pinacoteca, The Vatican (SCALA from Art Resource)

An Italian tapestry called *The Miraculous Draught of Fishes* was designed by the Renaissance artist Raphael. It was woven about 1519 by Pieter van Aelst, a Flemish craftsman. The scene, based on an episode in the New Testament, shows Peter kneeling before Jesus, *right,* in a boat on the Sea of Galilee.

A French tapestry woven during the late 1400's, *left,* has a *millefleurs* design in the background. Such a design consists of numerous flowers and leaves. A detail from the design appears above. This tapestry, called *The Unicorn at the Fountain,* is part of a famous series known as *The Hunt of the Unicorn.*

by packing the threads of each newly completed row against the previous row with a comblike tool called a *reed.*

A tapestry weaver works from the back of the tapestry and follows a pattern called the *cartoon,* which indicates the design and thread colors. When the tapestry is finished, its design is the reverse of the cartoon. Linen and wool have been the most common materials, along with gold and silver thread.

History. Tapestry is one of the oldest techniques in textile art. It probably originated in prehistoric times, but the oldest surviving cloth fragments and written accounts date from about 1500 B.C. They come from many parts of the ancient world, including Egypt, Babylonia, China, and Peru.

Tapestry flourished in Europe in the Middle Ages, especially from the 1300's to the 1500's. Professional workshops produced sets for castles and churches. Most weavers worked from a full-scale cartoon painted by another artist. Because most tapestries were wool, they helped insulate rooms as well as decorate them. Kings and nobles took tapestries with them when they traveled to create attractive and familiar surroundings, and sometimes hung them in their tents on the battlefield.

Paris became the first major tapestry-making center in Europe. The *Apocalypse of Angers,* one of the oldest sets of tapestries in existence, was produced there during the 1370's or 1380's. During the 1400's, Arras in France, and Brussels and Tournai in Belgium, became famous tapestry-making centers.

Most tapestries from the Middle Ages depict scenes from history, mythology, the Bible, or daily life. Many have a *millefleurs* design as background. Millefleurs is a French word that means *a thousand flowers.* The design consists of flowers and leaves in realistic detail scattered over a background, making the picture seem flat like the wall it decorates. One famous set of millefleurs tapestries is called *The Lady and the Unicorn.*

In the early 1500's, the Italian painter Raphael designed cartoons for a set of tapestries called the *Acts of the Apostles.* They looked like paintings with figures standing in a three-dimensional space. Their realistic compositions greatly influenced tapestry design.

Tapestry weaving continued to thrive in Europe during the 1600's and 1700's. The Gobelin factory in Paris was one of the most famous centers. Such famous artists as Peter Paul Rubens, François Boucher, and Francisco Goya designed cartoons for various factories.

The popularity of tapestry declined during the 1800's, when wallpaper became widely used in homes. The Industrial Revolution also contributed to the disappearance of such crafts. In the late 1800's, the Englishman William Morris founded the arts and crafts movement to revive the handcrafts displaced by the machine. He also rediscovered the handweaving and dyeing techniques of the Middle Ages. Morris' ideas greatly influenced artists of the 1900's.

In the early 1900's, French artist Jean Lurçat introduced the use of modern artists' designs at Aubusson, France, a tapestry center important since the Middle

Ages. A modern crafts revival occurred after the end of World War II in 1945. Since the 1950's, artists have experimented with materials and weaving to create many new forms of wall tapestry.   Nancy A. Corwin

See also **Animal** (picture: Animals that hunt); **Jesus Christ** (picture: Jesus was brought before Pilate).

Additional resources

Ackerman, Phyllis. *Tapestry: The Mirror of Civilization.* AMS, 1974. First published in 1933.
Verlet, Pierre, and others. *The Book of Tapestry: History and Technique.* Vendome, 1978.

Tapeworm is any of a group of tapelike flatworms that live as parasites. Adult tapeworms live in the intestines

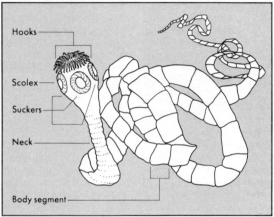

WORLD BOOK illustration by Zorica Dabich

A pork tapeworm has a flat, ribbonlike body. Its headlike scolex has both hooks and suckers, which the worm uses to attach itself to the intestines of people and animals.

of human beings or other animals. They have a headlike organ called a *scolex* and a series of blocklike segments in a flat body. A tapeworm has no mouth or intestine. It absorbs food through its body wall. Some tapeworms measure less than 1 inch (2.5 centimeters) long and have only a few segments. Others grow more than 30 feet (9 meters) long and have thousands of segments.

A tapeworm's scolex has suckers or hooks or both. The worm uses the scolex to attach itself to the intestine of the *host*—that is, the animal in which the worm lives. The rest of the worm's body grows from a necklike region behind the scolex. Numerous segments develop as the worm grows longer. Each segment contains male and female reproductive organs and produces many eggs. Segments filled with eggs may drop off the end of the worm's body. The segments then may pass out of the host's body with body wastes and release the eggs outside the host.

Almost all tapeworms have one or more *larval* (immature) stages and develop in two or three hosts. A newly hatched tapeworm is called an *oncosphere.* It is round and has small hooks. An oncosphere develops in a host that eats it or the egg it hatches from. The oncosphere burrows through the intestine of this host to muscles or other organs. If another animal eats this host, the oncosphere may develop into another larval stage or into an adult tapeworm. A person may be infected by a tape-

worm by eating improperly cooked fish, pork, or beef that contains tapeworm larvae.

Most adult tapeworms produce no bad effects in people. Sometimes they cause loss of appetite, abdominal discomfort, diarrhea, nausea, weakness, or anemia. Tapeworm larvae are much more dangerous to people. A person who accidentally eats eggs of the pork tapeworm may have young worms develop in almost every organ of the body, including the eyes, brain, and heart.

Scientific classification. Tapeworms belong to the class Cestoda of the phylum Platyhelminthes.   Seth Tyler

See also **Flatworm.**

Tapioca, *TAP ih OH kuh,* is a food starch that is widely used in making puddings. It is taken from the root of the cassava, a tropical plant of the same family as the castor bean. Tapioca pudding is healthful and easily digested.

Commercial tapioca comes chiefly from Brazil, Java, and the Malay Peninsula. A single plant may yield up to 10 pounds (5 kilograms) of starch. The roots are 2 to 8 inches (5 to 20 centimeters) thick, and 1 to 4 feet (30 to 120 centimeters) long. They are washed to remove the prussic acid they contain, and then reduced to a pulp. The pulp is strained until all the starchy particles are separated from the root fibers. The moist starchy pellets are then set on hot iron plates and left to dry. During the drying, the starch pellets form the small, uneven, milky white balls known as *pearl tapioca.* Pearl tapioca must be soaked in water for an hour before it can be cooked. A finer granular form, called *quick-cooking tapioca,* does not require soaking before cooking.

Tapioca swells and thickens the liquid in which it is cooked. A flour made from cassava root is also used as a thickening. This flour is one of the starches called *arrowroot.*   Margaret McWilliams

See also **Cassava.**

Tapiola, *tap ee OH luh,* a community in the city of Espoo, Finland, became world famous as a model for city planning. It lies in southern Finland. For the location of Espoo, see **Finland** (political map).

A private organization and its sponsors founded Tapiola as a new community, or *new town,* in the 1950's. The founders tried to create a community that blends completely with its natural surroundings. They also wanted Tapiola to offer its inhabitants many types of employment, housing, and services so the community would be entirely self-sufficient. Tapiola features a wide variety of architectural styles, and many walking paths that enable people to get around by foot. Some of Finland's best-known architects helped plan the community. Today, Tapiola is the largest business center of Espoo. But it does not yet provide jobs for all its inhabitants. Many of its approximately 35,000 people work nearby, especially in Helsinki.   Pekka Kalevi Hamalainen

See also **City planning** (picture: Tapiola, Finland); **Finland** (picture: The new town of Tapiola).

Tapir, *TAY puhr,* is related to the horse and rhinoceros, though it looks more like a pig. The tapir has a short, heavy body, and a thick neck. Its nose is drawn out to form a movable, short trunk. Its front feet have four toes, and the hind feet have three toes. The tail is short. Tapirs are wary creatures. They live in the depths of the forests, and near water, in which they love to swim. Tapirs feed on the twigs and foliage of trees and shrubs, and on fruit and other vegetable food.

Warren Garst, Tom Stack & Assoc.

The tapir resembles a pig but actually is related to the horse and rhinoceros. Tapirs have a sturdy body and a short movable trunk. They eat fruits, vegetables, and foliage.

There are two kinds of tapirs that live in South America. The most common one is found in the forest regions east of the Andes. The other makes its home high in these mountains. The two species of tapirs that live in Central America are the smallest of the family. All full-grown American tapirs are of a uniform dark-brown color, but young American tapirs are marked with yellowish streaks.

The Malayan tapir is found in Sumatra and the Malay Peninsula. It stands 3 to $3\frac{1}{2}$ feet (91 to 107 centimeters) high at the shoulder. The back, rump, and sides are white while the rest of the thinly haired body is glossy black or dark brown.

People hunt tapirs for their flesh and thick hides. As a result of both hunting and the cutting of forests, tapirs have become rare in many areas.

Scientific classification. Tapirs form the tapir family, Tapiridae. The South American tapir is *Tapirus terrestris.* The mountain tapir is *T. roulini.* The Central American tapir is *T. bairdi.* The Malayan tapir is *T. indicus.*   C. Richard Taylor

See also **Animal** (picture: Animals of the tropical forests); **South America** (Animals).

Tar is any of a group of thick, oily, dark-brown or black liquids. Most tars are by-products of the conversion of such organic matter as coal, petroleum, or wood into useful industrial products.

Coal tar, also called *high-temperature coke-oven tar,* is the most important industrial tar. It is condensed from vapors given off during the manufacture of coke from bituminous coal (see **Coke**). This tar is used as a raw material for such products as disinfectants, dyes, perfumes, plastics, roofing and water-proofing materials, and synthetic drugs. See **Coal tar.**

Coal gasifier tar is a by-product of certain manufacturing processes that convert coal into a high-energy gas. This gas can be used as a substitute for natural gas. Coal gasifier tar is a source of various organic chemicals.

Wood tar is a by-product of the *destructive distillation* of wood in the production of charcoal (see **Distillation** [Destructive distillation]). The tar is condensed from vapors given off during the process. It is an important source of acetic acid, methyl alcohol, pine oil, and turpentine.

Oil-gas tar and water-gas tar were once widely used in the manufacture of road-paving materials, wood preservatives, and other products. These tars are by-products of the conversion of petroleum oils into gas used for heating and lighting. They are seldom produced today because other sources supply energy for those purposes.   Frank A. Smith

See also **Pitch.**

Tar sands. See **Bituminous sands.**

Tarabulus. See **Tripoli.**

Tarantella, *TAR uhn TEHL uh,* is a popular folk dance that originated in southern Italy. It is a brisk and energetic dance performed in accelerating $\frac{6}{8}$ time. It usually is danced by couples, and it most often is accompanied by music featuring castanets and tambourines. The steps of the dance can be done in a variety of sequences. In some steps, the dancer moves forward and backward while hopping on one foot. Other steps feature heel-toe movements across the standing foot. The steps are linked by runs, skips, and movements with a partner.

The tarantella gets its name from the city of Taranto. According to folklore, the people there danced the tarantella as a cure for the bite of the tarantula spider. The tarantella is featured in the ballroom scene of the famous ballet *Swan Lake.*   Dianne L. Woodruff

Tarantula, *tuh RAN chuh luh,* is the common name of any one of a group of mostly large, hairy spiders. Tarantulas are found in warm climates such as those of the Southern and Western United States, and throughout the tropics. Some tarantulas live more than 20 years. Tarantulas get their name from a large wolf spider found around Taranto in southern Italy. People once believed this spider's bite caused a disease called *tarantism.* The victims supposedly leaped in the air and ran about making strange noises. According to superstition, the best cure was a lively Italian folk dance that became known as the *tarantella.*

One of the world's largest spiders, the *bird spider* of South America, is a tarantula. The bird spider has a body from 3 to $3\frac{1}{2}$ inches (7.6 to 8.9 centimeters) long and can

WORLD BOOK illustration by Oxford Illustrators Limited

The tarantula has a hairy body and looks fierce, but its bite is usually no more dangerous than that of other spiders.

spread its legs about 7 inches (18 centimeters). Some bird spiders live in trees and eat small birds. Some tarantulas in Brazil eat small reptiles and amphibians.

Tarantulas found in the United States are quiet creatures that live in burrows. Their bite is no more dangerous to people than the sting of a bee. Their chief means of defense consists of thousands of microscopic, irritating body hairs that can be flung into the air by rubbing motions of the hind legs. The bite of some South American tarantulas may be serious. An Australian species, which belongs to a group of tarantulas called *funnel-webs,* is more feared than the black widow spider. The *trap-door spider,* a tarantula found in the United States, grows about 1 inch (2.5 centimeters) long (see **Trap-door spider**).

Scientific classification. Tarantulas make up the suborder Orthognatha. Bird spiders form the bird spider family, Theraphosidae. Trap-door spiders form the trap-door spider family, Ctenizidae. Funnel-web tarantulas form the family Dipluridae.

Edwin W. Minch

See also **Spider** (Tarantulas; pictures); **Insect** (pictures).

Tarascan Indians, *tuh RAS kuhn,* were an important group in central Mexico. At the time of the Spanish Conquest in the 1500's, they controlled about the same area as the present state of Michoacán. The Tarascans developed an empire in a way similar to that of the Aztec, but on a smaller scale. Their capital, which was called Tzintzuntzan (*TSEENT soont SAHN*) or *place of the humming birds,* stood on the shore of Lake Pàtzcuaro.

The Tarascans were farmers, warriors, and craftworkers. They made copper tools, feather "paintings," and gold objects. They refused to join the Aztec against the Spanish, and were subjugated. Their descendants still live in the area. They farm, make fine lacquerware, fish from dugouts, and hunt.   Gordon F. Ekholm

See also **Mexico** (picture: Ancient ways of life).

Tarawa, *tah RAH wah* (pop. 22,148), is the capital of Kiribati, a country of many small islands in the southwest Pacific Ocean. Tarawa is an *atoll* (ring-shaped reef) composed of many coral islets that cover a total of 9 square miles (23 square kilometers).

The commercial and shipping center of Kiribati is Betio, a densely populated islet in the southwest area of Tarawa. Bairiki, east of Betio, is the government center. Bonriki, in the southeast, has an international airport.

In 1788, the British explorer Captain Thomas Gilbert became the first European to sight Tarawa. The British took control of Tarawa in the 1890's. In 1942, during World War II, Japanese troops seized the atoll. American forces captured Tarawa from the Japanese in 1943 in one of the bloodiest battles of the war. Britain then ruled Tarawa until 1979, when it became part of the independent nation of Kiribati.

Robert Langdon

See also **Kiribati; World War II** (Island hopping).

Tarbell, Ida Minerva (1857-1944), an American

Drake Well Museum, Titusville, Pa.

Ida M. Tarbell

author, led in the muckraking movement of the early 1900's which attacked dishonesty in politics and business. Her *History of the Standard Oil Company* (1904) exposed the practices of some great corporations, and strengthened the movement for outlawing monopolies. She also wrote biographies of Napoleon Bonaparte and Abraham Lincoln and an autobiography, *All in the Day's Work* (1929).

Ida Tarbell was born in Erie County, Pennsylvania. She was graduated from Allegheny College, and studied in Paris. Between 1883 and 1915, she was successively associate editor of *The Chautauquan, McClure's Magazine,* and *American Magazine.*   Merle Curti

Targum. See **Bible** (The first translations).

Tariff, *TAR ihf,* is a tax placed on goods that one nation imports from another. Many nations use tariffs to protect their industries from foreign competition. Tariffs provide protection by acting to raise the price of imported goods. Thus, tariffs encourage people to buy goods produced in their own country. Governments rarely place tariffs on exports because most nations want to sell as much as possible in other countries. A nation also may use tariffs to influence the political and economic policies of other countries. For example, a nation may raise its tariffs to protest increases by others.

Nations set their tariff rates in various ways. Two or more nations may sign a *reciprocal trade agreement* to set tariff rates for one another. Such an agreement may include a *most-favored-nation* clause. This clause requires the countries involved to use their lowest tariff rates on all products when dealing with one another. Nations also may set tariffs by forming a *free trade area,* a *customs union,* or a *common market.* The members of a free trade area have no tariffs among themselves, but each member may set its own tariffs on nonmembers. In a customs union, the members have no tariffs among themselves, but they establish a common set of tariffs for nonmembers. A common market has the same tariff policies as a customs union, but a common market provides for greater economic cooperation among its members.

Kinds of tariffs

Economists classify tariffs according to (1) the purpose of the taxes and (2) how the taxes are levied. A tariff levied in order to restrict imports is called a *protective tariff.* A tariff levied simply to raise the income of a government without protecting any industry is known as a *revenue tariff.*

In some cases, a revenue tariff may also serve as a protective tariff. For example, if domestic and foreign firms both produce woolen sweaters, a revenue tariff might give the domestic firms an advantage. Such a tariff could raise the price of the imported sweaters enough to reduce their sale—and thus protect domestic firms.

Through the years, many governments have used revenue tariffs to increase their income. But protective tariffs usually play a more important role in a nation's economy than do revenue tariffs.

Protective tariffs or revenue tariffs may be levied in any of three ways—as (1) specific duties, (2) ad valorem duties, or (3) compound duties.

Specific duties are placed on imported products according to a certain amount per unit of weight or volume. For example, a government might levy a specific duty of 10 cents per pound or 25 cents per liter of a product. Most specific duties are levied on raw materials, such as iron ore or rubber, or on bulk products, such as sugar or wheat.

Ad valorem duties are levied according to the value of a product. In most cases, governments levy ad valorem duties on manufactured goods. The rate may be as low as 5 per cent or less, or as high as 100 per cent or even higher.

Compound duties are a combination of specific and ad valorem duties. They are levied on certain manufactured products according to the weight of the raw material used and the value of the finished article. For example, a government might impose a compound duty on copper pipe. This duty could consist of a specific duty on the weight of the copper, plus an ad valorem duty on the value of the pipe.

Disagreements about tariffs

Many people believe that tariffs help a nation improve its economy. On the other hand, most economists argue that tariffs lower the standard of living in a country by forcing its citizens to pay higher prices for goods. Most economists also believe that tariffs lower the standard of living throughout the world by reducing trade.

Arguments for tariffs. Supporters of tariffs claim these taxes help provide (1) domestic job protection, (2) an aid to industrial development, and (3) a strong national defense.

Domestic job protection. Many people believe the workers of any nation cannot compete successfully with those of other countries who earn lower wages or produce more. To protect domestic jobs and industries, business companies and worker organizations may form

special interest groups that promote high tariffs. These groups argue that tariffs make up for the lower wages in other nations and keep wages high at home.

Aid to industrial development. Tariffs can help a country develop and maintain a variety of industries. Without tariffs, a nation might be able to produce only a few kinds of goods profitably. In many cases, a new industry cannot compete successfully with established industries in other countries. A protective tariff may help new industries survive until they have developed completely.

Tariffs also may stop foreign competitors from putting established domestic industries out of business. Some foreign suppliers use a practice called *dumping* to win an unfair share of a nation's markets. Dumping involves selling certain products at different prices in different countries—sometimes even at a loss. For example, radio manufacturers in one country may sell their products so cheaply in another country that radio firms in the importing nation cannot compete successfully. As a result, those radio firms may go out of business. The importing nation would then have to depend completely on foreign manufacturers for radios. The foreign companies could then raise prices far above their original levels. Many countries use *antidumping duties* to protect their industries against unfair competition from foreign countries. A nation may impose antidumping duties against certain products from certain countries even though regular tariffs would not apply to those products.

Strong national defense. Tariffs may help a nation develop industries needed for national defense. Many nations do not want to depend on other countries for such essential products as petroleum or steel. If a nation has no petroleum industry, an enemy might cut off its oil supply in time of war. Many economists believe that a

What protective tariffs do	Nations levy protective tariffs to guard their industries from foreign competition. The tariffs make imported products more expensive and thus encourage people to buy goods produced in their own country. But most economists believe tariffs reduce world prosperity by discouraging trade.

WORLD BOOK illustration

With tariffs Tariffs protect a nation's industries by increasing sales of domestic products. On the other hand, tariffs reduce international trade, raise prices to consumers, and deprive nations of the benefits of specialization.	Little international trade	High prices on imports	Large sales of domestic products
Without tariffs Each country can specialize in making the goods it produces best and most economically. Nations exchange a large volume of goods, and consumers buy many imported products because they are better or cheaper.	Much international trade	Low prices on imports	Large sales of imported products

nation should use tariffs to develop industries needed for national defense.

Arguments against tariffs include the belief that they result in (1) higher prices, (2) industrial inefficiency, and (3) unfair support for some industries. Tariffs may reduce trade, and so many economists believe they lower the standard of living in trading nations.

Higher prices. Many people believe tariffs waste a nation's supply of labor and natural resources and thus raise prices. A country wastes money if it tries to produce everything it needs. Therefore, it should produce chiefly what it makes best and most economically. If a country has excellent factories but poor farmland, for example, it should export manufactured products and import most of its food. If such a nation tries to expand its farming by placing a tariff on imported food, its people will have to pay higher prices for food.

Industrial inefficiency. Tariffs may encourage inefficiency by protecting industries from competition. Without competition, an industry has little need to become more efficient. If a nation's tariff policy encourages inefficiency, its industries will lose business to those of more efficient countries. Many economists claim that tariffs themselves cannot make—or keep—a nation prosperous by protecting inefficient industries.

Unfair support for some industries. Tariffs may help some industries—but only at the expense of others. If a high tariff protects a nation's aluminum industry, for example, aluminum might cost more in that country than it would without a tariff. All domestic industries that use aluminum would save money if they could buy the imported product at a lower price. But the tariff forces those industries to pay the higher price.

History

Tariff policies reflect the economic and political conditions within various countries. Throughout history, nations have changed their tariff policies to keep in step with their economic and political goals.

The first tariffs. In early times, nations did not have well organized foreign trade nor formal tariffs—but they did collect such taxes. Most tariff collectors simply charged merchants the highest duties they thought they could get.

From about 1100 to 1300, the Christian military campaigns called the Crusades brought increased trade between Europe and the Middle East. The rise in trade led to formal tariffs during this period. The first tariff agreements were made by Italian trading cities, such as Genoa and Venice, with various commercial partners in Africa and Asia. England levied a revenue tariff in 1303 that included an ad valorem duty on imported and exported goods. Collectors based this duty, called *poundage,* on the value in pounds of the goods.

Beginning in the 1490's, the explorations of Christopher Columbus, Vasco da Gama, and other Europeans resulted in a great increase in foreign trade. European trading nations began to follow an economic policy called *mercantilism.* This policy involved the use of high tariffs to limit imports, so that exports would exceed imports. An excess of exports over imports produced a *favorable balance of trade*—and boosted the size of a nation's treasury. Mercantilism flourished in Europe until the 1700's.

The changing role of tariffs. During the late 1700's, the beginning of industrialization in Europe led to a major change in the role of tariffs. The production of goods increased in the industrial nations, such as Belgium and Great Britain. As a result, these nations wanted to sell more and more products to other countries. Many industrial nations, in an effort to increase trade, sought lower tariffs with their trade partners. But nations that were just beginning to industrialize kept tariffs high to protect their new industries. Efforts to reduce tariffs increased as industrialization progressed during the 1800's and 1900's.

Modern tariff policies. By the mid-1900's, three major trading groups had developed, each with its own tariff policies. These groups were: (1) the non-Communist industrial nations, (2) the underdeveloped countries, and (3) the Communist nations. The non-Communist industrial nations sought to increase their trade by reducing tariffs. For example, the Western European countries formed the European Economic Community to eliminate tariffs on one another's goods. Many developing nations in Africa, Asia, and Latin America continued to use high tariffs to protect their industries. The Communist nations worked toward removing tariffs on one another's products.

United States tariffs have played a major role in the nation's history. The U.S. government has changed its tariff policies many times through the years.

The revolutionary period. Many people in the American Colonies resented the tariffs that Great Britain put on goods that they imported. They sought independence partly to free themselves from tariffs levied by the British.

Soon after the Revolutionary War ended in 1783, many Americans demanded that the government establish a tariff. They argued that a tariff would (1) protect the nation's industries, (2) raise government revenue, and (3) encourage other nations to grant fair tariffs to the United States. The first Congress passed the Tariff Act of 1789, which set up U.S. tariffs.

The 1800's. The nation's first tariffs were low, but most of them rose during the early 1800's. People in various parts of the country called for different tariff policies. For example, people in the New England and Middle Atlantic states sought high tariffs to protect their manufacturing industries. But Southerners, whose income came chiefly from agriculture, demanded low tariffs. They wished to buy European products, which were better and cheaper than those made in the United States. Westerners, whose income also came mostly from agriculture, at first opposed high tariffs. But they came to accept a plan called the "American System" proposed by Representative Henry Clay of Kentucky. This plan included a protective tariff. Clay believed that Westerners would benefit by supporting such a tariff for Eastern manufacturers. He thought it would bring increased prosperity for the East, which in turn would create a larger market for farm products produced in the West. In 1824, Congress boosted most tariffs as a result of Clay's proposals.

Many people, especially Southerners, protested the rising tariffs, particularly what they called the "Tariff of Abominations" of 1828. This tariff again increased the cost of foreign products needed by farmers. To satisfy those who wanted to eliminate all tariffs, Clay helped work out the Compromise Tariff of 1833. This law maintained some high duties but included a plan to reduce tariffs gradually until 1842. However, poor economic conditions resulted in a new and higher tariff in 1842. In 1846, after the economy had improved, Congress lowered tariffs with the Walker Tariff Act. Further reductions were made in 1857, but the Morrill Tariff Act of 1861 once again raised tariffs because of poor economic conditions.

The tariff disagreement between the North and South helped cause the Civil War, which began in 1861. Southerners felt betrayed when the Westerners and Northerners joined in support of high tariffs.

During the Civil War, the government raised tariffs to new highs. Most tariffs remained high throughout the 1800's. Several attempts to lower them failed. For example, the Mills bill of 1888 included President Grover Cleveland's proposal to lower tariffs. The House of Representatives passed the bill, but the Senate never voted on it. The McKinley Tariff Act of 1090 raised the average level of tariffs to a new high.

The 1900's. During the early 1900's, many people in the United States wanted to increase the nation's trade by lowering tariffs. The Payne-Aldrich Tariff of 1909 changed many tariff rates but failed to lower the average level of tariffs. In 1913, the Underwood Tariff Act generally reduced tariffs. But a decline in shipping during World War I (1914-1918) cut trade and limited the effects of the lower tariffs. In 1922, the Fordney-McCumber Tariff Act raised tariff rates sharply. United States tariffs reached an all-time high under the Smoot-Hawley Tariff Act of 1930.

In 1934, during the Great Depression, Congress passed the Reciprocal Trade Agreements Act in an effort to increase trade. This law made the most significant change in the history of the nation's tariffs. It authorized the President to cut tariffs for certain nations by as much as half. It also enabled him to make agreements setting the exact tariff rate for each product. Formerly, Congress had set the rates.

After World War II ended in 1945, a number of countries made further efforts to lower tariffs. In 1947, the United States and 22 other nations signed the General Agreement on Tariffs and Trade (GATT). This pact reduced tariffs and provided for the settlement of trade disputes. It also restricted its members from banning or limiting imports from other member nations. As a result of a series of meetings held under terms of the GATT, nations throughout the world lowered their tariffs. In 1967, more than 50 nations that had signed the GATT agreed on tariff concessions that covered more than $40 billion in world trade.

By the mid-1980's, about 90 nations had signed the GATT. In addition, Congress had passed several laws to help industries and labor unions adjust to increased competition attracted by lower tariffs. In 1955, an amendment to the Reciprocal Trade Agreements Act of 1934 provided for the gradual lowering of U.S. tariffs. Such action helps protected industries adjust to foreign competition. The Trade Expansion Act of 1962 provided financial and technical assistance to firms and workers harmed by the effects of lower tariffs. This law also gave the President authority to make trade agreements for lower tariffs without getting congressional approval.

The Trade Reform Act of 1974 made further efforts to lower tariffs and increase trade. It enlarged the President's authority to determine tariff rates within limits specified by Congress. The law also authorized the President to grant most-favored-nation benefits to Romania and the Soviet Union for the first time. In addition, the act increased financial assistance to U.S. workers, communities, and industries that suffered economic hardship caused by tariff reductions.   Harold J. Heck

Related articles in *World Book* include:

Balance of payments	General Agreement on Tariffs
Customs union	and Trade
Exports and imports	International trade
Free trade	Reciprocal trade agreement

Tariff Act of 1842. See Obscenity and pornography.
Tariff Commission, United States. See International Trade Commission, United States.
Tariff of abominations. See Adams, John Quincy (The "tariff of abominations").

Tarkenton, Fran (1940-   ), was one of the top quarterbacks in National Football League (NFL) history. He was noted for his passing and his ability to scramble—that is, to avoid tacklers. Tarkenton holds several NFL regular season career records, including most passes attempted, most passes completed, most yards passing, and most touchdown passes. During his 18-year professional career, he attempted 6,467 passes and completed 3,686 for 47,003 yards and 342 touchdowns. He also gained 3,669 yards by running, more than any other NFL quarterback.

Tarkenton won all-America honors while playing at the University of Georgia from 1958 to 1960. He

Minnesota Vikings
Fran Tarkenton

played for the Minnesota Vikings from 1961 to 1966 and was traded to the New York Giants in 1967. He returned to the Vikings in 1972. Tarkenton retired after the 1978-1979 season. Francis Asbury Tarkenton was born in Richmond, Va.   Bob Wolf

See also **Football** (picture).

Tarkington, Booth (1869-1946), was an American novelist and dramatist. His writings are considered one of the best mirrors of the wholesome aspects of life in the Middle West. Tarkington's works range from the sentimentally romantic *Monsieur Beaucaire* (1900) to the humor of *Penrod* (1914) and the realism of *Alice Adams* (1921). His trilogy of novels called *Growth* (1927) presents a cross section of city life such as it was in his home town, Indianapolis. The trilogy consists of *The Turmoil* (1915), *The Magnificent Ambersons* (1918), and *The Midlander* (1923). *Penrod, Penrod and Sam* (1916), and *Seventeen* (1916) portray the joys and problems of young people.

Tarkington also published plays, short stories, and essays. He was amiable, optimistic, and somewhat passive in emphasizing the smiling aspects of life and the joys of boyhood. Tarkington was awarded two Pulitzer Prizes for literature, in 1919 and 1922, for *The Magnificent Ambersons* and *Alice Adams.*

Tarkington was born on July 29, 1869, in Indianapolis, Ind. He was elected to the Indiana House of Representatives for the 1902-1903 term. He was a neighbor and admirer of the poet James Whitcomb Riley, and a devotee of William Dean Howells and Mark Twain. Tarkington

Huston, Pix

Booth Tarkington

also wrote some of the verses that were sung in the *Ziegfeld Follies* in the early 1900's.

Several of Tarkington's short stories dealing with political life were collected into one work entitled *In the Arena.* He also wrote *The Gentleman from Indiana* (1899), *The Beautiful Lady* (1905), *Beauty and the Jacobin, an Interlude of the French Revolution* (1912), and *The Plutocrat* (1927).   Bert Hitchcock

Tarnish. When a metal rusts, or combines with oxygen, it is tarnished. When a metallic or mineral surface loses its luster, it is also tarnished. The word *tarnish* is used for rust formed on metals other than iron, or *nonferrous* metals.

See also **Rust.**

Taro, *TAH roh* or *TA roh,* is a tropical plant used as food. The edible portion of the plant consists of one or more large, starchy underground stems. The taro is grown in many tropical regions, especially in Hawaii and on other Pacific Islands. Several different forms of the plant are cultivated. In the southern United States, the taro is called *dasheen.* In other countries, it is sometimes known by such names as *eddo, malanga,* and *yautia.* The taro is closely related to the ornamental plants called *elephant's-ear* and *caladium.*

Scientific classification. The taro belongs to the arum family, Araceae. It is *Colocasia esculenta.*   Alwyn H. Gentry

See also **Elephant's-ear.**

Tarot cards. See Magic (History; picture).

Tarpan, *TAHR pan,* was a wild horse that lived in the forests of Europe. The tarpan has been extinct since the 1800's. However, scientists believe that they have bred a horse that is exactly like the original European forest horse. These scientists worked at the Hellabrunn Zoo in Munich, Germany. They developed a process of backbreeding which produced a small horse in the 1950's that looks like the ancient tarpan.

See also **Horse** (Wild horses); **Przewalski's horse.**

Tarpeian Rock, *tahr PEE uhn,* was a famous cliff on the southwestern corner of the steep Capitoline Hill in Rome. According to the legend, this rock was named for Tarpeia, whose father commanded the Roman citadel in the time of Romulus. The story says that Tarpeia wanted the golden bracelets worn by the Sabine enemies of Rome. She treacherously opened the gate of the fortress for them after they promised they would give her what they wore on their left arms. Once inside the citadel, the Sabines crushed and killed her when they threw upon her the shields they wore on their left arms. Tarpeia was buried at the foot of the rock, which ever afterward bore her name. In later times, the Romans killed traitors by hurling them down from the top of the Tarpeian Rock.

Justin M. Glenn

Tarpon, *TAHR pahn,* is a large game fish that resembles a herring. It lives in the Atlantic Ocean from Long Island to Brazil, in the Gulf of Mexico, and in West Indian waters. It is abundant off the southern Atlantic Coast of the United States. It also is found off the coasts of Spain, Portugal, and the Azore Islands. The tarpon grows to a length of 8 feet (2.4 meters) and sometimes weighs 200 pounds (91 kilograms). Its flesh is coarse and not desirable for food. The large, tough, silvery scales are used in decorative designs. The tarpon is a popular sport fish in the United States because it is a strong, skillful fighter. Most fishing for tarpon is done off the south Atlantic Coast. Tarpon enter fresh waters and may be seen rolling, giving off bubbles of air as they dive. Sometimes they leap out of the water. Tarpon spawning sites are unknown.

Scientific classification. Tarpons belong to the tarpon family, Elopidae. The tarpon found near Florida is *Megalops atlanticus.*   John D. McEachran

See also **Fish** (picture: Fish of coastal waters).

Tarpon Springs, *TAHR pahn,* Fla. (pop. 13,251), is one of the world's largest sponge markets. It lies along the Gulf of Mexico on the western coast of Florida. For location, see **Florida** (political map).

The sponge industry began in 1905, when Greek fishermen arrived in the area. It grew to a fleet of more than

WORLD BOOK illustration by John D. Dawson

The taro plant has a large, starchy underground stem. The stem is used as food on many Pacific islands.

100 deep-sea boats, manned by fishermen of Greek descent. By the 1950's, disease and overfishing had depleted the supply of sponges. But the situation improved in the 1960's, and fishing began again. Tarpon Springs was founded in 1876.   Daniel P. Martin

Tarquinius, *tahr KWIHN ee uhs,* was the name of two of the seven legendary kings of Rome.

Lucius Tarquinius Priscus (reigned 616-578 B.C.) was the fifth king. According to legend, he was born in Etruria and was not of royal blood. He moved to Rome and became a good friend of the king, Ancus Marcius, who made him guardian for his children. When the king died, Priscus was elected to his place. His reign was very prosperous and successful. He made many conquests, and built many monuments and public works, including the Circus Maximus and the Temple of Jupiter. Legends claim that either Priscus or his son Superbus acquired the Sibylline books of prophecy. See **Sibyl.**

Lucius Tarquinius Superbus, the Proud (reigned 534-510 B.C.), was the son of Priscus, and the last of the seven legendary kings. He was the son-in-law of Servius Tullius, whom he murdered in order to gain the throne. Superbus was a tyrant and took away the rights of the lower classes. When his son, Sextus Tarquinius, committed a crime against Lucretia, the people revolted and drove Superbus from the throne. Then the people established the Roman Republic. They also put down several attempts to bring Superbus back. The most famous attempt, by Lars Porsena, inspired Thomas Macaulay's poem "Horatius at the Bridge."   Thomas A. Brady

Tarragon, *TAR uh gahn,* is a plant that provides leaves used to flavor meats, vegetables, sauces, dressings, vinegar, and cooking oil. It is related to American sagebrushes and the absinthe plant.

Scientific classification. Tarragon belongs to the composite family, Compositae. It is classified as *Artemisia dracunculus.*
      J. B. Hanson

Tarsal bones. See **Foot** (in anatomy).

Tarsier, *TAHR see uhr,* is a small mammal with a round head and unusually large owllike eyes. Like humans and apes, it belongs to the order *Primates* (see **Primate**). The tarsier lives in the East Indies and the Philippines. It has big ears and a long thin tail with a little tuft of fur on the end. Its fur is kinky and woolly. It has short front legs, and long hind legs that help it hop among the branches of its tree-home. All of its long fingers and most of its toes have nails, but the second and third toes have claws. The tarsier grows to be about as large as a rat. Its name comes from the long tarsal bones in the animal's feet. The tarsier moves through trees at night, feeding on insects, snails, and small lizards.

Scientific classification. The tarsier belongs to the tarsier family, Tarsiidae. It is genus *Tarsius.* Species include *T. spectrum, T. bacanus,* and *T. syrichta.*   George B. Schaller

Tarsus, *TAHR suhs* (pop. 121,074), a city in south-central Turkey, is an agricultural center. Tarsus was the birthplace of Saint Paul. Ancient Tarsus was an important trading center, surrounded by fertile land. The Cydnus River linked the city with a good harbor on the Mediterranean Sea, and an important trade road ran through Tarsus. For location, see **Turkey** (political map).

Tarsus was first mentioned in the records of the Assyrians, a group of people from western Asia. The Assyrians probably seized control of the city about 850 B.C.

from Greek colonists. After 104 B.C., the Romans took control of Tarsus, and the city was rich and prosperous while they controlled it.   Mary Francis Gyles

Tartan, *TAHR tuhn,* is a plaid cloth pattern that developed chiefly in Scotland. The design consists of stripes of various widths and colors. The stripes cross at right angles against a solid color background. The principal *clans* (tribes) in Scotland, especially in the Highlands, have their own tartans. Scottish regiments have also adopted tartans. In the United States, the word *tartan* also means a cloth or a garment with a tartan design.

The cloth that is used to make tartan is usually wool. A tartan design is called a *sett.* The sett may be made in any size, depending on the intended use of the cloth. Regardless of the size of the sett, the proportions of the stripes must remain the same. The colors of a sett may vary in shade from pale to dark.

A Scottish Highlander wears a tartan *kilt* (a knee-length pleated skirt) and may carry a *plaid* over the left shoulder. A plaid is a blanketlike mantle fastened at the shoulder with a brooch. Other parts of the costume include a *sporran* (pouch) hanging in front of the kilt, a *doublet* (jacket), and a *bonnet* (cap). The stockings may be of tartan pattern, and the *brogues* (shoes) are low-cut. Tartan *trews* (trousers) are sometimes worn as an alternative to the kilt, particularly by the Lowland Scottish regiments.

The use of checkered garments dates back to ancient times. The Irish, the Britons, the Caledonians of Scotland, and the Celts in Europe wore them. Scottish literature first referred to tartan in the 1200's. Originally, tartans in Scotland were associated with districts. Later, they were used to identify the chief clan or family of an area. Extra lines were added to some setts to show the wearer's rank.

Originally, the kilt and the plaid were part of a single large piece of tartan cloth. Wearers folded the tartan lengthwise and gathered it around the waist with a belt.

M. P. L. Fogden, Bruce Coleman Ltd.

The tarsier is a small Southwest Pacific animal with large eyes. Pads on its fingers and toes help it to grip branches.

Colorful Scottish tartans are favorite designs in many countries. The tartan developed chiefly in the Highlands of Scotland, where each clan and family designed its own pattern. Some Scottish clans wear a bright tartan on formal occasions, and a more restrained hunting tartan for everyday wear. There are hundreds of different tartans. Some of the best-known clan tartans are illustrated in this article. Because of the problem of matching dyes, the colors of different samples of the same tartan may vary in shade. The uniform of the famous Black Watch Royal Highland Regiment, *right,* includes the government tartan. The soldier is a drum major in the regiment, which was organized in 1725.

John Blomfield

Exclusive WORLD BOOK photos by Sidney H. Siegel; tartans courtesy Kinloch Anderson, Ltd., Edinburgh, Scotland

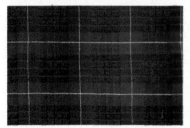

Buchanan

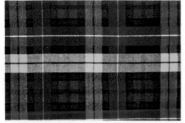

Cameron

Campbell

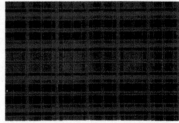

Cumming

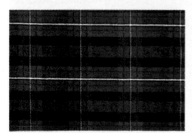

Ferguson

Graham

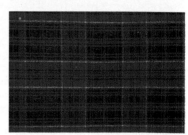

Grant

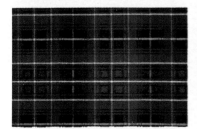

Innes

Lindsay

MacDuff

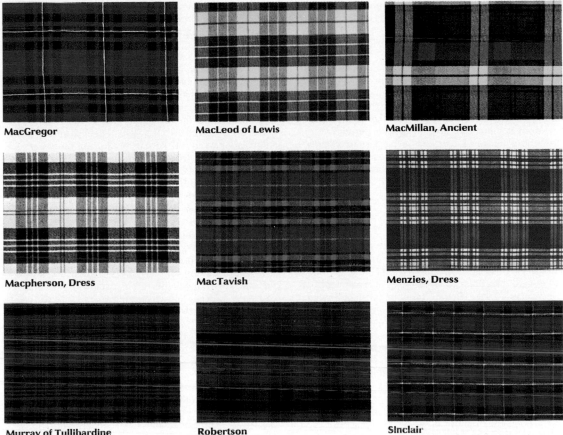

MacGregor

MacLeod of Lewis

MacMillan, Ancient

Macpherson, Dress

MacTavish

Menzies, Dress

Murray of Tullibardine

Robertson

Sinclair

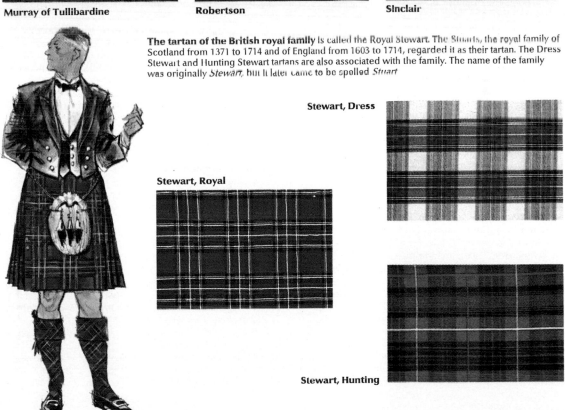

The tartan of the British royal family is called the Royal Stewart. The Stuarts, the royal family of Scotland from 1371 to 1714 and of England from 1603 to 1714, regarded it as their tartan. The Dress Stewart and Hunting Stewart tartans are also associated with the family. The name of the family was originally *Stewart,* but it later came to be spelled *Stuart*

Stewart, Dress

Stewart, Royal

Stewart, Hunting

They threw the rest over the shoulder and pinned it. In bad weather, they wore it over the head and shoulders. When sleeping outside, they used it as a blanket. Today, a smaller kilt called a *filibeg* and the plaid are worn separately.

After the Jacobite Rebellion in 1745, the British Parliament banned tartan and the use of Highland dress until 1782. Some old setts were lost, but many new ones were invented, especially about 1820, when the works of Scottish writer Sir Walter Scott awakened interest in Highlands traditions. Today, the tartan is popular throughout the world, particularly in the United States, where many people have Scottish ancestors. There are no rigid rules for its use, but people usually wear tartans associated with their name or ancestry.

Critically reviewed by the Royal Celtic Society

See also **Clan; Scotland** (Way of life; Traditions; picture: Bagpipes and kilts).

Tartar emetic, *TAHR tuhr ih MEHT ihk,* is a medicinal preparation which people once used to cause vomiting. It is now used to make patients cough up phlegm and mucus. Tartar emetic is prepared from antimony oxide and potassium tartrate. In large doses, it is a violent, irritating poison. Tartar emetic should be taken only when prescribed by a physician.

Tartaric acid, *tahr TAR ihk,* is an organic chemical that occurs naturally in grapes and several other fruits. It is commonly used in the production of jellies and carbonated grape beverages.

Most commercial tartaric acid is obtained as a by-product of the wine industry. The acid's colorless crystals are derived from potassium hydrogen tartrate, or *argol,* which collects on the walls of wine vats during the fermentation of grapes.

Three salts of tartaric acid—cream of tartar, tartar emetic, and Rochelle salt—are used by the food industry and other industries. Cream of tartar is an ingredient of some baking powders and is also used in making hard candies and taffy. Tartar emetic and Rochelle salt are used in some medicines. Crystals of Rochelle salt, which are *piezoelectric,* are also an important part of some microphones (see **Piezoelectricity**). In addition, tartaric acid and some of its salts are used in cleaning and polishing metals and in dyeing fabrics.

Tartaric acid was first isolated by Carl W. Scheele, a Swedish chemist, in 1770. The acid has a chemical formula of $C_4H_6O_6$.   Robert J. Ouellette

See also **Acid; Cream of tartar; Tartar emetic.**

Tartars, *TAHR tuhrz,* are a Turkic-speaking people of Europe and Asia. They live in the central and southern parts of the Soviet Union and in Romania, Bulgaria, Turkey, and China. The Tartars are Turks, and they are related to the people of Turkey. Typical Tartar groups living in the Soviet Union include the Crimean Tartars, the Siberian Tartars, and the Volga Tartars. Most Tartars are *Muslims* (followers of Islam).

The Tartars have traditionally called themselves *Tatars.* During the 1200's, they joined with other Mongol tribes and neighboring nomads to invade eastern Europe. Europeans incorrectly used the word *Tartar* to describe all the nomadic invaders.

Today, there are more than 6 million Tartars. They are no longer nomadic. More than $1\frac{1}{2}$ million of them live in the Tatar Autonomous Soviet Socialist Republic. This area forms part of the Russian Soviet Federative Socialist Republic, the largest state in the Soviet Union. Kazan, the capital of the Tatar republic, is a center of Tartar culture (see **Kazan**).   Andrew C. Hess

Tartarus, *TAHR tuhr uhs,* was a deep pit below the surface of the earth in early Greek mythology. It was as far below the surface as heaven was above the earth. High walls and a river of fire called Phlegethon (or Pyriphlegethon) encircled Tartarus. Zeus, ruler of the gods, imprisoned the rebellious gods called Titans there. Any god who swore a false oath by the River Styx in the Underworld was kept in Tartarus for nine years (see **Styx**). In later Greek and Roman belief, Tartarus was a place of punishment for the most wicked sinners, and was part of Hades, the kingdom of the dead (see **Hades**). In some ways, Tartarus resembled the Christian idea of hell.   Justin M. Glenn

Tartary, *TAHR tuh ree,* was once the name of a vast region in Europe and Asia which was inhabited by tribes of Tartars. The region lay outside the Great Wall of China. It included present-day northern China, Mongolia, Xinjiang, and the southern parts of Russia in Europe and Asia. Today, the name Tartary usually applies only to the area commonly known as Xinjiang, or Chinese Turkestan, plus western Mongolia. This is a rugged mountain area north of Tibet.   J. E. Spencer

Tartini, *tahr TEE nee,* **Giuseppe,** *joo ZEHP peh* (1692-1770), was a great Italian violinist, composer, and teacher. He influenced violin playing by introducing a system of violin bowing and fingering. He also started the use of thicker strings and lighter bows. In 1728, he founded a school of violin playing at Padua. Tartini's best-known composition for violin is the *Devil's Trill Sonata.* He also composed about 140 concertos, 40 trios, 150 violin sonatas, and wrote essays on violin playing methods and the theory of acoustics.   Stephen Clapp

Tartu, *TAHR too* (pop. 110,000), is the second largest city in Estonia, a republic of the Soviet Union. Only Tallinn has more people. Tartu lies along the Emajõgi River in eastern Estonia (see **Estonia** [map]).

Tartu is a major educational and cultural center. Tartu State University, founded in 1632, is the second oldest university in the Soviet Union. Only the V. Kapsukas State University in Vilnius, Lithuania, is older. Tartu is also the home of the Estonian Academy of Agriculture and other schools of higher education; and the Vanemuine, an old drama and musical theater. Tartu's industries include food processing and the production of leather and wood products, machine tools, and textiles.

The earliest settlement at Tartu was begun in the A.D. 400's. Tartu was founded as a city in 1030. It was part of the independent nation of Estonia from 1918 to 1940. In 1940, Russia seized Estonia and forced it to become part of the Soviet Union.   V. Stanley Vardys

Tarzan. See **Burroughs, Edgar Rice.**

Tasadays. See **Philippines** (The people).

Tashkent, *tahsh KEHNT* (pop. 1,986,000), is the capital of Uzbek Soviet Socialist Republic in the Soviet Union. The largest city in Soviet Asia, Tashkent lies north of Afghanistan, in the valley of the Chirchik River (see **Union of Soviet Socialist Republics** [political map]). The city is divided into two sections, the old Asiatic and the new Soviet. The Soviet section reflects modern city life. The Asiatic section resembles a dusty caravan town. Tashkent has railroad connections with Krasnovodsk and with the railroad lines in Siberia. The city has machinery plants and a cotton-textile mill. For the monthly weather, see **Union of Soviet Socialist Republics** (Climate).

Theodore Shabad

Tasman, *TAZ muhn,* **Abel Janszoon,** *AH buhl YAHN sohn* (1603-1659), a Dutch sea captain, explored the South Pacific. In 1642, he sailed southeast from Batavia, Java, and became the first European to reach the island now called Tasmania and to sight New Zealand. See **Tasmania** (History).

On this famous voyage, which lasted 10 months, he sailed completely around Australia without sighting it. As a result, the question of whether Australia or New Zealand were parts of a great southern continent remained unanswered until the voyages of Captain James Cook (see **Cook, James**). On his voyage in 1644, Tasman entered the Gulf of Carpentaria along northern Australia. Historians believe he was born at Hoorn (near Alkmaar), the Netherlands.   James G. Allen

Tasman Sea, *TAZ muhn,* is that part of the Pacific Ocean which lies between southeastern Australia, Tasmania, and New Zealand. It covers about 900,000 square miles (2,300,000 square kilometers). A submarine cable on the seabed provides communication between Australia and New Zealand. The Dutch navigator Abel Janszoon Tasman reached the sea in the mid-1600's.

W. B. Johnston

Tasmania, *taz MAY'nee uh,* is the island state of Australia. It is the smallest Australian state, and one of the most beautiful. Many Australians spend their vacations on the island.

Location, size, and description. Tasmania once formed the southeastern corner of the Australian mainland. But this heart-shaped chunk of land split off from the continent, and the rough waters of Bass Strait now separate Tasmania from the state of Victoria. For location, see **Australia** (political map).

Tasmania administers several small islands, including Macquarie, Maria, Flinders, Bruny, and King islands. Tasmania and its islands cover an area of 26,200 square miles (67,800 square kilometers). The mountains in eastern Tasmania form part of the Great Dividing Range that runs down the eastern edge of the Australian mainland. Western Tasmania has steep jagged mountains. Mount Ossa (5,305 feet or 1,617 meters) in western Tasmania is the highest point on the island.

Tasmania's lakes and rivers are the source of electricity for industry. Its swift rivers rise in the mountains of the central region. The chief rivers are the Derwent, Huon, Mersey, Arthur, Pieman, Gordon, and Tamar. The lakes include Great Lake, St. Clair, Sorell, Gordon, Pedder, and Echo. The coastline has many capes and bays.

Climate. Tasmania's temperature averages 60° F. (16° C) in January and 50° F. (10° C) in July. The annual rainfall averages 20 to 40 inches (51 to 100 centimeters) in eastern Tasmania and 40 to 60 inches (100 to 150 centimeters) in the west. The area of Lake Margaret, near the west coast, receives the most rain—140 inches (355 centimeters) annually.

Natural resources. Many mineral deposits are found in Tasmania. Most of Australia's petroleum and a large part of its natural gas are produced from huge offshore deposits in Bass Strait. The state's other minerals include coal, copper, gold, iridium, lead, osmium, silver, tin, and zinc. Large forests cover parts of the island. The seeds that produced California's first eucalyptus trees came from Tasmania. A small bearlike beast called the Tasmanian devil lives on the island.

The people. Tasmania has a population of about 436,000. Most of the people are of British descent, and most of them were born in Australia. In the early 1800's, European settlers hunted down and killed most of the Aborigines who lived in Tasmania (see **Aborigines**). Those who remained were taken to Flinders Island in Bass Strait for protection. The last surviving full-blooded Tasmanian Aborigine died in 1876.

Most of the important cities and towns of Tasmania lie on or near the coast. Tasmania has no large cities. Hobart is the capital and largest city, and Launceston ranks as the second largest city. Other important towns include Burnie-Somerset, Devonport, Glenorchy, and Ulverstone.

Agriculture. Farmers cultivate scattered areas because of Tasmania's mountains and rugged landscape. But the soil is rich and farm products include apples, hay, oats, potatoes, wheat, and vegetables. Farmers also raise such specialized crops as opium poppies, and lavenders and peppermint plants. The raising of sheep and dairy cattle is also important.

Mining and manufacturing. Important minerals taken from Tasmania's mountains include coal, copper, lead, silver, and zinc. Hobart has Australia's largest zinc-processing factory. Bell Bay is the site of an aluminum processing plant. Other industries include metal-working and the processing of fruit, dairy products, and wool. During World War II, Tasmania's wood pulp and paper industry at Burnie was greatly enlarged. Australia's largest newsprint mill operates at Boyer.

Transportation. Tasmania has about 700 miles (1,100 kilometers) of railroads for hauling freight. It has no passenger railroads. The island has about 12,000 miles (19,300 kilometers) of roads, and is served by international and Australian airlines and shipping companies.

Education. Children are required by law to attend school until they reach the age of 16. Education is free. The state has about 285 state schools and 60 private schools. The University of Tasmania is in Hobart.

Government. The British Crown appoints the governor of Tasmania. The voters elect a 19-member legislative council for six years, and a 35-member house of assembly for four years. Tasmania sends 10 senators and five representatives to the Australian Parliament.

History. In 1642, the Dutch navigator Abel Janszoon Tasman became the first European to reach Tasmania. He called the island Van Diemen's Land, in honor of the governor of the Dutch East Indies (later Netherlands Indies). British convicts settled on the island in 1803. Great Britain granted responsible government to the island in 1855, and its name was changed to Tasmania the following year. In 1901, it became part of the Commonwealth of Australia.   Rod C. Boucher

See also **Hobart; Tasman, Abel J.; Tasmanian devil; Tasmanian tiger.**

Tasmanian devil, *taz MAY nee uhn,* is a fierce animal that lives on the Australian island of Tasmania. It eats small mammals and reptiles, plus any dead animals it can find. It hunts mainly at night and spends the day in

Fritz Prenzel

The Tasmanian devil, a fierce animal of the Australian island of Tasmania, hunts small mammals and reptiles at night.

a cave, a hollow log, or some other shelter. Tasmanian devils measure from 3 to 4 feet (0.9 to 1.2 meters) long, including a tail of about 1 foot (30 centimeters). Most have black fur with white markings, but some are entirely black. Tasmanian devils are *marsupials.* Female marsupials give birth to tiny, poorly developed offspring. Like most marsupials, young Tasmanian devils are carried in a pouch on the mother's belly until they develop more completely.

Scientific classification. Tasmanian devils belong to the marsupial family Dasyuridae. They are *Sarcophilus harrisii.*

Michael L. Augee

Tasmanian tiger, *taz MAY nee uhn,* was a large animal of the Australian island of Tasmania. Most scientists believe it is extinct. The Tasmanian tiger, also called the *Tasmanian wolf,* measured about 5 feet (1.5 meters) long, including a tail of about 20 inches (51 centimeters). It had short brown fur and looked like a wolf. Dark stripes resembling those of a tiger crossed the rear part of its back. Australians sometimes call the animals *thylacines.*

The Tasmanian tiger was a *marsupial.* Female marsupials give birth to tiny, poorly developed young. Like the offspring of most living marsupials, young Tasmanian tigers were carried in a pouch on the mother's belly until they developed more completely.

Tasmanian tigers were fairly common until the early 1900's. European settlers hunted them—and probably

David Fleay

The Tasmanian tiger, which most scientists believe is extinct, had stripes along its back like those of a tiger. The photo above, taken in 1933, shows the last Tasmanian tiger in captivity.

killed them off—because the animals preyed on sheep and poultry.

Scientific classification. Tasmanian tigers make up the marsupial family Thylacinidae. They are *Thylacinus cynocephalus.*

Michael L. Augee

Tass, *tas* or *tahs,* is the official news agency of the Soviet Union. It distributes information to newspapers throughout the Soviet Union and in more than 100 countries around the world. The agency obtains news by means of a worldwide network of reporters and editors. Foreign correspondents for Tass also try to learn other countries' official secrets to pass on to the Soviet government. Tass is an abbreviation of *T*elegrafnoye *A*gentstvo *S*ovietskovo *S*oyuza (Telegraph Agency of the Soviet Union).

As the official news service of the Soviet Communist Party, Tass transmits news of party conferences, meetings, and discussions. Agency editors must be approved by party committees. Most editors are party members.

Tass was formed in 1925 as a reorganization of the Rosta Agency. Rosta had begun operating in 1918, replacing the czar's information service.   Michael Emery

See also **News service.**

Tasso, *TAS oh,* **Torquato,** *tawr KWAH taw* (1544-1595), was an Italian poet of the late Renaissance period. He was long connected with the court of Alfonso II, Duke of Ferrara. Tasso was one of the greatest masters of Italian poetry. He took full advantage of the sonorous beauty of the language, and gave his poems a gently mournful mood. His pastoral drama, *Aminta* (1573), concerns the victory of true love over base love in a make-believe world of loyal shepherds.

Tasso's masterpiece was his *Jerusalem Delivered* (1575), an epic about the first crusade and the delivery of the sacred tomb from the infidels. It is written, like Ludovico Ariosto's *Orlando Furioso,* in melodious, eight-line stanzas. It is more compact and regular than Ariosto's epic, though it is filled with valiant warriors, noble heroines, enchantresses, miracles, and dire dangers. But Tasso restrained his epic. He feared that the Roman Catholic Church might censor it because of its sensuousness and its evidence of pagan mythology.

Tasso's natural inclination toward morbidity finally induced him to rewrite his epic under the title of *Jerusalem Conquered.* During the last 20 years of his life, he became mentally ill and was in an insane asylum at times. Tasso was born in Sorrento.   Werner P. Friederich

Taste is an important sense in people and many animals. The taste of foods helps determine what and how much we eat. People may reject foods whose taste they dislike and so not have a proper diet. Our sense of flavor is affected by how things smell. When we have a cold and a stopped-up nose, some foods may taste alike (see **Smell**). Food must be moist to be tasted. If the tongue and food are dry, there is no taste.

Many people believe that there are four kinds of taste—salt, sour, sweet, and bitter. But the *receptor cells* that make up our *taste buds* do not have structural or functional differences that correspond to these tastes. The idea of the four categories of taste seems to be something that is learned. Taste categories may be only easily identified characteristics of taste. They tell us little about how the taste sense functions.

Taste buds are grouped on the tongue into small

mounds called *papillae*. The papillae on the front part of the tongue have their taste buds connected to one nerve. The papillae on the edges of the tongue—about halfway between front and back—and those at the back of the tongue are connected to a second nerve.

When we take food into our mouth, the taste buds transmit information about the chemicals in the food to the nerves. The nerves may respond differently to the same chemicals in foods. In addition, small amounts of some chemicals are more easily tasted on the front of the tongue, and others are more easily tasted on the back or sides of the tongue. The taste of still other chemicals changes little over the entire tongue.

The nerves from the papillae come together at the back part of the brain stem. Here, some taste signals carried by the nerves are separated according to the different chemicals they respond to. The taste signals then travel to the front of the brain stem, the *thalamus*. From the thalamus, the signals move to the *cerebral cortex* of the brain. Here, the signals are interpreted, and we become aware of taste.

The receptor cells that make up the taste buds are continually being replaced. The receptor cells develop from skin cells that surround the taste buds. The skin

How taste works

The sense of taste is sent to the brain through taste buds located in the tongue. In the diagrams below, each boxed-in section is enlarged in the following drawing.

WORLD BOOK diagram by Lou Bory Associates

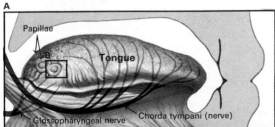

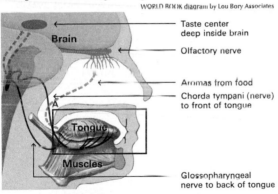

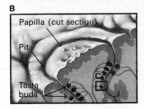

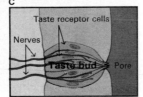

cells slowly move into the area of the taste buds. As the skin cells move, they turn into receptor cells. About half the receptor cells are replaced every 10 days.

Bruce P. Halpern

Tatars. See Tartars.

Tate, Allen (1899-1979), was an American poet and critic. Tate's writing stresses links between the present and the past. A major theme is a yearning for the rural, aristocratic way of life that was common in the South before the Civil War. Many of Tate's writings express dislike for what he regarded as the crowded, dehumanizing way of life in modern industrial society.

Tate is best known for his poetry, much of which is powerful, intense, and written in violent language. His early poem "Ode to the Confederate Dead" (1930) shows the influence of the poet T. S. Eliot. Tate's conversion to Roman Catholicism in 1950 led to an increased concern with religion and ethics in his work. His *Collected Poems: 1919-1976* was published in 1977.

As a literary critic, Tate became noted for his essays on the nature of the imagination and the value of literature. He became known for his essays about literary figures and for detailed analyses of poems. Many of his critical works were published in *Essays of Four Decades* (1969). Tate included both critical and autobiographical essays in *Memoirs and Opinions* (1975).

John Orley Allen Tate was born in Winchester, Ky. As a student at Vanderbilt University, he helped found the Fugitives, a group of Southern writers who hoped to preserve the cultural heritage of the South. Tate's ties with the South can be seen in his novel *The Fathers* (1938) and in his biographies *Stonewall Jackson: The Good Soldier* (1928) and *Jefferson Davis: His Rise and Fall* (1929). John B. Vickery

Tate, Nahum. See Poet laureate.

Tattooing is the practice of making permanent colored designs on the body. It is done by pricking small, deep holes in the skin and placing coloring matter in them. Tattooing is a popular custom among soldiers and sailors of many countries.

No one knows when or where tattooing started, but some Egyptian mummies of 1300 B.C. show blue tattoo marks under the skin. The Japanese and the Burmese have done the most elaborate tattooing in the world. Many Burmese have their entire bodies covered with colorful pictures of plants, animals, and human faces. The people of southeastern New Guinea regard tattoo marks on girls as signs of beauty.

Tattooing is not the only way of marking the body. The Bambara, Bamiléké, Mossi, and some other African peoples cut scars into their skin in a process called *scarification*. Each group has its own design, which serves to identify group members. The Maori of New Zealand once rubbed blue coloring into deep grooves in their faces. Wilfrid D. Hambly

Tatum, Art (1910-1956), ranks among the greatest piano soloists in the history of jazz improvisation. Tatum's light and delicate touch and swinging beat were perhaps unequaled among pianists of his time. His brilliant keyboard technique earned him the praise of many classical pianists.

Arthur Tatum was born in Toledo, Ohio. He was blind in one eye from birth and had only slight vision in the other eye. He arrived in New York City in 1932 as an accompanist for a singer. He soon became a favorite soloist in the small nightclubs along Manhattan's West 52nd Street, a hotbed of jazz during the 1930's and 1940's. Tatum led a trio for many years. However, he was one of the rare jazz pianists who needed no support from a rhythm section.   Leonard Feather

Tatum, *TAY tuhm,* **Edward Lawrie** (1909-1975), an American biochemist, shared the 1958 Nobel Prize for physiology or medicine for discovering that genes regulate specific chemical processes. He and George W. Beadle found that mutations caused by X rays and biochemical processes are passed on to successive generations. Tatum was born in Boulder, Colo. See also **Beadle, George W.; Heredity** (The study of the chemistry of genes).   Henry H. Fertig

Taunton Flag. See Flag (picture: Flags in American history).

Taurus, *TAWR uhs,* is the second sign of the zodiac. Taurus, an earth sign, is symbolized by a bull. Astrologers believe that the planet Venus, named for the ancient Roman goddess of love and beauty, rules Taurus.

According to astrologers, people born under the sign of Taurus, from April 20 to May 20, are loyal, patient, practical, and trustworthy. They appreciate beauty, comfort, and the countryside. Taureans move slowly and can be lazy, but they are determined to finish any task they

Taurus—The Bull

Symbol

Birth dates: April 20–May 20.
Group: Earth.
Characteristics: Affectionate, conservative, loyal, sensible, possessive, stubborn.

Signs of the Zodiac

Aries
Mar. 21–Apr. 19
**Taurus
Apr. 20–May 20**
Gemini
May 21–June 20
Cancer
June 21–July 22
Leo
July 23–Aug. 22
Virgo
Aug. 23–Sept. 22
Libra
Sept. 23–Oct. 22
Scorpio
Oct. 23–Nov. 21
Sagittarius
Nov. 22–Dec. 21
Capricorn
Dec. 22–Jan. 19
Aquarius
Jan. 20–Feb. 18
Pisces
Feb. 19–Mar. 20

begin. They have a down-to-earth personality and rely on their common sense.

Taureans, though not talkative, are affectionate, friendly, and warm-hearted. They are even-tempered but can become fierce when angered. They are stubborn, and tend to keep grudges.   Christopher McIntosh

See also **Astrology; Horoscope; Zodiac.**

Taurus Mountains. See Turkey (The land).

Taussig, *TOW sihg,* **Helen Brooke** (1898-1986), was an American physician who specialized in children's heart diseases. She discovered the major defect that causes the bluish tinge in the skin of *blue babies* (see **Blue baby**).

From 1930 to 1963, Taussig served as chief of the Cardiac Clinic of the Harriet Lane Home, the children's sec-

tion of the Johns Hopkins Hospital in Baltimore. She found that blue babies have a partial blockage of the pulmonary artery at birth. The heart pumps blood through this artery to the lungs, where oxygen enters the blood. A lack of oxygen in the blood gives the skin a bluish color. In 1944, Taussig and a surgeon, Alfred Blalock developed an operation that enables the blood to bypass the faulty artery.

Taussig was born in Cambridge, Mass. She graduated from the University of California in 1921 and received her M.D. degree from the Johns Hopkins University School of Medicine in 1927.   Miriam Schneir

WORLD BOOK photo by E. F. Hoppe
Helen Brooke Taussig

Tautog. See Blackfish.

Tawney, Richard Henry (1880-1962), was a noted British historian and social philosopher. His most famous work, *Religion and the Rise of Capitalism* (1926), related economic growth in the 1500's and 1600's to the spread of Protestantism. According to Tawney, such virtues as hard work and efficiency, stressed by the Protestants, contributed to the success of capitalism. In *The Acquisitive Society* (1920) and *Equality* (1931), Tawney argued for a more just and humane society based on the moderate and democratic socialism of the Fabian Socialists (see **Fabian Society**). Tawney was born in Calcutta, India, and attended Oxford University. He was an expert on English history between 1485 and 1715. He was a professor of economic history at London University from 1931 to 1949.   Roland N. Stromberg

Tax Court, United States, is a federal court that handles disputes involving income, estate, gift, and other taxes. Taxpayers who cannot reach an agreement with the Internal Revenue Service may file a petition with the U.S. Tax Court. The court has offices in Washington, D.C., but it holds sessions at locations throughout the country for the convenience of taxpayers.

Taxpayers may choose to take a case involving $10,000 or less to the court's Small Tax Division. This division provides simplified procedures for handling cases, and its decisions are final. All other Tax Court rulings may be appealed to the U.S. Court of Appeals and then to the Supreme Court of the United States.

The Tax Court was established in 1924 as the U.S. Board of Tax Appeals. It received its present name in 1969.   Critically reviewed by the United States Tax Court

Taxation is a system of raising money to finance government services and activities. Governments at all levels—local, state, and national—require people and businesses to pay taxes. Governments use the tax revenue to pay the cost of police and fire protection, health programs, schools, roads, national defense, and many other public services.

Taxes are as old as government. The general level of taxes has varied through the years, depending on the role of the government. In modern times, many governments—especially in advanced industrial countries—

have rapidly expanded their roles and taken on new responsibilities. As a result, their need for tax revenue has become great.

Through the years, people have frequently protested against tax increases. In these situations, taxpayers have favored keeping services at current levels or reducing them. Voters have defeated many proposals for tax increases by state and local governments.

Kinds of taxes

Governments levy many kinds of taxes. The most important kinds include *property taxes, income taxes,* and *taxes on transactions.*

Property taxes are levied on the value of such property as farms, houses, stores, factories, and business equipment. The property tax first became important in ancient times. Today, it ranks as the chief source of income for local governments in the United States and Canada. Most states of the United States and provinces of Canada also levy property taxes. Property taxes are called *direct taxes* because they are levied directly on the people expected to pay them. See **Property tax.**

Income taxes are levied on income from such sources as wages and salaries, dividends, interest, rent, and earnings of corporations. There are two main types of income taxes—*individual income taxes* and *corporate income taxes.* Individual income taxes, also called *personal income taxes,* are applied to the income of individuals and families. Corporate income taxes are levied on corporate earnings. Income taxes may also be levied on

the earnings of estates and trusts. Income taxes generally are considered to be direct taxes. The corporate income tax also may be described as a *shifted tax.* This is because corporations shift the cost of the tax to their customers by raising prices. See **Income tax.**

Most nations in the world levy income taxes. In the United States, income taxes are levied by the federal government, most state governments, and some local governments. Many people and businesses in the United States also pay special income taxes that help fund social security programs. These taxes are known as *social security contributions* or *payroll taxes.* In Canada, income taxes are levied by the federal government and by the country's 10 provincial governments. See **Social security** (Financing OASDHI).

Taxes on transactions are levied on sales of goods and services and on privileges. There are three main types of such taxes—*general sales taxes, excise taxes,* and *tariffs.*

General sales taxes apply one rate to the sales of many different items. Such taxes include state sales taxes in the United States and the federal sales tax in Canada. The *value-added tax* is a general sales tax levied in France, Great Britain, and other European countries. It is applied to the increase in value of a product at each stage in its manufacture and distribution. See **Sales tax; Value-added tax.**

Excise taxes are levied on the sales of specific products and on privileges. They include taxes on the sales of such items as gasoline, tobacco, and alcoholic bever-

Taxes in the United States This graph shows the amount of taxes paid in the United States. The amounts shown include tariffs and estate, excise, gift, income, and property taxes but exclude social security contributions.

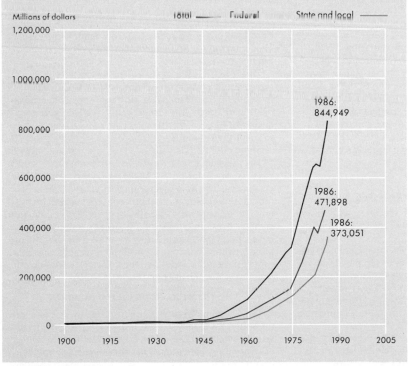

Year	Total tax (millions)	Total tax per person
1902	$ 1,373	$ 17.34
1913	2,271	23.35
1922	7,387	67.12
1927	9,451	79.39
1932	7,977	63.09
1934	8,854	70.06
1936	10,583	82.64
1938	12,949	99.74
1940	12,688	95.78
1942	20,793	154.18
1944	49,095	366.61
1946	46,380	329.67
1948	51,218	349.06
1950	51,100	336.90
1952	79,066	503.49
1954	84,476	521.83
1956	91,593	547.61
1958	98,387	567.86
1960	113,120	628.47
1962	123,816	666.32
1964	138,292	722.78
1966	160,836	820.86
1968	185,126	926.27
1970	232,877	1,145.98
1972	262,534	1,260.78
1974	314,785	1,489.12
1976	358,227	1,668.82
1978	468,161	2,146.89
1980	574,244	2,535.24
1982	671,424	2,963.73
1984	735,023	3,107.99
1986	844,949	3,504.89

Graph labels: Millions of dollars; Total ——; Federal ——; State and local ——

1,200,000
1,000,000
800,000
600,000
400,000
200,000
0

1986: 844,949
1986: 471,898
1986: 373,051

1900 1915 1930 1945 1960 1975 1990 2005

Source: U.S. Bureau of the Census.

The U.S. federal government dollar

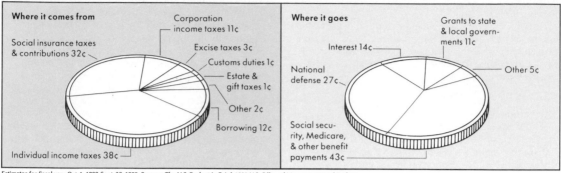

Where it comes from

Social insurance taxes & contributions 32¢

Corporation income taxes 11¢

Excise taxes 3¢

Customs duties 1¢

Estate & gift taxes 1¢

Other 2¢

Borrowing 12¢

Individual income taxes 38¢

Where it goes

Interest 14¢

National defense 27¢

Grants to state & local governments 11¢

Other 5¢

Social security, Medicare, & other benefit payments 43¢

Estimates for fiscal year Oct. 1, 1988-Sept. 30, 1989. Source: *The U.S. Budget in Brief, 1989,* U.S. Office of Management and Budget.

ages. Other excise taxes are the *license tax,* the *franchise tax,* and the *severance tax.* The license tax is levied on the right to participate in an activity, such as selling liquor, getting married, or going hunting or fishing. The franchise tax is a payment for the right to carry on a certain kind of business, such as operating a bus line or a public utility. The severance tax is levied on the processing of natural resources, such as timber, natural gas, or petroleum. See **Excise; Franchise.**

Tariffs are taxes on imported goods. Countries can use tariffs to protect their own industries from foreign competition. Tariffs provide such protection by raising the price of imported goods, thus making these goods more expensive than domestic products. See **Tariff.**

General sales taxes and taxes on gasoline and other products are called *indirect taxes* because they tax a service or privilege instead of a person. Manufacturers and business owners pay these taxes, but they add the cost to the prices they charge their customers. These taxes, like corporation taxes, are a form of shifted taxes.

Other taxes include *estate taxes, inheritance taxes,* and *gift taxes.* An estate tax is applied to the value of property before it has been given to heirs. An inheritance tax is levied on the value of property after it has been given to heirs. A gift tax is applied to the value of property that is given away during a donor's lifetime. The donor pays the tax. See **Inheritance tax.**

In the United States, the federal government and some state governments levy estate and gift taxes. Only state governments levy inheritance taxes. In Canada, only the province of Quebec levies gift and inheritance taxes. Canada has no estate taxes.

Principles of taxation

A good tax system must satisfy several general principles of taxation. The main principles include *productivity, equity,* and *elasticity.*

Productivity. The chief goal of a tax system is to generate the revenue a government needs to pay its expenses. When a tax system produces such revenue, it satisfies the principle of productivity. If a tax system fails to produce the needed revenue, the government may have to add to its debt by borrowing money in order to cover expenses.

Equity. Most people agree that a tax system should be *equitable* (fair) to the taxpayers. Economists refer to two kinds of equity—*horizontal* and *vertical.* Horizontal

equity means that taxpayers who have the same amounts of income should be taxed at the same rate. Vertical equity implies that wealthier people should pay more taxes than poorer people. This is sometimes called the principle of *ability to pay.*

Governments often try to achieve tax equity by making their taxes *progressive.* A progressive tax has a rate that depends on the sum to which it is applied. The rate increases as that sum increases. For example, the U.S. individual income tax is a progressive tax because it applies a higher rate to larger taxable incomes than it does to smaller ones.

Elasticity. A tax system should be *elastic* (flexible) so that it can satisfy the changing financial needs of a government. Under an elastic system, taxes help stabilize the economy. For example, taxes increase during periods of economic growth and thus help limit *inflation* (rapid price increases). Increasing taxes would leave less money for consumers to spend to send prices up. Similarly, taxes decrease during a decline in economic activity to help prevent a recession. This action would leave consumers more money to spend and encourage economic growth.

Other principles of taxation. People agree that taxes should be convenient and easy to pay, and that they should be inexpensive for governments to collect. In addition, taxpayers should know in advance when a tax has to be paid, so that they can save enough money to cover the payment.

Some economists believe a tax system should also satisfy the principle of *neutrality.* According to this principle, tax laws should not affect taxpayers' economic decisions, such as how to spend, save, or invest their money. But other economists believe a tax system must defy the principle of neutrality to achieve tax equity or to stabilize economic growth. Still other economists believe a tax system should play an active role in redistributing wealth. They support taxing the wealthy at highly progressive rates and using the collected revenue to finance services for the poor.

Taxation in the United States

The Constitution of the United States gives Congress the sole right to levy federal taxes. Congress first used its tax powers in 1789, when it began to levy a tariff. Tariffs were the chief sources of federal revenue until the outbreak of the Civil War in 1861. Then the cost of the war prompted the government to levy a series of excise taxes and other new taxes.

In 1894, the federal government levied a tax on individual incomes. But the tax was abolished in 1895 because it violated a section of the Constitution that required any direct tax to be *apportioned* (divided) among the states according to population. In 1913, the 16th Amendment removed this restriction. Later that year, the first modern income tax took effect.

During the early 1900's, the income tax became the main source of federal revenue. Local governments relied chiefly on property taxes. State governments also depended heavily on property taxes during the early 1900's. But by the 1930's, state governments received a rapidly growing percentage of their tax revenue from income taxes and sales taxes.

During the Great Depression of the 1930's, the role of the federal government grew tremendously. The New Deal program of President Franklin D. Roosevelt greatly increased federal services and activities in order to help bring economic relief to the country (see **New Deal**).

The federal government continued to expand its activities during and after World War II (1939-1945). As a result, the nation's tax system also grew to pay for the new federal programs. For example, during the 1920's, revenue from local taxes was about half of the total U.S. tax revenue. But today, local taxes account for only about a sixth of the country's tax revenue, while federal taxes account for about two-thirds of the total. The main federal taxes are individual and corporate income taxes and social security contributions. Some revenue from these taxes goes to state and local governments to finance such projects as roadbuilding and public housing.

Taxation in Canada

The individual income tax ranks as Canada's chief source of federal revenue. The federal government also levies corporate income taxes, a general sales tax, tariffs, and excise taxes on such items as gasoline, alcohol, and tobacco. Canada's 10 provincial governments also rely most heavily on individual and corporate income taxes. The provinces also levy property taxes, sales taxes, and excise taxes on gasoline, tobacco, and motor vehicle licenses. Some provinces tax gifts, logging, and health-care programs. Local governments get most of their revenue from property taxes.   Vito Tanzi

Related articles in *World Book* include:

Assessment	Internal revenue	Social security
Capital gains tax	License	(Financing
Congressional	Poll tax	OASDHI)
Budget Office	Property tax	Stamp
Excess-profits tax	Revenue sharing	Stamp Act
Excise	Road (How roads	Tariff
Franchise	and highways	Tithe
Gasoline tax	are paid for)	Turnpike
Income tax	Sales tax	Value-added tax
Inheritance tax	Single tax	

See also *Taxation* in the Research Guide/Index, Volume 22, for a *Reading and Study Guide.*

Additional resources

The Economics of Taxation. Ed. by Henry J. Aaron and M. J. Boskin. Brookings, 1980.
Minarik, Joseph J. *Making Tax Choices.* Urban Institute Press, 1985.
Sapinsley, Barbara. *Taxes.* Watts, 1986. Suitable for younger readers. A history of taxation in the United States.

Taxation without representation. See Revolutionary War in America (The Townshend Acts); Franklin, Benjamin (A delegate in London).

Taxco, *TAHS koh* (pop. 27,089), is a historic silvermining town 70 miles (113 kilometers) southwest of Mexico City. Its official name is Taxco de Alarcón (pronounced *day AH lahr KOHN*). For location, see **Mexico** (political map). Taxco looks like an old Spanish town. Narrow cobblestone streets climb the steep hills on which it stands. In order to preserve the town's appearance, the Mexican government has made Taxco a national monument. It is illegal to erect buildings in the contemporary style. The town's beauty, charm, crafts, and mild climate attract tourists, artists, and writers. Taxco has served as a mining center since Hernando Cortés founded it in 1529 (see **Cortés, Hernando**). Today, the town serves as the center of Mexico's silverware industry.   James D. Riley

Taxicab is an automobile for hire. It is an important part of the transportation system of a modern city. City law fixes the maximum rates for taxicabs. Almost all cabs have taximeters, which show the fare for the distance traveled. Some cities have zonal fares. Taxis charge additional fares when passing from one zone into another. About 260,000 taxis operate in the U.S.

The first motor-driven taxicab in the United States appeared about 1898. It had an electric motor. The first gasoline-engine taxicab and the first use of the taximeter came in 1907, in New York City. In 1914, the French Army organized the "taxicab army" to move troops from Paris to halt the Germans at the Marne (see **Automobile** [World War I]).   Franklin M. Reck

See also **Jinrikisha; Pedicab.**

Taxidermy, *TAK suh DUR mee,* is a technique for preserving animals and showing them as they looked when they were alive. The word taxidermy comes from two Greek words meaning *arrangement* and *skin.* Museums of natural history often exhibit birds, fish, squirrels, antelope, tigers, bears, and other wild animals in their natural settings.

Process of mounting. The taxidermist first takes accurate measurements of the anatomy of the dead animal. The animal's skin is carefully removed and treated with a preservative, such as arsenical soap. The taxidermist then makes a drawing of the animal's body structure, including the muscles, bones, and depressions. This copy becomes a guide. Next, the taxidermist makes a framework out of wood and metal. The skeleton of the animal also may be used. The taxidermist then adds clay to the framework and sculpts the animal's anatomy. The clay model is used to make a thin, hollow casting of plaster, papier-mâché, burlap, and sometimes mesh wire. This casting must correspond accurately with the figure of the animal. Finally, the taxidermist places the skin on the casting and sews and glues it together. Skins of large, heavy animals must be tanned before being mounted on the casting.

Taxidermists must add many other body features and use special materials to make the eyes and tongue. Taxidermists may use painted hollow globes instead of glass eyes to give the preserved animal a natural expression. They must also shape the ears.

Some museums use a *freeze-drying* technique to preserve specimens. This method is used mainly for small animals, such as songbirds and squirrels.

A taxidermist proceeds through several steps to create a lifelike model of a running cheetah. First, the skin is removed from the animal and tanned, *left.* A clay model of the animal is then sculpted, *center.* Next, a casting is made from a mold of the sculpture, *right.*

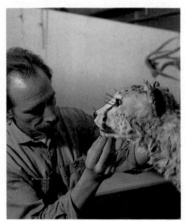

Field Museum of Natural History, Chicago (Taxidermy by
Paul O. Brunsvold; photography by Ron Testa and Diane Alexander White)

The taxidermist then places the tanned skin on the casting, *left.* Finally, the taxidermist sews, glues, and pins the skin into place, *center.* After other body features—such as eyes, ears, and a tongue—are added, the model is complete, *right.*

Careers in taxidermy. Taxidermy is a complicated art. It requires a knowledge of anatomy, natural history, drawing, sculpture, mechanics, tanning, and dyeing. Many museums have taxidermists on their staffs. Some museums hire commercial studios to mount their specimens. Most taxidermists learn their skills at a technical institute or by training under an experienced taxidermist. Further career information can be obtained from the National Taxidermists Association, 18626 St. Clair Avenue W., Cleveland, OH 44110.   Frank Greenwell

Additional resources

The Jonas Technique: Vol. 1, Bird Mounting; Vol. 2, Mammal Mounting; Vol. 3, Big Game Head Mounting; Vol. 5, Hints and Tips. Jonas Brothers (Denver, Colo.), 1974-1984.
McFall, Waddy F. *Taxidermy Step by Step.* Winchester, 1975.

Taxonomy. See Classification, Scientific.
Tay-Sachs disease is a hereditary disorder of the nervous system. It occurs chiefly among Jewish children

of eastern European ancestry. Tay-Sachs disease causes severe brain damage, enlargement of the head, convulsions, blindness, deafness, lack of energy, and eventually death. Victims develop a reddish spot on the retina of the eye. They begin to have symptoms when they are about 6 months old. There is no treatment for the disease, and most victims live only three or four years.

Tay-Sachs disease occurs in children who have too little of the enzyme *hexosaminidase A.* This enzyme controls the amount of *ganglioside* that accumulates in nerve cells. Ganglioside is a fat produced by normal cell growth. Nerve cells that store too much ganglioside become swollen and eventually die. A large number of damaged or dead nerve cells causes brain damage.

The symptoms of Tay-Sachs disease were first reported during the 1880's by two physicians, Waren Tay of Great Britain and Bernard Sachs of the United States. In 1969, researchers discovered that the lack of hexosaminidase A caused the disease. Today, scientists use

Tay-Sachs disease

Tay-Sachs disease is a hereditary brain disorder that occurs chiefly among Jews of eastern European ancestry. People who inherit the Tay-Sachs gene from both parents have the disorder.

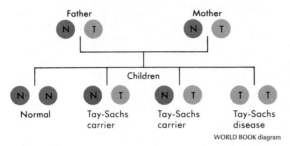

Father   Mother

Children

Normal | Tay-Sachs carrier | Tay-Sachs carrier | Tay-Sachs disease

WORLD BOOK diagram

In the chart above, each parent carries one normal gene and one Tay-Sachs gene. Such people are called *carriers.* A child of such parents has one chance in four of inheriting the Tay-Sachs gene from both parents—and thus having Tay-Sachs disease. People who inherit the Tay-Sachs gene from only one parent do not get the disease, but they may transmit the one abnormal gene to their children. The magnified photographs below show a normal brain cell, *left,* and an abnormal cell from the brain of a Tay-Sachs victim, *right.* The many dark, round bodies in the diseased cell are characteristic of the disorder.

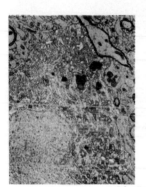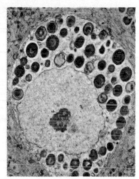

Robert D. Terry, M.D., Albert Einstein College of Medicine,
© *Journal of Neuropathology and Experimental Neurology*

a variety of tests to determine the activity of hexosaminidase A in samples of blood and various tissues. These tests can reveal whether unborn babies have Tay-Sachs disease. They also show whether adults are carriers of the disease. Carriers do not have the disease themselves. But if two carriers marry, their children may inherit it from them. Reuben Matalon

Taylor, Edward (1642?-1729), was the finest poet in colonial American literature. Taylor was born in Leicestershire, England. Unwilling to sign a loyalty oath to the Church of England, he sailed to New England in 1668. In 1671, he became a pastor in Westfield, Mass., a position he held the rest of his life.

Taylor's best poetry appears in *Preparatory Meditations,* a collection written for monthly communion in his church. In *God's Determination,* he used a debate between good and evil to emphasize God's mercy for people caught in the battle between Jesus Christ and Satan. Taylor achieved his complex thought in a few words. His work shows the influence of the intricate style of the English metaphysical poets of the 1600's. Although his language is complicated, Taylor's use of examples from everyday life makes his poetry understandable.
Edward W. Clark

See also **American literature** (Colonial poetry).

Taylor, Frederick Winslow (1856-1915), was an American engineer and efficiency expert. He joined Midvale Steel Works in Philadelphia in 1878 as a laborer, and left the company in 1890 as chief engineer. During this time, he conducted experiments to determine the maximum possible efficiency of people and machines. Taylor expanded his ideas into a detailed system for organizing and systematizing factory work. The best-known part of his system is the *time and motion study.* In this study an efficiency expert clocks each step in a job and looks for ways to reduce the time needed to do the job. Taylor's system was only one of many proposed in the early 1900's. However, the entire efficiency movement was often called *Taylorism* after 1910. Taylor was born in Germantown, Pa. Monte A. Calvert

Taylor, George (1716-1781), was a Pennsylvania signer of the Declaration of Independence. He served in the provincial assembly from 1764 to 1769 and in 1775. He became a colonel in the Pennsylvania militia in 1775. He also served as a member of the Continental Congress. Elected a member of the First Supreme Executive Council of Pennsylvania in 1777, he soon retired because of illness. Taylor was born in Ireland and came to Pennsylvania about 1736. Richard B. Morris

Taylor, Maxwell Davenport (1901-   ), gained fame as a United States general during World War II (1939-1945) and the Korean War (1950-1953). He later held important military and diplomatic positions under Presidents John F. Kennedy and Lyndon B. Johnson, and helped shape U.S. military strategy in the Vietnam War (1957-1975).

Taylor was born in Keytesville, Mo. He graduated from the U.S. Military Academy in 1922. During World War II, Taylor helped organize the Army's first airborne divisions and later served as artillery commander of the 82nd Airborne Division in Sicily and Italy. He was the first U.S. general to land in Normandy, France, during the Allied invasion on D-Day, June 6, 1944. Taylor commanded the 101st Airborne Division in 1944 and 1945. After the war, from 1949 to 1951, Taylor headed U.S. forces in West Berlin.

Taylor commanded the U.S. Eighth Army in the Korean War in 1953. From 1955 to 1959, he served as U.S. Army chief of staff. Taylor retired as a four-star general in 1959 but returned to active duty in 1961 to become Kennedy's military adviser. Taylor became chairman of the Joint Chiefs of Staff in 1962 and held that post until Johnson appointed him ambassador to South Vietnam in 1964, during the Vietnam War. Taylor served there for about a year and then became a special military and diplomatic consultant to Johnson. Taylor retired again in 1969. D. Clayton James

Taylor, Mildred, an American author of books for children, received the 1977 Newbery Medal for *Roll of Thunder, Hear My Cry* (1976). This novel tells of a black family's struggle against racial prejudice and poverty during the Great Depression of the 1930's. The story is set in rural Mississippi. Taylor also wrote an earlier novel about the same family, *Song of the Trees* (1975). Both books are based partly on events from her family. Taylor was born in Jackson, Miss. Zena Sutherland

**12th President of
the United States 1849-1850**

Polk
11th President
1845-1849
Democrat

Taylor
12th President
1849-1850
Whig

Fillmore
13th President
1850-1853
Whig

Millard Fillmore
Vice President
1849-1850

Oil painting by John Vanderlyn, Corcoran Gallery of Art, Washington, D.C.

Taylor, Zachary (1784-1850), served his country for 40 years as a soldier and for 16 months as President. His courage and ability during the Mexican War made him a national hero. Taylor showed the same courage while he was President, but he died before he could prove his full abilities as a statesman. He was succeeded by Vice President Millard Fillmore.

President Taylor was one of the large slaveowners of the South. But he did not oppose admitting California and New Mexico to the Union as free states. The South demanded that other slavery problems be settled before those territories became states, and threatened to secede. The President replied that he was ready to take his place at the head of the army to put down any such action. Taylor died at the height of this argument. President Fillmore's policies delayed the Civil War for 10 years.

Taylor made his greatest contribution to his country as a soldier. This quiet, friendly man was not a military genius. But he was a good leader. Taylor never lost a battle. His troops nicknamed him "Old Rough and Ready."

Early life

Childhood. Zachary Taylor was born near Barboursville, Va., on Nov. 24, 1784. He was the third son in a family of six boys and three girls. His parents, Richard and Sarah Strother Taylor, came from leading families of the Virginia plantation region. Richard Taylor served as an officer in the Revolutionary War. In 1783, he received a war bonus of 6,000 acres (2,400 hectares) of land near Louisville, Ky. He settled there in 1785.

Zachary grew up on "the dark and bloody ground" of Kentucky's frontier. There were no schools, but the boy

studied for a while under tutors, and gained much practical knowledge by working on his father's farm.

Perhaps it was natural that Zachary should turn to a military career. He grew up in the midst of Indian warfare, and heard tales of the Revolutionary War from his father. In 1808, Taylor received an appointment as a first lieutenant in the U.S. Army. Two years later, he was promoted to captain.

Taylor's family. Early in 1810, Taylor met Margaret Mackall Smith (Sept. 21, 1788-Aug. 14, 1852). She was the orphaned daughter of a Maryland planter. Taylor and Miss Smith were married on June 21, 1810. They had a son and five daughters, two of whom died as infants. Their daughter Sarah married Jefferson Davis, the future President of the Confederacy. She died three months after her wedding. The Taylors' son, Richard, served as a general in the Confederate Army.

Military career

Indian campaigns. During the War of 1812, Taylor won promotion to major for his defense of Fort Harrison in the Indiana Territory. He left the army briefly after the war, but returned and by 1829 had become a lieutenant colonel. He served in Wisconsin during the Black Hawk War, and received the surrender of Chief Black Hawk in 1832 (see **Black Hawk**).

Taylor was sent to Florida in 1837. There he defeated the Seminole Indians at Lake Okeechobee on Dec. 25, 1837. This victory brought him the honorary rank of brigadier general. In 1841, Taylor became commander of the second department of the western division of the U.S. Army, with headquarters at Fort Smith, Ark.

Mexican War. In 1846, Mexico threatened war with the United States over the annexation of Texas. Taylor

Revolutions swept Europe in the late 1840's. The uprisings led to increased immigration to the United States.

The California gold rush brought thousands of treasure seekers, called "Forty-Niners," to the West Coast in 1849.

The world of President Taylor

The Department of the Interior was established by Congress in 1849. The department took over duties in such areas as Indian affairs, public lands, and mining.

Amelia Jenks Bloomer began publishing a journal called the *Lily* in 1849 to promote temperance and women's rights. She became famous for wearing long, gathered pants called "bloomers" under her skirts.

Charles Dickens enjoyed a reputation as the most popular English writer of his time. He published *David Copperfield,* a semiautobiographical novel, in 1849-1850.

Overland mail service by wagon began in 1850, when a stagecoach route opened between Independence, Mo., and Santa Fe, N. Mex. It took about 30 days for mail to be delivered from one end of the route to the other.

The slavery issue led to some of the most memorable debates in the history of the United States Senate. Senator Henry Clay of Kentucky proposed a series of resolutions that became the basis for the Compromise of 1850. Such noted orators as Daniel Webster of Massachusetts, Stephen Douglas of Illinois, and John Calhoun of South Carolina led the historic debates.

The Scarlet Letter, published in 1850, brought international fame to American author Nathaniel Hawthorne. The novel dealt with sin and morality in Puritan Boston.

Popular uprisings against undemocratic governments in Europe won American sympathy. Hungarian revolutionary leader Lajos Kossuth toured the United States in 1849 and was hailed as the "Hungarian George Washington."

Bibliothèque Nationale, Paris; California Historical Society

was ordered to the Rio Grande with 4,000 troops. When Mexican forces crossed the river, Taylor defeated them in battles at Palo Alto and Resaca de la Palma. War was declared on May 13, 1846. Taylor then invaded Mexico, and captured Matamoros and Monterrey.

After these victories, Taylor seemed the best choice to lead an invading army into the central valley of Mexico. But President James K. Polk, a Democrat, knew that Taylor favored the Whig party. Partly because Polk feared the growth of a popular Whig leader, he named General Winfield Scott to lead the invasion.

On Feb. 22-23, 1847, Taylor's 5,000-man army was attacked by between 16,000 and 20,000 Mexican troops in the Battle of Buena Vista. Taylor's troops won a stunning victory over the forces of General Santa Anna. The triumph made Taylor a national hero. See **Mexican War; Santa Anna, Antonio López de.**

Nomination for President

Whig leaders decided that Taylor could easily win the presidency. Taylor hesitated to enter politics, but the Whigs nominated him anyway. They chose Millard Fillmore, comptroller of New York, for Vice President. The Democrats nominated Senator Lewis Cass of Michigan and General William O. Butler of Kentucky.

Important dates in Taylor's life

1784	(Nov. 24) Born near Barboursville, Va.
1810	(June 21) Married Margaret Mackall Smith.
1812	Defended Fort Harrison against Tecumseh.
1832	Received surrender of Black Hawk.
1847	Defeated Santa Anna in Battle of Buena Vista.
1848	Elected President of the United States.
1850	(July 9) Died in the White House.

During the campaign, both Whigs and Democrats avoided the slavery issue. Only the Free Soil Party, a group led by former President Martin Van Buren, campaigned on this issue (see **Free Soil Party**). Van Buren

Taylor's election

Place of nominating convention	....Philadelphia
Ballot on which nominated	.........4th
Democratic opponent	..............Lewis Cass
Electoral vote*	........................163 (Taylor) to 127 (Cass)
Popular vote	........................1,361,393 (Taylor) to 1,223,460 (Cass)
Age at inauguration	64

*For votes by states, see **Electoral College** (table).

The Granger Collection

The Battle of Buena Vista established Taylor as a hero of the Mexican War. Taylor, shown above on the white horse, led his outnumbered troops to a decisive victory over the Mexicans.

White House Historical Association

Courtesy Ruth C. Tate, from *Seventy-Five Years of White House Gossip,* by Edna M. Colman, Doubleday & Company, Inc.

Mary Elizabeth Bliss, *above,* the Taylors' youngest daughter, performed the duties of White House hostess. Margaret Smith Taylor, *left,* who had not favored her husband's candidacy for President, took little part in Washington social life.

did not carry a single state, but he drew many votes from Cass. Taylor and Fillmore won by 36 electoral votes. The presidential election of 1848 was the first to be held at the same time in all the states.

Taylor's Administration (1849-1850)

Taylor was inaugurated on March 5, 1849. He would normally have taken office on March 4, but declined to be inaugurated on Sunday. Some historians claim that David R. Atchison, president pro tempore of the Senate, served as acting President on March 4 because the presidency was vacant on that day.

Taylor leaned heavily on the advice of others, because he knew he lacked political experience. Taylor's friends learned that anyone could advise him, but no one could influence him to act against his conscience.

Vice President and Cabinet

Vice President	*Millard Fillmore
Secretary of state	*John M. Clayton
Secretary of the treasury	William M. Meredith
Secretary of war	George W. Crawford
Attorney general	Reverdy Johnson
Postmaster general	*Jacob Collamer
Secretary of the Navy	William B. Preston
Secretary of the interior	Thomas Ewing

*Has a separate biography in WORLD BOOK.

Life in the White House. Mrs. Taylor had not favored the idea of her husband running for President. She viewed it as a plot to deprive her of his company. Mrs. Taylor, a semi-invalid, took little part in the White House social life. Hostess duties passed to her daughter Mary Elizabeth, known as Betty. Betty's husband, Colonel William W. S. Bliss, was Taylor's secretary.

The Nicaragua Canal. The acquisition of territory on the Pacific Coast during President James K. Polk's administration revived the dream of a water route across Central America. American businessmen tried to obtain rights to build a canal across Nicaragua. The British were also interested in such a canal. In 1850, the United States and Britain signed the Clayton-Bulwer Treaty, which guaranteed the neutrality of any such canal. See **Clayton-Bulwer Treaty.**

Sectional quarrels. Controversy over the extension of slavery reached a new high in 1849, when California applied for admission to the Union as a free state. Taylor urged the admission of California, and expressed hope that New Mexico would also apply. Southerners angrily demanded the adjustment of other slavery problems before new states were admitted. During the next months, Congress had one of its greatest debates. Southerners threatened secession, and Northerners promised war to preserve the Union.

Many congressional leaders, including Senator Henry Clay of Kentucky, urged some kind of compromise. But Taylor scorned any compromise, and insisted that California be admitted to the Union. Those in favor of compromise eventually won their point, but not until Fillmore had succeeded to the presidency. Congress then adopted a series of laws called the Compromise of 1850. See **Compromise of 1850.**

Death. Before the slavery issue could be settled, Taylor became ill and died on July 9, 1850. He was buried in the family cemetery near Louisville, Ky. Mrs. Taylor died on Aug. 14, 1852, and was buried beside her husband.

Brainerd Dyer

Related articles in *World Book* include:

Outline

I. Early life
  A. Childhood   B. Taylor's family
II. Military career
  A. Indian campaigns   B. Mexican War
III. Nomination for President
IV. Taylor's Administration (1849-1850)
  A. Life in the White House   C. Sectional quarrels
  B. The Nicaragua Canal   D. Death

Questions

How did Taylor become a national hero?
What was one reason that President Polk did not choose Taylor to lead the invasion of Mexico City?
How may Taylor have become interested in the army?
How did President Taylor reply to a Southern threat to secede from the Union?
Why do some historians claim that an acting President served the first day of Taylor's term?

Additional resources

Bauer, K. Jack. *Zachary Taylor: Soldier, Planter, Statesman of the Old Southwest.* Louisiana State Univ. Press, 1985.
Hamilton, Holman. *Zachary Taylor.* 2 vols. Bobbs, 1941-1951.

Singletary, Otis A. *The Mexican War.* Univ. of Chicago Press, 1960.

Tayra, *TY ruh,* is a large member of the weasel family. It lives in tropical forests from Mexico to Argentina. Most tayras have black or dark brown fur, with a white or yellow patch on the chest. The fur on the head gradually turns brown or gray as the animal grows older. An adult tayra weighs about 10 pounds (5 kilograms) and measures about $3\frac{1}{2}$ feet (107 centimeters) long, including a tail 16 inches (41 centimeters) long.

Tayras wander the forests and are active both day and

© Fulvio Eccardi, Bruce Coleman Inc.

The tayra lives In tropical forests of the Americas.

night. They travel alone or in family groups. These graceful animals climb well and can run swiftly.

Tayras eat birds, small mammals, and fruits. The female tayra gives birth to two to four young in a nest she has built in a tree or on the ground.

Scientific classification. The tayra belongs to the weasel family, Mustelidae. Its scientific name is *Eira barbara.*

John H. Kaufmann and Arleen Kaufmann

TB. See Tuberculosis.

Tbilisi, *tuh BIHL uh see* (pop. 1,140,000), is the capital of the Georgian Soviet Socialist Republic, a republic of the Soviet Union. *Tbilisi* means *warm springs* in the Georgian language. The city used to be called *Tiflis,* its name in Russian. It lies on the Kura River (see **Union of Soviet Socialist Republics** [political map]). Tbilisi is one of the oldest cities in the Soviet Union. Part of the city is modern, and part looks like an ancient Oriental city. Tbilisi's products include cotton materials, felt, leather goods, machinery, metal products, and oil. Tbilisi is the junction for a highway network and a railroad network. Airlines link Tbilisi to other major cities in the Soviet Union.   Zvi Gitelman

Tchaikovsky, *chy KAWF skee,* **Peter Ilich,** *IHL yihch* (1840-1893), was the first Russian composer to gain international fame. He was a master of orchestration with a superb talent for blending instrumental sounds and for achieving rousing orchestral effects. He also had a remarkable gift for writing melody.

Tchaikovsky is often described as a composer of music that is basically melancholy. Some of his music is melancholy, especially the last movement of his *Symphony No. 6.* But he also wrote spirited music, as in *Marche Slave* and "1812" overture; lyrical music, as in

the symphonic poem *Romeo and Juliet;* lively ballet music, as in the *Nutcracker Suite;* and powerful symphonies.

Brown Bros.

Peter Tchaikovsky

His life. Tchaikovsky was born on May 7, 1840, in Votkinsk. He entered a law school in St. Petersburg (now Leningrad) in 1850. From 1862 to 1866, he studied music at the St. Petersburg Conservatory under Anton Rubinstein, a pianist and composer. Tchaikovsky was the first Russian composer to receive systematic training in music fundamentals.

From 1866 to 1877, Tchaikovsky taught at the Moscow Conservatory of Music. He began composing seriously about 1866. At this time, his early emotional sensitivity developed into long periods of depression. Curiously, he wrote some of his most cheerful music during these periods. He was married in 1877, but he and his wife separated within a few weeks. This experience brought him close to a nervous breakdown.

In 1876, Nadezhda von Meck, a wealthy widow, commissioned some works from Tchaikovsky. She admired his music and agreed to support him so he could compose at leisure. She insisted that they never meet, but they exchanged letters for years. Assured of an income, Tchaikovsky left the Moscow Conservatory and concentrated on composing. He traveled widely, and in 1891 took part in the opening of Carnegie Hall in New York City. He died on Nov. 6, 1893.

His works. Tchaikovsky's six symphonies stand out as landmarks in his artistic development. His first three symphonies are seldom performed today. His fourth, written in 1877, is his first masterpiece in the symphonic form. Tchaikovsky's *Symphony No. 5* (1888) is his finest from the standpoint of formal construction. *Symphony No. 6* (1893) is called the "Pathétique" ("Pathetic"). It departed from the traditional symphonic form by expressing a deeply emotional feeling of tragedy in the final movement. Tchaikovsky's other orchestral works include his *Italian Capriccio* (1880), his famous *Nutcracker Suite,* and four other suites.

Tchaikovsky's *Concerto for Piano and Orchestra No. 1 in B flat minor* (1874-1875) and his *Violin Concerto in D major* (1878) are classics of their types. Tchaikovsky also wrote an important work for violoncello—*Variations on a Rococo Theme for Violoncello and Orchestra* (1876). He composed vocal pieces and works for solo piano.

Tchaikovsky's three ballets have become classics. They are *Swan Lake* (1875-1876), *Sleeping Beauty* (1888-1889), and *The Nutcracker* (1892). Tchaikovsky wrote 11 operas, but only *Eugene Onégin* (1877-1878) and *Queen of Spades* (1890) are well known outside of Russia. Both have *librettos* (words) based on works by the Russian poet Alexander Pushkin. *Queen of Spades* is written on a larger scale than *Eugene Onégin.* It is a powerful psychological music drama dominated by the idea that fate rules human beings.

Tchaikovsky has often been described as a "Westerner" among Russian composers. He was the first Russian composer to write polished music in the Western manner and the first to win widespread popularity outside Russia. Some critics tend to see the melancholy strain in Tchaikovsky's music as almost the only trace of his Russian origin. But Tchaikovsky always claimed to be fully Russian in his feelings, and his works contain quotations from Russian folk melodies. He cited Mozart, a Westerner, and Mikhail Glinka, a Russian, as the composers who influenced him the most. Much of Tchaikovsky's work represents a blend of the spirits of these two widely different composers.   Miloš Velimirović

Additional resources

Abraham, Gerald E. H., ed. *The Music of Tchaikovsky.* Norton, 1974. Reprint of 1946 edition.

Brown, David. *Tchaikovsky: The Early Years, 1840-1874.* Norton, 1979. *Tchaikovsky: The Crisis Years, 1874-1878.* 1983. *Tchaikovsky: The Years of Wandering, 1878-1885.* 1986.

Strutte, Wilson. *Tchaikovsky: His Life and Times.* Two Continents, 1979.

Warrack, John H. *Tchaikovsky.* Scribner, 1973.

Te Kanawa, *teh KAH nah wah,* **Dame Kiri,** *KIHR ee* (1944-   ), a New Zealand opera singer, is one of the most praised sopranos in the world. She has sung major roles in the operas of Wolfgang Amadeus Mozart, Giacomo Puccini, Giuseppe Verdi, and Georges Bizet. Her voice is rich and lyric, and impresses with its freshness and warmth.

Te Kanawa was born in Gisborne, New Zealand. In 1971, she performed her first major operatic role as Countess Almaviva in Mozart's *The Marriage of Figaro* at Covent Garden in London. In 1974, she made her debut with the Metropolitan Opera in New York City. This appearance came on three hours' notice, when she substituted for an ailing performer as Desdemona in Verdi's *Otello.* Her performance made her an international star. In 1982, Te Kanawa was made Dame Commander of the Order of the British Empire.   Charles H. Webb

Lyric Opera of Chicago

Kiri Te Kanawa

Tea is a beverage prepared by pouring boiling water over dry processed tea leaves. It ranks as the most popular refreshing drink in more countries than any other beverage.

In 1985, about 5 billion pounds (2.3 billion kilograms) of dried tea were produced. India has always played a dominant role in world tea production. Today, India produces about $1\frac{1}{2}$ billion pounds (670 million kilograms) each year. China is the second largest producer with about 1 billion pounds (460 million kilograms) annually. Other tea-producing countries include Argentina, Bangladesh, Indonesia, Japan, Kenya, the Soviet Union, Sri Lanka, and Turkey.

The tea-producing countries themselves consume over one-half of the global tea crop. Great Britain imports the greatest amount of tea—about 400 million pounds (180 million kilograms) annually. On the average, about 7 pounds (3.2 kilograms) of tea are consumed per person each year in Great Britain. In the United States,

tea use is about $\frac{3}{4}$ pound (0.34 kilogram) per person per year.

From leaf to cup

The tea plant grows in tropical and subtropical climates. The plant, an evergreen, grows quickly at low altitudes where the air is warm. The finest tea comes from elevations of 3,000 to 7,000 feet (900 to 2,100 meters). The plant grows more slowly in cool air, adding to its flavor.

Tea plants have small, white, sweet-smelling flowers. Each flower produces three seeds that look like hazelnuts. On a tea estate or in a tea garden where tea plants are grown commercially, workers plant the seeds in a nursery bed. Another method involves planting cuttings of tea plants with desirable qualities, such as high yield or special flavor, in the bed. About a year later, when the plants are about 8 inches (20 centimeters) high, they are transplanted to the field. About 3,000 tea plants grow on 1 acre (0.4 hectare) of land.

Wild tea plants grow as high as 30 feet (9 meters). But a commercial tea plant is pruned to keep it from 3 to 4 feet (91 to 120 centimeters) high. The plant matures in three to five years and produces a *flush* (growth of new shoots). Each shoot consists of several leaves and a bud. At lower altitudes, tea plants may grow a flush every week. At higher altitudes, a plant needs as long as two weeks to grow a flush. No flushes grow in cold weather.

Workers called *tea pluckers* pick the flushes off the bush by hand. A plucker can harvest about 40 pounds (18 kilograms) of tea leaves a day, enough to make about 10 pounds (4.5 kilograms) of manufactured tea.

Mechanical pluckers are common in countries with flat land. These devices are tractorlike machines that can harvest as much tea leaf as up to 100 manual pluckers. However, tea of higher quality is generally produced from leaves that have been hand-plucked.

Processing tea. There are three main kinds of tea: (1) black, (2) green, and (3) oolong. They differ in the method used to process the leaves. The processing takes place in a factory on or near the tea estate. All tea-producing countries manufacture black tea. Most of the green and oolong tea comes from China, Japan, and Taiwan.

Black tea. To make black tea, workers first spread the leaves on shelves called *withering racks.* Air is blown over the leaves to remove excess moisture, leaving them soft and flexible. Next, the leaves are crushed between the rollers of a machine to release their flavorful juices. Then, in a *fermenting room,* the tea leaves change chemically under controlled humidity and temperature until they turn coppery in color. Finally, the leaves are dried in ovens and become brownish-black.

Green tea is made by steaming the leaves in large vats. The steaming prevents the leaves from changing color. The leaves are then crushed in a machine and dried in ovens.

Oolong tea is made by partially fermenting the leaves. This gives tea leaves a greenish-brown color.

Grades of tea vary only according to the size of the leaves. The size of a tea leaf has nothing to do with the quality of the tea.

To sort the processed tea leaves by grade, they are passed across screens with different size holes. The

Shostal

Tea pluckers on a plantation near Kandy, Sri Lanka, pick leaves from mature tea plants, *left.* The tea plants produce shoots called *flushes,* which consist of several leaves and a bud, *above.* After being picked, the flushes are processed into tea in a nearby factory.

Tea Council of the U.S.A., Inc.

largest leaves, selected for packaging as loose tea, are classified—in order of size—as *orange pekoe, pekoe,* and *pekoe souchong.* The smaller or broken leaves, generally used in tea bags, are classified as *broken orange pekoe, broken orange pekoe fannings,* and *fannings.*

Instant tea is made by brewing tea on a large scale and then removing the water by a drying process. When the process is completed, only a powder remains. The

Leading tea-growing countries

Annual tea production

Country	Production
India	1,477,000,000 pounds (670,000,000 kilograms)
China	1,025,000,000 pounds (465,000,000 kilograms)
Sri Lanka	471,800,000 pounds (214,000,000 kilograms)
Soviet Union	352,700,000 pounds (160,000,000 kilograms)
Kenya	324,100,000 pounds (147,000,000 kilograms)
Turkey	288,800,000 pounds (131,000,000 kilograms)
Indonesia	284,400,000 pounds (129,000,000 kilograms)
Japan	212,000,000 pounds (96,000,000 kilograms)
Bangladesh	94,800,000 pounds (43,000,000 kilograms)
Argentina	92,600,000 pounds (42,000,000 kilograms)

Figures are for 1985. Source: *FAO Production Yearbook, 1985,* Food and Agriculture Organization of the United Nations.

powdered tea combines easily with moisture, and so it must be packed under controlled humidity and temperature. People make instant tea at home by simply adding water to the powder.

Teas grown in different countries, or even in different parts of the same country, vary in taste, flavor, and quality. To obtain the best teas, each tea company employs *tea tasters* who select only certain teas for purchase. These teas, after being blended by the company, have a flavor for which the firm is known. The company then sells its blend of tea under its own brand name.

Brewing tea. Tea is brewed by pouring boiling water over one teaspoon of loose tea, or one tea bag, per cup. To obtain the best flavor, the tea should *steep* (soak) for three to five minutes before being served. People who prefer weak tea can add hot water.

Iced tea, the most popular form of the beverage in the United States, is prepared by first brewing a strong hot tea. For each two glasses, three teaspoons of tea or three tea bags should be used. After steeping for five minutes, the tea is cooled at room temperature and served over ice cubes.

History

According to legend, the use of tea was discovered by Emperor Shennong of China about 2737 B.C. The earliest known mention of tea appeared in Chinese literature of about A.D. 350. The custom of tea drinking spread to Japan around 600 A. D. The first shipment of tea to Europe was made in 1610 by Dutch traders who imported it from China and Japan. By 1650, the Dutch were importing tea into the American Colonies.

In 1657, tea was sold for the first time in coffee houses in England. It went on to become the national drink of Great Britain. In 1767, Britain placed a tax on the tea being used by the American colonists. Colonial resistance to the tax brought about the Boston Tea Party in 1773 and contributed to the American independence movement (see **Boston Tea Party**).

The use of iced tea and tea bags began in the United States. Richard Blechynden, an Englishman trying to increase the use of tea in the United States, first served iced tea at the Louisiana Purchase Exposition (also called the St. Louis World's Fair) in 1904. That same year, Thomas Sullivan, a New York City coffee and tea merchant, sent his customers samples of tea leaves in small silk bags instead of the usual tin containers. The customers began to order tea leaves in bags after finding that tea could be brewed easily with them. Instant tea was developed in the United States and first marketed in 1948.

Scientific classification. The tea plant is a member of the tea family, Theaceae. It is *Camellia sinensis*.   Philip Coggon

See also **Caffeine; Japan** (picture: Japanese agriculture); **Kenya** (picture: Kenya's highland); **Labrador tea; Maté.**

Additional resources

Pratt, James N. *The Tea Lover's Treasury.* Scribner, 1982.
Schafer, Charles and Violet. *Teacraft,* Random House, 1975.
Schapira, David, and others. *The Book of Coffee and Tea.* Rev. ed. St. Martin's, 1982.

Tea tax. See Revolutionary War in America (The Tea Act).
Teach, Edward. See Blackbeard.
Teacher. See Teaching; Education.
Teachers, American Federation of. See American Federation of Teachers.
Teachers College, Columbia University, is the graduate school of education at Columbia University in New York City. It prepares men and women for professional service at every level of education.

Through its 19 departments, Teachers College offers programs in all phases of teaching, curricular planning, computing technology, and administration for the training of educational personnel. It provides advanced work in psychology, counseling, and guidance. The university also prepares students for careers in nursing, health, and nutrition education. It conducts research in all these areas and provides field service to schools throughout the United States and abroad. Teachers College also sponsors many international activities in education.

Organization. Teachers College is financially independent, with its own charter, board of trustees, and president. It forms a division of Columbia University by formal agreement between the trustees of the college and the trustees of the university. Under this agreement, faculty members at the college are also members of the Columbia University faculty, and university courses are open to students of Teachers College. Degrees earned at the college are granted through the university.

Many research and service activities at Teachers College are conducted through various institutes and special projects. These activities concern such areas as the needs of handicapped children, higher education, the philosophy and politics of education, and the education of gifted students. They also deal with such areas as psychological services, motor learning, urban and minority education, health promotion, and curriculum development.

History. Teachers College was founded in 1887 as the New York College for the Training of Teachers. Sponsored by the Industrial Education Association, it prepared teachers in various fields, particularly home economics and industrial arts. The college greatly expanded its curriculum under the leadership of Nicholas Murray Butler, who served as president from 1887 to 1891, and Walter L. Hervey, the president from 1891 to 1897. In 1892, the New York State Regents granted the college a permanent charter. In 1898, Teachers College became part of Columbia University.

The college became a world leader in educational research and experimentation during the administrations of James E. Russell, its dean from 1897 to 1927, and William F. Russell, the dean from 1927 to 1949 and president from 1949 to 1954. These men—father and son—emphasized research and experimentation to advance knowledge about educational goals and processes and to improve teaching practices in schools, colleges, and other academic institutions. As a result of their efforts, many important educational developments were pioneered at Teachers College. For enrollment, see **Universities and colleges** (table [Columbia University]).

Critically reviewed by Teachers College

© Lee Snider

Teachers College offers graduate-level courses and is part of Columbia University in New York City. The college's campus, *left,* includes buildings that date from the late 1800's.

Gene Harris, Meyers Photo-Art

College professor giving a lecture

Jim Collins

Elementary-school teacher guiding a student

Kindergarten teacher introducing the alphabet

Teachers at all levels guide the learning of students in various ways. Sometimes, teachers help students individually. At other times, they instruct an entire group. At still other times, teachers guide students by asking questions or encouraging class discussion.

Teaching

Teaching is the process by which a person helps other people learn. It is one of our most important activities. Teaching helps people gain the knowledge and attitudes they need to be responsible citizens, earn a living, and lead a useful, rewarding life. It also provides the chief means of passing knowledge to the next generation. Without teachers, people would have to learn everything by themselves. Few people could learn enough on their own to get along in the world. The world would change greatly as humanity lost the knowledge, skills, and ideals inherited from past generations.

Much teaching takes place *informally*—that is, outside school. In the home, for example, parents teach their children everyday skills, as well as values and habits. Businesses and industries often teach their employees

Willard Abraham, the contributor of this article, is Professor of Education and Chairman of the Department of Special Education at Arizona State University.

necessary job skills. But when people speak of teaching, they usually mean *formal teaching*—the kind provided in schools by professional teachers.

More people belong to the teaching profession than to any other. About 32 million men and women throughout the world are teachers. The United States has about $3\frac{1}{4}$ million teachers, and Canada has more than 330,000.

The teaching profession has developed mainly since the early 1800's, when the first teacher-training schools began in western Europe. Before then, schoolteachers received little or no special training. Today, most countries require teachers to complete a professional training program and to meet professional standards.

This article deals chiefly with the teaching profession in the United States and Canada. It discusses teaching careers in both countries and current issues in U.S. teaching. For detailed information about the history of teaching, see **Education** (History).

A teacher's duties

A teacher's job involves four main duties. (1) Teachers must prepare for their classes. (2) They must guide, or

Jim Collins

WORLD BOOK photo

Preparing for class requires thought and effort on a teacher's part. This second-grade teacher is arranging a display of her pupils' artwork and poetry in preparation for a class discussion.

Teaching aids, such as the chalkboard and wall map above, help teachers guide learning. Teachers also use such aids as tape recordings, filmstrips, and special television programs.

assist, the learning of students. (3) They must check student progress. (4) Teachers must set a good example for their students. In carrying out these duties, teachers try to identify and respond to the needs of individual students.

A teacher's main duties also involve a number of related tasks, from keeping attendance records to marking papers. Also, many teachers take part in school-related activities after school hours and often outside school.

Since the 1950's, science and industry have developed many new devices and techniques for classroom use, including educational TV, language laboratories, and other advanced learning aids. Although these *technological* advances may assist the learning process, they have not greatly changed the teacher's basic role.

This section deals mainly with the duties of elementary- and secondary-school teachers.

Preparing for classes. Before each class session, a teacher must do such things as review subject matter, prepare learning activities, and plan special projects. This preparation is often called a *daily lesson plan.* Teachers have guidelines to help them plan their teaching. For example, local school boards usually decide the *curriculum* (courses of study and other learning activities) for students to follow. Many local school boards involve teachers in the process of planning the curriculum for the area's schools.

A state or local school board may also set general learning goals for students. Such learning goals include the acquiring of certain knowledge and skills and the development of certain values and attitudes. If a school board does not outline these goals, teachers and administrators must decide them. Many teachers involve their students in deciding learning goals. Within the guidelines, most teachers are free to plan the kinds of activities they think will help students meet the desired goals.

Guiding the learning of students. Most teachers use a variety of methods to guide their students' learn-

ing. For example, they sometimes guide students individually and sometimes as a group. But even when dealing with students as a group, a good teacher's basic concern is the individual development of each student. Many teachers believe that students should be given only enough guidance to help them learn to solve problems by themselves.

Teachers have long depended on textbooks to assist learning. Today, many teachers also use *audio-visual materials,* including tape recordings, filmstrips, and television programs (see **Audio-visual materials**). Some teachers utilize specially designed textbooks or audio-visual materials to give *programmed instruction.* In this method, a subject is broken down into a series of small steps called a *program.* A student must master each step before going on to the next one. Students can thus study at their own pace.

Although teachers generally use a variety of teaching methods and materials, they must suit them to the abilities, age, and needs of their students. Nursery-school teachers, for example, use such instructional materials and methods as toys and games to attract the interest of youngsters. In certain areas, including the poorer sections of large cities, some students may lack the basic communication and study skills they need to progress in school. To help these students acquire the necessary skills, a teacher may decide to use special methods and materials. For example, a teacher of reading in an inner-city school may find it helpful to use textbooks that relate directly to life in the inner city. In all of these cases, a teacher must also take into account the differing needs and abilities of individual students.

For more information on how teachers assist learning, see **Education** (The educative process).

Checking student progress. Most teachers give written or oral tests to help evaluate the progress of their students. By analyzing the test results of all the students in a group, teachers can discover which students

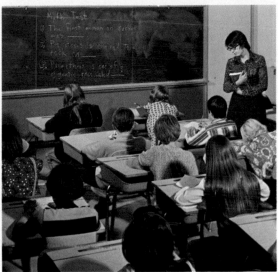

WORLD BOOK photo

A class test helps teachers check their students' progress. A teacher may use the test results to find out which students need extra help and what kind of help they need.

need special help and decide what kind of help they need. By evaluating the performance of the entire group, teachers can judge the effectiveness of their teaching methods and materials.

Most schools group students in various grades according to age. In these schools, teachers use test results to give students specific marks in their courses. *Nongraded* schools do not group students according to age. Instead, students advance in each subject at their own speed. They attend classes with other students who have reached the same level, regardless of age. In most of these schools, teachers give general evaluations rather than specific marks. The evaluations may be written, or a teacher may meet with each student and his or her parents to discuss the student's progress. For more information about school tests and how they are used, see the article Testing.

Setting a good example for students. Teachers often help students more by their example than they do in any other way. One of the most important ways that teachers set an example is by showing such qualities as patience, understanding, trustworthiness, and attention to work. Students who see these qualities in their teachers may be encouraged to develop similar qualities in themselves. In addition, students are more likely to cooperate with a teacher whom they respect and admire and so are more likely to benefit from the assistance of that teacher.

Other duties. Teachers often have certain duties after school hours. For example, many teachers act as advisers or sponsors of student groups, such as athletics teams or hobby clubs. Many teachers also serve as student counselors after school hours. Elementary school students ask chiefly for help with minor problems related to their schoolwork or outside activities. But a teacher sometimes faces difficult counseling problems. In high school, for example, some students regularly cut classes or consider dropping out of school alto-

gether. Whenever possible, teachers try to discourage such actions through talks with individual students and their parents.

Most teachers also take part in various professional activities outside school. These activities range from attending teachers' conferences and taking study trips to taking advanced courses in college.

Teaching as a career

A person who wants to become a teacher should like people and get satisfaction from helping them. It is also important to be well educated and to speak and write effectively. Although the brightest students do not necessarily make the best teachers, most teachers were good students.

Good teaching requires intense work on a personal level. Good teachers take an interest in their students and do all they can to help them. They realize that some students find learning difficult and so require extra patience and encouragement. The best teachers make learning enjoyable. They have a thorough knowledge of the subjects they teach and know how to arouse their students' interest in them.

Teacher-training programs. Almost all teacher-training programs in the United States and Canada are offered at general colleges or universities. Most U.S. teacher-training programs consist of three main areas of study: (1) general education, or liberal arts, courses; (2) advanced courses in a major area of study, such as English or mathematics; and (3) professional education courses. Canada's teacher-training programs are similar to those in the United States.

During their first two years in college, teachers-in-training take courses in history, language arts, mathematics, science, and other liberal arts. During their second two years, most students specialize in a particular subject, usually the subject that they plan to teach. Also during their second two years, teachers-in-training take such professional education courses as child development, teaching methods, and practice-teaching. In practice-teaching, a student does actual classroom teaching under the guidance of an experienced teacher.

Certification of teachers. Every state requires public elementary- and secondary-school teachers to obtain a *teaching certificate* before they may teach in the state. The state issues the certificate to persons who meet the state's basic teaching requirements. Some states also require certification to teach in a nursery school, private school, or public junior college. Teachers in four-year colleges and universities do not need a certificate. Instead, they must obtain an advanced degree and demonstrate their teaching ability through satisfactory on-the-job performance.

Almost all states issue separate certificates for elementary- and secondary-school teachers. Every state requires beginning teachers at both levels to be college graduates. Teachers at both levels must also have completed a professional training program that prepares them to teach in either elementary or secondary school. In addition, secondary-school teachers must be qualified to teach a particular subject. Many states also require such qualification for elementary-school teachers. Some teachers in special fields earn certificates that allow them to teach at both the elementary level and the

Age, sex, and education of U.S. public school teachers*

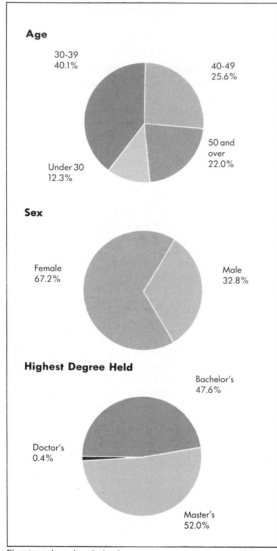

Age

- 30-39 40.1%
- 40-49 25.6%
- 50 and over 22.0%
- Under 30 12.3%

Sex

- Female 67.2%
- Male 32.8%

Highest Degree Held

- Bachelor's 47.6%
- Doctor's 0.4%
- Master's 52.0%

*Elementary- and secondary-school teachers.
Source: *Nationwide Teacher Opinion Poll, 1983,* copyright ©
1983 National Education Association. All Rights Reserved.

after they have taught a certain number of years. Many states also require additional college courses or a master's degree for advanced certification. A few states issue advanced certificates to new teachers who meet the necessary requirements. Some states issue advanced certificates on a permanent basis. Other states require teachers to renew their advanced certificate every few years. About half the states accept teaching certificates from other states. The rest require teachers from other states to take certain additional courses or to pass a special examination.

Public elementary- and secondary-school teachers in Canada must also have a teaching certificate. Each province issues its own certificates and sets the requirements for them. Most provinces require elementary- and secondary-school teachers to have a college degree plus, or including, a year or more of teacher-training courses.

Job opportunities. Schools in the United States and Canada need many thousands of new teachers each year. Teachers who retire or go into other lines of work create most of the openings.

The demand for teachers in the United States varies somewhat by teaching field, grade level, and locality. For example, there is generally a demand for teachers in the fields of mathematics; special education, which is designed for handicapped or gifted children; and vocational education, which prepares students for skilled jobs. There is also a demand for nursery-school teachers, school administrators, guidance counselors, librarians, and psychologists. The United States as a whole has an oversupply of elementary-school teachers and of secondary-school teachers in such subject areas as English, foreign languages, and social studies. But many small towns and the poor sections of large cities need teachers in these fields.

At one time, almost all elementary-school teachers in the United States were women, and almost all college and university teachers were men. But this situation has been slowly changing. Although women still far outnumber men as elementary-school teachers, men now make up about 15 per cent of the total. At the same time,

secondary level. These fields include art, music, and the education of handicapped children.

Most states issue special certificates for such positions as school principal, school librarian, and guidance counselor. In most cases, applicants must meet the basic requirements for a teaching certificate and also be specially trained in their field. *Teacher aides,* or *paraprofessional teachers,* do not need a professional teaching certificate. They mainly help professional teachers perform such duties as marking test papers and giving students individual guidance.

Most states issue an initial, or provisional, certificate to new teachers who meet the basic teaching requirements. Teachers may apply for an advanced certificate

Milt & Joan Mann

A teacher-training program includes courses in educational theory, *above.* Students must also do *practice-teaching*—that is, classroom teaching supervised by experienced teachers.

an increasing number of women have been hired to teach in U.S. colleges and universities, where they now fill about a fourth of the teaching positions. In U.S. secondary schools, slightly more teaching jobs are held by men than women.

Changes in the number of job openings for teachers depend largely on changes in the birth rate. For example, a sharp increase in the U.S. birth rate during the late 1940's led to rising enrollments and a teacher shortage in the 1950's and early 1960's. But the birth rate then dropped sharply, reducing school enrollments. As a result, many qualified college graduates could not find teaching jobs in the 1970's and the early 1980's.

Employment practices. In most public school districts, the local school board is responsible for hiring teachers. Most boards sign a contract with every teacher they hire. In the contract, the board agrees to pay a certain salary for the teacher's services. The contract covers a specified period of time, after which a new contract must be signed. In many school districts, a teachers' union or other professional organization also signs a *master contract* with the school board. This contract covers not only the teachers who belong to the organization but also all other teachers in the district, including any new teachers the school board hires. Before signing the contract, the organization tries to obtain from the board the highest salaries possible and other benefits for the teachers. The master contract is good for only a certain period of time. A new contract is then signed, after the teachers' organization and the board have again agreed to its terms.

Most colleges and universities in the United States and Canada grant teachers *tenure*—that is, they automatically renew a teacher's contract after a trial period of satisfactory service. Most school districts in the two countries also grant tenure to public-school teachers. A number of states have laws that prohibit school boards from dismissing tenured teachers except in proven cases of inefficiency or misconduct. In states without such laws, school boards can dismiss teachers when their contracts expire.

Rewards of teaching. One of a teacher's greatest rewards is to see his or her students succeed at their studies and develop into productive, responsible citizens. Nearly every teacher has this opportunity.

The salaries of U.S. teachers vary from district to district and from state to state. In the early 1980's, the national average was about $19,000 a year for elementary-school teachers, about $20,000 a year for secondary-school teachers, and about $25,500 a year for teachers in colleges and universities. During the early 1980's, the national average in Canada was about $27,000 a year for elementary-school teachers, about $31,500 a year for secondary-school teachers, and about $40,000 a year for university teachers.

In most U.S. school districts, teachers receive pay raises according to a *salary schedule*. The schedule grants salary increases for each additional year or other period of service and for additional professional training. Teachers' organizations generally seek to raise scheduled salaries when they work out a new master contract with a school board. Other U.S. school districts use a *merit pay system* or a *differentiated staffing system* to grant pay increases. The merit pay system bases

Photophile

A teacher aide, *right,* helps a professional teacher with certain duties, such as keeping class records. Unlike professional teachers, teacher aides do not need a teaching certificate.

raises mainly on how well teachers teach rather than on their experience and additional training. It requires a method of teacher evaluation. The differentiated staffing system divides the teaching positions in a school into various levels according to the amount of responsibility they involve. Teachers receive raises mainly by being promoted to a higher level.

Some school districts and many colleges and universities grant teachers a *sabbatical,* or *professional, leave* after a certain number of years of service. Many sabbaticals consist of a semester's leave of absence with full pay. Teachers are expected to use a sabbatical to further their professional growth.

Continuing education. All teachers are expected to continue their professional growth throughout their career. Many teachers use their vacation time to take advanced college courses or to attend conventions for teachers in their field. Many school districts provide *in-service* training for teachers. Such training may include conferences and workshops after school hours or special reading materials to be studied at home. A variety of journals and other publications help teachers keep informed about developments in their field.

Teachers' organizations. In the United States, teachers may join a number of professional organizations. The National Education Association of the United States (NEA) has the largest membership of teachers of any U.S. educational organization. It has branches in every state and in many cities and towns. The NEA works chiefly to raise educational standards and to improve the pay and working conditions of teachers. The American Federation of Teachers (AFT) is a national teachers' union that works mainly to improve teachers' salaries and working conditions. Hundreds of local teachers' unions throughout the United States are associated with the AFT. In the mid-1970's, the NEA and AFT discussed joining to form one organization.

Many U.S. teachers' organizations concentrate on a particular field, such as English, mathematics, or special education. For example, the National Council of Teachers of English is an organization for English teachers at all school levels. The National Catholic Educational Association offers membership to teachers and administrators in Roman Catholic schools. The Association of Teacher Educators works to promote quality programs for teacher education.

Canada has a number of large provincial and local teachers' organizations and unions with goals similar to those of the NEA and AFT. The Canadian Education Association is a small but important national organization that works to improve the quality of education throughout Canada.

Current issues in U.S. teaching

Teachers' strikes became common in the 1960's. Teachers went on strike for various reasons, but most often they struck for higher pay and better working conditions.

People have reacted in various ways to the pay demands of teachers. Some people doubt the right of teachers to strike for any reason. Other people feel that educational costs are already too high and that pay raises for teachers will drive such costs even higher. In many communities, voters have turned down tax increases for education, including raises for teachers.

The debate over teachers' pay has led to several other issues concerning teachers. Two of the most important issues deal with (1) the effectiveness of teaching and (2) the effectiveness of teacher training.

The effectiveness of teaching. Many taxpayers have urged that teachers be required to improve the quality of their teaching before being granted pay raises. As a result, cost-control systems called *accountability* have gained much public favor in the field of education. These systems were originally designed to hold workers in business and industry responsible for meeting production goals. In education, accountability systems hold teachers responsible for their students' level of achievement. The systems try to ensure that a certain amount of

Artstreet

Teachers' strikes have become common in many U.S. communities. In most cases, teachers have struck for higher pay and better working conditions.

learning results from a certain level of expenditure.

A number of states have passed laws setting up educational accountability systems. In many other states, state education agencies or local school districts have established such systems. The various systems differ somewhat, but most require a method of teacher evaluation. Some methods of evaluating teachers require the testing of students to see if they have achieved the desired learning goals. Others require the evaluation of teachers by administrators or supervisors. In most accountability systems, a teacher who continually receives a poor evaluation faces dismissal.

Many teachers oppose accountability. They argue that some of the most important results of teaching are difficult to measure. Such results include the acquiring of values and attitudes and the development of mental skills. Also, accountability systems indirectly result in the loss of tenure. Without a system of tenure, administrators can refuse to renew the contracts of teachers whose work they consider unsatisfactory. But many teachers consider tenure a right to which they are entitled.

The effectiveness of teacher training. Many people have complained that teacher-training programs concentrate too heavily on educational theory. These people propose a *competency-based,* or *performance-based,* program. Such a program would develop specific skills, or *competencies.* These competencies might include the ability to make decisions, provide leadership, and deal with disciplinary problems. To acquire such skills, teachers-in-training would spend more time gaining teaching experience and less time attending lectures.

A number of teacher-training programs have been experimenting with competency-based training. To complete such a program, education students must master the particular skills required by the program. They do so in most cases by working with groups of elementary or high school students. The students' achievements supposedly reflect the student teachers' degree of skill. Many states have approved granting teaching certificates to people who completed a competency-based program.

Some educators believe that competency-based programs concentrate so heavily on teaching methods that they neglect to train future teachers adequately in the subjects they plan to teach. Critics also argue that teachers who have mastered the required competencies might be just as effective had they mastered other teaching methods.   Willard Abraham

Related articles in *World Book.* See **Education** and its list of *Related articles.* See also the following articles:

Organizations

American Federation of Teachers
Canadian Education Association
Childhood Education International,
    Association for
National Catholic Educational Association
National Congress of Parents and Teachers
National Education Association of
    the United States
Parent-Teacher Organizations

Other related articles

Academic freedom

Audio-visual
    materials

Outline

I. A teacher's duties
   A. Preparing for classes
   B. Guiding the learning of
      students
   C. Checking student prog-
      ress
   D. Setting a good example
      for students
   E. Other duties

II. Teaching as a career
   A. Teacher-training
      programs
   B. Certification of teachers
   C. Job opportunities
   D. Employment practices
   E. Rewards of teaching
   F. Continuing education
   G. Teachers' organizations

III. Current issues in U.S. teaching
   A. The effectiveness of teaching
   B. The effectiveness of teacher training

Questions

What are the four main duties of teachers?
What is a *teaching certificate*? Who must have one?
Why do teachers give tests?
Of what three main areas of study do most teacher-training pro-
   grams consist?
What are some characteristics of a good teacher?
How do teachers continue their professional growth throughout
   their career?
Why were many qualified college graduates unable to find
   teaching jobs in the United States in the 1970's and early
   1980's?
What two national organizations work to improve the pay and
   working conditions of U.S. teachers?
What is *tenure*? A *sabbatical leave*?
What is an *accountability* system in education?

Additional resources

Barzun, Jacques. *Teacher in America.* Liberty Press, 1981. Reprint
   of 1945 edition.
Hartbarger, Neil. *Your Career in Teaching.* Arco, 1979.
Hentoff, Nat. *Does Anybody Give a Damn?* Knopf, 1977. Examines
   the problems of teaching in inner-city schools.
Highet, Gilbert. *The Immortal Profession: The Joys of Teaching
   and Learning.* Weybright & Talley, 1976.
Postman, Neil. *Teaching as a Conserving Activity.* Delacorte,
   1979.

Teaching machine is a device that presents instructional material to students and requires that they respond to it. Immediately after a student responds to a
question, the machine tells whether the answer was correct and then advances to the next step, which provides
additional material. Unlike television and motion pictures, which also may present educational material,
teaching machines require active participation by the
student. The student may push a button, type on a keyboard, or write on paper in the machine. Teaching machines are used in schools, homes, and businesses.

The educational material in a teaching machine is
called a *program.* The first teaching machines were testing machines, and their programs were tests. In the
1920's, the American psychologist Sidney L. Pressey designed a mechanical testing device that asked multiple-
choice questions, one at a time. The student answered
each question by pressing a lever. The machine did not
present a new question until the correct lever had been

© Richard Hutchings, Photo Researchers

Teaching machines use various methods to present information. This student uses a computer to progress through a series
of lessons. The computer also can test the user's knowledge.

pressed. Students prepared for the tests by studying
with a teacher. But they also learned from the tests because they could correct errors immediately.

Modern teaching machines use a technique developed by B. F. Skinner, another American psychologist.
During the 1950's, Skinner investigated the learning
process. He found that people efficiently learn complicated behavior if they receive an immediate reward for
each step toward that behavior. A person using a teaching machine is rewarded by knowledge of correct answers and by going on to new material.

How teaching machines work

Teaching machines are based on the view that a student learns best by working in small steps that gradually
increase in difficulty. The program of a teaching machine consists of a carefully planned series of statements and exercises. Each step in the program is called
a *frame,* and each frame builds on information already
provided. The early frames guide the student's thinking
so the learner makes few errors and is rewarded by success. The later frames provide less assistance, present
more difficult ideas, and require more sophisticated responses. This method of teaching is called *programmed
instruction.*

Kinds of programs. Teaching machines use *linear
programs* and *branching programs.*

A linear program is one in which every student works
through the frames in the same order, each at his or her
own pace. Each frame gives information and asks the
student to supply a word or phrase or to choose among
several answers. The machine gives the correct answer.
The table included with this article is a linear program.

A branching program is one in which the student's responses determine what frames are presented. The machine gives the student information and then asks a
question. If the student answers correctly, the machine

A linear program to teach word usage

The following questions and answers show a linear program that might appear in a teaching machine. The program first provides information and then asks the student to complete sentences based on that information. The student supplies a word to complete each sentence. The machine then gives the correct answer and presents the next sentence.

Information given

The word *can* means to have the ability to do something. The word *may* is used to ask for permission or to give permission. It also expresses the probability of something happening.

Sentences to be completed	Answers
1. _____we go to the library after school today?	May
2. She_____take a car apart and put it back together in one day.	can
3. Who_____remember when a candy bar cost 5 cents?	can
4. The weather forecast says that it _____rain tomorrow.	may
5. You_____borrow my bicycle.	may

presents new material and questions. If the student gives a wrong answer, the machine branches into additional frames that explain the error. If the student's answers show that the material is already known, the machine gives more advanced instruction. A branching program is designed to provide what each student needs in order to learn. Therefore, it allows more adaptation to differences among students than does a linear program.

Subjects of programs provide a variety of courses for students of all ages. Educators have developed programs to teach English and other languages, mathematics, reading, science, and sports. Training programs have been prepared for use by business, government, and the military. There are even programs to help bridge and chess players improve their skills.

Kinds of teaching machines

Teaching machines range from simple cardboard or paper devices to complex electronic equipment. The three major types are (1) programmed texts, (2) mechanical devices, and (3) computers.

Programmed texts are not actually machines at all. They are books arranged according to the principles of programmed instruction. Each page of the book may present one or more frames of a program. Students work through some programmed texts from beginning to end. Other texts direct students to turn to a certain page, depending on their response to a question.

Mechanical devices display one frame of a program at a time. The student presses one or more buttons or pulls a lever to bring a new frame into view.

Computers present lessons on a printed sheet, on a screen similar to a television screen, or by audio messages. Students respond by typing answers or by touching the screen with a lighted wand. Before instruction begins, the computer can test students to determine the best instructional material for each. During the session, it can check a student's progress to determine whether to provide extra help. At the end of the session, the computer can measure the student's achievement and report it to the student. This teaching method is called *computer-assisted instruction* (CAI).

There are three types of computer-assisted instruction: (1) drill-and-practice CAI, (2) tutorial CAI, and (3) dialogue CAI. Drill-and-practice CAI supplements study with a teacher. It gives practice in applying what the teacher has taught. It usually does not introduce new material. Tutorial CAI develops ideas and skills independent of a teacher. Dialogue CAI allows students to make up problems and have the computer show how to solve them. One system enables students to carry on a "conversation" with the computer and ask it questions.

The effects of teaching machines

The effects of teaching machines are much like those of tutors working individually with students. A constant exchange occurs between the student and the machine. The machine requires the student to participate. It does not simply present material to be memorized. Like a tutor, the machine makes sure the student understands the material presented at each step before going on. It also gives the student hints and suggestions, as a tutor does. In addition, the student does not have to wait for a final exam to know whether the material has been understood. The machine responds to every answer, so that students are informed of their progress. Also, each student works at his or her own rate. Students who need more time or help can get it. Those who master the subject quickly move on to new lessons.

Some people claim that teaching machines make teaching too mechanized. They argue that the human aspects of teaching are lost by using the devices. Others, however, consider teaching machines as tools that assist teachers, just as other tools assist other workers. The machines give large numbers of students the advantage of individual instruction. They also give a teacher more time to work with individual students.

Educators still need to know what subjects can be taught best by teaching machines. They are seeking ways to measure differences among students so that instruction can be adapted to each student. They also are exploring better ways to break down subjects into units of learning and to guide students through a series of instructional steps.   Phillip J. Sleeman

See also **Audio-visual materials; Educational psychology; Speed reading; Videodisc.**

Additional resources

Coburn, Peter, and others. *Practical Guide to Computers in Education.* Addison-Wesley, 1982.
Dorsett, Loyd G. *Audio-Visual Teaching Machines.* Educational Technology Pubs., 1971.
Hendershot, Carl H. *Programmed Learning and Individually Paced Instruction.* 5th ed. Hendershot, 1982. A resource guide to self-study materials.
Jackson, Philip W. *The Teacher and the Machine.* Univ. of Pittsburgh Press, 1968. A classic essay on the role of mechanical devices in the classroom.

Teagarden, Jack (1905-1964), was an American trombone player and blues singer. His intense, warm, blues-rooted trombone style was widely imitated. Teagarden was also the first successful nonblack blues singer. His most famous records are "I've Got a Right to Sing the Blues" and "Basin Street Blues." They illustrate his rich, deeply moving vocal style.

Teagarden was born in Vernon, Tex. He was partly American Indian in ancestry. His full name was Weldon

John Teagarden. Mainly a self-taught musician, Teagarden went to New York City in 1927 and toured with Ben Pollack's band from 1928 to 1933. He later performed with Paul Whiteman's band and recorded with Benny Goodman. He led his own band from 1939 to 1947, and worked four years with Louis Armstrong. He led small groups after 1951.　　Leonard Feather

Teak is a forest tree that comes from southeastern Asia. Its wood is highly valued for shipbuilding and for making furniture. Teakwood is strong and durable and resists water. It takes a high polish and contains an oil that helps it resist insects. The teak tree sometimes grows to a height of 150 feet (46 meters). The leaves often grow 2 feet (61 centimeters) long and 1½ feet (46 centimeters) wide. They yield a purple dye and are also used for thatch and for wrapping material.

Countries which produce teakwood commercially include India, Burma, and Thailand. Teakwood also is grown on plantations in some of these countries.

A tree known as *African teak,* or *African oak,* is also valued for its wood. However, the wood of this tree is less durable than teakwood.

Scientific classification. Teak is in the vervain family, Verbenaceae. It is *Tectona grandis.* African teak is in the spurge family, Euphorbiaceae. It is *Oldfieldia africana.*　　K. A. Armson

Peter Arnold

The cinnamon teal is a small North American duck. The male, *above,* has dark cinnamon-red plumage and blue patches on its wings. Teals live near ponds, streams, and marshes.

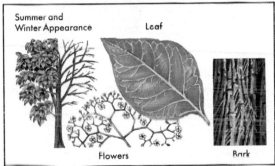

WORLD BOOK illustration by Chris Shilton

The teak tree grows in forests of southeastern Asia.

Chester B. Stem, Inc. (WORLD BOOK photo)　　WORLD BOOK photo

Teakwood is used in making ships, furniture, and other products. A panel of teakwood, *left,* has beautiful grain patterns. A statue of an elephant, *right,* was carved from teakwood.

Teal is a small duck that lives in many parts of the world. The most common teals in North America are the *green-winged,* the *blue-winged,* and the *cinnamon* teals. They are all surface-feeding ducks and never dip more than a short distance beneath the surface for food. They live mostly near ponds, streams, and marshes. Unlike diving birds, they keep their tail feathers completely out of the water when they swim, and can take to the air immediately when frightened. Teals usually breed in Can-

ada and the northern United States and migrate south in winter, often to Mexico.

The *green-winged,* the smallest teal, may reach only 13 to 15 inches (33 to 38 centimeters) in length. The male is gray with a brown head and a speckled breast. Green patches color the wings and the head. The female is more plainly colored. The male makes sharp and mellow whistles. The *blue-winged* teal is 15 or 16 inches (38 or 41 centimeters) long. Except for a blue patch on the front of its wing and a white spot on its face, the male is dull in color. The *cinnamon* teal is about 16 inches (41 centimeters) long. The male has dark cinnamon-red plumage and blue patches on its wings.

Scientific classification. Teals belong to the genus *Anas* of the family Anatidae. The green-winged teal is *Anas crecca.* The blue-winged teal is *A. discors.* The cinnamon teal is *A. cyanoptera.*　　Joseph J. Hickey

See also Bird (picture: Birds of inland waters and marshes); Duck.

Team handball is a fast and exciting sport for men and women in which players try to score goals by throwing a ball into their opponents' goal. Team handball can be played indoors or outdoors. Modern team handball at the international level is an indoor game. This article describes the indoor version that has been an event in the Summer Olympic Games since 1972.

Teams consist of seven players—six court players and a goalkeeper. A team handball court is 40 meters (131 feet) long and 20 meters (65½ feet) wide. A goal line runs the width of the field at each end. Side lines enclose the playing area lengthwise. A goal is centered lengthwise on each goal line. It consists of two posts 2 meters (6½ feet) high and 3 meters (9¾ feet) apart. The posts are connected by a horizontal bar. A net is attached to the posts and bar. The ball in men's competition is 58 to 60 centimeters (23 to 26½ inches) in circumference. The ball in women's games is slightly smaller.

Games are divided into two 30-minute periods. Many of the rules resemble soccer rules except that players can use their hands but cannot use their feet to pass and dribble the ball. Two referees supervise play.

Critically reviewed by the U.S. Team Handball Federation

Team teaching. See Education (Elementary).

Teamsters Union is the largest labor union in the United States. Its official name is International Brotherhood of Teamsters, Chauffeurs, Warehousemen, and Helpers of America. The Teamsters also has local unions in Canada and Puerto Rico. Its membership includes truckdrivers, chauffeurs, warehouse employees, and helpers; people who work with automotive vehicles, including salespeople; garage and service-station employees; dairy, brewery, food-processing, and soft-drink plant employees; and industrial workers and airline and public service employees.

The Teamsters has a total membership of about 2 million. It is organized primarily through its nearly 800 local unions in the United States, Canada, and Puerto Rico. It also has joint councils, and an international convention. The major responsibilities of the joint councils include adjusting jurisdictional disputes between local unions, approving or disapproving strikes or boycotts planned by locals, and evaluating wage scales that the locals plan to submit to employers. The convention is the supreme governing body of the union. It meets every five years. Each local's representation at the convention is based on the size of its membership. Only the convention amends the union constitution. It also elects the international officers, including the president, secretary-treasurer, 15 vice presidents, and 3 trustees.

The Teamsters Union was chartered by the American Federation of Labor (AFL) in 1899 as the Team Drivers' Union. The group split into two unions, which reunited at Niagara Falls, N.Y., in 1903, the official date of the founding of the Teamsters Union. The union grew rapidly under presidents David Beck and James Hoffa in the 1950's and early 1960's. It was expelled from the AFL-CIO in 1957, after its leaders were accused of unethical practices. The Teamsters Union was readmitted to the AFL-CIO in 1987. Headquarters are at 25 Louisiana Avenue NW, Washington, D.C. 20001. For membership, see **Labor movement** (table).   James G. Scoville

See also **Fitzsimmons, Frank E.; Hoffa, James; Williams, Roy L.**

Teapot Dome was one of the most notorious government scandals in United States history. It occurred in the Administration of President Warren G. Harding and contributed to his low standing among U.S. presidents.

Committees of the U.S. Senate and a special commission investigated the scandal from 1922 to 1928. The investigators found that Secretary of the Interior Albert B. Fall had persuaded Harding to transfer control of three naval oil reserves from the Department of the Navy to the Department of the Interior in 1921. Fall leased the reserves, at Elk Hills, Calif., and Teapot Dome, Wyo., mostly without competitive bidding to the private oil companies of Edward L. Doheny and Harry F. Sinclair in 1922. For helping to arrange the Elk Hills transfer, Fall received a "loan" of $100,000 from Doheny. For Teapot Dome, Fall received over $300,000 in cash, bonds, and valuable livestock from Sinclair. Fall resigned in 1923 and joined Sinclair's oil business.

In 1927, the government successfully sued to cancel the leases. In 1929, Fall was convicted of accepting a bribe, fined $100,000, and sentenced to a year in prison. He was the first Cabinet member ever to go to jail for crimes committed while in office. See also **Harding, Warren G.** (Government scandals).   Robert D. Parmet

Additional resources

Noggle, Burl. *Teapot Dome: Oil and Politics in the 1920's.* Greenwood, 1980. First published in 1962.
Werner, Morris R., and Starr, John. *Teapot Dome.* Augustus Kelley, 1973. First published in 1959.

Tear gas. See Chemical-biological-radiological warfare; Mace (gas).

Tears are the secretion of the lacrimal glands. The tears continually bathe the *cornea,* the tough outer layer of the eyeball. They help to clear it of foreign particles,

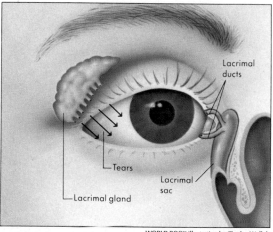

WORLD BOOK illustration by Charles Wellek

Tears are produced by the *lacrimal glands,* one of which lies above each eyeball. The tears wash across the eye and empty into the *lacrimal ducts,* which lead to the *lacrimal sac.* From there, they drain through a passage into the nose.

such as dust and hairs, and keep it from drying out, which would result in blindness.

Two lacrimal glands, one over each eye, lie behind the eyelid. They pour out their fluid through several small ducts in the underside of the lid. Each time the eyelid blinks, it sucks a little fluid from the glands. When a person feels some emotion such as grief or anger very strongly, the muscles around the lacrimal glands may tighten up and squeeze out the tear fluid. The same thing happens if a person laughs very heartily.

After the tears pass across the eyeball, they flow out through two lacrimal ducts that open at the inner corner of each eye. They lead to a lacrimal sac and then to the nasal duct. This duct runs the length of the nose and finally opens into it. Tears flowing through this opening make the nose run when a person cries.

Mostly a salt solution, lacrimal fluid also contains substances that fight bacteria and proteins that help make the eye immune to infection.   Nandalal Bagchi

Teasdale, Sara (1884-1933), was an American lyric poet. Much of her work anticipates modern feminist verse and the intimate, autobiographical style known as *confessional poetry.* Many of Teasdale's poems deal with love and death. The speakers in her lyrics are often women who face the death or desertion of a loved one. They also face the fact of their own mortality with disillusionment, but not as cynics. Nature plays an important part in Teasdale's poetry. She associated moral and spiritual beauty with the harmonies of the natural world.

Teasdale was born in St. Louis, Mo. In addition to writing her own poetry, she edited an anthology of love lyrics by women called *The Answering Voice* (1917, rev. ed. 1928). She also edited *Rainbow Gold* (1922), a collection of poetry for young people. Her *Collected Poems* was published in 1937.   Clark Griffith

Teasel, *TEE zuhl,* is the name of a group of plants that have one commercially valuable species. This species is the *fuller's teasel, clothier's teasel,* or *clothier's brush,* which comes from southern Europe and is now grown in America. It is used to raise the nap on cloth.

The plant is a thistlelike herb with long, stemless leaves, prickly stems, and stiff bracts surrounding the flower heads. The parts used are the dry flower heads, whose fresh flowers are tubular, and which are colored pale lilac or white. The heads are cut in two and attached to a cylinder which revolves against the cloth. The best heads are used for raising the nap on men's garments. The largest are used on blankets.

WORLD BOOK illustration
by Lorraine Epstein
Teasel flower head

Small heads are used for fine woolens and broadcloth. No mechanical device has ever been invented that can replace these heads satisfactorily.

Scientific classification. Teasels belong to the teasel family, Dipsaceae. They make up the genus *Dipsacus.* Fuller's teasel is classified as *D. fullonum.*   Paul C. Standley

Tebaldi, *tuh BAHL dee,* **Renata,** *ruh NAH tuh,* (1922-   ), an Italian singer, became one of the great operatic stars of her day. Her voice is noted for its velvety quality and even scale. Her early lyric roles include Desdemona in *Otello* and Mimi in *La Bohème.* She was able to progress to more dramatic roles, including the title roles in *Aida* and *Tosca,* which require a voice of larger size. She is not especially gifted as an actress, but beauty of tone and her personal appeal brought her success in the United States, especially at the Metropolitan Opera.

Renata Tebaldi was born in Pesaro, Italy. She made her operatic debut in Rovigo as Elena in *Mefistofele* in 1944. She made her debut at the Metropolitan Opera as Desdemona in 1955.   Max de Schauensee

Technetium, *tehk NEE shee uhm* (chemical symbol, Tc), was the first artificially created element. Its atomic number is 43. The most stable available isotope has a mass number of 98.906. In 1937, Carlo Perrier and Emilio Segrè isolated technetium in Italy. They produced it from a sample of molybdenum that had been bombarded with deuterons in the cyclotron of E. O. Lawrence in California (see **Cyclotron**). Perrier and Segrè proved that the bombardment left one proton in the molybdenum and formed technetium. Scientists first called

the element *masurium* and thought that it occurred in nature. However, only small quantities are produced naturally, so the name was changed to technetium, which means *artificial.* Technetium is now obtained in large quantities as a by-product from atomic fission. Its properties resemble those of manganese and rhenium. Its melting point is 2200° C, and its density is 11.5 grams per cubic centimeter at 25° C. There is no significant use for technetium, though one form has been found to be a good radiation source.   S. C. Cummings

Technical assistance is a form of foreign aid. Through technical assistance programs, people in developing countries learn skills that help increase production and raise living standards.

There are various forms of technical assistance. Experts from more prosperous countries may set up demonstrations or provide on-the-job training in developing countries. Workers, executives, and engineers from developing countries may go to prosperous countries for training. Technical assistance may be as simple as teaching a farmer to use a plow instead of a forked stick. It may be as involved as showing a government how to keep statistics on its economy.

President Harry S. Truman's Point Four Program of 1949 was an early technical assistance plan (see **Point Four Program**). Some private and public agencies gave such aid before 1949. The United Nations and its agencies also offer technical assistance programs. The United States Agency for International Development operates a major technical assistance program. Its aid ranges from short-term assistance to three-year projects.

Technical assistance may be used by a larger country to coerce a smaller country. The smaller, receiving country may be expected to support the larger country in world affairs in return for the aid.   Michael P. Sullivan

See also **Foreign aid, United Nations** (Economic and technical aid); **Colombo Plan; Agency for International Development; Developing country.**

Technical drawing. See Mechanical drawing.

Technical school. See Vocational education.

Technicolor is a patented process for making motion pictures in color. It involves producing three separate black-and-white negatives of the scene being filmed. Each negative is exposed to one of the *primary colors of light*—red, blue, or green—from the scene. The negatives are then developed into positive images on film. Technicians dye the positives to reproduce the red, blue, and green areas recorded on the negatives. Next, the dyed positive images are transferred onto blank film to make the final print. The transferred colors blend to produce all the original colors of the filmed scene. Technicolor results in color reproduction of high quality. But the process is difficult and costly to produce.

Herbert T. Kalmus, an American chemical engineer, developed Technicolor in the early 1900's. The first full-length film made with the process, *The Gulf Between,* appeared in theaters in 1917. Originally, Technicolor was a two-color system. The improved three-color process was introduced in 1932. Many Technicolor films were made in the 1930's and 1940's. Since then, however, Technicolor has largely been replaced by simpler and less expensive color film processes.

Robert A. Sobieszek

Timken Company, Canton, Ohio

An automated steel mill produces huge steel bars at the touch of a button. The computer-controlled machines that roll the glowing bars are products of modern technology. Other machines and methods will turn the bars into a variety of industrial and household products.

Technology

Technology refers to all the ways people use their inventions and discoveries to satisfy their needs and desires. Ever since people appeared on the earth, they have had to work to obtain food, clothing, and shelter. They have also had to work to satisfy their desire for leisure and comfort. Through the ages, people invented tools, machines, materials, and techniques to make work easier. They also discovered water power, electricity, and other sources of power that increased the rate at which they could work. Technology thus involves the use of tools, machines, materials, techniques, and sources of power to make work easier and more productive.

Many people call the age we live in the *age of technology.* Yet people have always lived in a technological age because they have always had to work to obtain most of life's necessities and many of its pleasures. Technology thus includes the use of both primitive and highly advanced tools and methods of work. But when people speak of technology today, they generally mean *industrial technology*—the technology that helped bring about our modern society.

Industrial technology began about 200 years ago with

Melvin Kranzberg, the contributor of this article, is Callaway Professor of the History of Technology at Georgia Institute of Technology and coeditor of Technology in Western Civilization.

the development of power-driven machines, the growth of factories, and the mass production of goods. As industrial technology advanced, it affected more and more aspects of people's lives. For example, the development of the automobile influenced where people lived and worked and how they spent their leisure time. Radio and television changed entertainment habits, and the telephone revolutionized communication. Today, industrial technology helps people achieve goals that few thought possible a hundred years ago. It gives people the means to conquer hunger and to cure or prevent many diseases. It enables them to transport goods and passengers swiftly and easily to any place on the earth. They can even leave the earth, soar through space, and set foot on the moon.

Science has contributed much to modern technology. But not all technology is based on science, nor is science necessary to all technology. Science attempts to explain how and why things happen. Technology is concerned with making things happen. For example, people made objects of iron for centuries before they learned about the changes that occurred in the structure of the metal during ironmaking. But some modern technologies, such as nuclear power production and space travel, depend heavily on science.

The word *technology* is sometimes used to describe a particular application of industrial technology, such as medical technology or military technology. Each of the various specialized technologies has its own goals and its own tools and techniques for achieving those goals. The engineering profession is responsible for much of

Assembly line production, an important method of technology, increases the amount of goods a worker can produce. Increased productivity provides more goods for more people.

Automobiles, like other inventions of technology, changed our way of life. The convenience of automobile travel influences where we live and work and how we use our free time.

today's industrial technology (see **Engineering**).

Industrial technology enables people to live in greater security and comfort than ever before. But only a small part of the world's population enjoys the full benefits of modern technology. In addition, nations with advanced technologies have found that certain undesirable side effects, such as air and water pollution, have accompanied technological growth. Technology also enables people to produce more powerful weapons, thus adding to the destructiveness of war.

This article describes technology's benefits and undesirable side effects. It also discusses the problems people face in trying to combat these side effects. The development of technology largely parallels the history of inventions and discoveries, which is traced in the article on **Invention**. Detailed information on the development of technology in specific areas can be found in the *History* sections of such articles as **Agriculture, Medicine,** and **Transportation.**

Benefits of technology

Technology has helped people gain control over nature and so build a civilized way of life. The first people had little control over nature. They had only simple tools. They did not know how to raise animals or plants and so had to search for wild animals and plants for food. They had no permanent homes. Animal skins were their only protection against the cold. The sun was their only source of light. Then people discovered how to make fire. This discovery helped them gain some control over nature. They could now carry heat and light

wherever they went. They next learned to raise animals and crops. The development of farming allowed them to build settlements. It also freed people for work other than producing food. Classes of priests, rulers, craftworkers, and merchants developed. This division of labor helped make civilization possible.

Through the ages, technology has benefited people in four main ways. First, it has increased their production of goods and services. Second, it has reduced the amount of labor needed to produce goods and services. Third, technology has made labor easier. Fourth, it has given people higher living standards.

Increased production. Through technology, people have achieved a tremendous increase in the production of goods and services. In the mid-1800's, for example, people and animals were the main source of power on farms in the United States. Farmers labored from dawn to dusk, yet one farmer produced enough food for only about four persons. In the early 1900's, more and more farmers began using tractors and other machines powered by gasoline or electricity. Today, machines do most of the work on U.S. farms. As a result of machinery, fertilizers, and other advances in agricultural technology, one U.S. farmer today produces enough food for 77 people. Similar developments have occurred in manufacturing, mining, and other industries. Most workers today produce many times more goods than workers did a hundred years ago.

Reduced labor. Powered machines have increased production. But they have also reduced the amount of labor needed to produce goods and services and so

Grant Heilman

Farm machines, such as these combines, and other advances in agricultural technology make farm work easier. Such machines and methods also help farmers produce larger amounts of food.

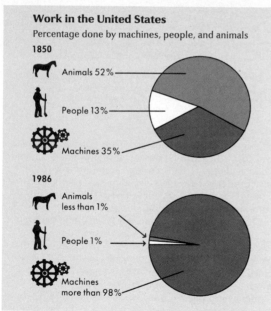

Work in the United States

Percentage done by machines, people, and animals

1850

Animals 52%

People 13%

Machines 35%

1986

Animals less than 1%

People 1%

Machines more than 98%

WORLD BOOK diagram

United States farm productivity

Number of persons each farmer supplies with food

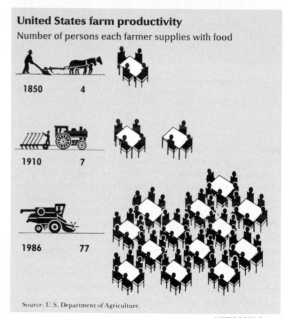

1850   4

1910   7

1986   77

Source: U.S. Department of Agriculture.

WORLD BOOK diagram

In 1850, machines did only 35 per cent of U.S. farm and industrial work, while people and animals performed the rest. The charts above show how the 1850 percentages compare with those of today, when machines do over 98 per cent of the work.

This chart shows the increase in U.S. farm productivity since 1850, when a farmer produced enough food for four people. Today, a farmer produces enough for 77 people. Advances in technology have been largely responsible for the increase.

have increased productivity. Increased productivity gives workers more leisure time. In the early 1800's, for example, most factory work was done by hand or hand-operated machines. Workers labored 12 to 16 hours a day, six days a week. Few people received a vacation. Today, powered machinery has largely replaced hand labor in factories. Many factories also use mass production techniques. As a result, the amount of labor needed to produce manufactured goods has decreased sharply. Today, most factory employees work only eight hours a day, five days a week. They also receive paid holidays and vacations.

Easier labor. Technology has enabled people to produce more goods and services with less labor. It has also made labor easier and safer. Coal mining provides an example. In the early 1900's, miners toiled all day with pick and shovel to produce a few tons of coal. The mines were dark, poorly ventilated, and dangerous. Today, mining is still dangerous. But better lighting and ventilation and improved safety devices have reduced the hazards. The work itself is easier and more productive. Machines perform most of the hard labor. The operator of a coal-mining machine can dig more than 1 short ton (0.9 metric ton) of coal a minute.

Higher living standards have resulted from the increased production of goods and services. The industrial nations produce more goods and services than other countries and have the world's highest standard of living. Most people in industrial nations are better fed, clothed, and housed and enjoy a healthier, more comfortable life than any other people in history. Above all, technology has increased human *life expectancy*—the number of years a person can expect to live. Improved public health practices have ended the plagues that once swept through many countries. Better health care and nutrition have also reduced the number of deaths among infants. In 1900, most people born in the United States did not live past the age of 50. Today, Americans live an average of about 75 years (see **Life expectancy**).

Side effects of technology

The advance of technology has benefited people in numerous ways, but it has also created serious problems. These problems have arisen mainly because technologies were put to use without considering the possible harmful side effects. For example, many people welcomed the development of the automobile in the late 1890's and early 1900's. They believed that automobiles would be quieter and less smelly than horses. But as more and more automobiles came into use, the noise of roaring traffic proved more annoying than the clatter of horse hoofs. Automobile exhaust fumes proved worse than the smell of horse manure. The fumes polluted the air with carbon monoxide gas and other impurities and so threatened human health. Also, automobiles created traffic jams, which often made automobile travel more time-consuming than travel on horseback. The ever-increasing production of automobiles used up iron and other natural resources.

This section discusses four major side effects of technology. They are: (1) environmental pollution, (2) the depletion of natural resources, (3) technological unemployment, and (4) the creation of unsatisfying jobs.

Environmental pollution ranks as one of the most harmful side effects of industrial technology. Most industrial countries face problems of air, water, soil, and noise pollution. Motor vehicles cause most of the air and noise pollution in these countries. But many other products as well as many processes of technology also pollute the environment. For example, certain insecticides pollute the soil and water and endanger plant and animal life. Factory smoke and wastes also contribute greatly to air and water pollution. In the United States, power plants that burn oil or other fuels to generate electricity add millions of tons of pollutants to the air annually. Junkyards, open-pit mines, logging operations, and freeways detract from the beauty of the natural environment. See the article on **Environmental pollution** for a further discussion of technology's harmful environmental effects.

The depletion of natural resources. The rapid advance of technology threatens the supply of resources. For example, the use of electrically powered machinery in the United States and other industrial countries has greatly increased factory production. But at the same time, it has reduced the supply of oil and other fuels used to produce electricity. These fuels cannot be replaced after they are used. As power production increases, the supply of fuels decreases. Since the 1950's, power production has increased so greatly in the United States that the nation began to experience a fuel and power shortage during the 1970's.

Technological unemployment is a type of unemployment that sometimes results from advances in technology. The most common type of technological unemployment occurs when machines take over workers' jobs. Since the late 1950's, many factories and offices have introduced automatic machines to perform tasks formerly done by workers. The use of such machines, which is called *automation,* has caused some unemployment. But it has not been so severe as some experts predicted. Automation has helped a number of industries expand. As a result, these industries have been able to provide new jobs for displaced workers. But technological unemployment nevertheless remains a threat to workers in many industries. For more information on technological unemployment, see **Unemployment** (Types of unemployment).

The creation of unsatisfying jobs. Some tasks required by industrial technology fail to give workers a feeling of accomplishment. For example, most factory workers make only a part of the finished product. As a result, they may lack the feeling of pride in their work that comes from creating an entire product. Many factory jobs also demand concentration. Although factory machines are safer today than in the past, many are

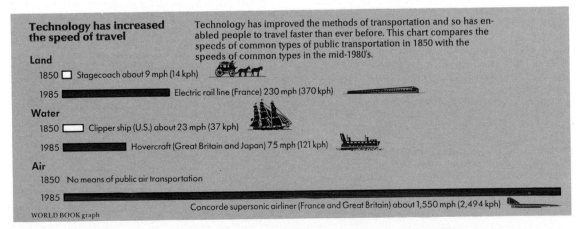

Technology has increased the speed of travel

Technology has improved the methods of transportation and so has enabled people to travel faster than ever before. This chart compares the speeds of common types of public transportation in 1850 with the speeds of common types in the mid-1980's.

Land
1850 ☐ Stagecoach about 9 mph (14 kph)
1985 ▬ Electric rail line (France) 230 mph (370 kph)

Water
1850 ☐ Clipper ship (U.S.) about 23 mph (37 kph)
1985 ▬ Hovercraft (Great Britain and Japan) 75 mph (121 kph)

Air
1850 No means of public air transportation
1985 ▬ Concorde supersonic airliner (France and Great Britain) about 1,550 mph (2,494 kph)

WORLD BOOK graph

Harmful effects of technology include the scarring of once-fertile land by surface, or strip, mining, *left.* Streams fill with mud, the soil becomes acid, and plant and animal life vanish.

E. R. Degginger

dangerous if not operated with extreme care. The operators must be constantly alert to make sure they are operating their machines properly. But constantly tending a machine or performing the same task again and again can be monotonous as well as demanding.

The challenge of technology

Modern technology presents enormous challenges. One of the chief challenges is to combat the undesirable side effects of existing technologies. Another is to prevent possible side effects in the development of new technologies. Still another challenge is to spread technology's benefits to the people of developing countries.

Combating side effects. Some of technology's side effects are extremely hard to remedy. For example, it is difficult to make an unsatisfying job satisfying. But automation will continue to free many workers from routine, monotonous jobs. Some of these workers may then face the hardships of unemployment. But with help from industry and government, they can be retrained to fill more highly skilled and possibly more interesting jobs. See **Automation** (Automation and jobs).

Industries can do much to combat environmental pollution and the depletion of natural resources. One way is by developing substitute technologies for those that produce harmful side effects. Automobile makers, for example, can help curb air pollution by finding a means of purifying automobile exhausts. Manufacturers can help conserve mineral and timber resources by a process called *recycling.* In recycling, raw materials are recovered from waste products and used to make new products (see **Environmental pollution** [Recycling]).

Developing a substitute technology can be costly. An industry may need to hire additional experts or invest in expensive equipment. Most industries that develop a substitute technology pass the cost on to buyers in the form of higher prices. Some industries choose not to spend the money to develop a substitute technology. But in many cases, the choice is too serious to be left to industries because the health of an entire community, state, or nation may be affected. In these cases, government agencies make and enforce the decision. For example, many local governments require factories to install pollution control devices.

Substitute technologies may also have side effects.

For example, nuclear power plants have several advantages over fuel-burning plants in producing electricity. Nuclear plants can produce tremendous amounts of electricity using only small amounts of raw materials. In addition, they do not pollute the air as do fuel-burning plants. But nuclear plants, like some fuel-burning plants, release hot water into lakes and rivers. The hot water may cause *thermal pollution,* which harms water plants and animals. But scientists and engineers are working to solve this problem. For example, many nuclear plants have installed *cooling towers,* which use air to cool the hot water they produce.

Preventing side effects. Some experts believe that most harmful side effects of technology can be prevented. According to this view, any proposed large-scale technology should be thoroughly tested and then evaluated before it is put into use. Such an evaluation is called a *technology assessment.* The findings of a technology assessment are usually published in a detailed report called an *environmental impact statement* (see **Environmental impact statement**).

The purpose of an assessment is to discover in advance all the possible good and bad effects that a new technology may have on society and the environment. An assessment might show that the benefits of a new technology outweigh any side effects. Or it might show that the side effects would be so harmful that they outweigh any benefits. In 1972, Congress created the Office of Technology Assessment to provide information on the impacts of new technologies.

Some experts doubt the value of technology assessment. They believe that it is not possible to discover all the side effects of a technology before it is put into use. They also fear that technology assessments will block scientific and technological progress.

Spreading the benefits of technology. Technology's benefits are limited largely to the industrially developed nations of Europe and North America. But even in these nations, the benefits of technology are not evenly distributed. Many families in the United States, for example, lack all but the bare necessities of life.

The developing nations of the world enjoy few of technology's benefits. Also, the people of these countries want the goods and services that technology has made available to industrialized nations. The transfer of

E. R. Degginger

Recycling recovers raw materials from wastes and so helps to conserve resources used by technology. This discarded material is being separated into iron and steel for recycling.

technological knowledge from developed to developing nations is one of today's chief challenges.

As technology advances in developing countries, it will probably produce some harmful side effects. Advanced technology will probably also continue to create problems in the industrialized countries. But technological achievements in the past show that people have the intelligence, imagination, and inventive skill to deal with present and future problems created by technology.

Melvin Kranzberg

Related articles in *World Book*. See **Engineering, Industry, Invention,** and **Manufacturing** with their lists of *Related articles* See also the following articles:

Agriculture	Labor force
Assembly line	Machine
Automation	Machine tool
Building trade	Mass production
Careers	Mining
Environmental pollution	Technology Assessment,
Factory	Office of
Industrial Revolution	

Outline

I. Benefits of technology
   A. Increased production   C. Easier labor
   B. Reduced labor   D. Higher living standards

II. Side effects of technology
   A. Environmental pollution
   B. The depletion of natural resources
   C. Technological unemployment
   D. The creation of unsatisfying jobs

III. The challenge of technology
   A. Combating side effects   C. Spreading the benefits of
   B. Preventing side effects   technology

Questions

In what four main ways has technology aided people?
How does technology differ from science?
What is *technology assessment*? What is its main purpose?
Why is less labor needed to manufacture goods today than in the past?

What are four of the major side effects of technology?
What challenges does modern technology present?
When did industrial technology begin?
What is technological unemployment?
What are some of the ways in which industrial technology has affected people's lives?
Why did many people welcome the development of the automobile in the late 1890's and early 1900's?

Additional resources

Kerrod, Robin. *The Way It Works: Man and His Machines.* Octopus Books, 1980.
Pursell, Carroll W., Jr., ed. *Technology in America: A History of Individuals and Ideas.* MIT Press, 1981.
Singer, Charles, and others, eds. *A History of Technology.* 7 vols. Oxford, 1954-1978.
Taylor, Paula. *The Kids' Whole Future Catalogue.* Random House, 1982. For younger readers. Includes facts and predictions of modern and future technology, and "send for" sections for additional information.

Technology Assessment, Office of, is an advisory agency of the United States Congress. The agency, often called OTA, gathers information on the ways that technology can affect people's lives. Many congressional committees ask OTA for studies evaluating the economic, environmental, social, and political effects of legislative decisions that affect uses of technology. The studies may involve a wide range of topics, including communications, energy, food, health, natural resources, transportation, and world trade.

OTA has a congressional board that establishes the policies of the agency. The board consists of six senators and six representatives, plus the OTA director. OTA also has a Technology Assessment Advisory Council that advises the board on technological matters. The council consists of experts in the fields of education, engineering, and science. Congress established OTA in 1972. The agency began operations in 1974.

Critically reviewed by the Office of Technology Assessment

Technology education. See Industrial arts.

Tectonics, *tehk TAHN ihks,* is the study of forces within the earth that form the earth's mountains and ocean basins. Although tectonic forces cannot be explained, earth scientists believe they are produced by heat energy.

The plate tectonic theory. In the 1960's, earth scientists proposed a tectonic theory that included two earlier ideas. These ideas involved *continental drift* and *convection currents* (see **Continental drift**). The new theory led many earth scientists to conclude that the earth's outer shell, called the *lithosphere,* consists of a number of rigid plates. Some of these plates do not follow continental boundaries, and some include both continents and oceans. The lithosphere is about 45 to 95 miles (72 to 153 kilometers) thick and appears to be in continual motion. The lithosphere plates slowly slide on a soft plastic layer of rock called the *asthenosphere.* The plates move from $\frac{1}{2}$ to 4 inches (1.3 to 10 centimeters) a year.

Tectonic activity seems to occur chiefly along the edges of the plates. If one plate pushes against another, it either crumples and forms mountains or bends downward into the earth's *mantle,* the layer beneath the crust and above the *core* (see **Earth** [Inside the earth]). These downward-bending plates, called *subduction zones,* generate earthquakes and volcanic activity. Two plates spreading apart form ocean floors and long underwater mountains called *oceanic ridges.* Major earthquakes and fractures in the earth's crust occur where two plates slide past each other. Such fractures are called *faults.*

Some of the earth's major crustal features occur at the edges of the lithosphere plates. Such features include mountains, ocean floor trenches, oceanic ridges, volcanoes, and volcanic islands that are called *island arcs.*

Most earth scientists believe convection currents create the power that moves the huge plates. According to this theory, convection currents in the earth's mantle carry molten rock up from the asthenosphere. The rising molten rock adds to the ocean floor at some of the oceanic ridges. Convection currents in the rock carry the newly formed crustal plate away from the ridge as if it were riding on a conveyor belt.

Some scientists do not accept various parts of the convection current theory. Other scientists want proof that convection currents even exist—and that they produce the enormous power needed to move the plates.

Other theories. Some earth scientists once thought that the earth began as a molten ball and has been cooling ever since. As the earth became cooler, it shrank. The shrinking produced tectonic forces.

Other earth scientists believe that the earth began as a cold mass and was warmed by heat from radioactive material inside the planet. As the earth became hotter, it expanded and created forces that fractured the crust into large blocks. These blocks became the continents, and the regions between the continents became the basins of the oceans.   Albert J. Rudman

Tecumseh, *tih KUHM suh* (1765?-1813), was an outstanding leader of the eastern American Indian tribes after the American Revolutionary War. He worked to unite all the American Indian tribes into a single alliance that would defend Indian lands against invasion by white people. Tecumseh means *shooting star* or *meteor.*

Tecumseh, the son of a Shawnee chief, is believed to have been born in the Scioto River Valley, south of Co-

Lithograph (1841) by Nathaniel Currier (Granger Collection)

Tecumseh was an Indian leader who fought to defend Indian lands against invasion by white people. He allied his Indian forces with the British army against the Americans during the War of 1812 and died at the Battle of the Thames River, *above.*

lumbus, Ohio. His father and two brothers were killed in battles with the American colonists.

White settlers were rapidly taking Indian lands, and Tecumseh and his brother, Tenskwatawa, began a crusade to keep Indian lands for the Indians. Tenskwatawa, known as the Shawnee Prophet, led a religious revival (see **Shawnee Prophet**). Tecumseh, a strong warrior and gifted orator, led in politics and war. He traveled tirelessly from his home in Ohio to almost every tribe east of the Rocky Mountains. The two men did much to lead the Indians back to the ways of their forefathers.

Tecumseh condemned a treaty that William Henry Harrison made with the Indians. His action led to the Battle of Tippecanoe in November 1811. See **Indian wars** (Other Midwestern conflicts [1790-1832]).

Tecumseh joined the British armies to fight the Americans in the War of 1812. He served as a brigadier general in command of Indian allies. He was killed while leading his forces in Canada after Commander Oliver H. Perry's victory at Lake Erie (see **War of 1812** [Chief battles of the war]).   E. Adamson Hoebel

Tedder, Arthur William (1890-1967), Baron Tedder of Glenguin, became a marshal of the Royal Air Force of Great Britain in 1945. Tedder served in the Royal Air Force during World War I and World War II. He was named deputy supreme commander to General Dwight D. Eisenhower, the supreme Allied commander, in World War II. He later became deputy supreme commander of the North Atlantic Treaty Organization (NATO) forces in Europe. He was born in Stirlingshire (now Central Region), Scotland.

Teen age. See Adolescent.

Teeth

Teeth are hard, bonelike structures in the upper and lower jaws of human beings and many kinds of animals. They are the hardest parts of the body.

People use their teeth chiefly to chew food. Chewing is the first step in the process of *digestion.* Digestion begins as the teeth chop and grind chunks of food into smaller pieces. As the teeth chew the food, it is mixed with *saliva,* a liquid produced in the mouth. The food becomes a moist pulp, which is easy to swallow. The food is further broken down in the stomach and the small intestine, where it is absorbed by the blood. The blood carries the digested food to all parts of the body. Without teeth, people could not eat foods that must be chewed. They could only swallow soft foods and liquids.

Teeth also play an important part in speech. The teeth and tongue are used together to form many sounds that make up words. To produce the *th* sound, for example, the tip of the tongue is placed against the upper front teeth. A person who lacks these teeth may be unable to make the sound.

Teeth also help support the muscles around the mouth and so contribute to a person's appearance. People who have lost their teeth lack this support. Unless they wear artificial teeth, they may have deep, saggy lines around the mouth.

Like human beings, most animals use their teeth to chew food. They also use their teeth to obtain food. Many animals that eat plants tear off the leaves or stalks of the plants with their teeth. Most meat-eating animals use their teeth to seize and kill prey.

This article chiefly discusses human teeth. The last section of the article describes the differences in the teeth of various kinds of animals.

Kinds of teeth

Human beings grow two sets of teeth: (1) deciduous teeth and (2) permanent teeth. The individual deciduous teeth appear and fall out gradually early in life. They are replaced, one by one, by the permanent teeth. See the table *Ages at which teeth appear* for the times the various kinds of deciduous and permanent teeth generally appear.

Deciduous and permanent teeth have the same basic structure. Each tooth has a *crown* and one or more *roots.* The crown is the part of the tooth that can be seen in the mouth. The root or roots are covered by the bone and gums. The roots hold the tooth in a socket in the jawbone.

Deciduous teeth are also called *baby teeth, milk teeth,* or *primary teeth.* They start to form about $7\frac{1}{2}$ months before a baby is born. They begin as oval or round swellings called *buds,* which gradually develop into teeth. When a baby is born, parts of all the deciduous teeth are present deep within the jaws. As the teeth grow, they push through the gums. This process is called *eruption* or *teething.* Babies begin to teethe at about 6 to 9 months of age. Most children have all their deciduous teeth by about 2 years of age.

There are 20 deciduous teeth, 10 in each jaw. They consist of three kinds of teeth: (1) incisors, (2) canines, and (3) molars. Each jaw has 4 incisors, 2 canines, and 4

molars. The incisors and canines are used to bite into food, and the molars to grind food. The positions of these teeth in the mouth are shown in the illustration *Kinds of teeth.*

The deciduous teeth help the permanent teeth erupt in their normal positions. Most of the permanent teeth form near the roots of the deciduous teeth. When a child is about 3 years old, the roots of various deciduous teeth begin to dissolve slowly. By the time a permanent tooth is ready to erupt, the root of the deciduous tooth has completely dissolved. The crown of the tooth then becomes loose and falls out.

Permanent teeth, like deciduous teeth, begin to develop before birth. But most of their growth occurs after birth. The permanent teeth begin to erupt after the deciduous teeth start to fall out.

The first permanent teeth appear when a child is about 6 or 7 years old. Between the ages of 6 and 12, a child has some permanent and some deciduous teeth in the mouth. The last permanent teeth erupt when a person is 17 to 21 years old.

There are 32 permanent teeth, 16 in each jaw. They are larger than the deciduous teeth and consist of four kinds of teeth. The four kinds are (1) incisors, (2) canines, (3) premolars, and (4) molars. Each jaw has 4 incisors, 2 canines, 4 premolars, and 6 molars. The following discussion describes the four kinds of permanent teeth. Their positions in the mouth are shown in the illustration *Kinds of teeth.*

Incisors are the chief biting teeth. They have a sharp, straight cutting edge. In most cases, incisors have one root. The central incisors of the lower jaw are the smallest permanent teeth.

Canines are used with the incisors to bite into food.

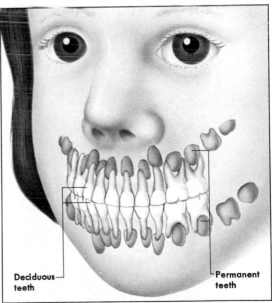

Deciduous teeth

Permanent teeth

The teeth of a child. By the time a child is about 4 years old, most of the permanent teeth have formed within the jaws near the roots of the deciduous teeth. The deciduous teeth, all of which have erupted by about age 2, will gradually fall out and be replaced, one by one, by the permanent teeth.

Kinds of teeth

The illustrations below show the kinds of deciduous and permanent teeth and their positions in the mouth.

WORLD BOOK diagrams by Charles Wellek

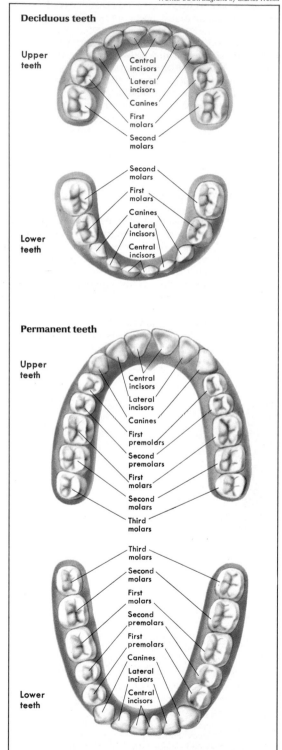

Deciduous teeth

Upper teeth
- Central incisors
- Lateral incisors
- Canines
- First molars
- Second molars

Lower teeth
- Second molars
- First molars
- Canines
- Lateral incisors
- Central incisors

Permanent teeth

Upper teeth
- Central incisors
- Lateral incisors
- Canines
- First premolars
- Second premolars
- First molars
- Second molars
- Third molars

Lower teeth
- Third molars
- Second molars
- First molars
- Second premolars
- First premolars
- Canines
- Lateral incisors
- Central incisors

Ages at which teeth appear*

Deciduous teeth:	Lower teeth	Upper teeth
Central incisors	6 months	7 months
Lateral incisors	7 months	9 months
Canines	16 months	18 months
First molars	12 months	14 months
Second molars	20 months	24 months
Permanent teeth:	**Lower teeth**	**Upper teeth**
Central incisors	6-7 years	7-8 years
Lateral incisors	7-8 years	8-9 years
Canines	9-10 years	11-12 years
First premolars	10-12 years	10-11 years
Second premolars	11-12 years	10-12 years
First molars	6-7 years	6-7 years
Second molars	11-13 years	12-13 years
Third molars	17-21 years	17-21 years

* The ages given are approximate. In many cases, individual teeth may erupt at an earlier or later age.

They are also used to tear off pieces of food. The name for these teeth comes from another word for *dog*—that is, *canine*. The canine teeth resemble a dog's fangs. They have a sharp, pointed edge and one root. Canines are also called *cuspids* or *dogteeth*. The upper canines are sometimes known as *eyeteeth*.

Premolars are used to crush and grind food. They have a broad, lumpy top instead of a sharp biting edge. The small surface lumps are called *cusps*. The cusps enable the teeth to mash pieces of food.

Premolars are sometimes called *bicuspids* because, in most cases, they have two cusps. The prefix *bi* means *two*. The first upper premolars normally have two roots. The other premolars have one root. The premolars erupt in the place of the deciduous molars.

Molars, like premolars, are used to grind food. They are shaped much like premolars but are larger. The various molars normally have three to five cusps and two or three roots.

The permanent molars do not form beneath any of the deciduous teeth. They develop as the jaws grow, which makes space for them. Some adults lack one or more of the third molars, which are commonly called *wisdom teeth.* In many cases, the jaws do not grow large enough to provide space for the wisdom teeth. As a result, the wisdom teeth may become *impacted*—that is, wedged between the jawbone and another tooth. The wisdom teeth must then be removed.

Parts of a tooth

A tooth consists of four kinds of tissues. They are (1) pulp, (2) dentin, (3) enamel, and (4) cementum. Connective tissue surrounds the root of the tooth. This tissue, called the *periodontal ligament,* holds the root in the socket in the jaw.

Pulp is the innermost layer of a tooth. It consists of connective tissue, blood vessels, and nerves. The blood vessels nourish the tooth. The nerves transmit sensations of pain to the brain.

The pulp has two parts, the *pulp chamber* and the *root canal.* The pulp chamber lies in the crown of the tooth. The root canal lies in the root of the tooth. Blood vessels and nerves enter the root canal through a small hole at the tip of the root. They extend through the root canal and into the pulp chamber.

Dentin is a hard, yellow substance that surrounds the pulp. It makes up most of a tooth. Dentin is harder than bone. It consists mainly of mineral salts and water but also has some living cells.

Enamel overlies the dentin in the crown of the tooth. It forms the outermost covering of the crown. Enamel is the hardest tissue in the body. It enables a tooth to withstand the pressure placed on it during chewing. Enamel consists of mineral salts and a small amount of water. Enamel is white but transparent. The yellow color of the dentin shows through the enamel, and so most teeth appear slightly yellowish.

As a person grows older, small amounts of enamel begin to wear away. This process, called *attrition,* results from the use of the teeth over a long period. As the enamel wears away, the dentin becomes exposed.

Cementum overlies the dentin in the root of the tooth. In most cases, the cementum and enamel meet where the root ends and the crown begins. As the surface of the tooth wears away, the tooth grows farther out of its socket, exposing the root. These areas may then become more sensitive to hot and cold liquids. Cementum is about as hard as bone. Like dentin and enamel, it consists mainly of mineral salts and water.

Periodontal ligament consists of small fibers. These fibers extend through the cementum and into the bony socket, which is called the *alveolus.* Besides anchoring the tooth in the alveolus, the periodontal ligament serves as a shock absorber during chewing.

Care of the teeth and gums

Most cases of tooth decay and gum disease could be prevented if people took proper care of their teeth and gums. Proper care requires (1) a good diet, (2) cleaning the teeth after eating, and (3) dental checkups.

A good diet. Dentists advise people to eat well-balanced meals. Such meals include a variety of foods and provide the *nutrients* (nourishing substances) needed by the teeth and gums. Nutrition experts divide foods into groups to make it easier for people to plan well-balanced meals. According to one system, foods are classified into four groups. Another system lists seven groups. The article **Nutrition** describes these food groups. For each group, the article gives the number of daily servings that experts advise people to eat.

Dentists also urge people to eat fewer sugary foods because these foods contribute to tooth decay. Bacteria in the mouth digest sugar and produce an acid as a result. The acid dissolves tooth enamel, forming a cavity.

Foods that have a large amount of sugar include candies, pastries, most breakfast cereals, and sweetened canned fruits. Many people eat sugary foods as snacks. In place of sugary foods, dentists advise people to snack on such foods as fresh fruits and vegetables, cheeses, and nuts. They also recommend that people drink milk or unsweetened fruit and vegetable juices instead of soft drinks and other sugar-sweetened beverages.

Dentists further recommend that children drink water that contains chemical compounds called *fluorides.* Fluorides are absorbed by the enamel as the teeth grow. They help the teeth resist the acid that forms cavities. Some communities have a water supply that naturally contains fluorides. Many other communities add fluorides to the water supply. However, some people oppose *fluoridation* (the addition of fluorides to water supplies). For information on the arguments for and against fluoridation, see **Fluoridation.**

Fluorides may be applied directly to a child's teeth during a dental checkup. In some cases, dentists prescribe a fluoride substance that children can apply at

WORLD BOOK diagram by Charles Wellek

Parts of a tooth

The *crown,* or visible part of a molar tooth, includes projections called *cusps.* The *root* extends into the bone of the jaw. A tissue called *dentin* makes up most of the tooth. A layer of *enamel* covers the dentin of the crown, and *cementum* overlies the dentin of the root. Within the dentin lies the *pulp,* including the *pulp chamber* and the *root canal,* through which blood vessels and nerves enter the tooth. The *periodontal ligament* surrounds the root and holds the tooth in its socket.

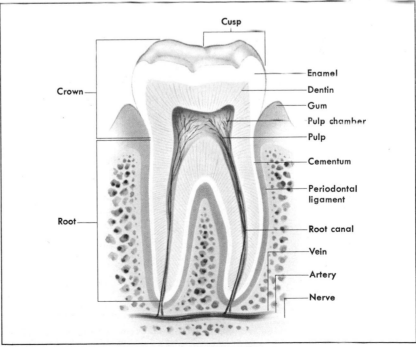

Cusp
Enamel
Dentin
Gum
Pulp chamber
Pulp
Crown
Cementum
Periodontal ligament
Root canal
Vein
Artery
Root
Nerve

home. Most dentists also advise children to brush their teeth with a toothpaste that contains fluorides.

Cleaning the teeth. Dentists advise people to clean their teeth by brushing after every meal and by using *dental floss* once a day. Dental floss is a thin thread that comes in a roll. It is used to clean the areas between teeth and under the gum line. Brushing and flossing remove trapped food particles and *plaque* from the teeth. Plaque is a sticky film that consists of saliva, food particles, and bacteria. The bacteria digest certain foods, particularly sugars, and form an enamel-dissolving acid.

To brush the teeth, you should use a small, soft toothbrush and a toothpaste that contains fluorides. There are several methods of brushing. You should use the one recommended by your dentist. One commonly recommended method is to place the brush against the teeth at a slight angle, with the bristles pointed toward the gums. Brush the upper teeth with a downward, sweeping motion. Brush the lower teeth with an upward, sweeping motion. Clean both the outside and the inside surfaces of the teeth in this way. Use a scrubbing motion to clean the biting surfaces of the premolars and molars. Lastly, brush the tongue to remove food particles and bacteria, which contribute to bad mouth odors. Then rinse the mouth thoroughly. Rinsing with water is just as effective as rinsing with mouthwash.

To floss the teeth, cut a piece of floss about 18 inches (46 centimeters) long from the roll. Wrap one end of the floss around each middle finger. Using the index fingers and thumbs, gently guide the floss between two teeth.

Then pull the floss up and down, cleaning the sides of both teeth and the areas around the gum line. Repeat this procedure on all the teeth.

Some people use *disclosing tablets* to determine if any areas of the teeth remain unclean after brushing and flossing. Disclosing tablets contain a red or purple dye. When you chew a tablet, the dye sticks to any unclean areas of the teeth. You can then rebrush and refloss these spots. You can obtain disclosing tablets from your dentist.

Dental checkups. Dentists advise people to have a dental checkup at least once a year. Children should start going to a dentist after all their deciduous teeth have erupted. Dentists can recognize and treat diseases of the teeth and gums at an early stage, before the diseases cause serious damage. Dentists also provide services that help prevent diseases of the teeth and gums. Many dentists employ a licensed *dental hygienist* to help them in their work.

During a checkup, the dentist looks at the teeth, gums, and other tissues inside the mouth for signs of diseases. The dentist—or the dental hygienist—also may X-ray the teeth. X rays can show the location of dental decay that cannot be seen. They also show any abnormal conditions of the jawbones and other tissues that support the teeth. Based on the examination, the dentist may decide to fill cavities or plan other treatment. The dentist or hygienist then cleans the teeth to remove plaque and *calculus,* a hard, yellowish substance formed by the buildup of plaque. Calculus is also called

How to brush your teeth   Use a small, soft toothbrush and a toothpaste that contains fluorides. Place the brush against the teeth at a slight angle, with the bristles pointed toward the gums. The illustrations below show one of the brushing methods commonly recommended by dentists.

WORLD BOOK diagrams by Charles Wellek

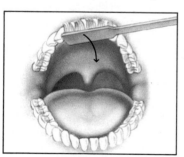

Outside surfaces of upper teeth. Use a downward, sweeping motion.

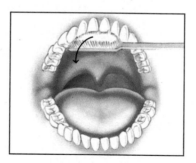

Inside surfaces of upper teeth. Use a downward, sweeping motion.

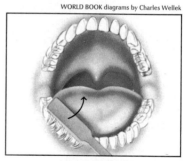

Outside surfaces of lower teeth. Use an upward, sweeping motion.

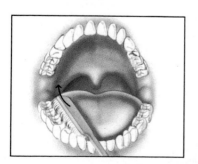

Inside surfaces of lower teeth. Use an upward, sweeping motion.

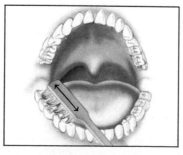

Biting surfaces of premolars and molars. Scrub back and forth.

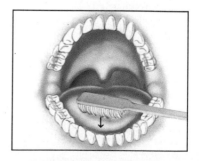

The tongue. Brush to remove food particles and bacteria.

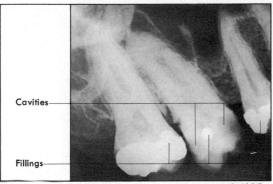

An X ray of the teeth shows cavities and fillings. Cavities appear as dark spots. Fillings show up as distinct white areas.

Patrick D. Toto

tartar. After the teeth have been cleaned, a fluoride substance is applied to help the teeth resist decay. Generally, only children and teen-agers receive applications of fluorides. Lastly, the dentist or hygienist may instruct the patient on how to brush and floss the teeth properly.

Diseases and defects of the teeth

Dental decay, also called *caries,* is the most common disease of the teeth. Most people under the age of 35 who lose their teeth do so because of dental decay. A defect in the position of the teeth, called *malocclusion,* is also a common problem among young people. Diseases of the gums and alveolus, called *periodontal diseases,* are the chief dental problem of people over the age of 35. A less common but very severe disease is *oral cancer,* which kills about 8,000 people in the United States each year. The following discussion describes the causes and treatment of (1) dental decay, (2) malocclusion, (3) periodontal diseases, and (4) oral cancer.

Dental decay is a complex process that involves plaque, bacteria, and food. Saliva produces an invisible film on the teeth. Bacteria and food particles stick to this film, forming plaque. The bacteria digest the *carbohydrates* (sugars and starches) in food and produce an acid. The acid dissolves enamel, causing a cavity. If the cavity is not treated, the decay will progress through the enamel and into the dentin. When the decay reaches the pulp, a toothache results.

The *occlusal* (biting) surfaces of the premolars and molars tend to decay easily because they have many small pits, which trap food. This type of decay may be prevented in deep pits by applying a *surface sealant.* The sealant is a plasticlike material and is bonded to the occlusal surface.

Dentists have several methods of treating dental decay, depending on the severity. The most common methods include (1) filling a cavity, (2) performing root canal therapy, (3) crowning a tooth, and (4) removing and replacing teeth. Before beginning any of these procedures, the dentist usually injects an *anesthetic* (painkilling drug) into the gums near the nerves of the tooth.

Filling a cavity. To fill a cavity, the dentist first removes the decayed and soft parts of the tooth, using small hand instruments or an electric drill. The dentist then makes tiny undercuts or ledges in the hole with a high-speed drill. These undercuts help hold the filling, which is not adhesive. The filling is packed into the hole and allowed to harden slightly. The dentist then carves the filling to restore the original shape of the tooth. In most cases, dentists fill cavities with *silver amalgam* or gold. Silver amalgam consists of silver and a small amount of copper and tin. Another method of filling cavities uses a plasticlike *resin* that is shaded to match the tooth color. This method is particularly useful in repairing decay or breaks in the front teeth. After any decay has been removed, a small amount of dilute acid is applied to the area to be filled. The acid etches or grooves the surrounding enamel surface and is left in place for about one minute. The acid is then rinsed off with water and the area is dried. The resin is then applied to the etched area and formed into the shape of the cavity or break. After hardening, the resin is shaped and polished with a drill.

Performing root canal therapy. Root canal therapy is the removal of the pulp of a tooth. It is performed if the pulp has become infected. When decay extends into the pulp, a small sac of pus, called an *abscess,* may form. An abscess can be extremely painful. If it is not treated, infection may spread to other parts of the body.

To perform root canal therapy, the dentist first anesthetizes the area and then drills a hole into the crown of

Filling a cavity

These illustrations show how a dentist fills a cavity. The dentist usually begins by injecting a drug called an *anesthetic* into the gums near the tooth. The anesthetic prevents the patient from feeling the pain that drilling might produce.

WORLD BOOK diagrams by Charles Wellek

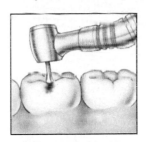

Drilling. The dentist uses a drill to remove decayed and soft parts of the tooth and to form undercuts or ledges that will help hold the filling.

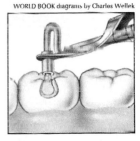

Filling. An instrument is used to place filling material into the hole. Silver amalgam, made from silver, copper, and tin, is a commonly used filling.

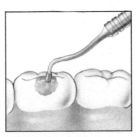

Packing. Using another instrument, the dentist firmly packs the filling into the hole. The filling is then allowed to harden slightly.

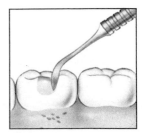

Shaping. The dentist carefully carves the filling to restore the original shape of the tooth. Finally, any rough edges are smoothed down.

the tooth. The dentist uses small files to reach through the hole and clean out the pulp. After removing the pulp, the dentist fills the empty space, usually with a rubberlike substance called *gutta-percha.* Sometimes, the hole in the crown of the tooth is then filled. But in the majority of cases, the tooth must be fitted with an artificial crown.

Crowning a tooth. Crowns are toothlike caps that may be made of metal, porcelain, or plastic. They are used when the natural crown is so badly damaged that it does not have enough healthy tissue to hold a filling.

To crown a tooth, the dentist first anesthetizes the area and then prepares the natural crown by grinding it down slightly. Next, the dentist covers the prepared tooth and the teeth next to it with a jellylike material. After this material hardens, it is removed from the patient's mouth and serves as an *impression* (mold). The dentist also makes an impression of the teeth in the opposite jaw that press against the prepared tooth and the teeth next to it. The impressions are used to make a plaster reproduction of the prepared tooth and other teeth. Dental technicians then produce a crown, using the plaster reproduction as a model. They must make sure that the crown not only fits the prepared tooth but also fits in place with the other teeth.

Crowning a tooth

A crown is a toothlike cap made of metal, porcelain, or plastic, which is cemented onto a damaged tooth. It is used when a tooth does not have enough healthy tissue to hold a filling.

WORLD BOOK diagrams by Charles Wellek

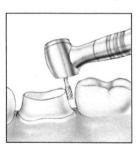

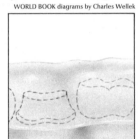

Preparing the tooth. The dentist uses a drill to remove damaged parts of the tooth and to shape the tooth so that a crown will fit over it.

Making a mold. The teeth are covered with a gel that forms a mold. Plaster teeth made in this mold serve as models for making the crown.

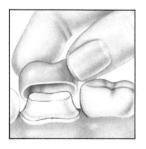

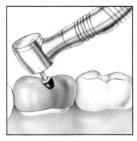

Cementing the crown. The crown must fit the prepared tooth and also fit in place with the teeth next to it and those in the opposite jaw.

Final fitting. The dentist may use a small grinding stone to make minor adjustments in the crown so that it will fit properly.

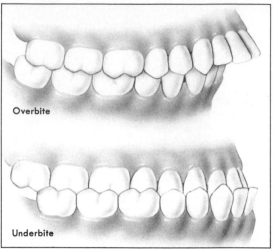

WORLD BOOK diagrams by Charles Wellek

Malocclusion is the failure of the upper and lower teeth to meet properly when a person bites. Two kinds of malocclusions are *overbite* and *underbite.* In overbite, the upper front teeth stick out farther than normal over the lower ones. In underbite, the lower front teeth extend in front of the upper ones.

Meanwhile, a temporary crown is placed on the tooth. When the permanent crown is ready, the dentist removes the temporary crown and cements the permanent one onto the tooth.

Removing and replacing teeth. In severe cases of dental decay, a dentist may remove one or more teeth and replace them with artificial ones. But artificial teeth do not function as well as natural teeth. Dentists therefore remove teeth only if no other method of treatment is considered possible.

To remove a tooth, a dentist first anesthetizes the area. The dentist uses an instrument that resembles a pliers to grip the crown of the tooth and loosen the root from the socket. Both the crown and the root are then removed. After the gums heal, the patient can be fitted with an artificial tooth.

Artificial teeth are made from impressions taken of the patient's mouth. In most cases, the teeth are made of plastic. The most common types of artificial teeth are *bridges, partial dentures,* and *full dentures.* Bridges are permanently fixed in the mouth, but partial dentures and full dentures are removable. Bridges are used when only a few teeth are missing. They consist of one or more artificial teeth with a metal or porcelain crown on each side. The crowns fit over the adjoining natural teeth, which must be prepared to hold the crowns. Partial dentures are also used to replace only a few missing teeth. A partial denture has metal clasps that hook around nearby teeth and hold the denture in place. Full dentures are used when all the teeth of one or both jaws are missing. In a full denture, the artificial teeth are attached to a plastic base that fits over the ridge left after the teeth have been removed. In the upper jaw, the plastic base also covers the roof of the mouth.

Malocclusion is the failure of the teeth in the upper and lower jaws to meet properly when a person bites. Normally, the upper front teeth should slightly overlap the lower front teeth. There are three main types of mal-

How braces work Braces consist of a system of metal brackets and wires. The brackets are bonded to the front surface of each tooth and connected by wires, *left.* A spring wire is tightened periodically, forcing the irregularly positioned tooth to move. In time, the tooth moves into its correct position, *right.*

WORLD BOOK diagrams by Charles Wellek

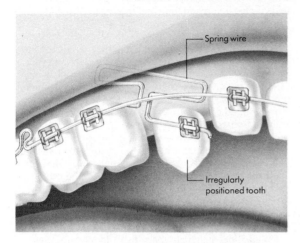
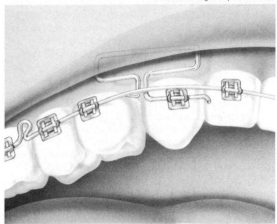

occlusions, *overbite, underbite,* and *crowding.* In overbite, the upper front teeth stick out too far over the lower front teeth. This defect is commonly called *buck teeth.* In underbite, the lower front teeth extend in front of the upper ones. Many people have the correct *occlusion* (bite), but their teeth are crowded. Crowding is the most common malocclusion.

Malocclusion has various causes. In some cases, a deciduous tooth falls out before a permanent tooth is ready to erupt. The nearby teeth then gradually move into the open space and prevent the permanent tooth from erupting in the correct position. In other cases, the permanent teeth are too large for the jaw and crowd one another. The edges of some teeth may then overlap, or one tooth may grow above another. In still other cases, the jaws do not grow properly.

Malocclusion prevents the teeth from functioning normally when a person chews food. It also may affect the way a person speaks. In addition, malocclusion contributes to the development of dental decay and periodontal diseases, partly because irregularly positioned teeth are hard to clean.

Most cases of malocclusion can be corrected with *braces.* Braces consist of metal brackets that are bonded on the front surface of each tooth and connected by wires. The wires are tightened periodically to force the teeth to move into the correct position. But the teeth must be moved slowly, and so the treatment may take a year or more. In some cases, one or more teeth must be removed to allow enough space for the others to move into a normal position.

Periodontal diseases are caused chiefly by the build-up of plaque and calculus between the gums and teeth. The plaque and calculus irritate the gums, causing them to become inflamed. In time, the jawbones may become infected. The best way to prevent plaque from building up under the gum line is by flossing daily. The gums can also become irritated by habitually breathing through the mouth, smoking or chewing tobacco, brushing improperly, or wearing ill-fitting dentures. Irregularly positioned teeth can also irritate the gums.

There are three main kinds of periodontal diseases. They are (1) gingivitis, (2) periodontitis, and (3) Vincent's infection.

Gingivitis is an inflammation of the *gingivae* (gums). The gingivae become red and swollen and bleed easily when brushed or prodded. Dentists treat gingivitis by cleaning the teeth and gums to remove plaque and calculus. They also instruct patients on how to brush and floss the teeth and on how to massage the gums. If gingivitis is not treated, it can lead to periodontitis.

Periodontitis, also called *pyorrhea,* is a severe infection of the gingivae, alveolus, and other tissues that support the teeth. The infection gradually destroys the bony walls of the sockets, and the teeth become loose. Periodontitis is difficult to cure. Treatment may involve surgical removal of the damaged tissues and repair of the re-

Periodontal diseases

The illustrations below show two kinds of periodontal diseases. In *gingivitis,* calculus builds up between gums and teeth, causing the gums to become inflamed. Gingivitis may lead to *periodontitis,* an infection that gradually destroys the bony socket.

WORLD BOOK diagrams by Charles Wellek

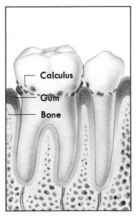
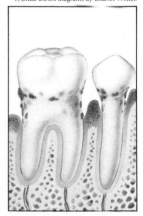

Gingivitis   **Periodontitis**

maining healthy tissues. Sometimes, loose teeth can be *splinted* (attached) to nearby teeth that are still firm. But in many cases, the loose teeth must be removed and replaced by artificial ones.

Vincent's infection, also called *trench mouth,* is a painful infection of the gingivae. The gums become red and swollen and bleed easily. The mouth has an extremely bad odor, and the victim may develop a fever. To treat Vincent's infection, a dentist cleans the teeth and gums thoroughly and instructs the patient on mouth care. In most cases, the dentist also prescribes antibiotics to combat the infection.

Oral cancer is a disease that destroys the tissues of the mouth and may spread to other parts of the body. Scientists do not know for certain what causes oral cancer. But many factors can contribute to its development. For example, people who smoke or chew tobacco or drink excessive amounts of alcoholic beverages increase the risk of developing oral cancer.

Oral cancer may be painless and unnoticeable in its early stages. The first symptom may be a small sore in the mouth that does not heal. To test for cancer, a dentist removes some tissue from the sore. The tissue is examined under a microscope to determine if it is cancerous. Oral cancer may be treated with drugs, radiation, or surgery.

Teeth of animals

Many kinds of animals have teeth. However, birds, toads, turtles, and some types of insects and whales do not have teeth.

Cats, dogs, and most other mammals have *heterodont teeth*—that is, they have at least two types of teeth, which have different uses. For example, they may have incisors for biting into food and molars for crushing or grinding food.

The teeth of various kinds of mammals differ in shape and size, depending chiefly on what the animals eat. For example, plant-eating mammals, such as elephants, giraffes, and sheep, have unusually broad, flat molars. They use the molars to chew and mash plants. Meat-eating mammals, such as lions, tigers, and wolves, have long, pointed canines. They use the canines to rip and tear the bodies of their prey.

Some mammals have teeth that grow continuously. The tusks of elephants are actually incisors that have become very long. The tusks have an open pulp, which enables them to keep growing. Beavers, rats, and other rodents also have teeth that grow continuously. But most of the growth is worn down by continual use of the teeth, and so the teeth of these animals do not lengthen greatly.

Unlike most mammals, many fish and most reptiles have *homodont teeth*—that is, all their teeth are about the same size and shape and have only one use. In general, animals that have homodont teeth use their teeth to catch prey. Fish and reptiles lose and replace their teeth continuously.

Snakes have teeth that curve back toward the throat. Snakes swallow their prey whole and use their teeth to pull the prey back into the throat. In poisonous snakes, certain teeth have a canal or a groove, through which

Some animal teeth   Animal teeth vary in size and shape. Most mammals have *heterodont teeth,* which consist of two or more types: incisors and canines for biting and tearing food, and molars for crushing it. Most reptiles and many fish have *homodont teeth,* a single type that generally is used to catch prey.

WORLD BOOK diagrams by Patricia J. Wynne

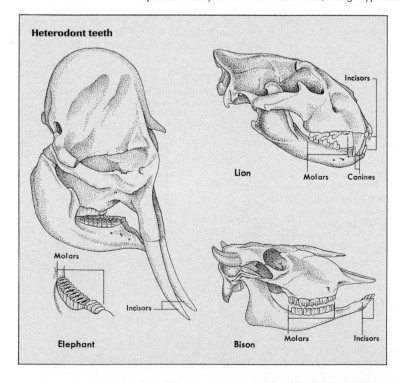

Heterodont teeth

Lion

Incisors

Molars   Canines

Molars

Incisors

Elephant

Molars   Incisors

Bison

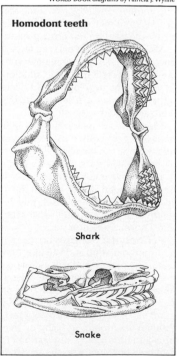

Homodont teeth

Shark

Snake

poison can be ejected. The poison comes from glands in the roof of the mouth. John P. Wortel

Related articles in *World Book* include:

Human teeth

Abscess	Mouth
Dental hygiene	Orthodontics
Dentistry	Periodontitis
Digestive system (From mouth to stomach)	Races, Human (picture: The upper front teeth)
Fluoridation	Saliva
Fluorine	Toothpaste and toothpowder
Mastication	Trench mouth

Animal teeth

Animal (Jaws and teeth)	Hog (Teeth)
Beaver (Teeth)	Horse (Teeth)
Cat (The body of a cat)	Insect (Mouth parts)
Cattle (Teeth)	Lion (The body of a lion)
Dog (Body structure)	Mammal (What mammals eat)
Elephant (Tusks and teeth)	Rodent
Fish (Digestive system)	Ruminant
Hippopotamus (The body of a river hippopotamus)	Shark (Teeth and scales)
	Snake (Skeleton)
	Whale (picture: Toothed whales)

Outline

I. Kinds of teeth
  A. Deciduous teeth
  B. Permanent teeth
II. Parts of a tooth
  A. Pulp   D. Cementum
  B. Dentin   E. Periodontal ligament
  C. Enamel
III. Care of the teeth and gums
  A. A good diet
  B. Cleaning the teeth
  C. Dental checkups
IV. Diseases and defects of the teeth
  A. Dental decay
  B. Malocclusion
  C. Periodontal diseases
  D. Oral cancer
V. Teeth of animals

Questions

How often should the teeth be brushed?
What are the incisors and canines used for? The molars and premolars?
What are the four kinds of tissues that make up a tooth?
When should children start going to a dentist?
What are some of the causes of malocclusion? How can malocclusion be corrected?
When does dental decay result in a toothache?
How does eating sugary foods contribute to dental decay?
What is dental floss used for?
What does the periodontal ligament do?
What is the chief cause of periodontal diseases?

Additional resources

Level I
Betancourt, Jeanne. *Smile! How to Cope with Braces.* Random House, 1982.
Gaskin, John. *Teeth.* Watts, 1984.

Level II
Goldberg, Hyman J. V., and others. *Your Mouth Is Your Business: The Dentists' Guide to Better Health.* Appleton-Century, 1980.
Guerini, Vincenzo. *History of Dentistry from the Most Ancient Times Until the End of the Eighteenth Century.* Longwood, 1977. First published in 1909.
Holt, Robert L. *Straight Teeth: Orthodontics and Dental Care for Everyone.* Morrow, 1980.
Marshall, Howard B. *How to Save Your Teeth: The Preventive Approach.* Thomas Nelson, 1980.
Woodforde, John. *The Strange Story of False Teeth.* Universe Books, 1970.

Tegu, *tay GOO,* also spelled *teju,* is the name of two species of ground-dwelling South American lizards. They weigh about 5 pounds (2.3 kilograms) and are about 3 feet (91 centimeters) long. Tegus are strong, swift, and aggressive. Tegus burrow in sand or under rocks. They eat plants, snails, insects, and small *vertebrates* (animals with backbones). In farming areas, tegus are considered pests because they eat eggs and chicks. Female tegus often lay their eggs inside termite mounds to protect the eggs from attack by other animals.

Scientific classification. Tegus belong to the family Teiidae. They are genus *Tupinambis.* Raymond B. Huey

Tegucigalpa, *teh GOO see GAHL pah* (pop. 571,400), is the capital of Honduras. The city's Indian name means *Silver Hill.* It lies on a fertile plain along the Choluteca River and is about 78 miles (126 kilometers) from the Gulf of Fonseca, an arm of the Pacific. For location, see **Honduras** (map). Mountains surround the city. Tegucigalpa is the center of a well-populated and rich farming and mining area. Important buildings include the cathedral and the National University. See also **Honduras** (picture). Rollin S. Atwood

Teheran, *teh uh RAHN* (pop. 5,734,199), also spelled *Tehran,* is the capital of Iran and the second largest city in the Middle East. Only Cairo, the capital of Egypt, has more people. Teheran is Iran's cultural, economic, and political center. It lies in northern Iran, at the foot of the Elburz Mountains. For location, see **Iran** (map).

The city. Teheran is one of the most modern cities in the Middle East. Large parts of it have been built or rebuilt since the 1920's. The city has many wide boulevards, which are lined with tall, modern buildings of

Marge Kathan

Teheran, the capital of Iran, is one of the most modern cities in the Middle East. The main downtown street, *above,* is lined by office and government buildings and fashionable shops.

Western-style architecture. The major business and government buildings and most of Teheran's fashionable shops are near the center of the city. In the same area is an old business section where merchants sell fabrics, jewelry, and other handmade products at a bazaar that is hundreds of years old.

Most of Teheran's middle-class residents live in apartment buildings. Large numbers of poor people live in run-down apartments and houses in the southern part of Teheran. Many wealthy people live in large, beautiful houses north of the city.

Teheran has many parks and theaters. Its museums include the Archaeological and Ethnological museums and the Golestan Palace, which feature many treasures from Iran's past. The city has several universities, the largest of which is the University of Teheran.

Economy. The Iranian government employs many of Teheran's people. The city's industries include banking, construction, and petroleum processing. Factories in Teheran make bricks, cigarettes, textiles, and other products.

Buses and taxis provide public transportation in Teheran. An international airport lies west of the city.

History. People probably lived on the site of what is now Teheran at least 3,000 years ago. Teheran was a small town until the 1200's, when it began to grow. The city became the capital of Iran in 1788.

During the 1920's, many of Teheran's old buildings were torn down and replaced by new ones. The city's population has increased from about 1,800,000 in 1960 to about 5,700,000. This rapid growth caused such problems as a housing shortage, pollution, and traffic jams. Since the 1970's, a number of construction projects have provided more residential and office buildings in Teheran.   Malcolm C. Peck

See also **Iran** (picture: A boulevard in Teheran).

Teheran Conference was the first meeting of the main Allied leaders during World War II. These leaders, called the Big Three, were Prime Minister Winston Churchill of Great Britain, President Franklin Delano Roosevelt of the United States, and Premier Joseph Stalin of the Soviet Union. The meeting was also the first summit conference involving the heads of the Soviet Union and the United States. It took place from Nov. 28 to Dec. 1, 1943, in Teheran, Iran's capital.

The two main military decisions made at the conference were that the United States and Britain would launch an invasion of France in 1944 and that the Soviet Union would enter the war against Japan after Germany's defeat. The leaders also discussed plans for establishing a United Nations organization, for dividing and disarming Germany, and for moving Poland's borders westward after the war. The Polish-Soviet border would be redrawn to add territory to the Soviet Union that had been part of Russia before World War I began in 1914. The cooperative spirit of the Teheran Conference paved the way for later agreements among the Allied war leaders at the Yalta Conference in 1945.
Diane Shaver Clemens

Tehran. See Teheran.

Tehuantepec, *tuh WAHN tuh PEHK,* **Isthmus of,** forms the narrowest part of Mexico. It lies between the Bay of Campeche and the Gulf of Tehuantepec, and includes parts of the states of Veracruz and Oaxaca. For lo-

cation, see **Mexico** (terrain map). The isthmus has large petroleum and sulfur deposits. It measures 130 miles (209 kilometers) wide at its narrowest point. Most of the land is tropical lowland. Foothills of the Sierra Madre mountains rise in the south.   John A. Crow

Teilhard de Chardin, *TAY YAR duh SHAR DAN,* **Pierre** (1881-1955), was a French *paleontologist* (expert in fossils). He helped discover Peking man, an early type of human being. Teilhard's greatest fame, however, rests on a theory that claims to unify cosmic evolution and Christianity.

Teilhard entered the Jesuit order in 1899 and was ordained a priest in 1911. He lectured for a time at the Catholic Institute in Paris. His theory of evolution in relation to the Catholic doctrine of original sin in his lectures was considered unorthodox. As a result, church authorities forbade him to continue teaching in Paris. Teilhard then lived in China from 1923 to 1946, where he was a consultant to the National Geological Survey. He began his fossil research in 1923. He wrote extensively in China. However, most of Teilhard's writings were controversial, and so they were not published until after his death.

According to Teilhard, "Evolution is a general condition to which all theories, all hypotheses, all systems must bow and which they must satisfy if they are to be thinkable and true." He placed humanity at the center of the universe and Christianity at the center of human history. Some theologians welcome Teilhard's extreme optimism as a balance to the fear and discouragement in the world. His best-known works include *The Phenomenon of Man* and *The Divine Milieu.*   John A. Hardon

Teju. See Tegu.

Tektite, *TEHK tyt,* is a glassy stone that may look like a teardrop, ball, disk, rod, dumbbell, or button. A few tektites are blocklike in appearance. Many tektites are nut-sized, but some are microscopic. Tektites are black, green, or amber, and they usually have grooved or pitted surfaces.

Some scientists think that tektites were formed when giant meteorites crashed into deposits of sandstone and other sedimentary rock on the earth's surface. Fragments of such rocks were melted by the heat of the impact and scattered over great distances. They solidified in flight and fell back to the earth as tektites. Other scientists have developed an entirely different theory about tektites. They believe tektites are the remains of lava masses that were hurled to the earth by volcanoes on the moon from 750,000 to 35 million years ago. The liquefied rock materials that were ejected during the violent eruptions solidified into stony glass on the way to the earth.   Robert W. Charles

Tel Aviv, *TEHL uh VEEV* (pop. 325,700; met. area pop. 1,350,000), is the second largest city of Israel and the nation's chief commercial and industrial center. Only Jerusalem has more people. Tel Aviv is one of the most modern cities in the Middle East. It lies on the eastern shore of the Mediterranean Sea. For the location of Tel Aviv, see **Israel** (map).

The heart of Tel Aviv is a major downtown intersection called Dizengoff Circle. Fashionable shops and sidewalk cafes line the nearby streets. The 37-story Shalom Tower stands in the center of the city's financial district, several blocks south of Dizengoff Circle. It is the tallest

Tel Aviv, Israel's chief commercial and industrial center, lies on the eastern shore of the Mediterranean Sea. Pleasure boats dock near modern buildings of the city, *above.*

building in Israel. The southwestern section of the city was formerly a separate town called *Jaffa (Yafo* in Hebrew). Jaffa, an ancient port area that dates back to Biblical times, has many historic sites that have been restored by archaeologists. Jaffa also has many art galleries, cafes, restaurants, and nightclubs. Most of the people of Tel Aviv live in apartment buildings.

Cultural attractions in Tel Aviv include the Museum Haaretz and the Tel Aviv Museum. Tel Aviv University is one of the city's several institutions of higher learning. Bar Ilan University is in Ramat Gan, a suburb of the city.

Tel Aviv is the center of Israel's chief manufacturing district. About half the nation's business companies are in the area. Their products include building materials, chemicals, clothing, electronic equipment, machine tools, and processed foods. The city is also the nation's leading center for such activities as banking, publishing, and trade. Israel's political parties have their headquarters in Tel Aviv.

In 1909, Jewish immigrants from Europe founded Tel Aviv northeast of Jaffa. Tel Aviv was administered as part of Jaffa at first, but it became a separate town in 1921. Tel Aviv grew rapidly as Jewish immigrants poured in, mainly from Europe. It became Israel's first capital when the nation was established in 1948. The capital was moved to Jerusalem in 1949, but the Israeli Ministry of Defense and many foreign embassies remained in Tel Aviv. In 1950, Tel Aviv and Jaffa merged to form the city of Tel Aviv-Yafo. Tel Aviv-Yafo remains the official name, but the city is almost always called Tel Aviv.

Tel Aviv continued to grow rapidly in the 1950's and early 1960's. Its population reached about 392,100 in 1965 and then began to decline, but the suburban population continued to rise. The rapid growth of the Tel Aviv area resulted in such problems as air pollution, slums, and traffic jams.   Saul B. Cohen

See also **Israel** (picture); **Jaffa.**

Telecommunication is the transmission and reception of messages over long distances. Visual signaling with flags, lamps, or smoke was the earliest form of telecommunication. Today, the term refers to a wide variety

of electrical and electronic communication systems that transmit information throughout the world. Modern telecommunication systems send and receive sound, printed materials, and visual images in a fraction of a second.

Common telecommunication systems include telephones, television sets, and radios. Other kinds of systems are used chiefly in industry. These systems can transmit such information as airline reservations, banking transactions, and stock market reports. Newspapers rely on teletypewriter and telephoto equipment to obtain news stories and photographs from all parts of the world. Communication between space stations and the earth also has been established through telecommunication.

Most telecommunication systems transmit messages by wire, radio, or satellite. Many telegraph messages and telephone conversations, especially local calls, travel over wires that are laid underground in cables. Cables on the ocean floor handle such communications that travel overseas. Television and radio broadcasts are sent through the air by radio waves. Radio waves called *microwaves* transmit television signals over extremely long distances. Microwaves are also used in most long-distance telephone communication. Communications satellites orbiting the earth transmit telephone, television, and other communications signals throughout the world.

There are two methods of telecommunication transmission, *analogue transmission* and *digital transmission.* Analogue transmission uses signals that are exact reproductions of the sound or picture being transmitted. For example, an analogue telephone system transmits an electric current that copies the pattern of sound waves of the speaker's voice. This current travels over wire and is converted back to sound waves in the telephone receiver.

In digital transmission, the signals are converted into a code. In most cases, the code has two elements, such as the dot-dash of Morse code or the on-off flashing of a light. In one type of digital telephone system, the coded signals are transmitted by a rapidly flashing beam of light and are decoded in the receiver. A device called a *laser* produces the light, which travels through thin strands of glass called *optical fibers.*

When transmitting a telephone conversation, the light in the system flashes on and off about 45 million times per second. This high rate enables two optical fibers to carry about 6,000 conversations at the same time. It would take 250 copper wires to handle as many conversations. Digital transmission also involves less noise and distortion than an analogue system. Many telecommunication systems are being converted from analogue to digital transmission.   Solomon J. Buchsbaum

Related articles in *World Book* include:

Telegram. See Telegraph.

David R. Frazier

A telegram is transmitted over wires to a telegraph office close to the receiver. There the message is removed from the telegraph's printer, *above,* and delivered to the receiver.

Telegraph was the first device to send messages by electricity. At one time, most telegraph messages were sent by tapping out a special code for each letter of the message with a telegraph key. The telegraph changed the dots and dashes of this code, which became known as the *Morse code,* into electrical impulses and transmitted them over telegraph wires.

Today, most long-distance electric or electronic communication signals are transmitted by such means as communications satellites, broadcasting antennas, and coaxial and fiber-optic cables. The telegraph is the common ancestor of these devices, but it is now rarely used where more advanced technology is available. However, the term *telegram* still applies to several kinds of communication in which an electronically transmitted message is delivered to the receiver in paper form.

For many years, the Western Union Telegraph Company controlled telegraph services in the United States. Today, any company may offer public message telegraphy. Telegraph rates are set by the Federal Communications Commission (FCC).

Sending a telegram

In the United States, a person may send a telegram by telephoning the message to a special telephone bureau of the telegraph company. A person also may go to a public telegraph office or telegraphic agent and write the message on a special form.

A message telephoned to the telephone bureau of a telegraph company is recorded by an operator on a *video display terminal,* a device that reproduces the message on a screen. The operator depresses a key to send the complete message to a message-switching computer, which routes the message to the circuit serving the point of destination. A message submitted at a message office may also be transmitted to the computer by a *teleprinter.* A teleprinter has a keyboard similar to that of a typewriter, and the message is sent by typing it. After reaching its destination, a telegram may be telephoned or delivered in person to the receiver.

Kinds of telegrams

Telegraph messages that travel over land are called *telegrams* or *wires.* Such messages are called *cablegrams* or *cables* if they go by underwater cables. Regu-

lar telegrams are transmitted and delivered within a few hours. A fixed rate is charged for a minimum number of words, and an extra fee for each additional word. In addition to regular telegrams, there are several special types, including *personal opinion messages* and *mailgrams.*

Personal opinion messages are telegrams sent to an elected official to express the sender's opinion on some issue. For example, the sender may wish to urge support of a certain bill. The message is limited to 20 words, for which a special rate is charged. Direct circuits deliver the message to the White House, the U.S. Capitol, or any of the state capitols.

Mailgrams combine the facilities of Western Union and the U.S. Postal Service to deliver messages. The sender phones the message to the telephone bureau of the telegraph company, and the message is electronically transmitted to the post office nearest the receiver. It is delivered with the next day's business mail.

Development of the telegraph

Before electric telegraphy, most messages that traveled long distances were entrusted to messengers who memorized them or carried them in writing. Such messages could usually be delivered no faster than the fastest horse. An exception was the *semaphore,* or *visual telegraph* system, in which a sequence of fire beacons or other markers signaled from point to point. In the 1790's, Claude Chappe, a French inventor, established a system of visual telegraph towers that relayed messages across France. However, visual telegraphs did not work well at night or in bad weather. Even in good weather, they could transmit only a small amount of information.

The electric telegraph makes use of the relationship between magnetism and electricity. During the 1790's, the Italian scientist Alessandro Volta invented an electrochemical cell that made a steady source of electric current available. In 1820, the Danish physicist Hans Christian Oersted discovered that an electric current will cause a magnetized needle to move. This principle is the basis of the telegraph, in which a current is varied systematically according to a code. The British electrician William Sturgeon invented the electromagnet in 1825. Three men used these discoveries to develop telegraphs and commercial applications for them. They were the physicists William F. Cooke and Charles Wheatstone, working together in Great Britain, and American inventor and painter Samuel F. B. Morse.

The Cooke-Wheatstone telegraph. In 1837, Cooke and Wheatstone patented a telegraph that worked by electromagnetism. Their receiving instrument had five or six magnetic needles mounted vertically on a dial on which the letters of the alphabet were printed. A separate wire and a coil that served as an electromagnet controlled each needle. When an electric current passed through one of these wires, it produced a magnetic field in the coil, causing the needle to move. Letters were signaled by pointing two needles toward the letter at the same time. In principle, the Cooke-Wheatstone telegraph was a miniature electric semaphore system. A single-needle version was patented in 1845 and was used in Great Britain until 1870.

The Morse telegraph was first publicly demonstrated in 1837. The sending device was a switch, called

© Bradley Smith — Granger Collection — Radio Times Hulton Picture Library

The first telegraphs. Samuel Morse's first telegraph, *left,* patented in 1837, had an electromagnet that caused a pen to make V-shaped marks on paper. Later, he developed the Morse code and a telegraph with a sounder to click out incoming messages, *center.* In 1837, two English inventors produced a telegraph, *right,* with needles that pointed to letters to spell out the message.

a *key,* that completed a circuit and allowed current to flow to a receiving *sounder.* In the sounder, the current caused an electromagnet to attract an iron bar, called an *armature.* The armature struck the electromagnet, making a clicking noise in Morse code, a dot-dash code developed by Morse. With each click, a pointed instrument attached to the armature also *embossed* (marked) the code on a strip of paper, creating a record of the transmission. When the key was released, the circuit was broken and no current flowed. This caused the electromagnet in the sounder to lose its magnetism, and a spring pulled the bar back to its original position. Morse also developed a relay device to lengthen the distance over which messages could be sent. Morse patented his telegraph in 1840.

In 1843, Morse received $30,000 from Congress to build an experimental telegraph line from Washington, D.C., to Baltimore, Md. When the Whig Party met in Baltimore in May 1844 to nominate a candidate for the presidency, the telegraph line was within 15 miles (24 kilometers) of Baltimore. News of the nomination of former Senator Henry Clay was rushed to the end of the telegraph line and transmitted instantly to Washington. An hour and a half later, the train from Baltimore arrived with verification. However, Clay had been most likely to win the nomination, and doubters were not impressed. When news of the vice presidential nomination also arrived ahead of the train, even doubters were converted. On May 24, 1844, Morse sat at a sending device in the Supreme Court chamber of the Capitol and tapped out the first official telegraph message, "What hath God wrought!"

Early expansion. In the United States, the Morse telegraph was successful for a number of reasons, including its simple operation and its relatively low cost. By 1851, the country had more than 50 telegraph companies. Most telegraph business was controlled by the Magnetic Telegraph Company, which held the Morse patents.

The Magnetic proprietors wanted to build a system of lines linking the main commercial routes of the nation. They assigned parts of this system to various partners. However, bitter arguments and competition arose, and some partners left to build rival systems. Rate-cutting and questionable investment practices were common. Lines and instruments were often built carelessly and with inferior materials. Several companies were bankrupted by such problems as fierce competition, lawsuits, and insufficient income. In the public's view, the telegraph did not work reliably. Messages often did not reach their destination, and rates were high and unpredictable.

Telegraphy and the railroad. Despite the difficulties, some businesses found the telegraph useful. For example, newspapers printed columns of "telegraph news." Stockbrokers used the telegraph to move important information rapidly. But the telegraph's most valuable and constant partner was the railroad.

Western Union Telegraph Company was one of the first telegraph companies to gain benefits from contracts with railroads. In these contracts, the railroad agreed to lay telegraph lines along railroad rights of way. The railroad also agreed to provide office space in depots for telegraphers employed by both the railroad and the telegraph company and free transportation for people who repaired the telegraph lines. In return, Western Union agreed to transmit messages relating to railroad business free of charge, and to give priority to messages concerning the movement of trains.

The telegraph helped coordinate train schedules and increase safety. Trains could be moved more quickly using a common time standard transmitted to every station at the same instant. The location of any train could be known with certainty. The telegraph made the railroad a safe and efficient national transportation network. The railroad offered the telegraph company a monopoly of protected routes.

Western Union. During the 1850's, competition between telegraph companies gave way to profitable mergers as the telegraph pushed west. Short, disconnected, broken-down lines were rebuilt and combined into extensive networks. By the 1860's, central telegraph offices existed in every major city.

By the beginning of the Civil War in 1861, there were two major telegraph companies in the United States: (1) Western Union, whose lines ran east and west, and (2) American Telegraph, whose lines ran north and south along the East Coast. The Civil War destroyed the north-south lines of American Telegraph and strengthened the east-west lines of Western Union, which connected states loyal to the Union. After the war, Western Union absorbed its only significant remaining rivals. Western Union was both the first industrial monopoly in the United States and the nation's largest corporation. It became the most successful of all the telegraph companies. See **Western Union.**

Across the Atlantic. Western Union had completed a transcontinental link by 1861. In 1866, a permanent transatlantic link was achieved. A cable 2,000 miles (3,200 kilometers) long was laid from the *Great Eastern,* the largest ship of its day. American businessman Cyrus W. Field and his British and American associates were largely responsible for the success. The British physicist Lord Kelvin offered essential scientific and technical advice. See **Cable** (The Atlantic telegraph cable).

Faster and better service. Improvements in telegraphy increased the message capacity of single wires and the speed of message handling and transmission. The *duplex system,* which could send two messages over one wire at the same time, one in each direction, began operating in the United States in 1872. Two years later, American inventor Thomas A. Edison developed a *quadruplex system,* which handled four messages at the same time. In 1875, Émile Baudot, a French telegrapher, developed a *multiplex system* that could handle five at once. In 1915, Western Union began using a system capable of multiplexing eight messages at a time.

Devices to send and receive messages in printed form instead of Morse code were also developed in the late 1800's and early 1900's. During the same time, methods of sending messages by means of a paper tape punched with holes were introduced. Multiplex systems used a punched-tape method of sending. Teleprinters, which can send electrical impulses directly over telegraph lines to similar printers at the receiving end, were generally adopted in the late 1920's. In 1925, a telephoto-

graph and facsimile telegraph system began operating in the United States. These systems can send and receive telegrams in picture form (see **Facsimile; Telephoto**). *Telex* and *TWX,* which are interconnected two-way dial teleprinter services, were introduced during the 1930's.

Effects of telegraphy. New management methods worked out in the partnership of wire and rail were applied to other businesses in the 1800's. With rapid telegraphic communication, it was possible to increase both the number of operating units in a single company and their distance from headquarters. Efficient supervision by means of cheap, fast long-distance telegraphy helped change the structure of business. Large, corporate structures began to replace small, separate businesses. The union of wire and rail also made possible the efficient organization of the entire United States as one national market. Information about products for sale could move quickly between producer and consumer.

Telegraphy also transformed the press. When the United States declared war on Mexico in 1846, the front was seven days away from the East Coast by the fastest government mails. In order to obtain the latest news quickly, six newspapers formed the New York Associated Press. This news service, which later became the Associated Press, used the telegraph to collect the news and sell it to other newspapers (see **Associated Press; News service**).

The telegraph today. For many years, the telegraph was a vital part of commerce, government, and the military. It greatly influenced the machines that came after it. The original backers of the American scientist Alexander

Making a simple telegraph set

Two-way communication can be achieved with two telegraph sets. Each set includes a key, a sounder, and a battery. The key of one set is connected to the sounder of the other. Directions for making a set are given below.

1. The base of the set is a flat piece of wood that holds the sounder. First, nail together the wood base, one of the smaller wood blocks, and the T-shaped piece of tin, as shown.

2. The sounder. Hammer two steel nails into one end of the base. Wind a piece of insulated wire around the nails—about 30 turns for each—to form coils. Connect the coils to the battery with one end of the wire. Leave the other end loose to connect the coils to the key. Hammer a bent aluminum nail next to, but not touching, the T-shaped piece of tin.

3. The key is the thin metal strip mounted on one of the small blocks. Push two thumbtacks halfway through the key. Scrape the insulation from one end of the wire attached to the sounder coils. Wrap the bare wire around the tacks and press down.

4. Bend the key upward about half an inch from the block. Press the third thumbtack under the raised end. Take a piece of wire and scrape the insulating material from each end. Connect the tack to the battery with the wire. The key should touch the tack when pressed and spring up when released.

5. Touching the key to the tack causes electricity to flow through the circuit. Electromagnets pull the metal T down, making a clicking sound. When the key is released, the T springs up and strikes the bent nail, making another clicking sound. These sounds form the dots and dashes of the telegraph code.

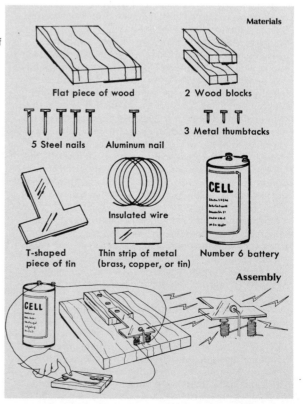

Materials

Flat piece of wood

2 Wood blocks

5 Steel nails   Aluminum nail

3 Metal thumbtacks

Insulated wire

CELL

Number 6 battery

T-shaped piece of tin

Thin strip of metal (brass, copper, or tin)

Assembly

CELL

Graham Bell believed the telephone he invented in 1876 was a talking telegraph that could compete with the Western Union monopoly. Radio, patented by the Italian inventor Guglielmo Marconi in 1896, was called *wireless telegraphy*. The distribution of telegraphic news from a central wire service to other newspapers was the original model for national network broadcasting of radio and television to associated stations.

The introduction of the telephone took away most of the short-distance communication business of the telegraph. The arrival of long-distance telephone communication threatened to eliminate the remaining telegraph business. Today, the telegraph has been largely replaced by such communications machines as computers and communications satellites. These machines are faster than the telegraph and can process many kinds of information.   Carolyn Marvin

Related articles. See the *Communication* section of the various country articles. Other related articles in *World Book* include:

Biographies

Cornell, Ezra	Henry, Joseph	Pupin, Michael I.
Edison, Thomas A.	Kelvin, Lord	Wheatstone,
Gray, Elisha	Morse, Samuel F. B.	Sir Charles

Other related articles

Associated Press	Morse code
Cable	News service
Common carrier	Radio (History)
Communication	Radiogram
Facsimile	Stock ticker
Federal Communications Commission	Telephone
	Telephoto
International Telecommunication Union	Teletypewriter
	Western Union

Additional resources

Cook, Cherri. *Telephone and Telegraph.* New Readers, 1975. For younger readers.

Math, Irwin. *Morse, Marconi and You.* Scribner, 1979. Explanations and building directions for telegraph, telephone, and radio. Suitable for younger readers.

Thompson, Robert L. *Wiring a Continent: The History of the Telegraph Industry in the United States, 1832-1866.* Ayer, 1972. First published in 1947.

Wells, Robert. *Messages, Men and Miles: Electronic Communications, How They Work.* Prentice-Hall, 1958. For younger readers.

Telegraph plant is an herb about 4 feet (1.2 meters) high. It is native to tropical Asia, and grows in greenhouses in many parts of the world. If the plant, or especially its leaves, is touched, the leaves quickly droop downward, like the arms of a railroad semaphore signal. The plant received its common name from these leaf movements. It bears small purple flowers. The seed pods are jointed and can be separated easily.

Scientific classification. The telegraph plant belongs to the pea family, Leguminosae. It is *Desmodium motorium.*

George H. M. Lawrence

Telemann, *TAY luh MAHN,* **Georg Philipp,** *gay AWRK* (1681-1767), was perhaps the most famous German composer of his day. Telemann wrote thousands of compositions in the popular forms of the 1700's. He wrote more than 1,000 cantatas as well as operas, concertos, oratorios, and chamber music. His music forms an important link between the baroque style of Johann Sebastian Bach and the classical style of Joseph Haydn.

Telemann's works show an understanding of melody and harmony with a strong sense of musical form. He was concerned that his music would be suitable for performance by amateurs. His best-known works include the operas *Der geduldige Socrates* (1721) and *Pimpinone* (1725), the cantata cycle *Harmonischer Gottes-Dienst* (1725-1726), and a three-part collection of orchestral pieces called *Musique de Table* (1733).

Telemann was born in Magdeburg and studied in Leipzig. In 1721, he became the music director for the five main churches in Hamburg, where he spent the rest of his life. From 1722 to 1738, he served as director of the Hamburg Opera.   Mary Vinquist

Telemetry, *tuh LEHM uh tree,* means *measuring at a distance.* Scientists and engineers use telemetry in many ways. Scientists send weather balloons as high as 20 or 30 miles (32 or 48 kilometers) into the air to measure the air temperature, pressure, and humidity above the earth. Radios attached to the balloons relay this information back to the earth.

Telemetry also helps people explore outer space. Rockets and spacecraft send information about their own performance and conditions in outer space to scientists and engineers on the earth. On manned flights, telemetry systems provide data on astronauts' physical condition by reporting their pulse rate, blood pressure, and temperature. To save space and weight, special miniature equipment is used in spacecraft.

A telemetry system consists of a measuring instrument, a transmitter, and a receiving station. For example, a telemetry system that records temperatures at remote locations uses an electrical thermometer as the measuring instrument. Signals produced by the thermometer are transmitted by radio or by wire to a receiving station. Instruments at the receiving station record the signals on magnetic tape and convert them into meter readings and graphs.   Arthur C. Aikin

Teleology. See Mechanist philosophy.

Telepathy, *tuh LEHP uh thee,* is the communication of thoughts, feelings, or knowledge from one person to another without the use of the senses of hearing, sight, smell, taste, or touch. Telepathy is sometimes called *mind reading* or *thought transference.* An example of telepathy would be if one person thought of something specific and another person stated or wrote the thought correctly. To be telepathic, however, the performance would have to be repeated and could not be explainable in any other way.

Telepathy is part of the subject matter of parapsychology and is studied by scientists called *parapsychologists.* Parapsychologists believe that neither distance nor time affects telepathy. Thus, a person's thoughts might be received by another person who is far away. Parapsychologists also believe that a person may know in advance the thoughts, feelings, or knowledge that another person will have at a later time. If true, this would be an example of *precognitive telepathy.*

Telepathy is considered a major form of *extrasensory perception (ESP),* an awareness of something without the use of the known senses. Telepathy is under scientific investigation. Its existence is still an open question, but many scientists doubt its reality.   James E. Alcock

See also **Extrasensory perception; Clairvoyance; Mind reading; Parapsychology; Psychical research.**

WORLD BOOK photo

An automatic telephone answering device records messages and gives tape-recorded information to callers.

Motorola (WORLD BOOK photo)

A car phone enables motorists to make and receive calls. Many airplanes, ships, and trains also have mobile telephone units.

Porta-TelTM (WORLD BOOK photo)

A special teletypewriter attachment, called a *TTY,* enables a deaf person to send and receive messages by telephone.

Bell Federal Savings (WORLD BOOK photo)

A telephone switchboard connects the phones within an office or building to one another and to outside lines.

Telephone

Telephone is an instrument that sends and receives sound, usually by means of electricity. Telephones provide the commonest method of talking to people at a distance. In just a few seconds, you can telephone a friend on the next block, in another part of the country, or nearly anywhere in the world. The word *telephone* comes from two Greek words meaning *far* and *sound.*

The telephone is one of our most valuable means of communication. A telephone call may cost only a few cents. But in an emergency, a telephone call can swiftly help bring a doctor, the police, or fire fighters. People can save time by phoning their grocer or pharmacist. Business people can phone out-of-town customers.

A telephone call can be made from almost anywhere. You can call from your home or from a phone booth in a store. Such telephones are connected to each other by wires that carry sound by electric current. *Radiotelephones* are used in cars, trucks, ships, trains, and airplanes. They carry sound by means of radio waves and are not directly connected to each other by wires.

Alexander Graham Bell invented the telephone in Boston in 1876. Today, about 425 million telephones serve people all over the world. The United States uses about two-fifths of this total amount, about 162 million telephones. Japan ranks second with about 51 million telephones, and Great Britain is third with 23 million.

Kinds of telephones

The most familiar type of telephone is the *desk telephone.* It stands on a desk, a table, or a shelf. A *wall telephone* can be a handy space-saver or it may be used where a desk phone would not be convenient.

Telephones in some offices have push buttons, with which a person can make, receive, hold, or transfer calls from two or more lines. The user can make a call to an *extension telephone* or on an *outside line.* An extension telephone is another phone connected to a telephone with the same number. An outside line connects a phone to any other phone with a different number. An *intercom telephone* enables the user to talk to someone in another room as well as to make outside calls.

A person who makes or receives many calls might use a phone called a *Call Director.* Some Call Director phones can control more than 100 outside and extension lines at one time. Each line is controlled by a button. *Speakerphones* have a microphone and a loudspeaker. With a speakerphone, several people in the room can participate in the conversation. *Cordless telephones* do not have a wire that connects the handset to the base of the phone. The handset can be carried 750 feet (229 meters) from the base and still be used to place or receive a call.

A device called an *automatic dialer* saves time for a person who dials the same numbers frequently. One type of automatic dialer has a prepunched plastic card for each of these numbers. The caller puts a card into a slot on the phone, then presses a bar to dial the number. Other automatic dialers use magnetic tape or electronic memory devices to store numbers.

Regular telephone services

A person can make three kinds of telephone calls—*local, long distance,* and *overseas.* More than 90 per cent of all calls in the United States are local calls.

Local service includes various types. One type allows the customer to make an unlimited number of calls for a fixed charge. Another type costs a basic amount for a set number of calls, plus an added amount for each additional call. Extended Area Calling permits local service dialing to nearby areas for a set rate.

Long distance service includes *station-to-station calls* and *person-to-person calls.* In a station-to-station call, the charge begins as soon as the telephone is answered. In a person-to-person call, the charge does not begin until a specific person or extension is reached. However, a station-to-station call costs less than a person-to-person call. The cost of both types of calls also depends on the distance called, the number of minutes talked, and the time and the day of the call. Day, evening, and night rates vary on all out-of-state calls and most long distance calls within states.

In the past, a telephone user could make a long distance call only through an operator. Today, nearly 99 per cent of the phones in the United States and Canada are equipped for Direct Distance Dialing (DDD). The two countries are divided into about 125 areas, each identified by a three-digit *area code.* To make a telephone call outside his or her own area, a person first dials 1, then the area code, and then the seven-digit local telephone number.

Overseas service. A person in the United States can make a telephone call to about 220 other countries and territories. Most overseas calls are made through a local or an international operator. In some areas, a person can dial directly overseas. Most overseas calls are transmitted by undersea cables or by communications satellites. A few overseas telephone calls are sent by radio waves. Telephone calls can be made to ships at sea by means of *high seas telephone service,* which uses radio waves.

Special telephone services

Private line services are used by organizations that send many messages between two or more places. For example, a company might receive daily reports from branch offices throughout the country. The company has private lines to each branch.

A number of special services are provided by private telephone lines. Typewritten messages can be sent over a private line by an instrument called a *teletypewriter*

(see **Teletypewriter**). A similar device, called a *teletypesetter,* receives messages over a line and sets them in type automatically (see **Teletypesetter**). Private telephone lines also are used to link radio and television stations into one large network. Drawings, photographs, and similar information can then be sent to each of the stations. Computers also send vast quantities of information over private telephone lines.

Answering services give and take phone messages for people who are away from their office or home. Some answering services inform a person that he or she has a message by beeping a signaling device carried by the person. An automatic answering device is an instrument that answers the phone automatically, gives recorded information to callers, and records messages.

Mobile telephone service provides two-way radio communication for travelers on land, on water, or in the air. In the United States, many automobiles, trucks, trains, ships, and airplanes are equipped with mobile phone units.

Conference calls enable three or more people anywhere in the world to talk together at the same time over the regular telephone network.

How a telephone works

When a person speaks into a telephone, sound waves created by the person's voice enter the mouthpiece. An electric current carries the sound to the telephone of the person being spoken to. A telephone has two main parts: (1) the *transmitter* and (2) the *receiver.*

The transmitter of a telephone serves as a sensitive "electric ear." It lies behind the mouthpiece of the phone. Like the human ear, the transmitter has an "eardrum." The eardrum of the telephone is a thin, round metal disk called a *diaphragm.* When a person talks into the telephone, the sound waves strike the diaphragm and make it vibrate. It vibrates at various speeds, depending on the variations in air pressure caused by the varying tones of the speaker's voice.

Behind the diaphragm lies a small cup filled with tiny grains of carbon. The diaphragm presses against these carbon grains. Low voltage electric current travels through the grains. This current comes from batteries at the telephone company. The pressure on the carbon grains varies as sound waves make the diaphragm vibrate. A loud sound causes the sound waves to push

How to make a simple telephone set   You can make a private telephone line with some string and two empty tin cans. First, cut off the tops of the cans and punch a small hole in the bottom of each can. Next, thread the ends of the string through the holes and tie a knot inside each can. Then, you and a friend each take a can and move apart, keeping the string straight and tight. Speak into the open end of your can. Your voice travels along the string and can be heard by your friend through the open end of the other can.

WORLD BOOK illustration by Jack Hagen

How a telephone carries sound

The transmitter, *below,* converts sound into a pattern of electric waves that can travel over wire. When a person speaks into a telephone, sound waves make the diaphragm vibrate against the carbon chamber. The vibrations vary according to the sound. They regulate the amount of electric current that flows through the chamber and out over the telephone wire.

Permanent magnet

Diaphragm

Electro-magnet

Diaphragm

Carbon chamber

The receiver, *above,* converts the pattern of electric waves back into sound. The varying electric current activates the electromagnet. The force of the electromagnet pulls on the diaphragm, opposing the steady pull of the permanent magnet. The changes in magnetic pull cause the diaphragm to vibrate, producing the sound waves heard by the listener.

WORLD BOOK illustration by Jack Hagen

hard on the diaphragm. In turn, the diaphragm presses the grains tightly together. This action makes it easier for the electric current to travel through, and a large amount of electricity flows through the grains. When the sound is soft, the sound waves push lightly on the diaphragm. In turn, the diaphragm puts only a light pressure on the carbon grains. The grains are pressed together loosely. This makes it harder for the electric current to pass through them, and less electricity flows through.

Thus, the pattern of the sound waves determines the pressure on the diaphragm. This pressure, in turn, regulates the pressure on the carbon grains. The crowded or loose grains cause the electric current to become stronger or weaker. The current copies the pattern of the sound waves and travels over a telephone wire to the receiver of another telephone.

The receiver serves as an "electric mouth." Like a human voice, it has "vocal cords." The vocal cords of the receiver are a diaphragm. Two magnets cause the diaphragm to vibrate. One of the magnets is a *permanent magnet* that provides a steady pull on the diaphragm. The other magnet is an *electromagnet.* It consists of a piece of iron with a coil of wire wound around it. When an electric current passes through the coil, the iron core becomes magnetized and it pulls on the diaphragm, opposing the pull of the permanent magnet. The pull of the electromagnet varies between strong and weak, depending on variations in the current. The changes in magnetic pull cause the diaphragm to vibrate.

The electric current that activates the electromagnet is sent by the transmitter of another telephone. The electric current becomes stronger or weaker according to the sound waves "heard" by the transmitter. Thus, the diaphragm in the receiver vibrates according to the speaker's voice. As the diaphragm moves, it pulls and pushes the air in front of it. The pressure on the air sets up sound waves that are nearly the same as those sent into the transmitter. The sound waves strike the ear of the listener, and the listener hears the words of the speaker.

How a telephone call travels

Telephone lines crisscross the United States and connect millions of telephones in a vast network. Most telephone lines consist of copper wires. Many long distance calls travel by radio systems. In the United States, almost all telephone wires are bound together in cables. Some cables have more than 4,000 wires.

Lines for local calls. When you make a local telephone call, the call travels over wires or by radio to a central office. There, switching equipment connects your telephone to the phone you are calling. The switching process is discussed in a later section of this article, *How a telephone call is made.*

Long distance lines. The same kind of cables used for local calls could be used for long distance calls. At great distances, however, the electric signals in the wire would become too weak. To overcome this problem, long distance lines are equipped with *repeaters* (amplifiers) that strengthen the electric current through such electronic devices as transistors.

A long distance call would be very expensive if only one call could be transmitted on a pair of wires at a time. Engineers have developed ways to send many telephone messages on the same pair of wires. A process called *carrier transmission* enables two pairs of wires to carry as many as 96 conversations at the same time. Each electric current carrying a conversation travels at a different *frequency* (rate of vibration). Electronic filters at each end of the line sort out the conversations.

Coaxial cables make it possible to send even more messages along the same route. A coaxial cable consists of up to 22 *coaxial conductors*—copper tubes about as big around as a pencil—that work on the carrier transmission principle. A pair of tubes can carry up to 13,200 telephone conversations. See **Coaxial cable.**

In the late 1970's, telephone companies began replacing coaxial cables with fiber-optic cables. A fiber-optic system uses bundles of extremely fine glass fibers to carry calls on a laser beam. The first long-distance fiber-optic cable was completed in 1983. Signals sent over long-distance fiber-optic cables need less amplification than signals sent over copper cables of equal length. Fiber-optic cables can also carry more information than copper cables, making them especially popular for heavily used long distance lines. See **Fiber optics.**

Both wires and cables must be strung on telephone poles or placed underground. To reduce the cost of long distance phoning, telephone companies use radio relay systems that send telephone calls by radio waves.

Radio relay systems use superhigh frequency radio waves called *microwaves* (see **Microwave**). Unlike radio broadcasting waves, microwaves do not follow the curve of the earth. They travel mostly in straight paths. Microwaves are concentrated in a narrow beam like that of a searchlight. They are focused from one relay station to another. The stations are about 30 miles (48 kilometers) apart. Each has antennas to transmit and receive microwaves. A microwave route can carry almost 36,000 telephone conversations.

The *over-the-horizon* radio relay system sends microwaves beyond the horizon. It uses powerful relay stations up to 200 miles (320 kilometers) apart. The stations send microwaves aimed at the horizon by means of antennas the size of outdoor motion-picture screens. Much microwave energy is lost in space. But enough scatters downward and carries the radio signals to the next station, much as the headlights of a car shine over a hill without being directly seen. Over-the-horizon systems operate between Florida and Nassau, Florida and Cuba, Japan and Korea in the Pacific, and Tortola and Trinidad in the Caribbean. Systems also serve Alaska and military bases in the Arctic.

How a telephone call is made

Before you can talk to another person on a telephone, the two telephones must be *switched* (connected). A pair of wires extends from each phone to switching equipment in the central office. Large cities have many central offices, all linked together by trunk cables. A *telephone exchange* designates the local area served by one or more central offices. Every telephone number has a prefix that stands for its central office. In the past, all prefixes consisted of letters and numbers. For example, in the telephone number "AB 7-6452," the prefix "AB 7" means the "ABerdeen 7 central office." Today, most areas have all-numeral telephone numbers, such as "257-6452." The prefix "257" stands for the "257 central office." Many more central office codes are possible with the all-number system than with the use of letters.

There are two main types of switching—*automatic* and *manual.* In automatic switching, used with rotary dial and push-button phones, special equipment makes the connections. In manual switching, a telephone operator makes connections by hand on a switchboard.

Automatic switching. More than 99 per cent of the telephones in the United States are rotary or push-button operated and switched automatically. The dialing equipment goes into action as soon as the phone is lifted. An electric signal flashes over the telephone line to the switching equipment in the central office. A humming sound called the *dial tone* tells the caller that the equipment is ready to handle a call. In a rotary dial phone, the dial returns to its starting position after each letter or number has been dialed. As the dial returns, an electric switch inside the phone opens and closes—once for number 1; twice for 2, A, B, or C; and so on. Each time the switch opens and closes, an electric signal goes to the switching equipment. A push-button phone works in a similar way. But musical tones, rather than an electric switch, create the electric signal.

Telephone companies use three chief types of auto-

How telephones are connected

A pair of wires extends from each subscriber's phone to equipment in a *central office.* Central offices are linked by *trunk cables*—either directly or by alternate routes through *tandem offices.*

WORLD BOOK diagrams

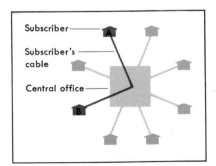

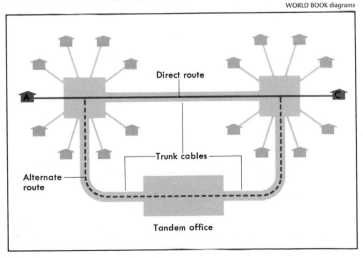

A telephone call between subscriber A and subscriber B, *above,* is simply *switched* (connected) by equipment in the central office that serves them both. However, a call between subscribers A and C, *right,* must travel along a trunk cable because they are served by different central offices.

matic switching: (1) step-by-step switching, (2) crossbar switching, and (3) electronic switching. Step-by-step and crossbar are older systems that operate by means of electro-mechanical switches and relays. An electronic switching system (ESS) uses tiny electronic, rather than mechanical, devices. ESS, which was introduced in 1965, is rapidly replacing other switching systems because it provides greater efficiency and speed. For example, an ESS central office can handle more than 200,000 calls per hour. A typical crossbar system can carry fewer than 10,000 calls an hour.

Step-by-step switching, which was developed in the late 1800's, was once common in small communities. In a step-by-step switching system, a call travels through a series of mechanical switches. Each switch has a vertical rod with a horizontal metal blade called a *contact arm.* Electromagnets move the arm up and down the rod and rotate it horizontally. Sets of *terminals* (electric contacts) are stacked one above the other within reach of the contact arm. The arm moves to a terminal in response to the electric signal created by the dialing of a number. When the arm touches the terminal, the call is connected to a second switch. This process is repeated for each number that is dialed until the connection is made to the phone of the person being called. Today, most step-by-step switches have been replaced by newer switches.

Crossbar switching, first used in 1938, makes connections faster than step-by-step switching. The crossbar system can be used in both large and small communities. It is fast because it uses a switch that moves only slightly. The switch has a rectangular frame with sets of horizontal and vertical bars. These bars operate electric contacts that are only $\frac{1}{100}$ inch (0.25 millimeter) apart. Electromagnets turn a horizontal bar and then a vertical bar to bring the contacts together in a split second.

Electronic switching works much like a huge computer. It operates by means of transistors, integrated circuits, and other miniature electronic devices. ESS has three major parts—the *central control,* the *memory,* and the *switching network.*

The central control directs all operations of the system. The memory consists of two sections that store information—the *program store* and the *call store.* The program store contains the exact instructions for all operations. The call store keeps track of which telephones are in use and what paths are available for connecting calls. The switching network provides thousands of paths on which calls can travel.

To make a connection between two telephones, the ESS central control selects a path based on information provided by the memory sections. It sends electrical commands to the proper switch contacts, causing them to close and complete the circuit. The entire switching process takes about 25-thousandths of a second.

In addition to speed, ESS provides several special features. It enables callers to abbreviate frequently called numbers to just two, rather than the usual seven, digits. It also allows customers to have their incoming calls temporarily forwarded to a number where they can be reached. Conference calls are also easy to arrange with ESS. Any change in the telephone service that a customer receives requires only a simple change of information in the program store, rather than the alteration of wiring and switches that is needed in other systems.

Manual switching is used in only a few small communities without dial telephones. A pair of wires from each phone connects with a switchboard. Each pair of wires has its own *jack,* a hole in the board into which the operator can insert a metal plug. The plugs are attached to the switchboard by a wire cord.

When a person lifts the phone to make a call, a light goes on at the caller's jack. The operator inserts an *answering plug* into the jack and the caller gives the operator the number of the person being called. The operator then puts a *calling plug* into the jack of the person being called and rings the phone. When the person answers the telephone, the electric circuit is completed.

The telephone industry

In the United States, private companies own and operate the telephone systems. However, the Federal Communications Commission (FCC), an agency of the United States government, regulates rates and services for interstate telephone communications. Telephone rates within the states are regulated by public utility commissions.

The American Telephone and Telegraph Company (AT&T), a private corporation, is the largest communications company in the world. It manages the nation's largest and oldest long-distance telephone network. It also includes AT&T Technologies, Incorporated (formerly called the Western Electric Company), which manufactures telephone equipment and supplies; and AT&T Bell Laboratories, a research organization.

In 1974, the United States government filed a lawsuit against AT&T, charging the company with hindering competition in the telephone industry. At the time, AT&T also included 22 local telephone operating companies. These companies operated about 80 per cent of the telephones in the United States. The rest of the phones were served by about 1,600 independent telephone companies.

In 1982, the government and AT&T agreed to settle the lawsuit. As a result of the settlement, in 1984, the local telephone companies became independent, and AT&T was allowed to enter the unregulated computer and information-processing businesses. Previously, AT&T had been prohibited from engaging in any businesses that were not regulated by the government.

In other countries, the government, as well as private companies, owns and operates the telephone systems. In West Germany, for example, a branch of the federal government provides telephone service for the entire nation. The central government also owns and operates the phone systems in Peru, Spain, Sweden, and Venezuela. Private companies provide all the telephone service in Italy. In Canada, the Bell Telephone Company of Canada, a private corporation, operates more than half the nation's telephones. Other private companies, government agencies, and cooperative businesses operate the rest. Other countries with some privately owned systems include Denmark, Finland, Portugal, and the Philippines.

History

Bell's invention. Alexander Graham Bell, a Scotsman who came to the United States in 1871, invented the telephone. Bell was a teacher of the deaf in Boston. At

How an electronic switching system (ESS) works

The memory is the information storage unit of an ESS central office. Its *program store* contains the instructions for the system's operations. The *call store* keeps track of calls in progress and of the paths that are available to connect calls.

The central control in an ESS office directs all operations based on information provided by the memory. To connect a subscriber's telephone to another phone, the central control selects the best path available through the switching network.

The switching network provides thousands of paths on which telephone calls can travel. Electrical commands from the central control cause certain switch contacts in the network to close. The electric circuit between two telephones is then completed.

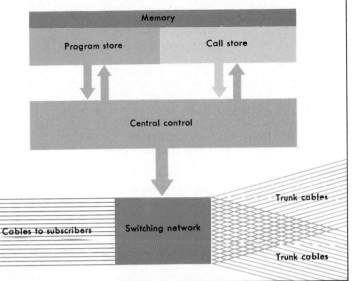

WORLD BOOK diagram

The call store includes electronic devices called *circuit packs.* A circuit pack, *above,* stores data about which telephones are being used, plus other temporary conditions in the system.

The program store provides the permanent information needed to operate and maintain the system. The data is electronically coded on *memory cards,* such as the one above.

The central control's computer, *above,* receives information from the program store and call store. It also sends commands to the switching network and regulates all other ESS operations.

Illinois Bell (WORLD BOOK photos)

The electric circuits that connect telephone calls travel through the switching network. The worker, *above,* is testing the line equipment linking a subscriber's phone to the network.

night, he experimented with a *harmonic telegraph,* a device for sending several telegraph messages at once over one wire. Bell developed the idea of the telephone in 1874, but he continued his experiments with the harmonic telegraph.

On June 2, 1875, one of the metal reeds of the harmonic telegraph stuck. Bell's assistant, Thomas A. Watson, snapped the reed to loosen it. Bell, who was in another room, heard the sound in his receiver. He realized that the vibrations of the reed had caused variations of electric current. In turn, the electric current had reproduced the same variations in the receiver he was using.

On March 10, 1876, Bell finally succeeded in speaking words over a telephone. He was about to test a new transmitter. In another room, Watson waited for the test message. Suddenly, Bell spilled some acid from a battery on his clothes. He cried out: "Mr. Watson, come here. I want you!"

Watson rushed into the room, shouting: "Mr. Bell, I heard every word you said—distinctly!" Bell had invented the first successful telephone.

In June 1876, Bell exhibited his telephone at the Centennial Exposition in Philadelphia. Scientists praised his work. But the public showed little interest until early in 1877, when Bell gave many telephone demonstrations.

Early telephones. In August 1876, Bell received the first one-way long distance call. This call came over an 8-mile (13-kilometer) line he had built between Brantford, Ont., and Paris, Ont. In October 1876, Bell and Watson held the first two-way long distance telephone conversation. They spoke between Boston and Cambridge, Mass., a distance of 2 miles (3 kilometers). In 1877, Roswell C. Downer, a banker, installed the first commercial telephone line. It extended 3 miles (5 kilometers) between Downer's home in Somerville, Mass., and his bank in Boston.

Also in 1877, E. T. Holmes, the owner of a burglar alarm system, began operating the first switchboard. It connected four banks and a factory in Boston. At night, the switchboard served as a burglar alarm. The first telephones used no switchboards. A pair of iron wires connected each pair of phones. One person called another

by pushing a knob on the telephone. This caused a hammer to make a thumping sound that went over the telephone line to the other phone. As more telephones came into use, each was connected to all the other phones. More than 1,000 connections were required to link only 50 telephones. Switchboards solved this problem by bringing together the wires from all telephones in an area.

The Bell System. Bell, Watson, Gardiner G. Hubbard, and Thomas Sanders formed the Bell Telephone Company in 1877. Hubbard was Bell's father-in-law, and Sanders was the father of one of Bell's pupils. They had helped pay for Bell's experiments.

In 1878, the first telephone exchange opened in New Haven, Conn. It had 21 customers. Soon exchanges opened throughout the United States and Canada.

Also in 1878, the Western Union Telegraph Company entered the telephone business. Western Union used transmitters developed by Thomas A. Edison, the great American inventor. Its receivers had been developed by Elisha Gray, another American inventor. The Bell company met the competition by using the improved transmitters of Emile Berliner, an American, and Francis J. Blake, a Britisher.

In September 1878, the Bell company sued Western Union to protect Bell's telephone patents. Western Union claimed that Gray, not Bell, had invented the telephone. But Gray had filed his patent a few hours after Bell had applied for his first patent on Feb. 14, 1876. The United States Patent Office had issued Bell his patent on March 7, 1876. During the lawsuit, in 1879, the Bell Telephone Company was reorganized as the National Bell Telephone Company. That same year, Western Union acknowledged Bell's patents and agreed to stay out of the telephone business. The Western Union case was the first of more than 600 lawsuits over Bell's patents. Many people claimed to have invented the telephone. In 1888, the Supreme Court of the United States upheld Bell's patents.

In 1880, the American Bell Telephone Company was formed. It combined the National Bell Telephone Company and the telephone activities of Western Union. The

Historical Pictures Service, Chicago

Illinois Bell (WORLD BOOK photo)

Telephone operators connected almost all calls manually through a switchboard until the early 1900's. The picture at the left shows the central telephone exchange of New York City about 1900. Today, operators assist callers when necessary, *right.* But almost all calls are switched automatically.

The development of the telephone

The first telephone was this device, invented in 1876 by Alexander Graham Bell.

An 1882 wall phone had a hand-held receiver and a crank to signal the operator.

A 1919 dial telephone required complex switching equipment.

The 1928 desk telephone combined receiver and transmitter in a handset unit.

The "300" model desk phone, introduced in 1937, contained a bell in its base.

The colored telephone of 1954 gained widespread popularity as a decorative item.

The "trimline" telephone of 1968 featured push buttons on the handset.

AT&T Corporate Archive

A touch-a-matic phone of 1973 dialed a number at the push of a button.

first commercial long distance line opened in 1881. This line extended 45 miles (72 kilometers) between Boston and Providence, R.I. A 292-mile (470-kilometer) commercial line between New York City and Boston opened in 1884. The following year, the American Telephone and Telegraph Company (AT&T) was organized to operate long distance lines. In 1899, AT&T took over American Bell and became the parent company of the Bell System.

Telephone improvements. Almon B. Strowger, an American inventor, patented an automatic step-by-step switching system in 1891. The first commercial switchboard based on his patent opened in La Porte, Ind., in 1892. The caller pressed buttons to get the number, then turned a crank to ring the phone. Also in 1892, phone service began between New York City and Chicago.

In 1896, the first dial telephones went into operation in Milwaukee. The American scientist Lee De Forest patented the electron tube in 1907, and it was adapted as an amplifier in 1912. Transcontinental telephone service began between New York City and San Francisco in 1915. Transatlantic radio-telephone service between New York City and London began in 1927. The first long distance coaxial cable linked New York City and Philadelphia in 1936.

In 1947, the transistor was invented by scientists of Bell Laboratories, the research and development organization of the Bell System. This electronic device is smaller than the electron tube and requires less power. Underseas telephone cables between the United States and Europe began operating in 1956. A cable between the U.S. mainland and Hawaii began operating in 1957, and a cable between Japan and the United States began in 1964. In 1961, Bell scientists developed the first continuously operating *laser,* a device that amplifies light. A

light beam from a laser can carry many more phone calls than wires or radio waves can. See **Laser.**

In 1960, the United States began launching communications satellites. The first, *Echo,* was a huge, shiny balloon that simply reflected radio signals from one ground station to another. *Telstar, Relay,* and *Syncom* satellites used electronic equipment to amplify the signals. The first commercial communications satellite, *Early Bird,* was launched in 1965. The *Early Bird* satellite provides 240 two-way telephone circuits between Europe and the United States.

Recent developments. In 1970, International Direct Distance Dialing (IDDD) began operating between New York and London. IDDD, which now serves several cities throughout the world, enables people to dial overseas directly. In 1980, a fiber-optic system for transmitting local calls was installed in Atlanta. In a fiber-optic system, telephone conversations travel on beams of laser light through hair-thin strands of glass (see **Fiber optics**). A fiber-optic system between New York City and Washington, D.C., began in 1983.

Since the late 1960's, a number of important decisions have been made by the Federal Communications Commission that may lead to greater competition in the U.S. telephone industry. In several cases, the FCC voted to permit independent communications companies to provide private long distance services. In another case, the FCC ruled that people could purchase and install their own telephones and other equipment. Previously, all phone equipment was leased to users by telephone companies for a fee.

In 1982, the FCC began granting licenses for companies to build and operate mobile telephone systems based on *cellular radio* technology. In these systems, a city is divided into districts called *cells,* each of which has a low-powered radio transmitter and receiver. As a phone-equipped car travels from cell to cell, a computer transfers a call from one transmitter and receiver to another without interrupting the conversation. Cellular mobile telephone service can handle many more calls than earlier systems, which used one high-powered transmitter and receiver for an entire city.

In 1982, the U.S. government and AT&T settled a lawsuit in which the government had charged the company with anticompetitive practices. AT&T agreed to give up ownership of its local telephone operating companies in return for being allowed to enter the computer services and information-processing businesses.

Career opportunities

About a million men and women work in the U.S. telephone industry. They work in offices, in factories that make equipment, and in research laboratories. Telephone operators are perhaps the best-known telephone employees. Telephone companies also employ secretaries, clerks, and sales and service representatives. Skilled workers install and maintain telephones. Engineers prepare plans for switching equipment and transmission systems. Physicists and mathematicians work on research and development.   Barry R. Campbell

Related articles in *World Book* include:

Biographies

Bell, Alexander Graham	Edison, Thomas Alva
Berliner, Emile	Gray, Elisha
De Forest, Lee	Pupin, Michael I.

Other related articles

American Telephone and	Electronics
Telegraph Company	Federal Communications
Cable	Commission
Communication	Headphones
Communications satellite	Intercom
Communications Satellite	Radio
Corporation	Sound-powered telephone
Computer	Telecommunication
Electromagnet	Television

Outline

Questions

Who invented the telephone?
What were the first words spoken over the telephone?
Who was Thomas A. Watson? Almon B. Strowger?
Where was the first telephone line installed?
What is a *conference call* ?
What is *carrier transmission*?

When and where was the first dial telephone used?
What country has the most telephones?
How are satellites used in telephone communication?
What are the two main parts of a telephone?

Additional resources

Boettinger, Henry M. *The Telephone Book: Bell, Watson, Vail and American Life, 1876-1983.* Rev. ed. Stearn, 1983.
Brooks, John N. *Telephone: The First Hundred Years.* Harper, 1976.
Chorafas, Dimitris N. *Telephony: Today and Tomorrow.* Simon & Schuster, 1984.
Kohn, Bernice. *Telephones.* Dandelion, 1979. For younger readers.
Math, Irwin. *Morse, Marconi, and You.* Scribner, 1979. For younger readers.

Telephoto is a way of sending pictures by wire or radio. The process is also known as *Wirephoto.* A scanning light at the sending station *scans* (passes back and forth over) a picture. The light reflected from the picture is converted into an electric current by a photoelectric cell (see **Electric eye**). At the receiving station, the electric current is converted into a light beam. The light beam then hits a film or photographic paper in proportion to the strength of the current. The picture is reproduced because the film or paper is sensitive to light.

After development, the photographic film may be used for contact printing or conventional enlarging. It may also be retransmitted by wire or radio. Telephoto differs from the system called *facsimile,* which reproduces pictures by passing an electric current through chemically treated paper (see **Facsimile**).

In the United States, news services operate nationwide telephoto networks. The Associated Press opened the first network in 1935.   James Hoge

Teleprompter. See **Television** (Talent; picture: Production preparations).

Telescope is an instrument that magnifies objects at a distance. Astronomers use telescopes to observe and photograph heavenly bodies.

The first telescope probably was made in 1608 by Hans Lippershey, a Dutch optician. After hearing of Lippershey's invention, Galileo, an Italian astronomer, built his first telescope in 1609. The most powerful instrument Galileo built magnified objects about 30 times. In addition, only a small field area, with a diameter less than one-fourth that of the moon, could be seen with this telescope. Nevertheless, Galileo made some outstanding discoveries with the instrument, including four of Jupiter's satellites and the rings of Saturn. However, he could not see the rings clearly and thought they were moons. Galileo also discovered that there are mountains and craters on the moon. Today, the simple principle of the Galilean telescope is used only in opera glasses.

Optical telescopes are used to observe visible light given off, or reflected by, other objects. Astronomers use two main types of optical telescopes—refracting telescopes and reflecting telescopes.

The refracting telescope is the simplest type of telescope. It was the kind used by Galileo. A refracting telescope consists chiefly of a long, heavy tube. At one end of the tube is a small *ocular* (eyepiece), which usually is made up of two lenses. The image is seen through and magnified by, the ocular. At the other end of the telescope is a large lens that in most cases is made from two or more pieces of glass. This lens is called the *ob-*

jective or *object lens.* It gathers light from the object that is being viewed. A refracting telescope is focused by changing the distance between the objective lens and the eyepiece.

When light from an object strikes the objective lens, the light rays are bent by the lens until they come to a point known as the *focal point.* A small representation of the object called an *image* is formed at the focal point. As the light passes through the eyepiece, the image is enlarged and looks as though it is closer than it really is. Because the light is bent as it goes through the objective lens, the image appears upside down.

Some telescopes have lenses between the objective lens and the eyepiece. These extra lenses cause the light rays to cross and form an image that is right side up. Telescopes that have these extra lenses are used to observe objects on the earth.

The reflecting telescope uses a mirror instead of a lens as the objective. Reflecting telescopes can be built larger than refracting telescopes, and they thus can have greater light-gathering power. For this reason, it is possible to see or photograph fainter objects with a reflecting telescope than with a refracting telescope.

One of the first reflecting telescopes was built by the English scientist Sir Isaac Newton. The type of telescope built by Newton is known as the Newtonian telescope. It consists of a heavy tube with one end open. At the other end of the tube is a large mirror that serves as the objective. The eyepiece is at the side of the tube, at a right angle to the tube. A tiny mirror is set inside the tube, near the eyepiece, and at a 45-degree angle to the objective. After the light waves enter the tube, the objective reflects them to the small mirror, which, in turn, reflects them into the eyepiece.

Another type of reflecting telescope is the Cassegrainian telescope, which was invented by N. Cassegrain of France. In this telescope, the eyepiece is set behind the objective, which has a small opening at its center. As the light waves strike the objective, they are reflected back to a small mirror that is set in front of the

Sir Isaac Newton's reflecting telescope, as shown in this reconstruction, included a small mirror, *upper right,* that reflected light waves from the objective into the eyepiece on the side.

objective. The small mirror reflects the waves, in turn, through the opening in the objective and into the eyepiece, which magnifies the image.

A combination refracting-reflecting telescope was invented in 1931 by Bernhard Schmidt, a German optician. Schmidt telescopes resemble Cassegrainian telescopes, but they have a thin, specially shaped lens at the front end of the tube. This lens enables Schmidt telescopes to give a view of a larger area of the sky than other optical telescopes can.

Recording images produced by optical telescopes. Astronomers can preserve the images seen through optical telescopes by using *photographic plates* or films or by using *photoelectric cells* (see **Electric eye**). Electronic image detectors called *charge-coupled devices* (CCD's) are also commonly used. Charge-coupled devices are far more sensitive to light than are photographic plates or films.

Magnification by optical telescopes. The degree to which an optical telescope magnifies an object can be determined by knowing the *focal length* of both the objective and the eyepiece. The focal length is the distance between the focal point and the center of the objective lens or mirror. The magnification (m) of an optical telescope can be found by dividing the focal length of the objective (f_1) by the focal length of the eyepiece (f_2). The formula for finding the magnification is

$$m = \frac{f_1}{f_2}$$

Other telescopes are used by astronomers to study forms of radiation from space other than visible light. These forms of radiation include radio waves, infrared rays, ultraviolet light, and X rays. Telescopes that detect these forms of radiation can tune in on stars and galaxies that give off a faint light or no light at all, and which therefore cannot be seen with optical telescopes. These nonoptical telescopes also can penetrate clouds

The Hubble Space Telescope, scheduled to be launched in 1989 or 1990, will serve as an observatory in the sky. It will produce images far more clearly than earth-based telescopes.

Celestron

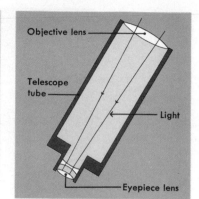

Celestron

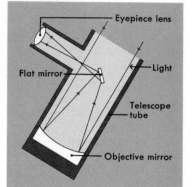

Celestron

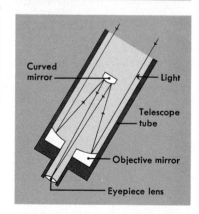

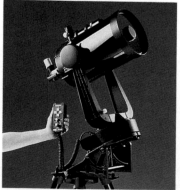

Celestron

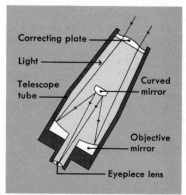

Types of telescopes

A refracting telescope is a tube with lenses at each end. Light enters the telescope through an objective lens at one end of the tube. This lens *refracts* (bends) the light toward the eyepiece at the other end of the tube. A lens in the eyepiece bends the light further and forms an enlarged image of the light source.

A Newtonian reflecting telescope uses a curved mirror instead of a lens as its objective. The mirror gathers light and focuses it on a flat mirror suspended in the center of the telescope tube. The flat mirror reflects the light through a hole in the side of the telescope tube to the eyepiece lens.

A Cassegrainian reflecting telescope has a curved mirror with a hole in its center as the objective. Light gathered by the mirror is reflected to a smaller curved mirror suspended above the objective. The small mirror focuses the light through the hole in the objective mirror and into the eyepiece lens below it.

A Schmidt-Cassegrainian telescope resembles a Cassegrainian telescope, but it has a correcting plate in front of the objective mirror. This plate is a lens that corrects irregularities in the image formed by the mirror. The lens and mirror combination can give a sharp picture of a larger area of the sky than other telescopes can.

WORLD BOOK diagrams

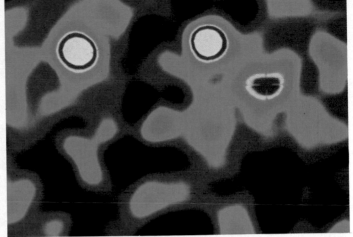

Infrared telescopes include the University of Hawaii's Infrared Telescope Facility, *left.* An infrared image, *right,* shows what astronomers believe to be a galaxy 17 billion light-years from Earth. The galaxy appears as a reddish area to the right of the two white circles, which are nearby stars.

of dust and gas that fill vast regions of outer space.

Radio telescopes were invented during the 1930's. They collect radio waves, in most cases with a huge saucer-shaped reflector. Radio telescopes can be used in any kind of weather because radio waves can travel through clouds in the earth's atmosphere. See **Radio telescope.**

Infrared telescopes are very similar to optical telescopes. Infrared telescopes use detectors that are especially sensitive to infrared rays. When possible, scientists place infrared telescopes high in the atmosphere aboard balloons or high-flying planes, or in orbit aboard artificial satellites, to escape interference from the earth's atmosphere.

Ultraviolet telescopes are also similar to optical telescopes, but they use a detector that is sensitive to ultraviolet light. Ultraviolet telescopes must be launched into outer space because much of the ultraviolet light that reaches the earth's atmosphere does not pass through it.

X-ray telescopes also must be launched into space. X-ray telescopes use special X-ray reflectors. These reflectors reflect X rays well only if the rays strike the reflector surface when they are moving almost parallel to the surface. For this reason, an X-ray reflector resembles a large collection of flattened rings, one inside another.

The Hubble Space Telescope is one of the newest and most important telescopes. Scientists plan to place it in orbit above the earth in 1989 or 1990. The telescope will be sensitive to both visible and ultraviolet light. In orbit, it will have a *resolving power* about 10 times greater than that of the best ground-based telescopes. Resolving power is the ability to produce distinguishable images.   Frank D. Drake

Related articles in *World Book* include:

Astronomy	Galileo	World, History of
(Observing with	Lens	the (picture:
telescopes;	Observatory	New scientific
pictures)	Radio telescope	devices)
Binoculars		

Additional resources

Asimov, Isaac. *Eyes on the Universe: A History of the Telescope.* Houghton, 1975.

Howard, Neale E. *The Telescope Handbook and Star Atlas.* Rev. ed. T. Y. Crowell, 1975.

Muirden, James. *How to Use an Astronomical Telescope: A Beginner's Guide to Observing the Cosmos.* Linden Press, 1985.

Yount, Lisa. *The Telescope.* Walker, 1983. For younger readers. Development of the telescope.

Teletext. See **Television** (Televised information services).

Teletypesetter (TTS) is an electrical machine somewhat like a teletypewriter (see **Teletypewriter**). It sends typewriter copy over long distances and at the same time it punches holes in a paper tape. When this tape is fed into a typesetting machine, the machine automatically sets the copy in type used to print a newspaper.

The leading news wire services began using TTS to send reports to newspapers in the early 1950's. Today, wire service copy is transmitted to most newspapers by satellite. It is then fed directly into a computer and stored there until it is edited on a video display terminal (VDT). This new system, though more expensive than the earlier TTS, is more than 20 times faster than it.
  Keith P. Sanders

Teletypewriter is an electromechanical typewriter that transmits impulses over a wire to a receiver which prints a message. As the typist strikes each key on the transmitter, it activates a certain combination of electrical impulses that makes a similar letter arm react at the receiving end. Teletypewriter machines are often connected in series, and many receivers in different parts of the world can be run from one transmitter at the same time.

News wire services pioneered the use of the teletypewriter in the early 1950's. Today, the teletypewriter is being rapidly replaced by computerized satellite transmissions that relay the news directly to newsroom computers.   Keith P. Sanders

The Olympic Games; Eiji Miyazawa, Black Star

Sports events

"Sesame Street"; Children's Television Workshop

Learning and fun for children

WMAQ-TV (WORLD BOOK photo by Steve Hale)

The latest news

"Wheel of Fortune" (Merv Griffin Enterprises)

Game shows

Television is sometimes called "the device that brings the world into the home." TV provides millions of home viewers with a wide variety of entertainment, information, and special events. The pictures on this and the following page show some examples of television's far-reaching coverage.

Television

Television, also called TV, is one of our most important means of communication. It brings pictures and sounds from around the world into millions of homes. People with a television set can sit at home and watch the President make a speech or visit a foreign country. They can see a war being fought, and they can watch government leaders try to bring about peace. Through television, viewers can see and learn about people, places, and things in faraway lands. Television even takes viewers out of this world with coverage of America's astronauts as the astronauts explore outer space.

In addition to all these things, television brings its viewers a steady stream of programs that are designed to entertain. In fact, TV provides many more entertainment programs than any other kind. The programs include action-packed dramas; light comedies; soap operas; sporting events; cartoon, quiz, and variety shows; and motion pictures.

About 89 million homes in the United States—or about 97 per cent of all the country's homes—have at least one TV set. About 60 per cent of American homes have two or more TV's. Altogether, there are about 214 million sets in the United States. On the average, a TV set is in use in each home for about 7 hours each day.

The contributor of this article is George Comstock, S. I. Newhouse Professor of Public Communications at Syracuse University.

As a result, TV has an important influence on how people spend their time and on what they see and learn.

Because of its great popularity, television has become a major way to reach people with advertising messages. Most TV stations carry hundreds of commercials each day. In the mid-1980's, about $24 billion a year was spent on television advertising in the United States. The use of television advertising has greatly changed the process of getting elected to public office in the United States. Before TV, candidates relied chiefly on public appearances to urge people to vote for them. Today, most candidates for high office reach many more people through TV than they reach in person.

The name *television* comes from a Greek word meaning *far* and a Latin word meaning *to see.* Thus, *television* means *to see far.* Most pictures and sounds received by a television set are beamed from a television station on electronic signals called *electromagnetic waves.* The television set changes these waves back into pictures and sounds.

Many scientists contributed to the development of television, and no one person can be called its inventor. Experiments leading to the invention of TV began in the 1800's, but progress was slow. Television as we know it today was not developed until the 1920's, and it had little importance in communication until the late 1940's. But during one 10-year period—the 1950's—it became part of most households in the United States. Since then, television has gained importance in most other countries. In addition, many organizations, including businesses, hospitals, and schools, now use television for their own special purposes.

Astronaut Aldrin reaches the moon (NASA)

Space exploration

"The Cosby Show" (Shooting Star)

Family comedy shows

"General Hospital" (Capital Cities/ABC, Inc.)

Soap operas

Special Report
TELEVISION
1990 Year Book, p. 70

Year Book Close-Up
TELEVISION
1990 Year on File (Television)

Uses of television

About three-fourths of the approximately 1,400 television stations that broadcast in the United States are *commercial stations*. The rest are *public stations*. Commercial stations are those that sell advertising time to pay for their operating costs and to make a profit. Public stations are nonprofit organizations that generally rely on business, government, and public contributions to pay their operating costs. In addition to receiving the programs of commercial and public stations, millions of homes subscribe to *cable television* systems. Viewers pay a fee for this subscription service.

Television also has many uses other than broadcasting programs to the home. For example, schools, businesses, hospitals, and many other organizations use *closed-circuit television*. In closed-circuit TV, signals are sent—by way of wires—to only certain television sets rather than to all sets within the area that broadcast signals could reach.

Since the late 1970's, such equipment as video cassette recorders, videodisc players, and personal computers have changed the way people use television in their homes. For example, TV sets may be used for such purposes as playing electronic games and receiving televised information services.

Commercial television. Commercial television stations broadcast many more entertainment programs than any other kind. These shows include light dramas called *situation comedies;* action-packed dramas about detectives, doctors, lawyers, and police officers; variety shows featuring comedians, dancers, and singers; and movies, including some made expressly for television. Entertainment programs also include quiz shows and *soap operas* (melodramatic plays), and cartoons and other children's shows.

Another kind of commercial television program is the *documentary.* A documentary is a dramatic, but nonfictional, presentation of information. Some TV documentaries entertain as well as inform. These include travel programs about people, animals, and things in faraway places. Television also presents documentaries about such serious social issues as alcoholism, drug abuse, poverty, and racial prejudice.

Commercial television stations broadcast many *discussion,* or *talk,* shows. On these shows, a host interviews people from many walks of life—including athletes, authors, motion-picture and TV stars, and politicians.

Commercial television stations cover almost every kind of sports event—from baseball and football to table tennis and skydiving. Every four years, TV brings its viewers the colorful Olympic Games—often from halfway around the world.

All commercial stations broadcast brief summaries of local, national, and international news every day. Also, stations often interrupt their regular program schedules to present extended coverage of special events, such as space shots, political conventions, and important presidential activities.

Advertising makes up an important part of commercial television. Television commercials appear between and during most programs. The vast majority of the commercials urge viewers to buy some kind of product —from dog food and hair spray, to cars and insurance policies. At election time, many political candidates buy advertising time on television to ask people to vote for them. A small percentage of TV advertising provides a *public service*. Public service ads include messages that tell people to drive carefully and follow other safety rules. They also include announcements about local community activities.

Commercial television attracts huge audiences. Often, more than 50 million people tune in to a top entertainment show or sporting event. On a typical day, about 32 million homes have a television set tuned to one of the three half-hour network evening news programs. Thus, it must be assumed that large numbers of people like what commercial television offers. Even so, many people criticize its coverage. They say that commercial TV shows too many programs designed only to entertain, and not enough programs that inform, educate, or provide cultural enrichment. The critics also claim that much of the entertainment is of poor quality because it aims at the largest possible audience. They criticize newscasts for being too brief to provide the real meaning of news stories.

The people responsible for deciding what appears on commercial television respond to such criticisms by pointing out that commercial TV can stay in business only by selling much advertising time at high prices. To do this, the programs must attract large numbers of viewers. Statistics show that many more people watch popular shows and brief news reports than watch more sophisticated shows and in-depth news reports.

Public television programming focuses chiefly on educational and cultural subjects. Because public television stations do not rely on advertising to stay in business, it is not necessary for them to attract huge audiences.

Public stations broadcast educational programs on a wide range of subjects, from literature and physics to cooking and yoga. In some cases, viewers can earn college credits by passing tests based on what the programs teach. Some educational programs on public TV take much the same form as classroom instruction. But others use a more entertaining approach. Examples include "Sesame Street" and "Mister Rogers' Neighborhood," two lively, yet educational, children's shows.

Public television stations offer many programs that combine entertainment and cultural enrichment. They telecast such things as plays by leading dramatists, ballets and symphonies, and surveys of art and history. Such television shows draw up to 2 million viewers—a small audience by commercial TV standards, but a much larger one than ever attended a theater or concert hall.

About 90 per cent of the public television stations in the United States carry an hour-long newscast on weekday evenings. In addition, public television often presents programs in which leading journalists and others who deal closely with current events participate in in-depth discussions of news developments.

Subscription television is television broadcasting paid for by the viewers. Most subscription TV is made up of cable systems. Cable television offers greater program variety than regular television stations alone.

Commercial and public television stations send signals over the airwaves. Cable television signals are delivered to home TV sets of most of their customers by way of cables. Some cable systems carry more than 100 channels—far more than can be broadcast over the airwaves even in the largest urban areas. Many cable channels are devoted exclusively to specific types of programming. For instance, there are cable channels that specialize in movies, news, sports, the arts, health, religion, or Spanish-language programs. In addition, many communities require cable operators to reserve channels for programs of local interest, such as city council meetings. See the section on *Cable television systems* in this article for more information on cable TV.

Closed-circuit television has a number of specialized uses. Many schoolrooms have TV sets that receive special lessons by way of closed-circuit television. Also, a lesson in one class can be shown simultaneously to students in other parts of the school through closed-circuit TV. Regular broadcast TV also brings into the classroom such events as government hearings and presidential press conferences.

Businesses use videotaped television programs extensively to train their employees. Many large corporations operate their own private TV studios. Some companies conduct nationwide meetings and conferences by live TV. This procedure, called *teleconferencing*, saves the time and expense of travel.

Closed-circuit TV in banks and prisons enables guards to observe many people at once. Hospitals use closed-circuit TV to *monitor* (keep track of) patients. Television cameras are placed in operating rooms to give medical students close-up views of actual surgical procedures.

Rush-Presbyterian-St. Luke's Medical Center;
WORLD BOOK photo by Stephen Feldman

Closed-circuit television enables hospital personnel to monitor the condition of many patients at the same time.

Video entertainment systems include video cassette recorders (VCR's), videodisc players, and electronic games.

Video cassette recorders enable people to tape television programs on blank video cassettes and play them back later. The VCR is attached to the user's television set. People also may buy or rent prerecorded videotapes. Many of these are tapes of movies, concerts, or sports events. With the use of a video camera, families can create their own videotaped television programs. See **Videotape recorder.**

Videodiscs resemble phonograph records, but they carry both sound and pictures. These prerecorded programs are transmitted by a videodisc player to an attached TV set. Videodiscs are used in the home primarily for viewing movies.

One type of videodisc, called an *optical videodisc,* is read by a tiny laser. This videodisc holds up to 54,000 pictures, or *frames,* per side and can store a vast amount of information. The images on these frames may be observed singly, like the pages of a book. They also may be played in sequence to produce a moving picture. An optical videodisc player provides instant access to any frame on the disc. This feature makes the optical disc a useful teaching device.

In an *interactive* optical system, the videodisc player is linked to a computer. When a student answers a test question incorrectly, the disc automatically responds with the appropriate information. Videodiscs have been used to teach economics to high school students and tank gunnery to soldiers. See **Videodisc.**

Electronic games use a television screen as a game board. Such games, which are also called *video games,* are played on a computer-controlled unit connected to a television set. Each video game has its own program on a cartridge that is inserted into the unit. Players operate controls that move electronic dots, lines, and other images that appear on the TV screen. See **Electronic game.**

Televised information services, sometimes called *electronic publishing,* were developed in Canada, Great Britain, and France during the 1970's. Televised information services provide viewers with televised newspaper stories, stock market listings, classified ads, calendars of local events, and other kinds of information. There are two main types of televised information services—*teletext* and *videotex,* or *videotext.*

Teletext is broadcast over the airwaves on regular television channels. An electronic control panel attached to the TV set decodes the broadcast signals and converts them into images on the screen. Teletext transmits its store of information over and over again. The user selects a particular "page" of information by typing in a code number on the control panel. Teletext is limited to about 200 to 300 pages of information.

Videotex, also known as *viewdata,* is brought into the home over television cables or telephone lines. The viewer uses a control panel to select the information to be transmitted. The information may be displayed over a television set or on the screen of a personal computer. Unlike teletext, videotex enables the user to conduct two-way transactions. In some communities, people can use videotex to do their shopping, banking, and pay their bills by TV.

Producing television programs

The *production* (putting together) of a television program is an extremely complicated process. A program requires careful planning, much preparation, and the combined efforts of many workers with artistic and technical skills.

Most television productions take place in television studios. But TV production companies also create shows in movie studios, on city streets, in stadiums, in deserts and jungles, and even underwater. Broadcasters telecast some programs *live* (as they happen). But most TV programs—including almost all entertainment shows—are prerecorded, and then telecast later. The recording may be done on videotape or on film.

Many prerecorded programs are produced from beginning to end, in the manner of a stage play. But television production companies also use the *piecemeal approach* of the motion-picture industry. In this approach, each scene is recorded separately, and *spliced* (connected together) later.

The first two parts of this section—*Planning and preparation* and *Putting a show on the air*—trace the development of an entertainment program produced straight

The photographs in this section were taken for World Book *at the production facilities of NBC-TV's "The Tonight Show Starring Johnny Carson" by John Hamilton, Globe Photos.*

through in a television studio and recorded on videotape. But much of the information under these headings applies to all TV productions. The last part of this section describes the differences involved in other production methods.

Planning and preparation

The planning of television shows begins in the programming department of the networks and stations that broadcast programs. Members of these departments decide what programs their companies will telecast. Networks and stations produce many programs themselves. Independent producers create others, and sell them to networks and stations. In either case, once a programming department approves an idea for a program, a *producer* takes responsibility for its production.

The producer usually begins by obtaining a script and choosing a director. Sometimes—especially for uncomplicated shows—producers write their own script. They may also serve as their own director—in which case they become a *producer-director.* But more often, the producer assigns the script-writing job to a professional writer or team of writers, and the directing job to a professional director. The producer and director select the *talent* (actors, actresses, or other people who will appear on the show). The producer also chooses

A TV production involves achieving an appearance of naturalness amid much activity. Viewers of "The Tonight Show" see Johnny Carson and Ed McMahon chatting in a relaxed atmosphere, *above*. But off camera, many workers are doing jobs that require split-second timing.

the production specialists needed to produce the show. These people may include an art director, a costume designer, and a composer. In addition, the producer works closely with the director throughout the production process.

Writers prepare the scripts for television programs. A television script is a written account of what is to be said and done during the program. The amount of detail a script contains varies, depending on the program. A talk show script, for example, may include only the host's opening remarks, some of the key questions to ask the guests, and directions for any special acts that may take place during the show. During most of the show, the host and the guests carry on *adlibbed* (unplanned) conversations. A script for a television drama, on the other hand, includes every word to be spoken by the actors and actresses. It also describes the actions they are to perform.

The director. As soon as the writers complete the script, the director reads it and tries to visualize ways to translate it into an actual television program. Directors get ideas about how the characters should speak, move, and generally behave. They decide what camera shots will be needed to create the effects they visualize. Sometimes, the director has an artist prepare a *storyboard* (a series of drawings) that shows how key parts of the program will look.

Production specialists. The producer and director call on many production specialists to help prepare for the program. An *art director* and artists and craftspeople who work with the art director design and build the show's scenery. A *costume designer* creates or obtains costumes needed for the production. A *property manager* gets special items called *props* for the show. These items include furniture, vases of flowers, and guns. Specialists in technical work also play a key role in the pro-

duction process. They advise the producer and director on what kinds of cameras, microphones, and lights will be needed. A *production manager,* or *production coordinator,* sees to it that all the required equipment is available when needed.

Talent is a technical term for all the people who appear on television programs. A talent may be a *performer,* or an *actor* or *actress.* The talent who appear as themselves on television are performers. A talent who plays someone else is an actor or actress. Television performers include newscasters, sports announcers, and talk show hosts. The people who play roles in TV dramas and situation comedies are actors and actresses.

Selection of talent ranks among the key steps in the planning of a television program. The producer and director do this important job. If the talent are big stars, they may get television roles because of their fame and proven ability. But usually, the talent must *audition* (try out) for the parts they want to play. During an audition, the director and producer may ask the talent to *take a screen test* (perform in front of a camera).

The talent who earn a job get a script so they can study their lines. An actor or actress may have less than a week to learn the lines for a one-hour drama. Those who perform on TV's daily soap operas have only a few hours each day to memorize their lines.

Some television productions make use of *cue cards* to help the talent with their lines. A cue card is a large piece of cardboard or similar material with writing on it. The writing may be a key word or phrase, or an entire passage from a script. An off-camera stagehand holds the card up so the talent can see it.

The *TelePrompTer* is another aid sometimes used in television productions. A TelePrompTer is a mechanical device that contains a roll of paper with words from a script printed on it. The roll moves continuously, giving

Production preparations may include setting up a *Tele-PrompTer,* a device that shows parts of a script. The TelePromp-Ter above shows lines of a commercial Ed McMahon will read.

Rehearsals are practice sessions of TV productions. During dress rehearsal for a comedy routine, the director (*holding script*) goes over the skit with Carson and other cast members.

the talent a line-by-line view of the script. Television performers who deliver commercials, news stories, and speeches often use a TelePrompTer.

Composers and musicians. Most television programs include music. A producer and director may decide they need an original musical composition for their show. If so, the producer hires a composer. The composer meets with the producer and director to discuss the theme, mood, and *climaxes* (dramatic high points) of the program. Composers base their compositions on what they learn about the show. Often, producers and directors use existing music for their programs. To do so, they must get permission from the holders of the copyright on the music, and pay them a fee.

The producer hires musicians and a conductor to perform the music. For prerecorded shows, the musicians often record the music after the actual program is produced. Then, technicians combine the music with the rest of the program.

Rehearsals are practice sessions for TV shows. Most TV productions require at least one rehearsal. Complicated productions often require many more.

During a rehearsal, the talent—under the director's guidance—practice their lines and their actions. The director also directs the actions of the camera operator and other off-camera workers.

Rehearsal for a dramatic production may begin with a *script reading.* Then, the director may call for a *dry run* (rehearsal without equipment or costumes). Many dry runs take place in a *rehearsal room.* This room has lines on the floor that indicate where such things as doors, chairs, and tables will be during the actual production. A director may watch a dry run through a *director's viewfinder.* This device resembles the viewfinder on a still camera. It enables the director to get an idea of how scenes will appear on television.

Finally, the director calls for a *dress rehearsal,* or *camera rehearsal,* in the studio. The goal of a dress rehearsal is to achieve a performance that is the same as the final production will be. In fact, directors sometimes record both the dress rehearsal and the actual production. In reviewing both recordings, directors may decide that parts of the dress rehearsal came out better than the actual production. They may then substitute the parts of the dress rehearsal they like for the corresponding parts of the actual production.

Television rehearsals stress the importance of split-second timing. A theater drama may run as much as five minutes more than its planned time. But a television show must be timed exactly. A show cannot run even a few seconds past its planned time, because that time is set aside for the next program.

Putting a show on the air

When the time comes to tape a program, everything needed for the process is brought together in a television studio. Workers put the scenery and props in place in the studio. Other workers put floodlights and spotlights in place. Technicians turn these lights off and on and brighten and dim them during the production to achieve the desired effect for various scenes. Often, a single televised scene requires as many as 20 different lighting instruments. One or more microphones are put in place. Workers bring television cameras—usually at least two and sometimes four or five—into the studio. The people responsible for the technical parts of the show's production get ready in the *control room.* This room lies off to the side of the place where the telecast occurs.

Some studios have rows of seats, very much like a theater. Visitors can come to these *audience areas* and watch shows being produced.

Putting a show on the air requires the skills of many behind-the-scenes workers. A "Tonight Show" audio engineer controls the program's sounds at an audio console, *left.* Monitors, *right,* show all the scenes the studio cameras are photographing. The director decides which scenes go on the air.

Before the show begins, makeup artists apply makeup to the talent who will appear on the show. Makeup helps people look natural on camera. The talent put on special costumes, if the show calls for such costumes. Finally, they come into the studio and perform the production before the cameras.

The cameras used for *shooting* (photographing) the production are big, heavy instruments. They are mounted on devices that have wheels so the camera operators can move them around the studio to change the direction of their shots. Many cameras can be lowered and raised mechanically to change the vertical angles. In addition, all broadcast cameras have a lens that allows the camera operator to vary televised scenes without moving the camera. This device is called a *zoom lens.* By pressing a button or turning a handle, the camera operator causes adjustments in the lens. These adjustments enable the camera operator to gradually change a scene from a close-up to a long-range view of an entire scene. *Zooming* (moving in and out on scenes) is a widely used TV production technique.

A broadcasting camera also has a *viewfinder* (tiny television set) on it. The viewfinder shows the camera operator the exact scene the camera is photographing.

Microphones. Most studio TV productions involve the use of one or more *boom microphones.* A boom microphone is attached to a *boom* (long metal arm). A worker called the *boom operator* uses mechanical devices to move the microphone above and in front of the person speaking. For dramatic productions, it is essential that the microphone be kept out of camera view. Imagine a dramatic scene in which an actor lies exhausted in a hot desert, crying for help. If suddenly the boom microphone that hangs above him dropped into camera view, the scene would look ridiculous. Sometimes, television makes use of *hidden microphones*—ei-

ther in addition to, or in place of, boom microphones. They may be hidden in or behind scenery or props.

Talk shows and other nondramatic productions may use boom microphones. But they also use microphones that viewers can see. These include *desk microphones,* which stand on desks or tables in front of performers; and *hand microphones,* which performers hold. Another kind of microphone, the *lavalier,* is hung around a performer's neck or attached to a performer's clothing. It may be in camera view, or hidden in the clothing.

The control room. During a television program, scenes from each of the studio's cameras will appear on the viewer's screen. Pictures from other video sources, including filmed commercials and slides that show titles, will also be seen. The job of determining which scene appears on the screen at a given time is performed in the control room. A program may also include sounds from several sources. Technicians in the *audio control* section of the control room regulate the sounds. In addition, engineers operate equipment that maintains the quality of the pictures and sounds.

The control room has several *monitors* (television sets). Each monitor shows the scenes from a different camera or other video source. The director watches the monitors when choosing which scenes to put on the air. The picture that is on the air at any given time appears on a monitor called the *master,* or *line, monitor.*

An important piece of equipment in the control room is the *switcher.* This instrument has many buttons, including buttons for controlling each studio camera and each other picture source. On command from the director, a technician called the *technical director* (T.D.) presses buttons to change the televised scene. If the director wants the scene being photographed by camera number 1 to be shown, the director tells the T.D. to press the button for camera number 1. To change to camera number 2, the T.D. presses button number 2, and so on. This switching process goes on throughout the program. But it is done so smoothly that viewers hardly realize it is happening.

The switcher also has levers. By moving levers in various ways, the T.D. can combine scenes from two or more cameras or other video sources. Such combinations are called *special effects*. They include the *dissolve*, the *super*, the *wipe*, and *matting*, or *keying*.

The *dissolve* is a gradual change from one picture to another in which the two pictures overlap briefly. A dissolve can take place slowly or rapidly, depending on how fast the T.D. moves the levers. Directors use the dissolve to move smoothly from scene to scene and, sometimes, to indicate a passage of time.

The *super*, or *superimposition*, is the blending together of two scenes. Television often uses this device to show dream scenes. One camera shows a close-up of the face of the sleeping person, and the other shows the scene about which the person is dreaming.

A *wipe* is a special effect in which one picture seems to push another picture off the screen. A wipe that is stopped halfway is called a *split screen*. TV productions use the split-screen technique to show scenes from two different locations at the same time. Other common wipes include the *circle* and the *diamond*, in which the second picture appears on the screen as an expanding circle or diamond.

The *matting*, or *keying*, technique is used to show titles and other objects over a scene. The letters of the titles come from a title card, title slide, or electronic letter-making machine. The picture on which the letters appear comes from a studio camera, or film or tape.

The switcher also enables television broadcasters to *cut* (switch instantly) from the program to filmed commercials, and back again.

The sound inputs of a television program are controlled by an instrument called an *audio console*. An *audio engineer* operates this instrument. The audio engineer pushes buttons and moves levers to choose and mix together various audio inputs. For example, a scene of two persons sitting in an automobile might require the audio engineer to mix the sounds of the persons' conversation with recorded sounds of the automobile engine, outside traffic, and mood music. The audio engineer also controls the volume of sounds.

Taping the program. The program produced in the studio and control room is immediately recorded on a videotape machine. This machine stands in or near a special part of the television studio called *master control*. The director reviews the finished tape, and tape editors correct any major errors in it. Then, the tape is stored until the time the program is scheduled for broadcasting. For technical information on videotape, see *Videotape recording* later in this article.

Master control is the electronic nerve center of a television station. Much of the electronic equipment that helps create television pictures is located there. A program goes from master control by cable or microwave to the transmitter. Then, the transmitter sends it on its way to the viewers. Master control also has equipment for switching from program to program. The programs include those that originate at the station, at network headquarters, and at remote locations.

Other production methods

A television production can differ from the method just described in four chief ways. (1) Television producers put some programs together piecemeal rather than straight through. (2) They create many programs with film cameras rather than with TV cameras. (3) They telecast many programs live instead of recording them first. (4) They create programs in locations away from studios. Such programs are called *remote telecasts*.

The piecemeal approach involves recording a program on videotape or film scene-by-scene with *stopdowns* (stops) between scenes. Each recorded scene is called a *take*. After each take, directors can play back the tape or film and judge its merits. If they like the take, they go on to another one. If they do not like it, they can call for a *retake* (shoot the scene over again). The piecemeal approach also allows directors to shoot scenes out of order. If, for example, the first and last scenes of a TV play happen in the same location, the director may shoot them one right after the other. Upon completion, film or tape editors splice all the scenes together in their proper order to create a continuous story.

Filming television programs. Film cameras can be carried around and operated more easily than can television cameras. As a result, many television producers use film cameras to create programs that take place at several locations. For example, television news programs, which report on widely scattered events, use film cameras. Programs shot at faraway locations usually use film. In addition, motion-picture studios create many entertainment programs with film cameras (see **Motion picture** [How a motion picture is made]).

After camera operators film a program, broadcasters telecast it from a telecine unit. For technical information, see *Telecine* later in this article.

Live telecasts include coverage of political conventions, speeches by the President, and sports events. The part of newscasts in which the announcers speak are also live. But most of the news scenes shown on these programs come from film or videotape recordings.

Broadcasters usually videotape live programs at the same time as they telecast them. This allows them to rerun all or parts of a show at a later time. For example, videotaped highlights of a live telecast of a speech by the President are often shown later on newscasts. Videotapes of live sports events allow sportscasters to rerun and analyze key plays immediately after they happen. This process is called *instant replay*.

Remote telecasts. Almost all remote telecasts are broadcast live. They include telecasts of sports events and political conventions. Producers of these programs use regular-sized television cameras. But they also use cameras small enough to be carried around. These *hand-held cameras* help TV crews cover the huge area of a sports field or convention hall. Broadcasters park a *remote truck* near the place of the telecast. This truck contains control room and master control equipment needed to create TV signals. The signals travel by microwave or wire from the truck to the transmitter.

The popularity of TV programs in the United States created a huge television industry in a short time. In 1946, there were only six television stations in the United States. In 1988, the country had 1,367 stations.

The number of TV stations accounts for only part of television's impact on the American economy. The manufacture and sales of television sets and broadcasting equipment became big businesses because of the rise of television. In addition, broadcasting, manufacturing, and sales created thousands of new jobs.

The national networks. About two-thirds of all commercial television stations in the United States are *affiliates* of one of the three major national networks. That is, they agree to carry programs provided by these networks. The major national television networks are those of the American Broadcasting Companies (ABC), CBS Inc., and the National Broadcasting Company (NBC). The networks create some of their programs and buy others from independent producers.

An affiliate agrees to carry programs provided by a network. The network pays the affiliate for carrying the programs. Sponsors, in turn, pay the networks for showing their commercials on the stations.

A network's success depends on its ability to select programs that attract large audiences. The bigger a program's audience, the more money sponsors will pay for the right to show commercials on it. For top-rated network shows during prime time, sponsors pay about $200,000 for 30 seconds of commercial time.

The TV executives who choose network programs know that famous entertainers and championship sports contests usually attract large audiences. But these executives cannot be certain how many viewers other shows are likely to attract. They are helped in choosing programs by specialists in *audience research.* Such specialists collect data about people's interests and the kinds of programs they like to watch. These specialists also gather the responses of audiences that are invited to view special "pilot" episodes of new programs. Such research has limited success in predicting a program's popularity for various reasons. For example, an audience's response to a single exposure to a program might differ from its response to a series. As a result, network executives must ultimately rely on their own intuition or "educated guesses" in choosing programs.

The success of a program is measured in ratings and shares. *Ratings* measure the percentage of all *TV homes* (homes that have television sets) that are tuned to a particular program. *Share* measures the percentage of TV homes with a set switched on that are tuned to a particular program. The A. C. Nielsen Company ranks as the most important national audience measurement service. It provides television stations and advertisers with information about ratings and share and with *demographic* data about audiences. Demographic data describe the makeup of an audience in terms of sex, age, income, education, race, place of residence, and other features. The Arbitron Ratings Company is the leading American audience measurement service at the local level.

A national audience survey typically consists of about 3,000 households that are paid a small fee for participating. The viewing habits in these households supposedly reflect the habits of the entire nation. Networks usually cancel a program that receives low ratings, often after only a few shows. The most advanced device to measure a TV audience is the "people meter," which resembles a TV remote-control unit. Family members each press an assigned key on the meter to indicate who is watching TV. In this way, the people meter registers the age and sex of a program's viewers for advertisers.

Commercial stations. In 1988, 1,033 local commercial stations operated in the United States. About two-thirds of them were affiliates of the three major networks. The rest operate independently or as affiliates of smaller networks.

An affiliate carries many hours of network programs daily. But in 1971, the Federal Communications Commission (FCC)—which regulates broadcasting in the United States—limited the amount of network programming affiliates can carry during *prime time.* Prime time refers to the evening hours, when television programs draw the largest audience. The FCC ruled that local stations in the nation's 50 largest television markets cannot broadcast more than 3 hours of network programs during prime time. This ruling was designed to force the stations to offer a wider variety of programs—especially programs of local interest—during the prime-time period.

In spite of this FCC ruling, most nonnetwork programs are old movies, talk shows, game shows, and reruns of old network shows. These programs are *syndicated*—that is, sold to the stations by independent organizations called *syndicates.* Affiliates or independent stations prefer to buy syndicated programs rather than produce new programs because it is far less expensive. In addition, syndicated programs are generally well known. Local stations fill some time with shows they produce themselves, especially newscasts. Both affiliates and independent stations sell time to advertisers to cover the costs of their programs. Affiliates sometimes refuse to carry a network program because they can make more profit by selling the time themselves.

Number of television sets in use

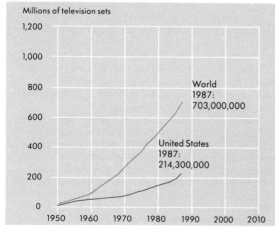

Sources: *Statistical Yearbook,* 1981 and earlier years, UN; *Television and Cable Factbook,* 1988 and earlier years, Television Digest, Inc.; *World Communications,* UN; Chinese government sources.

Public stations. In 1988, 334 public TV stations operated in the United States. These stations create many of the programs they show and buy programs from independent producers. Often, a program created by one public station is carried by many others. An agency called Public Broadcasting Service (PBS) serves as a distributor of locally produced public programs.

Public stations are nonprofit organizations, but they need money to cover their production and operating costs. The largest part of a station's funds come from viewer contributions. A viewer who contributes to a public television station becomes a member of the station. Businesses and foundations also help support public television. Local and state taxes help support many public stations. In addition, stations get funds from the Corporation for Public Broadcasting (CPB).

CPB, created by Congress in 1967, gets most of its funds from the federal government. CPB helps public stations serve their communities through grants for programming and technical facilities. It also finances the production of programs distributed by PBS and sets policies for a national public broadcasting service.

Cable television systems bring television to the home by means of cables rather than through the air. These systems are also known as *Community Antenna Television* (CATV) because the cables are connected to a powerful antenna that serves a large area.

Cable TV, which began in the early 1950's, is one of the fastest-growing parts of the television industry. Its original purpose was to bring network and local station programs to places that either cannot receive TV signals through the air, or can receive them only with much interference. Such places include isolated communities, mountain valleys, extremely hilly regions, and areas with heavy concentrations of tall buildings.

Improved reception of regular television programs still ranks as an important purpose of cable television. But since the 1960's, people have begun to use it for other purposes. A single cable system can carry more than 100 channels. Thus, a cable system can transmit regular network television programs and also provide a wide variety of special features. Some cable systems offer adult education classes; continuous news, weather, and stock market reports; programming from distant independent TV stations; first-run motion pictures; and special sporting events. In many communities, channels are set aside for coverage of such local activities as city council and school board meetings.

Today, there are about 8,500 cable television systems in the United States. The largest of these systems provides TV to about 300,000 homes. Others serve fewer than 100 homes. Altogether, cable TV serves more than 45 million homes in over 20,000 communities.

Cable TV has great economic potential despite the high cost of installing cable systems. Many operators charge an installation fee. Subscribers pay a monthly fee for the basic service plus additional fees for special services. Operators can also create their own programming and sell advertising time to sponsors.

Related industries. The spectacular growth of television broadcasting caused a similar growth in other industries. In 1946, manufacturers in the United States

Leading countries in number of TV sets

Country	Number of sets	Sets per 1,000 people
United States	214,300,000	887
Soviet Union	88,000,000	310
China	67,500,000	62
Japan	32,000,000	264
West Germany	25,300,000	416
France	25,000,000	453
Brazil	22,000,000	155
Great Britain	18,700,000	330
Mexico	14,700,000	177
Italy	14,500,000	254

Sources: *Television and Cable Factbook, 1988,* Television Digest, Inc.; China figure per official Chinese government source.

turned out only 56,000 television sets, and the American people spent about $1 million for sets. In the late 1980's, manufacturers produced more than 23 million sets a year, with a retail value of about $8 billion. Set sales have improved the business of many retail stores, including radio and phonograph shops, department stores, and appliance stores. Also, TV repair shops have sprung up throughout the country.

Television broadcasting requires much expensive equipment, including cameras, control boards, and transmitters. The manufacture of such equipment has become a multimillion-dollar industry.

The huge demand for television commercials has created a boom in the advertising industry. About 20 per cent of all the money now spent on advertising in the United States goes to television commercials.

Television awards are presented each year by a number of organizations. The best-known awards, the *Emmys,* are given by the Academy of Television Arts and Sciences and by the National Academy of Television Arts and Sciences. The two academies recognize achievements of the preceding year in various fields of the TV industry. Some local chapters of the National Academy also present Emmys for local programming.

Careers in television. The television industry has opened up thousands of job opportunities in a variety of fields. The industry needs such workers as writers, producers, directors, camera operators, engineers, electronic technicians, stagehands, lighting specialists, graphic artists, and set designers to help produce television shows. Actors, actresses, and performers are needed to appear in them. TV news departments provide a variety of jobs for journalists. TV broadcasting also creates many jobs for specialists in management, market research, and advertising.

The television industry also employs workers in technical fields outside of broadcasting. Scientists and engineers are needed to design television equipment. Factory workers manufacture television sets and other TV equipment. Technicians service home receivers.

Almost all careers in television require special training. Many colleges and universities have departments that train students in nontechnical broadcasting careers. Journalism schools teach courses in broadcast—and printed-media—journalism. Technological institutes and engineering departments of colleges offer training in technical areas of television. Information on television careers is available from the National Association of Broadcasters, 1771 N Street NW, Washington, DC 20036.

Television ranks as a major influence on American life. It affects the way people spend their time, what and how they learn, and such *institutions* (established parts of society) as politics, the other media, and sports. Some authorities believe that TV has an even greater influence on young people than on adults.

Effects on leisure time. A typical adult spends more time watching TV than doing anything else except sleeping and working. Watching television ranks as the most time-consuming leisure activity among adults. It takes time away from other activities, such as reading, conversation, social gatherings, and exercise.

Effects on learning. Television contributes greatly to what home viewers learn. It benefits people by widening their experience. On the other hand, TV also may contribute to harmful impressions of the world.

Enriched experience. No communication system has ever provided so many people with as wide a range of new experiences as television has. Without leaving their homes, TV viewers can watch government officials perform important functions, and see how people in far-off lands look and live. Television takes viewers to deserts, jungles, and the ocean floor. A TV viewer can see how a famous actor performs the role of Hamlet, and how top comedians draw laughter. Television gives its viewers a glimpse of real-life tragedy, as when it covers the victims of war, natural disasters, and poverty. It also captures moments of great triumph, such as when astronauts first set foot on the moon. However, some authorities question how much specific information viewers remember from watching television.

Harmful impressions. Many social scientists believe that people are likely to form two negative impressions from watching a lot of television. One of these impressions is that many people are better off than they are. The other is that the world is an unfriendly place, filled with untrustworthy people and risky circumstances.

Television programs often show people who lead more glamorous lives and have more material possessions than most viewers. In addition, TV commercials constantly urge viewers to buy various goods. Many sociologists believe that as a result, the material expectations of TV viewers are raised, sometimes to an unrealistic level. One harmful effect results when people fail to achieve the success they see on TV and become dissatisfied or bitter. Some people may even turn to crime to increase their material wealth.

The violent, crime-filled world shown on TV may contribute to an impression of an evil world. Studies indicate that people who watch a great deal of television are more likely to hold fearful or negative views of the world than those who watch less TV. However, some researchers argue that people who watch a lot of television already hold such views.

Effects on institutions. Television has brought about major changes in several American institutions. They include politics, motion pictures and radio, and sports.

Effects on politics. Every election year, thousands of political candidates use television in their campaigns. They buy commercial time to urge voters to support them. They also appear in debates with other candidates and answer interviewers' questions about their views.

Television plays its greatest role in presidential races. Before TV, presidential candidates tried to make personal appearances and speeches in as many cities and states as possible. Today, many candidates reach more voters through a single television appearance than through all the in-person campaigning they do.

The most widely used form of political advertising in television is the *spot announcement.* Spot announcements are political messages that last 10 to 90 seconds. These contrast sharply with the long political speeches that are typical of traditional in-person campaigning.

Television does much to promote interest in politics and political issues. But political advertising on TV also draws criticism. Critics say spot announcements are too short to allow candidates to discuss issues. Instead, candidates use the time to present oversimplified statements to win support or attack their opponents. Critics also claim that, because television time is so expensive, TV campaigning gives unfair advantage to the candidates with the most money. Another complaint about television campaigning is that it leads to the "selling" of candidates through advertising methods similar to those used to sell products.

Motion pictures and radio. From the 1920's through the 1940's, films and radio were the chief forms of entertainment for millions of Americans. Many people went to the movies at least once a week. They listened to comedies, dramas, and other entertainment programs on the radio almost every night. The rise of TV in the 1950's caused a sharp drop in movie attendance. Ever since, the movie industry has faced economic problems. Radio entertainment changed completely after TV became a part of American life. Almost every radio entertainment show went off the air. Recorded music became the chief kind of radio programming.

National magazines also suffered after the arrival of television. *Collier's, Life, Look,* and the *Saturday Evening Post* all had circulations of many millions. These magazines went out of business when advertisers shifted huge amounts of money to television.

Professional sports have long attracted millions of spectators yearly. But many more millions now watch the events on television. Television networks and stations pay team owners huge amounts of money for the right to televise games. These funds, in turn, help owners pay the huge salaries of today's professional athletes. Television also helps increase the popularity of sports. For example, the popularity of professional football has soared largely because of television. On the other hand, minor league baseball lost much of its audience after television brought major league games into the home.

Effects on young people. There is little agreement about how television affects young people. Parents have long been concerned about the amount of time young people spend watching TV. Studies have linked watching a lot of television with poor performance in school. However, these studies do not prove that TV viewing actually causes students to perform poorly. Watching television may simply be an activity preferred by young people who do poorly in school. Other studies suggest that television encourages aggressive behavior by showing so much violence.

A person looking directly at a scene sees the entire view all at once. But television cannot send a picture of an entire scene all at once. It can send only one tiny part of the picture after another until it has sent the complete picture. A TV camera divides a picture into several hundred thousand tiny parts by a process called *scanning.* As the camera scans the picture, it creates electronic signals from each part of the picture.

A TV set uses these signals in re-creating the picture on its screen. The scanning process puts the picture back together piece by piece. A person watching TV does not realize this is happening. The process works so quickly that the viewer sees only a complete picture.

Sending television pictures and sounds involves three basic steps. (1) The light and sound waves from the scene being televised must be changed into electronic signals. (2) These signals must be transmitted to the television receiver. (3) The receiver must unscramble the signals and change them back into copies of the light and sound waves that came from the original scene.

Creating television signals

A television signal begins when light from the scene being televised enters a television camera. The camera changes the light into electronic signals. At the same time, a microphone picks up the sounds from the scene and changes them into electronic signals. Television engineers call the signals from a camera *video* and the signals from a microphone *audio.*

This section describes how a TV camera creates video signals. It also explains how video signals are produced by *telecine* (television film) and videotape. TV audio signals are created in the same way as radio signals. For information on this process, see **Radio.**

The video signals broadcast by most TV stations are *compatible color signals.* These signals produce a color picture when received on a color set, and they produce a black-and-white picture on a black-and-white set.

Color TV uses the three *primary colors in light*—red, blue, and green—to produce full-color pictures. The proper mixture of these three colors can produce any color of light. For example, a mixture of red and green light produces yellow light. Equal amounts of red, blue, and green light produce white light.

The television camera. In producing a compatible color signal, the TV camera must: (1) capture the image of the scene being telecast; (2) create video signals from the image; and (3) encode the color signals for transmission. To perform these tasks, a television camera uses a lens, a system of mirrors and filters, camera tubes, and complex electronic circuits. Some of the electronic circuits used by the camera are located elsewhere in the TV station and connected to the camera by wires.

Capturing the image. The lens gathers the *image* (picture) of the scene in front of the camera. Like the lenses in other cameras and the human eye, the TV lens *focuses* (collects and bends) the light from the scene in order to form a sharp image. This image contains all the colors of the scene. However, in order to produce color signals, the camera must split the full-color image into three separate images—one for each primary color.

Most TV cameras use two *dichroic mirrors* to split the image into the primary colors. The first mirror reflects the blue image and allows red and green light to pass through it. The second mirror reflects the red image, leaving only the green image. Other mirrors reflect each image to a separate camera tube. In many cameras, this color separation is done by color filters and prisms contained in a small compartment called the *prism block.*

Creating the video signals. A camera tube changes the light image into video signals. A black-and-white camera has only one camera tube. Most high-quality color cameras have three such tubes. These tubes create a separate video signal for each of the three primary colors. Many small, lower-quality, portable cameras are equipped with a single tube. This tube has many thin red, blue, and green *filter stripes* on its surface. The stripes divide the light into the three primary colors, and the tube then converts each of the colors into a separate video signal.

The tubes in color cameras are improved versions of a tube called the *vidicon.* This section describes the working of one vidicon tube in cameras that have three.

A vidicon tube has a glass *faceplate* at its front end. In back of the faceplate is a transparent coating called the *signal plate.* A second plate, called the *target,* lies behind the signal plate. The target consists of a layer of *photoconductive material* that conducts electricity when exposed to light. At the rear of the tube is a device called an *electron gun.*

Light from the image reaches the target after passing through the faceplate and the signal plate. The light causes negatively charged particles called *electrons* in the photoconductive material to move toward the signal plate. This movement leaves the back of the target with a positive electric charge. The strength of the positive charge on any area of the target corresponds to the brightness of the light shining on that area. The camera tube thus changes the light image gathered by the lens into an identical electric image of positive charges on the back of the target.

The electron gun shoots a beam of electrons across the back of the target. The beam moves across the target in an orderly pattern called a *scanning pattern.* As the beam moves across the target, it strikes areas with different amounts of positive charge. Areas of the target that have the strongest charge attract the most electrons from the beam. This occurs because particles of unlike electric charge attract each other. Other areas of the target attract fewer electrons. The electrons from the beam move through the target and cause an electric current to flow in the signal plate. The voltage of this current changes from moment to moment, depending on whether the beam is striking a bright or dim part of the image. This changing voltage is the video signal from that camera tube.

The electron gun scans the target much as a person reads—from left to right, top to bottom. But unlike the way a person reads, the electron beam skips every other line on the target. After the beam scans the top line, it quickly snaps back to the left. Then, it scans the third line, fifth line, and so on. When the beam reaches the bottom of the target, it snaps back and then scans line two, line four, line six, and so on.

How color television is transmitted

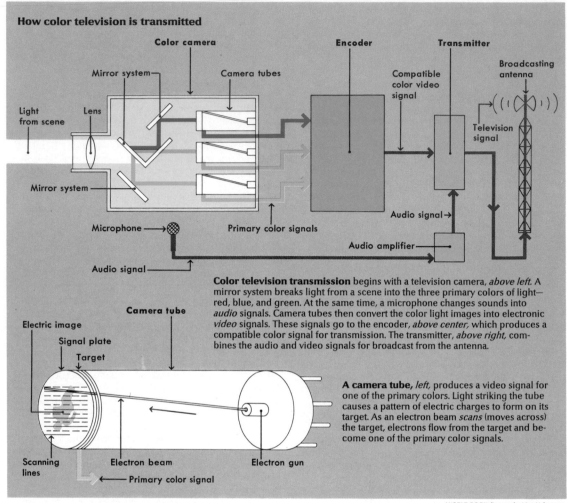

Color television transmission begins with a television camera, *above left.* A mirror system breaks light from a scene into the three primary colors of light—red, blue, and green. At the same time, a microphone changes sounds into *audio* signals. Camera tubes then convert the color light images into electronic *video* signals. These signals go to the encoder, *above center,* which produces a compatible color signal for transmission. The transmitter, *above right,* combines the audio and video signals for broadcast from the antenna.

A camera tube, *left,* produces a video signal for one of the primary colors. Light striking the tube causes a pattern of electric charges to form on its target. As an electron beam *scans* (moves across) the target, electrons flow from the target and become one of the primary color signals.

WORLD BOOK diagram by Mas Nakagawa

The scanning pattern of TV cameras in the United States is made up of 525 lines (262½ odd-numbered and 262½ even-numbered lines). The beam completes the scanning of one *field* each time it scans 262½ lines. Two fields make up a complete television picture, called a *frame.* The electron beam moves with such extreme speed that it produces 30 complete frames in a second. This speed is fast enough so the television picture shows moving objects smoothly.

Each of the three vidicon tubes converts its particular primary color to a video signal by means of the scanning process. Wires carry the signals to electronic circuits in the camera that *amplify* (strengthen) them. The three signals then go to the *encoder.*

Encoding the color signals. At the encoder, the three video signals are combined with other signals to produce a compatible color signal. The first step in this process involves combining the three video signals into two color-coded signals and a black-and-white signal. The two color-coded signals are called *chrominance signals* and the black-and-white signal is called a *lumi-*

nance signal. A circuit in the encoder, called the *matrix,* performs this function.

Another circuit in the encoder, the *adder,* combines the chrominance and luminance signals and, in the process, adds a *color burst* and a *synchronization signal.* The color burst enables a color TV set to separate the color information in the chrominance signals. This information, along with the luminance signal, produces a full-color picture on the TV screen. The synchronization signal locks the receiving set into the same scanning pattern as that used by the camera.

Telecine (pronounced *TEHL uh SIHN ee*) is equipment that transfers motion pictures or slides into TV signals. Telecine uses a combination of film and slide projectors and a single television camera to create such signals. A typical telecine unit, often called a *film chain,* consists of two motion-picture projectors, a slide projector, a *multiplexer,* and a telecine camera. The *multiplexer* is a system of mirrors that directs the images from film or slides into the telecine camera. The camera then converts these images into video signals.

How color television is received

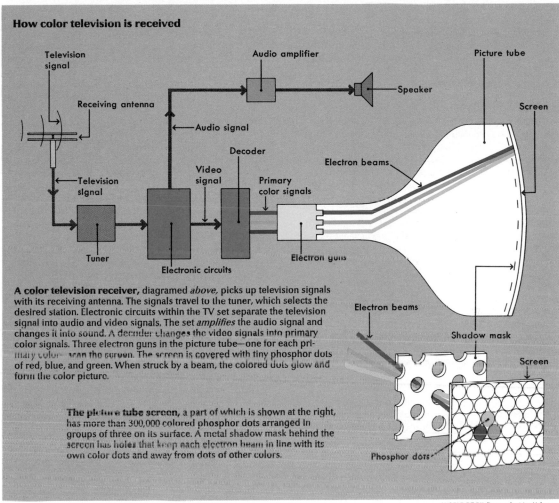

A **color television receiver,** diagramed *above,* picks up television signals with its receiving antenna. The signals travel to the tuner, which selects the desired station. Electronic circuits within the TV set separate the television signal into audio and video signals. The set *amplifies* the audio signal and changes it into sound. A decoder changes the video signals into primary color signals. Three electron guns in the picture tube—one for each primary color—scan the screen. The screen is covered with tiny phosphor dots of red, blue, and green. When struck by a beam, the colored dots glow and form the color picture.

The picture tube screen, a part of which is shown at the right, has more than 300,000 colored phosphor dots arranged in groups of three on its surface. A metal shadow mask behind the screen has holes that keep each electron beam in line with its own color dots and away from dots of other colors.

Videotape recording stores television pictures and sound as magnetic impulses on tape. The video signals are usually recorded as *diagonal* (slanted) tracks in the center of the tape, and sound and control signals are recorded along the tape's edge. Unlike film, which must be developed before showing, a videotape can be played back immediately.

Character generators produce writing and simple pictures directly on a television screen without the use of a camera. The generator works like a small computer. It can create, store, and animate letters and simple pictures of various sizes and colors.

Transmitting television signals

Most television signals are broadcast through the air. Engineers at a television station use a device called a transmitter to produce a TV signal from separate audio and video signals. The signal is then carried by wire to an antenna and broadcast. The signal is called an *electromagnetic wave.* Such waves can travel through the air at the speed of light, about 186,282 miles (299,792 kilo-

meters) per second. But the signal can be received clearly only up to a distance of about 150 miles (241 kilometers). To send TV signals farther, other means of transmitting must be used. These include coaxial cable and fiber optic cable, microwaves, and satellites.

Broadcasting. Before a television signal is broadcast, the transmitter boosts its *frequency* (rate of vibration). A television signal needs a high frequency to carry the picture information through the air. The transmitter amplifies the signal so it has enough power to reach a large area.

The transmitter increases the frequency of both the video and audio signals by a process called *modulation.* High-frequency electromagnetic waves, called *carrier waves,* are first generated by the transmitter. The transmitter uses the video signal to vary the *amplitude* (strength) of the carrier waves to produce the video part of the TV signal. This process is called *amplitude modulation* (AM). The video signal is then amplified to a power of 1,000 to 100,000 watts.

The transmitter uses the audio signals to modulate

another carrier wave, which becomes the audio part of the television signal. This process, called *frequency modulation* (FM), shifts the frequency of this carrier wave slightly. The transmitter then combines the modulated video and audio carrier waves to form the television signal.

A wire called the *transmission line* carries the television signal to the transmitting antenna, which releases the signal into the air. Television stations erect their antennas on high buildings or towers so the signal can reach as far as possible. The maximum range of most TV signals is from 75 to 150 miles (121 to 241 kilometers).

Television stations in the same area transmit on different frequencies so their signals do not interfere with one another. The group of frequencies over which one station broadcasts is known as a *channel.*

A total of 68 channels are available for television broadcasting in the United States. These channels are divided into two groups. Channels numbered 2 through 13 are called *very high frequency* (VHF) channels. VHF refers to signals with a frequency between either *54 megahertz* (54,000,000 vibrations per second) and 72 megahertz, 76 and 88 megahertz, or 174 and 216 megahertz. Channels numbered 14 through 69 are called *ultrahigh frequency* (UHF) channels. UHF signals have a frequency between 470 and 806 megahertz.

Coaxial cable and fiber optic cable are used to carry television signals for long distances or to areas that have difficulty receiving signals. The television networks often send programs to their affiliated stations throughout the country through coaxial cables. The affiliates then broadcast the programs to their viewers. Cable television systems use coaxial or fiber optic cables to carry signals to the homes of persons who subscribe to the service. See **Coaxial cable; Fiber optics.**

Microwaves are electromagnetic waves, similar to television signals. Tall relay towers spaced about 30 miles (48 kilometers) apart across the country carry programs from the networks to affiliate stations on these waves. Equipment in a tower automatically receives, amplifies, and then retransmits the microwave signal to the next tower. The affiliate stations change the microwave signals back into TV signals.

Satellites carry television signals between stations where cables or microwave towers cannot be built. For example, satellites relay signals across oceans. Satellites work like relay towers in space. They receive coded TV signals from a special earth station, amplify them, and send them on to another earth station. The two stations may be thousands of miles or kilometers apart.

Receiving television signals

The television signal from a transmitter is fed into a home television set through a *receiving antenna* or *aerial.* The set uses the signal to make copies of the pictures and sounds from the televised scene. In reproducing the television program, a TV set uses a tuner, amplifiers and separators, and a picture tube.

Receiving antenna. A good antenna collects a strong enough television signal for the receiver to produce a picture. A simple *dipole* (rabbit ear) antenna picks up a strong enough signal within a few miles or

kilometers of the transmitter. At greater distances, a more elaborate antenna mounted on the roof may be needed. The best reception results when the antenna is pointed toward the desired station. Some antennas can be rotated by remote control to align them with widely separated stations.

Tuner. Signals from the antenna are fed into the set's tuner. The tuner selects only the signal from the station the viewer wants to receive. It shuts out all others. Most TV sets have two tuning devices. One device selects the VHF channels, 2 through 13, and the other device selects the UHF channels, 14 through 69.

Amplifiers and separators. From the tuner, the television signal goes to a group of complicated electronic circuits in the set. These circuits amplify the signal and separate the audio and video portions of it. The audio signals are changed into sound waves by the speaker. The video signals go to the *picture tube,* or *kinescope,* where they re-create the picture.

A color set has circuits that use the color burst to separate the video signal into the two chrominance signals and the luminance signal. Another group of circuits, called the *decoder* or *matrix,* transforms these signals into red, blue, and green signals that duplicate the signals from the three camera tubes.

The picture tube transforms the video signals into patterns of light that duplicate the scene in front of the camera. One end of the picture tube is rectangular and nearly flat. This end forms the screen of the television set. Inside the set, the picture tube tapers to a narrow neck. The neck of a color picture tube holds three electron guns—one each for the red, blue, and green signals. A black-and-white tube has only one electron gun.

Each electron gun in a color picture tube shoots a separate beam of electrons at the screen. Each beam scans the screen just as the beam in each camera tube scanned its target. The synchronization signal, which is a part of the video signal, ensures that the picture tube's scanning pattern follows exactly the pattern used by the camera. The beams must be in step with each other in order to produce a picture.

The screen of most color tubes is coated with more than 300,000 tiny phosphor dots. The dots are grouped in triangular arrangements of three dots each—one red, one blue, and one green. These dots glow with their respective color when struck by an electron beam. A metal plate perforated with thousands of tiny holes lies about $\frac{1}{2}$ inch (13 millimeters) behind the screen of a color tube. This plate is called the *shadow mask.* Its holes keep the beams from hitting any color dots but their own.

The amount of light given off by the dots depends on the strength of the beam at the instant it strikes them. Since the strength of the beam is controlled by the video signal from the camera, the dots are bright where the scene is bright and dark where the scene is dark. When the television set shows a color program, the three colored dots blend together in the viewer's mind to produce all the colors in the original scene (see **Eye** [How we see]). The dots appear to produce only differing amounts of white light when showing a black-and-white program.

The Federal Communications Commission (FCC) regulates television—and also radio—broadcasting in the United States. An agency of the federal government, the FCC issues broadcasting licenses to stations and assigns frequencies on which the stations must broadcast. These regulations are needed to maintain order in the airwaves. If anyone who wanted to were allowed to broadcast and use any frequency, signals would interfere with each other and make broadcasting impossible.

The FCC also sets standards for broadcasters. The agency cannot censor programs, but it has the power to take away, or refuse to renew, a station's license if the station violates the standards too much. The FCC expects stations to avoid obscenity and pornography in their programs. The agency requires stations to provide public services and programs designed to meet the needs of their local communities. Another FCC standard requires television broadcasters to give equal time to all legally qualified candidates for public office. In addition, the FCC, along with the Federal Trade Commission (FTC), evaluates truthfulness in television advertising. Until 1987, the FCC insisted that stations permit oppos-

ing viewpoints to be heard when dealing with controversial subjects. That year, the FCC abolished the so-called Fairness Doctrine.

Congress can also regulate broadcasting. For example, it passed a law prohibiting cigarette advertising on television. The law was based on the government's conclusion that cigarette smoking is harmful to health. In 1973, Congress called for a change in the *blackout* policy of the National Football League (NFL). Under this policy, NFL games were not televised in areas where they were played. Congress ruled that games could not be blacked out if all the seats offered were sold 72 hours before game time. The law expired in 1975, but the NFL agreed to continue the policy.

Broadcasters and regulations. Broadcasters generally oppose government regulations. They say regulations that affect programming interfere with their rights to freedom of expression. Most members of Congress disagree, as do many citizens' groups. They claim that because the airwaves are public property, the government must create regulations that serve the public's interest.

Television in other lands

Television broadcasting developed more slowly in other parts of the world than it did in the United States. But beginning about 1960, a television boom began in many nations. Today, there are about 215 million sets in the United States, and nearly 500 million sets elsewhere. Television now reaches almost every part of the world that has electricity. Programming varies from one country to another. But in all nations, the programs provide entertainment, cultural enrichment, education, news, and special events.

The government of every country regulates broadcasters in some ways. But in general, democratic governments—such as those of Australia, Canada, Great Britain, and New Zealand—allow broadcasters much freedom. Communist and other undemocratic governments tightly control broadcasting. They use TV as a tool to promote the government's beliefs and policies.

In the United States, most television programs are paid for by the sale of advertising time. In some other countries, however, the government finances television broadcasts by means of taxes, fees paid by the owners of television sets, or commercial advertising.

Canada. The Canadian people own about 12 million television sets, or 474 for every 1,000 people. The only major country with a higher ratio is the United States, which has 887 television sets per 1,000 people.

The Canadian Broadcasting Company (CBC), a publicly owned corporation, operates about 100 television stations in Canada. About 300 stations are privately owned. Canada also has about 505 cable TV systems serving over 4 million subscribers. Most Canadian people speak English, but many speak French. Therefore, some Canadian stations broadcast in English, and some in French. Most Canadians live in the southern part of the country, close to the United States. As a result, many of Canada's TV viewers can also tune in U.S. programs.

Europe. World War II and the economic problems that followed it slowed the development of television in Europe. But since the 1960's, TV has grown at a rapid rate in Western Europe. Five West European nations each have over 10 million sets and rank among the world's leading nations in the number of sets. They are Great Britain, West Germany, France, Italy, and Spain.

The Soviet Union, the largest country in Eastern Europe, has about 88 million TV sets, or about 310 sets per 1,000 people. It ranks second to the United States in the total number of sets. Poland and East Germany follow the Soviet Union in the total number of sets among the Communist nations of Eastern Europe.

Asia. China has about 68 million television sets—about twice as many as any other Asian nation. Japan ranks fourth, after the United States, the Soviet Union, and China, in total number of sets. Television is still a small industry in much of Asia. But the industry is growing rapidly in some countries, including Israel, Kuwait, Malaysia, and the Philippines.

Africa has fewer television sets than any other continent except Antarctica. In Nigeria, the African nation with the most TV's, there are only 20 sets for every 1,000 people. About half of the African nations have fewer than 5 sets per 1,000 people.

Australia and New Zealand have thriving television industries. Australia has about 400 TV sets per 1,000 people, and New Zealand has about 300 per 1,000 people, high figures by world standards. But these countries have small populations, and neither one ranks among the leaders in total sets.

Latin America. Television is more widespread in Latin America than in Africa and much of Asia. But Latin America lags behind Europe and North America. Brazil has more television sets than any other Latin-American country. Mexico and Argentina rank next.

Early development. Many scientists contributed to the development of television, and no one person can be called its inventor. Television became possible in the 1800's, when people learned how to send communication signals through the air as electromagnetic waves. This process is called *radio communication.* For details on its development, see **Radio** (History).

The first radio operators sent code signals through the air. By the early 1900's, operators could transmit words. Meanwhile, many scientists had conducted experiments involving the transmission of pictures. As early as 1884, Paul Gottlieb Nipkow of Germany had invented a scanning device that sent pictures short distances. His system worked mechanically, rather than electronically as television does. In 1922, Philo T. Farnsworth of the United States developed an electronic scanning system. In 1926, John Logie Baird, a Scottish engineer, invented a television system that used infrared rays to take pictures in the dark. Vladimir K. Zworykin, a Russian-born American scientist, invented the *iconoscope* and the *kinescope* in 1923. The iconoscope was the first television camera tube suitable for broadcasting. The kinescope is the picture tube used in TV receivers. Zworykin demonstrated the first completely electronic, practical television system in 1929.

The start of broadcasting. Many experimental telecasts took place in the late 1920's and the 1930's. The British Broadcasting Corporation (BBC) in Great Britain, and CBS and NBC in the United States were leaders in experimental telecasts. World War II and the economic problems that followed the war caused Great Britain to abandon TV experiments. The United States moved far ahead of the rest of the world in TV broadcasting.

In 1936, the Radio Corporation of America (later RCA Corporation), which owned NBC, installed television receivers in 150 homes in the New York City area. NBC's New York station began experimental telecasts to these homes. A cartoon of Felix the Cat was its first program. NBC established the first regular TV broadcasts in the United States in 1939. The United States entered World

Important dates in television

1800's People learned how to send communication signals through the air as electromagnetic waves.
1929 Vladimir K. Zworykin demonstrated the first practical television system.
1939 NBC made the first regular telecasts in the U.S.
1946 A television boom began. It resulted in making television part of most American homes by 1960.
1951 The first coast-to-coast telecast showed President Harry S. Truman opening the Japanese Peace Treaty Conference in San Francisco.
1953 Color telecasts began.
1954 Television covered the Army-McCarthy hearings.
1960 Presidential candidates John F. Kennedy and Richard M. Nixon debated on TV before a nationwide audience.
1965 *Early Bird*, the first commercial communications satellite, relayed TV programs between the U.S. and Europe.
1967 Congress established the Corporation for Public Broadcasting to help finance public TV stations.
1969 TV viewers saw the first moon landing by astronauts.
1973 Television covered the Watergate hearings.
1974 A nationwide television audience watched President Richard M. Nixon's resignation speech.
1977 The miniseries became a popular TV format with the broadcast of "Roots" over eight nights.
1979 The U.S. House of Representatives began allowing TV broadcasts of daily sessions.
1985 A worldwide audience estimated at 1½ billion people—probably the largest audience in TV history—watched the "Live Aid" concert, a benefit for famine victims in Africa.

War II in 1941. Television broadcasting was suspended until after the war ended in 1945.

The television boom. The national networks—all based in New York City—resumed broadcasting shortly after the war. At first, their telecasts reached only the Eastern Seaboard between Boston and Washington, D.C. But by 1951, they extended coast-to-coast. TV stations sprang up throughout the country. Entertainment, news, special events, and sports contests replaced the simple, largely experimental, prewar shows.

The American people became fascinated with the idea of having so wide a range of visual events available in their homes. The demand for TV sets became enor-

RCA

An experimental telecast of the late 1920's showed a statue of the comic strip character Felix the Cat.

Culver

Milton Berle became the first big TV star. His zany comedy show drew a huge audience during the early 1950's.

CBS

"The $64,000 Question" was one of several television quiz shows of the 1950's that offered valuable prizes to contestants.

TV coverage of the Army-McCarthy hearings of 1954 brought a major historical event into millions of homes. The dramatic hearings included charges by U.S. Senator Joseph R. McCarthy, *right,* that the Army was "coddling Communists."

mous. In 1945, there were probably fewer than 10,000 sets in the country. This figure soared to about 6 million in 1950, and to almost 60 million by 1960. In TV's early days, people who had no set often visited friends who had one just to watch television. Also, many stores placed television sets in windows, and crowds gathered on the sidewalk to watch programs.

Early programs. Milton Berle became the first television entertainer to attract a huge, nationwide audience. His show, "The Texaco Star Theater," was filled with zany comedy routines. It ran from 1948 to 1956, and often attracted 80 per cent of the TV audience. "I Love Lucy," starring Lucille Ball, went on the air in 1951. This early situation comedy also attracted a huge following. Westerns such as "Gunsmoke" and "Have Gun Will Travel" became popular in the mid-1950's. Other popular early entertainment programs included Ed Sullivan's variety show, "The Toast of the Town"; professional wrestling matches; and quiz shows offering prizes of thousands of dollars. A major scandal hit TV in 1959, when it was

learned that quiz show producers had helped some contestants answer questions.

Coverage of special events did much to widen TV's appeal. In 1951, TV broadcast the Kefauver hearings, in which U.S. Senator Estes Kefauver and his Senate committee questioned alleged mobsters about organized crime. In 1954, TV covered the Army-McCarthy hearings. Viewers watched spellbound as Senator Joseph R. McCarthy accused the U.S. Army of "coddling Communists," and the Army charged McCarthy's staff with "improper conduct." The hearings reached a dramatic climax when Joseph Welch, a soft-spoken lawyer for the Army, and the outspoken McCarthy clashed in an emotion-filled argument (see **McCarthy, Joseph R.**).

The 1960's opened with a milestone of television broadcasting. During the fall of 1960, presidential candidates John F. Kennedy and Richard M. Nixon faced each other and the nation in a series of TV debates. It marked the first time presidential candidates debated on TV. Many people believe the debates made an important contribution to Kennedy's victory in the 1960 election.

Popular entertainment remained the major part of television's coverage during the 1960's. But TV also reflected the turmoil that marked American life. President Kennedy was assassinated on Nov. 22, 1963. Two days later, millions of viewers witnessed one of the most startling scenes ever shown on television. In full view of TV cameras, Jack Ruby shot and killed accused Kennedy assassin Lee Harvey Oswald as policemen were taking Oswald from one jail to another.

From the mid-1960's on, television regularly brought viewers battle scenes from the Vietnam War. The conflict was sometimes called "the first war to be fought on television." Television viewers also watched war protesters demonstrate—sometimes violently—and witnessed bitter debates over the war policy of the United States. Civil rights protests by blacks and other minority groups also became part of TV coverage.

Technological advances made during the 1950's and 1960's helped improve the physical quality of tele-

Vietnam War scenes first came on TV in the 1960's. They brought the horrors of war into millions of homes.

"All in the Family" became a hit show during the 1970's. The program combined comedy with the treatment of controversial topics.

Rock videos, which became popular in the 1980's, featured such performers as singer Michael Jackson, *above.*

casts. In TV's early days, most screens measured 7 or 10 inches (18 or 25 centimeters) diagonally. Today, 21- and 25-inch (53- and 64-centimeter) screens are common. In the 1970's, manufacturers introduced *projection television systems,* which beam programs onto a screen as large as 7 feet (2 meters) measured diagonally. Other TV sets, small enough to fit in a pocket, have screens measuring about 3 inches (7.6 centimeters) diagonally.

Improvements in broadcasting and receiving equipment provide much clearer pictures than were available in the past. In early days, all programs were telecast in black and white. Color television began in 1953. Today most programs are telecast in color. More than 90 per cent of American households have a color set.

At first, most telecasts were live productions or programs made from film. The film took time to develop. Also, the equipment and techniques used produced pictures and sounds of poor quality. Videotaping of programs began in the mid-1950's, and became a major production method. Videotapes can be played back immediately after taping. They produce good quality pictures and sounds, and allow flexibility in program scheduling. Later, scientists developed equipment and techniques that improved the quality of filmed shows.

Early Bird, the first commercial communications satellite, was launched in 1965. Satellites made worldwide television broadcasting possible. Today, viewers can see such events as the Olympic Games as they happen.

Recent developments. Television continues to be primarily a source of entertainment. But it also carries on its role of providing coverage of important events. For example, in 1973 networks canceled many regular programs to cover the Watergate hearings—a U.S. Senate investigation of charges of illegal campaign practices during the 1972 election (see **Watergate**).

Through the years, television broadcasters generally avoided controversial themes, such as abortion, alcoholism, divorce, drug abuse, political satire, racial prejudice, and sex. They feared that such themes would result in a loss of viewers. However, beginning in the late 1960's, broadcasters found that they could deal with controversial themes and still attract large audiences. The comedy show "Laugh-In" included many jokes about sex and much political satire, and it became the top-rated show of the late 1960's. "All in the Family," a situation comedy satirizing prejudice, gained top ratings in the early 1970's. "M*A*S*H," a popular situation comedy of the 1970's and early 1980's, satirized war. Such dramatic programs as "Little House on the Prairie" and "The Waltons" dealt with many moral and ethical problems. The success of such shows encouraged broadcasters to cover a wide range of topics.

Many people believe, however, that television has gone too far in its presentation of controversial themes. The amount of violence and sex on TV has especially drawn a great deal of criticism.

In the late 1970's, broadcasters began to present an increasing number of made-for-TV movies, serialized dramas called *miniseries,* and other special programs. The most popular such presentation was "Roots," an eight-part drama tracing the history of an American black family from slavery to freedom.

During the 1980's, videocassette recorders skyrocketed in popularity. Many viewers enjoyed renting pretaped movies and watching them at home. Also in the 1980's, satellites gained importance in distributing television programs to cable systems and broadcasting stations. Some viewers received satellite signals at home with a huge antenna called a *dish* because of its shape. As a result, some cable systems began to "scramble" their signals to prevent dish owners from picking up their programs without paying for the service. For a fee, they provided decoding devices to dish owners who wished to receive their programs.

By the late 1980's, *high definition television* (HDTV), which has extremely sharp picture and sound quality, appeared to offer the next advance in television technology. U.S. firms hoped to begin selling HDTV's in the early 1990's.   George Comstock

Study aids

Related articles in *World Book* include:

Biographies

Baird, John L.	De Forest, Lee	Murrow,
Carson, Johnny	Farnsworth, Philo T.	Edward R.
Cosby, Bill	Hertz, Heinrich R.	Zworykin,
Cronkite, Walter	McLuhan, Marshall	Vladimir K.

Equipment and physical principles

Antenna	Electron gun	Tape recorder
Audio-visual	Electronics	Transistor
materials (Television)	Frequency modulation	Ultrahigh frequency waves
Automatic frequency control	Image orthicon	Very high frequency waves
Coaxial cable	Microphone	Videodisc
Communications satellite	Microwave	Videotape recorder
Electromagnetism	Radio	
	Speaker	
	Static	

Other related articles

Advertising	Corporation for Public Broadcasting
British Broadcasting Corporation	Federal Communications Commission
Canadian Broadcasting Corporation	Medicine (with pictures)
Copyright	

Outline

I. Uses of television
  A. Commercial television
  B. Public television
  C. Subscription television
  D. Closed-circuit television
  E. Video entertainment systems
  F. Televised information services

II. Producing television programs
  A. Planning and preparation
  B. Putting a show on the air
  C. Other production methods

III. The television industry
  A. The national networks
  B. Commercial stations
  C. Public stations
  D. Cable television systems
  E. Related industries
  F. Television awards
  G. Careers

IV. Effects of television
  A. Effects on leisure time
  B. Effects on learning
  C. Effects on institutions
  D. Effects on young people

V. **How television works**
   A. Creating television signals
   B. Transmitting television signals
   C. Receiving television signals
VI. **Government regulations**
VII. **Television in other lands**
   A. Canada   C. Asia   E. Australia and
   B. Europe   D. Africa   New Zealand
                                  F. Latin America

VIII. **History**

Questions

What is the role of electromagnetic waves in television?
What is a dissolve? A super? A wipe?
How did Vladimir K. Zworykin help develop TV?
Who was the first major television entertainer?
What career opportunities are available in television?
What are the methods of transmitting TV programs?
What are some criticisms of television?
What are some specialized uses of television?

Reading and Study Guide

See *Television* in the Research Guide/Index, Volume 22, for a *Reading and Study Guide.*

Additional resources

Level I
Cheney, Glenn A. *Television in American Society.* Watts, 1983.
Greenfield, Jeff. *Television: The First Fifty Years.* Abrams, 1977.
Lachenbruch, David. *Television.* Raintree, 1985. Discusses the history, mechanics, and modern applications of television.

Level II
Barnouw, Erik. *Tube of Plenty: The Evolution of American Television.* Rev. ed. Oxford, 1982.
Levinson, Richard, and Link, William. *Stay Tuned: An Inside Look at the Making of Prime-Time Television.* St. Martin's, 1981.
Utz, Peter. *Video User's Handbook.* 2nd ed. Prentice-Hall, 1982. An amateur's guide to TV electronics.

Telex. See Telegraph (Faster and better service).
Telford, Thomas (1757-1834), a noted Scottish civil engineer, devised improved methods of road construction. The Telford method of using large flat stones for road foundations is named after him. Telford engineered bridges, canals, harbors, docks, and waterways. He built the Menai Strait suspension bridge which connects the Island of Anglesey and the mainland of Gwynedd County in Wales, and the Ellesmere Canal, connecting the Mersey, Severn, and Dee rivers in England. He also engineered the Caledonian Canal in Scotland. He was born in Eskdale, Scotland.   Robert W. Abbett

Tell, William, was a legendary hero of Switzerland. His story, though not verified by history, represents the spirit of the Swiss movement for independence from the Austrian Habsburgs in the 1300's. According to legend, Tell was a man of tremendous strength and the most skilled marksman in the whole *canton* (state) of Uri. The Austrian bailiff, Gessler, had ordered all Swiss to bow to a hat he had set up on a pole in the main square of Altdorf. When Tell refused to bow, he was arrested. Gessler knew of Tell's skill with the crossbow and promised to let him go free if Tell could shoot an apple off his own son's head. Tell hit the apple and then said if he had hurt his son, he would have killed Gessler. Gessler had him seized and chained.

While Tell was being taken across a lake in Gessler's boat, a storm broke. Gessler ordered Tell untied to help steer the boat safely to the shore. Tell escaped to the

Detail of a woodcut (Granger Collection)

William Tell was a legendary Swiss patriot. The character is known for shooting an apple off his son's head with a crossbow.

shore and shot an arrow through the tyrant's heart. This act led to a revolt by the Swiss, in which Tell played a leading role. This tale is the basis of Johann Friedrich Schiller's drama *William Tell* (1804). Gioacchino Rossini wrote the opera *William Tell* (1829).   Arthur M. Selvi

Teller. See Bank (Careers in banking).

Teller, Edward (1908-   ), an outstanding American atomic scientist, is often called the *father of the hydrogen bomb.* His work in nuclear physics led to the development of the H-bomb in 1952.

Teller was born on Jan. 15, 1908, in Budapest, Hungary. He received his doctor's degree in physics from the University of Leipzig, Germany, in 1932. He joined the wartime atomic bomb project in 1941. He worked with the Los Alamos (N. Mex.) National Laboratory until 1952. Then he joined what is now the Lawrence Livermore Laboratory, a research facility at Livermore, Calif., dedicated to designing nuclear weapons. Teller also served as professor of physics at the University of California from 1953 to 1975. He was director of the Livermore laboratory from 1958 to 1960 and associate director from 1972 to 1975.   Ira M. Freeman

Tellurium, *teh LUR ee uhm,* is a semimetallic chemical element. Pure tellurium is usually obtained as a byproduct of copper refining. In nature, the element most often occurs in combination with such metals as copper, gold, lead, mercury, and silver. Tellurium is important in the manufacture of certain alloys and in semiconductor research. It serves as a curing agent for rubber and as a catalyst in petroleum refining. It is also used to color glass and ceramics. Tellurium has the chemical symbol Te. Its atomic number is 52, and its atomic weight is 127.60. The crystalline form of tellurium melts at 449.8° C and boils at 989.9° C. Tellurium was discovered in 1782 by the Austrian chemist Franz Müller von Reichenstein.
      Marianna A. Busch

Telstar. See Communications satellite (History); Telephone (Telephone improvements).

Tempera. See Painting (Tempera; pictures).

Temperance Union, Woman's Christian. See Woman's Christian Temperance Union.

Temperature is how hot or cold something is as measured on a particular scale. The concept of temperature is closely related to the flow of heat between two connected objects of different temperatures. Heat always flows from the hotter object to the cooler one.

Instruments that measure temperature are called *thermometers.* A scale marked on the thermometer indicates each level of "hotness." The two most common temperature scales used on thermometers are *Fahrenheit* and *Celsius.* Temperatures on all scales are based on the *International Practical Temperature Scale of 1968* (see **Thermometer** [Temperature scales]).

Scientists often speak of *thermodynamic temperature,* a fundamental physical quality completely independent of the properties of a substance. The unit of thermodynamic temperature is the *kelvin,* indicated by *K.* This unit was agreed upon by scientists from many nations. All temperatures are based on their position above or below 273.16 K, a temperature called the *triple point of water.* At this temperature, water, ice, and water vapor all exist together. In common practice, a temperature is actually expressed in terms of its difference from the melting point of ice. Under one atmosphere of pressure, ice melts at a temperature 0.01 K lower than the triple point of water (see **Atmosphere**).

Temperature does not seem to have an upper limit. Scientists believe the temperature at the center of the sun is about 15 million degrees Celsius (27 million degrees Fahrenheit). However, the interior of any star larger than the sun is probably much hotter. On the other hand, there does seem to be a lower limit to temperature. This theoretical limit, called *absolute zero,* has a value of $-273.15°$ C or $-459.67°$ F. At this temperature, the molecules and atoms of a substance have the least possible energy.   Harmon H. Plumb

Related articles in *World Book* include:

Absolute zero	Climate	Heat	Sun (The
Air	Cryogenics	Melting point	sun's heat)
Boiling point	Freezing point	Pyrometry	Weather

Temperature, Body. Body temperature is a measurement of the heat in an animal's body. The body of an animal generates heat by burning food. But the animal also loses heat to—or gains heat from—its environment.

Birds and mammals, including human beings, are *warm-blooded animals.* Their body temperature almost always stays fairly constant, regardless of the temperature of their environment. The body of a warm-blooded animal balances the amount of heat it exchanges with the environment with the amount it produces by burning food. Nearly all other animals are *cold-blooded animals.* Their body cannot balance this heat exchange so accurately. As a result, their body temperature tends to vary with the temperature of their environment.

When taken orally, the average body temperature of a healthy, resting adult human being is 98.6° F. (37.0° C). Physicians consider a temperature within 1° F. (0.5° C) of this figure normal. A higher temperature may indicate a fever (see **Fever**). A lower temperature may be a sign of old age or of certain illnesses.

Warm-blooded animals make various physical and behavioral adjustments to regulate their heat exchange with the environment. In cold surroundings, they increase the production of body heat and decrease the amount of heat lost to the environment. In hot surroundings, they do just the opposite. A part of the brain called the *hypothalamus* controls these adjustments. Certain nerves in the skin and deep within the body send messages to the hypothalamus. The hypothalamus compares the temperatures of these areas with that of the brain. It triggers the necessary responses by nerves and glands to keep a normal body temperature.

Even with the various controls, the body temperature of a warm-blooded animal does not remain entirely constant. It changes slightly throughout the day. In a healthy human being, for example, the body temperature is lowest in the morning and then rises until late afternoon. It falls again during sleep. Strenuous activity can raise the body temperature. In cold surroundings, the temperature of the skin and limbs may drop far below the temperature deep within the body.

Each species of warm-blooded animal has its own normal body temperature. Each species also functions best when the temperature of its surroundings remains within a certain range. This range varies greatly from species to species, depending on such factors as the thickness of fur and the rate at which its body burns food. Some warm-blooded animals hibernate. During hibernation, their body temperature drops below normal. In fact, the body temperature of most hibernators drops almost to the temperature of their environment. See **Hibernation.**

Cold-blooded animals lack the precise temperature regulation abilities that characterize warm-blooded creatures. However, many cold-blooded animals can exercise some physical and behavioral control over body temperature. Reptiles, for example, can alter the amount of heat their body absorbs from the sun by changing their skin color. Moreover, many reptiles alternately warm themselves in the sun and cool themselves in the shade, thereby maintaining a fairly constant body temperature throughout the day.   James Edward Heath

See also **Warm-blooded animal; Cold-blooded animal; Hypothermia.**

Temperature-humidity index, also called THI, is a scale of values that serves as an estimate of how comfortable people feel in hot weather. The values of the scale depend on air temperature and *relative humidity*— that is, the actual moisture in the air compared to the most moisture the air could hold. They do not include the effects of wind and sunshine. However, the scale does help to indicate how some people may be affected when high temperature and humidity are combined.

The higher a temperature-humidity index reading is, the more uncomfortable people are. Most people will feel comfortable with a temperature-humidity index below 75. Half or more will feel uncomfortable when the index is between 75 and 80. When the index reaches 80, most people will be uncomfortable. Serious health hazards, such as tiredness, dizziness, heatstroke, and heat exhaustion, can occur when the index reaches 85 or more (see **Sunstroke**).

The temperature-humidity index was developed in 1959 by the United States Weather Bureau (now the National Weather Service). It was originally called the *discomfort index.*   David D. Houghton

Tempering is a process of hardening glass and metals, especially steel. Steel can be made very hard and strong by tempering. First, the steel is heated to a high temperature. Next, it is *quenched* (cooled rapidly) by plunging it into water, oil, or other liquid. Then, it is heated again to a temperature lower than that used before quenching it, and is allowed to cool slowly.

Tempering changes the internal structure of the steel. Different uses of steel require different properties, such as varying degrees of hardness, strength, and toughness. To obtain those properties, the structure of steel is changed by tempering it at various temperatures.

Thin films of iron oxide form on steel that is being heated in the tempering process. Those films have different colors, known as *temper colors,* which vary with the tempering temperature.

Glass is tempered in a somewhat similar way. It Is heated until it becomes almost soft, then chilled by blasts of air or by plunging it into oil or other liquids. Glass which has been tempered may be up to five times as hard as ordinary glass. It may be used to hammer nails into wood. A sheet of tempered glass can be struck by a hammer without breaking.   Joel S. Hirschhorn

See also **Annealing.**

Templars, Knights. See Knights Templars.

Temple is a house of worship. The word *temple* usually refers to Buddhist, Confucian, Hindu, Taoist, and ancient Near Eastern and European places of worship. In Christianity, it is generally used only for certain Mormon buildings. In Judaism, Reform houses of worship are commonly called temples, but Conservative or Orthodox ones are usually called synagogues. The word rarely refers to an Islamic house of prayer, called a *mosque,* or to a Shinto shrine.

Most temples are built to honor God, a god, or many gods. Many of these buildings are considered the homes of gods. Worship at temples often involves traditional ceremonies and may include sacrifices. Many people visit temples as individuals or in small groups, rather than as members of large congregations.

Temples range from small, simple huts to huge, elaborately decorated buildings. Many contain a picture or statue of the honored god. In a typical temple, the holi-

Milt and Joan Mann

A temple in Nara, Japan, called the Hall of the Great Buddha is the world's largest wooden building. A bronze statue of Buddha more than 50 feet (15 meters) high stands inside the temple.

est image or object of worship is in a central room. To reach this area, worshipers may have to pass through a series of gates or doors that symbolize a spiritual journey. In many temples, only the clergy may enter the room. An altar stands inside or in front of many temples.

Certain temples stand on sacred sites. For example, some were built where people believed that miracles or divine revelations occurred. King Solomon of ancient Israel erected a temple in Jerusalem at the place where God was believed to have stopped a plague. This temple, which served as the center of the Hebrew religion, is considered the most important one in the history of Western religion. Temples also have been built where people thought sacred forces flowed together in the most favorable way. Hindus and Taoists use an elaborate procedure involving the interpretation of divine signs to choose the most favorable location for a temple.

The temperature-humidity index

The chart at the right shows how the combination of temperature and relative humidity affects people. As the temperature and relative humidity rise, the index increases. When the temperature is below 75° F. (24° C), most people are comfortable even if the relative humidity is high (blue). An index of 85 or over—when the temperature and relative humidity are both high (dark yellow)—can cause serious health problems.

Air temperature (°F.)	Relative humidity (per cent) 10 20 30 40 50 60 70 80 90 100	How people are affected
	Temperature-humidity index	
65	62 62 62 63 63 64 64 65 65 65	Most are comfortable
70	64 65 65 66 67 67 68 69 69 70	
75	67 67 68 69 70 71 72 73 74 75	Half or more are uncomfortable
80	69 70 72 73 74 75 76 78 79 80	Most are uncomfortable
85	72 73 75 76 78 79 80 82 84 85	
90	74 76 77 79 81 83 85 87 88 90	
95	77 79 81 83 85 87 89 91 93 95	
100	79 82 84 86 89 91 93 95	Danger
105	82 84 87 90 92 95	
110	84 87 90 93 96	

The design of numerous temples is symbolic. In eastern Asia, for example, a number of Buddhist temples are towerlike buildings called *pagodas,* which have many stories. The stories represent the levels of the earth and heaven, or the various spiritual goals that a Buddhist must achieve to gain salvation.   Robert S. Ellwood, Jr.

Related articles in *World Book* include:

Abu Simbel, Temples of	Indonesia (picture)	Pantheon
Architecture (pictures)	Japan (pictures)	Parthenon
Greece, Ancient (pictures)	Mormons (picture: The Mormon Temple)	Sculpture (picture: Kailasanatha Temple)
	Pagoda	

Temple, Henry John. See Palmerston, Viscount.

Temple, Shirley (1928-   ), was the most popular child motion-picture star of the 1930's. She made her movie debut at the age of 3 and became a star in the 1934 film musical *Stand Up and Cheer.* Shirley Temple made about 25 movies during the 1930's, including *Little Miss Marker* (1934), *The Little Colonel* (1935), *The Littlest Rebel* (1935), and *Dimples* (1936). She played teen-age roles in many movies during the 1940's, but these films were not as popular as her earlier pictures.

Shirley Temple retired from motion pictures in 1949. She married Charles A. Black in 1950. In 1969, President Richard M. Nixon appointed her a U.S. representative to the United Nations General Assembly. In 1974, President Gerald R. Ford named her the U.S. ambassador to Ghana. In 1976 and 1977, she was chief of protocol in the Department of State, the first woman to hold that post. She was born in Santa Monica, Calif.   Gerald Bordman

Scene from *Just Around the Corner* (1938); Bettmann Archive

Shirley Temple, a child motion-picture star of the 1930's, appeared in several films with dancer Bill Robinson, *above.*

Temple of Artemis. See Seven Wonders of the Ancient World.

Temple of Solomon. See Solomon; Jerusalem (History).

Temple of Zeus. See Olympia.

Temples of Abu Simbel. See Abu Simbel, Temples of.

Ten Commandments are Biblical rules that state the basic religious and moral ideals of Judaism and Christianity. The commandments are also called the *Decalogue,* from two Greek words meaning *ten words.*

The Ten Commandments appear twice in the Old Testament—in Exodus 20:2-17 and Deuteronomy 5:6-21. The two versions differ slightly. The first group of commandments deals with duties toward God, and the second group concerns relations among persons. Judaism and various Christian denominations number them differently. The list below reflects the numbering most commonly used in English-language references to the Ten Commandments:

1. I am the Lord thy God. Thou shalt have no other gods before me.
2. Thou shalt not make unto thee any graven image, or any likeness of any thing that is in heaven above, or that is in the earth beneath, or that is in the water under the earth. . . .
3. Thou shalt not take the name of the Lord thy God in vain. . . .
4. Remember the sabbath day, to keep it holy. . . .
5. Honor thy father and thy mother.
6. Thou shalt not kill.
7. Thou shalt not commit adultery.
8. Thou shalt not steal.
9. Thou shalt not bear false witness against thy neighbor.
10. Thou shalt not covet thy neighbor's house, thou shalt not covet thy neighbor's wife, nor his manservant, nor his maidservant, nor his ox, nor his ass, nor any thing that is thy neighbor's.

In the Old Testament, the Ten Commandments appear as conditions of a *covenant* (agreement) between God and His chosen people, the Israelites. The Old Testament tells that the finger of God wrote the commandments on two stone tablets given to Moses on Mount Sinai. As Moses came down from the mountain, he saw the Israelites worshiping a golden calf. Enraged at the idol worship, Moses smashed the tablets. But at God's command, he carved the commandments into other stone tablets. The Israelites kept the tablets in a wooden ark (see Ark of the Covenant).

By the A.D. 200's, Christian teachers believed that God had stamped the commandments on the conscience of every human being, even before the laws were engraved on stone. Beginning in the A.D. 400's, everyone who became a Christian memorized the Ten Commandments. By the A.D. 800's, the laws had become a central part of church education. By the 1200's, the leading Christian scholars regarded them as principles of a universal natural law that governed human conduct. Protestant reformers of the 1500's included the Decalogue in their catechisms.   William A. Clebsch

See also **Moses.**

Tenant, in law, is a person who holds or possesses lands or buildings by any kind of title. In popular speech, a tenant is a person who has the right to occupy and use lands or buildings which belong to another person, known as the landlord. A *lease* (written agreement), signed by both owner and tenant, states the terms and period of time.

The relation of landlord and tenant had its origin in the feudal system of the Middle Ages. Some of the feudal obligations still survive in the present laws. The rights and duties of the *lessor* (landlord) and *lessee* (tenant) are generally defined in detail by the written lease. The terms of a lease bind the heirs, successors, or administrators of both tenant and landlord.

A *tenant at will* occupies property for an indefinite period, which may be ended at any time by either landlord or tenant. A tenant at will is entitled to a notice of removal. If there are crops growing on the land, the tenant may harvest them when they are ready.

A *tenant at sufferance* occupies property without the express consent of the owner or after the term of possession has expired. The tenant may be put off the property at any time by the landlord.   William Tucker Dean

See also **Eviction; Joint tenancy; Lease.**

Tenant farming is a common farming practice that involves raising crops and livestock on rented land. Farmers who rent the land they farm are called *tenants.* People who own the land are called *landlords.*

There are two basic types of leases used in tenant farming—(1) cash leases and (2) share leases. Under a cash lease, the tenant pays a fixed amount of rent. The landlord provides land and buildings, and the tenant pays all other production costs. Under a share lease, the tenant and landlord agree to share both the crop and the cost of producing it. For example, in a 50-50 share lease, the landlord may supply land and buildings and pay for half the necessary seed, fertilizer, and chemicals. The tenant furnishes labor, machinery, and the rest of the seed, fertilizer, and chemicals. The tenant and landlord each receive half the crop.   Warren F. Lee

See also **Asia** (Farm organization); **United States, History of the** (1870-1916 [The war-torn South]).

Tendon, *TEHN duhn,* also called *sinew, SIHN yoo,* is a strong white cord that attaches muscles to bones. Muscles move bones by pulling on tendons. A tendon is a bundle of many tough fibers . Some tendons are round, others long or flat. One end of a tendon arises from the end of a muscle. The other end is woven into the substance of a bone. The tendon may slide up and down inside a sheath of fibrous tissue, as an arm moves in a coat sleeve. The tendon and sheath are held in place by connective tissue called *ligaments.* A cut tendon can be *sutured* (sewed) together. Healing may take six weeks or more.   Bruce Reider

See also **Achilles' tendon; Hand; Human body** (picture: Ligaments and tendons); **Muscle** (Skeletal muscles).

Tenement is a term usually used to describe a crowded, decaying apartment building. But a tenement may refer to any dwelling that is rented to two or more families or tenants. A tenement can be an old residential building that has been divided to house low-income families at low standards. It can also be a new structure built for many low-income families—each in its own small apartment. An urban district that houses numerous tenements is often called a *slum.*

Tenements are strong income-producing properties. Each family may pay a low rent, but many people are crowded in small, poorly maintained areas. Thus, the rent per unit of area is often greater than that paid by middle-income people in larger and better apartments.

Historians believe tenements have existed since ancient times, when the Romans built them to house the poor and the slaves. Most tenements in the United States were built to house poor immigrants. Today, housing standards prevent construction of new tenements. But such standards do not prevent old buildings from being converted into tenements.   Oscar Newman

Teng Hsiao-p'ing. See Deng Xiaoping.

Tennent, Gilbert (1703-1764), was a colonial American religious leader. During the early 1700's, he played a major role in the Protestant religious movement called the Great Awakening. An important aspect of the Great Awakening was *revivalism,* an emotional approach to religion that emphasized individual religious experience rather than church doctrines.

As a Presbyterian minister in New Jersey from 1726 to 1743, Tennent became active in the Great Awakening. In 1739, he gave a sermon, "The Danger of an Unconverted Ministry," in which he attacked ministers who favored established church doctrines and opposed revivalism. The publication of this sermon in 1740 contributed to a split in the Presbyterian Church in America in 1741. Tennent eventually became more willing to compromise with his critics. He helped reunite the church in 1758.

Tennent was born in County Armagh, now a district in Northern Ireland. He came to America when he was about 15. His father, William Tennent, was also a well-known minister.   Sandra Sizer Frankiel

See also **Great Awakening; Tennent, William.**

Tennent, William (1673-1746), was an important Presbyterian minister in colonial America. In 1726, he became pastor of a church in Neshaminy, Pa., near Philadelphia. There he founded the Log College to train Presbyterian ministers according to the principles of *revivalism* (see **Revivalism**). Some church leaders' disapproval of revivalist training at the college contributed to a split in 1741 within the Presbyterian Church of America. Tennent ran the college until his death. The college closed, but its supporters later founded the College of New Jersey (now Princeton University).

Tennent was probably born in Ireland. He immigrated to America about 1718. His four sons—Gilbert, William, Jr., John, and Charles—also became Presbyterian ministers (see **Tennent, Gilbert**).   Sandra Sizer Frankiel

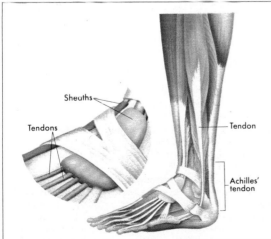

WORLD BOOK illustration by Leonard Morgan
Tendons connect bones and muscles, thus allowing the muscles to move the bones. Leg tendons include the Achilles' tendon at the heel. Foot tendons are covered by protective sheaths.

Sheaths
Tendons
Tendon
Achilles' tendon

Tennessee Tourist Development

The Great Smoky Mountains stretch across eastern Tennessee in the state's *Blue Ridge* region. The thickly forested mountains create a dense, humid atmosphere that looks like a smoky mist.

Tennessee *The Volunteer State*

Tennessee is one of the states that link the North and the South of the United States. Life in West and Middle Tennessee resembles life in the Deep South. East Tennessee is similar to parts of the North. Even during the Civil War, Tennessee loyalties were divided between the North and the South. Tennessee was the last Confederate state to leave the Union, and the first to return.

The lonely pioneer, wearing a coonskin cap and carrying a trusty flintlock rifle, is a symbol of Tennessee's great past. But a better symbol of the present and future is the nuclear physicist working in an Oak Ridge laboratory, or the technician who controls the robots on the assembly line of a motor vehicle manufacturing plant. Although some Tennesseans today work on farms, most are employed by business offices and factories.

Tennessee stretches all the way from North Carolina, one of the easternmost states, to Arkansas, one of the westernmost states in the South. At its eastern boundaries, Tennessee starts high in the Blue Ridge Mountains. The land becomes lower toward the west until it reaches the banks of the Mississippi River. Wholesale and retail trade and other service industries play a leading role in Tennessee's economy. Manufacturing is also an important source of income and jobs. Tennessee's fertile soil and abundant mineral deposits make it a rich agricultural and mining state.

The contributors of this article are Charles S. Aiken, Professor of Geography at the University of Tennessee at Knoxville, and C. Edward Skeen, Professor of History at Memphis State University.

Indians once roamed Tennessee's mountains and forests. Early explorers passed through the region, and people from Europe fought to decide who would own it. Pioneers crossed the mountains to settle in the wilderness. It was the pioneers who brought with them the spirit of independence and daring that has become a part of Tennessee's history. The pioneers formed their own governments in this region before any other independent governments existed in North America. In 1796, Tennessee became the 16th state in the Union. Such Tennesseans as John Sevier in the Revolutionary War, Andrew Jackson in the War of 1812, and Alvin C. York in World War I established a Tennessee military tradition of honor and bravery.

More Civil War battles were fought in Tennessee than in any other state except Virginia. Three Presidents of the United States—Andrew Jackson, James K. Polk, and Andrew Johnson—all distinguished themselves in Tennessee. Two great heroes of the Texas Revolution, Davy Crockett and Sam Houston, grew up in Tennessee, and served its people.

The name *Tennessee* comes from *Tanasie,* the name of a Cherokee village in the region. Tennessee is sometimes called the *Big Bend State,* because of the sudden bend in the Tennessee River that makes it flow through the state twice. However, Tennessee is usually called the *Volunteer State* because of its outstanding military traditions.

Nashville is the capital of Tennessee. Memphis is the state's largest city.

Bob Mooty, Shostal

Douglas Dam, on the French Broad River near Sevierville, is part of the Tennessee Valley Authority (TVA) system. It provides electric power and flood control and forms Douglas Lake.

David R. Frazier

Vanderbilt University, in Nashville, was founded in 1873. It was named after Cornelius Vanderbilt, an American business-man who donated $1 million to build and support the school.

Interesting facts about Tennessee

WORLD BOOK illustrations by Kevin Chadwick

The first guide dog for the blind in the United States was "Buddy," a female German shepherd that lived in Nash-ville with her owner, Morris Frank. Buddy was trained in Switzerland in 1928 by The Seeing Eye, the first organiza-tion to train guide dogs.

The State of Franklin occu-pied a section in northeastern Tennessee between the Cum-berland Mountains and the Blue Ridge Mountains from 1784 to 1788. Named after Benjamin Franklin, the state had its own constitution and governor beginning in 1785. North Carolina controlled the area in 1788 and 1789. Franklin became a part of Tennessee when it became a state in 1796.

First guide dog

Two brothers competed in a gubernatorial election for the first time on Nov. 2, 1886, in Tennessee. Robert Love Taylor, the Democratic candidate, defeated his brother Alfred Alexander Taylor, the Republican candidate, in the event known to Tennes-seans as the "War of the Roses."

Kingston was the capital of Tennessee for one day. In 1807, the state legislature voted to meet in Kingston on September 21. Its business, to discuss a treaty with the Cherokee Indians, was completed that day.

The first publications wholly devoted to abolish-ing slavery were written by Elihu Embree, a slaveholder living in Tennessee, a slave state. Embree called for the abolition of slavery in a weekly newspaper published in 1819 in Jonesborough, and later in the monthly magazine *The Emancipator,* published from April 30 to Oct. 31, 1820.

The Emancipator

David R. Frazier

Downtown Nashville in-cludes the Tennessee State Capitol, *left foreground.* Nash-ville is the second largest city in Tennessee in population. It is one of the nation's largest cities in area, covering 530 square miles (1,373 square kil-ometers).

Tennessee in brief

Symbols of Tennessee

The state flag, adopted in 1905, has three stars representing East, Middle, and West Tennessee. On the state seal, a plow, a sheaf of wheat, and a cotton stalk symbolize the importance of agriculture. The riverboat represents commerce. The date 1796 is the year the first state constitution was approved. The current state seal came into use during the term of Governor William G. Brownlow, who served from 1865 to 1869.

State flag

State seal

Tennessee (brown) ranks 34th in size among all the states and 8th in size among the Southern States (yellow).

General information

Statehood: June 1, 1796, the 16th state.
State abbreviations: Tenn. (traditional); TN (postal).
State motto: *Agriculture and Commerce.*
State songs: "Rocky Top." Words and music by Boudleaux and Felice Bryant. "The Tennessee Waltz." Words by Pee Wee King; music by Redd Stewart.

The State Capitol is in Nashville, Tennessee's capital since 1826. Earlier capitals were Knoxville (1792-1812, 1817), Nashville (1812-1817), and Murfreesboro (1818-1826).

Land and climate

Area: 42,114 sq. mi. (109,152 km²), including 989 sq. mi. (2,561 km²) of inland water.
Elevation: *Highest*—Clingmans Dome, 6,643 ft. (2,025 m) above sea level. *Lowest*—182 ft. (55 m) above sea level in Shelby County.
Record high temperature: 113° F. (45° C) at Perryville on July 29 and Aug. 9, 1930.
Record low temperature: −32° F. (−36° C) at Mountain City on Dec. 30, 1917.
Average July temperature: 78° F. (26° C).
Average January temperature: 38° F. (3° C).
Average yearly precipitation: 52 in. (132 cm).

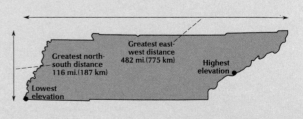

Greatest east-west distance 482 mi.(775 km)

Greatest north-south distance 116 mi.(187 km)

Highest elevation

Lowest elevation

Important dates

Charles Charleville set up a French trading post near the present site of Nashville.

Tennessee became the 16th state on June 1.

| 1540 | 1714 | 1780 | 1796 |

Hernando de Soto of Spain led the first white expedition into the Tennessee region.

Nashville settlers signed the Cumberland Compact.

State bird
Mockingbird

State flower
Iris

State tree
Tulip poplar

People

Population: 4,591,120 (1980 census)
Rank among the states: 17th
Density: 109 persons per sq. mi. (42 per km²), U.S. average 67 per sq. mi. (26 per km²)
Distribution: 60 per cent urban, 40 per cent rural

Largest cities in Tennessee

Memphis	646,174
Nashville	455,651
Knoxville	175,045
Chattanooga	169,728
Clarksville	54,777
Jackson	49,131

Source: U.S. Bureau of the Census.

Population trend

Millions

*All figures are census figures except 1985, which is an estimate.

Source: U.S. Bureau of the Census.

Year	Population*
1985	4,762,000
1980	4,591,120
1970	3,926,018
1960	3,567,089
1950	3,291,718
1940	2,915,841
1930	2,616,556
1920	2,337,885
1910	2,184,789
1900	2,020,616
1890	1,767,518
1880	1,542,359
1870	1,258,520
1860	1,109,801
1850	1,002,717
1840	829,210
1830	681,904
1820	422,823
1810	261,727
1800	105,602
1790	35,691

Economy

Chief products

Agriculture: beef cattle, milk, soybeans, tobacco, greenhouse and nursery products.
Manufacturing: chemicals, food products, nonelectrical machinery, electrical machinery and equipment, transportation equipment, clothing, fabricated metal products.
Mining: coal, stone, zinc.

Gross state product

Value of goods and services produced in 1985, $64,848,000,000. *Services* include community, business, and personal services; finance; government; trade; and transportation, communication, and utilities. *Industry* includes construction, manufacturing, and mining. *Agriculture* includes agriculture, fishing, and forestry.

Sources: U.S. Department of Agriculture and U.S. Department of Commerce.

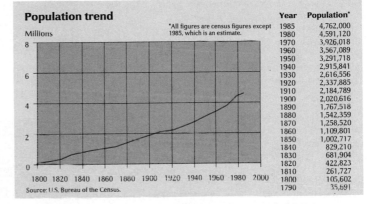

Industry 31%

Services 68%

Agriculture 1%

Government

State government

Governor: 4-year term
State senators: 33; 4-year terms
State representatives: 99; 2-year terms
Counties: 95

Federal government

United States senators: 2
United States representatives: 9
Electoral votes: 11

Sources of information

Tourism: Department of Tourist Development, 320 Sixth Avenue North, Nashville, TN 37219
Economy: Department of Economic and Community Development, Industrial Research Division, 320 Sixth Avenue North, Nashville, TN 37219
Government: Information Center, Tennessee State Capitol, Nashville, TN 37219
History: Department of Tourist Development, 320 Sixth Avenue North, Nashville, TN 37219

A yellow fever epidemic killed about 5,200 of the 19,600 people in Memphis.

The federal government began building the atomic energy center at Oak Ridge.

1878   **1933** **1942**   **1982**

The U.S. Congress created the Tennessee Valley Authority.

A world's fair was held in Knoxville.

Population. The 1980 United States census reported that Tennessee had 4,591,120 people. The population had increased 17 per cent over the 1970 census figure, 3,926,018. The U.S. Bureau of the Census estimated that by 1985 the state's population had reached about 4,762,000.

About three-fifths of the people of Tennessee live in urban areas and about two-fifths live in rural areas. About 66 out of 100 live in the seven metropolitan areas that lie chiefly within the state (see **Metropolitan area**). These metropolitan areas are, in order of population, Nashville; Memphis; Knoxville; Johnson City-Kingsport-Bristol, Va.; Chattanooga; Clarksville-Hopkinsville, Ky.; and Jackson. For the population of these areas, see the *Index* to the political map of Tennessee.

Memphis is the state's largest city, followed by Nashville, Knoxville, and Chattanooga. Each of these cities has over 100,000 people. The fifth largest city is Clarksville with about 55,000 people. Eight other cities in the state have populations of 25,000 or more. See the articles on Tennessee cities listed in the *Related articles* at the end of this article.

About 99 out of every 100 Tennesseans were born in the United States. About 16 out of every 100 Tennesseans are blacks, a lower percentage than in most southern states. About 45 per cent of the blacks in Tennessee live in Shelby County. Memphis is the county seat of Shelby County.

Schools. Education in Tennessee began with privately owned schools, usually controlled by churches. Samuel Doak, a Presbyterian minister, started the first

Walking Horse Owners Association

The International Grand Championship Walking Horse Show features walking horses bred in middle Tennessee. More than 800 horses take part in the competition, held each August.

David R. Frazier

The Cumberland Museum and Science Center in Nashville has an art gallery, a planetarium, and exhibits on natural history. The earth pendulum, *above,* demonstrates that the earth turns.

Tennessee Tourist Development

The National Storytelling Festival takes place each October in Jonesborough. Master storytellers from the United States and many other countries spin tales before fascinated listeners.

Population density

West Tennessee, Middle Tennessee, and East Tennessee each have densely populated areas. Thinly populated areas separate the three regions.

Persons per sq. mi.		Persons per km²
More than 100		More than 40
50 to 100		20 to 40
25 to 50		10 to 20
Less than 25		Less than 10

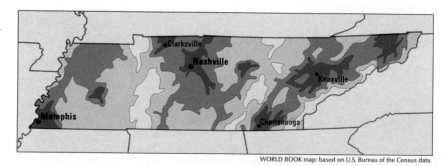

WORLD BOOK map; based on U.S. Bureau of the Census data.

school in about 1780. Public schools for children of the poor were established in the early 1800's. In 1873, free education was made available to all children in Tennessee.

The governor appoints a commissioner of education to a four-year term. The commissioner heads the state department of education and makes recommendations to the state board of education. The board is composed of 10 members appointed by the governor and confirmed by the General Assembly. Nine of the members represent the state's nine congressional districts and are appointed to nine-year terms. The remaining member is a student, who is appointed to a one-year term.

Children in Tennessee must attend school from ages 7 through 16. For the number of students and teachers in Tennessee, see **Education** (table).

Libraries. The state's first public library was opened in Nashville in 1813. Today, Tennessee has about 250 public libraries. The State Library and Archives in Nashville specializes in collections of Tennessee history, literature, and biography, and state and federal documents. The Vanderbilt University Library in Nashville and the University of Tennessee Library in Knoxville have the largest collections in the state.

Museums. The Tennessee State Museum in Nashville displays collections of the Tennessee Historical Society. The Cumberland Museum and Science Center in Nashville has an art gallery, a planetarium, and exhibits on natural history. The Museum of Appalachia is in Norris. It features exhibits on early American life. The Frank H. McClung Museum at the University of Tennessee at Knoxville displays Tennessee archaeological findings. The Memphis Pink Palace Museum has exhibits on the history of the mid-South. Other museums include the American Museum of Science and Energy in Oak Ridge and the Railroad Museum in Jackson.

Universities and colleges

Tennessee has 42 universities and colleges that grant bachelor's or advanced degrees and are accredited by the Southern Association of Colleges and Schools. Locations shown below refer to the schools' mailing addresses. For enrollments and further information, see **Universities and colleges** (table).

Name	Location	Name	Location
Austin Peay		Meharry Medical College	Nashville
State University	Clarksville	Memphis College of Art	Memphis
Belmont College	Nashville	Memphis State University	Memphis
Bethel College	McKenzie	Mid-America Baptist	
Bryan College	Dayton	Theological Seminary	Memphis
Carson-Newman College	Jefferson City	Mid-South Bible College	Memphis
Christian Brothers College	Memphis	Middle Tennessee	
Church of God School of Theology	Cleveland	State University	Murfreesboro
Cumberland University	Lebanon	Milligan College	Milligan College
David Lipscomb University	Nashville	Rhodes College	Memphis
East Tennessee		Scarritt Graduate School	Nashville
State University	Johnson City	South, University of the	Sewanee
Emmanuel School of Religion	Johnson City	Southern College	
Fisk University	Nashville	of Optometry	Memphis
Freed-Hardeman College	Henderson	Southern College of	
Harding Graduate		Seventh-Day Adventists	Collegedale
School of Religion	Memphis	Tennessee University of	Nashville
Johnson Bible College	Knoxville	Tennessee State University	
King College	Bristol	Tennessee Technological	
Lambuth College	Jackson	University	Cookeville
Lane College	Jackson	Tennessee Wesleyan College	Athens
Lee College	Cleveland	Trevecca Nazarene College	Nashville
LeMoyne-Owen College	Memphis	Tusculum College	Greeneville
Lincoln Memorial University	Harrogate	Union University	Jackson
Maryville College	Maryville	Vanderbilt University	Nashville

*For campuses and founding dates, see Universities and colleges (table).

David R. Frazier

The University of Tennessee has four campuses. The oldest and largest, *above foreground,* is in Knoxville. It was founded in 1794. The other campuses are in Chattanooga, Martin, and Memphis.

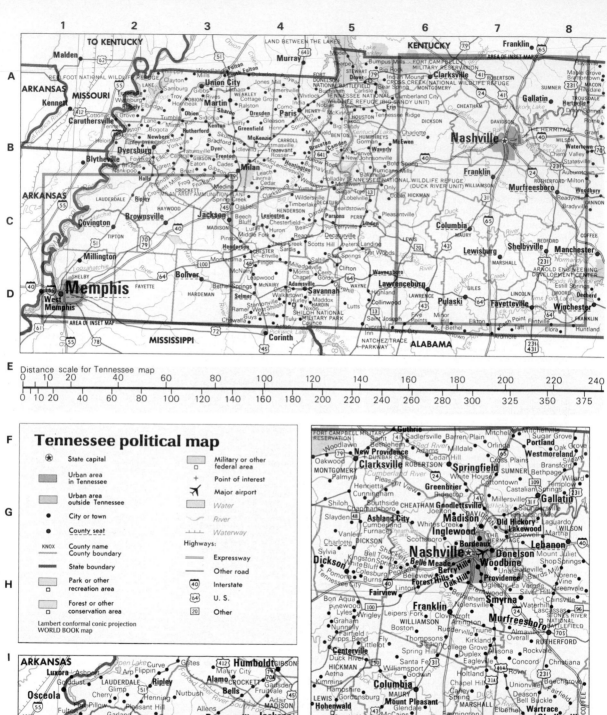
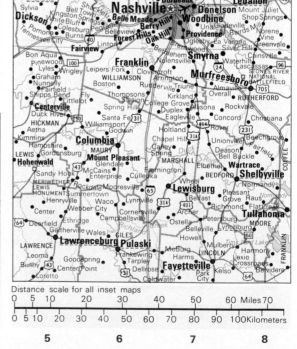

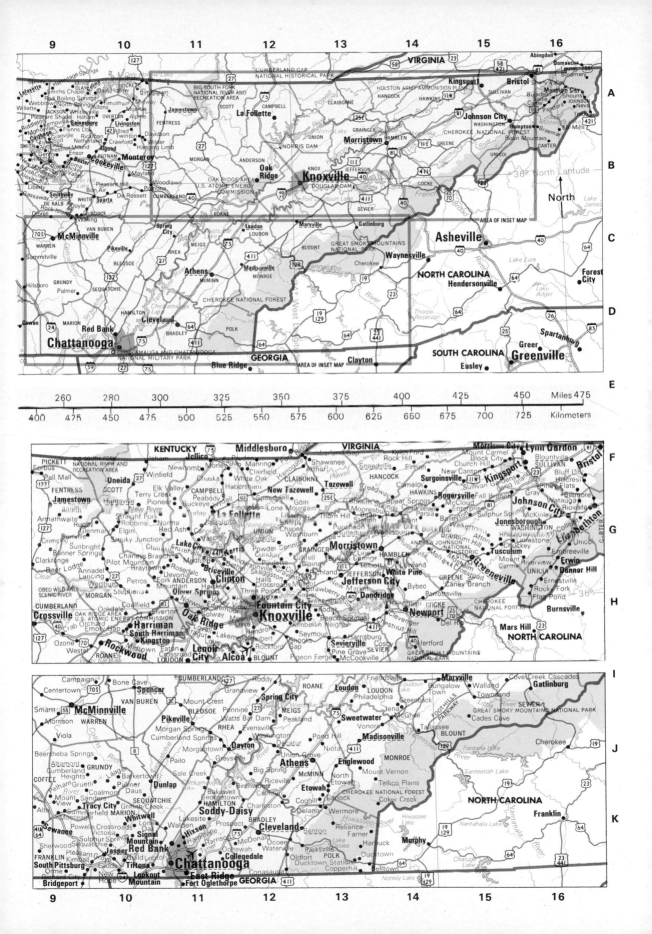

Tennessee map index

Joelton ..... G 6
John Sevier ..... H 12
Johnson City ..... 39,753. A 16
Jones Mill ..... A 4
Jonesborough ..... 2,829.°G 16
Joppa ..... G 13
Karns* ..... 1,173. B 12
Keeling ..... J 2
Kelso ..... K 8
Kempville ..... A 9
Kenton ..... 1,551. B 3
Kimball ..... 1,220. K 10
Kimberlin Heights ..... H 12
Kimmins ..... I 5
Kingsport ..... 32,027. A 15
Kingsport North* ..... A 15
Kingston ..... 4,441.°I 10
Kingston Springs ..... 1,017. H 6
Kirkland ..... I 7
Knoxville ..... 175,045.°B 12
Kodak ..... H 13
Kyles Ford ..... F 14
Laconia ..... K 3
Ladds ..... K 10
Lafayette ..... 3,808.°A 9
La Follette ..... 8,198. A 12
La Grange ..... 185. K 3
Lake City ..... 2,335. G 11
Lakeland ..... 612. K 2
Lakemont ..... I 12
Lakesite ..... 651. K 11
Lakewood ..... 2,325. G 7
Lancaster ..... B 9
Lancing ..... H 10
Lane ..... B 2
Lascassas ..... H 8
Latham ..... A 4
Laurel Bloomery ..... A 16
La Vergne ..... 5,495. H 7
Lavinia ..... B 4
Lawrenceburg ..... 10,184.°D 6
Leach ..... B 4
Leapwood ..... D 4
Lebanon ..... 11,872.°G 8
Leighton ..... J 4
Leipers Fork ..... H 6
Lenoir City ..... 5,446. I 11
Lenox ..... B 2
Leoma ..... K 5
Lewisburg ..... 8,760.°C 7
Lexie Crossroads ..... K 8
Lexington ..... 5,934.°C 4
Liberty ..... B 4
Liberty ..... 365. B 9
Liberty Hill ..... G 13
Limestone ..... G 15
Linden ..... 1,007.°C 5
Linton ..... H 6
Littlelot ..... I 5
Livingston ..... 3,372.°A 10
Lobelville ..... 993. C 5
Locke ..... K 1
Lone Mountain ..... G 13
Lone Oak ..... K 10
Long Island ..... F 16
Lookout Mountain ..... 1,886. K 11
Loretto ..... 1,612. K 5
Loudon ..... 3,943.°C 12
Louisville ..... I 11
Lovell ..... H 11
Lowland ..... G 14
Lupton City ..... K 11
Luray ..... C 4
Luttrell ..... 962. G 12
Lutts ..... D 5
Lyles ..... H 5
Lynchburg ..... 668.°K 8
Lynn Garden ..... 7,213. F 16
Lynnville ..... 383. J 6
Macon ..... K 2
Maddox ..... D 4
Madison ..... G 7
Madisonville ..... 2,884.°C 12
Malesus ..... J 4
Manchester ..... 7,250.°C 8
Manring ..... F 12
Mansfield ..... B 4
Maple Grove ..... A 8
Martha ..... G 8
Martin ..... 8,898. A 3
Maryville ..... 17,480.°C 12
Mascot ..... 2,203. H 12
Mason ..... 471. J 2
Mason Hall ..... B 3
Maury City ..... 989. I 3
Mayland ..... B 10
Maynardville ..... 924.°G 12
McBurg ..... K 7
McCains ..... J 6
McCloud ..... G 14
McCookville ..... I 13
McDonald ..... K 12
McEwen ..... 1,352. B 6
McGhee ..... J 14
McIllwain ..... B 5
McKenzie ..... 5,405. B 4
McKinley ..... G 16
McKinnon ..... A 5
McLemoresville ..... 311. B 4
McMinnville ..... 10,683.°C 9
McNairy ..... D 4
Medford ..... G 11
Medina ..... 687. C 3
Medon ..... 162. J 4
Memphis ..... 646,174.°D 1
Mercer ..... J 4
Michie ..... 530. D 4
Middle Fork ..... C 4
Middle Valley* ..... 11,420. D 10
Middleburg ..... K 4
Middleton ..... 596. K 4
Midtown ..... I 10
Midway ..... 2,754. A 10
Milan ..... 8,083. B 3
Milldale ..... F 7
Milledgeville ..... 392. D 4
Millersville ..... G 7
Milligan College ..... G 16
Millington ..... 20,236. D 1
Milton ..... B 8
Minor Hill ..... 564. D 6
Miston ..... B 2
Mitchell ..... F 7
Mitchellville ..... 209. F 7
Model ..... A 5
Mohawk Crossroad ..... G 14
Monoville ..... B 9
Monroe ..... A 10
Monteagle ..... 1,126. K 9
Monterey ..... 2,610. B 10
Montezuma ..... C 4
Mooresburg ..... G 14
Mooresville ..... J 6
Morgan Springs ..... J 11
Morgantown ..... J 11
Morley ..... F 11
Morris Chapel ..... D 4
Morrison ..... 587. J 9
Morrison City ..... 2,032. F 15
Morristown ..... 19,683.°B 14
Moscow ..... 499. K 3
Mosheim ..... 1,539. G 15
Moss ..... A 9
Mount Carmel ..... 3,764. F 15
Mount Carmel ..... G 16
Mount Crest ..... I 11
Mount Juliet ..... 2,879. G 7
Mount Olive ..... H 12
Mount Pleasant ..... 3,375. J 6
Mount Vernon ..... J 13
Mount View ..... K 9
Mountain City ..... 2,125.°A 16
Mulberry ..... K 8
Munford ..... 2,326. J 1
Murfreesboro ..... 32,845.°B 8
Nankipoo ..... B 2
Nashville ..... 455,651.°B 7
Netherland ..... B 10
Neubert ..... H 12
Neva ..... A 16
New Canton ..... F 15
New Hope ..... 681. K 10
New Johnsonville ..... 1,824. B 5
New Line ..... G 13
New Market ..... 1,216. H 13
New Middleton ..... B 9
New Providence ..... F 5
New River ..... G 10
New Tazewell ..... 1,677. F 13
Newbern ..... 2,794. B 3
Newcomb ..... F 11
Newport ..... 7,580.°H 14
Niota ..... 765. J 13
Nixon ..... D 4
Nobles ..... A 5
Nolensville ..... H 7
Norene ..... H 8
Norma ..... G 10
Normandy ..... 118. J 8
Norris ..... 1,374. G 11
North Etowah ..... K 13
North Springs ..... A 9
Norwood ..... H 11
Nunnelly ..... I 5
Nutbush ..... I 3
Oak Grove ..... 3,103. F 8
Oak Hill ..... 4,609. H 7
Oak Ridge ..... 27,662. B 12
Oakdale ..... 323. H 10
Oakfield ..... C 3
Oakland ..... 472. K 2
Oakwood ..... F 5
Obion ..... 1,282. A 3
Ocoee ..... K 12
Oglesby ..... H 7
Old Hickory ..... G 7
Oldfort ..... K 12
Olivehill ..... D 5
Oliver Springs ..... 3,659. H 11
Oneida ..... 3,494. F 10
Only ..... B 5
Ooltewah ..... K 11
Orebank* ..... 1,284. A 15
Orlinda ..... 382. F 7
Orme ..... 181. K 9
Orysa ..... J 2
Ostella ..... J 7
Overall ..... I 8
Ozone ..... I 9
Pailo ..... J 11
Pall Mall ..... F 9
Palmer ..... 1,027. D 9
Palmersville ..... A 4
Palmyra ..... G 5
Pandora ..... A 16
Paris ..... 10,728.°A 4
Park City ..... K 7
Parksville ..... K 13
Parrottsville ..... 118. H 14
Parsons ..... 2,422. C 5
Paulette ..... G 12
Peabody ..... G 11
Peakland ..... J 12
Pegram ..... 1,081. H 6
Pelham ..... K 9
Pennine ..... I 12
Perryville ..... C 5
Persia ..... G 14
Peters Landing ..... C 5
Petersburg ..... 681. J 7
Petros ..... 1,286. H 10
Philadelphia ..... 507. I 13
Phillippy ..... A 2
Pigeon Forge ..... 1,822. I 13
Pikeville ..... 2,085.°C 10
Pilot Mountain ..... G 10
Pine Crest* ..... 3,992. B 16
Pine Grove ..... I 13
Pinewood ..... H 5
Piney Flats ..... F 16
Pinson ..... C 3
Pioneer ..... G 11
Piperton ..... 746. K 2
Pittman Center* ..... 488. C 13
Pleasant Grove ..... K 10
Pleasant Grove ..... J 7
Pleasant Hill ..... 371. J 2
Pleasant Hill ..... B 10
Pleasant Shade ..... A 9
Pleasant View ..... G 6
Pleasantville ..... C 5
Pocahontas ..... K 4
Pomona ..... H 5
Pomona ..... B 10
Portland ..... 4,030. F 7
Powder Springs ..... G 12
Powell ..... 7,220. H 12
Powells Crossroads ..... 918. K 10
Prospect ..... K 12
Providence ..... H 7
Pruden ..... F 12
Pulaski ..... 7,184.°D 7
Puncheon Camp ..... G 13
Puryear ..... 624. A 4
Quebeck ..... C 9
Ralston ..... A 3
Ramer ..... 429. D 4
Raus ..... J 6
Readyville ..... C 8
Reagan ..... C 4
Red Ash ..... G 11
Red Bank ..... 13,129. D 10
Red Boiling Springs ..... 1,173. A 9
Reedtown ..... H 14
Reliance ..... K 13
Rheatown ..... G 15
Riceville ..... J 12
Richard City ..... 87. K 9
Richland ..... H 13
Richmond ..... J 7
Rickman ..... B 10
Riddleton ..... A 9
Ridgely ..... 1,932. A 2
Ridgeside* ..... 417. D 10
Ridgetop ..... 1,225. G 7
Riovista ..... G 16
Ripley ..... 6,366.°C 2
Riverview ..... H 16
Rives ..... 386. A 3
Roan Mountain ..... 1,108. B 16
Robbins ..... G 10
Rock Hill ..... F 14
Rock Island ..... C 9
Rockdale ..... J 5
Rockford ..... 567. I 12
Rockvale ..... I 7
Rockwood ..... 5,767. I 10
Rocky Fork ..... H 16
Roddy ..... J 12
Ro Ellen ..... B 2
Rogers Springs ..... K 4
Rogersville ..... 4,368.°G 14
Rome ..... B 8
Rosedale ..... H 11
Rosemark ..... K 2
Rosser ..... B 4
Rossville ..... 379. K 2
Routon ..... B 4
Rover ..... I 7
Rudderville ..... I 7
Rugby ..... G 10
Russellville ..... 1,069. G 14
Rutherford ..... 1,378. B 3
Rutledge ..... 1,058.°G 13
Sadie ..... A 16
Sadlersville ..... F 6
St. Bethlehem ..... F 5
St. Clair ..... G 14
St. Joseph ..... 897. D 6
Sale Creek ..... J 11
Saltillo ..... 434. D 4
Samburg ..... 465. A 2
Sanders ..... K 9
Sandy Hook ..... J 5
Santa Fe ..... I 6
Sardis ..... 301. C 4
Saulsbury ..... 156. K 3
Saundersville ..... G 7
Savannah ..... 6,992.°D 4
Scotts Hill ..... 668. C 4
Scottsboro ..... G 6
Selmer ..... 3,979.°D 4
Sequatchie ..... K 10
Sevierville ..... 4,556.°I 13
Sewanee ..... 2,298. K 9
Seymour ..... H 12
Shacklett ..... H 6
Shady Valley ..... A 16
Sharon ..... 1,134. B 3
Sharps Chapel ..... G 12
Shawanee, see Harrogate [-Shawnee]
Shelbyville ..... 13,530.°C 8
Sherwood ..... K 9
Shiloh ..... G 5
Shipps Bend ..... I 5
Shooks Gap ..... H 12
Shop Springs ..... H 8
Shouns ..... A 16
Sidonia ..... B 3
Signal Mountain ..... 5,818. K 10
Silerton ..... 100. K 4
Siloam ..... F 8
Silver Hill ..... H 8
Skaggston ..... H 12
Skullbone ..... B 3
Slayden ..... 69. G 5
Smartt ..... I 9
Smiths Chapel ..... A 9
Smithville ..... 3,839.°B 9
Smoky Junction ..... G 11
Smyrna ..... 8,839. H 7
Sneedville ..... 1,110.°F 14
Soddy-Daisy ..... 8,388. K 11
Solway ..... H 11
Somerville ..... 2,264.°K 3
South Carthage* ..... 1,004. B 9
South Cleveland* ..... 4,460. D 11
South Clinton* ..... 1,671. B 12
South Fulton ..... 2,735. A 3
South Harriman ..... H 10
South Pittsburg ..... 3,636. K 9
Southside ..... G 5
Sparta ..... 4,864.°B 10
Spear Springs ..... G 14
Speedwell ..... G 12
Spencer ..... 1,126.°I 10
Spivey ..... A 9
Spring City ..... 1,951. C 11
Spring Creek ..... C 4
Spring Hill ..... 989. I 6
Springfield ..... 10,814.°F 6
Springville ..... B 5
Spurgeon* ..... 3,006. A 15
Stainville ..... G 11
Stanton ..... 540. J 3
Stantonville ..... 271. D 4
Statesville ..... B 8
Stephens ..... H 10
Stewart ..... A 5
Strawberry Plains ..... H 13
Sugar Grove ..... F 8
Sugar Tree ..... C 5
Sullivan Gardens ..... 2,513. F 15
Sulphur Springs ..... K 10
Sulphur Springs ..... G 16
Summerfield ..... K 9
Summertown ..... J 5
Summit* ..... 8,307. D 10
Summitville ..... C 9
Sunbright ..... G 10
Surgoinsville ..... 1,536. F 15
Sweetwater ..... 4,725. J 13
Sylvia ..... G 5
Taft ..... D 7
Talbott ..... G 13
Tallassee ..... J 14
Tarpley ..... K 6
Tatumville ..... B 3
Tazewell ..... 2,090.°F 13
Tellico Plains ..... 698. J 14
Templow ..... G 8
Tennemo ..... B 2
Tennessee City ..... H 5
Tennessee Ridge ..... 1,325. A 5
Terry Creek ..... G 11
Tharpe ..... A 5
Thompsons Station ..... I 6
Thorn Hill ..... G 13
Three Points ..... H 12
Tiftona ..... K 10
Tigrett ..... B 3
Timberlake ..... C 4
Timothy ..... A 10
Tipton ..... J 1
Tiptonville ..... 2,438.°A 2
Toone ..... 355. K 4
Townsend ..... 351. I 15
Tracy City ..... 1,444. K 9
Trade ..... A 16
Treadway ..... G 14
Trenton ..... 4,601.°B 3
Trentville ..... H 12
Trezevant ..... 921. B 4
Trimble ..... 722. B 3
Triune ..... I 7
Troy ..... 1,093. A 3
Tullahoma ..... 15,800. J 8
Tulu ..... D 4
Turley ..... G 11
Tusculum ..... 1,242. G 15
Twinton ..... B 10
Tyner ..... K 11
Una ..... H 7
Unicoi ..... G 16
Union City ..... 10,436.°A 3
Union Grove ..... J 12
Unionville ..... I 7
Vale ..... B 4
Valley Forge* ..... 2,180. B 16
Valley View ..... H 11
Vanleer ..... 401. G 5
Vasper ..... G 11
Victoria ..... K 10
Vildo ..... K 3
Vine ..... H 8
Viola ..... 149. J 9
Vonore ..... 528. J 14
Waco ..... J 6
Walden ..... 1,293. K 11
Wales ..... K 6
Walkertown ..... D 4
Walkertown ..... G 15
Walland ..... I 15
Walling ..... C 9
Walnut Hill* ..... 3,288. A 15
Wartburg ..... 761.°H 10
Wartrace ..... 540. J 8
Washburn ..... G 13
Washington ..... J 12
Watauga ..... 376. G 16
Waterhill ..... H 8
Watertown ..... 1,300. B 8
Waterville ..... K 12
Watts Bar Dam ..... J 12
Waverly ..... 4,405.°B 5
Waynesboro ..... 2,109.°D 5
Webber City ..... J 5
Webbtown ..... A 9
West Johnson City* ..... 2,182. A 15
West Shiloh ..... D 4
Westel ..... I 10
Westmoreland ..... 1,754. F 8
Westport ..... B 4
Wetmore ..... K 13
Wheel ..... J 7
White Bluff ..... 2,055. H 5
White House ..... 2,225. F 7
White Oak ..... C 11
White Pine ..... 1,900. H 14
Whites Creek ..... G 7
Whitesburg ..... G 14
Whiteville ..... 1,270. K 3
Whitleyville ..... A 9
Whitlock ..... A 4
Whitwell ..... 1,783. K 10
Wilder ..... B 10
Wildersville ..... C 4
Wildwood Lake* ..... 1,642. D 11
Willard ..... G 8
Willette ..... A 9
Williamsport ..... I 6
Williston ..... 395. K 3
Winchester ..... 5,821.°D 8
Winfield ..... F 10
Woodbine ..... H 7
Woodbury ..... 2,160.°C 8
Woodland Mills ..... 526. A 3
Woodlawn ..... F 5
Woodlawn ..... B 10
Wrigley ..... H 5
Wynnburg ..... A 2
Yorkville ..... 272. B 3
Yuma ..... B 4

*Does not appear on map; key shows general location.
°County seat.

Source: 1980 census. Places without population figures are unincorporated areas.

Tennessee's rugged mountains, thick forests, and beautiful lakes and rivers are ideal for outdoor sports, camping, and sightseeing. The majestic beauty of Great Smoky Mountains National Park attracts several million visitors a year. Students of American history delight in the state's many sites of historic interest. Music lovers travel to Tennessee in order to hear outstanding per-

formances by bluegrass, blues, and country artists. The Memphis in May International Festival is one of the largest annual events in the United States. This month-long celebration honors a different nation each year and includes five major weekend festivals. The unique cultural heritage of Memphis is also featured during this popular celebration.

Jodi Cobb, Woodfin Camp, Inc.

Grand Ole Opry near Nashville

Places to visit

American Museum of Science and Energy, at Oak Ridge, features exhibits on energy, including displays on the peaceful uses of nuclear energy.

Casey Jones Home and Railroad Museum, in Jackson, is the restored home of the famous railroad hero. The home is maintained as a railroad museum.

Graceland, in Memphis, was the estate of Elvis Presley, the most popular American singer in the history of rock music. The estate features Presley's mansion and grave site, and a variety of memorabilia.

Grand Ole Opry House, near Nashville, features weekend performances of country music. It includes the world's largest broadcasting studio.

James K. Polk Ancestral Home, in Columbia, is the only one of the president's Tennessee homes still standing. Built in 1816, it contains furniture used by President and Mrs. Polk.

Lookout Mountain rises 2,146 feet (654 meters) above sea level at the Moccasin Bend of the Tennessee River near Chattanooga. There, Union forces won an important victory in the "Battle Above the Clouds" in November, 1863.

Rocky Mount, near Johnson City, is a log house that served as the first capitol of The Territory of the United States South of the River Ohio.

The Hermitage, the home of President Andrew Jackson, is about 10 miles (16 kilometers) east of downtown Nashville. It was first built in 1819, and rebuilt in 1835. Jackson and his wife are buried on the grounds.

The Parthenon, in Nashville, is the world's only full-scale reproduction of the ancient Greek temple. It has casts of the Elgin Marbles, sculptures from the original Parthenon.

National parks, forests, and historic sites. Almost half of the Great Smoky Mountains National Park lies in Tennessee. The rest of the park is in North Carolina. The Cherokee National Forest lies in southeastern Tennessee. The Andrew Johnson National Historic Site is located at Greeneville. The state has several national military parks, including Chickamauga and Chattanooga, which Tennessee shares with Georgia; and Shiloh, near Savannah. Fort Donelson National Battlefield lies near Dover. The Cumberland Gap National Historical Park lies in the area where Kentucky, Virginia, and Tennessee meet. The Big South Fork National River and Recreation Area lies in Tennessee and Kentucky.

State parks and forests. Tennessee maintains 51 state parks and 13 state forests. For information on the state parks in Tennessee, write to Director of State Parks, Department of Conservation, 701 Broadway, Nashville, TN 37203.

Tennessee Tourist Development

Crockett Tavern in Rutherford

Memphis Chamber of Commerce

Hall of Gold Records at Graceland

David R. Frazier

Great Smoky Mountains National Park

Annual events

January-March
Eagle watch tours at Reelfoot Lake near Tiptonville (January-March); National Field Trial Championships for bird dogs in Grand Junction (February).

April-June
Dogwood Arts Festival in Knoxville (April); Mule Day in Columbia (April); Spring Wildflower Pilgrimage in Gatlinburg (April); World's Largest Fish Fry in Paris (April); East Tennessee Strawberry Festival in Dayton (May); Iroquois Steeplechase in Nashville (May); Spring Music and Crafts Festival in Rugby (May); West Tennessee Strawberry Festival in Humboldt (May); Great River Carnival in Memphis (May-June); Dulcimer and Harp Convention in Cosby (June); International Country Music Fan Fair in Nashville (June); June Jaunt festival in Chattanooga (June); Rhododendron Festival in Roan Mountain (June).

July-September
Frontier Days in Lynchburg (July); Fiddlers' Jamboree and Crafts Festival in Smithville (July); Historic Rugby Pilgrimage of Homes in Rugby (August); International Grand Championship Walking Horse Show in Murfreesboro (August); Elvis International Tribute Week in Memphis (August); Tennessee Walking Horse National Celebration in Shelbyville (August-September); Agriculture and Industrial Fair in Knoxville (September); Tennessee State Fair in Nashville (September).

October-December
International Banana Festival in South Fulton (October); National Storytelling Festival in Jonesborough (October); Autumn Gold Festival in Coker Creek (October); Oktoberfest in Memphis (October); Fall Color Cruise and Folk Festival in Chattanooga (October); Christmas at Twitty City in Hendersonville (December).

Main Event, Inc.

Iroquois Steeplechase in Nashville

Land regions. Tennessee has seven main land regions. These are, from east to west: (1) the Blue Ridge; (2) the Appalachian Ridge and Valley Region; (3) the Appalachian Plateau; (4) the Highland Rim; (5) the Nashville Basin; and (6) the Gulf Coastal Plain.

The Blue Ridge region skirts the entire eastern edge of Tennessee. The region's elevation averages 5,000 feet (1,500 meters), the highest in the state. Clingmans Dome, the state's tallest peak, rises to 6,643 feet (2,025 meters). Several mountain ranges dot the region. They include the Bald, Chilhowee, Great Smoky, Holston, Iron, Roan, Stone, and Unicoi mountains. Rolling lowlands lie within the mountains. The region has a great deal of timber and some minerals.

The Appalachian Ridge and Valley Region stretches westward from the mountainous Blue Ridge for about 55 miles (89 kilometers). This region has fertile farm country in valleys that lie between parallel wooded ridges. The broad valleys and narrow ridges in the eastern part of the region make up an area called the *Great Valley*.

The Appalachian Plateau, or *Cumberland Plateau,* lies west of the Ridge and Valley Region. There, the land rises in rocky cliffs that range from 1,500 to 1,800 feet (457 to 549 meters) high. The plateau region consists of flat-topped mountains and V-shaped valleys. Most of Tennessee's coal comes from this region. The area also has deposits of petroleum and natural gas. From Lookout Mountain, in the southern part of the region, visitors can see seven states.

The Highland Rim is an elevated plain that surrounds the Nashville Basin. Steep slopes reach from the Rim to the Basin below. In the east, underground streams leave hollowed-out caves in the rocks that lie beneath the surface of the region.

The Nashville Basin lies within the Highland Rim. Most of the Basin drains toward the northwest. The Basin has rich farming areas where cattle graze in fertile pastures, and farms produce bumper crops. In addition, the region has phosphate deposits.

The Gulf Coastal Plain is part of an important land region that begins at the Gulf of Mexico and extends northward as far as southern Illinois. In Tennessee, the

Tennessee Tourist Development

Cane Creek Falls, near Pikeville, is in the Appalachian Plateau region of Tennessee. Rocky cliffs in this area rise from 1,500 to 1,800 feet (457 to 549 meters) high.

Plain has three parts. A hilly strip of land about 10 miles (16 kilometers) wide runs along the west bank of the Tennessee River. The second part is an area of low rolling hills and wide stream valleys called *bottoms.* This area slopes toward the Mississippi River, ending in steep bluffs that overlook the Mississippi Alluvial Plain, the third part of the region. The narrow plain lies along the western edge of the state. This flat strip along the Mississippi River averages less than 300 feet (91 meters) above sea level. It is the lowest part of the state and is sometimes called *The Mississippi Bottoms.* Farmers raise soybeans and other field crops on the Alluvial Plain.

Land regions of Tennessee

WORLD BOOK map

Map index

Map labels: Cumberland R. / Mississippi R. / Tennessee R. / GULF COASTAL PLAIN / NASHVILLE BASIN / APPALACHIAN RIDGE AND VALLEY REGION / BLUE RIDGE / HIGHLAND RIM / APPALACHIAN PLATEAU

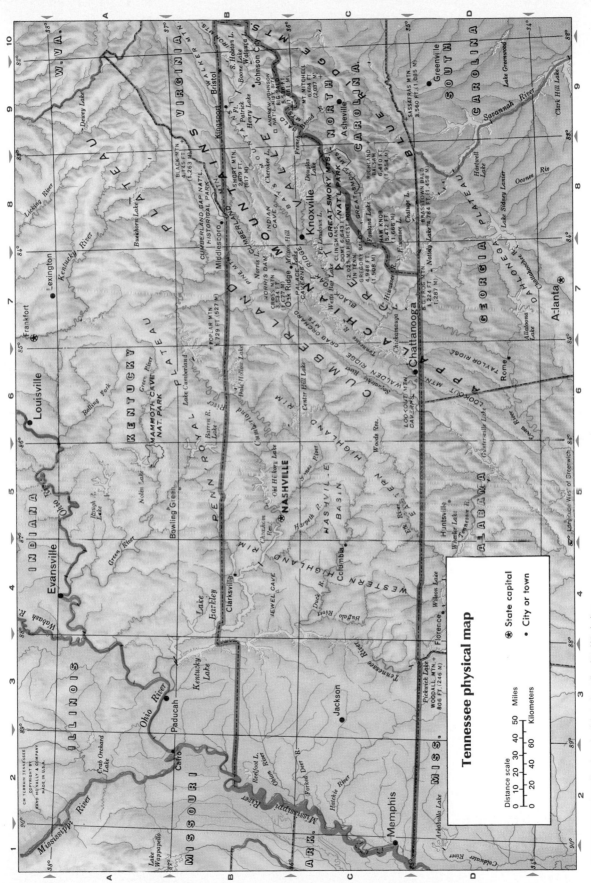

Tennessee physical map

⊛ State capital
• City or town

Distance scale

| Miles | 0 | 10 | 20 | 30 | 40 | 50 |
| Kilometers | 0 | 20 | 40 | 60 | |

Specially created for *The World Book Encyclopedia* by Rand McNally and World Book editors

Rivers and lakes. Three large river systems—the Mississippi, Cumberland, and Tennessee—drain the state. The Mississippi drains most of West Tennessee. Its largest tributaries in Tennessee include the Forked Deer, Hatchie, Loosahatchie, Obion, and Wolf rivers. The Cumberland and Tennessee drain most of the rest of the state. They rise in the Appalachian Mountains and join the Ohio River. Principal branches of the Tennessee include the Big Sandy, Buffalo, Clinch, Duck, Elk, French Broad, Hiwassee, Holston, Little Tennessee, Powell, and Sequatchie rivers. Tributaries of the Cumberland in Tennessee include the Caney Fork, Harpeth, and Stones rivers.

Since 1933, the Tennessee Valley Authority (TVA) and the U.S. Army Corps of Engineers have built many dams along the Cumberland and Tennessee rivers and their tributaries. Artificial lakes formed by these dams have more than doubled the inland water area of Tennessee. The largest of these artificial lakes is Kentucky Lake. Others include Boone, Cherokee, Chickamauga, Douglas, Fort Loudoun, Fort Patrick Henry, Norris, Pickwick, Watauga, and Watts Bar reservoirs. These artificially created lakes are often called the *Great Lakes of the South.*

Plant and animal life. Forests cover about half the state. Tennessee's most important trees include the hickory, shortleaf pine, red and white oaks, and yellow poplar. Other common trees include ash, cherry, elm, sycamore, maple, and walnut. Azaleas, mountain laurel, rhododendron, and other shrubs cover the mountain slopes. The passionflower and iris grow throughout the state. Common wild flowers in Tennessee include the dragonroot, hop clover, spring beauty, and yellow jasmine.

Tennessee's mountains, forests, and waters abound with wild game. Hunters seek deer, ducks, wild turkeys, and other game. Wild hogs roam remote parts of the Tennessee mountains. Beavers, muskrats, rabbits, raccoons, and skunks live in the fields and forests. Common songbirds in Tennessee include the mockingbird, robin, and wood thrush. Bass, crappie, trout, and walleyed pike are found in the lakes and streams.

Climate. Most of Tennessee has a humid, subtropical climate. Temperatures rarely go above 100° F. (38° C) or below 10° F. (−12° C). The lowlands and plains in West Tennessee generally are warmer than the mountainous eastern regions. Average temperatures in the west range from 40° F. (4° C) in January to 79° F. (26° C) in July. The east averages 37° F. (3° C) in January and 71° F. (22° C) in July. Tennessee's lowest recorded temperature, −32° F. (−36° C), occurred on Dec. 30, 1917, at Mountain City in the northeast. Its highest recorded temperature, 113° F. (45° C), occurred on July 29 and Aug. 9, 1930, at Perryville in the west. Eastern Tennessee averages about 10 inches (25 centimeters) of snow a year, while the west averages 4 to 6 inches (10 to 15 centimeters). Most of the state averages about 52 inches (132 centimeters) of *precipitation* (rain, melted snow, and other forms of moisture) a year.

Average monthly weather

	Knoxville						Nashville				
	Temperatures F° High Low		Temperatures C° High Low		Days of rain or snow		Temperatures F° High Low		Temperatures C° High Low		Days of rain or snow
Jan.	50	31	10	−1	13	Jan.	49	31	9	−1	12
Feb.	53	32	12	0	12	Feb.	52	33	11	1	11
Mar.	61	38	16	3	13	Mar.	60	40	16	4	12
Apr.	71	47	22	8	11	Apr.	71	49	22	9	11
May	79	56	26	13	12	May	79	57	14	14	10
June	87	65	31	18	12	June	88	66	31	19	10
July	89	68	32	20	12	July	91	69	33	21	10
Aug.	88	66	31	19	11	Aug.	89	68	32	20	9
Sept.	84	61	29	16	8	Sept.	85	62	29	17	8
Oct.	73	48	23	9	7	Oct.	74	50	23	10	7
Nov.	59	38	15	3	9	Nov.	59	39	15	4	9
Dec.	50	32	10	0	12	Dec.	50	33	10	1	11

Average yearly precipitation

Tennessee has a humid climate with the greatest amount of precipitation falling in the central and southeastern sections.

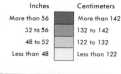

Inches	Centimeters
More than 56	More than 142
52 to 56	132 to 142
48 to 52	122 to 132
Less than 48	Less than 122

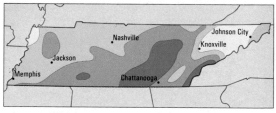

Average January temperatures

Tennessee has moderate winters. Temperatures throughout the state generally average well above freezing.

Degrees Fahrenheit	Degrees Celsius
Above 40	Above 4
38 to 40	3 to 4
36 to 38	2 to 3
Below 36	Below 2

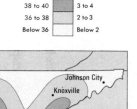

Average July temperatures

The lowlands and plains of the west usually remain warmer in the summertime than the mountainous eastern regions.

Degrees Fahrenheit	Degrees Celsius
Above 80	Above 27
78 to 80	26 to 27
75 to 78	24 to 26
Below 75	Below 24

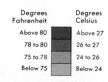

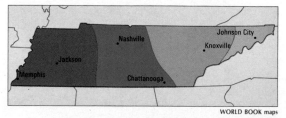

WORLD BOOK maps

Service industries, taken together, account for more than two-thirds of Tennessee's *gross state product*—the total value of all goods and services produced in a state in a year. However, manufacturing is the single most important economic activity. It accounts for more than a fourth of the gross state product.

Natural resources. Tennessee's fertile soil, temperate climate, vast water supply, and abundant minerals make the state rich in natural resources.

Minerals. Tennessee has a large variety of minerals. East Tennessee has large deposits of fluorite, marble, pyrite, and zinc. Middle Tennessee contains rich stores of limestone, phosphate rock, and zinc. The Appalachian Plateau has deposits of coal, petroleum, and natural gas. Ball clay and lignite are found in West Tennessee. The state also has barite, copper, sand and gravel, and other minerals.

Soil. The most fertile and productive soils lie in the Appalachian Ridge and Valley Region, the Nashville Basin, and the Gulf Coastal Plain. A limestone-based soil covers the mountain coves in the Blue Ridge region. A clay loam formed from weathered limestone covers the valley floors in the Ridge and Valley Region. The Appalachian Plateau and most of the Highland Rim have poor soils. A loam soil, formed from rich soluble limestone, covers the Nashville Basin. The Gulf Coastal Plain has light soils that produce well. Fertile sand, silt, and clay soil covers the Mississippi Alluvial Plain.

Service industries account for 68 per cent of the gross state product of Tennessee. Most of the service industries are concentrated in the state's seven metropolitan areas.

Wholesale and retail trade is the most valuable service industry in Tennessee. It makes up 18 per cent of the gross state product. Memphis is a wholesaling center and a major market for cotton and hardwood lumber. Much retail trade takes place in the Nashville area, which is also a major convention center. Knoxville is the trade center of eastern Tennessee.

Community, social, and personal services form the second most important service industry in Tennessee.

Production and workers by economic activities

Economic activities	Per cent of GSP* produced	Employed workers	
		Number of persons	Per cent of total
Manufacturing	25	489,300	25
Wholesale & retail trade	18	437,700	22
Community, social, & personal services	15	359,300	18
Finance, insurance, & real estate	13	89,300	5
Government	12	304,400	15
Transportation, communication, & utilities	10	91,300	5
Construction	5	82,100	4
Agriculture	1	114,200	6
Mining	1	7,500	†
Total	100	1,975,100	100

*GSP = gross state product, the total value of goods and services produced in a year.
† Less than one-half of 1 per cent.
Figures are for 1985.
Source: *World Book* estimates based on data from U.S. Bureau of Economic Analysis, U.S. Bureau of Labor Statistics, and U.S. Department of Agriculture.

This industry accounts for 15 per cent of the gross state product. It includes such economic activities as private schools and hospitals, advertising and data processing, and the operation of repair shops and cleaning establishments. Other service industries include finance, insurance, and real estate; government; and transportation, communication, and utilities.

Manufacturing accounts for 25 per cent of the gross state product of Tennessee. The state's manufactured goods have a *value added by manufacture* of about $18 billion a year. This figure represents the increase in value of raw materials after they become finished products. Leading industries, in order of importance, are (1) chemicals, (2) food products, (3) nonelectrical machinery, and (4) electrical machinery and equipment.

Chemicals. Tennessee ranks among the leading states in the production of chemicals. This industry has a value added of about $3 billion yearly, or about one-sixth of

Chemical products, including plastics and industrial chemicals, are produced at the Tennessee Eastman factory in Kingsport. Tennessee is among the leading states in the manufacture of chemical products.

the state's manufacturing income. Plants in various parts of the state manufacture such products as agricultural chemicals, industrial chemicals, paints, pharmaceuticals, plastics, and soaps.

Food products have a value added of about $2 billion a year. The state's largest stockyards are in Chattanooga and Nashville. Meat-packing plants operate in Chattanooga, Johnson City, Knoxville, Nashville, and Union City. Tennessee has several centers that freeze and can fruits and vegetables. Memphis has large shortening plants.

Nonelectrical machinery has an annual value added of more than $1½ billion. The industry's chief centers of production are Chattanooga and Memphis. Its leading products include refrigeration and heating equipment and general industrial machinery.

Electrical machinery and equipment has an annual value added of about $1½ billion. Factories throughout the state make household appliances, welding equipment, and motors and generators.

Other leading industries in Tennessee produce transportation equipment, clothing, fabricated metal products, and rubber and plastics products. Tennessee industries also manufacture paper products, primary metals, and printed materials.

East Tennessee plants produce aluminum in Alcoa and steel in Chattanooga. In the middle of the state, factories in the Nashville area make aircraft parts, automobiles and pickup trucks, and river barges. A refinery in Clarksville processes zinc ores. In the west, Memphis manufacturers produce furniture and structural steel. The state has a flourishing music publishing industry. Centered in Nashville, it specializes in country, folk, and western music.

Tennessee's textile industry is centered in the eastern part of the state, in Chattanooga, Cleveland, Greeneville, Harriman, Johnson City, Knoxville, and other cities. Many textile manufacturers make blankets and hosiery. Bemis, in western Tennessee, has a cotton mill.

Agriculture accounts for 1 per cent of the gross state product of Tennessee. Farm products supply a yearly net income of about $500 million. Farmland covers about 13 million acres (5.3 million hectares), or about half the state. Tennessee has about 98,000 farms. They average about 133 acres (54 hectares) in size.

Livestock accounts for about half the income re-

ceived from farm products. Tennessee is one of the South's leading dairy states. Farmers in most parts of the state raise beef cattle, dairy cattle, and hogs. Other livestock products in Tennessee are *broilers* (chickens between 5 and 12 weeks old) and eggs. The Nashville Basin is the home of the famous Tennessee Walking Horse (see **Horse** [Saddle horses; picture]). Most of Tennessee's sheep come from there.

Soybeans and tobacco are Tennessee's most valuable crops. Each brings in about 15 per cent of the income from farm products. Tennessee ranks among the leading states in the production of both of these crops. Soybeans are used primarily for vegetable oil and livestock feed. Most of Tennessee's soybeans are grown in the western part of the state. Tobacco is grown mainly in the central and eastern parts of the state. Burley tobacco is the most important type of tobacco grown in Tennessee. Burley tobacco is used to make cigarettes. Farms in northern Tennessee produce fire-cured tobacco, which is cured with heat and smoke.

Cotton is Tennessee's third most valuable crop, with 5 per cent of the income from farm products. Tennessee is among the leading cotton-producing states.

Other crops grown in Tennessee include corn, hay, and wheat. Corn is grown on farms in most parts of the state. Farmers feed most of the corn to livestock. Hay is also used primarily for livestock feed. Farmers grow wheat mainly in the eastern and central parts of the state. Tomatoes and snap beans earn the largest income among the *truck crops* (vegetables grown for market). Truck farmers also grow cabbage, potatoes, and sweet potatoes. Farmers raise valuable crops of apples, peaches, and strawberries. Other important agricultural products include wheat and hay.

Mining accounts for 1 per cent of Tennessee's gross state product. Mineral products provide an income of about $700 million a year. Coal accounts for the greatest income from mining. Stone ranks second and zinc third.

Mines that produce *bituminous* (soft) coal operate in 12 eastern counties and yield about 9 million short tons (8 million metric tons) a year. Blount, Grainger, and Union counties in the east are marble producers. About 65 counties, mainly in eastern and central Tennessee, produce limestone.

Tennessee leads the states in the production of zinc. Most of the zinc in Tennessee comes from Jefferson,

Farm, mineral, and forest products

This map shows where the state's leading farm, mineral, and forest products are produced. The major urban areas (shown on the map in red) are the state's important manufacturing centers.

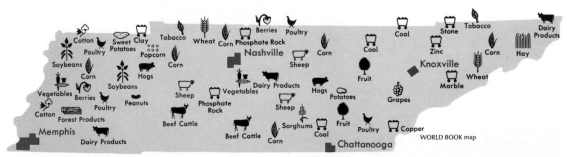

WORLD BOOK map

Knox, and Smith counties. Tennessee also produces phosphate rock. Miners dig most of the phosphate rock in Giles, Hickman, Maury, and Williamson counties in the central portion of the state. Tennessee is the only Southern state that mines copper. All of Tennessee's copper is produced from sulfide ores that are mined in Polk County. These sulfide ores support a large sulfuric-acid industry, and also yield some gold, iron, silver, and zinc.

Ball clays and other high-grade ceramic and pottery clays, mined in the northwestern section, support an important ceramics industry. Quality glass sands come from Benton County. Pits in about 30 counties produce sand and gravel.

Electric power. The Tennessee Valley Authority (TVA) generates almost all the state's electric power. The TVA produces more power than any other system in the country, and distributes it to local electric power systems (see **Tennessee Valley Authority**). About 65 per cent of the state's power comes from steam-generating plants that burn coal. About 20 per cent comes from nuclear plants, and hydroelectric plants provide about 15 per cent.

Transportation. Tennessee faced many problems in building its transportation systems. Many bridges and tunnels had to be built through hilly and mountainous areas. This raised the costs of railroad and highway construction. Between about 1800 and 1860, private companies built turnpikes and collected tolls to maintain them.

In 1913, the legislature authorized counties to issue bonds for highway construction. Tennessee now has about 84,000 miles (140,000 kilometers) of highways and roads, nearly all surfaced.

Tennessee's busiest airports are at Memphis and Nashville. Knoxville and Chattanooga also have important air terminals. Several rail lines provide freight services, and passenger trains link Memphis with Chicago and New Orleans. Barges float along the Cumberland, Mississippi, and Tennessee rivers. Memphis ranks as one of the busiest inland ports on the Mississippi River. The Tennessee-Tombigbee Waterway connects the Tennessee River to the Tombigbee River of Alabama and Mississippi and links Tennessee cities with ports on the Gulf of Mexico.

Communication. Tennessee has about 125 newspapers, of which about 30 are dailies. George Roulstone established the state's first newspaper, the *Knoxville Gazette,* in 1791. Papers with the largest daily circulations include the *Chattanooga News-Free Press, The Chattanooga Times, The Knoxville Journal, The Knoxville News-Sentinel, The* (Memphis) *Commercial Appeal, the Nashville Banner,* and *The* (Nashville) *Tennessean.* About 120 periodicals are published in the state.

Tennessee's first radio station, WNAV, began broadcasting at Knoxville in 1922. The first television station, WMCT-TV, started operations at Memphis in 1948. Today, Tennessee has about 280 radio stations and over 25 television stations.

Government

Constitution. Tennessee's Constitution was adopted in 1870. The state had two earlier constitutions. The first was adopted in 1796, the year Tennessee achieved statehood, and the second was adopted in 1834.

Either the state legislature or a constitutional convention can propose amendments to the Constitution. In the legislature, a proposed amendment first needs the approval of a majority of both houses. Then, during the next regular legislative session, it must be approved by two-thirds of both houses. Finally, a majority of people voting in an election for governor must approve the amendment.

Constitutional conventions cannot be held more often than once every six years. They may be called by a majority of the legislators with the approval of a majority of voters. Amendments proposed by a constitutional convention must be approved by a majority of voters.

Executive. Tennessee's governor holds office for a four-year term and may serve any number of terms, but not more than two in a row. The speaker of the state Senate has the title of lieutenant governor and is next in line after the governor.

The governor appoints the heads of Tennessee's 21 chief administrative departments. But the governor does not have the power to appoint the state's four top administrative officers. The legislature chooses the secretary of state, who serves a four-year term, and both the state treasurer and the state comptroller of the treasury, who serve for two years. The state Supreme Court selects the attorney general to serve an eight-year term. The voters elect the three members of the Public Service Commission. This board regulates intrastate carriers and privately owned utility companies.

Legislature, called the *General Assembly,* consists of a 33-member Senate and a 99-member House of Representatives. Senators serve four-year terms and house members serve two-year terms. They are elected from legislative districts.

The Assembly meets in odd-numbered years on the second Tuesday in January for an organizational session lasting no longer than 15 days. The regular session begins on the Tuesday following the end of the organizational session. The length of regular sessions is limited to 90 legislative days. Special sessions may be called by the governor or by two-thirds of the members of each house.

Courts. The highest court in Tennessee is the state Supreme Court. It has a chief justice and four associate justices, elected by the voters for eight-year terms. The court of appeals has 12 judges. It hears civil cases that have been transferred from lower courts. This court may serve as a complete body or in as many as three separate divisions. The court of criminal appeals has nine judges. It hears appeals from criminal trial courts.

Tennessee has 31 judicial districts for its circuit courts, 23 for its *chancery* (equity) courts, and 13 for its criminal courts. Circuit courts have *jurisdiction* (authority) over any matters where jurisdiction is not given to another court. Other trial courts are general sessions courts, probate courts, juvenile and domestic relations courts, and city or municipal courts. All judges in Tennessee are elected to eight-year terms.

Local government. County commissions govern almost all of Tennessee's 95 counties. Each commission consists of from 9 to 25 county commissioners. Either a county executive or the chairman of the commission presides over commission meetings. The commission must meet at least four times a year to perform such duties as setting the property tax rate, approving the county's budget, and authorizing bond issues. All counties have such officials as a sheriff, assessor of property, trustee, register of deeds, and county clerk.

Any of Tennessee's approximately 335 incorporated cities and towns may, by popular vote, adopt *home rule.* That is, a city may vote to frame and operate its own charter instead of remaining under the control of the state legislature. But only 12 cities have adopted home rule since a constitutional amendment made it available in 1953. About 200 Tennessee cities have a mayor-council government. Other cities in the state use either the council-manager or commissioner system. Davidson County and Nashville have combined their governments into a single unit governed by a mayor and metropolitan council.

Revenue. A state sales and use tax accounts for about 30 per cent of the state government's *general revenue* (income). Another 30 per cent of the revenue comes from federal grants and other U.S. government programs. Most of the state's remaining revenue comes from a variety of other taxes. The most important of these are a motor fuels tax and a corporation income tax.

Politics. Tennessee has been a Democratic stronghold for most of its history. During the 1960's, however, Republicans made strong gains in the state legislature. In 1966, Howard H. Baker, Jr., became the first Republican elected to the U.S. Senate from Tennessee since the 1860's. In 1970, Winfield Dunn became the first Republi-

can in 50 years to be elected governor of Tennessee. By the end of the 1970's, Tennessee had become a two-party state.

In presidential elections, Democrats have carried Tennessee about twice as often as Republicans have. But Republicans have won the state in most presidential elections after 1948. For a record of the state's electoral votes, see **Electoral College** (table).

Tennessee State Legislature

The Tennessee State Legislature, called the *General Assembly,* is made up of a 33-member Senate and a 99-member House of Representatives. The Senate chambers are shown above.

The governors of Tennessee

	Party	Term		Party	Term
John Sevier	* Dem.-Rep.	1796-1801	Robert Love Taylor	Democratic	1887-1891
Archibald Roane	Dem.-Rep.	1801-1803	John P. Buchanan	Democratic	1891-1893
John Sevier	Dem.-Rep.	1803-1809	Peter Turney	Democratic	1893-1897
Willie Blount	Dem.-Rep.	1809-1815	Robert Love Taylor	Democratic	1897-1899
Joseph McMinn	Dem.-Rep.	1815-1821	Benton McMillin	Democratic	1899-1903
William Carroll	Dem.-Rep.	1821-1827	James B. Frazier	Democratic	1903-1905
Sam Houston	Dem.-Rep.	1827-1829	John I. Cox	Democratic	1905-1907
William Hall	Democratic	1829	Malcolm R. Patterson	Democratic	1907-1911
William Carroll	Democratic	1829-1835	Ben W. Hooper	Republican	1911-1915
Newton Cannon	Whig	1835-1839	Tom C. Rye	Democratic	1915-1919
James K. Polk	Democratic	1839-1841	A. H. Roberts	Democratic	1919-1921
James C. Jones	Whig	1841-1845	Alfred A. Taylor	Republican	1921-1923
Aaron V. Brown	Democratic	1845-1847	Austin Peay	Democratic	1923-1927
Neill S. Brown	Whig	1847-1849	Henry H. Horton	Democratic	1927-1933
William Trousdale	Democratic	1849-1851	Hill McAlister	Democratic	1933-1937
William B. Campbell	Whig	1851-1853	Gordon Browning	Democratic	1937-1939
Andrew Johnson	Democratic	1853-1857	Prentice Cooper	Democratic	1939-1945
Isham G. Harris	Democratic	1857-1862	Jim McCord	Democratic	1945-1949
Andrew Johnson			Gordon Browning	Democratic	1949-1953
(Military governor)	Democratic	1862-1865	Frank G. Clement	Democratic	1953-1959
William G. Brownlow	** Whig-Rep.	1865-1869	Buford Ellington	Democratic	1959-1963
DeWitt Clinton Senter	Whig-Rep.	1869-1871	Frank G. Clement	Democratic	1963-1967
John C. Brown	† Whig-Dem.	1871-1875	Buford Ellington	Democratic	1967-1971
James D. Porter	Democratic	1875-1879	Winfield Dunn	Republican	1971-1975
Albert S. Marks	Democratic	1879-1881	Leonard Ray Blanton	Democratic	1975-1979
Alvin Hawkins	Republican	1881-1883	Lamar Alexander	Republican	1979-1987
William B. Bate	Democratic	1883-1887	Ned Ray McWherter	Democratic	1987-

*Democratic-Republican   **Whig-Republican   †Whig-Democratic

Indian days. Although Indians probably lived in what is now Tennessee at least 8,000 years ago, the earliest known groups of Indians were the Mound Builders. They settled the area about 1,000 years ago. The Mound Builders used mounds to support their temples and chiefs' houses. When the first white explorers came to the area, they saw some of the early Cherokee and Chickasaw peoples still building mounds. See **Mound Builders.**

The Cherokee claimed Middle Tennessee as their hunting ground. The Chickamauga Indians, a branch of the Cherokee, lived near the present site of Chattanooga. The Chickasaw occupied West Tennessee.

Exploration. In 1540, a party of Spanish explorers led by Hernando de Soto raided some Indian villages in the valley of the Tennessee River. Moving westward, De Soto became the first European to reach the Mississippi River. He came upon it in 1541. De Soto died in the spring of 1542, and was buried in the river he discovered. No other explorers entered the region until 1673, when James Needham and Gabriel Arthur of England explored the Tennessee River Valley. That same year, Louis Jolliet of Canada and Father Jacques Marquette of France sailed down the Mississippi River. In 1682, René-Robert Cavelier, Sieur de la Salle, claimed the entire Mississippi Valley for France. He built Fort Prud'homme on the Chickasaw Bluffs. But the post was so isolated that the French soon had to abandon it. French settlers began moving into the Mississippi Valley, which they called *New France.* In 1714, Charles Charleville set up a French trading post at French Lick, near what is now Nashville.

France, Spain, and Great Britain all claimed the Tennessee region. All three countries competed for the trade and the friendship of the Indians. The dispute eventually became a contest between the British and the French. In 1754, the French and Indian War broke out between British and French settlers. The French were outnumbered by about 20 to 1 but won decisive victories during the early years of the war. After nine bloody years, however, the British won out. In 1763, by the Treaty of Paris, the French surrendered to the British all claim to lands east of the Mississippi.

Early settlement. By 1769, permanent settlers lived in the Tennessee region. New settlers began to come into the area from Virginia and North Carolina.

The Tennessee region belonged to the British colony of North Carolina. But vast, rugged mountains separated settlers in Tennessee from the protection of the mother colony. In 1772, a group of settlers established law and order in the wilderness by forming their own government, the Watauga Association. They drew up one of the first written constitutions in North America. See **Watauga Association.**

A group called the Transylvania Company bought a large area of present-day Tennessee and Kentucky from the Cherokee in 1775. Daniel Boone, working for the company, blazed a trail from Virginia across the mountains at Cumberland Gap to open this land to settlement. Boone's trail, the famous Wilderness Road, became the main route to the new settlements.

Territorial years. In 1779, two groups of pioneers, led by James Robertson and John Donelson, pushed far into the wilds and settled around the Big Salt Lick on the Cumberland River. They built Fort Nashborough (later Nashville), which formed the center of the Middle Tennessee settlements. These pioneers drew up an agreement called the Cumberland Compact. It established representative government for all settlers, and created a court system to enforce its provisions.

In 1780, during the Revolutionary War, John Sevier led a group of pioneers from the Tennessee region across the Great Smoky Mountains into South Carolina. These men helped American forces win a victory over the British at the Battle of Kings Mountain on October 7.

Meanwhile, the settlers and Indians were trying to drive each other out of the Tennessee region. The settlers appealed for help to North Carolina. But help did not come. In 1784, three counties in East Tennessee revolted against North Carolina and formed the independent State of Franklin. They made John Sevier, the hero of Kings Mountain, their governor. North Carolina regained control of the area in 1788 (see **Franklin, State of**). In 1789, North Carolina gave the Tennessee region to the United States. The federal government made it into a new territory, and called it The Territory of the United States South of the River Ohio. William Blount became its first and only governor.

The Chickasaw owned nearly all West Tennessee until 1818, when they ceded their land to the federal government. But the Cherokee still held a large area in Middle Tennessee, and a smaller tract south of the Little Tennessee and Sequatchie rivers in the east.

Statehood. On Feb. 6, 1796, Tennessee adopted a constitution in preparation for statehood. It became the 16th state in the Union on June 1. Tennesseans elected John Sevier as their first governor. The new state had a population of about 77,000, and was the first state to be created out of government territory.

Black slaves toiled on West and Middle Tennessee farms before the Civil War. But most farmers in the eastern part of the state did not own slaves. Free blacks could vote in Tennessee until a new constitution, adopted in 1834, took that right away from them.

Building the state. Three men who became Presidents of the United States played key roles in the development of Tennessee. They were Andrew Jackson, James K. Polk, and Andrew Johnson.

Andrew Jackson helped draw up Tennessee's first constitution in 1796. He served as the state's first United States representative and later as a U.S. senator from Tennessee. He also served as a justice of the Tennessee Supreme Court. During the War of 1812, Jackson led his Tennessee troops to victory against the Creek Indians. He became a national hero by leading U.S. forces in an overwhelming defeat of the British Army at the Battle of New Orleans. Tennessee supported Jackson when he ran unsuccessfully for the presidency in 1824, and when he was elected in 1828.

James K. Polk was a close friend and supporter of Andrew Jackson. Polk served Tennessee for two years in the state legislature, for 14 years in the U.S. House of Representatives, and for a two-year term as governor. Polk was elected President in 1844 on a platform of expansionism. During his presidency, he led the country to victory in the Mexican War and nearly doubled the territory of the United States.

Andrew Johnson fought for the rights of the poor. As

a state senator, he courageously tried to reduce the voting power of the powerful slave owners. Johnson served as a U.S. representative, as governor of Tennessee, and as a U.S. senator. Although he did not oppose slavery, he believed strongly in the Union. Johnson pleaded with the people of Tennessee to remain in the Union.

Many Tennesseans were in favor of staying in the Union. But when Confederate troops fired on Fort Sumter, and war appeared inevitable, feelings in favor of seceding grew stronger. On June 8, 1861, about two months after the Civil War broke out, over two-thirds of the people voted to join the Confederacy. Tennessee was the last state to secede. Andrew Johnson was the only senator who did not secede with his state.

The Civil War. The people of Tennessee were divided in their sympathies between the North and the South. Most Union sympathy came from the eastern part of the state. Confederate forces moved into that region and held it captive for a good part of the war.

In 1862, the war spread across the state's middle and western regions. Union forces under General Ulysses S. Grant invaded Tennessee in February of that year and quickly captured Fort Henry and Fort Donelson, strong points on the Tennessee and Cumberland rivers. Grant then proceeded along the Tennessee River to Pittsburg Landing. There, one of the bloodiest battles of the war took place. It was called the Battle of Shiloh, after a church that stood on the battlefield. Despite enormous losses, Union troops won an important victory at Shiloh. Federal control of Middle and West Tennessee was established in 1862. President Lincoln appointed Andrew Johnson the military governor of Tennessee.

Union forces captured Chattanooga in September, 1863, but Confederate troops soon regained the area outside the city. In November, Grant attacked the Confederate positions. In the first day of fighting, Union General Joseph Hooker drove the Confederate forces from Lookout Mountain in the "Battle Above the Clouds." The Union troops won control of Chattanooga after two more days of fighting.

In 1864, General William T. Sherman's troops marched from Chattanooga into Georgia and captured Atlanta. In Tennessee, Confederate forces under General John B. Hood tried to draw Sherman back by attacking Franklin and Nashville. But General George H. Thomas defeated Hood's army at Nashville.

The National Union Party, consisting of Republicans and War Democrats, nominated Andrew Johnson to run for Vice President under President Lincoln in the 1864 election. They won the election. But on April 14, 1865, President Lincoln was assassinated. Andrew Johnson was inaugurated as President on April 15, 1865. He declared the rebellion in Tennessee at an end on June 13. But a strong group in Congress tried to block Tennessee's readmission to the Union. On July 24, 1866, after considerable debate, Tennessee became the first Confederate state to be readmitted.

Reconstruction. The years following the Civil War also were difficult ones for the people of Tennessee. The war had left much of the state in ruin and had left thousands of persons homeless.

A group of Union sympathizers, called *Radicals,* gained control of the Tennessee government after the war. This group included the governor and most of the

Bettmann Archive

Yellow fever swept through Tennessee during the 1870's. The epidemic hit especially hard in Memphis, where 5,200 of the city's 19,600 residents died from the disease in 1878.

state legislature. They imposed severe measures on those who had followed the Confederate cause. They gave black men the right to vote, but they took voting privileges away from a number of Confederate sympathizers. Most of these Radicals were voted out of office in 1869. Tennessee adopted a new Constitution in 1870. This Constitution reduced the power of the governor, set limits on legislative salaries, and extended the right to vote to all male citizens 21 or older.

Plantations in Middle and West Tennessee were divided into smaller farms. With slavery abolished, farmers had to plant their own cotton and other crops, and progress was slow. It took nearly 40 years for Tennessee's farms to recover from the war. But during that period the manufacturing and mining industries grew, creating jobs and speeding Tennessee's recovery.

Disease swept across the state during the 1870's. One of the worst yellow fever epidemics in U.S. history hit Memphis in 1878, killing about 5,200 of its 19,600 residents. Memphis lost its city charter after this disaster, and did not regain the charter until 1893.

Poor management of state funds in Tennessee banks left the state deeply in debt after the Civil War. In 1890, the Tennessee Banking Association began a campaign to reform the banking system. In 1913, a state banking department was set up to protect the public against bank mismanagement, fraud, and harmful speculation.

The early 1900's saw Tennessee in a period of change. New and better highways and railroads spread across the state. People began to move away from the farms and into the cities. By the mid-1930's, manufacturing was beginning to overtake farming as Tennessee's leading industry.

⸎Historic Tennessee

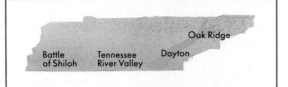

Oak Ridge

Battle of Shiloh   Tennessee River Valley   Dayton

The earliest known people in what is now Tennessee were Indians called Mound Builders who settled the area about 1,000 years ago. They built mounds to support temples and chiefs' houses.

Oak Ridge, begun in 1942, had the world's first nuclear reactor. The device was used to produce materials for the first atomic bomb.

The Battle of Shiloh in 1862 ended in a victory for the North when Confederate troops tried to stop a Union advance on Corinth, Miss. The Confederates lost more than 10,000 men. More than 13,000 Union soldiers died.

The Tennessee Valley Authority, created in 1933, built a network of dams to furnish electric power and control floods.

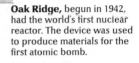

The Scopes trial in Dayton in 1925 centered on a Tennessee law that made the teaching of the theory of evolution illegal in state schools.

WORLD BOOK illustrations by Kevin Chadwick

Important dates in Tennessee

1540 Hernando de Soto of Spain led the first white expedition into the Tennessee region.

1673 James Needham and Gabriel Arthur of England, and Louis Jolliet of Canada and Father Jacques Marquette of France explored the region.

1682 Robert Cavelier, Sieur de la Salle, claimed the Mississippi River Valley for France.

1714 Charles Charleville set up a French trading post near the present site of Nashville.

1763 France surrendered to Great Britain all claim to lands east of the Mississippi River.

1772 The Watauga Association drew up one of the first written constitutions in North America.

1784 Three counties established the State of Franklin.

1796 Tennessee became the 16th state on June 1.

1818 The Chickasaw Indians sold all their land east of the Mississippi River to the U.S. government.

1838 The Cherokee were forced out of Tennessee.

1861 Tennessee became the last state to secede from the Union, on June 8.

1866 Tennessee became the first state to be readmitted to the Union, on July 24.

1870 A new constitution gave all male citizens 21 or older the right to vote.

1878 One of the worst yellow fever epidemics in U.S. history killed about 5,200 of the 19,600 persons in Memphis.

1925 John Scopes was convicted of teaching evolution in a Tennessee public school.

1933 Congress created the Tennessee Valley Authority.

1942 The federal government began building the atomic energy center at Oak Ridge.

1953 Tennessee voters approved eight amendments to the state constitution.

1962 The U.S. Supreme Court ruled, in a Tennessee case, that federal courts could challenge legislative apportionment.

1970 Winfield Dunn became the first Republican in 50 years to be elected governor of Tennessee.

1982 A world's fair was held in Knoxville.

AP/Wide World

Estes Kefauver waves to on-lookers in Memphis in 1948 during his successful campaign for U.S. Senator. In 1950, Kefauver won recognition for his role as head of the U.S. Senate committee for investigating organized crime. Kefauver was the Democratic candidate for Vice President in 1956.

In 1925, John T. Scopes, a high school teacher in Dayton, Tenn., was charged with teaching Darwin's theory of evolution, contrary to state law. The state brought Scopes to trial. William Jennings Bryan aided the prosecution. Clarence Darrow defended Scopes. The trial aroused enormous controversy. Scopes lost and was fined $100, but the conviction was reversed because of a minor legal error. Over 30 years later, Tennessee repealed the law under which he had been convicted.

In 1933, the federal government established the Tennessee Valley Authority (TVA) to conserve and develop the resources of the Tennessee River Valley.

The mid-1900's. In 1942, the federal government began to build an atomic energy plant in Oak Ridge. Scientists there worked on the development of the atomic bomb during World War II (1939-1945).

After the war, Tennessee continued to shift from an agricultural to an industrial economy. The TVA built more dams and steam plants to control floods, provide plentiful water supplies, and furnish cheap electric power. These facilities and the state's large labor force attracted new industries. Recreational areas built near scenic sites drew many tourists. A multimillion-dollar music industry grew up in Nashville, which became the nation's second largest recording center. The industry had its beginning in the Grand Ole Opry, a radio program featuring country and western music.

Tennessee's political life changed after the war, as many veterans became active in politics. This helped cause a revolt in the 1948 state elections against control by Memphis political boss E. H. Crump. In the elections, Crump began to lose power for the first time in over 20 years as Estes Kefauver won a seat in the U.S. Senate. Kefauver had run an anti-Crump campaign.

A constitutional convention was held in 1953, the state's first since 1870. Voters approved all eight of the convention's proposed amendments, which extended the governor's term from two to four years but prohibited two successive terms. Also during the 1950's, the Republican Party began to grow in the state. In 1966, Republicans won their first statewide office in Tennessee since 1920 with the election of Howard H. Baker, Jr., to the Senate. In 1970, the voters elected their first Republican governor in 50 years, Winfield Dunn.

Political control in Tennessee shifted from rural to urban areas. The shift resulted from an increase in city populations and from a ruling by the Supreme Court of the United States. In 1962, the Supreme Court ruled in *Baker v. Carr,* a Tennessee case, that federal courts have legal power over state legislative apportionment. In 1964, a federal court ordered Tennessee to redraw its legislative districts. The state did so in 1965, giving equal representation according to population.

Most social change in the state concerned desegregation. Tennessee's Constitution made it illegal for black and white children to attend the same schools. But in 1954, the U.S. Supreme Court ruled that compulsory segregation in public schools was illegal. Desegregation of state-supported schools began in 1956 in Clinton. State officials sent National Guardsmen to enforce the order. Since 1956, desegregation has taken place in all Tennessee schools.

A world's fair was held in Knoxville in 1982. The Sunsphere, a 266-foot (81-meter) tower, symbolized the fair's theme, "Energy Turns the World."

Jim Ayres, Black Star

On April 4, 1968, civil rights leader Martin Luther King, Jr., was murdered in Memphis. He had gone there to lead protests for striking garbage workers. James Earl Ray, an escaped convict, pleaded guilty to the crime and was sentenced to 99 years in prison. King's assassination in their state made many Tennesseans aware of the need to solve racial problems.

Recent developments. In 1974, the state legislature passed a *sunshine law* that allows the public to attend local and state government meetings. In 1978, voters approved an amendment to the state constitution that limits spending by the state government. Another amendment adopted in 1978 made governors eligible for reelection.

In 1982, a world's fair held in Knoxville helped promote tourism in Tennessee. Knoxville renovated 70 acres (28 hectares) of its downtown area for the event.

To increase its job opportunities, Tennessee is trying to attract new industry. In 1985, Spring Hill was chosen as the location for a new automobile plant. The new plant, scheduled to open in 1990, will create about 20,000 jobs. Also in 1985, the Tennessee River was connected to the Gulf of Mexico by the $2-billion Tennessee-Tombigbee Waterway project. The new water passage should stimulate future economic growth.

Despite the efforts to attract new industries and jobs, the living standard of many Tennesseans remains low. The state's economic growth is hampered by insufficient tax revenues and a low literacy rate among workers. However, since the early 1980's Tennessee has been a leader in educational reform.

Charles S. Aiken and C. Edward Skeen

Study aids

Related articles in *World Book* include:

Biographies

Acuff, Roy	Hull, Cordell
Arnold, Eddy	Jackson, Andrew
Baker, Howard Henry, Jr.	Johnson, Andrew
Bell, John	Kefauver, Estes
Blount, William	Polk, James K.
Crockett, David	Ross, John
Davis, Samuel	Sequoya
Driver, William	Sevier, John
Forrest, Nathan B.	White, Hugh L.
Houston, Samuel	York, Alvin C.

Cities

Chattanooga	Memphis
Knoxville	Nashville

History

Civil War	Tennessee Valley Authority
Franklin, State of	Watauga Association
Natchez Trace	Westward movement
Scopes trial	

Physical features

Blue Ridge Mountains	Cumberland River
Clingmans Dome	Great Smoky Mountains
Cumberland Gap	Mississippi River
Cumberland Mountains	Tennessee River

Other related articles

Great Smoky Mountains National Park
Oak Ridge National Laboratory

Outline

I. People
  A. Population
  B. Schools
  C. Libraries
  D. Museums
II. Visitor's guide
  A. Places to visit
  B. Annual events
III. Land and climate
  A. Land regions
  B. Rivers and lakes
  C. Plant and animal life
  D. Climate
IV. Economy
  A. Natural resources
  B. Service industries
  C. Manufacturing
  D. Agriculture
  E. Mining
  F. Electric power
  G. Transportation
  H. Communication
V. Government
  A. Constitution
  B. Executive
  C. Legislature
  D. Courts
  E. Local government
  F. Revenue
  G. Politics
VI. History

Questions

When and why did the people in the Tennessee region form the State of Franklin?

What are the leading minerals found in Tennessee?

Which three U.S. Presidents influenced Tennessee's development?

From what peak in Tennessee is it possible to see seven states?

Why did Memphis lose its city charter in the 1870's?

How does the way of life in East Tennessee differ from that in West and Middle Tennessee?

How can Tennessee's constitution be amended?

How is most electric power in Tennessee generated?

How did the Tennessee region come under British control in the 1700's?

How has the inland water area of Tennessee been doubled since 1933?

Additional resources

Level I

Carpenter, Allan. *Tennessee.* Rev. ed. Childrens Press, 1979.

Fradin, Dennis B. *Tennessee in Words and Pictures.* Childrens Press, 1980.

Schell, Edward. *Tennessee.* Graphic Arts Center, 1979.

Level II

Bergeron, Paul H. *Paths of the Past: Tennessee, 1770-1970.* Univ. of Tennessee Press, 1979.

Clark, Joe. *Tennessee Hill Folk.* Vanderbilt Univ. Press, 1972.

Connelly, Thomas L. *Civil War Tennessee: Battles and Leaders.* Univ. of Tennessee Press, 1979.

Corlew, Robert E. *Tennessee: A Short History.* 2nd ed. Univ. of Tennessee Press, 1981.

Dykeman, Wilma. *Tennessee: A Bicentennial History.* Norton, 1975.

Dykeman, Wilma, and Stokely, Jim. *Highland Homeland: The People of the Great Smokies.* U.S. National Park Service, 1978.

An Encyclopedia of East Tennessee. Ed. by Jim Stokely and J. D. Johnson. Children's Museum of Oak Ridge, 1981.

Greene, Lee S., and others. *Government in Tennessee.* 4th ed. Univ. of Tennessee Press, 1982.

Jones, Billy M., ed. *Heroes of Tennessee.* Memphis State Univ. Press, 1979.

Lamon, Lester C. *Blacks in Tennessee, 1791-1970.* Univ. of Tennessee Press, 1981.

Luther, Edward T. *Our Restless Earth: The Geological Regions of Tennessee.* Univ. of Tennessee Press, 1977.

Satz, Ronald N. *Tennessee's Indian Peoples: From White Contact to Removal, 1540-1840.* Univ. of Tennessee Press, 1979.

Tennessee, University of, is a coeducational, state-assisted institution. Its largest campus is in Knoxville. It also has campuses in Chattanooga, Martin, and Memphis. The university grants bachelor's, master's, and doctor's degrees.

The Knoxville campus includes colleges of agriculture, business administration, communications, education, engineering, human ecology, law, liberal arts, nursing, and veterinary medicine; and a graduate school. The campus is the headquarters for the university's statewide programs of agricultural research and extension, continuing education, and public service.

The Chattanooga and Martin campuses also offer a wide variety of programs, including business administration, education, engineering, and liberal arts. The Memphis campus has colleges of basic medical sciences, allied health sciences, dentistry, medicine, nursing, and pharmacy, and a graduate school of medical sciences.

The university also operates research facilities. The main agricultural experiment station is in Knoxville. Other facilities conduct studies in business and economics, engineering, the environment, health sciences, transportation, and water resources.

The university was founded in 1794 as Blount College. It received its present name in 1879. For the enrollment of the University of Tennessee, see **Universities and colleges** (table).

Critically reviewed by the University of Tennessee

Tennessee River is the largest tributary of the Ohio River. It begins at Knoxville, Tenn., where the Holston and French Broad rivers meet, and flows southwest through Tennessee and Alabama. Then the river curves northward. It flows back into Tennessee and northwest across Kentucky. At Paducah, Ky., it empties into the Ohio River. The Tennessee River drains an area of about 41,000 square miles (106,000 square kilometers).

Development of the Tennessee River's water power to generate electricity began in 1913 with the construction of Hales Bar Dam, near Chattanooga, Tenn. Nickajack Dam replaced Hales Bar Dam in 1968. Wilson Dam, near Muscle Shoals, Ala., began generating electricity in 1925. In 1933, the Tennessee Valley Authority began a series of dams that converted the Tennessee River into a chain of narrow lakes. The river's 650-mile (1,046-kilometer) course is now navigable. In 1985, the completion of the Tennessee-Tombigbee Waterway connected the Tennessee River with the Tombigbee River of Mississippi and Alabama (see **Tombigbee River**).

E. Willard Miller

Tennessee-Tombigbee Waterway. See Tombigbee River.

Tennessee Valley Authority (TVA) is a federal corporation that works to develop the natural resources of the Tennessee Valley. Congress created TVA in 1933 and gave it the overall goal of conserving the resources of the valley region. Congress also directed TVA to speed the region's economic development and, in case of war, to use the Tennessee Valley's resources for national defense.

Beginning in colonial times, the valley's forests had been cut down for lumber or to clear the land for farming and mining. The roots of trees and shrubs had held the soil in place and absorbed moisture. But when the forests were removed, the water ran off the land, carrying the topsoil with it. Farming became decreasingly productive, and flooding rivers caused loss of life and property.

Through the years, TVA has built dams to control floods, create electric power, and deepen rivers for shipping. TVA has also planted new forests and preserved existing ones, and it has developed highly effective fertilizers.

The valley. The Tennessee Valley covers 40,910 square miles (105,956 square kilometers). The valley includes parts of Tennessee, Kentucky, Virginia, North Carolina, Georgia, Alabama, and Mississippi. The land varies from peaks 1 mile (1.6 kilometers) high in the Great Smoky Mountains to the low, muddy plains near the mouth of the Tennessee River. The valley has rich deposits of coal, copper, gravel, iron, limestone, manganese, marble, sand, and zinc.

The achievements of the TVA program have been spread far outside the valley. Power from TVA dams and steam plants reaches homes, farms, factories, stores, and mines in an area of about 80,000 square miles (210,000 square kilometers). In addition, phosphate fertilizers developed and improved under the TVA program have been tested and demonstrated throughout the United States.

The dams. Thirty-nine dams on the Tennessee River and its branches work as a single system, making this one of the most effectively controlled waterways in the world. TVA built most of the dams. The agency also directs the storage and release of water and the genera-

© Gene Ahrens

TVA's Norris Dam on the Clinch River is 265 feet (81 meters) high and 1,860 feet (567 meters) long. Its reservoir stores over $2\frac{1}{2}$ million acre-feet (3.1 billion cubic meters) of water.

tion of power at four dams owned by the Aluminum Company of America (Alcoa). TVA also buys power from eight dams of the Cumberland River system, operated by the U.S. Army Corps of Engineers.

The dams are of two general types. On the main stream of the Tennessee River, long dams were built, making a continuous chain of lakes from Paducah, Ky., to Knoxville, Tenn. Each of these dams has a lock by which towboats and barges may be raised or lowered from one lake level to another.

On the branches of the Tennessee River, high dams were constructed to create great water reservoirs between the hills and mountains. The highest of these dams is Fontana Dam, 480 feet (146 meters) high, on the Little Tennessee River.

TVA dams on the Tennessee River itself are Chickamauga, Fort Loudoun, Guntersville, Kentucky, Nickajack, Pickwick Landing, Watts Bar, Wheeler, and Wilson. Kentucky Dam, the largest, measures 8,422 feet (2,567 meters) long and 206 feet (63 meters) high. It creates a lake about 185 miles (298 kilometers) long.

Electric power. The TVA region uses more than 100 billion kilowatt-hours of electricity a year, about 65 times as much power as it used in 1933. During TVA's early years, dams generated much of its power. But as the demand for electricity increased, the agency had to find other power sources. In the mid-1980's, water power supplied only about a sixth of the electricity generated in the TVA system. Most of the rest came from nuclear power plants and from large steam plants that generated power from coal.

TVA has taken several steps to control environmental damage related to producing electricity. In the past, for example, much of the coal used by TVA to generate electricity came from *strip mining.* Strip mining, a method of surface mining, usually scars the landscape, pollutes rivers, and destroys valuable timber. TVA was criticized for buying coal from strip mines. As a result, TVA has since 1965 required operators of the strip mines supplying coal to its power plants to reclaim any damaged land. TVA also manages one of the largest programs for controlling air pollution from coal-burning plants. Its engineers and scientists work to develop ways of burning coal that will be less harmful to the atmosphere.

In addition, TVA provides practical assistance and low-interest loans to homes and businesses to encourage them to conserve energy and to install solar-energy devices. This program aims to help cut overall energy costs and reduce the need for new power plants.

TVA was designed to provide abundant power for the region at the lowest possible rates. Household users of TVA power pay about a third less per kilowatt-hour than do consumers on the average in the United States. About 160 local nonprofit electric power distributors furnish TVA power for consumers.

River shipping. The Tennessee River provides a 650-mile (1,046-kilometer) route for boats of 9-foot (2.7-meter) draft. It connects with the inland waterway system (see **Inland waterway**). In the mid-1980's, barges on this system carried about 30 million short tons (27 million metric tons) of freight yearly.

Tennessee Valley Authority (TVA)

TVA provides electric power, flood control, water recreation, and navigable waterways in Tennessee and the surrounding states. It builds and operates power plants and dams and directs the operation of several Alcoa and Corps of Engineers dams.

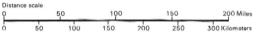

▨ Tennessee River watershed	—	TVA dam
▪ Coal-fired power plant	—E	Corps of Engineers dam
▪ Nuclear power plant	—A	Alcoa dam

WORLD BOOK map

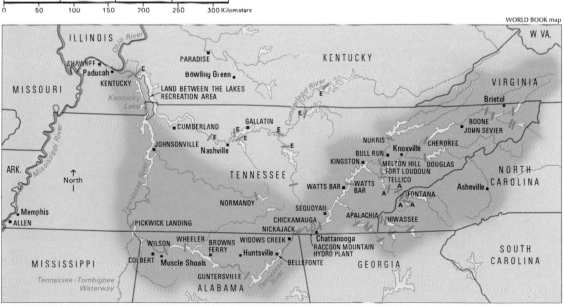

Flood control. Most floods on the Tennessee River occur in late winter and early spring. TVA lowers the lakes in the region during fall and early winter to create space for the expected floodwaters. As the flood season passes in late spring, TVA allows the lakes to fill gradually to high levels for the summer.

Other activities. TVA operates the National Fertilizer Development Center at Muscle Shoals, Ala. Scientists and engineers at the center seek to develop fertilizers and improve methods of producing them. TVA tests the products from the centers on farms nationwide and encourages the private fertilizer industry to mass produce the most successful ones.

In the Tennessee Valley, TVA helps sponsor demonstrations of farming devices and techniques designed to control soil erosion, increase crop yields, and improve farm management and income levels. TVA also works to promote better management of the region's forests. It encourages greater use of them as sources of lumber, furniture, paper, and other wood products.

The lakes created by damming the Tennessee River and its branches add to the beauty of the region. They also provide many recreational opportunities. States, counties, cities, and private organizations have developed many parks and other facilities. TVA itself developed the huge Land Between the Lakes recreational area between Kentucky Lake and Lake Barkley in Kentucky and Tennessee.

History. Congress established the Tennessee Valley Authority after about 15 years of debate on how to use the government's two nitrate plants and Wilson Dam at Muscle Shoals. These projects, built under the National Defense Act of 1916, had not been finished in time for use during World War I. The TVA Act transferred them from the War Department to TVA.

The new corporation represented a great change in national policy. Previously, responsibility for various projects in the valley had been divided among the Departments of Agriculture, the Army, and the Interior. The TVA Act recognized that all conservation problems were related. It gave one agency the responsibility of improving all types of conservation and development of resources.

The creation of TVA became a highly controversial issue and remained so for many years. Private power companies strongly opposed government production of electric power. State and local agencies in the Tennessee Valley feared that TVA would take over their functions. Political opponents of President Franklin D. Roosevelt's New Deal used the issue of the TVA's creation to embarrass him.

TVA pays no federal income taxes, but it pays more than $100 million a year in dividends and repayments to the U.S. Treasury. It also makes payments to states and counties in place of taxes.

A board of three members directs TVA. The President of the United States appoints them to nine-year terms with the consent of the Senate, and they report to the President.   John R. Moore

Related articles in *World Book* include:

Kentucky Lake	Tennessee River
Muscle Shoals	Willkie, Wendell L.
Norris, George W.	Wolf Creek Dam

Additional resources

Callahan, North. *TVA: Bridge over Troubled Waters.* A. S. Barnes, 1980.
Hubbard, Preston J. *Origins of the TVA.* Vanderbilt, 1961.
Morgan, Arthur E. *The Making of the TVA.* Prometheus, 1974. Written by the first director of the Tennessee Valley Authority.
The Economic Impact of TVA. Ed. by John R. Moore. Univ. of Tennessee Press, 1967.

Tennessee walking horse. See Horse (Saddle horses; picture).

Tennessee Wesleyan College. See Universities and colleges (table).

Tenniel, *TEHN yuhl,* **Sir John** (1820-1914), an English cartoonist and book illustrator, illustrated Lewis Carroll's *Alice's Adventures in Wonderland* (1865) and *Through the Looking-Glass* (1871). He also became famous for his political cartoons in *Punch,* a magazine for which he worked for about 50 years after 1850. His work was admired for its originality, dignity, and excellent technique. Tenniel and other artists of his time helped Great Britain keep leadership in the field of book illustration. He was born in London.   Elizabeth Broun

See also **Literature for children** (The rise of illustration; picture: *Through the Looking-Glass*); **Carroll, Lewis** (The *Alice* books).

Macmillan & Co., Ltd.; Radio Times Hulton Picture Library

Sir John Tenniel, *above,* became famous as the illustrator of Lewis Carroll's *Alice's Adventures in Wonderland.* His drawing of the mad tea party, *left,* expressed comic dignity.

Russ Adams Productions

Important tennis tournaments attract thousands of fans who come to watch the world's finest players compete against each other. The tournament held each summer in Wimbledon, England, *above,* ranks as the unofficial world championship for men and women players.

Tennis

Tennis is a game in which opposing players—one or two on each side—use rackets to hit a ball back and forth over a net. The game is played on a flat surface called a *court.* Each player tries to score points by hitting the ball so that the opposing player or players cannot return it over the net and inside the court.

Tennis may be played indoors or outdoors. If two people play, the game is called *singles.* If four people play, it is called *doubles.* In most singles and doubles matches, men play men and women play women. In *mixed doubles,* a man and a woman play on each side.

Millions of people throughout the world play tennis for exercise and recreation. They play on courts in public parks and in private tennis clubs. Players of almost any age can enjoy the sport. The United States Tennis Association (USTA), which governs American tennis, sponsors national tournaments for players as young as 12 and as old as 75.

Professional tennis players travel throughout the world to compete in tournaments that offer thousands of dollars in prize money. Many countries enter men's and women's teams that compete for international trophies. The most famous trophy is the Davis Cup, which represents the world's men's team championship.

Tennis ranks as one of the world's most popular spectator sports as well as a favorite participant sport. Thousands of fans attend the many tournaments held each year. Millions more watch important matches on TV.

Margaret Smith Court, the contributor of this article, won more major tennis titles than any other player in the history of the sport.

Tennis as it is played today developed in England during the late 1800's. The game quickly spread to the United States and other countries. By 1900, tennis had become a major international sport.

The court and equipment

The court is a rectangle divided into halves by a net stretched across the middle. The net measures 3 feet (91 centimeters) high at the center and $3\frac{1}{2}$ feet (107 centimeters) high at the side posts that support it. The court is 78 feet (23.7 meters) long. Almost all courts are marked off so that both singles and doubles games can be played on them. The singles court measures 27 feet (8.2 meters) wide. The doubles court is $4\frac{1}{2}$ feet (1.37 meters) wider on each side. Various lines divide the singles and doubles court into sections. For the names of these lines and the sizes and names of the sections, see the diagram of a court in this article.

For many years, major tennis tournaments were played on grass courts. In fact, the early name for the sport was *lawn tennis.* But grass courts cost much to maintain, and so nearly all of them have been replaced by other surfaces.

The most popular surfaces for outdoor courts are asphalt, clay, and concrete. Most indoor courts have a carpet-type surface laid over concrete or plywood. Several manufacturers have developed surfaces made of synthetic materials. Many of these surfaces can be laid on either indoor or outdoor courts.

Tennis balls are hollow. They are made of rubber and covered with a felt fabric woven of Dacron, nylon, and wool. A tennis ball must have a diameter of more than $2\frac{1}{2}$ inches (6.35 centimeters) but less than $2\frac{5}{8}$ inches (6.67 centimeters). It must weigh more than 2 ounces (56.7 grams) but less than $2\frac{1}{16}$ ounces (58.6 grams). Balls used in tournaments may be either white or yellow. Manufacturers also make balls in other colors.

Tennis rackets. No rules govern the size and weight of a tennis racket, and so the models of various manufacturers differ slightly. But nearly all rackets measure 27 inches (68 centimeters) long. Most men choose a racket that weighs about 14 ounces (397 grams). Most women select one that weighs about 13 ounces (369 grams). In general, young players use a racket that weighs about 9 ounces (255 grams). A typical racket frame is made of fi-

berglass and graphite. The most common striking surface is a net of tightly strung nylon or other synthetic material.

Tennis clothes should fit comfortably so that a player can move freely. During the late 1800's and early 1900's, men players wore long-sleeved shirts and trousers, and women wore ankle-length dresses. Such bulky clothing limited a player's movements. Today, men wear short-sleeved shirts and shorts. Women wear minidresses or blouses and short skirts.

Shoes are perhaps the most important item in a player's wardrobe. Tennis shoes are designed specially for the sport. They are made of cloth and have rubber soles and no heels. The shoes help keep players from slipping and do not damage the court.

How tennis is played

Before they begin to play tennis, the players must decide who serves first and which end of the court each player or team will defend. Most players make these decisions by means of a racket "toss." For example, they may use the manufacturer's markings on one side of a racket handle as "heads" and on the other side as "tails." One player stands the racket upright on the frame and spins it. The opposing player or team calls which side will land face up. If the call is correct, the player or team may either (1) choose to serve or receive first or (2) decide which end of the court to defend.

The court diagram in this article locates the various lines and playing areas discussed in this section.

Scoring. Tennis is scored in terms of points, games, and sets. A player or doubles team scores a *point* when the opposing side fails to return the ball properly or commits an error. To win a *game,* one side must score four points and lead by at least two points. The first

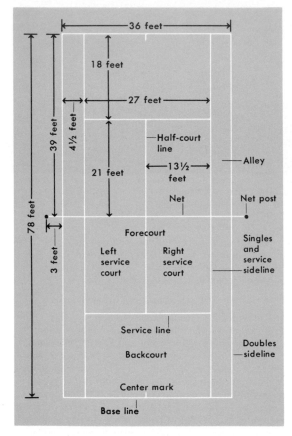

A tennis court is a rectangle divided into halves by a net. Various white lines further divide the court into sections.

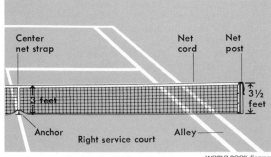

WORLD BOOK diagrams

The net is suspended across the court by a cable or cord. Two posts, one outside each doubles sideline, support the net. A narrow strap in the middle holds the net tight.

Terms used in tennis

Ace, or *service ace,* is a point scored by a server when the receiver is unable to touch a legal serve.

Deuce is a tie score after 6 points in a game or 10 games in a set.

Fault is called when a player serves into the net or outside the receiver's service court. A server commits a *foot fault* by stepping over the base line or changing position by walking or running before hitting the ball during a service. A server who makes two faults in a row commits a *double fault* and loses a point.

Game is the next highest unit of scoring after a point. To win a game, a player must score four points and lead by at least two points.

Ground stroke is any shot that a player uses after the ball bounces once on the court.

Let is a serve that hits the net and drops into the proper service court. A let does not count and is replayed.

Lob is a shot hit high into the air. It is intended to land behind an opponent, forcing the player to retreat from the net.

Love is the scoring term for zero.

Overhead smash is a hard swing at an opponent's shot from above the head.

Set is the highest unit of scoring in a match. To win a set, a player or team must win six games and lead by at least two games unless a tie breaker is played.

Tie breaker is a play-off of a certain number of points to decide the winner of a set. Most tie breakers are played after the game score reaches 6-6.

Volley is any shot made by hitting the ball before it bounces on the court.

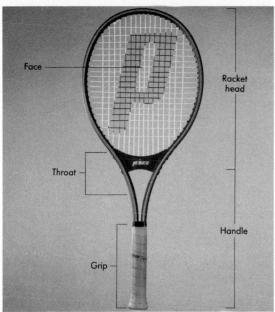

Face

Racket head

Throat

Handle

Grip

A typical tennis racket has a frame made of 85 per cent fiberglass and 15 per cent graphite. The racket's face is a net of nylon or other synthetic material. Leather covers the grip.

point is called *15*; the second, *30*; the third, *40*; and the fourth, *game point.* A score of zero is called *love.* Historians are not certain how this scoring system began.

The server's score is always given first. For example, if the serving side leads three points to one, the score is *40-15.* If the receiving side wins the first two points, the score is *love-30.* If both sides win three points, the score is *40 - 40,* which is called *deuce.* To win a deuce game, one side must lead by two points. The first point scored after deuce is called the *advantage* or *ad.* If the side with the advantage loses the next point, the game returns to deuce.

To win a *set,* one side must win six games and lead by at least two games. If the game score is 5-5—a deuce set—play continues until one side has a two-game margin. In some tournaments, if the score reaches 6-6, a *tie breaker* is played. It consists of a play-off of a certain number of points. The side that wins the tie breaker wins the set by a score of 7-6.

In most competitions, the first side to win two sets wins the tennis *match.* In some tournaments, the first side to win three sets takes the match.

The serve, or *service,* puts the ball into play at the start of each game and after each point is scored. The server must toss the ball into the air and hit it before it strikes the ground. The ball must then travel into the service court diagonally opposite. The server begins each game by serving from the right side of the court. The serve then alternates between the left and right sides following each point. The server must serve from behind the base line but may stand anywhere between the center mark and the singles sideline.

In a singles match, a player serves until a game is completed. Then the receiver becomes the server. The players continue to alternate serves after each game. In

a doubles match, the serve also changes sides after each game. But in addition, the members of each team alternate serves. If a team serves odd-numbered games, for example, one member would serve the first game, the other the third game, and so on. In both singles and doubles matches, the opposing players change ends of the court after the first, third, and all following odd-numbered games.

If a serve lands in the net or outside the receiver's service court, the server has committed a *fault.* A server commits a *foot fault* by stepping on or over the base line or changing position by running or walking before hitting the ball. A player who commits a fault or foot fault gets a second serve. But if this serve fails through a fault or foot fault, the player has committed a *double fault* and loses the point. If the ball hits the top of the net and drops into the proper service court, the serve is called a *let* and is replayed. A let is also called if a player serves before the receiver is ready.

A powerful, accurate serve can help a player win easy points. A player can serve an *ace,* which is a legal serve that the receiver is unable to touch. Even if the receiver manages to return a serve, the return may be so weak the server can easily hit a winning shot.

Receivers may stand anywhere on their end of the court during the service. A receiver often takes a position based on knowledge of an opponent's serve. If the server has a very fast serve, for example, the receiver will stand far back to allow enough time to sight the ball for the return shot.

The ball in play. After the serve, the receiver must hit the ball on the first bounce and return it over the net. The ball must land in the area bounded by the base line and the singles sidelines or, in team play, the doubles sidelines. A shot that lands on a sideline or base line is in play. A shot that hits the net and drops into the opposing court is also in play. After the ball has been served and returned, it may be hit either on the fly, which is called a *volley,* or after the first bounce, which is called a *ground stroke.* The players continue to *rally* (hit the ball back and forth) until one side scores a point. During play, a player or team wins a point if the opposing side (1) hits the ball into the net, (2) hits the ball outside the court, or (3) allows a ball to bounce twice.

Players may use a variety of ground strokes and volleys. The basic shots are the *forehand drive* and the *backhand drive.* Right-handed players hit a forehand drive on the right, or racket, side of the body. They hit a backhand drive by reaching across the body to the left side. Left-handed players hit a forehand drive on the left side and a backhand drive on the right.

To force an opponent away from the net, a player may hit a *lob*—a high shot deep into the opponent's court. The opponent must retreat from the net to reach the ball. If the lob is not hit deep enough, however, the opponent may reply with an *overhead smash.* This shot is made by hitting the ball from above the head. A smash often is so powerful that it cannot be returned.

By hitting the ball in a certain way, a player can give a shot *topspin* or *underspin.* Spin causes the ball to react in such a way that it is difficult to return. A lob hit with topspin will dart toward the rear of the court after it lands. A shot hit with underspin barely clears the net and stays low after it bounces.

The grip is the way in which a player holds the racket. Most players use a grip called the *Continental grip* to serve and a form of the *Eastern grip* to hit forehand and backhand drives. In each grip, the player places the palm and fingers on the handle as shown at the right.

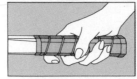 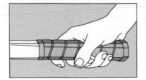 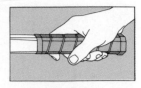

Continental serve   **Eastern forehand**   **Eastern backhand**

WORLD BOOK illustrations by James Curran

The serve. (1) The player, *right,* points his racket toward the net and places one foot comfortably behind the other. (2 and 3) He then tosses the ball into the air with his thumb and first two fingers and starts his backswing. (4) He next moves the racket back until it is behind him and pointing toward the ground. (5) The player then hits the ball with his arm fully extended and the ball slightly in front of him. (6) He ends the stroke with a strong follow-through.

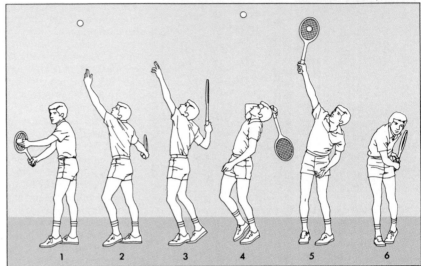

The forehand drive. (1) The player, *right,* stands behind the spot where the ball will bounce. (2 and 3) She pivots her body and starts her backswing as the ball strikes the court. (4) As the ball bounces, she begins to bring the racket forward. (5) She hits the ball when it reaches a height between her knee and waist, keeping the racket parallel to the court. (6) Finally, she shifts her weight to her front foot while following through after hitting the shot.

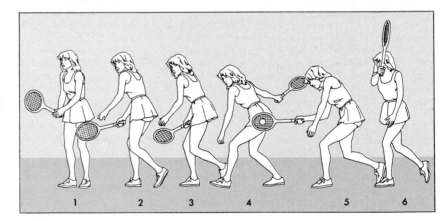

The backhand drive. (1) The player, *right,* holds the grip with one hand and lightly grasps the throat of the racket with the other hand. (2) As he sights the ball, he turns his shoulder toward the net, pivots, and begins his backswing. (3) He ends the backswing with the racket behind him. (4 and 5) He then swings the racket forward, hip high and parallel to the court, and strikes the ball while it is still rising. (6) He follows through to complete the stroke.

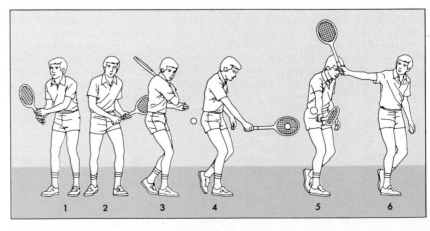

Officials. In most tennis matches, the players themselves act as officials and keep their own score. But in an important tournament, many officials may be used. The chief official is the tournament referee, who has charge of the entire tournament. On the court, the top official is the umpire. The umpire sits on a high chair alongside center court and announces the score to the crowd. The umpire also supervises as many as 13 linespersons. These officials are stationed at various spots around the court. They determine whether a ball has been served legally and whether shots are *good* (inside the court) or *out* (outside the court).

Organized tennis

Amateur tennis. Most of the world's tennis players are amateurs. They play for enjoyment and exercise and receive no pay. Many of them play in small organized interclub competitions, chiefly on weekends. High schools and colleges also sponsor tennis teams as part of their athletics programs.

The International Tennis Federation (ITF) governs tennis throughout the world. The ITF consists of the national tennis associations of about 100 countries. These associations include the U.S. Tennis Association, the Canadian Lawn Tennis Association, the Lawn Tennis Association of Australia, and the Lawn Tennis Association of Great Britain.

Professional tennis. For many years, nearly all the world's leading tournament players were amateurs. Professional tennis first became widely accepted in the late 1960's, and today all the top players are professionals. Professionals play tennis for money, or they are paid for coaching or teaching the game.

Both men and women professionals have formed organizations to represent them and supervise their tournaments. Men professionals established the Association of Tennis Professionals in 1972. The same year, women professionals formed the Women's Tennis Association.

Tennis tournaments. Only amateurs could play in major tournaments before 1968. That year, the member countries of the ITF voted to allow amateurs and professionals to compete in the same tournaments. These events became known as *open* tournaments. Today, almost all major tournaments are open.

The most important tournaments for individual players are the national championships of Great Britain, the United States, Australia, and France. The British meet, popularly called the Wimbledon, is the most highly regarded of the world's major championships. Together, the four championships make up the *grand slam.* Only two men have won all four in the same year. Don Budge of the United States won the grand slam in 1938. Rod Laver of Australia did it twice, in 1962 and 1969. Three women have won the grand slam—Maureen Connolly of the United States in 1953, Margaret Smith Court of Australia in 1970, and Steffi Graf of West Germany in 1988.

A number of organizations sponsor tournaments just for professional players. The leading male professionals play in a series of tournaments, called the Grand Prix Circuit, held throughout the world. Other tournaments are held for lower ranking players. Women professionals also compete in a series of tournaments.

Most amateur and professional tournaments use a system called *seeding* to prevent the top players from meeting each other in an early round. The best player would be seeded number one; the next best, number two; and so on. Players are seeded according to their records and reputations. In most tournaments, eight players are seeded. The matches are arranged so that seeded players do not face each other until the quarterfinal round, unless unseeded players defeat them.

Several tournaments are held for international team trophies. The best-known trophy is the Davis Cup, donated in 1900 by Dwight Davis, an American player. Competition for the cup takes place every year for teams of men players from 16 eligible nations. The teams meet in a series, called a *tie,* consisting of one doubles and four singles matches. For the winners of the trophy, see the article **Davis Cup.**

American and Australian men compete for the World Cup each year. The event began in 1970 and is held in Hartford, Conn. The competition consists of five singles and two doubles.

In 1923, Hazel Hotchkiss Wightman, an American player, donated the Wightman Cup as a trophy for competition between British and American women's teams. The annual Wightman Cup tournament consists of five singles and two doubles. In 1963, the ITF established the Federation Cup for teams of women representing member nations. Each round in this elimination tournament consists of two singles and one doubles.

History

Beginnings. Most historians agree that the French originated tennis during the 1100's or 1200's. The French called it *jeu de paume,* meaning *game of the palm.* The players batted the ball back and forth over a net with the palm of their hand.

Major Walter Clopton Wingfield of England is generally considered the father of modern tennis. In 1873, he introduced a version of the game closely resembling the modern sport. In 1874, he patented tennis equipment and rules for playing on grass courts. Wingfield called the game *sphairistike,* the Greek word for *playing ball.* But the name was soon replaced by *lawn tennis.* Some historians feel that Major Harry Gem of England should share credit as the sport's founder. Gem played a form of tennis in the 1860's.

Tennis soon replaced croquet as England's most popular outdoor sport. In 1877, the All England Croquet Club changed its name to the All England Croquet and Lawn Tennis Club. Also in 1877, the club sponsored the first major tennis tournament at its headquarters in Wimbledon, a suburb of London. This tournament has become the unofficial world championship for men's and women's singles and doubles.

The spread of tennis. Mary Ewing Outerbridge, an American sportswoman, introduced tennis into the United States. In 1874, she purchased tennis equipment from British army officers in Bermuda. Outerbridge used the equipment to set up the first U.S. tennis court. The court was on the grounds of the Staten Island Cricket and Baseball Club in New York City.

The United States National Lawn Tennis Association (now the United States Tennis Association) was established in 1881. That same year, the association sponsored the first U.S. men's championship tournament in Newport, R.I.

Bettmann Archive　　　　　　　　　United Press Int.　　　　　　　　　*Chicago Sun-Times*

Great women players include, *from left to right,* Hazel Hotchkiss Wightman and Helen Wills Moody of the United States and Margaret Smith Court of Australia. Wightman starred in the early 1900's, and Moody during the 1920's and 1930's. Court won many titles in the 1960's and 1970's.

In 1900, the American player Dwight Davis donated the Davis Cup to be awarded annually to the country that wins the world's men's championship. The trophy became recognized as the top prize in international team tennis.

Many of the greatest stars in tennis history played during the 1920's. But the period was dominated by Bill Tilden, an American who is generally considered the sport's finest player. Tilden won the U.S. singles title every year from 1920 through 1925 and again in 1929. He also won the Wimbledon title three times.

The top women players in the 1920's were Suzanne Lenglen of France and Helen Wills (later Helen Wills Moody) of the United States. Lenglen won six Wimbledon and six French championships. Moody won eight Wimbledon championships and seven U.S. titles.

Perhaps the outstanding individual player of the 1930's was Don Budge of the United States. In 1938,

All-England (Wimbledon) Championships

The All-England Championships are held annually in the London suburb of Wimbledon. Men's competition began in 1877, and women's competition in 1884. This table lists the Wimbledon singles champions since 1920.

Men's singles

Year	Winner	Country
1920	Bill Tilden	United States
1921	Bill Tilden	United States
1922	Gerald Patterson	Australia
1923	Bill Johnston	United States
1924	Jean Borotra	France
1925	René Lacoste	France
1926	Jean Borotra	France
1927	Henri Cochet	France
1928	René Lacoste	France
1929	Henri Cochet	France
1930	Bill Tilden	United States
1931	Sid Wood	United States
1932	Ellsworth Vines	United States
1933	Jack Crawford	Australia
1934	Fred Perry	Great Britain
1935	Fred Perry	Great Britain
1936	Fred Perry	Great Britain
1937	Don Budge	United States
1938	Don Budge	United States
1939	Bobby Riggs	United States
1940-45	No competition	
1946	Yvon Petra	France
1947	Jack Kramer	United States
1948	Bob Falkenburg	United States
1949	Ted Schroeder	United States
1950	Budge Patty	United States
1951	Dick Savitt	United States
1952	Frank Sedgman	Australia
1953	Vic Seixas	United States
1954	Jaroslav Drobny	Egypt
1955	Tony Trabert	United States
1956	Lew Hoad	Australia
1957	Lew Hoad	Australia
1958	Ashley Cooper	Australia
1959	Alex Olmedo	United States
1960	Neale Fraser	Australia
1961	Rod Laver	Australia
1962	Rod Laver	Australia
1963	Chuck McKinley	United States
1964	Roy Emerson	Australia
1965	Roy Emerson	Australia
1966	Manuel Santana	Spain
1967	John Newcombe	Australia

Year	Winner	Country
1968	Rod Laver	Australia
1969	Rod Laver	Australia
1970	John Newcombe	Australia
1971	John Newcombe	Australia
1972	Stan Smith	United States
1973	Jan Kodes	Czechoslovakia
1974	Jimmy Connors	United States
1975	Arthur Ashe	United States
1976	Bjorn Borg	Sweden
1977	Bjorn Borg	Sweden
1978	Bjorn Borg	Sweden
1979	Bjorn Borg	Sweden
1980	Bjorn Borg	Sweden
1981	John McEnroe	United States
1982	Jimmy Connors	United States
1983	John McEnroe	United States
1984	John McEnroe	United States
1985	Boris Becker	West Germany
1986	Boris Becker	West Germany
1987	Pat Cash	Australia
1988	Stefan Edberg	Sweden

Women's singles

Year	Winner	Country
1920	Suzanne Lenglen	France
1921	Suzanne Lenglen	France
1922	Suzanne Lenglen	France
1923	Suzanne Lenglen	France
1924	Kitty McKane	Great Britain
1925	Suzanne Lenglen	France
1926	Kitty McKane Godfree	Great Britain
1927	Helen Wills	United States
1928	Helen Wills	United States
1929	Helen Wills	United States
1930	Helen Wills Moody	United States
1931	Cilly Aussem	Germany
1932	Helen Wills Moody	United States
1933	Helen Wills Moody	United States
1934	Dorothy Round	Great Britain
1935	Helen Wills Moody	United States
1936	Helen Hull Jacobs	United States
1937	Dorothy Round	Great Britain
1938	Helen Wills Moody	United States
1939	Alice Marble	United States

Year	Winner	Country
1940-45	No competition	
1946	Pauline Betz	United States
1947	Margaret Osborne	United States
1948	Louise Brough	United States
1949	Louise Brough	United States
1950	Louise Brough	United States
1951	Doris Hart	United States
1952	Maureen Connolly	United States
1953	Maureen Connolly	United States
1954	Maureen Connolly	United States
1955	Louise Brough	United States
1956	Shirley Fry	United States
1957	Althea Gibson	United States
1958	Althea Gibson	United States
1959	Maria Bueno	Brazil
1960	Maria Bueno	Brazil
1961	Angela Mortimer	Great Britain
1962	Karen Hantze Susman	United States
1963	Margaret Smith	Australia
1964	Maria Bueno	Brazil
1965	Margaret Smith	Australia
1966	Billie Jean King	United States
1967	Billie Jean King	United States
1968	Billie Jean King	United States
1969	Ann Haydon Jones	Great Britain
1970	Margaret Smith Court	Australia
1971	Evonne Goolagong	Australia
1972	Billie Jean King	United States
1973	Billie Jean King	United States
1974	Chris Evert	United States
1975	Billie Jean King	United States
1976	Chris Evert	United States
1977	Virginia Wade	Great Britain
1978	Martina Navratilova	United States
1979	Martina Navratilova	United States
1980	Evonne Goolagong	Australia
1981	Chris Evert Lloyd	United States
1982	Martina Navratilova	United States
1983	Martina Navratilova	United States
1984	Martina Navratilova	United States
1985	Martina Navratilova	United States
1986	Martina Navratilova	United States
1987	Martina Navratilova	United States
1988	Steffi Graf	West Germany

United Press Int.

Great men players include, *from left to right,* Bill Tilden and Don Budge of the United States and Rod Laver of Australia. Tilden dominated international competition throughout the 1920's. Budge starred in the late 1930's, and Laver was the world's leading player during the 1960's.

Budge became the first player to win the grand slam.

The mid-1900's. Until the 1950's, France, Great Britain, and the United States produced almost all the world's major players. Then Australia became the leading country in men's competition. From 1950 through 1967, Australian teams won the Davis Cup 15 times. Such players as Roy Emerson, Lew Hoad, Rod Laver, John Newcombe, Ken Rosewall, Frank Sedgman, and Fred Stolle helped Australia maintain its top position in international men's tennis.

During the 1940's and 1950's, several American players achieved worldwide success. The most notable included Pancho Gonzales, Jack Kramer, Frank Parker, Ted Schroeder, and Tony Trabert.

United States Championships

The United States Championships are held annually in Flushing Meadow in New York City. Men's competition began in 1881, and women's in 1887. This table lists the U.S. singles champions since 1920.

Men's singles

Year	Winner	Country
1920	Bill Tilden	United States
1921	Bill Tilden	United States
1922	Bill Tilden	United States
1923	Bill Tilden	United States
1924	Bill Tilden	United States
1925	Bill Tilden	United States
1926	René Lacoste	France
1927	René Lacoste	France
1928	Henri Cochet	France
1929	Bill Tilden	United States
1930	John Doeg	United States
1931	Ellsworth Vines	United States
1932	Ellsworth Vines	United States
1933	Fred Perry	Great Britain
1934	Fred Perry	Great Britain
1935	Wilmer Allison	United States
1936	Fred Perry	Great Britain
1937	Don Budge	United States
1938	Don Budge	United States
1939	Bobby Riggs	United States
1940	Don McNeill	United States
1941	Bobby Riggs	United States
1942	Ted Schroeder	United States
1943	Joe Hunt	United States
1944	Frank Parker	United States
1945	Frank Parker	United States
1946	Jack Kramer	United States
1947	Jack Kramer	United States
1948	Pancho Gonzales	United States
1949	Pancho Gonzales	United States
1950	Art Larsen	United States
1951	Frank Sedgman	Australia
1952	Frank Sedgman	Australia
1953	Tony Trabert	United States
1954	Vic Seixas	United States
1955	Tony Trabert	United States
1956	Ken Rosewall	Australia
1957	Mal Anderson	Australia
1958	Ashley Cooper	Australia
1959	Neale Fraser	Australia
1960	Neale Fraser	Australia
1961	Roy Emerson	Australia
1962	Rod Laver	Australia
1963	Rafael Osuna	Mexico
1964	Roy Emerson	Australia

Year	Winner	Country
1965	Manuel Santana	Spain
1966	Fred Stolle	Australia
1967	John Newcombe	Australia
1968	Arthur Ashe	United States
1969	Rod Laver	Australia
1970	Ken Rosewall	Australia
1971	Stan Smith	United States
1972	Ilie Nastase	Romania
1973	John Newcombe	Australia
1974	Jimmy Connors	United States
1975	Manuel Orantes	Spain
1976	Jimmy Connors	United States
1977	Guillermo Vilas	Argentina
1978	Jimmy Connors	United States
1979	John McEnroe	United States
1980	John McEnroe	United States
1981	John McEnroe	United States
1982	Jimmy Connors	United States
1983	Jimmy Connors	United States
1984	John McEnroe	United States
1985	Ivan Lendl	Czechoslovakia
1986	Ivan Lendl	Czechoslovakia
1987	Ivan Lendl	Czechoslovakia
1988	Mats Wilander	Sweden

Women's singles

Year	Winner	Country
1920	Molla Bjurstedt Mallory	United States
1921	Molla Bjurstedt Mallory	United States
1922	Molla Bjurstedt Mallory	United States
1923	Helen Wills	United States
1924	Helen Wills	United States
1925	Helen Wills	United States
1926	Molla Bjurstedt Mallory	United States
1927	Helen Wills	United States
1928	Helen Wills	United States
1929	Helen Wills	United States
1930	Betty Nuthall	Great Britain
1931	Helen Wills Moody	United States
1932	Helen Hull Jacobs	United States
1933	Helen Hull Jacobs	United States
1934	Helen Hull Jacobs	United States
1935	Helen Hull Jacobs	United States
1936	Alice Marble	United States
1937	Anita Lizana	Chile
1938	Alice Marble	United States
1939	Alice Marble	United States
1940	Alice Marble	United States

Year	Winner	Country
1941	Sarah Palfrey Cooke	United States
1942	Pauline Betz	United States
1943	Pauline Betz	United States
1944	Pauline Betz	United States
1945	Sarah Palfrey Cooke	United States
1946	Pauline Betz	United States
1947	Louise Brough	United States
1948	Margaret Osborne duPont	United States
1949	Margaret Osborne duPont	United States
1950	Margaret Osborne duPont	United States
1951	Maureen Connolly	United States
1952	Maureen Connolly	United States
1953	Maureen Connolly	United States
1954	Doris Hart	United States
1955	Doris Hart	United States
1956	Shirley Fry	United States
1957	Althea Gibson	United States
1958	Althea Gibson	United States
1959	Maria Bueno	Brazil
1960	Darlene Hard	United States
1961	Darlene Hard	United States
1962	Margaret Smith	Australia
1963	Maria Bueno	Brazil
1964	Maria Bueno	Brazil
1965	Margaret Smith	Australia
1966	Maria Bueno	Brazil
1967	Billie Jean King	United States
1968	Virginia Wade	Great Britain
1969	Margaret Smith Court	Australia
1970	Margaret Smith Court	Australia
1971	Billie Jean King	United States
1972	Billie Jean King	United States
1973	Margaret Smith Court	Australia
1974	Billie Jean King	United States
1975	Chris Evert	United States
1976	Chris Evert	United States
1977	Chris Evert	United States
1978	Chris Evert	United States
1979	Tracy Austin	United States
1980	Chris Evert Lloyd	United States
1981	Tracy Austin	United States
1982	Chris Evert Lloyd	United States
1983	Martina Navratilova	United States
1984	Martina Navratilova	United States
1985	Hana Mandlikova	Czechoslovakia
1986	Martina Navratilova	United States
1987	Martina Navratilova	United States
1988	Steffi Graf	West Germany

Focus on Sports   Focus on Sports   © Bob Martin, Allsport

Modern women tennis stars include, *from left to right,* Chris Evert and Martina Navratilova of the United States and Steffi Graf of West Germany. Evert and Navratilova dominated the sport from the mid-1970's to the late 1980's, when Graf became the leading player.

The United States provided most of the top women stars from the mid-1940's through the mid-1960's. They included Louise Brough, Maureen Connolly, Margaret Osborne duPont, and Doris Hart. Connolly was probably the greatest woman player of this period. In 1953, she became the first woman to win the grand slam.

Althea Gibson of the United States became the first important black tennis player. She won the U.S. and Wimbledon titles in 1957 and 1958. In the late 1960's, Arthur Ashe of the United States became the first black male tennis star. In 1968, he won the U.S. singles championship.

Laver ranked as the top male star of the 1960's. The Australian became the only player to win the grand slam twice, in 1962 as an amateur and in 1969 as a professional. Other leading male players of the 1960's included Manuel Santana of Spain and Stan Smith of the United States. In the 1960's, Margaret Smith (later Margaret Smith Court) became the first Australian woman to win the U.S. and Wimbledon singles titles. She won the

grand slam in 1970. Maria Bueno of Brazil and Billie Jean King of the United States also ranked as important players of the period.

Tennis today. International tennis has largely been a professional sport since 1968. Professionals compete for millions of dollars in prize money annually. Television played an important role in increasing the popularity of tennis during the 1970's and 1980's. Major tournaments are televised to many countries.

Several highly publicized matches were arranged largely for television audiences. In 1973, Bobby Riggs, a top-ranked American player of the late 1930's and 1940's, defeated Margaret Smith Court in a televised "battle of the sexes." Later that year, Riggs played Billie Jean King in the Houston Astrodome before 30,472 spectators, the largest crowd ever to watch a tennis match. Millions more people watched on TV as King defeated Riggs.

The Davis Cup became a center of political dispute in the 1970's. In 1974, South Africa won the cup by forfeit from India. The Indian government refused to allow its

Focus on Sports   © Jacques M. Chenet, Woodfin Camp, Inc.   © Bob Martin, Allsport

Modern men tennis stars include, *from left to right,* Bjorn Borg of Sweden, John McEnroe of the United States, and Czech-born Ivan Lendl. Borg was the top player in the world in the 1970's. McEnroe and Lendl ranked among the top international players of the 1980's.

team to play because of South Africa's *apartheid* (racial separation) policies. The Davis Cup had already lost some of its importance because many professionals refused to play for their countries. These players claimed that the many weeks of cup play-offs would force them to miss too many tournaments. In 1981, Davis Cup competition was changed to attract more top players. It was compressed into a shorter period of time and the prize money was increased.

By the mid-1970's, a new generation of players had begun to dominate tennis. The most successful men players of the 1970's and early 1980's included Jimmy Connors, Arthur Ashe, and John McEnroe of the United States; Bjorn Borg of Sweden; Guillermo Vilas of Argentina; and John Newcombe of Australia. Leading women players included Tracy Austin, Chris Evert, Andrea Jaeger, and Martina Navratilova of the United States; and Evonne Goolagong of Australia. By the mid-1980's, another group of players began to dominate the sport. The leading men were Ivan Lendl of Czechoslovakia, Mats Wilander and Stefan Edberg of Sweden, Pat Cash of Australia, and Boris Becker of West Germany. The top women players included Evert, Navratilova, and Pam Shriver of the United States; Steffi Graf of West Germany; and Gabriela Sabatini of Argentina.

In 1987, Navratilova won the women's singles championship at Wimbledon for the sixth consecutive year. No one had ever won a men's or women's singles title at Wimbledon more than five straight times in the history of modern tennis.   Margaret Smith Court

Related articles in *World Book* include:

Ashe, Arthur	Evert, Chris	Navratilova, Martina
Badminton	Gibson, Althea	
Borg, Bjorn	Gonzales, Pancho	Platform tennis
Budge, Don	King, Billie Jean	Table tennis
Connors, Jimmy	Laver, Rod	Tilden, Bill
Davis Cup	McEnroe, John	Wills, Helen N.

Outline

I. **The court and equipment**
  A. The court   C. Tennis rackets
  B. Tennis balls   D. Tennis clothes
II. **How tennis is played**
  A. Scoring   C. The ball in play
  B. The serve   D. Officials
III. **Organized tennis**
  A. Amateur tennis   C. Tennis tournaments
  B. Professional tennis
IV. **History**

Questions

What is an open tournament?
How does a player hit a backhand drive?
What is a *tie breaker*?
Why have almost all grass courts been replaced by other surfaces?
What is a *fault*? A *double fault*?
When would a player hit a smash?
What is the Davis Cup? The Wightman Cup?
Where are the All-England Championships and the United States Championships held?
Who is considered the father of modern tennis?

Additional resources

Benjamin, David A. *Competitive Tennis: A Guide for Parents and Young Players.* Harper, 1979.
Braden, Vic, and Burns, William. *Teaching Children Tennis the Vic Braden Way.* Little, Brown, 1980.
Navratilova, Martina, and Carillo, Mary. *Tennis My Way.* Scribner, 1983.

United States Tennis Association. *Official Encyclopedia of Tennis.* Rev. ed. Harper, 1981.

Tennyson, Lord (1809-1892), *Alfred Tennyson,* was one of the most important English poets of the 1800's. He succeeded William Wordsworth as poet laureate of Great Britain in 1850. Tennyson earned his position in literature because of the remarkable range of his natural talents and his dedication throughout his long career to perfecting his art. Tennyson stands today both as a great national poet and as one of the supreme craftsmen in the English language.

His life. Alfred Tennyson was born on Aug. 6, 1809, in Somersby, Lincolnshire. His father was *rector* (clergyman in charge) of the parish there.

Tennyson entered Cambridge University in 1828, but he never received a degree. At Cambridge, he joined "The Apostles," a society of undergraduates that included several men who later became intellectual leaders of the age. Tennyson's most intimate friend in this circle was Arthur Henry Hallam. Hallam's sudden death in 1833 was a crucial event in the poet's generally uneventful life. Tennyson wrote his great *elegy* (poem mourning a death) *In Memoriam* (1850) in memory of Hallam.

Tennyson was the most popular British poet of the Victorian era, but he avoided public life. He married in 1850 and lived quietly in his country homes at Farringford on the Isle of Wight and Aldworth in Surrey. Tennyson's long list of works showed his consistent inspiration and creative vitality, beginning with *Poems, Chiefly Lyrical* (1830) and extending to *The Death of Oenone and Other Poems,*

Oil portrait by M. Arnault, National Portrait Gallery, London

Lord Tennyson

published after his death more than 60 years later. He was awarded the title of Baron Tennyson in 1883 by Queen Victoria. His full title was Baron of Aldworth and Farringford. Tennyson died on Oct. 6, 1892, and was buried in the Poets' Corner of Westminster Abbey.

His poems. Tennyson's influential place in the intellectual life of his age comes largely from his concern with the vital issues confronting Victorian England. He reveals his sense of political responsibility in such patriotic verses as "Ode on the Death of the Duke of Wellington" and his famous "The Charge of the Light Brigade," which was inspired by an incident in the Crimean War (see **Balaklava, Battle of**). *Maud,* a narrative in the form of separate lyrics, describes the withering effect of the materialistic spirit of his day on a sensitive young lover.

Tennyson's accurate and concrete descriptions of nature reflect his informed interest in science. The stars, for example, suggest to the unhappy speaker in *Maud:*

  A sad astrology, the boundless plan
  That makes you tyrants in your iron skies,
  Innumerable, pitiless, passionless eyes,
  Cold fires, yet with power to burn and brand
  His nothingness into man.

Tennyson's masterpiece, *In Memoriam,* consists of

133 individual poems composed between his friend Arthur Hallam's death in 1833 and their publication in 1850. The work ranks with John Milton's *Lycidas* and Percy Bysshe Shelley's *Adonais* as one of the greatest examples of the elegy in English poetry. *In Memoriam* is personal and specific in its focus on Tennyson's struggles as artist and thinker. The poem frequently offers general consolation to a troubled age:

> I stretch lame hands of faith and grope,
> And gather dust and chaff, and call
> To what I feel is Lord of all,
> And faintly trust the larger hope.

Perhaps no English poet had a more acute ear for fine shades of poetic expression or a greater range of verse style than Tennyson. His exquisite lyrics perfectly express emotions and experiences shared by all people. Among the most moving of these are many of the sections from *In Memoriam,* as well as "Break, Break, Break" and "Tears, Idle Tears." Following the author's wishes, "Crossing the Bar," the noble address to death, always ends collections of his poems.

Tennyson's most characteristic form of poetry was the idyl, a poem about country life developed by the ancient Greeks. These poems often take the form of dramatic *reveries* (daydreams) spoken by mythical figures. They tell a story, but depend primarily on the creation of mood through the power of richly described settings, as in "The Lotos-Eaters." Many of these stories indirectly urge Victorians to act heroically. The speakers commonly fall into two groups: the lovelorn maidens of "Mariana," "The Lady of Shalott," and "Oenone"; and the aged heroes and prophets of "Ulysses," "Tithonus," "Tiresias," and "Merlin and the Gleam."

Tennyson's lifelong fascination with King Arthur and his knights led to his most ambitious work, *Idylls of the King.* It is a series of 12 narrative poems that he published with constant revisions between 1842 and 1885. The work has an *allegorical* (symbolic) side, suggested by the many implied comparisons between Arthur and Queen Victoria's husband, Prince Albert, who had died in 1861. The work also ends with an allegorical *epilogue* (closing) to the queen with its invitation to:

> accept this old imperfect tale
> New-old, and shadowing Sense at war with Soul,
> Ideal manhood closed in real man . . .

Nevertheless, the poem is most likely to move a modern audience as the story of King Arthur's vision of the perfect state. This vision was tragically betrayed by the inability of the king's followers to live up to his heroic ideals.   Richard J. Dunn

See also **Galahad, Sir; January** (Quotations); **Poetry** (Introduction).

Additional resources

Martin, Robert B. *Tennyson: The Unquiet Heart.* Oxford, 1980.
Tennyson, Hallam. *Alfred, Lord Tennyson: A Memoir by His Son.* Longwood, 1977. Reprint of 1897 edition.

Tenochtitlan. See **Aztec** (introduction; History); **Indian, American** (Indians of Middle America; picture: The Aztec capital); **Cuauhtémoc.**

Tenpins. See **Bowling.**

Tense is a feature of verbs that indicates the time of an action. There are three divisions of time—present, past, and future. Within these divisions, English has six tenses—present, past, future, present perfect, past perfect, and future perfect.

Only two forms of English verbs can express time by themselves. These are the simple present, as in *She sees,* and the simple past, as in *She saw.* All other forms are phrases that include *helping verbs,* also called *auxiliaries.* Such forms combine helping verbs with the simple present (*see*), the present participle (*seeing*), or the past participle (*seen*). The following shows all six tenses:

Present	She sees.
Past	She saw.
Future	She will see.
Present perfect	She has seen.
Past perfect	She had seen.
Future perfect	She will have seen.

These tenses are written in the active voice and indicative mood. For a complete list of the tenses for all forms of a verb, see **Conjugation.**

The *progressive* forms of a verb indicate that an action is in progress at a particular time—for example, *She is seeing the picture for the first time.* The *emphatic* forms provide emphasis, as in *She does see.* However, this form is more commonly used to ask questions, such as *Does she see?* It is also used to make negative statements, such as *She does not see.*

The perfect tenses express time relationships other than simple present, past, and future. The present perfect expresses an action that belongs to the past but touches the present: *Until now, we have seen Paris three times.* The past perfect expresses an action completed at some past time: *In 1945, we had seen Paris only once.* The future perfect expresses an action to be completed at some future time: *By next year, we will have seen Paris for the fourth time.*

Perfect tenses sometimes express special kinds of action. For example, *We keep seeing ugly billboards* shows repeated action. *We used to see better times than we do now* expresses past continuing action. *We go on seeing what we want to see* shows present continuing action. *We are about to see an amazing feat* expresses action to come.

Future time is expressed by the auxiliaries *will* and *shall.* Current usage no longer distinguishes between the two, but *shall* is rapidly disappearing from use. Future time is also indicated by the present tense plus an adverbial expression: *He sails tomorrow.* In addition, future time can be expressed by other forms:

> He is sailing tomorrow.
> He is to sail tomorrow.
> He is going to sail tomorrow.

Literary uses of tense. Many writers, especially historians and storytellers, use the present tense to tell about the past. This technique, called the *historical present,* provides a quality of vividness and immediacy. The present tense also is often used to describe any published work—for example, *The story of* Alice in Wonderland *includes many fantastic characters and incidents.*

Tenses follow natural sequences, depending on the wishes of the author. A writer generally chooses a tense and maintains it unless a change seems desirable. For example, an author might want to discuss the working conditions in a particular industry. The writer could begin by describing conditions in past years, then follow with an account of present conditions, and end with ideas about developments in the future. The tenses would reflect these changes. *William F. Irmscher*

See also **Verb.**

Tenskwatawa. See Shawnee Prophet.

Tent is a portable shelter that many campers use for protection against the weather and insects. Most tents consist of a wooden or metal frame with a covering and floor made of nylon, canvas, or cotton.

Tents are made in a variety of sizes and styles. They range from small models for one person to large cabin tents for as many as six adults. Extremely large tents are used for such activities as carnivals, circuses, and church meetings. This article discusses camping tents.

Kinds of tents. There are more than half a million styles and sizes of camping tents. However, most of them are variations of one of three basic types: (1) A-frame tents, (2) umbrella tents, and (3) wall tents.

A-frame tents rise to a point at the top and resemble the letter *A*. One or two people can sleep in these small, lightweight tents, which are ideal for backpack trips. Most mountaineering tents designed for year-round camping are A-frame shelters.

Umbrella tents are larger and heavier than A-frame tents. An umbrella tent has slightly slanted walls and a pyramid-shaped top. Some models have a center pole that decreases the space inside the tent, but newer ones lack this pole. Umbrella tents have sleeping space for four to six people. They are sturdy shelters that can withstand high winds.

Wall tents resemble small houses. They have vertical walls and an A-frame roof. They provide more sleeping and standing room than A-frame or umbrella tents but are harder to pitch. One kind of wall tent, the *cabin tent,* offers the highest degree of camping comfort. Its spacious interior and high walls allow more room for standing, walking, and sleeping than any other kind of tent. Wall tents and most umbrella tents are too large and heavy to carry in a backpack. They are used mainly by campers who drive to campsites.

Most tents of all kinds are made of canvas or nylon. Canvas tents weigh much more but are less likely to leak. Most nylon tents are specially treated to prevent leakage. However, this treatment also seals moisture inside the tent and may cause the interior to become damp. Some nylon tents have a canvas roof that lets moisture escape. Others have a roof with an untreated nylon layer through which moisture can pass, plus a treated nylon covering that keeps rain out.

All tents provide some type of ventilation and protection against rain and insects. Cabin tents have large windows and a door, and smaller tents have vents and a door flap. In most tents, these openings are covered with netting that keeps insects out. Many tents have flaps that can be closed over the windows during a storm, and some have a storm flap that can be put over the entire tent.

Pitching a tent. Before setting up camp, campers should find a suitable spot to pitch their tent. The ideal campsite lies on high, level ground near trees and has firewood and fresh water nearby. Camping on high ground helps prevent the tent from being flooded during a storm. If a tent is pitched on low ground, a shallow

Some kinds of tents

Tents are manufactured in many sizes and styles. They range from small shelters for one or two people to larger tents that can hold six adults. Some popular tents are shown below.

WORLD BOOK illustrations by David Cunningham

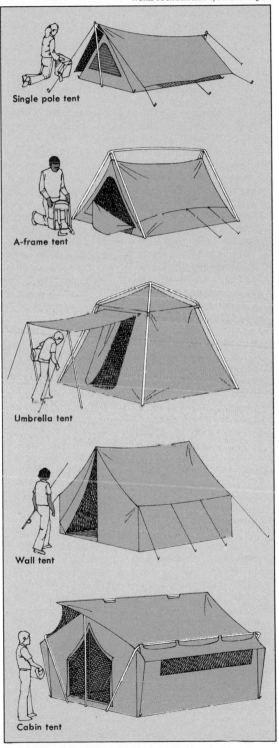

Single pole tent

A-frame tent

Umbrella tent

Wall tent

Cabin tent

trench should be dug around it to keep water out. Campers should not pitch a tent close to trees with dead branches that could break off easily in high winds and strike the tent.

In most cases, the first step in pitching a tent is to spread out the floor and secure it to the ground with stakes. The stakes are driven into the ground through small loops along the bottom edge of the tent. The pitching procedure then varies according to the design of the tent. If the tent has an interior frame, the frame is erected and the fabric draped over it. A tent with an exterior frame has hangers to which the fabric is attached. The fabric should be stretched enough to eliminate large wrinkles, but not so tightly that it will rip.

Wall tents and some A-frame tents are staked with ropes called *guy lines.* The guy lines of a wall tent are staked several feet from the tent. They are strung through holes along the top edges of the walls. Some A-frame tents have a guy line attached to the top of the tent at each end. Guy lines can be adjusted to assure the proper shape of the tent and tightness of the fabric.

Caring for a tent. A tent that receives proper care will provide years of use. The most important points in caring for a tent are to keep it as clean and dry as possible. Dirt, insects, and leaves should be wiped off the shelter each time it is taken down. If the tent is wet, it should be pitched and dried as soon as possible to avoid mildew and discoloration. After a camping trip, a tent should be thoroughly cleaned and dried before storage. Canvas and nylon tents can be washed in a mild detergent. In addition, poles and stakes should not be packed with the tent fabric because they could puncture it.   Samuel R. Thoreson

See also **Camping.**

Tent caterpillar is the larva of certain moths that damage trees. They get their name because they spin a loose, white web that looks like a tent. This web envelops tree twigs and is the home for a group of caterpillars.

In midsummer, the female moth lays brown egg masses on tree twigs. The eggs hatch the following spring. After feeding for about six weeks, the larvae enter the *pupa stage* in which they spin silky cocoons around themselves. After three weeks, they emerge as full-grown moths, mate, lay their eggs, and die.

Tent caterpillars damage trees because they eat the leaves. A nest of caterpillars has been known to eat most of the leaves on a single tree. The *eastern tent caterpillar* lives in tents in fruit and shade trees. It has a yellow line along its back. The *forest tent caterpillar* lives in forest trees but it does not build a tent. It has a row of yellow spots along its back. Both species are black and hairy with blue spots on the sides. Both kinds live in eastern and central North America. Other species are found in the West.

Tent caterpillars can be controlled by collecting the egg masses in winter, and by burning the larvae in their tents in spring. Spraying with lead arsenate gives effective control over large areas.

Scientific classification. Tent caterpillars are members of the tent caterpillar family, Lasiocampidae. They are in the genus *Malacosoma.*   Alexander B. Klots

Tentacle, *TEHN tuh kuhl,* is a slender leg or arm of certain animals. Tentacles are ordinarily used for protec-

Edward S. Ross

A group of tent caterpillars gather in their white, tentlike nest in an oak tree, *above.* Tent caterpillars can seriously damage trees because they eat the leaves.

tion or as feelers. Sea anemones and octopuses use tentacles to capture food.

See also **Coelenterate; Octopus** (picture); **Jellyfish** (with pictures); **Animal** (picture); **Mollusk** (Univalves or gastropods; Octopuses and squids).

Tenure of Office Act was passed by Congress in 1867 over the veto of President Andrew Johnson. From the time the United States government was founded, the custom had been to permit the President to dismiss presidential appointees at will. But discord arose between President Johnson and Congress on questions of Reconstruction after the Civil War. Congress passed the Tenure of Office Act for fear that Johnson might use his powers of dismissal to upset the congressional plan of reconstruction. The act in effect required the Senate's consent to the dismissal of any official whose appointment had required its consent.

The law was clearly contrary to American tradition, and Johnson believed it to be unconstitutional. In 1868, to test this point, Johnson removed Edwin M. Stanton from the office of secretary of war, a course of action which led to the President's impeachment. Johnson was not convicted, however, and the reason for the law ceased to exist. The Tenure of Office Act was repealed in 1887.

An act passed in 1821 also bore the name *Tenure of Office Act.* It limited the terms of many appointive officers to four years, and is said to have laid the foundation for the spoils system.   John Donald Hicks

See also **Johnson, Andrew** (Increased tension).

Tenzing Norgay. See Mount Everest.

Teotihuacán. See Mexico (picture: Ancient pyramids and temples).

Tepee, also spelled *tipi,* was the type of tent most commonly used by the Plains tribes of North American Indians. A tepee was made by stretching a buffalo-skin covering over poles. The poles were arranged in the shape of a cone. At the top, the ends of the poles crossed and stuck out of the covering. Two flap "ears" were opened at the top to let out smoke from the campfire. The tent was pegged to the ground all around the bottom. The front had a slit partly closed with wooden pins to form an entrance. W. Roger Buffalohead

See also **Indian, American** (pictures); **Tent; Wigwam.**

Tephra. See **Volcano** (Rock fragments; Kinds of volcanoes).

Terbium, *TUR bee uhm* (chemical symbol, Tb), is one of the rare-earth metals. Its atomic number is 65, and its atomic weight is 158.925. Swedish scientist Carl Mosander first discovered terbium in 1843. Georges Urbain of France first isolated it in an almost pure form in 1905. Terbium is best separated from the other rare earths by ion-exchange processes or by solvent extraction. It has a density of 8.253 grams per cubic centimeter at 25° C. Terbium resembles silver in appearance. It melts at about 1365° C and boils at 3230° C. Chemists believe that terbium has a valence of 3 in most compounds. The dark-brown oxide (Tb_4O_7) becomes the white oxide (Tb_2O_3) when heated in a stream of hydrogen. Terbium salts are white with a slight pink cast. Many terbium compounds glow with a green color and are used in phosphors. Larry C. Thompson

See also **Element, Chemical; Rare earth.**

Terek River. See **Caspian Sea.**

Terence, *TEHR uhns* (195?-159? B.C.), was a Roman comic playwright. His plays are essentially Latin versions of Greek plots, more refined than those of Plautus and marked by pure style, careful construction, and fine characterization. All six of his comedies survive. They are *The Woman of Andros, The Self-Tormentor, The Eunuch, Phormio, The Mother-in-Law,* and *The Brothers. The Brothers* is a thoughtful comedy about two brothers, a country man and a city man. Each brings up one of the sons of the country brother. The country man is strict and the city man is permissive. The resulting idea, that education must pay attention to human nature, perhaps reflects Terence's own experience.

Terence was born Publius Terentius Afer in Carthage. He came to Rome as a slave in the household of a senator who educated and freed him. Norman T. Pratt

Teresa, *tuh RAY suh,* **Mother** (1910-   ), is a Roman Catholic nun who received the 1979 Nobel Peace Prize for her work with the poor. She is known as the *saint of the gutters.* In 1950, Mother Teresa founded a religious order in Calcutta, India, called the Missionaries of Charity. The order provides food for the needy and operates hospitals, schools, orphanages, youth centers, and shelters for lepers and the dying poor. It has branches in about 50 Indian cities and about 30 other countries.

Mother Teresa, whose original name was Agnes Gonxha Bojaxhiu, was born in what is now Skopje, Yugoslavia. In 1928, she joined a religious order, which sent her to India. She took the name Teresa after joining the order. A few years later, she began teaching in Calcutta. In 1948, the Catholic Church granted her permission to leave her convent and work among the city's poor people. She became an Indian citizen that year.

Wide World
Mother Teresa

In addition to the 1979 Nobel Peace Prize, Mother Teresa has received other awards for her work with the needy. These awards include the Pope John XXIII peace prize, which she received in 1971, and India's Jawaharlal Nehru award for international understanding, given to her in 1972. James McGovern

Additional resources

Doig, Desmond. *Mother Teresa: Her People and Her Work.* Harper, 1980. First published in 1976.

Egan, Eileen. *Such a Vision of the Street: Mother Teresa-The Spirit and the Work.* Doubleday, 1985.

Leigh, Vanora. *Mother Teresa.* Bookwright, 1985. For younger readers.

Spink, Kathryn. *The Miracle of Love: Mother Teresa of Calcutta, Her Missionaries of Charity and Her Co-Workers.* Harper, 1981.

Tereshkova, *teh rehsh KAW vah,* **Valentina Vladimirovna,** *VAH lehn TEE nah vlah DEE mih RAWV nuh* (1937-   ), of the Soviet Union, became the first woman to travel in space. In the spacecraft *Vostok VI,* Tereshkova made 45 revolutions around the earth in a 70-hour and 50 minute space flight from June 16 to June 19, 1963. Soviet cosmonaut Valery F. Bykovsky was in orbit at the same time. He was launched almost two days before Tereshkova. The two spacecraft came within 3 miles (5 kilometers) of each other during the flight. According to Soviet officials, the dual flight was conducted for "simultaneous observation of the reactions of a man and woman flying in space."

Tereshkova orbited the earth once every 88 minutes during her historic journey. The *apogee* (highest point in the orbit) carried her about 130 miles (209 kilometers) above the earth. The *perigee* (lowest point in the orbit) was approximately 108 miles (174 kilometers) above the earth. Tereshkova operated her spacecraft by manual controls.

Tereshkova parachuted from the *Vostok VI* after reentering the earth's atmosphere. She landed approximately 380 miles (612 kilometers) northeast of Karaganda, Kazakhstan, in central Asia.

Tereshkova, the first space traveler with no experience as a test pilot, became interested in parachuting as a hobby. She made more than 125 jumps before volunteering for space flight training school. Tereshkova also received training as an airplane pilot.

Sovfoto
Valentina Tereshkova

Tereshkova was born in the village of Maslennikovo, near Yaroslavl. She went to work in a textile mill when she was 18 years old. Tereshkova became an active member of the Young Communist League while at the mill. In November 1963, she married cosmonaut Andrian G. Nikolayev. Cathleen S. Lewis

See also **Astronaut** (The cosmonauts; picture: First woman in space).

Term paper. See the section *A Student Guide to Better Writing, Speaking, and Research Skills* in the Research Guide/Index, Volume 22.

Terman, *TUR muhn,* **Lewis Madison** (1877-1956), was an American psychologist who became known for his studies of intelligence. In 1916, while teaching at Stanford University, Terman revised the Binet-Simon intelligence tests, which were in French, for English-speaking students. The revised examination, usually called the Stanford-Binet test, became one of the most widely used tests of learning ability. Terman worked with Maud A. Merrill, another Stanford psychologist, on two later revisions of the test published in 1937 and 1960.

Terman was especially interested in children of high intelligence. In the early 1920's, he began a study of the behavior and personality of about 1,500 extremely bright elementary and high school students. He observed them throughout their careers and reported on their development. Terman's study helped prove that most bright children are normal and well adjusted. The reports of his study were published in a five-volume series, *Genetic Studies of Genius* (1925-1959).

Terman was born in Johnson County, Indiana. He taught at Stanford from 1910 to 1942.   Richard M. Wolf

See also **Intelligence quotient** (History).

Termite is the common name of a group of chemically complex insects that live in communities somewhat as ants do. They have long been known as *white ants.* This name is incorrect, for termites are like ants only in their habits of living together and in their small size. Actually termites are more closely related to cockroaches and grasshoppers. Their mouth parts, antennae, thick waists, primitive wings, and other features resemble those of cockroaches. Ants have thin waists and elbowed antennae.

Life and habits. There are three *castes* (groups) in most termite colonies. Some reproduce, others are workers, and still others are soldiers. The highest is the *royal* or *reproductive* caste. This is made up of fully developed males and females. Of all the termites, these most closely resemble other insects. They are dark colored and have eyes, fairly hard bodies, and fully developed wings. Each colony of termites is founded by a pair of reproductives, which become the king and queen of the colony. Other and less completely developed kings and queens often develop in older colonies. In every mature colony, also, there develops an annual population of young winged reproductives that leave the parent nest, mate, and set out to start new colonies. They use their delicate, membranous wings for but one short flight. They break their wings off immediately afterward and just before they seek mates.

The *worker* caste consists of small, blind, wingless termites with pale or whitish soft bodies. Only the heads and feet of the workers are covered with a hard protective material. The workers are the most numerous individuals in a colony. They do all the work. They enlarge the nest, search for food and water for the colony, and make tunnels.

The *soldiers,* which are also wingless and blind, are larger than the workers. They have enormous hard heads, powerful jaws, and strong legs. Their bodies are soft and weak. The sole duty of the soldiers is to defend the termite colony against attack, principally against ants. The soldiers are strangely unable to care for themselves. They must be fed and groomed by the workers.

All termite castes contain both sexes, and the kings live as long as the queens. In wasp, ant, and bee colonies, *drones* (males) appear only in the reproductive caste and live for only a short time.

Termite eggs and newly hatched young appear to be alike in all the castes. Why some young develop into workers and others into soldiers or reproductives has not been entirely settled. With certain termites it seems development is governed by substances that are contained in skin secretions produced by the reproductives and soldiers. The workers lick off the secretions as they groom the reproductives and soldiers. These skin secretions are also given with food to the entire colony of termites.

Termites live most abundantly in warm regions, notably in Africa, Australia, and the Amazon regions. Some termites build huge mounds of bits of soil mixed with saliva. These nests may be 20 feet (6 meters) high. The inside of the mound is divided into numerous chambers and galleries. In the center is a closed cell, where the king and queen are kept. In the cell, the female undergoes an extraordinary change. Her body swells until it is large enough to hold many thousands of eggs. The queen lays the eggs at the rate of several thousand a day. The worker termites carry the eggs away to specially constructed cells in the nest. There the workers take care of the *larvae* (young) of the termites as they hatch from the eggs.

Termites digest wood, paper, and other material containing cellulose, with the aid of protozoa in their bodies. They do much damage in tunneling through the woodwork of houses, destroy books and furniture, and do great damage to sugar cane and orange trees. In tropical forests, where these insects occur in large numbers, railroad builders must import cast-iron or steel

© Giuseppe Mazza

Termites live in colonies where each *caste* (group) has a certain job. The queen, *top,* is a fully developed female whose sole job is to mate and reproduce. The soldier, *bottom left,* defends the colony against attack. The worker, *bottom right,* gathers food and cares for the young termites after they hatch.

A. Kerneis-Dragesco, Jacana

A termite nest may contain thousands of termites. It is made of wood particles and divided into chambers.

ties at great expense because the termites destroy wooden ties. Termites are also considered a serious pest in many parts of the United States because they damage houses and other wooden structures.

Kinds of termites. About 2,000 different species of termites are known. Only two species live in Europe. About 40 species live in North America. Though they do not build large mound nests, they do much damage by tunneling through fence posts, trees, timbers of wooden buildings, bridges, trestles, and other structures. In houses, they eat cloth, books, and paper. A few kinds attack and destroy living plants. Experts have estimated that termites cause as much property damage each year in the United States as fire does.

Termites in the United States fall into three groups, according to their habits. The *subterranean termites,* the smallest but most destructive, nest underground. They extend their burrows for considerable distances into wooden structures. The *damp-wood termites* live only in very moist wood. These termites cause trouble only on the Pacific Coast. The *dry-wood termites* need little moisture. They are destructive in the Southwest. Damp-wood and dry-wood termites have no true worker caste.

Termite control. The United States Department of Agriculture recommends the use of stone, brick, or concrete for foundations of bridges and trestles, and for support posts of buildings. Where timber has to be used, it should be treated with creosote or other wood preservative applied in large tanks under pressure, to make sure it penetrates the wood deeply. Most termites will die if their supply of moisture is cut off.

Scientific classification. Termites make up the order Isoptera. This order includes the families Mastotermitidae, Hodotermitidae, Kalotermitidae, Rhinotermitidae, and Termitidae. The family Rhinotermitidae includes the most important genus in the order. This is genus *Reticulitermes,* which has 10 species of subterranean termites that cover the entire country. *R. flavipes* is distributed widely in the East and Southwest. *R. hesperus* occurs chiefly from British Columbia to Lower California.

Sandra J. Glover

Tern is a subfamily of sea birds related to gulls. Terns are famous for their powers of flight. About 35 or more kinds of terns are found in different parts of the world. Fourteen kinds are native to North America. Most of them live along seacoasts, rivers, and lakes, rather than in the open sea. The *sooty tern* and some others often range far from land.

Terns have long, pointed bills and webbed feet. Their pointed wings can carry them through the air swiftly and for long distances. Their swift, graceful flight has given them the name *sea swallow.* Terns feed mainly on small fish. They seize the fish by darting quickly into the water from the air, with the bill pointing down.

Great colonies of terns inhabit islands during the nesting season. Usually, the nests are slightly hollowed-out places in the ground. Sometimes, the terns lay eggs on bare rock or sand. Some make nests of seaweed. The *fairy tern* lays its single egg on a hollow place on a small branch, or on a rock ledge with no nest whatever. The parents then carefully incubate the egg by sitting on it until it hatches.

One of the largest kinds is the *Caspian tern,* a handsome bird 21 inches (53 centimeters) long. It has a shining black crest, and pearl-gray back and wings. The smallest is the *least tern,* 9 inches (23 centimeters) long. Large numbers of the beautiful *common tern* live on the Atlantic Coast of North America. Once hunters almost killed off this species in seeking its eggs and plumes. All types of terns are now protected by law. The common

WORLD BOOK Illustration by Trevor Boyer, Linden Artists Ltd.

The Caspian tern has a black crest and gray feathers. Terns have pointed wings that can carry them over long distances.

tern has light, pearl-gray feathers, with a white tail and throat. It is about 15 inches (38 centimeters) long. The common tern lays three or four eggs, which vary in color from whitish to brownish and are thickly spotted with brown and lavender. A tern usually seen on inland marshes and lakes is the *black tern.* Other types include *gull-billed, royal,* and *arctic terns.* The arctic tern flies farther in its migration than any other bird known. Some arctic terns travel 22,000 miles (35,400 kilometers) in a year, from the Arctic Circle to the Antarctic Circle and back. See **Arctic tern.**

Scientific classification. Terns are in the gull family, Laridae, and make up the subfamily Sterninae. Most of them are genus *Sterna,* including the common tern, *S. hirundo;* the sooty tern, *S. fuscata;* and the arctic tern, *S. paradisaea.* The Caspian tern is *Hydroprogne caspia;* the royal tern, *Thalasseus maximus;* the gull-billed tern *Gelochelidon nilotica;* and the fairy tern, *Gygis alba.* The black tern is *Chlidonias niger.*

George L. Hunt, Jr.

Terpsichore. See Muses.

Terra cotta, *TEHR uh KAHT uh,* is a hard, durable kind of earthenware. Like other kinds of earthenware, terra cotta is a type of baked clay. It ranges in color from buff to brown to various shades of red and is usually unglazed. Terra cotta is widely used to make flowerpots, fountains, tiles, architectural ornaments, and decorative garden sculptures. Because terra cotta can be molded easily, many sculptors have used the material to make preliminary models of their works.

Terra cotta was developed during prehistoric times. The ancient Greeks and Romans used the material to make decorative objects, plus gutters, pipes, and other construction materials. The term *terra cotta* is Italian for "cooked earth." John W. Keefe

Enameled sculpture (early 1500's) by Andrea della Robbia; Bargello, Florence (SCALA/Art Resource)
Terra-cotta sculpture

Terracing. See **Conservation** (Soil conservation); **Philippines** (picture: Traditional and modern ways of life).

Terrapin, *TEHR uh pihn,* is the common name of certain freshwater or tidewater turtles. The common United States terrapins are the diamondback terrapins, of which there are several subspecies. Terrapins eat crabs, snails, and other water animals, as well as green plants. The female terrapin is the larger animal, with a lower shell that may measure over 7 inches (18 centimeters). Terrapins live along the Gulf and Atlantic coasts, but not north of Massachusetts.

Scientific classification. The turtles commonly known as terrapins belong to the class Reptilia. They are in the common turtle family, Emydidae. Clifford H. Pope

Terrarium, *tuh RAIR ee uhm,* is the name for a transparent container in which small plants or small land animals are kept. Terrariums reproduce as closely as possible a natural setting or habitat. People set up terrariums in glass or plastic containers of various sizes and shapes. The containers are usually covered to prevent the loss of moisture. The word *terrarium* comes from a Latin word that means *earth.*

To prepare a terrarium, place a layer of small pebbles on the bottom of the container for drainage. A layer of broken charcoal should be added to absorb odors and to provide additional drainage. Then add commercial potting soil or a mixture made up of garden loam, freshwater sand, and either peat moss or *leaf mold* (decomposed leaves). This mixture should be heated in an oven at 200° F. (93° C) for one hour to kill harmful bacteria and other soil pests. When the mixture is cool, place it into the container, handful by handful.

Plants that grow well together under the same conditions are best suited for a terrarium. Each plant should be carefully placed in the soil leaving enough space be-

How to make a terrarium

A terrarium can be made by placing pebbles, charcoal, and a soil mixture in a transparent container. Then add such plants as ferns and ivy, which grow well in a warm, humid atmosphere.

WORLD BOOK illustration by James Teason

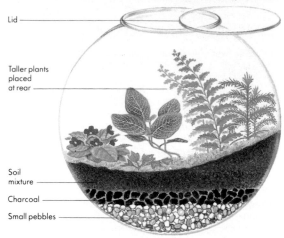

Lid

Taller plants placed at rear

Soil mixture

Charcoal

Small pebbles

tween plants to allow for growth. The soil should be moistened thoroughly, but not so much that it becomes soggy. Animals often kept in terrariums include lizards, small snakes, toads, and salamanders.

The completed terrarium should be placed in an area that is well-lit but out of direct sunlight. When covered, a balanced terrarium preserves temperature and moisture inside to provide excellent growing conditions. If the container clouds with moisture, the lid may be opened to decrease humidity. William H. Carlson

Additional resources

Evans, Charles M., and Pliner, R. L. *The Terrarium Book.* Random House, 1973.
Wilson, Charles L. *The World of Terrariums.* Jonathan David, 1975.

Terrell, *TEHR uhl,* **Mary Church** (1863-1954), joined the struggle to gain equal rights for black people in the United States in the 1890's. Terrell remained active in this equal rights movement until she died at age 90.

Mary Church Terrell was born in Memphis, Tenn. Her father was a former slave who became a millionaire through real estate and other business transactions. Mary graduated from Oberlin College in 1884, and then settled in Washington, D.C. She became a member of

S. C. Bisserot, Bruce Coleman Inc.

The diamondback terrapin gets its name from the shape of the pattern on its shell. The tasty meat of this small turtle is regarded as a delicacy.

the Washington school board in 1895, and helped found the National Association of Colored Women in 1896. Through most of her career, she advised government leaders on racial problems. In 1953, she led a committee that won a suit to end discrimination in Washington hotels, restaurants, buses, and other public facilities.

Collection of Phyllis T. Langston
Mary Church Terrell

C. Eric Lincoln

Terrier is the name of a group of breeds of dogs. The name comes from the Latin word *terra,* meaning *earth,* because these breeds were once used to drive game out of holes, or burrows, in the ground. Most terriers originated in England.

The 24 terrier breeds recognized by the American Kennel Club are the *Airedale terrier, American Staffordshire terrier, Australian terrier, Bedlington terrier, border terrier, bull terrier, cairn terrier, Dandie Dinmont terrier, Irish terrier, Kerry blue terrier, lakeland terrier, Manchester terrier, miniature schnauzer, Norfolk terrier, Norwich terrier, Scottish terrier, Sealyham terrier, Skye terrier, smooth fox terrier, soft-coated wheaten terrier, Staffordshire bull terrier, Welsh terrier, West Highland white terrier, and wire fox terrier.* Four other breeds are called terriers. But they are not members of the terrier group. The *Boston terrier* and the *Tibetan terrier* are classed as nonsporting dogs. The *Silky terrier* and the *Yorkshire terrier* are toy dogs. All of the terrier breeds have separate articles in *World Book.*

Critically reviewed by the American Kennel Club

See also **Dog** (table; pictures: Terriers)

Territorial waters are areas of the ocean where a nation has *sovereign rights.* These rights include control of fishing, navigation, and shipping, as well as the use of the ocean's natural resources.

A nation's territorial waters include its *internal waters* and its *territorial sea.* Internal waters include lakes, rivers, and the waters within such coastal areas as bays and gulfs. A country's territorial sea lies beyond its coast or the boundary of its internal waters. Nations have more authority over their internal waters than their territorial seas. The main difference is that ships of other countries can freely cross territorial seas in peacetime.

Various nations have set different outer limits for their territorial sea. Most of the approximately 120 coastal nations have a limit of 12 or fewer nautical miles. A nautical mile equals about 1.2 statute miles or 1.9 kilometers. The United States has a limit of 3 nautical miles. A few nations claim a limit of as much as 200 nautical miles. Many countries prohibit foreigners from fishing in their territorial sea. Many nations also claim exclusive fishing and other rights in an *exclusive economic zone,* which extends 200 nautical miles from shore.

Many disagreements have occurred about the extent and use of territorial waters. The United Nations sponsored a series of conferences to draw up an international treaty governing many uses of the ocean. In 1982, a Law of the Sea Treaty was adopted and signed by 117 nations. Among other things, the treaty provides for a territorial sea of 12 nautical miles. It will not become official until ratified by 60 nations, but most of its terms are already being followed.   George P. Smith II

See also **High seas.**

Territoriality is a form of animal behavior in which an individual animal or a group claims a certain area as its own. Such animals also defend the territory against other members of their species. Some animals hold long-term claims on large territories that they use as sources of food. Other species become territorial only during their breeding season, when they defend a small nesting area. Territoriality is most common among birds, fish, and lizards. Some species of amphibians and mammals also claim territories. Only a few kinds of invertebrates do so.

Animals claim territories in various ways. Songbirds establish their areas by vigorous singing. Some mammals signal territorial claims by leaving scents, such as that of urine or of secretions from special glands.

Various species also differ in how they defend their territories. Male fur seals fight intensely during the breeding season. Some fish push against each other until one retreats. But most animals rarely engage in physical combat. Instead, they make threatening movements to ward off intruders. For example, fiddler crabs signal their territorial rights by waving their large claw. The color of some fish brightens when they are in their own territory but fades rapidly if they swim away.

Territoriality serves different purposes among different kinds of animals. It may protect a female from males other than her mate. Or it might provide a male and a female a good nest site and a feeding area large enough to support their young. Among many species, individual animals without a territory do not breed. Thus, territoriality may prevent the population from becoming too large for the environment.   John A. Wiens

See also **Animal** (Animal homes; Communication); **Mammal** (Territoriality).

Additional resources

Cohen, Daniel. *Animal Territories.* Hastings, 1975. For younger readers.
Klopfer, Peter H. *Habitats and Territories: A Study of the Use of Space by Animals.* Basic Books, 1969.

Territory is a type of region that belongs to or is controlled by a country or other independent political unit. In countries with a federal government, such as Australia, Canada, Mexico, and the United States, territories rank below states or provinces. In these countries, the national government establishes separate governments for the individual territories. In most cases, the territories have no representation in the national government. The territories have varying degrees of self-rule, and may or may not become states or provinces.

In the United States

The United States has four main territories: American Samoa, Guam, the Virgin Islands, and various Pacific islands. It also governs an island area in the Pacific Ocean under a United Nations trusteeship. For many years, the United States had many more outlying territories. Two of them, Alaska and Hawaii, became states. One, the Philippines, became an independent country. Two others, Puerto Rico and the northern Mariana Islands, became U.S. commonwealths. See **Philippines** (History); **Puerto Rico** (Government); **Mariana Islands.**

In the United States, territorial government is an older institution than the U.S. Constitution. In 1787, under the Articles of Confederation, Congress passed the Northwest Ordinance, setting up the first American territory, the Northwest Territory (see **Northwest Territory**). This action set the pattern for congressional action in governing territories and providing for their eventual statehood. The United States Constitution, also written in 1787, provides that "new States may be admitted by the Congress into this Union." Accordingly, Congress has full control over the admission of territories. During the 1800's, Congress set terms for statehood and in many cases admitted territories on the basis of U.S. domestic politics. All but 19 states—the original 13 and six others—were once territories.

Up to 1867, Congress always set up territories in mainland areas on the frontiers of the United States. Alaska, bought in 1867, was the first area not directly connected with the rest of the states. Gradually, the United States gained other distant territories, most of them after the Spanish-American War. These new territories presented special problems: they were far away, and their peoples had little or no experience of democratic self-government. In addition, the territories contained large nonwhite populations. For these reasons, Congress was unwilling to consider the territories for statehood and was reluctant to extend to their residents all the protections provided by the Constitution.

As a result, in the Insular Cases of 1901, the Supreme Court drew a distinction between *incorporated* and *unincorporated* territories. It held that all rights guaranteed by the Constitution applied in incorporated territories. In unincorporated ones, only fundamental rights applied, as distinguished from formal or procedural rights such as the right to trial by jury. Congress has the power to decide whether a territory has incorporated or unincorporated status. Incorporated territories may become states. Unincorporated territories may not. A third class of territories includes *wholly unorganized and unincorporated* territories. These territories are controlled by executive-branch officials, not by Congress.

The territories have no regular representatives in Congress. Until it became a state, Hawaii elected one delegate to the House of Representatives. The delegate could serve on committees and take part in debates, but could not vote.

American territorial government

Alaska and Hawaii were the last fully incorporated U.S. territories. Unincorporated territories include the Virgin Islands and Guam. Unorganized and unincorporated territories include American Samoa, Wake Island, and other Pacific islands.

The Virgin Islands, purchased from Denmark in 1917, have a considerable measure of home rule. The people elect their own governor and legislature. But Congress can disallow acts passed in the Virgin Islands. The people do not take part in U.S. presidential elections. See **Virgin Islands.**

Guam, acquired from Spain in 1898, was governed by the Department of the Navy until 1950, when officials of the Department of the Interior took over. With author-

ization from Congress, Guam drew up a constitution in 1969. Since 1970, its people have elected their own governor and legislature. See **Guam.**

American Samoa, a group of islands ceded to the United States between 1900 and 1925, is controlled by the Department of the Interior. The people are regarded as *nationals,* but not citizens, of the United States. See **Samoa.**

Pacific islands. Several of these islands, including Wake and Midway islands, are governed by the Department of Defense. The others are governed by the Department of the Interior. See **Pacific Islands.**

Trust Territory of the Pacific Islands consists of the Palau Islands, which were taken from Japan during World War II (1939-1945). The Department of the Interior administers the trust. The trust operates under an agreement between the United States and the United Nations. See **Pacific Islands, Trust Territory of the; United Nations** (The Trusteeship Council).

Territories in Canada

Canada has two territories, each governed by a commissioner appointed by the federal government.

Northwest Territories, made up of three geographical districts, is governed by a commissioner, an executive council, and a 24-member assembly. The people elect all the council and assembly members as well as two representatives to the Canadian House of Commons. See **Northwest Territories** (Government).

Yukon Territory has a commissioner, an executive council, and a 16-member Legislative Assembly. The people elect the assembly members. They also elect one representative to the Canadian House of Commons. See **Yukon Territory** (Government).   Kinley J. Brauer

See also **Australia** (Government); **Canada, Government of; Enclave; Trust territory.**

Terrorism is the use or threat of violence to create fear and alarm. Terrorists murder and kidnap people, set off bombs, hijack airplanes, set fires, and commit other serious crimes. But the goals of terrorists differ from those of ordinary criminals. Most criminals want money or some other form of personal gain. But most terrorists commit crimes to support political causes.

The word *terrorism* first appeared during the French Revolution (1789-1799). Some of the revolutionaries who seized power in France adopted a policy of violence against their enemies. The period of their rule became known as the Reign of Terror.

Features of terrorism. Terrorist acts are committed for various reasons. Some terrorist groups support a particular political philosophy. Other terrorist organizations represent ethnic groups seeking liberation from governments in power. Dictators use violence to frighten or eliminate their opponents. Most terrorist groups have a small number of members. They believe the threat or use of violence to create fear is the best way to gain publicity and support for their causes.

Generally, terrorists attack people who oppose their cause or objects that symbolize such opposition. Common victims of terrorist kidnappings and assassinations include diplomats, business executives, political leaders, judges, and police. Terrorists also attack churches and synagogues, oil refineries, and government offices. At other times, terrorists simply choose any target certain to attract newspaper or TV coverage. Some terrorists hijack airplanes or seize public buildings. Then they hold the passengers or occupants hostage and make demands to further their cause. They often threaten to kill the hostages if their demands are not met. Bombings make up about half of all terrorist acts.

Terrorism may cross national boundaries. A quarrel in one nation may produce terrorist attacks in several other countries. Some governments secretly support certain terrorist groups by providing weapons, training, and money for attacks in other countries.

Most terrorist groups fail to achieve their long-range political goals. Governments fight terrorism by refusing to accept terrorist demands and by increasing security at airports and other likely targets. Some countries train special military units to rescue hostages.

History of terrorism. Terrorist tactics have been used for hundreds of years. An American group, the Ku Klux Klan, used violence to terrorize blacks and their sympathizers in the period following the end of the Civil War in 1865 and during the 1900's. In the 1930's, the dictators Adolf Hitler of Germany, Benito Mussolini of Italy, and Joseph Stalin of the Soviet Union used terrorism to discourage opposition to their governments.

Another wave of terrorism began during the 1960's. Terrorist groups that surfaced included the Red Brigades in Italy and the Red Army Faction in West Germany. Both groups seek the destruction of the current political and economic systems in their home countries and the development of new systems. Before the independence of Israel in 1948, a Jewish group used terror to speed the end of British rule in Palestine and create a Jewish homeland. Since the 1960's, various Palestinian groups have carried out a campaign of terrorism aimed at the destruction of Israel and the establishment of an independent Palestinian state.

The Provisional Irish Republican Army, established in 1970, uses violence in its fight to rid Northern Ireland of British rule. A Puerto Rican nationalist group called FALN committed numerous bombings in the United States during the 1970's. The group supported a campaign to win Puerto Rico's independence from the United States. Terrorists, especially those from the Middle East, continued to set off bombs and commit other crimes during the 1980's.   Brian Michael Jenkins

See also **Anarchism; French Revolution** (Terror and equality); **Guerrilla warfare; Hostage; Ku Klux Klan.**

Additional resources

Raynor, Thomas P. *Terrorism: Past, Present, Future.* Rev. ed. Watts, 1987.
Wilkinson, Paul. *Terrorism and the Liberal State.* Rev. ed. New York Univ. Press, 1986.

Terry, Dame Ellen Alicia (1848-1928), was considered the greatest actress on the English stage for almost 50 years. Her famous roles included such Shakespearean heroines as Portia in *The Merchant of Venice,* Desdemona in *Othello,* Juliet in *Romeo and Juliet.* Terry often appeared as Sir Henry Irving's leading lady. She was born in Coventry.   Richard Moody

Tertiary Period. See **Earth** (table: Outline of the earth's history).

Tesla, Nikola (1856-1943), an electrical engineer, is generally recognized as the inventor of the induction

motor. While still a student, he began to devise a motor free of the inconvenience of the commutator. Tesla invented a motor with coils arranged so that when out-of-step alternating currents energized them, the resulting magnetic field rotated at a predetermined speed. See **Electric motor.**

Tesla patented the rotating field motor in 1888. He introduced it at a time when advocates of alternating current were seeking such a motor. He sold it to George Westinghouse, whose company developed it into a commercial motor.

Tesla made advances in the fields of high voltage and frequency apparatus. He invented the Tesla coil, a system of arc lighting, a generator for high-frequency currents, and a system of wireless transmission.

Tesla was born in Smiljan, Austria-Hungary (now in Yugoslavia). He received a technical education at an engineering college in Graz and at the University of Prague. He moved to France and came to the United States in 1884. After 1900, Tesla engaged in independent research in his laboratory.   Ronald R. Kline

Test. See **Testing; Drug** (Testing with people).

Test Act. Certain religious laws passed by the English Parliament were known as Test Acts. The laws were intended to keep people who were not members of the Church of England from holding public office. One of the most important test acts was the Corporation Act of 1661, which stated that all judges must declare complete allegiance to the king and must receive communion according to the Church of England. The Test Act of 1673 made the same provisions for all other holders of public office. All test acts in Great Britain were finally repealed in 1828.   J. Salwyn Schapiro

Test Ban Treaty. See **Kennedy, John Fitzgerald** (Disarmament).

Test pilot is a person who flies new aircraft to test them for safety. There are two kinds of test pilots—experimental test pilots and production test pilots.

Experimental test pilots test the performance capabilities of newly designed aircraft. They become the first people to fly such aircraft. These pilots test the performance limits, called the *flight envelope,* of an aircraft by subjecting it to greater-than-normal flight stresses. Most experimental test pilots have at least a bachelor's degree in engineering, mathematics, or one of the physical sciences. The majority have also attended a military test-pilot school. Experimental test pilots know what to expect from an aircraft's design and what problems to anticipate. Most of these pilots have several thousand hours of flying time and can react calmly and quickly to unexpected situations.

Many U.S. astronauts and Soviet cosmonauts formerly served as experimental test pilots. Charles E. Yeager, an American experimental test pilot, became the first person to fly faster than the speed of sound.

Production test pilots test factory-produced aircraft before the aircraft are delivered to customers. The pilots make sure that the aircraft's engines, flight controls, and mechanical systems are functioning properly. The design of the aircraft has already passed through the experimental flight-testing phase. Production test pilots typically have a strong understanding of aircraft mechanics.   James P. Johnson

See also **Airplane** (Design and testing).

Testes. See Testicle.

Testicle is either of a pair of small oval glands in the male reproductive system. The testicles, also called *testes* (singular, *testis*), hang behind the penis in a sack called the *scrotum*. They have two main functions. (1) They produce sperm, and (2) they secrete male sex hormones, particularly *testosterone.*

In an adult man, each testicle measures about $1\frac{1}{2}$ inches (4 centimeters) long and about $1\frac{1}{4}$ inches (3 centimeters) wide, and each weighs about $\frac{2}{3}$ ounce (20 grams). The testicle is covered by a dense fibrous material. This material enters the rear of the gland and separates into sheets that divide the testicle into about 250 sections. Each section contains one to four twisting tubes called *seminiferous tubules,* in which sperm are produced. Larger tubes inside the testicles transport the sperm to the *epididymis,* a highly coiled tube at the rear of each testicle. In the epididymis, the sperm develop further before being released from the body during sexual arousal.

Testosterone is produced by the tissue between the seminiferous tubules. Testosterone controls the development during puberty of such male characteristics as a beard, enlarged muscle mass, a deep voice, and increased size of the sex organs. This hormone also stimulates male sexual behavior.   Earl F. Wendel

See also **Reproduction** (The male reproductive system; diagram: Human reproduction); **Penis; Prostate gland; Testosterone.**

Testimonial. See Advertising (Testimonials).

Testimony. See Witness.

Testing, in education and psychology, is an attempt to measure a person's knowledge, intelligence, or other characteristics in a systematic way. There are many types of tests. Teachers give tests to discover the learning abilities of their students. They also give tests to see how well students have learned a particular subject. Some tests help people choose a vocation, and other tests help them understand their own personality.

Standardized tests

Most printed tests taken by students and others are *standardized.* A test has been standardized after it has been used, revised, and used again until it shows consistent results and average levels of performance have been established. Firms that prepare standardized tests include information with them on how to give and score each test. The results of one person's performance may be compared with those of many others who have taken the same test. Most teachers also use *nonstandardized* tests that they make up themselves. The quality of a test is judged by three major standards: (1) validity, (2) reliability, and (3) practicality.

Validity reflects how well a test measures what it is intended to measure. For example, a test of reading comprehension could lose validity if it allows too little time for taking the test. It might actually measure reading speed rather than comprehension.

Reliability refers to the consistency of results achieved by the test. To establish reliability, a test may be given to the same group several times. If very similar results are obtained each time, the test may be considered highly reliable.

Practicality involves the cost and convenience of the test. If a test requires too much expense or effort, it may be impractical. It also may be impractical if the results are too difficult to interpret.

Kinds of tests

Most tests are designed to measure one of several characteristics: (1) learning ability, (2) learning achievement, (3) aptitude and interest, or (4) personality.

Tests of learning ability attempt to predict how well an individual will perform in a situation requiring intellectual ability. These tests are sometimes called *intelligence tests, mental ability tests, academic aptitude tests,* or *scholastic aptitude tests.*

A learning ability test consists of a standard set of tasks or questions. It enables a student to demonstrate the skills learned throughout the individual's life, both in and out of school. Tests of learning ability do not measure how "bright" a person is. Educators use the terms *intelligence* and *mental ability* simply to describe a person's ability to solve certain kinds of problems typically involved in schoolwork. These terms do not reflect a person's ability in all areas. See **Intelligence; Intelligence quotient.**

Achievement tests try to measure how much an individual has learned about a particular subject, rather than the general ability for learning. Schools use achievement tests more than any other kind of test. Throughout elementary school, high school, and college, most teachers rely on such tests when rating a student's progress. Special achievement tests are used to license people in such professions as law, medicine, and accounting.

Many teachers prepare achievement tests that closely follow their own method of instruction. They also use standardized achievement tests. These tests are available on many subjects or topics, including division of fractions, American history before 1776, and chemical equations. Some schools ask students to take standardized achievement tests, as well as scholastic ability tests, for admission or placement.

There are two types of achievement tests—*norm-referenced* and *criterion-referenced.* In norm-referenced tests, each person's performance is compared with those of others who took the test. A student who answers some questions incorrectly would still rank high if most other students answered a larger number of questions incorrectly. But in criterion-referenced tests, each person's performance is compared with a predetermined standard or criterion. For example, a teacher might decide that 90 per cent of the questions on a test must be answered correctly for a student to earn a passing grade.

Aptitude and interest tests reveal an individual's talents or preferences for certain activities. A person who likes to tinker with machinery would probably score high on a test of mechanical aptitude. Such a person has an aptitude for mechanical work—and at least a fairly good chance of succeeding at it.

Interest tests are also known as *interest inventories.* In them, a person indicates a preference among large groups of activities, ideas, and circumstances. One of these tests might ask, "Would you rather fix a broken clock, keep a set of accounts, or paint a picture?" Most individuals prefer certain types of activities over others.

SCHOOL LEARNING ABILITY TESTS

Verbal Reasoning

1. Which word below does *not* go with the others?
   a) red   b) green   c) dark   d) blue

2. Eye is to see as ear is to
   a) head   b) hear   c) talk   d) nose   e) cheek

Quantitative Reasoning

1. A boy bought 3 pencils at 5¢ each. How much did the 3 pencils cost?
   a) 5¢   b) 10¢   c) 20¢   d) 25¢   e) none of these

2. Which number is missing in this series?
   1   2   _   4   5   6   7

   a) 1   b) 3   c) 4   d) 8

Figural Reasoning

1. Which picture does not belong with the others?
   a) ⊘   b) ⊖   c) ⊕   d) ⊘

2. ◯ is to ◯ as ☐ is to
   a) ☐   b) ☐   c) ◯   d) ◯   e) ▭

Learning ability tests measure intellectual skills that an individual has learned from a variety of sources, including the home, school, and community. These tests are used to estimate a student's capacity for learning. They can help teachers instruct the student better and direct the student toward kinds of learning that best suit individual abilities.

The pattern of answers reveals the strength of a person's interest in various fields.

Personality tests attempt to measure an individual's personal traits scientifically. Some standardized personality tests consist of lists of personal questions requiring yes or no answers. The answers can be analyzed for various characteristics. For example, a person might score high in *social introversion,* which would indicate a strong preference for being alone. Such a person might find scientific research more satisfying as a career than teaching science in a classroom.

Another type of personality test, the *projective test,* requires individuals to tell what certain images mean to them. In a Rorschach test, for example, a person describes what he or she sees in a number of standardized inkblots. A trained counselor can often recognize behavioral tendencies in these descriptions. Psychologists use personality tests as clues for further study of an individual. They do not regard them as conclusive evidence about the individual's personality.

Most personality tests are less reliable and less valid than the other kinds of tests discussed here. Some people criticize their use as an invasion of privacy.

How to take a test

Knowing how to take tests does not increase anyone's learning ability or achievement. But it does help a person avoid losing points unnecessarily. Experts in testing offer the following suggestions:

1. Get all the experience you can in taking tests. The ability to take tests improves with practice.

2. Cramming before a test is better than no study at all. But a careful review spread over several days is better than cramming.

3. Be sure you understand the directions at the beginning of a test. You may get a lower score than you deserve because you failed to follow certain instructions.

4. Answer the questions that are easy for you, and then go back to the hard ones.

5. If there is no penalty for guessing, answer every question. If there is a penalty, you may still gain points by guessing some answers. On a multiple-choice question, for example, you may know enough about the subject to eliminate some answers. If so, your chance of guessing the correct answer improves considerably.

Interpreting test scores

There are several points to keep in mind about test scores. First, a test reflects only a sample of a person's skill or knowledge, not everything about an individual. A test score can tell only how well the person performed on one particular test on one particular day.

Second, a score on a standardized test compares one person's performance with the performance of others. Such a comparison may provide useful information if all the people taking the test are alike in some important way. Most standardized tests give scores for persons of the same age or in the same grade.

Third, every test score is an estimate rather than a precise measurement. To remind people of this, some scores are reported as bands rather than as a single number. The bands show the range in which a person's actual ability probably lies.

Testing often has far-reaching effects, and so it receives much attention from educators and social scientists. Criticism has been directed both at the limitations of tests and at their influence.

Some educators believe multiple-choice tests penalize a student who has an expert knowledge of a subject. Such a student may see flaws in the answer generally accepted as correct. Other critics say that standardized tests discriminate against disadvantaged and minority groups. These students may be unfamiliar with words, terms, and concepts used in the tests. To give these students an equal chance, educators have tried to prepare *culture-fair* or *culture-free* tests. Such tests might consist of pictures, symbols, and nonsense syllables that are equally unfamiliar to everyone taking the test. This type of test reduces the influence of cultural background on performance. Tests that use no words at all are called *nonverbal tests.*

The general effect of testing on education has also caused concern. Standardized tests sometimes lag behind educational thought and practice. If tests do not measure the content of new programs, they may fail to encourage educational progress.

Many educators believe there is at least some truth in criticisms of tests. But they also know that testing is necessary in teaching. Tests can determine whether one method of teaching works better than another. Tests can also tell a teacher what help a student needs most. No better way has been found to determine how much students have learned, what they seem able to learn, and how quickly they might learn it.   Richard M. Wolf

Related articles in *World Book* include:

College entrance examination
Competency-based education
National Assessment of Educational Progress
Personality
Study

Additional resources

Gilbert, Sara D. *How to Take Tests.* Morrow, 1983. Suitable for younger readers.
Mental Measurements Yearbook. Ed. by James V. Mitchell, Jr. Univ. of Nebraska Press. Published every 3-5 years. Lists and describes standardized tests.
Shelley, Douglas, and Cohen, David. *Testing Psychological Tests.* St. Martin's, 1986.

Testosterone, *tehs TAHS tuh rohn,* is a hormone that stimulates sexual development in male human beings. It belongs to a family of hormones called *androgens.* Androgens are produced primarily by the *testicles,* a pair of male sex glands (see **Testicle**). The ovaries in females and the adrenal glands in both sexes also yield small amounts of testosterone and other androgens.

During a boy's early teen-age years, his testicles are stimulated by a hormone from the pituitary gland to secrete increasing amounts of testosterone, particularly during sleep. Testosterone enters the blood and acts on certain tissues in the body to cause various physical changes. These changes include growth of hair on the face and in the genital area, muscle development, deepening of the voice, and maturation of the sex organs. Testosterone also helps in the production of sperm by the testicles. After a man reaches old age, the testicles produce smaller amounts of testosterone. In adult females, testosterone contributes to the formation of es-

trogens by the ovaries. Estrogens are hormones necessary for female sexual development. See **Estrogen.**

In many kinds of animals, testosterone influences male sexual behavior. For example, some deer breed in the fall. At this time, the testicles of male deer secrete large amounts of testosterone. As a result, the males spend much time pursuing females.

Drugs called *anabolic steroids* are made from testosterone. They are used by some athletes who feel such drugs increase strength and endurance. Most doctors believe the dangers of using anabolic steroids outweigh the benefits. See **Steroid** (The sex steroids).

P. Landis Keyes

See also **Elephant** (Musth).

Tetanus, *TEHT uh nuhs,* is a serious disease that affects muscles. It is also called *lockjaw* because severe *spasms* (violent muscle contractions) of the jaw muscles make it hard for victims to open their mouths.

Tetanus is caused by *toxins* (poisons) produced by a bacterium called *Clostridium tetani.* These germs thrive in dust and dirt, and need no air to live. They get into the body through breaks in the skin. Any dirt in a wound may contain tetanus germs. The germs grow quickly if no air gets to the wound.

Symptoms of tetanus usually start within several weeks after infection. The victim feels depressed, has headaches, and soon has trouble opening the mouth or swallowing. After a while, all of the body muscles tighten, and spasms may interfere with breathing. If not treated, the victim may die from exhaustion.

Tetanus can be prevented. All wounds should be cleaned thoroughly. People may be immunized against infection with injections of *tetanus toxoid,* a substance made from specially treated toxins of the bacillus. But if tetanus develops, doctors treat the disease with antitoxin injections. People with severe tetanus may need to undergo a *tracheotomy.* In this operation, surgeons make an artificial opening in the patient's windpipe to help the patient breathe.   Thomas J. Gill III

See also **Kitasato, Shibasaburo.**

Tetany, *TEHT uh nee,* is a disorder associated with overexcitability and spontaneous activity of the nervous system. It is characterized by periodic muscle spasms and small, fluttering tremors. Affected body parts may tingle or feel numb. The hands are usually affected first, but spasms may later spread to the face, body, and throat. The spasms are only painful in severe cases. Tetany results from a deficiency of calcium salts or a chemical imbalance in the body.   William J. Weiner

Teton, Grand. See **Grand Teton National Park.**

Teton Range, *TEET uhn,* is a rugged group of 10 Rocky Mountain peaks south of Yellowstone National Park in western Wyoming. The highest peak is Grand Teton (13,770 feet, or 4,197 meters). The range forms part of Grand Teton National Park. See also **Wyoming** (pictures).   John H. Garland

Tetra, *TEHT ruh,* is a type of small tropical fish that lives in rivers of South America and Africa. Tetras are also called *characins.* There are nearly 1,500 species of these fish. Tetras are popular aquarium fish because they can be raised in captivity and have beautiful colors. Most tetras grow 2 to 3 inches (5 to 8 centimeters) long and live 3 to 4 years.

Popular species for home aquariums include neon

Zig Leszczynski, Animals Animals

Neon tetras are popular aquarium fish.

tetras, bleeding-heart tetras, cardinal tetras, and diamond tetras. The neon tetra has a brilliant blue stripe along the side of its body. The bleeding-heart tetra has a red splotch on the middle of its side. The cardinal tetra is deep-red on the sides and the belly. The diamond tetra has a bright silver color.

Scientific classification. Tetras belong to the family Characidae.   John E. McCosker

Tetracycline, *TEHT ruh sy klihn,* is any of a family of antibiotics used to treat infections. The tetracyclines affect many kinds of bacteria and other microorganisms, including *rickettsias* (see **Rickettsia**). Doctors use tetracyclines to treat such serious diseases as typhus and Rocky Mountain spotted fever. They also use tetracyclines in the treatment of acne.

The first tetracycline became available in 1948. Since then, tetracyclines have been widely—and often inappropriately—used to treat a great variety of diseases. This widespread use caused many microorganisms to become resistant to the effects of these antibiotics. As a result, tetracyclines are no longer effective against diseases caused by these microorganisms.

All the tetracyclines fight most of the same microorganisms. They differ chiefly in how well they are absorbed by the body and in how long their effects last. Tetracyclines act by blocking the process by which bacteria make proteins. Although generally safe, tetracyclines can cause many side effects. For example, large doses of these antibiotics can seriously damage the liver and kidneys. In addition, tetracyclines can permanently discolor developing teeth. For this reason, doctors do not prescribe tetracyclines in treating children and pregnant women.   Eugene M. Johnson, Jr.

See also **Antibiotic.**

Tetraethyl lead, *TEHT ruh EHTH uhl,* is an ingredient added to gasoline to improve the performance of engines. It is called an *antiknock additive* because it reduces the "knocking" or "pinging" sound that an engine makes. An engine knocks if the gasoline in its cylinders begins burning too soon or too fast. The same conditions that cause knocking also reduce an engine's power and can damage the engine. A small amount of tetraethyl lead in the gasoline corrects these conditions.

An engine that burns *leaded* gasoline (gasoline containing tetraethyl lead) gives off an exhaust that includes chemical compounds containing lead. These compounds pollute the air. They also destroy the effectiveness of *catalytic converters,* devices installed in automobiles to remove pollutants from automobile exhaust.

Because of these problems, oil companies make *unleaded* gasolines. They also have decreased the amount of tetraethyl lead in their leaded gasolines. These unleaded and reduced-lead fuels contain a larger proportion of other ingredients that resist knocking. As a result, the amount of tetraethyl lead needed in these gasolines is reduced or eliminated.   Geoffrey E. Dolbear

See also **Gasoline; Octane number.**

Tetrahedron, *TEHT ruh HEE druhn,* in geometry, is a *regular pyramid* whose sides consist of four equilateral triangles. See **Pyramid.**

Tetzel, *TEHT suhl,* **Johann,** *YOH hahn* (1465-1519), was a Dominican monk who sold papal indulgences in Germany in 1517. He declared that anyone who bought an indulgence could choose a soul to be freed from purgatory. Tetzel's claim led Martin Luther to draw up his Ninety-Five Theses in protest (see **Luther, Martin**). Tetzel's action thus brought about the Protestant Reformation. Germans accused Tetzel of telling possible buyers of indulgences:

> When the coin in the coffer rings,
> A soul from purgatory springs.

Many Catholics criticized Tetzel for his vulgar conduct. He defended himself vigorously but clumsily.

Tetzel was born in Pirna, in what is now East Germany. In 1503, he began his long career of selling indulgences.   Richard Marius

Teutoburg Forest, Battle of. See Army (table: Famous land battles).

Teutonic Knights, *too TAHN ihk,* was the name of an organization of German crusaders that arose in Europe during the 1100's. The Teutonic Knights were organized for service in the Holy Land. They modeled their organization after two earlier crusading orders, the Knights Templars and the Knights Hospitalers (see **Knights Templars; Knights of Saint John**).

In the 1200's, the Teutonic Knights shifted their activities to central Europe, where they tried to convert and control the people of what became Prussia, Lithuania, Latvia, and Estonia. Their power and influence spread throughout central and eastern Europe. In the 1300's, they lost much of their power, and finally the Poles and Lithuanians overthrew them. In 1525, the Grand Master, Albert of Hohenzollern, embraced Protestantism, and changed the Order from a religious to a civil organization. In 1618, the Order's territory passed to the Hohenzollern Elector of Brandenburg.   Bryce Lyon

See also **Latvia** (History); **Lithuania** (History).

Teutons, *TOO tuhnz,* is a name sometimes given to the Germanic peoples. The term comes from the *Teutones,* or *Teutoni,* who, with the Cimbri, were the first "Germans" to threaten the power of ancient Rome. With their neighbors, the Ambrones, the Teutones left their homeland around the mouth of the Elbe River in the 100's B.C. In Gaul, they allied themselves with the Cimbri. The Roman general Gaius Marius routed them at Aquae Sextiae (Aix) in 102 B.C.

Later, the Teutones mixed with other early groups that wandered through Europe. They eventually gave their name to a whole group of *Teutonic languages.* These languages included the Scandinavian and Germanic tongues, and Low German (Dutch and Flemish) of Belgium and the Netherlands.   William C. Bark

Big Bend National Park lies within the great bend of the Rio Grande River in western Texas. The Chisos Mountains rise in the background. Texas, the second largest state in size, has vast regions of fertile lowlands, dry plains, and mountain ranges.

Texas   *The Lone Star State*

Texas is the second largest state in the United States. It has a greater area than Illinois, Indiana, Iowa, Michigan, and Wisconsin combined. Texas is more than 220 times as large as Rhode Island, the smallest state. Only Alaska is larger than Texas. But Texas has about 30 times as many people as Alaska.

Frontier cowboys with their 10-gallon hats have long been a symbol of Texas. Cowboys still ride across the plains driving great herds of cattle. And cowboy boots and hats still make up part of the everyday dress of many rural Texans. However, the Texans of today are just as likely to be workers in an oil field or scientists in a laboratory as they are to be cowboys. Or they might be engineers in a chemical plant, computer operators in a

The contributors of this article are John Edwin Coffman, Associate Professor of Geography at the University of Houston; and Clifford L. Egan, Professor of History at the University of Houston.

bank, or musicians in a symphony orchestra. Thousands of Texans are also employed in the aerospace industry. The Lyndon B. Johnson Space Center, located in Houston, serves as the headquarters for all manned spacecraft projects of the National Aeronautics and Space Administration (NASA).

The land of Texas has helped make the state rich. Many industries, such as trade and finance, benefit from the state's huge agricultural and mining production. Today, wholesale and retail trade is the state's leading economic activity. Vast plains and rolling hills provide fertile soil and rich grasslands. Texas has more farms and farmland than any other state. It leads the country in the production of cattle, sheep, and wool. Texas ranks behind only California and New York in the value of goods and services produced annually.

Many colorful people have played important roles in Texas history. Spanish adventurers began exploring the region about 450 years ago. Texas received its name from their pronunciation of the Indian word *Tejas*

Interesting facts about Texas

The Comal River, the shortest river in Texas, is only $2\frac{1}{2}$ miles (4 kilometers) long. The Comal originates in a spring at one end of New Braunfels and ends at the Guadalupe River, still within the city's limits.

Marshall served as the capital of Missouri during the Civil War from 1863 to 1865. Thomas C. Reynolds, the state's governor, fled to Texas when Union forces took Missouri. He rented two buildings, one of which served as the Missouri state capitol, the other as the Missouri governor's mansion.

Santa Gertrudis cattle, the first recognized beef breed in the Western Hemisphere, were developed between 1910 and 1940 at the King Ranch in southern Texas.

Texas has the right to divide into as many as five states under the terms of the 1845 annexation treaty that made the Republic of Texas one of the United States.

Santa Gertrudis cattle

WORLD BOOK illustrations by Kevin Chadwick

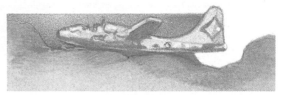

Lucky Lady II

The first round-the-world airplane flight originated from Carswell Air Force Base in Fort Worth. It began on February 26 and ended March 2, 1949. Captain James G. Gallagher, Lieutenant Arthur Neal, and Captain James Morris piloted the B-50 Superfortress *Lucky Lady II* on the flight, which took 94 hours, 1 minute. The airplane was refueled four times in the air by B-29 tanker planes.

The first play-by-play radio broadcast of a football game took place in College Station in November 1919. The game was played between the University of Texas and the Agricultural and Mechanical College of Texas, located at College Station.

© Walter Frerck, Odyssey Productions

Downtown Houston has many modern skyscrapers. Houston is the largest city in Texas and a major industrial center. Buffalo Bayou winds through Houston's Memorial Park in the foreground.

(friends or allies). The Tejas formed a group of united Indian tribes that lived in what is now the northeastern part of the state.

Texas was part of Mexico when the first Americans settled there in 1821. In 1836, Davy Crockett, Jim Bowie, and other famous heroes died at the Alamo fighting for independence from Mexico. Sam Houston led the Texans to their final victory against the Mexicans. One of his battle cries was "Remember the Alamo!" For nearly 10 years after the war with Mexico, Texas was an independent republic. After Texas became a state in 1845, the settlers fought Indians for many years to protect their families and homes.

Texas is called the *Lone Star State* because of the single star on its flag. Through the years, the flags of six nations have flown over Texas. Besides the United States, these nations were Spain, France, Mexico, the Republic of Texas, and the Confederate States of America. Austin is the capital of Texas, and Houston is the state's largest city.

Paul Conklin

Paseo del Rio (River Walk), a popular dining and shopping area, stretches along the San Antonio River in San Antonio.

Texas in brief

Symbols of Texas

The state flag, known as the Lone Star Flag, was adopted in 1839. The red stands for bravery, the white represents purity, and the blue is for loyalty. The front of the state seal, adopted in 1845, also has a lone star. The oak branch on the left symbolizes strength, and the olive branch on the right stands for peace. The reverse side of the seal was adopted in 1961. It displays the six flags that have flown over Texas.

State flag

State seal

Texas (brown) ranks 2nd in size among all the states and is the largest of the Southwestern States (yellow).

General information

Statehood: Dec. 29, 1845, the 28th state.
State abbreviations: Tex. (traditional); TX (postal).
State motto: *Friendship.*
State song: "Texas, Our Texas." Words by Gladys Yoakum Wright and William J. Marsh; music by William J. Marsh.

The State Capitol is in Austin, Texas' capital since 1845. Other capitals were Houston (1837-1840), Austin (1840-1842), and Washington-on-the-Brazos (1842-1845).

Land and climate

Area: 266,807 sq. mi. (691,030 km²), including 4,790 sq. mi. (12,407 km²) of inland water but excluding 7 sq. mi. (18 km²) of Gulf of Mexico coastal water.
Elevation: *Highest*—Guadalupe Peak, 8,751 ft. (2,667 m) above sea level. *Lowest*—sea level, along the Gulf of Mexico.
Coastline: 367 mi. (591 km).
Record high temperature: 120° F. (49° C) at Seymour on Aug. 12, 1936.
Record low temperature: −23° F. (−31° C) at Seminole on Feb. 8, 1933.
Average July temperature: 83° F. (28° C).
Average January temperature: 46° F. (8° C).
Average yearly precipitation: 27 in. (67 cm).

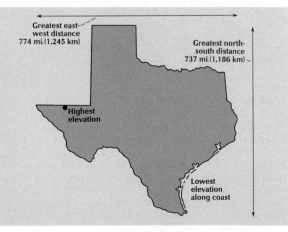

Greatest east-west distance 774 mi.(1,245 km)

Greatest north-south distance 737 mi.(1,186 km)

Highest elevation

Lowest elevation along coast

Important dates

Spanish missionaries built the first two missions in Texas, near present-day El Paso.

| 1519 | 1682 | 1835 |

Alonso Álvarez de Piñeda of Spain mapped the Texas coast.

The Texas Revolution against Mexico began.

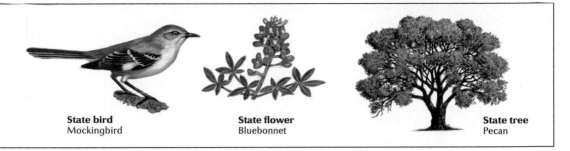

State bird
Mockingbird

State flower
Bluebonnet

State tree
Pecan

People

Population: 14,227,574 (1980 census)
Rank among the states: 3rd
Density: 53 persons per sq. mi. (20 per km²), U.S. average 67 per sq. mi. (26 per km²)
Distribution: 80 per cent urban, 20 per cent rural

Largest cities in Texas

Houston	1,595,138
Dallas	904,078
San Antonio	786,023
El Paso	425,259
Fort Worth	385,141
Austin	345,890

Source: U.S. Bureau of the Census.

Population trend

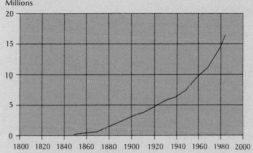

Millions

Source: U.S. Bureau of the Census.

Year	Population*
1985	16,370,000
1980	14,227,574
1970	11,198,655
1960	9,579,677
1950	7,711,194
1940	6,414,824
1930	5,824,715
1920	4,663,228
1910	3,896,542
1900	3,048,710
1890	2,235,527
1880	1,591,749
1870	818,579
1860	604,215
1850	212,592

*All figures are census figures except 1985, which is an estimate.

Economy

Chief products

Agriculture: beef cattle, cotton, milk, sorghum, grain, hay, wheat.
Fishing Industry: shrimp.
Manufacturing: nonelectrical machinery, chemicals, food products, petroleum and coal products, electrical machinery and equipment, fabricated metal products.
Mining: petroleum, natural gas, natural gas liquids, sulfur.

Gross state product

Value of goods and services produced in 1985, $292,870,000,000. *Services* include community, business, and personal services; finance; government; trade; and transportation, communication, and utilities. *Industry* includes construction, manufacturing, and mining. *Agriculture* includes agriculture, fishing, and forestry.

Sources: U.S. Department of Agriculture and U.S. Department of Commerce.

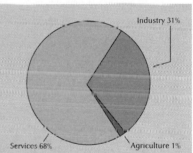

Industry 31%

Services 68%

Agriculture 1%

Government

State government

Governor: 4-year term
State senators: 31; 4-year terms
State representatives: 150; 2-year terms
Counties: 254

Federal government

United States senators: 2
United States representatives: 27
Electoral votes: 29

Sources of information

Tourism: Texas Tourist Development Agency, P. O. Box 12008, Capitol Station, Austin, TX 78711
Economy: Texas Economic Development Commission, P. O. Box 12728, Capitol Station, Austin, TX 78711
Government: Staff Services, P. O. Box 12428, Austin, TX 78711
History: Staff Services, P. O. Box 12428, Austin, TX 78711

Texas became the independent Republic of Texas.

The great Spindletop oil field was discovered.

President John F. Kennedy was assassinated in Dallas.

1836   1845   1901   1963   1964

Texas became the 28th state on December 29.

The Manned Spacecraft Center in Houston (now the Lyndon B. Johnson Space Center) became headquarters for U.S. astronauts.

People

Population. The 1980 United States census reported that Texas had 14,227,574 people. The population had increased 27 per cent over the 1970 figure, 11,198,655. The U.S. Bureau of the Census estimated that by 1985 the state's population had reached about 16,370,000.

About four-fifths of the people of Texas live in urban areas. About two-fifths live in the metropolitan areas of Dallas-Fort Worth, Houston, and San Antonio. In all, Texas has 28 metropolitan areas (see **Metropolitan area**). For the population of these areas, see the *Index* to the political map of Texas.

Texas has 15 cities with more than 100,000 persons. Houston is the largest city, followed by Dallas, San Antonio, El Paso, Fort Worth, Austin, and Corpus Christi. See the separate articles on the cities of Texas listed in the *Related articles* at the end of this article.

About 94 of every 100 Texans, including large numbers of Texas-born Mexicans, were born in the United States. Many Texans born elsewhere are Mexicans who work on farms and in factories in the state's southern and southwestern regions. Some Mexicans who live in the Rio Grande Valley speak Spanish and know only a few words of English. Many non-Mexicans who live in other sections of Texas where Mexicans have settled, especially in the San Antonio area, speak Spanish.

Schools. Texas had only a few public schools when it gained independence in 1836. Mexico had refused to establish a good public school system with English-

Population density

Texas ranks third among the states in population. About 80 per cent of the people live in urban areas. Most of the metropolitan centers lie in the eastern part of the state.

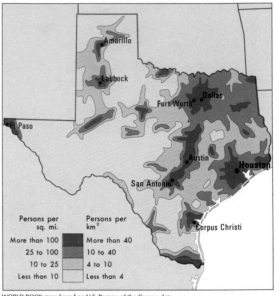

Persons per sq. mi.	Persons per km²
More than 100	More than 40
25 to 100	10 to 40
10 to 25	4 to 10
Less than 10	Less than 4

WORLD BOOK map; based on U.S. Bureau of the Census data.

© Joe Viesti

Schoolchildren listen to a lesson at the Alamo school in Galveston. Texas law requires children to attend school from the age of 7 until the end of the school year in which their 16th birthday occurs.

© Elliott Varner Smith

The Lyndon B. Johnson Presidential Library and Museum is located on the campus of the University of Texas in Austin. It has more than 30 million documents dealing with U.S. domestic policy and foreign relations, as well as many papers and souvenirs from Johnson's years as President.

speaking teachers. Teachers conducted classes only in Spanish. This was a major reason why American settlers objected to Mexican rule. In 1854, Texas established a school system for the entire state.

The Texas Education Agency supervises the public school system. It consists of the commissioner of education, the state board of education, and the state department of education. The board of education has 15 appointed members. It appoints the commissioner. Texas law requires children to attend school from age 7 until the end of the school year in which their 16th birthday occurs. For the number of students and teachers in Texas, see **Education** (table).

In 1985, a new law went into effect preventing high school students from participating in extracurricular activities if they failed a class. It was the first statewide law of its kind. Some Texans felt that school athletic programs would suffer, but a large majority supported the rule.

Libraries. Texas has over 450 public libraries and many college and special libraries. The Texas State Library, established in Austin in 1839 by the Republic of Texas, is Texas' oldest library. The libraries of the University of Texas at Austin have over 5 million volumes, the state's largest collection. These libraries include the Eugene C. Barker Texas History Center, the Harry Ransom Humanities Research Center, the Nettie Lee Benson Latin-American Collection, and the Tarlton Law Library.

The Lyndon Baines Johnson Library and Museum, also at the University of Texas at Austin, houses the papers and mementos of the nation's 36th president. The Armstrong Browning Library at Baylor University in Waco has the world's largest collection of material by and about the English poet Robert Browning.

Museums. Collections at the Museum of Fine Arts of Houston include jewelry from ancient Greece and Spanish sculptures of the 1400's. The museum also has works by Frederic Remington, the famous American painter of the old West. The Dallas Museum of Fine Arts has a collection of American paintings. The Kimbell Art Museum

In Fort Worth displays paintings by European masters.

The Witte Memorial Museum in San Antonio has a wide variety of displays, including exhibits on Texas wildlife and ecology, American Indians, archaeology, costumes, and paintings and furniture of early Texas and America. Other museums include the Texas Hall of State in Dallas, the Sam Houston Memorial Museum in Huntsville, and the Art Museum of South Texas in Corpus Christi.

© Bob Daemmrich

The University of Texas Longhorns play their home football games at Memorial Stadium in Austin. High school, college, and professional football games attract thousands of spectators in Texas each season.

Universities and colleges

Texas has 66 universities and colleges that offer bachelor's or advanced degrees and are accredited by the Southern Association of Colleges and Schools. Locations shown below refer to the schools' mailing addresses. For enrollments and further information, see **Universities and colleges** (table).

Name	Location	Name	Location	Name	Location
Abilene Christian University	Abilene	Howard Payne University	Brownwood	Southern Methodist University	Dallas
Amber University	Garland	Huston-Tillotson College	Austin	Southwest Texas State	
American Technological		Incarnate Word College	San Antonio	University	San Marcos
University	Killeen	Jarvis Christian College	Hawkins	Southwestern Adventist College	Keene
Angelo State University	San Angelo	Lamar University	Beaumont	Southwestern Baptist Theological	
Austin College	Sherman	LeTourneau College	Longview	Seminary	Fort Worth
Austin Presbyterian		Lubbock Christian University	Lubbock	Southwestern Christian College	Terrell
Theological Seminary	Austin	Mary Hardin-Baylor,		Southwestern University	Georgetown
Baptist Missionary Association		University of	Belton	Stephen F. Austin	
Theological Seminary	Jacksonville	McMurry College	Abilene	State University	Nacogdoches
Baylor College of Dentistry	Dallas	Midwestern State University	Wichita Falls	Sul Ross State University	Alpine
Baylor College of Medicine	Houston	North Texas State University	Denton	Texas, University of	*
Baylor University	Waco	Oblate School of Theology	San Antonio	Texas A&M University	
Concordia Lutheran College	Austin	Our Lady of the Lake University		System	*
Criswell College	Dallas	of San Antonio	San Antonio	Texas Chiropractic College	Pasadena
Dallas, University of	Irving	Pan American University	Edinburg	Texas Christian University	Fort Worth
Dallas Baptist University	Dallas	Paul Quinn College	Waco	Texas College	Tyler
Dallas Theological Seminary	Dallas	Rice University	Houston	Texas Lutheran College	Seguin
East Texas Baptist University	Marshall	St. Edward's University	Austin	Texas Southern University	Houston
East Texas State University	*	St. Mary's University		Texas Tech University	Lubbock
Episcopal Theological Seminary		of San Antonio	San Antonio	Texas Wesleyan College	Fort Worth
of the Southwest	Austin	St. Thomas, University of	Houston	Texas Woman's University	Denton
Hardin-Simmons University	Abilene	Sam Houston State		Trinity University	San Antonio
Houston, University of	*	University	Huntsville	Wayland Baptist University	Plainview
Houston Baptist University	Houston	Schreiner College	Kerrville	West Texas State University	Canyon
Houston Graduate School		South Texas, University		Wiley College	Marshall
of Theology	Houston	System of	*		

*For campuses and founding dates, see **Universities and colleges** (table).

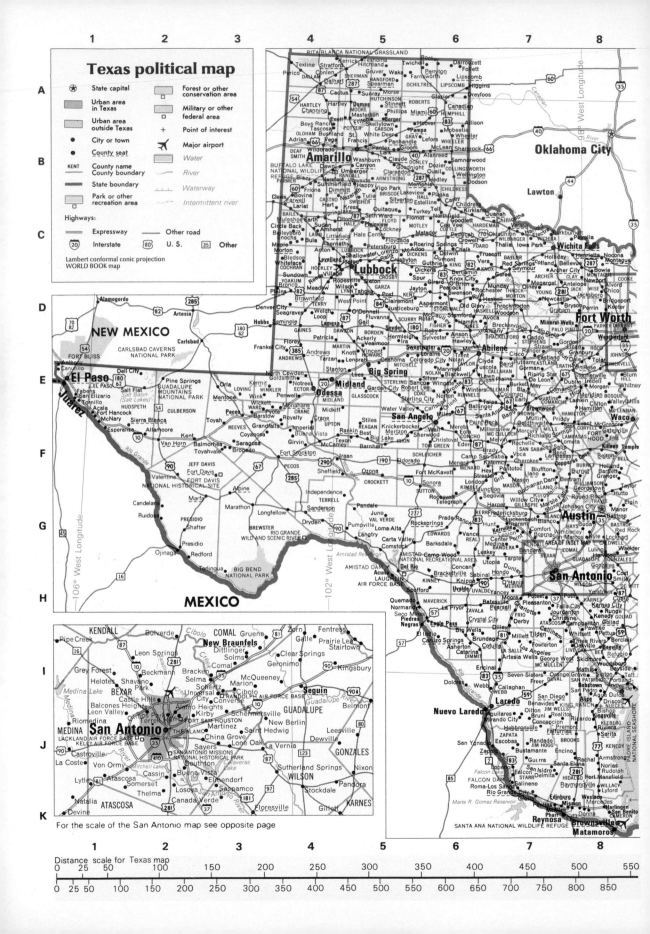

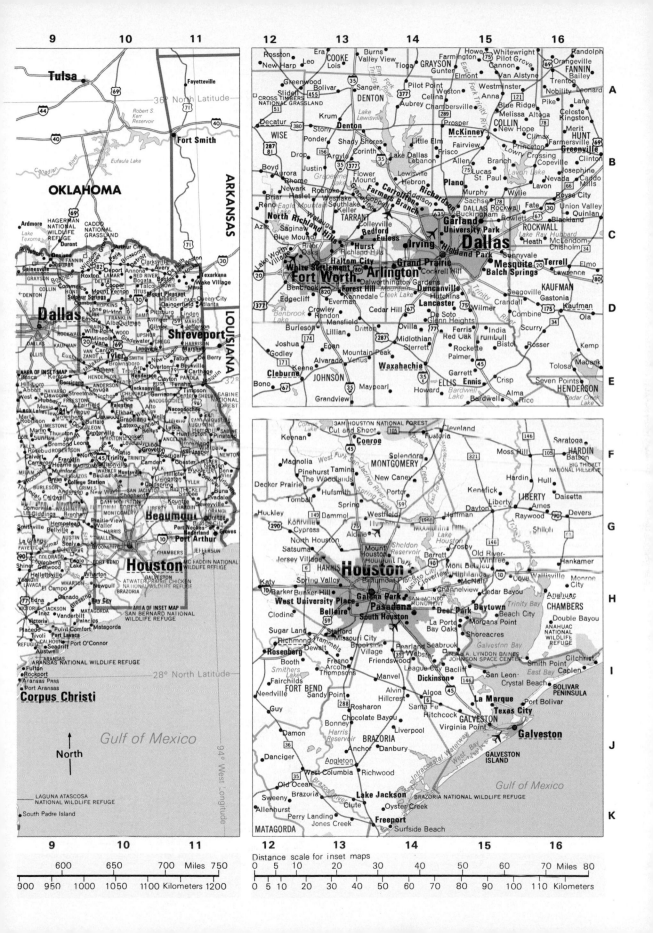

Texas map index

Metropolitan areas

Abilene 110,932
Amarillo 173,699
Austin 536,688
Beaumont-Port Arthur 375,497
Brazoria 169,587
Brownsville-Harlingen 209,727
Bryan-College Station 93,588
Corpus Christi 326,228
Dallas 1,957,378
El Paso 479,899
Fort Worth-Arlington 973,138
Galveston-Texas City 195,940
Houston 2,735,766
Killeen-Temple 214,656
Laredo 99,258
Longview-Marshall 151,752
Lubbock 211,651
McAllen-Edinburg-Mission 283,229
Midland 82,636
Odessa 115,374
San Angelo 84,784
San Antonio 1,071,954
Sherman-Denison 89,796
Texarkana-Texarkana (Ark.) 113,067 (75,301 in Tex.; 37,766 in Ark.)
Tyler 128,366
Victoria 68,807
Waco 170,755
Wichita Falls 121,082

Counties

Anderson 38,381 E 10
Andrews 13,323 E 4
Angelina 64,172 F 11
Aransas 14,260 I 9
Archer 7,266 D 7
Armstrong 1,994 B 5
Atascosa 25,055 H 7
Austin 17,726 G 9
Bailey 8,168 C 4
Bandera 7,084 G 7
Bastrop 24,726 G 8
Baylor 4,919 C 7
Bee 26,030 I 8
Bell 157,820 F 8
Bexar 988,798 G 7
Blanco 4,681 G 7
Borden 859 D 5
Bosque 13,401 E 8
Bowie 75,301 D 11
Brazoria 169,587 H 10
Brazos 93,588 F 9
Brewster 7,573 G 3
Briscoe 2,579 B 5
Brooks 8,428 J 8
Brown 33,057 E 7
Burleson 12,313 F 9
Burnet 17,803 F 8
Caldwell 23,637 G 8
Calhoun 19,574 I 9
Callahan 10,992 E 7
Cameron 209,727 K 8
Camp 9,275 D 10
Carson 6,672 B 5
Cass 29,430 D 11
Castro 10,556 C 4
Chambers 18,538 G 11
Cherokee 38,127 E 10
Childress 6,950 B 6
Clay 9,582 D 8
Cochran 4,825 C 4
Coke 3,196 E 5
Coleman 10,439 E 7
Collin 144,576 D 9
Collingsworth 4,648 B 6
Colorado 18,823 G 9
Comal 36,446 G 8
Comanche 12,617 E 7
Concho 2,915 F 6
Cooke 27,656 D 8
Coryell 56,767 F 8
Cottle 2,947 C 6
Crane 4,600 E 4
Crockett 4,608 F 5
Crosby 8,859 D 5
Culberson 3,315 E 2
Dallam 6,531 A 4
Dallas 1,556,390 D 9
Dawson 16,184 D 4
Deaf Smith 21,165 B 4
Delta 4,839 D 10
Denton 143,126 D 9
De Witt 18,903 H 8
Dickens 3,539 C 5
Dimmit 11,367 I 6
Donley 4,075 B 5
Duval 12,517 I 7
Eastland 19,480 E 7
Ector 115,374 E 4
Edwards 2,033 G 6
Ellis 59,743 E 9
El Paso 479,899 E 1
Erath 22,560 E 8
Falls 17,946 F 9
Fannin 24,285 C 9
Fayette 18,832 G 9
Fisher 5,891 D 6
Floyd 9,834 C 5
Foard 2,158 C 6
Fort Bend 130,962 G 10
Franklin 6,893 D 10
Freestone 14,830 E 9
Frio 13,785 H 7
Gaines 13,150 D 4
Galveston 195,738 H 10
Garza 5,336 D 5
Gillespie 13,532 G 7
Glasscock 1,304 E 5
Goliad 5,193 H 8
Gonzales 16,949 G 8
Gray 26,386 B 5
Grayson 89,796 D 9
Gregg 99,495 D 11
Grimes 13,580 F 9
Guadalupe 46,708 G 8
Hale 37,592 C 5
Hall 5,594 B 6
Hamilton 8,297 E 8
Hansford 6,209 A 5
Hardeman 6,368 C 6
Hardin 40,721 G 11
Harris 2,409,547 G 10
Harrison 52,265 D 11
Hartley 3,987 A 4
Haskell 7,725 D 6
Hays 40,594 G 8
Hemphill 5,304 A 6
Henderson 42,606 E 10
Hidalgo 283,323 J 8
Hill 25,024 E 8
Hockley 23,230 C 4
Hood 17,714 E 8
Hopkins 25,247 D 10
Houston 22,299 F 10
Howard 33,142 E 5
Hudspeth 2,728 E 1
Hunt 55,248 D 9
Hutchinson 26,304 A 5
Irion 1,386 F 5
Jack 7,408 D 8
Jackson 13,352 H 9
Jasper 30,781 F 11
Jeff Davis 1,647 F 2
Jefferson 250,938 G 11
Jim Hogg 5,168 J 7
Jim Wells 36,498 J 7
Johnson 67,649 E 8
Jones 17,268 D 6
Karnes 13,593 H 8
Kaufman 39,029 E 9
Kendall 10,635 G 7
Kenedy 543 J 8
Kent 1,145 D 5
Kerr 28,780 G 6
Kimble 4,063 F 6
King 425 C 6
Kinney 2,279 H 6
Kleberg 33,358 J 8
Knox 5,329 C 6
Lamar 42,156 D 10
Lamb 18,669 C 4
Lampasas 12,005 F 8
La Salle 5,514 I 7
Lavaca 19,004 H 9
Lee 10,952 G 9
Leon 9,594 F 10
Liberty 47,088 G 10
Limestone 20,224 F 9
Lipscomb 3,766 A 6
Live Oak 9,606 I 8
Llano 10,144 F 7
Loving 91 E 3
Lubbock 211,651 C 5
Lynn 8,605 D 4
Madison 10,649 F 9
Marion 10,360 D 11
Martin 4,684 E 4
Mason 3,683 F 7
Matagorda 37,828 H 10
Maverick 31,398 H 6
McCulloch 8,735 F 7
McLennan 170,755 E 8
McMullen 789 I 7
Medina 23,164 H 7
Menard 2,346 F 6
Midland 82,636 E 4
Milam 22,732 F 9
Mills 4,477 F 7
Mitchell 9,088 E 5
Montague 17,410 D 8
Montgomery 127,222 G 10
Moore 16,575 A 5
Morris 14,629 D 11
Motley 1,950 C 5
Nacogdoches 46,786 E 11
Navarro 35,323 E 9
Newton 13,254 F 11
Nolan 17,359 E 6
Nueces 268,215 I 8
Ochiltree 9,588 A 5
Oldham 2,283 B 4
Orange 83,838 G 11
Palo Pinto 24,062 D 7
Panola 20,724 E 11
Parker 44,609 D 8
Parmer 11,038 B 4
Pecos 14,618 F 4
Polk 24,407 F 10
Potter 98,637 B 5
Presidio 5,188 G 2
Rains 4,839 D 10
Randall 75,062 B 5
Reagan 4,135 F 5
Real 2,469 G 6
Red River 16,101 D 10
Reeves 15,801 F 3
Refugio 9,289 I 9
Roberts 1,187 A 5
Robertson 14,653 F 9
Rockwall 14,528 D 9
Runnels 11,872 E 6
Rusk 41,382 E 11
Sabine 8,702 F 11
San Augustine 8,785 F 11
San Jacinto 11,434 F 10
San Patricio 58,013 I 8
San Saba 5,841 F 7
Schleicher 2,820 F 6
Scurry 18,192 D 5
Shackelford 3,915 D 7
Shelby 23,084 E 11
Sherman 3,174 A 5
Smith 128,366 E 10
Somervell 4,154 E 8
Starr 27,266 J 7
Stephens 9,926 D 7
Sterling 1,206 E 5
Stonewall 2,406 D 6
Sutton 5,130 G 6
Swisher 9,723 C 5
Tarrant 860,880 D 8
Taylor 110,932 E 6
Terrell 1,595 G 4
Terry 14,581 D 4
Throckmorton 2,053 D 7
Titus 21,442 D 10
Tom Green 84,784 F 6
Travis 419,573 G 8
Trinity 9,450 F 10
Tyler 16,223 F 11
Upshur 28,595 D 10
Upton 4,619 F 4
Uvalde 22,441 H 6
Val Verde 35,910 G 5
Van Zandt 31,426 E 10
Victoria 68,807 H 9
Walker 41,789 F 10
Waller 19,798 G 10
Ward 13,976 E 3
Washington 21,998 G 9
Webb 99,258 I 7
Wharton 40,242 H 9
Wheeler 7,137 B 6
Wichita 121,082 C 7
Wilbarger 15,931 C 7
Willacy 17,495 K 8
Williamson 76,507 F 8
Wilson 16,756 H 8
Winkler 9,944 E 3
Wise 26,575 D 8
Wood 24,697 D 10
Yoakum 8,299 D 4
Young 19,083 D 7
Zapata 6,628 J 7
Zavala 11,666 H 6

Cities, towns, and villages

Abernathy 2,904 C 5
Abilene 98,315 °E 6
Addison 5,553 C 14
Agua Dulce 934 I 8
Alamo* 5,831 K 8
Alamo Heights 6,252 J 2
Albany 2,450 °D 7
Aldine 12,623 G 13
Aledo* 1,027 D 8
Alice 20,961 °I 8
Allen 8,314 B 15
Alpine 5,465 °G 3
Alto 1,203 E 10
Alton* 2,732 K 8
Alvarado 2,701 E 13
Alvin 16,515 I 14
Alvord 874 D 8
Amarillo 149,230 °B 5
Ames 1,155 G 16
Amherst 971 C 4
Anahuac 1,840 °H 16
Anderson °G 9
Andrews 11,061 °E 4
Angleton 13,929 °J 13
Anna 855 A 15
Anson 2,831 °D 6
Anthony 2,640 E 1
Anton 1,180 C 4
Aransas Pass 7,173 I 9
Archer City 1,862 °C 7
Argyle 1,111 B 13
Arlington 160,113 C 13
Arp 939 E 10
Asherton 1,574 I 6
Aspermont 1,357 °D 6
Athens 10,197 °E 10
Atlanta 6,272 D 11
Aubrey 948 A 14
Austin 345,890 °G 7
Azle 5,822 C 12
Bacliff 4,851 I 15
Baird 1,696 °E 7
Balch Springs 13,746 D 15
Balcones Heights 2,511 J 2
Ballinger 4,207 °E 6
Bandera 947 °G 7
Bangs 1,716 E 7
Barrett* 3,183 G 10
Bartlett 1,567 F 8
Bastrop 3,789 °G 8
Bay City 17,837 °H 10
Baytown 56,923 H 15
Beach City 977 H 15
Beaumont 118,102 °G 11
Beckville 945 E 11
Bedford 20,821 C 13
Beeville 14,574 °I 8
Bellaire 14,950 H 13
Bellmead* 7,569 E 8
Bellville 2,860 °G 9
Belton 10,660 °F 8
Benavides 1,978 I 7
Benbrook 13,579 D 12
Benjamin 257 °C 6
Bertram 824 F 8
Beverly Hills* 2,083 E 8
Bevil Oaks* 1,306 G 11
Big Lake 3,404 °F 5
Big Sandy* 1,258 E 10
Big Spring 24,804 °E 5
Big Wells 939 H 6
Bishop 3,706 I 8
Blanco 1,179 G 7
Blossom 1,487 C 10
Blue Mound 2,169 C 13
Boerne 3,229 °G 7
Bogata 1,508 D 10
Bonham 7,338 °C 9
Booker 1,219 A 6
Borger 15,837 A 5
Boston °D 11
Bovina 1,499 B 4
Bowie 5,610 C 8
Boyd 889 B 12
Brackettville 1,676 °H 6
Brady 5,969 °F 7
Brazoria 3,025 K 13
Breckenridge 6,921 °D 7
Bremond 1,025 F 9
Brenham 10,966 °G 9
Briar 1,810 B 12
Bridge City 7,667 G 11
Bridgeport 3,737 D 8
Bronte 983 E 6
Brookshire 2,175 G 10
Brookside Village 1,453 I 14
Brownfield 10,387 °D 4
Brownsville 84,997 °K 8
Brownwood 19,396 °E 7
Bruceville-Eddy* 1,038 F 8
Bryan 44,337 °F 9
Buffalo 1,507 F 9
Bunker Hill 3,750 H 13
Burkburnett 10,668 C 7
Burleson 11,734 D 13
Burnet 3,410 °F 8
Cactus 898 A 5
Caddo Mills 1,060 B 16
Caldwell 2,953 °G 9
Calvert 1,732 F 9
Cameron 5,721 °F 9
Canadian 3,491 °A 6
Canton 2,845 °E 10
Canyon 10,724 °B 5
Carrizo Springs 6,886 °I 6
Carrollton 40,595 C 14
Carthage 6,447 °E 11
Castle Hills 4,773 I 2
Castroville 1,821 J 1
Cedar Hill 6,849 D 14
Cedar Park* 3,474 G 8
Celina 1,520 A 14
Center 5,827 °E 11
Centerville 799 °F 10
Champion* 14,692 G 10
Chandler* 1,308 E 10
Channelview 17,471 H 14
Channing 304 °A 4
Charlotte 1,443 H 7
Chico 890 D 8
Childress 5,817 °C 6
Chillicothe 1,052 C 7
China* 1,351 G 11
Cisco 4,517 E 7
Clarendon 2,220 °B 5
Clarksville 4,917 °C 10
Claude 1,112 °B 5
Clear Lake Shores* 755 H 10
Cleburne 19,218 °E 12
Cleveland 5,977 F 14
Clifton 3,063 E 8
Clint* 1,314 E 1
Cloverleaf 17,317 H 14
Clute 9,577 K 13
Clyde 2,562 E 7
Coahoma 1,069 E 5
Cockrell Hill 3,262 C 14
Coldspring 569 °F 10
Coleman 5,960 °E 7
College Station 37,272 F 9
Colleyville 6,700 C 13
Colorado City 5,405 °E 5
Columbus 3,923 °G 9
Comanche 4,075 °E 7
Combes* 1,488 K 8
Comfort 1,226 G 7
Commerce 8,136 D 9
Conroe 18,034 °F 13
Converse 5,150 I 3
Cooper 2,338 °D 10
Coppell 3,826 C 14
Copperas Cove 19,469 F 8
Corinth 1,264 B 14
Corpus Christi 231,134 °I 8
Corrigan 1,770 F 11
Corsicana 21,712 °E 9
Cotulla 3,912 °I 7
Cove 645 H 15
Crandall 831 D 16
Crane 3,622 °F 4
Crockett 7,405 °F 10
Crosbyton 2,289 °C 5
Cross Plains 1,240 E 7
Crowell 1,509 °C 6
Crowley 5,852 D 13
Crystal Beach 776 I 16
Crystal City 8,334 °H 6
Cuero 7,124 °H 8
Cut and Shoot 568 F 13
Daingerfield 3,030 °D 11
Daisetta 1,177 G 16
Dalhart 6,854 °A 4
Dallas 904,078 °D 9
Dalworthington Gardens 1,100 D 13
Danbury* 1,357 H 10
Dawson 747 E 9
Dayton 4,908 G 15
Decatur 4,104 °A 12
Deer Park 22,648 H 14
De Kalb 2,217 C 11
De Leon 2,478 E 7
Del Rio 30,034 °H 5
Denison 23,884 C 9
Denton 48,063 °B 13
Denver City 4,704 D 4
De Soto 15,538 D 14
Detroit 805 C 10
Devine 3,756 K 1
Diboll 5,227 F 10
Dickens 409 °C 5
Dickinson 7,505 I 15
Dilley 2,579 H 7
Dimmitt 5,019 °B 4
Donna 9,952 K 8
Dublin 2,723 E 7
Dumas 12,194 °A 5
Duncanville 27,781 D 14
Eagle Lake 3,921 G 9
Eagle Pass 21,407 °H 6
Early 2,313 E 7
Earth 1,512 C 4
Eastland 3,747 °E 7
Edcouch* 3,092 K 8
Eden 1,294 F 6
Edgecliff 2,695 D 13
Edgewood* 1,413 D 10
Edinburg 24,075 °K 8
Edna 5,650 °H 9
El Campo 10,462 H 9
Eldorado 2,061 °F 6
Electra 3,755 C 7
Elgin 4,535 G 8
Elkhart 1,317 E 10
El Lago* 3,129 G 10
El Paso 425,259 °E 1
Elsa* 5,061 K 8
Emory 813 °D 10
Ennis 12,110 E 15
Euless 24,002 C 13
Everman 5,387 D 13
Fabens 4,285 E 1
Fairfield 3,505 °E 9
Fairview 893 B 15
Falfurrias 6,103 °J 8
Farmers Branch 24,863 C 14
Farmersville 2,360 B 16
Farwell 1,354 °C 4
Ferris 2,228 D 15
Flatonia* 1,070 G 8
Florence* 744 F 8
Floresville 4,381 °K 3
Flower Mound 4,402 B 13
Floydada 4,193 °C 5
Forest Hill 11,684 D 13
Forney* 2,483 E 9
Fort Bliss* 12,687 E 1
Fort Davis °F 3
Fort Hood 31,250 F 8
Fort Stockton 8,688 °F 4
Fort Worth 385,141 °D 8
Franklin 1,349 °F 9
Frankston 1,255 E 10
Fredericksburg 6,412 °G 7
Freeport 13,444 K 14
Freer 3,213 I 7
Friendswood 10,719 I 14
Friona 3,809 B 4
Frisco 3,499 B 14
Fritch 2,299 A 5
Fuller Springs* 1,470 F 11
Gail °D 5
Gainesville 14,081 °C 9
Galena Park 9,879 H 14
Galveston 61,902 °J 15
Ganado 1,770 H 9
Garden City °E 5
Garland 138,857 C 15
Garrison 1,059 E 11
Gatesville 6,260 °F 8
George West 2,627 °I 8
Georgetown 9,468 °F 8
Giddings 3,950 °G 9
Gilmer 5,167 °D 10
Gladewater 6,548 D 10

Place	Population	Key
Glenn Heights	1,033	D 14
Glen Rose	2,075	°E 8
Goldthwaite	1,783	°F 7
Goliad	1,990	°H 8
Gonzales	7,152	°H 8
Gorman	1,258	E 7
Graham	9,170	°D 7
Granbury	3,332	°E 8
Grand Prairie	71,462	C 14
Grand Saline*	2,709	D 10
Grandview	1,205	E 13
Granger	1,236	F 8
Grapeland	1,634	F 10
Grapevine	11,801	C 13
Greenville	22,161	°B 16
Gregory*	2,739	I 8
Grey Forest	442	I 1
Griffing Park*	1,802	G 11
Groesbeck	3,373	°F 9
Groom	736	B 5
Groves	17,090	G 11
Groveton	1,262	°F 10
Grulla	1,442	K 7
Gruver	1,216	A 5
Gun Barrel City*	2,118	E 9
Gunter	849	A 15
Guthrie		°C 6
Hale Center	2,297	C 5
Hallettsville	2,865	°H 9
Hallsville*	1,556	E 11
Haltom City	29,014	C 13
Hamilton	3,189	°E 8
Hamlin	3,248	D 6
Hardin	779	F 16
Harker Heights*	7,345	F 8
Harlingen	43,543	K 8
Hart	1,008	C 4
Haskell	3,782	°D 6
Hawkins*	1,302	D 10
Hearne	5,418	F 9
Heath	1,459	C 16
Hebbronville	4,684	°J 7
Hedwig Village*	2,506	H 13
Hemphill	1,353	°F 11
Hempstead	3,456	°G 10
Henderson	11,473	°E 10
Henrietta	3,149	°C 8
Hereford	15,853	°B 4
Hewitt*	5,247	F 8
Hickory Creek*	1,422	D 9
Hico	1,375	E 8
Hidalgo*	2,288	K 8
Hidalgo Park, see Las Milpas [-Hidalgo Park]		
Highland Park	8,909	C 14
Highland Village*	3,246	D 9
Highlands*	6,467	G 10
Hill Country Village*	972	C 7
Hillcrest	771	I 14
Hillsboro	7,397	°E 9
Hitchcock	6,142	J 15
Holland	863	F 8
Holliday	1,349	C 7
Hollywood Park*	3,231	H 8
Hondo	6,057	°H 7
Honey Grove	1,973	C 10
Hooks	2,507	D 11
Houston	1,595,138	°G 10
Howe	2,072	A 15
Hubbard	1,676	E 9
Hudson*	1,659	F 11
Hughes Springs*	2,196	D 11
Humble	6,729	G 14
Hunters Creek Village*	4,215	H 13
Huntington	1,672	F 11
Huntsville	23,936	°F 10
Hurst	31,420	C 13
Hutchins	2,837	D 15
Idalou	2,348	C 5
Ingleside*	5,436	I 9
Iowa Park	6,184	C 7
Iraan	1,358	F 4
Irving	109,943	C 14
Italy*	1,306	E 9
Itasca	1,600	E 9
Jacinto City	8,953	H 14
Jacksboro	4,000	°D 8
Jacksonville	12,264	E 10
Jasper	6,959	°F 11
Jayton	638	°D 6
Jefferson	2,643	°D 11
Jersey Village	4,084	H 13
Joaquin	917	E 11
Johnson City	872	°G 7
Jones Creek	2,634	K 13
Joshua	1,470	E 12
Jourdanton	2,743	°H 7
Junction	2,593	°G 6
Justin	920	B 13
Karnes City	3,296	°H 8
Katy	5,660	H 12
Kaufman	4,658	°D 16
Keene	3,013	E 13
Keller	4,156	C 13
Kemah*	1,304	H 11
Kemp*	1,035	E 16
Kenedy	4,356	H 8
Kenefick	763	G 15
Kennedale	2,594	D 13
Kerens	1,582	E 9
Kermit	8,015	°E 3
Kerrville	15,276	°G 7
Kilgore*	11,332	E 11
Killeen	46,296	F 8
Kingsland	2,241	F 7
Kingsville	28,808	°J 8
Kingwood*	16,261	G 10
Kirby	6,435	J 2
Kirbyville	1,972	F 11
Knox City	1,546	D 6
Kountze	2,716	°G 11
Kress	783	C 5
Krum	917	A 13
Kyle	2,093	G 8
La Coste	862	J 1
Lackland Air Force Base	14,459	J 2
Lacy-Lakeview	2,752	E 9
La Feria*	3,495	K 8
La Grange	3,768	°G 9
La Joya*	2,018	K 7
Lake Dallas	3,177	B 14
Lake Jackson	19,102	K 13
Lake Worth Village	4,394	C 12
Lakeport*	835	E 11
Lakeside*	957	D 8
Lakeway*	790	G 8
La Marque	15,372	I 15
Lamesa	11,790	°D 4
Lampasas	6,165	°F 8
Lancaster	14,807	D 15
La Porte	14,062	H 15
La Pryor	1,257	H 6
Laredo	91,449	°J 7
Las Milpas [-Hidalgo Park]*	3,039	K 8
Laughlin Air Force Base	2,994	H 5
La Villa*	1,442	K 8
League City	16,578	I 14
Leakey	468	°G 6
Leander*	2,179	F 8
Lefors	829	B 6
Leon Valley	9,088	J 2
Leonard	1,421	A 16
Levelland	13,809	°C 4
Lewisville	24,273	B 14
Lexington	1,065	G 9
Liberty	7,945	°G 15
Liberty City*	1,121	D 10
Lindale*	2,180	E 10
Linden	2,443	°D 11
Lipscomb		°A 6
Little Elm	926	B 14
Little River-Academy*	1,155	F 8
Littlefield	7,409	°C 4
Live Oak*	8,183	H 9
Livingston	[illegible]	°F 10
Llano	3,071	°F 7
Lockhart	7,953	°G 8
Lockney	2,334	C 5
Lone Star*	2,036	D 11
Longview	62,762	°F 11
Loraine	929	E 6
Lorenzo	1,394	C 5
Los Fresnos*	2,173	K 8
Lott	865	F 9
Lowry Crossing	443	B 15
Lubbock	173,979	°C 5
Lucas	1,371	B 15
Lufkin	28,562	°F 11
Luling	5,039	G 8
Lumberton*	2,480	G 11
Lyford	1,618	K 8
Lytle	1,920	K 1
Mabank	1,443	E 16
Madisonville	3,660	°F 10
Magnolia	867	F 12
Malakoff	2,082	E 9
Manor	1,044	G 8
Mansfield	8,102	D 13
Manvel	3,549	I 14
Marble Falls	3,252	F 8
Marfa	2,466	°G 3
Marlin	7,099	°F 9
Marshall	24,921	°D 11
Mart	2,324	E 9
Mason	2,153	°F 7
Matador	1,052	°C 5
Mathis	5,667	I 8
Maud	1,059	D 11
McAllen	66,281	K 8
McCamey	2,436	F 4
McGregor	4,513	F 8
McKinney	16,256	°B 15
McLean	1,160	B 6
McLendon-Chisholm	403	C 16
McQueeney	1,332	I 4
Memphis	3,352	°B 6
Menard	1,697	°F 6
Mentone		°E 3
Mercedes	11,851	K 8
Meridian	1,330	°E 8
Merkel	2,493	E 6
Mertzon	687	°F 5
Mesquite	67,053	C 15
Mexia	7,094	E 9
Miami	813	°A 6
Midland	70,525	°E 4
Midlothian	3,219	D 14
Mineola	4,346	D 10
Mineral Wells	14,468	D 8
Mission	22,653	K 8
Missouri City	24,423	I 13
Monahans	8,397	°E 4
Mont Belvieu	1,730	H 15
Montague	1,253	°C 8
Moody*	1,385	F 8
Morgan's Point Resort*	1,082	F 8
Morton	2,674	°C 4
Moulton*	1,009	H 9
Mount Pleasant	11,003	°D 10
Mount Vernon	2,025	°D 10
Muenster*	1,408	D 8
Muleshoe	4,842	°C 4
Munday	1,738	D 6
Murphy	1,150	B 15
Nacogdoches	27,149	°E 11
Naples*	1,908	D 11
Nash*	2,022	D 11
Nassau Bay*	4,526	G 10
Natalia	1,264	K 1
Navasota	5,971	G 9
Nederland	16,855	G 11
Needville	1,417	I 12
New Boston	4,628	D 11
New Braunfels	22,402	°I 3
New London	942	E 10
New Waverly	824	F 10
Newton	1,620	°F 11
Nixon	2,008	J 5
Nocona	2,992	C 8
Nolanville*	1,308	F 8
North Richland Hills	30,592	C 13
North San Pedro*	2,553	I 8
Northcrest*	1,944	F 8
O'Donnell	1,200	D 5
Oak Ridge North*	2,504	G 10
Odem*	2,363	I 8
Odessa	90,027	°E 4
Old River Winfree	1,058	G 14
Olmos Park	2,069	J 2
Olney	4,060	D 7
Olton	2,235	C 4
Orange	23,628	°G 11
Orange Grove	1,212	I 8
Ore City*	1,050	D 11
Overton	2,430	E 10
Ovilla	1,067	D 14
Oyster Creek	1,473	K 14
Ozona	3,766	°F 5
Paducah	2,216	°C 6
Paint Rock	256	°F 6
Palacios	4,667	H 9
Palestine	15,948	°E 10
Palmer	1,187	E 15
Palo Pinto		°D 7
Pampa	21,396	°B 5
Panhandle	2,226	°B 5
Panorama Village*	1,186	G 10
Pantego*	2,431	D 8
Paris	25,498	°C 10
Parker*	1,098	D 9
Pasadena	112,560	H 14
Patton*	1,050	G 10
Pearland	13,248	I 14
Pearsall	7,383	°H 7
Pecos	12,855	°E 3
Perryton	7,991	°A 6
Petersburg	1,633	C 5
Petrolia	755	C 8
Pharr	21,381	K 8
Phillips	1,729	A 5
Pilot Point	2,211	A 14
Pinehurst	2,928	F 12
Pineland	1,111	F 11
Piney Point Village*	2,958	H 13
Pittsburg	4,245	°D 10
Plains	1,457	°D 4
Plainview	22,187	°C 5
Plano	72,331	B 15
Pleasanton	6,346	H 7
Point Comfort	1,125	H 9
Port Aransas	1,968	I 9
Port Arthur	61,251	G 11
Port Isabel*	3,769	K 9
Port Lavaca	10,911	°H 9
Port Neches	13,944	G 11
Port O'Connor	1,031	I 9
Portland	12,023	I 8
Post	3,961	°D 5
Post Oak Bend City	878	D 9
Poteet	3,086	H 7
Poth	1,461	H 8
Pottsboro	895	C 9
Prairie View	3,993	G 10
Premont	2,984	J 8
Presidio	1,723	G 2
Primera*	1,380	K 8
Princeton	3,408	B 15
Quanah	3,890	°C 6
Queen City	1,748	D 11
Quinlan	1,002	C 16
Quitman	1,893	°D 10
Ralls	2,422	C 5
Ranger	3,142	E 7
Rankin	1,216	°F 4
Raymondville	9,493	°K 8
Red Oak	1,882	D 14
Refugio	3,898	°I 8
Reno*	1,059	C 10
Reno	1,174	C 12
Richardson	72,496	C 15
Richland Hills	7,977	C 13
Richmond	9,692	°I 12
Richwood	2,591	J 13
Rio Grande City	8,930	°K 7
Rio Hondo*	1,673	K 8
Rising Star	1,204	E 7
River Oaks	6,890	C 12
Roanoke	910	B 13
Robert Lee	1,202	°E 6
Robinson	6,074	F 9
Robstown	12,100	I 8
Roby	814	°D 6
Rockdale	5,611	F 9
Rockport	3,686	°I 9
Rocksprings	1,317	°G 6
Rockwall	5,939	°C 16
Rogers*	1,242	F 8
Rollingwood*	1,027	G 8
Roma-Los Saenz	3,384	K 7
Roman Forest*	929	G 10
Roscoe*	1,628	E 6
Rosebud	2,076	F 9
Rosenberg	17,833	I 12
Rotan	2,284	D 6
Round Rock	12,740	G 8
Rowlett	7,522	C 15
Royse City	1,566	B 16
Rule	1,015	D 6
Runge	1,244	H 8
Rusk	4,681	°E 10
Sabinal	1,827	H 6
Sachse	1,640	C 15
Saginaw	5,736	C 13
St. Jo*	1,071	D 8
San Angelo	73,240	°F 6
San Antonio	786,023	°H 7
San Augustine	2,930	°E 11
San Benito	17,988	K 8
San Diego	5,255	°I 8
San Elizario	1,540	E 1
San Juan*	7,608	K 8
San Leon	1,745	I 15
San Marcos	23,420	°G 8
San Saba	2,847	°F 7
Sanderson	1,241	°G 4
Sanger	2,574	A 13
Sansom Park Village*	3,921	D 8
Santa Anna	1,535	E 7
Santa Fe	6,172	I 14
Santa Rosa*	[illegible]	[illegible]
Sarita		°J 8
Savoy*	855	C 9
Schertz	7,262	I 3
Schulenburg	2,469	G 9
Seabrook	4,670	I 15
Seadrift	1,277	I 9
Seagoville	7,304	D 15
Seagraves	2,596	D 4
Sealy	3,875	G 9
Seguin	17,854	°I 4
Seminole	6,080	°D 4
Seth Ward	1,186	C 5
Seven Points	647	E 16
Seymour	3,657	°C 7
Shady Shores	813	B 14
Shallowater	1,932	C 4
Shamrock	2,834	B 6
Shavano Park	1,448	J 2
Shenandoah*	1,793	G 10
Shepherd	1,674	G 10
Sherman	30,413	°C 9
Shiner	2,213	H 9
Shoreacres	1,260	H 15
Sierra Blanca		°F 1
Silsbee	7,684	G 11
Silverton	918	°C 5
Sinton	6,044	°I 8
Skellytown	899	A 5
Slaton	6,804	D 5
Smithville	3,470	G 9
Snyder	12,705	°D 5
Somerset	1,102	K 1
Somerville	1,814	G 9
Sonora	3,856	°F 6
Sour Lake*	1,807	G 11
South Houston	13,293	H 14
South Padre Island	791	K 9
Southlake	2,808	C 13
Southside Place*	1,366	H 13
Spearman	3,413	°A 5
Spring Valley	3,353	H 13
Springtown	1,658	D 8
Spur	1,690	D 5
Stafford	4,755	H 13
Stamford	4,542	D 6
Stanton	2,314	°E 5
Stephenville	11,881	°E 8
Sterling City	915	°E 5
Stinnett	2,222	°A 5
Stockdale	1,265	K 4
Stratford	1,917	°A 4
Sudan	1,091	C 4
Sugar Land	8,826	I 13
Sulphur Springs	12,804	°D 10
Sundown	1,511	D 4
Sunnyvale	1,404	C 15
Sunray	1,952	A 5
Sunset Valley*	733	G 8
Surfside Beach	577	K 14
Sweeny	3,538	K 12
Sweetwater	12,242	°E 6
Taft	3,686	I 8
Tahoka	3,262	°D 5
Talco	751	D 10
Tatum	1,339	E 11
Taylor	10,619	F 8
Taylor Lake Village*	3,669	G 10
Teague	3,390	E 9
Temple	42,354	F 8
Tenaha	1,005	E 11
Terrell	13,269	C 16
Terrell Hills	4,644	J 2
Texarkana	31,271	D 11
Texas City	41,201	I 15
The Colony*	11,586	D 9
The Woodlands	8,443	F 13
Thorndale	1,300	F 9
Three Rivers	2,133	I 8
Throckmorton	1,174	°D 7
Tilden		°I 7
Timpson	1,164	E 11
Tomball	3,996	G 13
Tool*	1,464	E 9
Trinidad*	1,130	E 9
Trinity	2,620	F 10
Troup	1,911	E 10
Troy*	1,353	F 8
Tulia	5,033	°B 5
Tye*	1,394	E 6
Tyler	70,508	E 10
Universal City	10,720	I 2
University Park	22,254	C 14
Uvalde	14,178	°H 6
Valley Mills	1,236	E 8
Van	1,881	D 10
Van Alstyne	1,860	A 15
Van Horn	2,772	°F 2
Vega	900	°B 4
Vernon	12,695	°C 7
Victoria	50,695	°H 9
Vidor*	11,834	G 12
Waco	101,261	°E 8
Waelder	942	G 8
Wake Village	3,865	D 11
Waller	1,241	G 10
Wallis*	1,138	G 9
Waskom*	1,821	E 11
Watauga	10,284	C 13
Waxahachie	14,624	°E 14
Weatherford	12,049	°D 8
Webster	2,405	I 14
Weches	26	F 10
Weimar	2,128	G 9
Wellington	3,043	°B 6
Wells	926	F 10
Weslaco	19,331	K 8
West	2,485	F 9
West Columbia	4,109	J 13
West Lake Hills*	2,166	G 8
West Orange*	4,610	G 12
West University Place	12,010	H 13
Westworth*	3,651	D 8
Wharton	9,033	°H 9
Wheeler	1,584	°B 6
White Deer	1,210	B 5
White Oak*	4,415	E 11
White Settlement	13,508	C 12
Whitehouse*	2,172	E 10
Whitesboro*	3,197	C 9
Whitewright	1,760	A 16
Whitney	1,631	E 8
Wichita Falls	94,201	°C 7
Willis*	1,674	F 13
Willow Park*	1,107	D 8
Wills Point	2,631	D 9
Wilmer	2,367	D 15
Windcrest*	5,332	G 7
Wink	1,182	E 3
Winnsboro*	3,458	D 10
Winters	3,061	E 6
Wolfe City*	1,594	D 10
Wolfforth*	1,701	D 5
Woodsboro	1,974	I 8
Woodville	2,821	°F 11
Woodway*	7,091	E 8
Wortham*	1,187	E 9
Wylie	3,152	B 15
Yoakum	6,148	H 9
Yorktown	2,498	H 8
Zapata	3,831	°J 7

*Does not appear on map; key shows general location.

°County seat.

Source: 1980 census. Places without population figures are unincorporated areas.

Some of the most popular resort centers in Texas are on the Gulf Coast. Sandy beaches stretch along most of the coast, making it ideal for bathing and boating. Many deep-sea fishing enthusiasts sail from the coastal cities of Aransas Pass, Corpus Christi, and Galveston. They catch marlin, sailfish, and tarpon in the Gulf of Mexico.

In northeast Texas, rolling timberlands provide many recreational areas. The region's rivers and lakes offer fine fishing. Central and west Texas are popular deer-hunting sites.

Texas has more than 500 fairs, festivals, and expositions each year—more than any other state in the nation. The greatest event is probably the State Fair of Texas, held in Dallas for 16 days in October. Nearly 3 million people visit the State Fair of Texas every year, making it the largest annual fair held in the United States.

Kent and Donna Dannen

Malaquite Beach at Padre Island National Seashore

Places to visit

Following are brief descriptions of some of the many interesting places to visit in Texas.

The Alamo, a low, gray chapel of an old Spanish mission, stands in downtown San Antonio. A famous battle was fought there in 1836 during the Texas Revolution.

Aquarena Springs, at Spring Lake in San Marcos, features large springs that form the beginning of the San Marcos River. The attractions include glass-bottom boats, a re-created frontier village, and mission ruins.

Astroworld, in Houston, is one of the largest amusement and entertainment centers in the Southwest. It adjoins an attraction called Waterworld. The Astrodome stadium is nearby.

East Texas Oil Museum, in Kilgore, recreates an oil boom town of the 1930's. Exhibits include mementos of the area's early oil industry and a study of oil formations within the earth.

Fair Park, in Dallas, covers about 200 acres (81 hectares) and is the home of the State Fair of Texas. The park includes the Cotton Bowl stadium, the Health and Science Museum, the State Music Hall, an amusement park, recreational areas, livestock exhibition buildings, an aquarium, the Hall of State, the Museum of Natural History, the Museum of Fine Arts, the Museum of Natural Resources, and the Dallas Garden Center.

La Villita, in San Antonio, is a restoration and reconstruction of a little city of early Texas days. The community shows the influence of Spanish culture, and has a museum and arts-and-crafts shops.

Lyndon B. Johnson Library, in Austin, contains more than 30 million documents dealing with U.S. domestic policies and foreign relations. The library's collection also includes gifts that Johnson received while he was President.

Lyndon B. Johnson Space Center, at Houston, is the headquarters for all manned spacecraft projects of the National Aeronautics and Space Administration (NASA). A visitors' center displays spacecraft equipment and shows films about space flights and moon landings. See **Johnson Space Center.**

Mission San Jose, in San Antonio, is considered the most beautiful Texas mission. Established in 1720, the church is one of the marvels of Spanish architecture in North America. The mission is a national historic site and a state park.

Padre Island National Seashore extends about 80 miles (130 kilometers) along the Texas coast on Padre Island. It includes dunes and beaches. Congress established the seashore in 1962.

San Jacinto Monument, near Channelview, honors the Texans who fought in the Battle of San Jacinto. In this battle, Texas won independence from Mexico. The monument, one of the tallest in the world, rises 570 feet (174 meters).

Six Flags over Texas is an amusement park in Arlington. The park features the history of the state under the six flags of Spain, France, Mexico, the Republic of Texas, the Confederacy, and the United States.

Texas Memorial Museum, in Austin, has displays featuring Texas botany, geology, history, and zoology. The museum also exhibits many historical records and documents.

Texas Ranger Hall of Fame, in Waco, honors the Texas Rangers, a group of Texas law enforcers that has existed for more than 150 years. On the site is a museum that is a replica of an early Rangers outpost.

National parks and forests. Texas has two national parks. Big Bend National Park lies within the great bend of the Rio Grande. Guadalupe Mountains National Park, authorized in 1966, lies in Culberson and Hudspeth counties. See **Big Bend National Park; Guadalupe Mountains National Park.**

The state's four national forests are in east Texas. Sabine National Forest is the largest. The other national forests in Texas are Angelina, Davy Crockett, and Sam Houston.

State parks. Texas began its state park system during the 1920's, and now has about 100 state parks. For information on the parks, write to Director, Texas State Parks and Wildlife Department, 4200 Smith School Rd., Austin, TX 78744.

© Bob Daemmrich
Cinco de Mayo celebration in Austin

Annual events

January-March
Texas Citrus Festival in Mission (January or February); Southwestern Exposition and Fat Stock Show in Fort Worth (January or February); Charro Days Festival in Brownsville (February); San Antonio Stock Show and Rodeo (February); Houston Livestock Show and Rodeo Exposition (February-March); Texas Independence Day (March 2).

April-June
Fiesta San Antonio in San Antonio (April); Jefferson Historical Pilgrimage in Jefferson (April and May); Buccaneer Days in Corpus Christi (April or May); Cinco de Mayo Celebration in Austin (May 5); Texas State Arts and Crafts Fair in Kerrville (May); Watermelon Thump in Luling (June).

July-September
Texas Cowboy Reunion and Rodeo in Stamford (July); Aqua Festival in Austin (August); Texas Folklife Festival in San Antonio (August); Four States Fair in Texarkana (September); Rice Festival in Bay City (September or October).

October-December
East Texas Yamboree in Gilmer (October); Texas Rose Festival in Tyler (October); Confederate Air Sho in Harlingen (November); Fiesta de las Luminarias, or Festival of the Lights, in San Antonio (December).

Paul Conklin

Lyndon B. Johnson Space Center in Houston

© Bob Daemmrich
Memorial service at the Alamo in San Antonio

Francis M. Martin, Houston Livestock Show and Rodeo
Houston Livestock Show and Rodeo Exposition

Land and climate

Land regions. Texas has five main land regions. These are, from east to west: (1) the Gulf Coastal Plains, (2) the Prairie Plains, (3) the Rolling Plains, (4) the Great Plains, and (5) the Basin and Range Region.

The Gulf Coastal Plains of Texas are part of the fertile lowland that lies along the entire Gulf Coast of the United States. They range in elevation from sea level to about 300 feet (91 meters) above sea level. A subtropical region extends along a large part of the coast.

The southernmost part of the coastal plains consists of the fertile Rio Grande Valley. Just northwest of this valley lies the Middle Nueces Valley, part of the Nueces Plains. The two valleys are famous for their winter vegetables and fruits. The region along the eastern coast, from the Rio Grande Valley to Louisiana, has extremely rich soils. Cotton and several types of grain thrive in this region.

The northeastern part of the plain is a timberland with thick forests of oak, pine, sweet gum, and other trees. This area is often called the Piney Woods. Major lumber and paper companies own most of the land. Farmers in this area raise beef and dairy cattle and poultry. The region has many large mineral deposits.

The Prairie Plains lie west of the forest belt of the Coastal Plains. The Prairie Plains feature alternating belts of rugged hills and rolling hills. The rugged hills are covered with oak and hickory forests. The region includes the fertile Black Waxy Prairie. The prairie has rich soils for farming.

The Rolling Plains are a hilly area west of the Prairie Plains. The area's elevation increases as it approaches the Great Plains to the west. The Rolling Plains have scattered belts of fertile farmland. They also have rich petroleum deposits.

The Great Plains reach westward from the Prairie Plains and Rolling Plains into New Mexico. They form part of the series of treeless plains that extends northward through the western United States into Canada. The Great Plains of Texas rise from an altitude of about 700 feet (213 meters) above sea level in the east to over 4,000 feet (1,200 meters) above sea level in the west.

The Texas Panhandle, also called the *Llano Estacado* (Staked Plains) or the High Plains, makes up a major part of the Great Plains. It is the northwestern part of the state that juts northward between Oklahoma and New Mexico. This treeless grassland is a high plateau. The Panhandle is a rich farming region, and it produces more wheat, cotton, and grain sorghum than any other area of Texas. The southwestern portion of the Panhandle is called the Permian Basin. It has one of the richest petroleum and natural gas fields in the United States.

The Edwards Plateau forms the southern part of the Great Plains. The surface of the plateau is mainly bare limestone bedrock, but it is dotted with shrubs and sparse grasses. Thick grasses grow in the plateau's river valleys and basins. This region produces more sheep and goats than any other part of the United States.

The Basin and Range Region, commonly called the *Trans-Pecos Region,* makes up the westernmost part of Texas. It includes high, partly dry plains that are crossed by *spurs* (extensions) of the Rocky Mountains. These spurs include, from north to south, the Guadalupe, Davis, and Chisos mountains. The peaks that do not form continuous ranges are called *lost mountains.* Farmers use the level sections mainly for raising cattle, with some irrigated agriculture on the plains along the Rio Grande. Many beautiful mountain gorges are along the upper Rio Grande, which forms the region's western border. Santa Elena Canyon, in Big Bend National Park, is one of the most spectacular gorges.

Coastline. A series of narrow sand bars, enclosing shallow lagoons, lies along the Texas coast. These sand bars help protect the coast from ocean storms and tidal waves. Padre Island, the largest sand bar, is about 100 miles (160 kilometers) long. Other large sand bars include the islands of Galveston, Matagorda, and St. Joseph.

The Texas coast has 28 artificially created ports. They were once filled by *silt* (particles of earth) left by the many streams emptying into the Gulf of Mexico. Only small vessels could use them. By removing the silt and deepening the harbors, engineers built 13 deepwater ports and 15 ports for barges and small ships.

The general coastline of Texas is 367 miles (591 kilometers) long along the Gulf. The tidal shoreline, including bays, offshore islands, and river mouths, is 3,359 miles (5,406 kilometers) long.

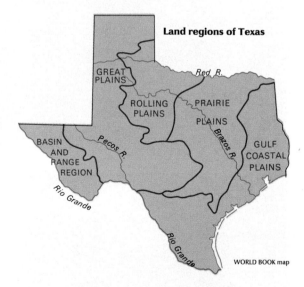

Land regions of Texas

WORLD BOOK map

Map index

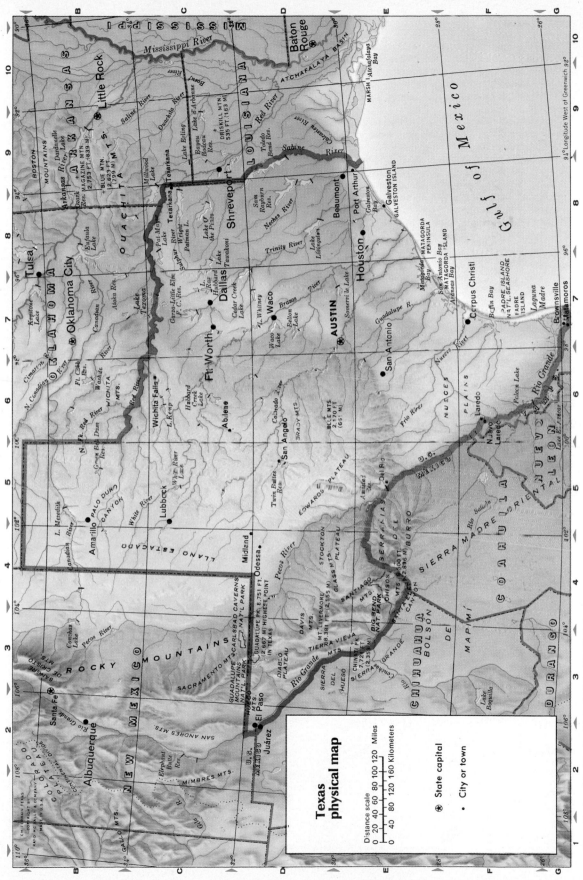

Texas
physical map

Distance scale

| Miles | 0 | 20 | 40 | 60 | 80 | 100 | 120 |
| Kilometers | 0 | 40 | 80 | 120 | 160 | | |

⊛ State capital

• City or town

Specially created for *The World Book Encyclopedia* by Rand McNally and World Book editors

Mountains. Texas' highest mountains rise in the Basin and Range Region. The chief ranges include the Chisos, Davis, and Guadalupe mountains. The main peak of the Guadalupe Mountains is Guadalupe Peak. It rises 8,751 feet (2,667 meters) above sea level and is the highest point in Texas.

Rivers and lakes. The Rio Grande, Texas' largest river, is one of the longest and most historic rivers in North America. For 1,241 miles (1,997 kilometers), it forms the boundary between the United States and Mexico (see **Rio Grande**). Other Texas rivers include the Brazos, Canadian, Colorado, Guadalupe, Neches, Nueces, Pecos, Red, Sabine, San Antonio, and Trinity.

Most of the state's rivers flow in a southeastward direction into the Gulf of Mexico. But the Canadian River drains into the Arkansas River, and the Pecos River flows into the Rio Grande. The Red River and its branches empty into the Mississippi River. In the dry western parts of Texas, many streams have water only after a rainstorm.

Texas has thousands of lakes that have been made or enlarged by human effort. Most of these lakes were created as part of the state's many programs for generating hydroelectric power, irrigating farmland, and storing water. The largest artificially created lake is Toledo Bend, which extends into Louisiana. The reservoir was created by Toledo Bend Dam, which crosses the Sabine River. Other artificially created lakes include Amistad, Buchanan, Falcon, Sam Rayburn, and Texoma.

Many saltwater lakes and ponds lie in the High

Big Thicket National Preserve, located north of Beaumont, was set aside to protect a variety of rare plant life. The preserve has 84,550 acres (34,220 hectares) of bayous and forests.

© Don Klumpp

Average monthly weather

	Corpus Christi						Dallas				
	Temperatures F°		C°		Days of rain or snow		Temperatures F°		C°		Days of rain or snow
	High	Low	High	Low			High	Low	High	Low	
Jan.	66	47	19	8	8	Jan.	55	36	13	2	8
Feb.	70	51	21	11	7	Feb.	60	40	16	4	8
Mar.	75	56	24	13	6	Mar.	68	47	20	8	7
Apr.	80	63	27	17	5	Apr.	77	56	25	13	9
May	86	69	30	21	6	May	84	64	29	18	9
June	90	74	32	23	5	June	92	72	33	22	6
July	93	75	34	24	4	July	95	76	35	24	5
Aug.	93	75	34	24	5	Aug.	96	76	36	24	6
Sept.	89	72	32	22	8	Sept.	89	69	32	21	5
Oct.	84	65	29	18	6	Oct.	80	58	27	14	6
Nov.	75	55	24	13	6	Nov.	66	45	19	7	7
Dec.	68	49	20	9	6	Dec.	58	39	14	4	6

Average January temperatures

Texas temperatures vary widely in winter. The south is the warmest and temperatures decline steadily to the north.

Degrees Fahrenheit	Degrees Celsius
Above 56	Above 13
50 to 56	10 to 13
44 to 50	7 to 10
38 to 44	3 to 7
Below 38	Below 3

Average July temperatures

Summers are hot in Texas with little variation in temperature. The northwest and southwest have the mildest summers.

Degrees Fahrenheit	Degrees Celsius
Above 86	Above 30
84 to 86	29 to 30
82 to 84	28 to 29
80 to 82	27 to 28
Below 80	Below 27

Average yearly precipitation

The western half of Texas is dry. However, the far eastern area receives more than 48 inches (122 centimeters) of rain.

WORLD BOOK maps

Inches	Centimeters
More than 48	More than 122
36 to 48	91 to 122
24 to 36	61 to 91
12 to 24	30 to 61
Less than 12	Less than 30

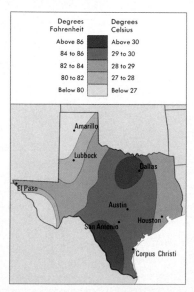

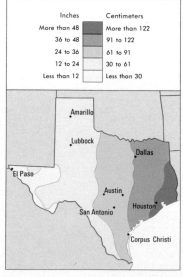

Plains, in the Basin and Range Region, and near the mouth of the Rio Grande. The largest include La Sal Vieja, Sal del Rey, and Salt Lake.

Plant and animal life. Forests cover about 14 per cent of the state. The most valuable trees commercially are gums, oaks, and pines. Other common trees that grow in Texas include cat's-claw, cypress, elm, juniper, magnolia, mesquite, mountain cedar, native pecan, and tupelo.

More than 500 kinds of grasses grow in Texas. They include bluestem, buffalo grass, curly mesquite, grama, and side oats. More than 4,000 kinds of wild flowers grow in the state. They include daisies, goldenrod, primroses, and sunflowers. The bluebonnet is the state flower. Many varieties of cactuses grow in the dry Basin and Range Region.

Much wildlife is found in the eastern forests and on the western plains. Deer, pronghorn, and wild turkeys are the chief game animals of Texas. Other animals include armadillos, bears, coyotes, mountain lions, and wild pigs. The state's large reptile population includes alligators, snakes, and lizards. The most common freshwater fish include bass, catfish, and sunfish. Crabs, menhaden, oysters, and shrimp thrive in the Gulf of Mexico.

Climate of Texas ranges from subtropical in the lower Rio Grande Valley to moderately temperate in the northwest. The lower Rio Grande Valley is the warmest region of the state. It has an average January temperature of 60° F. (16° C), and an average July temperature of 85° F. (29° C). The coldest area is the Panhandle, in the northwest. It has an average January temperature of 35° F. (2° C), and an average July reading of 79° F. (26° C). Texas' lowest temperature, −23° F. (−31° C), was recorded at Tulia on Feb. 12, 1899, and at Seminole on Feb. 8, 1933. The record high in the state was 120° F. (49° C), at Seymour on Aug. 12, 1936.

Along the Gulf of Mexico, the coast has a warm, damp climate. There, winds from the Gulf reduce the heat of summer and the cold of winter. Central Texas has a mild climate that makes it a popular resort area the year around. In the northeast, the weather is damp and cool. The northwest sometimes has long, cold winters. The west has a dry, cool climate.

Rainfall in Texas decreases from east to west. East Texas averages 46 inches (117 centimeters) of *precipitation* (rain, snow, sleet, and other forms of moisture) a year. Parts of west Texas average only 12 inches (30 centimeters) a year. Port Arthur, in the southeastern part of the state, gets about 45 more inches (114 centimeters) of rain a year than El Paso, in the far west. Along the coast, most of the rain falls in autumn.

Sleet, winds, and heavy rain from the north occasionally sweep across the state in the winter. Strong winds often blow throughout the High Plains. During periods of drought, these winds carry away the soil. Snow seldom falls in the south-central and central regions. But the High Plains have an average of more than 24 inches (61 centimeters) of snow a year.

Economy

The *gross state product* (GSP) of Texas is higher than that of all other states except California and New York. The GSP is the total value of all goods and services produced in the state in a year. The economy of Texas relies heavily on its extensive deposits of petroleum and natural gas.

A north-south line, drawn across Texas just west of Dallas, would divide the state into two great economic regions. The eastern section has most of the state's large, industrial cities. This section also includes cotton and rice farms, pine forests, and pecan groves. The western section, which also has cotton, forms part of the great oil, wheat, and cattle country of the Southwestern States.

Natural resources. The great natural wealth of Texas includes large mineral deposits, especially petroleum and natural gas. In addition, the state has fertile soils and rich grasslands.

Minerals. Texas is one of the world's great petroleum storehouses. About 8 billion barrels of petroleum lie beneath the Texas plains. The state's known petroleum deposits account for about a third of the country's known supply. The Panhandle natural-gas field takes in almost all of five northwestern counties. It is one of the largest known natural-gas reservoirs in the world. The Panhandle also has the greatest known helium supply in the United States.

Other mineral resources of Texas include large sulfur deposits in the Gulf Coastal Plains and the Basin and Range Region. Underground salt deposits occur in the Gulf Coastal Plains and in western Texas. Surface deposits are found in southern and western Texas. The state also has lignite coal deposits, totaling about 14 billion short tons (13 billion metric tons). Layers of rock containing beds of lignite cover about 75,000 square miles (194,000 square kilometers), extending from Laredo to Texarkana. Iron ore occurs in the northeastern part of the state.

Limestone occurs in a broad belt extending from the Red River to the Rio Grande, and across north-central

Production and workers by economic activities

Economic activities	Per cent of GSP* produced	Employed workers Number of persons	Employed workers Per cent of total
Wholesale & retail trade	18	1,703,700	25
Finance, insurance, & real estate	16	442,400	6
Community, social, & personal services	14	1,345,000	19
Manufacturing	14	1,004,600	15
Government	11	1,094,700	16
Mining	11	259,900	4
Transportation, communication, & utilities	9	383,300	6
Construction	6	447,800	6
Agriculture	1	211,000	3
Total	**100**	**6,892,400**	**100**

*GSP = gross state product, the total value of goods and services produced in a year. Figures are for 1985.
Source: *World Book* estimates based on data from the U.S. Bureau of Economic Analysis, U.S. Bureau of Labor Statistics, and U.S. Department of Agriculture.

Texas. Gypsum deposits lie in the southeastern part of the state. Gravel and silica sand are plentiful in many areas of Texas. The largest asphalt deposits in the state are near Uvalde. Potash occurs in a great bed of rock salt in the Basin and Range Region. Mercury, molybdenum, titanium, tungsten, and uranium are found in the southwestern part of the state. Texas also has deposits of basalt, fluorspar, fuller's earth and other clays, granite, lead, marble, mica, sandstone, tin, and zinc.

Soil. Texas has about 1,000 types of soil, in which farmers can grow a great variety of crops. A narrow belt along the state's Gulf Coast has marshy soils, mixed with clays. Rich soils lie along the banks of rivers throughout the state. Large sections of the interior of the Gulf Coastal Plains have soils composed of sands and clays. Rich, heavy, blackland clays make up a belt in the interior of the plains. The Prairie Plains Region has soils of clays, limestone, and sands. The High Plains and the Rolling Plains include clays, clay loam, and sandy loam soils. The Basin and Range Region has rough, stony mountain soils.

Service industries account for 68 per cent of the gross state product of Texas. Most of the service industries are concentrated in the state's 28 metropolitan areas.

Wholesale and retail trade is the most important industry in Texas. Houston is the leading center of trade in the Southwestern United States. The Port of Houston conducts much international trade. Fort Worth is a major center of wholesale trade in the Southwest. Oil trading is especially important in Beaumont, Dallas, Fort Worth, Houston, and Wichita Falls. San Antonio is a leading convention center. Amarillo is a leading livestock trading center in the United States.

Finance, insurance, and real estate is the second most important category of service industry in Texas. Dallas is a major U.S. banking center. It also is the headquarters of more insurance companies than any other Southern city. Other service industries in Texas include commu-nity, social, and personal services; government; and transportation, communication, and utilities.

Manufacturing accounts for about 14 per cent of the gross state product of Texas. Goods manufactured there have a *value added by manufacture* of about $53\frac{1}{3}$ billion a year. This figure represents the increase in value of raw materials after they become finished products. Texas is a leading manufacturing state. Its chief manufactured products, in order of importance, are: (1) nonelectrical machinery, (2) chemicals, (3) food products, and (4) petroleum and coal products.

Nonelectrical machinery has an annual value added of about $9\frac{1}{2}$ billion. It accounts for about 18 per cent of the state's manufacturing income. The industry's major products include construction machinery, oil-field machinery, and refrigeration and heating machinery. The industry also produces pumps and pumping equipment and farm machinery. Chief centers of production include the Dallas-Fort Worth area, Houston, Lubbock, Odessa, and San Antonio.

Chemicals have an annual value added of about $8\frac{1}{2}$ billion and account for about 16 per cent of the manufacturing income. Texas ranks first among the states as a chemical manufacturer. Important chemical products include benzene, ethylene, fertilizers, propylene, and sulfuric acid. The Texas chemical industry is located chiefly in cities along the Gulf Coast.

Food products have a value added of about $5\frac{1}{3}$ billion yearly. Beverages are the leading food product made in Texas. Meat products rank second. The Panhandle-Southern High Plains area is a center of the state's meatpacking industry, with large plants in Amarillo, Hereford, and San Antonio. Texas is a leading state in the cleaning and polishing of rice. Other food products that are processed in Texas include bakery products, dairy products, and grain mill products, such as flour, livestock feed, and pet food.

Petroleum and coal products have a value added of about $4\frac{3}{4}$ billion a year. Texas stands first among the

The Houston Ship Channel stretches 51 miles (82 kilometers) from the Gulf of Mexico to the Port of Houston. Ocean vessels use the channel to reach the port, which is one of the leading seaports in the United States. Houston's downtown skyscrapers rise in the distance.

states in oil refining. About 35 petroleum refineries operate throughout the state. The largest are along the Gulf Coast in Baytown, Beaumont, Houston, Port Arthur, and other port cities.

Other leading industries in Texas, in order of value, produce electrical machinery and equipment; fabricated metal products; transportation equipment; printed materials; and stone, clay, and glass products. Other important products made in Texas include primary metals and clothing.

Mining. Texas leads the states in value of mineral production, largely because of oil. Mining accounts for 11 per cent of the gross state product. Minerals have an annual value of about $40 billion in Texas.

Petroleum is the most valuable Texas mineral, earning about 60 per cent of the income from minerals. The state produces about 760 million barrels of crude oil annually and ranks first among the states in oil production. The oil wells of Texas account for about one-fourth of the nation's oil production.

Drillers first discovered oil in Texas near Nacogdoches in 1866. Large-scale production began with the opening of the Spindletop field near Beaumont in 1901. For several years, the Spindletop and other Gulf Coast fields formed the center of the Texas oil industry. Later, large fields were opened in the Panhandle, the Pecos Valley, and central, east, and north Texas. The greatest oil discovery in Texas occurred in 1930, when drillers brought in the famous East Texas oil field at Kilgore. This field was for a time the largest in the world.

Natural gas, the second most valuable Texas mineral, accounts for about 35 per cent of the mineral income. About one-third of all the natural gas produced in the United States comes from Texas. The state supplies about 6 trillion cubic feet (170 billion cubic meters) a year. Gas and natural gas liquids occur in all the oil-producing regions. Pipelines carry gas from Texas to Chicago and New York.

Other minerals. Texas furnishes about half the country's supply of sulfur. It is also the leading producer of asphalt, gypsum, magnesium chloride, and stone. Texas ranks second in the production of clay and salt. Lignite coal is mined in the eastern part of the state. Natural gasoline for fuel is made from Texas oil and gas. Helium occurs mixed with the natural gas found in the Panhandle. Valuable quantities of fluorspar, limestone, marble, sand and gravel, and sandstone also come from Texas. The state also produces gemstones, granite, iron ore, sodium sulfate, and talc.

Agriculture. Texas, with a yearly net farm income of about $2½ billion, is a leading agricultural state. Farm products account for about 1 per cent of the gross state product. Texas has about 184,000 farms, more than any other state. They average about 740 acres (296 hectares) in size. Texas farms cover about 136 million acres (54 million hectares), the greatest farming acreage of any state in the country. Of this total, about 6 million acres (2.4 million hectares) are irrigated. Most of the irrigated farmlands lie in the Rio Grande and Pecos valleys, near Lubbock, and along the coast.

Beef cattle are Texas' largest source of farm income, providing about 50 per cent of the annual income. Texas

© Robert Mitchell

Petroleum is Texas' most valuable mineral product. The state produces about one-third of the nation's crude oil and ranks first among the states in oil production.

Farm, mineral, and forest products

This map shows the areas where the state's leading farm, mineral, and forest products are produced. The major urban areas (shown in red) are the state's important manufacturing centers.

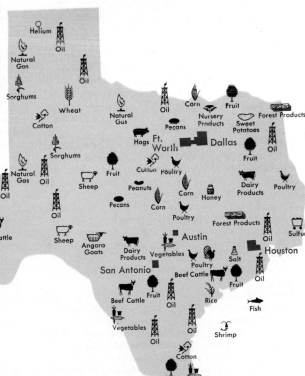

WORLD BOOK map

winters are usually so mild that cattle can graze out-doors all year around. As a result, Texans can raise cattle more cheaply than northern farmers. Texas leads the states in number of beef cattle, with about 14 million.

The United States range-cattle industry began in Texas with long-horned cattle. The ancestors of these *Texas longhorns* had been brought by early Spaniards and later settlers. After the Civil War, cattlemen drove cattle to Kansas and Missouri for shipment by railroad to northern and eastern markets. The most widely used cattle trails were the Chisholm Trail and the Western Trail. The Chisholm Trail ran from southern Texas to Abilene, Kans. The Western Trail connected west Texas and Dodge City, Kans. The colorful trail-drive period ended during the 1880's with the coming of railroads and the fencing of public lands.

Purebred cattle, such as the Aberdeen-Angus, Hereford, and Shorthorn breeds, gradually replaced the longhorns. During the early 1900's, the white-faced Herefords became the most popular breed in Texas. Ranchers bred Shorthorns with Brahman cattle from India and produced a breed unaffected by heat and insects. This breed, the Santa Gertrudis, was the first beef cattle variety developed in the United States.

Cotton is Texas' leading crop and the second-ranking farm product. It provides about 10 per cent of the income from farm products. Texas produces more cotton than any other state. Texas cotton thrives best on the coastal plain and on the central and northern prairies. Irrigated cotton grows in the Rio Grande Valley. Jared Groce, who is sometimes called the *Father of Texas Agriculture,* and other early settlers introduced commercial cotton growing. They planted cotton in the fertile valley of the Brazos River during the early 1820's. Today, Texas farmers produce about $4\frac{1}{2}$ million bales of cotton a year. These bales weigh a total of about $2\frac{1}{4}$ billion pounds (1 billion kilograms).

Grain sorghum is the second most valuable crop in Texas. The state's farmers produce about 88 million pounds (40 million kilograms) of grain sorghum a year. Texas and Kansas rank as the leading states in grain sorghum production. Grain sorghum can be raised on the dry plains and prairies because it can survive drought. It is used chiefly for livestock feed.

Other crops. Texas stands high among the states in the production of rice, which thrives along the Gulf Coast. Wheat and hay are also leading crops. Other important crops in the state include corn, cottonseed, hay, oats, soybeans, sugar beets, and sugar cane.

Vegetables. Texas is an important producer of vegetables. Farmers grow large crops in the lower Rio Grande Valley, around Laredo and San Antonio, and in the High Plains. The chief truck crops include cabbage, cantaloupes, carrots, cucumbers, lettuce, onions, peppers, potatoes, spinach, and watermelons (see **Truck farming**).

Fruits. Irrigation has made the lower Rio Grande Valley one of the country's finest fruit belts. Trainloads of grapefruit, oranges, and other citrus fruits travel from valley orchards to northern markets. Texas ranks high in the production of oranges and grapefruit. Farmers in the state also grow many peaches. Other fruits include apples, plums, and strawberries. Blackberries come from east Texas.

Nuts and honey. Texas is among the leading states in the production of nuts. Pecans and peanuts are the most important nuts harvested in the state. Pecan trees grow along the Colorado and Guadalupe rivers, and along streams throughout most of the state, except in the High Plains and the Basin and Range Region. Many farmers have large groves of various kinds of pecan trees. Farms in the eastern and central areas produce excellent crops of peanuts. Many Texas farmers keep colonies of bees, which produce much honey.

Poultry and dairy products. Texas ranks high in the production of *broilers* (chickens from 5 to 12 weeks old), eggs, and turkeys. The state has about 335,000 head of dairy cattle.

Horses, sheep, and other livestock. Texas ranchers raise saddle and race horses, cow ponies, polo ponies, and work horses. Texas raises more sheep than any other state—nearly 2 million a year. It also produces the most wool—about $17\frac{1}{2}$ million pounds (7.9 million kilograms) yearly. Almost all the mohair clipped in the United States comes from Texas goats. Most of them belong to the Angora breed. Most of the goats and sheep graze on the shrubbery of the Edwards Plateau. Farmers throughout the state raise hogs.

Fishing industry. Texas has an annual fish catch valued at about $180 million. It ranks among the leading states in the production of shrimp. The average yearly catch of shrimp in Texas totals about 80 million pounds (36 million kilograms). The state's fish catch also includes black drum, crabs, flounder, oysters, red snapper, red drum, and sea trout. Texas also produces farm-raised catfish.

Electric power. Texas ranks first in the nation in electric power production. The state has about 140 electric-power plants and stations. About 80 per cent of the electric power is produced by plants that burn gas. Most of the rest is produced by plants that burn coal or oil. About 1 per cent of the electric power is produced by 20 hydroelectric stations.

Transportation. Several famous trails crossed the Texas wilderness in the early days. During the period of Spanish rule, many of these trails served as transportation routes for missionaries and explorers in the Southwest.

Aviation. The Dallas-Fort Worth area and the Houston area each have two major airports. Other important airports in Texas are located at Austin, El Paso, and San Antonio.

Railroads in Texas operate on about 13,000 miles (20,900 kilometers) of track, more than in any other state. About 30 rail lines provide freight service in the state, and passenger trains link about 20 Texas cities to other cities.

Roads and highways. Texas has about 276,000 miles (444,000 kilometers) of roads and highways, about 80 per cent of which are surfaced. About 3,000 miles (4,800 kilometers) of the interstate highway system cross Texas. Seven United States highways in the state connect with roads in Mexico.

Shipping. Texas has 12 deepwater ports along the Gulf of Mexico. Houston is the busiest port. It also is one of the chief cotton-shipping centers in the country. The other deepwater ports are Bay City, Beaumont, Brownsville, Corpus Christi, Freeport, Galveston, Orange, Port

Arthur, Port Isabel, Port Mansfield, and Texas City. Fifteen shallow ports also lie along the coast. These shallow ports handle barges, fishing vessels, and other shallow-draft vessels.

Waterways. The Gulf Intracoastal Waterway runs the length of the Texas coast from Brownsville to Orange. This waterway is used by boats from the state's 15 shallow ports. The Gulf Intracoastal Waterway connects with the Mississippi River at New Orleans. See **Gulf Intracoastal Waterway.**

Communication. José Álvarez de Toledo, a Mexican, printed Texas' first newspaper, *Gaceta de Texas,* in Nacogdoches in 1813. Today, Texas publishers issue about

110 daily newspapers and about 345 weeklies. Texas newspapers with the largest circulations include the *Dallas News, Dallas Times Herald, Fort Worth Star-Telegram, Houston Chronicle, Houston Post, San Antonio Express-News,* and *San Antonio Light.* Texas publishers also issue about 350 periodicals. The *Texas Almanac,* which contains information about the state, has been published since 1857.

Texas' first radio station, WRR, began broadcasting in Dallas in 1920. The state's first television station, WBAP-TV (now KXAS-TV), started in Fort Worth in 1948. Texas has about 550 radio stations. It also has about 70 television stations.

Government

Constitution of Texas was adopted in 1876. The state had four earlier constitutions—those adopted in 1845, 1861, 1866, and 1869. An amendment to the Constitution must first be approved by two-thirds of the members of each house of the state legislature. Then, the amendment must get the approval of a majority of the voters in a statewide election.

Executive. The governor of Texas holds office for a four-year term and can serve an unlimited number of terms.

The governor has the power to appoint two of the top state officials—the secretary of state and the adjutant general. All others are elected, most to four-year terms. They include the lieutenant governor, attorney general, commissioner of agriculture, commissioner of the general land office, comptroller, and treasurer.

The voters also elect the three members of the Texas Railroad Commission. This important group controls the state's production of petroleum. It does this by deciding how much oil the Texas petroleum industry can pump from the earth each year.

Legislature consists of a Senate of 31 members and a House of Representatives of 150 members. Voters in each of the 31 senatorial districts elect one senator to a four-year term. Voters in each of the 150 representative districts elect one member of the House of Representatives to a two-year term. Both houses meet in odd-numbered years on the second Tuesday in January. By law,

regular sessions are limited to 140 calendar days. Special sessions can last only 30 days.

Courts. The highest civil court in Texas is the Supreme Court. It has a chief justice and eight associate

The governors of Texas

	Party	Term
J. Pinckney Henderson	Democratic	1846-1847
George T. Wood	Democratic	1847-1849
P. Hansborough Bell	Democratic	1849-1853
Elisha M. Pease	Democratic	1853-1857
Hardin R. Runnels	Democratic	1857-1859
Sam Houston	Independent	1859-1861
Francis R. Lubbock	Democratic	1861-1863
Pendleton Murrah	Democratic	1863-1865
Under federal military rule		1865
Andrew J. Hamilton	Conservative	1865-1866
James W. Throckmorton	Conservative	1866-1867
Elisha M. Pease	Republican	1867-1869
Under federal military rule		1869-1870
Edmund J. Davis	Republican	1870-1874
Richard Coke	Democratic	1874-1876
Richard B. Hubbard	Democratic	1876-1879
Oran M. Roberts	Democratic	1879-1883
John Ireland	Democratic	1883-1887
Lawrence S. Ross	Democratic	1887-1891
James S. Hogg	Democratic	1891-1895
Charles A. Culberson	Democratic	1895-1899
Joseph D. Sayers	Democratic	1899-1903
S. W. T. Lanham	Democratic	1903-1907
Thomas M. Campbell	Democratic	1907-1911
Oscar B. Colquitt	Democratic	1911-1915
James E. Ferguson	Democratic	1915-1917
William P. Hobby	Democratic	1917-1921
Pat M. Neff	Democratic	1921-1925
Miriam A. Ferguson	Democratic	1925-1927
Dan Moody	Democratic	1927-1931
Ross Sterling	Democratic	1931-1933
Miriam A. Ferguson	Democratic	1933-1935
James V. Allred	Democratic	1935-1939
W. Lee O'Daniel	Democratic	1939-1941
Coke R. Stevenson	Democratic	1941-1947
Beauford H. Jester	Democratic	1947-1949
Allan Shivers	Democratic	1949-1957
Price Daniel	Democratic	1957-1963
John B. Connally	Democratic	1963-1969
Preston Smith	Democratic	1969-1973
Dolph Briscoe	Democratic	1973-1979
Bill Clements	Republican	1979-1983
Mark White	Democratic	1983-1987
Bill Clements	Republican	1987-

© Bob Daemmrich

The Texas House of Representatives meets in the State Capitol in Austin. The Texas legislature consists of the House, which has 150 members, and the Senate, which has 31 members.

justices. The highest criminal court is the Court of Criminal Appeals. This court has nine judges, including a presiding judge. Members of both of these courts are elected to six-year terms.

Each of the 14 supreme judicial districts in Texas has a court of appeals. Each of these courts has a chief justice and a number of associate justices. The number of associate justices varies from 2 to 12. All justices for the courts of appeals are elected for six-year terms.

The chief trial courts are the district courts. The voters of each judicial district elect a district judge to a four-year term. Other trial courts include the county, municipal, justice of the peace, and criminal district courts. The voters elect judges of all these courts, except municipal courts, to four-year terms. Most municipal court judges are appointed to two-year terms.

Local government. Texas has 254 counties—more than any other state. Each one is governed by a county commissioners court made up of the county judge and four commissioners. This court performs such administrative duties as adopting the county budget and setting the county tax rate. County judges are elected to four-year terms. The commissioners are elected to four-year terms from each of four commissioner precincts in a county. Other county officials include the assessor-collector of taxes, the county attorney, the sheriff, and the treasurer.

Texas has more than 1,100 incorporated cities, towns, and villages. More than 200 cities have *home rule.* That is, they have adopted their own city charters. The Texas Constitution permits all cities with populations of more than 5,000 to adopt home rule. About 180 home-rule cities use either the council-manager or the commission-manager form of government. All other home-rule cities use the mayor-council system of government. Towns with populations of 5,000 or fewer are incorporated under general law.

Revenue. Taxes and license fees bring in about 60 per cent of the state's *general revenue* (income). Almost all remaining revenue comes from federal grants and other U.S. government programs. A retail sales tax on all items except food and medicine is the largest source of tax revenue. The second largest source of tax revenue in the state is a production and regulation tax on gas, petroleum, sulfur, and other minerals. Other sources of tax revenue include a corporation-franchise tax and a tax on motor-fuel use.

Politics. The Democratic Party has controlled Texas politics throughout most of the state's history. But the Republicans gained strength during the 1970's. In 1978, Bill Clements became the first Republican to be elected governor since 1869. In presidential elections, Republicans have won Texas' electoral votes only seven times, but four of the seven were after 1970. The state was carried by Republicans Herbert Hoover in 1928, Dwight D. Eisenhower in 1952 and 1956, Richard M. Nixon in 1972, Ronald Reagan in 1980 and 1984, and George Bush in 1988. Two United States Presidents were born in Texas. Eisenhower was born in Denison, and Lyndon B. Johnson was born near Stonewall. For Texas' electoral votes and voting record in presidential elections, see **Electoral College** (table).

History

Indian days. When the first Europeans arrived, about 30,000 Indians lived in what is now Texas. The largest group was the Caddo Indians, in the eastern part of the region. These Indians lived in permanent homes and were farmers. Some of the Caddo tribes, including the Nacogdoches, Nasoni, and Neche, formed a league called the *Hasinai Confederacy.* The Arkokisa, Attacapa, Karankawa, and other smaller tribes lived along the coast. The Coahuiltecan Indians occupied south Texas. Warlike Lipan Apaches lived on the Edwards Plateau in the west. Comanche and Tonkawa Indians roamed the Rolling Plains and the Prairie Plains.

Spanish exploration. Spanish adventurers, for "glory, God, and gold," began exploring Texas during the early 1500's. In 1519, the Spanish governor of Jamaica sent Alonso Álvarez de Piñeda to explore the Gulf Coast from Florida to Mexico. Piñeda mapped the coastline. Most historians believe he and his followers were the first white men in Texas. In 1528, a Spanish expedition that planned to explore the southern United States was shipwrecked on the Texas coast. Álvar Núñez Cabeza de Vaca, a leader of the expedition, and three companions traveled among the Indians. For eight years, they gradually made their way westward. They finally reached a Spanish settlement in Mexico near the Pacific Coast. The men brought to Mexico City stories of cities of great wealth that supposedly lay north of their westward route.

The Spaniards sent many expeditions to look for these golden cities, called the *Seven Cities of Cibola.* In 1540, Francisco Vásquez de Coronado led a party north from Mexico. He passed through Texas in 1541. But Coronado found only the grass-house villages of the Plains Indians and the adobe huts of the Pueblo Indians. In 1542, some members of an expedition originally led by Hernando de Soto entered northeast Texas after their leader died. They reached the vicinity of present-day Texarkana. Spain based its claims to Texas on these and other explorations, and on missions that Spanish friars built later. Franciscan missionaries built Texas' first two missions in 1682. These missions were located near the present site of El Paso.

French exploration in Texas began in 1685. That year, René-Robert Cavelier, Sieur de la Salle, landed at Matagorda Bay. He had intended to establish a colony at the mouth of the Mississippi River. Perhaps a storm on the Gulf of Mexico drove him to Texas. La Salle established a colony, Fort Saint Louis, inland, and made expeditions westward in search of gold and silver. One of La Salle's men killed him in a quarrel in 1687. Disease and Indians killed off the rest, and Fort Saint Louis was destroyed by the Indians.

La Salle's explorations in Texas alarmed the Spaniards. In 1689, an expedition led by Alonso de León set out from Mexico to destroy Fort Saint Louis. The party found the ruins of the fort and then traveled eastward as far as the Neches River. In 1690, a Franciscan friar with De León's expedition established the first mission in east

Historic Texas

Kingston ●

Houston ●

San Antonio ●

Lieutenant Audie Murphy won fame as the most decorated soldier of World War II. He was born in Kingston, near Greenville.

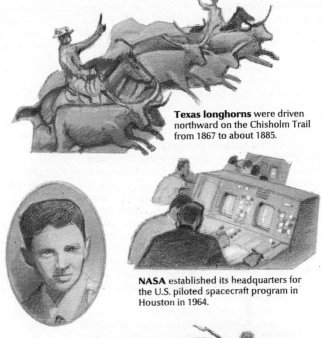

Texas longhorns were driven northward on the Chisholm Trail from 1867 to about 1885.

NASA established its headquarters for the U.S. piloted spacecraft program in Houston in 1964.

"Remember the Alamo" became the battle cry for Texans in their war for independence after they were defeated by Mexican forces at the famous San Antonio mission in 1836.

The last battle of the Civil War was fought at Palmito Hill on May 13, 1865. The soldiers had not heard that the war had ended on April 9.

WORLD BOOK illustrations by Kevin Chadwick

Important dates in Texas

1519 Alonso Álvarez de Piñeda of Spain mapped the Texas coast.

1528 Álvar Núñez Cabeza de Vaca and three other survivors of a shipwrecked Spanish expedition landed on the Texas coast and later explored parts of the region.

1541 Francisco Vásquez de Coronado traveled across part of west Texas.

1542 Hernando de Soto's expedition explored part of northeast Texas.

1682 Spanish missionaries built the first two missions in Texas, near present-day El Paso.

1685 René-Robert Cavelier, Sieur de la Salle, founded Fort Saint Louis, a French settlement, on the Texas coast.

1690 A Franciscan friar established the first mission in east Texas.

1718 The Spaniards established a mission and a fort on the site of present-day San Antonio.

1821 Texas became part of the new Empire of Mexico. The first colony of Americans settled in Texas under the sponsorship of Stephen F. Austin.

1835 The Texas Revolution began.

1836 Texas declared its independence from Mexico. The Alamo fell to Mexican forces. Sam Houston defeated the Mexicans in the Battle of San Jacinto. Texas became the independent Republic of Texas.

1845 Texas became the 28th state on December 29.

1861 Texas seceded from the Union and joined the Confederate States of America.

1870 Congress readmitted Texas to the Union.

1901 Oilmen discovered the great Spindletop field.

1925 Texas became the second state to have a woman governor—Mrs. Miriam A. Ferguson.

1947 A ship explosion in Texas City harbor killed about 500 persons and injured about 3,000.

1953 Congress restored Texas tidelands to the state.

1957 Texas' first toll highway opened, connecting Dallas and Fort Worth.

1963 President John F. Kennedy was assassinated in Dallas. Lyndon B. Johnson of Texas was sworn in as the 36th President at Dallas Love Field Airport.

1964 The Manned Spacecraft Center in the Houston area became the permanent headquarters of the U.S. astronauts.

1973 The Manned Spacecraft Center was renamed the Lyndon B. Johnson Space Center.

Texas, San Francisco de los Tejas. It stood near the present-day community of Weches.

The mission period. By 1731, Spain had sent more than 90 expeditions into what is now Texas. Spain also had established missions throughout central, east, and southwest Texas. The Spaniards built forts near some missions to protect them from Indians. In 1718, they built the fort of San Antonio de Bexar to guard the mission of San Antonio de Valero. This mission and fort stood on the site of present-day San Antonio. They were about halfway between the Spanish missions in east Texas and the Spanish *presidios* (forts) in northern Mexico. In 1772, San Antonio became the seat of Spanish government in Texas. Spanish colonization of Texas proceeded slowly. The region had only about 7,000 white settlers in 1793, after more than a hundred years of missionary effort.

President Thomas Jefferson of the United States purchased the Louisiana Territory from France in 1803. The United States then claimed all territory as far south as the Rio Grande on the basis of earlier French claims. In 1819, a treaty fixed the southwestern boundaries of the Louisiana Territory at the Sabine and Red rivers.

Mexico broke away from Spain in 1821, and Texas became part of the new Empire of Mexico. Mexico became a republic in 1824.

American settlement. In 1820, Moses Austin, a Missouri banker, asked Spanish officials in San Antonio to let him establish a colony of Americans in Texas. The Spanish government granted his request, but Austin died before he could organize the colony. His son, Stephen F. Austin, carried out the plan and brought 300 families to Texas. In 1821, Austin's group made its first settlements at Washington-on-the-Brazos and Columbus in southeast Texas. Austin arrived later and officially established the colony in 1822. It grew rapidly. In 1823, Austin laid out San Felipe de Austin in present-day Austin County as the colony's seat of government. Mexico soon issued new land grants to Austin, and he extended the boundaries of his colony.

Other Americans also received land grants from Mexico to establish colonies. The Mexicans called these American colonizers *empresarios.* The empresarios founded many colonies in Texas during the 1820's. From 1821 to 1836, the number of settlers grew to between 25,000 and 30,000. Almost all were Americans.

Mexican officials became alarmed by the increasing number of settlers from the United States. In 1830, they halted American immigration to Texas. From then on, relations between the American settlers and Mexican officials grew steadily worse. In 1834, General Antonio López de Santa Anna, a Mexican politician and soldier, overthrew Mexico's constitutional government and made himself dictator. The next year, the American colonists in Texas revolted against Mexico.

The Texas revolution. After a few battles with Mexican soldiers, Texas leaders met at San Felipe de Austin on Nov. 3, 1835. They organized a temporary government. Texas troops, led by Colonel Benjamin Milam, attacked San Antonio. The Mexicans there surrendered on December 11. The fall of San Antonio alarmed Santa Anna. He assembled a large army and marched on San Antonio. Texan rebels in the city withdrew behind the walls of the Alamo, the chapel of an old Spanish mission. Santa Anna's forces attacked the Alamo from Feb. 23 to March 6, 1836, when it finally fell. Some historians believe that all its defenders, including Jim Bowie, Davy Crockett, and William B. Travis, were killed in the battle. Other historians believe that a few men, perhaps including Crockett, survived the battle but were then executed by the Mexicans. Texas leaders met at Washington-on-the-Brazos on March 2. They issued a declaration of independence from Mexico and chose David G. Burnet as temporary president and Sam Houston as commander of the army. See **Alamo.**

After the fall of the Alamo, Santa Anna moved swiftly to put down the revolution. He ordered more than 330 Texas prisoners shot to death at Goliad after they had surrendered on March 27. But the Texans continued to fight, inspired by the battle cries of "Remember the Alamo" and "Remember Goliad." In April, after a long retreat, the smaller army of Sam Houston camped near Santa Anna's forces. On April 21, the Texans took the overconfident Mexicans by surprise. They captured

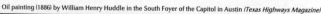

Oil painting (1886) by William Henry Huddle in the South Foyer of the Capitol in Austin *(Texas Highways Magazine)*

General Santa Anna surrendered to General Sam Houston and his army on April 22, 1836, ending the Texas Revolution against Mexico. Santa Anna, *standing center,* signed a treaty granting Texas its independence the day after Houston's forces won the Battle of San Jacinto. Houston, shown lying beneath the tree, was shot in the ankle during the battle.

Santa Anna and crushed his army in the Battle of San Jacinto. The victory ended the war, and guaranteed Texas
independence. See San Jacinto, Battle of.

The Republic of Texas faced serious problems. It
had no money, and raiding Indians and Mexicans threatened its people. In the new republic's first national election, Texans chose Sam Houston as president. They also
voted to join the United States. But the great powers of
Europe, especially France and Great Britain, wanted
Texas to remain independent. They feared the United
States would gain control of the Southwest. The South
wanted Texas to join the Union. But the North objected
because Texas allowed slavery.

During the nearly 10 years when Texas was an independent republic, its population increased rapidly. Most
of the people farmed for a living. In 1839, Texans passed
the first homestead exemption act, which many states
later adopted. This law prevented farms from being
seized for payment of debts.

Statehood and early progress. In 1844, the U.S.
Senate defeated a treaty to annex Texas to the United
States. The treaty failed to win the approval of two-thirds
of the senators voting. Texas finally joined the Union on
Dec. 29, 1845. It became the 28th state by a joint resolution of both houses of Congress. Passage of the resolution required the votes of only a majority of the members present in each house.

The statehood agreement provided that Texas could
keep its public lands and that it would pay its own public debts. The federal government would settle all
boundary disputes with other countries. J. Pinckney Henderson, a Democrat, became the first governor.

After Texas joined the Union, Mexico ended diplomatic relations with the United States. Disputes arose
over the boundary between Texas and Mexico. The
Mexican War between the United States and Mexico
began in 1846. Mexico surrendered in 1848. In the
Treaty of Guadalupe Hidalgo, Mexico gave up all claims
to Texas and other southwestern lands. See Guadalupe
Hidalgo, Treaty of; Mexican War.

Texas claimed much of the southwestern region that
Mexico turned over to the United States. In 1850, the

federal government agreed to pay the state $10 million
for its claims. The agreement also called for Texas to
give up other claims against the federal government.
Texas used part of this money to pay its public debts.
Settlers continued to flock to the state. During the
1850's, pioneers pushed the frontier westward, and
Texas organized 89 new counties. Northeast Texas and
the region east of Waco and Fort Worth attracted the
largest number of settlers.

The Civil War and Reconstruction. Texas *seceded*
(withdrew) from the Union and joined the Confederate
States of America in March 1861. The state seceded in
spite of strong Union feeling in some sections of Texas.
Governor Sam Houston refused to take an oath to support the constitution of the Confederate States. As a result, he was put out of office. More than 50,000 Texans
fought on the side of the Confederacy during the Civil
War (1861-1865). Texas also furnished the Confederacy
with great amounts of supplies. The Union navy blockaded the Texas coast and occupied Galveston for a short
time. The last battle of the Civil War was fought at Palmito Hill, near the mouth of the Rio Grande, on May 13,
1865. The soldiers had not heard that the war ended on
April 9.

After the war, Northern sympathizers called *Radicals*
rose to power in Texas state politics. Lawlessness
gripped the state as racial violence broke out and the Ku
Klux Klan became powerful (see Ku Klux Klan). During
the Reconstruction period, Texas was ruled by a military
government, an appointed governor, and three governors elected by the Radicals. Congress readmitted Texas
to the Union on March 30, 1870. Reconstruction ended
in the state when Democrat Richard Coke became governor in 1874. See Reconstruction.

Conquering the frontier. In the mid-1860's, Texans
began driving cattle along trails to railroad centers in
Kansas and Missouri. These trail drives continued during the 1870's and 1880's. Indian raids slowed the settlement of the western part of the state. The tribes were
subdued by 1880, and cattlemen began to occupy the
Panhandle and the western plains. Railroads crossed
Texas in the 1880's, ending the cattle drives and aiding
settlement. Pioneers followed the railroads west and
began farming the western regions of the state. The
Texas Rangers, organized in 1835, helped protect the far
western settlers from bandits such as Sam Bass. During
the 1890's, the state legislature passed various business-
reform laws, preventing some price and trade abuses by
the railroads and other large corporations.

The early 1900's. Between 1900 and 1920, Texas increased its railroad mileage and built a road system. The
state also developed irrigation and farming on land previously used for raising livestock.

The state's great oil and gas industries began in 1901
with the discovery of the Spindletop oil field near Beaumont. To develop the mineral resources, Texans built
great refineries and other manufacturing plants. They
deepened coastal harbors to help ship their oil and
other products. The annual value of manufactured
goods more than doubled between 1900 and 1910. Between 1900 and 1920, many Texans became city workers, and the number of cities and towns doubled. By
1920, a third of the people in Texas lived in cities. After
the United States entered World War I in 1917, the

Archives Division, Texas State Library
The Texas Rangers roamed the frontier during the 1800's
tracking murderers, train robbers, and other outlaws. They were
organized in 1835 to protect settlers against hostile Indians.

© 1902 F. J. Trost, Archives Division, Texas State Library

Spindletop oil field, near Beaumont, was the first gusher in North America. It sprayed more than 800,000 barrels of oil into the air in 1901 before it was first brought under control.

federal government set up many military training camps in Texas.

In the early 1920's, Governor Pat M. Neff improved education and prisons. He also led the push for a state park system. In 1925, Texas became the second state, after Wyoming, to have a woman governor. She was Miriam A. "Ma" Ferguson. Her husband, James E. Ferguson, had previously been governor.

Great highway construction took place in Texas during the 1920's and 1930's. New legislation helped ease hardships during the depression and droughts of the 1930's. This legislation included the establishment of old-age pensions and special relief programs. In 1936, the Texas Centennial Exposition at Dallas celebrated a hundred years of independence. In 1937, the Greater Texas and Pan American Exposition in Dallas promoted trade among nations of the Western Hemisphere.

The mid-1900's. During World War II (1939-1945), over a million servicemen trained in Texas military camps. Lieutenant Audie Murphy, who was born in Kingston, won fame as the most decorated U.S. soldier of the war.

After the war, manufacturing expanded rapidly in Texas. The aerospace, chemical, and electronics industries built many facilities in the state. Thousands of Texans moved from rural areas to cities to find jobs in new factories, and the state began to shift from a rural, farm economy to an urban, industrial economy.

Texas suffered one of its greatest disasters on April 16, 1947, when a French ship loaded with chemicals blew up in the harbor at Texas City. The explosion killed about 500 people, injured about 3,000, and caused about $70 million in damage.

In 1950, the Supreme Court of the United States ruled that Texas had lost ownership of its oil-rich *tidelands* (submerged offshore lands) when it entered the Union in 1845. The ruling meant that the U.S. government owned the oil beneath the tidewaters. After a dispute in Congress, President Dwight D. Eisenhower signed a bill in 1953 that restored the tidelands to Texas.

Like many other states, Texas faced racial problems in the 1950's and 1960's. The state had separate public schools for blacks and whites. In 1954, the U.S. Supreme Court ruled that compulsory segregation in public schools was unconstitutional. By the late 1960's, most school districts in Texas had been integrated.

Texas took a leading role in the U.S. space program during the 1960's. In 1962, the National Aeronautics and Space Administration (NASA) began building a Manned Spacecraft Center near Houston. The center became the headquarters of the U.S. piloted spacecraft program in 1964. In 1969, scientists and engineers at the center directed the Apollo 11 flight, in which astronauts made the first landing on the moon.

Texas also gained in national political importance during the 1960's. Rapid population growth made it a key state in national elections. In 1963, Lyndon B. Johnson of Texas became the first Southern President since the Civil War. Johnson became President on Nov. 22, 1963, after an assassin had killed President John F. Kennedy and wounded Texas Governor John B. Connally in Dallas. Vice President Johnson was sworn in as the 36th President aboard the presidential plane at Love Field in Dallas. Lee Harvey Oswald was accused of shooting President Kennedy. Two days after Kennedy's death, Jack Ruby, a Dallas nightclub owner, killed Oswald.

Recent developments. The Manned Spacecraft Center was renamed the Lyndon B. Johnson Space Center in 1973. It has made southeastern Texas a major center for space research. Besides NASA, several corporations design and test space equipment there. Universities conduct research in space medicine and other fields. In 1977, Houston annexed the area next to the space center.

The Republican Party gained strength in Texas during the 1970's. In 1972, Richard M. Nixon became only the fourth Republican presidential candidate to win Texas' electoral votes. In 1978, Bill Clements became the first Republican elected governor since 1869. Republican Ronald Reagan won the state's electoral votes in the 1980 and 1984 presidential elections, and Republican George Bush won them in 1988.

Texas is continuing the industrial expansion and urban growth that began after World War II. More Texans now work in manufacturing than in farming and mining combined. About four-fifths of the people live in urban areas. Texas has 28 metropolitan areas—more than any other state.

During the mid-1980's, however, the state's economy was deeply hurt by a sharp decline in oil and natural gas prices. This development emphasized the need to attract new types of industries to the state and to find new sources of tax revenue. In 1986, lawmakers agreed to raise the state sales tax and to cut the budgets for health, welfare, and higher education.

John Edwin Coffman and Clifford L. Egan

Related articles in *World Book* include:

Biographies

Austin (family)	Gutiérrez, José Angel
Autry, Gene	Hobby, Oveta C.
Baker, James A., III	House, Edward M.
Bass, Sam	Houston, Samuel
Bean, Judge Roy	Johnson, Lyndon B.
Bentsen, Lloyd M., Jr.	Jordan, Barbara C.
Bush, George H. W.	Long, Jane
Bowie, James	Maverick, Samuel A.
Connally, John B.	Murphy, Audie
Cortina, Juan Nepomuceno	Rayburn, Sam
Crockett, David	Travis, William B.
Dobie, J. Frank	Tyler, John
Eisenhower, Dwight D.	Wright, James Claude, Jr.
Garner, John N.	

Cities

Amarillo	Galveston
Austin	Houston
Beaumont	Laredo
Corpus Christi	Lubbock
Dallas	San Antonio
El Paso	Waco
Fort Worth	Wichita Falls

History

Alamo
Flag (pictures: Flags in American history [Texas flags])
Guadalupe Hidalgo, Treaty of
Jefferson, State of
Mexican War (Background of the war)
Mission life in America
San Jacinto, Battle of
Texas Rangers
Western frontier life
Westward movement (The southwest)

Physical features

Big Bend National Park	Lake Texoma
Colorado River	Padre Island
Dust Bowl	Pecos River
Guadalupe Mountains National Park	Red River
	Rio Grande
Gulf of Mexico	

Other related articles

Alibates Flint Quarries National Monument	Gulf Intracoastal Waterway
	Gulf of Mexico
Corpus Christi Naval Air Station	Johnson Space Center
Fort Bliss	Petroleum (picture: The first gusher)
Fort Hood	
Fort Sam Houston	Randolph Air Force Base

Outline

I. People
  A. Population
  B. Schools
  C. Libraries
  D. Museums
II. Visitor's guide
  A. Places to visit
  B. Annual events
III. Land and climate
  A. Land regions
  B. Coastline
  C. Mountains
  D. Rivers and lakes
  E. Plant and animal life
  F. Climate
IV. Economy
  A. Natural resources
  B. Service industries
  C. Manufacturing

  D. Mining
  E. Agriculture
  F. Fishing industry
  G. Electric power
  H. Transportation
  I. Communication
V. Government
  A. Constitution
  B. Executive
  C. Legislature
  D. Courts
  E. Local government
  F. Revenue
  G. Politics
VI. History

Questions

How did Texas win independence from Mexico?
What are the two major differences between the two great economic regions of east and west Texas?
What is Texas' most valuable crop?
Who established the first colony of Americans in Texas? When was it established?
Which six nations have flown flags over Texas?
Why was Governor Sam Houston put out of office during the Civil War?
What was the source of the name *Texas*?
What role does Texas play in the United States space program?
Which two minerals have contributed to making Texas a wealthy state?
Which political party has controlled Texas politics throughout most of the state's history?

Additional resources

Level I

Adler, Larry. *The Texas Rangers*. McKay, 1979.
Carpenter, Allan. *Texas*. Rev. ed. Childrens Press, 1979.
Fradin, Dennis B. *Texas in Words and Pictures*. Childrens Press, 1981.
Lawson, Don. *The United States in the Mexican War*. Harper, 1976.
McCall, Edith. *Stalwart Men of Early Texas*. Childrens Press, 1970.
Warren, Robert Penn. *Remember the Alamo!* Random House, 1958.

Level II

Anderson, James E., and others. *Texas Politics: An Introduction*. 4th ed. Harper, 1983.
Connor, Seymour V. *Texas: A History*. AHM, 1971.
Doble, J. Frank. *The Longhorns*. Little, Brown, 1941. *The Mustangs*. 1952. *Cow People*. 1964.
Fehrenbach, Theodore R. *Lone Star: A History of Texas and the Texans*. Macmillan, 1968.
Frantz, Joe B. *Texas: A Bicentennial History*. Norton, 1976.
The Handbook of Texas. Ed. by Walter P. Webb, and others. 3 vols. Texas State Historical Assn., 1952-1976.
Holmes, Jon. *Texas: A Self-Portrait*. Abrams, 1983.
Horgan, Paul. *Great River: The Rio Grande in North American History*. Rev. ed. Holt, 1960.
Nevin, David. *The Texans*. Time Inc., 1975.
Porterfield, Bill. *A Loose Herd of Texans*. Texas A&M Univ. Press, 1978. Two dozen biographical sketches.
Presley, James. *A Saga of Wealth: The Rise of the Texas Oilmen*. Putnam, 1978.
Richardson, Rupert N., and others. *Texas: The Lone Star State*. 4th ed. Prentice-Hall, 1981.
Samora, Julian, and others. *Gunpowder Justice: A Reassessment of the Texas Rangers*. Notre Dame, 1979.
Sharpe, Patricia, and Weddle, R. S. *Texas: The Newest, the Biggest, the Most Complete Guide to All of Texas*. Texas Monthly Press, 1983.
Tarpley, Fred. *1001 Texas Place Names*. Univ. of Texas Press, 1980.
Wooster, Ralph A., and Calvert, R. A., eds. *Texas Vistas: Selections from the "Southwestern Historical Quarterly."* Texas State Historical Assn., 1980.

Texas, University of, is a coeducational, state-supported system of higher education. Its official name is the University of Texas System. The system consists of seven academic institutions and six health-related institutions. The system's administrative offices are in Austin.

University of Texas at Austin grants bachelor's, master's, and doctor's degrees. It has colleges of business administration, communication, education, engineering, fine arts, liberal arts, natural sciences, nursing, and pharmacy; and schools of architecture and social work. Its graduate schools include business, law, library science, and public affairs. Major research facilities include the McDonald Observatory at Mount Locke and the Marine Science Institute at Port Aransas. The Austin campus library contains more than $3\frac{1}{2}$ million volumes, including many manuscripts, rare books, and special collections. The Lyndon B. Johnson Library is also on the Austin campus. The university was founded in 1883.

University of Texas at Arlington has colleges of business administration, engineering, liberal arts, and science; schools of nursing and of architecture and environmental design; and graduate schools. It also has an institute of urban studies and a center for professional teacher education. The university grants bachelor's, master's, and doctor's degrees. The campus opened in 1895 as a private college and became a state-supported college in 1917. It became part of the University of Texas System in 1965.

University of Texas at Dallas is located in the Dallas suburb of Richardson. The university offers upper-level programs that lead to the bachelor's degree, and graduate programs that lead to master's and doctor's degrees. It includes the Callier Center for Communication Disorders. Formerly a privately supported research institution, the University of Texas at Dallas was created in 1969.

University of Texas at El Paso grants bachelor's, master's, and doctor's degrees. It has colleges of business administration, education, engineering, liberal arts, nursing and allied health, and science. The school opened in 1913 as the Texas School of Mines and Metallurgy. It became part of the University of Texas in 1919.

University of Texas of the Permian Basin, in Odessa, offers courses at the junior, senior, and graduate levels. It grants bachelor's and master's degrees. The university was established in 1969.

University of Texas at San Antonio grants bachelor's and master's degrees. It has colleges of business, fine arts and humanities, sciences and mathematics, and social and behavioral sciences. The campus was established in 1969.

University of Texas at Tyler offers upper-level programs that lead to the bachelor's degree, and graduate programs that lead to the master's degree. It opened in 1971 as Texas Eastern University and became part of the University of Texas System in 1979.

Health-related institutions in the system are the three health science centers at Dallas, Houston, and San Antonio; a health center at Tyler; the Medical Branch at Galveston; and the University of Texas System Cancer Center, which has facilities in Houston and near Smithville.

For enrollments, see **Universities and colleges** (table). Critically reviewed by the University of Texas System

Texas A&I University. See Universities and colleges (table).

Texas A&M University System consists of four coeducational state universities in Texas. It also includes six agencies that provide service to the state. Its administrative offices are in College Station, Tex. The agencies in the system are the Texas Agricultural Experiment Station, Texas Agricultural Extension Service, Texas Engineering Experiment Station, Texas Engineering Extension Service, Texas Forest Service, and Texas Transportation Institute.

Texas A&M University, in College Station, is the oldest public institution of higher education in Texas. It was founded as the Agricultural and Mechanical College of Texas in 1871, and the first classes were held in 1876. In 1963, the school's name was changed to Texas A&M University. The university has colleges of agriculture, architecture and environmental design, business administration, education, engineering, geosciences, liberal arts, medicine, science, and veterinary medicine. It has a full graduate program.

Prairie View A&M University is in Prairie View. It has colleges of agriculture, arts and sciences, education, engineering, home economics, industrial education and technology, and nursing. Courses lead to bachelor's and master's degrees. The university was founded in 1876.

Tarleton State University, in Stephenville, has schools of agriculture and business, arts and sciences, and education. Courses lead to bachelor's and master's degrees. The institution was founded in 1899.

Texas A&M University at Galveston includes the Texas Maritime College and the Coastal Zone Laboratory. It was founded in Galveston in 1971 as Moody College, and it received its present name in 1979. Courses lead to bachelor's degrees in marine biology, marine engineering, marine sciences, marine transportation, maritime administration, and maritime systems engineering. The Texas Maritime College's program includes training on the ship *Texas Clipper.* Students who successfully complete the program qualify as officers in the United States merchant marine or as ensigns in the United States Naval Reserve.

For enrollments, see **Universities and colleges** (table). Critically reviewed by the Texas A&M University System

Texas annexation. See United States, History of the (Manifest destiny; map).

Texas Christian University is a private coeducational school in Fort Worth, Tex. It is related to the Disciples of Christ. The university has a college of arts and sciences, a college of nursing, a divinity school, and schools of business, education, and fine arts.

Courses at Texas Christian lead to bachelor's, master's, and doctor's degrees. The university offers several special programs. These include an honors program, a ranch management program, and foreign study programs in Europe and Mexico. The university operates a speech and hearing clinic and a school for children with learning disabilities. Texas Christian University was founded in 1873. For the school's enrollment, see **Universities and colleges** (table).

Critically reviewed by Texas Christian University

Texas fever. See Cattle tick.

Texas Rangers are special police officers of the state of Texas. They serve under the authority of the State De-

Texas Rangers are part of the state police of Texas. In their crime laboratory, *left,* specially trained Rangers use modern equipment to analyze bloodstains, fingerprints, and other evidence connected with the crimes they investigate.

Susan Hoermann, Texas Department of Public Safety

partment of Public Safety. One noted Ranger summarized their qualities in these words: "The Texas Rangers can ride like a Mexican, trail like an Indian, shoot like a Tennessean, and fight like a very devil." The Rangers have a tradition of individualism, resourcefulness, self-reliance, and politeness. They often "get their man" with quick thinking rather than by force. The Rangers wear no official uniforms. They furnish their own clothing. The state provides weapons and transportation. But Rangers may carry their own weapons, and they ride their own horses.

Early days. The Rangers were originally a band of mounted riflemen. Early in the 1800's, Stephen F. Austin formed bands of "rangers" to protect American settlers along the Brazos River from Indian warriors and Mexican bandits.

In 1835, the Texas general council formally organized the Rangers and assigned them the sole task of defending the frontier against Indians. One company of 25 men patrolled east of the Trinity River, another between the Trinity and the Brazos, and a third between the Brazos and the Colorado River. This was a large assignment. The Spaniards and Mexicans had never been successful in controlling the Plains Indian tribes.

The Rangers adopted the practices of their enemies in order to keep the peace. The Comanche Indians, with their cunning, speed, and courage, set the pattern of Plains warfare. The Rangers learned the Indian skills of horsemanship, woodcraft, and direction finding. They were excellent marksmen, and adopted the revolving six-shooter as their standard weapon. They always carried rifles, lariats, and bowie knives.

After Texas gained its independence in 1836, it faced a Mexican and Indian danger on a 1,000-mile (1,600-kilometer) frontier. With a population of about 400,000, it could not afford a standing army. Texas required a fighting force that was small and inexpensive, available in time of need but inactive when not needed. The Texas

Rangers, without uniforms, drill, or regular pay, met these requirements. They served as a mobile and efficient frontier defense organization.

After Texas joined the Union in 1845, the Rangers continued to play a major role in frontier defense. During the Mexican War (1846-1848), they performed valuable service as scouts and guerrilla fighters with the American armies in Mexico. When the federal government established forts along the Texas frontier and garrisoned them with regular troops, Texans still placed their faith in the Rangers. Sam Houston once said in the U.S. Senate: "Give us 1,000 Rangers, and we will be responsible for the defense of our frontier . . . We ask no regular troops; withdraw them if you please. I ask this not through any unkindness to them, but because they have not the efficiency for frontier service."

Later history. During the Reconstruction period that followed the Civil War, Texas suffered from lawlessness, murder, and Indian raids. In 1874, 450 Texas Rangers received commissions as peace officers. They continued to fight the Comanche along the northern border and Mexican cattle thieves along the Rio Grande. They also tracked down murderers, smugglers, bank and train robbers, and mine bandits. Within 10 years, they restored peace and quiet to the interior of Texas. In 1917 and 1918, they succeeded in clearing the rocky Big Bend region of outlaws. Since then, the Rangers have been greatly reduced in number.   Norman A. Graebner

Additional resources

Gillett, James B. *Six Years with the Texas Rangers, 1875 to 1881.* Univ. of Nebraska Press, 1976. First published in 1925.
Sterling, William W. *Trails and Trials of a Texas Ranger.* Univ. of Oklahoma Press, 1979. First published in 1959.
Webb, Walter P. *The Texas Rangers: A Century of Frontier Defense.* 2nd ed. Univ. of Texas Press, 1965.

Texas Tech University. See Universities and colleges (table).

Texoma, Lake. See Lake Texoma.

A wide variety of textile products—from carpeting, clothing, and towels to fire hoses, typewriter ribbons, and umbrellas—helps meet the needs of people throughout the world.

Textile

Textile has traditionally meant a woven fabric. The term comes from the Latin word *texere,* meaning *to weave.* Many fabrics are still made by weaving yarn on a loom. But today, all other types of fabrics are also considered textiles. They include knitted goods, felts, laces, nets, and braids. The textile industry also refers to the fibers and yarns used to make fabrics as textiles.

Textile mills produce an incredible variety of fabrics. They turn out huge rolls of soft cotton, warm wool, strong nylon, and other fabrics. The mills produce these textiles in every color imaginable and in countless patterns. The largest share of all textile production goes to garment manufacturers to be made into ready-to-wear clothing. The second-largest share is used to make such household products as draperies, blankets, sheets, and towels. In the United States, the textile industry manufactures about 25 billion square yards (21 billion square meters) of fabric a year. About 70 per cent of this output is used in making clothing and household goods.

Textiles are also used in thousands of other products. These products include basketball nets, boat sails, bookbindings, conveyor belts, fire hoses, flags, insulation materials, mailbags, parachutes, typewriter ribbons, and umbrellas. Automobile manufacturers use fabrics in the carpeting, upholstery, tires, and brake linings of cars. Hospitals use such textile products as adhesive tape,

bandages, and surgical thread. Surgeons replace diseased heart arteries with arteries knitted or woven from textile fibers.

Most textiles are produced by twisting fibers into yarns and then knitting or weaving the yarns into a fabric. This method of making cloth has been used for thousands of years. But throughout most of that time, workers did the twisting, knitting, or weaving largely by hand. With today's modern machinery, textile mills can manufacture as much fabric in a few seconds as it once took workers weeks to produce by hand.

Sources of textile fibers

Fibers are the raw materials for all fabrics. Some fibers occur in nature as fine strands that can be twisted into yarns. These *natural fibers* come from plants, animals, and minerals. Most natural fibers used for textile production measure $\frac{1}{2}$ to 8 inches (1.3 to 20 centimeters) or longer. Such short fibers are called *staple fibers.*

For most of history, people had only natural fibers to use in making cloth. But modern science has learned how to produce fibers by chemical and technical means. Today, these manufactured fibers account for more than two-thirds of the fibers processed by U.S. textile mills. Unlike most natural fibers, manufactured fibers are produced in long, continuous lengths called *filaments.* Many manufactured fibers also have certain qualities superior to those of natural fibers. For example, they may be stronger or more elastic.

Natural fibers. Plants provide more textile fibers than do animals or minerals. In fact, one plant, cotton, accounts for about 95 per cent of the natural fibers used in the United States. Cotton fibers produce soft, absor-

D. S. Hamby, the contributor of this article, is Dean of the School of Textiles at North Carolina State University.

Manufactured fibers

Fiber	Trade names	Characteristics	Uses
Acetate	Acele, Celaperm, Estron	Resists mildew, shrinking, stains, and stretching	Clothing; draperies; upholstery
Acrylic	Acrilan, Creslan, Orlon, Zefran	Soft; resists mildew, sunlight, and wrinkling	Blankets; carpeting; clothing; upholstery
Aramid	Kevlar, Nomex	Resists heat, chemicals, and stretching	Bulletproof vests; electrical insulation; rope; tires
Glass	Beta, Fiberglas, PPG, Vitron	Resists chemicals, flames, mildew, moisture, and sunlight	Draperies; electrical insulation; ironing board covers
Metallic	Brunsmet, Chromeflex, Fairtex, Lurex, Metlon	Resists insects, mildew, and tarnishing	Decorative trim for bedspreads, tablecloths, and upholstery
Modacrylic	Verel	Soft; resists chemicals, flames, and wrinkling	Artificial furs; blankets; carpeting; wigs
Nylon	Antron, Cumuloft, Enkaloft, Qiana	Strong; elastic; easy to launder; dries quickly; retains shape	Carpeting; hosiery; lingerie; parachutes; upholstery
Olefin	DLP, Herculon, Marvess, Vectra	Lightweight; resists insects, mildew, moisture, and sunlight	Automobile seat covers; filters; indoor-outdoor carpeting
Polyester	Dacron, Encron, Fortrel, Kodel	Resists wrinkling; easy to launder; dries quickly	Blankets; carpeting; clothing; fire hose; sewing thread
Rayon	Avril, Fibro	Absorbent; easy to launder; dyes easily	Carpeting; clothing; draperies; upholstery
Rubber (synthetic)	Contro, Lactron, Lastex	Strong; elastic; repels moisture	Mattresses; support hose; swimwear; underwear
Saran	Rovana, Velon	Resists acids, insects, mildew, moisture, and stains	Draperies; outdoor furniture; rainwear; upholstery
Spandex	Glospan, Lycra, Numa	Elastic; lightweight; resists sunlight and perspiration	Fitted sheets; slipcovers; support hose; swimwear; underwear
Triacetate	Arnel	Resists shrinking, stains, and wrinkling; dries quickly	Draperies; sportswear; blended with other fibers

bent fabrics that are widely used for clothing, sheets, and towels. Fibers of the flax plant are made into linen. The strength and beauty of linen have made it a popular fabric for fine tablecloths, napkins, and handkerchiefs. Fibers of the jute plant can be woven into burlap. Burlap is used for sacks and as backing for rugs and carpets.

The main animal fiber used for textiles is wool. Another animal fiber, silk, produces one of the most luxurious fabrics. Sheep supply most of the wool, but members of the camel family and some goats also furnish wool. Wool provides warm, comfortable fabrics for dresses, suits, and sweaters. Silk comes from cocoons spun by silkworms. Workers unwind the cocoons to obtain long, natural filaments. Fabrics made from silk fibers have great luster and softness and can be dyed brilliant colors. Silk is especially popular for scarfs and neckties.

The only natural mineral fiber used for textiles is asbestos, which comes from several varieties of rocks. Asbestos will not burn, though it melts at extremely high temperatures. Manufacturers use it in making brake linings, insulating wire, and fire-retardant hose.

Manufactured fibers. Most manufactured fibers are made from *wood pulp,* cotton *linters,* or *petrochemicals.* Wood pulp comes from trees and the waste products of the lumber industry. Linters are the short fibers remaining on the cottonseeds after the longer fibers have been removed by the cotton gin. Petrochemicals are chemicals made from crude oil and natural gas.

The fibers made from wood pulp and linters are rayon, acetate, and triacetate. Rayon and acetate are widely used for clothing, draperies, and upholstery. Rayon produces absorbent fabrics that dye easily. Fabrics of acetate resist shrinking and stretching. Triacetate has the desirable qualities of acetate and also resists wrinkling, making it especially popular for sportswear.

The chief fibers manufactured from petrochemicals include nylon, polyester, acrylic, and olefin. Nylon has exceptional strength, wears well, and is easy to launder. It is popular for hosiery and other clothing and for carpeting and upholstery. Such products as conveyor belts and fire hoses are also made of nylon. Polyester resists wrinkling and is widely used in permanent press clothing. Acrylic fibers produce soft, bulky, lightweight fabrics for blankets, carpeting, and children's snowsuits. Olefin cleans easily, dries quickly, and resists mildew. It is widely used for indoor-outdoor carpeting.

Other manufactured fibers include those made from glass and metals. Fabrics of glass fibers are used for insulation and to make boat hulls, molded products, and flame-resistant fabrics. Metallic fibers—chiefly aluminum, gold, and silver—provide decorative yarns for bedspreads, evening gowns, and tablecloths.

Kinds of fabrics

About 90 per cent of all fabrics produced in the United States are made by weaving or knitting. The rest are made by other processes. In producing fabrics by the various processes, textile mills may use yarns finer than sewing thread or as heavy as rug yarn.

Woven fabrics are made of two sets of yarns—a lengthwise set called the *warp* and a crosswise set called the *filling* or *weft.* The warp yarns are threaded into a loom through a series of frames called *harnesses.* During the cloth-making process, the harnesses raise some warp yarns and lower others. This action creates a space, or *shed,* between the yarns. A device called a *shuttle* carries the filling through the shed and so forms the crosswise yarns of the fabric. The pattern in which the harnesses are raised and lowered for each pass of the shuttle determines the kind of weave. There are three basic patterns: (1) the plain weave, (2) the twill weave, and (3) the satin weave.

The plain weave is the simplest and most common pattern. In this weave, the crosswise filling passes over one warp yarn and under the next alternately across the width of the fabric. The weave produces long-lasting, flat-textured cloth used in making such products as bedsheets, dresses, and upholstery. Plain-woven fabrics include gingham, percale, and taffeta.

The twill weave has a pattern of raised diagonal lines. The filling crosses over and then under two, three, or four warp yarns at a time, with each row following the same pattern. However, each row's pattern begins slightly to the right or left of the pattern in the previous row. This technique creates the diagonal lines. The twill weave produces strong, tightly woven cloth used in coats, sportswear, and work clothes. Popular twill fabrics include denim and gabardine.

The satin weave is the least common pattern. The filling may span as many as 12 warp yarns. The weave produces soft, luxurious cloth, but it may snag easily. Satin-weave fabrics are made into such products as draperies and formal clothes. Common satin weaves include damask and satin.

Knitted fabrics are made from a single yarn or a set of yarns. In making cloth, a knitting machine forms loops in the yarn and links them to one another by means of needles. The finished fabric consists of crosswise rows of loops, called *courses,* and lengthwise rows of loops, called *wales.* This looped structure makes knitted fabrics more elastic than woven cloth. Garment manufactur-

ers use knitted fabrics in producing comfortable, lightweight clothing that resists wrinkling. Textile mills manufacture knit goods by two basic methods: (1) weft knitting and (2) warp knitting.

Weft knitting is done with single lengths of yarn, which a knitting machine forms into the crosswise courses one row at a time. The loops of each course are pulled through the loops of the previous course. This process forms the wales at the same time as the courses. Weft knits can be made in the shape of a tube or as flat pieces of cloth.

Most weft-knitted fabrics are used in making hosiery, sweaters, and underwear. These fabrics are knitted in three basic stitches. In the *plain,* or *jersey, stitch,* the tops of the loops stand out on the face of the cloth, and the bottoms of the loops stand out on the back. The *purl stitch* produces crosswise ridges on both sides of the fabric. The *rib stitch* makes cloth with lengthwise ribs on the front and back. Another stitch, the *double knit,* produces a heavier, more tightly constructed fabric than do the other stitches. Double-knit dresses, men's suits, and sportswear are highly popular because of their wrinkle resistance.

Warp knitting requires hundreds of yarns fed as a sheet to a knitting machine. A separate needle for each yarn forms the wales of the fabric. At the same time, the needles interloop the wales crosswise and so form the yarns into a fabric. Almost all warp knits are produced in flat pieces.

Warp-knitted fabrics are tightly constructed and thus do not stretch as much as weft knits. In warp knits, the loops stand out on the face of the cloth, and the connecting yarns stand out on the back. Common warp-knitted fabrics include tricot and raschel. Tricot knits are lightweight fabrics that are widely used in making bedsheets, blouses, dresses, and women's underwear. Raschel knits are heavier fabrics and are used for a variety of products, including blankets, carpeting, men's suits, and swimwear.

Other fabrics include tufted fabrics, nets and laces, braids, and felt. None of these fabrics is woven. However, the textile industry produces another class of fabrics specifically called nonwoven fabrics.

Tufted fabrics are used in about 95 per cent of the carpeting produced in the United States. Such fabrics

WORLD BOOK photo by Steven Spicer

A woven fabric consists of two sets of yarns. The yarns are crossed over and under each other to form cloth.

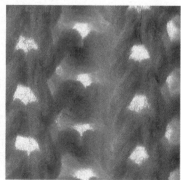

WORLD BOOK photo by Steven Spicer

A knitted fabric has a single yarn or a set of yarns. Loops are made in the yarn and linked together, forming cloth.

Larry Day

Felt is made chiefly from fibers of wool, fur, or animal hair. The fibers are matted together by moist heat and pressure.

consist of cut or uncut loops of yarn that have been punched through a backing material.

Nets and laces, which are called *open-mesh fabrics,* have wide spaces between the yarns. These fabrics can be produced on certain kinds of knitting machines. Netting is used for curtains, fishing nets, hammocks, and tennis nets. Laces have delicate designs and are popular as trim for clothing.

Braids consist of three or more interlaced yarns. Braided fabrics are used for such narrow items as ribbons and shoelaces.

Felt is chiefly produced from fibers of wool, fur, or animal hair. The fibers are matted together by moist heat and pressure. Felt is used in making billiard table covers, hats, and padding.

Nonwoven fabrics include *needle-punched fabrics* and fabrics produced by a process called *bonding.* Needle-punched fabrics, or *needle felts,* consist of fibers that have been tangled together by means of hooked needles. Such fabrics look like felt and are used in making blankets, indoor outdoor carpeting, and insulation. Fabrics produced by bonding are made by joining fibers with adhesives. Many of these fabrics are made into items that are used only once, such as disposable diapers and surgical gowns.

How fabrics are produced

Designing a fabric. Most fabric designers work for companies that manufacture fibers, fabrics, or clothing. Designers create new patterns and color combinations and decide what fibers and methods of construction to use in various fabrics. They must know enough about textile production to realize whether their ideas can be converted into actual products. Fabrics must also be designed so that they can be produced economically on standard textile machinery, such as looms, knitting machines, and tufting machines. In addition, a design has to appeal to a great many consumers for the fabric to be profitable.

Making the yarn. Yarn can be manufactured in various ways. Fiber companies may take filaments—that is, long, continuous fibers—and draw 15 to 100 of them together to make *multifilament* yarn. Or they may use a single filament to make *monofilament* yarn. Some filament yarns, including those made from nylon and polyester, can be *heat-set* to form *stretch yarns.* In one method of heat-setting, manufacturers tightly twist the yarn and heat it. After the yarn is untwisted, it tends to snap back like a spring. Such yarn is used in double-knit and stretch-woven fabrics. Other treatments can be applied to filament yarns to give them a bulky texture.

Filaments may also be cut into staple, or short, lengths that measure 1 to 3 inches (2.5 to 7.6 centimeters) long. Staple fibers cut from filaments produce yarn that is softer than filament yarn and not as lustrous. Yarn producers can also mix together natural fibers and manufactured fibers of staple length to form *blended yarns.* These yarns have the characteristics of each of the fibers used in their construction. For example, yarn produced from cotton and polyester is absorbent because it contains cotton and wrinkle resistant because it contains polyester.

Yarn made from natural fibers or manufactured fibers of staple length is called *staple yarn* or *spun yarn.* All

Burlington Industries, Inc.

Designing a fabric requires not only artistic ability but also knowledge of fibers and textile machinery. Designers must know whether their ideas can be converted into actual products.

staple yarns are manufactured in much the same way, whether they are blended or consist of only one kind of fiber. The fibers arrive at the mill in bales, which workers feed into a series of *opening machines.* These machines break up the large masses of fibers, remove some of the trash, and mix the fibers together. A *carding machine* then removes smaller impurities and some of the exceptionally short fibers and arranges the remaining fibers into a loose rope called a *sliver.* Next, as many as eight slivers at a time are drawn together into another sliver. This sliver is then formed into a thin strand called a *roving.* The roving is twisted on a *spinning frame* to form yarn. Some spinning frames produce yarn directly from slivers. Different kinds of fibers may be blended when the bales are opened, when the slivers are drawn together, or when the roving is spun.

After the yarn has been manufactured, it is wound onto large spools. Sometimes, two or more strands of yarn are twisted together for added strength. Each strand of such heavier yarn is referred to as a *ply.* Three-ply yarn, for example, consists of three strands of yarn. After the yarn has been spooled, it is ready to be woven or knitted.

Making the fabric begins when workers place the spools of yarn on a rack called a *creel.* The creel feeds the yarns onto a *beam* (roller) that is placed on a loom or a knitting machine. For a discussion of how looms and knitting machines make cloth, see the previous section, *Kinds of fabrics.*

Manufacturers produce woven and knitted fabrics in various lengths, depending on the orders of their customers. Woven fabrics made for clothing manufacturers are usually produced in widths of 36 to 60 inches (91 to 152 centimeters). Most woven *narrow goods,* which are used for such products as gauze bandages and labels, measure $\frac{1}{2}$ to 3 inches (1.3 to 7.6 centimeters) wide.

In general, a knitting mill specializes in one of four kinds of products—fabric; hosiery; underwear; or such outerwear as dresses, shirts, slacks, and sweaters. Most fabric produced in widths of 80 to 168 inches (200 to 427 centimeters) is sold to clothing manufacturers. Fabrics

Making yarn involves processing fibers through various machines. A carding machine, *above,* arranges the fibers into a loose rope called a *sliver.* The slivers are coiled into cans and fed into a spinning frame, *right,* which twists them into yarn.

made in the shape of tubes are used for the bodies of sport shirts and of T-shirts. Such cloth can also be cut and sewed together like flat-knitted fabrics to make garments.

Finishing the fabric. Fabrics that come directly from a loom or knitting machine are called *gray goods.* This term does not refer to the color of the cloth. It merely means that the fabric has not received any finishing treatments and so is unsuitable for most purposes. Gray goods are also called *greige* (pronounced *gray*).

Almost all gray goods are washed to remove dirt, grease, and other unwanted substances. Many fabrics are also bleached to whiten them or to prepare them for dyeing or printing. Cotton fabrics may be treated with

caustic soda before dyeing. This process, called *mercerizing,* swells the cotton fibers and thus increases the strength and luster of the cloth.

Some gray goods are made from dyed yarn. Such cloth may have brilliant colors and highly detailed designs. But most textiles are dyed a single color after the yarn has been made into cloth. Dyeing machines pull the fabric through a dyebath or force the dye into the cloth by means of pressure.

Designs are printed on fabrics by three chief methods. *Roller printing* uses rollers that have designs deeply engraved on their surface. Dye is applied to the raised areas and then transferred onto the cloth by the rollers. *Screen printing* is similar to using a stencil to

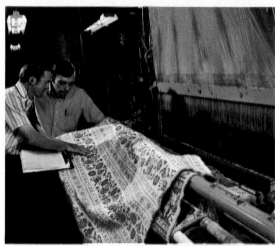

Weaving on a Jacquard loom, *above,* produces fabric with complex patterns for such items as towels and upholstery. Punched cards and other attachments guide the yarn.

Knitting on a circular knitting machine, *right,* produces fabric for hosiery, underwear, and many other garments. A device at the bottom of the machine rolls up the fabric as it is knitted.

form a design. Dye is pressed onto the cloth through a pattern on a screen. *Rotary screen printing* uses porous rollers that fit inside cylindrical screens. The rollers hold the dye and force it into the cloth through patterns on the screens. In another process, called *heat transfer printing* the design is printed on paper with special ink and then ironed onto the fabric. When the paper is peeled off, it leaves the design on the cloth. Some fabrics are dyed and then printed.

After the cloth has been dyed or printed, it may be dried and stretched on a machine called a *tenter frame.* Fabrics made from heat-set fibers may also be treated by this device to help the cloth resist shrinking and wrinkling. A patented process called *Sanforizing* pre-shrinks cloth to prevent it from shrinking or stretching more than 1 per cent in home laundering. Other finishing treatments help fabrics resist bacteria, fading, flames, mildew, moths, stains, static, and water.

The final step in manufacturing cloth is ironing it between heavy rollers, a process called *calendering.* The fabrics are then rolled onto bolts for shipment to clothing makers and other customers.

The textile industry

In the United States, the textile industry consists of about 5,500 companies that operate more than 7,000 plants. Many of these companies perform every step in the manufacturing process, from making the yarn to finishing the fabric. But some manufacturers specialize in only one operation. For example, a textile mill may produce cloth with yarn it buys from one company and then sell the fabric to another firm for finishing.

Textile producers use over 11 billion pounds (5 billion kilograms) of fibers yearly. Sales of the textile industry total over $50 billion a year. The largest textile companies, in order of sales, include Burlington Industries, Incorporated; J. P. Stevens & Company, Incorporated; West-Point Pepperell, Incorporated; and Springs Industries, Incorporated.

The textile industry employs about a million persons. Specialized workers include cloth inspectors, designers, dyeing supervisors, and loom technicians. Closely related industries, such as companies that manufacture fibers, clothing, and textile machinery, employ about $2\frac{1}{2}$ million persons. Two labor unions—the Amalgamated Clothing and Textile Workers Union (ACTWU) and the International Ladies' Garment Workers' Union (ILGWU)—represent over a fourth of the workers in the textile and related industries.

The U.S. government requires the textile industry to observe certain federal laws designed to protect consumers and give them information about the textiles they buy. The Wool Products Labeling Act of 1939 provides that all garments made of wool have a label telling the amount and kind of wool used. The Textile Fiber Products Identification Act of 1958 covers all other fibers. It requires that all clothing and most home furnishings have a label showing the fiber content by percentage. The Flammable Fabrics Act of 1953 prohibits the sale of fabrics that burn rapidly.

The Federal Trade Commission (FTC) and the Consumer Product Safety Commission (CPSC) are the government agencies chiefly responsible for enforcing the consumer protection laws. These agencies may also

Burlington Industries, Inc.

Dyeing processes may be used either to color fibers and yarns before they are made into cloth or to color the fabric itself. In *package dyeing, above,* tubes of yarn are dyed in large vats.

Burlington Industries, Inc.

Printing produces fabrics with beautiful designs and a variety of colors. In *rotary screen printing, above,* the dye is forced through patterns on cylindrical screens that fit around rollers.

Ferenc Berko, DPI

Weaving with a hand loom is still a major way of making cloth in many developing countries. This woman in Guatemala weaves a colorful fabric by an age-old method.

issue regulations of their own. Since July 1972, the FTC has required that all clothing be labeled with instructions regarding cleaning, ironing, and bleaching.

In Canada, about 1,210 textile mills sell about $5½ billion worth of goods annually. Canada's textile industry employs about 90,000 workers. Another 95,000 people work for clothing manufacturers. About a fourth of all the workers belong to local unions of the ACTWU and the ILGWU.

Canada's Textile Labeling Act requires a label on all

Leading textile-producing states and provinces

Value added by manufacture

North Carolina	$5,361,600,000
Georgia	$3,547,900,000
South Carolina	$2,940,100,000
Quebec	$1,417,500,000
Virginia	$1,126,800,000
Alabama	$1,098,700,000
Pennsylvania	$1,009,200,000
New York	$817,300,000
Massachusetts	$665,600,000

Figures are for 1985 for states and 1984 for provinces. All figures are in U.S. dollars. Sources: U.S. Bureau of the Census; Statistics Canada.

clothing to show the fiber content by percentage. The Department of Consumer and Corporate Affairs enforces the law. Labeling garments with instructions for their care is voluntary in Canada.

In other countries. Almost every country has a textile industry. In Japan and the countries of Western Europe, textile production is highly industrialized and centered on manufactured fibers. For example, England, Italy, Switzerland, and West Germany are leading exporters of textile machinery and manufactured fibers. Textile production is also highly mechanized in East Germany, Poland, the Soviet Union, and other Eastern European countries. But natural fibers have greater importance in these countries than in most Western nations.

In some developing nations, such as India and Pakistan, millions of workers still weave fabrics of cotton, silk, and other natural fibers in their homes. As the economies of developing countries advance, however, textile manufacturing often becomes one of the first industries to be mechanized. Textile production provides many jobs that can be filled by unskilled and semiskilled workers. It also supplies a nation's people with clothing, one of the basic human needs.

History

Prehistoric and ancient times. No one knows when people first made textiles. The earliest evidence of woolen textiles dates from about 6000 B.C. This evidence comes from what is now southern Turkey. Bits of linen from Egypt indicate that people there wove flax about 5000 B.C. Archaeologists have found Egyptian mummies from the 2500's B.C. wrapped in linen as well made as that produced today. By 3000 B.C., cotton was grown in the Indus River Valley in what are now Pakistan and western India. Cotton may also have been used for textiles in the Americas by this time. The Chinese began to cultivate silkworms about 2700 B.C. They developed special looms for silk filaments.

The ancient Greeks used chiefly woolen textiles. They also used some linen. In the 300's B.C., Alexander the Great's army brought cotton goods from what is now Pakistan to Europe. The ancient Romans developed an enormous trade in textiles. They imported woolens from Britain, Gaul, and Spain; linen from Egypt; cottons from India; and silks from China and Persia.

During the Middle Ages, from the A.D. 400's to the early 1500's, the textile industry gradually developed in Europe. The production of woolens centered in England; northern Italy; and Flanders, a region that now covers parts of present-day Belgium, France, and the Netherlands. As the textile industry expanded, production techniques improved, stimulating further growth. The spinning wheel came into use by the 1200's. Meanwhile, Italy had become the silk center of Europe. The invention of a machine to unwind silk from cocoons led to further expansion of Italy's silk industry.

In the large towns of Europe, associations of weavers and other craftworkers regulated textile production. These associations, called *guilds,* established prices and standards of quality for all products made by their members. But the *cottage industry,* also called the *domestic system,* produced most textiles during the Middle Ages. Under this system, merchants delivered raw materials to workers in their homes in rural areas. Later, the merchants collected the work and paid the workers for it by the piece.

The Industrial Revolution. Important developments in textile production continued after the Middle Ages. For example, an English clergyman named William Lee invented a machine for knitting hosiery in 1589. During the 1600's, textile workers in the Netherlands developed improved methods of dyeing and finishing cloth. But the greatest advances in the textile industry occurred during the Industrial Revolution, which began in England in the 1700's. In fact, the Industrial Revolution was largely a "textile revolution" created by a flood of English inventions that enormously increased the production of yarns and fabrics.

In 1733, John Kay, an engineer, invented the *flying shuttle.* This device enabled weavers to pass the filling through the warp yarns mechanically instead of by hand. About 1764, a weaver named James Hargreaves invented the *spinning jenny,* the first machine that could spin more than one yarn at a time. In 1769, Richard Arkwright, a former barber, patented the *water frame,* a spinning machine that ran on water power. A weaver named Samuel Crompton introduced the *spinning mule* in 1779. This machine combined the features of the spinning jenny and the water frame and gradually replaced them both. Edmund Cartwright, an Anglican clergyman, patented the first power loom in 1785.

In the United States, the New England region became the center of the textile industry. In 1790, an English textile worker named Samuel Slater built the first successful water-powered machines for spinning cotton in the United States. The machines were installed in a mill in Pawtucket, R.I. The production of cotton textiles in New England grew rapidly after the American inventor Eli Whitney developed the cotton gin in 1793. Before Whitney's invention, workers had to remove cotton fibers from the seed by hand. This slow process could not meet the textile mills' demand for cotton. The cotton gin separated the fibers far faster than workers could by hand. As a result, textile mills received ever-increasing

supplies of cotton. During the 1920's and 1930's, most of these mills moved to the Southern States, nearer to the supply of cotton.

The age of modern textiles began in 1884, when Hilaire Chardonnet, a French chemist, developed the first practical manufactured fiber. This fiber, now known as rayon, was first produced in the United States in 1910 under the name *artificial silk.* Wallace H. Carothers, an American chemist, developed nylon in 1935. During the 1940's and 1950's, polyester, acrylic, and other manufactured fibers were introduced.

In the 1960's, textile companies began making double-knit fabrics of textured polyester yarns. These fabrics were lighter in weight and more comfortable than double knits made of other materials. As a result, the popularity of knits greatly increased.

Today, new manufacturing processes and devices have made the textile industry one of the most modern of all industries. For example, knitting machines controlled by computers now produce fabrics with highly complex patterns at tremendous speeds. Many textile firms also use high-speed looms that have many tiny shuttles called *darts* instead of a single shuttle. Other looms weave with no shuttles at all. A jet of water or air carries the filling through the warp up to 1,000 times a minute, about four times faster than a shuttle works on a standard loom.   D. S. Hamby

Related articles in *World Book* include:

Biographies

Arkwright, Sir Richard	Hargreaves, James
Chardonnet, Hilaire	Jacquard, Joseph Marie
Crompton, Samuel	Slater, Samuel

Textiles

See the articles on clothing materials that are listed in the *Related articles* section of the **Clothing** article. See also the following articles:

Braiding	Flax
Burlap	Oilcloth
Cambric	Tapestry
Fiber	Twill

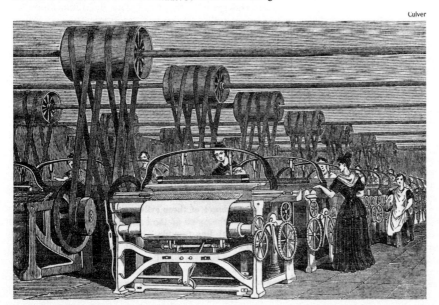

Culver

New textile machinery of the 1800's greatly increased fabric production. In textile mills like the one at the left, women operated looms powered by steam engines or water wheels.

Treatments and processes

Batik	Knitting	Tie dyeing
Bleach	Knitting machine	Waterproofing
Dye	Spinning	Weaving
Embroidery	Spinning jenny	

Other related articles

Brown lung	Guild
Clothing	Industrial Revolution
Cottage industry	Ireland (picture: Textile manu-
Garment Workers' Union, Inter-	facturing)
national Ladies'	Rugs and carpets

Outline

Questions

What two methods of making cloth account for about 90 per cent of all fabrics produced in the United States?

What was the first practical manufactured fiber?

Which industry consumes the largest share of all textile production?

What was the *domestic system*?

How are most carpeting fabrics made in the United States?

What are *gray goods*?

What is the most important natural fiber?

From what substances are most manufactured fibers produced?

How must clothing be labeled in the United States and Canada?

What is *blended yarn? Staple yarn*?

Textile engineering. See Engineering (Other specialized fields).

Texture. See Interior decoration (Pattern and texture; Choosing patterns and textures).

Tezel, Johann. See Tetzel, Johann.

Thackeray, William Makepeace (1811-1863), was one of the great novelists of the English Victorian Age. His *Vanity Fair* is one of the finest and best-known novels in English literature. Thackeray wrote in a colorful, lively style, with a simple vocabulary and clearly structured sentences. These qualities, combined with his honest view of life, give him an important place in the history of realistic literature.

Early career. Thackeray was born in Calcutta, India. In 1817, he was sent to England to live with relatives and begin his education. He later looked back on his school years with mingled affection and dislike. Said Thackeray, "I have the same recollection of Greek in youth that I have of castor oil." He entered Trinity College, Cambridge University, in 1829. No great scholar, he left after a year and a half to travel abroad.

Thackeray had trouble finding a career. He studied law for a short time, and went to art school in Paris. Meanwhile, he had spent his inheritance, losing part of it to professional gamblers. To make a modest living, he turned to writing book reviews, stories, and satirical sketches for magazines.

In 1836, Thackeray married Isabella Shawe. She became mentally ill following the birth of their third daughter in 1840. This tragedy affected Thackeray's natural good humor, making him lonely and depressed. But he needed money more than ever, and he continued turning out articles and stories.

Most of Thackeray's early writings were humorous, and were published under such ridiculous pen names as Michael Angelo Titmarsh. In 1848, he published *The Book of Snobs,* a collection of his magazine writings.

Later career. Thackeray ensured his fame with *Vanity Fair* (1847-1848), probably his best novel. Like most of his books, it was first published in monthly parts. The novel traces the fortunes of upper-middle-class Londoners of the early 1800's.

Thackeray called *Vanity Fair* "a novel without a hero," in keeping with his belief that most people are a mixture of the heroic and the ridiculous. He knew that men and women are complex, and he avoided oversimplifying them. He wrote with affection about kind and gentle Amelia Sedley. But he also called Amelia "a silly little thing." Becky Sharp, more clearly the "heroine," is selfish, cunning, and cynical. Becky is never bitter, however, and readers enjoy seeing her good-naturedly defeat people who are even less admirable than she.

The novel *Pendennis* (1848-1850) is partly autobiographical. It has the mellow, reflective quality that colors much of Thackeray's writing.

Henry Esmond (1852) is set in England in the early 1700's, a period that Thackeray loved. The book describes the loves and adventures of Esmond, who narrates the book. Henry is also only "part hero." Although well meaning, he is given to pious moralizing, which sometimes makes him a most unheroic bore.

The Newcomes (1853-1855) is the complex story of three generations of the Newcome family. Ethel Newcome is one of Thackeray's finest characters. She has gentleness and sympathy, but also intelligence and spirit. Thackeray's later novels show the diminished energy of an author who was ill and tired.

Thackeray's view of life. Thackeray disliked people who were unduly impressed by birth and rank. His skillful ridicule of snobs and hypocrites is even evident amid the broad humor of his early works. His realistic temperament enabled him to see and satirize inconsistencies in life. He once said of one of his characters that he "failed somehow in spite of a mediocrity which ought to have ensured any man a success." Thackeray knew that rogues sometimes do well while the innocent suffer, and that virtuous people can be dull and rascals lively. Such ironic twists in his books were misunderstood by some people, who accused him of being cynical.

Others complained that Thackeray's writings were sentimental. For example, he seemed to admire womanhood as an abstract ideal. When he wrote about young ladies who were gentle and affectionate but perhaps not very bright, he sometimes fell into a style of adoration. But his deep honesty made him show, at the same time, how these sentimental people were often stupid and dull. His critics often fail to see that Thackeray really hated cruelty and greed, and admired goodness and warm-heartedness.   John W. Dodds

Rus Arnold

The boats of merchants and shoppers jam a canal in Bangkok, Thailand's capital and largest city. This traditional "floating market" is one of the city's most picturesque features.

Thailand

Thailand, *TY land,* is a country in Southeast Asia. It is a wet, tropical land with many rivers, forests, and mountains. The people of Thailand are called *Thai.* Most of them live in villages and farm the land. But many villagers move to Thailand's cities each year, and so the urban areas are growing rapidly. Bangkok is the capital and largest city.

Thailand is the only nation in Southeast Asia that has never been ruled by a Western power. Local peoples established the first Thai nation in A.D. 1238. The country was called Siam from 1782 to 1939, when it became known as Thailand. Its name in the Thai language is *Muang Thai,* which means *Land of the Free.*

Government

National government. Thailand is a constitutional monarchy. The nation's Constitution of 1978 provides for a monarch, a prime minister, and a legislature called the National Assembly. Until 1980, only males could serve as monarch. But a law passed that year allows either males or females to hold the office.

Thailand's monarch has an advisory role as chief of state, but the prime minister actually heads the nation's government. The National Assembly nominates the

prime minister, who is then formally appointed by the monarch. The prime minister selects a cabinet, called the Council of Ministers, which may have a maximum of 44 members.

The National Assembly consists of a Senate of 225 members and a House of Representatives with 301 members. The senators are selected by the prime minister with the approval of the monarch and may be replaced at any time. The representatives are elected by the people to four-year terms.

Facts in brief

Capital: Bangkok.
Official language: Thai.
Official name: Muang Thai (Land of the Free).
Area: 198,500 sq. mi. (514,000 km²). *Greatest distances—* north-south, 1,100 mi. (1,770 km); east-west, 480 mi. (772 km). *Coastline—*1,635 mi. (2,631 km).
Elevation: *Highest—*Inthanon Mountain, 8,514 ft. (2,595 m). *Lowest—*sea level.
Population: *Estimated 1989 population—*54,835,000; density, 276 persons per sq. mi. (107 per km²); distribution, 77 per cent rural, 23 per cent urban. *1980 census—*44,824,540. *Estimated 1994 population—*59,481,000.
Chief products: *Agriculture—*rice, cassava, corn, cotton, rubber, sugar cane, tobacco. *Manufacturing—*automobiles, cement, drugs, electronic equipment, food products, paper, plywood, textiles. *Forestry and fishing—*teak, bamboo, rattan, anchovies, mackerel, shellfish. *Mining—*tin, bauxite, iron ore, lead, manganese, natural gas, precious stones, tungsten.
National anthem: "Pleng Chart" ("National Anthem of Thailand").
Money: *Basic unit—*baht. For its price in U.S. dollars, see **Money** (table: Exchange rates).

Herbert P. Phillips, the contributor of this article, is Professor of Anthropology at the University of California, Berkeley, and the author of Thai Peasant Personality.

Thailand's flag was adopted in 1917. The red represents the nation; the white, purity; and the blue, the monarchy.

The coat of arms, adopted in 1910, features the *garuda,* a birdlike creature from Southeast Asian mythology.

WORLD BOOK map

Thailand, a country in Southeast Asia, lies mostly on the Asian mainland. Southern Thailand extends along the Malay Peninsula.

Local government. Thailand is divided into 72 provinces, which, in turn, are divided into 576 districts. Each province has a governor, and every district has a district officer. All these officials are appointed by the minister of the interior. Thailand also has more than 5,300 smaller divisions called *communes,* which consist of a total of almost 50,000 villages. The people of each village elect their own headman. The headmen then choose a *kamnan* from among themselves to serve as the chief administrator of their commune. Every city in Thailand is governed by a mayor and a council, both elected by the people.

Politics. In most cases, a Thai political party comes into power through an election or by a *coup* (sudden revolt) against the ruling party. Thailand has several major political parties and a number of smaller parties. Citizens who are at least 18 years old may vote if they can read and write in Thai.

Courts. The Supreme Court, called the *Sarn Dika,* is the highest court in Thailand. It consists of a chief justice and 21 judges. The Court of Appeals, the second highest court, reviews decisions made by lower courts. All judges of the Supreme Court, and all head judges of the other courts, are appointed by the monarch on the advice of the prime minister.

The armed forces of Thailand consist of an army, a navy, an air force, a national police force, and a village defense corps. The forces have a total membership of

more than 200,000. Men from 21 to 30 years old may be drafted for at least two years of military duty.

The people

Population and ancestry. Thailand has approximately 55 million people. About three-fourths of the Thai live in rural areas. More than 5 million people make their homes in Bangkok.

The majority of the Thai are descendants of Thai-speaking peoples who migrated from southern China between the time period of the A.D. 100's and 900's. Chinese people make up the second largest population group. Most of the rest of the people are immigrants—or descendants of immigrants—from Burma, Kampuchea, Malaysia, or Vietnam. The population also includes some European, Indian, and Japanese people—most of whom live in Bangkok. Small groups of peoples who follow tribal ways of life live in the country's northern mountains.

Way of life. More than 75 per cent of Thailand's people make their living by farming. Large numbers of Thai also work in the fishing, lumbering, and mining industries. In the cities, many have jobs in factories. The nation's Chinese work mainly in commerce.

Most Thai live in villages that range in size from a few hundred to a few thousand people. The villagers raise almost all their own food, including corn, fruit, rice, and *cassava*—a tropical plant used in making tapioca. Every village has a school and a *wat* (Buddhist temple), which serves as the religious and social center of the community. The people enjoy village fairs, harvest celebrations, and other festive occasions.

Since the early 1960's, large numbers of Thai—especially young people—have moved from rural areas to cit-

Maurice G. G. Harvey, Alan Hutchison Library Ltd.

Modern stores and offices line the busy streets of the main business districts of Bangkok. The city is Thailand's chief commercial, cultural, and industrial center.

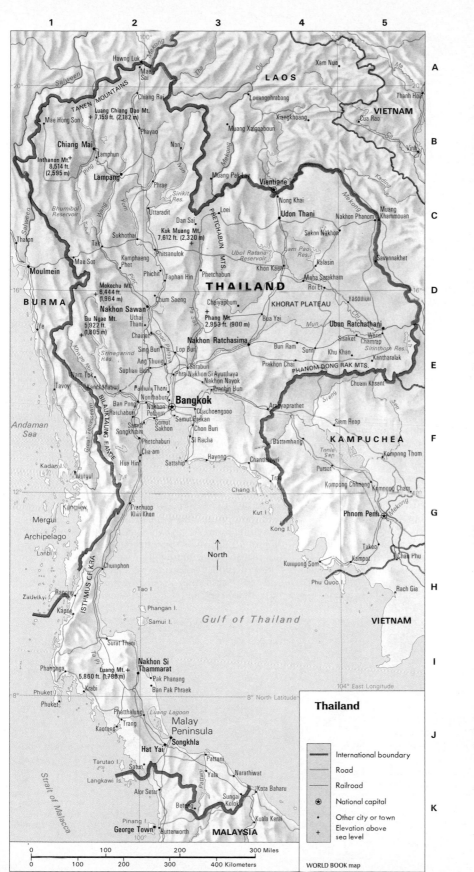

Cities and towns

Ban Pak		
Phraek	22,625	I 2
Ban Pong	25,047	E 2
Bangkok	5,153,902	E 2
Buri Ram	25,899	E 4
Chachoeng-		
sao	37,931	F 3
Chaiyaphum	20,932	D 3
Chanthaburi	30,242	F 3
Chiang Mai	100,146	B 2
Chiang Rai	40,641	A 2
Chon Buri	50,070	F 3
Hat Yai	98,091	J 2
Hua Hin	30,415	F 2
Kalasin	22,152	D 4
Kamphaeng		
Phet	20,200	D 2
Kanchanaburi	29,502	E 2
Khon Kaen	94,019	D 4
Lampang	43,112	B 2
Lop Buri	36,928	E 2
Mae Sot	18,719	C 1
Maha		
Sarakham	32,989	D 4
Nakhon		
Pathom	45,242	E 2
Nakhon		
Phanom	33,237	C 5
Nakhon		
Ratchasima	88,876	E 3
Nakhon Sawan	88,687	D 2
Nakhon Si		
Thammarat	66,558	I 2
Nan	22,564	B 3
Narathiwat	32,146	K 3
Nong Khai	25,032	C 4
Nonthaburi	30,940	E 2
Pattani	32,020	J 3
Phatthalung	29,948	J 2
Phayao	24,400	B 3
Phetchabun	23,763	D 3
Phetchaburi	34,597	F 2
Phichit	18,675	D 2
Phitsanulok	73,240	C 2
Phra Nakhon Si		
Ayutthaya	51,628	E 2
Phrae	19,872	B 2
Phuket	45,155	J 1
Prachin Buri	20,330	F 3
Ratchaburi	43,316	F 2
Rayong	37,305	F 3
Roi Et	31,223	D 4
Sakon		
Nakhon	24,491	C 4
Samut		
Prakan	48,960	F 2
Samut		
Sakhon	47,697	F 2
Samut		
Songkhram	30,419	F 2
Saraburi	46,251	E 3
Si Racha	21,651	F 3
Sisaket	19,823	E 5
Songkhla	72,326	J 2
Sukhothai	21,931	C 2
Sungai Kolok	21,917	K 3
Suphan Buri	22,903	E 2
Surat Thani	35,678	I 2
Surin	88,737	F 4
Tak	20,039	C 2
Trang	44,102	J 2
Ubon		
Ratchathani	48,537	D 5
Udon Thani	81,060	C 4
Uttaradit	33,311	C 2
Warin		
Chamrap	29,586	E 5
Yala	49,283	J 3
Yasothon	19,007	D 5

Physical features

Andaman Sea	F	1
Bilauktaung Range	F	2
Chang Island	G	3
Chao Phraya (river)	E	2
Chi (river)	D	5
Du Ngae Mountain	E	1
Gulf of Thailand	H	3
Inthanon Mountain	B	2
Isthmus of Kra	H	1
Khorat Plateau	D	4
Khwae Noi (river)	E	1
Kok Muang Mountain	C	2
Kut Island	G	4
Luang Mountain	I	2
Luang Chiang Dao		
Mountain	B	1
Luang Lagoon	J	2
Mekong (river)	C	4
Mokochu Mountain	D	2
Mun (river)	D	4
Nan (river)	B	3
Pa Sak (river)	D	3
Phang Mountain	D	3
Phangan Island	H	2
Phanom Dong		
Rak Mountains	E	4
Phetchabun		
Mountains	C	3
Phuket Island	I	1
Ping (river)	B	1
Samui Island	H	2
Ta Pi (river)	I	2
Tanen Mountains	A	2
Tao Island	H	2
Wang (river)	C	2
Yom (river)	C	2

Source: 1980 census.

Middle-class housing in Thailand consists mainly of small, neat, single-family dwellings. The houses in this photograph are in a suburb of Bangkok.

Saul Lockhardt, Advertasia Co., Ltd.

ies in search of jobs and educational opportunities. The rapid growth of Thailand's cities has led to unemployment, crowded living conditions, and other serious problems.

The women of Thailand have more freedom than those of many other Asian nations. Numerous Thai women have jobs in business, education, government, and medicine.

Most urban Thai people wear Western-style clothing. In rural areas, many people—both males and females— wear the traditional *panung,* a colorful cotton or silk garment. A panung, which consists of a piece of cloth, is wrapped tightly around the body. A male's panung extends from the hips to the ankles, and a female's from above the chest to the ankles. For pictures of other Thai clothing, see **Clothing** (Traditional costumes).

Housing. Most Thai villagers live in houses of wood or thatch that stand along rivers and canals. The homes are built on stilts to raise them above the ground for protection against flooding. Families use the area under their house as a shelter for farm animals. A high roof of tile or thatch helps keep the interior cool.

In the cities, many people live in small wooden or stucco houses. A number of the Chinese own shops and live in apartments above them. Some wealthy Thai have beautiful mansions. Poor communities in Thai cities consist either of slums or of housing projects built by the government.

Food. Thai people eat rice with almost every meal. Favorite foods served with rice include *curries* (spicy stews) and salads of meat, fish, and vegetables. The Thai take great pride in their *cuisine* (style of cooking and preparing food). Some communities are famous for their special dishes, and people often travel long distances just to taste these specialties.

Recreation. The Thai enjoy such sports as soccer and *Thai-style boxing,* in which opponents fight with both their hands and feet. In another popular sport,

© Horst Gossler, The Stock House

Thai-style boxing, in which opponents use their feet as well as their hands, is a popular sport throughout Thailand.

Orion Press from Katherine Young

Buddhist monks are dwarfed by a statue that guards the Temple of the Emerald Buddha in Bangkok.

Saul Lockhardt, Advertasia Co., Ltd.

Thai classical dancers act out traditional stories with religious themes. Jewels and embroidery decorate their costumes.

called *takraw,* the players try to keep a wicker ball in the air by using their heads, legs, and feet. Many Thai play *mak ruk,* a type of chess. Favorite forms of recreation involving gambling include cockfights and fish fights, in which male Siamese fightingfish attack each other in jars (see **Fightingfish**). Card games and betting on the national lottery are also popular.

Languages. About 90 per cent of Thailand's people speak Thai, the official language. Thai has four main regional dialects. The dialect of central Thailand is the most common form of the language. A small number of Thai speak Malay and various dialects of Chinese. Many of the nation's secondary schools teach English, but few of the nation's people actually use it.

Religion. More than 95 per cent of the Thai people are Buddhists. They are members of the Therevada school of Buddhism (see **Buddhism** [Buddhist schools]). According to Buddhist custom, men over the age of 20 are expected to serve in the Buddhist monkhood for at least a few months, and more than 40 per cent of them actually do. Most of the Chinese in Thailand practice Confucianism, and the majority of the Malays are Muslims. Hinduism is the main religion among the Indians of Thailand. Most of the Europeans in Thailand, as well as some of the nation's Chinese and Vietnamese, belong to a Christian faith.

Education. More than 85 per cent of Thailand's people 15 years of age or older can read and write. The Thai government operates free elementary schools throughout the country, and all children are required by law to attend school for at least six years. However, most of Thailand's high schools are privately owned and charge tuition. Only about 15 per cent of the people have graduated from high school. Thailand has 17 universities, 43 teachers colleges, and more than 200 vocational schools. But only about 1 per cent of the people are university or teachers college graduates.

The arts in Thailand are greatly influenced by Buddhism. The image of Buddha appears in many Thai paintings and sculptures. The nation's Buddhist temples rank among the best examples of Thai architecture, which combines traditional and modern styles. Modern Thai painting combines traditional religious themes and international styles.

Thai literature is divided into two groups, *wannakhadi* and *wannakam.* Wannakhadi consist of classical dramas and epic poems that were originally written and performed for royalty. Wannakam consist of novels, poems, and short stories about modern Thailand. Most of these works center on the problems and pleasures of everyday life.

The land

Thailand covers 198,500 square miles (514,000 square kilometers). The country has four main land regions: (1) the Northern Mountains, (2) the Khorat Plateau, (3) the Central Plain, and (4) the Southern Peninsula.

The Northern Mountains occupy northwest Thailand and extend along the country's western border to the Malay Peninsula. They are covered by thick forests of evergreen and teak trees, which provide valuable timber. The mountains include Inthanon Mountain, the tallest peak, which rises 8,514 feet (2,595 meters) above sea level.

Many streams flow south from the mountains to the Gulf of Thailand. These streams deposit mud and sand along their banks and help make the soil fertile. Farmers grow rice in the narrow mountain valleys. The region has deposits of copper, iron, and lead.

The Khorat Plateau, which lies in the northeastern part of Thailand, makes up about 30 per cent of the country's land area. It is also the country's most heavily populated region. The plateau is bordered by mountains on the south and west and by the Mekong River on the north and east.

Most of the plateau has sandy soil that holds little moisture. The Mekong, Chi, and Mun rivers provide irrigation water for the farming that takes place there. Rice is the principal crop.

The Central Plain extends between the foothills of the Northern Mountains region and the Gulf of Thailand. The fertile soil of the Central Plain enables farmers to raise more rice there than anywhere else in Thailand. Four rivers—the Nan, Ping, Wang, and Yom—unite in the northern part of the plain and become the Chao Phraya River, which is the country's chief transportation route.

The Southern Peninsula, which forms part of the Malay Peninsula, consists mainly of jungle, with some mountains and rolling hills. Many streams flow through the narrow valleys and flood small coastal plains. In the northern part of this region, Thailand and Burma share the Malay Peninsula. There, only a narrow strip of land belongs to Thailand.

The southern part of the region occupies the entire width of the Malay Peninsula. This mountainous area has fertile soil, and rubber trees thrive there. It also has large deposits of tin.

Animal life. Thailand's forest and jungle areas abound with boars, crocodiles, deer, tigers, and such poisonous snakes as banded kraits and cobras—including king cobras. In the past, many elephants lived in the

Edward S. Ross

The Northern Mountains region includes Thailand's highest peak, 8,514-foot (2,595-meter) Inthanon Mountain, *background.* In the foreground is a dwelling of the region's Meo people.

© Stephanie Colasanti

In Thailand's teak forests, elephants haul heavy logs to rivers to be floated downstream to sawmills. Strong and durable, teak is used mainly for shipbuilding and making fine furniture.

Charles Marden Fitch

Tin mining contributes greatly to Thailand's foreign trade. Most of the country's tin mines, including the one shown here, are in the mountains of the Southern Peninsula region.

wild in Thailand. However, today most of the country's elephants have been domesticated. They serve as beasts of burden.

Climate

Thailand has a tropical climate. Most of the country has three seasons—a hot dry spring, a hot wet summer, and a mild winter. Bangkok has an average temperature of 62° F. (17° C) in January and 98° F. (37° C) in May. The Northern Mountains region is cooler, with temperatures averaging 32° F. (0° C) in January and 90° F. (32° C) in May.

From July to December, winds called *monsoons* cause heavy rains throughout Thailand. The Southern Peninsula region receives an average of about 100 inches (254 centimeters) of rain yearly. Bangkok has an average annual rainfall of 55 inches (140 centimeters).

Economy

Thailand has a developing economy that depends mainly on agriculture and manufacturing. Over 75 per cent of the nation's workers make their living by farming, compared with only about 7 per cent in manufacturing. However, manufactured goods and agricultural products contribute about equally to the Thai economy. Large numbers of people have jobs in the fishing, forestry, and mining industries, and many work in commerce, government, and tourism. The economy operates as a free enterprise system, though the government sets prices for such important goods as rice and gasoline.

Agriculture. Thai farmers cultivate about 25 per cent of the nation's land, mostly to grow rice. Other leading crops include cassava, corn, cotton, pineapples, rubber, sugar cane, and tobacco. Thailand also produces bananas, coconuts, silk, soybeans, and *jute,* a fiber plant used in making rope. Farms in Thailand average about 6 acres (2 hectares), and more than 75 per cent of the farmers own their land.

Manufacturing has become increasingly important in Thailand since 1960. The nation's leading industries produce cement, food products, paper, plywood, and

textiles. Many international companies operate factories in the Bangkok area. These plants assemble automobiles and electronic equipment, and manufacture drugs and other products.

Forestry and fishing. Forests cover about 60 per cent of Thailand. Teak is the chief forest product. Elephants move the heavy teak logs to rivers, and the timber is floated downstream to lumber mills for sawing and shipping. Other important forest products include bamboo and *rattan,* a tough, stringy material that comes from the stems of certain palm trees.

Anchovies, mackerel, and such shellfish as crabs and shrimp are caught in Thailand's rivers and coastal waters. Most Thai farmers raise fish and shellfish in ponds that they build on their property.

Mining. Tin is Thailand's most important mineral, and the nation ranks among the world's leading tin producers. Mines in Thailand also provide large amounts of bauxite, iron ore, lead, manganese, precious stones, and tungsten. Natural gas is obtained from deposits in the Gulf of Thailand.

Tourism is an important source of income for Thailand. Tourists are especially attracted to the country's beaches and historical sites, and to the night life of the larger cities.

Foreign trade. Thailand's chief exports include rice, rubber, tapioca products, teak, and tin. The Thai also export corn, sugar, and tobacco. The nation imports such products as chemicals, fuels, and machinery. Thailand trades mainly with Japan, the United States, and China.

Transportation in Thailand ranks among the best in Southeast Asia. The country has about 8,100 miles (13,000 kilometers) of paved roads and more than 2,400 miles (3,800 kilometers) of railroad track. Rivers and canals in Thailand provide local transportation for passengers and cargo. Bangkok is the country's largest and busiest port.

Four international airports provide daily flights between Thailand and other Asian nations, various European countries, and Australia. Local airlines serve the nation's major cities.

Communication. Thailand has approximately 50 daily newspapers, about 20 of which are published in Bangkok. Most of the newspapers are published in Thai, and the rest in Chinese or English. Telegraph and telephone systems link the principal cities. The nation has 4 major television networks and more than 200 radio stations. The government owns and operates all the TV and radio stations.

History

Early days. People have lived in what is now Thailand for more than 5,000 years. Archaeological evidence indicates that people in what is now the northeastern Thai village of Non Nok Tha grew rice for food more than 5,000 years ago. The evidence is the world's first known record of the cultivation of rice—the most widely eaten of all human foods. The ancestors of most present-day Thai probably moved into the region from southern China between the time period of the A.D. 100's and 900's. They established many settlements, and in 1238, the Thai formed the first Thai nation. They named it *Sukothai,* which means *Dawn of Happiness.* King Ramkhamhaeng, one of the early rulers of Sukothai, invented the Thai alphabet. Sukothai expanded and prospered and, by 1350, occupied most of what became Thailand.

Invasions and wars. In 1350, a group of Thai people established the kingdom and the city of Ayutthaya in what is now the central region of Thailand. By the late 1300's, Sukothai had declined in importance. The Ayutthaya kingdom absorbed it. The city of Ayutthaya served as the Thai capital from the mid-1300's to the mid-1700's. During that period, the kingdom of Ayutthaya fought numerous wars with the Malays to the south, the Burmese to the west, and the Khmer of Kampuchea to the east. In 1431, Thai forces invaded Kampuchea and captured its capital, Angkor.

European contact for the Thai began when Portuguese traders came to Ayutthaya in the early 1500's. During the 1600's, Spain, England, France, Japan, and The Netherlands also established trade there. The Thai granted some nations—including France, England, and the Netherlands—*rights of extraterritoriality.* These rights allowed the people of the foreign nations to live in Ayutthaya under the laws of their own countries (see **Extraterritoriality**).

During the late 1600's, many young Thai began going to schools in Europe, where they learned Western ideas and customs. At the same time, European powers began to interfere in Ayutthaya's internal affairs. This interference angered the Thai. They forced all Europeans to leave the country, canceled the extraterritorial rights of some of the European nations, and resisted any contact with Western nations.

A new dynasty. Burmese troops invaded Ayutthaya in 1767 and destroyed the capital. But Thai forces, led by General Phya Taksin, soon drove the Burmese out of the country. Taksin became king and established a new capital at Thonburi.

In 1782, General Phya Chakri replaced Taksin as king. Chakri took the title Rama I and established the Chakri dynasty, which still reigns in Thailand. In 1782, the nation's name was changed to Siam and the Thai capital was moved from Thonburi across the Chao Phraya River to Bangkok.

King Mongkut (Rama IV), who ruled from 1851 to 1868, was one of Siam's most influential monarchs. He employed advisers from Western nations and encouraged his people to study Western languages and modern science. Mongkut also resumed trade relations with France, Great Britain, and other countries, and granted them extraterritorial rights.

King Chulalongkorn (Rama V), Mongkut's son, continued the social reforms started by his father. During his reign, from 1873 to 1910, Chulalongkorn abolished slavery in Siam, reorganized the government, and established a public education system designed to serve all the nation's children.

World War I and World War II. During World War I (1914-1918), Siam supported France and Great Britain against Germany and Austria-Hungary. Some Thai soldiers fought in Europe. In return for Siam's help in the war, France and Great Britain gave up their rights of extraterritoriality.

In 1932, a group of Thai who had been educated in France revolted against King Prajadhipok (Rama VII). They forced him to change the government from an absolute monarchy to a constitutional monarchy. In 1935, Prajadhipok gave up the throne in favor of his 10-year-old nephew, Ananda Mahidol (Rama VIII). A *regency* (group of temporary rulers) governed the country for the young king. Some members of the government were military officials, and others were civilians. The civilians held control at first, but the military officers took over in 1938. The country's name was changed to Thailand in 1939.

In 1940, during World War II, Thailand demanded the return of land that King Chulalongkorn had given French Indochina before World War I. Japan supported Thailand's demand and forced Indochina to return the land. In 1941, Japan invaded Thailand. The Thai resisted for a few hours but then signed a treaty of alliance with Japan. That same year, the Japanese attacked the United States military bases at Pearl Harbor in Hawaii, and the United States went to war against Japan. Thailand declared war on the United States and Great Britain in 1942. During the war, a Free Thai Movement worked against the Japanese within Thailand.

After World War II. Field Marshal Pibul Songgram, who had served as prime minister during the Japanese occupation, ruled Thailand from 1946 to 1957. Pibul was overthrown by Field Marshal Sarit Thanarat, who ruled the country until his death in 1963. Sarit brought widespread economic development to Thailand and strengthened the nation's ties with the United States. His successor, Field Marshal Thanom Kittikachorn, continued these policies. Thanom permitted the United States to build air bases in Thailand. In 1965, during the Vietnam War, United States forces began using the air bases to attack Communist forces in Vietnam, Kampuchea, and Laos. Thailand also sent troops to Vietnam to fight on the side of South Vietnam and the United States.

In 1967, Thailand, Indonesia, Malaysia, the Philippines, and Singapore formed the Association of Southeast Asian Nations (ASEAN). Brunei joined the organization in 1984. ASEAN promotes economic, cultural, and social cooperation among its members.

In 1973, university students in Thailand led a civilian revolt against the Thai government. For the next three years, Thailand had a series of democratically elected governments. This democratic period ended in October 1976 after conservative groups attacked radical students at Thammasat University in Bangkok. About 40 people died in the fighting, and thousands of others were arrested. The military then took control of the government until 1979, when general elections were held. Since then, all of Thailand's governments have been democratically elected.

Thailand today is one of the most prosperous nations in Southeast Asia, but it faces serious problems. Since 1975, after the end of the Vietnam War, thousands of refugees have moved to Thailand from Kampuchea, Laos, and Vietnam. The Thai government provides the refugees with food, clothing, and shelter, and the provision of such aid is a considerable drain on the nation's economy. In addition, continued conflicts between Vietnamese and Kampucheans near Thailand's borders represent a constant threat to the peace and security of the nation.   Herbert P. Phillips

Related articles in *World Book* include:

Asia (pictures: A Buddhist monk; River transportation)	Clothing (pictures: Religious clothing; Traditional costumes)
Association of Southeast Asian Nations	Mekong River
Bangkok	Southeast Asia Treaty Organization
Buddhism	Teak

Outline

I. Government
   A. National government
   B. Local government
   C. Politics
   D. Courts
   E. The armed forces
II. The people
   A. Population and ancestry
   B. Way of life
   C. Housing
   D. Food
   E. Recreation
   F. Languages
   G. Religion
   H. Education
   I. The arts
III. The land
   A. The Northern Mountains
   B. The Khorat Plateau
   C. The Central Plain
   D. The Southern Peninsula
   E. Animal life
IV. Climate
V. Economy
   A. Agriculture
   B. Manufacturing
   C. Forestry and fishing
   D. Mining
   E. Tourism
   F. Foreign trade
   G. Transportation
   H. Communication
VI. History

Questions

How does Buddhism influence the arts in Thailand?
What are some popular Thai dishes?
How did King Mongkut help promote the culture of Thailand?
How do elephants serve the Thai lumber industry?
What was the first Thai nation? When was it formed?
What is a *wat*? A *panung*? A *kamnan*?
What is Thailand's major rice-producing area?
How does Thai-style boxing differ from other boxing?
What is Thailand's principal crop? Chief mineral?
What is Thailand's name in Thai? What does it mean in English?

Additional resources

American University. *Thailand: A Country Study.* 5th ed. U.S. Government Printing Office, 1981.
Lewis, Paul and Elaine. *Peoples of the Golden Triangle: Six Tribes in Thailand.* Thames & Hudson, 1984.
Thailand. Ed. by Charles Levine and Hans Hoefer. Prentice-Hall, 1983. Guidebook with many photographs.
Wyatt, David K. *Thailand: A Short History.* Yale, 1984.

Thalassemia, *THAL uh SEE mee uh,* is a hereditary blood disease that causes anemia. It occurs chiefly among children whose ancestors came from the area near the Mediterranean Sea. Thalassemia also afflicts black Americans and some Asian and Middle Eastern peoples.

The bodies of children with thalassemia do not produce enough *hemoglobin,* a pigment that gives red blood cells their color. Hemoglobin also carries oxygen to body tissues. A shortage of hemoglobin deprives the victim's organs of the oxygen they need. Symptoms of thalassemia are present at birth or appear about six months later. They include pale skin, tiredness, irritability, poor appetite, and retarded growth. The child develops an enlarged heart, liver, and spleen. The disease also deforms and weakens certain bones, especially those in the face.

The severest form of the disease is *thalassemia major,* also called *Cooley's anemia.* It occurs in children who inherit the hemoglobin defect from both parents. Victims of thalassemia major may die in infancy if not properly treated. Many others die in early adulthood as a result of the build-up of iron, especially in the heart. A milder form, *thalassemia intermedia,* occurs in children who inherit a severe form of the defect from one parent or a mild form from both. It is not fatal in most cases. People who inherit the defect from only one parent usually get *thalassemia minor.* Such individuals are called *carriers* of the disease because they do not have its symptoms but may pass it on to their children.

Thalassemia cannot be cured, but it can be treated by blood transfusions given every three to six weeks. This treatment relieves the symptoms, but it causes excess iron to accumulate in the heart, pancreas, and other organs. The deposits of iron often lead to diabetes and heart failure. Researchers are working to develop drugs and techniques to remove the iron deposits from the body.   Dominick Sabatino

Thaler. See Dollar.

Thales, *THAY leez* (625?-546? B.C.), was the earliest known Greek philosopher. He was born in Miletus in Asia Minor. All that is known about Thales and his thought came from brief and scattered reports by later historians and philosophers.

According to the Greek philosopher Aristotle, Thales was the first philosopher to attempt to discover the underlying material source of all things. Aristotle wrote that Thales believed that this substance was water. He also reported that Thales believed that magnets have souls because of their ability to move iron.

Thales was perhaps the first individual to bring a philosophic and scientific approach to subjects that had previously been given mythological and supernatural explanations. He was the first to use reasoning and observation in attempting to answer questions about human beings and the universe. Thales may therefore be considered the founder of the philosophical and scientific tradition in the Western world.   S. Marc Cohen

See also **Pre-Socratic philosophy** (Early Pre-Socratic philosophers).

Thalia. See Graces; Muses.

Thalidomide. See Drug (Testing with people).

Thallium, *THAL ee uhm,* is a soft, bluish-gray metallic element that looks like lead. Most thallium comes from iron pyrites, in which traces of the element occur as an impurity. It also occurs in the minerals crookesite, hutchinsonite, and lorandite. Sir William Crookes, an English scientist, discovered thallium in 1861.

Thallium has an atomic number of 81 and an atomic weight of 204.383. Its chemical symbol is Tl. Thallium melts at 303.5° C and boils at 1457° ($\pm$10°) C. At 20° C, it has a density of 11.85 grams per cubic centimeter (see **Density**). Thallium is quite toxic to human beings. Its toxic effects are *cumulative*—that is, they build up over an extended period of time. Too much exposure to thallium may cause nerve damage, emotional change, cramps and convulsions, and eventually coma and death due to respiratory paralysis.

Thallium and its compounds have various uses. However, these uses are limited because of the chemical's highly toxic nature. A radioactive isotope of the element, Tl-201, is useful for diagnosing certain types of heart disease. The compound thallium sulfate is widely used in ant and rat poisons. Thallium bromide, thallium iodide, and thallium sulfide undergo changes when they are exposed to infrared radiation. As a result, they are used in devices for detecting and measuring such radiant energy.   Raymond E. Davis

Thallophyte, *THAL uh fyt,* is a plant in the subkingdom *Thallophyta.* This group includes the more primitive plants. They may consist of only one cell, or of many cells. But they do not have complex organs such as roots, stems, and leaves. Thallophytes include *algae,* or pond scums and seaweeds; *fungi,* or molds and mushrooms; and *bacteria.* See also **Algae; Bacteria; Fungi; Plant** (table: A classification)   George B. Cummins

Thames, *tehmz,* **River,** is the most famous and most important river in England. The Thames is also the longest river entirely within England. The Severn, partly in England and partly in Wales, is longer. The Thames flows 215 miles (346 kilometers) from the Cotswold Hills in south-central England to southeastern England, where it empties into the North Sea. The river serves as a major English trade route. For location, see **Great Britain** (terrain map).

A number of cities lie along the River Thames, including Oxford, Reading, Kingston upon Thames, London, Tilbury, and Southend-on-Sea. The river winds through

© Roger Markham-Smith, Vision Impact
The River Thames flows through the heart of London, past many famous landmarks. Tower Bridge, *background,* is one of 15 London bridges that span the Thames.

the center of London, passing such famous buildings as the Houses of Parliament and the Tower of London. The Thames measures about 5 miles (8 kilometers) wide at its mouth on the North Sea. The sea's tides affect the lower part of the Thames.

London owes its origin and much of its importance to the Thames River. In London, industries were established on the banks of the river and the city became England's most important trading port. The London docks were built on the river during the 1800's. However, in the 1900's, most of the shipping activity was moved from London to Tilbury. Oil refineries stand at the mouth of the river. A portion of the lower Thames has been *dredged* (deepened by digging up the river bottom) to allow large ships to sail inland from the North Sea.   Adrian Robinson

See also **Great Britain** (picture: The Houses of Parliament).

Thane is an Anglo-Saxon title which was used for many years in early England. The word thane had many meanings. At various times it meant servant, attendant, retainer, or official. Early England had a system of thanehood which was similar to the later system of knighthood. Thanehood was open to freemen, not of noble birth, who fulfilled the following conditions: gaining control of a certain amount of land, making three sea voyages, or doing military service.

A thane of ordinary standing received a manor from the lord he served. In time, a successful thane might become an *earl* (member of the higher nobility). In wartime, royal thanes formed the king's personal bodyguard. The title has not been used since the reign of William the Conqueror.   Robert S. Hoyt

Thanksgiving Day is a day set aside each year for giving thanks to God for blessings received during the year. On this day, people give thanks with feasting and prayer. The holiday is celebrated in the United States and Canada.

The first Thanksgiving Days in New England were harvest festivals, or days for thanking God for plentiful crops. For this reason, the holiday still takes place late in the fall, after the crops have been gathered. For thousands of years, people in many lands have held harvest festivals. The American Thanksgiving Day probably grew out of the harvest-home celebrations of England.

In the United States, Thanksgiving is usually a family day, celebrated with big dinners and joyous reunions. The very mention of Thanksgiving often calls up memories of kitchens and pantries crowded with good things to eat. Thanksgiving is also a time for serious religious thinking, church services, and prayer.

The first Thanksgiving observance in America was entirely religious and did not involve feasting. On Dec. 4, 1619, a group of 38 English settlers arrived at Berkeley Plantation, on the James River near what is now Charles City, Va. The group's charter required that the day of arrival be observed yearly as a day of thanksgiving to God.

The first Thanksgiving in New England was celebrated in Plymouth less than a year after the Plymouth colonists had settled in America. The first dreadful winter in Massachusetts had killed about half the members of the colony. But new hope arose in the summer of 1621. The settlers expected a good corn harvest, despite

Oil painting on canvas (1935); The Art Institute of Chicago, Mr. and Mrs. Frank G. Logan Purchase Prize

Thanksgiving, **a painting by the American artist Doris E. Lee, shows women preparing Thanksgiving dinner.**

poor crops of peas, wheat, and barley. Thus, in early autumn, governor William Bradford arranged a harvest
festival to give thanks to God for the progress the colony had made.

The festival lasted three days. The men of Plymouth
had shot ducks, geese, and turkeys. The menu also included clams, eel and other fish, wild plums and leeks,
corn bread, and watercress. The women of the settlement supervised cooking over outdoor fires. About 90
Indians also attended the festival. They brought five deer
to add to the feast. Everyone ate outdoors at large tables
and enjoyed games and a military review. Similar harvest Thanksgivings were held in Plymouth during the
next several years, but no traditional date was set.

Later Thanksgiving Days in the United States. The
custom of Thanksgiving Day spread from Plymouth to
other New England colonies. During the Revolutionary
War, eight special days of thanks were observed for victories and for being saved from dangers. In 1789, President George Washington issued a general proclamation
naming November 26 a day of national thanksgiving. In
the same year, the Protestant Episcopal Church announced that the first Thursday in November would be
a regular yearly day for giving thanks.

For many years, the country had no regular national
Thanksgiving Day. But some states had a yearly Thanksgiving holiday. By 1830, New York had an official state
Thanksgiving Day, and other Northern states soon followed its example. In 1855, Virginia became the first

Southern state to adopt the custom.

Sarah Josepha Hale, the editor of *Godey's Lady's Book,*
worked many years to promote the idea of a national
Thanksgiving Day. Then President Abraham Lincoln proclaimed the last Thursday in November 1863, as "a day
of thanksgiving and praise to our beneficent Father." See
Hale, Sarah Josepha.

Each year afterward, for 75 years, the President formally proclaimed that Thanksgiving Day should be celebrated on the last Thursday of November. But in 1939,
President Franklin D. Roosevelt set it one week earlier.
He wanted to help business by lengthening the shopping period before Christmas. Congress ruled that after
1941 the fourth Thursday of November would be observed as Thanksgiving Day and would be a legal federal holiday.

Thanksgiving Day in Canada is celebrated in much
the same way as in the United States. It was formerly celebrated on the last Monday in October. But in 1957, the
Canadian government proclaimed the second Monday
in October to be the holiday.   Joan R. Gundersen

Additional resources

Barth, Edna. *Turkeys, Pilgrims, and Indian Corn: The Story of the
Thanksgiving Symbols.* Seabury, 1975.
It's Time for Thanksgiving. Comp. by Elizabeth H. Sechrist and Ja-
nette Woolsey. Macrae Smith, 1957.
Jupo, Frank J. *The Thanksgiving Book.* Dodd, 1980.
Thanksgiving: Feast and Festival. Comp. by Mildred C. Luckhardt.
Abingdon, 1966.

Thant, *thahnt,* **U,** *oo* (1909-1974), a Burmese diplomat, served as secretary-general of the United Nations (UN) from 1962 to 1971. He had become acting secretary-general in 1961, filling the unexpired term of the late Dag Hammarskjöld. U Thant had only one name, as do most Burmese. *U,* a title of respect, has a meaning similar to *Mister.* U Thant was born in Pantanaw, Burma, and attended University College in Rangoon. From 1928 to 1947, U Thant taught school and worked as a journalist. He strongly opposed colonialism. In 1947, he became Burma's press director. He was named director of broadcasting in 1948. In 1957, U Thant became chairman of the Burmese UN delegation. See also **United Nations** (picture).

Thar Desert, *tuhr* or *tahr,* stretches northwest of the Aravalli Range in India across Rajasthan to the Indus River plain in Pakistan. It is also called the Indian Desert. The Punjab region forms its northern limits. For location, see **India** (physical map).

The Thar Desert covers 74,000 square miles (192,000 square kilometers). Less than 10 inches (25 centimeters) of rain falls there annually. Formerly, few people lived in the Thar Desert. They raised sheep where there was enough water for grass. In 1986, however, the Indira Gandhi Canal was completed and irrigation projects were begun. The projects have attracted some farmers to the area.

The Thar is rich in various types of precious minerals and stones. Pokharan, in the desert, is the site of India's nuclear test facilities. One of India's major nuclear power plants is located in the Thar at Kota. P. P. Karan

Tharp, Twyla, *TWY luh* (1941-), is an American dancer and *choreographer* (composer of dances). Her works feature a wide variety of movements from many types of dance, including ballet, social dances, and tapdancing. Tharp combines these movements to create dances that are filled with clever gestures and abrupt, unexpected changes in motion. Her choreography appears to be spontaneous, but actually it is carefully planned.

During the 1960's, Tharp created dances to be performed without music. But beginning with *Eight Jelly Rolls* (1971), she has used a wide variety of music to accompany her works. For example, *As Time Goes By* (1973) is performed to music by the Austrian composer Joseph Haydn. *Deuce Coupe* (1973 and 1974) is danced to the rock music of the Beach Boys. *Sue's Leg* (1975) has an accompaniment of music by the American jazz pianist and composer Fats Waller. Tharp also choreographed the motion picture *Hair* (1979).

Tharp was born in Portland, Ind. She formed her own dance company in 1965. It merged with the American Ballet Theatre (ABT) in 1988, and Tharp became resident choreographer and artistic associate of the ABT.
Dianne L. Woodruff

Thatcher, Margaret Hilda (1925-), became prime minister of Great Britain in 1979. She is the first woman ever to hold the office. Thatcher became prime minister after the Conservative Party—which she heads—defeated the Labour Party in parliamentary general elections in 1979. She remained in office after her party again won parliamentary elections in 1983 and 1987. She has held the office longer than any other British prime minister in the 1900's. A strong opponent of the Labour Party's socialist policies, Thatcher has worked to reduce government control over Britain's economy. Under Thatcher, the government has sold its interests in some industries to private citizens and businesses. Britain has experienced economic expansion.

Wide World
Margaret Thatcher

Thatcher was born Margaret Hilda Roberts in Grantham, Lincolnshire, England. She married Denis Thatcher, a London business executive, in 1951. She received a degree in chemistry from Oxford University, and worked as a research chemist in the early 1950's. She also studied law. In 1953, she became an attorney specializing in tax law. Thatcher was elected to the House of Commons in 1959. She was secretary of state for education and science from 1970 to 1974. In 1975, she became the first woman to head a British political party, when she was elected leader of the Conservative Party by the party's members of Parliament.
Richard Rose

Thayer, Sylvanus, *sihl VAY nuhs* (1785-1872), was an American Army officer who became known as father of West Point. From 1817 to 1833, Colonel Thayer served as superintendent of the United States Military Academy at West Point. His long service allowed him to impress his professional standards and his ideas of duty, honor, and loyalty on several generations of cadets. He was born in Braintree, Mass. H. A. DeWeerd

© Martha Swope
A Twyla Tharp dance, *Deuce Coupe,* presents dancers performing to the rock music of the Beach Boys. Tharp has choreographed works to classical music and jazz as well as rock.

A scene from *Macbeth* by William Shakespeare; Robert C. Ragsdale

The Stratford Festival in Canada annually presents classics of world theater.

Theater

Theater is an art form in which a series of events, usually a written play, is acted out by performers who impersonate the characters. It generally takes place in an auditorium before an audience.

Opening night—or any other night—in a theater is an exciting event, whether in a Broadway playhouse or a high school auditorium. Part of the excitement takes place in front of the stage where the audience waits eagerly for the performance. But the excitement is perhaps even greater backstage. There, the people involved in a play wait to see whether the audience approves of the result of weeks or even months of hard work.

The word *theater* comes from the Greek word *theatron,* meaning *a place for seeing.* In this sense, the word still refers to a building in which plays are performed. However, theater in a broader sense includes all aspects of play production. Theater also refers to a part of human culture that began in primitive times.

Although theater is not the same as *drama,* the words are often used interchangeably. Drama refers to the script of a play—the written work that is used as the basis for theatrical performances. Some critics believe that a play is not really a play until it has been performed

in a theater for an audience. Others argue that the script is only a blueprint that the director and other interpretive artists use as the basis for performance.

The theater is perhaps the most complex of the arts because it requires so many kinds of artists for its creation. These specialists include the playwright, performers, director, scene designer, costumer, and lighting designer. For many productions, musicians and a *choreographer* (dance composer) are needed. The theater is sometimes called a *mixed art* because it combines the script of the playwright, the scenic background of the architect and painter, and the speech and movement of the actors and actresses.

In the earliest theatrical performances, the dramatist performed all artistic functions, including acting. Gradually, specialists developed and the various theater arts took shape. The actor and the playwright gained recognition first, probably because they needed each other in order to bring their arts to life.

In the modern theater, a director is needed to settle differences between performers over such matters as interpretation of lines and movements on stage. The director also plans most of the stage action and coordinates it with the scenic background, costumes, lights, sound effects, music, dancing, and other elements.

This article describes how the theater arts are used to create a play. For a discussion of the history of written drama and theater practices, see **Drama.**

The contributor of this article is Oscar G. Brockett, Professor of Drama and Waggener Professor of Fine Arts at the University of Texas.

Every theater building has three basic parts: (1) the auditorium, (2) the stage, and (3) work areas.

The auditorium is where the audience sits. In the broadest sense, it also includes such facilities as the box office, lobby, entrances and exits, rest rooms, and refreshment stands.

A well-designed auditorium allows every person in the audience to see and hear without strain. It also permits the spectators to reach and leave their seats easily. The interior is decorated in a pleasing fashion that does not distract attention from the stage. Auditoriums may be large or small, and they vary in their basic characteristics. The seats are either all on the main floor, or on the main floor and in one or more balconies. The audience watches the action of the play from one, two, three, or all four sides. The distance between the closest spectators and the stage varies greatly from one auditorium to another.

The stage. Three basic types of stages are used in today's theater: (1) the proscenium stage, (2) the open or platform stage, and (3) the theater-in-the-round or arena stage. Each of these types creates a different relationship between the performers and the audience, and each requires certain adjustments in play production.

The *proscenium stage* is designed to be viewed only from the front. It is sometimes called a "picture frame" stage, because the opening through which the audience sees the action forms a frame for the performers and scenery. This frame is called a *proscenium arch*. Normally, the plays are performed behind it.

A proscenium stage has a curtain that is generally used to conceal or reveal the stage. The curtain may be closed to permit changes in scenery, to indicate the passage of time, or to mark the act or scene divisions of a play. Scenery can be placed on three sides of the stage. The performers enter or leave the stage by way of the *wings* (sides) or the back, depending on the location of doors or other openings in the set.

Most proscenium stages are farther from the audience than are open or arena stages. An orchestra pit or a forestage area may be between the seats and the acting area behind the proscenium arch. The scenery is in three dimensions, but is viewed only from the front.

Most *open stages* have seats arranged around three sides of a raised platform that extends into the auditorium. The purpose of the open stage is to bring audience and performers closer together than the proscenium stage can.

Because the audience sits on three sides of an open stage, little scenery can be used. Often, there is no curtain. An open stage has a limited capacity for realistic effects, but it is well suited for productions written for a theater with a large acting platform. Such plays include many by Shakespeare. The scenery, as well as the acting and other elements, must be planned so they can be seen from three sides at the same time. Large units of

Auditorium Theatre, Chicago (Hedrich-Blessing)

A proscenium stage permits the audience to see a play only from the front. Plays are usually performed behind a frame called the *proscenium arch,* which encloses the stage area.

The Stratford Festival Thrust Stage, Ontario, Canada

An open stage extends into the auditorium on three sides. This stage permits a close relationship between audience and performers, but limits large set pieces to the rear of the stage.

scenery can be used only at the back of the stage, or the audience's view will be blocked.

A *theater-in-the-round* has no stage as such. The performers act in an open space at floor level in the middle of the auditorium. The audience sits in seats arranged in bleacher fashion around all four sides of the acting area. Most theaters-in-the-round can seat only about 200 people. Thus, the performers and audience have a close relationship. Spectators sit near enough to see fine shadings of the performers' expressions and gestures.

A limited kind and amount of scenery can be used in a theater-in-the-round. Because the audience sits on all sides of the acting area, scenery must be low enough to allow the area to be seen from every angle. Most of these theaters do not have curtains, and so scene changes must be made either in darkness or in view of the audience. Pieces of scenery are moved through the aisles of the auditorium. Since the scenery is seen at close view, it must be built with great attention to detail. The performers turn often so each part of the audience can see them from the front as much as possible.

Work areas in a fully equipped theater include shops to make costumes and scenery, rehearsal and dressing rooms, storage space, lighting booths, and office space. Only such huge theaters as the Metropolitan Opera House have all these facilities. Most professional theaters do not have equipment to build scenery, and many nonprofessional groups work in limited space.

© Peter Gonzalez

A theater-in-the-round is an open area with the audience sitting on all four sides. The actors and actresses must adjust their performances so the entire audience can see and hear. Scenery must be low enough not to obstruct the view of anyone in the audience.

In the modern theater, the director is responsible for the artistic effectiveness of the production as a whole. He or she decides how the script is interpreted and coordinates the efforts of all the other artists. The director ordinarily has five major duties: (1) analyzing the play and determining the interpretation; (2) working with the playwright, technicians, and designers of scenery, lighting, and costumes in planning the production; (3) casting the performers; (4) supervising rehearsals; and (5) coordinating each element of the final production.

Interpreting the script. The director must be thoroughly familiar with the play in order to cast and rehearse the performers intelligently and guide the various designers. He or she studies the play's construction, noting its pattern of preparation, complications, crisis, and resolution. The director also examines the devices the author uses to tell the story and to build suspense. For this analysis, the play may be divided into short scenes separated by the entrance or exit of characters. Then the function of each scene is examined. Why do the characters behave as they do? What is the predominant mood? How is each scene related to those before and after it?

The director must understand each character as it functions in the play and what is demanded of the performer who will play the role. The director learns each character's physical characteristics, personality, emotional range, and vocal qualities. The scenic, costume, and lighting requirements must be visualized. The mood of the setting, its arrangement for the flow of action, and its suitability as background for the characters and events must also be pictured. The director also may study the background of the author and the period of the play.

Problems of interpretation vary according to whether the play is historical, a revival of a recent Broadway success, or an original drama. In producing historical plays, the director encounters special problems. Changes may be required in the script to make sure the play will be understood by a modern audience. The director might modernize the language or cut speeches or entire scenes. The director also might try to make a play more meaningful to modern audiences by changing its time and place. For example, *Hamlet* has been costumed in modern dress. Perhaps the director will change the emphasis of a play to give a new interpretation to a character. Shylock in *The Merchant of Venice* was played as a comic character during the 1600's, but most modern productions emphasize his pathetic aspects.

When working with a recent play, the director may be able to obtain a detailed account of how the original production was staged. In producing a new play, the director works directly with the playwright, suggesting changes and cuts. This process of rewriting may continue throughout the rehearsal period.

Working with the designers. Before beginning rehearsals, the director discusses the interpretation of the play with the scenic, costume, and lighting designers. These experts make suggestions about design, and the director may make specific requests. For example, doors may be needed at particular places on the stage.

The director makes sure that the proposed settings reflect the action, mood, theme, characters, and period of the play. The settings also must be functional in terms of the performers' movements.

Casting. One of the director's first tasks is to select the performers for all the roles in the play. An open tryout may be held, to which anyone may come. In the professional theater, however, many more performers seek work than are needed, and so closed or invitational tryouts are almost always used. Invitations to try out for parts are sent only to performers who are known to the director, producer, or playwright.

Performers trying out for a role may be given the play to read before the tryout. Perhaps they will be asked to read material they have never seen before. Some directors ask performers to memorize and act scenes from various plays. Others ask them to prepare pantomimes, or to respond to directions given during the tryout.

Many factors determine the final casting. Some roles demand specific physical or vocal characterizations. The director also considers the emotional range demanded in a role, and casts each part with the other parts in mind. Directors seek performers who are suited to their roles and who combine with others to make up a balanced and varied cast.

Rehearsing. During rehearsals, the director has three major concerns: (1) stage picture; (2) movements, gestures, and facial expressions; and (3) voice and speech.

Casting a Broadway play, *above,* may take place in a hotel ballroom. At a rehearsal, *below,* of Arthur Miller's play *After the Fall,* actor Jason Robards, *left,* Miller, *center,* and director Elia Kazan, *standing,* discuss the meaning of a scene.

Inge Morath, Magnum

To achieve a proper *stage picture,* the director makes sure that each moment of the performance presents an image that communicates silently with the audience. Each stage picture should have a center of interest and should express the dominant emotional tone and the relationships among the characters. The director's chief task is to focus the audience's attention on the important elements—usually one or two characters who are most important at the moment. This is done by manipulating the positions of the performers in relation to the audience and to each other. The stage picture is also strongly affected by the setting, costumes, and lighting.

The director uses *movement* to blend one stage picture into another, and to create a sense of flow and development. It is one of a director's most powerful tools. Movement must always be appropriate for the characters, situation, mood, and type of play. For example, surprise and anger tend to cause people to move closer together, but disgust and fear usually move people apart. *Gestures* and *facial expressions* supplement the effects of movement. Most problems of *voice* and *speech* are worked out by the performers, but the director makes sure that they speak clearly and expressively.

Most early rehearsals take place in a rehearsal room rather than on a stage. Chalk lines indicate the floor plan, and only basic furniture and props are used. Directors rarely have as much time as they would like for rehearsals. They carefully prepare their schedule to make the best possible use of the performers' time.

Most rehearsal schedules include the following steps, each of which takes from 5 to 10 rehearsals. First, the director and performers read and study the play. Then the director *blocks* the action. That is, he or she arranges the broad pattern of the performers' movements. Then detailed work begins on characterization, line readings, stage action, changes in mood, and blending the performers into a unit. Finally, in dress rehearsals, the director combines all elements of theatrical production.

The director's assistants include a rehearsal secretary, assistant director, and stage manager. The secretary sits near the director during rehearsals and takes notes. This job may be combined with that of the assistant director, who may rehearse certain scenes, coach performers, or act as a go-between for the director and designers. In the professional theater, the stage manager organizes tryouts. He or she attends all rehearsals, and records changes in dialogue and blocking in a master copy of the script. Later, during performances, the stage manager is in charge backstage.

Blocking a play, *above,* establishes the movements of the actors during the performance of each scene. Director Elia Kazan describes how he wants the performers to arrange their movements during one scene. A dress rehearsal, *below,* is the final step before a play opens before a paying audience.

Inge Morath, Magnum

Performers are among the few artists who cannot separate their means of expression from themselves. They create with their own bodies and voices, and their own psychological and mental qualities. Often it is difficult to separate talent and creativity from the performer's personality. But acting is an art, and, as with any art, natural ability, study, and practice are essential.

Body and voice. Performers need a flexible, disciplined, and expressive body. They must be able to use their bodies to represent a wide range of attitudes and reactions. They may be aided by courses in stage movement, dancing, fencing, and acrobatics, and by participating in sports that demand physical control and coordination. Dancing and fencing are particularly useful because they provide grace and body control. There are more opportunities for performers with these skills.

The same requirements of flexibility, control, and expressiveness apply to the voice as to the body. Performers learn how to breathe properly, to achieve variety in vocal rhythm and tone, and to make themselves heard and understood. They also learn dialects. Training in oral reading, acting, and singing is helpful. However, most performers require years of practice to change their voices significantly so they can speak higher, lower, louder, or softer—and still be understood.

Observation and imagination. To portray a role well, performers should know about human emotions, attitudes, and *motivations* (reasons for behavior). They must be able to express these elements so they can be understood by an audience. A good performer develops the habit of observing others and remembering how they behave. If an actor takes the role of an old man, for example, he may prepare by observing how old men walk, stand, and sit. He also learns how different people react to such emotions as happiness, grief, and fear.

Performers may try to develop *emotion memory,* so that in portraying a role they can recall how they felt in a similar situation. They thus learn to know others through knowing themselves, and they portray others partly by using their knowledge of themselves.

Concentration is particularly important for performers. They must be able to involve themselves in an imagined situation and shut out all distractions. Their goal is to give a performance that creates the illusion of something happening for the first time. To do so, they concentrate on listening to other performers in the play and responding appropriately.

Systems of acting. No matter how well trained performers are, they cannot use their skills effectively without some consistent working method. Performers should try as many approaches to acting as possible, and choose the one they consider to be most successful.

The differences among systems of acting are often described in terms of two extremes: *mechanical-external* and *psychological-internal.* The two differ on the question of whether a performer must be emotionally moved to act convincingly. Supporters of the external system argue that emotion may interfere with good acting.

Performers develop their imaginations at the Actors Studio in New York City. The students in this class are doing exercises in relaxation and in working with imaginary objects to stimulate the growth of their imaginations and emotions. Studio director Lee Strasberg stands in the center.

WORLD BOOK photo by Dan Budnick

Creating a role, students at the Actors Studio explain their intentions after doing a scene from a dramatization of a portion of Fyodor Dostoevsky's novel *Poor Folk.* This class helps the students analyze their roles to find the best method of expressing their desired characterizations.

They believe the performer should merely try to create the external signs of emotions. Supporters of the internal system claim that only through feeling can performers project themselves into a character and situation. This system is sometimes called the Stanislavski method, for the Russian director Konstantin Stanislavski.

Creating a role. Performers must solve several specific problems every time they play a new role. These problems include (1) analyzing the role, (2) movement and gesture, (3) vocal characterization, (4) conservation and build, and (5) ensemble playing.

Analyzing the role starts with a study of the play as a whole. Then performers concentrate on their own parts. First they analyze the various aspects of characterization—a character's appearance, occupation, social and economic status, basic attitudes, and general personality. They then examine the character's goals and behavior, both in the play as a whole and in individual scenes. Finally, they study how their role is related to the other characters and to the structure of the play. If the play takes place during an earlier time, performers may study the period and setting. They not only analyze their role independently, but also adjust their interpretation to that of the director.

Movement and gesture are the ways in which the performer portrays the character's walk, posture, gestures, and bodily attitudes. Although the director plans the broad pattern of movement, the performer fills in many details. The performer works to understand the purpose or emotional reason behind each movement so he or she can perform every action "in character."

Vocal characterization refers to the character's general vocal qualities. Performers decide what qualities are desirable, and adjust their voices accordingly. One character may require a high-pitched voice. Another may have a soft, soothing voice. The performer also notes the demands of each scene. Some scenes are relaxed, and others are emotionally high keyed. A change within a scene can be clarified by appropriate vocal patterns. For example, growing tension can be denoted by raised pitch, greater volume, and faster tempo.

Conservation and build include the ways performers conserve their powers and heighten the role to a climax. Every play builds in intensity and suspense, and every performance should also grow. The need to sustain and build a part is most important in highly emotional roles. If performers begin at an emotional pitch that is too intense, they soon may not be able to build the intensity any further. The rest of the performance will seem monotonous. They must pace themselves so the performance grows in strength and interest.

Ensemble playing is the sense of artistic unity that results from the cooperative efforts of the entire cast. No acting performance is fully effective unless it is integrated with all the other performances. Ensemble playing results when every performer adjusts to the needs of the play, and remains aware of the methods, strengths, and weaknesses of the other performers.

Scene design has two basic purposes—to aid the audience's understanding, and to express the distinctive qualities of a play. To aid understanding, the stage setting may define the time and place of the action, and help establish characterizations. The set creates an appropriate mood and expresses the play's dominant elements through design and color.

The scene designer begins a job by studying the play as a whole. He or she then analyzes its scenic demands. Consideration must be given to the number, size, and kinds of sets needed; their physical arrangement; the period, place, and social and economic background; and the type and style of the play. The designer also may do research to learn about typical manners and customs, decorative details, architectural forms, furnishings, and building materials of the period.

The designer meets with the director to discuss the requirements of the sets, where entrances and exits should be located, and how furnishings should be arranged. The designer also learns how much money can be spent and what type of stage will be used.

Next, the designer makes preliminary sketches of the set and discusses them with the director. Before the designs receive final approval, the designer draws them in perspective and in color. Floor plans are made of each set, and three-dimensional scale models may be built to show how each set will look. The designer also makes a series of working drawings that show how each set will be built. In the professional theater, where scenery is built by a scenic studio, every detail of construction, assembly, and painting must be indicated. In the nonprofessional theater, where the designer often supervises construction, fewer drawings are needed.

Kinds of scenery. The designer uses several basic scenic units when building sets. Most of these units may be classified as *standing* or *hanging*.

The basic standing unit is the *flat*. A flat is a rectangular wooden frame over which canvas or muslin is stretched, providing a lightweight structure. Flats vary in size from 8 to 16 feet (2.4 to 4.9 meters) high and 1 to 6 feet (30 to 180 centimeters) wide. A plain flat has no openings. A door flat, window flat, fireplace flat, and

WORLD BOOK photo by Vories Fisher

Flats are basic pieces in set construction. They are made of high-quality lumber and most are covered with cotton or muslin. Flats are often lashed together to create the walls of a room.

Sketch and model for George Farquhar's *The Recruiting Officer* at the Goodman Theatre, Chicago (WORLD BOOK photos by Vories Fisher)

Designing a production begins with a sketch of each set, *above.* The designer then may make a model for each set, *right,* to show how the scenery will look on stage. After the director and designer agree on the designs, construction begins.

arch flat all have appropriate openings. Other standing units include door and window frames, fireplaces, platforms, steps and staircases, rocks and built-up ground, tree trunks, and columns. A *ground row* is a low flat with a shaped edge that gives the appearance of distant hills or rows of buildings.

Hanging units include *ceilings, borders, drops, drapes, curtains, scrims,* and *cycloramas.* Most ceilings are made from two large rectangular flats hinged together. They are suspended above the set, and lowered to rest on the tops of flats representing walls. In most exterior settings, borders are substituted for ceilings. Borders are short curtains of black cloth or painted canvas hung parallel to the front of the stage. They may be shaped and painted to resemble such objects as trees.

Large pieces of canvas called drops usually extend the width of the stage. They are attached at top and bottom to lengths of wood called *battens.* The canvas can be painted to represent any scene. Most drapes or curtains are hung in a series parallel to the proscenium on each side of the stage to conceal offstage space. A scrim is a gauze curtain used for special effects. It appears transparent when lighted from the back, but opaque when lighted from the front. A cyclorama is a continuous stretched curtain suspended on a U-shaped batten. It encloses the stage on three sides. Most cycloramas are neutral in color, but can be made any color by lighting. They are often used to show the sky.

Changing scenery. After scenery has been built, it is assembled on stage. A one-set show can be set up permanently. However, a multiple-set production requires

Set construction, *above,* may be done in the theater's own shop or by an outside studio. Generally, each piece is designed so stagehands can move it easily during a performance.

Technical rehearsals, *below,* let the director and the various designers see how the sets, costumes, and lighting of a play look under conditions of an actual performance.

Photos of *The Recruiting Officer* at the Goodman Theatre by Vories Fisher

careful planning so that each unit can be set up and dismantled quickly and quietly during the show.

When scenery is changed by hand, each part is moved by one or more stagehands to a prearranged place offstage. New settings are then assembled onstage. Another common method of changing scenery is called *flying.* Suspended units overhead are raised and lowered as needed on the stage.

Rolling platforms called *wagons* are often used to change scenery. Scenery is placed on the wagons, which can be rolled on or off stage. One kind of wagon is called a *jackknife.* It has a platform approximately as wide as the proscenium and attached to the stage floor at one place. It can be rotated on or off stage, much as a jackknife opens and closes.

Scenery can also be changed by means of *revolving stages* or *elevator stages.* A revolving stage has a large circle of the stage floor mounted on a central supporting pivot that can be rotated. Several settings can be erected at one time and moved into view as needed by turning the stage. An elevator stage has sections of the stage floor that can be lowered to the basement of the theater. There, scenery can be changed while another set is being used.

Properties and decorations are added to the set after the scenery has been assembled. Properties are often divided into two categories. *Set props,* such as sofas, function as part of the design or are attached to the set. *Hand props,* such as guns, are used by the actors. Decorations include such items as pictures and drapes.

Flying scenic units such as the backdrop, *above,* are suspended backstage, ready to be lowered into place. The banks of lights below the backdrop have been lowered for cleaning.

Elevator stages permit a set to be assembled on a separate stage, which is lowered or raised into place. Only large theaters such as the Metropolitan Opera, *below,* can afford these stages.

WORLD BOOK photos by Donald Stebbing

Lighting methods. Lighting designers analyze a play for its dramatic values and then for its lighting needs. They note everything in the script concerning light. There might be such changes in intensity as a sunrise or lamps being lit. Perhaps variations in light are needed for various parts of the setting. The script may note the direction from which light enters the set, such as moonlight through a window. Colored light can suggest moonlight, sunlight, or firelight. Other special lighting effects include lightning.

The designers pay particular attention to mood because lighting helps establish stage atmosphere. They must understand the style of the play. For realistic drama, they will probably make the light come from specific sources. They will make sure there is a credible reason for each lighting change. In a nonrealistic play, lighting can be unmotivated.

The lighting designer confers extensively with the scene designer and the director. In the professional theater, he or she makes sketches showing how the stage will look when lighted. In most nonprofessional productions, the lighting designer and the director reach general agreement about lighting. Little can be done until the theater is available and the scenery is in place.

Lighting for the stage is divided into (1) specific illumination, (2) general illumination, and (3) special effects. *Specific illumination* concentrates on a limited area. It is used principally for lighting the acting areas, which require strong emphasis. *General illumination* is used to light the sets and background elements, and to blend the lighting of acting areas. It is also used to provide a gradual change between brilliantly lighted acting areas and less intense lighting on the background. *Special effects* refer to a variety of lighting techniques and instruments. Typical examples include projections of clouds and stars, fires, and rainbows.

In planning the lighting, the designer draws a *lighting plot* on a floor plan showing the entire stage, including the setting. A separate lighting plot is usually needed for each set, as well as a plot showing the lighting for all the sets at the same time. An *instrument schedule* provides a summary of all the technical information needed to set up the lights for a play. This schedule lists lighting instruments, mounting positions, areas to be lighted, color filters, and other technical data.

There are several types of lighting instruments. A *spotlight* illuminates a limited portion of the stage with a concentrated beam of light. Spotlights range in power from 100 to 10,000 watts. They have reflectors to increase their brightness, and lenses to give light a specific type of edge, either sharp or soft. Special frames enable the lighting designer to vary the color.

A *striplight* consists of a series of lamps set in a narrow, roughly rectangular trough. Striplights vary in length, wattage, and use. They can be divided into several categories. *Footlights* light the stage from the front. *Borderlights* are hung overhead to spread light to the set or background. Striplights may be placed on the floor or elsewhere on the stage to light a cyclorama or scenic units.

Many instruments are used to create special effects. Various kinds of projectors are among the most useful. An entire scenic background can be projected on a screen or on a cyclorama. Some projectors have rotating disks to create the effect of movement, as in clouds.

All lighting includes some method of controlling the light. A *control board* or *switchboard* permits some instruments to be used at maximum brightness while others are off or dimmed. A control board also allows the control of color by mixing the light from several instruments. *Dimmers* permit a gradual increase or decrease in the intensity of light. An *electronic control board* enables the lighting designer to preset all changes in lighting intensity for an entire production.

WORLD BOOK photos by Vories Fisher

A lighting control board, *left,* enables one technician to control all lighting changes from a single location. The lighting designer records lighting changes on a special cue sheet, *above.* The designer holds a gelatin, or *gel,* a thin, transparent colored sheet used to change colors on the stage lights.

Lighting establishes the mood of a play. Dylan Thomas' *Under Milk Wood* takes place during a 24-hour period. This play usually has a single simple set, but proper lighting can indicate the time of day. The picture above shows sunrise, and the one below shows late afternoon.

James Maronek

Sound production. Sound makes its greatest contribution when designed as a unit and carefully integrated into the production as a whole. Sound includes music, noises of no recognizable origin, and such realistic effects as thunder. In the professional theater, sound produced electrically is considered part of the stage lighting. Sound produced mechanically is regarded as a stage property.

Sound performs two basic functions: (1) to establish mood and style, and (2) to help tell the story. Music and abstract sound help indicate the proper atmosphere for each scene. Such realistic sounds as rainfall or a distant foghorn also contribute to mood. Sound helps tell the story through gunshots, ringing doorbells, and other realistic noises that either prepare the audience for on-stage action or indicate action supposedly occurring off-stage.

Sound is classified as *live* or *recorded*. Live sound is created fresh for each performance, and includes doorbells and telephones. Recorded sound includes noises made by a passing train and the sounds of a crowd off-stage.

Costume design shares the same broad purposes as scene design. It aids the audience's understanding and expresses the play's distinctive qualities. Costumes help identify the period and country in which the action takes place, and establish such specific locations as a farm. They suggest time of day, season, occasion, and information about the characters—ages, occupations, personalities, and social and economic status.

Costumes can also clarify the relationships among characters. For example, the warring sides in many Shakespearean history plays are identified by contrasting color schemes. Costumes also express the overall mood of the play, its style, and the emotional tone of individual scenes.

The costume designer studies the script in much the same manner as the actor does. The designs, like the actor's or actress's performance, express the characters and the play as a whole. The costumer uses line, mass, color, texture, and ornaments to create a visual equivalent of the dramatic action.

The costumer confers with the director, scenic designer, lighting designer, and principal performers to make sure his or her ideas fit the interpretation of the play. Like the scene designer, the costumer records ideas in color sketches. The sketches are usually accompanied by samples of material. They are given to the director for approval. The costumer also makes a chart indicating what each character wears in each scene of the play.

Costume design begins with a sketch of the proposed costume, *above.* Samples of the material are usually attached. The costume must be fitted correctly, *below left,* so the performer can move freely and comfortably. The costume shown in these pictures is worn by a fortuneteller, *below right,* in George Farquhar's *The Recruiting Officer,* a comedy of the early 1700's.

© Photri from Marilyn Gartman

Makeup helps establish character. For a role as Fagin in the musical *Oliver!*, an actor applies dark makeup to create hollows in his face, *upper left*. After he has painted on wrinkles, he daubs on more makeup, *left*. Finally, he makes up his hands to look as old as his face, *above*.

Costumes may be made new, assembled from an existing wardrobe, borrowed, or rented. In the professional theater, a professional costume house makes costumes to order. Nonprofessional theaters borrow costumes or rent them from a costume rental agency. Many permanent theater organizations, both professional and nonprofessional, make their own costumes. Most maintain a wardrobe of items from past shows.

The *dress parade* shows the performers separately and in groups under lights similar to those used during performances. The director and all the designers attend. The dress parade allows any necessary changes to be made during the rehearsal period. After performances begin, a wardrobe attendant works backstage and supervises costume changes, repairs, and adjustments.

Makeup techniques. Makeup is important in establishing characterization. The appearance of the face indicates the character's age, health, and race. The face also can suggest a general occupation and basic personality. Makeup serves the additional purpose of restoring the face's color and form, which may be affected by the stage lighting or distance from the audience.

For a *straight makeup,* the performer's appearance is not changed significantly. In a *character makeup,* it is changed greatly. The makeup may age the face; make it fat, thin, smooth, or wrinkled; or emphasize some peculiar facial characteristic.

Makeup effects can be achieved in two basic ways: (1) by painting, or (2) by using plastic pieces. Painting involves applying color, line, and shadow to the face or body. All makeup has some painted effects. Plastic makeup devices include beards, wigs, false noses, and warts or scars. Changing the shape of the nose with nose putty, and adding a beard and bushy eyebrows, alters the features of a performer more than painting alone.

Traditionally, makeup has been considered the performer's responsibility, though it also concerns the costumer. In the professional theater, performers are responsible for their own makeup, but they consult specialists for help with problems. In many nonprofessional theaters, makeup is considered part of the costumer's duties. Sometimes the director is responsible for makeup.

Broadway musical comedy has been called the major contribution of the United States to modern theater. In 1983, *A Chorus Line, above,* became the longest-running show in Broadway history.

Today, more groups than ever before are producing plays in the United States. Most of these groups are nonprofessional, and the process of theatrical production varies from one organization to another. However, the operation of the professional theater is basic for all theatrical organizations.

Broadway in New York City is the best-known center of the professional theater in the United States. But resident professional companies exist in many other U.S. cities. Several of these companies have contributed plays and musicals to Broadway.

The starting point for most theatrical productions, professional or nonprofessional, is the playwright's script. Good scripts are in great demand, but playwrights—unless well established—almost always have difficulty getting their plays performed. If they want a professional production, they must first find a producer. The producer has the overall responsibility of the entire show. He or she acquires the play, hires a director, rents a theater, and raises the money needed to finance the show. The producer may be either one person or a group of people.

A producer who is interested in a script may take an *option* on it. That is, he or she pays the playwright for exclusive production rights to the play for a certain period of time. An option does not guarantee production. A play may be placed under option many times without being produced. If the producer decides to present the play, a contract is drawn up specifying the amount of

the author's *royalty* (share of the profits). The contract also states the extent of the producer's control over the play. For example, the contract may require the playwright to be available for consultation and possible rewriting during the rehearsal period. Most contracts do not legally require playwrights to make changes in the script. But in most cases, they are under pressure to do so. Negotiations with producers can become so complex that most playwrights hire literary agents to represent them.

A producer who takes an option on a play then sets out to raise money to stage it. The cost of producing a play on Broadway has become increasingly high. A play with one set and a small cast may cost more than $500,000. Many musicals cost several million dollars and must run over a year to repay their investment. Few individuals can invest this much money, and so most producers seek funds from many people or groups. Investors may be influenced by the reputation of the playwright, director, or star of the show.

After raising the money to finance the play, the producer negotiates contracts with everyone involved in the production. In the Broadway theater, a producer deals with unions representing various employees. These employees include not only the director, actors, actresses, and designers, but also stagehands, musicians, dancers, and box office personnel.

Following the rehearsal period, many plays intended for Broadway are presented first in one or more theaters outside New York City, such as in Boston or Washington, D.C. Audience reaction and reviews by critics may lead to changes in the play. Since the 1960's, out-of-town tryouts often have been replaced by preview performances on Broadway. Tickets are sold, often at reduced prices, but the critics do not write reviews until after the official opening-night performance.

The final step in the production of a play—and the most vital from a dollars-and-cents standpoint—is opening night on Broadway. Drama critics from the leading newspapers in New York City, and from radio and television stations in the New York City metropolitan area, review the play immediately. Top magazines print reviews within the next week or two. The reviews, particularly those of the newspapers, greatly influence the commercial success of a play. If all or most of the reviews criticize the play severely, the producer normally will close the show. If the play is the work of a well-known playwright, or has a major star, the advance sale of tickets may save it despite bad reviews.

A play must be a big box-office hit to survive long on Broadway. Many productions close after only a few performances. Some run for years. The "hit" or "flop" pattern has created a situation in which a play must be a great success financially, or it is considered a failure. This pattern has hurt the range of plays offered. Producers limit themselves almost entirely to shows that indicate promise of success or that have been successful elsewhere. As a result, Broadway drama has less richness and variety than it might have. The number of plays presented outside New York City is also affected because only hit shows generally tour.

Each spring, many awards honor outstanding achievements in New York theater for the season that began the previous autumn. Among the best known are the "Tony" awards, named for Antoinette Perry, a pro-

Community theaters offer many fine productions of serious dramas for audiences outside New York City. Most operate on low budgets, using nonprofessional performers.

Scene from *The Indian Wants the Bronx* by Israel Horovitz at the Hull House Theater in Chicago (Larry Lowenthal)

ducer and director. Since 1947, Tonys have been presented to the best play and musical as well as the best authors, designers, directors, performers, and producers.

Off-Broadway theater developed in New York City about 1950 from dissatisfaction with conditions on Broadway. The people who founded off-Broadway theaters believed that Broadway was concerned basically with producing safe hit plays rather than works of artistic quality. Off-Broadway theaters tried to assist playwrights, directors, and performers who had been unable to find work in the Broadway theater. Most off-Broadway theaters were located in low-rent areas. Most had poorly equipped stages, limited seating, and few conveniences for the audience. The originality of the script, the creativeness of the performers, and the low cost of production made up for such disadvantages. By 1960, however, costs began to increase, and off-Broadway theater was encountering many of Broadway's problems and had lost most of its vitality.

With the decline of off-Broadway, a movement called *off-off-Broadway* developed in New York City. Off-off-Broadway theaters emphasized extremely inventive plays and staging. Since the mid-1960's, these theaters have become a major force in experimental drama. The most important groups include the La Mama Experimental Theatre Company, the American Place Theatre, the Circle Repertory Theatre Company, and the Public Theatre operated by the New York Shakespeare Festival. As such groups have gained public and critical acceptance, their operations have come to resemble the off-Broadway theaters of the 1950's.

Other professional theater. During the 1950's, resident acting companies began to be established in cities other than New York City. In the 1960's, with the financial aid of the Ford Foundation and other organizations, these companies increased in number and reputation. By the early 1980's, about 55 such companies were performing in the United States.

Most resident companies produce a season of plays each year. They present each play for a limited run, rather than for a long engagement. The theaters try to vary their programs with plays of a number of periods and styles. Occasionally, directors and performers are employed for the entire season. Most are hired for a single production. Many of these companies receive money from foundations or government agencies. However, few resident companies have any assurance of continuing financial aid and thus they must be cautious about making long-range plans. Several resident theaters have been particularly helpful to writers. These theaters include the Mark Taper Forum in Los Angeles and the Actors Theatre in Louisville, Ky.

A number of professional nonprofit companies comparable to off-off-Broadway groups are scattered throughout the United States. These groups are often called *alternative theaters* to distinguish them from more traditional professional resident theaters.

College and high school theater. Many colleges and universities have theater and drama departments. They produce plays as part of the education of their students, and as a service to the community. The best college theaters have the administrative organization of resident professional companies. Because their purpose is educational, such theaters usually present standard works from earlier periods as well as more recent plays. Many theaters also produce original plays. Occasionally, a professional performer may appear in a production, but all-student casts are customary.

Almost all U.S. high schools have some kind of theater production program, though relatively few offer courses in drama and theater. The production of plays may be assigned to people untrained in the theater, with poor results. But a number of high schools have developed theater programs of excellent quality, supervised by qualified staffs. Many schools have fine facilities and offer courses in play production, dramatic literature, and related areas.

Community theater developed between 1900 and 1920. Today, most towns of more than 30,000 persons have a community theater. The community theater not only provides entertainment for local audiences, but also furnishes an outlet for the creative talents of its members. Many community theaters employ a full-time director who supervises all productions. Many of these theaters are run by volunteers and cannot afford paid personnel. Others pay the director of each production, and also provide fees for the designer and chief technician. Most plays staged by community theaters are recent works. Community theaters present classics less frequently.

Children's theater operates within any framework—professional, educational, or community. Its chief characteristic is its intended audience. Only during the 1900's, and primarily since World War II ended in 1945, have programs been developed for child audiences. The plays are performed by adults or children.

Summer theater usually operates from late June until early September. Summer theater companies have greatly increased in number since World War II. Most are in resort areas. Some companies are entirely professional, and others have both professional and nonprofessional personnel. Still others are completely nonprofessional. Summer theater is also popular with college drama departments as a supplement to courses offered during the school year.

Most summer theaters present a season of recent plays or musicals. Groups connected with educational institutions often present both classic and commercial shows. A few companies perform a single work for the entire summer. Some groups present dramatizations of local history. Others perform in *repertory.* That is, the company prepares plays before the season begins and performs them in rotation throughout the summer. Several organizations specialize in the plays of Shakespeare. Occasionally, summer theaters try out new plays for producers who hope to present the plays elsewhere.

Government-supported theater, though common in Europe, has not yet gained full acceptance in the United States. Those who favor such support believe it can provide economic stability for theaters and enable them to charge lower ticket prices and present a wider range of plays. Opponents say it might lead to government control or censorship. They also believe that theater, like other businesses, should be self-supporting.

Many theaters today receive some assistance from government agencies. In 1965, Congress established the National Endowment for the Arts, which makes grants to groups or projects. Most states and many cities have arts councils that make grants to state or local groups. The amount of aid from such sources is small, however, and is not assured from one year to the next.

Theater in other countries

Nearly all major cities have theater districts resembling Broadway in organization and appeal. Many productions are commercial enterprises supported by private investment. However, the theaters with the highest reputations are permanent organizations.

Canada, most European countries, and some Asian and African nations, have several government-supported theaters. These *state theaters* are permanent organizations that employ staffs of directors, performers, designers, and others. Many state theaters also import performers, directors, and designers for single productions.

A number of theaters operate in government-owned buildings and pay no rent. The government gives them an annual sum of money called a *subsidy.* A subsidy usually does not cover all production costs, but it supplements the income from ticket sales. The subsidy enables a theater to charge lower admission prices and provides protection against financial loss. Most subsidized companies produce a season of plays annually. Each play is performed for a limited time or in rotation with other plays. Some plays are presented at regular intervals through the years.

Canada has two internationally known theater organizations. One, the Stratford Festival in Stratford, Ont., specializes in the plays of Shakespeare. The other, the Shaw Festival in Niagara-on-the-Lake, Ont., features plays by George Bernard Shaw. Montreal is the center of theater in French-speaking Canada. There are major resident companies in such cities as Halifax, N.S.; Toronto, Ont.; and Winnipeg, Man.

England. The British government started to give subsidies to the theater in 1945. The National Theatre, which was created in 1963, is one of the world's outstanding companies. The National Theatre succeeded the Old Vic company, one of England's finest troupes from 1914 until it was disbanded in 1963. In 1976, the National Theatre moved into a new theater center built especially for it.

Another subsidized theater, the Royal Shakespeare Company, was created from the organization that produced the Stratford-upon-Avon Shakespeare Festival. Since 1960, it has divided its company between London and the Shakespeare Festival Theatre in Stratford. Another major organization, the English Stage Society, has introduced the works of many new dramatists.

Several resident companies in cities outside London receive subsidies from the local governments.

France. The oldest state theater in the world still operating is the Comédie-Française in Paris. It was established in 1680. The Théâtre Nationale Populaire and several other notable French theaters also receive government support. The state supports dramatic centers in such cities as Lyon, Marseille, Nice, Rennes, St. Étienne, Strasbourg, Toulouse, and Tourcoing. The theatrical companies of many of these cities tour neighboring communities. The government also subsidizes touring companies and aids summer drama festivals.

Germany has the most extensive system of state-supported theaters in the world. Many of these theaters date back to the late 1700's. Although the nation has been divided since 1945, East Germany and West Germany have a similar organization of theaters. West Germany has about 330 professional theaters, of which about 245 are state-owned or city-owned. East Germany has about 150 companies, all performing in state-owned or city-owned theaters.

Almost every large German city has drama, opera, and ballet companies. All subsidized companies in a city generally are under one manager appointed by the city or state. All the companies share a staff of directors and designers. Outstanding organizations include the Berliner Ensemble in East Berlin and the Schiller Theater in West Berlin.

Italy. The Italian theater operates differently than that of most European countries. The most important Italian drama companies tour the larger cities of Italy. In addition, about eight resident theaters are subsidized by city or provincial governments. The leading resident theaters are in Genoa, Milan, Rome, and Turin.

The Soviet Union. Theater in the Soviet Union was generously subsidized before World War II. It suffered a severe blow in 1946 when many subsidies were withdrawn and tight censorship was imposed. After Premier Joseph Stalin died in 1953, the government relaxed its censorship and the variety of plays increased greatly. Today, despite state control and ownership, 98 per cent of the Soviet Union's theaters receive no direct subsidies from the government. Instead, they must support themselves from box-office receipts.

The Moscow Art Theater, founded in 1898, is perhaps the most respected company in the Soviet Union. It receives generous subsidies. Its company of about 140 actors may be the largest in the world. The Maly Theater and the Mayakovsky Theater are other leading companies. Two newer groups, the Sovremennik Theater and the Taganka Drama and Comedy Theatre, have aroused much interest in Moscow. In Leningrad, the Pushkin Theater ranks only slightly below the Moscow Art Theater in reputation. The Gorky Theater is also highly respected.

Training for the theater

There has been much dispute over the proper way to train theater artists. Some argue that these men and women should first get a general liberal arts education, with little or no theater training. Concentrated work in the theater arts would then follow. Those who favor this method believe that liberal arts training is especially valuable for the study of theater and drama, which deal with all aspects of human experience. Others believe a general education is unnecessary, and that professional training should be taken from the beginning. Still others think that liberal arts courses and professional theater training should be combined.

Colleges and universities. A large number of colleges and universities provide some training in the theater arts. However, many do not have such *performance courses* as acting or directing for undergraduates. These schools may offer courses in dramatic literature and theater history, but they leave specialized theatrical training to graduate schools or professional schools.

Other colleges and universities give academic credit for courses in playwriting; acting; directing; scene, costume, and lighting design; technical production; dance; and stage movement. The student must follow a course of study that provides a broad liberal arts education. But a fourth to a third of the course work may be devoted to the theater arts. Graduate programs may offer one to three additional years of intensive training.

Professional training programs are now offered by a number of universities. Such programs are also provided by conservatories and studios not connected with universities. Professional training programs normally allow students to spend most of their time on theater courses. Some schools give certificates for the completion of a prescribed program. Some programs offer academic degrees. Other programs do not lead to a certificate or degree. A student may simply enroll in any class for as long as he or she wishes.

Most professional training schools are in or near cities with professional theaters. Some of the best-known

Scene from Brecht's *Mother Courage.* Photo Pic, courtesy *The Drama Review,* New York University

Theater in Germany is heavily supported by the state. The Berliner Ensemble, *above,* of East Berlin is probably the best known. It was founded by playwright Bertolt Brecht in 1949.

programs are operated by the American Conservatory Theater, the California Institute of the Arts, the Juilliard School, and Yale University.

Professional training programs give performers intensive training but do not give any guarantee of employment. Many beginning performers seek work in resident or alternative theater companies, but many still go to New York City or Hollywood to find employment. The supply of performers always greatly exceeds the demand, and therefore most find it difficult to follow a career in the theater.   Oscar G. Brockett

Study aids

Related articles. See **Drama** with its list of *Related articles.* See also the following:

American actors and actresses

Adams, Maude	Gish, Lillian
Aldridge, Ira	Hayes, Helen
Barrymore (family)	Hoffman, Dustin
Booth, Edwin T.	Huston (Walter)
Booth, John W.	Ives, Burl
Booth, Junius B.	Jefferson, Joseph
Brando, Marlon	Laughton, Charles
Brice, Fanny	Lindsay, Howard
Cohan, George M.	Lunt, Alfred
Fiske, Minnie Maddern	Mansfield, Richard
Fonda, Henry	Robeson, Paul
Fonda, Jane	Rogers, Will
Forrest, Edwin	Russell, Lillian
Gillette, William	Waters, Ethel
Gish, Dorothy	Welles, Orson

British actors and actresses

Anderson, Dame	Gielgud, Sir John	Olivier, Laurence
Judith	Guinness, Sir Alec	Redgrave, Sir
Campbell, Mrs.	Gwyn, Nell	Michael
Patrick	Kean, Edmund	Siddons, Sarah K.
Coward, Sir Noel	Kemble, Fanny	Terry, Dame
Fontanne, Lynn	Langtry, Lillie	Ellen A.
Garrick, David	Lillie, Beatrice	Williams, Emlyn

Other actors and actresses

Barrault,	Boucicault, Dion	Roscius, Quintus
Jean-Louis	Dietrich, Marlene	Thespis
Bernhardt, Sarah	Duse, Eleonora	

Directors, producers, and designers

Bergman, Ingmar	Kazan, Elia
D'Oyly Carte, Richard	Nichols, Mike
Granville-Barker, Harley	Reinhardt, Max
Guthrie, Sir Tyrone	Stanislavski, Konstantin
Hammerstein, Oscar, II	Ziegfeld, Florenz
Kaufman, George S.	

Other related articles

Abbey Theatre	Ontario (Annual events)
Burlesque	Opera
Dancing	Operetta
Europe (picture: Ancient Greek	Pantomime
drama)	Puppet
Globe Theatre	Shadow play
Minstrel show	Shakespeare, William (The
Moscow Art Theater	Elizabethan theater)
Motion picture	Vaudeville
Musical comedy	

Outline

I. Modern theater architecture
  A. The auditorium   C. Work areas
  B. The stage

II. The director
  A. Interpreting the script   D. Rehearsing
  B. Working with the de-   E. The director's assistants
    signers
  C. Casting

III. The performer
  A. Body and voice   C. Concentration
  B. Observation and imagi-   D. Systems of acting
    nation   E. Creating a role

IV. Scene design
  A. The scene designer   D. Properties and
  B. Kinds of scenery   decorations
  C. Changing scenery

V. Lighting and sound
  A. Lighting methods   B. Sound production

VI. Costumes and makeup
  A. Costume design   B. Makeup techniques

VII. Theater in the United States
  A. Broadway   E. Community theater
  B. Off-Broadway theater   F. Children's theater
  C. Other professional the-   G. Summer theater
    ater   H. Government-supported
  D. College and high   theater
    school
    theater

VIII. Theater in other countries
  A. Canada   D. Germany
  B. England   E. Italy
  C. France   F. The Soviet Union

IX. Training for the theater
  A. Colleges and universities
  B. Professional training programs

Questions

What is a drop? a scrim? a cyclorama?
What is the difference between a proscenium stage and a theater-in-the-round?
What are the two chief systems of acting?
How can costumes help an audience understand a play?
What kinds of sound can be used in a play?
What is the role of the producer in staging a play?
What does the director need to know about a play?
What is the difference between *theater* and *drama*?
What is the oldest state theater in the world still operating?
What is a stage picture?

Reading and Study Guide

See *Theater* in the Research Guide/Index, Volume 22, for a *Reading and Study Guide.*

Additional resources

Bellman, Willard F. *Scene Design, Stage Lighting, Sound, Costume & Makeup: A Scenographic Approach.* Rev. ed. Harper, 1983. First published in 1977 as *Scenography and Stage Technology.*
Brockett, Oscar G. *The Theatre: An Introduction.* 4th ed. Holt, 1979. *History of the Theatre.* 4th ed. Allyn & Bacon, 1981.
Cheney, Sheldon. *The Theatre: Three Thousand Years of Drama, Acting, and Stagecraft.* 3rd ed. McKay, 1972.
Clurman, Harold. *On Directing.* Macmillan, 1972.
Green, Joann. *The Small Theatre Handbook: A Guide to Management and Production.* Harvard Common Press, 1981.
Greenberg, Jan W. *Theater Business: From Auditions Through Opening Night.* Holt, 1981. *Theater Careers: A Comprehensive Guide to Non-Acting Careers in the Theater.* 1983.

Thebes, *theebz,* is the Greek name of a city in ancient Egypt that served as a capital for many Egyptian kings. Thebes stood near the Nile River, at the site of what is now the city of Luxor (see **Egypt, Ancient** [map]).

Thebes was an unimportant village until a Theban prince became king of Egypt in 2052 B.C. During the Eighteenth Dynasty (1554-1304 B.C.), most Egyptian kings made Thebes their capital, and the Theban god, Amon-Re, became the most important god in Egypt. Some later

Egyptian kings made northern cities their capitals, but they still built tombs and temples at Thebes. The Romans destroyed Thebes in 29 B.C.

Theban temples still stand at Karnak and Luxor. The ruins of funeral temples of Egyptian kings and queens are across the Nile from Luxor. Tombs lie in cliffs along the river, in the so-called Valley of the Kings (see **Valley of the Kings**). Barbara Mertz

Thebes, *theebz,* was an ancient city in Boeotia, a region located in central Greece. At one time, it was the most powerful city-state in all Greece, and the head of the confederacy of cities known as the Boeotian League. The city lay in the southeastern part of Boeotia, about 30 miles (48 kilometers) north of Athens (see **Greece, Ancient** [map]). According to ancient legends, Cadmus, a king of Phoenicia, founded Thebes. The city appears in the Oedipus legends, which are almost as famous as the stories of Troy (see **Oedipus**).

The historical record of Thebes begins about 500 years before the birth of Christ, when the people of Thebes and of Plataea, another ancient Greek city, began to quarrel. Later, Thebes helped the Persians in their invasion of Greece in 480 B.C. Thebes fought frequent wars with Athens. The most important of these was the Peloponnesian War, which began in 431 B.C., when a Theban force attacked Plataea. After this war, the Boeotian League fell to pieces under the tyrannical rule of Sparta. It became important again between 379 and 374 B.C. through the patriotic efforts of Pelopidas. In 371 B.C. the Thebans, led by Epaminondas, won a victory over the Spartans at Leuctra, and thus gained control over Greece.

When Epaminondas died in 362 B.C., Theban control of Greece came to an end. The exhausted Greek states came under the rule of Philip of Macedon and his ambitious son, Alexander the Great. The Thebans revolted against Alexander, and he punished them by destroying their city. Thebes was rebuilt in 316 B.C., and was important under the later Roman Empire. The city flourished as a center of the silk trade during the A.D. 1000's and 1100's. Thebes began to decline when the Turks gained control of the city. The town of Thivai now stands on the site of Thebes. Donald W. Bradeen

See also **Cadmus; Pelopidas; Pindar.**

Theiler, Max. See **Yellow fever.**

Theine, another name for caffeine. See **Caffeine.**

Theism, *THEE ihz uhm,* is belief in a god or gods. The term comes from the Greek word *theos,* meaning *god.* Theism plays an important role in most religions, but various faiths differ in their teachings about a god or gods. The followers of ancient Greek and Roman religions were *polytheistic*—that is, they worshiped more than one god. Today, the followers of most major religions are *monotheistic.* They accept only one god.

The words *theism* and *theistic* are used principally in discussing religions that have one god. Such religions include Christianity, Islam, Judaism, and some forms of Hinduism. These faiths stress the existence of an all-knowing, all-powerful god. This god may provide ways of life for people to follow and may offer them salvation.

Theism is also a type of philosophical belief. It supports the existence of a god, as opposed to *atheism,* which argues that no god exists. Theism also states that a god exists apart from the world. This concept differs from *pantheism,* the belief that a god exists in all forces of nature and the universe. Nancy E. Auer Falk

See also **Atheism; Deism; God; Polytheism; Religion** (Belief in a deity).

Theme. See **Composition.**

Theme park. See **Amusement park.**

Themistocles, *thuh MIHS tuh KLEEZ* (514?-449? B.C.), was an Athenian statesman and soldier in the Persian Wars. He saved Greece by his statesmanship and laid the base for Athens' greatness with his naval policy.

Little is known of Themistocles' early life. He began his political career in 490 B.C. after the Battle of Marathon and the retreat of the Persians. Themistocles opposed Aristides, who was then leader of Athens. In 482 B.C., he defeated Aristides in a dispute about what was to be done with the silver from the mines at Laurium. Themistocles had always favored naval expansion, and proposed that Athens increase its fleet. Aristides was banished for opposing this plan, and Themistocles became the political leader of Athens.

Themistocles was certain that the Persians would attack again, but that this time the battle would be decided on the sea. Two years later the Persians returned. In a battle at Thermopylae, they overwhelmed a force of about 1,400 Greeks, led by the Spartans under Leonidas. Themistocles then moved the Athenians to Salamis, where he engaged the Persians in battle. He destroyed the Persian fleet and forced the Persians to leave Athens. The following year the allied Greeks completely defeated the Persians at Plataea.

Despite all Themistocles had done for Athens, the Athenians disliked him. They believed he had accepted bribes, and in 471 B.C., they banished him. He stayed awhile in Argos then went to Persia. The Persian king welcomed him and gave him an estate in Magnesia, where he remained until his death. Richard Nelson Frye

See also **Aristides; Greece, Ancient** (The Persian Wars); **Salamis.**

Theocracy, *thee AHK ruh see,* is a form of government in which the state is ruled by a priest or priests, and in which members of the priesthood have authority in civil and religious matters. The word *theocracy* comes from two Greek words, *theos,* which means *God,* and *kratein,* which means *to rule.*

Many ancient peoples believed that their god or gods had handed down laws for their government. The famous Code of Hammurabi was supposed to have been divinely revealed. The most famous theocracy was that of the Israelites, to whom God gave the Law through Moses.

The Puritan government of Massachusetts was called a theocracy. It was conducted for many years on the principle of obedience to divine law, as interpreted by the clergy. Alexander J. Groth

Theocritus, *thee AHK rih tuhs* (200's B.C.), was a Greek poet who originated *pastoral* (rustic) poetry. He wrote about 30 poems called *idyls.* Usually, they represent shepherds or goatherds (or poets masquerading as shepherds) talking to each other or competing in singing rustic songs on a summer day. Virgil imitated Theocritus in his *Eclogues.* Theocritus also influenced later poets, such as Lord Tennyson and Algernon Swinburne. Theocritus was born either at Syracuse, or on the Greek island of Kós. Moses Hadas

Theodolite, *thee AHD uh lyt,* is an instrument surveyors use to measure angles and directions. It is similar to the more commonly used transit. A theodolite gives more precise readings than does a transit. Some theodolites permit measurements to closer than one second of arc ($\frac{1}{3600}$ of a degree). Most theodolites are mounted on a *tripod* (three-legged stand). A theodolite has a telescope that permits accurate sighting in any direction. A horizontal plate below the telescope provides readings around the horizon in degrees, and in divisions of degrees called minutes and seconds. A vertical plate and scale, mounted to the left of the telescope, permit vertical readings.   Todd I. Blue

Theodora, THEE *uh DOHR uh* (A.D. 502?-548), was the wife of Justinian I, Byzantine (East Roman) emperor from 527 to 565. A beautiful and strong-willed woman, Theodora tried to influence Justinian's policies and to use her position to advance her friends and ruin her enemies. In 532, a rebellion in the capital city of Constantinople threatened to overthrow the empire. Theodora persuaded Justinian to stay and defend the city rather than to flee. Justinian crushed the rebels, thus securing his absolute power.

Theodora was probably born on Cyprus, to a poor family. She became an actress before marrying Justinian in 522, and was accused of numerous scandals, but many of them have been disproved. She founded homes for the care of poor girls.   William G. Sinnigen

See also **Justinian I.**

Theodore Roosevelt National Park is in western North Dakota. The park's outstanding feature is a scenic badlands area along the Little Missouri River. In this area, water and wind erosion have carved deep gullies and steep hills into the landscape. President Theodore Roosevelt owned two cattle ranches when he was a young man. The park includes the site of the headquarters of his Elkhorn Ranch. The restored cabin from Roosevelt's Maltese Cross Ranch is located at the park headquarters and is a popular tourist attraction. The area was established as a national memorial park in 1947 and became a national park in 1978. For the park's area, see **National Park System** (table: National Parks). For its location, see **North Dakota** (political map).

Critically reviewed by the National Park Service

Theodoric, *thee AHD uh rihk* (A.D. 455?-526), was an *Ostrogoth* (East Goth) king who governed Italy from A.D. 493 until his death. He won control of Italy from the barbarians who had taken it from the Romans 17 years earlier. Although a barbarian himself, Theodoric maintained a Roman form of government and Roman law in Italy. His rule was enlightened, peaceful, and just, and he won the praise of both barbarians and Romans. Theodoric let Romans hold high public office, and respected the senatorial class. He employed such prominent Romans as Boethius and Cassiodorus as his advisers and ministers of state. Theodoric believed in the Arian heresy, which denied the divinity of Christ. But he permitted his subjects to practice orthodox Christianity.

Theodoric was born in Pannonia, which covered parts of what are now Austria, Hungary, and Yugoslavia. He spent several years in Constantinople (now Istanbul, Turkey). Constantinople was the capital of the Byzantine (East Roman) Empire. When his father, Ostrogoth king

Theodemir, died in 471, Theodoric became king.

Theodoric alternately found himself an ally, then an enemy of the Byzantine emperors. He was a victim of a Byzantine plan to confuse and weaken barbarians by encouraging rivalries between them and then shifting support from one side to the other. In 489, Byzantine emperor Zeno commissioned Theodoric to attack Odoacer, the barbarian king of Italy. Theodoric defeated Odoacer in 493, then murdered him. Germanic peoples remembered Theodoric in their legends as the heroic Dietrich of Bern.   William G. Sinnigen

Theodosius I, THEE *uh DOH shee uhs* (A.D. 346-395), was the Roman emperor who prohibited all *pagan* (non-Christian) practices in the Roman Empire. For this, he became known to Christians as *The Great.* However, he was a shortsighted ruler who weakened the empire by creating many new government jobs and by raising taxes. His will divided the empire between his sons Honorius and Arcadius, splitting it permanently into eastern and western empires.

Theodosius was born in Spain. He became a distinguished soldier. In 379, Emperor Gratian made Theodosius co-emperor, responsible for the eastern provinces. The Visigoths had defeated a Roman army in the east in 378. In 382, a treaty between Theodosius and the Visigoths made the Visigoths the first independent barbarian nation within the Roman Empire.

Theodosius became senior co-emperor when Gratian died in 383. Gratian's brother, Valentinian II, became emperor of the western provinces. Valentinian died in 392, and pagans gained control of the western provinces. Theodosius crushed the pagans in 394 and ruled the entire empire until he died.   William G. Sinnigen

Theology, *thee AHL uh jee,* is the study and description of God. It may also be the expression of religious belief. The word *theology* comes from the Greek words *theos* (god) and *logos* (talk). Theology explores a wide range of questions, such as: "Does God exist? What is the nature of God? What is God's relation to the world and to its inhabitants? and How do human beings know or experience God?" Some branches of theology deal with the history of religion or the study of sacred writings. Other branches deal with the defense of religious doctrines against opposing views or the application of doctrine to daily life.

Approaches to theology vary from one religion to another. They also vary within a religious tradition. For example, some Christian theologians base their understanding of God on such authoritative sources as the Bible and the decrees of church councils. Others explain their understanding of God in terms of philosophy, psychology, or science. In most cases, a theologian's own religious experience plays an important part in his or her theological system.   Jerry A. Irish

See also **God; Religion.**

Theorem. See **Geometry; Binomial theorem; Pythagorean Theorem.**

Theosophy, *thee AHS uh fee,* is a system of philosophic and religious thought. Theosophy is based on claims of a mystic insight into the nature of God and the laws of the universe. The theosophist believes the truest knowledge comes not through reason or the senses, but through a direct communion of the soul with divine reality.

The term theosophy has been applied specifically to the beliefs and teachings of the Theosophical Society. This society was founded in the United States in 1875 by Madame Elena Petrovna Blavatsky and others. Hindu and Buddhist thought and doctrines have become prominent in theosophy. A characteristic feature is the belief in reincarnation, in accordance with the Hindu doctrine of Karma. This doctrine states that the spirit advances to its goal through a succession of earthly lives, and that the consequences of a person's actions in the present life are reaped by his or her successor on earth in a fresh incarnation. H. M. Kallen

See also **Besant, Annie Wood.**

Theotokopoulos, Domenikos. See Greco, El.

Therapy. See Chemotherapy; Drug; Occupational therapy; Physical therapy; Psychotherapy.

Theravada. See Buddhism (Buddhist schools).

Theremin, *THEHR uh mihn,* is a boxlike musical instrument that resembles a radio receiver. Musical tones are produced by two high-frequency electronic circuits inside the instrument. A player creates music by moving the right hand through the air in front of an antenna projecting from the instrument. The player controls the volume by means of a switch and by moving the left hand over a metal loop on the theremin. The Russian scientist Lev Theremin invented the instrument and first played it in public in 1920. The theremin is mainly a musical curiosity, but it has been used as a solo instrument. Composers of music for the theremin include Bohuslav Martinů and Edgard Varèse. Reinhard G. Pauly

Theresa, *tuh KEE suh,* **Saint** (1515-1582), also spelled *Teresa,* is a saint of the Roman Catholic Church. She was a Spanish nun, and is one of the patron saints of Spain.

Saint Theresa was born at Avila in Old Castile. Her study at an Augustinian monastery and her reading of the tales of ancient martyrs inspired her to seek martyrdom for herself. In 1533, she entered a Carmelite convent. The lack of asceticism and severity displeased her, but for many years she made no attempt to bring about reforms. A reading of the *Confessions* of Saint Augustine, combined with the death of her father and certain supernatural visitations, wakened in her a strong spirituality. She began to feel that it was her duty to restore the Carmelite order to the original austerity of its rule. Accordingly, she withdrew with a few followers in 1562, and set up a new convent to put her ideas into effect. Opposition to her plan was strong, but the Pope approved of the idea. At last, the general of the order asked her to introduce her reforms into other convents. She opened many new convents in Castile and even beyond its boundaries, and accomplished much in her efforts to reform existing Carmelite houses.

Several cities contended for her body after her death at Alba de Tormes, near Salamanca. The power of working miracles was believed to be in her relics, which were carried to various places. She was canonized by Pope Gregory in 1622. Saint Theresa wrote an autobiography and several treatises and letters, all published in 1587. Her feast day is October 15. Anne E. Carr

Thermal inversion. See Air pollution (Chief sources of air pollution).

Thermal pollution occurs when hot wastewater is discharged into rivers, lakes, oceans, or other bodies of water. The wastewater raises the temperature of the body of water above its normal level and can harm animals and plants living in the water. For example, warmer water may interfere with fish growth, reproduction, and food supply. In some cases, fish may be killed due to the sudden and rapid rise in temperature.

The major sources of thermal pollution are factories and power plants that use water to cool equipment or heat it to produce steam. In the United States, the Environmental Protection Agency (EPA) has issued regulations controlling the wastewater discharged by these facilities. Many factories and power stations attempt to reduce thermal pollution by cooling wastewater in cooling towers before releasing it, thereby allowing heat to escape into the air. Industries can also reduce thermal pollution by releasing hot water in scattered areas in order to prevent a dangerous temperature rise in any one place. Frank L. Parker

See also **Environmental pollution** (Water pollution; diagram).

Thermal springs. See Hot springs.

Thermocouple, *THUR moh KUHP uhl,* is an electric device that changes heat into electricity or electricity into heat. A thermocouple is made by twisting the ends of two different kinds of wire, such as iron and copper, together to form a *junction.* The opposite ends are also twisted together to form another junction. If one junction is heated, an ammeter connected to one of the wires between the junctions will show a *thermoelectric* (heat-generated) current flowing. The German physicist T. J. Seebeck discovered this effect in 1821. If a battery instead of an ammeter is connected to the thermocouple, one junction will become hot and the other will become cool. This effect was first noticed by the French physicist J. C. A. Peltier in 1834.

Thermocouples are used as thermometers and to generate electricity. Refrigeration devices have been made using them. In a thermocouple used as a thermometer, one of the junctions senses the temperature being measured, and the other is kept at a constant temperature. A voltmeter measures the voltage between the junctions and shows the temperature. Theodore Korneff

Thermodynamics, *THUR moh dy NAM ihks,* is the study of various forms of energy, such as heat and work, and of the conversion of energy from one form into another. Engineers, chemists, and physicists use the principles of thermodynamics in understanding events in nature and in such activities as designing machines and calculating the loss or gain of energy in chemical reactions.

Thermodynamics is based chiefly on two *laws* (principles). The first law states that energy in a *system,* which may be anything from a simple object to a complex machine, cannot be created or destroyed. Instead, energy is either converted from one form into another or transferred from one system to another. For example, a *heat engine,* such as a gas turbine or a nuclear reactor, changes energy from fuel into heat energy. It then converts the heat energy into mechanical energy that can be used to do work. The total amount of energy always remains the same. All systems also have internal energy that undergoes certain changes, but is never created or destroyed. Scientists study changes in this internal energy by measuring changes in such properties as the volume, temperature, and pressure of the system.

The second law of thermodynamics deals with the natural direction of energy processes. For example, according to this law, heat will, of its own accord, flow only from a hotter object to a colder object. The second law accounts for the fact that a heat engine can never be completely efficient—that is, it cannot convert all the heat energy from its fuel into mechanical energy. Instead, the engine transfers some of its heat energy to colder objects in the surroundings.   Robert F. Boehm

See also **Entropy; Heat** (Thermodynamics); **Clausius, Rudolf J. E.; Joule, James P.; Mayer, Julius R. von.**

Thermography, *thur MAHG ruh fee,* is a detection technique that converts invisible heat energy into a visible picture. A device called a *thermograph* is used to produce a *thermogram* (heat picture). Thermography is used in industry, medicine, and many other fields.

A thermograph looks like a TV camera connected to a TV screen. It "sees" temperature by sensing heat energy, called *infrared energy.* Infrared energy is radiated naturally by all objects, and hotter objects radiate more than cooler ones. Inside a thermograph, a solid-state detector converts infrared energy into electrical signals. The signals are displayed as pictures on the TV-like screen. The pictures show different temperature ranges by variations of brightness or color. These variations can be analyzed by scientists.

Industrial uses of thermography include detecting overheated parts in electrical distribution systems and energy losses in manufacturing processes. The technique also is used to find leaks in the insulation of homes and other buildings. In addition, thermography provides a means of inspecting blast furnaces. A weak spot in a furnace wall is hotter than the surrounding areas, and so it appears lighter on a thermogram.

In medicine, thermography can reveal arthritis, nerve damage, and blood circulation problems. Physicians also use thermography, along with other tests, to confirm the presence of breast tumors.

Military and police forces and firemen use thermography to see in the dark and through smoke. Pollution-control experts sometimes use the technique to determine the distribution of *thermal* (heat) pollution in bodies of water.   Cliff Warren

Thermometer is an instrument that measures the temperature of gases, liquids, and solids. The action of a thermometer is based on the fact that certain measurable physical characteristics of substances change when the temperature changes. These characteristics include the volume of a liquid and the length of a solid. Another is the *resistance*—that is, the opposition to the flow of electricity—in an electrical conductor.

There are three principal types of thermometers: (1) liquid-in-glass, (2) deformation-type, and (3) electrical. Many types of thermometers are made as both *digital* thermometers and *disposable* thermometers.

Liquid-in-glass thermometers are the best-known type of thermometers. They include those used to determine the temperature in or outside a building, to measure the temperature of the body, and for cooking. Mercury is the most common liquid in these thermometers. Alcohol is used in areas where the temperature frequently drops below the freezing point of mercury (−39° C or −38° F.). The liquid fills a glass bulb, which is connected to a sealed glass tube partially filled with liquid. When the temperature goes up, the volume of the liquid expands and the liquid rises. A temperature scale is on the outside of the thermometer.

Deformation-type thermometers change shape as a result of an increase or decrease in temperature. There are two kinds of deformation thermometers, *bimetallic* and *Bourdon tube.* Bimetallic thermometers, the most common type, consist of two strips of different metals, such as iron and brass. The strips are fastened together from end to end, forming a bar. When the temperature rises, each metal expands at a different rate, which causes the bar to bend. This motion of the bar causes a pointer to move up or down a scale, indicating a temperature change. A type of bimetallic thermometer called a *thermograph* includes a pen that makes a written record of temperature changes.

Bourdon tube thermometers have a curved, flexible metal tube filled with a liquid, such as glycerol or xylene. A rise in temperature makes the liquid expand. The tube straightens out to accommodate the increased volume of liquid. A pen or pointer attached to the end of the tube indicates the temperature.

Electrical thermometers include *thermocouples* and *resistance thermometers.* Thermocouples, the most widely used type, consist of two wires of different metals. Both ends of the two wires are twisted together to form junctions. One of these junctions, called the *reference junction,* is kept at a constant temperature—usually 0° C (32° F.). As the temperature of the other junction changes, a small voltage is generated between the two wires. The voltage is measured by an instrument called a *millivoltmeter,* which may have a temperature scale marked on it. Most thermocouples that measure the temperature of the air have wires made of copper and an alloy called *constantan.* Thermocouples with wires of other metals can measure temperatures up to 2800° C (5072° F.). See **Thermocouple.**

Resistance thermometers are made of such materials as copper, nickel, or platinum. A temperature change

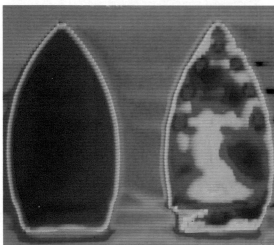

© Howard Sochurek

A thermogram of two irons shows the distribution of heat on their surfaces. The iron on the left has an even temperature. The iron on the right has hotter areas, which appear on the thermogram as light-orange, yellow, and purple.

causes a variation in the *electrical resistance* of these metals (see **Electric circuit** [Circuit mathematics]). The variation is measured and expressed as a temperature value. Scientists use *platinum resistance thermometers* to check the accuracy of all other types of thermometers. These extremely reliable thermometers are used to measure temperatures from −259.34° C (−434.81° F.) to 630.74° C (1167.33° F.) on the *International Practical Temperature Scale of 1968.* This scale provides a worldwide reference for temperature values.

Digital thermometers use electronic circuits and devices to show temperature measurements. These thermometers display the measurements as numbers. Digital thermometers measure temperature by means of a slender device called a *probe.* The probe is made of either a metal, such as copper or platinum, or a *semiconductor* (see **Semiconductor**). Temperature changes cause a large variation in the electrical resistance of these materials. Most semiconductors are more sensitive to temperature changes than are metals.

The probe is connected to an electronic circuit. The circuit receives temperature readings from the probe in the form of electrical signals. The signals are changed into numbers, which appear in a display window.

Disposable thermometers are frequently used in homes and medical clinics for measuring body temperature. They are cheaper than regular thermometers to manufacture and to buy. Most disposable thermometers lose their accuracy after a single use, but a few have been designed for repeated use.

Some disposable thermometers are made of materials that melt at certain temperatures. Others use substances called *liquid crystals,* which change appearance at specific temperatures (see **Liquid crystal**).

Temperature scales. Various manufacturers produce thermometers with a temperature scale in *Fahrenheit.* However, the National Bureau of Standards uses only the *Celsius* and *Kelvin* scales. The bureau is the federal agency that sets measurement standards for science, industry, and commerce in the United States.

On the Fahrenheit scale, 32° F. is the freezing point of water and 212° F. is the boiling point. On the Celsius scale, water freezes at 0° C and boils at 100° C. The Kelvin scale is used for scientific measurement. On this scale, water freezes at 273 K and boils at 373 K. See **Weights and measures** (Temperature).

All temperature scales are based on the International Practical Temperature Scale of 1968. On this scale, temperature is determined by means of six fixed points called *equilibrium states,* which have assigned values. Temperatures are expressed in Celsius and Kelvin units, but may be converted to other scales.

History. The first known thermometer was invented in 1593 by the Italian astronomer Galileo. It was called a *thermoscope* and had only fair accuracy. An accurate thermometer using alcohol was developed in 1641. In 1714, Gabriel D. Fahrenheit, a German physicist, built a mercury thermometer of the type used today.

Harmon H. Plumb

See also **Bolometer; Pyrometry; Temperature.**

Thermonuclear reaction. See **Nuclear energy** (Nuclear fusion); **Sun** (How long will the sun shine?; How the sun produces energy).

Thermoplastic materials. See **Plastics** (table).

Thermopylae, *thuhr MAHP uh lee,* was the name of a mountain pass in ancient Greece. The word *Thermopylae* means *Hot Gates.* The name comes from hot springs near the narrow pass. Greek history tells the story of the bravery that was shown at Thermopylae, where gallant Greek warriors fought against their enemies, the Persians. The mountain pass no longer exists. The area is now a wide, marshy plain. But the hot springs remain.

The narrow mountain pass lay between Mount Oeta and the Maliac Gulf. In ancient days, it provided the best way for an army to pass from northern into southern Greece. The pass was only about 50 feet (15 meters)

Types of thermometers

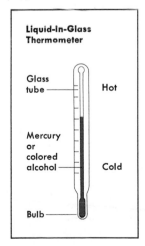

Liquid-In-Glass Thermometer

Glass tube — Hot

Mercury or colored alcohol — Cold

Bulb —

A column of liquid shows the temperature in a liquid-in-glass thermometer. The liquid in most such thermometers is mercury or colored alcohol.

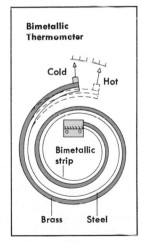

Bimetallic Thermometer

Cold / Hot

Bimetallic strip

Brass   Steel

A bimetallic strip, consisting of two metals, can show temperature. As the temperature changes, the strip bends, indicating the temperature.

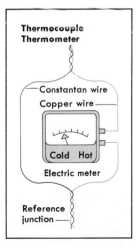

Thermocouple Thermometer

Constantan wire
Copper wire

Cold Hot

Electric meter

Reference junction —

An electric voltage from a device called a *thermocouple* can be measured to show the temperature. An electric meter measures the voltage.

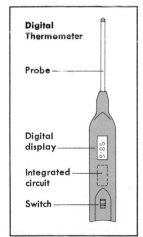

Digital Thermometer

Probe —

Digital display —

Integrated circuit —

Switch —

WORLD BOOK diagrams by Arthur Grebetz

A digital thermometer has a circuit that changes electric temperature signals into numbers. The numbers appear in a display window.

wide, and fairly small forces were able to defend it.

In 480 B.C., Xerxes led his Persian warriors in an attempted invasion of Greece. The Greek states united to meet the attack. Leonidas, the king of Sparta, led the Greek army of 6,000 men to hold the pass at Thermopylae. The Greek fleet at Artemisium protected the forces of Leonidas from a Persian attack by sea.

For two days, the Greeks held the Persian foe at bay. But on the evening of the second day, a Thessalian traitor named Ephialtes showed Xerxes a new path over the mountains. The Persians crossed and threatened the Greeks from the rear. To save them from death in the pass, Leonidas ordered most of the Greeks to leave. He held off the Persian warriors with a small force of about 300 Spartans and 1,100 other Greeks. But the Persians outflanked him and killed Leonidas and most of his forces.   Thomas W. Africa

See also **Greece, Ancient** (The Persian Wars); **Leonidas I; Xerxes I.**

Thermos bottle is a container that keeps liquids hot or cold for many hours. It is also called a *vacuum bottle* or *Dewar flask.* Thermos bottles vary widely in size, ranging in capacity from 2 ounces (59 milliliters) to 15 gallons (57 liters), and have many uses. They are commonly used to carry coffee, juice, milk, or soup. Vacuum bottles also are used in scientific and medical work to store chemicals and drugs, to transport tissues and organs, and to preserve blood plasma.

Sir James Dewar, a British chemist, invented the vacuum bottle in 1892. He developed it for storing liquefied gases. Although his flask was designed to prevent the entry of heat from outside the container, it worked

equally well in keeping liquids hot by reducing the loss of heat from the inside.

The modern thermos bottle has the same basic design as Dewar's flask. It blocks the three processes through which heat is transferred—*conduction, convection,* and *radiation* (see **Heat** [How heat travels]). A typical thermos bottle has an inner container that consists of two glass bottles, one within the other. Glass does not transmit heat well, and so reduces heat transfer by conduction. The bottles are sealed together at their lips by melting the glass. Most of the air between the bottles is removed to create a partial vacuum. This vacuum hinders heat transfer by convection because it has so few air molecules to carry heat between the bottles. The facing surfaces of the bottles are coated with a silver solution. They act like mirrors and reflect much of the heat coming from either the inside or outside of the container back to its source. In doing so, they prevent heat transfer by radiation.

Other features of thermos bottles help minimize both the loss or entry of heat. Most thermos bottles have a small mouth, which reduces heat exchange. The bottles are closed with a stopper made of cork, plastic, or some other material that conducts heat poorly. The fragile inner container of a thermos bottle is encased in metal or plastic for protection. A rubber collar around the mouth holds the inner container in place, and a spring at the base serves as a shock absorber.   W. David Lewis

Thermosphere, *THUR muh sfihr,* is the uppermost region of the earth's atmosphere. It begins at an altitude of about 53 miles (85 kilometers) and continues about 300 miles (480 kilometers) into space. The thermosphere has only a tiny fraction of the gases that are in the atmosphere. As a result, the atmospheric pressure in the lower thermosphere is a million or more times as low as the pressure at sea level.

The thermosphere is completely exposed to the sun's radiation. The radiation heats the thin atmosphere of the thermosphere to high temperatures. The temperature increases rapidly from about −135° F. (−93° C) at an altitude of 55 miles (89 kilometers) to more than 2700° F. (1500° C) in the *thermopause,* the upper region of the thermosphere.

Solar radiation, along with cosmic rays, changes the chemical composition of the atmosphere in the thermosphere. From 50 to 60 miles (80 to 97 kilometers) up, oxygen molecules are broken into atoms. Beyond 250 miles (400 kilometers) up, the thermosphere consists chiefly of helium and hydrogen atoms. The radiation also *ionizes* (charges electrically) atoms in the atmosphere. The region of ionized particles, called the *ionosphere,* extends into the thermosphere.

Veerabhadran Ramanathan

See also **Air; Troposphere; Stratosphere; Mesosphere; Ionosphere.**

Thermostat, *THUR muh stat,* is a device that helps control the temperature of an indoor area or of an appliance. Thermostats are used in many kinds of equipment, including air conditioners, heaters, electric blankets, ovens, and refrigerators.

A thermostat is set to keep an area or an appliance at a certain temperature. It measures temperature changes and automatically controls the heating or cooling unit of the equipment being used. For example, the thermostat

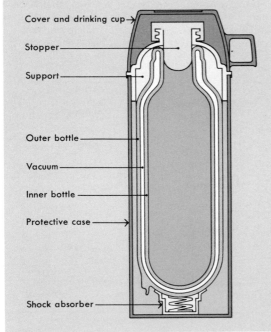

Cover and drinking cup

Stopper

Support

Outer bottle

Vacuum

Inner bottle

Protective case

Shock absorber

WORLD BOOK diagram

A thermos bottle is two bottles in one, as shown above. A vacuum in the space between the inner and outer bottles helps prevent heat from passing through the bottle.

in a home heating system turns on the furnace if the temperature drops below the desired level. It shuts off the furnace when the temperature reaches that level.

How thermostats work. Most metals, liquids, and gases expand when their temperature increases. They contract when their temperature decreases. Some thermostats use such expansion and contraction to measure and control temperature.

Most thermostats used in home heaters and air conditioners have a *bimetallic strip* that "senses" changes in temperature. This thin strip consists of two metals fastened together. When the temperature rises, each metal expands at a different rate, causing the strip to bend. The metals contract unequally when the temperature drops. These actions cause the strip to bend in the opposite direction. This bending action opens or closes the electric circuit that controls heating or cooling equipment. In some thermostats, the bending of the strip tilts a bulb filled with mercury. When the bulb tilts, it completes or breaks the circuit.

Some thermostats use the expansion or contraction of a gas or a liquid to control heating or cooling equipment. Other types use electric devices or infrared detectors that sense temperature changes.

Most thermostats turn heating or cooling equipment completely on or completely off. But some use a method called *proportional control*. These thermostats measure the difference between the actual temperature and the desired temperature. They change the amount of heating or cooling in proportion to this temperature difference. Proportional control thermostats can provide an extremely even temperature. They are used in industry and scientific research to control the temperature so that certain chemical processes can take place.

Uses. Thermostats that control air-conditioning and heating systems in houses and other buildings help keep the air comfortable for any activity. Some industries use thermostats to carefully control the temperature needed for manufacturing certain products or for scientific experiments.

Thermostats help keep refrigerators and freezers at the necessary temperature to keep food from spoiling. They control the temperature of household ovens and of industrial furnaces used in making such products as bricks and steel. In homes, thermostats are used in irons, hot water heaters, and heaters for fish tanks.

Thermostats also control the flow of water in automobile cooling systems. The thermostat operates a valve that opens when the water reaches a certain temperature. The open valve allows water to circulate through the radiator and through the water jacket that surrounds the engine.   Richard W. Henry

Theropod. See Dinosaur (Saurischians).

Theseus, *THEE see uhs* or *THEE soos,* was a great king of early Athens in Greek mythology. He was the son of King Aegeus and Aethra, a princess of Troezen. Aegeus left Aethra in Troezen and went back to Athens before Theseus was born. The king put his sword and sandals under a large rock and told Aethra that when their son could lift the rock, he should take the sword and sandals and come to him in Athens.

When Theseus was old enough to lift the rock, he set out for Athens. On the way, he killed many bandits and monsters. After he reached Athens, the sorceress Medea, now Aegeus' wife, tried to poison him. But Aegeus recognized Theseus' sword and saved his life.

According to the legend, Athens had to send seven youths and seven maidens to Crete every year in those days to be eaten by the Minotaur (see **Minotaur**). Theseus decided to go as one of the youths and try to kill the Minotaur. With the help of Ariadne, the daughter of King Minos of Crete, he succeeded, and saved his companions. Ariadne left Crete with him, but Theseus deserted her on the way back to Athens.

He had agreed with Aegeus that his ship would fly white sails if he should come back alive. Otherwise, the black sails with which the ship left Athens would not be changed. In his hurry to return home, Theseus forgot to fly white sails. When Aegeus saw black sails on the returning ship, he killed himself in his sorrow, thinking Theseus had perished. Theseus then became the king of Athens.   William F. Hansen

Thespis, *THEHS pihs,* a Greek actor and dramatist of the 500's B.C., helped to create drama as we know it. Today, actors are sometimes called *Thespians,* after his name.

Thespis was a real person. However, the ancient Greeks made him a legend and assigned several "firsts" to him. They said he was the first to use a speaker performing a role in dialogue with the choral group. Tragedy seems to have developed from this character-chorus dialogue, so the Greeks concluded that Thespis invented tragedy. The Greeks also credited Thespis with introducing makeup in the form of white lead paint and, later, masks to be worn by performers.

The famous "Parian Marble" tablet records that, in about 534 B.C. in Athens, Thespis became the first to produce a tragedy at the major festival honoring the god Dionysus. Competitions in playwriting were held regularly at the festival after this time.   Norman T. Pratt

How a home thermostat works

When the temperature in a room becomes too cold, the bimetallic strip of the thermostat uncoils. This action causes a drop of mercury to close a switch and start the heating system. After the temperature has risen to the desired level, the strip coils up and the mercury opens the switch, shutting off the heat.

WORLD BOOK diagram by Arthur Grebetz

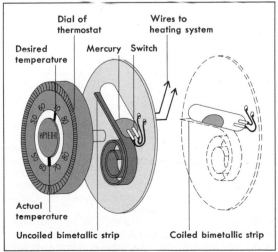

Dial of thermostat

Wires to heating system

Desired temperature

Mercury   Switch

Actual temperature

Uncoiled bimetallic strip

Coiled bimetallic strip

Thessalonians, THEHS uh LOH nee uhnz, **Epistles to the,** are the 13th and 14th books of the New Testament. They are both letters from the apostle Paul to Christians in Thessaloniki (now Salonika), Greece. Paul wrote the first letter from Corinth about A.D. 50. He wrote to encourage the Thessalonians in the midst of their struggles and to explain why he had been unable to return to visit them. Paul also explained that Christians who had died before the Second Coming of Jesus Christ would rise from the dead and be united with Jesus on the Coming. This letter is the earliest surviving letter of Paul and the earliest known Christian writing.

Some scholars doubt that Paul wrote the second letter. They believe it was written in his name by one of his followers. If Paul was the author, he wrote it shortly after writing the first letter. Its main purpose was to convince the Thessalonians that the Second Coming of Christ was not as near as they believed.   Terrance D. Callan

See also **Bible** (The New Testament); **Paul, Saint.**

Thessaloniki. See Salonika.

Thessaly, THEHS uh lee, is a region in northern Greece. It has an area of 5,368 square miles (13,903 square kilometers) and a population of about 700,000

WORLD BOOK map

Thessaly is a region in northern Greece. The map at the left shows the location of the region. A map of Thessaly itself appears at the right.

persons. For location, see **Greece** (map). Volos and Larisa are Thessaly's largest cities. Three mountains that border the region—Olympus, Pelion, and Ossa—are important in Greek history and legend (see **Olympus**).

In legend, Thessaly was the home of the great Greek warrior Achilles, and also of Jason, who led the Argonauts in search of the golden fleece. The ancient Thessalians were weak militarily because they never banded together. Philip of Macedon conquered Thessaly in 344 B.C. Later, the Romans took Thessaly, and added it to Macedonia in 146 B.C. The Venetians and the Turks controlled Thessaly for hundreds of years. In 1878, by order of the Congress of Berlin, Turkey gave Thessaly to Greece.   Norman A. Doenges

See also **Greece** (The land).

Thiamine. See Vitamin (Vitamin B); **Beriberi.**

Thibault, Jacques A. F. See France, Anatole.

Thiers, tyair, **Louis Adolphe,** lwee a DAWLF (1797-1877), was the first president of the Third Republic of France. His 10-volume *History of the French Revolution* (1823-1827) made him famous. He helped place Louis Philippe on the throne of France.

Thiers' political life included terms as foreign minister

and president of the council. He also wrote a *History of the Consulate and the Empire* (1845-1862). Emerging from retirement in 1870 during the Franco-Prussian War, he negotiated the peace treaty with Otto von Bismarck, Germany's chancellor. Thiers then put down the revolt of the Paris Commune, and led the new republic until he resigned in 1873. He was born in Marseille.
Francis J. Bowman

See also **Franco-Prussian War.**

Thinker, The. See Rodin, Auguste.

Thiopental, THY oh PEHN tal, is a barbiturate used to produce sleep for surgery. It is a *general anesthetic*—that is, a drug that causes unconsciousness and loss of feeling in the entire body. The trade name of thiopental is Pentothal or Sodium Pentothal.

The use of thiopental as an anesthetic was first publicly demonstrated in 1934 by John S. Lundy at the Mayo Clinic. Thiopental anesthesia soon came into wide use, largely because thiopental could be safely used in situations where flammable anesthetics, such as ether and cyclopropane, produced a danger of fire or explosion. Today, thiopental is used to bring about anesthesia for surgery throughout the world.

Thiopental is usually administered by injection into a vein. Because receiving an injection is more pleasant for most patients than breathing the vapors of an inhaled anesthetic, physicians use thiopental to begin anesthesia for surgery. After the patient is asleep, physicians usually maintain anesthesia with nitrous oxide, halothane, or other inhaled anesthetics.

Psychiatrists sometimes give patients small doses of thiopental. The drug helps patients discuss their thoughts and emotions more freely. For this reason, it is sometimes called a "truth serum."   Edwin S. Munson

Third International. See International, The.

Third Reich. See Germany (History); **Reich.**

Third World is a name sometimes given to economically developing countries, particularly those in Asia, Africa, and Latin America. The term *Third World* is also used for politically neutral countries. Such countries are also called *neutral nations* or *nonaligned nations* because they do not regularly support either the First World or the Second World. The First World is said to consist of the United States and other non-Communist industrial nations. The Second World refers to the Soviet Union and the Communist countries of Eastern Europe. Some political experts consider China a Third World country, but others disagree.

The Third World consists of about 120 countries, which have more than half the world's population. Most Third World countries are former colonies of Western European nations and have gained their independence since 1945. Although Third World countries frequently have similar goals, they actually represent different and sometimes opposing political and economic systems.

Most Third World countries have an economy based on agriculture and have developed few industries. Many export raw materials to industrial nations in exchange for manufactured goods. Most Third World countries are poor. About 60 per cent of the people in the Third World live in extreme poverty.

During the 1960's, Third World countries began to use the United Nations (UN) to promote their interests. Today, the Third World has a majority of the votes in the

UN General Assembly. Neither the Communist nor the non-Communist bloc can get a resolution adopted without the support of some Third World countries.

Since the mid-1970's, Third World countries increasingly have emphasized their economic problems. They demand financial aid and favorable trade agreements from the industrial countries to redistribute the earth's wealth. They consider the economic differences between developed and developing countries more important than the political differences between Communist and non-Communist ones. For this reason, they prefer the terms *North* for the wealthy nations and *South* for themselves, rather than First, Second, or Third World. Most industrial nations, both Communist and non-Communist, are in the North. Most Third World nations are in the South.

The World Bank, the United Nations Development Program, and other international organizations provide funds for development in the Third World. But progress has been slow because Third World countries continue to suffer from such problems as rapid population growth and high rates of disease and illiteracy. In addition, richer nations have been unwilling to accept the demands of many Third World countries for financial aid and other assistance.   W. Scott Thompson

See also **Developing country.**

Thirst is a sensation caused by the body's need for water. The body's *internal environment* (the organs and tissues) needs certain amounts of water and salts to function properly. Too much or too little water, or too much or too little salt, can damage or kill cells. Thus, people and animals must control their water intake.

People often describe thirst as a dry feeling in the throat. A lack of sufficient saliva can produce this kind of thirst, even when the internal environment has no need for water. In a similar way, the thirst sensation created by the internal environment's need will disappear briefly if water is drunk and wets the throat. But unless the water reaches the internal environment, thirst will recur after a short time.

The *sensory nerves* in the internal organs are affected by the volume of fluid in the internal environment. These nerves help regulate the amount of water drunk. The internal senses tell how much water and salt are inside and outside the body's cells (see **Senses**). One source of this information is a region of the brain stem called the *hypothalamus.* The hypothalamus is important in maintaining the internal environment. It contains nerve cells that respond to changes in the amount of salt in the blood. The salt concentration of the blood may indicate how much water is in body cells. For example, a decrease in body water produces an increase in the salt concentration in the blood. Thus, the amount of water in the internal environment also affects the amount of water eliminated from the body.   Bruce P. Halpern

Thirteen Colonies. See Colonial life in America; United States, History of the.

Thirteenth Amendment. See Constitution of the United States (Amendment 13).

Thirty-Nine Articles were a statement of doctrine issued in England in 1563 and approved by Parliament in 1571. The Articles were created to settle religious disputes caused by the Protestant Reformation. The Articles set forth religious positions that all English people were expected to accept. They remain the doctrine of the churches of the Anglican Communion.

The Articles set the Church of England on a middle ground between the Roman Catholic Church and various radical Protestant groups. The Articles condemned several Roman Catholic beliefs and practices, including purgatory, transubstantiation, reverence for saints and relics, indulgences, and the power of the pope. The Articles affirmed the doctrine of predestination—that people are saved solely by God's grace and cannot earn salvation by good deeds. The doctrine of free will was rejected. Contrary to the beliefs of the radicals, the Articles declared that Christians must obey *secular* (nonreligious) governments and could bear arms for the state. The Articles also affirmed infant baptism, rather than adult baptism, which was practiced by the Anabaptists (see **Anabaptists**).

Some Christians in England, later called Puritans, did not think the Thirty-Nine Articles went far enough in opposing Roman Catholic doctrine. But most of the English people accepted the Articles, and members of the clergy of the Church of England still endorse them today.   Richard Marius

Thirty Tyrants was the name given to the government of Athens after the city was captured by the Spartans in 404 B.C. The men who ruled at this time have also been called simply *The Thirty.* The brilliant Athenian politician Critias led this powerful group. They were appointed to reform the constitution of Athens along conservative lines. But Critias and some of his followers tried to set up a permanent military government. Their reign of terror ended in 403 B.C., when the old democracy was brought back to Athens and the Spartan forces left the city. A group of pretenders who tried to gain control of the Roman Empire around A.D. 260 were also called the Thirty Tyrants.   Donald Kagan

Thirty Years' War. The Thirty Years' War (1618-1648) was the last of the great religious wars of Europe. This conflict was really a series of wars. It began as a civil war between Protestants and Roman Catholics in the German states. But before the conflict ended, most European nations were involved, and the war had become a general struggle for territory and political power.

Causes of the war. The underlying cause of the war was the old deep-seated hostility between the German Protestants and the German Catholics. The two groups disagreed in their interpretation of the Peace of Augsburg (1555), which had been intended as a settlement of the religious question in Germany. Both groups had violated the peace. In addition, the Peace of Augsburg had recognized only Catholics and Lutherans. There were many Calvinists in southern and central Germany, and they also demanded recognition.

The Bohemian period (1618-1620). In 1608, the Protestants organized the Evangelical Union. In 1609, the Catholics founded the Holy League. The spark that set off the war came when the Archbishop of Prague ordered a Protestant church destroyed. In anger, the people appealed to Emperor Matthias, who ignored their protests. The Protestants rose in revolt. The event that marked the actual beginning of the Thirty Years' War is known in history as the Defenestration of Prague. (*Defenestration* is from the Latin word *fenestra,* which means *window.*) It was an old Bohemian custom for the people to punish offending officials by throwing them out of a window. The Protestant rebels punished two of their ruler's ministers in this way. Civil war began in Bohemia and spread throughout western Europe.

The Bohemian Protestants removed the Catholic king, Ferdinand, from the throne, and chose the Protestant Frederick, Elector Palatine, in Ferdinand's place. To make matters worse for the Bohemians, Ferdinand was chosen Holy Roman emperor. Ferdinand—who took the title Ferdinand II—had great power in this position. In 1620, his general, Johan Tserclaes, Count of Tilly, decisively defeated the Bohemians in the Battle of the White Mountain. This defeat cost the Bohemians their independence. The Protestant rebellion was stamped out, and Catholicism again became the state religion.

The Danish period (1625-1629). After Bohemia was defeated, the other Protestant countries began to realize their danger. The Protestant king of Denmark, Christian IV, aided by several other countries, opposed Ferdinand's forces in Saxony. But the emperor had received unexpected help from the famous general Albrecht Wenzel Eusebius von Wallenstein, who had a great army of hired soldiers and adventurers.

Wallenstein's army, aided by forces of the Holy League under the leadership of General Tilly, defeated the Danish king again and again. Christian IV finally signed the Treaty of Lübeck (1629) and withdrew from Saxony. Meanwhile, the emperor had issued the Edict of Restitution. This document provided that all Church possessions which the Protestants had acquired were to be returned to the Catholics. The Edict was a new source of friction in Germany.

The Swedish period (1630-1635). The Swedish king, Gustavus Adolphus, known as "the Lion of the North," next entered the war. He had two reasons for this entrance into conflict. He was sincerely devoted to the cause of Protestantism, and he was also ambitious for Sweden, which would be in danger if Emperor Ferdinand became too powerful. So, for the first time, a political issue entered the war.

In 1630, Gustavus Adolphus set sail from Sweden with 13,000 men to relieve the city of Magdeburg, which Tilly was besieging. The Swedish king had the best-trained and best-disciplined army in Europe, but he arrived too late to prevent the capture, looting, and destruction of Magdeburg. In 1631, the Swedish army defeated Tilly in the Battle of Breitenfeld. In 1632, the Swedish forces were victorious in another important battle, and Tilly was killed in the fighting.

Emperor Ferdinand now called back Wallenstein, whom he had previously dismissed. Another army of recruits was gathered together from many parts of Europe, and placed under Wallenstein's leadership. Ferdinand also made an alliance with Philip IV of Spain. Wallenstein's army met the Swedish forces in the famous Battle of Lützen (1632). The Swedes won, but Gustavus Adolphus was killed in the battle. The Swedes continued the struggle until 1634, when their army was destroyed in the Battle of Nördlingen. The emperor suspected that Wallenstein was negotiating with the Protestants and ordered his arrest. Wallenstein tried to escape, but was assassinated.

The Swedish-French period (1635-1648). The war now lost its religious character entirely and became purely political. Cardinal Richelieu, who was the real ruler of France, determined to block the growth of Habsburg power by interfering on the side of the Protestants. The war became a struggle between the French Bourbons and the Austrian Habsburgs. In 1635, Richelieu sent a French army into Germany, which joined with a new Swedish army. The Protestants and their French allies had excellent leaders, including the French Vicomte de Turenne and Louis II, Prince of Condé. The combined French and Swedish armies won a long series of victories, which gave new hope to the Protestants living in Germany.

The Peace of Westphalia (1648). For years the people of Germany had suffered misery and hardships because of the Thirty Years' War. In 1644, the European countries sent representatives to a peace conference. The Catholic and Protestant delegates met separately in two different cities of Westphalia. The negotiations dragged on for four years, until the Peace of Westphalia was signed in 1648. By this treaty, France acquired Alsace and Lorraine, Sweden got control of the mouths of the Oder, Elbe, and Weser rivers, and Calvinism was put on an equal footing with Catholicism and Lutheranism.

Results of the war. Germany was in a pitiable condition by the time the war finally ended. Many persons had been killed. Those who survived saw nothing but ruin wherever they looked. Whole cities, villages, and farms had disappeared, and much property had been destroyed. Art, science, trade, and industry declined. It took almost two hundred years for Germany to recover from the effects of the Thirty Years' War. Thousands of persons left Europe, especially Germany, and went to America to build a new life.   J. Salwyn Schapiro

See also **Gustavus Adolphus; Richelieu, Cardinal; Wallenstein, Albrecht W. E. von; Tilly, Count of.**

Additional resources

Langer, Herbert. *Thirty Years' War.* Hippocrene, 1980.
Maland, David. *Europe at War: 1600-1650.* Rowman & Littlefield, 1980.
Wedgwood, Cicely Veronica. *The Thirty Years War.* Methuen, 1981. First published in 1938.

Thisbe. See Pyramus and Thisbe.

Thistle is the name given to a group of plants that have sharp spines or prickles. Thistles are often troublesome weeds. They grow in many places throughout the world. The most common thistles are the *Canada thistle,* the *bull thistle,* the *tall thistle,* and the *pasture thistle.* The first two come from Europe, and the last two are native to North America. They grow in pastures and grain and hay fields, and along roads, where the soil is rich. The most troublesome, the Canada thistle, is a perennial. The other three species are biennial.

Thistles have tough, fibrous stems, prickly leaves with many lobes, and soft, silky flowers, usually purple or pinkish-purple in color. The flowers usually grow in round heads that form large, downy seed balls after the blossoms wither. The wind scatters the seeds, and this helps the thistles multiply rapidly. Some kinds have strong roots, and are hard to uproot. Root pieces left in the soil may produce new plants. Thistles are hard to remove from grain fields. Biennial species must be cut down before the flowers bloom. Chemicals that kill thistles but do not harm crops also can be used.

A number of plants similar to thistles are sometimes

WORLD BOOK illustration by Lorraine Epstein

The thistle has sturdy stems, prickly leaves, and purplish flowers. This weed thrives in grain fields and is a troublesome pest in large areas of North America.

called thistles. Included among these is the *Russian thistle* or *tumbleweed*. This plant has become a serious pest in large areas of North America.

Scientific classification. Thistles belong to the composite family, Compositae. The most important genera of thistles include *Carduus, Cirsium,* and *Onopordum.* The Canada thistle is *Cirsium arvense;* the bull, or common, thistle, *C. vulgare;* the tall thistle, *C. altissimum;* and the pasture thistle, *C. pumilum.*

Anton A. Reznicek

Related articles in *World Book* include:

Blazing star	Camomile	Composite	Sow thistle
Boneset	Canada	family	Tumbleweed
Calendula	thistle	Fleabane	

Thomas, Dylan, *DIHL uhn* (1914-1953), was a Welsh poet who wrote some of the most stirring, passionate, and eloquent verse in modern literature. From the publication of his first book, *Eighteen Poems* (1934), critics recognized him as a brilliant and original poet. The volume bewildered and fascinated readers with its extraordinary verbal and musical energy and with its exploration of emotional extremes. These extremes, alternately ecstatic and morbid, revealed Thomas' obsessions with love, death, religion, and the sound of words.

Thomas' high-spirited love of life and exuberant sense of humor are revealed in his prose fiction and drama as well as in his

Atlantic-Little, Brown & Co.
Dylan Thomas

verse. *Portrait of the Artist as a Young Dog* (1940) is a collection of stories about Thomas' youth in Wales. A group of his symbolic stories was published as *Adventures in the Skin Trade* in 1955, after his death. *The Collected Stories of Dylan Thomas* was published in 1984. Just before his death, Thomas completed a radio play, *Under Milk Wood.* This play describes with tender

humor a day in the life of eccentric residents of a Welsh village.

Thomas was born in Swansea. He gained great popularity through public readings of his works in Great Britain and the United States. Many of these readings are available on records and tapes. Thomas died of pneumonia aggravated by acute alcoholism while he was on a tour of the United States. William Harmon

Additional resources

Davies, Walford. *Dylan Thomas.* Taylor & Francis, 1985.
FitzGibbon, Constantine. *The Life of Dylan Thomas.* Little, Brown, 1965.
Moynihan, William T. *The Craft and Art of Dylan Thomas.* Cornell Univ. Press, 1966.
Tindall, William Y. *A Reader's Guide to Dylan Thomas.* Octagon, 1973. First published in 1962.

Thomas, George Henry (1816-1870), was a Union general in the Civil War. Because he held his line at the Battle of Chickamauga, he became known as "the Rock of Chickamauga." He served with the Army of the Cumberland, and succeeded Major General William S. Rosecrans as its commander. Thomas fought at Chattanooga and defeated an invading Confederate army at Nashville. A major general in the Army after the war, he died while commanding the Division of the Pacific. He was born in Southampton County, Virginia. See also **Civil War** (Battle of Chickamauga; Battle of Chattanooga).

T. Harry Williams

Thomas, Isaiah, *eyo ZAY uh* (1749-1831), was the leading printer and publisher in colonial America. His Boston newspaper, the *Massachusetts Spy,* printed strong attacks on the British government.

Thomas was born in Boston and became a printer's apprentice there. He began to publish the *Spy* in 1770. In 1775, the British tried to stop the publication of patriot newspapers. Thomas sent his printing equipment by night to Worcester, Mass., about 40 miles (64 kilometers) west of Boston. He arrived there a few days later. On the way, he aided Paul Revere in his famous midnight ride and fought at Lexington and Concord in the opening battles of the Revolutionary War.

Thomas later printed books and magazines in addition to his newspaper. He wrote a book, *The History of Printing in America* (1810), which still ranks as an important work on the subject. William Morgan Fowler, Jr.

See also **Mother Goose.**

Thomas, Martha Carey (1857-1935), was an American educator who fought for equal educational opportunities for women. In 1885, she became dean and English professor at Bryn Mawr College, a new women's college in Bryn Mawr, Pa. She served as president from 1894 to 1922 and worked to make Bryn Mawr as good as—or better than—the best men's college. She set up high entrance requirements and a demanding course of study, and she hired outstanding teachers.

Carey Thomas, as she preferred to be known, also worked to gain women the right to vote. She served as president of the National College Equal Suffrage League from 1908 to 1917.

Thomas was born in Baltimore and graduated from Cornell University. She went to Europe for further study because few United States graduate schools would admit a woman. In 1882, she earned a Ph.D. at the University of Zurich in Switzerland. Miriam Schneir

Thomas, Norman Mattoon, *muh TOON* (1884-1968), an American Socialist leader, was nominated six times for the presidency of the United States by the Socialist Party. His ardent pacifism during World War I (1914-1918) led him into the Socialist Party. He founded the periodical *World Tomorrow* (1918), and became active in the American Civil Liberties Union, an organization devoted to the defense of civil liberties.

During the 1920's, Thomas ran for mayor of New York City, state governor, and senator. He was first nominated for President in 1928, and received his largest popular vote in 1932. At first somewhat sympathetic to the Soviet experiment, by the middle 1930's he vigorously opposed Communism. He tried to keep the United States out of World War II (1939-1945).

Thomas wrote many books and articles that advocated "planning" in American economic and social relations. Thomas was born in Marion, Ohio.

Richard L. Watson, Jr.

Thomas, Saint, was one of the 12 apostles of Jesus Christ. He is mentioned often in the Gospel of John, where he is also called *Didymus,* which means *the Twin* in Greek. Thomas encouraged the apostles to go with Jesus into Judea, despite the danger of persecution (John 11:16). When Jesus spoke of His death and Resurrection at the Last Supper, Thomas wanted to know how he and the other apostles could follow Him (John 14:5). Thomas is also known as "Doubting Thomas" because he refused to believe the report of Jesus' Resurrection unless he could touch His wounds (John 20:24, 25). When Jesus allowed him to feel His hands and His side, Thomas became a believer, saying, "My Lord and my God" (John 20:26-29).

According to later traditions, Thomas preached in Parthia or India. He was reportedly martyred in India. His feast day in the Roman Catholic Church is July 3. The Eastern Orthodox Churches celebrate his feast on the first Sunday after their Easter celebration.

Richard A. Edwards

See also **Apostles.**

Thomas à Becket. See Becket, Saint Thomas à.

Thomas à Kempis (1380?-1471) was a medieval monk and religious writer. He is generally considered the author of *Imitation of Christ,* probably the most widely read work of Christian literature other than the Bible. *Imitation of Christ* has been translated into many languages. The work first appeared in manuscript form about 1424.

In *Imitation of Christ,* Thomas wrote that people can achieve grace only by trying to imitate the spirit and the actions of Jesus Christ. Thomas stated that grace could be attained through prayer, contemplation, the sacraments, and the rejection of worldly goods. He also emphasized the importance of humility, penitence, and self-discipline. In *Imitation of Christ,* Thomas drew on the writings of earlier Christian writers and the Bible. He also borrowed from the works of the Greek philosopher Aristotle and the Roman authors Ovid and Seneca.

Thomas was born in Kempen, Germany, near Krefeld. His given and family name was Thomas Hemerken. In school, he was called *Thomas from Kempen.* This eventually became *Thomas à Kempis.* Thomas completed his education in Deventer, the Netherlands. In 1399, he entered the Brethren of the Common Life at Mount St.

Agnes, near Zwolle, the Netherlands. He was ordained in 1413.   William J. Courtenay

Thomas Aquinas, Saint. See Aquinas, Saint Thomas.

Thomas Jefferson Memorial. See Jefferson Memorial.

Thompson, Man. (pop. 14,701), is one of the world's leading centers of nickel production. It lies on the Burntwood River, in north-central Manitoba (see **Manitoba** [political map]). Thompson is the province's third largest city, after Winnipeg and Brandon.

Thompson was founded in 1956, following the discovery of a huge deposit of nickel ore in the area by Inco Limited (then called the International Nickel Company of Canada, Limited). The city was named after John F. Thompson, chairman of the company at that time. The first permanent residents arrived in 1958.

Inco Limited built a huge nickel-producing complex in Thompson. This facility was the first in the world to handle all the processes of nickel production, from mining through refining. Production began in 1961. Inco Limited is Thompson's largest employer.

Thompson is also a government and transportation center for northern Manitoba. Airlines and freight and passenger trains serve the city. Thompson has a mayor-council form of government.   Grant Wright

Thompson, Benjamin (1753-1814), was an American-born scientist and political figure. He was best known for his observations on the apparent weightlessness of heat (at a time when heat was considered a material substance), and for his role in founding the British Royal Institution in 1800. His work to improve the living conditions of the poor in Munich, Germany, gained him the title of Count Rumford in 1791. Thompson was born in Woburn, Mass. He lived in Europe after the Revolutionary War. See also **Heat** (The caloric theory of heat); **Range** (History).   Robert P. Multhauf

Thompson, David (1770-1857), a Canadian geographer and explorer, traveled the Columbia River from its source to its mouth. He explored extensive areas of Canada, and surveyed the northernmost source of the Mississippi River. From 1816 to 1826, he was a surveyor on the U.S.-Canadian boundary.

Thompson was born in Westminster, England, and was apprenticed to the Hudson's Bay Company when he was 14 years old. He worked for the North West Company from 1797 until 1812.   William P. Brandon

Thompson, Ernest Seton. See Seton, Ernest Thompson.

Thompson, Francis (1859-1907), was a British poet. A deeply religious Roman Catholic, he wrote some of the best religious poems of his time. His greatest work was the mystical poem "The Hound of Heaven" (1893). Other works include *Poems* (1893), *Sister Songs* (1895), *New Poems* (1897), and *Essay on Shelley* (1909).

Thompson was born in Preston, Lancashire. He intended at first to become a priest, then chose to study medicine. But he was unable to pass the examinations. He settled in London, and began to write poems while living in poverty. He started taking opium, and became addicted to it. He was finally rescued by friends. They helped him publish his poems, and cared for him for the rest of his life.   C. L. Cline

Thompson, Frank. See Edmonds, Sarah E. E.

Sir John Sparrow David Thompson

**Prime Minister of Canada
1892-1894**

Abbott
1891-1892

Thompson
1892-1894

Bowell
1894-1896

Detail of a portrait by J. W. L. Forster;
Parliament Buildings, Ottawa (John Evans)

Thompson, Sir John Sparrow David (1844-1894), served as prime minister of Canada from 1892 until his death two years later. He was the first Nova Scotian to hold that office. Thompson, a Conservative, became prime minister during a period of difficulty for his party following the death of Sir John A. Macdonald. Macdonald, the first prime minister of the Dominion of Canada, had led the Conservative Party from 1867 until he died in 1891.

Thompson practiced law for several years before he entered politics in 1872. In 1882, he accepted Macdonald's offer of an appointment to the Nova Scotia Supreme Court. Three years later, after some persuasion, Thompson joined Macdonald's Cabinet as minister of justice.

Thompson's honesty and his ability to combine the roles of lawyer and statesman earned wide respect. He gained fame as a skillful diplomat and helped negotiate several international treaties. He also became known for a sarcastic sense of humor that sometimes offended people.

Early life. John Sparrow David Thompson was born on Nov. 10, 1844, in Halifax, N.S. His father, John Sparrow Thompson, had emigrated from Ireland in 1828. He had settled in Halifax and worked in the Nova Scotian Post Office. In 1829, he married Charlotte Pottinger, a Nova Scotian of Scottish descent.

John, the youngest of five children, went to school in Halifax. He then studied law as a clerk in a legal firm. Thompson was admitted to the Nova Scotia bar in 1865. In 1870, he married Annie Affleck of Halifax. She was a Roman Catholic, and Thompson, a Methodist, converted to Catholicism about a year after their marriage.

Early political career. Thompson entered politics in 1872, when Halifax voters elected him as a city alderman. He was elected to the Halifax Board of School Commissioners in 1874 and later served as board chairman. In 1877, the United States government asked Thompson to advise its delegation to the Halifax Fisheries Commission, which met to regulate international fishing rights off the Atlantic Coast. That same year, Conservative Party leaders urged Thompson to run for the Nova Scotia Legislative Assembly from Antigonish. He won the election and soon gained a reputation as an able legislator. In 1878, he became attorney general of Nova Scotia.

Thompson and other members of the legislature had supported reform laws aimed at Nova Scotia municipal government. These laws gave counties powers that had belonged to the provincial government. The new policies caused resentment, and many of the reform legislators were defeated in the election of June, 1882. Thompson, who served as premier of Nova Scotia for less than a month before the election, kept his seat in the legislature. But he had become tired of politics and, in July, accepted appointment by Macdonald to the Supreme Court of Nova Scotia.

Minister of justice. In the fall of 1885, Macdonald offered Thompson the office of minister of justice in his Cabinet. Thompson did not want to leave the provincial supreme court, but his wife persuaded him to do so. He became minister of justice in September and the next month was elected to the House of Commons from Antigonish, N.S.

Thompson's honesty and legal skill made him one of the most respected members of the government and of the Conservative Party. Macdonald declared that "the best thing I ever invented was Thompson." As minister of justice, Thompson defended some unpopular actions of the Macdonald administration. One such action involved the execution of Louis Riel, who had led an uprising of Canadian *métis* (people of mixed white and Indian ancestry). Many French Canadians had protested Riel's execution. See **Riel, Louis.**

In 1887 and 1888, Thompson helped draft a U.S.-Canadian treaty on fishing rights. Queen Victoria knighted him in 1888 for this service. Thompson also directed the revision of the Canadian Criminal Code, which set forth the nation's criminal laws.

Prime minister. Macdonald died in 1891, and the Conservatives asked Thompson to take over as party leader and as prime minister. Thompson refused because he feared that Protestant Canadians would not accept a Roman Catholic, particularly one who had converted from a Protestant faith. John J. C. Abbott succeeded Macdonald, and Thompson continued as minister of justice.

In 1892, Abbott became ill and resigned as prime minister. The Conservatives again offered Thompson the positions of party leader and prime minister, and this time he accepted. He was sworn in as prime minister on Dec. 5, 1892.

Thompson prevented a controversy involving Roman Catholic schools in Manitoba from becoming a major political issue during his term as prime minister. The controversy arose in 1890, when the Manitoba legislature passed a bill that abolished tax support for the province's Catholic schools. The legislature wanted to make all schools in the province part of the public school system. Catholics in Manitoba demanded that the federal government use its authority to *disallow* (reject) the legislation. Thompson thought the issue was a legal problem and decided to let the courts settle it. The dispute finally ended in 1896, when Prime Minister Wilfrid Laurier helped work out a compromise.

Thompson also worked to bring Newfoundland into the Canadian Dominion. He had almost succeeded at the time of his death. Newfoundland did not join the dominion until 1949.

As prime minister, Thompson continued to use his skill as a diplomat. In 1893, he represented Great Britain at the Bering Sea Convention in Paris. Partly as a result of his arguments, this conference ruled that the United States had to grant Britain fishing rights in the Bering Sea. See **Bering Sea controversy.**

In 1894, Thompson met in London with other British statesmen. They discussed publishing laws, commercial shipping regulations, and other issues involving members of the British Empire. At Windsor Castle, on December 12, Thompson was sworn in as a member of the Imperial Privy Council. This council consisted of leading statesmen of the empire. Immediately after the ceremony, Thompson suffered a heart attack and died within minutes. He was buried in Halifax.   P. B. Waite

Thompson, William Hale (1869-1944), became a controversial American political leader. Nicknamed "Big Bill," Thompson served as mayor of Chicago from 1915 to 1923 and from 1927 to 1931. His long term in office was largely due to his strict control of an efficient political *machine* (organization). Although a local leader, Thompson won fame for his stands on national issues.

During World War I, he opposed the sending of United States troops to fight against Germany. In 1919, Thompson ran on a "Freedom for Ireland" platform. In his 1927 campaign, he charged that British propaganda was creeping into American textbook treatment of the Revolutionary War in America. Thompson was born in Boston and moved to Chicago with his parents shortly after his birth.   Charles B. Forcey and Linda R. Forcey

Thomsen, Christian Jürgensen, *YOOR guhn suhn* (1788-1865), was a Danish archaeologist. He was one of the first to demonstrate that the vast history of humankind, before written records began, could be divided into a Stone Age, a Bronze Age, and an Iron Age. His interest in bringing this understanding to the public led him to organize the world's first ethnographical museum, in Copenhagen, in 1846.   David B. Stout

Thomson, Charles (1729-1824), served as secretary of the Continental Congress from 1774 to 1789, the entire period of its existence. As secretary, he signed the copy of the Declaration of Independence that the Congress adopted on July 4, 1776. Born in County Derry, Ireland, Thomson came to America at the age of 10 as an orphan. He became a schoolmaster and then a successful merchant. He published a translation of the Bible in 1808.   Richard B. Morris

Thomson, Charles Edward Poulett. See Sydenham, Baron.

Thomson, Charles Wyville. See Exploration (Deep-sea exploration).

Thomson, James (1700-1748), was the most celebrated Scottish poet of the 1700's until Robert Burns. In 1725, he traveled from Scotland to London where he published his masterpiece, *The Seasons* (1726-1730, revised 1744-1746). Thomson broke with the witty artificial poetic style of his day. He turned to nature for his subject matter and wrote fresh, vivid descriptions of natural scenes in rich blank verse. This style led to the romantic movement later in the 1700's.

Thomson was born in Ednam in the Scottish lowlands. He wrote tragedies, the poem *Liberty* (1735-1736), and an imitation of the poetry of Edmund Spenser, *The Castle of Indolence* (1748).   Martin C. Battestin

Thomson, Sir Joseph John (1856-1940), a British physicist, received the 1906 Nobel Prize in physics for his discovery of the electron. In 1937, his son and pupil, Sir George Paget Thomson (1892-1975), shared the Nobel Prize in physics with Clinton Davisson, an American physicist.

Thomson began in 1895 to investigate the mysterious rays that occurred when electricity was passed through a vacuum in a glass tube. Because the rays seemed to come from the *cathode* (negative electrical pole in the tube), they were called *cathode rays.* No one had succeeded in deflecting them by an electric force. It was assumed that cathode rays were like light waves. Thomson felt that they were really tiny particles of matter (see **Cathode rays**).

He built a special cathode-ray tube in which the rays passed between charged metal plates inside the glass. The rays became visible as a dot on a fluorescent screen placed inside the tube. By measuring the deflections of the dot, Thomson could determine the ratio of the charge to the mass of the particle (symbolized as e/m). From the direction of their deflection, he decided that they were negatively charged. Because their *e/m* was always the same, he felt sure that they were a fundamental part of all atoms. These particles were later called *electrons* (see **Atom** [diagram: Models of the atom]; **Electron**).

Thomson also discovered the first isotopes of the chemical elements, neon 20 and neon 22. This spurred the invention of the mass spectrograph by his pupil, Francis W. Aston (see **Mass spectroscopy**).

Thomson was born near Manchester, and was educated at Cambridge. Thomson's experimental work was invaluable to physics. His theoretical model of the atom, however, was discarded in 1911 for that of Ernest Rutherford.   Sidney Rosen

See also **Electronics** (picture: The discoverer of the electron).

Thomson, Tom (1877-1917), was a Canadian landscape painter. He was associated with, and greatly influenced, J. E. H. MacDonald, A. Y. Jackson, and the other Canadian artists who, after 1920, called themselves "the Group of Seven."

For eight months of each year, Thomson lived in Algonquin Park, Ont., painting and serving as a ranger. During the winters, Thomson lived in Toronto, where he painted from his sketches the few large pictures that he completed. The pictures portray the beauty and imposing grandeur of the Canadian wilderness. They are characterized by a brilliance of color and a free dashing treatment seldom equaled. His first work to be exhibited, *Northern Lake,* was purchased by the National Art Gallery at Ottawa. Thomson was born near Owen Sound, Ont. He accidentally drowned in Algonquin Park in 1917.   William R. Willoughby

See also **Canada** (The arts [picture]; **Group of Seven** (picture).

Thomson, Virgil (1896   ), is an American composer and music critic. He gained international fame for his simple compositions based on early American hymns and folk songs.

Thomson was born in Kansas City, Mo. From 1925 to 1940, he lived in Paris. There, he came under the influence of Erik Satie and other modern French composers. Thomson's *Missa Pro Defunctis* (1960), a religious composition for chorus, shows Satie's influence. In Paris, Thomson and the American writer Gertrude Stein became friends. They collaborated on two operas, *Four Saints in Three Acts* (1928) and *The Mother of Us All* (1947).

Thomson pioneered in writing music for motion pictures. He composed the music for two documentary films about the Great Depression of the 1930's, *The Plow That Broke the Plains* (1936) and *The River* (1937). Thomson won the 1949 Pulitzer Prize for his music for the documentary *Louisiana Story* (1948). His other works include such musical portraits as *The Mayor La Guardia Waltzes* (1942) and such descriptive pieces as *The Seine at Night* (1947).

From 1940 to 1954, Thomson served as music critic of the *New York Herald Tribune.* His literary style and insight into modern music made him one of the most respected critics of his time. Thomson wrote several books of music criticism, including *The State of Music* (1939) and *Music, Right and Left* (1951). He also wrote an autobiography, *Virgil Thomson* (1966).   James Sykes

Oil painting on canvas (1917); National Gallery of Canada

Tom Thomson's *The Jack Pine,* one of his brilliant landscapes, portrays the beauty of Canada's wilderness.

Thomson, William. See Kelvin, Lord.

Thor, the god of thunder and lightning, was the ruler of the sky in Norse mythology. He was the oldest and most powerful son of Odin, the king of the gods and goddesses. Thor had great strength and was a skilled fighter. His chief weapon was a hammer named Mjollnir, which he threw at his enemies. Mjollnir never missed its mark and always returned to Thor after hitting a target. Thor created lightning whenever he threw Mjollnir, and thunder was the rumbling of his chariot as it moved across the sky. The day Thursday was named for Thor.

Of all the Norse gods, Thor best represented the way of life of the ancient Vikings. For example, the Vikings held great feasts and glorified war. Several myths describe Thor's huge appetite. He once ate an ox and eight salmon and drank three barrels of an alcoholic beverage called mead. Another myth tells of a drinking contest in which Thor tried to drink the sea dry. He failed to do so, but he lowered the level of the sea slightly and thus created the first tides. The gods had several huge drinking horns, and only Thor could consume their entire contents.

Many myths tell of Thor's encounters with the giants, the chief enemies of the Norse gods and goddesses. One story describes his battle with Hrungnir, a giant, who hurled a huge stone at him. Thor threw his hammer, and it shattered the stone in the air and killed Hrungnir.

Someday, according to Norse mythology, the gods and goddesses will fight the giants in a great battle called *Ragnarok,* and the world will be destroyed. Thor and the Midgard Serpent, a vicious snake coiled around the world under the sea, will kill each other during the battle.   C. Scott Littleton

See also **Mythology** (Teutonic mythology).

Thoracic duct. See Lymphatic system.

Thorax. See Chest; Insect (The bodies of insects).

Thoreau, Henry David (1817-1862), was an American writer who is remembered for his attacks on the social institutions he considered immoral and for his faith in the religious significance of nature. The essay "Civil Disobedience" is his most famous social protest. *Walden,* a study of people in nature, is chiefly responsible for his literary reputation.

Henry David Thoreau by Samuel Rowse. Concord Public Library, Concord, Mass. (The Thoreau Society, Inc.)

Henry David Thoreau

His life. Thoreau was born in Concord, Mass., on July 12, 1817. Unlike most leading writers of his time, Thoreau came from a family that was neither wealthy nor distinguished. His father made pencils in a small shop. His mother took in boarders.

Thoreau graduated from Harvard College in 1837. He soon met the writer Ralph Waldo Emerson, who encouraged him to write, gave him useful criticism, and later employed him as a gardener and handyman. Emerson also taught Thoreau the philosophy of *transcendentalism,* with its emphasis on mysticism and individualism (see **Transcendentalism**).

Thoreau published only two books in his lifetime, *A Week on the Concord and Merrimack Rivers* (1849) and *Walden.* Many of the books published after his death were based on trips he had taken. These books include *Excursions* (1863), *The Maine Woods* (1863), *Cape Cod* (1865), and *A Yankee in Canada* (1866). The books are organized in a loose chronological form that takes the reader through the author's experiences.

His beliefs and works. Thoreau believed that people must be free to act according to their own idea of right and wrong, without government interference. In "Civil Disobedience" (1849), he said that people should refuse to obey any law they believe is unjust. Thoreau practiced this doctrine of *passive resistance* when, in 1846, he refused to pay poll taxes. He did so to express his opposition to slavery as it became an issue in the Mexican War. He spent a night in jail for his refusal.

Marmel Studios from FPG

Walden Pond, near Concord, Mass., inspired Thoreau's most famous book. He built a one-room cabin near the pond.

Thoreau summed up his idea of the role of government in "Civil Disobedience." He wrote, "There will never be a really free and enlightened State until the State comes to recognize the individual as a higher and independent power, from which all its own power and authority are derived, and treats him accordingly." The essay greatly influenced such reformers as Leo Tolstoy of Russia, Mahatma Gandhi of India, and the leaders of the present-day American civil rights movements.

Thoreau called for an end to slavery. He attacked it in the essay "Slavery in Massachusetts" (1854), and defended abolitionist John Brown's raid at Harpers Ferry in "A Plea for John Brown" (1859).

In 1845, Thoreau moved to the shore of Walden Pond near Concord, Mass. He lived there alone from July 4, 1845 to Sept. 6, 1847. *Walden* (1854) records Thoreau's observations of nature there, and tells how he built his house, paid his bills, and spent his time. It also tells about his visitors and reports what he read and thought. On a deeper level, the book is a celebration of people living in harmony with nature.

Thoreau insisted that his trip to Walden Pond was an experiment in simple living, not an idle withdrawal from society. He wrote, "The mass of men lead lives of quiet desperation." He appealed to people to economize, to simplify their lives, and thus to save the time and energy that will allow them "to live deep and suck out all the marrow of life. . . ."   John Clendenning

Additional resources

Burleigh, Robert. *A Man Named Thoreau.* Atheneum, 1985. For younger readers.
Harding, Walter R. *The Days of Henry Thoreau.* Princeton, 1982. First published in 1965.
Harding, Walter R., and Meyer, Michael. *The New Thoreau Handbook.* Rev. ed. New York Univ. Press, 1980.
Richardson, Robert D., Jr. *Henry Thoreau: A Life of the Mind.* Univ. of California Press, 1986.

Thorium is a radioactive chemical element. It is a soft metal with a silvery luster. Thorium has 12 isotopes, the most stable of which has a mass number of 232 and a half-life of 14 billion years. When thorium is bombarded with neutrons, it changes to uranium-233, a nuclear fuel. U-233 is used in bombs and nuclear reactors. Thorium is also used in making strong alloys. In addition, manufacturers use thorium in special photoelectric cells designed to measure ultraviolet light. The mantles of some camping lanterns are also made of thorium. The mantles give off a bright light when lit.

Thorium occurs in various minerals, including monazite and thorite. These minerals are mined chiefly in Brazil, India, and South Africa.

Thorium has the chemical symbol Th. The element's atomic number is 90 and its atomic weight is 232.038. Thorium metal melts at 1750° C and boils at about 4000° C. The Swedish chemist Jöns J. Berzelius discovered thorium in 1828. The element is named for the Norse god Thor.   Richard L. Hahn

See also **Uranium** (Uranium isotopes); **Monazite.**

Thorn, in botany, is a short, hard, sharp-pointed and leafless branch. Thorns develop on many different kinds of plants. Vines such as cat brier, bushes such as blackberries and roses, woody plants such as hawthorns and locusts, and nonwoody and desert plants such as cacti, all have thorns.

Thorn apple. See Hawthorn; Datura; Jimson weed.

Thorndike, Edward Lee (1874-1949), an American educational psychologist, made many contributions to the study of learning, teaching, and mental testing. He invented the puzzle-box to investigate how such animals as cats and dogs solve problems. He found that they tend to repeat only those movements that are successful. This leads them to a final quick solution.

Thorndike also studied learning in human beings. He found that being right helped the student to retain a correct response, but that being wrong did not seem to eliminate errors. He conducted large-scale statistical studies to show how the study of Latin, mathematics, and other subjects affects the later school performance of students. He was one of the first to devise tests to measure learning and aptitudes.

Thorndike was born in Williamsburg, Mass. He received a Ph.D. from Columbia University, and taught at Teachers College, Columbia University, for 41 years. He developed a method to determine which words are used most often. His data was used as a basis for the Thorndike-Century and the Thorndike-Barnhart school dictionaries. His *Teacher's Word Book* (1944) lists 30,000 words by their frequency of use. His other works include *Mental and Social Measurement* (1904), *The Measurement of Intelligence* (1926), *Fundamentals of Learning* (1932), and *The Psychology of Learning* (1941).

Richard M. Wolf

Thornton, Matthew (1714?-1803), was a New Hampshire signer of the Declaration of Independence. He served as president of the first New Hampshire Provincial Congress in 1775, and as speaker of the general assembly in 1776. In 1776 and 1778, he was a delegate to the Continental Congress. Thornton was born in Ireland, and came to America about 1718. He practiced medicine in Londonderry.

Richard B. Morris

Thoroughbred. See Horse (Saddle horses).

Thoroughwort. See Boneset.

Thorpe, Jim (1887-1953), was one of the greatest all-around athletes in history. He became an outstanding college and professional football player and won fame as an Olympic track and field champion. Thorpe also played major-league baseball.

In the 1912 Olympic Games, Thorpe became the first athlete to win both the pentathlon and the decathlon (see Track and field [The decathlon, heptathlon, and pentathlon]). But about a month later, Olympic officials took away his medals. Prior to the games, Thorpe had played baseball for a small salary. The Amateur Athletic Union ruled that Thorpe was therefore a professional athlete and ineligible to compete in the Olympic Games. In 1982, the International Olympic Committee restored Thorpe's gold medals and added his name to the list of 1912 Olympic champions.

James Francis Thorpe, an Indian, was born near Prague, Okla. His great-grandfather was Black Hawk, a famous Indian chief. Thorpe began his athletic career at the Carlisle (Pa.) Indian Industrial School. He led the small school to national fame in football. He was an outstanding runner, place kicker, and tackler and won all-America honors in 1911 and 1912.

From 1913 to 1919, Thorpe played baseball as an outfielder on three major league teams. Thorpe began his professional football career in 1915 and played on seven

United Press Int.

Jim Thorpe became one of the first men to be admitted to the National Football Foundation's Hall of Fame in 1951.

teams during the next 15 years. Thorpe helped establish professional football as a popular sport. In 1920, Thorpe became the first president of the American Professional Football Association, now known as the National Football League.   Bob Wolf

Additional resources

Hahn, James and Lynn. *Thorpe! The Sports Career of James Thorpe.* Crestwood, 1981. For younger readers.
Newcombe, Jack. *The Best of the Athletic Boys: The White Man's Impact on Jim Thorpe.* Doubleday, 1975.
Richards, Gregory B. *Jim Thorpe: World's Greatest Athlete.* Childrens Press, 1984. For younger readers.

Thorvaldsen, TOOR VAHL suhn, **Bertel,** BAIR tuhl (1770-1844), was a Danish sculptor. His name is also spelled *Thorwaldsen.* During his lifetime, many people considered him the greatest sculptor in Europe. Thorvaldsen was a leader of the *neoclassical* movement. Neoclassical artists based their style and subjects on the classical traditions of ancient Mediterranean civilizations, particularly Greece. Like many painters and sculptors of his time, Thorvaldsen believed that imitation of ancient classical works of art was the surest way of becoming a great artist.

Thorvaldsen was born in Copenhagen. He lived in Rome from 1797 to 1837, where he studied classical art firsthand. Thorvaldsen took many of his subjects from ancient literature and mythology. Like the ancient Greek artists, he tried to sculpt human figures with clear contours, smooth surfaces, pleasing proportions, and a feeling of tranquillity. Thorvaldsen created most of his works in white marble. They included relief sculptures, monuments, and portrait busts.   Sarah Burns

See also **Sculpture** (1600-1900; picture).

Thoth, *thohth* or *toht,* was an ancient Egyptian moon god. He was a patron of civilization and such intellectual arts as writing, astronomy, mathematics, law, magic, and healing. He is most often shown in art with a human body and the head of an ibis bird. He is also portrayed as a dog-headed baboon.

Thoth's most important role in the underworld was to oversee the scales on which the souls of the dead were weighed to determine innocence or guilt. He was also related to many other gods. He was considered the scribe of the sun god Re and even Re's chief administrative officer. In the creation myth from Memphis, Thoth became the tongue of the creator god Ptah, through whom the world was created.   Orval Wintermute

See also **Mythology** (Egyptian mythology).

Thothmes III. See Thutmose III.

Thousand and One Nights. See Arabian Nights.

Thousand Islands is a group of more than a thousand islands in the Saint Lawrence River. No complete count has ever been made, because some of the islands are only small points of rock above the water. But at least 1,700 islands compose the group. A few of the islands extend as much as 4 to 5 miles (6 to 8 kilometers) in length. The islands lie in a 40-mile (64-kilometer) stretch of the Saint Lawrence where the river runs from 4 to 7 miles (6 to 11 kilometers) wide as it leaves Lake Ontario. They are formed where the river flows over the low hills of the Canadian Shield, which extends southeast into New York (see **Canadian Shield**).

These rocky islands are noted for their beautiful scenery and mild summer climate. Many have popular public summer resorts. Several have luxurious summer homes. Seventeen of the islands are included in Saint Lawrence Islands National Park. The park has been made into a recreational center and game preserve.

The Thousand Islands International Bridge, completed in 1938, spans some of the islands. It consists of two main suspension structures, three smaller bridges, and roadways across two islands. Its total length is about 6½ miles (10.5 kilometers).   John Brian Bird

See also **Ontario** (picture: Thousand Islands area in the St. Lawrence River).

Thrace, *thrays,* was the ancient Greek name for a large region in the Balkan Peninsula. It stretched from Macedonia north to the Danube River, and eastward as far as the Black Sea. Under the Romans, Thrace included only the southern half of this region. The mountains of Thrace contained valuable deposits of gold and silver. Its broad plains were used for farming and for raising horses and cattle. Some historians believe that Greece owes the foundation of its music, its mythology, and its philosophy to the people of early Thrace.

The people of Thrace were savage Indo-Europeans who liked warfare and looting. Their rulers acted like kings. Greek trading cities occupied the coast of Thrace in early days. The Greeks established the cities with the consent of Thracian kings. Persians conquered this coast in the time of Darius (550?-486 B.C.). Later it belonged to the Athenian state and then to Macedonia. Philip II conquered all of Thrace, and the region was held by his son, Alexander the Great. Thrace later became a province of the Roman Empire.

The most important Greek cities of Thrace were Abdera, Sestos, and Byzantium. Ancient Byzantium was the foundation of the modern city of Istanbul (Constantinople). The fall of Constantinople in 1453 brought all Thrace under Turkish rule.

After the Russo-Turkish War of 1877-1878, northern Thrace became known as Eastern Rumelia and was united with Bulgaria in 1885. Greece took western Thrace during World War I. Turkey and Bulgaria control the rest of the region. German troops overran Greek Thrace in 1941, but it was given back to Greece after World War II. Greek Thrace includes the departments of Evros and Rhodope. Turkish Thrace corresponds to Turkey in Europe.   Donald W. Bradeen

Thrasher is the name of a group of brownish, long-tailed birds found from southern Canada through South America. There are about 17 species of thrashers. The best-known species is the *brown thrasher* of eastern North America (see **Brown thrasher**). Most thrashers have a brown head and back, and a pale underside with brown streaks. The largest thrashers grow more than 1 foot (30 centimeters) long.

Thrashers spend most of their time on the ground searching for food. They eat insects and worms, as well as fruit and seeds. These birds have a loud, repetitive song. They build cup-shaped nests, usually in low bushes and shrubs, and lay from two to six eggs.

Eight species of thrashers range from western North America to Central America. Most of these thrashers have a long, curved bill. Species that inhabit arid re-

Four by Five

The Thousand Islands occupy a 40-mile (64-kilometer) stretch of the St. Lawrence River as it leaves Lake Ontario. The rocky islands are noted for their beautiful scenery and mild summer climate.

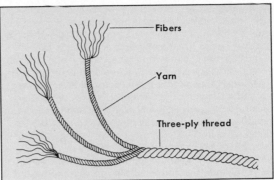

WORLD BOOK diagram by Art Grebetz

Thread consists of many fibers that have been spun into yarns. The yarns are *plied* (twisted together) to form thread.

Sandy Sprunt, Photo Researchers

The pearly-eyed thrasher, *above,* is common in the West Indies. These thrashers have a long, curved beak and live in trees. About 17 species of thrashers live in North and South America.

gions of the Southwest also have longer legs and shorter wings than other thrashers. These species do more running than flying and nest in thorny shrubs or cactuses.

Four species live only in the West Indies. Two of them, the *white-breasted thrasher* and the *trembler,* are in danger of extinction. Both of these species are nervous ground-dwellers. The trembler was named for its nervous behavior. The other West Indian species, the *pearly-eyed thrasher* and the *scaly-breasted thrasher,* dwell in trees. The pearly-eyed thrasher is the most common West Indian species. It nests in holes in trees.

Scientific classification. Thrashers belong to the mockingbird family, Mimidae. The brown thrasher is *Toxostoma rufum.*

Donald F. Bruning

Thread is a fine cord. It is used chiefly to join two or more pieces of material or to sew an object to a piece of fabric. Thread is made of such fibers as cotton, flax, nylon, polyester, rayon, silk, or other textile material. Thread has numerous uses. These uses include sewing

clothing, mending tears, and attaching buttons.

Most thread is made by spinning many fibers into a single yarn. Several yarns are then twisted tightly together to form thread. Each yarn, called a *ply,* adds strength and thickness to the thread. Some thread consists of only a single yarn.

Thread is made from three kinds of fibers: (1) plant, (2) animal, and (3) manufactured. Plant and animal fibers are called *natural fibers.* Almost all natural fibers grow in short lengths known as *staple.* For example, cotton staple measures from $\frac{1}{2}$ inch to $1\frac{3}{8}$ inches (1.3 to 3.5 centimeters) long or longer. Cotton ranks as the most widely used natural fiber for making thread. Manufactured fibers, such as nylon and polyester, are produced in long, continuous strands called *filaments.* Silk is the only natural fiber that begins as filament. Silk fibers average from 1,000 to 1,300 yards (914 to 1,189 meters) long.

Most natural and manufactured thread goes through some kind of chemical treatment that improves its quality. One such process, called *mercerization,* treats cotton thread in a saltlike solution. This treatment strengthens the thread and gives it a silky finish. Most thread is also bleached or dyed before being packaged.

Making thread from natural fibers. Natural fibers, such as cotton or flax, are first cleaned. Then they are straightened and further cleaned in a process called *carding.* The next step, called *combing,* smooths the

How thread is made   Thread may be made from natural or manufactured fibers. After preliminary processing, the fibers are drawn into strands, spun into yarn, and plied. Most thread is dyed or bleached before packaging.

WORLD BOOK diagrams by Art Grebetz

Natural fibers used in making thread include cotton and flax. The carding and combing processes straighten the fibers and smooth them into a sheet before drawing begins.

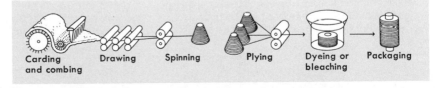

Carding and combing — Drawing — Spinning — Plying — Dyeing or bleaching — Packaging

Manufactured fibers, such as nylon and polyester, are made in long continuous strands called *filaments.* To make thread, the filaments are cut into fiber-sized pieces before drawing.

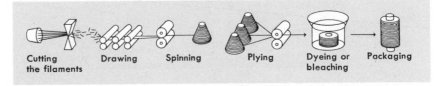

Cutting the filaments — Drawing — Spinning — Plying — Dyeing or bleaching — Packaging

staple and removes some of the exceptionally short fibers. The combed fibers pass between sets of powerful rollers, which draw many pieces of loosely joined staple into continuous strands of increased strength. The strands are then spun into yarn and wound on bobbins. Several yarns are *plied* (twisted together) to form thread.

Making thread from manufactured fibers involves few steps. Filaments need little preliminary processing because they are specifically produced to be made into thread. A single filament can be used as *monofilament thread,* or many filaments may be twisted together to form *multifilament thread.* Filaments may also be cut into staple lengths, which are drawn into strands and then spun into yarn and plied. This process produces a softer thread than that made directly from filaments.

One type of manufactured thread, called *core thread,* combines the qualities of two kinds of fibers. An example of such a thread is a blend of cotton and polyester. This thread is made by combining a core of multifilament polyester with a protective cotton *wrap.* The resulting strand is plied with two or more similar strands. This process gives the thread the smoothness of cotton and the strength of polyester. Core threads can be sewn on a machine faster than other manufactured thread without heating up and breaking. Core threads are ideal for sewing such textiles as knits, permanent-press fabrics, and fabrics that are made from two or more kinds of fibers.   Richard James DeMasse

See also **Spinning.**

Threadworm. See Pinworm.
Three-day measles. See German measles.
Three-dimensional picture. See Holography; Stereoscope; also the Trans-Vision three-dimensional pictures with the **Human body** article.
Three Mile Island. See Nuclear energy (Safety concerns).
Three-mile limit. See Territorial waters; Right of search.
Three Wise Men. See Magi.
Threshing machine is a machine that farmers once used to *thresh* (separate) kernels of grain from stalks. The machine also *winnowed* (blew) the husks from the kernels. Andrew Meikle of Scotland built the first practical threshing machine in the 1780's. Before then, farmers had threshed and winnowed by hand—a hard, slow task. Threshing machines enabled farmers to process grain much faster than they could by hand. Since the 1930's, combines have replaced most threshing machines (see **Combine**).

Modern threshing machines were based on a type designed in the 1830's by two brothers, Hiram and John Pitts of Winthrop, Me. Horses walking on a treadmill produced power for early threshers. A revolving cylinder knocked the kernels off the stalks, and a fan blew away the husks. The machine was stationary during operation. It cost so much that a group of farmers bought one thresher and shared it in harvesting their crops. By the late 1800's, steam engines powered most threshers. Later, farmers used their tractor motors to power threshing machines.   Melvin E. Long

Thrift institution. See Bank (Kinds of banks).
Thrips are short, slender insects with sucking mouthparts. Most species feed on plants, but a few prey on other thrips. Adult thrips are usually less than $\frac{1}{25}$ inch (1 millimeter) long. They have two pairs of narrow, fringed wings. Thrips are serious plant pests.   John R. Meyer

WORLD BOOK illustration by Oxford Illustrators Limited
Thrips

Scientific classification. Thrips make up the order Thysanoptera.

Throat is a term loosely applied to the part of the neck in front of the backbone. The throat contains structures important in breathing and eating. It includes the pharynx, the larynx, part of the esophagus, and part of the trachea. A sore throat results when any of these parts becomes inflamed.

When a person breathes, air enters the nose and travels through a passage called the *pharynx.* From the pharynx, it passes into the *larynx* (voice box), then through the *trachea* (windpipe), and into the lungs. Food, on its way from the mouth to the stomach, passes through the pharynx before it enters the *esophagus,* the tube that leads to the stomach. Thus, part of the pharynx is a common passage for both food and air. The routes of food and air cross one another in this passage, and it is possible for food to enter the wrong tube.

Normally, when a person swallows, two actions take place to block off the air passage. The *soft palate* presses against the back of the pharynx, closing the opening to the nose. At the same time, the larynx rises and is covered by the *epiglottis,* a leaf-shaped lid. These actions force the food into its own passage, the esophagus, and muscular waves carry it to the stomach. When a person laughs or talks while swallowing, food may enter the larynx and choke the person until it is removed by coughing.

The largest muscle of the throat region is the *sternocleidomastoid.* It moves the head. This muscle looks like a cord in the side of the neck when the head is turned.

Historical Pictures Service, Chicago

Early threshing machines, such as the one at the left, were powered by horses walking on a treadmill. The clean kernels poured out of the machine into a bucket, and a conveyor belt carried the stalks away.

It runs diagonally across each side of the neck from the breastbone to the skull behind the ear. Smaller muscles in the throat help in the actions of breathing, speaking, and swallowing.

Large arteries and veins pass through the neck. They carry blood to and away from the face, scalp, and brain. Unconsciousness may result from blockage of the arteries on each side of the trachea.   James M. Toomey

Related articles. See the Trans-Vision three-dimensional picture with **Human body.** See also:

Esophagus	Larynx	Tonsil
Gargle	Pharynx	Windpipe

Thrombosis. See Blood (Blood clotting); **Coronary thrombosis; Stroke.**

Throttle. See Airplane (Flying an airplane); **Carburetor.**

Thrush is the name of a group of songbirds that live in most parts of the world. Many of the thrushes are plain brown birds, with whitish and usually spotted breasts. Robins, wheatears, and bluebirds are all thrushes. These birds are migratory. They fly to warmer countries as winter approaches. They live in wooded regions and spend much time on the ground.

The largest and best-known North American type of thrush, except for the American robin, is the *wood thrush.* This bird has bright cinnamon-colored upper parts and spotted white breast and sides. It is noted for its clear, flutelike songs. The wood thrush nests in the eastern United States and southeastern Canada, and winters in Central America. It builds its nest 5 to 20 feet (1.5 to 6 meters) up in a bush or tree. The bird arranges a base of dead leaves and coarse grass, plasters the nest with mud, and lines it with roots or grasses. The female wood thrush lays from three to five greenish-blue eggs.

Other common North American thrushes are the *veery,* the *hermit thrush,* the *varied thrush,* and *Swainson's thrush.* In Europe, the most common thrushes are the *redbreast,* or *robin;* the *song thrush,* or *mavis;* the *mistle thrush;* the *blackbird;* and the *nightingale.*

Scientific classification. Thrushes make up the subfamily Turdinae of the family Muscicapidae. (Some authorities consider the thrushes a separate family, Turdidae.) The wood thrush is *Hylocichla mustelina.* The veery is *Catharus fuscescens;* the hermit thrush is *C. guttatus;* and Swainson's thrush is *C. ustulatus.*

Donald F. Bruning

Related articles in *World Book* include:

Bird (table: State birds; pictures: Birds of inland waters and marshes; Birds' eggs)	Nightingale
	Robin
Bluebird	Stonechat
	Veery

Thrush is a contagious disease of infants. It is sometimes called *parasitic stomatitis, white mouth, oral moniliasis,* and *infantile sore mouth.* Thrush causes the mouth to become sore. It is particularly frequent in weak and undernourished infants.

Thrush is an infection. It appears in the form of small, roundish, white patches, called *aphthae,* on the lining membrane of the mouth and throat, and also on the tongue. These patches are slightly raised. They cover drops of watery fluid, and contain a fungus growth. When the patches peel off, a raw, red surface is left. As fresh patches of aphthae continue to appear, the victim's mouth becomes sore. At the start, thrush is usually accompanied by fever, colic, diarrhea, restlessness, no desire for food, and difficulty in swallowing.

WORLD BOOK illustration by Trevor Boyer, Linden Artists Ltd.

WORLD BOOK illustration by Trevor Boyer, Linden Artists Ltd.

Some members of the thrush family are the European blackbird, *top above,* the wood thrush, *above,* and the veery thrush, *below.* The European blackbird looks like a black robin. The wood thrush has a spotted white breast. The veery thrush, also called Wilson's thrush, is a shy bird found in forests.

WORLD BOOK illustration by Trevor Boyer, Linden Artists Ltd.

Preventive treatment for thrush requires absolute cleanliness of nipples and nursing bottles, with sterilization of milk and other foods. Physicians treat thrush by swabbing the throat with certain drugs.   Austin Smith

Thrust. See Airplane (Drag and thrust); **Jet propulsion; Space travel** (table: Space travel terms).

Thucydides, *thoo SIHD ih DEEZ* (460?-400? B.C.), a Greek historian, became the world's first historian who aimed to write an unbiased and accurate history that would also reveal the workings of human nature in society. His subject was the great war between the Greek city-states Athens and Sparta. The war took place from 431 to 404 B.C. Thucydides' famous account, the *History of the Peloponnesian War,* ends at 411 B.C. To ensure accuracy, Thucydides worked hard to record events as they happened each year and spoke to participants on both sides. His brilliant accounts of speeches and his descriptions and analyses of dramatic actions are written in a style that earns him a distinguished place in literature.

Thucydides was born in Athens into a prominent family. In 424 B.C., he served as a general in the war and commanded a naval fleet in the Aegean Sea. That year, Thucydides was blamed for the loss of Amphipolis, a city on the north Aegean coast. As a result, he was exiled from Athens. In exile, he gathered materials for his book. Thucydides remained in exile until 404 B.C.

Donald Kagan

See also **Greek literature** (Historical literature).

Thug is a member of an old society in India, the members of which killed in the name of religion. The term comes from the Hindustani *thag,* meaning a *cheat* or *rascal.* The thugs committed murders and robbed their victims in honor of Kali, the Hindu goddess of destruction and wife of Shiva. The thugs always murdered by strangling. One of their chief principles was not to spill blood. According to legend, the thugs believed that Kali disposed of the bodies by devouring them. But one member of the society pried into Kali's actions. So the angry goddess condemned them to bury their victims in the future. The local Indian and British governments tried many times to stop *thuggee*—the practice of the thugs. In 1831, the British began a drive to end the practice, and it is now almost wiped out. Today, people commonly refer to robbers and other criminals as thugs.

George Noel Mayhew

Thulium, *THOO lee uhm* (chemical symbol, Tm), is one of the rare-earth elements. Its atomic number is 69. Its atomic weight is 168.934. The name comes from *Thule,* the Latin word for the northernmost part of the inhabitable world.

The Swedish scientist Per Cleve first discovered thulium in 1879. Thulium occurs with other rare earths in the minerals gadolinite, euxenite, xenotime, and others. Thulium is best separated from the other rare earths by ion-exchange processes or by solvent extraction. It melts at 1545° C, and boils at 1950° C. It has a density of 9.318 grams per cubic centimeter at 25° C. Portable X-ray units use radioactive thulium. Such units require no electrical equipment, and they need to be recharged with thulium only once every few months.   Larry C. Thompson

See also **Element, Chemical** (tables); **Rare earth.**

Thumb. See Hand.

Thumb, Tom. See Stratton, Charles S.

Thunder. Prehistoric people thought that thunder was the sound of the gods roaring in anger when they were displeased with the people of the earth. Today, scientists know that thunder is caused by the violent expansion of air that has been heated by lightning.

Air is heated instantly when an electrical charge of lightning passes through it. The heat causes the molecules of air to expand, or fly out, in all directions. As the molecules seek more room, they collide violently with layers of cool air, and set up a great air wave that has the sound of thunder.

Thunder has many different sounds. The deep, rumbling roar of thunder is caused by the air wave from the lightning trunk that is farthest away from an observer. The sharp crackle of thunder is set up when the large

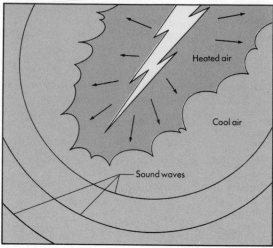

WORLD BOOK illustration by Arthur Grebetz

Thunder is the sound caused by lightning. Lightning heats the nearby air, causing it to expand. The expanding hot air collides with cool air, creating sound waves that we hear as thunder.

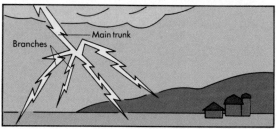

WORLD BOOK illustration by Arthur Grebetz

Different sounds of thunder come from different parts of a bolt of lightning. The main trunk of lightning causes the loudest crash. The branches produce the sharp, crackling sound.

trunk of lightning forks out into many branches. The loud crash of thunder is caused by a main trunk of lightning that is near an observer. The sound of thunder reaches us after we have seen the lightning. That is because light travels 186,282 miles (299,792 kilometers) per second, while sound travels at a rate of only about 1,100 feet (335 meters) per second. The number of seconds between seeing the lightning flash and hearing the thunder, divided by five, yields the distance of the lightning from the observer in miles.   Wayne M. Wendland

See also **Lightning; Jupiter; Thor; Zeus.**

Thunder Bay, Ont. (pop. 112,272; met. area pop. 122,217), is a city on the northwest shore of Lake Superior. Its excellent harbor makes it an important shipping center. For location, see **Ontario** (political map). Thunder Bay was formed in 1970 by the merger of the cities of Fort William and Port Arthur and the townships of McIntyre and Neebing.

Thunder Bay is an international port. It is the shipping center for much of the grain produced in western Canada and for potash and coal. Large ships reach Thunder Bay by the St. Lawrence Seaway and the Great Lakes. Thunder Bay has pulp and paper mills, building-board mills, and sawmills. Other industrial activities include railroad car manufacturing, ship repair, and tourism.

Thunder Bay is the home of Lakehead University and Confederation College of Applied Arts and Technology. The city has five public libraries, a museum, and a public art gallery. The Thunder Bay Community Auditorium hosts a variety of entertainment performances.

In 1679 and 1717, the French built forts at what later became Fort William. After 1805, Fort William served as headquarters for fur traders of the North West Company. Another settlement, Prince Arthur's Landing, grew up alongside Fort William. Fort William was designated a transcontinental rail point in 1875. Prince Arthur's Landing developed as a starting point for the road to western Canada. It was also the center of regional silver mining activity. Prince Arthur's Landing became the town of Port Arthur in 1882, and Fort William was incorporated as a town in 1884. Both became cities in 1907. The port cities flourished, especially after the St. Lawrence Seaway opened in 1959. Thunder Bay has a mayor-council form of government.   Michael D. Grieve

Thunderstorm. See Cloud (Storms); Hail.

Thurber, James (1894-1961), was a celebrated American humorist. He became famous both for his comic writings and his cartoonlike drawings.

Thurber's works describe the anxieties of the average individual in modern society. He wrote chiefly about oversensitive, dissatisfied men who feel trapped by the complications of the modern world. The men in his stories are frustrated by their domineering wives and rebellious children. They often fear such machines as automobiles and dread the pressures of their jobs. They try to escape from their problems through alcohol or daydreams. Thurber's short story "The Secret Life of Walter Mitty," for example, portrays a man who finds relief from his nagging wife through daydreams. In his daydreams, Mitty always plays the fearless hero.

Many of Thurber's works include cartoons of frightened men, menacing women, wicked children, and sad dogs. Many of his stories, essays, and drawings appear in such collections as *The Middle-Aged Man on the Fly-*

Illustration by the author from *The Thurber Carnival* by James Thurber, published by Harper and Row. © 1945 James Thurber, renewed 1973 Helen W. Thurber and Rosemary Thurber Sauers. Originally printed in *The New Yorker* magazine.

A Thurber cartoon illustrates one of his favorite subjects, a timid middle-aged man married to a domineering woman.

ing Trapeze (1935) and *The Thurber Carnival* (1945). He wrote his first book, *Is Sex Necessary?* (1929), with E. B. White and co-authored a play, *The Male Animal* (1940), with Elliott Nugent. Thurber also wrote an autobiography, *My Life and Hard Times* (1933). Much of his work first appeared in *The New Yorker* magazine. He wrote about Harold Ross, the first editor of *The New Yorker,* in *The Years with Ross* (1959). James Grover Thurber was born in Columbus, Ohio. He was blind for the last 15 years of his life.   Joseph N. Riddel

Additional resources

Bernstein, Burton. *Thurber: A Biography.* Arbor House, 1985. First published in 1975.
Morsberger, Robert E. *James Thurber.* Twayne, 1964.

Thurman, Allen Granberry (1813-1895), was the Democratic candidate for Vice President of the United States in 1888. He and President Grover Cleveland lost to Republicans Benjamin Harrison and Levi P. Morton. Thurman served as a U.S. senator from Ohio from 1869 to 1881. He was chief justice of the Ohio Supreme Court from 1854 to 1856, and served in the U.S. House of Representatives from 1845 to 1847. He was born in Lynchburg, Va.   Irving G. Williams

Thurmond, Strom (1902-   ), a U.S. senator from South Carolina, is known for his strong support of states' rights. He served as chairman of the Senate's powerful Judiciary Committee from 1981 to 1987.

Thurmond withdrew from the Democratic Party in 1964 and became a Republican. In 1948, he also left the Democratic Party to run as the States' Rights Democratic (*Dixiecrat*) candidate for President (see Dixiecrat Party). He carried four states and received 39 electoral votes. Thurmond felt that the federal government was taking over many duties and powers that rightfully belonged to state and local governments. At one time, he favored racial segregation. But he changed his views and supported some civil rights legislation.

Thurmond served as governor of South Carolina from 1947 to 1951. He was elected to the U.S. Senate in 1954 as a write-in candidate. James Strom Thurmond was born in Edgefield, S.C. He graduated from Clemson College.   William J. Eaton

Thursday is the fifth day of the week. The ancient Norsemen considered the day sacred to Thor, the Teutonic god of thunder. The name means *Thor's day.* This is probably a translation of the Latin *dies Jovis,* meaning *Jove's day,* for Jove, or Jupiter, the Roman god of thunder. In the United States, Thanksgiving Day is on the fourth Thursday in November. See also Thor; Week.

Grace Humphrey

Thurstone, Louis Leon (1887-1955), an American psychologist, played a major role in the development of psychological tests. One of his most significant achievements was the creation of a statistical technique called the *centroid method of factor analysis.* This technique helped Thurstone and other psychologists study such psychological characteristics as ability and personality. By applying the method to the results of intelligence tests, Thurstone determined that intelligence consists of separate abilities, among them reasoning and numerical aptitude. His findings differed from the common belief of the time that intelligence was a single factor.

Thurstone also developed tests to measure attitudes.

He wrote several books, including *Primary Mental Abilities* (1938) and *Multiple-Factor Analysis* (1947).

Thurstone was born in Chicago. He received a Ph.D. degree in psychology from the University of Chicago in 1917. Thurstone taught psychology at Carnegie Institute of Technology from 1915 to 1923 and at the University of Chicago from 1924 to 1952.   Richard M. Wolf

Thutmose III, *thoot MOH suh* (reigned about 1490-1436 B.C.), ranks among the greatest of all the kings of ancient Egypt. He is also known as Thothmes III. Thutmose succeeded his father, Thutmose II, but was kept in the background by his stepmother, Queen Hatshepsut. After Hatshepsut died, Thutmose III ordered her name erased from monuments and statues.

Thutmose III became a brilliant general and also a capable administrator. By his well-planned campaigns, mainly in Palestine and Syria, he greatly expanded Egypt's imperial boundaries. The rich booty and many captives taken in his wars provided the means and labor for extensive building operations in Egypt. He greatly enlarged the vast temple at Karnak. Its walls still bear the hieroglyphic records of his wars, long lists of captured cities in Asia and Africa, and pictures of plants and animals collected on his campaigns. Thutmose erected granite *obelisks* (giant stone pillars) in Karnak and Heliopolis. The two he erected at Heliopolis are now known as *Cleopatra's Needles.* One stands in Central Park in New York City, and one on the Thames Embankment in London.   Leonard H. Lesko

See also **Egypt, Ancient** (The New Kingdom).

Thyme, *tym* or *thym,* is a fragrant garden herb. An oil in the leaves and stems causes its scent. The drug thymol is prepared from this oil. The plant grows from 6 to 8 inches (15 to 20 centimeters) high, and has square, hairy stems, narrow leaves, and small lilac or purplish flowers, borne in separate whorls. It grows well in dry places and poor soils.

Scientific classification. Thyme belongs to the mint family, Labiatae. Common or garden thyme is genus *Thymus,* species *T. vulgaris.*   Harold Norman Moldenke

Thymus is a flat, pinkish-gray organ that plays an important part in the immune system of the body. It is located high in the chest cavity behind the breastbone and extends into the lower neck below the thyroid gland.

The thymus aids in the development of white blood cells called *lymphocytes,* which help the body fight disease. There are two kinds of lymphocytes, both of which are formed from cells in the bone marrow. Some lymphocytes, called *B cells,* probably mature in the bone marrow itself (see **Immunity** [Cells of the immune system]). The *B* stands for *bone marrow derived.* The other lymphocytes travel to the thymus, where they are changed into *T cells.* The *T* stands for *thymus derived.* The thymus produces a substance called *thymosin,* which scientists believe plays an important part in the change into T cells.

The T cells leave the thymus and inhabit the blood, lymph nodes, and spleen. There, they attack bacteria, cancer cells, fungi, viruses, and other harmful organisms. T cells are sometimes called "killer cells" because of their ability to find and destroy such organisms.

When a person is born, the thymus weighs about $\frac{1}{2}$ ounce (15 grams). By the age of 12, it has grown to about twice its original size. At that time, the lymph nodes and

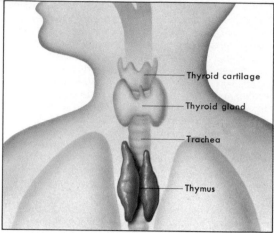

WORLD BOOK diagram by Charles Wellek

The thymus is in the upper chest, behind the breastbone. It aids in the formation of white blood cells called *lymphocytes,* which protect the body from disease.

the spleen take over the task of producing lymphocytes. The thymus then begins to shrink and produces fewer T cells. By adulthood, the organ has shrunk so much that it may be hard to distinguish from the fatty tissue that surrounds it.

Disease or injury may require the removal of the thymus. The loss of the thymus has little effect in an adult. But in a person under 12 years old, removal of the thymus may lead to difficulties in growing properly and in developing immunities.   Don H. Nelson

Thyroid gland is a body organ located in the front of the neck. It has two *lobes* (parts), one on each side of the *trachea* (windpipe). The lobes are connected by a thin band of tissue. A network of blood vessels surrounds the gland. The thyroid takes iodine from the blood and uses it to make the active hormones *thyroxine,* also called *tetraiodothyronine,* and *triiodothyronine.* An inactive form of thyroid hormones is stored inside the lobes in small chambers called *follicles.*

Thyroid hormones control the body's *cell metabolism.* When thyroid hormones are released into the bloodstream, cells increase the rate at which they convert oxygen and nutrients into energy and heat for the body's use. During a child's development into adulthood, thyroid hormones stimulate an increase in growth rate. Release of thyroid hormones also stimulates mental activity and increases the activity of the other hormone-producing glands.

Thyroxine and triiodothyronine are released into the bloodstream in response to such conditions as stress, pregnancy, and low levels of thyroid hormones in the blood. These conditions activate a hormone in the pituitary gland called *thyroid-stimulating hormone* (TSH). TSH regulates the thyroid's production of hormones.

The thyroid gland produces another hormone, *calcitonin,* in response to high levels of calcium in the blood. Calcitonin causes the kidneys to discharge more calcium into the urine, and it raises the amount of calcium stored in the bones.

Underactive thyroid, called *hypothyroidism,* is a defect that results in the low production of thyroid hor-

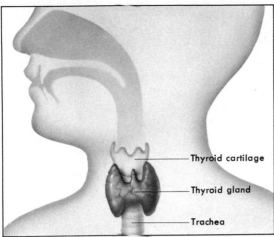

WORLD BOOK diagram by Charles Wellek

The thyroid gland is in the neck. This gland produces and stores a hormone called *thyroxine,* which is essential for mental development and physical growth.

mones. This deficiency causes an overall decrease in both physical and mental activity. Symptoms appear in almost every organ system of the body. The skin becomes dry and puffy. Hair thins and becomes brittle. Slow speech, slow reflexes, poor memory, constipation, and fatigue can all result from hypothyroidism. In adults, hypothyroidism is called *myxedema.* If the condition goes untreated in infants, it causes physical and mental retardation (see **Cretinism**). When hypothyroidism is detected in a newborn child, thyroid hormones can be replaced or supplemented by drugs to prevent retardation. A myxedemic adult can also be treated with drugs.

Overactive thyroid, called *hyperthyroidism,* results in an overproduction of thyroid hormones. Excessive thyroid hormones in the blood cause an increase in the rate of most biological reactions. This leads to a higher rate of physical and mental activity. Symptoms of hyperthyroidism include sweating, excessive nervousness, insomnia, diarrhea, and *exophthalmos.* Exophthalmos is a condition in which the amount of tissue behind the eyes increases, causing them to bulge abnormally. Treatment of hyperthyroidism sometimes involves surgery to remove a portion of the thyroid gland. Drugs can also be prescribed to decrease thyroid production.

Charlotte H. Greene

See also **Gland; Goiter; Hormone.**

Thysanoptera. See **Insect** (table); **Thrips.**

Thysanura. See **Insect** (table).

Tiahuanaco Indians. See **Bolivia** (History).

Tian Shan, *tyehn shahn,* also spelled *Tien Shan,* is a mountain system in central Asia. It runs for nearly 1,500 miles (2,410 kilometers) northeast from The Pamirs (see **Pamirs, The**). Tian Shan means *Heavenly Mountains.* The system is the highest mountain system north of Tibet. Pobeda Peak, the highest peak, rises 24,406 feet (7,439 meters) above sea level. Rivers flow north from Tian Shan into the Soviet Union, and south into China. The system includes some of the world's largest glaciers. Roads follow passes through Tian Shan. For location, see **Union of Soviet Socialist Republics** (terrain map).

J. E. Spencer

Tianjin, *tyehn jihn* (pop. 7,764,141), is a trading center in northern China. Its name is also spelled *Tientsin* or *T'ien-chin.* In 1860, the Chinese opened the city and its port to foreign trade. Nine countries received *concessions* (tracts of land). All of these concessions have been given back to China.

Tianjin is 85 miles (137 kilometers) southeast of Beijing, near the mouth of the winding Hai River (see **China** [political map]). Chinese emperors did not allow foreign merchants to live in Beijing, the rich capital. So traders who wanted to sell goods to Beijing settled in Tianjin. As a result, Tianjin became an important center of foreign trade. Railroads connect Tianjin with Beijing, Nanjing, Shanghai, and the cities of Manchuria. Tianjin lies at the northern end of the Grand Canal, a water route that leads to southern China.

Tianjin is the chief port for Beijing and a center for foreign and domestic trade for northeastern China. Since the 1970's, the production of goods in Tianjin has expanded from textiles and handicrafts to a wide range of consumer goods and industrial products. For example, Tianjin has become an important center for petrochemical products since the discovery of offshore oil fields nearby. Much new construction has taken place in the city since the 1970's. Tianjin has more than 25 universities and technical schools.

Fighting between Japan and China in 1937 badly damaged Tianjin. Japan then gained control of the city and held it until World War II ended in 1945. In 1976, an earthquake struck Tianjin, Beijing, and the area around the cities. About 240,000 people died in the disaster and property damage was extensive.   Norma Diamond

Tiber River, *TY buhr,* is the third largest river in Italy. Only the Po and the Adige are larger. The Tiber rises in the Apennine Mountains in central Italy, 4,160 feet (1,268 meters) above sea level. The river flows for about 245 miles (394 kilometers), first through the Sabine Mountains, a range of the Apennines, then through Rome and into the Tyrrhenian Sea (see **Italy** [physical map]). It flows into the sea through branches at Ostia and Fiumicino. The Tiber has often overflowed its banks. Flood embankments have been built at Rome.   Shepard B. Clough

Tiberias, Lake. See **Galilee, Sea of.**

Tiberius, *ty BEER ee uhs* (42 B.C.-A.D. 37), was the emperor of Rome during the life of Jesus Christ. His full name was Tiberius Claudius Nero. The second emperor of Rome, Tiberius succeeded his stepfather, Emperor Augustus.

Tiberius became a successful army commander for Augustus. The emperor forced Tiberius to divorce his wife and marry his stepsister—Augustus' daughter, Julia. But Tiberius and Julia were unhappy, and he left her and went to live on the island of Rhodes. By A.D. 4, both of Augustus' grandsons and Tiberius' brother, Drusus Claudius, had died. Augustus then recalled Tiberius to Rome and made Tiberius his heir and successor. When Augustus died in A.D. 14, Tiberius became emperor.

Tiberius was a fine administrator. He carefully supervised tax collections and balanced the budget. He chose efficient governors for the provinces of Rome and maintained friendly relations with the neighboring kingdoms of Parthia and Armenia.

When Germanicus, a possible successor to Tiberius, died, his widow accused Tiberius of causing his death.

Tibet

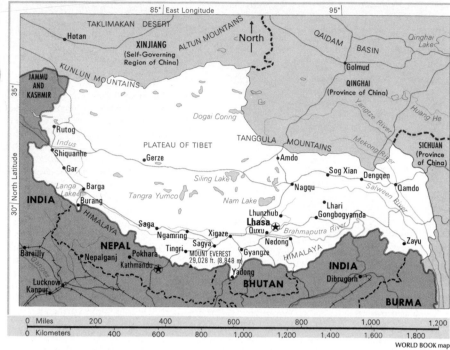

* ★ Capital
* • Other city or town
* ----- Road
* +++++ Railroad
* ▲ Mountain
* ⌒ River

WORLD BOOK map

Because of difficulties with the Senate, Tiberius retired to the island of Capri. He named Sejanus, captain of his personal guard, to govern Rome.

Tiberius became unpopular during his last years because of his poor relations with the Senate and opposition to the gladiator games. But he left a peaceful and prosperous empire to his heir Caligula, a descendant of Augustus.   Mary Francis Gyles

See also **Caligula**.

Tibet, *tih BEHT,* is a land in south-central Asia. It is often called the *Roof of the World.* Its snow-covered mountains and a windswept plateau are the highest in the world. The world's highest mountain, Mount Everest, towers along the southern mountain wall of Tibet. Ka-erh, in western Tibet, is believed to be the highest town in the world. It is more than 15,000 feet (4,570 meters) above sea level. Valley bottoms in Tibet are higher than the mountains of most countries. Lhasa is Tibet's capital.

Tibet has been a part of China since the 1950's. However, for many years Tibet was an independent or semi-independent state. Although it carried on some trade with other lands, its mountain ranges generally isolated it from outside peoples. The Tibetans are sometimes called the *hermit people.* Tibet was traditionally a *theocracy* (religious kingdom). Buddhist monks had a strong voice in the rule of Tibet before China took control.

The land. Tibet has an area of 471,662 square miles (1,221,600 square kilometers). A high, cold plateau called the Plateau of Tibet covers much of the land. High mountain walls border the plateau. Along the southern end of the plateau, the snowy Himalaya rises higher than any other mountain chain in the world. Mount Everest (29,028 feet, or 8,848 meters, above sea level) is in the

Himalaya. In the north, many peaks of the Kunlun range rise more than 20,000 feet (6,000 meters). Tibet has an average elevation of 16,000 feet (4,880 meters).

Large parts of Tibet are wastelands of gravel, rock, and sand. Most of the land cannot be farmed because of poor soil and cold climate. But there are some fertile valleys and other areas suitable for farming. Tibet also has areas of grasslands and forests. More than 5,000 different kinds of plants grow in Tibet. Tibet's wild animals include deer, gazelles, tigers, bears, monkeys, pandas, and wild horses. Tibet has hundreds of lakes and streams, but many of them have barren shores and a high salt content. Some of the great rivers of Asia begin in the mountains of Tibet. These include the Brahmaputra, Indus, Mekong, Salween, and Yangtze rivers.

Climate. Much of Tibet receives less than 10 inches (25 centimeters) of rain annually. The Himalaya shuts out moisture-bearing winds from India. Sudden blizzards and snowstorms are common. Violent winds sweep Tibet in all seasons. January temperatures average 24° F. (−4° C). July temperatures average 58° F. (14° C).

The people and their work. Tibet has a population of about 2 million. About 96 per cent of the people are Tibetans. Most of the rest are Chinese. Most of the people live in southern Tibet, where there is land that is fertile enough for farming and raising livestock. Nomads who raise sheep and yaks live in the northern grasslands. About 84,000 people live in Lhasa, Tibet's largest city. Many of these people are employed in jobs in government, light industry, or tourism.

The Tibetans belong to the Asian geographical race. The main traditional language is Tibetan. All Tibetans speak Tibetan at home. However, Mandarin Chinese is the official language of Tibet. Both Tibetan and Mandarin Chinese are taught in the schools. All government documents are written in both languages.

Before China seized Tibet, the nobility and monks called *lamas* owned the farmland and governed the country. Most farmers were serfs. The serfs were not free to leave the land, and they had to give much of what they produced to the landowners. China, a Communist country, broke up the large estates of the monks and the nobility and distributed them among farmers.

Tibetan homes have stone or brick walls and flat roofs. Few houses have more than two floors. But houses built for the wealthy have three or four floors. The ground floor is used to house animals.

Barley is Tibet's chief crop, and barley flour is the main food. Tibetans mix barley flour with tea and butter. Milk and cheese are also important parts of the diet. Chinese tea is the chief beverage. Tibetans flavor the tea with salt, soda, and yak butter.

The yak, a hairy ox, serves many purposes in Tibet. It provides cloth, meat, milk, and transportation. It is also used as a beast of burden. Its hair is used for tents, and its hide for shoe leather and boats.

Typical clothing of Tibetan men and women includes a long robe with long sleeves and a high collar. Wealthy people wear silk robes. Wool, felt, and sheepskin are common clothing materials for the cold weather. Lighter garments are made of hemp and cotton.

Cloth weaving and carpet making are household industries in Tibet. Wool is a major export. Other traditional exports include furs, mules, musk, and ponies.

Religion and culture. Tibetans are intensely religious. People turn prayer wheels and recite prayers on the streets. Religious rites are an important part of life. Festivals are religious in character. Long pilgrimages to important temples in Lhasa or Xigaze are popular.

Tibet's religion is a branch of Buddhism called *Lamaism*. The religion recognizes two Grand Lamas. The Dalai (High) Lama is regarded as the ruler of Tibet and its highest spiritual ruler. The Panchen Lama is regarded as a leading spiritual authority. Tibetans regard both Grand Lamas as Buddha, born again. When the Dalai or Panchen Lama dies, his spirit is thought to enter the body of a baby boy. Monks search the country for a boy who was born about the same time as the death of the lama. The boy thus selected becomes the lama's successor. The Chinese Communists ended the authority of the Dalai Lama and Panchen Lama after they took control of Tibet.

There are several different sects of Lamaism. The chief sect is the Yellow Hat, headed by the Dalai Lama, who has lived in exile in India.

In the past, large numbers of Tibetan men became monks and every town and valley had a monastery, called a *lamasery*. Before the Chinese take-over, as many as 20 per cent of all Tibetan males were monks. Many Tibetans became monks because they were sent to the monasteries as children by poor parents who could not pay their debts or taxes. Others went because the monasteries were the only places that provided an education.

During the 1960's and 1970's, the Chinese Communists closed or destroyed most of the monasteries in Tibet. As a result, the religious emphasis of life in Tibet decreased a great deal. During the 1980's, some monaste-

A Tibetan family, at their highland camp, wear traditional clothing made from material they weave themselves.

ries were allowed to reopen and recruit new monks.

Today, Tibet has far fewer monasteries than it had in the past, and only a few thousand males are monks. Many monks engage in agriculture and handicrafts. The monasteries are centers of education, art, and public worship. Tibetan art reflects Chinese and Indian influences, and presents Buddhist themes.

Cities. Lhasa is the political and religious center of Tibet. The Potala Palace is the most impressive landmark in Lhasa. It is a grand, castlelike structure with gold roofs and more than 1,000 rooms. Formerly a residence of the Dalai Lama and other monks, it now houses a museum that has many art treasures. Other cities include Gyangze, Xigaze, and Yadong.

History and government. During the A.D. 600's, Tibet became a powerful kingdom. Buddhism and writing were introduced from India, and Lhasa was founded. The Dalai Lama became the ruler of Tibet in the 1600's. In the early 1700's, Tibet fell under the control of China. A British mission arrived in Lhasa in 1904. The British and Tibetans signed a treaty, setting up trading posts in Tibet.

Tibet remained in Chinese hands until 1911, when Tibetans forced out the Chinese troops stationed there. Even after 1911, China claimed Tibet as an area within the Chinese domain. In the 1920's, rivalry grew between the Dalai and Panchen lamas over political affairs. The Panchen Lama fled to China with his court. He remained there until his death in 1937. A new Panchen Lama was enthroned in China in 1944, but he was not officially recognized in Tibet until 1949. The Dalai Lama died in 1933. According to custom, a boy was chosen as his successor. The successor, a peasant boy, was officially installed as Dalai Lama in 1940.

Communists gained control of China's government in 1949. In 1950, Chinese forces entered Tibet. In 1951, Tibetan representatives signed an agreement with China in which Tibet surrendered its sovereignty to the Chinese government but kept its right to regional self-government. The agreement promised no immediate change in the political system of Tibet and guaranteed the Tibetans freedom of religious belief. Committees made up of both Tibetans and Chinese were established as local governments in various parts of the country. In 1956, the Preparatory Committee for the Tibetan Autonomous Region was formed with the Dalai Lama as chairman, and a Chinese general and the Panchen Lama as two of the vice chairmen. This committee was founded to establish Tibet as an *autonomous* (self-governing) region.

But also in 1956, China began tightening its control of Tibet. The Dalai Lama fled to India in 1959. The Panchen Lama became head of the Preparatory Committee. By 1965, when Tibet officially became an autonomous region, the large estates of landlords and monks had been broken up. Peasants were required to sell a fixed amount of grain to the government and were forced to grow wheat rather than barley to feed the Chinese soldiers. The Chinese government took control of the radio stations, newspapers, banks, and shops that sold food. Chinese people took over a majority of such jobs as local government administrators and teachers. Tibetans faced discrimination by Chinese soldiers and settlers. Many Tibetans believed their lives were getting more difficult rather than better. In the 1950's and 1960's, Tibetans staged riots against Chinese rule.

In the 1980's, the Chinese government adopted a more liberal policy toward Tibet. Some religious shrines were opened to worshipers, as were some surviving monasteries. Farmers were again allowed to decide which crops to grow and to sell them as they chose. But in 1987, riots by Tibetans against Chinese rule broke out in Lhasa. Many observers believe the riots were protests against the slow pace of reform and the discrimination by Chinese against Tibetans.   Norma Diamond

Related articles in *World Book* include:

Tibetan spaniel is a breed of dog that originated in Tibet hundreds of years ago. Buddhist monks kept these dogs as pets and as watchdogs for monasteries. The dogs were also companions to Tibet's rulers. Visitors to Tibet first brought the breed to Europe in the 1800's, but it was not officially introduced into the United States until 1967. Tibetan spaniels are not actually spaniels, despite their name. Although Tibetan spaniels have keen eyesight and a nose for scent, they are not hunters or retrievers. Their alert personalities and intelligence make them useful as watchdogs.

The thick, silky coat of a Tibetan spaniel lies flat against the body. The coat may be almost any color or combination of colors. The bushy tail curls over the back, and the shoulders are covered with a *ruff* (frill) slightly longer than the rest of the fur. The dogs stand from $9\frac{1}{2}$ to 11 inches (24 to 28 centimeters) high at the shoulder and normally weigh between 10 and 12 pounds (4.5 and 5.4 kilograms).   Joan McDonald Brearley

Tibetan terrier is a breed of dog that originated in Tibet, where Buddhist monks raised it in monasteries.

Louise Van der Meid, T.F.H. Publications

The Tibetan terrier has a heavy coat of long hair.

The Tibetans once believed these dogs were holy, and monks gave them to important people for good luck.

Tibetan terriers stand from 14 to 16 inches (36 to 41 centimeters) high and resemble miniature Old English sheep dogs. They have a thick, shaggy coat that may be black, cream, gold, gray, or white, or a combination of those colors. The Tibetan terrier has a fluffy tail that curls over the dog's back.   Joan McDonald Brearley

Tic is a term used to describe repetitive, brief, rapid, involuntary movements of various muscle groups. Tics occur at random intervals. Examples of simple tics include shoulder shrugging, eye blinking, facial twitching, head and neck jerking, kicking and bending movements of the waist. Tics are most commonly seen in the face, head, and neck. See also **Neuralgia; Tourette syndrome.**   William J. Weiner

Tick is the name of a small animal which is related to mites, spiders, and scorpions. The tick is oval in shape. It is a parasite, which means that it lives on other animals. Ticks and mites cause various diseases in human beings and in domestic animals. Ticks often carry certain disease germs in their bodies and transfer these germs to

Tibetan Spaniel Club of America, Inc.

A Tibetan spaniel has a thick coat and a curly tail.

the blood of their victims. Sometimes the bites of ticks are poisonous. Cases of paralysis are known to have followed their attacks. However, such effects are not common, and the victim usually recovers rapidly once the tick is removed.

Spotted fever tick

Ticks and mites look much alike in body structure, but ticks are larger. Ticks look somewhat like insects but are not. Most kinds of ticks can be seen without a magnifying glass. They live only on animal fluids. But some mites feed on plant juices and tissues, on decaying matter, and on small insects and other mites.

The bodies of ticks seem to be all in one piece. But some have a groove behind the head. The head of a tick is a movable part at the front end of the body. Ticks draw blood through a beak. Other body parts help ticks cling tightly to their host. Adult ticks have eight legs which stick out on the sides like those of a crab.

The tick lays eggs in dead leaves or other ground rubbish. The eggs hatch into flat, six-legged larvae. These larvae wait on grass stalks and shrubs for passing

R. A. Mendez, Animals Animals
A female tick may lay up to 10,000 eggs at one time. After hatching, the larvae attach themselves to passing animals.

Kim Taylor, Bruce Coleman Ltd.
The sheep tick sucks the blood of animals and people. Its body becomes swollen with blood after it has eaten, *above.*

animals. Once attached, they gorge on the blood of these animals and swell up. Then, they cease to eat and begin to *molt* (shed their outer covering). After this, they become eight-legged nymphs. The nymphs resume feeding, molt again, and then are adults.

While the various kinds of ticks have special names, such as *chicken, cattle, dog,* or *sheep* tick, few of them are limited to one kind of animal. Many which attack animals also annoy human beings. Eight species are pests on cattle in the United States. Only one of these, the Texas fever tick, is of major importance.

The American dog tick and the Rocky Mountain wood tick transmit *Rocky Mountain spotted fever* to humans. The disease causes a few deaths each year in the United States. Deer ticks transmit *Lyme disease* to humans. If untreated, this disease can lead to chronic arthritis and heart and nerve disorders. The common English sheep tick, which lives in America, infests dogs and cattle.

Wood ticks often trouble people walking and camping in the woods. If this pest is pulled out forcibly, a portion of the head often will break off and remain inside the flesh and may cause a festering sore. To remove a wood tick, cover it with rubbing alcohol, with petroleum jelly, or with a heavy oil such as mineral oil, salad oil, or machine oil. Wait until the tick relaxes its grip. Then carefully remove it using tweezers. Wash the affected area of the skin thoroughly with soap and water.

Scientific classification. Ticks belong to the class of arachnids. Together with mites, they make up the order Acarina. The Rocky Mountain wood tick is *Dermacentor andersoni.* The American dog tick is *D. variabilis.* Edwin W. Minch

See also **Cattle tick; Lyme disease; Mite; Tick fever; Rocky Mountain spotted fever.**

Tick fever is a name for several diseases carried by the bite of ticks. They include Colorado tick fever, relapsing fever, Rocky Mountain spotted fever, and Texas fever. Texas fever is a disease of cattle. These diseases are infections by different microbes, which enter the body through the tick bite. See also **Relapsing fever; Rocky Mountain spotted fever.** Thomas P. Monath

Ticking is a strong fabric used chiefly to cover mattresses and pillows. It is woven closely of stout yarn so that cotton felt, feathers, curled horsehair, and other fillings for bedding cannot pass through. Ticking may be made of cotton, synthetic fibers, or a blend of cotton and synthetic fibers in a twill, herringbone twill, or jacquard weave. Phyllis Tortora

Tickseed. See Coreopsis; Flower (picture: Flowers of prairies and dry plains).

Ticonderoga, Battle of. See Fort Ticonderoga; Allen, Ethan.

Tidal wave is a destructive wave that sweeps in from the ocean like a huge tide. However, tidal waves are not related to true tides. Instead, they are caused by undersea earth movements called *seaquakes* or by hurricanes, cyclones, or other large storms at sea.

Tidal waves caused by seaquakes are called *seismic sea waves.* They also are known as *tsunamis,* a name given them by the Japanese. Scientists using seismographs can accurately predict when a tsunami will arrive at a given seacoast. For example, they know that a seaquake off the Aleutians may cause a tsunami that will hit the coast of Hawaii. If seismographs in Hawaii show that a seaquake has occurred off the Aleutians, the fore-

E. R. Degginger

Tides rise and fall in a cycle that is regulated by the moon's gravity. When the water is at *low tide, left,* it rises gradually for about 6 hours, until it reaches *high tide, right.* Then it falls gradually for about 6 hours until it is at low tide again.

caster calculates the number of minutes that it took for the earth tremor to reach Hawaii. It will take about the same number of hours for the tsunami to hit Hawaii. This conclusion is based on the fact that earthquake tremors travel 350 miles (563 kilometers) or more per minute, while a tsunami travels 400 to 500 miles (640 to 800 kilometers) per hour. The exact speed of the tsunami depends on the depth of the water. Most tsunamis go undetected at sea. However, a tsunami may form a wall of water more than 80 feet (24 meters) high when it approaches shallow water near shore.

Tidal waves caused by large storms at sea are called *storm surges.* The size of a storm surge depends on the wind velocity, the duration of the storm, the ocean distance over which the wind blows, and the barometric pressure. Storm surges are especially destructive if they hit the shoreline during high tide.

In 1900, Galveston, Texas, suffered great damage from a storm surge caused by hurricanes at sea. In 1946, a tsunami severely damaged Hilo, Hawaii. In 1970, a cyclone and storm surge struck East Pakistan (now Bangladesh), killing about 266,000 people. Another cyclone and storm surge struck Bangladesh in May 1985, killing about 10,000 people.   Peter P. Sakalowsky

See also **Krakatoa; Seiche.**

Tide is the rise and fall of ocean waters, on a definite time schedule. Tides regulate the day for the people who live along the seacoasts of the world. The tide is important to the boy or girl who swims along the wharves when the tide is "in" and digs clams on the uncovered tidal flats when the tide is "out." The tide signals the start and end of the working day to people who fish and need high water to leave or enter the harbor.

All bodies of water, large or small, are subject to the tide-producing forces of sun and moon. But it is only where oceans and continents meet that tides are great enough to be noticed. In the inland bodies of water the regular rise and fall of the tide is so small that it is completely masked by changes in level due to wind and weather. Lake Superior, for example, has a tide that rises and falls only about 2 inches (5 centimeters).

Great harbors and seaports make use of the tides in many ways. The tidal currents help to sweep out the main channels and keep them deep. Ocean liners and cargo steamers use high tide to pass shallow harbor entrances, for at that time there is deep water to float them. Tides help to keep harbors clean and healthful. They pick up waste material from the coastlines and carry it to deep water where it settles to the bottom.

Tides also occur on land and in the atmosphere, but they are much harder to observe than ocean tides. Land and atmospheric tides can only be detected by highly-sensitive scientific instruments.

Tides follow the moon in its apparent motion around the earth. The tides rise and fall twice in the time between two rising moons, about 24 hours and 50 minutes. The time between two rising moons is determined by two motions: (1) the rotation of the earth on its axis, and (2) the revolution of the moon around the earth. As the earth turns on its axis, the moon appears to sweep across the sky once a day. But relative to the sun, the moon revolves around the earth once in about $29\frac{1}{2}$ days. Therefore, the moon moves about 12° around the earth each day. Between risings of the moon, the earth makes a complete rotation and then turns this additional 12°. The extra 12° of turning takes about 50 minutes.

Causes of ocean tides

Tides in the ocean are caused mainly by the pull of the moon on the earth. The moon's gravity pulls up the water directly below the moon, forming a high tide there. High tide also occurs on the other side of the earth, because the moon pulls the solid earth away from the water. As the earth turns, high tide occurs at each place on the ocean twice a day.

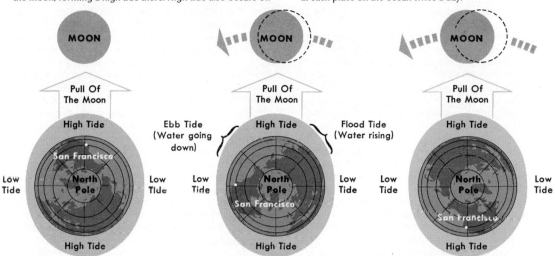

High tide occurs directly below the moon and on the opposite side of the earth. When the earth is in the position above, San Francisco has a high tide.

As the earth turns, the tides rise and fall at each place on the ocean. About 6 hours and 13 minutes after high tide, San Francisco has a low tide, *above.*

The next high tide at San Francisco occurs about 12 hours and 25 minutes after the first. The earth has turned 186° in this time. The moon has moved 6°.

Spring tides

Spring tides result when the pull of the sun combines with the pull of the moon to produce tides that are higher than normal. Spring tides occur about twice a month near the times of the full and new moons. The moon then lies either between the earth and the sun, as shown *below,* or on the opposite side of the earth from the sun.

Neap tides

Neap tides result when the pull of the sun is at right angles to the pull of the moon. Neap tides do not rise as high as normal tides. They occur about twice each month, when the moon is near its first and third quarters. At these times, the moon is either on the side of the earth shown *below,* or on the opposite side of the earth,

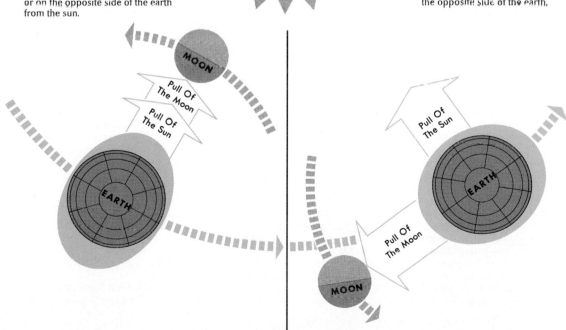

People have known for thousands of years that the moon has some relationship to the tides. Before the year A.D. 100, the Roman naturalist Pliny wrote of the moon's influence on the tides. But the physical laws of tides were not worked out until after the English scientist Sir Isaac Newton discovered the law of gravitation in the 1600's.

The moon's gravity pulls the water nearest the moon slightly away from the solid part of the earth. At the same time, the moon pulls the solid earth slightly away from the water on the opposite side of the earth. In this way, the moon's gravity produces two bulges on the ocean. These bulges are the positions of high tide.

As the earth turns on its axis, the land and water rotate together. But one tidal bulge always stays under the moon, and the other tidal bulge always stays on the opposite side of the earth. Therefore, the earth's rotation brings a high tide to most places on the ocean about twice a day. The two high tides at a given place do not usually rise equally high, because the centers of the tidal bulges usually lie on opposite sides of the equator. The centers are located there instead of on the equator because the moon is usually located either north or south of the plane of the equator.

Both the sun and the moon exert a pull on the earth called *gravitation*. The force of this pull depends on the body's *mass* (amount of matter) and on the distance of the body from the earth. The force is proportional to the mass of the body. Therefore, if the body's mass could be doubled, the body would exert twice as much force on the earth. The force is inversely proportional to the *square of the distance* (the distance multiplied by itself) between the body and the earth. Thus, if the distance of the body from the earth could be doubled, the body would exert only one-fourth as much force on the earth.

The sun and the moon pull harder on the side of the earth nearest them than they do on the center of the earth, because the center of the earth is farther away. It is this difference in pull that produces the tides. The difference is inversely proportional to the *cube of the distance* (the distance multiplied twice by itself) between the body and the earth. Therefore, if the distance of a body from the earth could be doubled, the body would exert only one-eighth as much tide-producing force on the earth.

The sun has about 27 million times as much mass as the moon. Therefore, if the sun and the moon were the same distance from the earth, the sun would exert about 27 million times as much tide-producing force as the moon. But the sun is about 390 times as far from the earth as the moon. So the tide-producing force of the sun is only 46 per cent as great as that produced by the moon. As a result, the tides caused by the sun are only 46 per cent as high as those caused by the moon. The tides caused by the sun and by the moon combine to produce the tides seen along the seacoast.

Differences in the coastline and in the channels of the sea bottom may make a difference in the times that the tide wave hits the different ports along the same coastline. The governments of most seacoast nations print tide tables showing the times of the tides for the whole year at main ports of the country. Ships are brought to the entrance of a port when the tide is high enough to carry them and is on the flood to help them in. Ship cap-

tains find tide tables dependable—for tide times never change their regular pattern.

High tides and low tides. One tide acts very much like another. From its lowest point, the water rises gradually for about six hours, until it reaches *high tide* (high water). Then it begins to fall for about six hours, until it reaches *low tide* (low water). The cycle then begins again. The difference between high water and low water is called the *range* of the tide. As the water rises and falls, it moves toward and away from the coast. This movement is called the *tidal current*. When the water moves toward the coast or inland, it is the *flood current*. When it flows seaward, it is called the *ebb current*.

The range of the tide differs from day to day according to the position of the sun and the moon. When the moon and the sun are pulling along the same line, as they do at full moon and new moon, the tide rises higher than usual and is called a *spring tide*. When the sun and moon pull at right angles, as when the moon is in its first and third quarters, the tide does not rise as high as usual and is called a *neap tide*.

The formation of the seacoast itself also makes a great difference in the range of the tide. In funnel-shaped estuaries and bays, the range may be very high. In the Bay of Fundy, the difference between high and low tide is sometimes more than 50 feet (15 meters). Here, the tide rushes into the Petitcodiac River in a *bore* (high wall) that usually rises about 2 feet (0.6 meter) high.

The shape, size, and depth of seas or oceans make differences in the way the tide acts. For example, the Atlantic Ocean has tides that flow and ebb regularly twice a day. But some Pacific islands have *mixed tides,* such as two high tides daily, with only a little ebb between, and then a very low tide. At Saint Michael, Alaska, and certain places along the Gulf of Mexico, there is only a *daily tide*—one high tide and one low tide each day. The Mediterranean Sea has little tide.

Tides in the air are similar to those in the ocean. At the earth's surface, the speed of these tides, called *lunar winds,* is about $\frac{1}{20}$ mile (0.08 kilometer) per hour. Although they are too low to be felt, scientists detect them by studying variations in weather statistics. High and low tides in the air come twice daily. There also are high stages that are equivalent to the ocean's spring tide. Lunar winds blow eastward in the morning and westward in the evening.   Peter P. Sakalowsky

See also **Bay of Fundy; Bore; Energy supply** (Tidal energy); **Ocean** (The tides); **Sea level; Seashore; Tidal wave.**

Tie. See **Railroad** (The rails and crossties).

Tie dyeing is a method of dyeing cloth to produce a design. Tie dyeing is one of the oldest methods of printing designs on fabric, and various techniques are found in many cultures. Typically, parts of a woven material are bunched together in a design and knotted or tied with a cord or string. The fabric is then submerged in dye. The tied sections are protected from absorbing the dye, thus creating the design. The fabric can be retied and submerged into dyes of other colors to create new patterns and color combinations.   Patrick H. Ela

Tien Shan. See **Tian Shan.**

Tientsin. See **Tianjin.**

Tiepolo, *tee EHP uh LOH,* **Giovanni Battista,** *joh VAH nee baht TEES tah* (1696-1770), was the last important Italian painter of the Venetian group. He began as an admirer of Paolo Veronese, but he soon developed a grand, colorful mural style that became popular in Europe during the 1700's. Many of his murals portray historical scenes and fantastic allegories. They show active figures painted in lively pastel colors. His painting *Allegory of the Marriage of Frederick Barbarossa and Beatrice of Burgundy* is reproduced in the **Painting** article.

Tiepolo was born in Venice. After 1750, he worked mainly in Germany and Spain. His works include decorations for the archbishop's palace in Würzburg, Germany, and the Royal Palace in Madrid. Some of Tiepolo's small oil sketches for his large murals are displayed in the Metropolitan Museum of Art in New York City.

Vernon Hyde Minor

See also **Painting** (Painting as decoration).

Tierra del Fuego, *tih EH ruh dehl foo AY goh,* is the name of a group of islands lying off the extreme southern tip of South America. The name *Tierra del Fuego* means *Land of Fire.* In 1520, Ferdinand Magellan named the region when he sighted large fires blazing along the shore. He was trying to find a passage to the Pacific. The Indians who lived there usually kept many fires burning to warm themselves.

The islands cover 26,872 square miles (69,598 square kilometers). The Strait of Magellan separates them from the mainland. The largest island, also called Tierra del Fuego, covers 19,280 square miles (49,935 square kilometers). The city of Ushuaia, the world's southernmost seat of government, lies on this island. The islanders are called *Fuegians.* The population is about 36,000.

Argentina owns the eastern part of Tierra del Fuego Island, while Chile controls the western part. In 1948, an Italian settlement was made in the Argentine section. Each country also owns several of the smaller islands. Chile controls the Strait of Magellan, and maintains a naval base on Navarino Island. Cape Horn is at the

Tierra del Fuego is a group of islands at the southern tip of South America. The islands are divided between Argentina and Chile.

WORLD BOOK map

southern tip of the islands.   Arthur P. Whitaker

See also **Cape Horn; Clothing** (introduction).

Tiffany, *TIHF uh nee,* **Charles Lewis** (1812-1902), was an American dealer in precious stones. His reputation as a jeweler became so great that his name now stands for the highest quality in jewelry.

Tiffany was born in Killingly, Conn. He went to New York City in 1837 and opened a small notions store. He soon was specializing in jewelry, glassware, and china. Later he imported European crown jewels. He also set up factories to make some products he sold. Louis Comfort Tiffany, his son, created the famous Tiffany glass (see **Tiffany, Louis Comfort**).   John S. Lizzadro

Tiffany, Louis Comfort (1848-1933), was a major stained-glass designer of the late 1800's and early 1900's. He was an important American figure in the establishment of an international art style called *art nouveau.* The style flourished from about the 1890's to about 1910 (see **Art nouveau**).

Tiffany was born in New York City. Charles Lewis Tiffany, his father, founded a famous jewelry business. Tiffany began his career as a painter, but soon developed an interest in the decorative arts, especially stained glass. In 1879, he formed a partnership with several modern artists. The firm specialized in contemporary interior design. In 1880, Tiffany took out a patent for colored glass that was *iridescent*—that is, it changed colors when viewed from different angles. In 1885, he formed his own glass company. In 1894, Tiffany registered the name *Favrile* to describe his handmade works in iridescent glass.   John W. Keefe

See also **Glass** (picture: Stained-glass windows).

Tiflis. See Tbilisi.

Tiger is the largest member of the cat family. People admire the tiger for its strength and beauty, but they fear it because it has been known to kill and eat human beings. Yet almost all wild tigers avoid people. Probably only 3 or 4 of every 1,000 tigers ever eat people, and some of these are sick or wounded animals that can no longer hunt large prey.

Wild tigers are found only in Asia. Until the 1800's, many lived throughout most of the southern half of the continent. Tigers still live in some of this area, but only a few are left. People have greatly reduced the number of tigers by hunting them and by clearing the forests in which they lived. Today, wildlife experts consider the tiger an endangered species.

Tigers can live in almost any climate. They need only shade, water, and prey. They are found in the hot rain forests of Malaya, the dry thorn woods of India, and the cold, snowy spruce forests of Manchuria. They also live in oak woods, tall grasslands, swamps, and marshes. Tigers prefer to be in the shadows and seldom go into open country as lions do. Many tigers also live in zoos. In the past, wild tigers were captured for zoos. Today, enough tigers for zoos are born in captivity.

The body of a tiger. Adult male tigers weigh about 420 pounds (191 kilograms) and are 9 feet (2.7 meters) long, including a 3-foot (0.9-meter) tail. Tigresses weigh about 300 pounds (136 kilograms) and are 8 feet (2.4 meters) long. The tiger's coat ranges from brownish-yellow to orange-red and is marked by black stripes. The stripes vary greatly in length, width, and spacing. The fur on the throat, belly, and insides of the legs is whitish.

Ylla, Rapho Guillumette

The tiger's coloration helps conceal the animal in its natural surroundings. This female tiger could easily go unseen because her stripes blend with the tall grasses.

Many tigers have a ruff of hair around the sides of the head, but the hair is not so long as the mane of lions. The tigers of Manchuria, where the winters are bitter cold, have long, shaggy, winter coats.

The tiger looks different from the lion because of its stripes and more colorful coat. But the two animals have similar bodies. In fact, tigers and lions have mated in zoos. The offspring are called *tiglons, tigons,* or *ligers.*

How a tiger hunts. Tigers prefer large prey, such as deer, antelope, wild oxen, and wild pigs. Some tigers attack elephant calves. They also eat small prey, such as peafowl, monkeys, tortoises, and frogs. Tigers especially like porcupines, but their quills may stick in a tiger's body and cause painful wounds. In parts of Asia, some tigers prey on domestic cattle and buffalo because hunters have reduced the number of wildlife.

The tiger usually hunts at night, wandering over animal trails and along stream beds. A tiger depends on its sharp eyes and keen ears, but it may also use its sense of smell. The tiger, waiting in cover, rushes at its prey in a series of bounds. Using its sharp claws, the tiger grasps the victim by the rump or side and pulls it to the ground. The tiger's teeth are well suited both for holding prey and for tearing off chunks of meat.

Tigers are extremely swift for short distances and can leap nearly 30 feet (9 meters). But if a tiger fails to catch its prey quickly, it usually will give up because it soon tires. As long as a week may go by without a successful hunt. After a kill, the tiger drags the *carcass* (dead body) to thick cover, preferably near water. The muscles of the tiger's neck, shoulders, and forelegs are very powerful. A tiger may drag the body of a 500-pound (230-kilogram)

young water buffalo $\frac{1}{4}$ mile (0.4 kilometer). The tiger stays near the carcass until it has eaten everything except the bones and stomach. A tiger may eat 50 pounds (23 kilograms) of meat in a night. A long drink and a nap often follow a meal.

Tigers are good swimmers and may swim across rivers or from one island to another in search of prey. On hot days, they may go into the water to cool off. Tigers can climb trees, but they do not usually do so.

The life of a tiger. Adult tigers usually live alone, but they are not unfriendly. Two tigers may meet on their nightly rounds, rub heads together in greeting, and then part. Several tigers may share a kill.

Many adult males claim a territory as their own and keep other males out. The territory may cover from 25 to 250 square miles (65 to 647 square kilometers) or more, depending on the amount of prey available. The tiger marks a path with urine and with fluids from glands at the base of the tail. The scent lets other tigers know that

Facts in brief

Names: *Male,* tiger; *female,* tigress; *young,* cub.
Gestation period: 98 to 109 days.
Number of newborn: 1 to 6, usually 2 or 3.
Length of life: Up to 20 years.
Where found: Chiefly in Bangladesh, India, Nepal, and Southeast Asia, including Sumatra; also a few in China, Iran, Java, and Korea, and along the Siberian-Manchurian border.
Scientific classification: Tigers belong to the class Mammalia and the order Carnivora. They are in the cat family, Felidae, and the genus *Panthera.* All tigers are of the same species, *P. Tigris.*

Marc & Evelyne Bernheim, Rapho Guillumette

The male tiger has heavier patches of fur around its face than the female. This male is taking a dip on a hot day.

The skeleton of a tiger

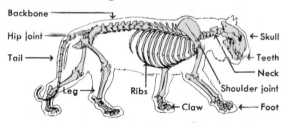

Backbone
Hip joint
Tail
Leg
Ribs
Skull
Teeth
Neck
Shoulder joint
Claw
Foot

Tiger tracks

Front feet
Hind feet

WORLD BOOK diagram

Where tigers live

The yellow areas in the map below show the parts of the world where tigers are found. Most tigers live in southern Asia.

the territory is occupied. A male's large territory includes the smaller territories of two or more females, each wandering alone but aware of one another. Tigers communicate by many sounds, including a roar that can be heard for 2 miles (3 kilometers) or more.

A tigress can bear her first cubs when she is $3\frac{1}{2}$ to 4 years old. The cubs are helpless and weigh about 3 pounds (1.4 kilograms) at birth. Tiger cubs, like kittens, are playful. But their life is hazardous, and about half die before they are a year old. The cubs cannot kill enough for themselves until they are more than a year old. Even then, they cannot kill a large animal. The mother may teach her cubs how to kill by providing a live animal for them to attack. Cubs become independent when about 2 years old.   George B. Schaller

See also **Animal** (Animals of the tropical forests [picture]); **Lion; Saber-toothed cat.**

Additional resources

Hunt, Patricia. *Tigers.* Dodd, 1981.
Mountfort, Guy. *Saving the Tiger.* Viking, 1981. For older readers.
Schaller, George B., and Selsam, M. E. *The Tiger: Its Life in the Wild.* Harper, 1969.

Tiger, Tasmanian. See Tasmanian tiger.

Tiger lily is a tall garden flower that originally grew in eastern Asia. It received its name because it has reddish-orange flowers splashed with black. People in China, Japan, and Korea serve tiger lily bulbs as food.

The stem of the tiger lily is greenish-purple or dark brown, and many grow from 2 to 6 feet (0.6 to 1.8 meters) tall. Tiny black bulblets appear where the long, spear-shaped leaves join the stalk. The bulblets finally drop off, producing new plants.

Tiger lilies grow best in bright sunlight, in a loose, fertile soil. They can withstand cold weather but need some protection in winter. The bulbs should be planted about 4 inches (10 centimeters) in the ground, with a little sand or gravel under each. After being planted, tiger lilies bloom from year to year with little care.

Scientific classification. The tiger lily belongs to the lily family, Liliaceae. It is *Lilium tigrinum.*   August A. De Hertogh

Tiglath-pileser, *TIHG lath pih LEE zuhr,* was the name of three kings of Assyria, an ancient land in what is now northern Iraq.

Tiglath-pileser I (reigned 1115-1077 B.C.) expanded Assyrian power by military victories. He conquered lands as far north as what is now Turkey, as far east as the Zagros Mountains in what is now Iran, and as far west as the Mediterranean Sea. To avenge a Babylonian raid on his territory, he captured the city of Babylon in what is now Iraq, but spared its temples.

Tiglath-pileser II (reigned 967-935 B.C.) is relatively unknown. But scholars believe his reign was a stable one, because it lasted so long.

Tiglath-pileser III (reigned 744-727 B.C.) conquered parts of what are now Turkey, Iraq, and Syria. He founded the Assyrian Empire, which ruled this region for over 100 years. In 728 B.C., he became king of Babylonia and ruled it under the name *Pulu.*

Jacob J. Finkelstein

Tiglon. See Lion (Cubs).

Tigris River, *TY grihs,* is a major river of southwestern Asia. It is about 1,180 miles (1,899 kilometers) long and forms part of the historic Tigris-Euphrates river system.

The Tigris rises in mountainous terrain in eastern Turkey, flows southeast to the border between Turkey and Syria, and then enters Iraq. The river winds through Iraq and gradually descends to low, flat land. At the town of Al Qurnah, Iraq, it joins with the Euphrates River to form the Shatt al Arab. The Shatt al Arab flows into the Persian Gulf. For the location of the Tigris, see **Iraq** (map); **Euphrates River** (map).

The area near and between the Tigris and Euphrates rivers has Iraq's most fertile soil, and the rivers provide water for irrigation. Most of Iraq's people live in this area. Baghdad, the country's largest city, lies on the Tigris. Dams along the river in Iraq store water used to generate hydroelectric power. Small boats sail on the Tigris, but much of the river is too shallow for large vessels.

The Tigris-Euphrates region was the site of the world's first civilization, which developed in Sumer about 3500 B.C. Assyria and other early civilizations also flourished in the region. The ruins of the Assyrian capital of Nineveh lie along the Tigris River.   John Kolars

See also **World, History of the** (The Tigris-Euphrates Valley); **Mesopotamia; Nineveh.**

Tijuana, *tee WHAN uh* or *tee uh WAH nuh* (pop. 534,993; met. area pop. 535,535), is a city in the Mexican state of Baja California Norte. It lies at Mexico's border with the United States, about 15 miles (26 kilometers) south of downtown San Diego (see **Mexico** [political map]).

Tijuana is a modern city with attractive public buildings and luxury hotels. Tourists from the United States spend millions of dollars in Tijuana each year. The city's attractions include gift shops, fine restaurants, nightclubs, bullfights, and horse races. Tijuana is in a *free trade zone,* where shoppers may buy items imported from outside Mexico without paying a Mexican import tax. Tijuana produces electronic products and clothing. It is an export center for grapes, tomatoes, and onions.

Tijuana's name may be derived from an Indian name for the region, or from a huge ranch in the area called the *Tia Juana* (Aunt Jane). During the early 1900's, Tijuana was a small village of about 200 people. Since 1940, the city has grown rapidly because of its booming tourist trade.   Julian C. Bridges

Tikhonov, *TEE khuhn uhf,* **Nikolai Aleksandrovich,** *nyih kuh LY uh lyih KSAN druh vyihch* (1905-   ), served as premier of the Soviet Union from 1980 to 1985. The premier—officially chairman of the Council of Ministers—is the chief administrator of the Soviet government. However, the general secretary of the Soviet Communist Party is actually the most powerful person in the government.

Tikhonov was born in Kharkov. He earned an engineering degree in Dnepropetrovsk and worked as an engineer and plant manager in factories. Tikhonov joined the Communist Party in 1940. Beginning in 1950, he held various industrial management positions in government. From 1957 to 1960, he headed the Dnepropetrovsk economic council. During the 1960's and 1970's, Tikhonov rose through the ranks of the Soviet government's Council of Ministers. He became a full member of the powerful Politburo of the Communist Party in 1979. He resigned as premier and from the Politburo in 1985 for reasons of health.   John A. Armstrong

Tilden, Bill (1893-1953), was the United States men's singles tennis champion from 1920 to 1925, and in 1929. He was the first American to win the Wimbledon, England, championship. He won it in 1920, 1921, and 1930. He led the United States team in winning the Davis Cup from 1920 to 1926. Tall and slender, Tilden was known for his powerful forehand and serve. Tilden left amateur tennis competition in 1930, and became a professional player for 10 years. William Tatem Tilden, Jr., was born in Philadelphia.   Pat Harmon

See also **Tennis** (picture: Great men players).

Tilden, Samuel Jones (1814-1886), an American lawyer, became famous as the leader of the attack on the "Tweed Ring" of New York City. This group of politicians, led by William Tweed, had stolen millions of dollars through city improvement schemes (see **Tweed, William M.**).

Tilden was born in New Lebanon, N.Y. He earned his law degree in 1841 from the University of the City of New York. He practiced law in New York City. In 1845, Tilden was elected as a Democrat to the New York state assembly. He became governor of New York in 1875, and in 1876 became the Democratic candidate for President. Tilden received a majority of the popular votes, but the electoral vote was in doubt. An electoral commission created by Congress decided the election in favor of the Republican nominee, Rutherford B. Hayes. Hayes was declared elected by a margin of one electoral vote (see **Electoral Commission**). Tilden left $6 million, half of which was used to found the New York City Public Library.   W. B. Hesseltine

Tile. All the several kinds of clay tile are made in much the same way. Thin sheets of clay are pressed, molded, and baked in kilns in the same process as is used for making brick. The tile may be left in its rough state. It may also be given a smooth surface, called *glazing,* by throwing salt into the kiln or by treating the clay with a chemical wash.

Tile pipe is used for sewage-disposal systems and for draining fields of excess water. A continuous tile line is formed by fitting together short sections, each of which has one end enlarged to form a bell into which the small end of the next section fits. Drain tiles are generally laid with uncemented butt ends through which the drainage water may seep. Sewer pipes are laid with tight cement joints.

Finer grades of clay are used in making tiles for roofs, for walls, and for floors. Roofing tiles are made in various shapes and colors. Hollow clay tile blocks are used in load-bearing walls and partitions.

Home builders use decorative tiles for interior floors and walls. They obtain artistic effects by using tiles of different colors. Mosaics are small, unglazed tiles that are combined to form a design in colors. White and colored glazed tiles are popular for the walls of kitchens and bathrooms. *Encaustic tiling* is the trade name for decorative tiles used in such a way that there is a background of one color and a pattern of another, contrasting color.

Floor tiles are made of rubber, linoleum, terrazzo, cork, asphalt, plastic, and terra cotta and other ceramics. Acoustic ceiling tiles are made of asbestos, cork granules, wood fiber, and mineral fiber.   George W. Washa

See also **Clay; Terra cotta.**

Tilefish are deep-sea fish that live along the New England coast. The tilefish is the most colorfully decorated ocean fish in northern waters. The upper parts of the side are a bluish or olive-green color, blending into yellow or rose on the lower part. The head is reddish and

WORLD BOOK illustration by James Teason

The tilefish lives along the coast of New England.

is pure white below. The upper sides are thickly dotted with small yellow spots. Large tilefish are about 3 feet (91 centimeters) long and weigh about 30 pounds (14 kilograms) or more. Tilefish feed chiefly on crabs and other fish. They can be caught on trawl lines and hand lines, with any kind of bait.

    Scientific classification. The tilefish belongs to the tilefish family, Branchiostegidae. It is classified as *Lopholatilus chamaeleonticeps*.   Leonard P. Schultz

Till Eulenspiegel. See Eulenspiegel, Till.

Tillage. See Farm and farming (Preparing the soil; illustration: Tillage and planting equipment).

Tilley, Sir Samuel Leonard (1818-1896), served as premier of the Canadian colony of New Brunswick from 1861 to 1865, and again in 1866. He represented New Brunswick at three conferences at which the delegates agreed on the terms of a Canadian union. These conferences were the Charlottetown and Quebec conferences of 1864 and the London Conference of 1866. The delegates became known as the Fathers of Confederation.

    In the mid-1860's, many New Brunswickers opposed a plan for confederation because they feared they would lose political rights. Tilley helped persuade the people to join the Dominion of Canada by assuring them that the larger provinces would not control the smaller ones.

    In 1867, Tilley became minister of customs in the Cabinet of Sir John A. Macdonald, the first prime minister of Canada. Tilley was promoted to minister of finance in 1873 and held that office under Macdonald again from 1878 to 1885. Tilley prepared a program to develop Canadian industries by putting a tariff on many imported products. This program was called the National Policy. Tilley was knighted in 1879. He was born in Gagetown, N. B.   C. M. Wallace

Tillich, *TIHL ihk,* **Paul** (1886-1965), was an important German-born theologian. Tillich was a brilliant student of culture. In *Theology of Culture* (1959), he analyzed the forms of culture, showing the religious dimension in all cultural activities. Tillich developed a theory of religious symbols and myths, which he discussed in *Dynamics of Faith* (1957). His masterpiece is the three-volume *Systematic Theology* (1951, 1959, 1963). In this work, Tillich interpreted the meaning of God and Jesus Christ in correlation with philosophical questions of modern life and thought.

Paul Johannes Tillich was born in Starsiedel, near Leipzig. His thought and life were transformed by his experiences as a Lutheran chaplain in World War I (1914-1918). He encountered what he called "the power of nonbeing" in wartime anxieties concerning death, guilt, and loss of meaning. In *The Courage to Be* (1952), he understood God to mean "the power of being itself" in the experience of courageously conquering anxiety.

    Tillich left Germany in 1933 after the rise of Nazism. He settled in the United States, teaching at Union Theological Seminary, Harvard University, and the University of Chicago.   David E. Klemm

Tilly, Count of (1559-1632) was a leading Roman Catholic general during the Thirty Years' War, a struggle between European Catholics and Protestants. Tilly devoted his life to trying to restore the influence of Roman Catholicism in central Europe.

    When the Thirty Years' War broke out in 1618, Tilly took command of the Catholic Holy League. He won important early victories over both the Bohemians and Danes. But he was defeated at the Battle of Breitenfeld by King Gustavus Adolphus of Sweden in 1631. Tilly then raised a new army to oppose the advancing Protestants. He was wounded during a battle with Swedish forces along the Lech River in Germany, and died soon afterward in Ingolstadt, Germany.

    Tilly was born in Gembloux, Belgium. His given and family name was Johan Tserclaes. In 1843, a statue of Tilly was placed in the Hall of Generals in Munich, Germany.   Theodore S. Hamerow

    See also Thirty Years' War.

Timber. See Forest products; Forestry.

Timber line. See Forest (Mountain evergreen forests).

Timber wolf. See Wolf (with picture).

Timbuktu, *tihm BUHK too* (pop. 20,483), is a small trading town in central Mali. Its official name is Tombouctou (pronounced *tawn book TOO*). From the 1200's to the 1500's, it was one of the richest commercial cities of Africa and a center of Muslim learning.

    Timbuktu was founded about 1100. It lies near the southern edge of the Sahara, about 8 miles (13 kilometers) from the Niger River (see **Mali** [map]). Timbuktu came to be known as the "meeting point of camel and canoe." Goods from North Africa were exchanged there for products from the forests and grasslands of West Africa. Camel caravans from North Africa carried salt, cloth, copper, cowrie shells that were used as money, dates and figs, and metal manufactures to Timbuktu. The merchants of Timbuktu traded gold, ivory, kola nuts, and slaves—all from the south. A school in Timbuktu became a center of scholarship in history, law, and Islam, the Muslim religion.

    Timbuktu's location left it open to attack, and control of the city changed hands many times. It has been controlled by the Mali Empire, the Songhai Empire, Tuareg nomads, Morocco, the Tukulor Empire, and then by France from 1893 to 1960. Since the 1600's, Timbuktu has declined in both importance and population. Many of its mud and brick buildings have crumbled or lie half-buried in the shifting sands. But the arrival of the camel caravans from the northern salt mines is still an important event.   Leo Spitzer

    See also **Mali** (picture); **World, History of the** (picture; The Sankore Mosque).

Time is one of the world's deepest mysteries. No one can say exactly what it is. Yet, the ability to measure time makes our way of life possible. Most human activities involve groups of people acting together in the same place at the same time. People could not do this if they did not all measure time in the same way.

One way of thinking about time is to imagine a world without time. This timeless world would be at a standstill. But if some kind of change took place, that timeless world would be different "now" than it was "before." The period—no matter how brief—between "before" and "now" indicates that time must have passed. Thus, time and change are related because the passing of time depends on changes taking place. In the real world, changes never stop happening. Some changes seem to happen only once, like the falling of a particular leaf. Other changes happen over and over again, like the breaking of waves against the shore.

Any change that takes place again and again stands out from other changes. The rising and setting of the sun are examples of such change. The first people to keep time probably counted such natural repeating events and used them to keep track of events that did not repeat. Later, people made clocks to imitate the regularity of natural events. When people began to count repeating events, they began to measure time.

Measuring time

Units of time measurement. For early peoples, the only changes that were truly regular—that is, repeated themselves evenly—were the motions of objects in the sky. The most obvious of these changes was the alternate daylight and darkness, caused by the rising and setting of the sun. Each of these cycles of the sun came to be called a *day.* Another regular change in the sky was the change in the visible shape of the moon. Each cycle of the moon's changing shape takes about $29\frac{1}{2}$ days, or a *month.*

The cycle of the seasons gave people an even longer unit of time. By watching the stars just before dawn or after sunset, people saw that the sun moved slowly eastward among the stars. The sun made a full circle around the sky in one cycle of the seasons. This cycle takes about $365\frac{1}{4}$ days, or a *year.*

For hundreds of years, people tried to fit days and months evenly into a year or a period of several years. But no system worked perfectly. Today, the calendar is based entirely on the year. Although the year is divided into 12 so-called months, the months have no relation to the moon's actual cycle. See **Calendar.**

There is no regular change in the sky that lasts seven days, as does the *week.* The seven-day week came from the Jewish custom of observing a *Sabbath* (day of rest) every seventh day.

The division of a day into 24 *hours,* an hour into 60 *minutes,* and a minute into 60 *seconds* probably came from the ancient Babylonians. The Babylonians divided the imaginary circular path of the sun into 12 equal parts. Then they divided the periods of daylight and darkness into 12 parts each, resulting in a 24-hour day.

The Babylonians also divided the circle into 360 parts called *degrees.* Other ancient astronomers further divided each degree into 60 minutes. Later, clocks became accurate enough to need smaller units than the hour.

Clockmakers, following the astronomers' division of the degree, divided the hour into 60 minutes and the minute into 60 seconds. In this way, the face of a clock could easily show hours, minutes, and seconds. A clock face has 12 divisions. Each of these divisions equals one hour for the hour hand, five minutes for the minute hand, and five seconds for the second hand.

Some clock faces are divided into 24 hours. On such a clock, 9 a.m. would be shown as 0900 and 3 p.m. would be 1500. This system avoids confusion between the morning and evening hours.

Measuring time by the sun. Directly above every spot on the earth, an imaginary curved line called the *celestial meridian* passes through the sky. As the earth rotates on its axis, the sun crosses every celestial meridian once each day. When the sun crosses the celestial meridian above a particular place, the time there is noon. Twelve hours later, the time at that place is midnight. The period from one midnight to the next is called a *solar day.* The length of a solar day varies because of the tilt of the earth's axis, the oval shape of its orbit, and its changing speed along the orbit.

To make all solar days the same length, astronomers do not measure solar time with the *apparent* (real) sun. Instead, they use an imaginary *mean* (average) sun that moves at a steady speed around the sky. *Local mean solar noon* occurs when the mean sun crosses the celestial meridian above a particular place. The time between one mean solar noon and the next is always the same. Thus, all *mean solar days* are the same length.

Measuring time by the stars. Astronomers also measure time by the earth's rotation in relation to the stars. This time is called *sidereal time.* Each day, as the earth rotates on its axis, an imaginary point among the stars called the *vernal equinox* crosses the celestial meridian above every place on the earth. The time when this happens is *sidereal noon.* The time between one sidereal noon and the next is one *sidereal day.* A sidereal day is shorter than a mean solar day by 3 minutes and 56 seconds. See **Star** (Measuring time).

Devices that measure time. The *sundial* was one of the earliest devices for measuring time. But it can work only in uncloudy daylight. Early peoples also used ropes with knots tied at regular intervals or candles marked with regularly spaced lines. When burned, such devices measured time. An *hourglass* or *sandglass* tells time by means of sand trickling through a narrow opening. A *water clock,* or *clepsydra,* measures time by allowing water to drip slowly from one marked container into another. By the 1700's, people had developed clocks and watches that told time to the minute. Modern electronic and atomic clocks can measure time with far greater accuracy. See **Measurement** (Measuring time).

Time zones

Local and standard time. Clocks in various parts of the world do not all show the same time. Suppose they all did show the same time—3 p.m., for example. At that time, people in some countries would see the sun rise, and people in other lands would see it high in the sky. In still other countries, the sun could not be seen because 3 p.m. would occur at night. Instead, clocks in all locations show 12 o'clock at midday.

Every place on the earth that is east or west of another place has noon at a different time. The time at any particular place is called the *local time* of that place. At noon local time in one town, the time might be 11 a.m. in another place west of the town or 1 p.m. in a place to the east. The local time in the other places depends on how far east or west they are from the town.

If every community used a different time, travelers would be confused and many other problems would be created. To avoid all such problems, *standard time zones* were established. These zones were set up so there would be a difference of one hour between a place on the eastern edge of a time zone and a place on the western edge if each were on its own local time. But under the time zone system, each of these places is not on its own local time. The local time at the *meridian* (line) of longitude that runs through the center of the zone is used by all places within the zone. Thus, time throughout the zone is the same.

Time zones in the United States and Canada. The United States and Canada within within eight standard time zones. Each of these zones uses a time one hour different from its neighboring zones. The hours are earlier to the west of each zone and later to the east. The boundaries between the zones are irregular so that neighboring communities can have the same time.

The United States has not always had standard time zones. Every locality once set its own time by the sun. Various railroads tried to make their schedules simpler by establishing *railroad time* along sections of their routes. But in 1883, there were still about 100 different railroad times. That year, all the railroads divided the United States into four standard time zones.

Each zone is centered on a meridian of longitude 15° apart. In the United States and Canada, the Eastern Time Zone is centered on the 75° west meridian, and the Central Time Zone on the 90° west meridian. The Mountain

Standard time zones in the United States and Canada

The United States and Canada each have six standard time zones. This map does not show the Hawaii-Aleutian time zone, which includes Hawaii and the western Aleutian Islands (part of Alaska). The rest of Alaska is in the Alaska time zone. Major zones differ from neighboring zones by one hour. Zone boundaries are irregular so that places near the zone's edge can have the same time.

WORLD BOOK map

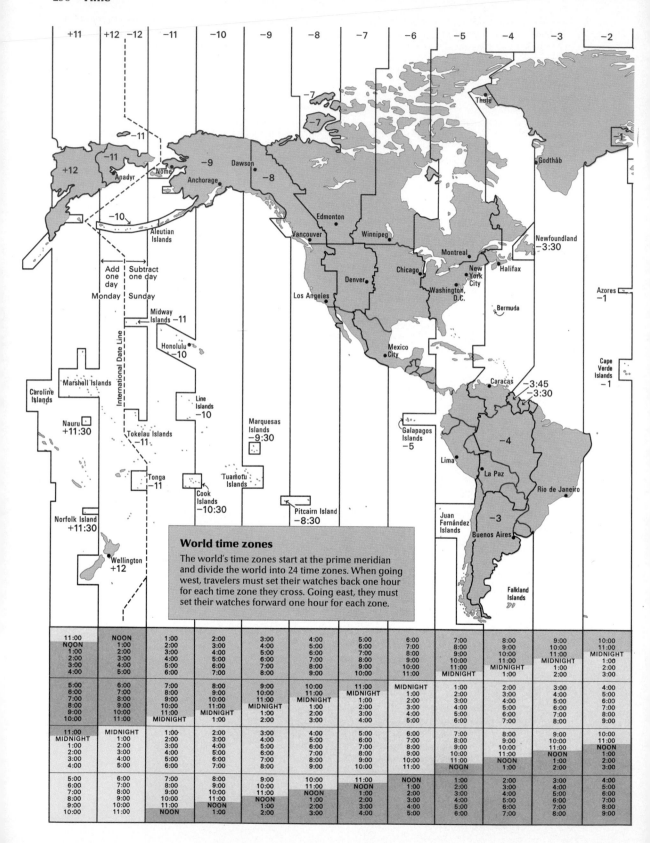

+11	+12	-12	-11	-10	-9	-8	-7	-6	-5	-4	-3	-2

-7

-7

Thule

Godthåb

+12

-11

-11

Anadyr

Nome

-9

Dawson

-8

Anchorage

Newfoundland
-3:30

Edmonton

Vancouver

Winnipeg

Montreal

Denver

Chicago

New
York
City

Halifax

Los Angeles

Washington,
D.C.

Bermuda

Add
one
day

Subtract
one day

Monday Sunday

Midway
Islands -11

Mexico
City

Azores
-1

Honolulu
-10

International Date Line

Caroline
Islands

Marshall Islands

Line
Islands
-10

Cape
Verde
Islands
-1

Nauru
+11:30

Marquesas
Islands
-9:30

Galapagos
Islands
-5

Caracas -3:45
-3:30

Tokelau Islands
-11

Lima

-4

Tonga
-11

Tuamotu
Islands

Cook
Islands
-10:30

Pitcairn Island
-8:30

La Paz

Rio de Janeiro

Norfolk Island
+11:30

Juan
Fernández
Islands

-3

Buenos Aires

World time zones

The world's time zones start at the prime meridian
and divide the world into 24 time zones. When going
west, travelers must set their watches back one hour
for each time zone they cross. Going east, they must
set their watches forward one hour for each zone.

Wellington
+12

Falkland
Islands

11:00	NOON	1:00	2:00	3:00	4:00	5:00	6:00	7:00	8:00	9:00	10:00
NOON	1:00	2:00	3:00	4:00	5:00	6:00	7:00	8:00	9:00	10:00	11:00
1:00	2:00	3:00	4:00	5:00	6:00	7:00	8:00	9:00	10:00	11:00	MIDNIGHT
2:00	3:00	4:00	5:00	6:00	7:00	8:00	9:00	10:00	11:00	MIDNIGHT	1:00
3:00	4:00	5:00	6:00	7:00	8:00	9:00	10:00	11:00	MIDNIGHT	1:00	2:00
4:00	5:00	6:00	7:00	8:00	9:00	10:00	11:00	MIDNIGHT	1:00	2:00	3:00
5:00	6:00	7:00	8:00	9:00	10:00	11:00	MIDNIGHT	1:00	2:00	3:00	4:00
6:00	7:00	8:00	9:00	10:00	11:00	MIDNIGHT	1:00	2:00	3:00	4:00	5:00
7:00	8:00	9:00	10:00	11:00	MIDNIGHT	1:00	2:00	3:00	4:00	5:00	6:00
8:00	9:00	10:00	11:00	MIDNIGHT	1:00	2:00	3:00	4:00	5:00	6:00	7:00
9:00	10:00	11:00	MIDNIGHT	1:00	2:00	3:00	4:00	5:00	6:00	7:00	8:00
10:00	11:00	MIDNIGHT	1:00	2:00	3:00	4:00	5:00	6:00	7:00	8:00	9:00
11:00	MIDNIGHT	1:00	2:00	3:00	4:00	5:00	6:00	7:00	8:00	9:00	10:00
MIDNIGHT	1:00	2:00	3:00	4:00	5:00	6:00	7:00	8:00	9:00	10:00	11:00
1:00	2:00	3:00	4:00	5:00	6:00	7:00	8:00	9:00	10:00	11:00	NOON
2:00	3:00	4:00	5:00	6:00	7:00	8:00	9:00	10:00	11:00	NOON	1:00
3:00	4:00	5:00	6:00	7:00	8:00	9:00	10:00	11:00	NOON	1:00	2:00
4:00	5:00	6:00	7:00	8:00	9:00	10:00	11:00	NOON	1:00	2:00	3:00
5:00	6:00	7:00	8:00	9:00	10:00	11:00	NOON	1:00	2:00	3:00	4:00
6:00	7:00	8:00	9:00	10:00	11:00	NOON	1:00	2:00	3:00	4:00	5:00
7:00	8:00	9:00	10:00	11:00	NOON	1:00	2:00	3:00	4:00	5:00	6:00
8:00	9:00	10:00	11:00	NOON	1:00	2:00	3:00	4:00	5:00	6:00	7:00
9:00	10:00	11:00	NOON	1:00	2:00	3:00	4:00	5:00	6:00	7:00	8:00
10:00	11:00	NOON	1:00	2:00	3:00	4:00	5:00	6:00	7:00	8:00	9:00

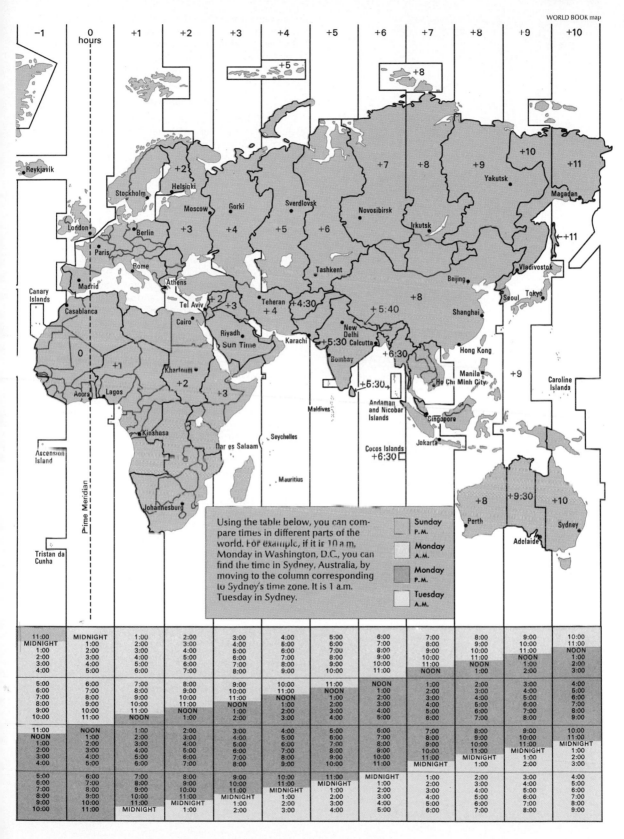

WORLD BOOK map

Using the table below, you can compare times in different parts of the world. For example, if it is 10 a.m. Monday in Washington, D.C., you can find the time in Sydney, Australia, by moving to the column corresponding to Sydney's time zone. It is 1 a.m. Tuesday in Sydney.

Sunday P.M.
Monday A.M.
Monday P.M.
Tuesday A.M.

−1	0	+1	+2	+3	+4	+5	+6	+7	+8	+9	+10
11:00	MIDNIGHT	1:00	2:00	3:00	4:00	5:00	6:00	7:00	8:00	9:00	10:00
MIDNIGHT	1:00	2:00	3:00	4:00	5:00	6:00	7:00	8:00	9:00	10:00	11:00
1:00	2:00	3:00	4:00	5:00	6:00	7:00	8:00	9:00	10:00	11:00	NOON
2:00	3:00	4:00	5:00	6:00	7:00	8:00	9:00	10:00	11:00	NOON	1:00
3:00	4:00	5:00	6:00	7:00	8:00	9:00	10:00	11:00	NOON	1:00	2:00
4:00	5:00	6:00	7:00	8:00	9:00	10:00	11:00	NOON	1:00	2:00	3:00
5:00	6:00	7:00	8:00	9:00	10:00	11:00	NOON	1:00	2:00	3:00	4:00
6:00	7:00	8:00	9:00	10:00	11:00	NOON	1:00	2:00	3:00	4:00	5:00
7:00	8:00	9:00	10:00	11:00	NOON	1:00	2:00	3:00	4:00	5:00	6:00
8:00	9:00	10:00	11:00	NOON	1:00	2:00	3:00	4:00	5:00	6:00	7:00
9:00	10:00	11:00	NOON	1:00	2:00	3:00	4:00	5:00	6:00	7:00	8:00
10:00	11:00	NOON	1:00	2:00	3:00	4:00	5:00	6:00	7:00	8:00	9:00
11:00	NOON	1:00	2:00	3:00	4:00	5:00	6:00	7:00	8:00	9:00	10:00
NOON	1:00	2:00	3:00	4:00	5:00	6:00	7:00	8:00	9:00	10:00	11:00
1:00	2:00	3:00	4:00	5:00	6:00	7:00	8:00	9:00	10:00	11:00	MIDNIGHT
2:00	3:00	4:00	5:00	6:00	7:00	8:00	9:00	10:00	11:00	MIDNIGHT	1:00
3:00	4:00	5:00	6:00	7:00	8:00	9:00	10:00	11:00	MIDNIGHT	1:00	2:00
4:00	5:00	6:00	7:00	8:00	9:00	10:00	11:00	MIDNIGHT	1:00	2:00	3:00
5:00	6:00	7:00	8:00	9:00	10:00	11:00	MIDNIGHT	1:00	2:00	3:00	4:00
6:00	7:00	8:00	9:00	10:00	11:00	MIDNIGHT	1:00	2:00	3:00	4:00	5:00
7:00	8:00	9:00	10:00	11:00	MIDNIGHT	1:00	2:00	3:00	4:00	5:00	6:00
8:00	9:00	10:00	11:00	MIDNIGHT	1:00	2:00	3:00	4:00	5:00	6:00	7:00
9:00	10:00	11:00	MIDNIGHT	1:00	2:00	3:00	4:00	5:00	6:00	7:00	8:00
10:00	11:00	MIDNIGHT	1:00	2:00	3:00	4:00	5:00	6:00	7:00	8:00	9:00

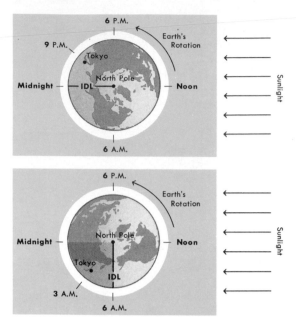

6 P.M.

9 P.M.

Earth's Rotation

Tokyo

North Pole

Midnight — IDL — Noon

Sunlight

6 A.M.

6 P.M.

Earth's Rotation

North Pole

Midnight — — Noon

Sunlight

Tokyo

IDL

3 A.M.

6 A.M.

WORLD BOOK diagram

The time and date at any place on the earth change as the earth rotates on its axis in relation to the sun. When the International Date Line (IDL) is on the opposite side of the earth from the sun, *top diagram,* it is midnight there and 9 p.m. in Tokyo. At this instant, every place on the earth has the same date. Six hours later, *bottom diagram,* as the earth continues to rotate, it is 6 a.m. at the IDL. A new day, *shown in red,* has begun in the area between the IDL and midnight. The time in Tokyo is 3 a.m.

Time Zone is centered on the 105° west meridian, and the Pacific Time Zone on the 120° west meridian. The central meridians of the other U.S. and Canadian zones are 60° west for the Atlantic Time Zone, 135° west for the Yukon Time Zone, and 150° west for the Alaska-Hawaii Time Zone. Western Alaska uses Bering Standard Time, which is centered on the 165° west meridian.

Worldwide time zones were established in 1884. The meridian of longitude passing through the Greenwich Observatory in England was chosen as the starting point for the world's time zones. The Greenwich meridian is often called the *prime meridian.* The mean solar time at Greenwich is called *Greenwich Mean Time* (GMT) or *Greenwich Civil Time* (GCT).

An international conference in 1884 set up 12 time zones west of Greenwich and 12 to the east. These zones divide the world into 23 full zones and two half zones. The 12th zone east and the 12th zone west are each half a zone wide. They lie next to each other and are separated by an imaginary line called the *International Date Line.* The line is halfway around the world from Greenwich. A traveler crossing this line while headed west, toward China, loses a day. A traveler who crosses it traveling eastward gains a day. A few places do not use standard time zones. For example, the polar regions have weeks of constant sunlight or darkness.

In the 1940's, experts began to realize that time based on astronomical measurements was not completely smooth, since the earth slowed down and speeded up in an irregular fashion. As a result, in 1958, the length of

the second was redefined in terms of the natural vibration frequency of the cesium atom. However, the length of the year continued to be determined from astronomical observations. This time scale based on both atomic and astronomical measurements is called *Universal Time Coordinated* (UTC).

Scientific ideas about time

Physical time. Scientists think of time as a fundamental quantity that can be measured. Other fundamental quantities include length and mass. The noted physicist Albert Einstein realized that measurements of these quantities are affected by *relative motion* (motion between two objects). Because of his work, time became popularly known as the *fourth dimension.* See **Relativity** (Special theory); **Fourth dimension.**

Many physicists believe that the apparent nonstop, forward flow of time is not a property of the basic laws of nature. They consider it a result of the fact that the universe is expanding and becoming more disorganized. Some physicists have considered the possibility that, under certain circumstances, time might flow backward. But experiments have not supported this idea.

Biological time. The activities of many plants and animals are timed to the cycle of day and night. These natural rhythms are called *circadian rhythms.* The most obvious example is the sleep cycle.

Many plants and animals are sensitive to other natural time cycles. Certain plants do not start their next step of growth until daylight each day lasts a certain time. Some sea animals time their activities to the changing tides. These creatures even seem to know such times away from their home waters.

Geological time. Geologists have found clues in the earth's crust that indicate how many billions of years ago it was formed. One of these indicators is the element uranium. Uranium changes slowly into the element lead by means of radioactive decay. By measuring the amount of lead in a sample of uranium ore, scientists can estimate when the rock was formed.

A second clue to geological time is radioactive carbon. This form of carbon is absorbed by every living plant and animal. The rate of the carbon's decay can help a geologist estimate how long ago the plant or animal died. See **Radiocarbon.**   James Jespersen

Related articles. See **Calendar** and **Clock** with their lists of *Related articles.* Other related articles include:

Biological clock	Meridian	Standard time
Day	Naval Observatory,	Time capsule
Daylight saving	United States	Weights and
Greenwich Meridian	Radiogeology	measures
Hour	Ship (Nautical terms	
International Date	[Ship's bell])	
Line	Sidereal time	

Time capsule is a container of items sealed to preserve a record of a particular civilization. Time capsules were buried at the New York World's Fair of 1939-1940 and of 1964-1965. In 1975 and 1976, Americans buried time capsules throughout the United States in honor of the nation's 200th anniversary of independence. The capsules contain articles of clothing, letters, photographs, and other items representing American life in the 1900's. A huge time capsule in Seward, Nebr., even holds an automobile and a motorcycle. It is not to be opened until 2025.   W. David Lewis

Time lock. This type of combination lock cannot be opened before a certain hour to which the lock has been set. There are two general types of time locks. The first kind is used mainly in bank vaults. This lock is set to a certain hour. At that hour, but at no other time, the lock can be opened by dialing the combination.

The second type of time lock is called a time-recording lock. It has several keys. When the lock is opened, it registers the number of the key and the time that the lock was opened.   E. A. Fessenden

Time zone. See Time (Time zones; map).

Timed-release medicine. See Microencapsulation.

Times Square. See New York City (Manhattan; picture: Times Square in the 1930's).

Timor, *TEE mawr,* is an island in Southeast Asia. For location, see **Asia** (political map). Timor covers 11,946 square miles (30,939 square kilometers) and has a population of about 1,558,337.

The western half of Timor has been part of Indonesia since that country was formed in 1949. The eastern half became a territory of Portugal in the 1500's. In 1975, Timorese people there demanded independence from Portugal. Fighting broke out among groups of Timorese who wanted to control the territory. The Portuguese rulers left eastern Timor. In 1975, Indonesian troops occupied eastern Timor. In 1976, Indonesia claimed the region and declared it an Indonesian province. Since then, fighting has occurred off and on between the Indonesian troops and Timorese guerrillas. The fighting caused a sharp decline in farm production, and during the late 1970's, food shortages resulted. Many people in eastern Timor died from starvation or suffered from malnutrition.   Justus M. van der Kroef

Timothy was one of the friends of Saint Paul. He was probably born in Lystra, in Asia Minor. His father was Greek and his mother was Jewish (Acts 16:1, II Timothy 1: 5) He is thought to have converted to Christianity when Paul made his first missionary journey and talked with him. Timothy joined Paul on his second journey and is said to have been his trusted friend and companion until Paul's death. Later, he took Paul's place as bishop of the church of Ephesus. It is believed he died as a martyr, about A.D. 100.

The First and Second Epistles to Timothy and the Epistle to Titus are known as the Pastoral Epistles. This is because they contain advice to pastors concerning church government, church officers, teaching, and Christian faithfulness and endurance. Critics debate whether or not Paul wrote these epistles. Some believe that a later author wrote them, using Paul's ideas. The epistles may have been written between A.D. 90 and 110, or even later.   Frederick C. Grant

Timothy is an important grass crop grown primarily for hay. It grows in tufts $1\frac{1}{2}$ to $3\frac{1}{2}$ feet (46 to 107 centimeters) high. The slender, leafy stems bear round spikes of tiny, tightly packed flowers. Timothy is a cool season plant native to northern Europe and Asia. Timothy is also called *herd's-grass.* The English call it *cat's-tail.*

Timothy is a *perennial*—that is, it grows year after year without replanting. However, the crop does not live long if animals graze on it continually, or if it is harvested in an immature stage. The quality of timothy hay is improved when the plant is grown with clover or alfalfa. In the United States and Canada, the first cutting of

timothy is frequently harvested for hay or silage. Later cuttings are left in the pasture for grazing.

Timothy is widely grown in the Northern United States and in Canada. New York ranks as the leading state in the production of timothy hay, and Ohio leads in the production of commercial timothy seed.

Scientific classification. Timothy is a member of the grass family, Gramineae. Its scientific name is *Phleum pratense.*

Vern L. Marble

See also **Grass** (picture: Common grasses).

Timpanogos Cave National Monument, *TIHM puh NOH guhs,* is in northern Utah. It contains limestone caverns with hundreds of stalactites, stalagmites, and helictites in varied colors. The cavern has passageways that lead back into Mount Timpanogos, highest peak in the Wasatch Range. The monument was established in 1922. For area, see **National Park System** (table: National monuments).

Critically reviewed by the National Park Service

Timur the Lame. See Tamerlane.

Tin is a white metallic element that people have used since ancient times. The earliest known use of tin occurred about 3500 B.C. in the city of Ur in southern Mesopotamia (now Iraq). The people of Ur made articles from bronze, an alloy of tin and copper. Today, tin is used chiefly in the production of *tin plate.* Tin plate consists of steel coated on both sides with an extremely thin film of tin. Most tin plate is made into tin cans for packaging food and other products.

Tin has the chemical symbol Sn. Its atomic number is 50, and its atomic weight is 118.71. At 20° C, tin has a density of 7.2984 grams per cubic centimeter (see **Density**). The difference between its melting point, 231.9° C, and its boiling point, 2270° C, is one of the widest of any metal. Tin is also very *malleable*—that is, it can easily be formed into complex shapes. These and other properties of tin enable it to be used in the manufacture of an extremely wide variety of products.

Uses. The coating on tin cans protects the steel in the cans from rust and provides an attractive appearance. Tin also prevents the weak acids in food from damaging the inside of the cans. See **Tin can.**

How tin is used

Tin's unusual chemical and physical properties enable it to be used in a wide variety of products for the home and industry.

WORLD BOOK illustration by David Cunningham

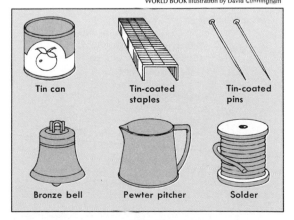

Tin can

Tin-coated staples

Tin-coated pins

Bronze bell

Pewter pitcher

Solder

Cameramann International, Ltd.

A tin mine near Kuala Lumpur, Malaysia, provides tin ore for refining. Malaysia is the world's leading producer of tin.

Tin coatings also protect many other items. Most paper clips, safety pins, straight pins, and staples are made of steel or brass coated with tin. Many food-preparation containers and utensils have tin coatings.

The second most important use of tin is in *solders,* which are alloys used to join metal surfaces. Solders

Leading tin-mining countries

Annual tin production

Country	Production
Malaysia	●●●●●●●●●●●●●●●● 40,700 short tons (36,900 metric tons)
Soviet Union	●●●●●●●●●● 25,400 short tons (23,000 metric tons)
Indonesia	●●●●●●●●● 24,400 short tons (22,100 metric tons)
Brazil	●●●●●●●●● 24,300 short tons (22,000 metric tons)
Thailand	●●●●●●●● 22,000 short tons (20,000 metric tons)
Bolivia	●●●●●●● 19,800 short tons (18,000 metric tons)
China	●●●●●● 16,500 short tons (15,000 metric tons)
Australia	●●● 7,700 short tons (7,000 metric tons)
Great Britain	●●● 5,800 short tons (5,300 metric tons)
Peru	●● 4,200 short tons (3,800 metric tons)

Figures are for 1985.
Source: *Minerals Yearbook, 1985,* U.S. Bureau of Mines.

made primarily of tin and lead are called *soft solders* and melt at relatively low temperatures. Other important tin alloys include bronze and pewter. See **Solder; Bronze; Pewter.**

The malleability of tin enables manufacturers to make tin into extremely thin foil. One use for such foil is as a moistureproof wrapping. *Terneplate* is iron coated with an alloy of lead and tin. Sheets or strips of terneplate are used for roofing and in making such products as fuel tanks and fire extinguishers.

Manufacturers improve the properties of various metals by adding small amounts of tin. For example, cast iron that contains only 0.1 per cent tin is much more durable and easier to work with than ordinary cast iron. Many other products, including bearings, dental fillings, and printing alloys, also contain small amounts of tin, which improves their properties.

Tin combines with other elements to form a great number of useful compounds. Many toothpastes contain *stannous fluoride,* a compound of tin and fluorine that helps prevent tooth decay. Certain compounds that contain tin and carbon are used as pesticides.

Where tin is found. Tin makes up only about 0.001 per cent of the earth's crust. As a result, the amount of tin mined annually is very small compared with other common metals. Most known deposits of tin are in the Southern Hemisphere. The United States has none large enough to mine.

The principal tin ore is a compound of tin and oxygen called *cassiterite* (see **Cassiterite**). Some tin ores contain sulfur and small amounts of such other metals as copper, iron, and lead. Tin deposits sometimes occur as narrow veins that run through granite. Most tin ore, however, is found in plains, where flowing water has deposited bits of eroded granite and ore.

Malaysia is the world's leading producer of tin. Other important tin-producing countries include Australia, Bolivia, Brazil, China, Great Britain, Indonesia, Peru, the Soviet Union, and Thailand.

Refining tin. Processors produce tin by heating cassiterite with coal and limestone in a special furnace. After this process, called *smelting,* the processors refine the tin—usually to a purity of 99.8 per cent. For details on refining, see **Metallurgy** (Extractive metallurgy). Most pure tin is cast into *ingots* (bars) that weigh about 100 pounds (45 kilograms).   Paul E. Davis

See also **George Town.**

Tin can is a container used for packaging, transporting, and marketing hundreds of food and nonfood items for home and industry. Most tin cans are made of steel covered with a thin coat of tin. But millions of cans contain no tin at all and many are made entirely of aluminum. The first tin cans were handmade and sealed with solder. Today, manufacturers make and seal them on a series of machines called a *can line* that produce more than 500 a minute. The shape, size, and construction of cans differ to meet the specific need of the product they contain. But cylindrical cans are most commonly used. Many tin cans have enamel on the inside to prevent discoloration of the food. Perishable foods are preserved by heating the sealed can. In 1963, an Ohio man received a patent on a "tab-opening" tin can. The user opens the can by pulling off a strip of aluminum on top. In the 1960's, steel companies began making *thin tin* for tin cans. It is thinner and lighter than the usual tin plate used in tin cans. The United States produces over 62 billion tin cans a year. See also **Canning** (Tin cans).

James A. Clum

Tinbergen, Jan (1903-   ), a Dutch economist, shared the first Nobel Prize in economics with Ragnar Frisch of Norway in 1969. Tinbergen and Frisch received the award for their work on the development of mathematical models used in *econometrics* (mathematical analysis of economic activity).

Tinbergen was born in The Hague and graduated from the University of Leiden. In 1933, he became a professor at the Netherlands School of Economics in Rotterdam. From 1936 to 1938, Tinbergen worked with the League of Nations and developed the first econometric model of a national economy. He also served with the Dutch government's Central Bureau of Statistics and its Central Planning Bureau. In 1955, Tinbergen became an adviser to other governments and international organizations. He became chairman of the United Nations Committee for Development Planning in 1965.

Leonard S. Silk

Tinbergen, Nikolaas (1907-1988), was a Dutch-born zoologist who studied how the behavior of animals is adapted to their environment. He also investigated the evolution of this behavior over millions of years by comparing the actions of various species. Tinbergen shared the 1973 Nobel Prize for physiology or medicine with Austrian naturalists Konrad Lorenz and Karl von Frisch. They received the award for their studies of animal behavior. Tinbergen worked with birds, butterflies, fish, wasps, and other animals in their natural surroundings. His best-known research concerns the social behavior of gulls.

Tinbergen, the brother of the economist Jan Tinbergen, was born in The Hague. He earned a doctorate from Leiden University in 1932. Tinbergen joined the faculty of Oxford University in England in 1949 and became a British citizen in 1955. Tinbergen's *The Study of Instinct* (1951) summarized scientific knowledge of animal behavior. He also wrote *The Herring Gull's World* (1953) and *Curious Naturalists* (1958).   John A. Wiens

Tinnitus, *tih NY tuhs,* is the sensation of hearing sounds that seem to come from within the head. Most people with tinnitus hear ringing, buzzing, or hissing noises. Others hear sounds like a cricket's chirping or the ocean's roar. The noise may be continuous or come and go. It may be heard in one or both ears. Tinnitus can be extremely distracting, and in some cases it is loud enough to keep the person awake. Many victims also have some hearing loss, ear pain, or dizziness.

Some cases of tinnitus can be traced to a specific condition, such as a blocked ear canal, an ear infection, or the use of certain medicines. Other cases of tinnitus include blood vessel disease, head injury, aging, and exposure to loud noises. However, in most cases of tinnitus, no cause can be identified. Doctors suspect that such cases are due to abnormal functioning of the inner ear or its nerve connections to the brain.

When physicians can identify the cause of a person's tinnitus, they often can relieve it by treating the underlying condition. In cases with no obvious cause, certain medicines or surgical procedures may reduce the noise. Some people who suffer from tinnitus use a device similar to a hearing aid, which masks the noise with more pleasant sounds.   James M. Toomey

Tintoretto, *tihn tuh REHT oh* (1518-1594), was a Venetian painter during the late Italian Renaissance. He became a leading artist of the period for the churches and wealthy families of Venice.

Tintoretto created works noted for their dramatic action. His paintings show the influence of the rich colors used by Titian and the vigorous, muscular forms drawn by Michelangelo. Tintoretto achieved a unique style through exaggeration. He sometimes distorted the proportions of his figures for dramatic effect. The figures move energetically through deep space and changing light.

Tintoretto planned his compositions by placing wax or clay figures in a box—like actors on the stage of a theater—and using candles for lighting effects. He studied these arrangements and drew sketches before beginning to paint. The theatrical character of Tintoretto's paintings can be seen in one of his most famous works, *Saint Mark Rescuing a Slave* (1548), which appears in the Painting article. The figures bend, gesture, and turn. Tintoretto achieved dramatic contrast by spotlighting some forms with intense color and painting others in softer tones and shadows.

Tintoretto's real name was Jacopo Robusti. He was nicknamed *Il Tintoretto,* which means *the little dyer,* because his father was a dyer. Scholars believe Tintoretto taught himself to paint. He opened his first studio at the age of 21.   David Summers

See also **Moses** (picture).

Tipi. See Tepee.

Tippecanoe, Battle of. See Indian wars (Other Midwestern conflicts).

Tipperary, *TIHP uh RAIR ee* (pop. 5,030), is a town in southern Ireland. It lies on the Ara River, in an area that has many dairy farms. For location, see **Ireland** (map). Tipperary serves as a market town and a processing center for dairy products.

Tipperary was founded in the late 1100's. It developed as a small town that surrounded a castle built by Prince John (later King John) of England. The name Tipperary is known in many parts of the world because of the song "It's a Long, Long Way to Tipperary." This tune was a favorite marching song of Allied troops during World War I (1914-1918).   Desmond A. Gillmor

Tiranë, *tee RAH nuh* (pop. 260,000), is the capital and largest city of Albania. Tiranë, also spelled *Tirana,* lies on a coastal plain about 20 miles (32 kilometers) east of the Adriatic Sea. For location, see **Albania** (map).

Tiranë's central district has wide avenues lined by attractive stone buildings. The city is Albania's educational and cultural center. The State University and several research institutes, museums, and theaters are there. Tiranë is the home of Albania's major publishing and broadcasting companies and of several light industries.

The Ottoman commander Barkinzadeh Suleiman Pasha founded Tiranë in the early 1600's. Tiranë became the capital of Albania in 1920. In the early 1920's, only about 12,000 people lived in the city. A Communist government gained control of Albania in 1944. It has expanded Tiranë's boundaries, and many Albanians have moved to the city to work in industries and the government.   Wayne S. Vucinich

Many types of tires are made for today's automobiles. The side view of a steel belted tire is shown above with the front views of, *left to right,* a steel belted tire, a radial ply tire, a mud tire, and a low profile tire. Tread patterns differ for various types of tires.

Tire is a covering for the outer rim of a wheel. Most tires are made of rubber reinforced with some kind of fabric and are *pneumatic* (filled with compressed air). They are used on airplanes, automobiles, bicycles, buses, earth-moving and mining machinery, motorcycles, recreational vehicles, tractors, trucks, and many other kinds of vehicles. Some rubber tires, such as those used on many wagons and wheelbarrows, are solid rubber.

The main feature of rubber tires is their ability to absorb the shock and strain created by bumps in the road. Tires help provide a comfortable ride and help protect many kinds of cargoes. The air in a rubber tire supports the weight of a vehicle.

Another important feature of rubber tires is their ability to grip the road. The face of a tire, called the *tread,* has many deep grooves. These grooves and many smaller slits called *sipes* make up the *tread pattern.* The tread provides the traction that enables the tires to grip the road. The tire body is composed of the rubber *side*

walls (sides), which cover and protect the rest of the body and are made of high-strength bundles of wire for holding the tire on the wheel rim. The body also contains layers of rubberized cord fabric. Each layer is called a *ply.*

How tires are made

Preliminary operations. Before a tire can be manufactured, several operations must be performed. They include mixing the rubber with sulfur and other chemicals, coating cord fabric with rubber, and cutting the rubberized fabric into strips.

A machine called a *Banbury machine* mixes the rubber with the chemicals. The chemicals strengthen the rubber and increase its resistance to wear. The rubber comes from the machine in the form of sheets.

Cord fabric is made of nylon, polyester, rayon, or steel. A *calendering machine* coats it with the rubber sheeting. The triple rollers of this machine squeeze the cords and the rubber together, producing a rubberized

Parts of a tire

The parts of a tire, shown below in cross section, are assembled one by one. Starting with the inner liner, a worker assembles the tire on a slowly turning *drum* (roller). Later, the process of *vulcanization* shapes the tire, seals the parts together, and molds the tread pattern of grooves and sipes into the tread.

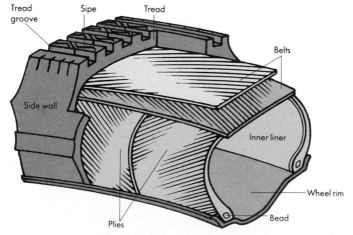

Tire belts improve traction and stability and reduce wear by putting as much tread as possible on the road, as shown in the diagram below.

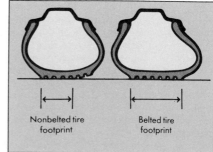

fabric. A cutting machine then slices the rubberized cord fabric into strips of the necessary size.

Assembling a tire. A tire is assembled by hand on a slowly rotating roller called a *drum*. The drum has the same diameter as the wheel on which the tire will be used. As the drum turns, a worker called a *tire builder* wraps an *inner liner* around the drum. The inner liner consists of a band of special rubber that makes the casing airtight. The tire builder then wraps the rubberized cord fabric around the drum, ply by ply. Most of today's automobile tires have two *belts* of fabric between the plies and the tread. The belts are made of steel or manufactured fibers that resist stretching, such as aramid, fiberglass, or rayon.

After putting on the plies, the tire builder adds two *beads.* Each bead consists of several steel wire strands that have been wound together into a hoop and covered with hard rubber. A bead is put on the outside of the tire on each side. It is inserted at the point where the tire will come into contact with the rim of the wheel. The two ends of each ply are wrapped around the bead, securing the bead to the tire.

Next, the builder adds the rubber side walls, the belts, and the tread. The various parts of the tire are then pressed together by a set of rollers in a process called *stitching*.

The *green* (uncured) tire is now ready to be *vulcanized*. The vulcanization process combines chemicals with the raw rubber and makes a rubber product strong, hard, and elastic. The tire is taken off the drum and placed in a *curing press*. The press contains a large rubber bag called a *bladder* and a mold that has the sipes and large grooves of the desired tread pattern in it. The press operates like a giant waffle iron. It is closed, heat is applied, and the bladder is filled with steam. The steam presses the tire against the mold. The bladder and the mold squeeze the tire into its final shape, complete with tread pattern. See **Rubber** (Vulcanization).

Today, more and more of these steps are performed by specially designed machinery. Eliminating hand operations improves productivity and product uniformity.

Retreading tires. After the original tread pattern has worn down, a tire—if it is in good condition—can be *retreaded*, or *recapped*. First, a machine rubs away the old tread. Then a worker applies new tread rubber and puts the tire into a mold. The new tread and tread pattern are then vulcanized to the old tire. Sometimes a new tread with a pattern that has already been vulcanized is cemented to the prepared tire body.

Types of tires and tread patterns

There are three basic kinds of automobile tires: (1) *bias;* (2) *bias belted;* and (3) *radial*, or *radial-ply.*

Bias tires are built with the fabric cord running diagonally—that is, on the bias—from one rim to the other. Each ply is added so that its cords run at an angle opposite to the angle of the cords below it.

As a vehicle moves, the plies of its tires rub against each other and against the tread in an action called *flexing and squirming.* This action produces inner heat, one of the major causes of tire wear. Extreme heat can separate the tread or split the plies.

Bias belted tires are made in the same way as bias tires, but cord fabric belts are placed between the plies and the tread. The belts help prevent punctures and tight tread squirm.

Radial tires are built with the body fabric cord running straight across the tire from one rim to the other. All radial tires are belted. The combination of radial ply and belting produces a tire with longer tread life than either bias or bias belted tires. Radial tires give longer wear because they have less flex and squirm than bias ply tires. They also roll more easily and thus save fuel.

Low profile tires are used on many high-performance cars. These tires look pudgier than regular tires. They are wider (from side wall to side wall) than they are high (from tread to wheel rim). They put more tread into contact with the road than standard tires. This additional

Tire size comparison   The size of a car's tires depends on the type and weight of the vehicle as well as the size of its wheels. Almost all new automobiles have standard tires. Some cars, including many high-performance cars, use low profile or ultra-low profile tires.

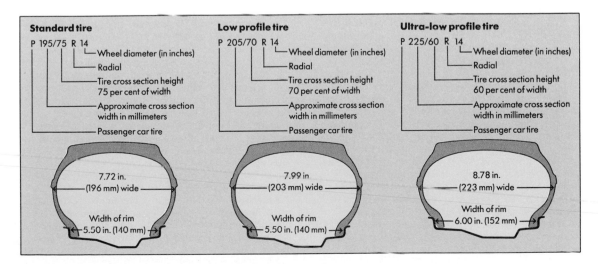

tread creates a wider *footprint* (track), which increases traction. The added stability provided by the tire shape gives a driver more control of a car at high speeds and around curves than standard tires give.

Tire tread patterns are designed for a variety of special purposes. For example, *snow tires* have a tread with extra-deep grooves. This tread bites into snow and mud, providing exceptional traction. A snow tire is not so effective on ice and hard-packed snow because even the deep grooves cannot gain traction. *Studded snow tires* have metal spikes called *studs,* which stick out of the tire like small, sharp fingernails. They dig into ice, providing added traction. Some states of the United States have banned these tires because studies have shown that studs can damage road surfaces. In the 1980's, manufacturers developed tires designed for use in any kind of weather. These tires are usually called *all-season tires.* Special tread patterns are also made for the tires of racing cars, trucks, and various construction, farming, and military vehicles.

History

The pneumatic tire was invented in 1845 by Robert W. Thomson, a Scottish engineer. At that time, most vehicles had wooden wheels and steel tires. The steel tires preserved the wood and wore well. Thomson's tires gave a smoother ride but were not strong enough. In 1870, the first solid rubber tires appeared in England. These tires were used on cars, bicycles, and buggies.

John B. Dunlop, a Scottish veterinarian, improved on Thomson's invention in 1888. Dunlop developed air-filled rubber tubes for his son's tricycle. These pneumatic tires provided a smoother ride and made pedaling easier than did solid rubber tires. Bike manufacturers in Europe and the United States soon began to use them.

Pneumatic tires appeared on automobiles in 1895. Like bicycle tires, they were single air-filled tubes. But as cars became heavier and were driven faster, the single tube tires could not hold enough air pressure for more than a short time. In the early 1900's, two-part tires were developed. They consisted of a casing and a flexible rubber tube that fit inside the casing and held the air. This *inner tube* held from 55 to 75 pounds per square inch (3.9 to 5.3 kilograms per square centimeter) of air pressure. These tires were called *high-pressure tires.*

Then tire manufacturers learned that less air in the tires would not only support the weight of an automobile but also add comfort to the ride. In 1922, *low-pressure tires,* or *balloon tires,* were introduced. They held from 30 to 32 pounds per square inch (2.1 to 2.2 kilograms per square centimeter) of air pressure.

The tubeless tire was introduced in 1948. Its casing was made airtight by an inner liner. Since 1954, most new cars have been equipped with tubeless tires. In 1966, the U.S. Congress passed the National Traffic and Motor Vehicle Safety Act. The act called for minimum safety standards and a system of grading auto tires according to heat resistance, traction, and tread wear. Manufacturers were required to begin labeling tires with performance grades in 1979. Labeling for tread wear was suspended in 1983. It resumed in 1985.

In the 1970's, manufacturers developed thin, "temporary use" spare tires that are much lighter and take up less trunk space than standard tires. Manufacturers also introduced tires that would seal themselves if punctured and experimented with tires that would work even when flat.   James A. Thiese

See also **Dunlop, John B.; Firestone, Harvey S.; Goodyear, Charles; Rubber.**

Tiros. See Space travel (Artificial satellites).

Tirso de Molina, *TEER soh day moh LEE nah,* was the pen name of Gabriel Téllez (1584-1648), a Spanish playwright. His masterpiece *The Deceiver of Seville* (1630) introduced the legend of Don Juan in literature (see **Don Juan**). Tirso probably wrote nearly 400 plays, of which 86 survive. They include historical and religious dramas, light comedies about palace society, and romantic tragedies. Tirso had a good understanding of psychology and showed greater skill in creating characters than any other Spanish playwright of his time. He also wrote light-hearted tales, *The Gardens of Toledo* (1624); and the more serious *Pleasure with Profit* (1635), a collection of stories, short plays, and verse. Tirso was born in Madrid. He was a friar and an important official in the Order of Mercy.   Peter G. Earle

Tishah be-av, *TIHSH ah buh AHV,* is a Jewish day of mourning observed on the ninth day of the Hebrew month of Av (approximately August). On that day, Jews commemorate the destruction of the First Temple in Jerusalem in 587 or 586 B.C. and the destruction of the Second Temple in A.D. 70. The day also commemorates other tragic events in Jewish history, including Nazi Germany's campaign of mass murder of Jews called the Holocaust. For three weeks before Tishah be-av, Jews observe partial mourning and hold no weddings or celebrations. Many Jews fast throughout the day.

The Biblical Book of Lamentations is recited in the synagogue the evening that begins the holiday. During the morning service, a collection of poems is added that mourn the destruction of the temples and other tragic occasions.   B. Barry Levy

Tisiphone. See Furies.

Tisquantum. See Squanto.

Tissue is a group of similar cells that work together to perform a particular function in an organism. Groups of tissues, in turn, form the organs of animals and plants.

Animal tissues are generally divided into four groups: (1) connective tissue, (2) epithelium, (3) muscle, and (4) nervous tissue.

Connective tissue is composed of cells and an abundant *intercellular material.* In most connective tissue, the intercellular material consists of fibers and a transparent, jellylike *ground substance.* Some connective tissues surround and connect other tissues and organs. Bone and cartilage are connective tissues that support and protect the body. Blood and lymph are connective tissues in which the intercellular material is a fluid.

Epithelium consists of tightly packed cells. The two main types of epithelium are membranes and glands. Epithelial membranes form the outer layer of the skin. They also line such internal body surfaces as those of the digestive tract and of the blood vessels. Glands produce secretions, such as hormones and perspiration.

Muscle consists of cells that alternately contract and relax. These actions allow the muscles to move parts of the body and to move substances through the body.

Nervous tissue consists of highly specialized cells that conduct nerve impulses throughout. Nervous tissue enables the body to coordinate many of its functions and to respond to a wide variety of stimuli.

Plant tissues. The cells of simple plants, such as algae and fungi, are not organized into tissues. Other plants have two major types of tissues, *meristematic* and *permanent.* Meristematic tissues consist of immature cells that divide continuously. The growing tips of roots and shoots are composed of meristematic tissue. Permanent tissues consist of mature cells that have specialized functions. Types of permanent tissues include *epidermis, parenchyma, xylem,* and *phloem.* Epidermis forms a plant's protective outer covering, and parenchyma stores food. Xylem conducts water from the roots to other parts of a plant, and phloem transports food throughout the plant.   Charles G. Crispens, Jr.

Related articles in *World Book* include:

Connective tissue	Life (diagram: Struc-	Muscle
Epithelium	tural units)	Nervous system
Histology	Membrane	

Tissue transplant is any tissue or organ permanently transferred from one part of the body to another, or from one person to another. Transplanted tissues and organs replace diseased, damaged, or destroyed body parts. They can help restore the health of a person who might otherwise have died or been disabled.

Types of transplants. Transplants of tissues from one part of the body to another are called *autografts.* They have a high success rate because the body does not recognize the transferred tissue as foreign. Skin, bone, and hair tissues are frequently autografted. For example, surgeons routinely use skin autografts to repair damage from severe burns (see **Skin grafting**).

Transplants from one person to another are called *allografts.* In many cases, the recipient's body rejects an allograft. Rejection occurs because the immune system, the body's chief defense against diseases, recognizes the cells of the transplanted tissue as foreign. White blood cells called *T cells* then attack the transplant. If this process is not controlled, the transplant eventually will fail. Rejection poses a major problem in the transplantation of tissues and organs that consist mainly of living cells—such as the heart, kidneys, lungs, liver, and bone marrow. But some tissues—including cartilage, hard layers of the bones, and the cornea of the eyes—can be allografted easily. These tissues contain relatively few living cells, and so are less likely to be recognized as foreign by the recipient's immune system.

Matching tissues. To help overcome rejection of transplanted tissue, researchers have developed methods for matching donor and recipient tissues. These methods include identifying certain proteins—called *HLA antigens*—on the surface of the cells. Scientists have identified a number of HLA antigens. Each person inherits eight HLA antigens—four on one chromosome inherited from the father, and four on one chromosome inherited from the mother. The greater the number of HLA antigens in common between the donor and recipient, the better the chances for a successful transplant.

About 1 in 4 pairs of *siblings* (brothers and sisters) have exactly the same HLA antigens, because they have inherited the same pair of chromosomes. Transplants between HLA-identical siblings have the best chance of success. Kidney transplants often involve HLA-identical siblings. Such transplants are possible because the

donor and the recipient can function with one kidney.

Combating rejection. Many transplant candidates have no HLA-identical siblings. Furthermore, such organs as the heart and liver can only be obtained from a deceased donor because their removal would kill a living donor. The chances of an exact HLA match between a transplant candidate and an unrelated deceased donor are poor. In these cases, physicians match the donor and recipient tissues as closely as possible, and then administer drugs to limit the immune system's reaction. In so doing, however, they weaken the body's chief means of fighting infections. During the 1980's, physicians began using *cyclosporine* to combat rejection. This drug interferes less than other antirejection drugs with the immune system's ability to fight infections. Researchers also have developed drugs which act against the T cells that cause rejection. One of these drugs is a type of *monoclonal antibody* (see **Monoclonal antibody**).
          Bruce A. Reitz

See also **Bone bank; Cyclosporine; Immunity; Lymphatic system** (Rejection of transplanted tissue).

Titanic, *ty TAN ihk,* was a British steamer. On the night of April 14-15, 1912, during its first trip from England to New York City, it struck an iceberg and sank. Experts had considered the ship unsinkable.

The *Titanic* sighted the iceberg just before the crash, but too late to avoid it. The collision tore a 300-foot (91-meter) gash in its hull. The lifeboats held less than half of the approximately 2,200 persons, and took on mostly women and children. The ship sank in about $2\frac{1}{2}$ hours. The liner *Carpathia* picked up 705 survivors.

The *Titanic* had been the largest ship in the world. It was 882.5 feet (269 meters) long, with a gross tonnage of 46,328. Death reports varied. A British inquiry reported 1,490 dead, the British Board of Trade, 1,503, and a U.S. Senate investigating committee, 1,517.

In 1985, researchers from France and the United States found the wreckage of the *Titanic.* The team refused to give the exact location of the ship, but reports indicated it was about 500 miles (800 kilometers) southeast of Newfoundland.   Walter Lord

Additional resources

Eaton, John P. and Haas, C. A. *Titanic, Triumph and Tragedy: A Chronicle in Words and Pictures.* Norton, 1986.

Drawing from *Le Petit Journal,* Paris (Granger Collection)
The "unsinkable" *Titanic* was believed to be the safest ship afloat. It sank on its first voyage after striking an iceberg.

Lord, Walter. *A Night to Remember.* Rev. ed. Holt, 1976. *The Night Lives On.* Morrow, 1986.

Titaniferous ore, *TY tuh NIHF uhr uhs,* is an iron ore rich in the metal titanium. It is usually a black, granular mixture of the minerals ilmenite and magnetite. See also **Ilmenite; Titanium.**

Titanium, *ty TAY nee uhm* (chemical symbol, Ti), is a lightweight, silver-gray metal. Its atomic number is 22, and its atomic weight is 47.88. The density of titanium lies between that of aluminum and stainless steel. It melts at 1667° C ($\pm$10° C) and boils at 3287° C.

Titanium resists seawater and sea-air corrosion or rust as well as platinum and better than stainless steel. Many highly corrosive acids and alkalies do not affect titanium. It is a *ductile* metal—that is, it can be drawn into wire. It also has a higher strength-weight ratio than steel. All these qualities make it a metal of great importance.

Uses. The first commercial use of titanium was as an oxide to substitute for white lead in paint. Titanium dioxide, or titanium combined with oxygen, is produced as a white pigment that has superior power to cover surfaces in painting. Titanium dioxide is also used in the manufacture of floor coverings, paper, plastics, porcelain enamels, rubber, and welding rods. Barium titanate, a compound of barium and titanium, can be used in place of crystals in television and radar sets, microphones, and phonographs. The gem *titania* is made from crystals of titanium oxide. When cut and polished, titania is more brilliant than the diamond, though not quite so hard. Titanium tetrachloride, or titanium combined with chlorine, has been used for smoke screens, and is the starting point for making the metal.

Titanium metal serves as an important alloying element. The armed forces use large amounts of titanium in aircraft and jet engines, because it is strong but light. It also withstands operating temperatures up to about 427° C (800° F.), which makes it useful in many types of machinery. Because of its superior qualities, titanium has a number of potential uses, such as armor plate for ships, steam-turbine blades, surgical instruments, and tools. The transportation industry would use large amounts of titanium in buses, railroad trains, trucks, and automobiles, if the price of titanium could be lowered enough to compete with the price of stainless steel.

Location of deposits. Titanium ranks as the ninth most plentiful element. But the difficulty of processing the metal makes it expensive. Titanium is never found in a pure state. It usually occurs in ilmenite or rutile. But it may be found in titaniferous magnetite, titanite, and iron (see **Ilmenite; Rutile; Titaniferous ore**).

The leading titanium-producing countries are Australia, Brazil, Canada, Finland, Malaysia, Norway, and the United States. The Soviet Union also has large titanium deposits, but production figures are not available. Florida, Idaho, New Jersey, New York, and Virginia are the chief titanium-producing states. Quebec is the only Canadian province that produces the metal.

Discovery and manufacture. Titanium was discovered by William Gregor of England in 1791, and named by Martin Klaproth of Germany in 1795. It was not until the 1930's, however, that a refining method adaptable to large-scale production was worked out by William Kroll of Luxembourg. The Du Pont Company first produced the metal commercially in 1948. At the present time, pro-

duction remains low because of the difficulty and expense of separating titanium from the ores with which it is found. The United States manufactures most of the refined metal. Japan and Great Britain also manufacture titanium. Research is being conducted to increase its supply and lower its cost.   Robert J. Doedens

Titans were the first gods in Greek mythology. Most of them represented, in human form, such natural phenomena as the earth, sky, and sun. Previously, the universe had existed in a state of emptiness called *Chaos.*

The first Titan was Gaea, the earth. She emerged from Chaos and gave birth to Uranus, the sky. She then married him. Gaea and Uranus had many offspring. The youngest and most important was Cronus, who married Rhea, his sister. Cronus deposed Uranus and became the king of the gods.

Rhea bore Cronus many children, but he swallowed them as soon as they were born to prevent one of them from overthrowing him. Rhea was determined to save Zeus, her youngest son. She tricked Cronus into swallowing a stone wrapped in baby clothes instead. Then she hid Zeus on the island of Crete.

After Zeus grew up, he tricked his father into vomiting up all the offspring. Zeus then led his brothers and sisters in a war against Cronus and overthrew him. Zeus banished Cronus and the Titans who had supported him to Tartarus, an underground region. The defeat of Cronus established Zeus as the supreme ruler of the universe and thus played an important role in the religion of the ancient Greeks.   C. Scott Littleton

See also **Mythology** (Greek mythology); **Atlas; Cronus; Prometheus; Tartarus; Uranus; Zeus.**

Tithe. The word *tithe* comes from the Anglo-Saxon word *teotha,* which means a *tenth part.* The term usually means a tax of one-tenth laid on the profits of a piece of land. In the Bible, the tithe was primarily for the support of the priesthood (Num. 18: 20-32). There was also tithing for the poor.

In the 500's, councils of the Catholic Church began to ordain the payment of taxes. In Charlemagne's time, such payment became state law. In England, tithes were demanded by Pope Adrian I from all lands except those belonging to the Church and the Crown. A *tithe rent* is still charged in a few parishes of the Church of England. In Quebec, Canada, the Roman Catholic Church is supported by tithes. Members of some Protestant churches also contribute a tenth of their income to the church.

William F. McDonald

Titi, *tih TEE,* is a type of small South American monkey. Titis live in the tropical rain forests of the Amazon, in the Orinoco River Basin, and in eastern Brazil. Male and female titis are about the same size. They weigh about $2\frac{1}{4}$ pounds (1 kilogram) and have gray, reddish-brown, or black fur. Titis live in trees and occasionally come to the ground. They feed mainly on fruits but also eat many types of leaves and insects.

Titis live in family groups that consist of an adult male and female pair and their offspring. A family group uses many different calls to defend its territory against other titi groups. Titis have one breeding season each year. Both parents care for the newborn. At 2 to 3 years of age, a titi leaves its parents to start its own family.

Titi monkeys often demonstrate a curious social behavior called *tail-twining.* Two, three, or four titis sit on a

Michael Dick, Animals Animals

The titi is a small South American monkey. The animal lives in trees in tropical rain forests. The titi feeds mainly on fruits but also eats many kinds of leaves and insects.

branch and wrap their tails in a spiral. Titis exhibit this behavior while resting or sleeping.

People hunt many types of South American monkeys for food. However, hunters usually do not kill titi monkeys because of their small size. The greatest enemies of titis are hawks and other predatory birds.

Scientific classification. Titis belong to the New World monkey family, Cebidae. They are genus *Callicebus*.

Randall L. Susman

Titian, *TIHSII uhn* (1487?-1576), was a Venetian painter of the Italian Renaissance. During his long career, which lasted about 70 years, he became one of the most influential and successful painters in the history of art.

Titian's works include portraits and paintings of myths and religious scenes. He developed a style that strongly influenced European painting for more than 200 years. Titian used bright colors, applied his paint in bold brushstrokes, and made one color seem to blend into another. His style is shown in *The Rape of Europa* (1562), which appears in the **Painting** article. This style of painting influenced many great artists, including El Greco, Rembrandt, and Peter Paul Rubens.

Titian painted portraits of royalty and aristocrats. He portrayed his subjects as elegant but spirited. Titian skillfully showed the human side of his subjects through facial expressions and gestures. The works of many great portrait painters, including Anton Van Dyck and Diego Velázquez, show his influence.

Titian was born in Pieve di Cadore, near Venice, Italy. His real name was Tiziano Vecellio. Titian moved to Venice as a boy to study painting. He was apprenticed to two artists, Gentile Bellini and then to his brother Giovanni Bellini. Titian's early works show the influence of Giovanni Bellini and of his artist friend Giorgione.

About 1515, Titian began to produce masterpieces. Titian's success led most of Europe's leading art patrons to buy and pose for his paintings. Titian's clients included Holy Roman emperors Charles V and Ferdinand I, Pope Paul III, King Francis I of France, King Philip II of Spain,

and many of the most important Italian nobles.

David Summers

See also **Drawing** (picture: A pen-and-ink drawing); **Painting** (Venetian painting).

Titicaca, Lake. See Lake Titicaca.

Title is a legal term that is often used to describe ownership of property. The term began with transfers of land. A history of the ownership of land is called a *chain of title*.

The term *title* is properly used to describe the way an owner obtains lawful possession of property. It usually refers to a legal document that describes the interest of the owner. Such documents include deeds to real property, a title to an automobile, the patent for an invention, or the copyright held by an author.

A title to property may be acquired in many ways. If a person buys property from another person, or receives it as a gift or through a will, the title is *derivative*. A title is *original* if the property is not obtained from someone else. For example, trappers may capture wild animals and make them their property. Title by *adverse possession* is a title acquired against the consent of the owner. It is obtained by wrongful entry and continuous possession for a time fixed by state law—10 years in most cases. Suppose, for example, that Jones farms Smith's land for over 10 years against Smith's consent, but Smith does not take legal action against Jones for using the land. Jones then has an original title by adverse possession. A title to land can be acquired by *letters patent.* This term refers to a title transferred from the United States government to a private citizen.

Robert E. Sullivan

See also **Abstract; Deed; Torrens system.**

Titmouse is any of a family of small woodland birds found throughout much of the world. Some species of titmice are known as *tits*. In North America, certain lit-

© The Frick Collection, New York City

Titian's *Man in a Red Cap* reflects the subject's personality through his pose and expression. Titian probably completed the portrait in 1516, at the beginning of his mature period.

WORLD BOOK illustration by Trevor Boyer, Linden Artists, Ltd.
The plain titmouse has brownish-gray feathers.

mice are called *chickadees*. Titmice are active and noisy during much of the day. They feed mainly on insects and also eat seeds, nuts, and berries. These birds measure about 4 to 6 inches (10 to 15 centimeters) long. Some titmice have a pointed crest of feathers on the head.

There are about 65 species of titmice. The *tufted titmouse* is the most common North American species. It is found in the eastern half of the United States and in Canada. This bird has a gray crest and back, a whitish belly, and brownish flanks. The *plain titmouse* is the most common species in the Western United States. Its crest is smaller than that of the tufted titmouse. The *great tit* lives throughout Europe and Asia. This species has a black forehead, breast, and belly, and a yellow back and flanks.

Titmice often nest in old woodpecker holes. They line their nests with fur, feathers, moss, or other soft materials. Most females lay five to eight eggs that are whitish with brown spots and blotches. Titmice travel in groups. They call loudly to one another to signal their location and thus keep the flock together. They also call to alert other birds to such enemies as hawks and owls.

Titmice are highly intelligent birds. In the 1700's, French kings kept titmice in cages and trained them to do tricks.

Scientific classification. Titmice make up the family Paridae. The tufted titmouse is classified as *Parus bicolor*. The plain titmouse is *P. inornatus,* and the great tit is *P. major*.

Richard F. Johnston

See also **Bird** (picture: Birds of forests and woodlands); **Chickadee; Verdin.**

Tito, *TEE toh,* **Josip Broz,** *YOH seep brohz* (1892-1980), established a Communist government in Yugoslavia after World War II and then became the country's ruler. In 1948, he declared Yugoslavia's independence from Soviet control. This act set an example that China and some Eastern European Communist nations later followed. Tito was the first Communist leader to permit his people some economic and social freedom.

Early life. Tito was born Josip Broz, the son of a peasant family, in Kumrovec, Croatia. Croatia is now part of Yugoslavia, but then it was part of Austria-Hungary. Broz became a metalworker. He was drafted into the Austro-Hungarian Army in 1913. In 1915, in World War I, he was

wounded and captured by Russian troops. In 1917, the Communists released him from prison after they had taken power in Russia. He joined the Communist Party.

In 1920, Broz returned to his homeland, which had gained independence after World War I ended in 1918. He helped organize the Yugoslav Communist Party, but it was outlawed and Broz was sent to jail in 1928. He used the name *Tito* to confuse the police after his release in 1934. He later added *Tito* to his real name. He was secretary-general to the Yugoslav Communist Party from 1937 until 1966 when he became party president.

During World War II, Tito organized and led the *Partisans,* guerrillas who fought Germans occupying Yugoslavia. Another resistance group, the anti-Communist *Chetniks,* fought the Partisans, but lost. After the war, Tito had Chetnik leader, Draža Mihailovich, executed.

Yugoslav leader. Tito set up a Communist government in Yugoslavia in 1945, and it was recognized by the United States, Great Britain, and the Soviet Union. Tito became prime minister and defense minister. But Soviet efforts to control Yugoslavia led to a split between Stalin and Tito. Stalin expelled Yugoslavia from the Soviet bloc in 1948. Tito became the first independent Communist leader. Later, he became a spokesman for nations that refused to take sides in the Cold War.

But Tito kept tight control over the Yugoslav people, and tolerated no opposition. He had his close associate, Milovan Djilas, jailed for criticizing the government. In 1963, Tito made himself president for life. Later, Tito released Djilas, limited the power of the secret police, and encouraged some economic and political freedom. In 1968, Tito supported Czechoslovakia's liberalization program, and he criticized the Soviet Union for sending troops into the country to stop the reforms. In 1971, he became head of a presidential council formed to rule Yugoslavia. As chairman, Tito retained much of his power until his death.   Walter C. Clemens, Jr.

See also **Yugoslavia** (History).

Additional resources

Auty, Phyllis. *Tito: A Biography*. Rev. ed. Penguin, 1974.
Djilas, Milovan. *Tito: The Story from Inside.* Harcourt, 1980.
Franchere, Ruth. *Tito of Yugoslavia.* Macmillan, 1970. For younger readers.

Titus, *TY tuhs* (A.D. 41-81), a Roman emperor, was noted for his generosity and his regard for the people's welfare. He was born in Rome, the oldest son of Emperor Vespasian (see **Vespasian**). Titus served in civil and military posts in many parts of the empire. He captured Jerusalem in A.D. 70 after a long siege. Soon after, he was made co-ruler with his father, and succeeded him in 79. The tragic destruction of Pompeii and Herculaneum, when Mount Vesuvius erupted, occurred during the first year of his reign.

The *Arch of Titus* was begun by Vespasian as a triumphal arch for his son's victory at Jerusalem. It was finished in A.D. 81 and is located on the Sacred Way by the Forum of Rome.   Mary Francis Gyles

Titus was an early Christian who was a companion of Saint Paul. Titus was often mentioned in Paul's letters and served as Paul's special representative to the church in Corinth. According to tradition, Titus was the first bishop of Crete. His feast day is January 26.

The Epistle to Titus is a letter addressed to Titus that

is the 17th book of the New Testament. The letter is traditionally attributed to Paul, but most modern scholars believe the letter was actually written by one of Paul's followers. Richard A. Edwards

Titus, Epistle to. See Titus.

Tivoli Gardens. See Denmark (Recreation; picture: Tivoli Gardens).

Tlingit Indians, *TLIHNG giht,* live in southeastern Alaska. The word *Tlingit* is also spelled *Tlinkit.*

Before Europeans arrived in Alaska, the Tlingit occupied an area that extends from present-day Ketchikan to what is now Yakutat. They divided the area into 13 territories called *kwans,* also spelled *quans.* Each kwan belonged to a particular group of Tlingit.

During most of the year, the groups moved about their kwans and hunted and fished. They hunted deer and seals; caught halibut, salmon, and other fishes; and gathered berries, bird eggs, and clams. In winter, the Tlingit lived in villages that consisted of large wooden buildings, each of which housed several families.

Tlingit society consisted of two groups, the *Raven* and the *Eagle* or *Wolf.* Children belonged to their mother's group. Men and women from the same group were not permitted to marry each other. Tlingit woodworkers carved symbols called *totems* into tall poles. Totem poles represented the history of a family or clan. To raise their standing in the community, rich members tried to outdo one another by hosting feasts called *potlatches.* At the feast, the host gave gifts to his guests.

Today, many Tlingit work in the logging and fishing industries. The tribe's economy has improved as a result of the Alaska Native Claims Settlement Act of 1971. This law called for payment of 962\frac{1}{2}$ million to the Tlingit and other original inhabitants of Alaska. It also provided for the return of more than 40 million acres (16 million hectares) of land to the original Alaskans. The Indians, in turn, agreed to abandon their claims to the rest of the state. The Tlingit established the Sealaska Corporation, an investment firm, to handle their share of the money. Each of the approximately 13,000 Tlingit owns a share in the corporation. Sam Stanley

TM. See Transcendental meditation.

TNT is short for trinitrotoluene, a powerful solid explosive. TNT is made up of the chemical elements nitrogen, hydrogen, carbon, and oxygen. The chemical formula for TNT is $CH_3C_6H_2(NO_2)_3$.

The explosive is made by nitrating the chemical compound toluene. The resulting explosive forms in pale yellow crystals that may darken to brown. These crystals of TNT can be handled safely and may even be melted at low heat without igniting. TNT is used alone and in mixtures with other explosives, such as PETN and RDX. It is chiefly used as the explosive charge for shells and bombs. James E. Kennedy

See also **Explosive.**

Toad is a small, tailless animal that closely resembles the frog. Toads and frogs both belong to a class of animals called *amphibians* and live part of their life in water and part on land. But toads have broader bodies, drier skin, and shorter, less powerful back legs than do most frogs.

Many toads are dull brown or gray. But some have vivid coloring, such as green stripes or red spots. The skin of most toads is dry, rough, and covered with warts.

Despite superstition, a person cannot get warts by touching a toad. But a pair of large *parotoid glands* on top of a toad's head give off a poison that can irritate the eyes or cause illness. The poison also has an unpleasant taste that helps protect the toad from enemies.

A toad uses its long, sticky tongue to prey on insects and other small animals. It can flip out its tongue, seize an animal, and swallow it—all in an instant.

Toads and frogs make up a scientific order known as Anura or Salientia. Members of several families in this order are commonly called toads. But zoologists consider only members of the family Bufonidae to be *true toads.* This article describes the true toads. For information on other members of the order Anura, see the section *Kinds of frogs* in the **Frog** article.

The life of a toad. Toads grow up in water but spend most of their adult life on land. They return to water to breed. Temporary pools resulting from spring or summer rain are typical breeding sites. In most toads, the male attracts the female with a mating call. A few kinds of toads do not have a mating call.

Almost all female toads lay eggs. Some females lay more than 30,000 eggs at a time. As the female deposits

S. C. Bisserot, Bruce Coleman Inc.

The striped toad of South America, like most species of toads, has dry, warty skin. Glands in a toad's skin contain a poisonous liquid that the animal releases if attacked.

Runk/Schoenberger from Grant Heilman

A fowler's toad flips out its sticky tongue to capture a cricket. A toad's tongue is attached to the front of its lower jaw. Fowler's toads are found in the Eastern United States.

Alvin E. Staffan

A male American toad puffs out its throat to utter a loud, flutelike mating call. The soft-voiced females cannot swell their throat. American toads live in the Eastern United States.

eggs in the water, the male clings to her body and fertilizes them. Toad eggs look like tiny, black spots enclosed in long strings of clear jelly. The jellylike substance helps protect the eggs.

Within a few days, small tadpoles hatch from the eggs. The tadpoles remain in the water as they go through a process called *metamorphosis.* In this process, the tadpoles gradually develop the characteristics of the adult toad. In most toads, metamorphosis takes from three to eight weeks. The young toads then leave the water and begin their life on land. Young toads grow rapidly. Some reach adult size in a year or less.

Toads avoid direct sunlight and heat. They are most active at night or on rainy days. During hot, dry spells, toads dig deep into the ground and remain there. This behavior is called *estivation.* Toads that live in areas with harsh winters hibernate during the cold weather.

Many animals prey on tadpoles and young toads. In North America, a chief enemy of adult toads is the hognose snake. A toad's poison does not affect this snake.

Scientists do not know how long toads live in the wild. Toads in captivity have lived more than 10 years.

Kinds of toads. There are about 300 species of toads. About 18 of them live in North America. The *American toad* is common in fields, gardens, and woods of the Northeastern United States. It is about the size of a person's fist. The *Southern toad,* a slightly smaller species, is common in the Southeast. Males of both species have a pleasant, high-pitched call. One of the most widespread North American species is *Woodhouse's toad.* It lives throughout most of the United States and in parts of northern Mexico. The call of the male Woodhouse's toad sounds somewhat like the bleat of a sheep.

The *giant toad,* also called the *marine toad,* ranks as one of the largest toads. It may grow more than 9 inches (23 centimeters) long. This toad once lived only in southern Texas and tropical regions of North and South America. It is now also found in other regions, including Australia, the Philippines, and southern Florida. Two of the smallest toads are *Rose's toad* of South Africa and the *oak toad* of the Southeastern United States. The adults measure only about 1 inch (2.5 centimeters) long.

The *African live-bearing toads* are the only toads that do not lay eggs. Females give birth to live young.

Scientific classification. True toads make up the toad family, Bufonidae. The American toad is *Bufo americanus,* the Southern toad is *B. terrestris,* and Woodhouse's toad is *B. woodhousei.*   J. Whitfield Gibbons

See also **Midwife toad; Surinam toad; Tadpole.**

Toadfish is the name of a group of large-headed fish that live on the bottom of tropical and temperate seas. There are about 65 species of toadfish. Most measure less than $1\frac{1}{2}$ feet (46 centimeters) long. Some species, such as the *midshipmen,* can produce light called *bioluminescence* (see **Bioluminescence**). Most toadfish make grunting or toadlike noises.

Female toadfish commonly make nests for their eggs. The males guard the nest and can be extremely aggressive if the eggs are threatened. Certain species of toad-

WORLD BOOK illustration by John F. Eggert

The toadfish lives on the bottom of the ocean.

fish are popular aquarium pets.

Scientific classification. Toadfish make up the toadfish family, Batrachoididae. Species commonly kept in home aquariums belong to either of two genera, *Opsanus* or *Porichthys.*
    Leighton R. Taylor, Jr.

Toadflax, also called *butter-and-eggs,* is a weed with yellow flowers and pale green leaves. It grows in central North America, as far west as the Rocky Mountains. The flowers cluster along the upper part of the stem. They are tube-shaped, with the edge cut into an upper and lower lip. The upper lip has two lobes, and the lower lip has three. A thick, orange-colored ridge on the middle lobe covers the mouth of the tube. The weight of a bee

WORLD BOOK illustration by Lorraine Epstein

Toadflax has clusters of yellow, tube-shaped flowers.

looking for nectar forces the mouth of the tube open. Toadflax was brought to America from Europe. It is sometimes grown in gardens.

Scientific classification. Toadflax is in the figwort family, Scrophulariaceae. It is *Linaria vulgaris.*　　Earl L. Core

Toadstool. See Mushroom.

Tobacco is a plant whose leaves are used chiefly in making cigarettes and cigars. Other tobacco products include smoking tobacco for pipes, chewing tobacco, and snuff. Inferior grades of tobacco leaves are used in making insecticides and disinfectants. The stalks and stems of the plant serve as an ingredient for some types of fertilizer.

Tobacco ranks as an important crop in more than 60 countries. During the mid-1980's, the annual worldwide production of tobacco totaled about $7\frac{1}{4}$ million short tons (6.6 million metric tons). China leads in tobacco production, followed by the United States, India, Brazil, and the Soviet Union.

Farmers in the United States harvest about 1 million short tons (900,000 metric tons) of tobacco annually. Crop sales total about $3\frac{1}{2}$ billion. North Carolina is the leading tobacco-producing state, followed by Kentucky, Tennessee, and South Carolina. Ontario produces most of Canada's tobacco.

The tobacco industry in the United States produces about 670 billion cigarettes and about 4 billion cigars yearly. About 160 million pounds (73 million kilograms) of tobacco are manufactured annually for smoking to-

Charles Gupton, Southern Light

Tobacco is *cured* in a special barn before being sent to market. In a modern curing barn, *above,* a furnace heats the air, which fans force through the drying leaves.

bacco, chewing tobacco, and snuff. The annual value of tobacco products amounts to about $17 billion. Most of this income comes from domestic sales.

The taxes on tobacco products provide a major source of revenue for the United States government. Tobacco products are also taxed by all the state governments and some local governments. Taxes on tobacco total about three times the amount that the growers receive for their crops.

Tobacco contains small amounts of nicotine, a substance that acts as a stimulant on the heart and other organs. Nicotine also stimulates the nervous system, causing many people to become addicted to it. Physicians believe these stimulating effects of nicotine help make smoking pleasurable. However, concentrated amounts of nicotine are poisonous. The nicotine that people consume from cigarettes may contribute to the occurrence of heart attacks and stomach ulcers. Other substances in the smoke aerosol may cause lung cancer. See **Smoking; Drug abuse.**

The tobacco plant

Cultivated tobacco is an *annual* plant—that is, it lives only one growing season. The plant reaches a height of 4 to 6 feet (1.2 to 1.8 meters). It produces about 20 leaves, which measure from 24 to 30 inches (61 to 76 centimeters) long and 15 to 18 inches (38 to 46 centimeters) wide. The tobacco plant ranges from light green to dark green in color. A vigorous, mature plant can produce a million seeds yearly—enough to plant about 100 acres (40 hectares) of tobacco.

Kinds of tobacco

In the United States, tobacco is classified into four main groups: (1) air-cured tobacco, (2) fire-cured tobacco, (3) flue-cured tobacco, and (4) cigar leaf tobacco. The first three kinds are classified according to the

WORLD BOOK illustration by James Teason

The tobacco plant, *above,* lives for only one growing season. It stands from 4 to 6 feet (1.2 to 1.8 meters) high and ranges in color from light green to dark green. The plant has about 20 leaves and grows light pink flowers.

method used in *curing* (drying) the leaves. More information on these methods appears in the *Curing tobacco* section. Cigar leaf tobacco is air cured, but it is classified according to its use.

Air-cured tobacco consists of two varieties, light air-cured and dark air-cured. Most cigarettes contain the two major types of light air-cured tobacco, burley and Maryland. Burley tobacco accounts for about 30 per cent of the tobacco production in the United States. Dark air-cured tobacco is used primarily for chewing tobacco and snuff.

Fire-cured tobacco has a distinctive smoky aroma and flavor. It is used to make smoking tobacco, chewing tobacco, snuff, and strong-tasting cigars.

Flue-cured tobacco is also called *bright tobacco* because the curing process turns it yellow to reddish-orange. It accounts for more than 60 per cent of the tobacco produced in the United States. Most flue-cured tobacco is used in cigarettes.

There are three types of cigar leaf tobacco: (1) cigar filler tobacco, (2) cigar binder tobacco, and (3) cigar wrapper tobacco.

Cigar filler tobacco is used in the body of cigars because it has a sweet flavor and burns evenly. Cigar binder tobacco was once used to hold filler tobacco together, but most cigar manufacturers now use *reconstituted tobacco sheets* instead. These sheets are made from coarse or damaged tobacco leaves. Today, cigar binder is used primarily in making chewing tobacco.

Cigar wrapper tobacco is used for the outside cover of cigars. It must have high-quality leaves that are smooth, thin, and uniform in color. To grow leaves with these characteristics, farmers surround the tobacco with a framework covered by cloth. Producing this tobacco is difficult and expensive, and many manufacturers use reconstituted tobacco sheets to cover their cigars.

Raising and marketing tobacco

Planting and cultivation. The soil and climate conditions that favor tobacco growth vary according to the kind of tobacco being raised. However, most tobacco grows best in a warm climate and in carefully drained and fertilized soil.

Tobacco seeds are planted in seed beds in late winter or early spring and covered with cloth or plastic. The plants grow 6 to 8 inches (15 to 20 centimeters) tall in 8 to 12 weeks and are then transplanted into the field.

Farmers cultivate the soil several times to keep it loose and to eliminate weeds and grasses. The last cultivation occurs after the plants reach a height of 18 to 24 inches (46 to 61 centimeters).

The upper part of the plant is *topped* (cut off) when it begins to produce flowers. This process allows the remaining leaves to become larger and heavier.

Harvesting tobacco. Farmers harvest tobacco from 70 to 90 days after it has been transplanted. They use two harvesting methods, *priming* and *stalk-cutting.*

Priming involves picking the individual tobacco leaves as they ripen. The leaves were once picked by hand, but most farmers now use priming machines. The priming method is used to harvest cigar wrapper, flue-cured, and some cigar filler tobaccos.

Stalk-cutting consists of cutting the entire plant with a hatchetlike tool. The stalks are then placed on sticks and left in the field for a day or two to wilt. Growers use the stalk-cutting method to harvest air-cured, fire-cured, and most cigar leaf tobaccos.

Diseases and pests. Diseases that attack tobacco include *black shank* and *black root rot.* Many farmers raise newly developed types of tobacco that resist black shank and various virus diseases. Crop rotation is the most effective way to control black root rot.

Budworms, flea beetles, grasshoppers, and other insects also damage tobacco plants. Farmers use insecticides to control these pests.

Curing tobacco involves drying the sap from newly harvested leaves. This process produces various chemical changes in tobacco that improve its flavor and aroma. There are three methods of curing tobacco: (1) air curing, (2) fire curing, and (3) flue curing. Each type of tobacco responds most favorably to one of these methods. Curing takes place in curing barns that are built specifically for the method used.

Air curing uses natural weather conditions to dry tobacco. Air-curing barns have ventilators that can be opened and closed to control the temperature and hu-

Leading tobacco-growing countries

Annual tobacco production

Country	Production
China	●●●●●●●●●●●●●●●●●●●●●●●●●●●● 2,244,000 short tons (2,036,000 metric tons)
United States	●●●●●●●●● 774,000 short tons (702,000 metric tons)
India	●●●●●◀ 521,000 short tons (473,000 metric tons)
Brazil	●●●●● 453,000 short tons (411,000 metric tons)
Soviet Union	●●●●◀ 419,000 short tons (380,000 metric tons)
Turkey	●● 194,000 short tons (176,000 metric tons)
Italy	●◀ 173,000 short tons (157,000 metric tons)

Figures are for 1985.
Source: *FAO Production Yearbook, 1985,* Food and Agriculture Organization of the UN.

Leading tobacco-growing states and provinces

Annual tobacco production

State/Province	Production
North Carolina	●●●●●●●●●●●●●●●●●●●●●●●●●●●● 278,700 short tons (252,800 metric tons)
Kentucky	●●●●●●●●●●●●●●●●●●●●●●◀ 223,300 short tons (202,600 metric tons)
Ontario	●●●●●●●● 85,800 short tons (77,800 metric tons)
Tennessee	●●●●●◀ 69,300 short tons (62,900 metric tons)
South Carolina	●●●● 49,500 short tons (44,900 metric tons)
Virginia	●●●◀ 45,900 short tons (41,600 metric tons)
Georgia	●●●◀ 41,100 short tons (37,300 metric tons)

Figures are for 1985.
Source: U.S. Department of Agriculture; Statistics Canada.

midity. This process takes from four to eight weeks.

Fire curing dries tobacco with low-burning fires. The smoke gives fire-cured tobacco its distinctive taste and aroma. Farmers regulate the heat, humidity, and ventilation in the curing barns in order to avoid scalding the tobacco leaves. Fire curing requires from three days to six weeks.

Flue curing dries tobacco by heat from *flues* (pipes) connected to furnaces. The temperature is gradually raised from 90° F. (32° C) to 160° F. (71° C) until the leaves and stems are completely dry. The flue-curing method takes about a week.

Marketing tobacco. Farmers sell tobacco by two major methods, *loose leaf auctions* and *country sales.*

Loose leaf auctions handle about 95 per cent of the tobacco sales in the United States. The term *loose leaf* refers to the practice of displaying and selling tobacco in leaf form rather than packed in containers.

Auction warehouses operate in cities and towns throughout tobacco-growing regions. In the United States, federal inspectors examine tobacco before it is sold and grade it according to government standards.

Buyers from tobacco companies bid on the tobacco, which is usually sold to the highest bidder. The government has *price supports* that guarantee the seller a certain price for tobacco. Government-sponsored organizations known as farmer *cooperatives* buy the tobacco if no bidder offers this amount.

Country sales involve the direct sale of tobacco from farmer to buyer outside the auction system. Most cigar leaf tobacco is sold directly. This system is also called *barn-door marketing* because the buyers usually come to the farm to inspect the crop.

Manufacturing tobacco products

Freshly cured tobacco has a sharp aroma and bitter taste. Therefore, most tobacco is put into storage and allowed to age before being used in manufacturing tobacco products.

Prior to storage, most tobacco goes through a redrying process, during which it is completely dried and cooled. Manufacturers then restore some water throughout the leaves to ensure uniform moisture content. This practice prevents the leaves from breaking.

Next, tobacco is stored for two or three years in barrellike containers. During storage, it ages and undergoes a chemical change called *fermentation.* Fermentation gives tobacco a sweeter, milder flavor and aroma and reduces its nicotine content. Tobacco also loses moisture and becomes darker during aging.

A somewhat different procedure is used to age cigar leaf tobacco, which does not require redrying. Bales of this tobacco are placed in heated rooms or are simply hung up to ferment before storage.

Cigarettes account for about 85 per cent of the tobacco consumed in the United States. The remainder is used in making cigars, smoking tobacco, chewing tobacco, and snuff.

Cigarettes contain blends of burley, Maryland, flue-cured, and imported Turkish tobaccos. Manufacturers add such flavorings as honey, licorice, menthol, and sugar to the blended tobacco. A chemical called *glycerine* is often added to preserve moisture.

Various machines handle the entire process of mak-

Charles Gupton, Southern Light

A tobacco auction enables buyers to inspect the tobacco and bid on it. Federal inspectors grade most U.S. tobacco.

ing and packaging cigarettes. Cigarette-making machines can produce about 4,000 cigarettes each minute.

Cigars consist of about 85 per cent cigar filler, 10 per cent cigar binder, and 5 per cent cigar wrapper tobaccos. Most cigars are made by machines, but the more expensive kinds are hand-rolled.

Most smoking tobacco is used in pipes, but some people smoke it in the form of cigarettes that they roll by hand. For flavor, manufacturers add tonka beans, vanilla leaves, and other substances. Tobacco flavorings are called *saucing compounds.*

Chewing tobacco is made from various types of inferior grade tobacco. Most chewing tobacco is treated with such saucing compounds as honey or licorice.

Snuff consists of a coarsely ground mixture of tobacco leaves and stems that has been pressed into a fine powder. The powder is strained through cloth and flavored with oils and spices.

History

American Indians smoked tobacco in pipes long before Christopher Columbus sailed to the New World in 1492. Columbus brought some tobacco seeds back to Europe, where farmers began to grow the plant for use as a medicine that helped people relax. In 1560, a French diplomat named Jean Nicot—from whom tobacco receives its botanical name, *Nicotiana*—introduced the use of tobacco in France.

Commercial production of tobacco began in North America in 1612, after an English colonist named John Rolfe brought some tobacco seeds from South America to Virginia. The Virginia soil and climate were excellent for tobacco, and it became an important crop there and in other parts of the South.

Most of the tobacco grown in the American Colonies was exported to England until the Revolutionary War began in 1775. Manufacturers in the United States then began to produce smoking tobacco, chewing tobacco, and snuff for domestic use. Cigars were first manufactured in the United States in the early 1800's.

Spaniards and some other Europeans began to

smoke hand-rolled cigarettes in the 1600's, but few people in the United States used them until the 1850's. Cigarette smoking became increasingly popular after the first practical cigarette-making machine was invented in the early 1880's.

The use of tobacco products has been a controversial issue for many years. During the 1500's, European physicians declared that tobacco should be used only for medicinal purposes. The Puritans in America considered it a dangerous narcotic. During the 1960's, scientists established that smoking tobacco products—especially cigarettes—could cause lung cancer, heart disease, and other illnesses.

Some cigarette manufacturers reacted to the medical findings by reducing the tar and nicotine content of cigarettes. However, doctors state that these measures have not eliminated the dangers of smoking.

Various federal laws have been passed in the United States regarding the sale of tobacco products. Since 1966, manufacturers have been required to include a health warning on all packages and cartons of cigarettes. Another law, which went into effect in 1971, banned radio and television commercials advertising cigarettes. In 1972, manufacturers agreed to include a health warning in all cigarette advertising. Some states prohibit smoking in various public places.

Scientific classification. The tobacco plant belongs to the nightshade family, Solanaceae. The major kind is genus *Nicotiana,* species *N. tabacum.*   J. H. Smiley

Related articles in *World Book* include:

Cigar	Kentucky (picture)
Cigarette	Nicotine
Colonial life in America (Crops)	Pipe
Drug abuse	Snuff
Filter	Virginia (picture)

Additional resources

Brooks, Jerome E. *Mighty Leaf: Tobacco Through the Centuries.* Little, Brown, 1952.
Robert, Joseph C. *The Story of Tobacco in America.* Univ. of North Carolina Press, 1967. First published in 1949.
Sullivan, George. *How Do They Grow It?* Westminster, 1968. For younger readers. Includes section on tobacco.
The Tobacco Industry in Transition: Policies for the 1980s. Ed. by William R. Finger. Lexington Books, 1981.

Tobago. See Trinidad and Tobago.

Tobey, *TOH bee,* **Mark** (1890-1976), was an American artist who painted elaborate linear abstract pictures, often on a small scale. Tobey's delicately colored compositions have dense patterns of lines and small symbols. They have been compared to *calligraphy* (the art of fine handwriting). Tobey used the term *white writing* to describe his style. Tobey developed his calligraphic style after a trip to the Orient in the 1930's. Later he ordered his images into highly complex groupings of tiny forms. Tobey's paintings were admired by Europeans, who saw in them an American blend of Eastern and Western styles. Tobey was born in Centerville, Wis.

Dore Ashton

Tobogganing, *tuh BAHG uhn ihng,* is the winter sport of coasting on snow or ice by means of toboggans, which are sleds without runners. A toboggan is made of strips of hickory, ash, or maple, with the front ends curved back. The strips are fastened together by crosspieces into one compact unit. The under surface is highly polished. The sled is usually 6 to 8 feet (1.8 to 2.4

Bruce M. Wellman, Stock, Boston

Tobogganing is a popular winter sport. Participants coast down a snowy or icy hill on a sled called a toboggan. A typical toboggan has no runners and its front end is curved forward.

meters) long and $1\frac{1}{2}$ feet (46 centimeters) wide. Four people usually make up a toboggan team. The one at the rear steers the sled. Tobogganists have attained a speed of 900 yards (823 meters) in 30 seconds, or more than 61 mph (98 kph).

Indian hunters first built toboggans to carry game over the snow. These were made of bark. The Eskimos used to make toboggans of whalebone. Bobsledding, an offshoot of tobogganing, has become a feature of the Winter Olympic Games. A bobsled can reach a speed of about 80 mph (128 kph). Both two-seat and four-seat bobsleds have a standard length of 9 to 12 feet (2.7 to 3.7 meters).   Robert M. Hughes

See also **Bobsledding; Sled.**

Tocopherol. See Vitamin (Vitamin E).

Tocqueville, *TOHK vihl* or *tawk VEEL,* **Alexis de,** *ah lehk SEE duh* (1805-1859), was a French historian and political philosopher. He became famous for his book *Democracy in America* (1835-1840), a study of political and social institutions in the United States. His other classic work, *The Old Regime and the Revolution* (1856), describes how government policies and conflicts between the upper class and other classes caused the French Revolution (1789-1799).

Unlike many thinkers of his time, Tocqueville believed the spread of some form of democratic government was inevitable. In *Democracy in America,* he analyzed what made free societies work and discussed the good and bad aspects of social equality. He warned that the "tyranny of the majority" would put great pressure on people to act like everyone else. As a result, democracy would tend to smother individuality and personal freedom. Tocqueville wrote the book after visiting the United States in 1831 and 1832.

Tocqueville was born in Paris into an aristocratic family. He served in the French legislature from 1839 to 1851 and briefly held the post of foreign minister in 1849.

Seymour Drescher

Todd, Mary. See Lincoln, Mary Todd.

Toddler. See **Child** (The toddler stage).

Toe. See **Foot**.

Tofu, *TOH foo,* is a food made of soybean curds pressed into cakes or blocks. Tofu originated in China more than 1,000 years ago. Today, it is a major source of protein throughout east Asia.

Tofu, formerly known as *bean curd,* resembles custard or a soft white cheese. It has little taste of its own, but it picks up the flavors of the foods it is cooked with. Tofu contains no cholesterol, and it is low in salt and calories.

Many Western-style dishes may be made with tofu, and since the mid-1970's, it has become increasingly popular in the United States. Tofu may be substituted for sour cream in dips and dressings, for ground beef in hamburgers, and for ham or cheese in sandwiches. It also may be used in place of cream cheese in cheesecake and cream in ice cream. *William Shurtleff*

Toga, *TOH guh,* was the loose, draped wrap, or outer garment, worn by the citizens of ancient Rome. They wrapped it about the entire body and allowed it to fall in graceful folds. Originally, both men and women wore the toga. But gradually the women began to wear the *stola* instead. Later, only Roman citizens could wear the toga. They wore it on all formal occasions.

Shape and size. The Romans changed the shape of the toga and draped it differently from time to time. It became more elaborate with each period. Originally, the shape was probably oblong. However, usually the toga was almost as wide as the height of the wearer. It was long enough to go around the body at least two times.

Colors and styles. Romans used wool fabrics to make togas. The ordinary citizen usually wore a white toga. But colored borders or a different colored material showed the rank or station of the wearer. For example, youths of from 14 to 17 years of age exchanged their purple-bordered togas for all-white togas, called the *toga of manhood,* or the *toga virilis.* Because of its pure white color, they also called it the *toga pura.* Magistrates and high priests wore a purple-bordered white toga, called the *toga praetexta.* A candidate for office wore a white toga known as the *toga candida.*

At first, Romans used a richly embroidered purple toga, called the *toga picta* or *toga palmata,* to honor victors. Later, emperors adopted it as their official dress. During the imperial period, the toga became elaborate and heavy. It required such careful drap-

Marble statue (A.D. 68-96) by an unknown artist; Galleria Borghese, Rome (SCALA/Art Resource)

A Roman toga was worn by Emperor Augustus, *above.*

ing that Romans probably wore it only on formal occasions. The toga never proved to be a practical garment, but it gave protection against dampness.

The Romans wore a type of shoe called the *calceus* with their togas. Different styles of shoes showed the rank or station of the wearer. *Mary Evans*

See also **Tunic.**

Togo is a small country in western Africa. Togo is long and narrow. It extends about 365 miles (587 kilometers) inland from the Gulf of Guinea, an arm of the Atlantic Ocean. It is only 40 miles (64 kilometers) wide at the coast and 90 miles (145 kilometers) wide at its widest point.

Most of the people of Togo work as farmers. But farm production is small, and many people grow only enough food to feed their families. Lomé, which has a population of about 229,400, is the capital and the only large city. Togo's name in French, the official language, is *République du Togo* (Republic of Togo). *Togo* means *behind the sea* in Ewe, the most commonly used language in Togo.

Government. In 1967, army officers led by Lieutenant Colonel Gnassingbe Eyadema overthrew Togo's civilian government. They suspended the Constitution and dissolved the National Assembly (parliament). Eyadema be-

Togo

	National park (N.P.) or reserve
	International boundary
	Road
	Railroad
✪	National capital
•	Other city or town
+	Elevation above sea level

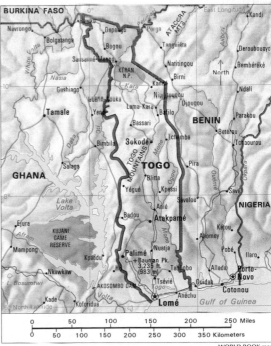

| 0 | 50 | 100 | 150 | 200 | 250 Miles |
| 0 | 50 | 100 | 150 | 200 | 250 | 300 | 350 Kilometers |

WORLD BOOK map

Facts in brief

Capital: Lomé.
Official language: French.
Area: 21,925 sq. mi. (56,785 km²). *Greatest distances*—north-south, 365 mi. (587 km); east-west, 90 mi. (145 km). *Coastline*—40 mi. (64 km).
Population: *Estimated 1989 population*—3,345,000; density, 153 persons per sq. mi. (59 per km²); distribution, 74 per cent rural, 26 per cent urban. *1981 census*—2,705,250. *Estimated 1994 population*—3,898,000.
Chief products: *Agriculture*—cacao, cassava, coffee, corn, cotton, millet, palm kernels and oil, peanuts, sorghum, yams. *Mining*—phosphates.
Flag: The flag has five horizontal stripes, three green and two yellow, with a white star on a red square in the upper left corner. Green symbolizes hope and agriculture; yellow, faith; white, purity; and red, charity and fidelity. See **Flag** (picture: Flags of Africa).
Money: *Basic unit*—franc. See **Money** (table).

Lomé, the capital of Togo, lies at the far southern end of the country. Many southerners, including the people in this market place, wear long loose-fitting garments of colorful fabric.

came president and set up a government made up of himself, other army officers, and civilians. In 1969, he created Togo's only legal political party, The Rally of the Togolese People.

Togo is divided into 21 administrative districts. Each is directed by a *chef de circonscription* (district head).

People. The ways of life in Togo reflect the fact that several different groups of people have settled the country. But the people are similar in physical type, occupation, and religion. Almost all of them are black Africans. About four-fifths of the people live in rural areas and work on family-owned farms. About three-fifths practice traditional African religions. But dress, language, and other ways of life differ throughout Togo, especially between the south and the north.

The ancestors of the people in southern Togo came from Benin and Ghana. The traditional life of southern Togo is similar to that of those two countries. Many southerners wear a toga, a full-length, loose-fitting gar-

A farm worker in Togo carries a basket of food on her head. Major food crops include cassava, corn, and millet.

ment. Many live in *compounds* (groups of huts inside walls). They speak the Ewe language.

European influence has been greater in the south than in the north. It has affected dress, occupation, and religion. Many southerners wear European-style clothes. Some work for the government, and others have small businesses. Most of Togo's 800,000 Christians, mostly Roman Catholics, live in the south.

Northern Togo was settled by people from the West African savanna region, and its way of life is similar to that of Burkina Faso and Niger. Northerners live in villages made up of adobe houses with cone-shaped thatched roofs. Most wear a white cotton smock. Many languages are spoken in northern Togo. Most of Togo's 250,000 Muslims live in the north.

About 70 per cent of Togo children attend primary school. Only about 20 per cent go to secondary school. Togo has one university, the University of Bénin in Lomé. Many students study abroad, especially in France.

Land. The Togo Mountains divide Togo into two major regions. The mountains stretch from southwest to northeast and cover much of western Togo. Bauman Peak (3,235 feet, or 986 meters) is Togo's highest point.

East and south of the Togo Mountains, the land descends across a sloping plateau to a low, sandy coastal plain. The plateau is covered with tall grass and clumps of hardwood trees. It is drained by the Mono River. The densely populated coastal plain is dotted with swamps, lagoons, and coconut and oil palm forests.

North of the Togo Mountains, the land descends through rolling grasslands to the border of Burkina Faso. The Oti River drains the region. Few people live there. Thorny trees are scattered across the grasslands.

Togo has a hot, humid climate. The temperature averages 81° F. (27° C), and rainfall averages about 40 inches (100 centimeters) a year in the north and 70 inches (180 centimeters) in the south. Rainy seasons last from March to July and September to November in the south, and from April to October in the north.

Economy. Togo is an agricultural country. But good land is scarce, harvests are small, and income is low.

Food crops are the most important farm products. They include cassava, corn, millet, sorghum, and yams. The principal crops raised for export are coffee and cacao. Togo also exports peanuts, cotton, *copra* (dried coconut meat), and the *kernels* (nuts) and oil from oil palms. Most of the farms that raise crops for food are owned in common by a group of families. Most of the crops that are sold are raised on small farms owned by individuals. Many Togolese work on these farms as *sharecroppers.* That is, they farm the land and give the landowner part of the receipts in payment for using the land. Fishing is an important coastal industry. Togo has one of the world's largest phosphate reserves, and phosphate is Togo's most valuable export.

Togo has little manufacturing. A cement plant, a petroleum refinery, and a large textile mill operate there.

Togo has about 325 miles (525 kilometers) of railroads and 4,880 miles (7,850 kilometers) of roads. The chief airport and seaport are at Lomé.

History. Scholars believe that the ancestors of the central mountain peoples were the original inhabitants of Togo. In the 1300's, the Ewe-speaking people began to move into what is now southern Togo and Ghana. Invaders from the north and refugees from wars in Ghana and Dahomey (now Benin) settled in Togo between the 1500's and 1800's.

Portuguese explorers and traders arrived on the coast in the late 1400's. Between the 1600's and 1800's, European slave-traders raided the coast to capture slaves, and Togo became known as the *Coast of Slaves.*

German traders and missionaries went to Togo in the mid-1800's. In 1884, Germany set up a small protectorate on the coast. By 1899, German Togo included what is now Togo and part of what is now Ghana.

British and French troops occupied German Togo in 1914, after World War I began. In 1919, Great Britain gained control of the western one-third of German Togo and France gained control of the eastern two-thirds. In 1922, the League of Nations confirmed a *mandate* (authority to govern) for Great Britain over British Togoland and for France over French Togoland. The United Nations changed the mandates to *trusteeships* (UN authority to govern) in 1946. In 1956, the people of British Togoland voted to join the Gold Coast. When the Gold Coast became independent as Ghana in 1957, it incorporated British Togoland.

After World War II, an independence movement developed in French Togoland. Sylvanus Olympio, leader of the Committee for Togolese Unity Party (CTU), wanted complete independence from France. Nicolas Grunitzky, leader of the Togolese Party for Progress, wanted to remain in the French Union.

In 1956, France made French Togoland a republic within the French Union and gave it internal self-government. France appointed Grunitzky prime minister. The Togolese approved the republic in an election, but the UN refused to accept this method of ending the trusteeship. In a UN-supervised election in 1958, the CTU won control of the legislature and Olympio became prime

minister. The UN approved this action. On April 27, 1960, French Togoland became the independent Republic of Togo with Olympio as president.

Rivalry between northerners and southerners has always been important in Togo's politics. In 1963, a group of northern army officers assassinated Olympio, a southerner. They made Grunitzky president. Grunitzky was from the south, but he opposed Olympio and the Committee for Togolese Unity Party. Southern CTU members tried unsuccessfully in 1966 to oust Grunitzky.

Army officers led by Gnassingbe Eyadema overthrew Grunitzky's government in January 1967. They suspended the Constitution and set up a government with Eyadema as president. The people endorsed him as president in a vote taken in 1972 and reelected him in 1979.   Immanuel Wallerstein

See also **Lomé.**

Toilet. See **Plumbing.**

Tojo, *toh joh,* **Hideki,** *hee deh kee* (1884-1948), was the general who, as premier, led Japan into war with the United States in 1941. He achieved national influence after 1937 as chief of staff of the Kwantung Army, the force that guarded Japan's holdings in South Manchuria. He was one of a group of militarists who objected to democratic developments within Japan.

By provoking "incidents," the militarists tried to commit their home government to decisive steps. In this manner, they had engineered the Manchurian Incident of 1931, which inaugurated the train of aggression leading to a conflict called the second Chinese-Japanese War (1937-1945). Thereafter, young officers also assassinated civilian leaders in Japan. After the collapse of civilian government, military men were named to high political office.

United Press Int.

Hideki Tojo

Tojo rose rapidly during the confusion of the 1930's. In 1940, he became minister of war. German dictator Adolf Hitler seemed to be winning World War II, and Tojo threw his weight behind Hitler and Benito Mussolini and against the democracies. As American embargoes on oil to Japan began to strain the Japanese economy, Tojo insisted that if an agreement with the United States could not be reached, Japan would have to fight. In October 1941, Tojo succeeded Prince Konoye as premier. When the Washington talks failed to bring results, Tojo decided on war.

Tojo was born the son of a general in Tokyo. His background, training, and interests were exclusively military. Tojo's popularity in Japan was high after the early victories of World War II, but his influence waned as American victories in 1943 and 1944 began to turn the tide. He was forced to resign as premier in 1944 after the fall of Saipan. He was arrested and convicted as a war criminal after Japan's surrender and was hanged on Dec. 23, 1948.   Marius B. Jansen

See also **Japan** (History).

Tokamak. See **Nuclear energy** (Present-day research).

Tokyo's Imperial Palace Plaza, *foreground,* adds beauty and charm to the busy downtown section of the city. Tokyo, the world's third largest city, ranks among the most crowded places on earth. But it has many scenic open areas like the plaza.

Tokyo

Tokyo, the capital of Japan, is the third largest city in the world. Only Mexico City and the South Korean city of Seoul have more people. About $8\frac{1}{3}$ million people live in Tokyo. Many countries have fewer inhabitants than this city has.

Tokyo is the main business center of Japan as well as the home of the Japanese emperor and the headquarters of the national government. The city's many banks, commercial establishments, and industries help make Japan one of the richest nations in the world.

In many ways, Tokyo seems like an American city. It has tall buildings, freeways jammed with traffic, and more neon signs than any other city in the world. Tokyo teen-agers dance to American hit tunes, and the city's restaurants offer everything from hamburgers to the finest European dishes. Many residents of Tokyo go to baseball games and watch movies and television shows from Western countries. But in spite of such outside influences, Japanese tradition remains strong in Tokyo. Many of the people enjoy going to city parks to admire their beautiful cherry trees and lotus blossoms. These

The contributor of this article is Kenneth B. Pyle, Professor of History and Director of the School of International Studies at the University of Washington.

and other gorgeous sights in the city reflect the Japanese trait of love of beauty. Large numbers of Tokyo's people take part in dances and parades during the city's many traditional festivals, some of which are hundreds of years old. They visit historic shrines and temples and attend old-style plays and wrestling matches.

Tokyo traces its beginning to 1457, when a powerful warrior built a castle there. It became the Japanese capital in 1868. Tokyo has twice been almost destroyed—by a terrible earthquake in 1923 and by air raids in the 1940's during World War II.

About 7 per cent of Japan's people live in Tokyo. The city has become so crowded that it has a severe housing shortage. Tokyo's rapid growth also created other problems, including some of the world's worst pollution and heaviest traffic.

Facts in brief

Population: *City proper*—8,353,674. *Metropolitan area population*—11,618,281.
Area: *City proper*—223 sq. mi. (578 km²); *Metropolitan area*—832 sq. mi. (2,156 km²).
Altitude: 80 ft. (24 m) above sea level.
Climate: *Average temperature*—January, 39° F. (4° C); July, 76° F. (24° C). *Average annual precipitation* (rainfall, melted snow, and other forms of moisture)—58 in. (147 cm).
Government: *Chief executive*—governor (4-year term). *Legislature*—126-member assembly (4-year terms).
Founded: 1457.

The city of Tokyo, called the *city proper,* covers 223 square miles (578 square kilometers) and has a population of 8,353,674. The city is part of a large metropolitan area called the *Metropolis of Tokyo.* The Metropolis includes many communities west of the city. It covers 832 square miles (2,156 square kilometers) and has a population of 11,618,281.

The entire metropolitan area operates under the same government. In this way, it differs from most U.S. metropolitan areas, which have completely separate governments for each community within them. Due to its single government, the Metropolis of Tokyo is often considered a single community. But this article describes the city proper and outlying areas separately.

The city proper is the busiest, most heavily populated part of the Metropolis. It lies at the northwest end of Tokyo Bay on the Kanto Plain, Japan's largest lowland. The city is bordered by the Edo River on the northeast and the Tama River on the south.

The city proper is divided into 23 units called *wards.* The Japanese word for *ward* is *ku,* and so the city proper is called the *ku area,* or the *ward area.* The Imperial Palace, where the emperor lives, stands amid beautiful parklike grounds on high land near the center of the city. Eastward, from the palace to the bay, the land is low and flat. Many of Tokyo's chief business, commercial,

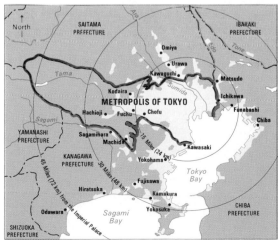

Tokyo lies on Honshu Island in central Japan. The map below shows the Metropolis of Tokyo which covers the same area as Tokyo Prefecture. Prefectures in Japan are similar to states in the United States. The map shows built-up areas in yellow.

HOKKAIDO

Sea of Japan

HONSHU

Tokyo

North Pacific Ocean

KYUSHU   SHIKOKU

North

SAITAMA PREFECTURE

IBARAKI PREFECTURE

Omiya
Urawa
Kawaguchi
Matsudo
Kodaira
Ichikawa
METROPOLIS OF TOKYO
Hachioji   Fuchu   Chofu
Funabashi
Chiba
YAMANASHI PREFECTURE
Sagamihara
Machida
Kawasaki
KANAGAWA PREFECTURE
Yokohama
Tokyo Bay
Fujisawa
Hiratsuka
Kamakura
Odawara
Yokosuka
Sagami Bay
CHIBA PREFECTURE
SHIZUOKA PREFECTURE

15 Miles (24 km)
30 Miles (48 km)
45 Miles (72 km) from the Imperial Palace

Tama
Sagami
Ara
Sumida
Edo
Tone

WORLD BOOK map

and industrial districts are in these low-lying areas. Part of eastern Tokyo is jammed with office and apartment buildings made of concrete and steel. For a picture of Tokyo's business center, see the start of the **City** article. Tokyo's oldest and poorest residential sections are also in the eastern part of the city.

Much of far eastern Tokyo is filled-in land on what had been part of Tokyo Bay. Some of this land lies below sea level. The low-lying areas are always in danger of floods, especially during heavy rains. Dikes have been built along the waterfront and the river banks. But the filled-in land sinks lower every year, mainly because of the removal of large amounts of ground water for industrial use. The dikes sink along with the land, making flood control difficult.

West of the Imperial Palace, the land becomes hilly. The chief residential sections of the city proper are in the west. The houses include large apartment buildings like those in Western cities and simple one- or two-story wooden buildings, the traditional Japanese houses. Many of the wooden houses are small and plain by Western standards. In some sections, rich families and poor families live in the same neighborhood, and their houses are plain and look much alike. But the western part of the city proper also has luxurious residential sections where the wealthy live.

Tokyo, unlike most other Japanese cities, no longer has large numbers of buildings in the ancient Japanese style that is most familiar to Westerners. This style features low, graceful lines and roofs turned up at the edges. Most of the remaining buildings in this style are religious shrines or temples.

Several well-known districts, each with its own characteristics, lie near the Imperial Palace. The Marunouchi district, an area of tall office buildings southeast of the palace, is Tokyo's business and financial center. The Ginza district lies farther south. It ranks as one of Tokyo's liveliest and most colorful districts and is famous for its stores and nightclubs. The Kanda district, northeast of the palace, is famous for its many bookstores. The Asakusa district, north of Kanda, is one of Tokyo's oldest entertainment sections. It features amusement parks, theaters, and restaurants.

Only main streets in Tokyo have names. Instead of street names, Tokyo addresses give the names of wards and other districts. A ward, called a *ku,* is divided into sections or neighborhoods, each of which has a name. These sections are divided into *subdivisions* (groups of blocks) called *chome,* which are numbered. Each block in a chome has a number, as does each house or cluster of houses in a block. The address *2-7, Yamabuki 1-chome, Shinjuku-ku* stands for *block 2, house 7, subdivision 1 in the Yamabuki section of Shinjuku ward.*

Outlying areas. In addition to the city proper, the Metropolis of Tokyo includes 26 suburban cities and 1 county area. The suburban cities extend westward from the city proper. The county area, which lies in the westernmost part of the Metropolis, includes several towns and villages as well as farms and forests. Two small island groups in the Pacific Ocean are also part of the Metropolis. They are the Izu Islands and the Bonin Islands. The islands have a few towns and villages.

Tokyo

The map at the right shows central Tokyo and its major landmarks. The map below shows the Metropolis of Tokyo, which includes the city proper and the suburban and county areas. Each area appears on the map in a different color. The red circles show distances from the Imperial Palace.

————	Metropolis boundary
––––	Prefecture boundary
———	Highway or street
⊢⊢⊢⊢	Rail line
•	City or town
■	Point of interest
▢	City proper
▨	Suburban area
▨	County area
▨	Park or garden
▨	National park

WORLD BOOK maps

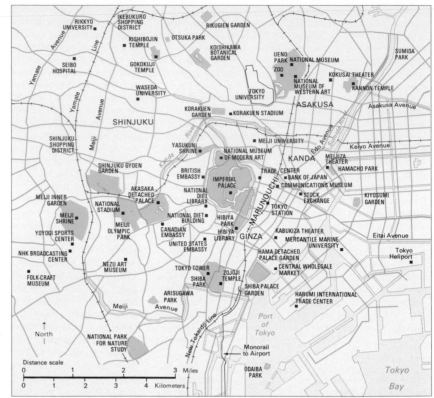

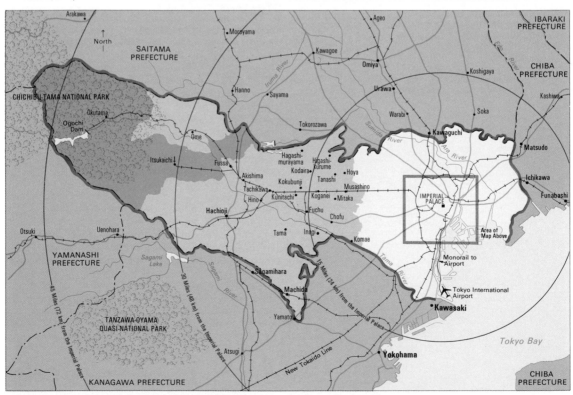

More jobs and educational and cultural opportunities are available in Tokyo than anywhere else in Japan. As a result, the city constantly attracts people—especially the young—from other parts of the country. Between 1960 and 1980, the Metropolis gained nearly 2 million people. Today, Tokyo proper has an average of about 37,000 persons per square mile (14,000 persons per square kilometer)—nearly twice as many as New York City has.

Housing. Tokyo's soaring population has created a serious housing shortage. In the past, most Tokyo residents lived in small, one- or two-story wooden houses, each with its own yard or garden. As the population grew, many apartment buildings were constructed in the city proper in an attempt to provide housing for all the people. Even so, the housing shortage continued. The shortage of housing and of land in the city proper drove up rents and land prices. Many people—even if they could find housing in the city proper—could not afford to pay for it. As a result, a building boom began in Tokyo's outlying areas during the mid-1900's.

The city government has begun financing the construction of low-rent housing projects. One such project, called Tama New Town, will house 400,000 persons after its completion in the late 1980's. But Tama New Town, like many other Tokyo housing developments, is far from the city proper. Some workers who live in outlying areas spend up to four hours a day traveling to and from their jobs in downtown Tokyo.

Food and clothing. Many Tokyo residents enjoy traditional Japanese foods. Popular Japanese dishes include *sukiyaki* (beef cooked with vegetables), *tempura* (fish and vegetables fried in batter), and *sushi* (rice flavored with vinegar and mixed with other food, such as fish or vegetables). Western and Chinese foods are also popular in Tokyo.

On the streets and at work, most of the people wear Western-style clothing. Some older people still put on a *kimono* when they get home. The kimono, a traditional Japanese garment of both men and women, is a long robe tied with a sash. Most Tokyo young people wear a kimono only on holidays or other special occasions. Many elementary and some high school students wear uniforms to school. The boys' uniform is a suit with a jacket that fits tightly around the neck. Girls wear skirts and pullover blouses.

Education. The Metropolis of Tokyo has about 1,200 elementary schools, 700 junior high schools, and 400 senior high schools. Most of these schools are in the city proper. Some parts of Tokyo do not have enough schools for the rapidly growing population. However, in some old sections of the city that are now largely occupied by businesses, many of the schoolhouses stand nearly empty.

Tokyo has about 100 four-year colleges and universities and 90 junior colleges. About half of Japan's college students attend these institutions.

Social problems, such as poverty and crime, exist in Tokyo. But they are not so severe as they are in many other large cities. Because of Tokyo's strong economy, most people can find jobs. In addition, the local and national governments provide aid for people who cannot support themselves. Tokyo's crime rate is much lower than the crime rate in most Western cities. The robbery rate in New York City, for example, is more than 150 times greater than that in Tokyo. Tokyo has no large minority groups, and so the city is not troubled by conflicts that stem from racial or other social differences.

Demonstrations are often held in Tokyo to protest such matters as political and educational policies. They have sometimes resulted in violence.

Eiji Miyazawa, Black Star

Sven Samelius from Carl Östman

Life in Tokyo combines the old and the new. Some people, like the woman above, wear the traditional kimono. But most wear Western clothes. Housing in the city includes both old frame houses and modern high-rise apartment buildings, *right.*

Few cities in the world can match Tokyo as a *cosmopolitan* (international) cultural center. Tokyo's art galleries, concert halls, museums, and other cultural institutions reflect the culture of both the East and the West.

The arts. Many of Japan's finest artists and craftworkers live and work in Tokyo. Some still use the styles and methods of their ancestors to create beautiful paintings on paper or silk and colorful woodblock prints. But many Tokyo artists create paintings and sculptures using Western styles and methods.

Tokyo is the center of Japan's performing arts, such as drama and music. Two traditional types of Japanese drama, *no* and *kabuki,* rank as favorite forms of entertainment in Tokyo. For descriptions of these colorful plays, see **Drama** (Japan). Five professional symphony orchestras that specialize in Western music perform in Tokyo. Other Tokyo musical groups present concerts of traditional music, featuring such Japanese instruments as the three-stringed *samisen,* or *shamisen,* and a kind of harp called a *koto.* Japan's motion-picture industry is also centered in Tokyo. Japanese movies have been praised by audiences throughout the world.

Museums and libraries. Some of Japan's finest museums and libraries are in Tokyo. The Tokyo National Museum, the largest museum in Japan, has a valuable collection of Asian art objects. The National Museum of Modern Art specializes in works by modern Japanese artists. The National Museum of Western Art houses a large collection of works by Western artists.

Tokyo's public library system includes a central library and more than 70 branch libraries. The National

Minoru Aoki, Rapho Guillumette

Sports events rank among Tokyo's chief forms of entertainment. Many people, like those above, are baseball fans. Many also enjoy sumo wrestling and other ancient Japanese sports.

Diet Library, which is part of the headquarters of Japan's national government, ranks as the country's largest library. It owns about 6 million volumes, and its functions resemble those of the U.S. Library of Congress (see **Library of Congress**).

Entertainment and recreation. Tokyo offers a wide variety of leisure-time activities. Concerts, motion pictures, and plays attract large audiences. Exhibitions of *judo* and *sumo,* which are Japanese forms of wrestling, rank as favorite sporting events. Western sports, including baseball, bowling, golf, ice skating, tennis, and track and field, are also popular. Baseball is the most popular sport in Tokyo. Home games of the Tokyo Giants professional baseball team and many other sports events are held in the 35,000-seat Korakuen Stadium. Tokyo's largest stadium, the National Stadium, is the site of many important track and field events. It seats about 72,000 spectators.

Tokyo also has many amusement parks and nightclubs. At some of the older Japanese-style restaurants, talented young women called *geishas* entertain patrons with singing, dancing, and conversation.

Almost all Tokyo families own a TV set. Both Japanese programs and American and European programs with Japanese sound tracks appear on Tokyo TV.

Religion. Shinto and Buddhism are the chief religions throughout Japan. Tokyo has hundreds of historic Shinto shrines and Buddhist temples. But most Tokyo residents visit these places of worship only for public festivals or such special occasions as weddings and funerals. Less than 2 per cent of the residents of the Metropolis are Christians.

Toshio Watanabe, DPI

Japan's performing arts are centered in Tokyo. Traditional art forms, such as the *no* drama, *above,* are popular. However, Western-style drama and music also draw large crowds.

Large numbers of tourists visit Tokyo the year around. In early April, the city's famous cherry trees are in bloom. Autumn in Tokyo usually brings pleasantly mild weather. The city's many festivals are other tourist attractions. These include the exciting parade of Tokyo's firemen on January 6 and the lively festival of the Asakusa Shrine in mid-May.

Tourists can choose from many fine hotels and restaurants in Tokyo. Many of the hotels are built and furnished in Western style. Others are Japanese-style hotels called *ryokan.* They have such traditional features as sliding paper-paneled doors, *tatami* mats that cover the floors, and heavy quilts that serve as beds. Tokyo has an unusually large number of restaurants—more than 60,000. Some of these restaurants specialize in Western or Chinese foods, and others serve only Japanese dishes.

This section of the article describes a few of the interesting places to visit in Tokyo. Other sections discuss additional places of interest.

The Imperial Palace is the home of Japan's emperor. It stands near the center of the city proper and consists of several low buildings and beautiful parklike grounds. Stone walls and a series of wide moats separate it from the rest of the city. The palace is open to the public only two days of the year—January 2 and the emperor's birthday. Thousands of Japanese come to pay their respects to the emperor on these two days.

The National Diet Building, a concrete and granite structure with a tall central tower, stands southwest of the Imperial Palace. It is the meeting place of Japan's *Diet* (parliament) and is open to visitors.

Tokyo Tower, a 1,092-foot (333-meter) steel tower, stands about 1½ miles (2.4 kilometers) south of the Impe-

Milt and Joan Mann

The Imperial Palace attracts thousands of visitors on January 2 and the emperor's birthday, when it is open to the public. A family poses for a photograph near the palace grounds, *above.*

rial Palace. The city's tallest structure, Tokyo Tower, houses radio and television broadcasting studios and has two observation platforms.

Parks and gardens of Tokyo attract many visitors. Ueno Park, about 2 miles (3 kilometers) northeast of the palace, is one of the city's most popular parks. Its spring displays of cherry blossoms and summer displays of lotus blossoms are outstanding. The park includes Tokyo's largest concert hall, several museums and art galleries, a zoo, a temple and shrine built during the 1600's, and tombs of Japanese rulers.

Several Japanese-style gardens in Tokyo are open to the public. Korakuen Garden and Rikugien Garden—both a little north of the palace—are two of the oldest and most famous gardens. Many people visit Tokyo's gardens to admire their beautifully landscaped grounds and relax at their teahouses.

Shrines and temples attract millions of worshipers and tourists yearly. The shrines are Shinto places of worship, and the temples are Buddhist. Meiji Shrine, about 3 miles (5 kilometers) southwest of the Imperial Palace, is one of the best-known shrines in Japan. Many Japanese visit it on New Year's Day, one of the few times when most Japanese women wear traditional dress in public. The Yasukuni Shrine stands northwest of the palace. It is dedicated to Japan's war dead and draws huge crowds of worshipers for special festivals in April and October. Tokyo also has a number of famous Buddhist temples, including the historic Kannon Temple in the Asakusa district. The temple traces its origins to the 600's, though the present buildings were constructed in the 1950's. Colorful souvenir shops line the approach to the temple.

Milt and Joan Mann

At Tokyo's famous Meiji Shrine, Shinto priests greet visitors with a bow. This shrine and other historic places of worship are among Tokyo's leading tourist attractions.

Tokyo ranks as one of the world's centers of economic activity. Since the end of World War II in 1945, Japan's economy has grown faster than that of any other country. Tokyo has played a major role in this growth. It is the main center of Japan's commercial, financial, and industrial activities and of its transportation industry. About a fourth of Japan's business corporations have their headquarters in the Metropolis. About 15 per cent of all the factories in Japan are also there.

Industry. The Tokyo Metropolis has more than 80,000 factories. Most of them are small and employ fewer than 20 people. However, some are gigantic plants that have from 10,000 to 20,000 workers. Nearly $1\frac{1}{2}$ million industrial workers hold jobs in the Tokyo Metropolis.

Tokyo's two leading industries are (1) the manufacture of electrical machinery and (2) publishing and printing. Several huge companies and many small ones in the Metropolis make computers, phonographs, radios, television sets, tape recorders, and other electrical machinery. Many of these products are exported to the United States and other countries. About four of every five Japanese publishing companies have their headquarters in Tokyo. The Tokyo area's newspaper companies publish more than 25 daily papers and sell a total of about 25 million copies daily. Much of the material published in Tokyo is also printed there. Other important products of Tokyo include chemicals, food, furniture, and paper. Several Tokyo companies rank among the 25 largest manufacturing firms in the world.

Finance. Businesses and industries throughout Japan depend on Tokyo banks for loans. The Bank of Japan,

the nation's central bank, has its headquarters in Tokyo. Controlled by the national government, the Bank of Japan regulates the nation's entire banking system. Tokyo also has many commercial banks. The largest commercial banks have branches or offices in many Japanese and foreign cities.

The Tokyo Stock Exchange is one of the world's leading stock exchanges. It has about 100 members and lists about 1,070 stocks.

Trade. Nearly 3,000 companies in the Tokyo Metropolis deal in foreign trade. These firms handle almost half of Japan's export business and more than half of the nation's import business. The 40-story Tokyo Trade Center displays various types of Japanese goods for foreign buyers.

About 173,000 wholesale and retail establishments are in the Metropolis. The 41,000 wholesale companies, which sell to buyers throughout Japan, employ more than 600,000 people. The 132,000 retail stores employ more than 550,000 workers. Most of the retail stores are small shops. But Tokyo has department stores and shopping centers as large and modern as any in the United States.

Transportation. About 2 million motor vehicles are registered in the Metropolis. Most are automobiles. In the mid-1900's, the metropolitan government built a system of freeways to speed traffic through the city. Even so, there are many more motor vehicles than the freeways and streets can handle, and severe traffic jams occur frequently. The metropolitan government is trying to provide more public transportation as a substitute for automobile travel.

© Jerry Cooke

The Tokyo Stock Exchange, *above,* is one of the world's leading stock exchanges. The exchange and the city's many banks help make Tokyo the financial center of Japan.

The manufacture of electrical machinery is Tokyo's leading industry. Many electrical products made in Tokyo, including video recorders, *above,* are exported to other countries.

Norma Morrison

Tokyo's public transportation system is a complicated network of railroad, subway, and bus lines. Railroads extend from the city proper to most outlying areas and to other parts of Japan. Japanese National Railways operates some of the lines, and the rest are privately owned. Tokyo's commuter trains rank among the fastest and most efficient in the world. Nearly 10 million passengers cram aboard them each day and about 3 million use the trains of the city's seven subway lines daily. Employees called *pushers* work at some train stations. Their job involves shoving passengers into crowded trains to make more room (see **City** [picture: Travel in cities]). One of the world's few successful *monorails* (single-rail trains) carries passengers between central Tokyo and Tokyo International Airport, in the far southern part of the city. Buses carry about 6 million passengers daily.

About 20 major airlines offer scheduled flights between Tokyo International Airport, also called Haneda Airport, and foreign cities. Air travel in and out of Tokyo is heavy, and so a much larger airport had to be built. The New Tokyo International Airport, also called Narita Airport, is located about 40 miles (64 kilometers) northeast of central Tokyo. It was completed in 1973. However, the opening of the airport was delayed because of strong, sometimes violent, protests by nearby residents and others who objected to the airport's presence. The airport opened in 1978.

The Port of Tokyo is not one of Japan's leading ports. Other ports, including those of Kobe and Yokohama, have deeper harbors and therefore can handle larger ships. Much of Tokyo's ocean trade passes through the nearby Port of Yokohama. Railroads, trucks, and barges carry large quantities of freight between the two cities.

Organization. The Metropolis of Tokyo is treated like one of Japan's *prefectures.* A prefecture is somewhat like a state of the United States. The government of the Metropolis serves as the government for the prefecture and for the city proper and the rest of the metropolitan area. It is a large, complicated organization.

The governor of Tokyo serves as the chief government official of the Metropolis of Tokyo. The people elect the governor to a four-year term. Tokyo's chief lawmaking body is the Metropolitan Assembly. It has 126 members, whom the voters elect to four-year terms. Each ward, city, and other community in the Metropolis has at least one representative in the Assembly. The metropolitan government also includes the board of education, the police and fire departments, and many other agencies. Together, they employ more than 220,000 people.

The wards, cities, towns, and villages of the Metropolis all have some form of local government. Each elects a council and a mayor or other administrator, but the powers of these officials are limited by the metropolitan government. The metropolitan government makes *ordinances* (rules) for all the communities in the Metropolis. It also provides police protection and certain other public services for the entire Metropolis. But it provides some services, including fire protection and sanitation facilities, for the city proper only. Local governments must provide services not supplied by the metropolitan government. They may collect some tax money for these projects, and they receive additional funds from the metropolitan and national governments.

Problems. Tokyo, like cities everywhere, faces enormous problems. The metropolitan government must deal with such problems as a severe housing shortage, air and water pollution, overcrowded streets and highways, and danger from floods and earthquakes. Tokyo's complicated government organization and a shortage of money make solutions to the problems difficult. The metropolitan government has a responsibility to both the national government and the people of the Metropolis. This double responsibility complicates the metropolitan government's work. In addition, much of the tax money collected in the Metropolis goes to the national government. Many Tokyo government officials believe that the national government should make the duties of the metropolitan government simpler and give the Metropolis more control over its finances.

Symbols of Tokyo. The flag of the Metropolis of Tokyo, *left,* and the coat of arms, *right,* feature a design made from the *kanji* characters used to write the word *Tokyo.* Kanji are Chinese characters used in the Japanese language. The design also represents the sun casting its rays throughout the city.

Early development. During most of its history, Tokyo was called *Edo.* The first historical record of a settlement in the area shows that a powerful family named Edo lived there about 1180. The area had military importance because it overlooked both Tokyo Bay and the Kanto Plain. In 1457, a warrior named Ota Dokan built a castle at Edo. Dokan worked in the service of a powerful warrior family, one of several who ruled parts of Japan. He built his castle where the Imperial Palace now stands, and so Tokyo marks 1457 as the year of its beginning. A town named Edo grew up around the castle. But the development that made the town Japan's chief city did not begin until 1590. In that year, a warrior named Tokugawa Ieyasu made Edo his headquarters. In 1603, Ieyasu became *shogun* (military ruler) of Japan, and so Edo became the nation's political center. But Kyoto, a city southwest of Edo and the home of the emperor, remained the official capital. By the early 1800's, Edo had grown into a city of over a million people—more than 15 times larger than New York City at that time. Ieyasu and his descendants ruled as shoguns in Edo until 1867.

Western influence. Beginning in the early 1600's, Japan closed itself off from normal contact with the rest of the world. This is known as the *sakoku* (closed country) policy. The government allowed ships from Holland and from China to trade in Japan, but only occasionally and only at the port of Nagasaki. It prohibited Japanese people from traveling to other countries. In 1853, Commodore Matthew C. Perry arrived at Tokyo Bay on a mission for the U.S. government to open relations with Japan. Perry sailed into Tokyo Bay with four warships and began talks with Japanese rulers. He returned with more warships the next year and reached a partial agreement with the rulers. Partly as a result of Perry's efforts, Japan signed trade treaties with the United States and other Western countries in 1858. The treaties marked the start of modern Western influence in Japan.

Emperor Mutsuhito—also known as the Meiji Emperor—did much to further Westernization. He took control of Japan from the shogun in 1867. He transferred the capital from Kyoto to Edo in 1868 and moved into the Edo castle. Edo was renamed *Tokyo,* which means *eastern capital.* After 1868, Japan—especially Tokyo— rapidly adopted Western styles and inventions. By the late 1800's, Tokyo began to look like a Western city.

Earthquake and reconstruction. On Sept. 1, 1923, a violent earthquake shook the Tokyo-Yokohama area. Buildings collapsed and fires broke out throughout Tokyo. About 59,000 residents of the city proper died in the disaster, and most of central Tokyo was destroyed. The city was rebuilt during the next 20 years.

At the time of the earthquake, Tokyo consisted of 15 wards in the vicinity of the Imperial Palace. After the tragedy, areas outside the 15 wards began to develop. In 1932, the city took over many of the areas and made them wards, establishing the present ward area.

World War II brought destruction to Tokyo again. American bombers first attacked the city in April 1942. The heaviest raids occurred from March to August of 1945, when Japan announced its intention to surrender. The bombs ruined about 97 square miles (251 square kilometers) of Tokyo. Over 250,000 people were killed or listed as missing. Thousands fled the city. Tokyo's population dropped from about 7,350,000 in 1940 to about 3,500,000 in 1945. In 1943, Tokyo and communities west of it formed the Metropolis of Tokyo.

Rebuilding the city. The people of Tokyo began to rebuild their city after the war, but without much planning. Buildings went up wherever there was room. Tokyo's economy began booming a few years after the war. Population growth accompanied economic growth, and the population of the city proper more than doubled between 1945 and 1960. In 1964, Tokyo was host to the summer Olympic Games. In preparation for the games, the city started a construction program that included new freeways and hotels, and the monorail.

Recent developments. Tokyo's continued growth has made it one of the world's largest cities and has given it a strong economy. But this growth, along with the lack of planning, has helped cause such problems as the housing shortage, pollution, and traffic jams.

In 1969, the metropolitan government started a series of three-year plans to help solve Tokyo's problems. The plans set goals for improving public housing, purifying the polluted air and river water, reducing street noise and traffic jams, and increasing sanitation facilities. Parts of the Metropolis have been set aside for public housing and other community projects. To ease overcrowding, the government encourages the development of new suburban towns. A number of such towns in and around Tokyo Prefecture are growing rapidly.

In 1985, an international exposition called "Tsukuba Expo '85" was held at Tsukuba, a new town about 30 miles (50 kilometers) northwest of Tokyo. Tsukuba has about 50 research institutes and two universities dedicated to technological studies.   Kenneth B. Pyle

Study aids

Questions

In what ways does Tokyo resemble an American city? What is the *ward area?*

What is the most popular sport in Tokyo?

Why is Tokyo's government unusually complicated?

What kind of clothing do many Tokyo students wear?

What are Tokyo's two leading industries?

How large a part of Japan's population lives in Tokyo?

Why do parts of Tokyo face the danger of flooding?

What are Tokyo's main kinds of public transportation?

When was Tokyo made the capital of Japan?

Additional resources

Seidensticker, Edward G. *Low City, High City: Tokyo from Edo to the Earthquake.* Random House, 1983. Describes the beginnings of modern Tokyo, from 1867 to 1923.

Waley, Paul. *Tokyo Now & Then: An Explorer's Guide.* Charles Tuttle, 1984.

Tokyo Rose. See World War II (Propaganda).

Toledo, *tuh LEED oh* or *toh LAY thoh* (pop. 57,769), is on a high hill 41 miles (66 kilometers) southwest of Madrid, Spain. The Tagus River flows in a deep ravine around the hill. The city is the capital of Toledo province. For location, see **Spain** (political map).

Toledo is a medieval city of narrow, steep, winding streets. There are many historic works of architecture in Toledo, and the Spanish government has declared the entire city a Spanish national monument. Its architecture shows a strong Moorish influence. Houses rise straight up, many of them without windows facing the streets. A magnificent Gothic cathedral dominates the city. Its tower rises 300 feet (91 meters). Beautiful chapels inside contain many fine paintings and statues. El Greco lived in Toledo, and his home is now a museum for some of his paintings.

Toledo has little industry, but is famous for sabers, firearms, Toledo ware (inlaid steel), and textiles. Its founding date is unknown. Arabs destroyed the city in the 700's. Alfonso VI, king of León and Castile, seized Toledo in 1085 and made it his capital. Philip II made Madrid the capital in 1561.   Stanley G. Payne

Toledo, *tuh LEE doh* (pop. 354,635; met. area pop. 616,864), is a leading industrial and transportation center in northwestern Ohio. It is also a major Great Lakes port. For location, see **Ohio** (political map). Toledo lies on both banks of the Maumee River. At Toledo, the river widens into Maumee Bay at the western end of Lake Erie. For many years, the city was a key glass-manufacturing center and was often called the Glass Capital of the World. However, several of the firms that specialized in glassmaking now make other kinds of products. Toledo also ranks as one of the largest producers of automotive parts in the United States.

The first permanent white settlers in what is now the Toledo area arrived in 1817. The settlers chose the site because of its location on the Maumee River. The city was named for Toledo, Spain, but no one knows why.

Description. Toledo, the county seat of Lucas County, covers about 81 square miles (218 square kilometers). Its business district and most of its homes are west of the Maumee River. Toledo's glass plants lie east of the river. The port is on Maumee Bay.

Institutions of higher education in Toledo include the Medical College of Ohio and the University of Toledo. The Toledo Museum of Art owns one of the largest collections of rare glass objects in the world. Toledo is also the home of the Toledo Symphony Orchestra and the Toledo Opera Association. The Toledo Zoo ranks among the finest zoos in the nation. Several historical

monuments lie near the city. They commemorate General Anthony Wayne's victory over Indians in the Battle of Fallen Timbers in 1794 and General William Henry Harrison's defeat of British forces in the War of 1812.

Economy. The Toledo metropolitan area has more than 1,000 manufacturing plants. These firms employ over 25 per cent of the area's workers. The production of transportation equipment is the chief industrial activity. Champion Spark Plug Corporation, the world's largest spark plug manufacturer, has headquarters in Toledo. Other industries, in order of importance, produce glass products, nonelectrical machinery, petroleum and coal products, food products, and metal goods.

The port of Toledo handles about 21 million short tons (19 million metric tons) of cargo annually. It is one of the world's leading shippers of coal. Toledo serves as a trade center for the rich agricultural region in northwestern Ohio, and its port handles a huge volume of corn, wheat, and other grain grown in the area. Several freight railroads help bring cargo to Toledo for lake shipment. Toledo Express Airport also serves the city.

Government and history. Toledo has a council-manager form of government. The voters elect a mayor and eight other council members, all to two-year terms. The council hires a city manager to carry out its policies.

Erie Indians lived in the Toledo area before white people came there. In 1615, Étienne Brulé, a guide for the French explorer Samuel de Champlain, became the first white person to see the area. In 1817, land speculators established a settlement on the site of Fort Industry, a stockade built about 1795. They called this settlement Port Lawrence. Port Lawrence and the nearby village of Vistula united in 1833 to form Toledo. The community received a city charter in 1837.

The city's growth as a transportation center began in 1836, when railroads first reached Toledo. The Wabash and Erie Canal in Indiana and the Miami and Erie Canal in Ohio began operating during the 1840's. They had a joint outlet in Toledo. The city, with its natural lake port, became an important water gateway to the western United States.

In 1888, Edward Libbey, a glass manufacturer from East Cambridge, Mass., brought skilled workers to the Toledo area and founded the Libbey Glass Company. He was later joined by Michael Owens. The glass industry helped increase the city's population from 3,829 in 1850 to 131,822 in 1900. An automobile plant opened in 1908. By 1930, 290,718 people lived in the city.

In the 1970's and 1980's, parts of Toledo's riverfront were redeveloped. The Portside Festival Marketplace, a collection of shops and restaurants, opened in 1984 at the north end of Promenade Park, which stretches along the river. Fort Industry Square, an office and restaurant complex, opened in 1979 at the opposite end of the park. These restored buildings are among the oldest in the city.   Lawrence A. Keeler

Toleration Act is a law permitting people to believe in any religion they choose. One famous toleration act, passed by the colony of Maryland in 1649, gave religious liberty to all Christians. The most famous Toleration Act was that of 1689, passed by the English Parliament. It granted religious freedom to the Protestant dissenters from the established Anglican Church. This law did not apply to Roman Catholics, Jews, and Unitarians. But the dissenters continued to suffer until the 1800's.   J. Salwyn Schapiro

Tolkien, *TOHL keen,* **J. R. R.** (1892-1973), an English author and scholar, wrote a popular series of novels about an imaginary people called *hobbits.* Tolkien introduced the dwarflike hobbits in *The Hobbit* (1937). He continued their story in three related novels called *The Lord of the Rings.* These novels are *The Fellowship of the Ring* (1954), *The Two Towers* (1954), and *The Return of the King* (1955).

Hobbits are industrious and good-natured. They live in a world called Middle-earth, along with elves, goblins, wizards, and human beings. In *The Hobbit,* Bilbo Baggins, a hobbit, discovers a ring that has evil powers. The hero of *The Lord of the Rings* is Frodo Baggins, Bilbo's cousin. After many adventures, Frodo and eight companions destroy the ring so that Sauron, the evil Dark Lord, cannot use it against the hobbits. Many critics have interpreted *The Lord of the Rings* as a symbolic moral or religious story about the battle between good and evil. But Tolkien insisted that he wrote the novels only as fantasies to entertain readers.

In 1917, Tolkien began to write *The Silmarillion,* a history of Middle-earth before the hobbits appeared. He died before completing it, and his son Christopher finished the novel. It was published in 1977. A collection of previously unpublished material about Middle-earth and the legendary island of Númenor appeared in 1980 as *Unfinished Tales.*

John Ronald Reuel Tolkien was born in Bloemfontein, South Africa, of English parents. From 1925 to 1959, he taught at Oxford University in England, where he specialized in medieval languages and literature. He wrote several scholarly works in this field. Tolkien's hobbit stories show the influence of the medieval English, German, and Scandinavian languages and literature.

Harry Oster

Additional resources

Carpenter, Humphrey. *Tolkien: A Biography.* Houghton, 1977.
Purtill, Richard L. *J. R. R. Tolkien: Myth, Morality, and Religion.* Harper, 1984.
Shippey, T. A. *The Road to Middle-Earth.* Houghton, 1983.

Toll. See Road (State and local financing).
Toll road. See Turnpike.
Tolman, Edward Chace (1886-1959), was an American psychologist known for his theory of how human beings and other animals learn. Tolman rejected the learning theory of John B. Watson and other behavioral psychologists of the time. These psychologists maintained that learning occurs through a random trial-and-error process. Tolman argued that learning is a systematic process guided by goals and expectations. He believed that learners develop what he called *cognitive maps*—that is, mental images of the probable paths to their goals. He explained his theory in a book called *Purposive Behavior in Animals and Men* (1932).

Tolman was born in Newton, Mass. He taught psychology at the University of California at Berkeley from 1918 until his death.   Richard M. Wolf

Tolstoy, Alexei (1882-1945), Count Tolstoy, won great popularity and wealth in Russia as a writer of novels and plays. His name is also spelled *Tolstoi.* He wrote *Road to Calvary* (1921-1941), a trilogy portraying Russian life just before, during, and after the Russian civil war of 1918-1920. He also wrote *Peter I* (1929-1945), an unfinished novel about that czar.

Alexei Nikolaevich Tolstoy was born in the province of Samara (now Kuybyshev). He studied engineering at the Saint Petersburg Technological Institute, but gave up this career for writing. During the Revolution of 1917, Tolstoy fled from Russia, but he returned in 1922. He gave up his title of count and wrote propaganda for the Soviet Union. He was a distant relative of Leo Tolstoy.

Ernest J. Simmons

Tolstoy, *TAHL stoy* or *TOHL stoy,* **Leo** (1828-1910), a Russian writer, ranks among the greatest novelists in world literature. Tolstoy was also an important moral and religious thinker and social reformer. His name is sometimes spelled *Tolstoi.*

Early life and works. Leo Nikolaevich Tolstoy was born at Yasnaya Polyana, his family's estate near Tula. Both of his parents died when he was young, and he was raised by relatives. Tolstoy received his elementary education from foreign tutors. He entered the University of Kazan in 1844, but he became bored with university instruction and did not earn a degree. He returned to Yasnaya Polyana in 1847 to manage the estate and devote himself to his own study. He wrote three semiautobiographical novels that reflect his formative years—*Childhood* (1852), *Boyhood* (1854), and *Youth* (1857).

As a young man, Tolstoy spent considerable time among the high society of Moscow and St. Petersburg (now Leningrad). His diaries reveal that he became restless and dissatisfied with this life, and thus decided to volunteer for the Russian Army.

Tolstoy was a soldier during the Crimean War (1853-1856). He distinguished himself for bravery at the Battle of Sevastopol. He wrote several Sevastopol sketches for magazines in 1855, depicting war as an unglamorous bloodbath and attacking romantic ideas of war heroes. Another work based on Tolstoy's travels with the army was the highly praised short novel *The Cossacks* (1863). Olenin, the central character of the novel, is a refined aristocrat. He finds much to admire in the wild, free life of the Cossacks of the Caucasus region in southwestern Russia.

Tolstoy retired from military service in 1856. Between 1857 and 1861, he made two trips to western Europe, where he took a keen interest in educational methods. After returning to his estate, he opened a school for peasant children there. Tolstoy was successful as a progressive educator who believed that teaching should be adapted to the needs of each pupil. He published a journal, called *Yasnaya Polyana,* explaining his educational theories.

His masterpieces. In 1862, Tolstoy married Sonya Behrs. At first the two had a happy marriage, though it became troubled in later years. During this period, Tolstoy wrote *War and Peace* and *Anna Karenina,* his greatest works.

AP/Wide World
Leo Tolstoy

The epic novel *War and Peace* was published in its complete form in 1869. Like many other works of Russian realism, *War and Peace* is a family chronicle. It shows the lives of five families as they go through the universal experiences and stages of life that always concerned Tolstoy—birth, growing up, marriage, sex, childbirth, maturity, old age, and death. *War and Peace* is also a historical novel, describing the political and military events that occurred in Europe between 1805 and 1820. It focuses in particular on Napoleon's invasion of Russia in 1812. In the novel, Tolstoy rejected the "Great Man" theory of history. According to Tolstoy's theory, prominent people or heroes actually have no significant impact on the course of history.

Tolstoy's second masterpiece, *Anna Karenina,* was published in installments from 1875 to 1877. Its plot concerns the open infidelity of a Russian princess, Anna Karenina, to her husband, Karenin. The novel examines Anna's romance with Count Vronsky. Anna and Vronsky show contempt for the disapproving opinions of the members of the high society to which they belong. The difficulties of their relationship eventually lead to Anna's suicide. But *Anna Karenina* is more than a tragic love story. The novel explores broad social, moral, and philosophical issues of Russia and its aristocracy in the 1870's. These issues include the hypocritical attitude of the upper class toward adultery and the role of religious faith in a person's life. Many of these vital issues are raised through the thoughts and actions of Konstantin Levin, the novel's second most important figure. Through Levin, Tolstoy expresses many of his own views.

His conversion. During the years that Tolstoy was writing *Anna Karenina,* he became obsessed with the questions he had always pondered concerning the meaning and purpose of life. Tolstoy described his agonizing moral self-examination and his quest for life's meaning in the essay "My Confession" (1882).

Tolstoy changed dramatically as a result of his spiritual crisis. Rejecting the authority of the Russian Orthodox Church, he developed his own version of Christianity, which he later detailed in the essay "The Kingdom of God Is Within You" (1894). Tolstoy believed that people are able to know and affirm the good in themselves if they engage in self-examination and willingly reform themselves. Tolstoy also believed that any use of violence or force is harmful, and that force should be opposed nonviolently. Tolstoy objected to all forms of force, including that represented by organized government and religion, private property, and the bonds of oaths.

Tolstoy produced no fiction between 1878 and 1885, writing instead on his religious beliefs and social themes. In his zeal to live in conformity with his religion, he gave up his property and sex life. He left his estate to his family, and his wife obtained the copyrights to all his works written before 1881. Tolstoy dressed as a peasant and often worked in the fields. He tried to be as self-sufficient as possible. Tolstoy's great fame as a novelist sparked a public interest in his religion that spread quickly. People made pilgrimages from all over the world to visit him. His authority was so great that the Russian Orthodox Church excommunicated him in 1901 in an effort to minimize his influence.

In his essay "What Is Art?" (1898), Tolstoy denounced all of the works he created before his conversion. The essay advances the idea that art should help to morally instruct and improve people. Tolstoy also wrote that art should communicate its ideas to even the simplest people. By these standards, Tolstoy judged most of his earlier works as "aristocratic art" written for vain purposes and not intelligible to the common person.

Later works. Tolstoy returned to writing fiction with the tale "The Death of Ivan Ilyich" (1886). In the story, Ivan Ilyich is the victim of a fatal disease. While he is dying, he sees the emptiness of his life, and he can only accept the inevitability of death. Tolstoy also wrote several plays. His best-known drama, *The Power of Darkness* (1888), is a tragedy about a peasant whose adulterous passion drives him to commit terrible crimes. Tolstoy was interested in the stage for its potential to reach a wide-ranging audience, but his dramas seldom reached the heights of his novels and short stories.

The major novel of Tolstoy's later period is *Resurrection* (1899), the story of the spiritual reformation of a young nobleman. The stories "The Devil" (1889) and "The Kreutzer Sonata" (1891) focus on love, jealousy, and the destructive component of the sex drive. The novel *Hadji Murad,* published after Tolstoy's death, tells the tale of a tribal leader in the Caucasus Mountains. In this story, Tolstoy again shows himself as the masterful psychologist and great literary craftsman of his earlier years.

While important and influential as a moralist, Tolstoy was, first and foremost, a creative writer. Tolstoy's religious and moralistic works are flat when compared to the beauty of his greatest works of fiction.

Anna Lisa Crone

Additional resources

Christian, Reginald F. *Tolstoy: A Critical Introduction.* Cambridge, 1970.
Rowe, William W. *Leo Tolstoy.* Twayne, 1986.
Tolstaia, Aleksandra L'vovna. *Tolstoy: A Life of My Father.* Octagon, 1973. First published in 1953.
Troyat, Henri. *Tolstoy.* Octagon, 1980. First published in 1967.

Toltec Indians, *TAHL tehk,* were the dominant people in the central Mexican highlands from about A.D. 900 to 1200. Their language and way of life influenced the Aztec, who followed them. The Toltec also probably affected the Maya of Yucatán. Buildings at the Mayan city of Chichén Itzá closely resemble Toltec architecture, and may have been built under the Toltec. See **Maya** (The Mexican period).

Aztec legends referred to the Toltec as ancient heroes who brought civilization to Mexico, and who built a majestic capital called Tula, or Tollan, "Place of the Reeds." The word *Toltec* means *people of Tula.* The ruins of the city lie near the present town of Tula, 60 miles (97 kilometers) north of Mexico City.

The ruins of Tula contain several pyramids surmounted by temples, in the usual Mexican fashion. One was the temple of Quetzalcóatl, "The Plumed Serpent," who according to legend, had founded Tula. He was a major god of both the Toltec and the Aztec Indians. Great columns in the form of serpents and human beings supported the roof of the temple. Nomadic Mexican tribes gradually overran Tula and the Toltec empire and founded the greater empire of the Aztec.

Gordon F. Ekholm

Toluene, *TAHL yu een,* is a colorless liquid related to benzene. Toluene is also called *methylbenzene* (pronounced *MEHTH uhl BEHN zeen*). It belongs to a group of compounds called *aromatic hydrocarbons.* Its chemical formula is $C_6H_5CH_3$. A molecule of toluene has its six carbon atoms arranged in a ring with five hydrogen atoms and a *methyl* (CH_3) group attached.

Manufacturers make toluene by treating petroleum or distilling coal tar. Chemists use toluene as a raw material to produce other chemicals. For example, they sometimes make benzoic acid from it. Benzoic acid is used as a preservative for foods, beverages, and cosmetics. An antiseptic known as chloramine-T is also made from toluene. Makers of explosives use toluene to make trinitrotoluene, commonly called TNT. Paint manufacturers use toluene as a lacquer solvent. Toluene is also used in the manufacture of many dyes and perfumes. Federal regulations require manufacturers to limit the amount of toluene in the air breathed by workers. Excessive exposure to toluene can damage the skin, the eyes, and the central nervous system.

Donald L. Stinson

See also **Benzene; TNT.**

Tom Sawyer. See Twain, Mark.

Tom Thumb. See Stratton, Charles Sherwood.

Tom Thumb was the name of the first American-built steam locomotive to be operated on a common-carrier railroad. Peter Cooper designed and built it in 1830. It operated on the Baltimore and Ohio Railroad in Baltimore in the summer of 1830. It pulled one of the first passenger trains. See also **Cooper, Peter; Railroad** (Developments in the United States).

Tom-tom is a musical instrument that belongs to the drum family. Most tom-toms consist of a cylinder with a thin sheet of plastic or calfskin called a *head* stretched across the top, bottom, or both. The tom-tom measures from 6 to 18 inches (15 to 46 centimeters) in diameter and stands from 6 to 20 inches (15 to 51 centimeters) high. It has a dull, hollow sound and may be tuned with a *drum key,* which adjusts the tightness of the heads. Musicians play the tom-tom with felt mallets, drumsticks, or with their hands.

Tom-toms date back to ancient times. The earliest tom-toms consisted of an animal skin stretched across

Craig Kersten

The tom-tom is an important rhythm instrument, especially in rock and jazz bands. This drummer is playing a bass tom-tom, *left.* Another tom-tom is mounted above the large bass drum.

the opening of a hollowed log. Today, tom-toms form part of the drum set used in many jazz and dance bands. Sets of four one-headed tom-toms are used in concert bands, orchestras, and percussion groups.   John H. Beck

Tomahawk was a small ax that the Indians of North America used as a tool and a weapon. Most tomahawks measured less than 18 inches (45 centimeters) long and were light enough to be used with one hand. Early tomahawks consisted of a *head* (top part) made of stone or bone mounted on a wooden handle. Some tomahawks ended in a ball or knob instead of a flat blade. After Europeans arrived in America, the Indians traded with them for iron tomahawk heads.

The Indians used tomahawks to chop wood, to drive

Some kinds of tomahawks

The Indians of North America used many different types of tomahawks. Some ended in a ball or knob, and some in a flat blade. Early tomahawks had stone or bone heads, and later ones were made of iron. Pipe tomahawks had a pipe bowl on the head and a hollow handle, so that they could be smoked.

National Museum of Natural History, The Smithsonian Institution, Washington, D.C.

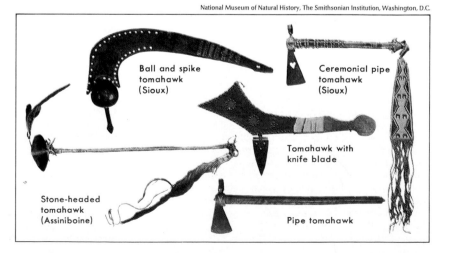

Ball and spike tomahawk (Sioux)

Ceremonial pipe tomahawk (Sioux)

Tomahawk with knife blade

Stone-headed tomahawk (Assiniboine)

Pipe tomahawk

stakes into the ground, and for many other purposes. In battle, warriors used their tomahawks as clubs or threw them at their enemies. Tomahawks also served as hunting weapons.

The Indians used a *pipe tomahawk* in religious ceremonies. This special kind of tomahawk had a pipe bowl on the head and a hollow handle, and it could be smoked as a ceremonial pipe. The Indians decorated their pipe tomahawks with feathers or with dyed porcupine quills.

Some people think the expression *bury the hatchet* came from an Indian custom of burying a tomahawk to pledge peace. However, many scholars doubt that the Indians ever had such a custom. W. Roger Buffalohead

Tomato, *tuh MAY toh* or *tuh MAH toh,* is a plant grown for its smooth, round, juicy fruit. The word *tomato* refers both to the fruit, which people eat, and to the entire plant. The fruit has a slightly acid taste. There are more than 4,000 varieties of tomatoes.

Botanists classify tomatoes as fruits. However, most people consider tomatoes vegetables because fresh tomatoes are used in much the same way as lettuce, onions, cauliflower, and many other vegetables. Fresh tomatoes are eaten raw or cooked and are generally served in salads and other dishes. Most tomatoes grown in the United States are processed for use in making a variety of food products. These products include catchup, tomato juice, tomato soup, tomato paste, tomato sauce, and canned whole tomatoes. Tomatoes are an important source of vitamins A and C and of certain minerals.

About $59\frac{1}{2}$ million short tons (54 million metric tons) of tomatoes are grown throughout the world annually. The United States produces more tomatoes than any other nation, followed by the Soviet Union, China, and Italy. Growers in the United States raise a commercial

Leading tomato-growing states and provinces

California	●●●●●●●●●●●●●●●● 6,325,000 short tons (5,738,000 metric tons)
Florida	●◖ 665,000 short tons (603,000 metric tons)
Ontario	●◖ 458,000 short tons (415,000 metric tons)
Ohio	● 419,000 short tons (380,000 metric tons)
Michigan	◖ 203,000 short tons (184,000 metric tons)

*One box equals 32 pounds (14.5 kilograms); figures are for 1983.
Sources: U.S. Department of Agriculture; Statistics Canada.

tomato crop of about $8\frac{1}{2}$ million short tons (7.5 million metric tons) yearly. About three-fourths of the crop comes from California, but tomatoes are grown in almost every area of the country. Ontario leads the Canadian provinces in tomato production.

The tomato plant has a strong smell and has small hairs on its stems. It spreads out while growing and produces clusters of small yellow flowers. The flowers develop into ripe tomatoes in 40 to 75 days, depending on the variety. Tomatoes are green at first, but most turn red, orange, or yellow as they ripen.

Tomatoes thrive in fertile, warm, well-drained soil and in locations that receive at least six hours of direct sunlight each day. Tomatoes are a favorite of home gardeners, because they can be grown in nearly any kind of soil. In addition, a large crop requires relatively little space. Many varieties produce 10 to 15 pounds (4.5 to 7 kilograms) of fruit per plant.

WORLD BOOK illustration by Kate Lloyd-Jones, Linden Artists Ltd.

Grant Heilman

Tomatoes, *left,* are smooth, round, juicy fruits that grow in almost any soil. They are a favorite of home gardeners and are also widely grown commercially. In the United States, much of the commercial tomato crop is harvested by machine, *above.*

Researchers and growers have bred tomatoes to increase the number of fruits per plant and to improve their quality and other features. For example, the leading variety of tomato grown in California, *VF 145,* was developed especially for harvesting by machines. Other types commonly grown in the United States include cherry tomatoes, *Sunray,* and *Big Boy Hybrid.* Another common variety, the *Ponderosa,* may produce tomatoes that weigh over 3 pounds (1.4 kilograms).

Growing, harvesting, and processing. Tomato seeds require 75 to 85 days to develop into mature plants with ripe fruits. In California and other areas that have a long growing season, the seeds can be planted outdoors. They are planted indoors in areas where the growing season is too short for outdoor development. Young tomato plants obtained from the seeds are transplanted outdoors when the seedlings are four to six weeks old. The transplanting takes place about two weeks after the last frost of spring, because tomato plants can be damaged by cold temperatures.

In gardens and greenhouses, most tomato plants are supported with stakes or trellises to keep them from spreading on the ground. Such supports allow the plants to be placed closer together, thus increasing the yield of each unit of land. The supports also help produce a better quality fruit and prevent a disease called *fruit rot* by keeping the fruits off moist ground.

The most common diseases of the tomato are *bacterial wilt, fusarium wilt,* and *verticillium wilt* (see **Wilt**). Several kinds of insects and worms also attack tomatoes. Plant breeders have developed varieties of the plants that resist some diseases and pests. Many growers also use chemicals to fight the enemies of tomatoes.

Most tomatoes raised to be eaten fresh are picked by hand, but an increasing number of growers use machines to harvest the crop. In the United States, machines harvest most tomatoes grown for processing.

Home gardeners pick tomatoes when they are ripe. Commercially grown tomatoes are picked before they ripen. Then they are shipped to warehouses in market areas. Unripe tomatoes are less easily damaged while being shipped. Tomatoes ripen in the warehouses.

Tomatoes grown for processing are harvested when ripe. They are then washed and scalded. Scalding loosens the skins and makes peeling easier. After the tomatoes have been peeled, they undergo different processes, depending on the final product. For example, tomatoes may be cooked or strained. The product is packed into containers, which are heated to destroy harmful bacteria. Finally, the containers are cooled and labeled, and then stored for shipping.

History. Tomatoes originated in South America, and Spanish priests probably brought them to Europe from Mexico in the mid-1500's. People in Spain and Italy then began to grow tomatoes as food. However, many people considered them poisonous because they are related to several poisonous plants. As a result, tomatoes did not become widely accepted as food until the early 1800's. Tomatoes were sometimes called *love apples,* perhaps because of a superstition that eating them made people fall in love.

Scientific classification. The tomato belongs to the nightshade family, Solanaceae. Its scientific name is *Lycopersicon esculentum.*   William L. George, Jr.

Tomb is any chamber in which the dead are buried. Some tombs are cut out of rocks, and others are built aboveground. Ancient peoples used tombs to keep the bodies of the dead safe. The Egyptians believed the departed person's spirit visited the burial place. They built the Pyramids, the world's greatest tombs, for their kings (see **Pyramids; Valley of the Kings**). Many ancient tombs contained personal possessions. Scholars have learned much about earlier cultures from the discovery of ancient tombs.

The Jews cut tombs out of rock. Christ was said to have been placed in a new rock tomb belonging to Joseph of Arimathea. Most Greek tombs were simple, but those in the colonies of Asia Minor were elaborate. The most famous of these was the tomb of Mausolus at Halicarnassus in Caria. The word *mausoleum* comes from the name of this tomb. The Romans built stately tombs which lined the roads leading to the city, because burial within the city was not allowed. Ruins of Roman tombs still line the Appian Way. The early Christians built tombs in underground rooms called *catacombs* (see **Catacombs**). Islamic tombs are often large buildings, sometimes with a dome. One of the most famous of these is the Taj Mahal in Agra, India (see **Taj Mahal**).

The Tomb of the Unknowns at Arlington National Cemetery in Virginia, Grant's tomb in New York City, and that of George and Martha Washington at Mount Vernon are perhaps the best known in the United States (see pictures with **Grant, Ulysses S.; Unknown soldier**).

Richard A. Kalish

See also **Crypt; Funeral customs; Megalithic monuments; Sarcophagus.**

Tombigbee River, *tahm BIHG bee*, rises in northeastern Mississippi and flows southeastward into western Alabama. In southwestern Alabama, the Tombigbee and Alabama rivers meet and form the Mobile River. The Mobile River flows into Mobile Bay at the deepwater port of Mobile. The bay is an inlet of the Gulf of Mexico (see **Alabama** [physical map]). The Tombigbee is about 400 miles (640 kilometers) long and the Mobile is 38 miles (61 kilometers) long (see **Mobile River**).

The Black Warrior River is the Tombigbee's chief tributary. It provides a water route from the Tombigbee to the Birmingham area in north-central Alabama.

The Tennessee-Tombigbee Waterway connects the Tombigbee and Tennessee rivers. Construction of the waterway involved building a canal from the east fork of the source of the Tombigbee north to the Tennessee River. It also involved deepening and widening the Tombigbee from its source southward to Demopolis, Ala., and constructing 10 locks and dams along the rivers. The 234-mile (377-kilometer) Tennessee-Tombigbee Waterway was completed in 1985. Often called the Tenn-Tom Waterway, it ranks among the world's largest navigational projects.   Howard A. Clonts, Jr.

Tombouctou. See Timbuktu.

Tombstone (pop. 1,632) is a town in southeastern Arizona that was the center of a rich silver-mining district in the late 1800's (see **Arizona** [political map]). Tombstone was named by its founder, prospector Ed Schieffelin. His friends feared he would be killed by Indians, and warned him he would find a tombstone, not a mine. Today, Tombstone attracts many tourists to its museums, historic sites, and mine tours.

Tombstone was founded in 1879. By 1882, its population had grown to an estimated 5,500 because of the silver-mining boom nearby. Lawlessness was widespread in Tombstone, and the famous gunfight at the O.K. Corral took place there in 1881. In 1883, underground water flooded the mine shafts. Mining activities slowed, and practically ended by 1893. The population decreased steadily. But residents promoted tourism and kept Tombstone alive.   Harwood P. Hinton

Tomlin, Bradley Walker (1899-1953), was an American abstract expressionist painter. His best-known works contain strong lines arranged in a rhythmical order that suggest hieroglyphics. They maintain a balance between carefully structured, overlapping forms and such random elements as curving symbols, letters, and numerals. Tomlin's sense of order and his preference for harmonious colors set him slightly apart from most other abstract expressionists. His works are more lyrical and restrained than those of other artists in the movement.

Self-Portrait (1932); collection of the Whitney Museum of American Art, New York City, Gift of Henry Ittleson, Jr.

Bradley Walker Tomlin

Tomlin was born in Syracuse, N.Y. In 1921, he moved to New York City where he earned a living for a time designing magazine covers. From 1925 to the late 1930's, he painted in a moderate realistic style. From 1939 to about 1944, he concentrated on cubistic blends of still-life elements and abstract forms. This style led to the simplification and abstraction of Tomlin's later works. In 1957, the Whitney Museum of American Art presented a definitive exhibition of his works.

Dore Ashton

Tompkins, Daniel D. (1774-1825), served as Vice President of the United States from 1817 to 1825 under President James Monroe. He was governor of New York from 1807 to 1817. He favored the War of 1812, and defended New York from the British as commander of the state militia.

He was handicapped by inadequate accounting methods during this trying period. During most of the rest of his life, Tompkins fought rumors that he had misappropriated funds entrusted to him as wartime governor. These false charges affected him as Vice President. He became despondent during his vice presidency, left Washington for long periods, and wasted his energies defending his character against his critics. Tompkins was born in Fox Meadows (now Scarsdale), N.Y. He served as associate justice of the Supreme Court of New York from 1804 to 1807.   Irving G. Williams

See also **Vice President of the U.S.** (picture).

Ton is the name of three different units used to measure weight and capacity. The units are the *long ton, short ton,* and *metric ton.* The long and short tons are units most often used in the United States, but the metric ton is used by nearly all other countries. The long ton equals 2,240 pounds (1,016 kilograms), the short ton equals 2,000 pounds (907 kilograms), and the metric ton equals 1,000 kilograms, or 2,204.6 pounds. Custom houses in the United States use the long ton in weighing. Coal and iron ore are weighed and sold at the mines by the long ton, and sold by the short ton to customers.   E. G. Straus

See also **Measurement** (Measuring weight); **Metric system; Weights and measures.**

Tone, in music, is the sound made by the vibration of a musical instrument or of the human voice. Tones differ in quality, pitch, intensity, and duration. Musicians use the word *tone* to describe the sound of each key on the piano, symbolized by a *note.* They also use it to describe the intervals on a keyboard. An interval between a white key and the nearest white or black key, is a *half,* or *minor, tone.* Two half tones (as from C to D on the keyboard) create the interval of a *whole,* or *major, tone.*

Raymond Kendall

See also **Harmonics; Music** (Tone); **Piano** (The strings); **Sonometer; Sound** (Sound quality).

Tonga, *TAHNG guh,* is a country made up of about 150 islands in the South Pacific Ocean. The islands lie about 3,000 miles (4,800 kilometers) southwest of Honolulu. The British explorer Captain James Cook, who first visited the islands in 1773, called them the *Friendly Islands.* In 1789, Captain William Bligh and 18 crewmen of the British ship *Bounty* floated through the islands after being cast adrift by mutineers.

Tonga is the only remaining kingdom of Polynesia,

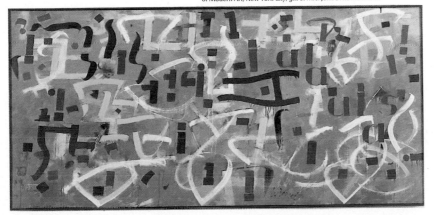

Number 9: In Praise of Gertrude Stein (1950; an oil painting on canvas; Museum of Modern Art, New York City, gift of Mrs. John D. Rockefeller III

A Tomlin painting shows repeated rhythmic lines and muted colors that are typical of his later style. Tomlin became a leading member of the movement in American painting called *abstract expressionism.*

Tonga

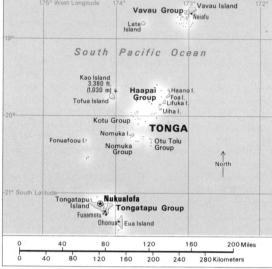

Airport	✈
National capital	⊛
Other city or town	•
Elevation above sea level	+

WORLD BOOK map

one of the three main groups of the Pacific Islands. It became independent in 1970 after being a protectorate of Great Britain since 1900. It is a member of the Commonwealth of Nations.

Most of Tonga's people raise crops. Over half the people live on Tongatapu, the largest island. Nukualofa, Tonga's capital, chief port, and commercial center, lies on Tongatapu. Nukualofa has a population of about 18,000.

Government. Tonga is a constitutional monarchy. The king appoints a premier and a Cabinet to assist him. The Cabinet consists of the premier and six other mem-

Facts in brief

Capital: Nukualofa.
Official language: Tongan.
Official name: Kingdom of Tonga.
Area: 289 sq. mi. (748 km²).
Elevation: *Highest*—Kao, an extinct volcano in the Haapai group, 3,380 ft. (1,030 m) above sea level. *Lowest*—sea level, along the coasts.
Population: *Estimated 1989 population*—108,000; density, 374 persons per sq. mi. (144 per km²); distribution, 72 per cent rural, 28 per cent urban. *1976 census*—90,085. *Estimated 1994 population*—115,000.
Chief products: bananas, copra, sweet potatoes, tapioca.
National anthem: "'E 'Otua Mafimafi" ("O God Almighty").
Flag: The flag has a red field and a white canton. A red cross in the canton symbolizes the Christian faith of the Tongans. Adopted in 1866. See **Flag** (picture: Flags of Asia and the Pacific).
Money: *Basic unit*—pa'anga. The pa'anga approximately equals the Australian dollar. See **Money** (table: Exchange rates (Australia)).

bers. The Legislative Assembly is composed of the Cabinet, seven nobles elected by Tonga's hereditary nobility, and seven commoners elected by the people. Elections take place every three years. Tongans who are at least 21 years old and can read and write may vote.

The Legislative Assembly meets for two or three months a year. When the assembly is not in session, the privy council has the power to make laws. The privy council, headed by the king, consists of the premier, the Cabinet, and the governors of two major island groups —Haapai and Vavau. The Legislative Assembly may change laws passed by the privy council. The king appoints the governors of Haapai and Vavau.

People. Almost all the people of Tonga are Polynesians and are Methodists. Tonga's Constitution prohibits work or recreation on Sunday, and the people follow this law strictly. Most Tongans live in small villages and raise crops. The people also fish for such seafood as shark and tuna. Most of the islands have no running water, and many have no electricity.

The law requires all Tongan children from 6 to 14 years old to go to school. Tonga has about 125 elementary schools and 45 high schools. The government operates about 60 per cent of the schools, and the churches direct about 40 per cent. The country's official language is Tongan, but the children also learn English. Tongan schoolchildren enjoy many sports, especially Rugby football. The country has no universities, but there is a teacher-training college in Nukualofa. Some Tongans attend universities in Australia, Fiji, and New Zealand.

Land. Tonga is made up of three main island groups —Haapai, Tongatapu, and Vavau. Most of the islands in these groups are coral reefs. Most of Tonga's people live on these islands. A chain of higher, volcanic islands lies west of the coral islands. Some of the volcanoes are active. Fertile clay soils cover most of Tonga. Strips of sandy soil lie along the coasts. Forests cover about 14 per cent of the land.

Tonga has a warm, wet climate with high humidity. Temperatures average 78° F. (26° C). The average annual rainfall varies from 70 inches (180 centimeters) on Tongatapu to 100 inches (250 centimeters) on some northern islands. Most rain falls from December through March. Cyclones sometimes hit Tonga.

Economy. Fertile soils and a warm climate have made agriculture the basis of the Tongan economy. About three-fourths of the workers are farmers. The government owns all the land. Every male who is 16 or over is entitled to a plot of land, which he rents from the government. The government has helped establish small-scale manufacturing, especially in Nukualofa. Tourism is also important to the economy.

Tonga's crops include bananas, breadfruit, sweet potatoes, tapioca, and yams. The chief exports are fruits, vegetables, and *copra* (dried coconut). Most exports go to New Zealand. Australia and New Zealand supply most of the imports, including flour, meat, petroleum, sugar, textiles, and tobacco.

Tonga has over 200 miles (320 kilometers) of roads, mostly on Tongatapu. Shipping services operate among the many islands. Government-owned shipping services connect Tonga with Australia, New Zealand, Hawaii, and other places in the Pacific. Neiafu and Nukualofa are Tonga's chief ports. The most important airport operates

Tongan farmers shell coconuts to obtain copra, one of the nation's chief exports. Copra, the dried meat of the coconut, is used in making soap, margarine, and other products.

C. D'Hotel, Explorer

at Fuaamotu on Tongatapu. Tonga has no railroads. The government publishes a weekly newspaper in both Tongan and English. The government operates the country's one radio station.

History. The first people to settle in Tonga were Polynesians who probably came from Samoa. Although much of Tonga's early history is based on myths, records of Tongan rulers go back to the A.D. 900's. The early rulers held the hereditary title of *Tu'i Tonga*. The people believed the Tu'i Tonga were sacred representatives of the Tongan gods. About 1470, the ruling Tu'i Tonga gave some governing powers to a nonsacred leader. Through the years, the Tu'i Tonga became only a figurehead. By 1865, after the death of the last Tu'i Tonga, the nonsacred king held all the ruling power.

Two Dutch navigators, Willem Cornells Schouten and Jakob le Maire, became the first Europeans to visit Tonga. They landed on some of the northern islands in 1616. In 1643, Abel Tasman, a Dutch sea captain, visited Tongatapu and other southern islands.

Methodist missionaries from Great Britain settled in Tonga during the early 1800's and converted most of the people to Christianity. But civil war spread throughout Tonga. One of the most powerful chiefs, Taufa'ahau, united the islands in 1845. He was crowned King George Tupou I, the first monarch of Tonga. Tupou I developed legal codes that became the basis of the Tongan Constitution, which was adopted in 1875.

After Tupou I died in 1893, his great-grandson, George Tupou II, took the throne. Tonga became a protectorate of Great Britain in 1900. Queen Salote succeeded Tupou II in 1918 and ruled until her death in 1965. Salote worked to improve education and health in Tonga. Her son became King Taufa'ahau Toupou IV in 1967.

In 1970, Tonga gained independence from Great Britain. Since independence, Tonga—with British aid—has worked to modernize its agriculture and build wharves and airstrips. It has also encouraged foreign investment. Through these efforts, the government hopes to vary the economy and provide more jobs for Tonga's growing population.   Stuart Inder

Tongue is the chief organ of taste. It also helps in chewing and swallowing, and plays an important part in forming the sounds of words.

The tongue is made up of many groups of muscles that a person can consciously control. This type of muscle is called *skeletal* muscle. The tongue muscles run in many different directions. They arise from the hyoid bone, and the inner surfaces of the lower jaw and temporal bones. As a result, a person can move the front part of the tongue many different ways. The tongue can move food about, push it between the teeth, and roll it into small masses. It helps clean the mouth by removing

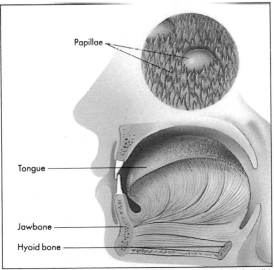

WORLD BOOK illustration by Charles Wellek

The tongue consists of bundles of muscles that run in several directions. It is covered by a mucous membrane, and its upper surface has round and cone-shaped projections called *papillae*.

food from between the cheeks and teeth. In swallowing, the tongue pushes the food back into the *pharynx* (throat). In doing this, the tongue presses against the *palate* (roof of the mouth) and also spreads against the sides of the mouth. This action prevents the food from moving in any direction except back into the pharynx.

The tongue is covered with a mucous membrane. The undersurface of the tongue is smooth. But many *papillae* (small projections) give the tongue a rough surface on the top.

Four types of taste buds, found in the papillae, enable us to distinguish between sweet, sour, salty, and bitter tastes (see **Taste**). The tip of the tongue is more sensitive to the feeling of touch than any other part of the body (see **Touch**).

The tongue is a highly useful organ to many animals. Frogs and some birds use their tongues to catch insects. Hummingbirds use their long tongues to lap up plant nectar. Dogs, cats, and other animals use their tongues for many purposes, such as to lap up water or milk, to clean their fur, or to express affection.   Raymond L. Burich

See also **Chameleon; Snake** (picture); **Toad.**

Tonsil is any of several masses of specialized tissue found in the throat. The term commonly refers to a pair of deep pink, almond-shaped structures, one of which is on each side of the back of the throat. These are the *palatine,* or *faucial,* tonsils. There are two other kinds of tonsils—the *pharyngeal* tonsils and the *lingual* tonsils. Pharyngeal tonsils, commonly called *adenoids,* grow in the back of the throat near the nasal passage. Lingual tonsils are found at the back of the tongue. Together, the three types of tonsils form a continuous ring around the back of the throat.

No one really knows the purpose of tonsils, but many medical scientists believe they aid in protecting the respiratory and digestive systems from infection. Tonsils consist of a type of tissue called *lymphoid tissue.* This tissue produces white blood cells, known as *lymphocytes,* that help fight infection. For example, lymphocytes release antibodies that destroy invading bacteria and viruses or make them harmless (see **Lymphatic sys-**

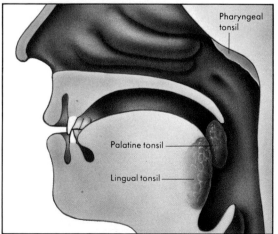

Palatine tonsil
Lingual tonsil
Pharyngeal tonsil

WORLD BOOK illustration by Charles Wellek
Tonsils form a continuous ring around the back of the throat. Medical scientists believe that tonsils help protect the respiratory and digestive systems from infection.

tem [Lymphoid tissue]). In addition, the surface of the palatine tonsils has many deep pits, called *crypts,* in which bacteria and food particles collect. Each lingual tonsil has a crypt, but the pharyngeal tonsils have none.

Sometimes the palatine or pharyngeal tonsils become badly inflamed and must be removed by a surgical operation. As children grow older, their tonsils tend to decrease in size.   James M. Toomey

See also **Tonsillitis; Adenoids.**

Tonsillitis is a painful disease resulting from inflamed tonsils. It is caused by bacteria or viruses that infect one or both of the palatine tonsils. Most attacks of tonsillitis occur in persons between the ages of 10 and 40. An attack begins with swelling and pain in the throat and difficulty in swallowing. Fever, headache, backache, stiff neck, and nausea occur in severe cases. Sometimes an *abscess* (collection of pus) forms next to the tonsil in the throat.

Physicians generally recommend bed rest, aspirin, and saltwater gargles to relieve the symptoms of tonsillitis. If the infection is bacterial, doctors can cure it with antibiotics. Antibiotics are not effective against viral tonsillitis. Some people suffer from long-lasting or repeated attacks of tonsillitis. Doctors may recommend that the tonsils be removed in such cases. The operation to remove the tonsils is called a *tonsillectomy.* A tonsillectomy is a relatively simple operation.

James M. Toomey

Tonti, *TAHN tih,* Henri de, *ahn REE duh,* also spelled *Tonty,* (1650-1704), was a French explorer who helped open the midwestern part of what is now the United States. He was the companion of Sieur de la Salle in 1682, when they traveled all the way down the Mississippi River to its mouth.

Tonti, the son of Italian parents, was probably born in Paris, France. In 1678 he went to Canada with La Salle, and two years later they traveled together into what is now Illinois. Tonti took command of Fort Crèvecoeur, near the present city of Peoria, Ill. He soon retraced his route toward Canada and met La Salle at Mackinac Island in the spring of 1681.

After exploring the Mississippi Valley, Tonti took charge of Fort St. Louis, a stronghold built at Starved Rock, Ill. This was one of the earliest white settlements in what was to become the United States. Until 1702, Tonti was the leader of the Illinois Indians. Then he joined the French-Canadian explorer Sieur d'Iberville (Pierre le Moyne) in Louisiana.   Franklin L. Ford

See also **Iberville, Sieur d'; La Salle, Sieur de.**

Tonto National Monument in south-central Arizona contains two pueblo cliff dwellings. Indians who farmed in the Salt River Valley lived in these dwellings during the 1300's. For the monument's area, see **National Park System** (table: National monuments).

Tony Award. See **Theater** (Broadway).

Tool is any instrument that a worker uses to do work. Tools that do their tasks on a machine are called *machine tools* (see **Machine tool**). Small *power-driven* tools are similar to both hand tools and machine tools. The two main kinds of tools are *woodworking tools* and *metalworking tools.*

Woodworking tools. The tools of the carpenter and cabinetmaker include such measuring tools as the *rule* for measuring lengths; the *square* and *protractor* for measuring angles; *compasses* for marking circles and arcs; and *carpenter's levels* and *plumb lines* for ensuring that carpentry work will be straight and true. *Vises* and *clamps* hold material in place while it is being shaped. Shaping tools include *saws, chisels, planes, files,* and *boring bits.* Woodworkers also use *hammers, hatchets, screw drivers,* and *pliers.* See **Woodworking.**

Metalworking tools. The work of the machinist and toolmaker ordinarily requires much greater precision than that of the woodworker. For this reason, measuring tools for metalworking must be extremely accurate. Many *micrometers* and *calipers* can measure distances as small as $\frac{1}{10,000}$ inch (0.0025 millimeter). The *hacksaw* used for cutting metal is much thinner and harder than the woodworking saw. Machinists use *taps* and *dies* to cut threads in screws, bolts, and machine parts. Machinists use *wrenches* for repair work and in assembling machinery. Most forming operations on metal parts are done by machine tools such as lathes, milling machines, shapers, and grinders.

History of tools. Prehistoric people learned that rocks and sticks of certain shapes could help them do things they could not do with their bare hands. They later improved the natural stones they used. They shaped them into knives, hatchets, and hammers, and attached wooden handles to them. Stone-Age people developed a drill for drilling soft stone and wood. Bronze-Age people developed new tools, such as tongs for holding hot objects. Agricultural civilizations later developed new tools such as the hoe and the simple plow. See **Prehistoric people.**

After people learned to work iron and steel, they developed newer and more improved tools. Tools became stronger, sharper, and more durable. The development of steam engines, gasoline engines, and electric motors made it possible to replace hand tools with machine tools. Today, much work once done by hand is done by small, power-driven hand tools.   Arthur C. Ansley

Related articles in *World Book* include:

Ax	Indian, American	Plumb line
Die and diemaking	Knife	Pneumatic tool
Drill	Level	Saw
Farm and farming	Machine tool	Steam hammer
Forging	Pioneer life in	Trip hammer
Hammer	America (Tools)	

Toolmaking chiefly involves the making of precision devices and parts for power-driven machines used to shape metal. Such machines are called *machine tools.* Toolmakers also produce a number of special tools and measuring instruments. Toolmaking is one of the most important and highly skilled crafts in the manufacturing industry.

The main products of toolmaking include *fixtures, jigs,* and *dies* for machine tools. Fixtures hold a *workpiece* (the metal being worked) in place while a manufacturing process, such as boring, cutting, or drilling, is performed on it. Jigs both hold a workpiece in place and guide a machine's cutting tool. Dies are used to mold, punch, bend, and cut out a workpiece. They range in size from huge blocks of steel for shaping automobile bodies to tiny precision devices for making watch gears. See **Die and diemaking.**

Toolmakers not only help produce machine tools but also use a variety of them in their work. For example,

they use *lathes* to cut metal into round or cylindrical shapes, *milling machines* to cut flat surfaces, *grinding machines* to smooth metal, and *boring machines* to bore holes in metal. They also use a number of hand tools, including handheld drills and grinding machines.

Toolmakers, sometimes called *tool and diemakers,* must complete a training program that lasts at least four years and combines practical toolmaking experience with classroom learning. Training programs enable toolmaking students to learn about the machines, processes, and materials involved in their work. For example, they learn to set up and operate many types of machines, ranging from power saws to sophisticated computer-controlled machines. Toolmaking students study mechanical drawing and geometry, and they learn to use micrometers and other precision measuring instruments. They also receive instruction concerning the properties of metals.   R. G. Fenton

See also **Cast and casting; Machine tool; Tool.**

Toombs, Robert Augustus (1810-1885), served in the United States Congress before the Civil War and then became Confederate Secretary of State. Toombs did not regain his U.S. citizenship after the war because he refused to swear allegiance to the United States government. He represented Georgia in the House of Representatives from 1845 to 1853 and in the Senate from 1853 to 1861. Toombs served as Secretary of State in the Confederacy in 1861 and as brigadier general of the Army of Northern Virginia from 1861 to 1862. He was born in Wilkes County, Georgia.   Kenneth Coleman

Toomer, Jean (1894-1967), was a black American writer. He is best known for *Cane* (1923), a book of poems, short stories, and a novelette about black people in the North and the South. In *Cane,* he describes people frustrated by their conflicts with social customs and by psychological conflicts within themselves. The work is noted for its poetic and sensitive descriptions. *Cane* established Toomer as a leading American writer of the 1920's. It inspired authors of the Harlem Renaissance, an important period in black literary history.

Most of Toomer's writings after *Cane* examine philosophical and psychological problems he saw in Americans. He wrote *Essentials* (1931), a collection of thoughts on these problems. Toomer also wrote book reviews, essays, poems, short stories, and a novelette. Some of them were collected in *The Wayward and the Seeking,* published in 1980, 13 years after Toomer's death.

Toomer was born in Washington, D.C. His full name was Nathan Eugene Toomer.   Darwin T. Turner

See also **American literature** (The Harlem Renaissance).

Tooth. See Teeth.

Tooth shell. See Mollusk (Tooth shells; picture); **Indian, American** (Money; picture).

Toothache tree. See Prickly ash.

Toothbrush. See Brush; Teeth.

Toothpaste and toothpowder are substances used with a toothbrush to clean teeth. Both contain a mildly abrasive substance, such as finely powdered chalk (calcium carbonate), and a *detergent* (soaplike material). Some sweetening agent other than sugar, and flavoring oils, are included to make the agent taste good. Glycerol or a similar material is added to these basic ingredients to make toothpaste. Many toothpastes contain *fluoride,* a chemical that helps prevent decay.

Top is the name for a child's toy. Most tops have cylindrical or pear shapes. They are made of wood, metal, or plastic, and usually spin on a metal tip.

Kinds of tops. The best-known top receives its motion from a string that has been wrapped around it and suddenly pulled. This makes the top spin around and stay erect without being held up. Other tops spin when a center stem is twirled between the thumb and forefinger. *Mechanical* tops receive power to spin from an inside spring that is wound with a key. In *musical* tops, holes, reeds, or whistles inside the top produce sounds when the top spins. Scientists use this spinning force in a type of gyroscopic top that helps stabilize boats and airplanes (see **Gyroscope**).

History of tops. No one knows exactly when people first began to use tops. But children in ancient Greece played with them, and tops have been a popular amusement in China and Japan for hundreds of years. In the 1800's, people in the Orient often became professional top spinners. They made tops do a great variety of tricks, such as jumping steps and walking up an inclined board.

Tops became popular in Europe during the 1700's. In a game called *diabolo,* the player whipped a top into the air. Sometimes the player tried to see how high the top could be sent. Other times, the top was caught in the hand from various bodily positions. Many types of

© Peter Gonzalez

Tops are popular toys. The red and blue tops, *top,* were made in the United States. The small finger tops, *center,* are from India. A Mexican top, *bottom left,* has colorful stripes. An Austrian craftworker carved the yellow top, *bottom right.*

self-winding tops were used in the 1800's. The *bandilor* top unwinds itself while going up an incline, and rewinds as it comes down. The top can be manipulated to wind and unwind itself many times. Tops were among the first toys patented in the United States. The *torpedo* top contained a ball that shot into the air when a paper cap exploded.   Philip L. Kirkham

Topaz, *TOH paz,* is a mineral composed of aluminum, silicon, oxygen, and fluorine. Topaz occurs in many colors, including deep golden-orange, yellow, brownish-yellow, pink, red, and various shades of blue. It may also be colorless. Topaz is often used as a gemstone. In the mineral table of hardness, topaz has a hardness of 8. Topaz can scratch quartz, but not corundum, the hardest mineral next to diamond. See **Hardness; Corundum.**

The most valuable topaz is golden-orange in color and is known as *imperial topaz.* Colorless and pale-blue topaz are much less expensive and more abundant. The color of topaz may be enhanced by various techniques, such as heating and *irradiation* (exposure to nuclear radiation). For example, some brown topaz may turn pink when heated. Colorless or pale-blue stones may become a dark blue when treated by a combination of heating and irradiation.

Topaz is found in many parts of the world, especially Brazil, the Soviet Union, Namibia, Nigeria, Pakistan, and Australia. Most fine-quality imperial topaz comes from Brazil. Some topaz crystals have been found that weigh several hundred pounds or kilograms. Large, beautiful topaz stones are the pride of many museums.

Yellow or brownish quartz is sometimes sold as a substitute for topaz. It can be produced by heating amethyst. In addition, blue topaz may be sold as an imitation of aquamarine. Topaz is the birthstone for November.

Robert I. Gait

See also **Gem** (picture).

Topeka, *tuh PEE kuh* (pop. 115,266; met. area pop. 154,916), is the capital and third largest city of Kansas. Only Wichita and Kansas City have more people. Topeka is located in northeastern Kansas on the Kansas River. For location, see **Kansas** (political map). Topeka is an important trade center. It is also the home of the Menninger Foundation, which conducts psychiatric research, trains psychiatrists, and treats mentally ill patients.

Topeka lies in a region of gently rolling hills. The city has many wide streets lined with tall shade trees. The Capitol towers above Topeka's downtown area. The building, much of which dates from the late 1800's, is topped by a pale green copper dome.

Many Topeka residents work for federal, state, or local government agencies. Hospitals and other medical institutions also rank among the city's chief employers. Topeka factories produce agricultural machinery, cellophane, pet foods, potato chips, steel products, and tires. Other Topeka industries include grain storage, printing and publishing, and the manufacture and repair of railroad cars.

The Topeka area was once occupied by the Kansa (Kaw) Indians. In 1842, Louis Papan, one of the area's first European settlers, began operating a ferry on the Kansas River. Papan's ferry transported people who were traveling westward to such places as California and Oregon.

Topeka was founded in 1854 by a small group of pio-

Karl Kummels, Shostal

The State Capitol in Topeka stands in a 10-acre (4-hectare) park. Topeka has been the capital of Kansas since 1861.

neers at the place where Papan had operated his ferry. The pioneers were led by Cyrus Holliday, a businessman from Pennsylvania. Holliday later helped found the Atchison, Topeka, and Santa Fe Railroad (now the Atchison, Topeka and Santa Fe Railway Company). In 1878, he helped establish the railroad's headquarters in Topeka. Today, the railroad is one of the largest in the United States. Topeka was incorporated in 1857, and it became the state capital in 1861.

Topeka is the home of Washburn University of Topeka. The city is the seat of Shawnee County and has a mayor-council form of government. For the monthly weather, see **Kansas** (Climate).   Stannie Anderson

See also **Curry, John Steuart; Kansas** (picture: The State Capitol); **Menninger Foundation.**

Topelius, *tu PAY lee UHS,* **Zachris,** *SAK rihs* (1818-1898), was a Finnish short-story writer and poet. His best-known work is *Tales of an Army Surgeon* (1853-1867), a classic of Scandinavian literature. It is a multivolume series of historical romances that stress the role of common people in Finnish-Swedish history. The stories cover the period from the Thirty Years' War (1618-1648) to the reign of Gustavus III in the late 1700's. Topelius wrote two series of children's stories, *Tales* (1847-1852) and *Readings for Children* (1865-1896).

Topelius was born near Nykarleby. He edited a Helsinki newspaper, and was professor of history, and then became president of the University of Helsinki. He was a champion of Finnish nationalism, but he wrote in Swedish.   Richard B. Vowles

Topiary work, *TOH pee EHR ee,* is the art of training and cutting plants into ornamental shapes. Topiary work is usually done on shrubs, evergreen trees, and lawns, but decorators make topiary trees from crepe paper and wire.

Topiary work was a favorite hobby of the Romans, who made plants grow in geometrical forms such as cubes, cones, and pyramids. Later topiary designs included giraffes, dogs, pigs, and peacocks. Topiary workers also imitated such useful objects as chairs, fountains, and sundials. One design was a long row of trees shaped like elephants, with the trunk of one elephant holding the tail of the one ahead.   Stephen F. Hamblin

Topography, *tuh PAHG ruh fee,* is the natural and artificially created surface features of the land. These include hills, valleys, streams, lakes, bridges, tunnels, roads, and cities. Topography is also the science of making an accurate and detailed drawing of such features. See also **Map; Photogrammetry; Surveying.**

Topology, *tuh PAHL uh jee,* is a branch of mathematics that explores certain properties of geometrical figures. The properties are those that do not change when the figures are deformed by bending, stretching, or molding. Topology makes no distinction between a sphere and a cube, because these figures can be deformed or molded into one another. Topology makes a distinction between a sphere and a *torus* (a doughnut-shaped figure) because a sphere cannot be deformed into a torus without being torn. Topology is often called *rubber-sheet geometry* because its figures can be deformed.

Unlike high school geometry, topology ignores straightness, parallelism, and distance, because deformation can alter them. Instead, topology studies such problems as the number of intersections made by a curve with itself, whether a surface is closed or has boundaries, and whether or not a surface is connected.

Topology makes up theorems and tries to prove them, just as high school geometry does. For example, the *four-color theorem* applies to maps. The theorem states that four colors are sufficient to color any map so that, in any group of adjacent countries, each country is a different color. The American mathematician Kenneth Appel and the German-born mathematician Wolfgang Haken proved the theorem in 1976.   Alan Shuchat

Topsoil is the surface layer of soil. It is usually 4 to 10 inches (10 to 25 centimeters) deep. The structure and consistency of topsoil encourages the growth of plants' root systems. Topsoil is rich in a substance known as *humus,* an important food source for such plants as small grains and grasses (see **Humus**). Topsoil also contains bacteria that are necessary for plant growth. Because fertile topsoil is required for agriculture, landscaping, and gardening, it ranks as one of our most important natural resources. Hundreds of years may be needed for topsoil to develop. For this reason, the preservation of topsoil is one of the chief goals of soil conservation. See also **Conservation** (Soil conservation); **Lawn** (Preparing the soil).   Raymond K. Moore

Torah, *TAWR uh,* is the Hebrew name for the *Pentateuch* (first five books of the Bible). See **Pentateuch.**

Torch is the term used in Great Britain and Commonwealth countries for a flashlight. See **Flashlight.**

Torino. See Turin.

The development of a tornado is shown in the four pictures at the left. First, a dense, dark cloud forms, *upper left.* Rotating air at the bottom of the cloud then forms into a narrow cloud called a *funnel, upper right.* The funnel extends toward the earth's surface, *lower left.* If the funnel touches the surface, it raises a huge dust cloud, *lower right,* and destroys almost everything in its path.

© Howard Bluestein, Photo Researchers

Tornado is a powerful, twisting windstorm. The winds of a tornado are the most violent winds that occur on the earth. They whirl around the center of the storm at speeds of more than 200 miles (320 kilometers) per hour. Most tornadoes measure several hundred yards or meters in diameter, and many have caused widespread death and destruction.

A tornado is a rotating funnel cloud that extends downward from a mass of dark clouds. Some funnels do not reach the earth. Others may strike the surface of the earth, withdraw into the dark clouds above, and then dip down and strike the earth again. In the United States, most funnel clouds tend to travel toward the northeast.

The winds of a tornado whirl in a counterclockwise direction in the Northern Hemisphere and clockwise in the Southern Hemisphere. People in some regions call a tornado a *twister* or a *cyclone.* A tornado that occurs over a lake or ocean is called a *waterspout* (see **Waterspout**).

Most tornadoes last less than an hour. These storms travel a distance of about 20 miles (32 kilometers) at a speed of 10 to 25 miles (16 to 40 kilometers) per hour. Some tornadoes last several hours and measure up to 1½ miles (2.4 kilometers) in diameter. They may travel 200 miles (320 kilometers) or more at a speed of up to 60 miles (97 kilometers) per hour. Such tornadoes are especially destructive.

Tornadoes occur throughout the world, but mostly in the United States. Those in the United States hit chiefly

Where tornadoes occur

Tornadoes frequently hit the Midwestern and Southern States. The Western States have few tornadoes. The map shows the number of tornadoes that occurred in each region during a 12-year period.

Less than 10

10-50

50-100

100-200

More than 200

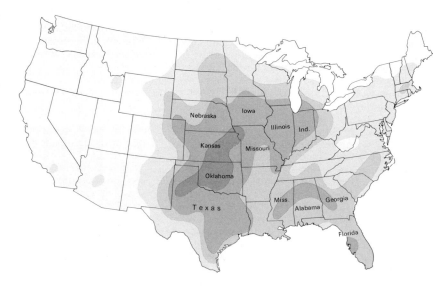

WORLD BOOK map

in spring and early summer. No one knows how many tornadoes occur yearly because many of the storms occur in thinly populated areas and may not be reported. About 700 tornadoes have been reported annually in the United States since the mid-1950's.

The greatest killer tornado in history roared through Missouri, Illinois, and Indiana on March 18, 1925, and killed 689 persons. This tornado was one of the largest and fastest tornadoes ever recorded. Its path measured about 220 miles (354 kilometers) long and up to a mile (1.6 kilometers) wide. The storm traveled at a speed of about 60 miles (97 kilometers) per hour.

The story of a tornado. Most tornadoes in the United States strike the Midwest and the states that border the Gulf of Mexico. Scientists do not know exactly why tornadoes develop.

Most tornadoes form along a *front* (boundary) between cool, dry air from the north and warm, humid air from the Gulf of Mexico. A narrow zone of *cumulonimbus* (thunderstorm) clouds develops along such a front. This zone of clouds, called a *squall line,* produces violent weather. See **Cloud** (picture: Some cumulonimbus clouds).

The violent weather produced by a squall line results when a mass of warm, humid air rises extremely rapidly. As this air rises, more warm air rushes in to replace it. The inrushing air also rises and, in some cases, begins to rotate. The rotating air then forms into a tornado.

Most tornadoes occur in spring on a hot, humid day in the afternoon or in the early evening. Large thunderclouds appear in the sky, and thunder begins to rumble in the distance. A nearby cloud becomes dark and dense. Rounded masses at the bottom of the cloud start to twist. One of the twisting masses then forms a funnel cloud that gradually extends downward. Heavy rain and some hail begin to fall, and flashes of lightning occur. A hissing sound begins as the funnel cloud extends toward the earth. If the funnel touches the ground, it stirs up dirt and debris. The hissing becomes a loud roar.

The violent, rotating winds of a tornado blow down almost everything in its path. In addition to the force of the wind, the explosive force of a tornado can demolish a small building. It does so primarily by causing a difference in air pressure between the inside and outside of the building. When a tornado passes over a house, it sucks up air from around the structure. The air pressure outside the house drops suddenly, but the air pressure inside remains the same. As a result, the pressure inside the house is greater than that outside. Because the pressure difference cannot equalize quickly enough, the building explodes outward.

The tremendous lifting force of a tornado results from a powerful updraft of air inside the funnel. Tornadoes have uprooted large trees, overturned railroad cars, and carried such heavy objects as automobiles hundreds of feet or meters.

Protection against tornadoes. Scientists of the National Weather Service constantly gather weather information from all parts of the United States. If weather conditions indicate that tornadoes or severe thunderstorms may occur, the agency issues an *advisory bulletin* that is broadcast on television and radio. If a tornado is spotted, the Weather Service warns communities in the path of the storm. The *warning* gives the location

George M. Cassidy, Shostal

A tornado strikes with terrible force. Its violent winds can destroy buildings, uproot huge trees, and carry automobiles and other large objects long distances. A tornado flattened parts of Marion, Ill., *above,* in 1982, killing 10 people.

and size of the tornado and the course the storm is following. Police in the endangered areas may also use sirens to warn the people to take cover. Tornadoes may be spotted by observers, or by special equipment, such as radar. One type of radar, *Doppler radar,* can indicate the location of tornadoes and can also determine the speed of the wind.

A storm cellar provides the best protection against a tornado. A basement is the next best place to take shelter. In a basement, people should crouch under a table on the side of the room from which the tornado is approaching. In a building that has no basement, they should lie flat under a table or bed on the ground floor, away from any windows. Some windows should be kept open to reduce the difference in air pressure inside and outside the building and thus help to prevent the building from exploding. Mobile homes should always be vacated if a tornado is approaching. They offer almost no protection and can be easily overturned by a tornado. Outside, people should lie face down in a ditch or ravine if possible. This action would provide some protection against flying debris but would not prevent a tornado from lifting a person into its funnel.

Wayne M. Wendland

See also **Cyclone; Hurricane; Weather.**

Torne River, *TAWR nuh,* also called the Tornio River, rises in Lake Torne in northern Sweden and flows eastward through northern Sweden. Then it turns southward, and forms part of the boundary between Sweden and Finland until it empties into the Gulf of Bothnia.

The Finnish people call the part of the river that forms the boundary the Tornio. But in Sweden, the river is called the Torne. The Torne River is more than 250 miles (402 kilometers) long.   John H. Wuorinen

Toronto is the capital of Ontario and Canada's chief center of industry. Toronto landmarks include the modern City Hall, *left.* Toronto's city seal, *above,* bears the city's coat of arms. The Missisauga Indian represents the area's early inhabitants. The Britannia figure indicates Canada's bond with Great Britain. The beaver stands for Toronto's industry and its Canadian identity. The city seal was adopted in 1961.

E. Otto, Miller Services

Toronto, *tuh RAHN toh,* is the capital of Ontario. Toronto has Canada's largest metropolitan area population. However, more people live within the city proper of Montreal than within the city proper of Toronto. Some people consider Toronto the country's largest city, while others give that distinction to Montreal. Toronto lies on the northwest shore of Lake Ontario. It is one of the busiest Canadian ports on the Great Lakes.

Toronto is the chief manufacturing, financial, and communications center of Canada. About a third of Canada's manufacturing industries are within 100 miles (160 kilometers) of the city. The Toronto Stock Exchange ranks first in the nation in daily trading volume. Toronto leads all Canadian cities in printing, publishing, and television and film production. It also ranks as a leading Canadian cultural center. The city has Canada's largest museum and public library system.

During the 1600's and 1700's, Indians used the Toronto area as a *portage* (overland route) between Lake Ontario and Lake Huron. In 1791, John Graves Simcoe became lieutenant governor of the new British colony of Upper Canada (now Ontario). He chose the site of present-day Toronto for a new colonial capital to replace Newark, which was then the capital. In 1793, Simcoe established a settlement on the site and named it *York.* In 1834, the town was renamed *Toronto,* a Huron Indian term meaning *meeting place.* During the late 1800's, Toronto began to grow as a center of manufacturing and transportation.

In 1954, the Municipality of Metropolitan Toronto became North America's first metropolitan government federation. The Municipality, commonly called *Metropolitan Toronto,* consisted of Toronto and 12 of its suburbs. The Ontario legislature created the federation to provide a way for Toronto and the suburbs to solve various problems they had in common. In 1967, the 13 members of the federation were merged to form Toronto and 5 boroughs—East York, Etobicoke, North York, Scarborough, and York. Since 1979, all but East York have become cities. But they remain in the federation.

Facts in brief

Population: *Toronto*—612,289; *Municipality of Metropolitan Toronto*—2,192,721; *Toronto Census Metropolitan Area*—3,427,168.

Area: *Toronto*—43 sq. mi. (111 km²); *Municipality of Metropolitan Toronto*—241 sq. mi. (624 km²); *Toronto Census Metropolitan Area*—1,401 sq. mi. (3,629 km²).

Altitude: 356 ft. (109 m) above sea level.

Climate: *Average temperature*—January, 24° F. (−4° C); July, 71° F. (22° C). *Average annual precipitation* (rainfall, melted snow, and other forms of moisture)—32 in. (81 cm). For the monthly weather in Toronto, see **Ontario** (Climate).

Government: *Toronto*—Mayor-council (3-year terms for the mayor and 22 council members). *Municipality of Metropolitan Toronto*—Metropolitan Council (3-year terms for a chairman and 39 council members).

Founded: Early 1700's. Incorporated as a town in 1793; as a city in 1834.

Each of the federation's six units has its own government to handle local needs.

The city

Near the center of Toronto's downtown business district stands the $30-million City Hall, which opened in 1965. This unusual structure consists of two curved office buildings and, between them, the oyster-shaped city council chambers. The three buildings stand in 12-acre (5-hectare) Nathan Phillips Square, which is named for the mayor who served from 1955 to 1962. Nearby Bay Street is the center of Toronto's financial district.

Toronto Eaton Centre, a huge downtown complex on Yonge Street, includes Eaton's, Toronto's largest department store. It also has about 300 other stores, a 36-story office building, and a 26-story office building. Downtown Toronto also has three of the world's tallest buildings. The Bank of Montreal Tower, a 72-story bank and office building, rises 935 feet (285 meters). The 68-story Scotia Plaza building is 906 feet (276 meters) tall. Another office building, Commerce Court West, has 57 stories and rises 784 feet (239 meters). Nearby is the CN (Can-

City of Toronto

The map at the right shows the Municipality of Metropolitan Toronto, which includes the City of Toronto. The map below shows the city and many of its major points of interest.

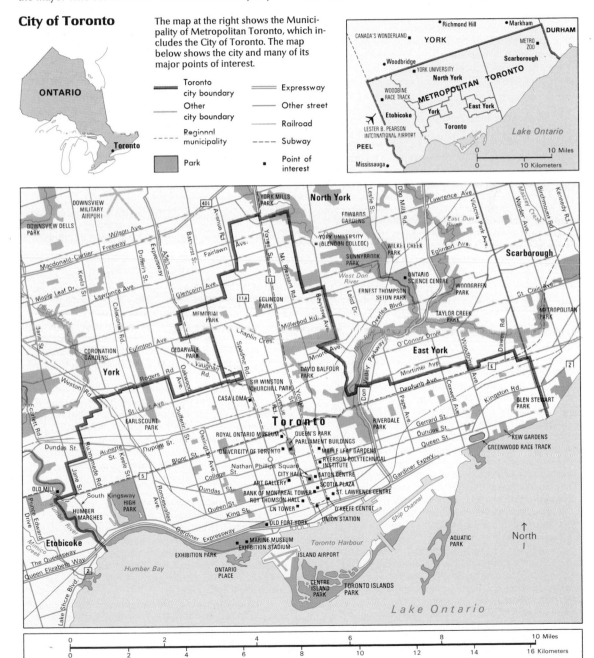

WORLD BOOK map

adian National) tower. This concrete-and-steel shaft rises 1,815 feet (553 meters) and is the world's tallest free-standing structure. The tower includes a large antenna and an observation deck. Ontario Place, a recreation center in Toronto's harbor, has an exhibition area, a marina, and a theater.

The Ontario Parliament Buildings stand at the head of University Avenue in Queen's Park, just north of downtown Toronto. The campus of the University of Toronto lies west of the park.

Toronto itself covers 43 square miles (111 square kilometers). The Municipality of Metropolitan Toronto covers 241 square miles (624 square kilometers). About a fourth of Ontario's people and about a tenth of the Canadian population live in the municipality. The official Toronto metropolitan area, called the Toronto Census Metropolitan Area, occupies 1,401 square miles (3,629 square kilometers).

The people

About two-fifths of the people of Toronto trace their roots to the British Isles. At the end of World War II in 1945, many Europeans immigrated to Toronto. People of Italian and Portuguese ancestry now make up the two largest ethnic groups. Other large groups include those of Chinese, French, and Greek ancestry.

The heavy immigration from other countries and from other areas of Canada to Toronto has greatly reduced the supply of affordable housing. The federal, provincial, and municipal governments have worked to build more public housing and to provide aid for private housing to people with low incomes. Despite their efforts, the situation remains critical.

Economy

Manufacturing. The Toronto metropolitan area ranks as Canada's chief industrial center. More than 5,700 factories in the area produce over $7 billion worth of goods yearly. About a third of the workers in the metropolitan area have manufacturing jobs. The major manufacturing activities are food processing and printing and publishing. Other leading products include clothing; electronics and electrical equipment; and paper, rubber, and wood products.

Finance. Toronto is Canada's leading banking and financial center. More Canadian banks, insurance companies, mining firms, trust companies, and loan companies have headquarters in Toronto than in any other city. The Toronto Stock Exchange ranks as the fourth largest exchange in North America in value of shares traded.

Transportation and communication. Toronto is also a major transportation center. The region's varied products travel to many parts of the world by air and by ship via the St. Lawrence Seaway. Toronto's port handles about 2 million short tons (1.8 million metric tons) of cargo a year. Leading railways that serve the city include the Canadian National and the CP Rail (formerly Canadian Pacific). Lester B. Pearson International Airport (formerly Toronto International Airport), about 15 miles (24 kilometers) northwest of the city, is Canada's busiest airport. The Toronto Island Airport in Lake Ontario has a seaplane base and runways. A domestic commuter service flies to Ottawa, Montreal, and Hamilton.

The Toronto subway, which opened in 1954, was Can-ada's first underground rapid transit railway. The first line ran under Yonge Street. Several new rapid transit lines and extensions opened during the 1960's and early 1970's. A line serving Scarborough opened in 1985, and several other lines were planned for construction during the next 20 years.

Toronto has three daily newspapers, the *Toronto Star,* the *Globe and Mail,* and the *Toronto Sun.* The city has about 15 radio stations and 5 television stations. One of Canada's first two TV stations was CBLT, which started broadcasting from Toronto in 1952.

Education

The public school system of the Municipality of Metropolitan Toronto has over 550 elementary and high schools, with about 280,000 students. About 94,000 children in Toronto attend Roman Catholic and other private elementary schools.

The University of Toronto, which was founded in 1827, has more than 50,000 students, one of the largest enrollments of any Canadian university. Other schools include the National Ballet School, the Ontario College of Art, the Royal Conservatory of Music, Ryerson Polytechnical Institute, and York University in nearby North York.

The Toronto Public Library, near the University of Toronto, has more than a million books. The library also owns the Osborne Collection of early children's books. The library has 27 branches that serve the city. Each of the metropolitan municipalities has its own library system.

Cultural life and recreation

The arts. The Toronto Symphony Orchestra and the Mendelssohn Choir perform in Roy Thomson Hall. The O'Keefe Centre for the Performing Arts presents programs by the Canadian Opera Company and the National Ballet of Canada. The St. Lawrence Centre for the Arts, St. Lawrence Hall, the Royal Conservatory of Music, and the Canadian Music Centre are also in Toronto. The Art Gallery of Ontario owns the country's second largest collection of Canadian paintings. The National Gallery of Canada in Ottawa has the largest.

Museums. The Royal Ontario Museum is the largest museum in Canada. It offers exhibits of archaeology, ethnology, mineralogy, and paleontology. The museum has one of the world's finest collections of Chinese objects. The Marine Museum of Upper Canada shows the development of shipping on the Great Lakes and the St. Lawrence River.

Parks. The Toronto park system covers more than 6,000 acres (2,400 hectares). It includes more than 100 parks. Toronto Islands Park, the city's largest park, occupies 612 acres (248 hectares) in Lake Ontario. The Metro Toronto Zoo lies just northeast of the city.

Sports. The Toronto Maple Leafs of the National Hockey League play their home games in Maple Leaf Gardens. The Hockey Hall of Fame is in Exhibition Park. The Toronto Argonauts of the Canadian Football League play in Exhibition Stadium. The Toronto Blue Jays of the American League play baseball in Exhibition Stadium.

Other interesting places to visit include:
Casa Loma, about 2 miles (3 kilometers) northwest of downtown Toronto. Sir Henry Pellatt, a Toronto stockbroker, built

this 98-room castle in the early 1900's at a cost of about $3 million.

Exhibition Park, on the Toronto lakefront. The Canadian National Exhibition, the world's largest annual fair, is held there from mid-August to Labor Day. The fair features exhibits and sports events.

Old Fort York, near Exhibition Park. This fort, which has been restored, was burned by invading United States forces during the War of 1812.

Ontario Place, on the lakefront near the downtown area, is a cultural and recreational complex. It includes a movie theater and a picnic area.

Ontario Science Centre, 6 miles (10 kilometers) northeast of downtown, consists of three buildings that house nine main exhibit halls.

Government

Metropolitan Toronto has a two-level system of government. This system consists of the Metropolitan Council of the Municipality of Metropolitan Toronto and the separate city and borough councils. The Metropolitan Council provides most of the area's major government services, including ambulance services, highway, police, public transportation, urban development, and welfare services. A separate council, the Toronto City Council, handles other services for the city. These services include fire protection, garbage collection, and public health.

The Metropolitan Council has a chairman and 39 members—including the mayors—each of whom is also a member of a city council or borough council. Each city or borough has its own election process. Toronto began direct election of its members of the Metropolitan Council in 1985. The other cities and the borough send members of their councils. In Scarborough and North York, the council members elect their representatives. Etobicoke, York, and East York send those council members who received the most votes in the election.

The Toronto City Council has a mayor and 22 other members. The voters elect all these officials to three-year terms. The mayor serves as head of the Executive Committee, which includes four other members of the City Council. This committee is the council's executive branch. However, all council members form its legislative branch.

History

Early settlement. Iroquois Indians lived in the Toronto area before white people arrived. The area lay at the southern end of an Indian trail that ran between Lake Huron and Lake Ontario. During the early 1700's, the French set up a mission, a fur-trading post, and a fort opposite the peninsula that helps form Toronto's harbor. In 1759, they burned Fort Toronto—also called Fort Rouillé—to keep the British from seizing it. In 1763, the Treaty of Paris gave all Canada to Great Britain.

In 1787, the Canadian government bought land on the peninsula from the Missisauga Indians. No permanent settlement began until 1793, when John Graves Simcoe chose the site to replace Newark as the capital of the colony of Upper Canada (now Ontario). He named the settlement York after the Duke of York.

The 1800's. During the War of 1812, United States troops captured and burned York. In 1834, York was renamed Toronto and received its city charter. The city had a population of about 10,000. In 1837, William Lyon Mackenzie, a printer who became Toronto's first mayor, led a revolt against the colony's British government (see Mackenzie, William L.).

Manufacturing expanded rapidly in Toronto during the late 1800's, when Canada's federal government adopted policies to protect new Canadian industries from American competition. Also during this period, the federal government opened new areas in the western prairies to grain growing and livestock raising. Toronto became the chief banker and market of the West and grew in importance as a railroad center.

The 1900's. The demand for war materials during World War I (1914-1918) and World War II (1939-1945) brought great industrial expansion to the Toronto area. The end of World War II saw a rapid population growth as well. Hundreds of thousands of European immigrants settled in Toronto. The city's population overflowed into 12 suburbs. This growth caused numerous problems throughout the area, including poor transportation, a housing shortage, and—in some communities—a lack of water. But the city and the suburbs often refused to work together to solve their common problems. Also, some of the suburban governments could not afford to pay for some improvements.

These problems led the Ontario legislature to create the Municipality of Metropolitan Toronto in 1953. The

E. Beldowski, Canapress

The CN Tower, a communications and observation tower, rises 1,815 feet (553 meters). Glass-walled elevators carry visitors to the Sky Pod, a seven-story restaurant and observation center. The tower, completed in 1976, is the world's highest free-standing structure.

federation of Toronto and 12 of its suburbs came into being on Jan. 1, 1954. The city and the suburbs each had self-government in local matters and sent representatives to a 25-member Metropolitan Council. In 1967, the legislature merged the 13 units into 6—Toronto and the boroughs of East York, Etobicoke, North York, Scarborough, and York. Since then, all the boroughs except East York have become cities. But all remain in the federation. In 1980, the Metropolitan Council was enlarged to 39 members and a chairman. The council has brought improvement in several fields. For example, it put into operation the first computer-controlled traffic system in the world. The council built public housing for the elderly and moderate rental housing for younger families. It also doubled the area's water supply.

Recent events. In October 1968, the Metropolitan Council approved the Metropolitan Waterfront Plan, a renewal program for the Toronto waterfront area. The first part of the plan, construction of Ontario Place, was completed in 1971. The CN Tower, the world's highest free-standing structure, was completed in 1976. It rises 1,815 feet (553 meters). A convention center opened in 1984. The entire waterfront program is expected to be completed in the early 2000's.

In the 1970's, construction began on Toronto Eaton Centre, a huge shopping-office complex in downtown Toronto. By 1979, about 300 stores and a 26-story office building had been completed. A 36-story office building was completed in 1981. In 1986, construction began in the downtown area on a covered sports stadium with a retractable roof. The project is scheduled for completion in 1989.　　Lou Clancy

See also **Ontario** (pictures).

Toronto, *tuh RAHN toh,* **University of,** is one of Canada's largest universities. It is coeducational and supported chiefly by the province of Ontario. The main campus is in downtown Toronto. The university also operates two colleges of arts and science—Erindale and Scarborough —near the city.

The university has 11 undergraduate divisions. The largest division, arts and science, offers more than 1,600 courses. The school of graduate studies consists of over 75 departments, institutes, and other divisions. The university operates more than 50 libraries, with a total of over 5 million volumes. It also administers an astronomical observatory, several research centers, and the University of Toronto Press.

The University of Toronto awards arts and science degrees for three other universities—the University of St. Michael's College, the University of Trinity College, and Victoria University. It also grants degrees for the Ontario Institute for Studies in Education. Three theological colleges—Emmanuel, Knox, and Wycliffe—are associated with the university but grant their own degrees. All seven associated institutions are in Toronto.

The university was founded in 1827 as King's College. It received its present name in 1850. For enrollment, see **Canada** (table: Universities and colleges).

Critically reviewed by the University of Toronto

Torpedo is a self-propelled, cigar-shaped, underwater weapon used to blow up ships. It is highly complicated and designed to combat fast-moving warships and merchant ships. Modern torpedoes are difficult to detect and are extremely versatile. They can be launched from submarines, surface vessels, or aircraft. They can even ride piggy-back on a rocket to distant targets.

Torpedoes vary in size, weight, and mechanical apparatus, according to the purpose for which they are intended. Some are designed for attacking large groups of cargo vessels shielded by warships. Other torpedoes are used in hunting deep-running submarines and aircraft carriers, or in unique battle situations.

How a torpedo operates. A conventional torpedo usually has four sections. The *nose* contains acoustic and electronic devices by which the torpedo hunts and pursues an enemy vessel. The *warhead* includes the explosive charge and the mechanism that makes it explode. The *energy* section holds the battery and the electric motor or engine. The *afterbody* houses the control and propulsion units.

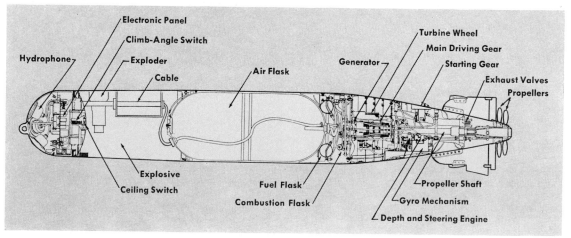

U.S. Navy

A modern torpedo carries power, steering, and detonation equipment and a high explosive charge. The hydrophone detects sound vibrations from a ship's engines and guides the torpedo to the source of the sound. An air flask supplies *oxygen,* or air, needed to burn the fuel in the engine. The small engine turns propellers that push the torpedo through the water.

Some torpedoes are launched from a tube or rack that points the torpedo toward a target or target area. As the torpedo leaves the launcher, a starting lever in the torpedo puts the energy section into action. At the same time, power flows to the propulsion unit that drives the torpedo forward, and to the control units that stabilize the torpedo. As the torpedo speeds toward the target zone, the explosive mechanism in the warhead automatically becomes armed. Acoustic "ears" or hydrophones hunt for the sounds made by the propellers or machinery of a distant ship. When the hydrophones pick up an enemy ship by its noises, the torpedo is within *acquisition range.* At this point, it leaves its hunting course and goes straight to the target. It explodes either *magnetically,* when it nears the ship's hull, or *upon impact,* when it strikes the hull.

A special-purpose torpedo with most of these features can be guided by wire to its target. The torpedo unwinds a reel of wire as it travels to the target area. The attacking ship sends steering signals over the wire, aiming the torpedo at a target at close range.

Another special type of torpedo is the antisubmarine rocket or *ASROC.* This weapon system detects a submarine at long ranges and quickly computes its course and speed. Then it launches a rocket-propelled *ballistic* missile containing either an *acoustic-homing,* or sound-detecting, torpedo or a depth charge. The rocket and other parts of the missile fall away in the air. In the water, the acoustic-homing device guides the torpedo to its target. A depth charge explodes at a predetermined depth. A similar weapon is the submarine rocket, or *SUBROC.* It is launched by one submerged submarine to attack another.

On the outside, present-day torpedoes resemble earlier ones. On the inside, the torpedo is vastly different. Modern warfare demands weapons that can operate on a broad scale and that have a high degree of reliability. Torpedoes used during World War II (1939-1945) were of simple mechanical or electrical design. They were aimed at surface vessels only, and they ran a straight course. They left a telltale wake of air bubbles behind them, and made a detectable noise as they traveled. These torpedoes could easily be evaded by a maneuvering ship. Today's torpedoes leave no wake behind them and can track ships making evasive maneuvers.

History. Until the 1900's, the word *torpedo* was applied to mines or any other explosive device used against ships. At first, none of these devices had means of propulsion. Those carried by surface vessels or submarines were intended to be rammed against an enemy ship or secretly attached to its hull. David Bushnell, an American, tried unsuccessfully to blow up British warships with torpedoes in 1776. In the early 1800's, the great American inventor, Robert Fulton, successfully blew up several ships with his torpedo, but there was little interest in it. During the Civil War (1861-1865), two large ships were sunk by *spar torpedoes.* These charges, which were mounted at the end of a pole sticking out from the attacker's bow, exploded on contact with another vessel.

In 1864, a Captain Luppis of the Austrian Navy took a plan for a torpedo to the famous Scottish engineer, Robert Whitehead. By 1868, Whitehead had developed the first real torpedo. Powered by compressed air, the tor-

pedo was completely self-propelled. Today's torpedo designs involve so many fields of science and are so complicated that it is not possible to credit the modern torpedo to any one person.   Jack Sweetman

See also **Depth charge; Guided missile; PT boat; Submarine.**

Torpedo, also called *electric ray,* is the name of a particular kind of ray which lives in warm seas. The name of this fish comes from its ability to give off electricity from glands just behind its head and gills. The body of the fish is flat and broad, and ends in a slender tail. The torpedo uses its strange power to stun small fish and to defend itself. The shock from a full-grown, healthy torpedo is powerful enough to stun a person for a moment. Scientists do not understand exactly how the electric organs in this fish become charged.

Scientific classification. The torpedo belongs to the electric ray family, Torpedinidae. The Atlantic Coast torpedo, also called the *crampfish,* is *Torpedo nobiliana.* The Pacific Coast torpedo is *T. californica.*   Leonard P. Schultz

Torpedo boat. See **PT boat; Torpedo.**

Torque, *tawrk,* is the amount of twisting effort that a force or forces exert on an object. The torque around any *axis* (reference line) is calculated by multiplying the force by the distance between the line of force and the axis. The torque increases as the force moves farther from the axis. For this reason, a wheel turns more easily when the force is applied farther from the center. In the English system of measurement, torque is measured in pound feet.   James D. Chalupnik

See also **Force; Lever.**

Torquemada, *tawr kay MAH dah,* **Tomás de,** *toh MAHS day* (1420-1498), a Roman Catholic priest, was *inquisitor-general* (chief official) of the Spanish Inquisition for 15 years. During that time, 2,000 people were executed by the Inquisition for *heresy* (beliefs contrary to those of the church).

Torquemada used the Inquisition for both religious and political reasons. He believed punishment of Christian heretics, and non-Christians—chiefly Jews and Muslims—was the only way to achieve political unity in Spain. He was partly responsible for the royal edict of 1492 that expelled 200,000 Jews from Spain. Many people admired him, but feared his power. King Ferdinand and Queen Isabella of Spain were among his supporters.

Torquemada was born in Valladolid. He became a friar in the Dominican monastery there, and later was prior of the monastery of Santa Cruz, at Segovia, for 22 years. He served as confessor to Isabella after she became queen of Spain. Torquemada became assistant to the inquisitors in 1482, and inquisitor-general for most Spanish lands in 1483. He laid down rules of procedure and established branches of the Inquisition in various cities. He retired to a Dominican monastery at Avila in 1496, but continued to direct the Inquisition until his death.   Raymond H. Schmandt

See also **Inquisition.**

Torrens, Lake. See **Lake Torrens.**

Torrens system, *TAWR uhnz* or *TAHR uhnz,* is a system of registering titles to real estate. It is named for Sir Robert Torrens, who introduced it in South Australia in 1858. It has not been widely used in the United States. But nations of the British Commonwealth and Europe have adopted it. The purpose of the system is to make the transfer of real property as simple and safe as the transfer of other property, and to end repeated examination of titles.

A bureau or court of registration, supervised by a registrar, operates the system. An examiner of titles usually works with the registrar. The system substitutes public registration for *conveyancing* (transferring property by deeds and other written documents).

Under the Torrens system, the owner of a piece of land files a petition with the registrar to have the land registered. Searchers make a full inquiry into the title. If they find no flaw, the registrar issues a certificate of title, which a court cannot set aside or overcome. Thereafter, the certificate will always show the state of the title and the person who holds it. Any claim or other legal restriction on the property is listed on the certificate. If someone later has a just claim against the property, an insurance fund pays the person. Registration fees maintain the fund.

In the United States, the first Torrens Act was passed by the legislature of Illinois in 1897. From time to time, other states in the nation have adopted the system. Since each state has its own system of registering titles, the Torrens acts vary. Few states use this system today.

In Canada. In 1861, Vancouver Island adopted a system of land registration based upon the Torrens system. When Vancouver became a part of British Columbia, in 1866, the entire province continued the system. The provinces of Alberta, Manitoba, Nova Scotia, Ontario, and Saskatchewan also use the Torrens title system.

Linda Henry Elrod

Torricelli, *TAWR ih CHEHL ee,* **Evangelista,** *eh VAHN jeh LEE stah* (1608-1647), was an Italian mathematician and physicist. He became known for his discovery of the principle of the barometer in 1643. He also improved the microscope and telescope. Torricelli wrote *Opera Geometrica* (1644). He was born in Faenza. See also **Barometer; Hydraulics** (Laws of hydrodynamics).

Carl T. Chase

Torsion balance, *TAWR shuhn,* is a device for measuring small forces of push or pull. A torsion balance sets an unknown force against the resistance to axial twist in a wire or fiber of small diameter, measuring the twist.

In practice, a torsion balance consists of a fine strand of quartz or sometimes a fine wire of steel or gold. This wire is mounted on a holding mechanism that can be rotated in a horizontal plane, to bring the torsion balance to its zero setting. Suspended from the lower end of the fiber is a horizontal pendulum arm. Each end of the arm carries a ball of a heavy substance that resists corrosion, generally gold, lead, or stainless steel. When the force to be measured is permitted to act on these balls, they swing about, twisting the fiber. A tiny mirror mounted at the junction of fiber and pendulum reflects a beam of light. By noting how much this reflection moves from zero as the force acts, one measures the amount of force in dynes or other convenient units. It is necessary to calibrate the instrument first by twisting it with known forces. These tests must be repeated often, because molecular changes in the fiber may occur.

James D. Chalupnik

Torsion bar suspension, *TAWR shuhn,* is a method of absorbing the shock, or energy, that results when an automobile travels over uneven road surfaces and bumps. When a car with coil springs strikes a bump, the coils press closer together and absorb the energy. In torsion suspension, a torsion bar replaces the coils in the front end of the car. A torsion bar is actually a coiled spring that has been straightened. Whereas a spring presses together to absorb energy, a torsion bar is subjected to *torsion* (twisting).

A torsion bar consists of a steel rod attached to an arm from the front wheel. When the car strikes a bump, the torsion bar twists to absorb the energy. Torsion bars take up less room than coil springs.   William H. Haverdink

See also **Automobile** (The suspension system); **Shock absorber; Spring** (metal).

Tort is a harmful act against a person that gives the person the right to collect money to pay for damage he or she has suffered. The branch of law that deals with such offenses is called *tort law.* Tort law is concerned mainly with injuries to your person, your reputation, and your property or business. For example, if someone harms your reputation by making false statements about you, you have a right to be paid for damages caused you. Other torts include someone's trespassing on your land or using your idea for a movie script. Most dam-

How torsion bar suspension works

Torsion bars are used in some cars instead of coil springs to help absorb shocks. One end of the torsion bar is attached to an arm connected to the wheel. The other end is attached to the car's frame. When the wheel hits a bump, the bar twists to absorb the jar, *upper right.* It then untwists, *lower right,* to help hold the wheel on the road and keep the car level.

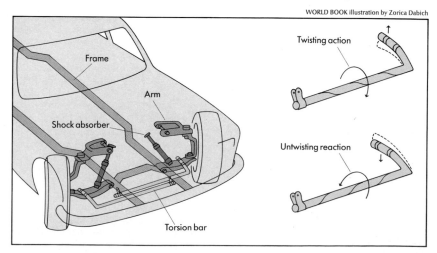

WORLD BOOK illustration by Zorica Dabich

Frame

Arm

Shock absorber

Twisting action

Untwisting reaction

Torsion bar

ages that result from a failure to keep a promise or to perform a contract are covered under a branch of law called *contract law.*

A tort may take place even though one person does not intend to harm another person. Many tort cases today result from injuries and damage in automobile accidents. The careful use of dynamite may be a tort if someone is injured by the explosion. Also, a tort may be committed by a corporation as well as by a person.

A tort may also be a crime. If someone punches you in the nose, you can be paid for the injury. The state may also punish the person for breaking a criminal law. In tort law, the injured party normally is an individual who sues to recover damages for the harm done. In criminal law, the injured party is the government, which takes legal action to punish the wrongdoer for a crime against the public.   Harry Kalven, Jr.

Related articles in *World Book* include:

Assault and battery	Libel	Slander
Damages	Negligence	Trespass

Tortilla. See Mexico (Food; picture: Corn is the chief food); Aztec (Food).

Tortoise is a turtle that lives only on land. Tortoises have stumpy hind legs that look like those of an ele-

Erwin and Peggy Bauer, Bruce Coleman Ltd.

The tortoise has stumpy, clublike legs and feet. When threatened, this turtle seeks safety inside its high, domed shell.

phant, quite different from the flippers and webbed feet of aquatic turtles. They eat plants, and some have lived more than a hundred years. In the United States, tortoises live in the deserts of the Southwest, in dry areas of the Southeast, and in southern Texas. At night and during the winter, they remain in holes that they dig.

The *desert tortoise* lives in parts of California, Nevada, Utah, Arizona, and Mexico. The *Texas tortoise* ranges from San Antonio into Mexico. The *gopher tortoise* lives in the Southeastern States.

Scientific classification. Tortoises belong to the class Reptilia, order Testudinata, family Testudinidae. The desert tortoise is *Scaptochelys agassizi;* the Texas tortoise, *S. berlandieri;* and the gopher tortoise, *Gopherus polyphemus.*   Laurie J. Vitt

See also Turtle; Animal (picture).

Tortoise shell. See Turtle (Turtles and human beings).

Tortugas. See Dry Tortugas.

Torture is the use of physical pain to make persons confess something or to punish them. Great cleverness

has been shown in the invention of instruments of torture such as the thumbscrew, scourge, and rack.

Some primitive peoples tortured their captives, but the most elaborate methods of torture were developed by civilized nations in Europe and Asia. The church and the state used torture in the Middle Ages. They made prisoners suffer terrible pain so that they would give information or change their religious beliefs. Savonarola and John Hus were both tortured before they were killed. Torture was a favorite method of the Inquisition in Spain. In colonial America, torture was practiced during witchcraft trials in Salem, Mass.

In the 1500's, public opinion began to turn against the use of torture. A papal bull in 1816 forbade the practice in Catholic countries. The Fascist governments of the 1900's revived its use on a large scale. In World War II, the Japanese and Germans tortured war prisoners and civilians. During the Korean War, Communist forces used an emotional and mental reconditioning process called *brainwashing.* Many view brainwashing as a modern form of torture.   Marvin E. Wolfgang

See also **Brainwashing; Pillory; Rack; Stocks.**

Tory Party was a conservative political party in Great Britain. The term came from a Gaelic word meaning *pursued* or *pursued man,* and was used in the mid-1600's to mean an Irish outlaw. The word was first used in English politics in 1679 to refer to those who wanted James, Duke of York, to succeed to the throne.

Eventually, the Tory Party became one of the two chief political parties in Great Britain. The Tories favored maintaining the legal privileges of the Church of England and the powers of the king. Their chief opponents, the Whigs, wanted to increase the power of the people in the House of Commons. After 1832, the name *Conservative* began to replace *Tory.*

During the American Revolutionary War, those colonists who remained loyal to King George III were called Tories.   James L. Godfrey

See also **Conservative Party; Liberal Party.**

Toscanelli, Paolo. See Columbus, Christopher (What Columbus wanted to do).

Toscanini, *TAHS kuh NEE nee,* **Arturo,** *ahr TOOR oh* (1867-1957), was perhaps the most influential symphony orchestra and opera conductor of his time. When Toscanini began his career, standards of musical performance were set by conductors and musicians of the romantic school. The romantics regarded music as a means for expressing their own emotions, ideas, and performance skills. But Toscanini regarded the performer as the servant of the composer. He insisted that an analytic study of the music should form the basis of a performance. In this way, the composer's intentions could best be understood and would dominate the performance. Toscanini's approach became widely accepted in the 1900's.

As a young conductor, Toscanini emphasized the music of Italian composers of his day and the works

Wide World

Arturo Toscanini

of such internationally known modern composers as Claude Debussy and Richard Wagner. In later years, his performances stressed the established music of the 1700's and 1800's. Toscanini was especially respected as an interpreter of the works of the composers Ludwig van Beethoven and Giuseppe Verdi.

Toscanini was born in Parma, Italy. He attended the local music conservatory, where he studied cello and piano. Toscanini began his conducting career at the age of 19, when he led a performance of Verdi's opera *Aida* with a traveling Italian opera company in Rio de Janeiro, Brazil. His reputation increased rapidly. In 1898, he became artistic director of La Scala, Milan, the most important opera house in Italy.

Toscanini's American career began in 1908 when he became a conductor of the Metropolitan Opera. He left that position in 1915. From 1921 to 1929, he again was artistic director at La Scala. Toscanini's hatred of Italy's Fascist government led him to return to the United States. From 1929 to 1936, he was principal conductor of the New York Philharmonic Orchestra. From 1937 to 1954, Toscanini directed the National Broadcasting Company Symphony Orchestra, which NBC formed especially for him. He retired at the age of 87.   Robert C. Marsh

Totalitarianism, *toh* TAL *uh* TAIR *ee uh* NIHZ *uhm,* is a form of government in which the state has absolute control over almost every aspect of people's lives. The individual is considered a servant of the state and is allowed almost no freedom of choice or expression.

A totalitarian government is ruled by one political party headed by, in most cases, a dictator. The party sets certain economic and social goals for the state, and it outlaws any activity that could interfere with the achievement of these goals. Most totalitarian governments prohibit such groups as labor unions and trade associations. Religious practices are forbidden unless they promote the policies of the state.

Under a totalitarian system, the government uses terror tactics to suppress individuals or groups who oppose the state. These tactics are carried out by a secret police force and the armed services. The government also uses censorship to silence anyone who criticizes its policies. The media spread government propaganda, and the schools teach absolute loyalty to the state.

A totalitarian government controls the nation's economy through ownership or management of farmland and industry. Thus, it determines the type and quantity of crops and goods that are produced.

Various totalitarian governments have developed throughout history. In the 1920's and 1930's, however, technological advances in communication and detection systems aided the rise of extreme types of totalitarianism. Totalitarian governments of that period included those of Fascist Italy under Benito Mussolini, Nazi Germany under Adolf Hitler, and Communist Russia under Joseph Stalin. Today, many governments have some totalitarian policies. These governments are especially common in developing nations that are working to build their economies.   Michael Hurst

See also **Communism; Fascism; Government** (Totalitarianism).

Additional resources

Archer, Jules. *Police State: Could It Happen Here?* Harper, 1977.

Arendt, Hannah. *The Origins of Totalitarianism.* Harcourt, 1966. Originally published in 1951.
Buchheim, Hans. *Totalitarian Rule: Its Nature and Characteristics.* Trans. by Ruth Hein. Wesleyan, 1968.
Curtis, Michael. *Totalitarianism.* Transaction, 1979.

Totem, *TOH tuhm,* is a symbol for a tribe, clan, or family. The Chippewa, or Ojibwa, Indians first used the term

Government of British Columbia

Totem poles, such as the ones pictured above, were wood carvings made by the Indians of the Northwest Coast.

for the animals or birds associated with their clans. The clan totem may be a bird, fish, animal, plant, or other natural object. Some groups consider the totem as an ancestor of the clan. A clan may have rules against killing or eating the species to which the totem belongs. Clan members are often known by the name of the totem. Some clans consider the totem holy and pray to it. Totemism, as a form of religion, may have been widespread among American Indians and black Africans.

Many American Indian tribes, particularly those of the Pacific Northwest, carved the family and clan emblems on totem poles. The tribe held a *potlatch,* or feast, when the totem poles were put up.

Totem poles may be seen in Vancouver and Victoria, B.C.; Seattle, Wash.; in the Field Museum of Natural History in Chicago; and in the American Museum of Natural History in New York City.   Michael D. Green

See also **British Columbia** (pictures); **Alaska** (picture).

Additional resources

Brindze, Ruth. *Story of the Totem Pole.* Vanguard, 1951. For younger readers.
Keithahn, Edward L. *Monuments in Cedar.* Rev. ed. Superior, 1963.
Smyly, John and Carolyn. *The Totem Poles of Skedans.* Univ. of Washington Press, 1976.
Wherry, Joseph H. *The Totem Pole Indians.* Funk, 1964.

Toucan, *TOO kan* or *too KAHN,* is an unusual-looking bird with an enormous and, in most species, brilliantly colored bill. Toucans live in the tropical and subtropical forests of Central and South America.

The bill of a toucan may be black, blue, brown, green, red, white, yellow, or a combination of colors. Toucans probably use their colorful bill to attract their mates. The toucan's huge bill looks heavy, but it actually weighs little because it contains a number of air pockets.

There are about 40 kinds of toucans. The largest species, the *toco toucan,* measures about 25 inches (64 centimeters) long. The smallest toucans, called *aracaris* and *toucanets,* grow 13 to 14 inches (33 to 36 centimeters) long. Toucans have a bristly, narrow tongue that resembles a feather. They feed mainly on various small fruits. They sometimes use their bill, which has sawlike edges, to tear off pieces of larger fruits as well.

Most toucans live in small flocks that sleep in hollow trees. When toucans sleep, they turn their head around and place their bill down the center of their back. Then they fold their tail over their head.

Most kinds of toucans mate once a year. They build a nest in a hollow tree, and the female lays from two to four white eggs. The parents take turns sitting on the eggs. The eggs hatch after about 15 days, and the parents care for the young in the nest for about 8 weeks.

Scientific classification. Toucans belong to the toucan family, Ramphastidae. The toco toucan is *Ramphastos toco.*

James M. Dolan, Jr.

Touch is the sense which gives us notice of contact with an object. It is also called the *tactile sense.* We learn the shape and hardness of objects through this sense. Touching an object can give rise to feelings of warmth, cold, pain, and pressure. Free nerve endings in the tissue give the sense of pain. Touch, warmth, cold, and pain are also called *cutaneous senses.*

Touch was formerly considered one of the five special, or exterior, senses. Now it is considered a common, or general, sense because the touch organs are found all over the body.

Kinds of touch organs. There are several kinds of touch organs, called *tactile corpuscles,* in the skin and mucous membranes. One kind is found near hairs, another in hairless areas, and still another kind in deeper tissues. The sensation occurs when an object comes in contact with the sense organs and presses them out of shape, or touches a nearby hair. Nerves from the organs then carry nerve impulses to the brain.

Touch is more sensitive in some parts of the body than in others. This difference is due to the fact that the end organs for touch are not scattered evenly over the body, but are arranged in clusters. The feeling of pressure is keenest where there are the greatest number of end organs. It is most highly developed on the tip of the tongue, and is poorest on the back of the shoulders. The tips of the fingers and the end of the nose are other sensitive areas.

Measurement. Scientists can easily measure keenness of touch with the *esthesiometer.* This instrument looks like a drawing compass with two needle points. The tip of the tongue can feel both points when they are only 1.1 millimeters apart—about $\frac{1}{25}$ inch. Less-sensitive areas feel only one point at this distance. The back of the shoulders feels the two points as a single one until they are 66 millimeters apart—about 2.6 inches.

The end organs for warmth, cold, and pain are also

Emerald toucanet
Aulacorhynchus prasinus
Found from Mexico to Peru
(Body length 14 inches, or 36 centimeters)

Toco toucan
Ramphastos toco
Found in Guianas and Brazil
(Body length 25 inches, or 64 centimeters)

WORLD BOOK illustrations by Albert Gilbert

Green aracari
Pteroglossus viridis
Found from Colombia through Brazil
(Body length 13 inches, or 33 centimeters)

distributed unevenly. This can be discovered by running a pointed metal instrument over the skin. The instrument is colder than the skin, but it feels cold only at some points. At other points it is simply felt as pressure. Many objects act on several senses at once. For example, a hot iron that touches a person's skin would cause the sensations of pain, heat, and touch.

Scientists know there are several million points on the body that register either cold, heat, pain, or touch. It is possible to map these points for the four cutaneous senses on any area of skin.   W. B. Youmans

See also **Pain; Insect** (Touch).

Touch football. See Football (introduction).

Touch-me-not is a yellow wild flower which grows in low, damp land in the eastern and central parts of the United States. Its ruffle-edged petals spread downward from the stem, somewhat like an orchid. Behind the blossom and growing from the base of the petals is a long spur in the form of a hollow tube. It curves inward on the spotted touch-me-not, but spreads outward on the pale touch-me-not. The plant is probably named *touch-me-not* because its seed pods fly open at the slightest touch.

Scientific classification. The touch-me-not belongs to the balsam family, Balsaminaceae. It is genus *Impatiens.* The spotted touch-me-not is *I. biflora;* the pale touch-me-not is *I. pallida.*

Marcus Maxon

See also **Flower** (picture: Flowers of woodlands and forests).

Toulon, *too LAWN* (pop. 179,423; met. area pop. 410,393), is a seaport city on the southeast coast of France. For location, see **France** (political map). Excellent docks along Toulon's coast can accommodate large ships. Toulon is the site of France's second largest naval base, after Brest. It is also the capital of the Var *department* (administrative district).

Toulon's landmarks include Ste. Marie-Majeure, and other old churches; and the Poissonnerie (fish market), which dates from the 1500's. Toulon's main industries include shipbuilding and the production of chemicals and electric machinery.

Roman soldiers established a colony on the site of what is now Toulon in the 100's B.C. In 1942, during World War II, the French Navy destroyed many of its own ships in the Toulon harbor to prevent the ships from being captured by the Germans.   Mark Kesselman

Toulon, Siege of. See Napoleon I (Early years).

Toulouse, *too LOOZ* (pop. 347,995; met. area pop. 541,271), is a city in southwestern France. It lies along the Garonne River. For location, see **France** (political map). Toulouse has many medieval buildings, including the Romanesque Church of St. Sernin and the Gothic Cathedral of St. Etienne. The University of Toulouse, founded in 1229, is the second oldest in France, after the University of Paris. The city is the site of the tomb of the medieval philosopher and theologian Saint Thomas Aquinas.

Toulouse serves as the capital of the Midi-Pyrénées region and the Haute-Garonne *department* (administrative district). It is also the center of the French aircraft construction industry. Other economic activities include electronics, printing, food processing, and the manufacture of chemicals.

Roman soldiers established a settlement on the site of

what is now Toulouse in the 100's B.C. During the Middle Ages, the city served as an artistic and literary center of Europe.   Mark Kesselman

Toulouse-Lautrec, *too LOOZ loh TREHK,* **Henri de,** *ahn REE duh* (1864-1901), was a French painter who also became known for his lithographs and posters. He won fame for his lively pictures of Paris night life and the Paris underworld.

Essentially, Toulouse-Lautrec's paintings are superb line drawings. He was a skilled draftsman and worked hard to give his pictures the appearance of sketches done with little effort. His work shows the influence of Japanese prints and impressionist paintings, especially the works of Edgar Degas (see **Impressionism**). A detail of a water color, *Trapeze Artist at the Medrano Circus,* by Toulouse-Lautrec is reproduced in color in the **Painting** article.

Toulouse-Lautrec lived among the dance halls, nightclubs, restaurants, and theaters of Montmartre, the Paris entertainment district. He immortalized many entertainers, including Jane Avril, May Belfort, Chocolate, La Goulue, and Yvette Guilbert. He portrayed them at work, catching each in a characteristic gesture and then exaggerating it.

Toulouse-Lautrec was born in Albi and moved to Paris with his parents in 1873. When he was 14 years old, he broke both legs in separate accidents. His legs healed but stopped growing, though the rest of his body matured normally. Toulouse-Lautrec's deformed, dwarfish appearance made him extremely sensitive. He sought the company of outcasts and rejects, including prostitutes. But when he painted them, he was neither sentimental nor critical. A museum in Albi has a collection of works by Toulouse-Lautrec.   Robert F. Reiff

See also **Poster** (picture).

Toupee. See Wig.

Touraco, *TUR uh KOH,* or *turaco,* is any member of a family of African birds that live south of the Sahara.

Anthony Mercieca, NAS

The red-crested touraco and many other forest species of touracos have brightly colored feathers and long tails.

Toulouse-Lautrec's works portray night life in the cafes and music halls of the Paris district called Montmartre. The artist became particularly noted for his skill in capturing the gaiety of the district.

At the Moulin Rouge (1892), an oil painting on canvas; The Art Institute of Chicago

These birds measure from 15 to 30 inches (38 to 76 centimeters) long. Many of them have bright green, red, and violet-blue feathers. Touracos are the only birds that produce a green *pigment* (coloring matter) in their feathers. The green color in other birds results from the reflection of sunlight by the feathers.

Scientists classify touracos into four groups: (1) crested touracos, (2) go-away birds, (3) great blue touracos, and (4) violet plantain-eaters. Most touracos live in pairs or small groups in thick forests, but go-away birds live in dry, open areas.

Touracos are weak fliers. They climb and run along tree branches somewhat as squirrels do. Touracos eat fruits and insects and nest chiefly in trees. The females lay two or three white or greenish eggs.

Scientific classification. Touracos make up the touraco family, Musophagidae. The family has 4 genera and about 19 species.   James M. Dolan, Jr.

Touré, *too RAY,* **Sékou,** *SAY koo* (1922-1984), became Guinea's first president in 1958 and held that position until his death. Touré maintained Guinea's neutrality in international politics. He supported independence movements in Africa and worked to strengthen ties among African nations. Touré rose in politics as a trade union leader in French Guinea, then a French territory. He led French Guinea to independence in 1958. Touré was born in Faranah.   Immanuel Wallerstein

Tourette syndrome, *tu REHT SIHN drohm,* is a disorder of the central nervous system characterized by involuntary utterances and body movements. It tends to run in families and affects three times as many men as women. It was named for Georges Gilles de la Tourette, a French doctor who described the symptoms in 1885.

The symptoms of Tourette syndrome begin between the ages of 2 and 15, usually at age 7. In most cases, the first symptom is an involuntary eye blink. Most patients soon develop other *tics* (involuntary muscle twitches), which may affect the face, neck, shoulders, trunk, or limbs. Patients also begin to make uncontrollable sounds. They may bark, grunt, repeatedly clear their throats, or speak unintelligibly—in many cases, using vulgar words. Some patients also have short attention spans and are hyperactive. The number and severity of a patient's symptoms tend to rise and fall. Although the disorder is not psychological, some patients develop emotional problems trying to deal with it.

Researchers suspect that Tourette syndrome results from an abnormality in the *neurotransmitters,* the chemicals that carry signals between nerve cells. There is no cure for Tourette syndrome, but certain drugs can help relieve the symptoms. Early diagnosis and treatment can help prevent the development of emotional problems.

Elaine Shapiro and Arthur K. Shapiro

Tourmaline, *TUR muh lihn* or *TUR muh leen,* is a mineral commonly found in rocks called *granitic pegmatites.* Tourmaline is slightly harder than quartz, and it wears well as a gemstone. The chemistry of tourmaline is extremely complex. The mineral consists of various elements combined with boron and silicon.

The word *tourmaline,* though widely used as a gem name, actually refers to at least six mineral species. Most of the gemstones in the tourmaline group are cut from the minerals *elbaite* and *liddicoatite.*

The minerals in the tourmaline group display the broadest range of colors of all gemstones. Tourmalines range from *achroite* (colorless) to *schorl* (black), and various shades and combinations of red, pink, green, blue, violet, yellow, and brown are known. Blue and violet tourmalines are called *indicolite*. Tourmaline crystals may also be *color-zoned* along their length to form *bicolor stones*. Bicolor stones have a different color at each end. For example, some have green at one end and red at the other. *Watermelon tourmalines* are color-zoned from the center outward and so may have a red center and green outer rim. The change in color may be very sharp and dramatic.

Tourmaline has several unusual properties. For example, it becomes electrically charged when subjected to changes in heat or pressure. As a result, it is used in various kinds of electrical instruments. Tourmaline also has a property called *pleochroism* or *dichroism*—that is, tourmaline crystals show a darker color when viewed lengthwise than at right angles.

Tourmalines are found in many parts of the world, including Brazil, Madagascar, southern Africa, and south-central Asia. In the United States, fine stones have come from Maine and California.   Robert I. Gait

See also **Gem** (picture); **Polarized light**.

Tournament. See **Knights and knighthood** (Tournaments).

Tourniquet, *TUR nuh keht,* is the name for a device used to check bleeding in a wound, or to stop the flow of blood during an amputation. In an emergency, a tourniquet can be made from a stocking, handkerchief, triangular bandage or other piece of cloth, and a short stick. It should be used only when a bleeding wound threatens a person's life, and when the bleeding cannot be controlled by another method (see **First aid**).

To apply a tourniquet, place a firm pad over the artery that supplies the wound and tie the tourniquet over the pad. Tie the cloth loosely around the limb, close to the wound but between the wound and the body. Then slip a short stick under the cloth and twist the stick, tightening the tourniquet, until the bleeding is checked. Only a doctor should remove a tourniquet, because the doctor can check the bleeding by other means. Also, a note stating the time the tourniquet was applied should be tied to the patient.   Benjamin F. Miller

Tours, *toor* (pop. 132,209; met. area pop. 262,786), is a historic city and important economic center in western France. It lies in the scenic Loire Valley, along the Loire and Cher rivers (see **France** [political map]).

The area around Tours has many old castles. The city's landmarks include the ruins of the Old Basilica of Saint Martin, completed about 470; and the Cathedral of Saint Gatien, which dates from the 1200's. Tours is the capital of the *department* (administrative district) of Indre-et-Loire. The city's industries include banking, insurance, and the production of electric equipment, farm machinery, machine tools, medicines, and wine.

Roman soldiers founded the town of Caesarodunum on the site of what is now Tours in the 50's B.C. In A.D. 732, the Christian Franks, a European people, defeated invading Muslim armies in a great battle that began near Tours and ended near Poitiers (see **Army** [Famous land battles]). During World War II (1939-1945), German bombers heavily damaged parts of Tours. These areas were soon rebuilt.   Mark Kesselman

Toussaint L'Ouverture, *too SAN loo vair TOOR* (1743-1803), Pierre Dominique Toussaint-Bréda, was a black revolutionist and general who became ruler of Haiti. His parents were black slaves. He was a slave himself until he was almost 50 years old. His name, L'Ouverture (The Opening), was taken from a remark by the French governor of Haiti, that "this man finds an opening everywhere," referring to his ability to break through enemy lines.

After the news of the Revolution in France reached the French colony of Haiti, various uprisings took place. A slave revolt broke out in 1791, in which Toussaint soon became a leader. The black army first fought against France. But in 1793 the National Convention in France proclaimed freedom for all the slaves. Toussaint then came to the aid of the French against the Spanish and the British, who were fighting the French in Haiti.

In 1799, a civil war broke out between the blacks and the *mulattoes* (people of mixed black and white parentage). Toussaint, as leader of the blacks, became ruler of the island. Haiti prospered under his rule.

In 1802, Napoleon signed the Peace of Amiens, which freed his hands in Europe. He decided to subdue Haiti, and announced the reestablishment of slavery. Toussaint resisted, and Napoleon sent an expedition against him. Toussaint was captured. But he was freed on condition that he would not work against the French again. He was later caught in a plot against the French and taken to France. Toussaint died in prison.   Donald E. Worcester

Consulate of Haiti

Toussaint L'Ouverture

Additional resources

Parkinson, Wenda. *'This Gilden African': Toussaint L'Ouverture*. Horizon Press, 1979. A biography.
Syme, Ronald. *Toussaint: The Black Liberator*. Morrow, 1971. For younger readers.

Towboat. See **Tugboat**.

Tower is an architectural structure whose height is much greater than its width or its thickness. Towers are generally taller than their surrounding structures. They may stand alone or be attached to walls or buildings. The first towers were for military or religious purposes, but over the centuries towers have assumed other uses.

Towers were rare in ancient times. One of the most famous early towers was the Lighthouse of Alexandria, Egypt, built during the reign of Ptolemy II (283-246 B.C.). During the Middle Ages in Europe, people erected masonry towers along the walls of castles and cities for military defense. The Tower of London is a prominent example of this type of structure. In the late Middle Ages, many European cities built tall slender bell towers on their city halls. They also served as watchtowers.

Towers are important in religious architecture. People who worshiped the sun and stars built towers so that their priests could be closer to the heavens. Buddhists build towers called *pagodas*. A crier calls Muslims to prayer from a tower called a *minaret*. In the 500's, Christians began to build free-standing bell towers beside their churches. These are called *campaniles,* from the Italian word for *bell.* After about 1000, Christians built steeples and other towers attached to the church itself.

Today, skyscrapers are often called towers. Towns use water towers to create the pressure needed to pipe water to homes and businesses. Broadcasting towers support radio or TV antennas. The world's tallest self-supporting structure is the CN (Canadian National) Tower in Toronto, Ont. This 1,815-foot (553-meter) broadcasting tower was completed in 1976.

William J. Hennessey

Related articles in *World Book.* See pictures with the **Architecture** article. See also:

Campanile
Eiffel Tower
Leaning Tower of Pisa
Lighthouse
Minaret
Pagoda

Seven Wonders of the Ancient World (The Lighthouse of Alexandria)
Singing Tower
Tower of London

Tower of Babel, *BAY buhl* or *BAB uhl,* was a tower in Babylon, a city in ancient Mesopotamia. It was shaped like a pyramid with terraces—a design known as a *ziggurat.* The tower had seven stories plus a small shrine on top. The Babylonians called the tower *Etemenanki,* which meant *the house of the foundation of heaven and earth. Babel* is the Hebrew name for *Babylon. Babylon* meant *gate of the god* in the Babylonian language.

Scholars know little about the tower. But a story of its construction is told in the Bible, in Genesis 11: 1-9. According to the Bible, Noah's descendants settled in southern Mesopotamia after the great Flood. They started to build a great city, including a tower that would reach to heaven. But God did not want the city completed, so He made the builders speak different languages. The builders then could not understand one another, and so they stopped working and scattered over the earth. The ancient Hebrews used this account to explain the origin of languages. John A. Brinkman

See also **Babylon.**

Tower of London is a group of stone buildings in the East End of London. It includes an ancient fortress, a dark prison, and a former royal residence. It stands on the north bank of the Thames River.

A shallow *moat* (ditch) and a high stone wall surround this group of buildings. The buildings have great thick walls. The structure is so strong that in former days it could have held off a whole army. The British War Department now uses the buildings chiefly as a showplace and museum. The armor collection in the museum was started by Henry VIII in the 1500's.

Many famous people were imprisoned in the tower's damp, dark cells. Lady Jane Grey came up through the Traitor's Gate on the Thames to be beheaded. The young Edward V and his brother, the Duke of York, were put in the tower after their uncle, Richard III, became king in 1483. The boys were never heard of again. Sir Roger Casement, a leader of the Irish Rebellion of 1916, was imprisoned in the tower until his execution.

The Tower of London also houses the royal jewel office. Here the crowns, scepters, and other glittering royal treasures of the English rulers, known as the *regalia,* are closely guarded. Tower of London guards are called *Yeomen Warders* (see **Yeoman**). Talbot Hamlin

See also **London** (picture).

Towhee, *TOH hee* or *TOW hee,* is any of several small North American birds related to the sparrows. The rufous-sided towhee, the most widespread species, lives in much of North America, from southern Canada to Mexico. This bird is about 8 inches (20 centimeters) long. Its sides are a chestnut color. Its belly is white. The head and back are black in males and brown in females. Rufous-sided towhees that live in western North America have white bars on their wings and white spots on their back.

The rufous-sided towhee makes its home in open woods and bushy fields. It usually builds its nest on the ground, using dead leaves and twigs. There, the female lays two to six whitish eggs with brown speckles. The birds scratch among leaves and grass, searching for insects, spiders, earthworms, berries, and seeds.

Three other species of towhees—Abert's towhee, the

Bettmann Archive

The Tower of Babel was a terraced pyramid, called a *ziggurat,* in the ancient city of Babylon. The Flemish artist Pieter Bruegel the Elder painted this rendition of the tower in 1563.

WORLD BOOK illustration by Trevor Boyer, Linden Artists Ltd.

The rufous-sided towhee lives mainly on the ground.

brown towhee, and the green-tailed towhee—are found in the western United States. These birds resemble the rufous-sided towhee in size and habits.

Scientific classification. Towhees belong to the finch family, Fringillidae. The rufous-sided towhee is *Pipilo erythrophthalmus.* Herbert Friedmann

See also **Bird** (picture: Birds' eggs).

Town is a community of closely clustered dwellings and other buildings in which people live and work. It may be large or small. Most people in the United States and Canada use the word *town* to refer to a municipal unit which is larger than a village and smaller than a city. In New England, the town is the principal unit of local government, combining the roles of both city and county. This unit consists of one or more settlements and the surrounding rural area. Susan H. Ambler

Related articles in *World Book* include:

Boom town	Local government	Township
Borough	Town meeting	Village

Town crier was a person appointed to make public announcements. The town crier was important in Europe, particularly in England, before newspapers were common, and was the "walking newspaper" of the American Colonies during the 1600's. The crier sang out the latest news at every corner, and announced the time of town meetings and other events of public interest. The town crier largely disappeared when the printing press, newspaper, and other forms of communication came into general use after the 1750's. Today, some British communities have a town crier. Robert J. Taylor

Town meeting is held once a year by the voters of a town. The first town meetings were held in colonial days. Such a meeting is the purest form of democratic government known, because it is government by the people rather than by their elected representatives. Today, citizens 18 years of age or older may participate in town meetings. At the meetings, the township makes its decisions for the year to come. It passes ordinances, discusses improvements, levies taxes, and elects officers. The town clerk makes and keeps a record of the meeting. The officers run the town between meetings. The town system is a typical New England institution, but it has been adopted elsewhere. Susan H. Ambler

Town planning. See City planning.

Townes, Charles Hard (1915-   ), is a United States physicist. In 1951, he explained the basic principles that led to the development of the maser. A *maser* is a device that uses the energy of molecules or atoms to amplify radio waves. Townes helped build the first maser in 1953 (see **Maser**). In 1958, Townes and Arthur L. Schawlow proposed the *laser,* a device for amplifying light waves (see **Laser**). For his work, Townes shared the 1964 Nobel Prize in physics with two Soviet scientists who also developed and improved masers.

Townes was born in Greenville, S.C. He taught at Columbia University from 1948 to 1961, when he became a professor and provost at the Massachusetts Institute of Technology. In 1967, he became a professor at the University of California in Berkeley. R. T. Ellickson

See also **Basov, Nikolai; Prokhorov, Alexander.**

Townsend, *TOWN zuhnd,* **Willard Saxby** (1895-1957), was one of the first black American labor leaders. He improved the wages and working conditions of *redcaps* (railroad baggage porters). Townsend

helped redcaps gain a fixed salary, plus retirement and insurance benefits.

Townsend was born in Cincinnati, Ohio, and began working as a redcap there when he was 19 years old. In 1936, he was elected the first president of the Auxiliary of Redcaps, a union that belonged to the American Federation of Labor (AFL). In 1937, he became the first president of

© *Chicago Sun-Times*
Willard Townsend

an independent union, the International Brotherhood of Redcaps. It became the United Transport Service Employees in 1940 and joined the Congress of Industrial Organizations (CIO) in 1942. Also in 1942, he became the first black member of the CIO executive board. When the AFL and CIO merged in 1955, he was named a vice president of the AFL-CIO.

Townsend was a vice president of the Urban League and an officer of the National Association for the Advancement of Colored People (NAACP). He was coauthor of *What the Negro Wants* (1944). James G. Scoville

Townsend Plan, *TOWN zuhnd,* is an old-age pension plan proposed in 1934 by Dr. Francis E. Townsend of Long Beach, Calif. It provided that all U.S. citizens over 60 years of age be paid $200 a month. The funds were to come from a 2 per cent tax on the transfer or sale of goods. Supporters believed it would stabilize American prosperity, because those receiving pensions would be obligated to spend the money within a month. A modified version of the Townsend Plan was presented to the U.S. House of Representatives on June 1, 1939, but it was voted down. Robert J. Myers

Townshend, Peter. See Who, The.

Townshend, *TOWN zuhnd,* **Viscount** (1674-1738), pioneered in improving English agriculture. He retired to a Norfolk estate in 1730 after a successful political career. Townshend then introduced the turnip to English farms, for which he is known as "Turnip" Townshend. He practiced *marling* (fertilization) and *enclosure* (the use of fences). He showed the productivity of better cultivation in one of England's poorest farming districts. His given and family name was Charles Townshend. C. B. Baker

Townshend Acts. See Revolutionary War in America (The Townshend Acts).

Township in the United States is a division of a county. It may be entirely rural, or include cities or towns. A township's governing body is usually a board of commissioners, supervisors, or trustees. It can pass ordinances and resolutions that have the force of law in the township. Routine administration is generally handled by a township clerk. In New England, most townships are called *towns,* and have more elaborate powers. See also **Local government; Town.** H. F. Alderfer

Toxemia of pregnancy, *tahk SEE mee uh,* is a disease that attacks women during the later months of pregnancy or just after giving birth. It is also called *preeclampsia* (pronounced *pree eh KLAMP see uh*). The disease may result in the death of the mother, the fetus, or both. Its cause is unknown.

Toxemia occurs in about 5 per cent of all pregnancies. It usually strikes in the final month of pregnancy. The disease is characterized by a rise in blood pressure, excessive protein in the urine, and body swelling. Unless treated, toxemia may progress to *eclampsia,* a life-threatening condition in which the victim suffers convulsions. Eclampsia is usually preceded by such symptoms as headache, severe pain over the liver, and extremely high blood pressure. But convulsions may appear without warning. The victim may also suffer other major complications, including loss of kidney function, liver disease, and *cerebral hemorrhage* (bleeding in the brain). Deaths from toxemia most often occur in developing countries. In developed countries, early diagnosis and treatment usually prevent severe cases.

Toxemia affects the fetus by restricting circulation of the mother's blood to the *placenta,* the organ that provides the fetus with food and nourishment. As a result, the fetus may not develop normally and it may die.

Treatment of toxemia consists of hospitalizing the victim and controlling her blood pressure. If symptoms of eclampsia appear, doctors administer drugs to prevent convulsions. They also end the pregnancy, either by removing the fetus surgically or by using drugs to bring about early delivery. After the pregnancy ends, the victim usually recovers rapidly.   Marshall D. Lindheimer

Toxic shock syndrome, *SIHN drohm,* or *TSS,* is a rare disease that most frequently occurs in young women who are having a menstrual period. It can, however, strike men and women of any age. Symptoms include a high temperature, vomiting, diarrhea, low blood pressure, and a sunburnlike rash.

TSS is caused by a bacterium called *Staphylococcus aureus,* which can produce infection anywhere on or inside the body. Scientists do not understand exactly how these infections cause TSS. They suspect the bacteria release a *toxin* (poison) that spreads through the body, probably by way of the bloodstream, and causes TSS.

Fewer than one-thousandth of 1 per cent of all menstruating women are likely to develop TSS each year. Most victims are teen-agers and women in their twenties who use a *tampon*—a roll of absorbent material inserted into the vagina—during the menstrual period. Physicians do not know why women who wear tampons run a greater risk of developing TSS than those who wear sanitary napkins. Public health doctors have not advised women to stop using tampons, but they do recommend that tampon-users recognize the symptoms of TSS. A woman who develops symptoms should remove the tampon and call a doctor immediately.

Physicians treat TSS with antibiotics and with fluids given through a vein. A female patient not treated with antibiotics may become ill again during her next menstrual period. Most patients recover and have no further problems. But some lose their hair, fingernails, or toenails about three months after developing TSS. About 4 per cent of TSS cases are fatal.   Kathryn N. Shands

Toxic wastes. See Hazardous wastes.

Toxin, *TAHK suhn,* is a poison produced by a living organism. Toxins may cause many diseases and even death. Some toxins remain inside the organism that produces them. They are called *endotoxins.* They cause poisoning only when the organism is broken up and the poison escapes. Other toxins, called *exotoxins,* are se-

creted into the substance surrounding the organism.

Bacteria (small organisms) that infect the human body may produce toxins that cause diphtheria, tetanus (lockjaw), gas gangrene, and scarlet fever. Some bacteria and fungi secrete toxins into the foods in which they grow. Such serious diseases as botulism, ergotism, and alimentary toxic aleukia may result if such food is eaten.

Some tropical fish produce toxins that remain in their bodies. These toxins do not harm the fish, but they can cause illness or death to a person who eats the fish. The venoms of poisonous snakes, spiders, and insects are toxins. Doctors prescribe *antitoxins* to fight toxins. Antitoxins are serums or substances formed in the body to neutralize a toxin.   Solomon Garb

See also **Serum; Antitoxin; Disease** (Bacterial diseases).

Toy is an object children can use as a plaything. Children throughout the world play with similar toys, such as balls, dolls, games, and puzzles. Since ancient times, toys have played an important role in children's lives. Some toys enable children to have fun while learning about the world around them. Games can help teach children to get along with others. Toys may also help them learn and develop special skills.

Manufacturers make thousands of different toys. A child plays with toys of increasing sophistication at each stage of his or her development. Toys can be divided into three main groups: (1) toys for infants, (2) toys for early childhood, and (3) toys for late childhood.

Toys for infants. An infant's first toys are often soft musical toys and *mobiles* (colorful, moving structures hung above a crib). These toys begin to stimulate vision and hearing. Later, when babies can hold or grasp toys on their own, they play with rattles, plastic blocks, and stuffed animals. Unbreakable mirrors help infants recognize themselves. As they begin to walk, youngsters like to play with push toys that help them balance. They also push themselves along with their feet on automobiles and other wheeled riding toys. Infants are mentally stimulated by simple puzzles and picture books.

Paul Robert Perry

Puzzles teach children patience and logic in putting things together. Some kinds, such as map puzzles that show countries and continents, also help young people obtain information.

David R. Frazier

Stacking blocks of various shapes helps this child learn to balance objects and to make many kinds of structures. Youngsters like to use their imagination to arrange blocks in creative ways.

Toys for early childhood. After children learn to walk and run, they become more interested in exploring the world around them. In these years, from ages 2 to 6, children need more physical play to develop the muscles in their arms and legs. Play with large building blocks and wagons helps strengthen these muscles.

Children use their imagination when they play with small plastic people or farms. Other toys help children develop mentally by encouraging them to count, speak, read, tell time, and work at a table or desk. These toys include plastic letters and numbers, toy telephones, picture story books, and pegboards. Puzzles challenge children to take things apart and put them back together. At this time, children often learn about emotions and caring through play with special dolls or stuffed animals.

Toys for late childhood. In late childhood, from ages 6 to 12, toys become part of more elaborate imaginative play. In doll play, children pretend that they are parents and use strollers, doll beds, and feeding equipment. Children also enjoy playing with action figures, such as robots, soldiers, and space aliens. In these years, children may learn to use clay, paints, and pastels as their artistic ability grows. Board and computer games help develop a child's mind. In many of these games, children must plan their own strategies and also guess what their opponents will do.

Near the end of childhood, boys and girls enjoy building model cars and ships and working with hobby kits. Kits, such as woodburning or embroidery, help develop discipline and patience. Children who like science may spend hours with chemistry sets or microscopes. These activities may persist as adult hobbies.

History. Children have played with toys for thousands of years. In ancient Africa, children enjoyed balls, toy animals, and pull toys. Children of ancient Greece and Rome had fun with boats, carts, hoops, and tops. During the Middle Ages in Europe, popular toys included clay marbles, rattles, and puppets.

Before the development of large toy factories, parents or craftworkers made toys. By the 1800's, most children in the United States played with homemade toys or imported toys from Europe. Toy manufacturing became an important U.S. industry in the early 1900's.

In 1969, Congress passed the Child Protection and Toy Safety Act, which enabled the government to recall or prohibit the sale of toys that were shown to be harmful. Such toys may contain poisonous substances, catch fire easily, have loose parts a child can swallow, or have unprotected points or sharp edges. During the mid-1980's, the U.S. toy industry sold about $40 billion worth of toys annually.   Doris McNeely Johnson

Related articles in *World Book* include:

Airplane, Model	Kaleidoscope	Rocket, Model
Automobile, Model	Kite	Ship, Model
Doll	Play	Skateboard
Dollhouse	Puppet	Top
Frisbee	Railroad, Model	Yo-yo
Hobby		

Additional resources

Fowler, Virginie. *Folk Toys Around the World and How to Make Them*. Prentice-Hall, 1984. Suitable for younger readers.
Kaye, Marvin. *The Story of Monopoly, Silly Putty, Bingo, Twister, Frisbee, Scrabble, Etcetera*. Stein & Day, 1977. First published as *A Toy Is Born* in 1973.

Toy dog is the name of a group of small dogs. Many are relatives of larger dogs. For example, the toy poodle is a tiny poodle. Other toys, such as the Chihuahua, are separate breeds. The recognized toy breeds include the affenpinscher, Brussels griffon, Chihuahua, English toy spaniel, Italian greyhound, Japanese chin, Maltese, miniature pinscher, papillon, Pekingese, Pomeranian, pug, shih tzu, silky terrier, and Yorkshire terrier. *World Book* has separate articles for each of the breeds listed here. See also **Dog** (pictures: Toy dogs).

Critically reviewed by the American Kennel Club

Toy Manchester terrier. See Manchester terrier.

Toynbee is the family name of two men, uncle and nephew, who contributed to sociology and history.

Arnold Toynbee (1852-1883) was interested in the problems caused by poverty. An enthusiastic social reformer, he lived in a shabby dwelling in Whitechapel, a London slum district. He worked for uplift of the poor, changes in the poor laws, and freedom of work. He urged prevention of waste by an equalization of supply and demand. He thought the church should work for social progress, and taught that imitation of Jesus' life of service to humanity was true Christianity. His best-known book was *The Industrial Revolution* (1884).

Toynbee was born in London, and was educated at Oxford University. His hard work to improve conditions ruined his health. Shortly after his death, Toynbee Hall, the first settlement house in the world, was set up in Whitechapel to help the poor.

Arnold Joseph Toynbee (1889-1975) was a famous historian. His outline of civilizations, *A Study of History*, was published in 12 volumes from 1934 to 1961. Toynbee divided world history into 26 civilizations, and traced their rise, decline, and fall. He declared that the one hope for the survival of Western civilization lies in a rebirth of the Christian spirit.

Toynbee's original and bold approach to world history, that of "an ancient historian, looking at the Western World from the outside," had a wide appeal. A two-volume abridgment of his great work sold widely in the United States and Europe. His writings include a number of volumes dealing with social-historical problems, such as *Nationality and the War* (1915), *Civilization on Trial* (1948), and *The World and the West* (1953).

Toynbee was born in London. He studied at Balliol College, Oxford, and at the British Archaeological School at Athens, Greece. Toynbee became a professor of international history at the University of London in 1925. See also **Civilization** (Why civilizations rise and fall).   Francis J. Bowman

Toyota Motor Corporation is the largest automobile manufacturer in Japan and one of the largest automakers in the world. It produces passenger cars, buses, trucks, vans, and automobile parts. In addition, Toyota owns companies that manufacture such products as rubber, steel, and textiles. Toyota also manages real estate and import and export firms.

Toyota has automobile plants in 17 countries. In the United States, Toyota and General Motors Corporation operate a car assembly plant in Fremont, Calif., through a joint venture. Toyota also plans to complete an automobile plant in Georgetown, Ky., during the late 1980's. This plant is expected to produce about 200,000 automobiles a year.

Toyota was founded in 1933. During the 1960's, the company became Japan's largest automobile manufacturer after it acquired several rival manufacturing firms. Toyota's headquarters are in Toyota City, Japan. For the sales, assets, and number of employees of Toyota, see **Manufacturing** (table: 25 leading manufacturers outside the U.S.).   William H. Becker

Trace elements are minerals needed in small amounts by plants, animals, and human beings. Such major elements as calcium, carbon, chlorine, hydrogen, magnesium, nitrogen, oxygen, phosphorus, potassium, sodium, and sulfur are part of the makeup of all living things. The trace elements are also necessary to life. Scientists know the uses of only a few of the trace elements. However, scientists do know that they are necessary for the work of such vital bodily compounds as enzymes and hormones (see **Enzyme; Hormone**).

The trace elements include chromium, cobalt, copper, fluorine, iodine, iron, manganese, molybdenum, selenium, and zinc. The body needs copper so it can use iron to build hemoglobin, an important part of red blood cells. Cobalt, contained in vitamin B_{12}, protects against a blood disease called *pernicious anemia*. Only $\frac{1}{15,000,000}$ ounce (0.000002 gram) of this vitamin each day keeps people with pernicious anemia healthy. Iodine is needed to form the hormone *thyroxine*. A lack of iodine in the diet results in *goiter*, a disease characterized by excessive growth of the thyroid gland. Manganese and zinc are required for the normal action of certain enzymes. Without these two minerals, certain reactions in the body cells would stop. Human beings and all animals need the same trace elements, but plants have different requirements. For example, plants do not need iodine or fluorine. Human beings get the required trace elements from their food in a balanced diet.

Mary Frances Picciano

See also **Nutrition.**

Tracery, in architecture, originally was the framework of light ornamental stone bars dividing a large window

G. R. Richardson, Taurus

Tracery is the ornamental stone or wooden patternwork that decorates arches and vaults in medieval Gothic buildings.

into smaller areas so that the stained glass could be easily placed and supported. Usually tracery took the form of tall, narrow, arched divisions below, with circles, cusps, and other shapes filling the upper part of the window. Later, these shapes were used to decorate wall panels, buttresses, vaulting, and furniture.

Builders first used tracery in the late 1100's, when church windows grew too large to be glazed in one unbroken area. It developed rapidly in delicacy and became a marked feature of nearly all Gothic architecture. The earliest tracery was called *plate* tracery, because the upper circles were pierced through a plate of stone in the upper part of the main window arch. *Geometric* tracery, a complete pattern of thin stone bars, later replaced this pierced "plate." In it, all the openings between the bars are simple geometric forms. Still later, *flowing* and *flamboyant* tracery was used, so called because of its flowing and swaying flamelike shapes. In the late 1300's and the 1400's in England, *perpendicular* tracery was the rule. In it, the vertical bars between the lower openings are carried up the whole height of the window, making small vertical panels.   William J. Hennessey

Trachea. See **Windpipe.**

Trachoma, *truh KOH muh,* is a contagious eye disease caused by a form of *Chlamydia trachomatis* bacteria. Trachoma is relatively rare in the United States because of treatment with antibiotics or sulfonamides. But in Egypt, India, Saudi Arabia, and other developing countries in warm parts of the world, trachoma is still a major cause of blindness. It affects the *conjunctiva* (membrane of the eyeball and lids) and *cornea,* the window of the eye (see **Eye** [Parts of the eye]). Symptoms of conjunctivitis develop and the disease may last for years (see **Conjunctivitis**).

Doctors must report cases of trachoma because the disease spreads easily. People in contagious areas are warned not to use public towels, or rub their eyes with unwashed hands. Severe cases may require an operation to repair deformed eyelids or to replace damaged corneal tissue.   Ramesh C. Tripathi and Brenda J. Tripathi

Track. See **Railroad** (Tracks).

Focus on Sports

A hurdle race is a track event in which competitors run over fencelike obstacles called *hurdles*. The women shown above are competing in an indoor high-hurdle race.

© Steven E. Sutton, Duomo

The steeplechase includes hurdles and water jumps. At a water jump, runners step on the hurdle and then leap into the shallow end of the water pit to soften the landing.

Track and field

Track and field is a sport in which athletes compete in running, walking, jumping, and throwing events. *Track events* consist of running or walking races of various distances. *Field events* are contests in jumping or throwing. Track and field meets can be held indoors or outdoors. Men and women compete separately in a meet.

Track and field is one of the most popular sports in the world. About 180 nations belong to the International Amateur Athletic Federation (IAAF), the governing body of track and field. The IAAF recognizes world records in 65 men's and women's events. The organization accepts world records in metric distances only, except for the mile run. The table in this article lists the major men's and women's records.

The track and the field

The track. Outdoor running tracks are oval in shape and usually are laid out in a stadium. IAAF rules specify that an outdoor running track should measure no less than 400 meters around—and most modern outdoor tracks are exactly that length. (One meter equals about $3\frac{1}{4}$ feet.) Older tracks consist of dirt or cinders, but most new tracks are made of a waterproof synthetic material and can be used in rainy weather.

Indoor tracks have a wooden or synthetic surface, and they usually have banked turns. According to IAAF rules, the preferred measurement for an indoor track is 200 meters.

Outdoor tracks are divided into six or eight lanes. Runners must stay in their lanes for all races up to 400 meters and until they pass the first curve of 800-meter races. IAAF rules state that a lane should measure from 1.22 to 1.25 meters (48 to 49 inches) in width.

The field. Most field events take place in an area enclosed by the track. But in some meets, one or more throwing events are held outside the stadium to protect other athletes and spectators who crowd the field area

or to avoid damaging the artificial turf that covers many athletic fields. The field includes runways for the jumping events. It also has circular areas of material such as concrete or asphalt for most of the throwing events.

Track events

Track events include a variety of races. Short races, called *sprints,* stress maximum speed, while distance races require more endurance. In certain running races, such as the hurdles and steeplechase, runners must go over barriers. Other races, called *relays,* involve teams of runners.

Running races on an outdoor track cover distances from 100 meters to 10,000 meters. Indoors, races may measure from 50 meters to 5,000 meters. *Cross-country races* and *road races* are run outside the stadium. Cross-country competitors run over terrain such as hills and fields. Most U.S. and Canadian schools and colleges compete in cross-country races in the fall. Most road races are open to all runners, and many races award prize money to the winners. The most common distance for road races is 10 kilometers.

Hurdle races are events in which the competitors run over obstacles called *hurdles.* Most of these races have 10 hurdles spaced at equal intervals. There are two types of hurdle races, intermediate and high. Intermediate hurdles are 36 inches (91 centimeters) high for men and 30 inches (76 centimeters) high for women. Men's high hurdles are 42 inches (107 centimeters) high. Women's high hurdles are 33 inches (84 centimeters) high. Intermediate-hurdle races cover 400 meters or 440 yards in men's and women's competition. Most outdoor high-hurdle races are 110 meters or 120 yards for men and 100 meters for women. Runners can knock over hurdles without penalty, but contact with a hurdle normally slows down the runner.

The steeplechase is a race, usually of 3,000 meters, over two kinds of obstacles, hurdles and *water jumps.* Runners must clear 36-inch (91-centimeter) hurdles 28 times. These hurdles are sturdier than the ones used in hurdle races, and runners may put a foot on top of them as they pass over them. Runners must cross water jumps seven times. A water jump consists of a hurdle and a water-filled pit 12 feet (3.66 meters) square. The steeple-chaser steps onto the hurdle and leaps across the water. The pit is $27\frac{1}{2}$ inches (70 centimeters) deep at the foot of the hurdle and slopes up to the track level. Most stee-plechasers come down in the water at the shallow end of the pit to soften their landing.

Walking races are events in which athletes must fol-low certain rules of walking technique. The front foot must touch the ground before the rear foot leaves the ground. While the foot is touching the ground, the leg must be unbent for at least one moment. Walkers are entitled to one warning for improper form before they are disqualified. Walking races, also called *race walking,* may take place on a track or a road. Most men's walking races cover distances of 20,000 meters or 50,000 meters. Women's world records are recognized for two dis-tances, 5,000 meters and 10,000 meters.

Relays are run by teams of four runners. The first runner carries a baton about 1 foot (30 centimeters) long. After running a certain distance, called a *leg,* the athlete hands the baton to the next team member. This exchange must occur within a zone 20 meters long. If the runners do not exchange the baton within this zone, their team is disqualified.

The most common relays are run at distances of 400 meters or 1,600 meters. The IAAF also keeps world rec-ords for relays of 800 meters, 3,200 meters, and—for men only—6,000 meters. In these relays, all four mem-bers of a team run an equal distance. Most U.S. relay meets include *medley relays,* in which the athletes run different distances. In the *sprint medley,* two members of the team run 220 yards each, another runs 440 yards, and the final runner covers 880 yards. In the *distance medley,* the members of the team run distances of 440 yards, 000 yards, $\frac{3}{4}$ mile, and 1 mile.

Field events

Field events take place in specially prepared areas, usually within the oval track. Typical field competition consists of four jumping events and four throwing events. The jumps are the long jump, triple jump, high jump, and pole vault. The throwing events are the dis-cus, hammer, javelin, and shot-put. Women do not com-pete in the pole vault or hammer throw. The IAAF does not recognize the women's triple jump.

Jumping events. In the long jump and triple jump, the athletes jump as far forward as they can. In the high jump and pole vault, they leap over a bar as high as pos-sible.

The long jump, once called the *broad jump,* is com-pleted in a single jump into a pit filled with sand. To begin the long jump, the competitor sprints down a long runway and leaps from a take-off board. If the ath-lete steps past the board before jumping, the jump is a foul. A jump's length is measured from the front edge of the take-off board to the nearest mark the athlete makes in the sand. When there are many competitors, each one is allowed three jumps, and a certain number of leaders qualify for three more. When fewer athletes compete, each one is allowed six jumps. If two jumpers leap the same distance, the winner is the one with the next-best jump.

John McDonough, Focus on Sports

In the long jump, athletes speed down a runway and leap from a board into a sand pit. A jump is measured from the near edge of the board to the closest mark the jumper makes in the sand.

The triple jump, originally called the *hop, step, and jump,* consists of three continuous jumps, the first two completed on the runway. On the first jump, the athlete takes off on one foot and lands on the same foot. On the second jump, the athlete lands on the other foot. At the end of the third jump, the athlete lands on both feet in a pit of sand.

High-jumpers and pole-vaulters try to propel them-selves over a long thin crossbar held up by two posts called *uprights.* The athletes land on a cushion of foam rubber. If a jumper knocks the crossbar off the uprights, the jump counts as a miss. Three consecutive misses eliminate the jumper. The winner is the one who clears the greatest height. In case of a tie, the winner is the one with the fewest misses at that height. If still tied, the win-ner is the one with the fewest overall misses.

A high jumper runs toward the bar from any angle within a large, semicircular runway. The athlete may

© Heinz Kluetmeier, *Sports Illustrated,* Time Inc.

The high jump requires an athlete to leap over a bar that rests on and between two poles. This jumper will kick her legs out and up to complete her headfirst leap.

use any style of jumping, but he or she must take off from one foot. In the most popular modern style, called the *Fosbury flop,* jumpers go over with their back to the bar and their head clearing first. The style was named for American high-jumper Dick Fosbury, who introduced it in the late 1960's.

A pole vaulter uses a long pole usually made of fiberglass. He begins his vault by sprinting down a runway, carrying the pole with both hands. As he nears the vaulting pit, he rams the far end of the pole into a wood or metal box imbedded in the ground. The pole bends while he hangs with his back to the ground and his feet up. As the pole straightens, helping to thrust him into the air, he pulls himself higher and turns his body to face the ground. Before he releases the pole, he gives a final push with his arms to add to his height.

Throwing events require athletes to propel an object as far as they can. Competitors in the discus, hammer, and shot-put all throw from inside a circle. In the discus and hammer events, athletes throw from an enclosure, called a *cage,* to protect spectators from wild throws. In the javelin event, the athlete runs down a runway marked on the field and throws the javelin before reaching a foul line. In each event, the thrown object must land within a marked area. If two competitors throw the same distance, the tie is decided by the next-best throw.

A discus is a saucer-shaped object usually made of wood with a metal rim. The men's discus measures about 22 centimeters ($8\frac{2}{3}$ inches) in diameter and weighs at least 2 kilograms (4 pounds $6\frac{1}{2}$ ounces). The women's discus is about 18 centimeters ($7\frac{1}{8}$ inches) in diameter and weighs at least 1 kilogram (2 pounds 3 ounces). The athlete grips the discus with one hand, spins around about $1\frac{1}{2}$ times, and releases it with a sidearm motion to make it sail through the air.

A hammer consists of a steel wire with a metal ball attached to one end and a handle fastened to the other end. The entire hammer weighs 7.26 kilograms (16 pounds) and measures about 120 centimeters (47 inches) long. Using both hands, the thrower grasps the handle and spins around three or four times before releasing it.

A javelin is a spear made of metal or wood. The men's javelin measures from 2.6 to 2.7 meters (8 feet 6 inches to 8 feet 10 inches) long and weighs at least 800 grams (28 ounces). Women throw a javelin that is 2.2 to 2.3 meters (7 feet 3 inches to 7 feet 7 inches) long and weighs at least 600 grams (21 ounces). The thrower holds the javelin by a cord grip near the center, runs with it, and then releases it with an overhand throw while running.

A shot is a metal ball. The men's shot measures about 12 centimeters ($4\frac{3}{4}$ inches) in diameter and weighs at least 7.26 kilograms (16 pounds). The women's shot measures about 10 centimeters (4 inches) in diameter and weighs at least 4 kilograms (8 pounds 13 ounces). Competitors *put* (push) the shot rather than throw it. The shot must be held against the neck to prevent any throwing motion. The athlete begins with a strong shove from one leg and finishes with a powerful push of the arm.

The decathlon, heptathlon, and pentathlon

The decathlon, heptathlon, and pentathlon are *combined competitions,* in which an athlete competes in several different events over a period of one or two days. The athletes receive a score for their performance in each event, based on IAAF scoring tables. The winner is the athlete who receives the highest total score. Thus, the champion is the best all-around athlete, not necessarily the best competitor in any single event.

The decathlon is a 10-event competition for men. On the first day, the participants compete in the 100-meter run, long jump, shot-put, high jump, and 400-meter run. On the second day, they compete in the high hurdles, discus, pole vault, javelin, and 1,500-meter run.

The heptathlon is a seven-event competition for women. On the first day, they begin with the high hurdles, followed by the high jump, shot-put, and 200-meter run. On the second day, they compete in the long jump, javelin throw, and the 800-meter run.

The pentathlon, a one-day competition of five events, is rarely held today. The heptathlon replaced the pentathlon for women in 1981. The men's pentathlon events include the long jump, javelin throw, 200-meter run, discus throw, and 1,500-meter run.

Competition

Organizations. The IAAF governs international track and field. It conducts the World Championships and cooperates with the International Olympic Committee in staging the track and field events of the Olympic Games. Other organizations conduct international meets, national championships, and restricted championships, such as college, regional, and high school meets.

In the United States, The Athletics Congress (TAC) is the governing body for track and field. The Canadian Track and Field Association (CTFA) governs the sport in Canada. The National Collegiate Athletic Association (NCAA) and the National Association of Intercollegiate Athletics (NAIA) govern U.S. college championships. The National Federation of State High School Associations regulates U.S. high school competition.

Types of competition. The most important international meets are the Olympic Games, which started in 1896, and the World Championships, which began in 1983. The Olympics are held every four years. The World Championships were held in 1983 and 1987 and

© Rich Clarkson, *Sports Illustrated,* Time Inc.

The shot-put is a throwing event in which the athletes *put* (push) a metal ball called a *shot.* They hold the heavy shot against their neck and release it with a powerful push.

are planned for 1991. Other major international meets include the African Championships, the Commonwealth Games, the European Championships, the Pan American Games, and the World Cup. Many nations compete against each other in annual *dual meets* (competitions between two teams).

In U.S. and Canadian schools and colleges, local meets may lead to regional, state, or provincial meets and, on the college level, to national meets. Much competition takes place in *open meets,* which any athlete may enter. Some private organizations sponsor *invitational meets.* Only the athletes invited by the organizers may compete in these meets. International *Grand Prix* meets allow athletes to score points for placing high in certain meets. At the end of the season, the athletes with the most points win prize money. Some meets are restricted to a certain age group, such as competitions for children 10 and under and adults 60 and over.

Track and field meets. A typical track meet is like a three-ring circus, with several events taking place at the same time. Officials conduct each event according to its particular rules. A race requires a starter, several judges at the finish line, and sometimes as many as a dozen timers. Electronic equipment is normally used in place of some judges and timers in major meets. In field events, judges measure jumps and throws, and watch for fouls. In some events, judges also check to see that athletes are using the legal form.

Most meets take place in a single day, but the Olympics and the World Championships schedule events over more than a week. Large meets include so many athletes that they cannot all compete at once. In these meets, the athletes must qualify for the finals in *preliminaries.* Eight competitors normally qualify for the finals of track events run in lanes. Most field-event preliminaries reduce the number of finalists to 12.

History

Beginnings. The first footrace probably took place thousands of years ago. A footrace is described in the Greek epic poem the *Iliad,* which was probably composed in the 700's B.C. A footrace was the only event in the first Olympic Games, held in Greece in 776 B.C. Track and field was introduced in England in the 1100's but did not become popular until the 1800's.

Revival in the 1800's. Footraces along the roads became common in England during the 1500's, but races on measured tracks did not begin until well into the 1800's. Modern track and field began in the schools of England. Eton held an interclass meet in 1837. In 1864, Cambridge competed against Oxford in the first intercollegiate track and field meet. The annual English championships began in London in 1866.

The first U.S. amateur meet took place indoors in 1868. The New York Athletic Club sponsored the meet. U.S. collegiate meets and the first national championships began in 1876. Several other nations held championship meets before 1900. In 1895, the New York Athletic Club met the London Athletic Club in the first notable international meet. In 1896, Athens, Greece, hosted the first modern Olympic Games. Although the track and field performances at Athens were not outstanding, the Olympics stimulated great interest in the sport. Women's competitions, which were not part of the first Olympic Games, also began during the late 1800's.

The early and mid-1900's. In 1912, 16 countries agreed to form the IAAF to govern men's track and field. An international organization for women's competitions was formed in 1917. Separate international women's championships were held until 1928, when women were admitted to Olympic competition.

During the 1920's, long-distance runner Paavo Nurmi of Finland raised track to international popularity. He broke world records 35 times and won 9 Olympic gold medals and 3 silver medals. Babe Didrikson of the United States popularized women's track and field. Didrikson won two gold medals and a silver medal in the 1932 Olympic Games. In the 1936 Olympics, Jesse Owens of the United States won four gold medals and retired with world records in seven events. Early in the 1940's, Cornelius "Dutch" Warmerdam of the United States captured the imagination of the track and field world by pole-vaulting higher than 15 feet a total of 43 times.

During the 1950's, athletes broke all previous world records except Owens' 1935 long-jump mark. Among the greatest athletes in this midcentury surge were long-distance runner Emil Zatopek of Czechoslovakia, and shot-putter Parry O'Brien and discus thrower Al Oerter of the United States. Zatopek won 4 Olympic gold medals and held 10 world records at the same time. O'Brien broke the shot-put record 13 times and won 2 firsts, a second, and a fourth in the Olympics. Oerter won the Olympic discus throw four times.

Track and field today. The sport has changed greatly since the mid-1900's. Performances once thought to be impossible are common today. In 1954, the British runner Roger Bannister became the first person to run the mile in less than four minutes. Within the next 20 years, more than 200 men had run the mile in under four minutes. In the late 1980's, the 50 all-time best performances in each event included only a few from before 1980.

There are a number of reasons for this remarkable progress in track and field. They include increased competition, especially in Europe, as well as improved training methods, equipment, and techniques. Traditionally, track and field has been an amateur sport. However, the rules have been broadened to allow athletes to receive large sums of money for endorsing athletic shoes or other products and for appearing in invitational meets. The opportunity to earn money has increased the level of competition.

Improved training methods help today's athletes perform well. Training with weights gives athletes greater strength for throwing, jumping, and even running. New equipment has raised performance levels. Synthetic tracks, which have more spring, cut a runner's time by as much as one second per lap. The use of fiberglass vaulting poles instead of wooden ones has reduced Warmerdam's once amazing heights to high-school performance levels. New techniques also help. In the high jump, for example, the use of the Fosbury flop adds about 6 inches (15 centimeters) to most jumps.

Current track-and-field champions reflect the international popularity of the sport. The biggest names in men's track and field in the 1980's included hurdler

World track and field records

Event	Record	Holder	Country	Date

Men's records

Running

100 meters	9.83 s.	Ben Johnson	Canada	Aug. 30, 1987
200 meters	19.72 s.	Pietro Mennea	Italy	Sept. 17, 1979
400 meters	43.29 s.*	Butch Reynolds	United States	Aug. 17, 1988
800 meters	1 min. 41.73 s.	Sebastian Coe	Great Britain	June 10, 1981
1,000 meters	2 min. 12.18 s.	Sebastian Coe	Great Britain	July 11, 1981
1,500 meters	3 min. 29.46 s.	Said Aouita	Morocco	Aug. 23, 1985
1 mile	3 min. 46.32 s.	Steve Cram	Great Britain	July 27, 1985
2,000 meters	4 min. 50.81 s.	Said Aouita	Morocco	July 16, 1987
3,000 meters	7 min. 32.1 s.	Henry Rono	Kenya	June 27, 1978
5,000 meters	12 min. 58.39 s.	Said Aouita	Morocco	July 22, 1987
10,000 meters	27 min. 13.81 s.	Fernando Mamede	Portugal	July 2, 1984
20,000 meters	57 min. 24.2 s.	Jos Hermens	Netherlands	May 1, 1976
25,000 meters	1 hr. 13 min. 55.8 s.	Toshihiko Seko	Japan	March 22, 1981
30,000 meters	1 hr. 29 min. 18.8 s.	Toshihiko Seko	Japan	March 22, 1981
1-hour run	13 miles 24 yards (20,944 meters)	Jos Hermens	Netherlands	May 1, 1976
3,000-meter steeplechase	8 min. 5.4 s.	Henry Rono	Kenya	May 13, 1978

Hurdles

110-meter hurdles	12.93 s.	Renaldo Nehemiah	United States	Aug. 19, 1981
400-meter hurdles	47.02 s.	Edwin Moses	United States	Aug. 31, 1983

Relays

400-meter relay	37.83 s.	U.S. national team (S. Graddy, R. Brown, C. Smith, C. Lewis)	United States	Aug. 11, 1984
800-meter relay	1 min. 20.26 s.	Univ. of Southern California (J. Andrews, J. Sanford, B. Mullins, C. Edwards)	United States	May 27, 1978
1,600-meter relay	2 min. 56.16 s.	U.S. national team (V. Matthews, R. Freeman, L. James, L. Evans)	United States	Oct. 20, 1968
		*U.S. national team (D. Everett, S. Lewis, K. Robinzine, B. Reynolds)	United States	Oct. 1, 1988
3,200-meter relay	7 min. 3.89 s.	Great Britain national team (P. Elliott, G. Cook, S. Cram, S. Coe)	Great Britain	Aug. 30, 1982
6,000-meter relay	14 min. 38.8 s.	West German national team (T. Wessinghage, H. Hudak, M. Lederer, K. Fleschen)	West Germany	Aug. 17, 1977

Race walking

20,000-meter walk	1 hr. 18 min. 40.0 s.	Ernesto Canto	Mexico	May 5, 1984
30,000-meter walk	2 hr. 8 min.	Jose Marin	Spain	Aug. 4, 1979
50,000-meter walk	3 hr. 41 min. 39 s.	Raul Gonzales	Mexico	May 25, 1979
2-hour walk	17 miles 881 yards (28,165 meters)	Jose Marin	Spain	Aug. 4, 1979

Jumping

High jump	7 ft. 11$\frac{1}{4}$ in. (2.42 meters)	Patrik Sjoberg	Sweden	June 30, 1987
Pole vault	19 ft. 9$\frac{1}{4}$ in. (6.03 meters)	Sergey Bubka	Soviet Union	June 23, 1987
Long jump	29 ft. 2$\frac{1}{2}$ in. (8.90 meters)	Bob Beamon	United States	Oct. 18, 1968
Triple jump	58 ft. 11$\frac{1}{2}$ in. (17.97 meters)	Willie Banks	United States	June 16, 1985

*Record pending

Event	Record	Holder	Country	Date

Men's records (continued)

Throwing

Event	Record	Holder	Country	Date
Shot put	75 ft. 2 in. (22.91 meters)	Alessandro Andrei	Italy	Aug. 12, 1987
Discus throw	243 ft. 0 in. (74.08 meters)	Jurgen Schult	East Germany	June 6, 1986
Hammer throw	284 ft. 7 in. (86.74 meters)*	Yuriy Syedikh	Soviet Union	Aug. 30, 1986
Javelin throw	287 ft. 7 in. (87.66 meters)	Jan Zelezny	Czechoslovakia	May 31, 1987

Decathlon

Event	Record	Holder	Country	Date
Decathlon	8,847 points	Daley Thompson	Great Britain	Aug. 8-9, 1984

Women's records

Running

Event	Record	Holder	Country	Date
100 meters	10.49 s.*	Florence Griffith Joyner	United States	July 16, 1988
200 meters	21.34 s.*	Florence Griffith Joyner	United States	Sept. 29, 1988
400 meters	47.60 s.	Marita Koch	East Germany	Oct. 6, 1985
800 meters	1 min. 53.28 s.	Jarmila Kratochvilova	Czechoslovakia	July 26, 1983
1,500 meters	3 min. 52.47 s.	Tatyana Kazankina	Soviet Union	Aug. 13, 1980
1 mile	4 min. 16.71 s.	Mary Decker Slaney	United States	Aug. 21, 1985
2,000 meters	5 min. 28.69 s.	Maricica Puica	Romania	July 11, 1986
3,000 meters	8 min. 22.62 s.	Tatyana Kazankina	Soviet Union	Aug. 26, 1984
5,000 meters	14 min. 37.33 s.	Ingrid Kristiansen	Norway	Aug. 5, 1986
10,000 meters	30 min. 13.74 s.	Ingrid Kristiansen	Norway	July 5, 1986

Hurdles

Event	Record	Holder	Country	Date
100-meter hurdles	12.25 s.	Ginka Zagorcheva	Bulgaria	Aug. 8, 1987
400-meter hurdles	52.94 s.	Marina Stepanova	Soviet Union	Sept. 17, 1986

Relays

Event	Record	Holder	Country	Date
400-meter relay	41.37 s.	East German national team (S. Gladisch, S. Rieger, I. Auerswald, M. Göhr)	East Germany	Oct. 6, 1985
800-meter relay	1 min. 28.15 s.	East German national team (M. Göhr, R. Muller, B. Wockel, M. Koch)	East Germany	Aug. 9, 1980
1,600-meter relay	3 min. 15.18 s.*	Soviet national team (T. Ledovskaia, O. Navarova, M. Piniguina, O. Bryzguina)	Soviet Union	Oct. 1, 1988
3,200-meter relay	7 min. 50.17 s.	Soviet national team (N. Olizarenko, L. Gurina, L. Borisova, I. Podyalovskaya)	Soviet Union	Aug. 5, 1984

Race walking

Event	Record	Holder	Country	Date
5,000-meter walk	21 min. 10.27 s.	Yan Hong	China	March 29, 1987
10,000-meter walk	44 min. 26.5 s.	Xu Yongiu	China	March 31, 1987

Jumping

Event	Record	Holder	Country	Date
High jump	6 ft. 10¼ in. (2.09 meters)	Stefka Kostadinova	Bulgaria	Aug. 30, 1987
Long jump	24 ft. 5½ in. (7.45 meters)	Heike Drechsler	East Germany	June 21, 1986
		Heike Drechsler	East Germany	July 3, 1986
		*Jackie Joyner-Kersee	United States	August 13, 1987

Throwing

Event	Record	Holder	Country	Date
Shot put	74 ft. 3 in. (22.63 meters)	Natalya Lisovskaya	Soviet Union	June 7, 1987
Discus throw	244 ft. 7 in. (74.56 meters)	Zdenka Silhava	Czechoslovakia	Aug. 26, 1984
Javelin throw	258 ft. 10 in. (78.90 meters)*	Petra Felke	East Germany	July 29, 1987

Heptathlon

Event	Record	Holder	Country	Date
Heptathlon	7,291 points*	Jackie Joyner-Kersee	United States	Sept. 23-24, 1988

*Record pending.
Source: *1988 Competition Rules*, The Athletics Congress.

Edwin Moses and sprinter Carl Lewis of the United States, distance runners Said Aouita of Morocco and Sebastian Coe of Great Britain, pole vaulter Sergey Bubka of the Soviet Union, and decathlon athlete Daley Thompson of Great Britain. In women's events, sprinter Marita Koch and sprinter and long jumper Heike Drechsler of East Germany were major figures in the 1980's, as were sprinter Florence Griffith Joyner and long jumper and heptathlon competitor Jackie Joyner-Kersee of the United States.   Cordner Nelson

Related articles. See the separate article on **Olympic Games.** See also the following articles:

Outline

I. **The track and the field**
  A. The track
  B. The field
II. **Track events**
  A. Running races   D. Walking races
  B. Hurdle races   E. Relays
  C. The steeplechase
III. **Field events**
  A. Jumping events
  B. Throwing events
IV. **The decathlon, heptathlon, and pentathlon**
V. **Competition**
  A. Organizations   C. Track and field
  B. Types of competition   meets
VI. **History**
  A. Beginnings
  B. Revival in the 1800's
  C. The early and mid-1900's
  D. Track and field today

Questions

What is one function of a judge in a field event?
Where did modern track and field begin?
Which running races do not take place on a track?
Who was Cornelius Warmerdam?
How is the winner of a combined competition determined?
What is the U.S. governing organization for high school track and field?
How do medley relays differ from other relays?
What are a few causes of the progress in track and field performances since the mid-1900's?
In what way do open meets differ from invitational meets?
What was the triple jump originally called?

Additional resources

Diagram Group. *Enjoying Track and Field Sports.* Paddington, 1979. For younger readers.
Doherty, J. Kenneth. *Track and Field Omnibook.* 3rd ed. Tafnews, 1980.
Jacoby, Ed. *Applied Techniques in Track & Field.* Leisure Press, 1983.
Sullivan, George. *Better Track for Girls.* Dodd, 1981.

Tracking. See Space travel (Communications with the earth; Artificial satellites).

Tractor is a machine that pulls or pushes a tool or a machine over land. Tractors provide the chief source of power on most farms. They are also used for industrial and military purposes, for logging, highway construction, and snow clearance. Tractors have either gasoline or diesel engines (see **Gasoline engine; Diesel engine**).

Parts of a tractor. The modern tractor has several built-in features that enable it to provide power for other farm machines. These features include the drawbar, a hydraulic system, and a power take-off.

The drawbar is a device for fastening equipment to the tractor for pulling. The drawbar enables a tractor to pull such equipment as plows, wagons, harrows, combines, and hay balers.

The hydraulic system controls the working position of implements hitched to or mounted onto the tractor. An engine-driven hydraulic pump and cylinder provide power to raise and lower these implements. Many rear-wheel-drive tractors have hydraulic systems with a mechanism that shifts weight from the front to the rear wheels of the tractor. The weight shift increases traction for pulling mounted implements.

The power take-off, or *PTO,* provides power for machines that are either mounted on or pulled by the tractor. The coupling device between the PTO and the equipment usually consists of two universal joints, one on each end of a telescoping shaft. The flexible action of the joints and the telescoping action of the shaft allows sharp turning and movement over rough surfaces without harming the power system. The PTO drives the moving parts of mowing machines, hay balers, combines, potato diggers, and spray pumps.

Types of tractors. There are two major types of tractors: the wheel tractor and the tracklayer tractor, known as a *crawler.*

Wheel tractors make up the majority of farm tractors in the United States. Many farmers use an *all-purpose* tractor because it does a variety of jobs, such as planting, cultivating, and harvesting. It has high rear wheels. It has either one or two small front wheels placed close together or two front wheels spaced the same as the rear wheels. The spacing of the wheels enables the tractor to be driven between rows of crops. Wheel tractors may have either two-wheel or four-wheel drive. Two-wheel-drive models range in weight from about 3,000

Case IH
A general-purpose tractor performs many jobs on a farm, including plowing, planting, fertilizing, and cultivating.

A crawler tractor, sometimes called a *caterpillar tractor,* does such work as moving earth for construction jobs, *above.*

pounds (1,400 kilograms) to more than 20,000 pounds (9,000 kilograms). Four-wheel-drive tractors may weigh as much as 60,000 pounds (27,000 kilograms). The demand for larger tractors has increased as the average size of farms has increased.

Crawler tractors are driven on two endless tracks. They are steered by stopping or slowing one of the tracks. Crawler tractors are used for heavy jobs, for land clearing, and for work on soft or rugged land. The smallest crawlers weigh about 3,800 pounds (1,720 kilograms). The largest of these tractors weigh more than 70,000 pounds (32,000 kilograms).

History. Tractors were first used during the 1870's. These tractors, called *traction engines,* were large, four-wheeled machines driven by steam. They provided enough power to pull as many as 40 plows, but they were too awkward to be practical. Smaller machines with internal-combustion engines soon replaced them. But the new machine had only a kerosene engine mounted on a four-wheeled frame. Later, kerosene or gasoline engines were built as part of the tractor frame. The tractors could do almost all the field work, but were too low to pull a cultivator through tall crops. Then, in the 1920's, the all-purpose tractor was developed.

Early manufacturing companies usually made only one tractor model or size. But modern companies make a complete line. Modern tractors have both speed and power, and are easy to operate. Most have power steering and power brakes. Many also have enclosed cabs with heating and air-conditioning systems and special structures that protect the operator if the tractor accidentally turns over. Gerald E. Rehkugler

See also **Agriculture** (picture: An early gasoline-powered tractor); **Bulldozer.**

Tracy, Spencer (1900-1967), was an American motion-picture actor. He became famous for his roles as a strong man of action and conviction in such films as *Bad Day at Black Rock* (1955) and *The Old Man and the Sea* (1958). He also won fame as a sophisticated comedian in several films, including *Woman of the Year* (1942) and *Father of the Bride* (1950). Tracy won Academy Awards for his performances in *Captains Courageous* (1937) and *Boys Town* (1938). He received seven other Academy Award nominations.

Tracy was born in Milwaukee. He made his stage debut in 1922. A 1930 stage performance led Tracy to a film contract, and he made his movie debut that year in *Up the River. The Power and the Glory* (1933) established him as a star. Tracy made more than 70 films, including *Woman of the Year* (1942), *State of the Union* (1948), *Adam's Rib* (1949), *Inherit the Wind* (1960), *Judgment at Nuremberg* (1961), and *Guess Who's Coming to Dinner* (1967). Rachel Gallagher

United Press Int.
Spencer Tracy

Trade is buying and selling goods and services. Trade occurs because people need and want things that others produce or services others perform.

People must have such necessities as food, clothing, and shelter. They also want many other things that make life convenient and pleasant. They want such goods as cars, books, and television sets. They want such services as haircuts, motion pictures, and bus rides. As individuals, people cannot produce all the goods and services they want. Instead, they receive money for the goods and services they produce for others. They use the money to buy the things they want but do not produce.

Trade that takes place within a single country is called *domestic trade. International trade* is the exchange of goods and services between nations. It is also called *world trade* or *foreign trade.* For detailed information on international trade, see **International trade.**

Trade has contributed greatly to the advance of civilization. As merchants traveled from region to region, they helped spread civilized ways of life. These traders carried the ideas and inventions of various cultures over the routes of commerce. The mixing of civilized cultures was an important development in world history.

Trade and specialization

Trade is vital both in developed and in developing nations. The economic systems of most countries have a high degree of *specialization,* or *division of labor.*

Specialization means that each worker concentrates on one job, such as being a farmer, mechanic, or doctor. Factories concentrate on making one product, such as washing machines, canned soup, or shirts. Countries, cities, and regions also concentrate on producing certain goods and services. For example, Australia specializes in raising livestock, and Japan in industrial products. Oregon specializes in producing lumber, Pittsburgh in steelmaking, and Florida in growing oranges.

Specialization makes trade necessary. Because people do not produce everything they need themselves, they become dependent on others. They sell their labor or products for money, and use the money to buy other goods and services that they need.

Trade helps people enjoy a higher standard of living. People can obtain more goods and services at lower cost through specialization and exchange. If workers concentrate on the job they are best fitted to perform, they can produce more than if they try to do several different jobs. If factories specialize, they can use mass-production methods and complicated machines and tools to produce more (see **Mass production**). If regions specialize, they can use their most plentiful resources. They can build up a supply of skilled labor and specialized *capital* (goods used to produce other goods).

Carrying on trade

The use of money. To make trading easier, people have developed *monetary systems.* Large-scale trade is possible only if money is used as a medium of exchange. Without money, people would have to exchange certain goods and services directly for other goods and services. This system of trade is called *barter.* Using barter, a banana grower who wanted a horse would have to find a horse owner who wanted some bananas. The two traders would then have to agree on how many bananas a horse was worth.

People will accept money for things they want to sell because they know it will be accepted by others in exchange for the things they want to buy. The amount of money exchanged for a particular product is the *price* of that product. The price of something is the value placed on it by those who are buying and selling it. See **Money** (How money developed); **Price.**

The use of markets. Trade takes place in *markets.* In earlier days, buyers and sellers actually met and bargained with one another at markets. In Europe during the Middle Ages, for example, farmers came to town with their produce on market day. The townspeople shopped around the market and negotiated directly with the seller. Today, most trade is more complicated.

Often, producers and consumers do not deal directly with one another. Instead, goods are passed on from producers to consumers by people called *middlemen.*

Two kinds of middlemen are *wholesalers* and *retailers.* Wholesalers buy goods from producers and sell them mainly to other business firms. For example, a wholesaler of vegetables buys large amounts of vegetables from the growers and then sells them to grocers. This kind of trade is called *wholesale trade.* The grocers sell the vegetables to customers who eat them. This type of trade in which merchants sell goods mainly to the final consumer is called *retail trade.* See **Marketing.**

It is no longer necessary for buyers and sellers to meet face-to-face. Goods and services can be bought and sold by mail, telephone, or teletype. Often, buyers and sellers do not even see the product being traded. They transact their business on the basis of description or sample. For example, a buyer of drapes will usually examine a small *swatch* (sample) of cloth before making a purchase. Cotton, wheat, and many other farm products are classified by grade. Buyers know exactly what they will get if they specify a particular grade, such as "Number 2 hard ordinary wheat." Agricultural goods are often traded at organized markets called *commodity exchanges* (see **Commodity exchange**).

Carrying on trade   Trade takes place because people need or want the things that other people produce or can do. Trade may be carried on in a number of ways. The illustrations below show trade at local markets, between nations, and at organized markets known as commodity exchanges.

© Marc Bernheim, Woodfin Camp, Inc.

A local market in Morocco

E. R. Degginger

A freight dock in New Jersey

© Robert Frerck, Woodfin Camp, Inc.

A commodity exchange in Chicago

The geographical extent of trade varies widely. In some cases, the buyers and sellers are from all parts of the world. Trade in such basic foods and raw materials as coffee, sugar, wheat, copper, oil, and rubber is international in scope. For example, the United States is a leading producer of wheat. It sells large amounts of wheat to India, Pakistan, Japan, Brazil, the Netherlands, and many other countries.

Trade in other products may be conducted on a local, regional, or national basis. For example, the trade in hominy grits is concentrated in the Southern States of the United States. The market for such familiar products as automobiles, clothing, furniture, and television sets is usually national in scope.

In earlier days, local trade was much more important than it is today. This was partly because transportation facilities were limited and goods could not be moved on a large scale. Also, perishable food could not be preserved for very long. Perishable items had to be consumed near their place of production. But technological advances have removed these trade barriers. Trains, trucks, airplanes, and pipelines make it possible to move large quantities of goods easily and cheaply. Vegetables, meats, and other perishables can be refrigerated or frozen and shipped all over the world. Even flowers can be flown by airplanes to distant markets.

Also in earlier days, people's tastes and preferences varied more from one locality to another. Today, mass advertising in magazines and newspapers and on radio and television has persuaded people all over the nation to use the same products. Millions of people drink the same kinds of soft drinks, use the same detergents, drive the same cars, and wear the same kinds of clothes and shoes. Thus, technological advances have created national markets, and nationwide trade has taken the place of much purely local trade.

Trade in the United States is carried out mainly by private persons and businesses. Government plays a less important role than do private individuals and groups, and is more important as a buyer than as a seller. The sellers of goods range from such giant businesses as the General Motors Corporation, which sells millions of automobiles and trucks each year, to small neighborhood shops that sell such goods as bakery products or flowers.

Large amounts of goods and services are purchased by individual consumers, who buy such things as dresses, transistor radios, food, and haircuts. Businesses buy the raw materials and capital equipment they need for production from other businesses. The various governments in the United States also buy many goods and services. For example, purchases of the federal government include interstate highways, missiles, and the services of members of the armed forces.

The way in which trade is organized and carried on in the United States is the nation's economic system. This system is often called *capitalism, free enterprise,* or *private enterprise* (see **Capitalism**). Trade—buying and selling goods and services in the market—is an essential part of a free economy. In the free market, consumers help determine prices and thus what will be produced. Their willingness to pay for what they want indicates to producers what ought to be produced. In the Soviet Union and other countries with *centrally planned economies,* government planners make the basic economic decisions about what will be produced and about the prices of the products.

The development of trade

Early trade. For thousands of years, families produced most of the things they needed themselves. They grew or hunted their own food, made their own simple tools and utensils, built their own houses, and made their own clothes. Later, people learned that they could have more and better goods and services by specializing and trading with others. As civilization advanced, exchanges became so common that some individuals did nothing but conduct trade. This class became known as *merchants.* The most famous early land merchants were the Babylonians and, later, the Arabs. These traders traveled on foot or rode donkeys or camels. The Phoenicians were the chief sea traders of ancient times.

Trade was very important during the hundreds of years the Roman Empire ruled much of the world. Roman ships brought tin from Britain, and slaves, cloth, and gems from the Orient. For more than 500 years after the fall of the Roman Empire in A.D. 476, little international trade took place.

The expansion of trade began in the 1100's and 1200's, largely because of increased contacts between people. The crusades encouraged European trade with the Middle East (see **Crusades**). Marco Polo and other European merchants made the long trip to the Far East to trade for Chinese goods (see **Polo, Marco**). Italians in Genoa, Pisa, and Venice built great fleets of ships to carry goods from country to country.

A great period of overseas exploration began in the 1400's. Trade routes between Europe and Africa, India, and Southeast Asia were established as a result of the explorations. In the 1500's and 1600's, private groups formed companies, usually with governmental approval, to trade in new areas.

Trade between Europe and America was carried on by the chartered companies that established the earliest American colonies. The colonists sent sugar, molasses, furs, rice, rum, potatoes, tobacco, timber, and cocoa to Europe. In return, they received manufactured articles, luxuries, and slaves. Trade also pushed American frontiers westward. Trading posts sprang up in the wilderness. Many of these posts later grew into cities.

Trade today affects the lives of most people. Improved transportation permits trade between all parts of the world. Through specialization, more and better goods and services are produced. Increased production has led to higher incomes, enabling people to buy more of these goods and services.   Robert M. Stern

Related articles in *World Book.* See the trade section of various country articles, such as **Italy** (Foreign trade). See also:

Additional resources

Caves, Richard E., and Jones, R. W. *World Trade and Payments: An Introduction.* 3rd ed. Little, Brown, 1981.

Miller, William J. *Encyclopedia of International Commerce.* Cornell Maritime Press, 1985.

Trade, Board of. See Commodity exchange.

Trade association is a nonprofit organization that represents a group of business firms. Businesses join their associations voluntarily and manage them cooperatively. The companies work together to accomplish goals that no single firm could reach by itself.

A trade association may have only a few members, as in the ironmaking and steelmaking industry. Or it may have thousands of members, as in an association of retail grocers. The size of the trade association's membership has little to do with the effectiveness of the organization. It is more important that the association include most of the companies in the industry. About 3,600 trade associations operate on the national level in the United States.

Trade association activities include promoting business for the industry; encouraging ethical practices in the industry; cooperating with other organizations; and holding conventions. Such associations also work to obtain good relations with the government, the industry's employees, and the general public.

Trade associations sponsor much of the industrial research work in the United States. This research helps improve the quality of goods or services sold by individual firms. Setting industry standardization is another important trade association activity. By obtaining agreements among firms, the trade association sets standards of size and quality for articles and services.

A trade association acts as a source of information about its industry. It may issue bulletins on business trends and provide statistical information. Some publish magazines which are distributed to the public. Trade associations date back to the *guilds* formed in Europe during the Middle Ages.   R. William Taylor

Related articles in *World Book* include:

Better business bureau	Jaycees
Chamber of commerce	National Association
Guild	of Manufacturers
Iron and Steel Institute, American	Railroads, Association of American

Trade Commission, Federal. See Federal Trade Commission.

Trade publication is a periodical devoted to a specific professional, business, industrial, or trade field. Trade journals form an important field of publishing in the United States. Most are weekly or monthly magazines, but there are a number of newspaper-style weeklies, as well as some dailies. These publications carry news items and articles designed to inform the reader about the particular trade or industry. See also **Advertising** (Magazines); **Magazine** (Kinds).   Van Allen Bradley

Trade route. Trade routes have always been the means of bringing new goods into the home and community. In early times, the luxuries of the Orient poured into Western Europe. Later, various countries exchanged raw materials and manufactured goods. Commerce gave rise to great cities along the routes. Trade routes have also increased contacts between peoples and resulted in an exchange of ideas and ways of doing things. Trade routes greatly affected the entire growth of civilization. Trade with Muslims of the Middle East brought new goods and new knowledge to Europe during the Middle Ages. Marco Polo's famous travels revealed knowledge of China and the Mongol Empire.

Early trade routes existed among primitive peoples. They expanded greatly as people became more civilized. Early Sumerians traveled by caravans throughout western Asia to the Mediterranean Sea. The Phoenicians traded by water routes connecting Egypt, Greece, Asia Minor, Italy, and the British Isles.

Rich commerce flowed from the Far East to Europe by three major routes. The northern route, or Great Silk Route, cut from China across central Asia to the Caspian and Black seas, ending at Byzantium (now Istanbul). But, as this overland route was expensive and dangerous, much of the silk commerce traveled by the middle route. It passed through the Persian Gulf and Euphrates Valley and ended either on the Black Sea coast or in such Syrian cities as Damascus. The southern route, by water, led from China around the southern tip of India, up the Red Sea, and overland to the Nile and northern Egypt. Merchants used it to carry spices and pearls from Ceylon; cotton, spices, precious stones, and drugs from India; and cinnamon and incense from Arabia.

Merchants of the Roman Empire carried on a vast amount of trade throughout the then known world. After the fall of the Western Roman Empire, Roman roads were completed and extended. They crossed the Alps, and branched out into Spain, France, and Germany. Water transportation also played a large part in European trading. Early traders shipped goods on the Seine, Rhine, and Danube rivers in Western Europe, and on the Volga and Don in Eastern Europe. Through such seaports as Bordeaux and Nantes on the Atlantic Ocean, they exchanged the wine, grain, and honey of Gaul for metals from Great Britain, and oil and lead from Spain.

Medieval routes. Cities trading with the eastern Mediterranean, such as Venice and Genoa, built powerful commercial empires. Ships brought goods from the Far East. Then Italian fleets carried the products to ports in Spain, England, and Flanders. Other goods crossed overland through Italy and across the Alps to France and to German cities along the Rhine and Danube. Merchants of the Hanseatic League bought these goods in Flanders or Germany, and carried them, along with their own products, to England, the Baltic countries, Poland, and Russia.

The search for new routes led to a great age of exploration and discovery. During the 1400's, European nations began to search for new routes to the East in order to avoid the expensive tolls and the many hazards of the long journey from the Orient. In addition, Italian city-states had a complete trade monopoly, which resulted in high prices and low profits to northern European merchants.

The voyages of Columbus and other explorers opened people's eyes to a whole new world. Many new all-water trade routes grew up. Nations set up trading companies to govern and control trade. The Portuguese first developed trade between India and the East Indies and Europe. The Spanish, Dutch, French, and English followed. Their commercial empires led to colonial empires.

Trade winds are strong winds that occur chiefly in the earth's Tropical Zone. They blow steadily toward the equator from both the northeast and the southeast. Trade winds blow mostly over the oceans because the weather there is more uniform than over the continents.

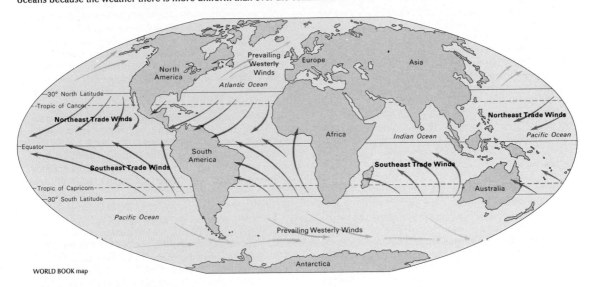

WORLD BOOK map

Today's trade routes are almost numberless, and cover the entire world. Highways and networks of railroads cover continents. Airplanes have connected distant points on the globe. Ships carry goods on the world's oceans and waterways.

The United States government lists 30 trade routes over which it believes adequate ship service is essential to the national interest. In some cases, the government gives *subsidies* (grants of money) to shippers for maintaining this service. Harold J. Heck

See also Exploration, Trade; Colonial life in America (maps: Colonial trade routes); **Colonialism.**

Trade school. See Vocational education; Smith-Hughes Act.

Trade union. See Labor movement.

Trade wind is a strong wind that blows toward the equator from the northeast or southeast. In the days of sailing ships, sailors depended greatly on trade winds. The paths of these winds were so regular, especially over the oceans, that early navigators named them *trade winds,* which meant *course,* or *track,* winds.

The trade winds are part of a great system of winds that blow over the earth. The winds blow toward the equator from about the 30th parallels of north and south latitude.

Differences between the temperature in low latitudes and the temperature in the polar regions cause trade winds. The heating of the air in low latitudes makes it expand and become light. Then it rises. This creates an area of low pressure near the surface. Cooler and heavier air from the polar regions then tends to flow in to fill the area of low pressure. These polar winds do not blow due north or due south, because of the eastward whirling of the earth. Instead, these winds blow from the northeast and from the southeast.

The belt of rising air between the trade winds is a region of mild winds and calms. This region is often called the *doldrums* because it is so calm. Sailing ships of early days were often stranded for many weeks in the doldrums.

Trade winds have a great deal to do with rainfall on land. When trade winds blow against mountain ranges, they are forced upward. As the warm air rises, it cools. Its moisture condenses and falls as rain on the mountain slopes. James E. Miller

See also Calms, Regions of; Doldrums.

Trademark is a word or words, a name, a design, a picture, a sound, or any other symbol that distinguishes the products of one company from those of another. A trademark also may consist of any combination of these identifications. Most trademarks appear on the product, on its container, or in advertisements for the product. A *service mark* identifies the source of a service rather than a product. For example, an electric company may use a lightbulb as a symbol of the service it offers.

A *strong trademark* consists of a word that has no recognizable meaning, such as Kodak. Strong trademarks receive broad protection from being used by other companies in a manner that is likely to cause confusion, mistake, or deception. *Weak trademarks* consist of a common word, such as Premier, or a word that suggests some characteristic of the product, such as Wet 'n Wash. They receive less protection, unless the public identifies them with a certain manufacturer as a result of wide advertising and long, continuous use.

Trademarks, also called *brand names,* provide an easy way to determine who makes a certain product. They help consumers identify brands they liked in the past so they can purchase them again. A trademark represents the manufacturer's reputation, called *good will.*

Most countries have laws that protect the rights of trademark owners. A firm must establish its rights in each country in which it seeks protection.

In the United States, the first company to use a trademark has certain rights to that trademark. The firm may prevent others in the same geographic area from using the same trademark or a similar one for related products. But unless the trademark is very strong, its owner cannot prevent other firms from using the trademark for unrelated products or in another area where it would not cause confusion.

Trademark rights are not limited in duration, and they are not dependent upon any registration. These rights, which form part of the broader law of unfair competition, protect the good will of the trademark owner. They also protect the public from fraud and deceit. Violation of trademark rights is called *infringement.* An infringing trademark is one that is likely to confuse or deceive consumers because of its similarity to a trademark in use.

A company may register its trademark in each state in which it uses the trademark. Trademarks also may be registered in the U.S. Patent and Trademark Office in Washington, D.C. Registration of a trademark serves as notice to everyone of a company's claim of ownership. A trademark owner does not have to register the mark to sue for infringement. But registration gives the owner much stronger rights if a suit is brought.

In other countries, trademark laws differ from those of the United States. Many governments allow a company to register a trademark before using it. Some require registration before any trademark rights can be enforced.   David Pressman

See also **Counterfeiting.**

Trades Union Congress (TUC) is a national organization of British trade unions. It was founded in the 1860's. It is similar to the American Federation of Labor and Congress of Industrial Organizations (AFL-CIO).

Trading post is a type of market place where people bring products to sell or to exchange for other goods. In the United States, many posts serve Navajo Indians who live on a large reservation in Arizona, New Mexico, and Utah. At these posts, the Indians sell goods and buy food, clothing, and farm equipment.

In ancient times, trading posts operated in the Near East. Later, Europeans set up trading posts as they ex-

Detail of a line engraving (1877); Granger Collection
A trading post of the Hudson's Bay Company served as a place where Indians and whites could exchange goods.

plored various parts of the world. At first, before the development of money, traders usually *bartered* with one another—that is, they exchanged items for other items.

The first trading posts in North America were established during the late 1400's in what is now Newfoundland, Canada. By the mid-1800's, trading posts had been set up throughout North America. Indians traded furs and hides to whites for such items as cloth, glass beads, guns, gunpowder, liquor, and metal goods.

Private companies and individuals set up many trading posts. The Hudson's Bay Company opened posts along Hudson Bay in Canada after 1670 (see **Hudson's Bay Company**). In 1796, the U.S. government created a system of government trading posts, hoping to keep private traders from cheating the Indians. The government abolished these posts in 1822 because private traders opposed them. Many white traders later opened posts on Indian reservations and charged unfair prices, but the Indians there had nowhere else to buy goods.

Many settlements that grew up around trading posts developed into large U.S. and Canadian cities. These communities included Chicago; Detroit; Kansas City, Mo.; Montreal; and Quebec.   Merwyn S. Garbarino

Trading stamps are *premiums* or *bonuses* that a retailer gives with a cash purchase of goods. The usual rate is one stamp for every 10 cents spent. People collect the stamps to exchange them for some item of value or to receive a discount on the retailer's merchandise. Trading-stamp companies sell the stamps to retailers. They also *redeem* (exchange) them for various products, such as appliances, housewares, or sports equipment. Some states prohibit trading stamps. The American businessman Thomas Sperry set up the first independent trading-stamp company in 1896. Though use of trading stamps has declined, they are still given by some companies to stimulate sales.   Jay Diamond

Trafalgar, *truh FAL guhr,* is a low, sandy cape on Spain's southern coast, at the western entrance to the Strait of Gibraltar. Admiral Horatio Nelson's British fleet defeated a combined French and Spanish fleet there on Oct. 21, 1805, in one of the greatest naval battles in history. The victory gave England undisputed control of the sea. Nelson was wounded and died during the battle.

The battle occurred during Great Britain's war against Napoleon Bonaparte (see **Napoleon I**). Napoleon hoped to draw the British fleet away to the West Indies so his armies could invade England. But Napoleon's admiral, Villeneuve, failed in this, and decided to attack the British fleet with a French and Spanish fleet. His fleet outnumbered Nelson's, 33 ships to 27.

But Nelson surprised the enemy by having his ships cut through the French battle line. The British fleet did not lose a ship in the battle, but it destroyed or captured over half the French and Spanish ships. Trafalgar Square in London was named in memory of Nelson's victory at Trafalgar.   Robert B. Holtman

See also **London** (picture; map); **Nelson, Horatio.**

Traffic is the movement of people and goods from one place to another. This article deals with traffic on streets and highways. For a discussion of other kinds of traffic, see **Transportation** with its list of *Related articles.*

The United States has about 4,000,000 miles (6,400,000 kilometers) of streets, roads, and highways. Canada has about 550,000 miles (885,000 kilometers). U.S. drivers travel about 1 trillion miles (1.6 trillion kilometers) each year in private and commercial motor vehicles. Passenger cars driven on city streets account for about half of this distance. The average U.S. passenger car covers about 9,200 miles (14,800 kilometers) each year.

Traffic problems

The millions of automobiles in the United States cause many traffic problems. In the morning and evening rush hours, city streets are often jammed with automobiles. On holidays and weekends, many highways are too full for comfort or safety. Freeways and expressways have been built to replace the horse-and-buggy-day streets, roads, and highways. They are constantly being maintained and improved to relieve crowded conditions. The main streets of many small towns are overburdened with through traffic, making it difficult for local people to get to the stores. Bypasses around these towns ease the pressure and help local business. It is hard to find a parking place in the business sections of cities and towns. Parking at the curb is being prohibited in more and more places in order to make additional street space available for traffic. Off-street parking areas are being provided in large numbers.

Improved mass transit systems help relieve congestion when the service is convenient, comfortable, and inexpensive. Better provision for truck loading and unloading at stores, office buildings, and factories eases the problem of truck interference on streets. It also reduces cost of delivery and distribution of goods. More efficient use of existing streets is obtained in several ways. These include: (1) creating one-way streets; (2) changing traffic lanes to one-way operation during hours of heavy traffic; (3) prohibiting curb parking; (4) installing modern coordinated traffic-signal systems, turn controls, and pedestrian controls; and (5) developing through-street systems to move traffic faster.

Traffic control

In the mid-1980's, about 46,000 people were killed and about 3 million people were injured in traffic accidents each year in the United States. Drivers and pedestrians can reduce the number of traffic accidents, injuries, and deaths by watching and obeying traffic control signs, signals, and pavement markings. Special control devices, such as electric signs that tell when to cross streets and highways, are often used to aid pedestrians. These signs operate in conjunction with vehicle traffic signals.

Signals, signs, and markings. There is no clear record of who invented or first used traffic control devices. It is generally agreed, however, that automatic traffic signals first appeared in Detroit in the early 1920's. The Wayne County (Michigan) Road Commission developed the use of a white center line for separating driving lanes on highways. Traffic signs date back to the early Roman roads.

Traffic controls are increasingly necessary for regulating, warning, and guiding motor vehicle and pedestrian traffic. The law requires signs to indicate how certain traffic regulations apply. Adequate use of warning signs, and well-designed and well-located route markings have great value, too, in helping the flow of traffic. Pavement and curb markings and traffic islands, when prop-

erly designed and located, also help guide traffic.

Modern traffic lights are made so that they can be set to change when traffic demands it. In most places, the changes are automatic every so many seconds or minutes. Where there are different amounts of traffic on intersecting highways and streets, the light can be set so that it will remain green longer for the highway or street with the most traffic. Some traffic lights also are arranged so that the traffic itself will cause them to change. This is done by placing switches or magnets on the roadway. These are called *detectors.* When cars pass over the detectors, the light changes to let the cars go through the intersection. Where there is a great deal of pedestrian cross-traffic but little motor vehicle cross-traffic to change the lights, the signals frequently work from a switch operated by the pedestrian.

Many warning and guide signs are covered with luminous paint, or glass or metal beads or buttons, which reflect beams from headlights. This makes the signs easier to see at night. Traffic lanes, pedestrian crosswalks, turn markings, and warning signs frequently are painted or otherwise marked. Sometimes, various types of reflector buttons or white material are embedded in the surface of the street or highway.

Control devices must be located in the right places or they can cause delay and congestion, and lead persons to disregard them. Good traffic control devices must be based on sound engineering principles. Studies of types and flow of traffic, accidents, speeds, delays, and physical conditions show the exact nature of a traffic difficulty and indicate the particular devices or methods of control that are needed.

Traffic regulations are the rules of the road governing the actions of pedestrians and drivers on public roads and streets. Regulations should be uniform, so that drivers everywhere will know exactly what actions to take under like conditions.

Parking meters were first used in Oklahoma City in 1935. The purpose of these traffic-control devices is to measure mechanically time-limit parking regulations. Originally located only at the curb, parking meters now frequently are placed in parking lots. There the parking meters are used to restrict the length of time vehicles are allowed to park, or to collect parking fees.

Traffic police enforce traffic-control measures and regulations, and control traffic emergencies. Development of street and highway facilities and traffic-control plans are the responsibilities of highway or traffic engineers.   Jack D. Bakos, Jr.

Related articles in *World Book* include:

Automobile	Police	Road
Bicycle	Radar (In controlling	Safety
Bus (Importance of	automobile speed	Street
buses)	and traffic)	

Tragacanth, *TRAG uh kanth,* is a true gum obtained from various shrubs (Astragalus) of the pulse family. These shrubs grow mainly in Asia Minor, Iran, and Syria. Tragacanth is dull white or yellowish in color, and clear and hornlike in texture. It is usually sold in thin flakes or ribbons which swell into a jellylike mass when soaked in water. The use of tragacanth in pharmacy dates back to Biblical times. Today, it is used in preparing pills, emulsions, and creams. It is also occasionally used in making printing gums for textiles.   Charles L. Mantell

Tragedy is a form of drama that deals with serious human actions and issues. Tragedy explores questions about morality, the meaning of human existence, relationships between people, and relationships between people and their gods. By the end of most tragedies, the main character has died or lost his or her loved ones.

Playwrights have written tragedies throughout the history of drama. The most famous were written during three periods—the 400's B.C. in Greece, the late 1500's and early 1600's in England, and the 1600's in France.

The greatest writers of Greek tragedy were Aeschylus, Euripides, and Sophocles. They took most of their plots from Greek mythology. William Shakespeare was the principal tragic dramatist of the English period. His tragedies are noted for their suspenseful plots, insights into human nature, and powerful poetic dialogue. Other leading English playwrights of the period included Christopher Marlowe and John Webster. Jean Racine dominated tragic drama during the French period. His tragic heroes and heroines are victims of violent passions they cannot control. Pierre Corneille was another important French tragic playwright of the 1600's.

Until the 1700's, almost all tragedies dealt with royalty, famous historical figures, or other notable people. Playwrights did not consider the lives of common men and women important enough to provide material for tragedies. After 1700, a number of dramatists wrote *domestic tragedies,* plays with middle-class people as heroes and heroines. Perhaps the most important of these playwrights was Gotthold Ephraim Lessing of Germany.

Notable tragedies of the late 1700's and early 1800's were written by Friedrich Schiller of Germany and Victor Hugo of France. Most of their works dealt with famous or powerful characters.

Critics disagree about whether any true tragedies have been written since the late 1800's. Some argue that serious plays of this period lack the moral, philosophical, or religious significance required for genuine tragedy. Other critics believe several playwrights have created works that can be considered tragedies. These playwrights include Georg Büchner of Germany, Henrik Ibsen of Norway, and Arthur Miller and Eugene O'Neill of the United States.   Oscar G. Brockett

Each playwright discussed in this article has a separate biography in *World Book.* See also **Drama; Aristotle** (Literary criticism).

Tragopan, *TRAG uh pan,* is a handsome quaillike bird of the pheasant family. It lives in forests high on mountain slopes of southern and central Asia. The male has a bright-colored *lappet* (loose-hanging skin) on his throat, and a pair of blue, fleshy, erectile horns on each side of his head. Both lappet and horns become enlarged and brilliant during the mating season.

Tragopans eat insects, leaves, fruits, and seeds. They nest in trees. Their white eggs are slightly speckled with dull lilac. These birds are shy. Hunters usually snare them by driving them slowly toward nooses.

Scientific classification. The tragopan belongs to the family Phasianidae and makes up the genus *Tragopan.* The best known of the five species is *T. satyrus,* the satyr tragopan of the Himalaya.   Joseph J. Hickey

Trail of Tears. See **Indian, American** (The fall of Indian America [In the United States]); **Oklahoma** (The Indian nations).

Coachmen Recreational Vehicle Company

Travel trailers, such as the one above, are popular for family vacations and for fishing and hunting trips. Trailers have comfortable interiors with room to store an assortment of gear.

Trailer is a wheeled vehicle that is pulled by an automobile or truck. Trailers are designed to be used chiefly (1) as temporary living quarters for either recreational travel or camping, or (2) for cargo hauling. *Mobile homes,* on the other hand, are designed to be used for permanent, year-round living (see **Mobile home**).

Recreational trailers include *travel trailers* and *camping trailers.* A travel trailer provides a dwelling for people on an automobile, fishing, or hunting trip. Travel trailers can be moved easily and serve as comfortable living quarters. Most travel trailers are sold with furniture and a completely equipped kitchen and bathroom. These trailers range in size from 12 to 35 feet (3.7 to 10.7 meters) long and from 6 to 8 feet (1.8 to 2.4 meters) wide. Popular models are about $7\frac{1}{2}$ feet (2.3 meters) wide.

Camping trailers are smaller and more compact than travel trailers. A camping trailer has collapsible walls of heavy fabric, plastic, or some other material. The trailer folds out into a tentlike structure in which four to eight people can sleep. It may have a kitchen and bathroom.

Hauling trailers range from 6 to 14 feet (1.8 to 4.3 meters) long, or longer. They are used to carry loads that may be too large to fit in an automobile trunk. They

WORLD BOOK illustration by Trevor Boyer, Linden Artists Ltd.

The tragopan, a colorful member of the pheasant family, has handsome markings. Tragopans live in mountain forests of Asia.

may also be used to transport farm animals to market or to a livestock show. Most hauling trailers look like boxes without tops. Canvas or another material may be spread over the top to protect the load.

Trailers with tops, called *vans,* open from the rear. Some, such as marine vans, used for hauling boats, also open on the sides. Some small vans can be hitched to a car, but large trucks pull most vans. Highway trucks use special trailers to haul various kinds of cargoes, such as automobiles, food, and logs.   F. M. Radigan

See also **Recreational vehicle.**

Trailing arbutus. See **Arbutus.**

Train. See **Electric railroad; Locomotive; Railroad.**

Training, Military. See **Military training.**

Training school. See **Reformatory.**

Trait. See **Heredity** (Human heredity; The physical basis of heredity).

Traitor. See **Treason.**

Trajan, *TRAY juhn* (A.D. 53?-117), was a Roman emperor and an important military leader. He expanded the empire by conquest and carried out extensive building programs. He tried to reduce poverty in Italy, and to improve the financial affairs of cities and towns across the empire. Trajan conquered Dacia (now parts of Romania and Hungary) and Arabia, and he won victories in Parthia (now part of Iran). He founded new cities, including Thamugadi (now Timgad, Algeria). Trajan also built bridges and harbors. These included bridges across the Danube River in Dacia and the Tagus River in Spain, and a harbor at the port of Rome.

Trajan was born Marcus Ulpius Trajanus in Italica, Spain, of Roman parents. His father was a soldier who became governor of an eastern province. Trajan received a military education and won fame in Spain, Syria, and Germany. In A.D. 97, Emperor Nerva adopted Trajan as his heir and successor. When Emperor Nerva died in A.D. 98, Trajan was declared emperor.

Trajan's Column is a monument built in the emperor's honor after he conquered Dacia. It was dedicated in A.D. 113. The well-preserved column, 100 feet (30 meters) high, stands in Trajan's Forum in Rome. A spiral stair-case inside the column leads to the top. The column and its pedestal are covered with carvings portraying events of the Dacian wars. The ashes of Trajan are said to have been placed in the column, but no trace of them has ever been found.   Ramsay MacMullen

See also **Rome** (picture: Trajan's Column); **Sculpture** (picture: Trajan's Column [detail]); **Library** (Libraries of papyrus).

Tram is the term used in Britain and other Commonwealth countries for a streetcar. See **Streetcar.**

Trampoline, *TRAM puh LEEN* or *TRAM puh lihn,* is a device that a person bounces or jumps on to perform aerial tumbling exercises. People can use trampolines for recreation or for organized competition.

Trampolines may be circular or rectangular. They consist of a bed of solid or woven material that is suspended from a steel frame by rubber cords or steel springs. The frame and the cords or springs should be covered with a pad for safety. Trampolines are supported by legs about 3 feet (0.9 meter) high. Trampolines used in national and international competition are rectangular and have beds that are 7 feet (2.1 meters) wide and 14 feet (4.3 meters) long.

A number of safety rules should be followed to avoid injury while using a trampoline. At least one qualified supervisor should always be present when a trampoline is in use. Only one person should perform on the device at a time. Somersaults should be prohibited except in competitive programs with qualified instructors. Trampolines should be inspected often for damage and kept locked when not in use.   Jeff T. Hennessy

Trance is a term that is generally used to describe any kind of unnatural sleep or partly conscious state. The term may be used to describe the condition of hypnotized persons, spiritualist mediums, and some persons with mental disorders. In some cases, trances continue for long periods of time. Usually, however, they last for only brief periods of time. The word *trance* was first used to describe conditions in which the soul was believed to have withdrawn from the body of a person for a period of time.

David R. Frazier

The trampoline allows an individual to perform exciting aerial tumbling exercises. Users should follow strict safety rules. Only one person should perform on the device at a time. At least one qualified person should always be present while the trampoline is being used.

There are no physical signs that always indicate a trance. But in many cases, the pulse and breathing rate slow down. A person in a trance is less responsive to changes in surroundings, and may not know what is happening. The person may appear to be responding to forces not actually present.

The best-known type of trance is probably that of the spiritualist medium who appears to have fallen into a deep sleep, but can still speak and write. Such a trance may be similar to a deep hypnosis, and it may involve hallucinations. James E. Alcock

See also **Hypnotism**.

Tranquilizer is a drug that calms a person by acting on the nervous system. Tranquilizers belong to a group of drugs called *depressants*.

There are two types of tranquilizers—*major tranquilizers* and *minor tranquilizers*. Major tranquilizers are used to treat patients with *psychoses* (severe mental illnesses). These tranquilizers are also called *antipsychotic drugs*. Minor tranquilizers are used to treat various emotional problems, particularly anxiety. They are also called *anti-anxiety drugs*.

Major tranquilizers include such drugs as chlorpromazine (commonly known by the trade name Thorazine), fluphenazine, and trifluoperazine. Physicians prescribe these drugs to treat *schizophrenia,* a mental illness that is characterized by illogical, unpredictable thinking. The drugs reduce the confusion and excitement experienced by the patient.

Minor tranquilizers include alprazolam, diazepam, and lorazepam, which are commonly known by the trade names Xanax, Valium, and Ativan, respectively. They relax the muscles and reduce tension. Minor tranquilizers are prescribed mainly for the treatment of anxiety. Physicians also use minor tranquilizers to calm children who must undergo surgery. In addition, these drugs are used to treat *delirium tremens,* a disorder that results from alcoholism.

Some tranquilizers have undesirable side effects. For example, meprobamate may cause muscle weakness and general fatigue. Some people become addicted to tranquilizers. In addition, tranquilizers may cause drowsiness, especially if a person drinks alcoholic beverages before or after taking the drugs. A person should not drive a motor vehicle for several hours after taking a tranquilizer. N. E. Sladek

See also **Depressant; Drug** (Depressants).

Transactional analysis is a method of psychotherapy. In this method, therapists treat emotional problems by helping people analyze their relationships in social situations. Such situations are called *transactions*. Eric L. Berne, a Canadian-born psychiatrist, developed the method during the 1960's. Interest in transactional analysis, or TA, was stimulated by two best-selling books—*Games People Play* (1964), written by Berne, and *I'm OK—You're OK* (1969) by Thomas A. Harris, an American psychiatrist.

Berne regarded the human personality as consisting of three "selves"—the *Child,* the *Parent,* and the *Adult.* According to Berne, any of these "selves" may be in control of a person during a transaction. The Child is dependent, impulsive, fun loving, and creative. The Parent is stern and critical. The Adult is capable of logical thinking. TA is based on the idea that people can learn to use the Adult to think and make decisions for themselves.

Berne thought that transactions can be understood by analyzing *games* in communication. A game is a transaction in which people deceive themselves or others. For example, people who blame their problems on others may be playing a game that Berne called "See What You Made Me Do." Berne believed that people use *scripts*—that is, life plans that they learn in childhood and later feel forced to act out. The games are part of the script. David L. Krantz

Trans-Alaska Pipeline System. See Pipeline (Major pipelines of the world).

Transatlantic cable. See Cable.

Trans-Canada Highway stretches about 5,000 miles (8,000 kilometers) across Canada and links the 10 provinces. It runs from St. John's, Nfld., on the Atlantic coast to Victoria, B.C., on the Pacific coast. The tollfree, two-lane highway cost more than $1 billion. It was begun in 1950 and officially opened in 1962.

The all-weather highway made many areas, especially in western Canada, easier to reach and opened them to new economic development. It also has attracted larger numbers of tourists to Canada's national parks. The route goes through Glacier, Mount Revelstoke, and

Trans-Canada Highway

The Trans-Canada Highway, shown as a red line on the map, runs from Victoria, B.C., to St. John's, Nfld. It provides a direct and scenic route across all 10 Canadian provinces.

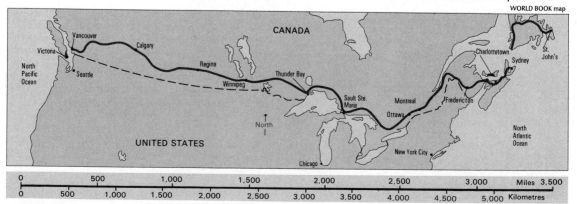

WORLD BOOK map

Yoho national parks in British Columbia; Banff in Alberta; and Terra Nova in Newfoundland.

Motorists driving westward along the Trans-Canada Highway travel through the Atlantic Provinces; Montreal, Canada's largest city; Ottawa, the Canadian capital; the upper Great Lakes region; the western prairie wheat fields; and the Rocky Mountains to Vancouver Island.

Allan R. Turner

Transcendental Meditation (TM) is a method of relaxing the body that became popular in many countries during the 1970's. It was developed in the 1950's by the Maharishi Mahesh Yogi, a Hindu monk from India. He used the word *transcendental* to describe the process of reaching a state of *pure consciousness,* where the mind is not aware of anything in particular. He declared that people who used this technique became happier and more relaxed and creative. Centers that teach TM operate in many countries, including the United States and Canada. Followers of the Maharishi call TM the Science of Creative Intelligence.

People practice TM by sitting quietly in a comfortable position. They close their eyes and silently repeat their *mantra,* a pleasant-sounding word from the Hindu scriptures. Teachers of TM select a personal, secret mantra for each student. A person who practices TM meditates for 15 to 20 minutes in the morning and evening, before meals.

Scientific studies show that certain bodily changes occur during meditation. For example, the rate of breathing and the amount of oxygen taken in by the body decrease. The blood pressure and the rate of heartbeat also decrease while a person meditates.

In addition, scientists found that *alpha waves* (brain waves that become prominent when a person is relaxed) increase in intensity during meditation. Psychologists report that many people who practice TM feel less anxious and aggressive than before and can handle stress more easily. Some scientists believe TM causes these changes because people have faith in the method and expect it to help them.

The Maharishi claimed that people cannot meditate effectively without training from a TM teacher and the use of a mantra. However, many scientists declare that other forms of meditation and relaxation can produce the same results as TM. Gary E. Schwartz

Additional resources

Benson, Herbert, and Klipper, Miriam Z. *The Relaxation Response.* Avon, 1976. First published in 1975. Presents an alternative to the TM technique.
Bloomfield, Harold H., and others. *TM: Discovering Inner Energy and Overcoming Stress.* Delacorte, 1975.

Transcendentalism was a philosophy that became influential during the late 1700's and 1800's. It was based on the belief that knowledge is not limited to and solely derived from experience and observation. It thus opposed the philosophy of empiricism—that knowledge comes from experience. Transcendentalism also stated that the solution to human problems lies in the free development of individual emotions.

According to transcendentalism, reality exists only in the world of the spirit. What a person observes in the physical world are only appearances, or impermanent reflections of the world of the spirit. People learn about the physical world through their senses and under-

standing. But they learn about the world of the spirit through another power, called *reason.* The transcendentalists defined reason as the independent and intuitive capacity to know what is absolutely true.

Elements of transcendentalism can be found in the Neoplatonic philosophy of ancient Greece (see **Neoplatonism**). But the chief source of transcendentalist ideas was the *Critique of Pure Reason* (1781) by the German philosopher Immanuel Kant.

In the United States, transcendentalism became both a philosophy and a literary, religious, and social movement. It began among Unitarians in New England and reached its peak during the 1840's. Ralph Waldo Emerson was the leading American transcendentalist. He taught that the physical world is secondary to the spiritual world. But, said Emerson, the physical world serves humanity by providing useful goods and by making human beings aware of beauty. Emerson believed that people should learn as much as possible through observation and science. But he insisted that they should adjust their lives primarily to the truths seen through reason.

Emerson and his followers believed that human beings find truth within themselves, and so they emphasized self-reliance and individuality. They believed that society is a necessary evil. They argued that to learn what is right, a person must ignore custom and social codes and rely on reason. The transcendentalists believed that the doctrines and organized churches of orthodox Christianity interfered with the personal relationship between a person and God. The transcendentalists said that individuals should reject the authority of Christianity and gain knowledge of God through reason.

The American transcendentalists never became numerous, but their writings greatly influenced American intellectual history and literature. Besides Emerson, the leading American transcendentalists included Bronson Alcott, Margaret Fuller, Theodore Parker, and Henry David Thoreau. John Clendenning

Each person discussed in this article has a biography in *World Book.*

Additional resources

Koster, Donald N. *Transcendentalism in America.* Twayne, 1975.
The Transcendentalists: An Anthology. Ed. by Perry G. E. Miller. Harvard, 1950.

Transcontinental railroad. See Railroad (The first transcontinental rail lines; picture: The meeting of two railroads).

Transcontinental Treaty. See Adams-Onís Treaty.

Transducer is a device that converts one form of energy into another. Many transducers convert electric waves into mechanical vibrations—or vice versa. Loudspeakers, microphones, and phonograph pickup cartridges are all transducers. *Sonar transducers* send and receive sound waves in water. *Ultrasonic transducers* generate and detect vibrations above the frequency range of human hearing. They are used to cut hard materials, to clean delicate instruments, to drill oil wells, and to measure the level of liquids in the fuel tanks of space vehicles.

Transducers work in various ways. Some phonograph cartridges use *piezoelectric* materials, which produce a voltage when squeezed. Loudspeakers use moving coils that vibrate when current moves through them. The vibrations result from an interaction between the coils and powerful permanent magnets. Some ultrasonic transducers use *magnetostrictive* materials, which contract in a magnetic field.   Douglas M. Lapp

See also **Ultrasound.**

Transexualism. See **Transsexualism.**

Transfer of training. See **Learning** (Efficient learning).

Transfiguration was the change in physical appearance that came over Jesus Christ on one occasion during His ministry. It is described in the Gospels of Matthew, Mark, and Luke. According to these Gospels, Jesus took Peter, James, and John up on a mountain, and permitted them to see Him in splendor, with His face shining like the sun, and His garments bright with light. Then the Old Testament figures of Moses and Elijah came to talk with Christ. Raphael's altarpiece *The Transfiguration,* said by many to be one of the world's greatest paintings, now hangs in the Vatican (see **Raphael**).

Stanley K. Stowers

Transformational grammar. See **Chomsky, Noam.**

Transformer is a device that increases or decreases the voltage of alternating current. Transformers provide a simple, inexpensive way to change such voltage. They enable electric power companies to transmit alternating current easily and efficiently. They also ensure the proper voltage for the circuits of home appliances, lights, industrial machinery, and other electric equipment.

Most transformers consist of two coils of insulated wire. One coil, known as the *primary winding,* is connected to the source of the voltage that is to be changed. This voltage is the *input voltage* of the transformer. The other coil, called the *secondary winding,* supplies the *output voltage* to the desired circuit. In most transformers, the primary and secondary windings are wound around a hollow core made of thin iron or steel sheets. Most cores have the shape of a ring or a square. The two coils are not connected to each other.

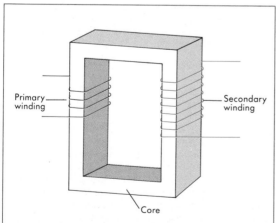

WORLD BOOK diagram by Linda Kinnaman

A typical transformer consists of two coils of wire wound around the sides of a core of thin iron sheets. The ends of the primary winding are connected to the source of the voltage that is to be changed. The ends of the secondary winding are connected to the circuit to which the electricity is to be transferred.

Transformers work by means of *electromagnetic induction* (see **Electromagnetism**). When the input voltage is applied to the primary winding, it generates alternating current in the coil. As the current flows, it sets up a changing magnetic field in the core of the transformer. When this magnetic field cuts across the secondary winding, it produces alternating voltage in the coil. If the secondary winding is connected to a circuit, the output voltage causes alternating current to flow through the circuit.

The ratio between a transformer's output voltage and input voltage equals the ratio of the number of turns in the secondary winding to the number in the primary winding. If E represents the voltage and N stands for the number of turns, then $\dfrac{E \text{ output}}{E \text{ input}} = \dfrac{N \text{ secondary}}{N \text{ primary}}$. The output voltage will be greater than the input voltage in a transformer whose secondary winding has more turns than the primary winding. Such a transformer is called a *step-up transformer.* If the secondary coil has fewer turns than the primary, the output voltage will be less than the input voltage. This type of transformer is called a *step-down transformer.*

In power plants, step-up transformers increase the voltage of the alternating current produced by generators. High voltages make it possible to transmit the current over long distances with only a small loss in power. When the current reaches the area where it will be used, step-down transformers lower the voltage to the level needed by local consumers (see **Electric power** [Transmitting and distributing electric power]).

Some transformers have special uses. For example, *air-core transformers* and *powdered iron-core transformers* are designed to handle high-frequency alternating currents. *Instrument transformers* are used in measuring extremely large alternating voltages and currents. *Variable transformers* vary the amount of output voltage delivered to a circuit.   Douglas M. Lapp

See also **Induction coil.**

Transfusion, Blood. See **Blood transfusion.**

Transistor is a tiny device used in computers, radios, television sets, and other electronic equipment. Transistors control the flow of electric current in such equipment. A typical transistor, together with its protective case, is about as large as the eraser on a pencil.

Electronic equipment has been revolutionized by transistors. In modern electronic equipment, most transistors are packaged inside devices called *integrated circuits.* There may be hundreds of thousands of transistors in just one integrated circuit about the size of a postage stamp (see **Integrated circuit**). Without transistors, manufacturers could not make pocket calculators or high-speed computers. Battery-operated radios and television sets would be much larger and cost more to operate. The small size and light weight of transistors also led to the development of communications satellites that link continents through telephones and television.

How transistors are made. Manufacturers make transistors from silicon, which is a solid material called a *semiconductor.* Semiconductors conduct electricity, but not so well as do true conductors, such as copper or iron. The atoms of the semiconductor material used in a transistor must be in the form of crystals.

Transistor manufacturers add small amounts of certain impurities to the crystals of the semiconductor. The impurities control the way electricity flows in the silicon. Some impurities add *free* (extra) electrons to the crystals. Other impurities do not supply the crystals with enough electrons. This lack of electrons causes empty spaces, known as *holes,* in the crystals. A semiconductor material is called *n-type* if it has extra electrons, and *p-type* if it has holes. Electricity flows as a movement of electrons in n-type material and as a movement of holes in p-type material.

Transistors consist of layers of n-type and p-type materials. To make a transistor, manufacturers may *grow* (make) pure crystals and cut them into thin slices. They heat these slices and expose them to impurities to form n-type and p-type layers. They then attach wires to the layers. Finally, the finished transistor is put into a tiny case to protect it.

How transistors work. There are two main types of transistors—*junction transistors* and *field effect transistors.* Each works in a different way. But the usefulness of any transistor comes from its ability to control a strong current with a weak voltage. For example, transistors in a public address system *amplify* (strengthen) the weak voltage produced when a person speaks into a microphone. The electricity coming from the transistors is strong enough to operate a loudspeaker, which produces sounds much louder than the person's voice.

Junction transistors. A junction transistor consists of a thin piece of one type of semiconductor material between two thicker layers of the opposite type. For example, if the middle layer is p type, the outside layers must be n type. Such a transistor is an *NPN transistor.* One of the outside layers is called the *emitter,* and the other is known as the *collector.* The middle layer is the *base.* The places where the emitter joins the base and the base joins the collector are called *junctions.*

The layers of an NPN transistor must have the proper voltage connected across them. The voltage of the base must be more positive than that of the emitter. The voltage of the collector, in turn, must be more positive than that of the base. The voltages are supplied by a battery or some other source of direct current.

The emitter supplies electrons. The base pulls these electrons from the emitter because it has a more positive voltage than does the emitter. This movement of electrons creates a flow of electricity through the transistor.

The current passes from the emitter to the collector through the base. Changes in the voltage connected to the base modify the flow of the current by changing the number of electrons in the base. In this way, small changes in the base voltage can cause large changes in the current flowing out of the collector.

Manufacturers also make *PNP junction transistors.* In these devices, the emitter and collector are both a p-type semiconductor material and the base is n-type. A PNP junction transistor works on the same principle as an NPN transistor. But it differs in one respect. The main flow of current in a PNP transistor is controlled by altering the number of holes rather than the number of electrons in the base. Also, this type of transistor works properly only if the negative and positive connections to it are the reverse of those of the NPN transistor.

Parts of a transistor

An NPN junction transistor, shown at the lower left, consists of a tiny silicon chip in a protective case. The chip has a layer of one type of material between two layers of the opposite type, as shown in the cross-section drawing at the lower right. Lead wires are attached to each of these layers by metal contacts.

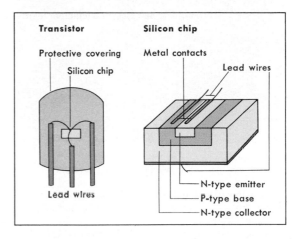

How a transistor works

The emitter of an NPN transistor has a negative voltage and produces electrons. The collector has a positive voltage and attracts the electrons. A weak current applied to the base enables the electrons to move across the base from the emitter to the collector and create a flow of electricity. The weak base current controls the main flow of current through an NPN transistor.

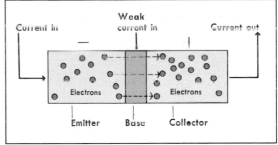

WORLD BOOK diagrams by Arthur Grebetz

Field effect transistors. A field effect transistor has only two layers of semiconductor material, one on top of the other. Electricity flows through one of the layers, called the *channel.* A voltage connected to the other layer, called the *gate,* interferes with the current flowing in the channel. Thus, the voltage connected to the gate controls the strength of the current in the channel. There are two basic varieties of field effect transistors— the *junction field effect transistor* (JFET) and the *metal oxide semiconductor field effect transistor* (MOSFET). Most of the transistors contained in today's integrated circuits are MOSFET's.

History. Three American physicists—John Bardeen, Walter H. Brattain, and William Shockley—invented the transistor in 1947. They shared the 1956 Nobel prize in physics for their work. The first transistor was called a *point-contact transistor.* In 1948, Shockley developed the theory of the junction transistor. Within a few years,

David R. Frazier

Transistor circuits occupy little space. In this photograph of a computer circuit board, a pencil points to a transistor.

junction transistors had replaced the point-contact type. In 1952, Shockley published the theory that led to the field effect transistor.

During the early 1960's, manufacturers developed the technique of making many transistors on a single piece of semiconductor material. This technique led to the development of integrated circuits on one piece of semiconductor material. Since that time, researchers have learned how to put ever increasing numbers of transistors and other components on each semiconductor chip. They have thereby reduced the average cost per transistor to a small fraction of what it was in the early 1960's.   Richard W. Henry

See also **Electronics; Semiconductor.**

Additional resources

Lenk, John D. *Handbook for Transistors*. Simon & Schuster, 1976.
Pearce, William E., and Klein, A. E. *Transistors and Circuits: Electronics for Young Experimenters*. Doubleday, 1971. For younger readers.

Transistor radio. See Radio (diagram: Main parts of an AM transistor radio).
Transit. See Surveying.
Transit, in astronomy, is the crossing of one heavenly body over the disk of a larger one, as seen from the earth. The transits of Venus and Mercury have been studied with much interest because they can be used to measure the size of the solar system. The orbits of these planets are between the sun and the earth's orbit. Mercury passes directly between the sun and earth at intervals from 3 to 13 years. It then appears as a black spot against the sun. Transits of Venus are much rarer, occurring in pairs every 122 years.

The term *transit* also means the passage of any celestial body, such as sun, moon, planet, or star, across an observer's meridian.   Lee J. Rickard

See also **Mercury** (Phases).
Transjordan. See Jordan.
Transkei, *trans KAY* or *trans KY,* is a region within the Republic of South Africa. It is one of the 10 *homelands* established by the white South African government for the country's *African* (black) people. The Transkei is the homeland of the Xhosa people.

In 1959, the South African government established a policy of granting independence to the homelands. In 1976, the Transkei became the first homeland to be declared an independent nation by the government. But neither the United Nations (UN) nor the Organization of African Unity (OAU) recognizes the Transkei as independent. Most critics of South Africa claim that the independence was granted to reduce criticism of South Africa's racial segregation policy, called *apartheid*. They believe the Transkei is too dependent on South Africa to be considered truly independent.

The Transkei consists of three separate sections of land in southeastern South Africa. It covers 16,070 square miles (41,620 square kilometers) and has a population of about $2\frac{1}{2}$ million. Umtata is the largest city of the region and the seat of its government.

Government. In 1987, the military overthrew the civilian government of the Transkei. Military leaders took control of the government. The Transkei had a legislature called the National Assembly. It consisted of 75 appointed chiefs and 75 elected members.

People. All African citizens of the Transkei are generally called Xhosa. Most of them actually belong to the Xhosa ethnic group. A small percentage of these people are members of related groups that also speak the Xhosa language. About 5,000 whites live in the Transkei, but most of them are citizens of South Africa.

The majority of Xhosa in the Transkei are a rural people, and many live much as their ancestors did. Many Xhosa people still live in cone-shaped huts, tend cattle, and grow crops. Many find it difficult to produce enough food for their own needs.

About half of all of the Xhosa people live in the Transkei. The others live in white-dominated areas of South Africa, where they work in white-owned industries. These Xhosa lost their South African citizenship when

Transkei

The Transkei consists of the three separate areas shown in white on the map below.

⊛   Capital
•   Other city or town
——— Road
┄┄┄ Rail line

WORLD BOOK map

Hutchison Library

In a rural area of the Transkei, clusters of small huts border a dirt road. Most people in the Transkei make their living by growing crops and raising cattle.

the Transkei was declared independent. They became citizens of the Transkei, even though many have never been in the region and do not intend to move there.

Land and climate. Most of the Transkei consists of rolling grasslands. Elevations range from sea level along the coast to about 9,800 feet (2,990 meters) in the mountains of the northwest. Several rivers in the Transkei have carved out beautiful valleys and canyons.

The Transkei has a mild climate, with rainy summers and dry winters. Temperatures average about 70° F. (21° C) in January and 60° F. (16° C) in July. About three-fourths of the Transkei receives more than 30 inches (76 centimeters) of rain yearly, and no area gets less than 20 inches (51 centimeters).

Economy of the Transkei depends heavily on South Africa. More than 70 per cent of the region's income consists of wages earned by Xhosa who work in South Africa. South Africa also provides about three-fourths of the budget for the Transkeian government.

Farming is the chief economic activity in the Transkei. Farmers grow chiefly corn, and other crops include coffee and tea. Many also raise cattle. The government is working to improve agriculture, but the region has serious problems of overgrazing, soil erosion, and low production. It produces relatively small amounts of manufactured goods and minerals. But manufacturing and mining have grown in importance since the mid-1960's. The region has deposits of coal, copper, and nickel.

History. During ancient times, Bushmen and Hottentots lived in what is now the Transkei. By the A.D. 1500's, the Xhosa and other related peoples had migrated into the region. During the 1800's, the Xhosa fought a series of wars, called the Kaffir Wars, against Dutch and British settlers. By 1894, all the Transkei had come under European domination. It became part of South Africa in 1910. South Africa granted the Transkei limited self-government in 1963 and declared it independent in 1976. The

Transkei claims control of East Griqualand, a small area that lies between its central and eastern sections. But South Africa considers the area its own territory. In 1978, the Transkei broke diplomatic relations with South Africa over the dispute. The diplomatic relations were reestablished in 1980, after South Africa agreed to consider the Transkei's claim. In the early 1980's, political corruption caused unrest among the people. In 1987, military leaders overthrew the government of the Transkei. The leaders claimed to have staged the coup in an attempt to end political corruption.   L. H. Gann

See also **Apartheid; South Africa; Xhosa.**

Transmigration of the soul. See Reincarnation.

Transmission is a series of parts that transmit power from the engine of a motor vehicle. The power goes from the engine to the *drive shaft,* which carries it to the *final drive.* The power is delivered by the final drive to the vehicle's drive wheels. The transmission, drive shaft, and final drive make up the *drive train* of the vehicle. Automobiles, trucks, buses, bulldozers, and other motor vehicles have drive trains. This article discusses automobile drive trains.

The diagram on this page shows the drive train of what automobile manufacturers call a *conventional car.* Conventional cars have the engine in front and the drive wheels in the rear. The parts of the drive train are arranged differently in cars that have a front-wheel drive or a rear-mounted engine. There are two main kinds of transmissions, *manual* and *automatic.*

What a transmission does

The power of an engine consists of *torque* and *speed.* Torque is the twisting force of the engine's crankshaft. Speed refers to the rate of rotation of the crankshaft. The transmission can adjust the proportions of torque and speed that it delivers from the engine to the drive shaft. When it increases the torque, it decreases the speed; and when it increases the speed, it decreases the torque. Thus, the transmission provides the high torque and low speed that a car needs to start moving. It also delivers the low torque and high speed needed for cruising on a highway. The transmission also reverses the torque so a car can back up.

Almost all transmissions vary torque and speed by means of *gears.* A gear is a wheel with projections called *teeth* around the edge. The teeth fit together with the teeth of another gear. Suppose that a small gear with 12 teeth drives a large gear with 24 teeth. The large gear rotates with half the speed, but twice the torque, of the small gear. This relationship is called *reduction.* The amount of reduction is expressed numerically by the *gear ratio.* The gear ratio in the above example is 2 to 1 because the small gear rotates twice for each rotation of the large gear.

Parts of a drive train

WORLD BOOK diagram by Richard Fickle

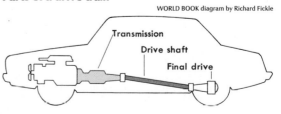

Transmission

Drive shaft

Final drive

The gears in a transmission can be combined in different ways to produce various gear ratios and thus various proportions of torque and speed. The gear ratios are often called simply *gears* or *speeds.* The process of changing from one gear ratio to another is called *shifting gears.*

How a manual transmission works

The driver shifts the gears of a manual transmission by means of a hand-operated lever called a *gearshift.* Most manual transmissions have a neutral position; three, four, or five forward gears; and a reverse gear. The driver puts the transmission into neutral when the engine is being started, or when a car is parked with the engine left running.

To put a car into forward motion, the driver shifts into *first,* or *low gear.* This gear provides the highest torque and the lowest speed. As the car picks up speed, the driver shifts into *second gear,* then into *third gear,* and so on, until the transmission is in the highest gear desired. If extra torque is needed, the driver may *downshift* from a higher gear to a lower one. This situation might occur when the car goes up a steep hill. The reverse gear is used to make the car go backward.

The clutch. The driver of a car with a manual transmission must operate the *clutch* along with the gearshift. The clutch, which is operated by a pedal, is a device that connects the engine to the transmission. When the driver presses the pedal, the clutch is *disengaged* (disconnected from the engine), and no power is sent to

the transmission. When the driver releases the pedal, the clutch is *engaged,* sending power to the transmission. The driver must disengage the clutch when shifting gears.

The clutch consists basically of two disks, the *flywheel* and the *clutch plate.* The flywheel is connected to the crankshaft and turns whenever the engine is running. The clutch plate is connected to the *input shaft,* which leads to the transmission. When the clutch is engaged, springs press the clutch plate against the flywheel. Friction forces the two disks to turn at the same speed. When the clutch is disengaged, the springs are released and the disks separate.

The gears. Power travels to the transmission through the input shaft. A gear at the end of this shaft drives a gear on another shaft called the *countershaft.* A number of gears of various sizes are mounted on the countershaft. These gears drive other gears on a third shaft, the *output shaft,* which leads to the drive shaft.

The transmission produces various gear ratios by engaging different combinations of gears. Only one combination can be engaged at a time. In a typical three-speed transmission, first gear has a ratio of 3 to 1; second gear, 2 to 1; and third gear, 1 to 1. Some four- and five-speed transmissions have a high-gear ratio of less than 1 to 1. For reverse, an extra gear called an *idler* operates between the countershaft and the output shaft. This extra gear turns the output shaft in the opposite direction of the input shaft, thus making the car go backward.

How a manual transmission works

What gears do

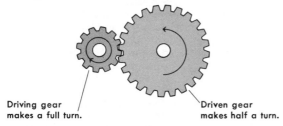

Driving gear makes a full turn.

Driven gear makes half a turn.

Reduction occurs when a small gear drives a large one, *above.* The driving gear makes a full turn for each half turn of the driven gear. Thus, speed is cut in half and torque is doubled.

Parts of a manual transmission

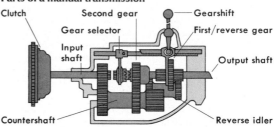

Clutch — Second gear — Gearshift

Gear selector — First/reverse gear

Input shaft — Output shaft

Countershaft — Reverse idler

A manual transmission contains a system of gears controlled by a gearshift. A clutch connects it to the engine. When the transmission is in neutral, *above,* no power is transmitted.

What happens when gears are shifted

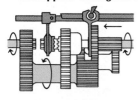

In first, or low, gear, the first/reverse gear slides forward and meshes with its mate on the countershaft. Power (green) flows to the output shaft through these gears. The output shaft turns a third as fast as the input shaft.

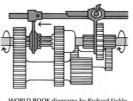

In third, or high, the gear selector slides forward and connects the output shaft to the input shaft. Power flows directly through the two shafts. No reduction occurs, and the output shaft turns at the same speed as the input shaft.

WORLD BOOK diagrams by Richard Fickle

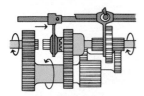

In second, the gear selector slides back to engage the second gear, which always meshes with its mate on the countershaft. Power flows to the output shaft through these gears. The output shaft turns half as fast as the input shaft.

In reverse, the first/reverse gear slides back and meshes with the reverse idler. The idler, an extra gear, turns the output shaft in the opposite direction of the input shaft, thus making the vehicle go backward.

In early manual transmissions, gears became engaged by sliding along the output shaft until they meshed with their mates on the countershaft. The gears often clashed because they turned at different speeds when they were being meshed. Most modern transmissions overcome this problem by having their forward gears always meshing. When these gears are not engaged, they turn freely on their shaft. They are engaged by a mechanism, called a *synchronizer,* which slides against a gear and locks it onto its shaft. The synchronizer forces the gear and the shaft to rotate at the same speed before locking them together.

How an automatic transmission works

An automatic transmission contains special devices that automatically provide various gear ratios as they are needed. Instead of a gearshift, the driver operates a lever called a *selector.*

Most automatic transmissions have selector positions for *park, neutral, drive, low,* and *reverse.* The engine can be started only if the selector is in either the park or neutral position. In park, the drive shaft is locked so that the drive wheels cannot move.

For ordinary driving, the driver moves the selector to the drive position. The transmission starts out in the lowest gear and automatically shifts into higher gears as the car picks up speed. The driver uses the low position of the transmission for going up or down steep hills or driving through snow or mud. When in low, the transmission remains in the lowest gear. Some transmissions

have a position between low and drive. This position prevents the transmission from shifting above second gear. The reverse position makes the car move backward.

The torque converter is a device that most automatic transmissions have instead of a clutch. A torque converter delivers power from the engine to the transmission and also increases the torque.

A torque converter resembles a large doughnut sliced in half. One half, called the *pump,* is bolted to the flywheel. The other half, called the *turbine,* is connected to the transmission input shaft. Each half is lined with *vanes* (blades). The pump and the turbine face each other in a case filled with oil. A bladed wheel called a *stator* is between them.

The engine drives the pump. As the pump rotates, it throws oil against the vanes of the turbine. The force of the oil tends to make the turbine rotate and send power to the transmission. After striking the turbine vanes, the oil travels back to the pump, passing through the stator along the way. When the pump turns much faster than the turbine, torque is increased. A complex reaction between the oil and the stator creates the increase in torque.

When the engine is running slowly, the oil may not have enough force to rotate the turbine at all. As a result, the driver can have the transmission in gear and the engine running slowly but can prevent the car from moving by simply applying the brakes lightly. When the driver releases the brakes and presses the accelerator

Parts of an automatic transmission

The diagram at the right shows a typical automatic transmission. It contains a *torque converter* rather than the clutch used in a manual transmission. It also has two sets of *planetary gears.* Some automatic transmissions have only one set of these gears. Special devices in the transmission shift the gears automatically.

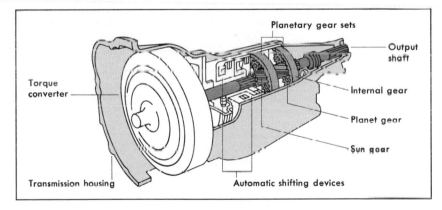

How planetary gears work

The parts of a planetary gear set can be held from turning or locked together to achieve a variety of gear ratios. The illustrations at the right show a few possible combinations. In all three cases, the internal gear is driving the other parts of the gear set. The effects can be multiplied by two gear sets arranged in line.

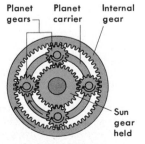

Reduction. Sun gear held. Planet gears "walk" around sun gear, causing planet carrier to rotate more slowly than internal gear.

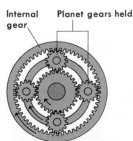

Direct drive. Internal gear and planet carrier locked together. Planet gears cannot turn. Entire gear set rotates as a unit.

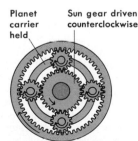

WORLD BOOK diagrams by Richard Fickle

Reverse. Planet carrier held. Internal gear rotates clockwise. Planet gears turn and act as idlers. Sun gear driven counterclockwise.

pedal, the engine runs faster and so does the pump. The action of the pump increases the force of the oil. This force gradually becomes strong enough to rotate the turbine—and move the car.

The planetary gears are a special kind of gears that are part of most automatic transmissions. A set of planetary gears consists of three elements. The first element is a *sun gear,* located in the center. The second element, called a *carrier,* surrounds the sun gear. The carrier holds two, three, or four *planet gears,* which mesh with the sun gear and revolve around it, much as the planets travel around the sun. The third element is an *internal gear,* a ring with teeth on the inside. It surrounds the planet gears and meshes with them.

Any element of a set of planetary gears can be held stationary, or locked to one of the others, to produce different gear ratios. Most automatic transmissions have two sets of planetary gears arranged in line. The gears are shifted by a system of automatic devices inside the transmission. These devices are controlled by the position of the selector, the speed of the car, and other factors.

The drive shaft

The drive shaft carries power from the transmission to the final drive. In conventional cars, the drive shaft is a metal tube called the *propeller shaft.*

When a car travels over an uneven surface, its drive wheels and final drive move up and down in relation to the transmission. To allow for this movement, the propeller shaft is fitted with flexible couplings called *universal joints.* These joints have a wristlike action that lets the propeller shaft flex up and down. Without them, the propeller shaft would bend or break as the car traveled over bumpy ground. Most propeller shafts have two universal joints, one at each end. Others have only one universal joint.

A car that has its engine and drive wheels at the same end does not need a propeller shaft. A short drive shaft carries the power from the transmission to the final drive. Such a shaft needs no universal joints because the transmission and final drive are bolted together. Universal joints on the axles permit up-and-down motion between the drive wheels and the final drive.

The final drive

The final drive transmits power from the drive shaft to axle shafts connected to the drive wheels. In a conventional car, the propeller shaft and the axle are at a right angle to each other. The final drive must carry power through this angle to drive the wheels. In addition to carrying the power to the drive wheels, the final drive divides the torque evenly between those two wheels. The final drive contains two sets of gears: (1) the ring gear and pinion and (2) the differential.

The ring gear and pinion are *bevel gears*—that is, they mesh at a right angle to each other. Thus, they carry power through a right angle to the drive wheels. The ring gear is driven by the pinion, which receives power from the propeller shaft.

In most cars, the ring gear is two to four times as large as the pinion. Therefore, these gears reduce the speed from the propeller shaft and increase the torque. The reduction in the final drive multiplies the reduction

that has already taken place in the transmission. For example, suppose a car has a first-gear ratio of 3 to 1 and a final-drive ratio of 3 to 1. The total reduction is 9 to 1. In other words, when the car is in first gear, the engine crankshaft rotates 9 times for each rotation of the drive wheels.

Some cars have a *transverse* engine, which is mounted across the car and between the drive wheels. In such cars, the power of the engine does not have to be carried through a right angle to the drive wheels. Therefore, the final drive contains ordinary reducing gears rather than a ring gear and pinion.

The differential is a set of gears that divide the torque evenly between the two drive wheels. The differential also enables one wheel to rotate faster than the other when necessary. For example, when a car goes around a corner, the outside drive wheel travels farther than the inside one. The outside wheel must rotate faster than the inside one to cover the greater distance in the same time.   Howard E. Chana

See also **Automobile** (The drive train; illustrations); **Gear.**

Transmitter. See **Radio** (How radio works; pictures: Building a radio transmitter); **Telephone** (How a telephone works); **Television** (Transmitting television signals).

Transmutation of elements is the conversion of one element into another through changes in an atom's nucleus. All atoms of the same element have the same number of protons in their nuclei. Any change in the number of protons in the nucleus produces an atom of a different element. An atom can change the number of protons in its nucleus by giving off or taking in atomic particles. Transmutation can occur naturally or it can be produced by artificial means.

Most natural transmutations occur when a nucleus of a radioactive atom spontaneously *emits* (gives off) certain particles through *alpha decay* or *beta decay.* In alpha decay, a nucleus emits an alpha particle, which consists of two protons and two neutrons. For example, the nucleus of an atom of radium has 88 protons. After the nucleus emits an alpha particle, 86 protons are left and an atom of radon has been formed.

In beta decay, a nucleus emits a beta particle. In most cases, the beta particle is a negatively charged electron that is produced by the transformation of a neutron in the nucleus. This change also results in the formation of a proton. As a result, after it emits the beta particle, the nucleus contains one more proton and one less neutron. For example, a nucleus of the isotope carbon 14 has six protons and eight neutrons. After the nucleus emits a beta particle, nitrogen 14, which has seven protons and seven neutrons in its nucleus, is formed.

In some cases, the beta particle is a *positron.* This positively charged electron is formed by the transformation of a proton. A neutron is formed at the same time. After it emits a positron, a nucleus has one less proton and one more neutron. For example, carbon 11, which has six protons and five neutrons, emits positrons. After a carbon 11 nucleus emits a positron, an atom of boron 11—which has five protons and six neutrons—is formed.

Most artificial transmutations are produced by bombarding nuclei with alpha particles or other high-energy particles in a nuclear reactor or a particle accelerator (see **Particle accelerator**). In a transmutation produced with alpha particles, a nucleus gains a proton and two neutrons. The nucleus first absorbs the alpha particle, which contains two protons and two neutrons. However, the nucleus formed by this absorption is unstable, and it ejects a proton.

Processes called *fission* and *fusion* also produce transmutation. Fission occurs when the nucleus of an atom splits into the nuclei of two lighter elements. In most cases, such splitting is caused by the absorption of a neutron by the nucleus. Fusion results from the joining of the nuclei of two lighter elements to form the nucleus of a heavier element. See **Fission; Fusion.**

John W. Poston

See also **Radioactivity; Transuranium element.**

Transnational corporation. See Multinational corporation.

Transpiration is the giving off of water by the leaves of a plant. Plants give off water chiefly through tiny pores called *stomata* on the surface of the leaves. The amount of water they give off depends somewhat upon how much water the roots of the plant have absorbed. The amount given off also depends upon such environmental conditions as sunlight, humidity, winds, and temperature. A plant should not be transplanted in full sunshine because it may lose too much water and wilt before the damaged roots can supply enough water.

Linda B. Brubaker

See also **Leaf** (Transpiration).

Transplant, in medicine. See **Tissue transplant.**

Transplanting, in gardening, is the process of removing a plant from one place and planting it in another. Many plants are started from seeds in protected areas, such as greenhouses and hotbeds, where growing conditions are ideal. When the seeds have grown into seedlings, the seedlings are transplanted to a garden. Seeds grown this way have a better chance of sprouting and will sprout more quickly than those planted outdoors. In addition, transplanting enables gar-

deners to space the seedlings properly in the ground. Plants also may be transplanted from one place in a garden to another. House plants are transplanted by a process called *repotting* (see **Gardening** [Cultivating an indoor garden]).

Seedlings for transplanting are grown by planting seeds in shallow wooden boxes called *flats,* or in individual containers. Plants for transplanting are also produced by using cuttings from the stems of older plants. Gardeners usually transplant seedlings two to three weeks after the seeds have sprouted. If seedlings are transplanted when they have grown bigger, their disturbed root system will not be able to supply enough water to the large leaves and stem. The seedlings should be watered several hours before transplanting to reduce the danger of fatal water loss.

Gardeners transplant a seedling by carefully digging underneath its roots and lifting it out. The seedling is immediately replanted in its new location, with the soil pushed firmly around it. If the roots are allowed to lie in the sun, they will dry out and the plant will die. The seedling should be watered as soon as it has been replanted. Gardeners may transplant seedlings with or without soil attached to the roots. Older plants should always be transplanted with a ball of soil around the roots.

Transplanting seedlings from an indoor protected area to an outdoor garden is a shock to the system of the plants. To decrease this shock, gardeners place the seedling flat outdoors in a warm, sheltered area, such as a cold frame or a porch, for several days before transplanting the seedlings.   William H. Carlson

See also **Cold frame; Gardening; Hotbed; Nursery; Tree** (Planting the tree).

Transport. See Air Force, United States (Other aircraft); Airplane (Airplanes of today).

Transport is the term used in Britain and other Commonwealth countries for transportation. See **Transportation.**

Steps in transplanting seedlings

Transplanting involves removing a plant from one place and planting it in another. Many plants are started indoors and then transplanted to a garden after the seeds have grown into seedlings. When transplanting the seedlings, gardeners follow several steps to prevent injury to the plants.

WORLD BOOK illustrations by Leon Bishop

Growing the seedlings indoors protects them from harsh outside conditions. Seedlings are often grown in boxes called *flats.* Flats are placed in sunny areas only after the seeds have sprouted.

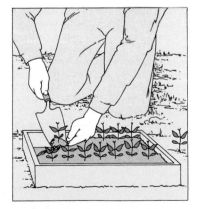

Removing the plants from a flat involves carefully digging around the roots and lifting out the seedling. The seedlings should be watered several hours before they are removed from the flat.

Replanting the seedlings is a fast and delicate process. The seedlings must be replanted quickly so the roots do not dry out, and they must be handled gently so they are not damaged.

Automobiles on an expressway interchange

Passengers alighting from a transoceanic airliner

A ship passing through the Panama Canal

Modern transportation involves the use of engine-powered vehicles, such as those pictured above and on the next page. Fast, dependable transportation is essential to the economy and way of life in industrially developed countries.

Transportation

Transportation is the act of moving people or goods from one place to another. Transportation takes people where they need or want to go, and it brings them the goods they need or want. Without transportation, there could be no trade. Without trade, there could be no towns and cities. Towns and cities are traditionally the centers of civilization. Therefore, transportation helps make civilization possible.

Throughout most of history, transportation was extremely slow and difficult. Prehistoric people traveled mainly on foot. They transported goods on their backs or heads or by dragging them along the ground. About 5000 B.C., people began to use animals to haul loads. By 3000 B.C., wagons and sailing vessels had been invented. The use of animals, wagons, and sailing vessels enabled people to transport loads farther and more easily than before. But the speed of transportation improved only slightly over the centuries.

Inventors produced the first engine-powered vehicles

Melvin Kranzberg, the contributor of this article, is Callaway Professor of the History of Technology at Georgia Institute of Technology and coeditor of Technology in Western Civilization.

during the late 1700's and early 1800's. This development marked the beginning of a revolution in transportation that has continued to the present. Today, jet airliners carry travelers nearly as fast as, or faster than, the speed of sound. Trains, trucks, and giant cargo ships haul a steady flow of goods to buyers in almost all parts of the world. Automobiles provide convenient transportation for many millions of people.

Although engine-powered transportation has benefited people in many ways, it has also created problems. For example, it uses great quantities of fuel and so strains the world's energy supplies. Automobiles jam many streets and highways, making travel slow. In addition, their exhaust fumes pollute the air. Such problems are so difficult to solve that governments have become increasingly involved in transportation.

This article discusses the kinds of transportation, the history of their development, and today's systems of engine-powered transportation. The article also discusses the transportation industry and current developments in transportation. Vehicles are also used for recreation, warfare, and space exploration. These uses are described in such articles as **Air Force, Balloon, Boating, Navy, and Space Travel.**

A snowmobile about to pull cargo in the far north

Steve McCutcheon

A train speeding workers to their jobs

Photri

Boeing Marine Systems

A hydrofoil ferrying passengers across a bay

Photri

School buses ready to take students home

Kinds of transportation

There are three main kinds of transportation: (1) land, (2) water, and (3) air. Land transportation depends mainly on wheeled vehicles, especially automobiles, trains, and trucks. Ships and boats are the most important water vehicles. Air transportation depends almost entirely on airplanes.

Each kind of transportation can further be classified according to whether the vehicles are engine powered or engineless. Most engine-powered vehicles have gasoline, diesel, or jet engines. The majority of engineless vehicles are powered by the muscles of human beings or animals or by natural forces, such as the wind or flowing water.

Engine-powered transportation has many advantages over engineless transportation. It is quick, convenient, and dependable, and can carry far greater loads. However, such transportation is costly. Most kinds of engine-powered vehicles cost from several thousands to many millions of dollars, depending on the type of vehicle. In most cases, each type of vehicle also requires certain *supporting facilities.* Automobiles require roads. Trains must have tracks. Airplanes require airports. Ships need ports and harbors. All these facilities are expensive to build and maintain. Every form of engine-powered trans-

portation also requires a source of energy. The combined cost of the vehicles, supporting facilities, and energy makes engine-powered transportation extremely expensive.

Engine-powered vehicles are the chief means of transportation in industrially developed countries, such as the United States, Canada, and most European nations. Engine-powered transportation costs too much to play such an important role in developing countries, which include many African, Asian, and Latin-American nations. Many people in these countries still rely on the kinds of transportation their ancestors used hundreds or thousands of years ago.

Land transportation is the most common kind of transportation by far. In many cases, it is the only suitable or available transportation.

Engine-powered land transportation. Automobiles, buses, motorcycles, pipelines, snowmobiles, trains, and trucks are the chief engine-powered land vehicles. All these vehicles except pipelines and snowmobiles ride on wheels.

Automobiles, buses, and trucks are the main modern road vehicles. In areas well served by roads, they can provide a variety of transportation services. Automo-

Edward S. Ross

© Robert Frerck, Dimensions

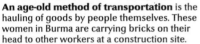

© Jean-Claude Lejeune

An age-old method of transportation is the hauling of goods by people themselves. These women in Burma are carrying bricks on their head to other workers at a construction site.

Pack animals are used to transport goods in many mountainous regions, deserts, and other areas that lack modern roads. In Afghanistan, nomads use camels as beasts of burden, *above top.* In Nepal, Asian oxen called *yaks* carry goods through the high, rugged passes of the Himalaya, *above bottom.*

biles enable people to travel whenever they choose and by the quickest route. Buses carry passengers between and within cities. Trucks can provide door-to-door freight service. In Europe and Japan, many people drive motorcycles to and from work. In the United States, people use motorcycles mainly for recreation.

Unlike road vehicles, trains ride on tracks. As a result, most trains cannot provide door-to-door freight service like trucks or convenient connecting services like buses. But trains can haul far heavier loads than trucks can. They can also carry many more passengers than buses can.

Snowmobiles skim across ice or snow. The vehicles have rotating tracks or skis at the front and a rotating track at the rear. The track or tracks propel the vehicle. People use snowmobiles for transportation mainly in far northern regions that are snow covered during much of the year.

Pipelines, unlike other forms of transportation, do not move. Most pipelines are built across land, but some span rivers or other bodies of water. Pipelines transport chiefly liquids and gases, especially petroleum and natural gas. Engine-powered pumps force the liquid or gas through the pipes.

Engineless land transportation. Walking is the most elementary means of transportation. Carrying a load on one's back or head or using animals to carry loads is also elementary. Animals used for this purpose are called *pack animals* or *beasts of burden.* They include camels, donkeys, elephants, horses, llamas, and oxen.

People use pack animals mainly in regions that lack modern roads. Such regions include many deserts, mountainous areas, and jungles.

People use their muscle power to move such wheeled vehicles as carts, bicycles, and pedicabs. A cart is a small box-shaped vehicle with two or four wheels and an open top. A person may either push or pull a cart, whichever is more convenient. Bicycles are two-wheeled vehicles that the rider powers by means of two pedals. Many people in European and Oriental countries ride bicycles to and from work. A pedicab resembles a bicycle but has two rear wheels instead of one. It also has a passenger carriage at the front or rear. Pedicabs are used as taxicabs and even as school buses in some Oriental countries.

Animal-drawn carts and wagons are a major means of transportation in rural areas of developing countries. Carts may be pulled by dogs, donkeys, horses, or oxen. Wagons are large four-wheeled carts that can carry heavy loads. Therefore, they must be pulled by exceptionally strong animals, such as oxen or draft horses.

Water transportation depends mainly on boats, ships, and rafts. Any small tub-shaped watercraft is classed as a boat. People use boats chiefly on rivers, canals, and lakes. A ship is a large vessel sturdy enough for ocean travel. A raft is a floating platform constructed of such materials as logs or barrels.

Engine-powered water transportation. Nearly all ships and many boats are powered by engines. Most ships specialize in hauling cargo. Cargo ships travel mainly on ocean waters and on bodies of water linked to the ocean, such as the Mediterranean Sea and the Baltic Sea. Some cargo ships operate on large inland waterways, such as the Great Lakes.

Few ships specialize in transporting passengers. However, various types of motorboats carry passengers locally. Some engine-powered boats, especially tugboats, are used in hauling freight. Tugboats have powerful engines that enable them to tow heavily loaded barges. Barges are actually large rafts. Most barges must be pushed or towed. Others have engines and so move under their own power. Barges are used mainly to haul freight along inland waterways.

In general, ships and boats are the slowest engine-powered vehicles. However, engineers have developed two fast-moving water vehicles—*hydrofoils* and *hovercraft.* Hydrofoils skim across the water on skids or runners. Hovercraft, or *air cushion vehicles,* ride above the water on a cushion of air. One or more powerful fans inside the vehicle create the air cushion. Because hydrofoils and hovercraft ride out of the water, they can travel faster than other watercraft of equal horsepower. Most hydrofoils and hovercraft are too small for ocean travel and so are classed as boats. They are used mainly to carry passengers locally. Some larger hydrofoils and hovercraft are used to haul cargo along inland and coastal waters.

Engineless water transportation. Engineless water vehicles include dugouts, canoes, rowboats, sailboats, and rafts. People use paddles or oars to propel dugouts, canoes, and rowboats. Sailboats are powered by the wind. Rafts may be propelled by paddles, poles, sails, or water currents.

Broad-bottomed sailboats and rowboats are widely used to haul freight in the Far East. The sailboats are called *junks,* and the rowboats are known as *sampans.*

Large junks have as many as five sails and can carry 100 short tons (91 metric tons) or more. Most sampans haul light cargo. However, many larger sampans have a sail, which enables them to haul heavier loads. In the tropical rain forests of Africa, Asia, and South America, many villagers use dugouts or rafts for transportation along the rivers. Many people of the Pacific Islands use dugouts for travel between islands. Some of the dugouts are equipped with outriggers and sails.

Air transportation depends almost entirely on engine-powered craft, especially airplanes. Engineless vehicles, such as gliders and hot-air balloons, are used mainly for recreation.

Airplanes provide the world's fastest practical means of transportation. Only spacecraft travel faster, but they are not yet a practical form of transportation. Big airliners routinely fly 500 to 600 miles per hour (mph), or 800 to 970 kilometers per hour (kph). Most private planes and some older airliners are powered by gasoline engines and driven by propellers. Nearly all newer airliners and some private planes have jet engines. *Supersonic* jets fly faster than the speed of sound. These planes travel at about 1,500 mph (2,410 kph). Most airliners chiefly carry passengers. Even the biggest planes can carry only a fraction of the weight that a ship or train can haul. Air freight rates are high as a result. The high cost limits the shipment of goods by air to expensive, lightweight, or perishable cargo. Such goods include electronic equipment and fresh flowers.

Helicopters, like airplanes, are powered by engines. But helicopters are smaller than most airplanes and cannot fly as fast or as far. Nor can they carry as many passengers as airplanes. Helicopters therefore play a secondary role in air transportation. However, they have certain special uses. For example, helicopters are used in rescue work and in fighting forest fires.

History

Prehistoric times. Transportation developed slowly during prehistoric times, which lasted until about 3000 B.C. Throughout most of the period, people lived by hunting, fishing, and gathering wild plants. They had no beasts of burden, wheeled vehicles, or roads. People traveled on foot and carried their infants and belongings strapped to their backs or heads. Loads too heavy for one person to carry were strapped to a pole and carried by two people.

In time, prehistoric people learned that they could drag loads along the ground on *sledges.* They made sledges from logs, poles, rawhide, or anything else that could hold a load and be dragged by one or more persons. During late prehistoric times, people began to build sledges with runners. These vehicles slid along the ground more easily than runnerless sledges, especially if the runners were greased. In far northern regions, people built lightweight sledges with runners for use on snow and ice. These vehicles became the first sleds.

By about 8000 B.C., various Middle Eastern peoples had developed agriculture and begun to establish per-

manent settlements. Trade between settlements then started to develop, which created a need for better means of transportation. The donkey and the ox, which had been *domesticated* (tamed) for farm work, helped meet this need. Between about 5000 and 3500 B.C., people began to use donkeys and oxen as pack animals. Next, they invented harnesses so that the animals could pull sledges. The use of donkeys and oxen as beasts of burden enabled people to transport heavier loads than they could before.

People also began to develop water transportation during prehistoric times. They built rafts of such materials as logs or reeds. Later, prehistoric people learned how to make dugouts and canoes. All these early craft were propelled by paddles or poles and were used on streams and lakes. The craft were too fragile for ocean travel.

The first wheeled vehicles and sailboats appeared near the end of prehistoric times. The wheel was invented about 3000 B.C. The invention probably took place in Mesopotamia, a region of the Middle East. The Egyptians invented sailboats about 3200 B.C. During the following centuries, wheeled vehicles and sailing vessels revolutionized transportation.

The first great civilizations arose in Mesopotamia and Egypt between 3500 and 3000 B.C. From these two centers, civilization gradually spread westward along the shores of the Mediterranean Sea. Sailing vessels played a vital role in the spread of civilization. Sea voyagers, for example, transmitted the ideas and inventions of civilized cultures to less developed societies as they sailed the Mediterranean.

The early Mediterranean civilizations flourished from about 3000 to 500 B.C. During this period, improvements in sailing vessels and wheeled vehicles accounted for the chief advances in transportation.

Early development of sailing vessels. By 3000 B.C., the Egyptians had learned to build sailing vessels sturdy enough to put out to sea. Some of these ships ventured onto the Mediterranean and Red seas on short trading missions. Between 2000 and 1000 B.C., other Mediterranean peoples developed bigger and sturdier vessels. By 1000 B.C., the Phoenicians, who lived along the eastern shores of the Mediterranean Sea, had built a large fleet of merchant ships. The Phoenicians sailed the length of the Mediterranean, from their home waters to Spain. They traded everything from pottery to cattle for various other goods at ports along the Mediterranean.

Sea travel remained slow and difficult throughout ancient times. Sailors lacked navigation instruments. As a result, they usually stayed within sight of land. The ships were hard to steer because they had no rudder. Sailors steered their ships by means of one or two oars at the stern. In addition, the ships could not depend entirely on the wind for power. The earliest ships had a single sail, which worked well only when the wind blew from behind. The sail did not work well in sailing against the wind and was useless when there was no wind. Many ships had teams of oarsmen, who rowed the vessels when the wind failed.

Early development of wheeled vehicles. The Mesopotamians built the first known wheeled vehicles about 3500 B.C. But such vehicles were not widely used until after 300 B.C. The technique of making wheels and wheeled vehicles slowly spread from Mesopotamia. It reached India about 2500 B.C., Europe about 1400 B.C., and China about 1300 B.C.

The first wheeled vehicles were four-wheeled carts. They were pulled by oxen or, after about 3000 B.C., by donkeylike animals called *onagers.* Each wheel on a cart was a wooden disk made from three rectangular boards. To construct a wheel, a wheel maker fastened the boards together edge to edge with wooden braces to make a square. The square was then rounded at the corners to form the disk. The three-piece construction prevented the wheels from being perfectly round. The early carts bumped along at a snail's pace and probably had to be stopped frequently for repairs. The wheelbarrow was not invented until the Middle Ages.

At the first, the Mesopotamians used carts mainly as funeral cars. After 3000 B.C., carts drawn by onagers carried Mesopotamian troops into battle. In time, carts were occasionally used to carry passengers and to haul grain, sand, and other goods that were difficult to load

Transportation in prehistoric times   Nearly all the methods of transporting goods or people during prehistoric times depended on the muscles of either human beings or animals. Some of these methods are pictured below. Similar methods are still used in many parts of the world.

WORLD BOOK illustrations for the *History* section by Robert Addison

Sledge

Travois

Carrying pole

Dugout

onto sledges or pack animals. However, wheeled vehicles could not compete with sledges and pack animals until the design of the wheels was improved.

Wheels continued to be made of three solid pieces of wood until about 2000 B.C. Between 2000 and 1500 B.C., the first spoked wheels appeared. These wheels consisted of a rim, a hub, and spokes. The three parts were constructed separately. Spoked wheels provided smoother riding than solid wooden wheels, and they were lighter and faster. The first spoked wheels were probably made for chariots.

Chariots with spoked wheels were light enough for horses to pull. Horses had been tamed for riding by about 2000 B.C. But they could not be used to pull heavy loads because a suitable harness had not yet been invented. The harnesses then in use pressed against a horse's windpipe. If a horse had to pull too heavy a load, the harness cut off the animal's breathing. However, two or more horses could pull a lightweight chariot easily. Horse-drawn chariots, used chiefly by warriors, became the swiftest vehicles of ancient times.

Ancient Greece. During the 400's B.C., Greece became the chief power in the Mediterranean area. The Greeks expanded the sea trade begun by the Phoenicians. They also pioneered in the building of two-masted vessels and increased the number of sails from one to four.

Greek cargo ships sailed from home with huge jars of olive oil and wine. These products were exchanged for wheat and other grain at various ports on the Mediterranean and Black seas. The grain trade was extremely important to the Greeks. Wheat was the principal food during ancient times, and the Greeks had to import most of their supply. Many Greek grain ships were seized by enemy or pirate vessels. Many others sank in storms. But almost every year, enough ships returned home to prevent famine for another year.

The ancient Greeks developed a highly advanced civilization. Greek merchant ships helped spread Greek civilization westward. As civilization spread, trade and shipping increased. By 400 B.C., about 300 ports lay on the Mediterranean and several thousand trading ships of various countries crisscrossed the sea.

Ancient Rome. From the 100's B.C. to the A.D. 400's, Rome ruled the mightiest empire of ancient times. At its peak, the Roman Empire included all the lands bordering the Mediterranean. It also extended as far north as the British Isles and as far east as the Persian Gulf. To help hold their vast empire together, the Romans built a highly advanced system of roads.

People had built roads long before Roman times. By about 1000 B.C., the Chinese had begun to construct roadways between their major cities. The Persians built a similar road network during the 500's B.C. But most of the early intercity roads were little more than dirt tracks. The Romans constructed the first extensive system of paved roads. The best Roman roads measured 16 to 20 feet (5 to 6 meters) wide and 3 to 6 feet (0.9 to 1.8 meters) thick. They had a base that consisted of several layers of crushed stone and gravel. The roads were paved with stone blocks.

The Romans used their roads chiefly to transport

Vehicles of ancient times   Wheeled vehicles and sailing vessels were invented during the 3000's B.C. They became the most widely used means of transportation during ancient times. But many people also continued to use earlier forms of transportation, such as pack animals.

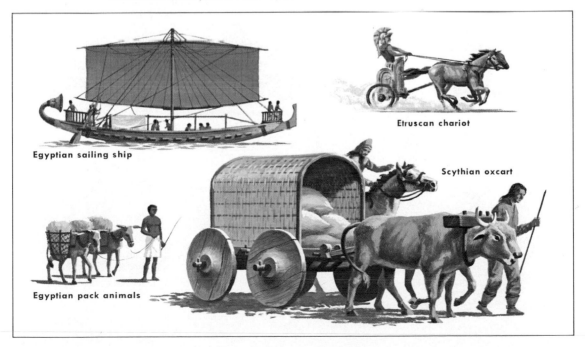

Egyptian sailing ship

Etruscan chariot

Scythian oxcart

Egyptian pack animals

troops and military supplies. But the roads also served as a major communications link between Rome and its provinces. Messengers in horse-drawn carts used the roads to carry government communications. By the A.D. 200's, more than 50,000 miles (80,000 kilometers) of paved roads connected Rome with almost every part of its empire.

During the 400's, Germanic tribes conquered most of the Roman territories in western Europe. The majority of Roman roads fell into ruin during the following centuries. However, a few are still used.

The Romans also built the largest fleet of cargo ships in ancient times. Like the Greeks, the Romans could not survive without sea trade. Roman cargo ships supplied the city of Rome with most of its grain supply.

The Middle Ages, which lasted from the 400's to the 1500's, brought great improvements in land and water transportation. These improvements resulted largely from three remarkable inventions—the rigid horse collar, the iron horseshoe, and the whiffletree. Scholars do not know exactly when or where these devices were invented. But all three had appeared in Europe by the end of the 1000's.

The rigid horse collar appeared about 800. Before this invention came into common use, horses wore a harness that fit across the neck. The harness choked a horse if it pulled a heavy load. The rigid horse collar shifted the weight of a load to a horse's shoulders. Horses collared in this way could pull four or five times as much weight as before.

The iron horseshoe appeared in Europe about 900.

Horses without shoes often suffered from damaged hoofs if they traveled long distances at top speed. Iron shoes protected a horse's hoofs from damage and so enabled the animal to travel farther and faster than it could without them.

The whiffletree, which appeared during the 1000's, made it possible for wagons to be pulled by teams of horses. A whiffletree is a pivoted crossbar at the front of a wagon to which a team's harnesses are fastened. It equalizes the pull of the horses. Without such a device, a wagon may be thrown off balance and may even be overturned.

The invention of the rigid horse collar, iron horseshoe, and whiffletree stimulated overland trade in Europe. They made it possible for horses to pull as much weight as oxen—and for longer distances and at twice the speed.

The increased speeds of horse-drawn vehicles also encouraged greater use of wagons for passenger transportation. But wagon rides were extremely bumpy. Wagon makers tried to correct this problem by building vehicles with *suspension systems,* which provided a certain amount of cushioning against bumps. However, only rich people could afford such vehicles. Most of the people of the Middle Ages traveled on foot or on horseback, just as people had done in the past.

The design and construction of ships improved greatly during the Middle Ages. The triangular *lateen sail* appeared in the 500's. Unlike square sails, which were widely used at the time, lateen sails worked well when ships sailed into the wind. The first ships with

Transportation in early modern times   Beginning in the 1400's, Europeans built ships capable of making long ocean voyages. Stagecoaches became widely used in Europe during the late 1600's and early 1700's. In other parts of the world, such as China, people continued to use older forms of transportation.

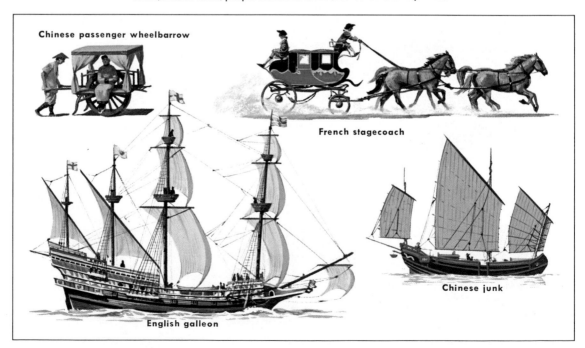

Chinese passenger wheelbarrow

French stagecoach

Chinese junk

English galleon

a rudder rather than steering oars at the stern appeared in Europe about 1300. Rudders could steer much bigger ships than could be steered with oars. During the 1400's, shipbuilders began to produce ships four times as large as any built before. All these ships had a rudder, and most had three masts and three sails.

Several important navigation instruments were also developed during the Middle Ages. One such instrument, called a *mariner's compass,* allowed voyagers to navigate their ships even when the sky was overcast. By the late 1400's, the advances in ship construction and navigation aids helped make long ocean voyages possible.

The age of overseas expansion. During the late 1400's and the 1500's, such European explorers as Christopher Columbus, Ferdinand Magellan, and Sir Francis Drake made great ocean voyages. As a result of these and later voyages, European civilization continued to spread westward—first to North and South America and then to Australia and New Zealand. However, this expansion of European culture took several hundred years. In spite of the improvements in ship construction, ocean travel remained extremely slow.

Overseas trade began to increase rapidly during the 1600's. Shipbuilders launched bigger and bigger cargo vessels to handle the growing trade. The bigger ships had to have more sails, and the added sails helped increase speeds. By the mid-1800's, the fastest merchant ships had as many as 35 sails and traveled at speeds up to 20 knots. These *clipper ships* could sail from New York City, around South America, to San Francisco in

three to four months. The overland journey from New York to California took twice as long.

Development of inland transport. By the 1600's, most people used horse-drawn wagons to haul goods locally. But they seldom used wagons for long hauls because of the poor condition of the roads. Until the mid-1800's, horse-drawn boats and barges were the chief means of long-distance inland transport. The animals trudged along the banks of rivers and canals and pulled the vessels with ropes.

Hundreds of canals were built in Europe from the late Middle Ages through the early 1800's. The first major American canal, the Erie Canal, opened in New York in 1825. It connected Albany and Buffalo and provided a vital link in an all-water route between New York City and Great Lakes ports. At that time, the overland journey between Albany and Buffalo took about 20 days. After the Erie Canal opened, horse-drawn barges made the trip in 8 days. The success of the Erie Canal led to a great burst of canal building in the United States. By 1850, the United States had about 4,500 miles (7,240 kilometers) of canals. These waterways carried most of the nation's intercity freight.

During the 1700's, France and England constructed the first well-built paved roads since Roman times. By the mid-1800's, the first major United States highway, the National Road, had been completed. The highway connected Cumberland, Md., and Vandalia, Ill. It was a gravel road and interior to the best French and English roads of the time. American pioneers traveling west from the Mississippi River crossed a wilderness without

Transportation in the 1800's   The steam engine provided a completely new source of power for transportation during the 1800's. It was used to propel locomotives and paddlewheel boats and ships. However, people also continued to use older sources of power, such as animals and the wind.

Horse-drawn streetcar

Clipper ship

Stern-wheel steamboat

Steam locomotive

Ox-drawn covered wagon

roads. They drove their covered wagons along well-traveled dirt paths, such as the Santa Fe Trail and the Oregon Trail.

The basic design of wagons and coaches changed little from the late Middle Ages through the 1800's. The first city coach line started in Paris during the 1660's. It was the ancestor of today's mass transit systems. The first long intercity coach line began service between England and Scotland about 1670. The line operated between the cities of London and Edinburgh, a distance of 392 miles (631 kilometers). The coaches were called *stagecoaches* because they traveled in stages, stopping at scheduled places on a route for changes of horses. The first stagecoach lines in the American Colonies began service during the 1730's.

The steam age. The invention of the steam engine marked the beginning of the greatest revolution in transportation since the invention of the wheel and the sailboat. British inventors developed the steam engine during the 1700's. In 1807, the first commercially successful steamboat service began in the United States. The first successful steam railroad began service in England in 1825. By the late 1800's, ships powered by steam engines had for the most part replaced sailing ships on the world's shipping lanes. However, steam-powered trains played the leading role in the transportation revolution.

By the late 1800's, steam locomotives traveled at speeds never imagined possible—up to 60 mph (97 kph) and faster. They could haul loads hundreds of times heavier than a team of horses could pull. By 1900, rail lines had been built throughout Europe and North America and in many parts of Africa, Asia, Australia, and South America. The overland journey by train from New York City to San Francisco took less than a week. In comparison, the trip took weeks or months by stagecoach or covered wagon.

As more and more steamships and steam-powered trains went into service, passenger fares and freight rates dropped. The lower costs encouraged travel, trade, and the growth of cities. In addition, many people became accustomed to fast movement and rapid change. The quickening pace of life created a demand for still faster transportation.

The beginnings of modern transportation. The first electric trains and streetcars appeared in Europe and the United States during the 1800's. In the 1890's, the German engineer Rudolf Diesel invented the engine that was later named after him. In time, diesel engines replaced steam engines on many ships and on most trains. But of all the inventions of the 1800's, the gasoline engine was the one that brought about the most far-reaching changes in transportation.

German inventors built the first gasoline engines during the 1800's and used them to power bicycles. The bicycle had been developed in Europe earlier in the 1800's. During the 1890's, French engineers built the first gasoline-powered vehicles with automobile bodies. The first gasoline-powered buses and trucks were built in Germany during the 1890's. In 1903, two American bicycle makers, Orville and Wilbur Wright, used a gasoline engine to power a small airplane that they had built. The

Vehicles of the early 1900's　By the early 1900's, engine-powered vehicles had revolutionized transportation. Oceangoing steamships, giant airships, electric streetcars, powerful steam trains, and the first mass-produced automobiles were carrying people farther and faster than they had ever traveled before.

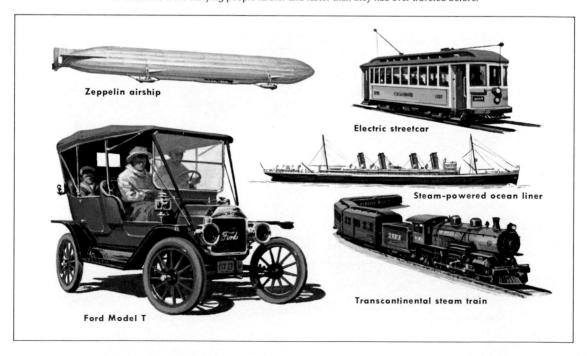

Zeppelin airship

Electric streetcar

Steam-powered ocean liner

Ford Model T

Transcontinental steam train

Wright brothers' plane became the first one to lift a person into the air and fly successfully.

Automobiles became the chief means of passenger transportation in the United States during the 1920's. As the number of automobile owners increased, so did the demand for more and better roads. About 700,000 miles (1,100,000 kilometers) of surfaced streets and highways were built in the United States between 1900 and 1930.

The first commercial airlines began service in Europe in 1919. Airlines began operations in many other parts of the world during the 1920's. By the late 1930's, the world's airlines carried $3\frac{1}{2}$ million passengers annually. All airplanes had propellers and gasoline engines. During the late 1930's, German engineers built the first planes with jet engines. All the early jet aircraft were warplanes. The first jet airliners began service during the 1950's.

The great advances in transportation during the 1900's have brought about enormous changes in people's lives. The development of commercial air travel has made long journeys routine. As a result of improvements in ocean shipping and in refrigeration, goods that were once available only in certain regions are now distributed worldwide. The development of the automobile has led to the growth of sprawling suburbs around big cities. Many suburbanites depend on their cars for shopping and other personal business. They may also use their cars to get to and from work in the central cities. Without this convenient means of private transportation, suburban living would be impractical or impossible for many people.

Important dates in transportation

c.5000 B.C. People began to use donkeys and oxen as pack animals.

c.3000 B.C. The Mesopotamians built the first wheeled vehicles.

c.3200 B.C. The Egyptians invented sails and produced the first sailboats.

300's B.C.—A.D. 200's The Romans built the first extensive system of paved roads.

c.800 The rigid horse collar appeared in Europe.

1100's Wagon makers in Europe built the first traveling carriages. Carriages with spring suspension systems became known as *coaches* during the 1400's.

1490's Improvements in ship construction helped make long ocean voyages possible.

1660's The first city coach line opened in Paris.

1700's British inventors developed the steam engine.

1807 The first commercially successful steamboat service began in the United States.

1825 The first successful steam railroad began operations in England.

1880's German inventors built the first gasoline engines and used them to power bicycles.

1890's French engineers built the first gasoline-powered vehicles with automobile bodies.

1903 An airplane built by Orville and Wilbur Wright of the United States became the first one to lift a person into the air and fly successfully.

1920's Automobiles became the chief means of passenger transportation in the United States.

1950's The first commercial jet airliners began service.

1970's Declining petroleum reserves throughout the world led to shortages of transportation fuel in the United States and other developed countries.

1976 The first supersonic passenger airliner, the Concorde, began service between Europe and the United States.

Transportation in the 1930's   Most of today's forms of public transportation had taken shape by the 1930's. Railroads were the chief form of intercity public transportation at the time. But intercity bus lines and commercial airlines were beginning to carry more and more passengers. Ferries carried many passengers locally

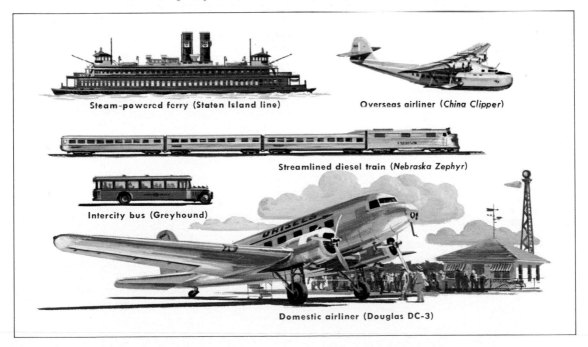

Steam-powered ferry (Staten Island line)

Overseas airliner (*China Clipper*)

Streamlined diesel train (*Nebraska Zephyr*)

Intercity bus (Greyhound)

Domestic airliner (Douglas DC-3)

Transportation today

Before the development of engine-powered vehicles, nearly all transportation involved the shipment of goods. Passenger transportation was relatively uncommon. The development of engine-powered transportation changed this situation dramatically. Today, passenger transportation is an essential part of everyday life in developed countries. Workers in these countries live much farther from their places of employment than workers did in the past. As a result, they need quick, dependable transportation each workday. Many children need transportation to and from school. Families depend on transportation for shopping and other errands. Many people travel long distances on vacations. In the United States today, more money is spent on the various means of passenger transportation than on the shipment of freight.

This section deals mainly with engine-powered passenger and freight transportation in developed countries. In developing countries, many people still rely on age-old transportation methods. For a discussion of these methods, see the section *Kinds of transportation.*

Passenger transportation

There are two main types of passenger transportation: (1) private transportation and (2) public transportation. People who use private transportation operate their own vehicles. Those who use public transportation pay to ride on vehicles owned and operated by private companies or the government.

Private transportation in industrial countries is provided mainly by automobiles, bicycles, motorcycles, and private airplanes. Automobiles are by far the most important means of private transportation.

Most people in the United States travel chiefly by car. Americans use their cars largely for local transportation. But automobiles are also the leading means of travel between U.S. cities. Intercity travel is usually measured in *passenger-miles.* A passenger-mile represents one passenger transported 1 mile (1.6 kilometers). Automobile transportation accounts for about 85 per cent of all the intercity passenger-miles traveled in the United States each year. Travel by motorcycle and travel by private airplane account for less than 1 per cent each.

Automobiles are also the chief means of passenger transportation in Australia, Canada, Japan, New Zealand, and most of the nations of Western Europe. People in these countries and in the United States own about 82 per cent of the world's automobiles. Americans own by far the largest share—about 40 per cent of the world total. The countries with the most automobiles also have the best road systems. There are about 12 million miles (19 million kilometers) of roads throughout the world. About one-third of this mileage is in the United States. Most of the rest is in the other countries that have a large number of automobiles.

Highway travel is far less important in developing countries than in developed ones. But a growing number of city dwellers in these developing countries own a car. The biggest cities have had to build more expressways to handle the ever-increasing flow of automobile traffic.

Public transportation. Any organized passenger service that is available to the general public can be classed as public transportation. There are three main types of public transportation service: (1) urban, (2) intercity, and (3) overseas.

Urban service. Most large urban areas provide some means of public transportation for people who do not own a car or who prefer to avoid city driving whenever possible. Public transportation in urban areas is called *mass transit.* Mass transit between cities and their suburbs is often called *commuter service.*

Average speeds of some kinds of passenger transportation

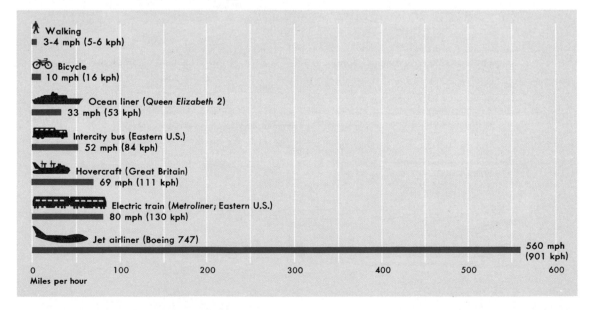

Buses are the chief mass transit vehicles. About 950 cities in the United States have a mass transit system. Almost all these systems provide bus service only. However, most of the world's big cities offer rail service in addition to bus service. About 50 cities throughout the world, including 9 U.S. and 2 Canadian cities, have both subway and surface rail lines. Many big cities throughout the world also have elevated trains, which run on tracks above the streets. In addition, a growing number of large cities have a mass transit system that includes *light-rail vehicles.*

A light-rail vehicle is an electrically powered railroad passenger car that runs on tracks at street level. The car gets its power from an electrified third rail or overhead trolley wire. Streetcars are a type of light-rail vehicle. During the late 1800's and early 1900's, streetcars were the chief mass transit vehicles. But most streetcar tracks ran down the middle of the street, and the vehicles interfered with auto traffic. Streetcars have been replaced by buses in nearly every American city where they operated.

Today's light-rail lines differ from streetcar lines mainly in the location of the tracks. Instead of running down the middle of the street, the tracks lie alongside the roadway. This arrangement eliminates interference with automobile traffic. In addition, it speeds up rail service.

Trains are the chief means of public commuter transportation. Many U.S. intercity railroads run commuter trains between big cities and their suburbs. About 75 per cent of all railroad passengers in the United States are commuters.

Intercity service is provided mainly by airplanes, buses, and trains. Riverboats and ferryboats carry an extremely small share of intercity passengers.

Milt & Joan Mann

Bicycles are an important form of private transportation in various European countries, including the Netherlands, *above.* Many Europeans ride bicycles to and from work.

© B. Kliewe, ICON

Automobiles are by far the chief means of private transportation in industrial countries. Big cities require large parking lots for the great number of cars driven by workers each day.

Jack Novak, Photri

High-speed trains carry much of the intercity passenger traffic in Japan and Western Europe. The sleek, bullet-shaped train above is part of a large fleet of Japanese superexpresses.

Commercial air, bus, and rail transportation account for about 15 per cent of the intercity passenger-miles traveled in the United States each year. Airlines handle the biggest share of this traffic, and railroads the smallest. The airlines' share increases with the length of the trip. In the case of especially long trips, nearly as many Americans travel by air as by automobile. Rail and bus travel are more important in other countries than in the United States. They are the chief modern means of intercity travel in most developing nations. Japan and most Western European countries have many high-speed passenger trains.

High-speed trains can compete with airliners for passengers on runs up to about 500 miles (800 kilometers). Most big airports are on the outskirts of central cities. For short and medium-length flights, the trip to and from the airport may take longer than the flight itself. Trains, on the other hand, take passengers all the way into central cities. Passengers on a high-speed train may thus complete their entire journey in less time than it would take by air.

Overseas service. The first overseas airlines began operations during the 1930's. But the planes had to stop frequently during a flight for refueling, and the flights were uncomfortable and even hazardous. Most overseas travelers continued to go by ship until the late 1950's, even though it took far longer to sail than to fly. The voyage across the Atlantic Ocean, for example, took four days or more. The first nonstop transoceanic airliners appeared during the late 1940's. These propeller-driven planes could carry passengers across the Atlantic safely and comfortably in hours rather than days. As these planes became more common, overseas travel increased. The first transoceanic jet airliners began service during the 1950's, leading to a tremendous increase in overseas air travel.

Today, the great majority of overseas travelers go by plane. Few ocean liners remain in operation. Most of those that do operate make regular runs during the summer and operate as cruise ships during the winter. Cruise ships specialize in taking vacationists to the Caribbean, Mediterranean, and other warm areas.

In 1976, the first supersonic airliner, the Concorde, began service between Europe and the United States. The Concorde travels between New York City and London or Paris—a distance of about 3,500 miles (5,630 kilometers)—in approximately $3\frac{1}{2}$ to 4 hours. However, the Concorde has not been efficient to operate because it uses fuel uneconomically.

Freight transportation

Pipelines provide the cheapest means of transporting freight. However, their use is largely limited to petroleum and natural gas. The cheapest way to move general cargo is by water. Rail transportation costs about 3 times as much as water transportation, and truck transportation costs about 10 times as much. Air transportation is by far the most expensive way to move freight. It costs nearly 40 times as much as water transportation. As a result, cargo planes usually carry only expensive, lightweight, or perishable merchandise.

The various means of moving cargo are used for both (1) domestic freight and (2) international freight.

Domestic freight. Most domestic freight traffic involves the transport of cargo between cities within a country. The cargo is carried by airplanes, barges, pipelines, railroads, ships, and trucks. Freight shipments within cities consist mainly of pickups and deliveries. Trucks carry nearly all such local freight.

Intercity freight traffic is usually measured in *ton-miles.* A ton-mile represents 1 short ton (0.9 metric ton) transported 1 mile (1.6 kilometers). Rail shipments account for about 35 per cent of the ton-miles of freight hauled in the United States yearly. Shipments by truck and by petroleum pipeline account for about 25 per cent each. Barges and ships carry about 14 per cent, and airplanes less than 1 per cent.

Freight transport in other developed countries is

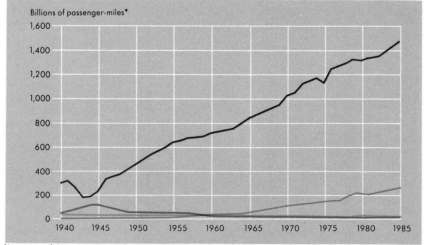

Growth of intercity passenger traffic in the United States

Billions of passenger-miles*

Volume of traffic by type of transportation

—— Automobiles
—— Airways
—— Buses
—— Railroads

*A passenger-mile is one passenger carried 1 mile (1.6 kilometers).
Sources: U.S. Interstate Commerce Commission; Transportation Policy Associates.

similar to that in the United States. However, railroads carry an even greater share of the intercity traffic in European countries than in the United States. Canal traffic is also greater in Europe.

In many cases, a particular freight shipment must be switched from one type of carrier to one or more other types to reach its destination. For example, many coal shipments travel by train, barge, and truck on their way to the buyer. The movement of freight by more than one method is called *intermodal transport.*

A type of intermodal transport known as *containerization* has become increasingly common since the mid-1900's. Freight is packed into big crates called *containers.* The containers are designed to ride on truck trailers and railroad flatcars. They can easily be transferred between the two types of carriers and to specially designed *container ships.* Containerization is used mainly to transport such goods as machinery and household appliances. The method reduces shipping costs, speeds deliveries, and cuts losses due to breakage. Some domestic freight is containerized. But the method is used mainly in international trade.

International freight is transported mainly by ships. Many of today's merchant ships are designed to carry containers or a particular kind of cargo, such as petroleum, grain, or iron ore. In numerous cases, the ships require specialized port facilities. Most large ports have been equipped to handle containers. Giant cranes and other lifting devices transfer the containers between container ships and truck trailers or railroad flatcars. Some of the world's busiest seaports specialize in handling oil tanker traffic. These ports have exceptionally deep harbors to accommodate giant tankers. They also have pumping systems and pipelines for loading and unloading the oil.

Some international freight moves by highway, rail, pipeline, inland waterway, or airplane. European countries, especially, depend on these methods in their trade with one another.

Milt & Joan Mann

Intermodal transport is the movement of freight by more than one method. For example, containers loaded with freight may be transferred from truck trailers to railroad flatcars, *above.*

John Launois, Black Star

Barge transportation is one of the cheapest ways to haul such cargo as coal, grain, and gravel. These barges are being pushed by a tugboat. Some barges, however, have built-in engines.

Growth of intercity freight traffic in the United States

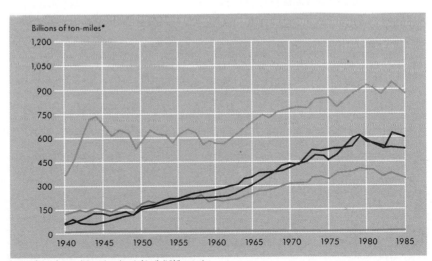

Billions of ton-miles*

Volume of traffic by type of transportation

——— Railroads

——— Oil pipelines

——— Trucks

——— Inland waterways

——— Airways

*A ton-mile is 1 short ton (0.9 metric ton) carried 1 mile (1.6 kilometers).
Sources: U.S. Interstate Commerce Commission; Transportation Policy Associates.

Transportation is one of the leading industries in the world. Many of the world's biggest industrial firms earn all or much of their income from the sale of equipment or fuel for transportation. The transportation industry employs many millions of people in countries throughout the world. In the United States alone, about 10 per cent of all workers are directly or indirectly involved in providing transportation.

The transportation industry consists of (1) equipment manufacturers, (2) passenger and freight carriers, and (3) related industries. The equipment manufacturers and passenger and freight carriers are the key organizations. However, the related industries play a vital role in transportation by providing fuel and various services and facilities. In addition, governments throughout the world are involved in transportation. The extent of the involvement of governments varies according to the political and economic systems of different countries.

Equipment manufacturers produce the vehicles on which modern transportation depends. They also supply the equipment needed to operate the vehicles, such as railroad tracks and airplane communications systems. The manufacture of transportation equipment is the second leading manufacturing industry in the United States in terms of *value added by manufacture*. The leader in the United States is the nonelectric machinery industry. Value added by manufacture measures the increase in value of raw materials after they become a finished product.

Companies that make automobiles, buses, and trucks are by far the largest producers of transportation equipment. The two leading U.S. producers of such motor vehicles are General Motors Corporation and Ford Motor Company. They rank among the top five manufacturing firms in the world.

Passenger and freight carriers include airlines, intercity bus lines, mass transit companies, pipeline companies, railroads, shipping lines, and trucking firms. In most countries, the central government owns and operates all the airlines and railroads and some or all of the intercity bus lines. The United States is the chief exception. Private companies own and operate all the airlines and nearly all the railroads in the United States. Canada has two major airlines and two major railroads. The Canadian government owns and operates one of the airlines and one of the railroads. The other airline and the other railroad are privately owned and operated. In addition, all of Canada's intercity bus lines are privately owned.

In Communist countries, the central government also owns the intercity bus lines, pipelines, and shipping and trucking lines. In most other countries, including the United States and Canada, these services are provided by privately owned firms, which are subject to various forms of government regulation. In nearly every country, all or most mass transit services are controlled by local governments.

The leading carrier groups in the United States, in order of income, are (1) trucking companies, (2) railroads, (3) airlines, (4) shipping lines, (5) pipeline companies, and (6) intercity bus lines. There are more companies in the trucking group than in any other category.

Steve McCutcheon

The Trans-Alaska Pipeline, *above,* is part of a vast network of oil pipelines that crisscrosses the United States. Pipeline companies, which transport gas and other products as well as oil, are among the nation's leading freight carriers.

The intercity bus group has the smallest number of companies.

Related industries include glass, petroleum, steel, and tire production; road construction; the selling of new and used automobiles; and the servicing of automobiles. Petroleum production is the leading transportation-related industry in terms of value. About half the petroleum processed in the United States is made into fuel for automobiles, airplanes, and other engine-powered vehicles. More than half of the world's 10 largest manufacturing firms are oil companies.

Government and transportation. Governments are most deeply involved in transportation in countries where all or much of the industry is publicly owned. But even in the United States, where nearly all transportation companies are privately owned, government plays a major role in the transportation industry. This role consists primarily of (1) providing funds for certain transportation facilities and (2) regulating certain aspects of transportation.

Government funding. Four kinds of transportation facilities in the United States depend almost entirely on public funds. They are (1) air traffic control centers, (2) airports, (3) public roads, and (4) river and harbor facilities. About 85 per cent of the money spent on the four types of facilities is used for the building and upkeep of roads. State and local governments provide the majority of the funds for airports, roads, and river and harbor facilities. The federal government finances all air traffic control operations. It also helps pay the expenses of Amtrak, a semipublic corporation that operates nearly all the passenger trains that run between the nation's cities.

Mass transit systems in every country depend heavily on government financial support. Few of the systems earn enough from passenger fares to pay all their expenses. Governments must provide whatever additional funds are needed to keep the mass transit systems in operation.

In the United States, the Department of Transportation distributes most of the federal funds for transportation. Most states and a majority of large metropolitan areas have transportation agencies that distribute state funds and local funds. In Canada, the Canadian Ministry of Transport handles the federal funding of transportation.

Government regulation deals chiefly with transportation safety and the business practices of transportation companies. Governments throughout the world establish safety rules for the various methods of transportation.

In the United States, agencies within the Department of Transportation set and enforce safety standards for the design and manufacture of transportation equipment. These agencies also set and enforce safety standards for the operation of airplanes and trains.

The Canadian Transport Commission sets and enforces safety standards in Canada. State, provincial, and local governments regulate traffic safety on roads and waterways under their control.

Several federal agencies regulate the freight rates and other business practices of U.S. transportation companies. The Interstate Commerce Commission oversees the railroad and domestic shipping industries and interstate trucking. The overseas shipping industry is regulated by the Federal Maritime Commission. The Federal Energy Regulatory Commission oversees natural gas pipeline companies. The commission also regulates those oil pipeline companies that provide commercial service. In Canada, the business practices of transportation companies are regulated chiefly by the Canadian Transport Commission.

The airline, railroad, and trucking industries have long been among the most heavily regulated industries in the United States. The federal government began its regulation of these companies to prevent them from charging unfair passenger and freight rates. Regulation also helped protect the companies from unfair competition.

Many people, however, believe that heavy government regulation discouraged the airline and trucking industries from improving their services. These people further believe that both industries would operate more efficiently if they were more competitive. With this end in view, the federal government began to relax some of its controls over the airline and trucking industries during the late 1970's.

Since the mid-1900's, governments throughout the world have become increasingly involved in regulating the environmental aspects of transportation. The following section, *Current developments,* discusses this type of regulation.

Problems of modern transportation include (1) traffic safety, (2) declining fuel reserves, (3) environmental problems, and (4) inadequate public transportation. These problems are most severe in countries that depend heavily on automobile transportation.

Traffic safety. Most types of high-speed, engine-powered transportation involve traffic safety problems. But automobile drivers have an especially poor safety record. In the United States, more people are killed in automobile accidents every year than in all other transportation accidents combined. Most automobile accidents could be prevented if every driver obeyed all traffic laws and all the rules for safe driving.

Airlines have one of the best safety records in the field of transportation. But heavy air traffic at major airports has increased the hazards of commercial flying. When many airliners await clearance to land or take off, airport approaches and runways become dangerously overcrowded. In addition, large airports have a growing amount of private plane traffic, which makes traffic control even more difficult. This problem could largely be eliminated if private planes were prohibited from flying near large commercial airports.

Railroads in the United States are increasingly plagued by train derailments. Worn-out or damaged tracks cause the majority of the derailments. Most railroad companies have track replacement programs. However, the railroad companies claim that they need federal financial help to replace all their worn-out or damaged tracks.

Declining fuel reserves. Gasoline and other fuels made from petroleum supply nearly all the energy for engine-powered transportation. Energy experts warn that the world's supply of petroleum is being used up rapidly. At the current rate of use, the supply may be exhausted by the early 2000's. Developed countries therefore face a difficult problem. On the one hand, they must ensure that their major transportation systems have enough fuel to function normally. On the other hand, these nations must do all they can to conserve fuel. Fuel conservation is necessary not only because of the threat of a serious fuel shortage but also because of the high price of petroleum. Higher petroleum prices result in higher transportation costs, and higher transportation costs drive up the prices of transported goods. During the 1970's, petroleum prices rose sharply, contributing to an increase in the costs of many goods.

Automobiles consume about half the energy used for transportation in the United States. They therefore contribute heavily to the nation's energy supply problems.

Energy use in intercity passenger transportation

Kind of vehicle	Average number of passengers per trip	Miles vehicle travels per gallon of fuel*	Passenger-miles per gallon of fuel
Diesel train	146	0.56	81.8
Bus	20	5.9	118.0
Automobile	2.3	22.5	51.8
Jet airliner	91	0.29	26.4

*One mile equals 1.6093 kilometers. One gallon equals 3.7854 liters. A passenger-mile is one passenger carried one mile.
Figures are for 1983. Source: Center for Transportation Research, Argonne National Laboratory.

To help reduce automobile fuel consumption, the U.S government sets gasoline-mileage standards for new cars. These standards encourage American automakers to produce smaller, lighter cars, which travel farther per gallon of gasoline than earlier methods.

Environmental problems. Automobiles are the chief cause of traffic congestion in urban areas, and their exhaust fumes contribute heavily to urban air pollution. Many cities plagued by traffic jams and air pollution have taken steps to reduce automobile traffic in their downtown areas. In addition, the U.S. government has established increasingly strict pollution-control standards for new automobiles. These standards require automakers to manufacture cars that give off cleaner exhausts than earlier models.

Inadequate public transportation. Except for airline facilities, most public transportation facilities in the United States have been neglected since the 1940's. Today, few of the nation's intercity passenger trains and mass transit systems provide adequate service. Greater use of public transportation would help ease the problems caused by heavy dependence on automobiles. But public transportation must be improved before more automobile drivers can be persuaded to use it.

Improvements in public transportation chiefly involve expanding and upgrading (1) mass transit service and (2) intercity train service.

Improvements in mass transit service. Most cities today cannot afford to build extensive new mass transit facilities. But many cities are trying to improve their existing facilities. For example, a number of cities have speeded up bus service by reserving certain traffic lanes for buses only. More and more communities provide *paratransit services.* Such services include public car and van pools and subscription bus services. The schedules and routes of paratransit vehicles are arranged to suit the passengers' convenience.

A new type of mass transit facility is the *people mover.* People movers carry passengers along specially constructed guideways in driverless, electrically powered cars. The cars operate automatically. They move along the guideways and stop at designated point to take on and discharge passengers. The U.S. Department of Transportation is helping to finance extensive people-mover systems in the downtown areas of Cleveland, Houston, Jacksonville, and Los Angeles. A number of short-distance people movers are in operation in such places as parks and airports.

Improvements in intercity train service. Most developed countries are trying to improve railroad passenger service along heavily traveled intercity routes. Trains use less energy per passenger than do automobiles, airplanes, and buses. Thus, railroads could help conserve energy if they attracted passengers away from air and highway travel.

The only high-speed passenger trains in the United States are *Metroliners,* which run between New York City and Washington, D.C. They average about 80 mph (130 kph) on their 225-mile (362-kilometer) run. Worn-out tracks and inadequate signal systems prevent most other U.S. intercity trains from traveling as fast.

Amtrak, which operates the *Metroliners,* plans to

Orion Press

The magnetic levitation vehicle (MLV) is a high-speed passenger train being developed in Japan, France, and West Germany. A magnetic force holds the vehicle above a guide rail and drives it forward. MLV's are expected to travel as fast as 300 miles (480 kilometers) per hour.

West Virginia University

People movers are mass transit vehicles that carry passengers along guideways in driverless, electrically powered cars. The cars operate automatically and stop at designated stations.

start similar high-speed service between New York City and Boston. It also has long-range plans to provide such service along heavily traveled routes in other parts of the United States. But before any of these plans can be carried out, the federal government must replace worn-out tracks and modernize signal systems along the routes. Congress has granted the money to make these improvements on the New York City-Boston route. But Amtrak has had great difficulty getting enough federal funding to start high-speed train service on other heavily traveled routes.

Japanese, French, and West German engineers are perfecting a new type of high-speed passenger train called a *magnetic levitation vehicle* (MLV). An MLV track consists of a single guide rail, which the vehicle straddles but does not touch when in motion. MLV's are powered by *linear electric motors.* Magnets on both the motor and the guide rail create a powerful magnetic force. This force holds the vehicle 4 to 6 inches (10 to 15 centimeters) above the guide rail and drives the train forward. MLV's are expected to travel up to 300 mph (480 kph).   Melvin Kranzberg

Study aids

Related articles in *World Book.* See the *Transportation* section of the state, province, country, and continent articles. See also the following articles:

Land transportation

Ambulance	Escalator	Recreational vehi-
Amtrak	Fire department	cle
Aqueduct	(Fire trucks)	Road
Automobile	Jinrikisha	Snowmobile
Bicycle	Monorail	Streetcar
Bridge	Motorcycle	Subway
Bus	Pedicab	Taxicab
Carriage	Petroleum (Trans-	Tractor
Coach	porting petro-	Travois
Conveyor belt	leum; diagram)	Truck
Electric railroad	Pipeline	Tunnel
Elevated railroad	Railroad	Viaduct
Elevator		Wagon

Water transportation

Air cushion vehicle	Lighthouse	Ship
Barge	Merchant marine	Submarine
Canal	Port	Tanker
Harbor	Raft	

Air transportation

Airmail	Airport	Aviation	Helicopter
Airplane	Airship	Balloon	

Beasts of burden

Camel	Elephant	Ox
Carabao	Horse	Reindeer
Donkey	Llama	Water buffalo
Dromedary	Mule	Yak

Other related articles

Careers (Transportation)	Interstate Commerce Com-
Coast Guard, U.S.	mission
Common carrier	Navigation
Communication	Rocket
Containerization	Space travel
Exploration	Transportation, Department
Industrial Revolution	of

Outline

I. **Kinds of transportation**
 A. Land transportation
 B. Water transportation
 C. Air transportation
II. **History**
III. **Transportation today**
 A. Passenger transportation
 B. Freight transportation
IV. **The transportation industry**
 A. Equipment manufacturers

 B. Passenger and freight carriers
 C. Related industries
 D. Government and transportation
V. **Current developments**
 A. Problems of modern transportation
 B. Improvements in public transportation

Questions

In what countries are automobiles the chief means of passenger transportation?

Why is engine-powered transportation expensive?

Which kinds of transportation facilities in the United States depend almost entirely on government funds?

Who were the first people to build an extensive system of paved roads?

What are the chief mass transit vehicles?

How do pipelines differ from other forms of transportation?

What was the chief means of freight transportation in the United States before the mid-1800s?

Why is the shipment of goods by air limited to expensive, light weight, or perishable cargo?

Why are most developed countries trying to improve their intercity passenger train service?

What two inventions of late prehistoric times revolutionized transportation during the following centuries?

Reading and Study Guide

See *Transportation* in the Research Guide/Index, Volume 22, for a *Reading and Study Guide.*

Additional resources

Level I

The Complete Junior Encyclopedia of Transportation. Ed. by A. M. Zehavi. Watts, 1973.

Hamer, Mick. *Transport.* Watts, 1982. Focuses on energy and transportation.

Hilton, Suzanne. *Faster Than a Horse: Moving West with Engine Power.* Westminster, 1983.

Humberstone, Eliot. *Things That Go.* Hayes Publishing, 1981.

Moolman, Valerie. *The Future World of Transportation.* Watts, 1984.

Level II

Dunn, James A. *Miles to Go: European and American Transportation Policies.* MIT Press, 1981.

Meyer, John R., and Gómez-Ibáñez, J. A. *Autos, Transit, and Cities.* Harvard, 1981.

Money, Lloyd J. *Transportation Energy and the Future.* Prentice-Hall, 1984.

Paradis, Adrian A. *Opportunities in Transportation.* VGM Career, 1983.

Schaeffer, K. H., and Sclar, Elliott. *Access for All: Transportation and Urban Growth,* Penguin, 1975.

Transportation in America. Ed. by Donald Altschiller. H. W. Wilson, 1982. Collection of articles on contemporary transportation issues.

Transportation, Department of, is an executive department of the United States government. The department develops and promotes national transportation policies and programs. It coordinates programs that provide safe, economical, and efficient transportation on land and sea and in the air. The secretary of transportation, a member of the President's Cabinet, heads the department. Congress established the department in 1966. It began operating in 1967.

Functions. The Department of Transportation includes most of the government agencies and bureaus that administer federal transportation programs. Its chief officials are responsible for coordinating the work of these organizations. The department promotes safety in all methods of transportation. It carries on research and development programs in cooperation with private industry. It conducts studies to identify and solve transportation problems, and to strengthen the weakest parts of the transportation system. It encourages high-quality, low-cost service to the public.

The department also grants licenses for commercial uses of space vehicles and regulates economic aspects of international civil aviation. The department determines the economic fitness of U.S. airlines providing domestic or international service.

Organization. The secretary of transportation, who directs the department, is appointed by the President, with the advice and consent of the Senate. Besides directing the department, the secretary serves as the President's chief adviser on transportation matters.

The deputy secretary of transportation is the secretary's chief assistant and serves as acting secretary in the secretary's absence. The secretary is aided by a general counsel and assistant secretaries for administration, budget and programs, governmental affairs, policy and international affairs, and public affairs.

The Department of Transportation has nine major operating divisions, each headed by an administrator who is responsible directly to the secretary. These divisions are the Federal Aviation Administration, the Federal Highway Administration, the Federal Railroad Administration, the Maritime Administration, the National Highway Traffic Safety Administration, the St. Lawrence Seaway Development Corporation, the United States Coast Guard, the Urban Mass Transportation Administration, and the Research and Special Programs Administration.

The Federal Aviation Administration (FAA) operates air traffic control and navigation systems; certifies civilian pilots, aircraft, and aviation schools; and directs the program of federal aid to airports.

Secretaries of transportation

Name	Took office	Under President
Alan S. Boyd	1967	Johnson
John A. Volpe	1969	Nixon
Claude S. Brinegar	1973	Nixon, Ford
*William T. Coleman, Jr.	1975	Ford
Brock Adams	1977	Carter
Neil E. Goldschmidt	1979	Carter
Andrew L. Lewis, Jr.	1981	Reagan
*Elizabeth H. Dole	1983	Reagan
James H. Burnley	1987	Reagan

*Has a separate biography in WORLD BOOK.

The Federal Highway Administration manages a program that provides financial assistance for states to build highways and bridges. The agency's Office of Motor Carriers has jurisdiction over the safety performance of motor carriers in interstate and foreign commerce.

The Federal Railroad Administration sets and enforces safety standards for railroads. The agency also conducts research on improved and advanced rail systems, and provides a subsidy for Amtrak, the nation's passenger rail system.

The Maritime Administration promotes a strong and efficient United States merchant marine. It also operates the U.S. Merchant Marine Academy.

The National Highway Traffic Safety Administration works to reduce the number of traffic deaths and injuries that occur on the nation's highways. The agency sets standards for vehicle and traffic safety programs.

The St. Lawrence Seaway Development Corporation operates the St. Lawrence Seaway in cooperation with the St. Lawrence Seaway Authority of Canada.

The United States Coast Guard inspects and certifies merchant vessels and licenses civilian sailors. It provides navigational aids, enforces maritime laws, and conducts searches and rescues at sea. In wartime, the Coast Guard becomes an active part of the United States Navy.

The Urban Mass Transportation Administration makes federal grants to cities to help provide and improve mass transportation facilities. The administration encourages the establishment of urban transportation systems.

The Research and Special Programs Administration has responsibility for research and development and for safety regulations covering transportation of hazardous materials.

History. The federal government took an active part in transportation long before the Department of Transportation was created. About 100 agencies, bureaus, and divisions have administered federal transportation programs. Congress created the Department of Transportation on Oct. 15, 1966.

The department took over several agencies and duties from other executive departments. From the Department of Commerce, it received the Bureau of Public Roads, the Great Lakes Pilotage Administration, the Saint Lawrence Seaway Development Corporation, and the office of the undersecretary for transportation. The Coast Guard was transferred from the Department of the Treasury. The Federal Aviation Agency, which had been an independent agency, became the Federal Aviation Administration in the new department.

Several agencies that regulate the economic affairs of transportation companies remain outside the department as independent agencies. These include the Federal Maritime Commission and the Interstate Commerce Commission (ICC).

Critically reviewed by the Department of Transportation

Related articles in *World Book* include:

Coast Guard, U.S.
Federal Aviation Administration
Federal Highway Administration
Flag (picture: Flags of the U.S. Government)
Maritime Administration
Merchant Marine
Saint Lawrence Seaway Development Corporation

Mid Hunt

The Department of Transportation works to develop convenient, economical, and safe transportation throughout the nation. The department's headquarters, *right,* are at 400 Seventh Street SW, Washington, DC 20590.

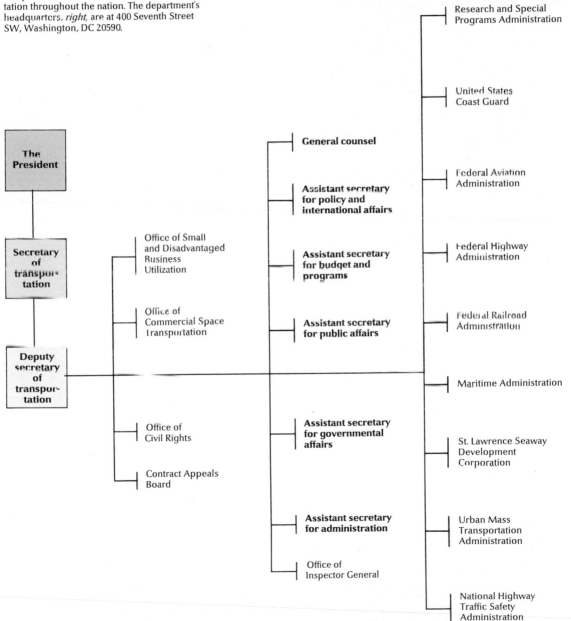

The President

Secretary of transportation

Deputy secretary of transportation

Office of Small and Disadvantaged Business Utilization

Office of Commercial Space Transportation

Office of Civil Rights

Contract Appeals Board

General counsel

Assistant secretary for policy and international affairs

Assistant secretary for budget and programs

Assistant secretary for public affairs

Assistant secretary for governmental affairs

Assistant secretary for administration

Office of Inspector General

Research and Special Programs Administration

United States Coast Guard

Federal Aviation Administration

Federal Highway Administration

Federal Railroad Administration

Maritime Administration

St. Lawrence Seaway Development Corporation

Urban Mass Transportation Administration

National Highway Traffic Safety Administration

Transsexualism is a condition in which a person who has the anatomy of one sex views himself or herself as a member of the opposite sex. People who view themselves this way are called *transsexuals.* They feel a strong need to act like and be treated as a member of the opposite sex. Transsexualism, also spelled *transexualism,* occurs in more males than females.

Scientists are uncertain about the causes of transsexualism. Some believe that a tendency toward the condition is established before birth. They suspect that hormones within the mother's or the baby's body may affect the sexual development of the unborn child. However, most researchers agree that even if such a tendency exists, a transsexual must have learned to identify with the other sex during early childhood.

Psychotherapy is generally ineffective in treating transsexualism. Some transsexuals seek *reassignment sex-organ surgery* in order to change their external anatomy to that of the opposite sex. People considering such surgery are advised to live and dress as a member of the opposite sex for up to two years. By doing so, they confirm that they can succeed as members of the other sex. During this time, they take hormones of the opposite sex to change their sexual characteristics. A woman's breasts may also be removed. If a transsexual has adjusted to living as a member of the opposite sex, reassignment surgery is performed. John Money

Trans-Siberian Railroad was the first railroad built across Siberia, the vast area that makes up most of the Asian part of the Soviet Union. When completed, it was the longest railroad in the world, extending over 5,000 miles (8,000 kilometers) from Yekaterinburg (now Sverdlovsk) and Chelyabinsk in the Ural Mountains to Vladivostok, east of China on the Sea of Japan. It was originally called the Great Siberian Railroad. No railroad in the Soviet Union today is officially named the Trans-Siberian Railroad. Today, a train called the Trans-Siberian Express travels from Moscow to Vladivostok in seven days. It runs from Moscow to Sverdlovsk, where it joins the original Trans-Siberian Railroad line. It has been electrified between Moscow and Irkutsk.

Construction of the Trans-Siberian marked the beginning of a new era in the development of Siberia. Industries and trade began to develop, and the population grew. The railroad was a valuable asset to the country during a war with Japan in the early 1900's and during World Wars I and II. It was used to transport troops and supplies across a vast territory.

The Trans-Siberian was built in several sections. It was begun in 1891 and finished in 1916. The section in eastern Siberia, between Vladivostok and Khabarovsk, had been completed about 1897. From 1892 to 1912, other sections were built across western and central Siberia.

Between 1897 and 1903, Russia built the Chinese Eastern Railway across Manchuria, in northeast China. This railroad connected Vladivostok with the sections of the Trans-Siberian in western and central Siberia. By 1904, a continuous railroad stretched from Vladivostok across China and Siberia to the Ural Mountains.

The Russians wanted a railroad route that did not cross China. They built a line north of China from Khabarovsk to Kuenga. Completed in 1916, it was the last link in a continuous railroad on Russian soil between Vladi-

vostok and the Ural Mountains. Another railroad led from the Urals west to Moscow. Since the 1920's, the Trans-Siberian has been joined to other railroads in the Soviet Union. The lines along the Trans-Siberian route are part of the rail network that links all parts of the country. See also **Asia** (picture). Theodore Shabad

Transubstantiation, *TRAN suhb STAN shee AY shuhn,* is a doctrine of the Roman Catholic Church. It explains the belief that bread and wine are changed into the body and blood of Jesus Christ during the sacrament of the Eucharist, or Mass. Transubstantiation indicates that Jesus is present in a real way under the appearance of bread and wine.

The word was first adopted by the church at the Fourth Lateran Council in 1215, and reaffirmed by the Council of Trent in 1551. The term had been in widespread use since the 1100's. Some Eastern Orthodox Christians accept transubstantiation as one of several explanations for the transformation of bread and wine. Some Protestant churches have similar doctrines concerning real presence. Richard L. Schebera

See also **Roman Catholic Church** (The Eucharist, or Mass); **Communion; Mass.**

Transuranium element, *TRANS yu RAY nee uhm,* is a radioactive element that has an atomic number higher than 92, the atomic number of uranium. Transuranium elements are also called the *transuranic elements.* The known transuranium elements have atomic numbers from 93 to 109. They are neptunium (Np), plutonium (Pu), americium (Am), curium (Cm), berkelium (Bk), californium (Cf), einsteinium (Es), fermium (Fm), mendelevium (Md), nobelium (No), lawrencium (Lr), and elements 104, 105, 106, 107, 108, and 109. Each element has a separate article in *World Book.* Scientists produce these elements artificially through a process called the *transmutation of elements* (see **Transmutation of elements**). In general, the known transuranium elements are considered unstable because they tend to undergo *radioactive decay* (loss of atomic particles). See also **Radioactivity.**
Richard L. Hahn

Transvaal, *trans VAHL,* is the name of one of the provinces of South Africa. It lies in the northern part of the country. The name *Transvaal* means *beyond the Vaal.* The first Boer settlers in the early 1800's gave this name to the region because it lay beyond the Vaal River. The Transvaal covers 109,621 square miles (283,917 square kilometers) and has about 11,885,000 people. A large majority of the people are black Africans, mostly of the Sotho and Tswana groups. Almost 2 million are white. Johannesburg is Transvaal's largest city. Pretoria, the capital and second largest city, is also the administrative capital of South Africa.

Wide and generally treeless plains called the *veld* cover most of the Transvaal. Plains in the eastern and southern parts lie up to 6,000 feet (1,800 meters) above sea level. In the east, the Drakensberg Mountains rise to over 11,000 feet (3,400 meters). The Vaal River and its branches water the southwestern Transvaal, a fertile farming area. The *Witwatersrand* (White Waters Ridge), a district in the southern part of the Transvaal, is South Africa's chief industrial area. It has many factories and the world's richest gold mines. Bruce Fetter

See also **Boer War; Johannesburg; Pretoria; South Africa** (History; map).

Transverse arch. See Foot (The arches).

Transylvania, *TRAN sihl VAY nee uh* or *TRAN sihl VAYN yuh,* is a geographical region of Romania near the Hungarian border. It covers about 39,000 square miles (101,000 square kilometers). The majority of its 7½ million people are Romanians. But about 1½ million Magyars also live there. Magyars make up the largest ethnic group in Hungary. The Carpathian Mountains and Transylvanian Alps separate the region from the rest of Romania. See **Romania** (map).

Transylvania has rich deposits of iron, lead, lignite, manganese, natural gas, and sulfur. The surrounding mountains are covered with beech and oak trees. Transylvania's high plains make good grazing grounds for cattle and sheep. Its valleys produce large bean, corn, potato, tobacco, rice, and wheat crops. The region's largest city is Cluj-Napoca.

For years, Romanians and Hungarians quarreled over Transylvania. Magyars conquered the region in the 900's. From 1526 to 1699, Transylvania was part of the Ottoman (Turkish) Empire. It was under Hungarian control from 1699 to 1867, when it once again became part of Hungary. During World War I, Romania joined the Allies after being promised Transylvania. After the war, Transylvania became part of Romania. In August 1940, Germany and Italy forced Romania to give northern Transylvania to Hungary. After World War II, Transylvania was returned to Romania, and lost its political identity.

Transylvania is the main site of the legend about the famous vampire Dracula. The character of Dracula is based on Vlad Tepes, a cruel prince of the 1400's who lived in Walachia, a region south of Transylvania. Vlad executed many of his enemies by driving a sharpened pole through their bodies. A belief in vampires formerly held by many Romanian peasants added details to the legend. *Dracula* (1897), a novel by the English author Bram Stoker, made the legend internationally famous. This immensely popular book has inspired numerous plays and motion pictures.   Vojtech Mastny

See also **Dracula; Romania** (Land regions).

Trap-door spider digs a burrow in the ground and covers the entrance with a lid, or trap door. It lives in warm climates, including the southern and western United States. It is harmless to human beings. Some grow over 1 inch (2.5 centimeters) long.

Trap-door spiders use their burrows for protection and as nests in which to raise young. The burrows are lined with silk. Some burrows are more than 10 inches (25 centimeters) deep and over 1 inch (2.5 centimeters) wide. Some trap-door spiders dig simple, tubelike burrows. Others dig burrows that have a branch tunnel. The branch tunnel, sometimes hidden by a second trap door, serves as an extra hiding place.

The trap doors are made of silk and mud, and are attached to the lining of the burrows by silk hinges. Some trap-door spiders build thin, waferlike doors that cover the burrow entrance loosely. Others construct thick doors, like corks, that fit so snugly into the tunnel entrance they are watertight. Still others build circular folding doors that open in the middle.

Trap-door spiders eat insects, including many kinds that damage valuable plants and flowers. The spider waits behind its door until its prey walks by. Then it quickly opens the door, seizes and poisons its victim,

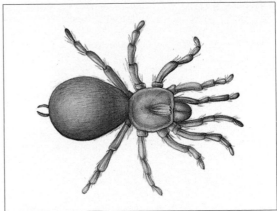

WORLD BOOK illustration by Oxford Illustrators Limited.

The trap-door spider is harmless to human beings.

Oxford Scientific Films

The trap-door spider's home is a silk-lined burrow. At the top is a hinged door made of silk and mud. The spider uses the burrow for protection and as a nest for its young.

Jen and Des Bartlett, Bruce Coleman Inc.

A female trap-door spider's abdomen, *left,* contains many eggs. The eggs are placed in the burrow to hatch.

and drags it into the burrow. Trap-door spiders are timid, and the females seldom leave their nests. These spiders are a type of *tarantula* (see **Tarantula**).

Scientific classification. Trap-door spiders make up the trap-door spider family, Ctenizidae. The most common trap-door spiders in the United States are genus *Ummidia.*

James E. Carico

Trapezoid. See Quadrilateral.

Beaver trapping was a profitable occupation for many pioneers during the 1700's and 1800's in North America. They used steel traps held in place by a chain and stake. The trappers sold the pelts or traded them for food and other supplies. Most beaver pelts were made into hats and sold in Europe.

Detail of a water color (1858) by Alfred Jacob Miller; Walters Art Gallery, Baltimore, Md.

Trapper. See Trapping.

Trapping is the capture or killing of wild animals in traps. It was one of the first methods by which people obtained animals for food and clothing. Later, people began to trap for profit. In North America, many pioneers of the 1700's and 1800's became wealthy by trapping fur-bearing animals. They sold the pelts for use in making fashionable fur garments.

Today, much of the fur supply comes from the manufacture of artificial furs and from farms that raise fur-bearing animals. But many people trap for sport and profit. Popular fur-bearing animals of the United States and Canada include beavers, martens, minks, muskrats, opossums, otters, raccoons, and skunks. Methods of trapping may be found in books at many libraries and in pamphlets published by state agencies.

In some parts of the world, people still trap animals for food and clothing. Some African tribes, for example, trap antelope and monkeys for food. People also trap for other reasons. For example, scientists trap wild animals unharmed to study their habits. Farmers and ranchers use traps to catch such animals as coyotes and foxes, which kill chickens and sheep. These animals that prey on other animals are called *predators.* Many homeowners trap mice, moles, and other pests that ruin lawns or invade cupboards looking for food.

Kinds of traps. There are three main types of traps: (1) arresting traps, (2) enclosing traps, and (3) exterminating traps. Bait can be used in any trap, but it may not be necessary.

Arresting traps grip animals but do not kill them. The most common arresting trap is the *steel trap.* Manufacturers make steel traps of various sizes and shapes to catch such animals as raccoons and skunks. Steel traps have jaws that operate with a steel spring and grip an animal by the foot or leg. Some have teeth that can hurt an animal badly if it struggles to get free. Great Britain

considers steel traps inhumane and bans them. Some states of the United States forbid steel traps with teeth.

Enclosing traps hold animals unharmed. A common type is the *box* or *cage* trap. The trapper uses bait to lure an animal into a box trap, and a door then closes and imprisons it. Animal collectors and scientists often use box traps to catch animals for zoos or research. Scientists

Mark Sherman, Bruce Coleman Inc.

An enclosing trap captures animals alive. These members of the Bureau of Wildlife Management have trapped a black bear. They will examine and tag the animal before releasing it.

Kinds of traps The type of trap a person uses depends on the kind of animal being trapped and on whether the animal is to be unharmed or killed. Bait can be used in any trap, but it may not be necessary. For example, trapping minks and muskrats seldom requires bait. The trapper simply conceals the traps in areas where the animals live and waits for them to trap themselves.

Enclosing traps

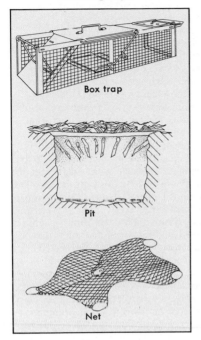

Box trap

Pit

Net

Arresting traps

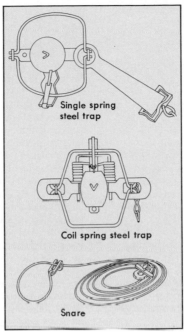

Single spring steel trap

Coil spring steel trap

Snare

Exterminating traps

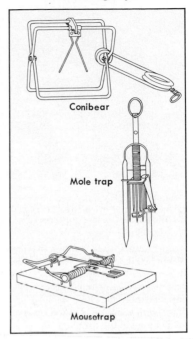

Conibear

Mole trap

Mousetrap

may trap an animal and tag it so they can follow the creature's movements after freeing it from the trap. Many people use box traps to catch raccoons, squirrels, or other animals in their gardens or homes. They then release the animals in an unpopulated area.

Exterminating traps grip animals and kill them. They include the *mousetrap* used in many homes and barns. A mousetrap has metal rods that snap shut by means of a coiled spring and break the victim's neck. Another exterminating trap, widely used for catching beavers and muskrats, is the *Conibear*. Its metal rods clutch the animal in a "scissors" grip and crush it to death instantly.

Trapping and wildlife conservation. Wildlife conservation groups often criticize any trapping that involves killing animals. They fear that certain animals may become extinct if people continue to hunt them.

Some people believe that trapping predators upsets the balance of nature (see **Balance of nature**). They feel that killing predators will in time result in an oversupply of rodents and other animals that predators eat. But others point out that when some animal species become too numerous, the population of predators increases because the predators have a larger food supply.

In the United States, many states have tried to preserve wildlife with various laws, including total bans on the trapping of certain animals. Some states, for example, forbid bear trapping. Trapping laws vary from state to state. Each state issues trapping licenses and determines where and when animals may be trapped. State agencies also decide what species may be trapped and what number of animals may be trapped at one time.

The federal Endangered Species Act of 1973 forbids the hunting and trapping of any endangered species in the United States. It also prohibits the importation of any endangered species or of products made from any such species. Supporters of this law believe that fewer of these animals will be trapped and hunted in other countries if there is no United States market for them. Special permits may be issued to exclude animals to be used for research.   John W. Peterson

See also **Fur.**

Additional resources

Bateman, James A. *Animal Traps and Trapping.* Stackpole, 1971.
Geary, Steven M. *Fur Trapping in North America.* Rev. ed. Winchester, 1984.

Trappists are Roman Catholic monks who belong to the Order of Cistercians of the Strict Observance. This branch of the Cistercians dates from a reform begun in 1664 at La Trappe Abbey in Normandy, France, by the abbot Armand-Jean le Bouthillier de Rancé. He restored rules of the original Cistercian abbey that no longer were followed, including almost complete silence, four to six hours of manual labor a day, and seclusion. He added other rules, such as abstaining from meat, except for the infirm. Orders of Cistercian Nuns of the Strict Observance, called Trappistines, were founded in 1794 by the monk Dom Augustin de Lestrange. Their first convent was La Sainte Volonté de Dieu, near Fribourg, in Switzerland. See **Cistercians.**   David G. Schultenover

Trapshooting is a sport in which a person shoots at clay disks that are thrown into the air by a machine.

© Tony Tomsic, *Sports Illustrated,* Time Inc.

Trapshooting is a sport in which a person shoots at clay disks with a shotgun. A machine called a *trap* throws the disks into the air. The traps are in low structures called *traphouses, top.*

Trapshooters use a shotgun that fires shells holding about 500 lead pellets. The disks measure no more than $4\frac{5}{16}$ inches (11 centimeters) in diameter. A machine called a *trap* hurls the disks into the air at speeds of almost 60 miles (97 kilometers) an hour. The trap is housed in a structure called a *traphouse,* which is partially beneath the ground.

A trapshooter stands behind the traphouse in one of five lanes, called *stations.* When the shooter calls out "pull," a disk is launched, and the shooter fires at it once. A disk is called "dead" if a visible piece falls from it. If the shooter misses, the disk is called "lost." Most competitions consist of 100 disks shot in groups of 25. The shooter fires five times from each of the five stations.

Trapshooters compete in *singles, doubles,* and *handicap* events. In singles, one disk at a time is launched. In doubles, competitors shoot at two disks launched simultaneously. In both singles and doubles, shooters stand 16 yards (15 meters) behind the traphouse. In a handicap event, the greater the shooters' ability, the farther they must stand behind the traphouse. The distance varies from 18 to 27 yards (16 to 25 meters).

A related sport called *skeet shooting* has eight stations and two traphouses aboveground.   Bonnie Nash

Trauma, *TRAW muh,* in psychiatry, is an unpleasant emotional experience of such intensity that it leaves a lasting impression on the mind. Psychoanalysts believe that childhood traumatic experiences sometimes lead to later emotional symptoms. The study of such childhood traumas plays an important part in the psychotherapeutic treatment given to the emotionally ill (see **Psychotherapy**).

Traumas that occur during adulthood also may have effects that require psychiatric treatment. Such traumas may be physical—such as a serious injury or illness—or psychological. In some cases, an unusually severe trauma may result in a type of mental disorder called a *post-traumatic stress disorder.*   Nancy C. Andreasen

Trauma center, *TRAW muh,* is a specialized area of a hospital that treats only persons suffering from *trauma*

(serious accidental injury). Some hospitals are devoted entirely to trauma care. In the United States, trauma kills an average of about 110,000 people annually. From 20 to 50 per cent of these people die because they do not promptly receive suitable medical care.

Trauma centers have specialized equipment and permanent staffs of physicians, nurses, and paramedics who are skilled in emergency lifesaving techniques. Staff members provide first aid at the accident site and rapid transportation by ambulance or helicopter to the center itself. Trauma centers developed from military hospitals that provided such service during the Korean War (1950-1953) and the Vietnam War (1957-1975).

Pioneer civilian trauma care systems were established by Maryland and Illinois. In 1969, Maryland opened a statewide trauma hospital in Baltimore called the Maryland Institute for Emergency Medical Services. Helicopters pick up accident victims and fly them directly to the institute. One of the most extensive trauma care systems was established in Illinois in 1971. This statewide system has four kinds of trauma centers: (1) local, (2) areawide, (3) regional, and (4) specialized. Local centers serve rural areas. After receiving basic treatment in a local trauma unit, the most seriously injured accident victims may be transferred to an areawide, regional, or specialized center. Areawide centers have such facilities as blood banks, intensive-care units, laboratory services, operating rooms, and specialized X-ray units. Regional centers are located within university medical centers. They have highly trained staffs and can provide sophisticated treatment for seriously injured patients. Specialized trauma centers treat such problems as spinal cord injuries and children's trauma. By the mid-1980's, every state had begun efforts to establish a statewide trauma and emergency medical services system. In addition, almost every U.S. city with a population of more than 50,000 had a trauma center.   David R. Boyd

Travel. See **Airplane** (Airplanes of today); **Automobile; Bus; Railroad** (pictures); **Recreational vehicle; Ship** (Passenger vessels); **Space travel; Transportation;** also the *Places to visit* section in *World Book* state and province articles, such as **Texas** (Places to visit).

Travel agency is a business that helps people arrange trips by handling many travel arrangements. It makes reservations for hotel rooms and transportation and arranges sightseeing tours. It offers customers guidance in obtaining passports and visas, which travelers need for foreign travel. A travel agency also provides customers with information on the travel regulations of the United States and other governments. Travel agencies arrange tours for individuals and for groups.

Most of the income of travel agencies comes from commissions paid by airlines, car rental companies, hotels, tour operators, and other businesses that serve travelers. These businesses pay a commission on each reservation that an agency makes or on each ticket it sells. Travelers pay nothing for most services. But agencies may charge a fee for planning special individual tours that require much of their time and effort.

Travel agencies operate in most countries of the world. In the mid-1980's, the United States and Canada had about 20,000 agencies. In the Soviet Union and some Eastern European countries, the government owns and runs all travel agencies.

During the 1980's, several states passed laws setting rules that travel agencies must follow in order to operate in that state. These rules, plus regulations instituted by the industry itself, helped establish standards of ethical conduct for travel agents. Milton A. Marks

Travelers Aid Association of America is a nationwide network that provides professional services to individuals and families who have experienced problems related to homelessness or traveling. Travelers Aid assists approximately 2 million people each year. Such people include elderly persons, runaway children, disabled or mentally ill persons, immigrants, jobseekers, stranded travelers, and travelers who encounter unexpected illness or accidents.

Travelers Aid agencies are located throughout the United States and Puerto Rico. These agencies offer such services as food, clothing, and shelter; financial aid; short-term professional counseling; information and referral about psychiatric and other medical care; and employment information. Travelers Aid was founded in 1917. Its headquarters are at 125 S. Wilke Road, Arlington Heights, IL 60005.

Critically reviewed by Travelers Aid Association of America

Traveler's check is a check that can be used as money or as a letter of credit. Banks and travel agencies issue traveler's checks. The purpose of traveler's checks is to protect the money carried by travelers. People sign the checks when they buy them and again when they spend them.

Marcellus F. Berry, general agent of the American Express Company, originated the system of traveler's checks in 1891. Today people buy millions of dollars' worth of these checks every year.

In the United States, such checks are issued in denominations of $10, $20, $50, and $100. Almost any bank, or any travel or express agency, sells them and adds a small fee. People can redeem them in foreign currencies abroad at the rate of exchange when converted. Thus, travelers bear the risk of exchange fluctuation. If travelers plan to be chiefly in one country, such as Great Britain or France, they may buy checks denominated in pounds sterling or French francs to avoid this risk. Traveler's checks are accepted the world over in payment for accommodations or merchandise, or in exchange for currency. Joanna H. Frodin

See also Letter of credit.

Traveller. See Lee, Robert Edward (picture).

Travers, Morris William. See Krypton; Neon.

Travers, *TRAV urz,* **Pamela** (1906-   ), an Australian writer, is best known for her books about Mary Poppins, a favorite children's character. These works include *Mary Poppins* (1934) and *Mary Poppins Comes Back* (1935). Travers was born of Irish parents in North Queensland, Australia, and began writing stories when she was seven years old. When she was 17, she wrote poetry which was first published in *The Irish Statesman*. From 1923 to 1936, she acted in Shakespearean plays in England. Jean Thomson

Travertine, *TRAV uhr tihn* or *TRAV uhr teen,* is a dense, closely compacted form of limestone found mostly in banded layers. Most travertine is white or cream colored. It consists mainly of calcium carbonate and has the chemical formula $CaCO_3$. It forms when calcium carbonate separates from water through evapora-

tion. Travertine is often used as decorative building stone because it is easy to cut.

Travertine occurs in areas where limestone is common and where circulating ground water contains calcium carbonate. It often forms around the mouths of hot springs and in streams. Rock formations called *stalactites* and *stalagmites,* which are found in caves, consist primarily of travertine (see Stalactite; Stalagmite).

The word *travertine* comes from an old Roman name for Tivoli, a town in Italy where large deposits of travertine occur. In the United States, travertine forms around the Mammoth Hot Springs in Yellowstone National Park. Mary Emma Wagner

Travis, *TRAV ihs,* **William Barret** (1809-1836), was a hero of the Alamo. He commanded the Texas patriots who died defending the Alamo against the Mexicans in 1836. Travis was born near Red Bank, S.C. He taught school and practiced law in Alabama before he moved to Texas in 1831. He also led troops at Anahuac and San Antonio. See also Alamo. H. Bailey Carroll

Travois, *truh VOY,* is a device used by American Indians and other peoples for carrying loads. It consists of two poles, a net or platform lashed between, and a harness for hitching the device to a horse or dog. A travois has no wheels. The ends of the poles drag on the ground. See also Transportation (picture: Transportation in prehistoric times). Franklin M. Reck

Trawl. See Fishing industry (Nets).

Treadmill, *TREHD mihl,* is a wheeled mechanism rotated by people or animals walking on or inside the wheel. A treadmill with an axle is called a *wheel and axle* (see Wheel and axle). The movement of the wheel turns the axle and any mechanical device to which it is attached.

The ancient Romans used treadmills for such tasks as grinding grain, lifting water out of mines, and powering cranes that hoisted construction materials. People and such animals as cows and horses provided the power for these devices. Treadmills were used for heavy work until the 1700's and 1800's, when they were replaced by steam and hydraulic engines. Today, many people exercise indoors by jogging on a device that resembles a treadmill. Tiny treadwheels provide exercise for hamsters and other small pets in cages. Melvin Kranzberg

Treason, *TREE zuhn,* once meant disloyalty to a sovereign ruler, such as a king. People who criticized the ruler's policies and actions might find themselves convicted of treason. But today, the meaning of treason has changed. The people in the United States or other democratic countries can criticize the government, and work as freely as they like for the election of a new government. The United States Constitution clearly defines treason as:

"Treason against the United States shall consist only in levying war against them or in adhering to their enemies, giving them aid and comfort." See Constitution of the United States (Article III [Section 3]).

This definition protects the right of citizens to oppose the actions of their government in all reasonable ways. Congress determines by law what the penalties shall be for treason against the United States. Many states have laws against treason. Death or life imprisonment is the usual penalty. A person convicted of treason is usually called a *traitor.*

A famous case of treason involved John Brown, an abolitionist who led a raid against the U.S. arsenal at Harpers Ferry in western Virginia (now West Virginia). The raid occurred in October 1859, and Brown was captured soon afterward. He was convicted of charges of treason and hanged. Another famous U.S. trial for treason was that of Aaron Burr, the third Vice President. Burr was found not guilty.   Douglas L. Wheeler

Related articles in *World Book* include:

Arnold, Benedict	Burr, Aaron	Quisling, Vidkun
Brown, John	Dreyfus, Alfred	Sedition

Treasure Island. See Stevenson, Robert Louis.

Treasury, Department of the, is an executive department of the United States government. Among its important jobs are collecting federal taxes and customs duties. It receives all money paid to the government, serves as custodian of the government's revenues, pays federal government expenses, and keeps accounts of government revenues and expenditures.

The Treasury Department prepares all paper money, coins, and federal securities, and prints all postage stamps. The department also supervises the operation of national banks. Upon authorization from Congress, the Treasury Department borrows money for the United States government and manages the national debt.

The department makes and carries out policies relating to the international economic, financial, and monetary field. For example, it has responsibilities in U.S. balance of payments problems. The department also enforces antismuggling laws, prevents counterfeiting, and protects the President and Vice President.

The secretary of the treasury heads the department. The secretary is appointed by the President with the approval of the Senate, and is a member of the President's Cabinet. The secretary advises the President on financial policies and reports to Congress each year on the nation's finances. Chief staff members include a deputy secretary, an undersecretary, a general counsel, and nine assistant secretaries.

The department's operating bureaus include:

Bureau of Alcohol, Tobacco, and Firearms supervises the production and distribution of alcohol and tobacco. It also checks the illegal possession and use of firearms and explosives.

Bureau of Engraving and Printing prints money, postage stamps, and securities.

Bureau of the Public Debt administers and keeps records of the public debt.

Federal Law Enforcement Training Center trains law enforcement agents of the Treasury Department and

Secretaries of the treasury

Name	Took office	Under President	Name	Took office	Under President
* Alexander Hamilton	1789	Washington	Walter Q. Gresham	1884	Arthur
* Oliver Wolcott, Jr.	1795	Washington, Adams	Hugh McCulloch	1884	Arthur
			Daniel Manning	1885	Cleveland
Samuel Dexter	1801	Adams, Jefferson	Charles S. Fairchild	1887	Cleveland
* Albert Gallatin	1801	Jefferson, Madison	William Windom	1889	B. Harrison
			Charles Foster	1891	B. Harrison
George W. Campbell	1814	Madison	John G. Carlisle	1893	Cleveland
Alexander J. Dallas	1814	Madison	Lyman J. Gage	1897	McKinley, T. Roosevelt
* William H. Crawford	1816	Madison, Monroe			
Richard Rush	1825	J. Q. Adams	Leslie M. Shaw	1902	T. Roosevelt
Samuel D. Ingham	1829	Jackson	George B. Cortelyou	1907	T. Roosevelt
Louis McLane	1831	Jackson	Franklin MacVeagh	1909	Taft
William J. Duane	1833	Jackson	William G. McAdoo	1913	Wilson
* Roger B. Taney	1833	Jackson	* Carter Glass	1918	Wilson
Levi Woodbury	1834	Jackson, Van Buren	David F. Houston	1920	Wilson
			* Andrew W. Mellon	1921	Harding, Coolidge, Hoover
Thomas Ewing	1841	W. H. Harrison, Tyler	Ogden L. Mills	1932	Hoover
Walter Forward	1841	Tyler	William H. Woodin	1933	F. D. Roosevelt
John C. Spencer	1843	Tyler	* Henry Morgenthau, Jr.	1934	F. D. Roosevelt, Truman
George M. Bibb	1844	Tyler			
Robert J. Walker	1845	Polk	* Frederick M. Vinson	1945	Truman
William M. Meredith	1849	Taylor	John W. Snyder	1946	Truman
Thomas Corwin	1850	Fillmore	George M. Humphrey	1953	Eisenhower
James Guthrie	1853	Pierce	Robert B. Anderson	1957	Eisenhower
Howell Cobb	1857	Buchanan	Douglas Dillon	1961	Kennedy, L. B. Johnson
Philip F. Thomas	1860	Buchanan			
John A. Dix	1861	Buchanan	Henry H. Fowler	1965	L. B. Johnson
* Salmon P. Chase	1861	Lincoln	Joseph W. Barr	1968	L. B. Johnson
* William P. Fessenden	1864	Lincoln	David M. Kennedy	1969	Nixon
Hugh McCulloch	1865	Lincoln, A. Johnson	* John B. Connally	1971	Nixon
			* George P. Shultz	1972	Nixon
George S. Boutwell	1869	Grant	* William E. Simon	1974	Nixon, Ford
William A. Richardson	1873	Grant	W. Michael Blumenthal	1977	Carter
Benjamin H. Bristow	1874	Grant	G. William Miller	1979	Carter
Lot M. Morrill	1876	Grant	Donald T. Regan	1981	Reagan
* John Sherman	1877	Hayes	* James A. Baker III	1985	Reagan
William Windom	1881	Garfield, Arthur	Nicholas F. Brady	1988	Reagan, Bush
Charles J. Folger	1881	Arthur			

*Has a separate biography in *World Book*.

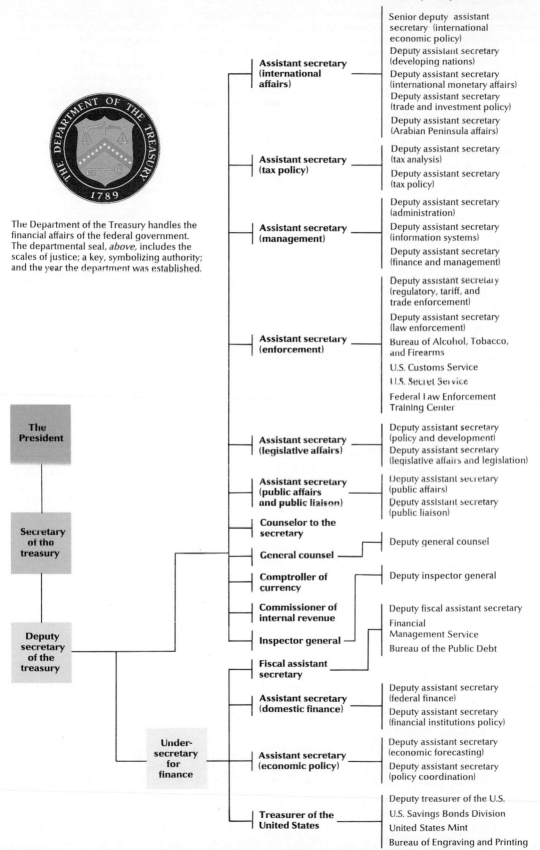

The Department of the Treasury handles the financial affairs of the federal government. The departmental seal, *above,* includes the scales of justice; a key, symbolizing authority; and the year the department was established.

of other agencies of the federal government.

Financial Management Service issues checks for most government agencies, records receipts and expenditures of all public funds, and supervises the issue and redemption of U.S. currency.

Internal Revenue Service assesses and collects taxes imposed by federal law. See **Internal Revenue Service.**

Office of the Comptroller of the Currency charters the national banks. It also directs a periodic inspection of these banks. See **Comptroller of the Currency.**

United States Customs Service collects duties on imports and prevents illegal entry of goods. See **Customs Service, United States.**

United States Mint manufactures coins. See **Mint.**

United States Savings Bonds Division promotes the sale of the savings bonds issued by the United States government. See **Savings bond.**

United States Secret Service guards against counterfeiting. It protects the President, the President's family, the Vice President, and certain other people. See **Secret Service, United States.**

History. The Department of the Treasury, established on Sept. 2, 1789, was the second executive department created by the first Congress. Alexander Hamilton was the first secretary of the treasury, and his department had five employees. The department now employs about 120,000 people.

Critically reviewed by the Department of the Treasury

See also **Flag** (picture: Flags of the U.S. government); **Mint; Money.**

Treaty is a formal agreement between two or more independent governments. It is usually a written docu-

ment, but it may be a verbal statement agreed to by representatives of the countries. The history of treaty making goes back many hundreds of years. As early as 3000 B.C., rulers of ancient countries signed treaties with neighboring kingdoms. The treaties served various purposes. Some treaties ended wars, and others settled boundary disputes. But through the history of the world, treaties have played an important part in the relations between countries.

Today, only sovereign states are able to make treaties. A sovereign state is one that is free from outside control. For example, Great Britain is a sovereign state because its government is free to make its own decisions. But the British colony of Gibraltar is not free to make its own decisions. It is therefore not a sovereign state, and cannot make its own treaties.

A treaty is much like a contract between private individuals. In both cases, the signing parties promise to do or not do some act. But there are important differences between treaties and contracts. A contract is not binding if one of the parties has forced the other party into agreement. But the use of force does not make a treaty void unless the force is actually used against the government representative who is working out the treaty terms. Unlike a private contract, a treaty does not go into effect until it is *ratified*. For example, a treaty between the United States and Great Britain is not official until it is approved by the United States Senate and by the British Crown.

There are several kinds of international agreements that have the force of treaties. One of these is called a *convention*. This is usually an agreement between states relating to a single topic, such as extradition. A *concor-*

A treaty signed by William Penn established friendship between colonists and Indians in Pennsylvania. Penn agreed to pay the Indians for most of the land he claimed in their territory.

dat is an agreement between the pope and a sovereign state. An agreement between two monarchs on a private matter is not a treaty.

Kinds of treaties. Treaties may be divided into several classes according to their purposes, although international law recognizes no formal distinctions among treaties. A single treaty may include clauses under several classes. Some of the classes are described below.

Political. A peace treaty is one kind of political treaty. For example, the Treaty of Ghent in 1814 ended the War of 1812. Others deal with alliances between countries and settle disputes. The Clayton-Bulwer Treaty in 1850 gave the United States and Britain equal protection rights in a future canal through Central America.

Commercial. These treaties include agreements on tariffs, navigation, fisheries, and consular services.

Confederation. Confederation treaties set up such international organizations as the Universal Postal Union.

Extradition. These treaties deal with escaped criminals. For example, let us suppose that two countries have signed an extradition treaty. If a criminal from one country flees to the other for safety, the criminal must be returned, or *extradited,* to stand trial for the crime.

Civil justice. These treaties protect a country's trademarks, copyrights, and patents in foreign countries. Some civil-justice treaties deal with the rights of aliens.

Negotiation. In monarchies, the king or queen and his or her legal agents have the power to make treaties and are represented at negotiations by a diplomatic agent, or *envoy.* For example, in Great Britain neither house of Parliament has any power over treaties. That power is reserved for the British Crown or Cabinet.

In republics, the chief executive usually has treaty-making power. This power is often subject to various restrictions. In the United States, the President may enter into a treaty with "the advice and consent" of the Senate. Two-thirds of the senators present must agree to the treaty terms. Separate states in the United States may not make treaty agreements. The Department of State carries on treaty negotiations. Sometimes the President enters into an *executive agreement* with a foreign country. This kind of agreement has the force of a treaty in international law, but it does not require the approval of the Senate.

Language used. Until the 1700's, all treaties were written in Latin. Then French became the official language. Today, most treaties are written in the various languages of the treaty-making nations.

Enforcement of treaties. In ancient times, a country had to "back up," or guarantee, its treaty promises. One way of doing this was to exchange hostages. Each country that signed the treaty would send one or more important people to the other countries that had agreed to the treaty. Hostages were held as prisoners. They could be killed if the terms of the treaty were not carried out.

The hostage system has not been used for many years. Today, most countries rely on the good faith of other countries, and on international public opinion. In many countries, including the United States, treaties have the force of law. As a result, treaty provisions become legal requirements for officials. At the same time, however, nations may repeal or abolish these treaties, as they do their own laws. But such actions are generally subject to certain international consequences.

Termination. Treaties may be ended in many ways. They may end upon the agreement of all parties concerned. Sometimes a treaty clause permits either party to cancel the agreement after due notice. The failure of one country to carry out its part of the agreement may cause the other country or countries to refuse to observe the treaty terms. A treaty becomes void when the physical conditions of the agreement become impossible to fulfill. War nullifies many treaties.

Ecclesiastical treaties deal with the religious rights of people who are living in a foreign country. Among Western nations, people may worship as freely in foreign lands as in their homelands. In several non-Christian parts of the world, Christian missionaries are permitted by treaty to teach the beliefs of Christianity. In some countries, ecclesiastical treaties permit foreign residents to practice their own religions but forbid them to try to convert others.   Robert J. Pranger

Related articles. The principal treaties among nations are listed in *World Book* under their respective titles, such as Clayton-Bulwer Treaty; Ghent, Treaty of. See also the following articles:

Arbitration	International relations
Extradition	Protocol
International law	

Treaty of 1783. See Revolutionary War in America (The Treaty of Paris).

Treaty port. Through the years, foreign powers have used different methods to gain trading rights in China. One of these methods was to persuade the Chinese government to open certain Chinese seaports to foreign trade. These cities were known as treaty ports because trade with foreign countries was carried on under treaty agreement at these ports.

In 1842, China entered into a treaty-port agreement with Great Britain. This treaty opened five Chinese ports to British trade. The ports open to Britain were Guangzhou (Canton), Xiamen (Amoy), Fuzhou (Fu-chou), Ningbo (Ningpo), and Shanghai. Later, China signed treaty-port agreements with many other countries, including the United States, Germany, Russia, and Mexico. By 1894, there were more than 60 treaty ports in China. Most treaty-port agreements were forced upon China by foreign pressure or wars. Treaty ports gave many special privileges to foreign countries. The foreigners who enjoyed privileges in treaty ports could not even be punished under Chinese laws.

In 1912, China began to object to treaty-port agreements. After World War I, Russia gave up its rights in China, and in 1929 Mexico did the same. In 1943, both Great Britain and the United States signed treaties giving up their special rights in China. Today, China no longer has treaty ports.   Robert M. Stern

See also **Extraterritoriality; Fuzhou; Guangzhou; Xiamen.**

Treble, *TREHB uhl,* is the upper, or highest, part in choral music of two or more parts. It is often called the *soprano* part, and is sung by women or boys. The treble part in instrumental music is played by such instruments as the violin, flute, clarinet, and oboe. It is also played on the higher keys of the piano or organ, roughly above middle C. *Treble clef* or *G clef* (𝄞) is the sign used to mark the five-line staff from which treble voices or instruments read.   Raymond Kendall

David Muench

The magnificent giant sequoias of California rank among the world's oldest and largest living things. Some of these trees are thousands of years old and over 200 feet (61 meters) tall.

Tree

Tree is the largest of all plants. The tallest trees grow higher than 30-story buildings. Many trees also live longer than other plants. Some trees live for thousands of years. They are the oldest known living things.

People do not think of trees the way they think of other plants, most of which grow only a short time and then die. People think of trees as permanent parts of the landscape. Year after year, large, old trees shade houses

Richard H. Waring, the contributor of this article, is Professor of Forest Ecology at Oregon State University.

and streets from the sun. Their buds and flowers are a sign of spring each year, and their colorful leaves brighten in autumn in many areas.

Trees continue to grow as long as they live. A tree's leaves make food that keeps the tree alive and helps it grow. Where winters are cold, many trees lose their leaves in autumn. Other trees keep their leaves during the winter and so stay green all year long. Trees that shed their leaves in autumn rest during the winter. In spring, they grow new leaves and flowers. The flowers grow into fruits, which contain seeds for making new trees. Some tree fruits, such as apples and oranges, taste good. Fruit growers raise large amounts of these fruits for sale. Trees also make new wood each year

Theodore F. Welch, Van Cleve Photography

Dwarf trees never reach full size. Some, such as this miniature cypress tree, are deliberately kept small by a special pruning process. But many dwarf trees grow naturally in arctic regions.

WORLD BOOK illustration by James Teason

Coconut

Coconut palm

The coconut palm provides wood and other building materials. The tree's nuts provide sweet-tasting milk and meat. Oil from dried coconut meat is used in making such products as margarine and soap.

Interesting facts about trees

The world's largest living thing is the General Sherman Tree, a giant sequoia in Sequoia National Park in California. It towers more than 275 feet (83.8 meters) and has a trunk about 37 feet (11 meters) wide. It probably dates from before 200 B.C.

The traveler's-tree, which grows in Madagascar, stores up to 1 pint (0.5 liter) of water inside the base of each of its long leaf stalks. The tree received its name because it provides thirsty travelers with fresh drinking water.

Traveler's-tree

The tallest trees are California's redwoods, which may tower more than 360 feet (110 meters). Australia's eucalyptuses may grow more than 300 feet (91 meters) tall.

The thickest tree trunk is that of a Montezuma baldcypress near Oaxaca, Mexico. Its diameter exceeds 40 feet (12 meters).

The baobab tree of Africa is one of the most useful trees. It has a huge trunk, which people hollow out to store water in or to live in. They eat the tree's leaves, fruit, seeds, and roots and use its parts in many other ways.

Baobab

The oldest trees are California's bristlecone pines and giant sequoias. Some bristlecone pines have lived between 4,000 and 5,000 years. The oldest sequoias are about 3,500 years old.

The banyan tree of India spreads by growing trunklike roots from its branches. In time, a banyan may cover acres of ground.

The ombu tree of Argentina is one of the hardiest trees. It can live with little water and can survive insect attacks, violent storms, and intense heat. The tree's wood is so moist it will not burn and so spongy it cannot be cut down.

Ombu

The largest seeds are the nuts of the coco-de-mer, or double coconut palm, of the Seychelles, an island group in the Indian Ocean. A nut may weigh up to 50 pounds (23 kilograms).

when the weather turns warmer. Wood is one of the most valuable parts of a tree. Mills and factories use wood to make lumber, paper, and many other products.

A tree differs from other plants in four main ways. (1) Most trees grow at least 15 to 20 feet (4.6 to 6.1 meters) tall. (2) They have one woody stem, which is called a *trunk.* (3) The stem grows at least 3 to 4 inches (8 to 10 centimeters) thick. (4) A tree's stem can stand by itself. All other plants differ from trees in at least one of these ways. For example, no plant with a soft, juicy stem is a tree. Most of these plants, called *herbs,* are much shorter than most trees. *Shrubs,* like trees, have woody stems. But most shrubs have more than one stem, and none of the stems grows so thick or so tall as a tree

trunk. Some jungle *vines* grow more than 200 feet (61 meters) long and have a woody stem. But the stems of most vines cannot support themselves. Some seaweeds called *kelp* have stems that grow 200 feet (61 meters) tall, but they cannot stand—or even live—out of water.

There are thousands of kinds of trees. But most trees belong to one of two main groups—the broadleaf trees and the needleleaf trees. These two types of trees grow in Europe, North America, and many other parts of the world. Most other types of trees, such as palms and tree ferns, grow mainly in warm regions.

E. R. Degginger

Wood is one of the most useful tree products. In the above picture, a circular saw strips bark from a log at a sawmill. The stripped log will be cut into boards and other lumber.

David R. Frazier Photolibrary

A forester checks young trees that were planted as part of a forest conservation project. These trees will replace trees that were cut down for timber.

For thousands of years, trees have provided people with foods, fibers, and medicines. Above all, they have provided people with wood. Prehistoric people used wood to make the first spear, the first boat, and the first wheel. Throughout history, people have used wood to make tools, construct buildings, and create works of art. They have also used it for fuel. Living trees are as valuable to humankind as are tree products because they help conserve natural resources.

Wood products. Each year, loggers cut down millions of trees in the world's forests. Logs from these trees are shipped to sawmills and pulp mills. Sawmills cut the logs into lumber, which the building industry uses for many types of construction work. Manufacturers use lumber to make everything from furniture to baseball bats. Pulp mills break down the logs into wood pulp, the main raw material for making paper. The chemical industry uses wood pulp to make alcohol, plastics, and other products. See **Forest products; Lumber.**

Food products. People throughout the world eat fruits, nuts, and other tree products. The greatest variety of fruit trees grow in tropical and subtropical regions. These trees produce such fruits as avocados, grapefruits, mangoes, and oranges. A number of these fruits serve as basic foods in some tropical lands. Cooler, temperate regions—such as most of the United States and Europe—have fewer kinds of fruit trees. But several kinds are widely grown. For example, orchards in the United States produce vast amounts of apples, cherries, and peaches. The most important nut tree of warm regions is the coconut palm, which produces coconuts. Nut trees of temperate regions include almonds, pecans, and walnuts. Trees also supply chocolate, coffee, maple syrup, olives, and such spices as cinnamon and cloves. See **Fruit; Nut.**

Other tree products are used by people in a variety of ways. The rubber tree produces *latex,* a milky fluid used to make natural rubber. Pine trees produce a sticky *resin,* used in making turpentine. The bark of oak and some other trees contains a compound called *tannic acid.* The tanning industry uses this compound to change animal hides into leather. The spongy bark of a type of oak that grows in Mediterranean countries provides cork. Some trees produce substances used as medicines. For example, the bark of the cinchona tree contains *quinine,* which doctors use to treat malaria and other diseases.

Trees in conservation. Trees help conserve soil and water. In open country, trees act as windbreaks and keep the wind from blowing away topsoil. Their roots prevent soil from being washed away by heavy rains. Tree roots also help store water in the ground. In mountain regions, forests prevent sliding snow from causing avalanches. Forests also provide shelter for wildlife and recreation areas for vacationists. See **Conservation.**

Trees help preserve the balance of gases in the atmosphere. A tree's leaves absorb carbon dioxide from the air. They also produce oxygen and release it into the atmosphere. These two processes are necessary for people to live. People could not survive if the air had too much carbon dioxide or too little oxygen.

There are about 20,000 kinds of trees. More than 1,000 kinds grow in the United States. They range from mighty forest trees to fragile ornamentals. The greatest variety of trees grow in wet tropical regions.

Scientists who study plants divide plants with similar characteristics into various groups (see **Plant** [Kinds of plants]). These scientists, called *botanists,* do not put trees in a separate group of plants. Instead, each kind of tree is grouped with other plants that have certain features in common with it. Therefore, a group of plants

may include certain trees, certain shrubs or vines, and certain herbs. For example, locust trees, broom plants, and clover all belong to the same *family.* These plants are grouped together because they reproduce in the same way and have similar flowers. On the other hand, some trees that look much alike, such as tree ferns and palms, belong to different groups of plants.

Trees also can be divided into six groups according to various features they have in common. These six groups are: (1) broadleaf trees; (2) needleleaf trees; (3)

The six main groups of trees

Trees can be divided into the six main groups illustrated below. All the trees in each group are similar in appearance and have other features in common.

Silver maple

Fruit   Leaf

Red, or Norway, pine

Needles and cone

Royal palm

Fruit

Broadleaf trees are known for their autumn colors, bare winter branches, and spring flowers, which develop into fruits.

Needleleaf trees have needlelike or scalelike leaves and bear their seeds in cones. Most are evergreen.

Palms and pandanus and lily trees form a group of mainly tropical trees. Most palms have huge leaves and no branches.

South African cycad

Leaves and cones

West Indies tree fern

Leaflet and spore cases

Seeds   Ginkgo   Leaf

WORLD BOOK illustrations by James Teason

Cycad trees live only in warm, moist regions. They bear heavy cones that may grow 3 feet (91 centimeters) long.

Tree ferns are the only trees that have no flowers, fruits, or seeds. They reproduce by means of *spores.*

Ginkgo trees are a single species. They bear seeds but not fruits or cones. The seeds have an unpleasant odor.

palm, pandanus, and lily trees; (4) cycad trees; (5) tree ferns; and (6) ginkgo trees.

Broadleaf trees are the most numerous and varied of the world's trees. They include ashes, elms, maples, oaks, walnuts, willows, and many other familiar trees of the United States and Canada. They also include most trees of the tropics, such as mahogany trees and mangrove trees.

In addition to their broad, flat leaves, broadleaf trees have other features in common. Almost all broadleaf trees of temperate regions are *deciduous*—that is, they lose their leaves each autumn. A few kinds of broadleaf trees in temperate regions do not lose their leaves in the fall. These broadleaf *evergreens* include the holly trees and live oaks of the Southeastern United States. Some tropical broadleaf trees are deciduous, but most are evergreen. See **Deciduous tree; Evergreen.**

Foresters call broadleaf trees *hardwoods* because many of these trees, such as beeches, maples, and oaks, have tough, hard wood. Such wood makes excellent furniture. Some broadleaf trees, including basswoods and cottonwoods, have soft, lightweight wood.

Broadleaf trees belong to a large *class* of plants called *angiosperms.* These plants have flowers which develop into *fruits* that completely surround the seeds. Fruits are the seed or seeds of a plant together with the parts in which they are enclosed. Botanists divide angiosperms into two subclasses—*monocotyledons* and *dicotyledons.* Monocotyledons produce seeds that contain one leafy structure called a *cotyledon* (see **Cotyledon**). These plants include palm, pandanus, and lily trees. Dicotyledons produce seeds with two cotyledons. These plants include broadleaf trees. A few kinds of trees that do not have broad, flat leaves also belong to the dicotyledon group. An example is the saguaro cactus of the Southwestern United States, which has prickly spines. See **Angiosperm.**

Needleleaf trees include such familiar trees as firs, hemlocks, pines, redwoods, and spruces. There are about 500 species of needleleaf trees. Most of them have narrow, pointed, needlelike leaves. But a few types, such as cedars and junipers, have narrow, scalelike leaves.

Most needleleaf trees are evergreen, though they produce new needles each year. The oldest needles turn yellow or brown and drop, but the youngest needles remain green and do not fall. A few species of needleleaf trees are deciduous. One kind is the larch, which grows in northern forests throughout the world. Another deciduous needleleaf tree is the baldcypress that grows in swamps of the Southeastern United States.

Foresters call needleleaf trees *softwoods* because most of them have softer wood than broadleaf trees have. But the wood of Douglas-firs, yews, and some other needleleaf trees is hard.

Needleleaf trees belong to a class of plants called *gymnosperms.* Gymnosperms do not have flowers and their seeds are not enclosed to form fruits. Most gymnosperm trees bear their seeds in cones composed of hard scales. The seeds lie open on the surface of the scales. Botanists call such trees *conifers.* See **Conifer; Gymnosperm.**

Most conifers grow north of the equator. They belong to four families—the pine, yew, cypress, and taxodium families. The *pine family* is by far the largest. It includes not only pines, but also such trees as firs, hemlocks, larches, and spruces. Pine trees make up a large *genus* (group of species) within the pine family. Loblolly pines, ponderosa pines, and white pines are a few North American members of this genus. The *yew family* includes such well-known ornamental trees as English yews and Japanese yews. Although yews are classified as conifers, they do not produce cones but cup-shaped "berries." Many members of the *cypress family,* such as

Trees of the states

Baldcypress Louisiana	**Holly** (American) Delaware	Iowa Maryland (White oak) New Jersey (Red oak)	Montana (Ponderosa pine) North Carolina
Birch New Hampshire (White birch)	**Horsechestnut** Ohio (Buckeye)	**Palm** (Sabal) Florida	**Piñon** (Nut pine) Nevada (Single-leaf piñon) New Mexico
Cottonwood Kansas Nebraska Wyoming	**Kentucky coffeetree** Kentucky **Kukui** Hawaii	**Palmetto** South Carolina	**Redbud** Oklahoma
Dogwood (Flowering) Missouri Virginia (American)	**Magnolia** Mississippi	**Paloverde** Arizona	**Redwood** California (California redwood)
Douglas-fir Oregon	**Maple** New York (Sugar maple) Rhode Island (Red maple) Vermont (Sugar maple)	**Pecan** Texas **Pine** Alabama (Southern pine)	**Spruce** Alaska (Sitka spruce) Colorado (Blue spruce)
Elm (American) Massachusetts North Dakota	West Virginia (Sugar maple) Wisconsin (Sugar maple)	Arkansas Idaho (Western white pine) Maine (White pine)	South Dakota (Black Hills spruce) Utah (Blue spruce)
Hemlock Pennsylvania Washington (Western hemlock)	**Oak** Connecticut (White oak) Georgia (Live oak) Illinois (White oak)	Michigan (White pine) Minnesota (Norway, or red, pine)	**Tulip tree** Indiana Tennessee (Tulip poplar)

Each tree listed in boldface type has a separate article in WORLD BOOK. All state trees are shown in color in the state articles.

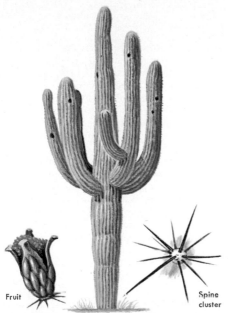

Fruit

Spine cluster

WORLD BOOK illustration by James Teason

The saguaro, or giant cactus, is a tree that has spines instead of leaves. It grows 25 to 50 feet (8 to 15 meters) tall. The saguaro has a thick, woody stem and bears sweet fruit.

Josef Muench

A prehistoric log in the Petrified Forest National Park of Arizona turned to stone millions of years ago. Scientists study such *petrified* logs to learn about the ancestors of today's trees.

arborvitae and junipers, have scalelike leaves and give off a spicy fragrance. The *taxodium family* includes bald-cypresses and the largest of all trees—the redwoods and giant sequoias.

Two conifer families—the *podocarpus family* and the *araucaria family*—grow mainly south of the equator. Podocarpus trees are tall evergreens with broader leaves than those of most needleleaf trees. The araucaria family includes the Chile pine. This strange-looking tree has snakelike branches covered with sharp, scaly leaves. It is sometimes called the monkey puzzle tree because its sharp leaves make it difficult to climb.

Palm, pandanus, and lily trees belong to the large group of flowering plants called monocotyledons. These trees grow mainly in warm climates. Of the three types of trees in this group, palms are the most important.

There are about 2,500 kinds of palm trees. They range from the coconut palms of tropical islands to the date palms of desert oases. Most palm trees have no branches. The trunk has a crown of enormous leaves. The leaves are either feather-shaped or fan-shaped. See **Palm.**

Unlike most palms, pandanus and lily trees have branches. Each branch has a crown of sword-shaped leaves. Most pandanus trees have tall *stilt roots* that extend into the ground from high on the trunk or branches. Lily trees are closely related to the garden flowers called lilies, and many of the trees have attractive, fragrant flowers. The yucca trees of Mexico and the far Southern United States are lily trees. The best-known yucca is the colorful Joshua tree found in the deserts of the Southwestern United States.

Cycad trees look much like palm trees. They have a trunk without branches and a crown of long, feathery leaves. But cycads are more closely related to pine trees

than to palms. They produce seeds in cones that look like large pine cones. Millions of years ago, cycads grew in nearly every part of the world. Today, they grow mainly in a few warm, moist sections of Africa, Asia, and Central America. See **Cycad.**

Tree ferns. Ferns are best known as rather short plants with feathery, green *fronds* (leaves). But in the tropics and some areas with mild climates, many relatives of these plants are trees. Tree ferns look much like palm trees, but they belong to a different group of plants. Tree ferns do not have flowers or cones and so do not reproduce by seeds. They reproduce by means of tiny bodies called *spores,* which develop on the undersides of their fronds. See **Fern.**

Ginkgo trees are an extremely old species of tree. Millions of years ago, various kinds of ginkgoes existed. Only one species survives today. The ginkgo, like needleleaf trees, is a gymnosperm. But unlike other gymnosperm trees, the ginkgo has fan-shaped leaves. These leaves look like the fronds of a fern called the *maidenhair.* Ginkgoes are sometimes called *maidenhair trees.* They are natives of Asia, but many are grown in the United States and Europe.

Fossil trees. About 300 million years ago, there were whole forests of trees unlike most of the trees that grow today. Huge club-moss trees and horsetail trees grew along with tree ferns in steaming hot swamps. Over millions of years, the trees and other plant life in the swamps died, became buried, and turned into coal. In other places, buried forests became *petrified* (turned into stone). Coal deposits and petrified forests contain fossils of many trees that died out more than 100 million years ago (see **Fossil**). Two of these extinct trees are the club moss tree and horsetail tree of the coal-forming swamps. The club mosses and horsetails living today are herbs.

The parts of a tree

A tree has three main parts: (1) the trunk and branches; (2) the leaves; and (3) the roots. The branches and leaves together are called the *crown*. The trunk supports the crown and holds it up to the sunlight. Tree ferns, cycads, and most palms have no branches. Their crowns consist only of leaves. The roots of most trees are hidden in the ground, but they may take up as much space as the trunk and crown do above the ground. Other important parts of a tree include the seeds and the seed-forming structures.

Trunk and branches give a tree its shape. The trunks of most needleleaf trees grow straight up to the top of the tree. The branches grow out from the trunk. On most needleleaf trees, the branches near the top are shorter than those farther down, which gives the crown a spirelike shape. The trunks of most broadleaf trees do not reach to the top of the tree. Instead, the trunk divides into spreading branches near the base of the

crown, giving the crown a rounded shape. The trunks of a few broadleaf trees, such as black willows and white poplars, sometimes divide so close to the ground that the trees seem to have more than one trunk.

The trunks, branches, and roots of broadleaf and needleleaf trees consist of four layers of plant tissue wrapped around one another. These layers, from innermost to outermost, are: (1) the *xylem,* (2) the *cambium,* (3) the *phloem,* and (4) the *cork.*

The xylem is the woody, central part of the trunk. It has tiny pipelines that carry water with a small amount of dissolved minerals from the roots to the leaves. This water is called *sap.* The cambium, which surrounds the xylem, is a thin layer of growing tissue. Its job is to make the trunk, branches, and roots grow thicker. The phloem, also called the *inner bark,* is a layer of soft tissue surrounding the cambium. Like the xylem, the phloem has tiny pipelines. The food made by the leaves

Parts of a tree

These diagrams show the three main parts of a tree: (1) the leaves, (2) the trunk and branches, and (3) the roots. The branches and leaves together make up a tree's *crown.* The diagrams also show the main types of tissue that compose most trees.

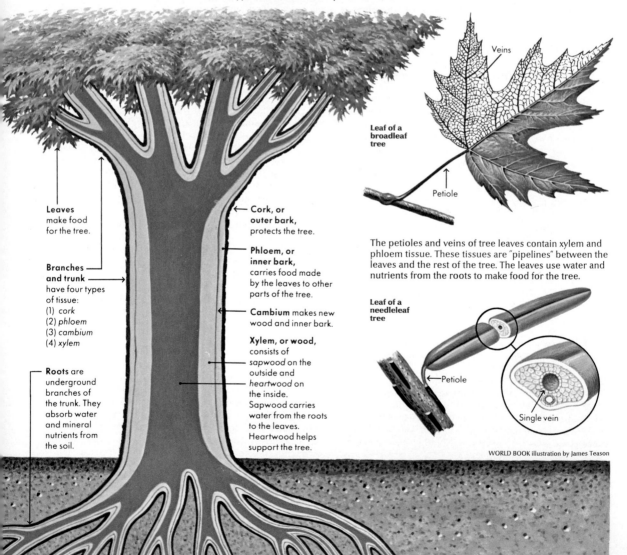

Veins

Leaf of a broadleaf tree

Petiole

Leaves make food for the tree.

← **Cork, or outer bark,** protects the tree.

Branches and trunk have four types of tissue:
(1) *cork*
(2) *phloem*
(3) *cambium*
(4) *xylem*

Phloem, or inner bark, carries food made by the leaves to other parts of the tree.

Cambium makes new wood and inner bark.

Xylem, or wood, consists of *sapwood* on the outside and *heartwood* on the inside. Sapwood carries water from the roots to the leaves. Heartwood helps support the tree.

Roots are underground branches of the trunk. They absorb water and mineral nutrients from the soil.

The petioles and veins of tree leaves contain xylem and phloem tissue. These tissues are "pipelines" between the leaves and the rest of the tree. The leaves use water and nutrients from the roots to make food for the tree.

Leaf of a needleleaf tree

Petiole

Single vein

WORLD BOOK illustration by James Teason

Seeds of broadleaf and needleleaf trees

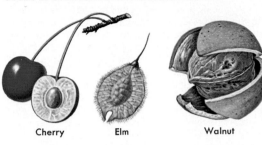

Cherry   Elm   Walnut

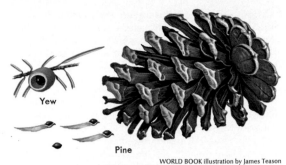

Yew   Pine

WORLD BOOK illustration by James Teason

Seeds of broadleaf trees, or *angiosperm seeds,* have protective coverings. The seed and covering together are called a fruit. Cherry and walnut seeds are enclosed in a pit or shell with a fleshy outer covering. Elm seeds have thin, winged coverings.

Seeds of needleleaf trees, or *gymnosperm seeds,* do not have protective coverings. The seeds of most needleleaf trees lie in cones and are released after the cones ripen. The yew and a few other coneless needleleaf trees have berrylike seeds.

moves through the phloem to the other parts of a tree. In palms and tree ferns, the xylem and phloem are not separate layers. Instead, bits of xylem and phloem are connected and form small double pipelines scattered throughout the trunk.

The cork layer is the *outer bark* of a tree. It forms a "skin" of hard, dead tissue that protects the living inner parts from injury. The bark stretches to let the trunk and branches grow thicker. The bark of some trees, such as beeches and birches, is smooth because it stretches easily. But the bark of most other trees does not stretch so well. As the trunk and branches grow thicker, they push against the bark. It finally cracks and dries and so becomes grooved and rough. Most trees replace old bark from time to time with a new layer.

Leaves of various species of trees differ greatly in size and shape. Palms have leaves over 20 feet (6 meters) long. The leaves of some needleleaf trees are less than ½ inch (13 millimeters) long. Some broadleaf trees have *compound leaves* made up of small leaflets.

The main job of the leaves is to make food for the tree. Every leaf has one or more *veins,* which consist of xylem and phloem tissue. The tissue that surrounds the veins contains tiny green bodies called *chloroplasts.* Water from the roots passes through the xylem of the trunk, branches, and leaves to the chloroplasts, which use the water to make food sugar. Only a small amount of the water carried to the leaves is used to make sugar. The leaves lose most of the water to the atmosphere through *transpiration* (evaporation). Like the water and dissolved minerals carried from the roots, the food made by the leaves is also called *sap.* It travels through the phloem of the leaves, branches, and trunk to parts of the tree where it is needed. See **Sap.**

Almost all leaves are green in the spring and summer. Their color comes from chlorophyll, a green substance in the chloroplasts. Most trees also have reds and yellows in their leaves. But the green conceals these colors. In late summer and early autumn, the chlorophyll in the leaves of many broadleaf trees breaks down. The leaves then die. But before the leaves fall, they reveal their hidden reds and yellows. After the chlorophyll breaks down, the leaves of many trees also develop scarlets and purples. See **Leaf** (The leaf changes color).

Roots are long, underground branches of the trunk. They have the same layers of tissue as the trunk. The roots anchor a tree in the ground and absorb water with dissolved minerals from the soil. The main roots branch out into small roots, which, in turn, branch out into still smaller roots. The main roots of most trees begin to branch out 1 or 2 feet (30 or 61 centimeters) under the ground. Some trees have one main root larger than the others. This root, called a *taproot,* extends straight down 15 feet (5 meters) or more.

A tree develops millions of small roots. Each root grows longer at its tip, which is as small as a thread. As a root tip grows, it pushes through particles of soil. Thousands of fine, white *root hairs* grow just back of the root tip. When the tip comes in contact with drops of water in the soil, the hairs soak up the water and dissolved minerals. The xylem layer of the roots, trunk, and branches carries this sap to the leaves.

Fungi grow on the roots of most trees in a helpful relationship called *mycorrhiza.* The fungi aid the roots in absorbing water and mineral nutrients. They also protect the roots from some diseases.

Seeds are the means by which all trees except tree ferns reproduce. Tree ferns reproduce by spores.

Angiosperms—broadleaf trees and palm, pandanus, and lily trees—produce seeds by means of flowers. Some broadleaf trees, such as horsechestnuts and magnolias, produce large, showy flowers. Many others have small, plain-looking flowers. Most palm, pandanus, and lily trees have small flowers that grow in bunches. Sometimes these are brightly colored and fragrant.

The seeds of angiosperms are enclosed to form a fruit. The fruits of some broadleaf trees, such as apples and cherries, have a fleshy outer covering. The fruits of other broadleaf trees, including acorns and beechnuts, are hard nuts. Ashes, elms, and maples have thin, winged fruits. Palm, pandanus, and lily trees have a variety of fruits, ranging from nuts to berries.

Gymnosperms—needleleaf trees, cycads, and ginkgoes—do not have flowers or fruits. Their seeds are produced in cones or similar structures. The seeds of needleleaf trees and cycads have no protective coverings. Ginkgo seeds have a fleshy outer covering, but the covering is not a true fruit.

Most trees begin life as a seed. The young tree that develops from this seed is called a *seedling*. After a tree reaches a height of 6 feet (1.8 meters) or more and its trunk becomes 1 to 2 inches (2.5 to 5 centimeters) thick, it is called a *sapling*. Many trees reach a height of more than 100 feet (30 meters). Some old trees have trunks more than 10 feet (3 meters) in diameter.

Trees need great amounts of water. A large apple tree in full leaf may absorb 95 gallons (360 liters) from the soil daily. Most of the water goes to the leaves. On a sunny summer day, some trees move water up through their trunks at the rate of 3 feet (91 centimeters) per minute. A tree's wood is about half water.

How seeds sprout into trees. A seed contains parts that develop into the trunk and roots of a tree. It also has one or more cotyledons and a supply of plant food. After a seed has left the parent tree, it rests for a while on the ground. Water, air, and sunshine help the seed *germinate* (begin to grow). The part of the seed that develops into the trunk points upward toward the sunlight. As the seed absorbs water, the root part swells and bursts through the seed's shell. As the root grows, it pushes down into the soil. The food stored in the seed nourishes the tree. As the root begins to soak up water from the soil, the trunk begins to develop leaves.

How leaves make plant food. As a leaf develops, it gets sap from the roots. It also absorbs carbon dioxide from the air. The leaf uses the energy of sunlight to change the sap and carbon dioxide into sugar process called *photosynthesis*. The sugar provides food for the trunk, branches, and roots. During photosynthesis, the leaves also produce oxygen and releases it into the atmosphere. See **Leaf** (How a leaf makes food).

How trees grow taller. Trees grow taller only at the tips of their trunk and branches. Each year, the tip of the trunk and of each branch develop a *bud*. The bud contains a tiny leafy green stem called a *shoot*. The bud is wrapped in a protective covering of *bud scales*. After a period of rest, the buds swell and open. The shoots that were inside the buds begin to grow and so make the trunk and branches taller. Another type of bud grows on the sides of the trunk and branches. These buds contain a shoot that develops into a leaf-bearing *twig* after the bud opens. As a twig grows larger, it becomes another branch of the tree. Some tree buds develop into flowers. Still others develop into twigs that bear both leaves and flowers. In warm climates, trees produce buds frequently during the year or continue to grow without forming buds. In colder climates, trees produce buds only in the summer. These buds rest through the winter and open after warm weather arrives in spring.

Trees without branches—cycads, most palms, and tree ferns—grow somewhat differently. For example, a young palm tree does not grow taller for a number of years. Its short trunk thickens and larger leaves each year. After the trunk and crown reach adult size, the tree begins to grow taller. The trunk stays about the same thickness for the rest of the tree's life.

How trunks and branches grow thicker. The trunk and branches of a broadleaf or needleleaf tree grow thicker as long as the tree lives. The cambium tissue just underneath the inner bark causes this thickening. It uses the sugar produced by the leaves to make new plant tissue. On its outside, the cambium makes new phloem, or inner bark, and on its inside, new xylem, or wood.

Wood consists largely of *cellulose*, a tough substance made from sugar. The xylem has two kinds of wood—*sapwood* and *heartwood*. The wood nearest the cambium is the sapwood. It is living wood and contains the tiny pipelines that carry sap. In tropical climates, the

How a tree reveals its history

Most trees in temperate regions grow a layer of wood each year. After such a tree has been cut down, the layers can be seen as rings in the trunk. These *annual rings* reveal the tree's life story. The pine log in this drawing has 72 annual rings, showing that the tree lived for 72 years.

Narrow center rings indicate that other trees shaded the young tree, depriving it of moisture and sunlight.

Wider rings on the log's lower side after the 30th year show that the tree was slightly bent in this direction. The tree then began to grow more wood on this side than on the other to keep from falling. Most rings after the 38th year are wider than the center rings. This indicates that many surrounding trees had been removed, giving the tree more moisture and sunlight. Differences in the width of rings after the 38th ring were caused mainly by varying amounts of rainfall from year to year.

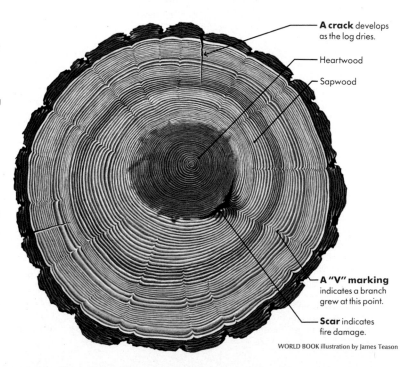

A **crack** develops as the log dries.

Heartwood

Sapwood

A **"V" marking** indicates a branch grew at this point.

Scar indicates fire damage.

WORLD BOOK illustration by James Teason

How most trees reproduce

Most trees reproduce by means of sex organs in their flowers or cones. Pollen from male organs produces sperm, which *fertilize* (unite with) eggs in female organs. This union produces seeds.

Fruit-bearing trees, or *angiosperms,* have flowers with an *ovary,* which becomes the outer part of the fruit.

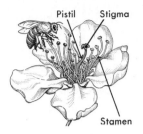
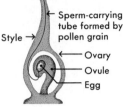
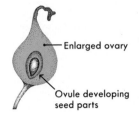
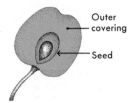

A cherry flower has male *stamens* and a female *pistil.* The top, or the *stigma,* of the pistil receives pollen grains from the stamens.

The pistil has an immature seed, or *ovule,* in an *ovary.* A sperm from a pollen grain moves down the *style* and fertilizes the egg.

After fertilization, the ovule develops into a seed, and the ovary grows larger. The other parts of the pistil and flower wither and die.

The fruit has an outer covering formed from the ovary. The seed or seeds are inside. A seed will develop into a new tree.

Cone-bearing trees, or *gymnosperms,* have cones without an ovary.

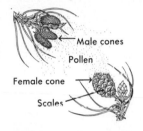
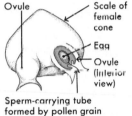
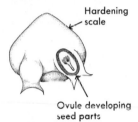
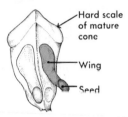

Pine cones are male or female. The wind carries pollen from male cones to the *scales* of a female cone.

A scale has two ovules, which are not enclosed in ovaries. Pollen enters the ovules and produces sperm.

After pollination, the scales harden. Fertilization occurs as a sperm in each ovule unites with the egg.

The seed produced from each fertilized ovule has the parts for a new tree. The seeds develop long wings.

WORLD BOOK illustration by Mary Ann Olson

sapwood thickens all year. In cooler climates, a new layer of sapwood usually forms only in early summer. As a tree ages, the wood nearest the center dies. This dead wood is the heartwood. It helps support the tree.

In regions where trees make a new layer of wood once a year, the layers form a series of *annual rings.* Each ring represents one year's growth. After such a tree has been cut down, a person can count the rings to determine the tree's age. Scientists have also found that slight changes in the composition of a tree's cellulose reveal the kind of weather that a tree experienced.

How trees reproduce. Most trees reproduce sexually. That is, seeds are produced only after sperm unite with eggs. Sperm are produced by pollen, which forms in the tree's male reproductive parts—either the male part of the flower or the male cone. Eggs form in the female part of the flower or in the female cone. Among many angiosperm species, the flowers have both male and female parts. The pollen from the male part can simply drop onto the female part. Other angiosperms and all gymnosperms have separate male and female flowers or cones, which may grow on the same tree or on separate trees. The pollen of these species is carried to

the female flower or cone by insects, the wind, or other means. After contacting the female flower or cone, pollen produces sperm. The sperm then unite with eggs, and one or more seeds develop within a fruit or cone.

When the fruit or cone has ripened, the seeds are ready to leave the tree. The wind scatters the seeds of needleleaf trees and the winglike seeds or fruits of such broadleaf trees as ashes, maples, poplars, and willows. Birds, squirrels, and other animals scatter seeds contained in nuts or fleshy fruits. Ocean currents sometimes carry the seeds of coconut palms and mangroves.

Trees can also reproduce by a process called *vegetative reproduction.* After a tree has been cut or blown down, the stump may develop green sprouts. In time, one or several of these sprouts can grow into trees. A clump of birches or tulip trees may be produced in this way. The roots of apple trees, aspens, and some other trees sometimes develop shoots called *suckers* that may also grow into trees. Some spruces found in bogs grow roots from their branches. This method of reproduction is called *layering.* In addition, nursery workers often grow trees from *cuttings*—that is, twigs cut from older trees. The twigs are planted and develop roots.

This section illustrates some of the chief characteristics of 58 North American broadleaf and needleleaf trees. The drawings show the summer and winter appearance, the leaf, the fruit or other seed-bearing structure, and the bark of each species. In some cases, the flower also is shown. The set of drawings for each tree includes information about the tree's native geographic range—that is, the part of North America where the tree is most likely to be found. But a number of the species shown have spread or have been planted outside their native range. The average height of adult trees of each species is given in feet and in meters alongside the illustration of the tree's shape.

The drawings and other information in this section can help in identifying trees. For example, if the leaf and bark of a tree match the leaf and bark of one of the trees shown here, the tree should be fairly easy to identify. Tree guidebooks can provide additional help in identifying trees. Several guidebooks are listed in the *Study aids* at the end of this article.

Broadleaf trees

WORLD BOOK illustrations by Donald Moss

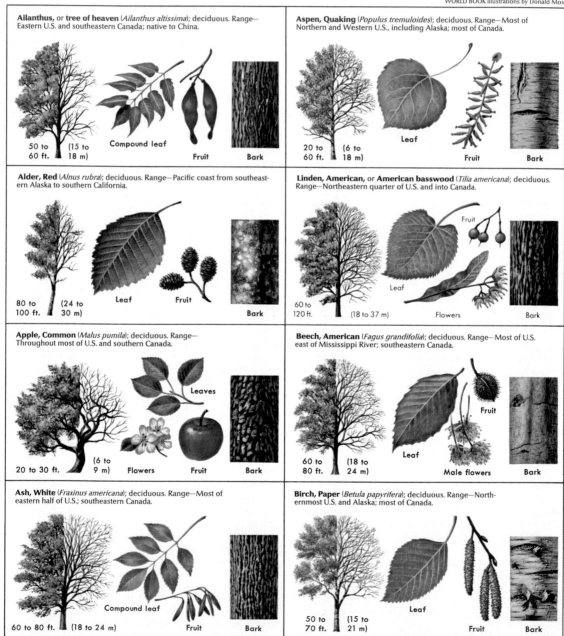

Ailanthus, or **tree of heaven** (*Ailanthus altissima*); deciduous. Range—Eastern U.S. and southeastern Canada; native to China.
50 to 60 ft. (15 to 18 m) Compound leaf Fruit Bark

Aspen, Quaking (*Populus tremuloides*); deciduous. Range—Most of Northern and Western U.S., including Alaska; most of Canada.
20 to 60 ft. (6 to 18 m) Leaf Fruit Bark

Alder, Red (*Alnus rubra*); deciduous. Range—Pacific coast from southeastern Alaska to southern California.
80 to 100 ft. (24 to 30 m) Leaf Fruit Bark

Linden, American, or **American basswood** (*Tilia americana*); deciduous. Range—Northeastern quarter of U.S. and into Canada.
60 to 120 ft. (18 to 37 m) Fruit Leaf Flowers Bark

Apple, Common (*Malus pumila*); deciduous. Range—Throughout most of U.S. and southern Canada.
20 to 30 ft. (6 to 9 m) Leaves Flowers Fruit Bark

Beech, American (*Fagus grandifolia*); deciduous. Range—Most of U.S. east of Mississippi River; southeastern Canada.
60 to 80 ft. (18 to 24 m) Fruit Leaf Male flowers Bark

Ash, White (*Fraxinus americana*); deciduous. Range—Most of eastern half of U.S.; southeastern Canada.
60 to 80 ft. (18 to 24 m) Compound leaf Fruit Bark

Birch, Paper (*Betula papyrifera*); deciduous. Range—Northernmost U.S. and Alaska; most of Canada.
50 to 70 ft. (15 to 21 m) Leaf Fruit Bark

Broadleaf trees

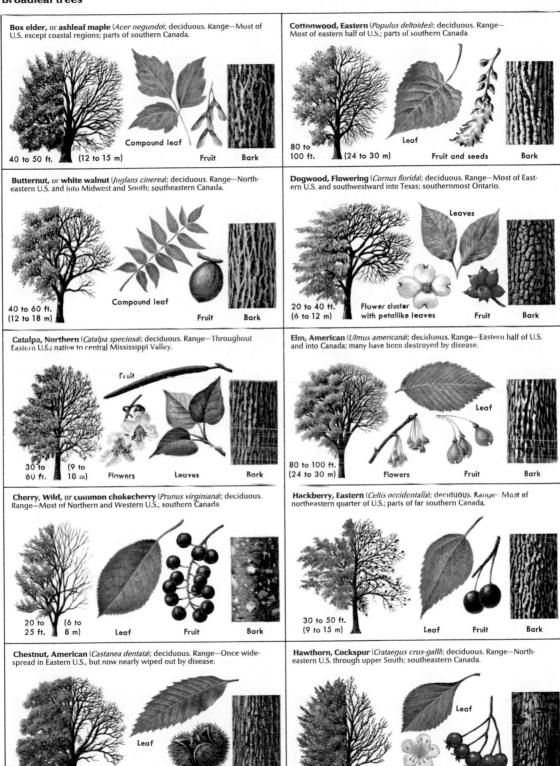

Box elder, or **ashleaf maple** (*Acer negundo*); deciduous. Range—Most of U.S. except coastal regions; parts of southern Canada.

Compound leaf
40 to 50 ft. (12 to 15 m) Fruit Bark

Cottonwood, Eastern (*Populus deltoides*); deciduous. Range—Most of eastern half of U.S.; parts of southern Canada.

Leaf
80 to 100 ft. (24 to 30 m) Fruit and seeds Bark

Butternut, or **white walnut** (*Juglans cinerea*); deciduous. Range—Northeastern U.S. and into Midwest and South; southeastern Canada.

Compound leaf
40 to 60 ft. (12 to 18 m) Fruit Bark

Dogwood, Flowering (*Cornus florida*); deciduous. Range—Most of Eastern U.S. and southwestward into Texas; southernmost Ontario.

Leaves
20 to 40 ft. (6 to 12 m) Flower cluster with petallike leaves Fruit Bark

Catalpa, Northern (*Catalpa speciosa*); deciduous. Range—Throughout Eastern U.S.; native to central Mississippi Valley.

Fruit
30 to 60 ft. (9 to 10 m) Flowers Leaves Bark

Elm, American (*Ulmus americana*); deciduous. Range—Eastern half of U.S. and into Canada; many have been destroyed by disease.

Leaf
80 to 100 ft. (24 to 30 m) Flowers Fruit Bark

Cherry, Wild, or **common chokecherry** (*Prunus virginiana*); deciduous. Range—Most of Northern and Western U.S.; southern Canada.

20 to 25 ft. (6 to 8 m) Leaf Fruit Bark

Hackberry, Eastern (*Celtis occidentalis*); deciduous. Range—Most of northeastern quarter of U.S.; parts of far southern Canada.

30 to 50 ft. (9 to 15 m) Leaf Fruit Bark

Chestnut, American (*Castanea dentata*); deciduous. Range—Once widespread in Eastern U.S., but now nearly wiped out by disease.

Leaf
70 to 90 ft. (21 to 27 m) Fruit Bark

Hawthorn, Cockspur (*Crataegus crus-galli*); deciduous. Range—Northeastern U.S. through upper South; southeastern Canada.

Leaf
20 to 25 ft. (6 to 8 m) Flower Fruit Bark

Familiar broadleaf and needleleaf trees of North America (continued)

Broadleaf trees

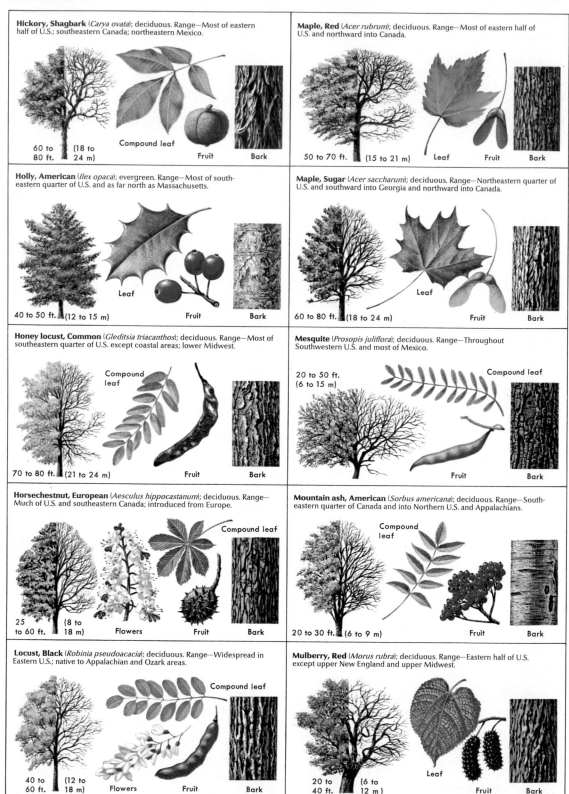

Hickory, Shagbark (*Carya ovata*); deciduous. Range—Most of eastern half of U.S.; southeastern Canada; northeastern Mexico.

60 to 80 ft. (18 to 24 m)   Compound leaf   Fruit   Bark

Maple, Red (*Acer rubrum*); deciduous. Range—Most of eastern half of U.S. and northward into Canada.

50 to 70 ft. (15 to 21 m)   Leaf   Fruit   Bark

Holly, American (*Ilex opaca*); evergreen. Range—Most of southeastern quarter of U.S. and as far north as Massachusetts.

40 to 50 ft. (12 to 15 m)   Leaf   Fruit   Bark

Maple, Sugar (*Acer saccharum*); deciduous. Range—Northeastern quarter of U.S. and southward into Georgia and northward into Canada.

60 to 80 ft. (18 to 24 m)   Leaf   Fruit   Bark

Honey locust, Common (*Gleditsia triacanthos*); deciduous. Range—Most of southeastern quarter of U.S. except coastal areas; lower Midwest.

70 to 80 ft. (21 to 24 m)   Compound leaf   Fruit   Bark

Mesquite (*Prosopis juliflora*); deciduous. Range—Throughout Southwestern U.S. and most of Mexico.

20 to 50 ft. (6 to 15 m)   Compound leaf   Fruit   Bark

Horsechestnut, European (*Aesculus hippocastanum*); deciduous. Range—Much of U.S. and southeastern Canada; introduced from Europe.

25 to 60 ft. (8 to 18 m)   Flowers   Compound leaf   Fruit   Bark

Mountain ash, American (*Sorbus americana*); deciduous. Range—Southeastern quarter of Canada and into Northern U.S. and Appalachians.

20 to 30 ft. (6 to 9 m)   Compound leaf   Fruit   Bark

Locust, Black (*Robinia pseudoacacia*); deciduous. Range—Widespread in Eastern U.S.; native to Appalachian and Ozark areas.

40 to 60 ft. (12 to 18 m)   Compound leaf   Flowers   Fruit   Bark

Mulberry, Red (*Morus rubra*); deciduous. Range—Eastern half of U.S. except upper New England and upper Midwest.

20 to 40 ft. (6 to 12 m)   Leaf   Fruit   Bark

Broadleaf trees

Oak, California white (*Quercus lobata*); deciduous. Range— Widespread throughout most of California.

50 to 90 ft.   (15 to 27 m)

Leaf   Fruit   Bark

Redbud, Eastern, or **Judas tree** (*Cercis canadensis*); deciduous. Range— Most of eastern half of U.S., southern Ontario; northern Mexico.

20 to 25 ft. (6 to 8 m)

Leaf   Flowers   Fruit   Bark

Oak, Live (*Quercus virginiana*); evergreen. Range—Atlantic and Gulf coastal plains and northward into central Texas.

40 to 50 ft.   (12 to 15 m)

Leaf   Fruit   Bark

Sassafras (*Sassafras albidum*); deciduous. Range—Southern U.S. and into parts of Northeast, Midwest, and Southwest.

20 to 50 ft.   (6 to 15 m)   Leaves   Fruit   Bark

Oak, Northern red (*Quercus rubra*); deciduous. Range—Most of eastern half of U.S., except far South, and northward into Canada.

60 to 80 ft.   (18 to 24 m)   Leaf   Fruit   Bark

Soapberry, Western (*Sapindus drummondii*); deciduous. Range— South-central and Southwestern U.S.; northern Mexico.

20 to 40 ft.   (6 to 12 m)   Compound leaf   Fruit   Bark

Pecan (*Carya illinoensis*); deciduous. Range—Southeastern quarter of U.S., though native only to western portion.

90 to 120 ft.   (27 to 37 m)   Compound leaf   Fruit   Bark

Sweet gum, or **red gum** (*Liquidambar styraciflua*); deciduous. Range— Southern U.S. and surrounding areas; parts of Mexico.

80 to 120 ft.   (24 to 37 m)   Leaf   Fruit   Bark

Persimmon, American or **common** (*Diospyros virginiana*); deciduous. Range—Southeastern quarter of U.S. and surrounding areas.

30 to 50 ft.   (9 to 15 m)   Leaf   Fruit   Bark

Sycamore, American (*Platanus occidentalis*); deciduous. Range—Eastern half of U.S., except far North and far South; southern Ontario.

80 to 120 ft.   (24 to 37 m)   Leaf   Fruit   Bark

Familiar broadleaf and needleleaf trees of North America (continued)

Broadleaf trees

Needleleaf trees

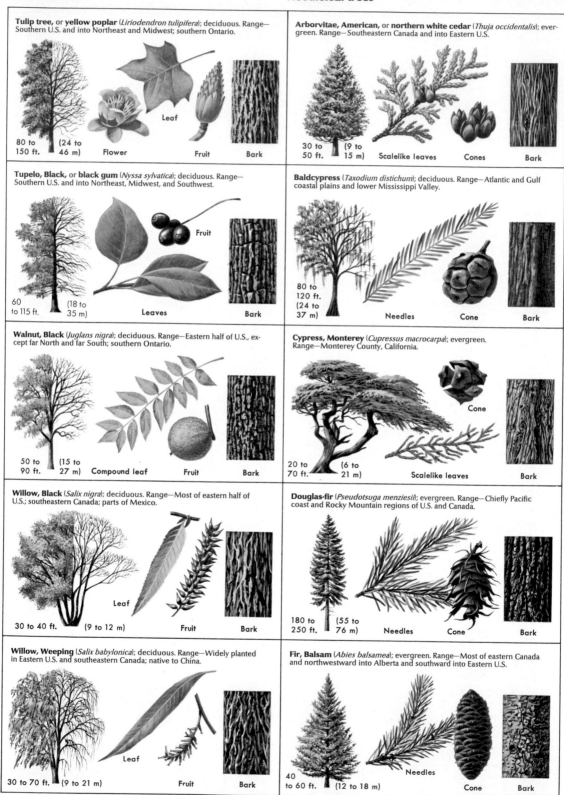

Tulip tree, or **yellow poplar** (*Liriodendron tulipifera*); deciduous. Range—Southern U.S. and into Northeast and Midwest; southern Ontario.

80 to 150 ft. (24 to 46 m)   Leaf   Flower   Fruit   Bark

Tupelo, Black, or **black gum** (*Nyssa sylvatica*); deciduous. Range—Southern U.S. and into Northeast, Midwest, and Southwest.

60 to 115 ft. (18 to 35 m)   Fruit   Leaves   Bark

Walnut, Black (*Juglans nigra*); deciduous. Range—Eastern half of U.S., except far North and far South; southern Ontario.

50 to 90 ft. (15 to 27 m)   Compound leaf   Fruit   Bark

Willow, Black (*Salix nigra*); deciduous. Range—Most of eastern half of U.S.; southeastern Canada; parts of Mexico.

30 to 40 ft. (9 to 12 m)   Leaf   Fruit   Bark

Willow, Weeping (*Salix babylonica*); deciduous. Range—Widely planted in Eastern U.S. and southeastern Canada; native to China.

30 to 70 ft. (9 to 21 m)   Leaf   Fruit   Bark

Arborvitae, American, or **northern white cedar** (*Thuja occidentalis*); evergreen. Range—Southeastern Canada and into Eastern U.S.

30 to 50 ft. (9 to 15 m)   Scalelike leaves   Cones   Bark

Baldcypress (*Taxodium distichum*); deciduous. Range—Atlantic and Gulf coastal plains and lower Mississippi Valley.

80 to 120 ft. (24 to 37 m)   Needles   Cone   Bark

Cypress, Monterey (*Cupressus macrocarpa*); evergreen. Range—Monterey County, California.

20 to 70 ft. (6 to 21 m)   Cone   Scalelike leaves   Bark

Douglas-fir (*Pseudotsuga menziesii*); evergreen. Range—Chiefly Pacific coast and Rocky Mountain regions of U.S. and Canada.

180 to 250 ft. (55 to 76 m)   Needles   Cone   Bark

Fir, Balsam (*Abies balsamea*); evergreen. Range—Most of eastern Canada and northwestward into Alberta and southward into Eastern U.S.

40 to 60 ft. (12 to 18 m)   Needles   Cone   Bark

Needleleaf trees

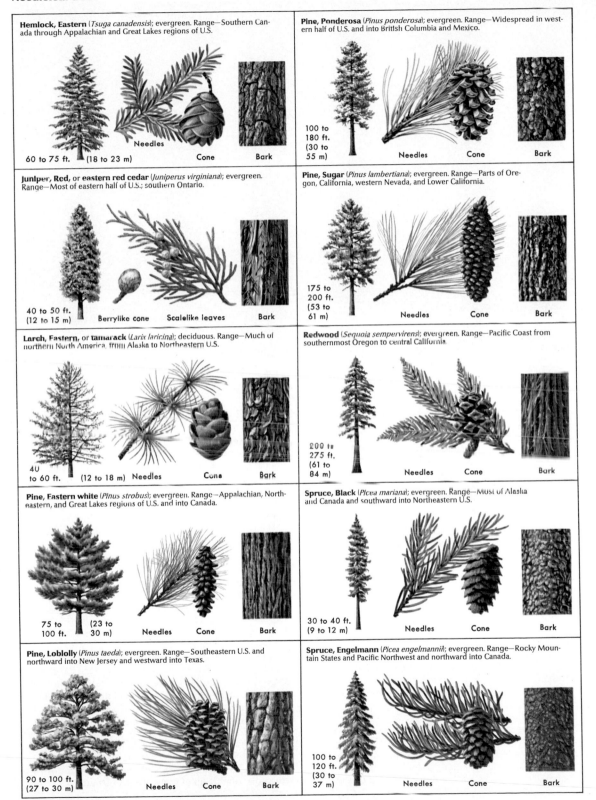

Hemlock, Eastern (*Tsuga canadensis*); evergreen. Range—Southern Canada through Appalachian and Great Lakes regions of U.S.

60 to 75 ft. (18 to 23 m)   Needles   Cone   Bark

Juniper, Red, or **eastern red cedar** (*Juniperus virginiana*); evergreen. Range—Most of eastern half of U.S.; southern Ontario.

40 to 50 ft. (12 to 15 m)   Berrylike cone   Scalelike leaves   Bark

Larch, Eastern, or **tamarack** (*Larix laricina*); deciduous. Range—Much of northern North America, from Alaska to Northeastern U.S.

40 to 60 ft. (12 to 18 m)   Needles   Cone   Bark

Pine, Eastern white (*Pinus strobus*); evergreen. Range—Appalachian, Northeastern, and Great Lakes regions of U.S. and into Canada.

75 to 100 ft. (23 to 30 m)   Needles   Cone   Bark

Pine, Loblolly (*Pinus taeda*); evergreen. Range—Southeastern U.S. and northward into New Jersey and westward into Texas.

90 to 100 ft. (27 to 30 m)   Needles   Cone   Bark

Pine, Ponderosa (*Pinus ponderosa*); evergreen. Range—Widespread in western half of U.S. and into British Columbia and Mexico.

100 to 180 ft. (30 to 55 m)   Needles   Cone   Bark

Pine, Sugar (*Pinus lambertiana*); evergreen. Range—Parts of Oregon, California, western Nevada, and Lower California.

175 to 200 ft. (53 to 61 m)   Needles   Cone   Bark

Redwood (*Sequoia sempervirens*); evergreen. Range—Pacific Coast from southernmost Oregon to central California.

200 to 275 ft. (61 to 84 m)   Needles   Cone   Bark

Spruce, Black (*Picea mariana*); evergreen. Range—Most of Alaska and Canada and southward into Northeastern U.S.

30 to 40 ft. (9 to 12 m)   Needles   Cone   Bark

Spruce, Engelmann (*Picea engelmannii*); evergreen. Range—Rocky Mountain States and Pacific Northwest and northward into Canada.

100 to 120 ft. (30 to 37 m)   Needles   Cone   Bark

Forests of broadleaf trees, or *hardwood forests,* grow in many parts of the world. This forest is in Germany. In temperate regions, most broadleaf trees lose their leaves each fall.

Trees around the world

In some parts of the world, trees grow in thick forests. In other regions, they do not grow at all. To grow, trees need a period of more than two months without frost each year. The few trees that grow in the Arctic never reach full tree size. No trees can grow in the ice and bitter cold of Antarctica. Most trees also need at least 15 to 20 inches (38 to 51 centimeters) of rainfall a year. Only a few trees, such as the Joshua tree and some types of palms, can survive in deserts.

Most broadleaf trees grow best in regions that are warm and moist at least three or four months of the year. Colder, dryer climates are better suited to most needleleaf trees. But some broadleaf trees, such as birches and willows, grow well in cool climates. Some needleleaf trees, including baldcypresses and various types of pines, need fairly warm climates. Palm trees grow in warm areas throughout the world, especially the wet and the dry tropics. Pandanus trees, cycads, and tree ferns grow mainly in the wet tropics and other warm, moist regions. Lily trees also thrive in warm areas, but they do not need so much moisture as do pandanus trees, cycads, and tree ferns.

Different kinds of trees also require different soils. Many needleleaf trees grow well in poor, sandy soil. But most broadleaf trees need more fertile soil.

Some trees grow alone or in small groups. Where moisture is scarce, trees may grow only along riverbanks. Tree seeds carried by ocean currents may take root along shorelines. People plant individual trees in such places as parks and gardens. But most trees by far

grow in forests. The world's forest regions consist chiefly of broadleaf and needleleaf trees.

Broadleaf forests grow in regions that have a fairly long growing season and plentiful rainfall. Every continent except Antarctica has broadleaf forests, which are also called *hardwood forests.* In areas with cold, snowy winters, almost all the trees in broadleaf forests lose their leaves each autumn. In tropical areas, most broadleaf trees are evergreen.

Before the 1800's, broadleaf forests covered much of the Eastern United States. They included such trees as ashes, birches, maples, and oaks. During the 1800's, most of the trees in these forests were cut down to provide lumber and fuel and to make room for farms and cities. Today, only a few parts of the Eastern United States have large broadleaf forests. Western Europe also had great forests of broadleaf trees, including ashes, beeches, and oaks. But most of these forests have been cut down.

Broadleaf forests made up largely of quaking aspens and balsam poplars cover parts of southern Canada and large areas of southern Siberia. Forests of birches and oaks grow in the central part of the European section of the Soviet Union and along the Yellow Sea coast of China and Korea. Southeastern Australia has valuable forests of eucalyptus trees. These broadleaf trees grow nearly as tall as California's needleleaf giants, the redwoods. Some eucalyptuses are more than 300 feet (91 meters) tall. About 600 kinds of eucalyptus trees grow in Australia. Almost all of them are evergreen.

Forests of needleleaf trees, or *softwood forests,* cover huge areas in the far north as well as the slopes of such mountain ranges as the Italian Alps, *above.* Most of the trees are evergreen.

In many areas, *mixed forests* of broadleaf and needleleaf trees grow alongside broadleaf or needleleaf forests. Central Canada, the Eastern United States, central and southern Europe, and eastern Asia all have large mixed forests.

Remarkable broadleaf forests grow in tropical regions where the weather is always hot and rain falls regularly every month of the year. In these *tropical rain forests,* many of the trees look alike. They are tall, and many tower more than 150 feet (46 meters). The trees have leathery, dark-green leaves. Because the trees receive plenty of moisture throughout the year, most of them are evergreen. The trees may thus look alike, but they belong to many species. Many palms grow among the broadleaf trees in the tropical rain forests. The largest rain forests are in South and Central America, central Africa, and Southeast Asia.

Needleleaf forests grow mainly in regions that have long, cold winters. These forests, which are also called *softwood forests,* stretch across Canada, northern Europe, and Siberia. Many firs, larches, and spruces grow in these northern forests, along with a few broadleaf trees, such as birches and willows. Some willows grow even farther north than needleleaf trees do. But they seldom reach more than shrub size. Needleleaf forests also blanket slopes in such mountain ranges as the Alps and the Rocky Mountains.

The Canadian needleleaf forests extend southward into the Western United States, where they include many of the world's largest trees. Many California redwoods tower over 300 feet (91 meters). Tall Douglas-firs also grow in the Western United States.

A few needleleaf forests grow in warmer regions. For example, the Southeastern United States has large forests of pines, such as loblolly pines and longleaf pines. These forests provide great quantities of wood for lumber and wood pulp.

How forests spread. Many forests did not always grow where they are growing now. These forests have spread from other areas. For example, broadleaf forests grow today in parts of the Northeastern United States where only needleleaf forests grew several thousand years ago. The spread of forests from one area to another is called *migration.* The wind helps trees migrate by carrying their seeds beyond the forests. Animals also help spread the seeds. Trees that grow from these seeds produce their own seeds, which may be spread in the same ways. Over hundreds or thousands of years, a particular kind of tree may thus spread to surrounding areas if the climate and soil are suitable.

Several hundred thousand years ago, glaciers moved down across much of North America and Europe. These glaciers caused the forests of needleleaf and broadleaf trees to migrate south. Thousands of years passed, and the ice began to melt. As the glaciers retreated northward, forests of needleleaf trees grew up again on the land that the glaciers had covered. The glaciers moved still farther north, and the climate became warm enough for broadleaf trees. Broadleaf trees usually crowd out needleleaf trees in areas where both are able to grow. As a result, broadleaf forests replaced needleleaf forests in many regions.

Forests can migrate over fairly level land but not across oceans or mountain ranges. Yet similar types of forest trees grow in areas separated by oceans or mountains. For example, the United States has oak trees much like those that grow in Europe. Most scientists believe that many millions of years ago, all the continents were connected. Needleleaf trees developed and spread across much of the earth. Broadleaf trees developed next and also spread. Over millions of years, the continents became separated—along with their trees and other forms of life—by the oceans. Mountain ranges rose up on the continents and separated the trees on each side of the mountains. In time, many of the trees on each continent and on each side of the mountain ranges developed into different species.

How people help trees spread. People have transplanted many species of trees across oceans and mountain ranges. Transplanted trees may grow well in a new region with a climate like that of their native lands. In time, these *introduced species* may spread and become native trees in their new surroundings. A kind of rubber tree that once grew only in Brazil was introduced into the Far East during the late 1800's. Today, whole forests of these trees grow in the Far East. About 100 years ago, Australian eucalyptus trees were planted in California. Today, many thousands of eucalyptuses shade streets and parks in several Western states. Monterey pines originally grew only in a small area of California. They now cover large areas in Australia and other countries south of the equator.

Alan Pitcairn, Grant Heilman

Joshua trees, such as this one at California's Joshua Tree National Monument, are among the few kinds of trees that grow in deserts. Most trees need more water than deserts provide.

Norman Meyers, Bruce Coleman Inc.

Tropical rain forests grow in Uganda, *above,* and in other hot, wet areas. Most of the trees are broadleaf and evergreen. Although they look alike, they belong to many different species.

Homeowners plant various kinds of trees on their property. They plant shade trees for protection from the sun and ornamental trees for beauty. They may also plant trees as windbreaks. Many people enjoy having fruit trees in their yard or garden to provide shade and beauty as well as fruit.

Selecting the right tree. To grow well, a tree must be suited to the region where it is planted. Trees from faraway places should be planted only in regions with similar climates. A tree's special characteristics must also be considered. For example, trees with wide-reaching roots should not be planted near houses because the roots may damage drains and foundations, or plug sewage pipes.

Trees with full, leafy crowns make the best shade trees. These trees include ashes, basswoods, maples, and oaks, all of which are popular in the Eastern United States. Trees with showy flowers, such as the catalpa and the crab apple, are popular ornamental trees in the Eastern United States. In fairly warm areas west of the Rocky Mountains, such trees as acacias and pepper trees are planted as both shade and ornamental trees. Needleleaf trees are grown as ornamentals in many parts of the United States and Canada. They also make good windbreaks. Various broadleaf trees, including cottonwoods and Lombardy poplars, are also planted as windbreaks. Apple and cherry trees are popular fruit trees in temperate climates. In warm climates, many people grow citrus trees.

Planting the tree. A tree should be planted where it will have enough room when fully grown. The soil should be fertile and should drain well so that water does not collect and drown the roots.

It takes much time and effort to grow a tree from seed. Most people prefer to buy a tree at a nursery. If a nursery tree is taller than 15 feet (4.6 meters) or if its trunk is thicker than 3 inches (8 centimeters), special transplanting equipment may be needed.

The best time to transplant a tree is when it is resting —that is, in the fall, winter, or early spring. The roots of a deciduous tree can be dug up without a covering of soil. But they must be kept moist while out of the ground. The roots of an evergreen should be dug up with a ball of soil around them. The hole for any new tree should provide room for all the roots below ground level. A small tree may need to be supported by stakes to keep the wind from blowing it over.

Caring for the tree. A young tree should be kept moderately watered until it is well rooted. It usually takes about a year for a tree to become firmly rooted.

Pruning improves the shape of trees. Cutting off some of a young shade tree's lower buds will keep it from developing many low branches. But enough buds should be left so that the tree has a full, leafy crown. As the tree develops upper branches, more lower branches may be removed. See **Pruning.**

Insects and diseases may attack a tree. With normal care, it can overcome most minor attacks. But if a tree fails to develop as many leaves as usual or if the leaves look pale, the tree may require the professional care of a tree surgeon. In some areas, air pollution threatens the health of trees. Richard H. Waring

How to plant a tree

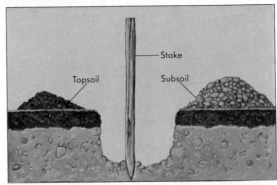

Digging the hole. Dig the hole big enough so all the roots can be spread out. Pile the topsoil and subsoil separately. A supporting stake, if needed, can be inserted at this time.

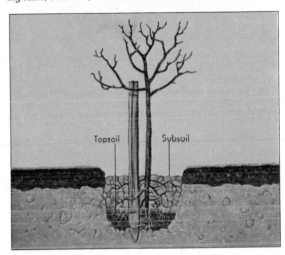

Planting the tree. Carefully spread out the roots in the hole and cover them with topsoil. Use the subsoil, which is less fertile, to fill the top part of the hole.

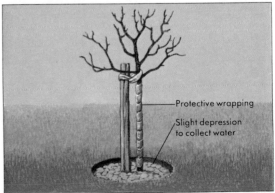

WORLD BOOK illustrations by John D. Dawson

Caring for the tree. Water the tree moderately during the first year. The trunk may be wrapped in burlap or heavy paper for the first two years to protect it from sunburn and insects.

Trees belong to the subphylum *Pteropsida,* a major grouping within the plant kingdom. The sub-phylum is divided into three *classes* of plants, according to various characteristics they have in common. The classes, in turn, are divided into *orders,* and the orders into *families.* A few plant families consist largely of trees or shrubs, but some families have no trees at all. This table lists the families with the most species of trees or with one or more outstanding species. The classes, sub-classes, orders, and families are arranged in the probable order of evolutionary development.

Class Filicineae (ferns)
Order Filicales
Family Cyatheaceae—tree ferns
Family Dicksoniaceae—tree ferns

Class Gymnospermae (cone-bearing and related plants)
Subclass Cycadophytae
Order Cycadales
Family Cycadaceae—cycads
Subclass Coniferophytae
Order Ginkgoales
Family Ginkgoaceae—ginkgo

Order Coniferales
Family Taxaceae—torreyas, yews
Family Podocarpaceae—podocarpuses
Family Pinaceae—deodar cedar, Douglas-firs, firs, hemlocks, larches, pines, piñons, spruces
Family Taxodiaceae—baldcypresses, giant sequoia, redwood
Family Cupressaceae—cypresses, junipers, western redcedar
Family Araucariaceae—Chile pine, kauri pine, paraná pine

Class Angiospermae (flowering, or fruit-bearing, plants)
Subclass Dicotyledoneae
Order Casuarinales
Family Casuarinaceae—beefwoods, or Australian pines
Order Salicales
Family Salicaceae—aspens, cottonwoods, poplars, willows
Order Myricales
Family Myricaceae—wax myrtles, or bayberries
Order Juglandales
Family Juglandaceae—butternut, hickories, pecan, walnuts
Order Fagales
Family Betulaceae—alders, birches, hazels, hornbeams
Family Fagaceae—beeches, chestnuts, chinquapins, oaks
Order Urticales
Family Ulmaceae—elms, hackberry, planer tree, sugarberry
Family Moraceae—banyan, figs, mulberries, Osage orange
Order Proteales
Family Proteaceae—macadamias, silky oak, silver tree
Order Santalales
Family Santalaceae—sandalwoods
Order Centrospermae
Family Phytolaccaceae—ombu
Order Ranales
Family Magnoliaceae—magnolias, sweet bay, tulip tree
Family Annonaceae—cherimoya, pawpaw, ylang-ylang
Family Myristicaceae—nutmegs
Family Lauraceae—avocado, cinnamon, laurels, sassafras
Order Rhoeadales
Family Moringaceae—horseradish tree
Order Rosales
Family Pittosporaceae—lemonwood, Victoria box
Family Hamamelidaceae—sweet gums, witch hazels
Family Platanaceae—sycamores, or plane trees
Family Rosaceae—almonds, apples, apricots, cherries, crab apples, hawthorns, loquat, medlar, mountain ashes, nectarine, peaches, pears, plums, quinces, serviceberries
Family Leguminosae—acacias, brazilwoods, carob, cassias, honey locusts, laburnums, locusts, logwood, mesquite, mimosa, paloverdes, poincianas, rain tree, tamarind
Order Geraniales
Family Zygophyllaceae—lignum vitae
Family Rutaceae—citruses, hop trees, prickly ashes

Family Simaroubaceae—ailanthus, bitter ashes, bitterbushes
Family Burseraceae—gumbo limbo, Java almond
Family Meliaceae—cedrelas, chinaberry, mahoganies
Family Euphorbiaceae—kukui, manchineel, rubber tree
Order Sapindales
Family Anacardiaceae—cashew, mango, pistachio, sumacs
Family Aquifoliaceae—hollies, mountain winterberry
Family Celastraceae—canotia, eastern wahoo, maytens
Family Aceraceae—box elder, maples
Family Hippocastanaceae—buckeyes, horsechestnut
Family Sapindaceae—butterbough, litchi, soapberries
Order Rhamnales
Family Rhamnaceae—buckthorns, jujubes, raisin tree
Order Malvales
Family Tiliaceae—basswoods, or lindens
Family Bombacaceae—balsa, baobabs, kapok
Family Sterculiaceae—bottle tree, cacao, kola
Family Theaceae—loblolly bay, mountain stewartia, wild tea
Family Guttiferae—copey, mammee apple, mangosteens
Family Tamaricaceae—tamarisks
Family Caricaceae—papayas
Order Opuntiales
Family Cactaceae—prickly pears, saguaro
Order Myrtales
Family Lythraceae—crape myrtles
Family Lecythidaceae—Brazil-nut, cannon-ball tree
Family Rhizophoraceae—dove tree, mangroves
Family Nyssaceae—tupelos
Family Combretaceae—Indian almond, oxhorn bucida
Family Myrtaceae—bay rum tree, bottlebrushes, clove tree, eucalyptuses, guavas, pimento, turpentine tree
Order Umbellales
Family Araliaceae—devil's walkingstick, lancewood
Family Cornaceae—cornelian cherry, dogwoods
Order Ericales
Family Ericaceae—madroñas, mountain laurel, sorrel tree
Order Ebenales
Family Sapotaceae—bumelias, gutta-percha tree, sapodilla
Family Ebenaceae—ebonies, persimmons
Family Styracaceae—epaulette tree, silverbells, snowbells
Order Gentianales
Family Oleaceae—ashes, devilwood, fringe tree, olives
Family Loganiaceae—strychnine trees
Family Apocynaceae—devil tree, frangipani, yellow oleander
Order Tubiflorae
Family Boraginaceae—anaqua, geiger tree, strongbarks
Family Verbenaceae—Florida fiddlewood, teak
Family Bignoniaceae—calabash tree, catalpas, desert willow, jacaranda, royal paulownia, sausage tree
Order Rubiales
Family Rubiaceae—buttonbush, cinchonas, coffee trees
Family Caprifoliaceae—black haw, elders, viburnums
Subclass Monocotyledoneae
Order Pandanales
Family Pandanaceae—pandanuses, or screw pines
Order Palmales
Family Palmae—palmettos, palms
Order Liliales
Family Liliaceae—aloes
Family Agavaceae—dragon tree, Joshua tree, Spanish bayonet
Order Zingiberales
Family Musaceae—traveler's-tree

Related articles in *World Book* include:

Common broadleaf trees

Alder	Elm	Linden	Poplar
Ash	Eucalyptus	Live oak	Prickly ash
Aspen	Gum tree	Locust	Sorrel tree
Beech	Hackberry	Madroña	Sweet gum
Birch	Honey locust	Maple	Sycamore
Bitternut	Horsechestnut	Myrtle	Tulip tree
Box elder	Ironwood	Oak	Willow
Catalpa	Kentucky cof-	Osage orange	
Chestnut	feetree		
Cottonwood	Laurel		

Common needleleaf trees

Arborvitae	Cypress	Juniper	Sequoia
Bristlecone	Douglas-fir	Larch	Spruce
pine	Fir	Pine	Yew
Cedar	Hemlock	Redwood	

Fruit trees

Apple	Date palm	Loquat	Pawpaw
Apricot	Fig	Mango	Peach
Avocado	Grapefruit	Mangosteen	Pear
Breadfruit	Guava	Mulberry	Persimmon
Cherimoya	Kumquat	Nectarine	Plum
Cherry	Lemon	Olive	Pomegranate
Citron	Lime	Orange	Quince
Crab apple	Litchi	Papaya	

Edible-nut trees

Almond	Cashew	Hickory	Pistachio nut
Brazil nut	Coconut palm	Pecan	Walnut
Butternut	Hazel	Piñon	

Trees that yield special products

Balsa	Camphor	Cork	Rubber
Bayberry	Carob	Kapok	Sapodilla
Betel	Cinchona	Kola nut	Sassafras
Brazilwood	Cinnamon	Mesquite	Tallowtree
Cacao	Clove	Nutmeg	Witch hazel
Calabash	Coffee	Palm	

Ornamental trees

Acacia	Holly	Mimosa	Poinciana
Box	Laburnum	Myrtle	Redbud
Fringe tree	Magnolia	Pepper tree	Rhododen-
			dron

Tropical trees

Baobab	Manchineel	Tamarind
Jacaranda	Mangrove	Teak
Mahogany	Rain tree	

Unusual trees

Banyan tree	Bottle tree	Ginkgo tree
Beefwood	Cannon-ball tree	Upas
Bo tree	Cycad	

Parts of trees

Bark	Flower	Root	Stem
Bud	Fruit	Sap	Wood
Cell	Leaf	Seed	

Maps

See the plant life maps with the following articles:

Africa	Australia	North America
Asia	Europe	South America

Other related articles

Bonsai	Conservation	Environmental pol-
Cellulose	Cotyledon	lution
Chlorophyll	Ecology	Evergreen

Forest	Lumber	Plant
Forest products	Nursery	Pruning
Grafting		

Outline

I. The importance of trees
   A. Wood products   C. Other tree products
   B. Food products   D. Trees in conservation
II. Kinds of trees
   A. Broadleaf trees   D. Cycad trees
   B. Needleleaf trees   E. Tree ferns
   C. Palm, pandanus, and lily F. Ginkgo trees
      trees   G. Fossil trees
III. The parts of a tree
   A. Trunk and branches
   B. Leaves
   C. Roots
   D. Seeds
IV. How a tree grows
   A. How seeds sprout into trees
   B. How leaves make plant food
   C. How trees grow taller
   D. How trunks and branches grow thicker
   E. How trees reproduce
V. Familiar broadleaf and needleleaf trees of North America
VI. Trees around the world
   A. Broadleaf forests   D. How people help trees
   B. Needleleaf forests   spread
   C. How forests spread
VII. Planting and caring for trees
   A. Selecting the right tree C. Caring for the tree
   B. Planting the tree
VIII. Scientific classification of trees

Questions

What is *sapwood*? *Heartwood*?
What is the main job of a tree's leaves?
In what climate do most needleleaf forests grow?
What do root hairs do?
How do forests spread?
How do *deciduous* trees differ from *evergreen* trees?
When is the best time of year to transplant a tree?
How do trees help conserve soil and water?
In what four ways do trees differ from all other plants?
How do trees grow taller?

Additional resources

Level I
Dowden, Anne O. *The Blossom on the Bough: A Book of Trees.* T. Y. Crowell, 1975.
Earle, Olive L. *State Trees.* Rev. ed. Morrow, 1973.
Nelson, Cora A. *Trees: Nature Stories for Children.* Hyperion (Winnipeg), 1986.
Norris, Louanne, and Smith, H. E. *An Oak Tree Dies and a Journey Begins.* Crown, 1979.

Level II
Collingwood, George H., and Brush, W. D. *Knowing Your Trees.* Rev. ed. American Forestry Assn., 1978.
Edlin, Herbert L. *The Tree Key: A Guide to Identification in Garden, Field, and Forest.* Scribner, 1978.
Elias, Thomas S. *The Complete Trees of North America: Field Guide and Natural History.* Van Nostrand, 1980.
Leathart, Scott. *Trees of the World.* Hamlyn, 1977.
Line, Les, and others. *The Audubon Society Book of Trees.* Abrams, 1981.
Little, Elbert L. *The Audubon Society Field Guide to North American Trees: Eastern Region.* Knopf, 1980. *The Audubon Society Field Guide to North American Trees: Western Region.* 1980.
The Oxford Encyclopedia of Trees of the World. Ed. by Bayard Hora. Oxford, 1981.
Petrides, George A. *A Field Guide to Trees and Shrubs.* 2nd ed. Houghton, 1972.

Tree farming. A tree farm is a privately owned area used to grow forest crops for a profit. Tree farms range in size from 10 acres (4 hectares) to nearly 1 million acres (400,000 hectares). The American Forest Institute sponsors the national tree-farm program.

The owner of a tree farm must have the land certified by a local forest-practices agency of a forest industry association. The owner must show that the timber will be grown and harvested in such a way that crops can also be grown on the land in the future. The owner must also agree not to harvest more mature timber than can be regrown, and to protect the crop from fire, insects, disease, excessive grazing, and other damage.

The Weyerhaeuser Company originated the first tree farm in 1941 in Montesano, Wash. The company began a tree-management project to plant seedlings and to develop a fire-control system. There are over 37,000 tree farms covering more than 80 million acres (32 million hectares).   Harry W. Lee

See also **Forestry; Washington** (Natural resources).

Tree fern. See Tree (Tree ferns; picture: Tree ferns).

Tree frog, also called *tree toad,* spends much of its life in trees. There are several hundred kinds of tree frogs. Most have sticky pads called *adhesive disks* on their feet, and can climb trees and leap through the treetops. Tree frogs are from less than 1 inch (2.5 centimeters) to about 5 inches (13 centimeters) long. They eat insects and other small animals. Most tree frogs can change color.

Tree frogs are common in North and South America. Probably more people hear them than ever see them. In the early spring and sometimes on mild winter days, types of tree frogs called *peepers* may be heard near waterways or marshes throughout the eastern half of North America. The males produce a high-pitched peep to attract females. Male peepers sometimes form a large, noisy group known as a *chorus.*

Other kinds of tree frogs give their call through much of the summer. They may be heard evenings or before rains in woodlands. Male tree frogs do all the calling. When a male calls, its throat swells until it looks like a bubble about to burst. Then it makes the call that is characteristic of its species. This sound is hard to locate, even though it may be nearby.

Tree frogs may be kept in aquariums or terrariums, and fed chopped earthworms and insects. In this way, they will be active through the winter and will not hibernate, as do the frogs that live outdoors.

Scientific classification. Tree frogs belong to the tree toad family, Hylidae. American tree frogs make up the genera *Acris, Pseudacris,* and *Hyla.*   Don C. Forester

See also Frog.

Tree of heaven. See Ailanthus.

Tree of life. See Eden.

Tree of wisdom. See Bo tree.

Tree shrew is a small, swift-moving mammal that lives in the forests of India, Southeast Asia, and southern China. Tree shrews look and act like small squirrels with long noses. They grow less than 8 inches (20 centimeters) long, not including their tails, and weigh less than 1 pound (0.5 kilogram). Tree shrews dart about in trees and bushes and on the ground. Their food consists mostly of fruits, insects, and worms.

Zoologists disagree on what animals are the tree

© Tom McHugh, Photo Researchers

The tree shrew is a mammal that resembles a small squirrel with a long nose. It lives in trees and bushes and on the ground.

shrew's closest relatives. Some zoologists believe that tree shrews belong to the order of animals called *primates,* which include monkeys. Tree shrews, like primates, have relatively large brains and eyes. Other zoologists classify tree shrews as members of the order of *insectivores,* which includes shrews and moles. Like insectivores, tree shrews have claws on all their fingers and toes. Primates have at least one nail on each foot. Still other zoologists put tree shrews in an order of their own. Experts do agree that the tree shrew is related to both primates and insectivores.

Scientific classification. Tree shrews belong to the tree shrew family, Tupaiidae. A common species is *Tupaia glis.*
Neil C. Tappen

Tree surgery is the care of trees, chiefly by pruning, bracing, filling hollows, and removing decayed wood. Large operations may call for a tree surgeon who is an expert in these methods. Tree surgeons also treat cuts and wounds in trees. They spray trees with chemicals to protect against insects and diseases and they provide the proper fertilizers and moisture conditions for trees. Many communities employ tree surgeons to care for trees in parks and recreation areas.

WORLD BOOK illustration by Richard Lewington, The Garden Studio

The tree frog uses its sticky foot pads to climb trees. Most tree frogs can change color to blend with their surroundings.

Trees decay when fungi enter through wounds in the bark, and spread in the wood. An important part of tree surgery is to cover such cuts. Pruning cuts should be painted with shellac, grafting wax, or tree paint. The expert makes a pruning cut flat with the limb or tree trunk, and cuts off stubs of branches. The bark easily grows over the smooth cut. In cutting off large branches, the branch is first cut a distance away from the trunk, then the stub is removed. This method keeps the heavy limb from tearing bark from the tree when it falls.

Removing decayed wood is known as cavity work. It is rather expensive, and often not worth while unless the tree is large and beautiful or has sentimental or ornamental value. This type of surgery is most successful with sapwood, which is near the surface. Cavities in the heartwood are often large, and weaken the tree. The tree surgeon tries to remove all the decayed wood, and shape the hollow so it will not hold stagnant water. The cut part of the bark and cambium is painted with shellac and the rest of the hollow is coated with a dressing like tar. The tree sometimes looks better if the hollow is filled, but filling does not strengthen the tree. It is often just as well to brace the tree with bolts or cables.

Some types of trees tend to split at the crotches of heavy limbs, especially in winter. The right way to prevent this type of split is to connect the limbs with a metal rod running through them and bolted at each end. The rod does not injure the tree, for it passes through a very small section of the living cambium. Cables or metal bands around a limb cut through the cambium as the limb grows, and strangle it. Harry W. Lee

See also **Pruning**.

Tree toad. See Tree frog.

Trefoil, *TREE foyl,* meaning *three-leaved,* is the name generally applied to various plants having compound leaves with three leaflets, like the clover. It is specifically applied to the lotus group, which belongs to the pea family. Several members of this group are found in the temperate parts of the Northern Hemisphere. *Bird's-foot trefoil* is so called because it bears clusters of pods somewhat resembling a crow's foot. Other *species* (kinds) of trefoil include *marsh bird's-foot,* common in damp meadowland, and *coralgem deervetch,* often planted in California. See also **Bird's-foot trefoil.**

Scientific classification. The trefoils belong to the pea family, Leguminosae. Bird's-foot trefoil is *Lotus corniculatus.* The marsh bird's-foot is classified as *L. uliginosus,* and the coralgem deervetch as *L. bertholeti.* Alfred C. Hottes

Trek, The Great. See Boers.

Trench foot. See Immersion foot.

Trench mouth, also called *Vincent's infection,* is a disease which centers in the mouth and throat. It was given the name *trench mouth* during World War I, when thousands of soldiers got it while fighting in the trenches. Doctors are not sure what causes trench mouth, though they think it may be a bacterial infection. Poor oral hygiene and poor nutrition are frequently found in people with trench mouth and may contribute to the development of the disease. The disease does not seem to be contagious.

The first symptoms of trench mouth are mouth pains and bad breath. The disease most often occurs in the gums, which swell, bleed, and eventually are destroyed. Occasionally, it may affect the tonsils and other areas of the mouth and throat. A person who has the disease may find it difficult to chew or swallow food. Trench mouth is uncommon among people who have had all their teeth extracted. Raymond L. Burich

Trent, Council of, was a series of conferences held by the Roman Catholic Church in Trent, Italy, between 1545 and 1563. The council attempted to define Catholic beliefs and to counteract Protestant teachings. The council also established many reforms in church practices. Its work became a major force in the Counter Reformation, the renewal movement in the Catholic Church during the 1500's and 1600's (see **Counter Reformation**). The doctrines issued by the council have greatly influenced the church ever since.

Pope Paul III called the council in 1542, and it opened on Dec. 13, 1545. The council met during three separate periods, and wars and religious disputes often interrupted its work. During the first period, from 1545 to 1547, the council declared that Scripture and tradition were equally valid sources of the Catholic faith. The council decreed that the church had the sole right to interpret Scripture. Tradition includes the writings of the apostles, the decrees of popes and councils, and the customs practiced by Catholics throughout church history. The council also rejected Protestant views on salvation and sin.

During the second period, from 1551 to 1552, the council defined the nature of the seven sacraments. The council also reaffirmed the doctrine of *transubstantiation,* the belief that bread and wine are changed into the body and blood of Jesus Christ during Communion.

During its final period, from 1562 to 1563, the council defended the granting of *indulgences* (pardons from some of the penalty for sins). It also approved prayers to the saints and defined the sacrifice of the Mass and many other Catholic doctrines. The council passed such reforms as the establishment of seminaries to train priests and the requirement that each bishop live in his own area. Pope Pius IV confirmed all the council's decrees on Jan. 26, 1564, and they became part of Catholic doctrine. William J. Courtenay

Trent Affair was a naval incident in the first year of the Civil War. It almost brought England into the conflict on the side of the South. In the fall of 1861, two men representing the Confederacy, James M. Mason and John Slidell, set sail for Europe. Their mission was to enlist the aid of neutral France and England to the Southern cause. Since Northern ships were blockading Southern ports, they boarded a British ship, the *Trent,* in Havana. Charles Wilkes, commander of the U.S.S. *San Jacinto,* stopped the British ship without orders to do so. He took Mason and Slidell prisoner and brought them to Boston. This act violated the principle of freedom of the seas, because England was a neutral nation.

The people of the North rejoiced, but the British government furiously demanded an apology and the immediate release of Mason and Slidell. To back up these demands, it ordered 8,000 troops to Canada. President Abraham Lincoln and Secretary of State William Seward realized that Wilkes was wrong. The United States government ordered the prisoners released, and made a formal apology. Mason and Slidell went on to Europe, but their mission failed. John Donald Hicks

See also **Mason and Slidell; Wilkes, Charles.**

Trenton (pop. 92,124; met. area pop. 307,863) is the capital of New Jersey and an important manufacturing center of the state. The city lies in west-central New Jersey, where the Assunpink Creek flows into the Delaware River (see **New Jersey** [political map]).

In 1679, Quaker farmers led by Mahlon Stacy established the first permanent white settlement in what is now the Trenton area. In 1714, Mahlon Stacy, Jr., sold part of his father's property to William Trent, a merchant who later became chief justice of the New Jersey colony. The community was named *Trent's Town* in 1719, and its name later became *Trenton.*

Description. Trenton, the county seat of Mercer County, covers about 8 square miles (21 square kilometers). The golden dome of the State Capitol rises above the downtown area (see **New Jersey** [picture: The State Capitol]). The New Jersey Cultural Center is near the capitol. It consists of the state library and museum, and a planetarium. The Battle Monument, 150 feet (46 meters) high, marks the site of a famous Revolutionary War battle (see **Revolutionary War in America** [Trenton and Princeton]). Other landmarks include the 1719 home of William Trent and the Old Barracks, built in 1758 to house British troops. Rider College, Trenton State College, and Princeton University are near Trenton. Fort Dix, a large Army post, is also nearby (see **Fort Dix**).

Economy. The state government employs about 30 per cent of Trenton's workers. The city has about 180 factories. Major industries produce electrical goods, fabricated metal products, machinery, and rubber products. The printing and publishing industry is also important. The city's slogan, *Trenton Makes—The World Takes,* refers to Trenton's history as a manufacturing center.

Government and history. Trenton has a mayor-council form of government. The voters elect the mayor and the seven city council members to four-year terms.

Delaware Indians lived in what is now the Trenton area before the British occupied New Jersey in the 1660's. During colonial times, Trenton became a major stopping place on the stage line between New York City and Philadelphia. George Washington made his famous crossing of the Delaware River near Trenton in December 1776, during the Revolutionary War. Washington's troops defeated the Hessians in the battle that followed (see **Hessians**).

Trenton served as the nation's capital in November and December 1784. It became the capital of New Jersey in 1790 and received a city charter in 1792. During the 1800's, Trenton developed into an industrial and trade center. An increase in river traffic, combined with the construction of railroads, brought the city great industrial growth. Thousands of factory workers moved to Trenton, and the city's population rose by about 90,000 from 1880 to 1920. By 1920, Trenton was the leading U.S. pottery producer. It also ranked high in the production of rubber goods, steel, and wire cable.

After 1920, many of Trenton's residents and largest businesses began to move to the suburbs. This relocation continued through the years. Since 1950, the population of Trenton has declined. To reverse this decline, Trenton started a modernization program. In 1974, the city barred traffic from two blocks of its main street and created a pedestrian mall called Trenton Commons. The state of New Jersey began an ambitious office building program in Trenton, beginning with a law enforcement center that opened in 1982. The construction of additional state buildings followed.   George E. Amick, Jr.

See also **New Jersey** (pictures).

Trenton, Battle of. See Revolutionary War in America (Trenton and Princeton).

Trepang, *trih PANG,* is the commercial name of the dried bodies of certain *species* (kinds) of marine animals called *sea cucumbers* (see **Sea cucumber**). Trepang is also called *bêche-de-mer* (pronounced *BEHSH duh MAIR*). It is used as food in the Far East. Sea cucumbers have soft, wormlike bodies. They vary from a few inches or centimeters to 2 feet (61 centimeters) in length. To prepare the edible species, the inner parts are removed and the bodies are boiled. Then they are soaked in fresh water and smoked or dried in the sun. This produces a rubberlike substance used to thicken and flavor soups.

The chief center of the trepang industry is Ujung Pandang, a seaport of Sulawesi, in Indonesia. California also has a trepang industry.   Robert D. Barnes

Trephining, *trih FYN ihng,* is a surgical operation that involves cutting out a small, button-shaped piece of the skull. The operation is done with an instrument called a *trephine.* Trephining is used in the treatment of certain head injuries. It relieves pressure on the brain caused by bleeding between the skull and the brain. Trephining is also used to remove blood clots and to gain entry to the brain for certain surgical procedures.

Trephining is the earliest-known surgical treatment. Evidence of trephining has been found in human skulls that date to prehistoric times. Anthropologists have found trephined skulls throughout much of the world. Ancient peoples probably used trephining to release spirits that were believed responsible for headaches, mental disorders, and epilepsy. Some ancient warriors trephined the skulls of people they killed in battle. The warriors wore the piece of bone as a trophy or to ward off evil spirits. The Inca and other Indians of South America practiced trephining.   James D. Whiffen

See also **Medicine** (History; picture: Trephining).

Trespass, in law, is most commonly known as the unlawful entrance upon the property of another. The term also means injury to the person of another. "No trespassing" signs are seen commonly where owners of groves, private estates, and club grounds desire to protect their property from intrusion. Failure to regard such notices is an unlawful act. False imprisonment and assault and battery are examples of trespass to the person. Trespass makes a person liable to a civil suit for damages. See also **Assault and battery; False imprisonment; Tort.**
          George T. Felkenes

Trestle, *TREHS uhl,* in engineering, is a structure used to support a roadway over a valley or crossroad. A wooden trestle, made of *bents* (tall posts connected by ties and braces), usually costs less to build than a bridge. In carpentry, a trestle is a beam on legs. It is used to support work. Some tables and drawing boards are supported by a frame called a trestle.   Todd I. Blue

Trevelyan, *trih VEHL yuhn,* **George Macaulay** (1876-1962), was a famous British historian. His two best-known books are *History of England* (1926) and *English Social History* (1942). Trevelyan's vivid descriptions of social life and his dramatic and imaginative writing style appealed to the general public. In his writings, he promoted the views of the Whig Party, which was important in British politics from the 1600's to the mid-1800's, and of its successor, the Liberal Party. Whigs and Liberals believed the common people had a more positive effect on history than did royalty and that democratic government would bring about steady social progress.

Trevelyan was born near Stratford-upon-Avon. His father was Sir George Otto Trevelyan, a politician and historian. The younger Trevelyan first won wide praise for a three-volume biography of the Italian military hero Giuseppe Garibaldi, published between 1907 and 1911. Trevelyan taught modern history at Cambridge University from 1927 until 1940, when he became master of Trinity College. He also wrote *England Under Queen Anne* (1930 to 1934) and *The English Revolution, 1688-1689* (1938).   Joseph Martin Hernon, Jr.

Trevino, *truh VEE noh,* **Lee** (1939-   ), is an American golfer. Few people had heard of Trevino before he won the U.S. Open in 1968. But he soon gained fame as one of the most colorful and popular figures in sports. During tournaments, Trevino often joked with his many followers, who became known as "Lee's fleas."

In 1971, Trevino accomplished one of the most remarkable winning streaks in golf history. Within 16 weeks that year, he won five tournaments and finished among the top five money winners in four other tourneys. No other golfer had ever won the U.S., Canadian, and British opens during the same year. Trevino also won the Professional Golfers' Association (PGA) tournament in 1974 and 1984. Lee Buck Trevino was born in Dallas, Tex.

Herman Weiskopf

Pictorial Parade

Lee Trevino

Trevithick, *TREHV uh thihk,* **Richard** (1771-1833), was an English inventor and engineer. He contributed to the development of the steam locomotive.

Trevithick was born in Cornwall, a tin-mining region of England. As he grew up, he became interested in the steam engines that pumped water from the mines. By the early 1800's, he had developed a new engine that was soon used in most of the local mines. This high-pressure engine was the model for most later steam engines.

In 1801, Trevithick designed and built a steam-powered carriage that ran on the road. In 1804, he built the first steam locomotive to run on rails. It pulled a load of iron along a railway for horse-drawn cars. In 1808, he exhibited a large locomotive in London. None of his locomotives were financially successful, because they were too heavy for the roads and railways of his time. But Trevithick did prove that steam-powered locomotives could be built.   Michael M. Sokal

See also **Locomotive** (picture); **Railroad** (History).

Triage, *tree AHZH,* is a French word that means *choosing* or *sorting.* The word is frequently used to refer to a proposed method of distributing limited food supplies among the world's nations. Under a triage system, nations that were temporarily short of food—but seemed likely to become self-sufficient in food production eventually—would receive help. But those that seemed incapable of ever producing enough food for their people would be left to starve.

Supporters of triage believe we will not be able to produce enough food to keep up with the growing world population. Opponents consider it ruthless and unethical to deliberately deprive the neediest nations of food. Despite fears of a food shortage, the world food supply has so far kept pace with population growth.

The word *triage* was introduced into English during World War I (1914-1918) to describe a system of classifying wounded soldiers. Physicians divided the soldiers into three groups: (1) those too severely wounded to survive, (2) those who would recover even without treatment, and (3) those who would survive only with immediate help. If medical resources were limited, only the third group received treatment.   Jean Mayer

Trial is a method of settling disputes verbally in a court of law. In most cases, the people on each side of the dispute use a lawyer to represent their views, present evidence, and question witnesses. About half the trials held in the United States are jury trials. In the other trials, the defendant chooses to be tried by a judge or a panel of judges instead of a jury.

There are two types of trials, *civil trials* and *criminal trials.* Civil trials settle noncriminal matters, such as contracts, ownership of property, and payment for personal injury. The jury decides who is at fault and how much money must be paid in damages. In a criminal trial, the jury decides the legal guilt or innocence of a person accused of a crime.

A jury trial begins with the selection of the jurors. Then the *prosecutor,* who argues the state's case against the defendant in a criminal trial, and the *defense attorney* make their opening statements to the jury. In a civil trial, one side is represented by the attorney for the *plaintiff* (the person who began the lawsuit). The other side is represented by the defense attorney. In their opening statements, the lawyers for both sides declare what they intend to prove during the trial.

Presenting evidence. Each lawyer presents evidence to support his or her side of the case. The evidence may include documents, such as letters or receipts; or objects, such as weapons or clothing. In most cases, the evidence consists of testimony given by witnesses who are sworn to tell the truth. Witnesses generally give their testimony in response to questions asked by an attorney. Then the opposing attorney cross-examines the witnesses and attempts to find mistakes in their testimony. A witness who is suspected of deliberately lying may be accused of *perjury.*

The admission of evidence in a trial is governed by certain rules. In general, information is admitted as evidence only if it is (1) relevant, (2) material, and (3) firsthand. Relevant information is related to a question in the case and helps answer the question. Material information helps settle the main issue of the trial. Firsthand information comes from the witness's personal knowledge, not from hearsay.

Following the testimony and cross-examination, the lawyers for each side summarize the case. Then, in a *charge to the jury,* the judge gives instructions concerning the laws that apply to the case.

The judge in each trial decides what evidence will be admitted. He or she may declare a *mistrial* if improper evidence is heard by a jury or if the fairness of a trial is jeopardized in some other way. A mistrial results in a new trial with new jurors. The judge may also hold in *contempt of court* any person who shows disrespect for the court by disrupting a trial. Such a person may be fined or imprisoned, or both.

Reaching a verdict. The jury is taken to a private room to discuss the case and reach a verdict. In cases that have received much publicity, the jurors may be *sequestered* (isolated) from other people, including their families, throughout the trial. Sequestered jurors may read newspapers and magazines only if articles about the trial have been cut out. Depending on the nature of the trial, the judge may order that the jurors not be allowed to watch television. These restrictions prevent jurors from reading or hearing anything that could influence their opinions about the trial.

In a criminal trial, the prosecutor tries to prove the defendant's guilt "beyond a reasonable doubt," which is the standard required by law. If the jurors do not feel the prosecutor has done so, they must *acquit* the defendant—that is, find him or her not guilty. If the jury finds the defendant guilty, the judge sets a date for sentencing. In a civil trial, the attorney for the plaintiff must prove the plaintiff's claim by a "fair *preponderance* (the greater weight) of the evidence."

A *hung jury* is one in which the required number of jurors cannot agree on a verdict. A new trial—with new jurors—is then held.

In some trials, the evidence points without question to the defendant's innocence. In such cases, the judge may order the jury to return a *directed verdict* of not guilty. The jury does not discuss a directed verdict. A judge cannot order a guilty verdict.

The defendant's rights. The Constitution of the United States guarantees accused people many rights concerning a fair trial. For example, it specifies the right to a jury trial. Other guarantees are included in the Bill of Rights, the first 10 amendments to the Constitution. The first guarantee is in the Fifth Amendment. It ensures by the right of *due process* that each trial will be conducted according to the law.

The Sixth Amendment sets forth the most important rights of a defendant in a criminal trial. These include the right to "a speedy and public trial." The right to a speedy trial means that a person must be tried as soon as possible after being accused. But the large number of cases awaiting trial may prevent the courts from trying every defendant promptly. Many courts put time limits on criminal prosecution to ensure prompt trials. The right to a public trial means a defendant cannot be tried in secret. Each trial must be open to public observation.

The Constitution states that a criminal trial must be held in the community in which the crime occurred. The Sixth Amendment requires that the jurors be chosen from that community. In some situations, many local residents have formed an opinion about a case, and so the defendant cannot receive a fair trial there. The defense may then request a *change of venue*—that is, a change in the locality of the trial.

The Supreme Court of the United States has issued many decisions that provide additional rights for accused persons. In 1963, for example, the court guaranteed the right to free legal counsel in all felony cases. In 1972, the court extended that right to persons accused of any offense involving a jail sentence.

A defendant who has been tried and convicted can use his or her right to *appeal.* In an appeal, the defendant asks that the case be retried by a higher court called an *appellate court.* Some cases have an automatic right of appeal. In others, the defendant must show some reason for retrying the case, such as the discovery of new evidence. In such cases, the appellate court may refuse to hear the appeal. But it must retry the case if the judge feels there has been a violation of federal law or of the defendant's constitutional rights. An appellate court does not use a jury. Lawyers present the appeal by written arguments called *briefs* and by oral arguments.

The United States legal system is based on the belief that a person is considered innocent until proven guilty. But only a small percentage of the legal disputes in the United States are settled by a trial. The defendant pleads guilty in most cases, and so no trial is needed.

Many cases are settled by *plea bargaining.* In this procedure, the prosecuting attorney agrees to dismiss certain charges, substitute a less serious charge, or recommend a shorter sentence if the defendant pleads guilty. The state saves time and money by plea bargaining rather than putting a defendant on trial. Critics of plea bargaining feel that it weakens the nation's system of justice. They point out that the defendant's guilt is assumed instead of proven, as it would be in a trial.

History. The Saxons, who lived in England during the Middle Ages, gave accused people a *trial by ordeal* rather than by jury. The defendant was perhaps required to hold a piece of red-hot iron or was deliberately injured in some other way. The Saxons believed that God would heal the accused person's wounds within three days if he or she was innocent. After the Norman Conquest in 1066, two persons fought if they disagreed about a matter. They believed that God would grant victory to the one who was right.

The present trial system in the United States and Canada developed from English *common law* and *equity.* Common law is a group of rulings made by judges on the basis of community customs and previous court decisions. Equity is a set of standards based on broad principles of justice. English colonists brought their legal system with them to North America.   Jack M. Kress

Related articles in *World Book* include:

Appeal	Criminal justice	Law
Constitution of the	system	Perjury
United States	Due process of law	Plea bargaining
Contempt	Evidence	Sentence
Court	Judge	Trial by combat
	Jury	Witness

Trial by combat, also called *trial by battle* or *wager of battle,* was a way of settling legal disputes in the Middle Ages. Noblemen used it for many years. Trial by combat differed from a fight or duel because people believed that God would interfere and help the righteous person to win. The general procedure was for the accused to fight the accuser. Noblemen sometimes appointed champions to do their fighting for them.

Women and priests were generally represented by others. Trial by combat was introduced into England by William the Conqueror. Trial by jury gradually took its place.

Trial by ordeal was another way of determining a person's innocence or guilt during the Middle Ages. In trial by ordeal, a person was subjected to various forms of physical torture. If the injuries healed within three days, the person was considered innocent.   Bryce Lyon

See also **Divination.**

Triangle, in plane geometry, is an enclosed figure that has three line segments for sides. The sides meet at three points called *vertices,* and each vertex forms an *angle* with two of the sides. The sum of the three angles of a triangle is always 180°. A triangle is a type of polygon (see **Polygon**).

Kinds of triangles. Triangles can be classified according to the relationships of their sides. A *scalene* triangle is a figure with three unequal sides. An *isosceles* triangle has at least two equal sides. A triangle with all three sides of equal length is called an *equilateral* triangle. Therefore, every equilateral triangle is also an isosceles triangle, but not every isosceles triangle is an equilateral triangle.

Triangles are also classified by their angles. A triangle in which every angle is smaller than 90° is an *acute* triangle. An *obtuse* triangle has one angle larger than 90°. A *right* triangle has one right—that is, 90°—angle. No triangle can have more than one obtuse angle or one right angle.

Properties and relationships of triangles. The parts of a triangle have many interesting characteristics and relationships. Sometimes a useful relationship between two or more triangles can also be established. Some of the most notable of these properties and relationships are discussed below.

Perimeter and area. The *perimeter* of a triangle is the sum of the lengths of its sides. To find the *area* of a triangle, we must know the *altitude,* or *height,* which is the perpendicular distance from a vertex to the opposite side, or *base.* The area is calculated by multiplying the base by the altitude and then dividing by 2. Even if the perimeters of several triangles are the same, the areas of those triangles may differ.

Right triangles and the Pythagorean Theorem. The sides of a right triangle have a special relationship to each other. This relationship is expressed in a mathematical statement called the *Pythagorean Theorem* (see

The parts of a triangle

A triangle is a plane figure that has three sides and three angles. The line segments that form the sides meet at three points called *vertices.* Each vertex forms an angle with two of the sides.

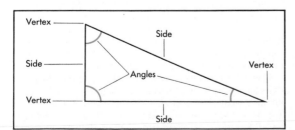

Kinds of triangles

Triangles can be classified by their angles or by the relationships of their sides. In the diagrams below, the blue lines indicate equal sides of a triangle. The red symbols mark equal angles. The gray box marks a *right angle*—that is, an angle of 90°.

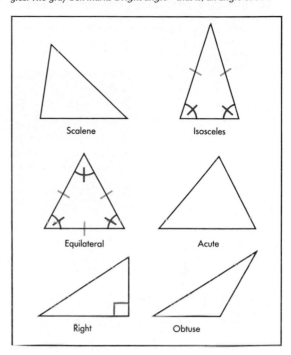

Scalene   Isosceles   Equilateral   Acute   Right   Obtuse

Pythagorean Theorem). This theorem was known in ancient civilizations, but it is credited to Pythagoras, a Greek philosopher and mathematician. According to the Pythagorean Theorem, a triangle is a right triangle if and only if the sum of the squares of the two shorter sides equals the square of the longest side, called the *hypotenuse.* This statement can be written as a formula: $a^2 + b^2 = c^2$. For example, if the sides of a triangle are 6, 8, and 10, it is a right triangle because $36 + 64 = 100$. The formula enables us to find the length of any side of a right triangle if we know the lengths of the other two sides.

Congruence. Two triangles are *congruent*—that is, they have exactly the same size and shape—if all their corresponding sides and angles are equal. Mathematicians have formulated specific sets of conditions for determining congruence. For example, two triangles are congruent if the sides of one equal the corresponding sides of the other. Using *S* to represent *side,* this statement can be abbreviated as $SSS=SSS$. Other sets of conditions for congruency involve angles as well as sides, with *A* standing for *angle.* These sets are $AAS=AAS$, $SAS=SAS$, and $ASA=ASA$.

Similarity. Triangles that are *similar* have equal corresponding angles and proportional corresponding sides. Similar triangles have the same shape but not necessarily the same size. For example, if the sides of one triangle are 3, 4, and 5, and those of another are 6, 8, and 10, the sides are proportional.

The similarity of two triangles, like the congruence of two triangles, can be established without knowing all the sides and angles. If two sets of corresponding angles are equal, for example, the triangles are similar. If all three corresponding sides of the triangles are proportional, the triangles are also similar. In a right triangle, the altitude from the right angle divides the triangle into two triangles that are similar to each other and to the parent triangle.   Arthur F. Coxford, Jr.

Triangle is a percussion instrument that consists of a steel bar bent in a triangular shape with one open corner. The player strikes the instrument with a short rod called a *beater* to produce a high sound with indefinite pitch. The quality of the tone can be varied by using metal beaters of different thicknesses or by using a wooden, rather than a metal, beater. A musician usually holds the triangle in one hand by a clip at the top and grasps the beater in the other hand. But the triangle can also be clipped to a stand and played with two beaters, one in each hand.

Northwestern University (WORLD BOOK photo by Ted Nielsen)

A triangle is a steel percussion instrument shaped like a triangle and open at one corner. A player hits it with a rod.

John H. Beck

Triangular trade. See Black Americans (Beginning of the slave trade).

Trianon, *TREE uh nahn* or *tree ah NAWN,* **Treaty of,** was signed by Hungary and the Western Allies after World War I. The treaty was signed in the gallery of the Grand Trianon, a palace at Versailles, in France, on June 4, 1920. It severely punished Hungary for its part in the war. The United States, which signed the treaty but never ratified it, made a separate peace with Hungary in 1921.

The Trianon treaty reduced Hungarian territory from 125,609 square miles (325,326 square kilometers) to 35,184 square miles (91,126 square kilometers). The country's population dropped from about 21 million to about 8 million, and it was left with no seaports. Hungary's bitter complaints against the treaty brought few results.

The Treaty of Trianon forced Hungary to recognize the new boundaries of Austria, Czechoslovakia, Romania, and what became Yugoslavia. Hungary had to give up its claims to the port of Fiume, and was allowed to keep an army of only 35,000 men. All Hungarian merchant ships had to be surrendered to the Allies. Hungary lost Slovakia, Transylvania, and Croatia to neighboring countries. About 3 million Magyars were separated from their fellow Hungarians.   Dwight E. Lee

Triassic Period. See Earth (table: Outline of earth history).

Tribe is a term used to describe certain human social groups. Some scholars dislike the term because it lacks a precise meaning and has been applied to many widely different groups. In addition, many of the peoples called tribes consider the term offensive or inaccurate. Most prefer such terms as *ethnic group, nation,* or *people.*

The first use of the word *tribe* in English referred to the Hebrews. Until about 1000 B.C., the Hebrews were loosely organized into 12 groups, each of which traced its descent to one of the 12 sons of Jacob. These groups were called the 12 Tribes of Israel. The term *tribe* was soon extended to mean any group of families who traced themselves to a common ancestor.

Beginning in the 1400's, many European nations established colonies in Africa, Asia, and North and South America. The Europeans often described the peoples of those areas as tribes, though the groups varied greatly in their economic, political, and social organization. Some of the so-called tribes consisted of unrelated groups. Others were more accurately called nations. Most Europeans regarded the colonized peoples, whose technology was less advanced than theirs, as primitive. In time, the word *tribe* acquired the broad meaning of "primitive group."

Anthropologists have added other characteristics to the definition of tribe, though different scholars emphasize different features. Many define a tribe as a group with a sense of shared identity and ties of ancestry, customs, language, and territory. Others believe a tribe also must have some form of political organization, such as a means of making decisions for the group and of settling disputes between its members. Some scientists regard only groups without a written language as tribes. Others define a tribal economy as one that operates to produce only enough food and other necessities for members of the group, with little or no surplus. Almost no groups have all these characteristics, though the Tiv of Nigeria and the Zuñi Indians of the United States come close.

Today, many black Africans and other peoples consider the word *tribe* insulting because they believe it implies that they are primitive. Other so-called tribes consider the term inaccurate because they regard themselves as separate groups. For example, the Yoruba, Nigeria's largest ethnic group, are sometimes called a tribe. But they include the Egba, the Ife, the Oyo, and other peoples, each with their own culture and political organization.

On the other hand, several American Indian groups have struggled since the mid-1900's to gain or regain legal status as tribes. These Indians declare that they need tribal status to get the protection and benefits that have been promised them by treaties.

Some scholars also use the term *tribe* to refer to an early stage in the development of political systems, about 10,000 years ago. The tribe came after the family or band and before the appearance of more centralized and specialized governmental systems, such as chiefdoms and kingdoms.   Jennie Keith

See also Clan; Ethnic group; Nation.

Triborough Bridge, *TRY bur oh,* connects three boroughs of New York City—Manhattan, the Bronx, and Queens. This great structure is actually a series of bridges forming three steel and concrete arms which form a rough Y in plan. The total length of the three arms is $17\frac{1}{2}$ miles (28.2 kilometers), of which about $3\frac{1}{2}$ miles (5.6 kilometers) consist of bridges and viaducts. The four overwater spans cross the East and Harlem rivers, the Bronx Kills, and Little Hell Gate.

Parts of the structure rest on Wards Island and Randalls Island, in the East River. The suspension span between Wards Island and Queens is the most important arm. It is 1,380 feet (421 meters) long. There is a vertical-lift bridge between Manhattan and Randalls Island.

The Triborough system includes crossings, highways, streets, park and parkway constructions, and 12 land bridges. The Triborough was the first project to give direct connection between the Bronx and Queens. It was opened to traffic on July 11, 1936.   Archibald Black

Tribune, *TRIHB yoon,* was an official in ancient Rome. There were two kinds of tribunes, *military tribunes* and *tribunes of the people.*

The first military tribunes were leaders of the soldiers which the various Roman tribes furnished to serve in the army of the republic. There were six tribunes to each *legion* (group of soldiers). They ranked next after the commander in chief. The early tribunes were appointed by *consuls* (chief government officials). Later, the people elected them. During the Roman Empire period, military tribunes lost much of their importance.

Tribunes of the people were officials elected to protect the rights of *plebeians* (commoners). According to one account, the plebeians left Rome in 494 B.C. and refused to return until they were allowed to elect their own defenders. Historians believe that at first there were only two tribunes. Later there were four or five, and then 10. They held office for a term of one year, but could be reelected. The tribunes could defend citizens against unfair acts by officials. In the Senate, they could veto bills. In their own assembly, they could introduce *plebiscites* (resolutions made by the plebeians). They could not be imprisoned. Tribunes became the most powerful civil officers in the state, although their powers did not extend beyond the city limits of Rome. Largely because of the work of the tribunes, the plebeians gradually took over many of the political rights which had once belonged only to *patricians* (aristocrats). In 23 B.C., Emperor Augustus received the powers of a tribune. These powers enabled Roman emperors to add civil authority to their military power.

In the A.D. 1300's, an Italian patriot named Cola di Rienzi took the title of tribune when he led the common people in their fight for freedom from the nobles. Those who defend the common people are often called tribunes. See Rienzi, Cola di.   Frank C. Bourne

See also Legion; Rome, Ancient (Government).

Tributary. See River (The source of a river).

Triceps. See Arm.

Trichina, *trih KY nuh,* is a small roundworm that causes the disease *trichinosis.* The worm is a *parasite.* That is, it lives in and feeds on other animals.

The trichina infects human beings and other animals, especially hogs, bears, and rats. Most infections of trichinosis in the United States and Canada result from eating infected pork that has not been cooked enough. Trichinosis in hogs, bears, and rats usually results from eating infected meat and infected garbage.

The *larvae* (early form of the worms) live in microscopic *cysts* (sacs) in the muscles of animals they infect. They usually live in the animal's chest and neck muscles. If an animal infected by the larvae is allowed to live, the cysts eventually harden and the larvae die. But sometimes infected animals are killed for meat. In such cases, the larvae can be killed by thoroughly cooking or freezing the meat. However, if the larvae are not killed and the meat is eaten, the larvae are freed from the cysts during digestion. The larvae attach themselves to the intestine of the person who eats the meat. They become

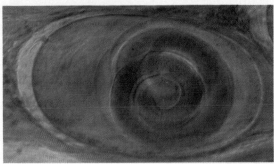
© Robert Mitchell

A trichina cyst forms in the muscle tissue of an infected person. Each cyst measures about $\frac{1}{50}$ inch (0.5 millimeter) long.

adult worms in about 3 or 4 days. The largest are only about $\frac{1}{4}$ inch (6 millimeters) long.

The adult females burrow into the wall of the intestine, where they produce large numbers of active larvae. The larvae enter the blood and are carried to many parts of the body. They eventually leave the blood and form new cysts in the muscles.

Some people carry trichina worms in their bodies for many years and never have severe symptoms. But in other people, the worms irritate the intestine and cause diarrhea, nausea, and vomiting. When they pass through the blood, fever, headache, and muscular pain occur. After they reach the muscles, they cause swelling of the face and other parts and bleeding under the skin. The worms may form their cysts in the *diaphragm* (chief muscle used for breathing) and make breathing painful. The disease is seldom fatal.

The prevention of trichinosis involves several steps. Garbage may carry trichina worms, so it should be cooked before it is fed to hogs. Meat packers should freeze pork to kill any worms the pork may carry. Finally, cooks should be sure the central section of pork is held at a temperature of at least 137° F. (58° C) for 5 minutes or more. The number of trichinosis infections is low in places where these preventive measures are followed.

Scientific classification. The trichina is in the trichina family, Trichinellidae. It is *Trichinella spiralis.*   James A. McLeod

Trichinosis. See Trichina.

Trichoptera. See Insect (table).

Tricolor, *TRY kuhl uhr,* is the French national flag. It has equal red, white, and blue vertical sections. The three colors were first used as a French emblem on July 17, 1789, during the French Revolution. King Louis XVI had come to Paris after the fall of the Bastille. He put a tricolor knot of ribbons on his hat as a patriotic gesture. Red and blue were the official colors of Paris, and white was the color of the royal family. After the royal family was restored to power in 1814, it rejected the tricolor. But the tricolor again became the French national flag in 1830. See France (picture).   Isser Woloch

Trier, *treer* (pop. 93,472), is the oldest city in Germany. It lies on the Moselle River in the state of Rhineland-Palatinate (see Germany [political map]). Trier is the center and market area of a famous wine district. The city makes leather goods, steel products, and textiles. The city is also an important railroad junction. Trier has a theological seminary that dates back to 1773, a university, and a school of *viticulture* (vine cultivation).

Trier was founded by the Romans, probably around 15 B.C. It was named for the Treveri, a people of ancient Gaul. A number of Roman monuments, including an amphitheater, baths, and the celebrated *Porta Nigra* (fortified north gate), stand in the city. Trier's cathedral dates from Roman times, and houses a garment believed to be the seamless coat of Jesus Christ. The city has been an important center of Roman Catholic tradition since the Middle Ages. It has many beautiful examples of church architecture, including the St. Simeon monastery and the St. Paulin baroque church. Trier came under French control in 1806 and was awarded to Prussia by the Congress of Vienna in 1814-1815. The French occupied Trier after World War I ended in 1918.

Peter H. Merkl

Trieste. See **Exploration** (Deep-sea exploration; picture: The bathyscaph *Trieste*).

Trieste, *tree EHST* or *tree EHS tee* (pop. 251,380), is a city in northeastern Italy. Several nations use Trieste's free port, which does not tax imported goods. The city produces clothing, iron and steel, machinery, and paint. Trieste lies at the northern end of the Adriatic Sea. For location, see **Italy** (political map).

Trieste was a Roman colony from the 100's B.C. to about A.D. 500. Austria gained control of the area in the late 1300's. Treaties following World War I (1914-1918) gave Trieste to Italy.

In 1946, after World War II, the United Nations (UN) took over Trieste and a large area surrounding the city. The UN set up the Free Territory of Trieste there and divided the total of 293 square miles (759 square kilometers) into two zones. United States and British troops occupied Zone A, which included the city of Trieste and an area to the north. Most of the people of this zone were Italians. Yugoslav forces occupied Zone B, an area south of the city. This zone had a largely Slavic population. In 1954, the city and most of Zone A came under Italian control. Yugoslavia continued to administer Zone B. In 1975, Italy took formal possession of Zone A, and Zone B became part of Yugoslavia.   Anthony James Joes

Triggerfish is a type of colorful fish that lives in coastal waters of warm and tropical seas. Most triggerfish are less than $1\frac{1}{2}$ feet (46 centimeters) long and have a roundish body with flattened sides.

The first three spines of a triggerfish's dorsal fin are specialized. The fish uses these spines to enlarge its body when threatened. The first spine is long and strong. It can be locked in place by the second, smaller spine, which lifts up and acts as a "trigger." When frightened, the fish hides in a crack or crevice and locks its spine. The fish then cannot be removed by predators. It returns to its normal size by releasing its second spine.

Triggerfish are closely related to filefish. There are about 120 species of triggerfish and filefish. Sixteen species of triggerfish and filefish live along the Atlantic Coast of the United States. Three species of triggerfish live along the mainland Pacific Coast. The state fish of Hawaii, the Humuhumunukunukuapuaa, is a triggerfish.

Scientific classification. Triggerfish and filefish belong to the family Balistidae.   John E. McCosker

See also **Fish** (pictures: Fish of the coral reefs).

Trigonometry, *TRIHG uh NAHM uh tree,* is a branch of mathematics that deals with the relationships between the sides and angles of triangles. It also provides methods of measuring these sides and angles. Trigonometry has applications in such theoretical sciences as physics and astronomy, and in such practical fields as surveying and navigation. The word *trigonometry* comes from two Greek words meaning *triangle* and *measure.*

There are two kinds of trigonometry—*plane trigonometry* and *spherical trigonometry.* Plane trigonometry is used to determine the unknown sides and angles of triangles that lie in a plane. Spherical trigonometry can be used to find the unknown sides and angles of triangles that lie on a spherical surface.

Both types of trigonometry are based on relationships that exist between the six parts—three sides and three angles—of any triangle. Because of these relationships, in almost all cases any three parts whose measures are known can be used to find the measures of the other three parts, if at least one of the known parts is a side. It is necessary to know the length of at least one side because the corresponding sides of two triangles may be unequal even though all their corresponding angles are equal.

Trigonometry is based on a type of geometry called *Euclidean geometry.* Euclidean geometry was developed from a set of assumptions spelled out about 300 B.C. by the Greek mathematician Euclid (see **Geometry** [Types of geometry]). Spherical trigonometry was first described about A.D. 150 in a work by Ptolemy of Alexandria called the *Almagest.* Plane trigonometry was developed in the 1400's by the German mathematician Johann Müller, who was also known as Regiomontanus.

Plane trigonometry

To understand trigonometry, it is necessary first to study the properties of *similar triangles.* Two triangles are said to be similar when all the corresponding angles of the triangles are equal. For example, the triangles *GHI* and *JKL* shown below are similar if angle *G* = angle *J,*

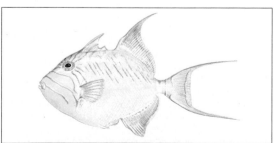

WORLD BOOK illustration by John F. Eggert

The triggerfish lives in warm coastal waters. It is a colorful fish with a roundish body and flattened sides.

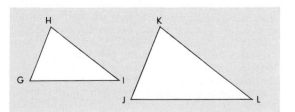

angle H = angle K, and angle I = angle L. The corresponding sides of similar triangles need not be equal. However, they are in proportion. Therefore, if triangles GHI and JKL are similar, the ratio $GH:GI$ will equal the ratio $JK:JL$. Suppose that GH = 3 units, GI = 5 units, and JK = 9 units. Then JL = 15 units, because $\frac{3}{5} = \frac{9}{15}$.

Right triangles. Trigonometry is largely derived from the study of similar *right triangles*. A right triangle is any triangle in which one of the angles equals 90°. The three angles in any triangle total 180°. Therefore, every right triangle has two acute angles that total 90°. If we know one of the acute angles, we can find the other one by subtracting the known angle from 90°. In addition, if an acute angle of one right triangle equals an acute angle of a second right triangle, then the two triangles are similar. In the right triangles ABC and DEF below, for example, angle C and angle F are right angles and angle A equals angle D. Therefore, the two triangles are similar. And because they are similar, their sides must

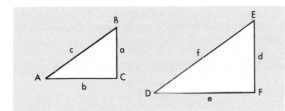

be in proportion, so that $\frac{a}{c} = \frac{d}{f}$, $\frac{b}{c} = \frac{e}{f}$, and $\frac{a}{b} = \frac{d}{e}$.

The ratios that make up these proportions will equal the ratios for the corresponding sides of any right triangle that has an acute angle equal to angle A. Each of the possible ratios between the sides of a right triangle has been given a special name. In the illustration above, for example, the ratio $\frac{a}{c}$ is called the *sine* of angle A, and is written sin A. The ratio $\frac{b}{c}$ is called the *cosine* of angle A. It is written cos A. The ratio $\frac{a}{b}$ is called the *tangent* of angle A, and is written tan A. Mathematicians have compiled tables that contain the values of these three ratios for all the possible angles of a right triangle. Such tables are programmed into scientific calculators.

Trigonometric tables also include three rarely used ratios called the *secant, cosecant,* and *cotangent*. The secant of angle A, written sec A, is $\frac{c}{b}$. The cosecant of angle A, written csc A, is $\frac{c}{a}$. The angle's cotangent, written cot A, is $\frac{b}{a}$.

Following are formal definitions of the six trigonometric ratios:

sine	=	side opposite the angle / hypotenuse
cosine	=	side adjacent to the angle / hypotenuse
tangent	=	side opposite the angle / side adjacent to the angle
secant	=	hypotenuse / side adjacent to the angle
cosecant	=	hypotenuse / side opposite the angle
cotangent	=	side adjacent to the angle / side opposite the angle

The trigonometric ratios make it possible to find all three sides of the right triangle ABC if we know the measure of one of the acute angles and the length of any side. For instance, if angle A is 30°, then we can use a table or calculator to determine that sin A = $\frac{1}{2}$. And if sin A = $\frac{1}{2}$, then $\frac{a}{c} = \frac{1}{2}$. Thus, if side c is 9 units long, then side a must be $4\frac{1}{2}$ units long.

This method has many applications. For example, suppose you are standing at point O on the bank of a river and looking at a tree at point N on the opposite shore (see the figure below). You can use this method to find the distance from O to N without crossing the river. First, place a marker at point O. Then, walk along a line at right angles to the line NO until you come to a convenient point M, thus forming the right triangle MNO. Next, measure the length of the line MO. If MO is, say, 75 units long, and angle M measures 40°, you can use a

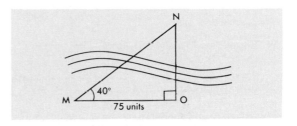

calculator or table to determine that tan $40°$ = 0.8391. Because tan M = NO/MO, NO = (MO) (tan 40°) = (75 units)(0.8391) = 62.93 units.

The law of sines. For some applications, you must determine the unknown parts of a triangle that is not a right triangle. If you know two angles and one side of such a triangle, you can find the other two sides and the other angle by using the *law of sines*. This law says:

> For a triangle ABC with sides $a, b,$ and c (see figure below),
> $$\frac{a}{\sin A} = \frac{b}{\sin B} = \frac{c}{\sin C}$$

If we know angle A and angle B, we can determine angle C, because angle C = 180° − (angle A + angle B). If we know side c, we can then find sides a and b, be-

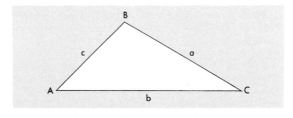

cause from the law of sines we know that

$$b = \frac{c\,(\sin B)}{\sin C} \quad \text{and} \quad a = \frac{c\,(\sin A)}{\sin C}$$

The law of cosines. If we know two sides of a triangle that is not a right triangle, and the angle between them, the remaining parts of the triangle can be found by using the *law of cosines*. The law of cosines states:

> For a triangle *ABC* with sides *a, b,* and *c,*
> $$c^2 = a^2 + b^2 - 2ab(\cos C).$$

For example, if we know sides *a* and *b* and angle *C,* we can find side *c* by the law of cosines. We can then use the law of sines to find the other two angles. Thus, if side *a* = 5 units, side *b* = 7 units, and angle *C* = 52°, we can solve for the unknown side and angles of the triangle. Using a table or a calculator, we can determine that cos 52° = 0.6157. We can then use the law of cosines to solve for c²:

$$c^2 = [(25 + 49) - (70 \times 0.6157)]$$
$$= 30.90$$

Then, we calculate that $c = \sqrt{30.901} = 5.56$ units. Next, because we know from the law of sines that

$$\frac{b}{\sin B} = \frac{c}{\sin C},$$ we find that $(\sin B)\, c = b\,(\sin C).$

Therefore, $$\sin B = \frac{b(\sin C)}{c} = \frac{7(\sin 52°)}{5.56} = 0.9922.$$

Using a table or a calculator, we can then determine that angle *B* = 82.8°. Finally,
angle *A* = 180° − (82.8° + 52°) = 45.2°.

A special case. There is only one case in which we must know more than the measures of three parts of a triangle to solve for the triangle's unknown sides and angles. This case occurs when we know two sides and one angle, but the known angle is not between the two known sides. In such a case, the triangle could take two possible forms. In the figure below, for example, if we

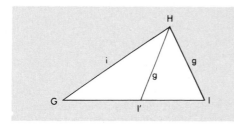

know only angle *G* and sides *g* and *i,* then the triangle may be either triangle *GHI* or triangle *GHI'.*

The two possibilities for the angle opposite side *i* are *GIH* and *GI'H.* These two angles are *supplementary*—that is, they total 180°. Sines of supplementary angles are equal, so **sin** angle *GIH* = **sin** angle *GI'H.* Thus, we cannot use the law of sines to determine which angle is part of the unknown triangle. To solve the triangle, we must know whether the triangle has an obtuse angle or whether all its angles are acute. If it has an obtuse angle, the triangle is *GHI'.* If all its angles are acute, the triangle is *GHI.* Once this extra information is provided, we can use the law of sines to determine the remaining parts of the triangle.

Spherical trigonometry

On the surface of a sphere, the shortest path between two points is an arc of the circle that contains those two

points and whose center is the center of the sphere. Such a circle is called a *great circle.* On a globe, the circles of longitude, which pass through the North Pole and the South Pole, are great circles. The circles of latitude, except for the equator, are not great circles because their centers lie above or below the center of the sphere. Arcs of circles are measured in degrees. A complete circle measures 360 degrees. The circumference of a great circle on the earth is about 24,860 miles (40,008 kilometers). Thus, each degree of arc of a great circle on the earth extends about 69.06 miles (111.13 kilometers). The angle between two great circles is the angle between their *tangents* at the point of intersection. A tangent is a line that touches an arc at one point only, without intersecting it. A *spherical triangle* is formed by the intersections of three great circles.

Because both the angles and the sides of a spherical triangle are measured in degrees, the formulas of spherical trigonometry differ somewhat from the formulas of plane trigonometry. Also, spherical triangles differ from plane triangles in that the angles of a spherical triangle always total more than 180°. However, spherical trigonometry uses the same tables that plane trigonometry uses.

The basic formulas in spherical trigonometry are the law of sines for spherical triangles, which reads:

$$\frac{\sin a}{\sin A} = \frac{\sin b}{\sin B} = \frac{\sin c}{\sin C}$$

and the law of cosines for spherical triangles, which reads:

$$\cos c = (\cos a)(\cos b) + (\sin a)(\sin b)(\cos C).$$

The figure below shows how these laws are applied. The distance from New York City to Paris is calculated

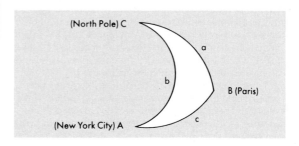

by drawing a spherical triangle whose vertices are New York City, Paris, and the North Pole.

Because the longitude of Paris is 2.20° east and the longitude of New York City is 73.58° west, angle *C* is 2.20° + 73.58°, or 75.78°. Because the latitude of Paris is 48.51° north, arc *a* is 90° − 48.51°, or 41.49°. Because the latitude of New York City is 40.40° north, arc *b* is 90° − 40.40°, or 49.60°. By the law of cosines for spherical triangles, the measure of arc *c* can be found by using the equation:

$$\cos c = (\cos 41.49)(\cos 49.60) +$$
$$(\sin 41.49)(\sin 49.60)(\cos 75.78)$$
$$= (.74907)(.64812) + (.66249)(.76154)(.24565)$$
$$= .60942$$

We can use a table or calculator to determine that .60942 is the cosine of a 52.45° arc. Therefore, arc *c* is 52.45°, and the distance from New York City to Paris is 69.06 miles (111.13 kilometers) × 52.45, or 3,622 miles (5,829 kilometers).

To find the direction in which Paris lies in relation to New York City, we find the measure of angle *A* by using the law of sines for spherical triangles:

$$\frac{\sin a}{\sin A} = \frac{\sin c}{\sin C}$$
$$(\sin A)(\sin c) = (\sin a)(\sin C)$$
$$\sin A = \frac{(\sin a)(\sin C)}{\sin c}$$
$$= \frac{(.66249)(.96936)}{.79282}$$
$$= .81000.$$

We can use a table or calculator to determine that angle *A* is 54.1°. From New York City, therefore, the compass direction to Paris is 54.1° east of north. But the angle between the direction to Paris and the north changes as a person travels along the great circle from New York City to Paris. Therefore, a person cannot reach Paris by simply traveling in this compass direction.   Roger Cooke

Related articles in *World Book* include:

Algebra	Geometry	Navigation	Triangle
Angle	Mathematics	Surveying	

Trilling, Lionel (1905-1975), was a major American literary critic. In his essays, Trilling used literature as a starting point for examining the moral responsibility of the "self," or individual, to society. He explored the ideas expressed in literature, and how they reflect or challenge the society that produced them. Trilling was influenced by the theories of the Viennese psychologist Sigmund Freud and wrote extensively about him.

Trilling's collections of essays include *The Liberal Imagination* (1950), *The Opposing Self* (1955), *Beyond Culture* (1965), and *Sincerity and Authenticity* (1972). He also wrote critical studies of the English authors Matthew Arnold and E. M. Forster. Trilling wrote one novel, *The Middle of the Journey* (1947), and he also wrote several short stories. He was born in New York City and taught literature at Columbia University from 1932 to 1975.   Samuel Chase Coale

Trillion is a thousand billion in the United States and France. One trillion is written 1,000,000,000,000. It has 12 zeros. In Great Britain and Germany, a trillion is a billion billion, so it has 18 zeros. See also **Decimal system** (The decimal system and number words).

Trillium, *TRIHL ee uhm,* is a wild flower that grows in damp, wooded places in the United States, Canada, and Asia. There are about 40 kinds. The flowers have three sepals, three petals, and six stamens. Each stem bears one flower and three leaves. Trilliums are often called *wake-robins* because some kinds bloom when the robins return north. The best-known trillium is the *white trillium.* It grows from New England to the Carolinas and west to Minnesota. The *painted trillium* is the most colorful. Its white flowers have deep pink or purple stripes. It grows from Quebec to Georgia and as far west as Michigan and Tennessee.

Scientific classification. Trilliums belong to the lily family, Liliaceae. The white trillium is *Trillium grandiflorum;* the painted trillium is *T. undulatum.*   Anton A. Reznicek

See also **Flower** (picture: Flowers of woodlands and forests).

Trilobite, *TRY luh byt,* was a prehistoric sea animal. It lived throughout the *Paleozoic Era,* which lasted from about 600 million years ago to about 230 million years ago. Trilobites lived in all parts of the world, and scientists have identified over 10,000 species from fossils. A soft shell covered much of the animal's body. Most trilo-

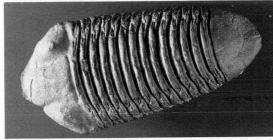

© W. H. Hode from Peter Arnold

A fossil of a trilobite

bites were under 4 inches (10 centimeters) long. Two grooves divided the animal's shell lengthwise into three *lobes* (sections). The name *trilobite* means *three lobes.* The body had three main parts: the head, the thorax, and the tail. The thorax had many segments, each bearing legs. The trilobite breathed through gills on the legs. See also **Fossil** (picture: A trilobite fossil).

Scientific classification. Trilobites belong to the phylum Arthropoda.   Keith Stewart Thomson

Trinidad and Tobago is a country that consists of two islands in the West Indies. It lies in the Caribbean Sea, near the northeast coast of South America. Trinidad, the larger island, is 7 miles (11 kilometers) east of Venezuela. Tobago is about 20 miles (32 kilometers) northeast of Trinidad.

Trinidad and Tobago covers 1,980 square miles (5,128 square kilometers) and has a population of about 1,263,000. Trinidad accounts for about 95 per cent of the country's land area, and approximately 95 per cent of the people live there. Port-of-Spain, on Trinidad, is the nation's capital, largest city, and chief port.

Government. Trinidad and Tobago is a republic. A prime minister, who is the leader of the majority party in Parliament, serves as the head of the government. The prime minister appoints a Cabinet of any number of members for assistance. A president, elected by the Parliament, serves as head of state. The Parliament consists of a 31-member Senate and a 36-member House of Representatives. Leading government officials appoint the senators. The people elect the members of the House of Representatives. The People's National Movement (PNM) is the largest political party.

People. Over a third of the people of Trinidad and Tobago have black African ancestry, and about a third are descendants of people from India. People of mixed European and black African ancestry, plus groups of Europeans and Chinese, form the rest of the population.

English is the country's official language, but French, Spanish, and Hindi are also spoken. Most of the poorer people speak *Trinidad English,* a form of standard English with French and Spanish influences. About 95 per cent of the people can read and write. The law requires all children from 6 to 12 years old to go to school. Roman Catholics make up the largest religious group, followed by Anglicans and Hindus.

Many people in the country play native musical instruments called *pans,* which are made from empty oil drums. Trinidad is the home of a form of folk music called *calypso* and of the *limbo* dance (see **Calypso**). Calypso music is featured at the Trinidad Carnival, an event held just before Lent that attracts many tourists.

Land and climate. Tropical forests and fertile flatlands cover much of Trinidad. A mountain range extends east and west across the northern area, and hills rise in the central and southern sections. Tobago has a central mountain ridge and scenic beaches.

Trinidad and Tobago has a warm, moist climate. Temperatures range from 64° F. (18° C) to 92° F. (33° C). The average annual temperature is 78° F. (26° C) on Trinidad and slightly lower on Tobago. The average annual rainfall is about 80 inches (203 centimeters).

Economy of Trinidad and Tobago is based on oil production and refining. The nation produces more than 50 million barrels of crude oil annually and imports about twice as much for refining. Petroleum accounts for about 80 per cent of the country's export income.

Pitch Lake, on Trinidad, is the world's chief source of natural asphalt, a tarlike substance that is used to make paving materials. This lake provides more than 100,000 short tons (91,000 metric tons) of asphalt yearly.

Other major industries of Trinidad and Tobago include agriculture and tourism. Sugar, the chief export crop, is also used to produce molasses and rum.

Trinidad and Tobago has about 4,000 miles (6,400 kilometers) of roads, and an airport operates on each island. The country has two daily newspapers, a television station, and two major radio stations.

History. Christopher Columbus claimed Trinidad for Spain in 1498, during his third voyage to the New World. The Arawak and the Carib Indians then lived there. The Spaniards set up a permanent settlement on the island in 1592, but the population did not begin to grow rapidly until 1783. That year, Spain offered land grants in Trinidad to any Roman Catholic settlers willing to develop the island's economy. Many planters of French ancestry then went there from Haiti and other nearby islands. They established thriving sugar cane plantations, and the island prospered. The British captured Trinidad in 1797 and ruled it for over 150 years.

A British sea captain named Lawrence Keymis reported seeing Tobago in 1596, and the Dutch settled there in 1632. Great Britain, France, and the Netherlands fought for possession of the island until 1814, when Britain took control of it. Through the years, thousands of black slaves had been brought from Africa to work on the islands' plantations. Labor shortages occurred after Britain abolished slavery in 1834, and many workers were brought from India.

In 1888, Trinidad and Tobago became one colony under British rule. During the Great Depression of the 1930's, the colony suffered severe economic setbacks. The people then began to demand a greater voice in their government. Britain allowed a gradual increase in self-government during the 1940's and 1950's, and the colony became an independent nation in 1962.

In the early 1970's, black-power supporters protested against widespread unemployment and what they considered social and economic inequality in Trinidad and Tobago. Violent demonstrations broke out, and the government twice declared a state of emergency. Racial tensions eased in the mid-1970's, but unemployment continued to be a major problem in the country.

Since the early 1970's, there has been a political movement on Tobago island to make the island independent from the rest of the country. In 1980, as a result

Trinidad and Tobago

▬▬▬	International boundary
───	Road
───	Railroad
⌒⌒	Swamp
⊛	National capital
•	Other city or town
+	Elevation above sea level

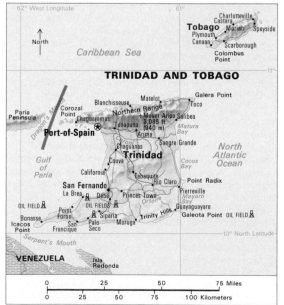

WORLD BOOK map

Facts in brief

Capital: Port-of-Spain.

Official language: English.

Total land area: 1,980 sq. mi. (5,128 km²). *Coastline*—292 mi. (470 km).

Elevation: *Highest*—Mt. Aripo, 3,085 ft. (940 m). *Lowest*—sea level.

Population: *Estimated 1989 population*—1,263,000; density, 638 persons per sq. mi. (246 per km²); distribution, 55 per cent rural, 45 per cent urban. *1980 census*—1,079,791. *Estimated 1994 population*—1,359,000.

Chief products: Asphalt, oil, sugar.

National anthem: "Forged from the Love of Liberty."

Flag: A black stripe, bordered by white stripes, runs across a red field from the upper left to the lower right corner. See **Flag** (picture: Flags of the Americas).

Money: *Basic unit*—West Indies dollar. See **Money** (table: Exchange rates).

Hutchison Library

Port-of-Spain is the chief port of Trinidad and Tobago. Small interisland vessels and large oceangoing ships dock at the busy harbor of the city.

of this movement, the national government allowed a local governing council to be established on Tobago island. The council has some control of local affairs.

Eric Williams, the founder and leader of the PNM, served as prime minister of Trinidad and Tobago from independence until his death in 1981. George Chambers of the PNM succeeded him.   Archibald W. Singham

See also **Port-of-Spain.**

Trinitrotoluene. See TNT.

Trinity, *TRIHN uh tee,* is a term used to express the belief that in the one God there are three Divine Persons—the Father, the Son, and the Holy Spirit (or Holy Ghost). The idea is based on various passages in the New Testament. Belief in Father, Son, and Holy Spirit was defined by early general councils of the Christian church. The Council of Nicea in 325 and the Council of Constantinople in 381 declared that the Son is of the same essence as the Father, and that the three Persons are one God. The East and West branches of the church later disagreed as to how the Holy Spirit proceeds from the other Divine Persons. The Eastern Church held that the Son comes from the Father, and that the Spirit comes from the Father through the Son. The Western Church held that the Spirit comes from Father and Son together. A special activity has been ascribed to each of the Persons. The Father creates, the Son became human, and the Spirit makes holy.   Joseph M. Hallman

See also **Nicene councils; Arianism.**

Trip. See LSD.

Trip hammer is a high-speed, power-driven hammer. Machinists use it to shape small forgings, such as edged tools, ornamental ironwork, and small, light machine parts. The trip hammer gets its name from the way it operates. A *cam* (projection on a wheel) raises it, then loosens its hold on it (*trips*), and releases the hammer.

Tripe is a meat that comes from the stomach walls of cattle. Such animals have stomachs that consist of four compartments. Tripe is produced from the first two compartments. Most tripe is white, and the meat has little taste. *Honeycomb tripe,* which comes from the lining of the second compartment, has a netlike appearance.

Tripe is sold canned, fresh, frozen, or pickled. People bake, broil, or fry tripe, or they cook it in water. Meatpackers sometimes use tripe as one of the ingredients of sausage.   Donald H. Beermann

Triple Alliance was a defense agreement among Austria-Hungary, Germany, and Italy. It lasted from 1882 until World War I. The three nations agreed to help one another in case of attack by two or more great powers. Austria-Hungary and Germany also agreed to help Italy in case of attack by France, and Italy agreed to help Germany if France attacked that nation. The three countries renewed the alliance several times, the last time in 1912. See also **Bismarck, Otto von** (Bismarck's diplomacy); **World War I** (A system of military alliances).

Stefan T. Possony

Triple Entente, *ahn TAHNT,* means *triple,* or *three-fold, agreement.* When World War I broke out in 1914, the chief powers of Europe formed two opposing groups. Germany, Austria-Hungary, and Italy made up the Triple Alliance, while Great Britain, France, and Russia formed the Triple Entente (see **Triple Alliance**).

The Triple Entente was only an informal grouping when first formed. But between 1912 and 1914, it became an effective diplomatic combination. After the outbreak of war, the Entente Powers signed the Declaration of London, in which each power agreed not to make a separate peace. This act transformed the Triple Entente into a formal union.   Dwight E. Lee

See also **World War I** (A system of military alliances).

Triple jump. See Track and field.

Triplets. See Multiple birth.

Tripoli, *TRIHP uh lee* (pop. 175,000), is the second largest city in Lebanon. Only Beirut has more people. Tripoli's name in Arabic is Tarabulus. A seaport and industrial center, Tripoli lies on Lebanon's northwest coast, at the eastern end of the Mediterranean Sea. For location, see **Lebanon** (map). The city's chief industries include trade and services; petroleum refining; the manufacture of furniture, soap, and textiles; and sponge fishing. Citrus fruits are grown in and around Tripoli.

The Castle of St. Gilles, built by crusaders before A.D. 1200, overlooks the city. The Teylan Mosque, a Tripoli landmark built in the traditional Arab style, dates from 1336. Tripoli's name, which means *Three Cities,* is related to its founding. Colonists from three Phoenician cities—Aradus, Sidon, and Tyre—founded the city in the 300's B.C.   Elsa Marston Harik and Iliya Harik

Tripoli, *TRIHP uh lee* (pop. 551,477), is the capital and largest city of Libya. Its Arabic name is Tarabulus. Tripoli lies in northern Libya, along the Mediterranean Sea. For location, see **Libya** (map).

Tripoli has a fine harbor and is a shipping center. It is also a trading center for a farming region. Tripoli's industries include oil refining, food processing, and the production of such handicrafts as woven carpets and leather goods. The old city center of Tripoli is surrounded by stone walls. It features a Roman arch that dates from the A.D. 100's and a palace and garden built in the 1500's. Since the 1970's, many modern high-rise buildings have been constructed in the city.

Tripoli was founded by Phoenicians, probably in the 600's B.C. It was originally called Oea. It was later renamed Tripoli, which means *Three Cities.* The name refers to the ancient district of Tripoli, which included three cities—Oea, Leptis Magna (now Lebda), and Sabrata. From the mid-1500's to 1911, Tripoli was part of the Ottoman Empire—which was centered in what is now Turkey—and the capital of the surrounding province called Tripolitania. But the local rulers in Tripoli had almost complete freedom during much of the period. Attacks by Barbary pirates of North Africa on U.S. shipping led to a war between the United States and Tripoli in 1801. Italy conquered Tripoli in 1911 and ruled it until World War II (1939-1945). Leon Carl Brown

See also **Barbary States; Jefferson, Thomas** (War with Tripoli).

Triticale, *TRIHT uh KAY lee,* is a grain produced by crossbreeding wheat and rye. It has a high nutritional content because it contains more usable protein than either wheat or rye. The plant stands from 18 to 41 inches (45 to 105 centimeters) tall and has 6 to 10 long, narrow leaves. The head consists of many spikelets, each of which holds three to five kernels of grain.

Botanists first crossbred wheat and rye in 1876. This process yielded a hybrid plant that could not produce seeds. In 1937, scientists discovered that treating seedlings of wheat-rye crosses with a chemical called *colchicine* made the plants fertile.

The first triticale breeding program was set up in Sweden in the mid-1930's. By the 1950's, many countries, including the United States and Canada, had such programs. These programs have developed many varieties of the grain. Someday, triticale may become an important food in countries not suited for wheat production. Some varieties can grow in cold climates and in sandy or acid soils. Others resist rust better than wheat does and produce a higher yield than rye. At higher latitudes, triticale grain yields increase at a greater rate than do wheat yields.

Triticale will probably be used in many countries mainly as an animal feed. It can also serve as a pasture crop. Food companies may use triticale to make flour for bread and cake. Other potential uses for the grain include cereal products and beermaking.

Scientific classification. Triticale is a member of the grass family, Gramineae. It makes up the genus *Triticosecale.*

Robert D. Wych

Tritium, *TRIHT ee uhm,* is a hydrogen isotope used in the release of nuclear energy through fusion, as in the hydrogen bomb. It is three times as heavy as ordinary hydrogen. The name *tritium* comes from the Latin *tri,* meaning *three.* Tritium decays to form helium; half the tritium disintegrates in about 12 years.

See also **Hydrogen; Nuclear weapon.**

Triton, *TRY tuhn,* was a sea god in Greek mythology. He was a *merman,* a creature often portrayed with the body of a man from the waist up and a fish from the waist down. Triton lived with his parents, the sea god Poseidon and his wife, Amphitrite, in their golden palace at the bottom of the sea. Triton often blew his conch shell horn to stir up or calm the seas and rivers.

According to early myths, Triton often befriended passing sailors. He guided the Argonauts, companions of the Greek hero Jason, and gave one of them a clod of earth that later became the island of Thera in the Aegean Sea. In later myths, Triton appeared as a menacing sea monster. The Roman poet Virgil told how Triton drowned Misenus, a human trumpeter who challenged his skill on the conch shell. In some Greek myths, members of a group of minor sea gods who served Poseidon were called Tritons. Nancy Felson-Rubin

See also **Poseidon.**

Triumph, in ancient Rome, was the highest honor given to a victorious general. The word *triumph* probably came through the Etruscan language from *thriambos,* a Greek word that means a procession honoring the god Bacchus.

When a victor received a triumph, he entered Rome in a triumphal car drawn by four horses, and proceeded along the *Via Sacra* (Sacred Way) to the capitol. The senators walked at the head of the procession. Behind them came trumpeters, carriages bearing the spoils of war, oxen to be sacrificed, and captives in chains. Then came the general, crowned with laurel, and his children and friends. The general's soldiers were at the end of the procession, cheering and singing as they marched. In a triumph given to honor a naval commander, nautical trophies were carried.

Under the Empire, only the emperor could receive a triumph. A great general might receive a minor celebration called an *ovation.* Frank C. Bourne

Triumph, Arch of. See Arc de Triomphe.

Triumvirate, *try UHM vuhr iht.* In Roman history, a triumvirate was a group of three men who seized control of the government. Rome had two triumvirates. The first was formed in 60 B.C. It was made up of Julius Caesar, Pompey the Great, and Marcus Licinius Crassus. The second triumvirate was formed in 43 B.C., after Brutus and Cassius had murdered Julius Caesar. Its members were Octavian (Augustus), Marcus Lepidus, and Mark Antony.

The Roman republican form of government almost disappeared while the triumvirates lasted. Both triumvirates ended in civil war to determine the supremacy of one member of the group. In the first war, Caesar defeated Pompey the Great. In the second civil war, Mark Antony was overcome by Octavian, who became Emperor Augustus. Chester G. Starr

See also **Antony, Mark; Augustus; Caesar, Julius; Crassus, Marcus Licinius; Pompey the Great.**

Trogon, *TROH gahn,* is a family of birds. Trogons live in warm regions of both the Eastern and the Western hemispheres. The feathers of adult males shine like metal. The underparts of their bodies are colored red, orange, or yellow. The trogon has a short, strong bill. Two of its toes point forward and two backward. Its feet are small and weak. The female lays two to four white, pale blue, or pale green eggs. The nestlings are naked when hatched. African and Asian trogons feed mostly on insects. American trogons eat fruits and insects. See also Quetzal.

Scientific classification. Trogons make up the trogon family, Trogonidae. The collared trogon is genus *Trogon,* species *T. collaris.* Rodolphe Meyer de Schauensee

Troika, *TROY kuh,* is a Russian word that means *a group of three.* A light, Russian sleigh that is pulled by three horses is called a troika. The term *troika* was applied to a 1960 plan by the Soviet Union to have the United Nations headed by three secretaries-general instead of one. See also **Cold War** (The troika proposal).

Trojan horse. See Trojan War; Mythology (picture).

Trojan War was a conflict in which ancient Greece defeated the city of Troy. The war, which probably took place during the mid-1200's B.C., inspired many leading works of classical literature. Some of the events that occurred during and after the Trojan War became the subject of three great epic poems. These poems are the *Iliad* and the *Odyssey,* attributed to the Greek poet Homer, and the *Aeneid* by the Roman poet Virgil. The heroes and victims of the war were portrayed in such Greek tragedies as *Agamemnon* by Aeschylus, *Ajax* by Sophocles, and *The Trojan Women* by Euripides.

Scholars know little about the actual Trojan War. Their knowledge of the war comes chiefly from the epics of Homer and Virgil, which are largely fictional. These poetic accounts combine historical facts with material from Greek legends and myths. But archaeologists have found historical evidence in the ruins of Troy and other cities that confirms certain events described by the poets.

The beginning of the war. According to ancient Greek myths, the Trojan War resulted from an incident at the wedding feast of Peleus, the king of Thessaly, and Thetis, a sea goddess. All the gods and goddesses of Mount Olympus had been invited except Eris, the goddess of discord. Eris was offended and tried to stir up trouble among the guests at the feast. She sent a golden apple inscribed "For the most beautiful." Three goddesses—Hera, Athena, and Aphrodite—each claimed the apple, and a quarrel began. Paris, the son of King Priam of Troy, judged the dispute. He awarded the apple to Aphrodite because she had promised him Helen, the most beautiful woman in the world.

Helen was already married to King Menelaus of Sparta. But when Paris visited her, she fled with him to Troy. Menelaus and his brother, Agamemnon, organized a large Greek expedition against Troy to win Helen back. The Greek army included such heroes as Achilles, Ajax the Greater, Nestor, and Odysseus (Ulysses in Latin).

The siege of Troy. The Greek army laid siege to Troy for 10 years but could not conquer the city. The *Iliad* describes some of the events that occurred during the last year of the struggle. The war began to go badly for the Greeks after Achilles, their bravest warrior, left the battlefield. Achilles refused to fight because Agamemnon, the Greek commander, had insulted him. The Trojans, led by Hector, drove the Greeks back to their ships. Achilles finally returned to combat after his best friend, Patroclus, had been slain by Hector. Achilles killed Hector to avenge Patroclus' death.

The *Iliad* ends with Hector's burial, and Greek legends relate events that followed. The Trojans received help from their allies, the Ethiopians and an army of women warriors called Amazons. But Achilles enabled the Greeks to defeat their enemies by killing Penthesilea, the queen of the Amazons, and Memnon, the king of the Ethiopians. Paris, aided by the god Apollo, later wounded Achilles fatally.

The fall of Troy is described in the *Aeneid.* The Greeks built a huge wooden horse, which has become known as the *Trojan horse,* and placed it outside the walls of Troy. Odysseus and other warriors hid inside the horse while the rest of the Greek army sailed away.

The prophetess Cassandra and the priest Laocoön warned the Trojans against taking the horse into their city. But Sinon, a Greek prisoner, persuaded them that the horse was sacred and would bring the protection of the gods. The Trojans then pulled the horse into Troy. That night they fell asleep after celebrating their apparent victory. Odysseus and his companions then crept

out of the horse and opened the city gates for the rest of their warriors, who had returned from a nearby island.

The Greeks took back Helen, slaughtered almost all the Trojans, and burned Troy. According to the *Aeneid,* the few Trojan survivors included the warrior Aeneas, whose descendants founded Rome.   Robert J. Lenardon

Related articles in *World Book* include:

Additional resources

Coolidge, Olivia E. *The Trojan War.* Houghton, 1952.
Wood, Michael. *In Search of the Trojan War.* Facts on File, 1985. For older readers.

Troll. See Fairy.
Trolley. See Electric railroad; Streetcar.
Trollope, Anthony (1815-1882), was a popular English novelist of the 1800's. He was over 30 years old when he published his first book. But after he started, he wrote with such regularity that his novels and tales fill more than 50 volumes.

Trollope's most famous books are the "Barsetshire Novels." These six stories about life in the imaginary county of Barsetshire, and especially the cathedral city of Barchester, are mildly satirical. But their tone shows Trollope's affectionate tolerance for the weaknesses of his basically generous and well-meaning characters. Trollope had so clear an idea of his creation that he could draw a map of Barsetshire.

The Barsetshire novels are *The Warden* (1855), *Barchester Towers* (1857), *Doctor Thorne* (1858), *Framley Parsonage* (1861), *The Small House at Allington* (1864), and *The Last Chronicle of Barset* (1867). Trollope's other works include social satire novels, such as *The Bertrams* (1859) and *The Way We Live Now* (1875); political novels, such as *The Eustace Diamonds* (1873); and novels of psychological analysis, such as *Cousin Henry* (1879).

Trollope was born in London. In his autobiography, he described his unhappy childhood. His family was poor, and his education was often interrupted by lack of money. Frances Trollope, Anthony's mother, was also a famous writer. She wrote *Domestic Manners of the Americans* (1832) after a visit to the United States. The book sold well, but did not provide enough money to pay the family bills. The Trollopes moved to Bruges, Belgium, to escape their creditors. All his life, Trollope remembered the humiliation of those early years.

Trollope returned to London in 1834. He became a clerk in the post office, where he worked for many years. He designed the red mail boxes that are still used in England. His last years were happy. He died in London of a stroke brought on, it is said, by over-hearty laughter.   James Douglas Merritt

Additional resources

Anthony Trollope. Ed. by Tony Bareham. Barnes & Noble, 1980. A collection of criticism.
Snow, C. P. *Trollope: His Life and Art.* Scribner, 1975.
Trollope, Anthony. *An Autobiography.* First published in 1883, after his death. Now available in many editions.
The Trollope Critics. Ed. by N. John Hall. Barnes & Noble, 1981. A collection of criticism.

Trombone is a brass instrument that consists chiefly of an oblong tube expanded into a bell at one end. It is played by blowing into a cup-shaped mouthpiece and vibrating the lips. Most trombones have a long slide. The player changes tones by tightening the lips and by moving the slide back and forth. A *valve trombone* has three valves instead of a slide. The *tenor trombone* is the most popular type of trombone. The *bass trombone* is larger. It has, in addition to the slide, one or two rotary valves for extending the range downward.

Northwestern University (WORLD BOOK photo by Ted Nielsen)

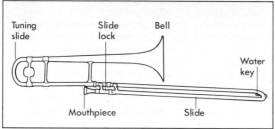

WORLD BOOK illustration by Oxford Illustrators, Ltd.

The trombone is an important brass instrument in both popular and classical music. It has a long slide attached to a tube. A musician plays different notes by moving the slide.

A primitive type of trombone was used as early as 1495 in England. The trombone became a part of symphony orchestras during the 1800's. Today, the instrument is popular in concert, marching, and military bands, and in popular music and jazz.   John Keil Richards

Trona, *TROH nuh,* is one of the most important natural soda minerals. It consists of sodium carbonate, sodium bicarbonate, and water and has the chemical formula $Na_2CO_3 \cdot NaHCO_3 \cdot 2H_2O$. Trona is the main source of soda ash, which is used in the manufacture of chemicals, glass, and paper. Trona is gray or yellowish-white and forms fibrous crystals. It dissolves easily in water, and so it is found at the earth's surface in solid form only in dry regions. Trona also occurs underground and is extracted from *brine* (extremely salty water). The largest pure deposit of trona in the United States lies underground near Green River, Wyo. See also **Wyoming** (The mid-1900's).   Maria Luisa Crawford

Trondheim, *TRAWN haym* (pop. 134,654), is the third largest city in Norway. It lies on the southern shore of Trondheims Fiord, where the Nid River empties into the fiord (see **Norway** [map]).

Trondheim is an important export center for copper

and iron ores, pyrites, wood pulp, timber, and fish. The city was founded in A.D. 998 by King Olav I. The Nidaros Cathedral, one of the finest Norman Gothic buildings in the world, dates back to A.D. 1070. The modern Technical University of Norway is also in Trondheim.
Oscar Svarlien

Tropic bird. See Tropicbird.

Tropic of Cancer is an imaginary line that traces the northern boundary of the earth's Tropical Zone. It marks the farthest limit north of the equator where the sun can appear directly overhead. The line lies 23° 27′ north of the equator. The vertical rays of the sun shine down on the Tropic of Cancer at noon on the day of the summer solstice, which is June 20 or 21.

The Tropic of Cancer passes through many lands with a variety of climates. It crosses Mexico, passes between Florida and Cuba, and crosses the Sahara, Arabia, north-central India, and southern China. It crosses the Pacific Ocean immediately north of the main islands of Hawaii (see **World** [map]). The word *Cancer* means *crab* in Latin, and refers to a constellation. This group of stars is one of the 12 constellations of the zodiac. The position of the Tropic of Cancer on the map was first marked by its location directly beneath the constellation of Cancer. The inclination of the earth to the plane of its orbit determines the position of the constellation. To an observer on the Tropic of Cancer, the North Star appears at an angle of 23° 27′ above the horizon.   Stephen S. Birdsall

See also **Tropics.**

Tropic of Capricorn is an imaginary line that traces the southern boundary of the earth's Tropical Zone. It marks the farthest limit south of the equator where the sun can appear directly overhead. The Tropic of Capricorn lies 23° 27′ south of the equator. The vertical rays of the sun shine on the Tropic of Capricorn at noon on the day of the winter solstice, which is December 21 or 22.

The Tropic of Capricorn crosses northern Chile and Argentina, Paraguay, and southern Brazil in South America. In Africa, it crosses Namibia, Botswana, South Africa, Mozambique, and Madagascar. The Tropic of Capricorn also passes through the middle of Australia (see **World** [map]). The Tropic of Capricorn separates the southern tropics from the South Temperate Belt. The word *Capricorn* comes from the Latin *caper,* meaning *goat,* and *cornu,* meaning *horn.* It refers to a group of stars representing the sign of the zodiac known as Capricorn. The Tropic of Capricorn used to lie directly below this constellation.   Stephen S. Birdsall

See also **Tropics.**

Tropical fish. Many kinds of fish live in the freshwater and saltwater habitats of the tropics. However, the term *tropical fish* is applied particularly to small, brightly colored varieties that breed very rapidly and are popular for home aquariums. Tropical fish are often a little smaller than goldfish, but tropical fish usually range in size from 1 to 12 inches (2.5 to 30 centimeters). About 600 different kinds of tropical fish are kept in home aquariums. Even beginning aquarium hobbyists can keep many kinds of fishes.

Most tropical fish will eat food made from grains, dried shrimp, fish, insects, and aquatic plants. Such food can be purchased in any pet shop. Small pieces of shrimp, oyster, crab, canned fish, boiled fish, and other kinds of fish may also be given. Many tropical fish are *carnivores* (meat-eaters), but sometimes plant-eating fish can be trained to eat such food. Some "hard-to-keep" saltwater fishes require special foods, such as sponges and live coral, but many species eat a wide variety of foods. Some people raise small worms to feed their pet fish. A good rule is to feed only the amount that the fish will clean up promptly because uneaten food drops to the bottom and decays. This makes the water foul and may kill the fish.

A tropical fish aquarium should be covered with a flat pane of glass to control the temperature. This also keeps the fish from leaping out of the aquarium. Water plants should be grown because they keep the water in better condition and produce oxygen for the fish to breathe.

The most common and best-known tropical fish is the *guppy*. It comes from fresh waters of the West Indies and South America. The female guppy is about $1\frac{1}{2}$ inches (3.8 centimeters) long, and the male is even smaller. The female is gray, but the male is brilliantly rainbow-hued. Guppies breed when they are about 3 months old and bear their young alive. Each female guppy produces from 20 to 50 young. See **Guppy.**

Other popular, freshwater tropical fish that bear live young are the *swordtail,* the *platyfish,* and the *black molly.* Some tropical fish that bear their young in eggs are the *barbs, danios, rasboras, characins,* and *cichlids.* The various *labyrinth fishes* are so named because they have a cavity with many branches in their head, usually above the gills. The fish store air in this cavity and use it as an accessory breathing organ. Some saltwater fish, such as *clownfish* and some *damsels,* have been successfully bred and raised in home aquariums.

Scientific classification. Most live-bearing, freshwater tropical fish belong to the live-bearer family, Poeciliidae. The guppy is *Poeciliidae reticulata.* Leighton R. Taylor, Jr.

See also **Fish** (pictures: Fish of coral reefs; Fish of tropical fresh waters); **Angelfish; Flyingfish, Aquarium.**

Additional resources

Halstead, Bruce W., and Landa, B. L. *Tropical Fish: A Guide for Setting Up and Maintaining an Aquarium for Tropical Fish and Other Animals.* Western Publishing, 1975. Suitable for younger readers.
Popular Tropical Fish for Your Aquarium. Ed. by Cliff Harrison. TAB, 1982.

Tropical fruit. See Fruit (How horticulturists classify fruits).

Tropical plant. See Tropical rain forest.

Tropical rain forest is a forest of tall trees in a region of year-round warmth and plentiful rainfall. Almost all such forests lie near the equator. They occupy large regions in Africa, Asia, and Central and South America, and on Pacific islands. The largest tropical rain forest is the Amazon rain forest, also called the *selva.* It covers about a third of South America. Tropical rain forests stay green throughout the year.

A tropical rain forest has more kinds of trees than any other area in the world. Scientists have counted 179 species in one $2\frac{1}{2}$-acre (1-hectare) area in South America. Most forests of this size in the United States have fewer than seven species. About half of the world's species of plants and animals also live in tropical rain forests. More species of amphibians, birds, insects, mammals, and reptiles live in tropical rain forests than anywhere else.

The tallest trees of a rain forest may grow as tall as 200 feet (61 meters). The *crowns* (tops) of other trees form a covering of leaves about 100 or 150 feet (30 to 46 meters) above the ground. This covering is called the *upper canopy.* The crowns of smaller trees form one or two *lower canopies.* All the canopies shade the forest floor so that it receives less than 1 per cent as much sunlight as does the upper canopy.

Most areas of the forest floor receive so little light that few bushes or herbs can grow there. As a result, a person can easily walk through most parts of a tropical rain forest. Areas of dense growth called *jungles* occur within a tropical rain forest in areas where much sunlight reaches the ground. Most jungles grow near broad rivers or in former clearings. See **Jungle.**

The temperature in a rain forest rarely rises above 93° F. (34° C) or drops below 68° F. (20° C). In many cases, the average temperature of the hottest month is only 2° to 5° F. (1° to 3° C) higher than the average temperature of the coldest month. At least 80 inches (200 centimeters) of rain falls yearly in a tropical rain forest. Thundershowers may occur more than 200 days a year. The air beneath the lower canopy is almost always humid. The trees themselves give off water through the pores of their leaves. This process, called *transpiration,* may account for as much as half of the rain in the Amazon rain forest.

All tropical rain forests resemble one another. But each of the three largest ones—the American, the African, and the Asian—has a different group of animal and plant species. For instance, each rain forest has many species of monkeys, all of which differ from the species of the other two rain forests. In addition, different areas of the same rain forest may have different species. For example, many kinds of trees that grow in the mountains of the Amazon rain forest do not grow in the lowlands of that forest. For illustrations of rain forests, see **Plant** (Where plants live) and **Tree** (Trees around the world). For illustrations of some of the animals that live in rain forests, see **Animal** (Animals of the tropical forests).

Plant life. A tropical rain forest is always green. Most trees in the forest lose old leaves and grow new ones throughout the year. But certain species of trees may lose all of their leaves for a short time during the year. Different kinds of trees bear flowers and fruit at various times of the year. Thus, some kind of tree is in bloom or in fruit at any time of the year. Some short trees bear fruit on the trunk or on large, low branches. Some tall trees bear large fruit on long, drooping, ropelike stalks.

Tropical rain forest trees include some species of great beauty and others that provide fruit, timber, and other useful products. Cassias, dhaks, shellseeds, and tabebuias bear bright-colored flowers. But most rain forest trees have smaller, less noticeable flowers, and the canopy always appears mostly green. Brazil nuts, cashews, durians, mangosteens, sapodillas, and many kinds of figs and palms yield fruit. Valuable timber comes from balsas, brazilwoods, lauans, logwoods, mahoganies, and rosewoods. Kapoks bear fruits that contain a fluffy fiber used to stuff life jackets and upholstery. Cinchonas provide the drug quinine. Curare, another important drug, comes from various woody vines that grow in a tropical rain forest.

In a tropical rain forest, many plants grow on tree branches, where they receive more sunlight than they

Squirrel monkeys live only in the tropical rain forests of Central and South America. These monkeys scamper along tree branches and climbing vines.

Huge growths called _buttresses_ extend from the trunk to the roots of many trees in tropical rain forests. The buttresses may help support the trees. Yagua Indians hunt small birds with blowguns in the upper Amazon Valley of South America, *right.*

would on the ground. Such plants, called *epiphytes* or *air plants,* include ferns, mosses, orchids, and bromeliads. Climbing plants called *lianas* twine around tree trunks and branches. Some lianas form loops and knots as they grow toward the sunlight. See **Epiphyte.**

Several kinds of *strangler* trees grow in rain forests. These trees start life as air plants. But unlike other species of air plants, they develop roots that reach down to the ground. The roots surround the tree on which the strangler lives. In time, the strangler may kill the other tree by depriving it of food, light, and water.

In a tropical rain forest, most plant *nutrients* (the chemicals necessary for growth) are locked up in the liv-

Tropical rain forests

Tropical rain forests lie chiefly near the equator. These areas receive some of the world's heaviest rainfall.

ing vegetation. Small amounts of nutrients are stored in a thin layer of soil near the surface, where decaying vegetation mixes with the soil. The roots of most rain forest trees remain close to the supply of nutrients near the surface. In some species, the roots form large growths called *buttresses* that extend between the roots and the trunk. The buttresses may help keep the trees upright.

A tropical rain forest has no dominant species of trees. Most kinds of trees are widely scattered throughout the forest and depend on animals for pollination. By contrast, in nontropical forests, certain tree species dominate and pollination occurs chiefly by wind.

Animal life. A great variety of animals lives in a tropical rain forest. Many of these animals spend their lives in the trees and never descend to the ground. The fruits and nuts of the upper and lower canopy furnish food for bats, gibbons, monkeys, squirrels, parrots, and toucans. Sloths and some monkeys feed on the leaves. Hummingbirds and sunbirds sip nectar from flowers. Frogs, lizards, and snakes also dwell among the branches. Large birds and large snakes prey on the smaller animals.

Many canopy animals are especially suited to treetop life. Flying lemurs and flying squirrels glide from tree to tree. Galagos and marmosets jump from branch to branch. Several kinds of anteaters, monkeys, opossums, and porcupines sometimes hang by their tail.

Antelope, deer, hogs, tapirs, and many kinds of rodents roam the forest floor. They feed on roots, seeds, and leaves, and also on fruit that drops to the ground.

Chimpanzees, coatis, and several members of the cat family live on the floor and in the trees. Ants may be found at all levels in a rain forest. Bees, butterflies, mosquitoes, moths, termites, and spiders are also abundant.

People and the rain forests. Through the years, few people have dwelt in tropical rain forests. Most such people clear small areas and plant crops there. They chop down the trees, burn them, and plant seeds among the ashes. But after a few years, the thin layer of soil no longer provides good harvests. The farmers then move elsewhere and begin the process all over again. Such farming, called *slash-and-burn cultivation*, can support only a small population.

A few groups of rain forest people practice no agriculture. For example, the Pygmies of the Central African rain forest live by hunting wild animals, gathering wild plants, and trading with agricultural tribes.

Today, the rapid growth of the world population and the increasing demands for natural resources threaten many tropical rain forests. People have destroyed large areas of rain forests by clearing land for farms and cities. Huge mining, ranching, and timber projects also have caused much damage. Scientists estimate that from $13\frac{1}{2}$ million to 55 million acres (5.5 million to 22 million hectares) of tropical rain forests are destroyed yearly. They fear that further forest destruction will lead to the elimination of hundreds of thousands of species of plants and animals.   Thomas E. Lovejoy

See also the sections on plant and animal life in the articles on **Africa, Asia, North America,** and **South America.**

Additional resources

Batten, Mary. *The Tropical Forest: Ants, Ants, Animals and Plants.* T. Y. Crowell, 1973.
Forsyth, Adrian, and Miyata, Kenneth. *Tropical Nature.* Scribner, 1984.
Ross, Wilda S. *The Rain Forest: What Lives There.* Coward, 1977. For younger readers.

Tropicbird is any of three species of sea birds found in tropical regions. Tropicbirds are also called *boatswains.* They eat fish, which they catch by diving straight down into the water from the air.

Tropicbirds' feathers are mainly white. They have two extremely long, slender middle tailfeathers. The *red-billed tropicbird* lives in tropical parts of the Atlantic, Indian, and Pacific oceans. It has a coral-red bill, black wing tips, and many black bars across its back. The bird

is nearly 40 inches (100 centimeters) long, including its middle tailfeathers, which measure about 24 inches (61 centimeters). Other kinds of tropicbirds are the *white-tailed* and the *red-tailed.*

Tropicbirds nest in holes, in cracks in rocks, or on sand. On land, a tropicbird shuffles along on its breast with outstretched wings because it cannot stand.

Scientific classification. Tropicbirds make up the family Phaethontidae. The red-billed tropicbird is classified as *Phaethon aethereus;* the white-tailed is *P. lepturus;* and the red-tailed is *P. rubricauda.*   James J. Dinsmore

See also **Bird** (picture: Birds of the ocean).

Tropics are the regions of the earth that lie within about 1,600 miles (2,570 kilometers) north and 1,600 miles south of the equator. Two imaginary lines, the Tropic of Cancer and the Tropic of Capricorn, form the boundaries of the tropics. The Tropic of Cancer is 23° 27' north of the equator, and the Tropic of Capricorn is 23° 27' south of the equator. These lines mark the northernmost and southernmost places on the earth where the sun ever shines directly overhead.

Most places in the tropics have warm to hot temperatures the year around. Tropical places near sea level are hot because every day the sun's rays shine almost straight down at noon. Such direct rays produce higher temperatures than do slanted rays.

The temperature does not change much in the tropics because the amount of daylight differs little from season to season. At the equator, the sun shines about 12 hours a day. At the edges of the tropics, daylight varies from about $10\frac{1}{2}$ hours a day in winter to about $13\frac{1}{2}$ hours a day in summer. Places at the edges of the tropics have cool periods in winter. Tropical places at high altitudes are cool because the temperature drops about $3\frac{1}{2}$° F. per 1,000 feet (2° C per 300 meters) of elevation.

Many tropical areas have definite rainy and dry seasons. Most places near the equator get much rain during all seasons and are covered by tropical rain forests (see **Tropical rain forest**). Farther to the north and south, one or two short dry seasons occur yearly. Such areas have forests of trees that lose their leaves during these dry seasons. Areas even farther from the equator have one long dry season each year. These areas are covered by *savannas* (grasslands with scattered trees and shrubs).   Stephen S. Birdsall

For information on how people live in the tropics, see **Africa** (Ways of life south of the Sahara); **Asia** (Way of

WORLD BOOK map

The tropics

The tropics, shown on the map at the right, lie on both sides of the equator. They are bounded by two imaginary lines called the Tropic of Cancer and the Tropic of Capricorn. Most tropical places are warm to hot the year around.

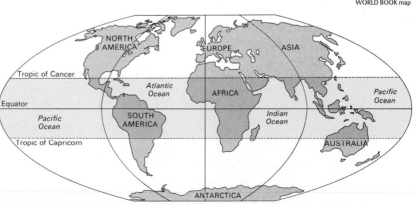

life in Southeast Asia); **Indian, American** (Indians of the tropical forest); **Latin America** (Way of life). See also **Fish** (pictures); **Jungle; Savanna; Tropic of Cancer; Tropic of Capricorn.**

Tropism, *TROH pihz uhm,* is a bending movement in living things caused by an outside *stimulus* (signal). For example, sunlight causes plant leaves and stems to bend toward it. A tropism results from differences in the growth rate of various parts of an *organ* (a body structure) when the stimulus is present. The bending usually is slow. For example, some tropisms in plants take from one hour to several days for completion. They occur only in young tissues.

Tropisms are named for the stimulus that causes them. For example, *geotropism* is bending caused by gravity, *phototropism* is bending caused by light, and *hydrotropism* is bending caused by moisture. Tropisms may be *positive* (bending toward the stimulus) or *negative* (bending away from the stimulus). Studies of tropisms led to the discovery of *auxins,* the plant hormones that control growth (see **Auxin**).   Neal D. Buffaloe

Troposphere, *TROH puh sfihr,* is the layer of the atmosphere closest to the earth. We live there, and nearly all the earth's weather occurs there. The upper boundary of the troposhere is the *tropopause.* The height of the tropopause varies. The tropopause lies about 10 miles (16 kilometers) over the equator and about 6 miles (10 kilometers) over the North and South poles. The *stratosphere* lies above the tropopause, followed by the *mesosphere* and the *thermosphere.*

Within the troposphere, the temperature of the air generally decreases as the altitude increases. The temperature of the troposphere also varies with latitude. The temperature averages about 59° F. (15° C) near the earth's surface and drops to about −85° F. (−65° C) at 10 miles (16 kilometers) above the surface. At the equator, the tropopause can become as cold as −112° F. (−80° C). Above the tropopause, the temperature stops decreasing with altitude.

The temperature decrease at higher altitudes in the troposphere plays an important part in changes in the weather. Air in the troposphere can mix because cold, *dense* (heavy) air lies above warmer, less dense air. If the air starts moving upward, it continues to rise because it remains warmer and less dense than its surroundings. Sinking air remains colder than its surroundings and continues to sink. These tropospheric mixings are the major weather systems of the earth. Rising air forms clouds and rain, and sinking air brings fair weather.

The troposphere helps maintain the earth's climate and helps keep the earth warm. Most sunlight passes through the troposphere to heat the earth's surface. This heat energy then radiates from the surface and escapes into space. But some energy is trapped by tropospheric gases—mainly water vapor and carbon dioxide—and by clouds. This trapping of heat energy is called the *greenhouse effect* (see **Greenhouse effect**).

Veerabhadran Ramanathan

See also **Air; Mesosphere; Stratosphere; Thermosphere.**

Trotsky, *TRAHT skee,* **Leon** (1879-1940), also spelled *Trotzky,* was a leader of the Bolshevik revolution in Russia (see **Bolsheviks**). While Lenin lived, Trotsky was the second most powerful man in Russia. After Lenin's

death, Trotsky lost the leadership to Joseph Stalin. Trotsky was later exiled. Until his violent death, Trotsky waged a bitter fight against Stalin from abroad. See **Lenin, V. I.; Stalin, Joseph.**

Trotsky was born Lev Davidovich Bronstein in the Ukraine of well-to-do parents. After two years of revolutionary activity as a Social Democrat, he was arrested in 1898. He escaped from Siberian exile in 1902 and went to London, where he met Lenin. He returned to Russia to take an active part in the revolution in 1905.

United Press Int.

Leon Trotsky

Trotsky was jailed for his leadership in the Saint Petersburg (now Leningrad) Soviet of 1905. But he escaped in 1907. For 10 years he was a revolutionary writer and editor in western Europe. During World War I, he was expelled from France and Spain, and came to New York, where he received the news of the czar's downfall in 1917. He returned to Russia. With Lenin, he successfully plotted the seizure of power that brought about a Bolshevik government in November 1917 (October on the old Russian calendar). Trotsky became the first Soviet commissar of foreign affairs, and was soon the commissar of war.

In the civil war of 1918-1920, Trotsky was an efficient organizer of the triumphant Red army. After Lenin's death, many believed that Trotsky would be the new head of the Soviet government, but he was outsmarted by Stalin. Trotsky was expelled from the Communist Party in 1927, and the next year was exiled to Soviet Central Asia. He was deported to Turkey in 1929. He later moved to Norway and then to Mexico.

By 1940, Stalin apparently regretted his "leniency" with Trotsky. His secret police sent an agent to Mexico, and Trotsky was murdered there. Trotsky died on Aug. 21, 1940. See also **Union of Soviet Socialist Republics** (The October Revolution).   Albert Parry

Additional resources

Ali, Tariq. *Trotsky for Beginners.* Pantheon, 1980. For younger readers.
Deutscher, Isaac. *The Prophet Armed: Trotsky, 1879-1921.* Oxford, 1954. *The Prophet Unarmed: Trotsky, 1921-1929.* 1959. *The Prophet Outcast: Trotsky, 1929-1940.* 1963.
Howe, Irving. *Leon Trotsky.* Viking, 1978.

Troubadour, *TROO buh dawr,* was one of a large group of poet-musicians who flourished in southern France in the 1100's and 1200's. The word comes from the Latin *tropare* (to compose). Many scholars believe the troubadours may have modeled their lyric verse on the works of Spanish Arab poets and classical Roman poets such as Ovid.

Troubadours composed poetry in a Romance language called Provençal, or *langue d'oc.* The *canso d'amor* (love song) was one of the rich and varied poetic forms used by troubadours. In the *canso,* the poet imagines the lady of his desires as the model of virtue, and dedicates his talents to singing her praises. The troubadours' praise of physical love stood in direct contrast to

Some kinds of trout

True trout

All true trout, also known as black-spotted trout, have dark markings on a light background. The rainbow trout, *below,* like every true trout of North America, originally lived only in the waters of the western half of the continent.

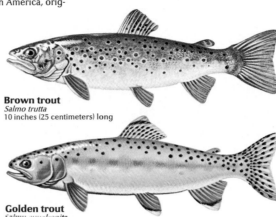

Brown trout
Salmo trutta
10 inches (25 centimeters) long

Golden trout
Salmo aguabonita
10 inches (25 centimeters) long

Bill Noel Kleeman, Tom Stack & Assoc.

Other trout

Other trout are distinguished from true trout by their light red, pink, or cream-colored spots. These fish include the brook trout, *below,* a traditional favorite of anglers; the bull trout, *top right;* and the lake trout, *bottom right.*

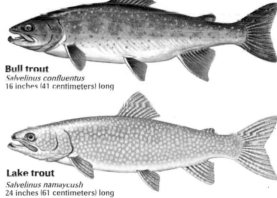

Bull trout
Salvelinus confluentus
16 inches (41 centimeters) long

Lake trout
Salvelinus namaycush
24 inches (61 centimeters) long

Treat Davidson, NAS

WORLD BOOK illustrations by James Teason and John F. Eggert

traditional Christian morality. Their ideal of love and their praise of women influenced many writers, including Dante and Petrarch.   Richard O'Gorman

See also **Knights and knighthood** (Knighthood in literature); **Minnesinger; Storytelling** (The Middle Ages); **Trouvère.**

Trout is a fish closely related to salmon, whitefish, and chars. Trout are native to cool waters of the Northern Hemisphere and have been introduced to cool waters throughout the world. Most species of trout spend their entire lives in freshwater streams and lakes. Some species migrate to the ocean to feed and grow and return to fresh water to *spawn* (lay eggs). Trout are prized both as sport fish and as food fish.

Kinds of trout

About 10 species of fish in North America are commonly called trout. All trout have strong teeth and streamlined bodies with small scales. A small, fleshy fin called an *adipose fin* grows on the back near the tail fin. True trout belong to the fish *genus* (group) known as *Salmo.* Atlantic salmon are also members of this genus. Other trout belong to the genus *Salvelinus,* which also includes chars.

True trout have dark spots on their bodies. The best-known species is the *rainbow trout.* This fish is native to western North America and has been introduced to many other areas. It has black spots on the upper body and the tail and a brilliant reddish band along each side. Rainbow trout that live in the ocean and return to fresh water to spawn are called *steelhead trout.* In the sea, these fish become a steely blue.

Several species of true trout live only in waters of western North America. The *cutthroat trout* ranges from southern Alaska to northern California and in the Rocky Mountains region from Canada to New Mexico. It gets its name from a red-orange slash on each side of the lower jaw. Other Western species include the *golden trout* of the California mountains, the *Apache trout* of Arizona, and the *Gila trout* of Arizona and New Mexico.

The *brown trout* has been introduced throughout North America. It is native to Europe and western Asia. The brown trout's body has dark brown or black spots, many of which are surrounded by pale halos. The tail is only slightly forked. This trout may have red or orange spots, surrounded by pale halos, along the sides of the body.

Other trout include the *brook trout,* the *bull trout,* and the *lake trout.* These fish generally have light red, pink, or cream-colored spots. The front edge of the lower fins is white. The brook trout has dark, wavy lines or blotches on the upper fins and tail. It originally was found only in streams in eastern North America. The bull trout lives in waters of the Pacific Northwest. The lake trout inhabits deep lakes and rivers in northern North America. It generally has a gray-green body and a deeply forked tail. Lake trout are the largest species of trout. A lake trout measuring 4 feet 2 inches (1.27 meters) long and weighing 102 pounds (46.3 kilograms) was taken from Lake Athabaska in Saskatchewan, Canada. It is the largest trout ever caught.

The life of a trout

Most trout spawn in streams or rivers, but some spawn in lakes with gravel bottoms and good water flow. Trout spawn in spring or autumn depending on the species.

The spawning behavior of rainbow trout is typical of that of other trout species. In early spring, rainbow trout move upstream to a spawning area. The female chooses a suitable site, usually a shallow, gravel area at the beginning of a stretch of choppy water. There, the female turns on her side and beats her tail up and down, scooping out a shallow nest called a *redd.* After the redd is prepared, the female positions herself over it. The male courts her by swimming closely alongside her and quivering his body. When the female is ready to spawn, she moves to the bottom of the redd and presses her belly against the gravel. The male positions himself close to her. As the female releases eggs, the male releases sperm that fertilize the eggs.

After the eggs have been fertilized, the female covers them with gravel. The eggs usually hatch in about 2 months. After the young hatch, they move up through the gravel into the water.

Young trout eat mainly *invertebrates* (animals without backbones), including insects. Mature trout also feed on other fish and on crayfish. They occasionally eat young birds, lizards, or other animals that fall into the water. The life span of trout varies among species. Rainbow trout live up to 11 years and lake trout up to at least 25 years.

Trout fishing

All trout species are valued as sport fish. The rainbow trout and the cutthroat trout are especially prized because of their fighting ability and their spectacular leaps when hooked. The brook trout, another spirited fighter, also is a favorite among fishing enthusiasts. Lake trout are usually taken by *trolling* (trailing a line behind a

boat) or by dropping a line through the ice in winter.

Some trout species are important commercially as food. Each year, commercial fishing crews catch great numbers of lake trout and steelhead trout. Rainbow trout and brook trout are raised in hatcheries and sold for food.

Scientific classification. Trout belong to the trout family, Salmonidae. True trout are in the genus *Salmo,* and other trout belong to the genus *Salvelinus.* The rainbow trout is *Salmo gairdneri.* The brook trout is *Salvelinus fontinalis.*

David W. Greenfield

See also **Fish** (Pictures: A leaping trout; Fish of temperate fresh waters; How a fish develops; How fish reproduce).

Trout lily. See Dogtooth violet.

Trouvère, *troo VAIR* or *troo VEHR,* was one of a group of lyric poets who flourished in northern France in the 1100's and 1200's. The word comes from an Old French word meaning *to compose.* The Trouvères composed their poems in an Old French dialect, called *langue d'oïl.* They were strongly influenced by the style and subject matter of the troubadours of southern France. Like the troubadours, the trouvères wrote *chansons d'amor* (love songs).   Richard O'Gorman

See also **Troubadour.**

Trovatore, Il. See Opera (*Trovatore, Il*); Verdi, Giuseppe.

Troy, also called Ilium, was an ancient city in Asia Minor (now Turkey) that was made famous in the legends of early Greece. The *Iliad* and the *Odyssey,* epics attributed to the Greek poet Homer, and the *Aeneid,* an epic written by the Roman poet Virgil, tell a story about Troy that is probably only partly true. The city's two names come from Ilus, its legendary founder, and Tros, the father of Ilus.

The legendary Troy was a mighty city ruled by King Priam. The king's son Paris judged a beauty contest between the goddesses Hera, Athena, and Aphrodite. He chose Aphrodite as the winner because she promised to give him the most beautiful woman in the world as his wife. Soon after the contest, Paris visited Menelaus, the king of Sparta. Paris fell in love with Menelaus' wife, Helen, who was known as the most beautiful woman in the world. Paris took Helen to Troy, and thereby angered Menelaus.

The people of the mainland of Greece, called *Achaeans* by Homer, swore revenge on Paris and the people of Troy. The Greeks sent a great naval expedition to Troy. The expedition was led by Agamemnon, Menelaus' brother, and included Achilles, Odysseus (Ulysses in Latin), and many other Greek heroes.

The Greeks besieged Troy for 10 years. But they could not capture the city, which was protected by high stone walls. Finally, Odysseus ordered workers to build a huge wooden horse, in which some Greek soldiers hid. The rest of the Greeks then pretended to sail away, leaving the horse standing outside the city walls.

The curious Trojans dragged the wooden horse inside the city, though Laocoön, a Trojan priest, warned them not to do so. That night, the Greek soldiers crept out of the horse, opened the city gates, and let the rest of the Greek forces into Troy. The Greeks massacred the people of Troy and looted and burned the city. Only Aeneas, the hero of Virgil's *Aeneid,* and a few other Trojans escaped. Paris was killed in the war, and Helen returned to Menelaus.

The real Troy. Apart from the legends, little is known about the history of Troy. Archaeologists have learned that Troy was founded in the early Bronze Age, which began about 3000 B.C. in Asia Minor. The city stood on a high point of a fertile plain in what is now northwestern Turkey. It was near the southern end of the *Hellespont,* a strait now called the Dardanelles. Archaeologists have discovered that nine cities were built on the site of Troy. Each successive city was built on the ruins of the one before it.

The second Troy and the sixth one were especially wealthy cities. The Trojans farmed, bred and raised horses, herded sheep, and produced woolen goods. They traded with the Mycenaeans, who lived in Greece, and with other people who lived along the Aegean coast of Asia Minor.

Scholars know little about the actual Trojan War. Archaeologists have found evidence that the Greeks may have attacked and destroyed Troy in a great expedition similar to the one described in the *Iliad.* However, no one knows the cause of the war. Greek scholars believed that Troy fell about 1184 B.C. Many archaeologists think that the seventh city on the site of Troy was the one written about in ancient Greek literature. These scholars believe that the city was destroyed about 1250 B.C.

The archaeological Troy. The first archaeologist to study Troy was a German named Heinrich Schliemann. Other persons had noted that a small mound about 4 miles (6 kilometers) from the Dardanelles seemed to fit the geographical location of Troy described in the *Iliad.* The mound was called *Hissarlik.* Schliemann began digging there in 1870. He found evidence that several cities had been built on the site over a long period. Near the bottom of the excavation, he discovered the ruins of an ancient city with massive walls, well-built houses, and hidden treasures of gold and silver. Schliemann mistakenly believed this city, which he called Troy II, was the Troy described by Homer.

The German archaeologist Wilhelm Dörpfeld, who had assisted Schliemann, conducted further

WORLD BOOK map

Troy was an ancient city in Asia Minor. Ruins of Troy have yielded historical relics nearly 5,000 years old.

excavations at Troy in the 1890's. He was the first researcher to recognize that nine cities had stood on the site. Dörpfeld believed the sixth was the city of Homer's *Iliad.* This city, called Troy VI, was larger than the earlier ones and was protected by high walls. The houses were large and rectangular and were probably built around a central palace.

In 1932, Carl Blegen, an American scholar from the University of Cincinnati, began a new research expedition at Troy. His study lasted six years and confirmed the findings of Dörpfeld, except that Blegen believed the seventh city was the legendary Troy. According to Blegen, Troy VI represented a major stage in the development of the city, even though it was not the Troy of Greek legends. This stage was marked by the arrival of immigrants who shared many cultural characteristics with the Mycenaeans in Greece. Troy VI was destroyed by an earthquake about 1300 B.C. The next city, which archaeologists called Troy VIIa, had small, crude houses

Detail of *The Burning of Troy* (early 1600's), an oil painting on canvas by an unknown French artist; Blois Museum, France (Lauros/Giraudon)

The fall of Troy was made famous in legends. Greek soldiers hid in a huge wooden horse, and curious Trojans dragged it into the city. The Greeks later crept out and attacked Troy.

Peter Loud,
Robert Harding Picture Library

The site of Troy has the remains of nine successive cities. The stone walls above are from Troy VI, destroyed by an earthquake about 1300 B.C. It was probably not the Troy of legend.

that were crowded together. The city was less prosperous than the earlier Troys. Around 1250 B.C., Troy VIIa was looted and burned. Although Blegen believed that Troy VIIa was the legendary city, archaeologists have not been able to prove that it was.

From about 1100 B.C. to 700 B.C., no one lived at Troy. Some Greek settlers then established a small village there about 700 B.C. The last city on the site, Troy IX, was built in the late 300's B.C. It was called Ilium by the Greeks and Romans. Ilium lasted about 700 years. It was abandoned about A.D. 400, and remained undisturbed until Schliemann discovered it.   Norman A. Doenges

See also **Trojan War** and its list of *Related articles;* **Homer; Schliemann, Heinrich.**

Additional resources

Blegen, Carl W. *Troy and the Trojans.* Praeger, 1963.
Edmonds, I. G. *The Mysteries of Troy.* Thomas Nelson, 1977.
Schliemann, Heinrich. *Ilios: The City and Country of the Trojans.* Arno, 1976. First published in 1881.
Ventura, Piero, and Ceserani, Gian P. *In Search of Troy.* Silver Burdett, 1985. For younger readers.

Troy weight is a standard system used in weighing gold, silver, platinum, and coins. It is also used to weigh jewels, except pearls and diamonds, which are weighed in carats. The name *Troy* comes from *Troyes,* a French town. In the 1300's, Troyes had its own system of weights and measures. In the system of troy weight, the pound contains 12 ounces. The ounce equals 20 pennyweights, and the pennyweight equals 24 grains. The troy pound and the apothecaries' pound both contain 5,760 grains. The pound avoirdupois equals 7,000 grains. The grains in all three systems are equal. The troy pound equals 0.3732 kilogram.   E. G. Straus

See also **Pennyweight; Weights and measures; Apothecaries' weight; Avoirdupois.**

Truce is a short suspension of hostilities between opposing sides in a war. A truce may be called to allow each side to remove wounded from the battlefield, bury the dead, exchange prisoners, or observe a religious holiday. A truce may also be used for brief negotiations. In such cases, the negotiations are usually conducted under a white *flag of truce,* which indicates the peaceful intentions of the participants.

During the early 1000's, Christian clergy of France instituted a custom called the Truce of God. This custom prohibited warfare on weekends and during certain religious observances. Opponents often ignored the truce.

A truce is different from an *armistice.* An armistice is an agreement to stop fighting that covers a longer period of time than a truce. It may even bring a permanent end of the fighting. Often, an armistice leads to a peace treaty that provides a political settlement of the war. The fighting in World War I (1914-1918) ended with an armistice followed by peace treaties. In the Korean War, truce talks were held from July 1951 to July 1953, when an armistice was signed and the fighting stopped. However, negotiations following the armistice failed to result in a final political settlement. Thus, the armistice did not lead to a peace treaty. In January 1973, a cease-fire agreement occurred during the Vietnam War. But it failed to lead to a peace treaty, and the war continued until 1975.   Richard Rosecrance

See also **Flag of truce; Peace** (The Middle Ages).
Trucial states. See United Arab Emirates.

Truck is a motor vehicle used to carry freight. Trucks transport a wide variety of cargo. They carry food to grocery stores and gasoline to service stations. Trucks haul manufactured products from factories to stores and, in some cases, to consumers' homes. In fact, trucks help transport nearly everything we eat, wear, and use. Some kinds of trucks are commonly called vans. The British word for truck is *lorry.*

Trucking is one of the most important industries in the United States. The nation spends about $110 billion yearly to transport goods by truck. The U.S. has about 34 million trucks. Canada has over 3 million trucks. Trucking is also important in many other countries.

Trucks vary greatly in size. Some kinds of trucks are smaller than certain automobiles. The largest trucks are *tractor trailers,* which have two main parts. The tractor is the front part of the truck and includes the engine and cab. The trailer is the rear part and holds the cargo. In some Western states, tractor trailers, also called *18-wheelers,* may weigh as much as 120,000 pounds (54,400 kilograms) fully loaded.

Trucks are sturdily built for rugged work. Most trucks have more powerful engines than automobiles have because trucks must carry heavy loads, often over long distances. The engines of large trucks have from about 200 to more than 400 horsepower. In comparison, the engines of automobiles have from about 75 to 225 horsepower.

Some trucks have as many as 20 forward driving gears and 10 reverse gears. These gears enable a truck to reach and maintain desired speeds under various conditions through the most efficient use of the engine. For example, certain gears on a truck make it possible to travel up an icy hill with a huge load. Trucks also have strong brakes and wide tires that grip the road. Many trucks have special devices on the rear wheels to prevent skidding on hills and curves.

Some trucks are powered by diesel fuel. Others operate on gasoline. In the United States, trucks use over 40 billion gallons (151 billion liters) of fuel annually. After the nation experienced periodic fuel shortages during the 1970's, many truck manufacturers and trucking firms began to seek ways to conserve fuel. For example, some manufacturers redesigned the engines of trucks for greater fuel efficiency.

Uses of trucks

Trucks are a vital part of the transportation system of the United States. They haul about 75 per cent of the nation's industrial products, and carry most of the goods moved short distances.

Trucks are often used in combination with other forms of transportation in a method called *piggybacking.* For example, a loaded trailer can be separated from a truck tractor and moved onto a railroad flatcar. The trailer is then transported to a railroad terminal, where it is reconnected to another truck tractor. The truckdriver then delivers the goods. Truck trailers can also be carried by ship. See **Containerization.**

Trucks have a wide variety of industrial, agricultural, and governmental uses. In addition, trucks have certain special uses.

Industrial uses. Many industries use trucks to haul raw materials to factories and to carry manufactured products to warehouses and stores. Trucks also transport manufactured parts to *assembly plants,* where finished products are made. For example, the parts for a car may be produced at several factories and then trucked to an assembly plant.

Agricultural uses. Trucks are used to transport almost all fruits, vegetables, and livestock from farms to markets. They thus help make it possible for American supermarkets to offer a wide variety of foods, some of which are grown in distant areas. Farmers can truck perishable crops, such as fruits and vegetables, to market while the foods are fresh. During winter, people who live in cold areas can eat fresh fruits and vegetables that are transported from warm areas where the foods are grown.

Farmers also transport other crops, such as hay and various grains, by truck. In addition, they use trucks to haul fertilizer, livestock feed, farm machinery, and other items. Many farm trucks have *power take-off,* a mechanism that provides power for other machines. Farmers use the mechanism to pump water, grind feed, saw wood, and perform other tasks.

Governmental uses. Federal, state, and city governments in the United States own or lease more than $1\frac{1}{4}$ million trucks. The federal government uses more trucks than any single industry. Many federal trucks are used to transport mail. The U.S. armed forces use trucks to carry equipment, troops, and weapons. Some huge army trucks even serve as missile launchers. State governments use trucks in the construction and maintenance of bridges, roads, and parks. In cities, police and fire departments require trucks. Trucks are also used in cities to sweep streets, clear away snow, and collect garbage.

Special uses. Many people use trucks to move their furniture, household goods, and personal belongings from one apartment or house to another. Some large trucks can even be used to move houses. Trucks called *bookmobiles* serve as traveling libraries. Similar trucks transport art exhibits. Some trucks carry medical equipment and workers who use the equipment to collect blood from the public or take various kinds of X rays. Trucks used as ambulances have lifesaving equipment and serve as mobile emergency rooms. Some types of *recreational vehicles* are used as temporary mobile homes by people who are camping or traveling (see **Recreational vehicle**).

Kinds of trucks

Truck manufacturers build more than 3 million trucks yearly. They produce thousands of kinds of trucks. A large manufacturer may offer customers a choice of nearly 500 designs. Many trucks are equipped with air conditioning and other comforts that are found in automobiles. The cabs of some tractor trailers are equipped with a small bed, in which drivers can sleep during long trips.

Trucks are classified into three main groups, *light, medium,* and *heavy.* Heavy trucks are sometimes further categorized as *light heavy* and *heavy heavy* trucks. The groups are based on *gross vehicle weight,* the combined weight of the truck and of the load it carries. Light trucks weigh less than 10,000 pounds (4,500 kilograms). Medium trucks weigh from 10,000 to 20,000 pounds (4,500 to 9,100 kilograms). Light heavy trucks weigh from 20,000 to 26,000 pounds (9,100 to 11,800 kilograms), and heavy heavy trucks weigh more than 26,000 pounds (11,800 kilograms).

Most trucks in the United States are light. Pickups and tow trucks are familiar light trucks. Many of these vehicles have transmissions similar to those in automobiles and can carry a load weighing about $1\frac{1}{2}$ short tons (1.4 metric tons). Most light trucks have gasoline engines. In 1977, some manufacturers began to produce light trucks with diesel engines.

Medium trucks are wider and higher than light trucks and are commonly used as commercial vehicles. They include multistop, or parcel delivery, trucks and bottlers. Multistop trucks are designed so the driver can stand behind the steering wheel and easily step on and off the vehicle. Bottlers have racks to carry bottled goods. Most medium trucks are equipped with diesel engines.

Heavy trucks perform a wide variety of rugged tasks. These vehicles include dump trucks and tractor trailers. Dump trucks are designed so the rear of the truck tilts for easy unloading. Tractor trailers have a powerful tractor that pulls a separate trailer with a full set of wheels. Almost all heavy trucks have diesel engines, which convert fuel to energy more efficiently than gasoline engines. Diesel engines enable trucks to haul heavier loads. Heavy trucks have stronger brakes and a better *suspension system* than other kinds of trucks. The suspension system is a set of devices that protect a vehicle from the jolts of travel.

Another way of grouping trucks is according to where they are used. Trucks may be classified as *highway trucks* or *off-the-highway trucks.*

Highway trucks. The three most popular types of trucks used on the road are panels, pickups, and tractors and semitrailers. A panel is a small, fully enclosed truck. A pickup has an enclosed cab and open-topped cargo compartment. A tractor and semitrailer has a trailer with only rear wheels. The front of the trailer rests on a wheeled extension of the tractor.

Other kinds of highway trucks include flatbed trucks and tank trucks. Flatbed trucks have an enclosed cab and a trailer that consists of a platform with rear wheels. The platform may have brackets along its side so that stakes can be inserted to help hold a load. Such trucks are also called platform or stake trucks. They are used to haul large pieces of equipment and other bulky cargo. Tank trucks have a trailer with a large tank. They are used to carry compressed gas or such liquids as gasoline or milk.

Several kinds of highway trucks are called vans. Light vans are commonly used for recreation. Heavier vans transport furniture or bulky goods. Refrigerated vans called reefers are used to carry perishable food and other products that require cooling.

Off-the-highway trucks are built for use on rugged terrain, rather than for highway driving. They are used on construction sites and in lumber camps, mines, oil fields, and quarries. These trucks can haul loads that weigh more than 200 short tons (180 metric tons). The largest truck used in North America is the off-the-highway vehicle that measures 67 feet long and $25\frac{1}{2}$ feet wide (20.4 meters long and 7.77 meters wide). This huge truck is used at mining sites and can transport loads weighing 350 short tons (317 metric tons). Some off-the-highway trucks are equipped with machinery that is used for earth-moving, hoisting, or pumping. Small electric-powered trucks that are used to carry loads inside factories are also a kind of off-the-highway truck.

The trucking industry

In the United States, truckers provide the only commercial land transportation for most communities without railroad or waterway service. Most U.S. trucking firms are either *local* or *intercity carriers.* Local carriers conduct more than half their business in one metropolitan area. Intercity carriers, also known as *line-haul* or *over-the-road carriers,* work in more than one metropolitan area.

Trucking firms may be (1) private carriers or (2) for-hire carriers. Both kinds of carriers are subject to government regulation.

Private carriers are businesses that either own or lease trucks and use them to transport their own goods. For example, a chain of supermarkets would use its trucks to deliver food from warehouses to stores. The company makes its profit on the sale of the food, not on the trucking.

For-hire carriers are trucking companies that earn profits by transporting freight for other businesses or for individuals or groups. For-hire carriers operate in local areas, *intrastate* (within one state), and *interstate* (between states). The United States has about 32,000 for-hire trucking firms, and Canada has more than 4,000 firms.

There are three types of for-hire carriers: (1) common, (2) contract, and (3) exempt. Common carriers are required by law to transport the goods of any shipper who can pay for the service. Such carriers charge set rates, haul specific types of freight, and operate only on certain routes (see **Common carrier**). Contract carriers work for a limited number of customers. They agree to deliver only the products of these customers. Exempt carriers transport only special kinds of goods or use their trucks only for specific purposes. Exempt carriers include firms that haul certain agricultural products or

carry newspapers. These carriers are exempt from certain government regulations.

Government regulation. In the United States, the trucking industry is regulated by federal, state, and local governments. The Interstate Commerce Commission (ICC), a federal agency, has responsibility for common and contract carriers that travel interstate. Intrastate and local carriers are regulated by state and local governments.

The ICC must approve an interstate carrier's rates and routes. It also checks the types of services offered and the kinds of goods carried.

All interstate carriers must obey the safety regulations of the U.S. Department of Transportation (DOT). These rules set standards for certain types of truck equipment, such as lights and brakes. The regulations also govern the operation of trucks. For example, the DOT specifies the number of hours a driver can work without rest. The DOT also regulates the interstate transport of chemicals and other hazardous cargoes.

The Surface Transportation Assistance Act of 1982 established uniform size and weight limits for the trucking industry nationwide. Under the law, trucks that use interstate highways and other designated highways may not weigh more than 80,000 pounds (36,000 kilograms). However, some states have higher weight limits for state highways not covered by federal law. The Surface Transportation Assistance Act also prohibited states from setting overall length limits on tractor-semitrailer and twin-trailer combinations. Twin trailers consist of two short trailers that are pulled by one tractor.

Trucking firms must pay taxes to use highways. The federal and state governments collect about $9 billion in such taxes annually. The money is used to construct and repair roads.

History

No one knows who manufactured the first truck. But by the mid-1890's, trucks were being made in the United States. By 1904, the trucking industry in the United States had only about 700 trucks. Many of these early trucks were poorly designed and weighed more than the loads they carried. Most were powered by steam or electrical engines. They had solid rubber tires and crude springs, which made traveling over the bumpy roads of the time uncomfortable for the driver and rough on the cargo. Sometimes, a truck was gradually shaken apart during a trip. Nevertheless, the early trucks were more efficient and less costly than the horse-drawn vehicles they replaced.

Such improvements as gasoline engines and air-filled tires were introduced during the early 1900's. These improvements enabled trucks to carry heavier loads at greater speeds. The trucking industry then grew rapidly. Trucks proved especially valuable during World War I (1914-1918). At that time, the railroads were unable to carry all the necessary war supplies to the Atlantic seaports for shipment overseas. Convoys of trucks helped move the supplies.

By 1918, the number of trucks in the United States had risen to about 605,000. During the 1920's, the federal and state governments began building a national system of highways. The improved roads enabled trucks to travel between cities more quickly.

Historical Pictures Service

A coal truck, *above,* was used as early as 1905. Today, trucks carry about 75 per cent of the goods handled by United States shippers and play a major role in the nation's economy.

Some kinds of trucks

Thousands of kinds of trucks perform specialized work. They range from small pickup trucks that carry relatively light loads to huge log carriers with tremendous hauling power. The United States has more than 30 million trucks.

WORLD BOOK illustrations by Robert Keys

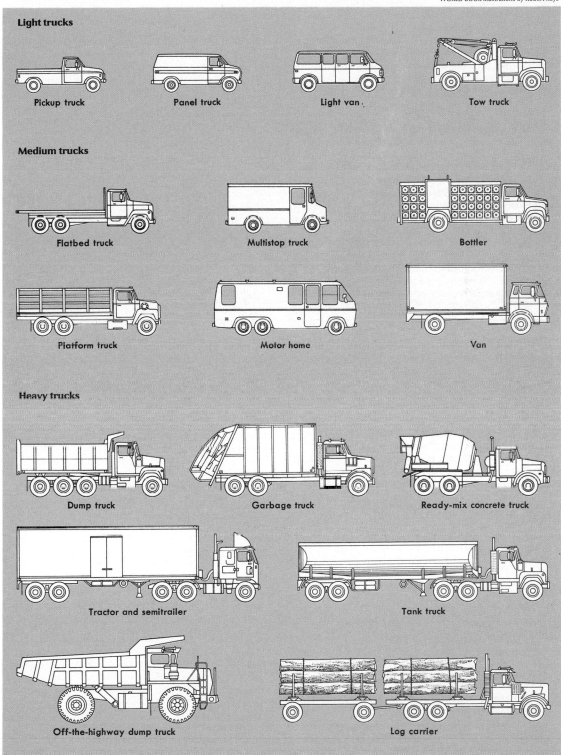

Light trucks

Pickup truck

Panel truck

Light van

Tow truck

Medium trucks

Flatbed truck

Multistop truck

Bottler

Platform truck

Motor home

Van

Heavy trucks

Dump truck

Garbage truck

Ready-mix concrete truck

Tractor and semitrailer

Tank truck

Off-the-highway dump truck

Log carrier

In 1935, Congress passed the Motor Carrier Act. This law gave the Interstate Commerce Commission authority to regulate the motor carriers and drivers involved in interstate commerce. At the time, many people believed government regulation was necessary to protect shippers and the trucking industry from various abuses that had become common practice. Today, some critics charge that regulation makes the establishment of new trucking firms difficult and raises shipping costs. Supporters claim that regulation lowers costs, provides trucking services to areas that might not have such services otherwise, and helps keep the industry stable.

Careers

The trucking industry employs over 9 million persons, more than any other private industry in the United States. About 2 million of these workers are drivers. Those who operate tractor trailers must pass a driving test and receive a special state license.

The trucking industry employs many kinds of workers besides drivers. For example, dispatchers are needed to direct trucks to the right destination with the right cargo. Freight handlers and loading-dock and warehouse workers load and unload trucks. Mechanics repair and maintain trucks. Trucking firms require various office workers, such as shipping clerks and computer programmers. Truck manufacturers employ engineers and factory workers. Companies that produce engines, tires, and other parts for trucks also offer employment opportunities.   Bennett C. Whitlock, Jr.

See also **Automobile** with its list of *Related articles.*
Truck farming is raising vegetables or fruit, or both, for market. Truck farmers do not usually need as much land for growing vegetables as they would for grain crops, and truck farms often are simply large gardens. But some truck farms cover large areas.

The terms *truck farm* and *truck garden* mean the same thing. They come from an old use of the word *truck,* which meant *to exchange or barter goods.* People speak of vegetables raised for sale as *garden truck.*

Kinds of truck farms. In general, there are two kinds of truck farms. Some truck farms are near cities, and supply the city dwellers with vegetables or fruit in season. They often also have greenhouses for growing tomatoes and other kinds of produce out of season. In most cases, such farms are small, and raise many different kinds of produce.

The other kind of truck farm may be far from any city. It depends on railroad, truck, or airplane transportation to carry the produce to market. Such a farm is usually large, and specializes in growing only one or a few kinds of produce. Some of these truck farms are in warm regions where they can produce certain fruits or vegetables in winter months and ship them to cold northern regions where they are out of season. Examples include the great winter vegetable gardens of southern Florida, southern California, Texas, and Arizona. Other truck farms can be far from market because they grow a particular fruit or vegetable that is in demand throughout the country and which can easily be shipped. Examples include the large onion, head lettuce, and celery farms of Idaho and Utah. Special conditions of soil and climate needed to grow certain kinds of produce also may influence the location of truck farms far

from market. For example, most of the head lettuce produced in the United States grows in the West and the South, where conditions are most favorable. But the largest market for head lettuce is the Northeastern United States.

Some truck farms are *part-time farms.* These farms are operated by farmers who spend less than half their work time on the farm. Farms operated by farmers who spend at least half their work time on the farm are called *primary farms.*

How truck farms operate. Many truck farmers ship and market their produce through cooperatives (see **Cooperative**). This method usually is cheaper and more convenient than for the growers to ship their crops separately. Truck farmers also sell produce at roadside stands and, in urban areas, at outdoor markets called *farmer's markets.* Sometimes, the farmers sell their produce directly to such middlemen as processors, wholesalers, and retailers.

Truck farming is hard work. Vegetables and fruit require more constant and careful cultivation than do field crops. They also are more difficult to harvest. Truck farming produces quick profits, but is risky.

Truck farmers usually rotate their crops every three or four years to keep the soil productive. Most land for truck gardening is expensive, because it must be rich and fertile, and it is often near big cities.

History. There was little need for truck farming when the United States was largely an agricultural country. Most people could raise their own vegetables or fruit in the summer and store them in the winter. But the growth of urban areas brought a great need for truck farming. Many city dwellers have no place to grow vegetables or fruit.

The building of railroads and highways throughout the country allowed the truck farmer to locate in nearly any part of the country that offered good growing conditions and good soil. The railroads and trucks also brought out-of-season produce to many people. The invention of refrigeration for railroad cars and trucks made it possible for fruits and vegetables to arrive at market almost as fresh as when they were harvested. It also made possible the distribution of perishable produce in city markets throughout the country during most of the year.

Truck farm products are the second largest food group in the United States in terms of volume and consumption. Only milk and milk products exceed them. The leading truck farming states are California, Florida, Texas, Arizona, and New York.   Donald M. Nixon

Trudeau, *TROO doh,* **Edward Livingston** (1848-1915), was a famous pioneer in the antituberculosis movement in the United States. Trudeau himself contracted the disease at the age of 25. He became convinced of the need for adequate sanitariums, and established the Adirondack Cottage Sanitarium at Saranac Lake, N.Y. It later became the Trudeau Sanitarium, which achieved a worldwide reputation.

Trudeau also founded the Saranac Laboratory in 1894, the first U.S. tuberculosis research laboratory. The sanitarium was closed in 1957 because of the great strides made in antituberculosis therapy. Trudeau was born in New York City. He studied medicine at Columbia College (now Columbia University).   Noah D. Fabricant

Pierre E. Trudeau

Prime Minister of Canada
1968-1979
1980-1984

Pearson	Trudeau	Clark	Trudeau	Turner
1963-1968	1968-1979	1979-1980	1980-1984	1984

Trudeau, *troo DOH,* **Pierre Elliott** (1919-   ), served as prime minister of Canada from 1968 to 1979 and from 1980 to 1984. He was the third French-Canadian prime minister. Like the first two—Sir Wilfrid Laurier and Louis S. St. Laurent—he was a Liberal.

The energetic and wealthy Trudeau generated great interest among Canadians, particularly the nation's youth. But during the late 1970's, his popularity and that of his party declined as Canada's economic problems worsened. The Progressive Conservatives defeated the Liberals in May 1979, and the Conservative leader, Charles Joseph Clark, succeeded Trudeau as prime minister. However, Clark's government fell from power at the end of the year, and Trudeau led the Liberals to an easy victory in February 1980.

Before his first term as prime minister, Trudeau had worked as a lawyer and law professor and had had only three years of experience in public office. Trudeau's social life had made him famous. He often wore colorful clothes; drove fast cars; and enjoyed skiing, skin diving, and canoeing.

As prime minister, Trudeau worked to broaden Canada's contacts with other nations and to ease the long-strained relations between English- and French-speaking Canadians. He achieved a personal goal in 1970, when Canada and China agreed to reestablish diplomatic relations. At home, Trudeau faced such problems as rapid inflation, high unemployment, and a movement to make the province of Quebec a separate nation. Trudeau achieved another major goal in 1982, when the Canadian constitution came under complete Canadian control. Previously, constitutional amendments required the British Parliament's approval.

Early life

Boyhood. Joseph Philippe Pierre Yves Elliott Trudeau was born in Montreal on Oct. 18, 1919. His father's family had gone to Canada from France in the 1600's. His mother's family was descended from British colonists in America who remained loyal to Great Britain at the time of the Revolutionary War in 1775 (see **United Empire Loyalists**). Trudeau, his sister Suzette, and his brother Charles learned to speak French and English with equal ease. Trudeau's father became wealthy as owner of a chain of service stations.

Education. Trudeau grew up in Montreal, where he attended a Jesuit college, Jean-de-Brébeuf. He received a law degree from the University of Montreal in 1943. While at the University of Montreal, he enlisted in the Canadian Officer Training Corps. He later completed his training with an army reserve unit.

In 1945, Trudeau earned a master's degree in political economy at Harvard University. He then studied at the *École des Sciences Politiques* (School of Political Sciences) in Paris and at the London School of Economics and Political Science in Great Britain.

His travels. In 1948, Trudeau set out to tour Europe and Asia. He traveled by motorbike or hitchhiked with a knapsack on his back. First he visited Germany, Austria, and Hungary. Then he traveled through Eastern Europe.

Important events during Trudeau's administration

Dennis Brack, Black Star

Prime Minister Trudeau met with Soviet Premier Aleksei N. Kosygin, *left,* in Ottawa in 1971. The two men agreed to broaden contacts between Canada and the Soviet Union.

Bettmann Archive

A crisis broke out in 1970 when French-Canadian separatists kidnapped two government officials. Trudeau is shown leaving an emergency meeting of Parliament.

WORLD BOOK illustration
by David Cunningham

The Election Act, passed in 1970, reduced the minimum voting age in national elections from 21 to 18.

In Jerusalem, the Arabs arrested him as an Israeli spy. But he continued on to Pakistan, Afghanistan, India, Burma, Thailand, Indochina, and China. He returned to Canada from China in 1949.

Next, Trudeau worked in the Privy Council office in Ottawa as a junior law clerk. He returned to Montreal in 1951 and began to practice law. In 1960, Trudeau and five other Canadians toured China. They were the first Westerners admitted to China since the Communists conquered the country in 1949. Trudeau became a law professor at the University of Montreal in 1961.

Entry into public life

During the late 1940's and the 1950's, Trudeau became concerned about the political situation in Quebec. The province was governed by Premier Maurice Duplessis and the Union Nationale Party. Trudeau and a group of youthful liberal friends set out to expose what they saw as dishonesty in the provincial government. They believed this corruption had resulted from political, religious, and business leaders working together to prevent reforms. To express their ideas, Trudeau and his group established the magazine *Cité Libre* (Community of the Free).

Trudeau worked in many ways for reform in Quebec. The most publicized event took place in 1949 when miners went on strike in the town of Asbestos. Premier Duplessis ordered the provincial police to aid the company and the nonunion men it tried to hire during the strike. The strikers blockaded the roads into Asbestos and kept

the strikebreakers from entering. Trudeau spent more than three weeks encouraging the strikers and speaking at their rallies. The police and many ministers called him an "outside agitator."

In 1956, Trudeau helped organize *Le Rassemblement* (The Gathering Together). The group's 600 members worked to explain democracy to the people of Quebec and to persuade them to use it. Trudeau later served as president of the group. In 1960, the Union Nationale Party was voted out of office.

French Canadians demanded more than democratic reform for Quebec. They had always struggled against what they believed was discrimination by Canada's English-speaking majority. Many French Canadians told of being refused jobs in government and industry because they spoke French. They feared that the French language would disappear in Canada if they were required to use English. They also feared that with the loss of their language they would lose their national identity and their culture and customs. Some demanded full equality. Others called for Quebec to become a separate country. During the 1960's, demands for separation from Canada became even stronger.

Trudeau favored preserving the French culture in Canada. But he opposed the creation of any country in which nationality was the only major common bond.

Member of Parliament. In 1965, Trudeau decided to enter national politics and run for a seat in the House of Commons as a member of the Liberal Party. He wanted to show French Canadians they could play a useful role

Duncan Cameron, Public Archives of Canada

Trudeau visited China in 1973, three years after Canada and China reestablished diplomatic relations. Chinese Premier Zhou Enlai welcomed the Trudeaus to Beijing.

Canada's bill of rights is called the Canadian Charter of Rights and Freedoms. It was adopted as part of the Constitution Act of 1982.

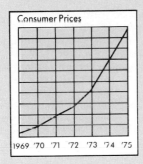

Rapid inflation became one of Canada's chief problems in 1969. To combat inflation, the Trudeau administration set limits on price and wage increases from 1975 to 1978.

Canapress

The Constitution Act was signed by Trudeau and Queen Elizabeth II on April 17, 1982. The act ended the need for British approval of amendments to Canada's constitution.

in the federal government. He also wanted to show the people of Quebec they were better off as part of Canada. In November 1965, he was elected to Parliament from Mont-Royal, a Montreal suburb.

Parliamentary secretary. In January 1966, Prime Minister Pearson appointed Trudeau as his parliamentary secretary. Trudeau used this position to influence the government's policy on constitutional issues. He wanted the constitution changed to provide a stronger federal government and to promote more cooperation among the provinces. For example, Trudeau believed the wealthy provinces should help support the poorer ones. He favored a tax program that would divide tax money more fairly among the provinces. In March 1966, the government adopted this kind of plan.

Minister of justice. In April 1967, Pearson named Trudeau to the Cabinet as minister of justice and attorney general. In this post, Trudeau introduced legislation to strengthen gun-control laws and to reduce restrictions on abortion, divorce, gambling, and homosexuality. He believed that individuals should be free to do whatever they wished if they did not endanger society as a whole. The government sponsored similar legislation after Trudeau became prime minister.

Prime minister

In December 1967, Pearson announced his intention to retire. Trudeau was elected leader of the Liberal Party on April 6, 1968, and he became prime minister on April 20. He called a general election for June 25, and the Ca-

nadian voters strongly supported him in that election.

Foreign affairs. Trudeau wanted to strengthen Canada's independence in world affairs. Early in his term, he changed the nation's defense arrangements and expanded its relations with China and the Soviet Union.

New defense policy. Trudeau adopted a defense policy that emphasized the protection of Canadian territory. In 1969 and 1970, he withdrew about half of the 9,800 Canadian troops serving with forces of the North Atlantic Treaty Organization (NATO) in Europe.

Foreign relations. In 1970, Canada and China agreed to reestablish diplomatic relations. These ties had ended

Important dates in Trudeau's life

1919	(Oct. 18) Born in Montreal.
1943	Earned law degree at University of Montreal.
1945	Earned master's degree at Harvard.
1961	Named professor of law at University of Montreal.
1965	Elected to House of Commons.
1966	Named parliamentary secretary to prime minister.
1967	Appointed minister of justice.
1968	Elected leader of Liberal Party and prime minister.
1971	(March 4) Married Margaret Sinclair.
1979	Progressive Conservatives defeated Liberals. Trudeau resigned as prime minister on June 4.
1980	Liberals defeated Progressive Conservatives. Trudeau became prime minister again on March 3.
1984	Trudeau resigned as prime minister on June 30.

Trudeau and his three sons, Michel, *left,* Justin, *top,* and Alexandre, *right,* posed for this photograph in 1982. Trudeau and his wife separated in 1977 and obtained a divorce in 1984.

Canapress

when the Communists gained control of China in 1949. The agreement had been one of Trudeau's chief goals. Trudeau visited China in 1973. He traveled to the Soviet Union in May 1971, and Premier Aleksei N. Kosygin of the Soviet Union toured Canada five months later. Trade increased with both China and the Soviet Union.

The national scene. Trudeau worked hard to help preserve the French heritage in Canada. For example, he greatly expanded the use of the French language in government services. Trudeau hoped his efforts would strengthen national unity. But relations between English- and French-speaking Canadians remained tense.

Domestic legislation. Parliament passed several far-reaching bills that were supported by Trudeau. In 1969, Parliament approved the Official Languages Act. This law requires courts and other government agencies to provide service in French in districts where at least 10 per cent of the people speak French. It also requires service in English in districts where at least 10 per cent of the people speak that language. The Election Act, passed in 1970, reduced the minimum voting age in national elections from 21 to 18. In 1971, Parliament extended unemployment insurance benefits to cover nearly all Canadian workers. In 1976, Parliament abolished the death penalty.

The October Crisis. Terrorism by French-Canadian separatists in October 1970 forced Trudeau to make his most difficult decision as prime minister. Members of the *Front de Libération du Québec* (FLQ), an underground separatist group, kidnapped Pierre Laporte, the labor minister of Quebec, and James R. Cross, the British trade commissioner in Montreal. Trudeau suspended civil liberties and sent thousands of federal troops to Quebec. He invoked Canada's War Measures Act, which permits police to search and arrest without warrants and to deny bail.

Laporte was murdered, and four men were charged with the crime. All the defendants were later sent to prison. The government let Cross's kidnappers go to Cuba in return for his release. Trudeau's firm stand received strong popular support.

The economy. Inflation became one of Canada's chief problems in 1969. To halt rising prices, Trudeau reduced government spending and eliminated thousands of civil service jobs. These policies contributed to a sharp increase in unemployment in 1970.

Economic conditions in Canada worsened in August 1971, when the United States placed a 10 per cent *surcharge* (extra tax) on many imports. The surcharge affected about a fourth of Canada's exports. In September, unemployment reached 7.1 per cent, the highest level since 1961. To encourage spending and help create jobs, Trudeau ordered cuts in individual and corporation income taxes. He also made available several hundred million dollars in loans for construction projects. The U.S. surcharge was ended in December.

The 1972 election. Trudeau called a general election for Oct. 30, 1972. He promised to seek new ways to reduce unemployment if he were returned to office. In the election, the Liberal and Conservative parties each won about 110 seats in the House of Commons. The Liberals failed to win a parliamentary majority, but Trudeau remained prime minister. Canada's economy expanded in 1973. But rapidly rising prices for clothing, food, fuel, and shelter caused hardship for many Canadians.

The 1974 election. On May 8, 1974, the House of Commons passed a motion expressing no-confidence in Trudeau's government. This motion, which forced a new general election, came on a vote concerning Trudeau's proposed budget. It was the first time that a Canadian government was defeated over its budget.

In the election of July 1974, Trudeau led the Liberal Party to victory. This time, the party gained a majority in the House of Commons, winning 141 of the 264 seats.

New economic policies. The cost of energy continued to rise sharply during the mid-1970's, largely because of increasing Canadian demand for oil and the nation's decreasing petroleum reserves. In 1974, the government adopted a plan to reduce oil exports to the United States and to end them entirely by the early 1980's. But a slump in Canada's economy prevented Trudeau from carrying out the plan.

Trudeau was also concerned about the influence of foreign companies on the Canadian economy. In the mid-1970's, for example, U.S. firms controlled over half of Canada's manufacturing. Trudeau supported establishment of a Federal Investment Review Agency to ensure that foreign investments in Canada serve Canada's best interests. This agency, which was approved by Parliament in 1973, began to operate in 1974.

Inflation continued to soar in 1975. Late that year, the Trudeau administration set limits on price and wage increases. The controls expired in 1978.

The separatist challenge to Canada's national unity became more serious in 1976. The Parti Québécois, a political party that favored the separation of Quebec from Canada, won control of the province's government. Trudeau spoke out strongly against separatism.

The 1979 election. In March 1979, Trudeau called a general election for May 22. During the campaign, the Conservatives criticized Trudeau and the Liberals for their failure to solve Canada's economic problems. In the election, the Conservatives won 135 seats in the House of Commons, the Liberals won 115, and the remaining 32 seats went to smaller parties. Charles Joseph Clark, the leader of the Conservatives, replaced Trudeau as prime minister. On November 21, Trudeau announced his intention to resign as party leader.

Return to power. The Liberals planned to select Trudeau's successor in a party convention in March 1980. But on Dec. 13, 1979, the House of Commons passed a motion of no-confidence in Clark's government. The vote came during consideration of the government's proposed budget, which called for tax increases.

As a result of his government's defeat, Clark called a general election for Feb. 18, 1980. Trudeau led the Liberals in the campaign. He climaxed an amazing political comeback when the Liberals won a majority of the seats in the House of Commons. Trudeau became prime minister again on March 3.

Trudeau's new administration soon faced a serious challenge. The government of Quebec called a vote for May 20 to give it the authority to negotiate for Quebec's political independence. Trudeau campaigned against the proposal, and the voters of Quebec rejected it.

Trudeau achieved a major goal in 1982 when the British Parliament approved an act giving Canada complete control over the Canadian constitution. The act, called the Constitution Act of 1982, set up a procedure for approving constitutional amendments in Canada instead of in Great Britain. Previously, all amendments required the British Parliament's approval.

A recession struck Canada during the early 1980's. The economy began to recover in 1983. But unemployment remained high, and public support for Trudeau's economic policies steadily declined. On June 30, 1984, Trudeau resigned as prime minister. He had held office for 15 years, longer than almost any other prime minister. W. L. Mackenzie King served for 21 years and Sir John Macdonald for almost 19 years. Trudeau was succeeded by his former finance minister, John N. Turner.

Trudeau's family. On March 4, 1971, Trudeau married Margaret Sinclair, the daughter of a former member of Parliament. The marriage surprised the nation because the couple's romance had received no publicity. The Trudeaus had three children, Justin (1971-   ), Alexandre (1973-   ), and Michel (1975-   ). In 1977, Trudeau and his wife separated. Trudeau received custody of their children. The couple obtained a divorce in 1984.

Jacques Monet

See also **Canada, History of; Clark, Charles J.; Pearson, Lester B.; Prime minister of Canada.**

Additional resources

Radwanski, George. *Trudeau.* Macmillan, 1979.
Thordarson, Bruce. *Trudeau and Foreign Policy: A Study in Decision-Making.* Oxford, 1972.

Truffaut, *troo FOH,* **François,** *frahn SWAH* (1932-1984), was a leading French motion-picture director. He directed several partly autobiographical films, beginning in 1959 with *The 400 Blows.* The character Antoine Doinel reflects Truffaut's almost delinquent youth. Truffaut continued the story in *Stolen Kisses* (1968) and *Bed and Board* (1971). Truffaut's *Day for Night* won the 1973 Academy Award as best foreign language film.

Truffaut began his career in the 1950's as a film critic and developed a deep respect for American suspense and action movies. His *Shoot the Piano Player* (1960) resembles an American gangster film. Two other Truffaut movies, *The Bride Wore Black* (1967) and *Mississippi Mermaid* (1969), show the influence of the American director Alfred Hitchcock. Truffaut was born in Paris. His other major motion pictures include *Jules and Jim* (1961) and *The Wild Child* (1970). He also directed a film in English, *Fahrenheit 451* (1966).   Roger Ebert

Truffle is a fungus that is used as a food and a flavoring. Truffles grow on or near the roots of trees, usually oaks. Most truffles are found from 3 to 12 inches (8 to 30 centimeters) belowground. They vary from $\frac{1}{4}$ to 4 inches (0.6 to 10 centimeters) in diameter. Truffles have a fleshy interior and a round, warty exterior. They may be black, brown, or white.

Truffles grow in Europe and the United States. The tastiest ones come from the Périgord region of southwestern France. White truffles found in Italy are also prized. Truffles have a strong odor, and trained dogs and pigs are often used to locate them. Wild truffles have declined in number, and most attempts to grow them commercially have failed. As a result, truffles are an extremely expensive delicacy.

Scientific classification. Truffles belong to the truffle family of ascomycete fungi, Tuberaceae. The Périgord variety, found in France, is *Tuber melanosporum.*   J. B. Hanson

Trujillo Molina, *troo HEE yoh moh LEE nah,* **Rafael Leonidas,** *RAH fah EHL LAY oh NEE thahs* (1891-1961), was the ruling force in the Dominican Republic for over 30 years. He was president from 1930 to 1938 and from 1942 to 1952. Even when he was not president, he controlled the country. Politically, his rule was severe. There were many plots against him, often spurred by exiles, chiefly after World War II. Trujillo was assassinated in 1961. He was born in San Cristóbal.   Donald E. Worcester

Truk Islands, *truhk,* form a large island group in the western Pacific about 1,800 miles (2,900 kilometers) southeast of Manila (see **Pacific Islands** [map]). They are part of the eastern Carolines. About 48 of them lie inside a barrier coral reef that forms a lagoon 40 miles (64 kilometers) wide. About 50 small islets lie along the reef. About 38,000 people live on the islands.

The French navigator Louis Duperrey first explored the islands in 1825. Germany bought them from Spain in 1899 but lost them to Japan in World War I. The United States took control in 1947 as part of a United Nations trusteeship. In 1980, Truk and other Carolines formed the Federated States of Micronesia. In 1986, these islands became a self-governing political unit in free association with the United States.   Edwin H. Bryan, Jr.

**33rd President of
the United States 1945-1953**

F. D. Roosevelt
32nd President
1933-1945
Democrat

Truman
33rd President
1945-1953
Democrat

Eisenhower
34th President
1953-1961
Republican

**Alben W.
Barkley**
Vice President
1949-1953

Harris & Ewing

Truman, Harry S. (1884-1972), became President at one of the most critical moments in American history. He had been Vice President for only 83 days when President Franklin D. Roosevelt died on April 12, 1945. World War II still had to be won. Plans to establish the United Nations organization had just been started.

When Truman became President, he was known mainly for his work as chairman of a wartime Senate investigating committee that had saved millions of dollars in military contracts. The Missouri Democrat met the challenges of his presidency with courage, determination, and imagination. During the first few weeks of his Administration, the Allies won victory in Europe. Truman then made one of the most awesome decisions ever considered by one human being—to use the powerful new atomic bomb against Japan to end World War II.

Truman faced other great problems throughout his years in the White House. The United States had to reorganize its economy from a wartime to a peacetime basis. Many war-torn countries needed large relief programs. Western nations faced Communist subversion and aggression in a Cold War that divided the world. To meet these challenges, Truman's Administration created such far-reaching programs as the Truman Doctrine, the Marshall Plan, the Point Four Program, and the North Atlantic Treaty Organization (NATO).

When Communist forces from North Korea invaded South Korea in 1950, Truman faced another grave decision. If he sent armed forces to intervene without waiting for United Nations action, he risked war with the Soviet Union, a Communist ally of North Korea. But if he delayed, help might be too late. Within two days, the President ordered American armed forces to aid South Korea. His action preserved South Korean independ-

ence and demonstrated that the United States would support and defend its allies.

Truman's strong personality and fighting spirit won him loyal friends and bitter enemies. Blunt and outspoken, he often lashed out with strong language at those who opposed him. His opponents said he was too undignified. His friends loved him as a straightforward man of the people.

Early life

Childhood. Harry S. Truman was born in Lamar, Mo., on May 8, 1884. He was the oldest of the three children of John Anderson Truman and Martha Ellen Young Truman. His parents named him Harry in honor of his uncle, Harrison Young. They chose the middle initial "S." But they gave him no middle name so that both his grandfathers, Solomon Young and Anderson Shippe Truman, could claim that he was named for them.

When Harry was 6 years old, his family moved from a farm near Grandview, Mo., to Independence, Mo. Harry went to elementary school and high school in Independence. Severely nearsighted, he began wearing glasses when he was 8. "I was so carefully cautioned by the eye doctor about breaking my glasses and injuring my eyes," he later wrote, "that I was afraid to join in the rough-and-tumble games in the schoolyard and back lot. My time was spent in reading, and by the time I was 13 or 14 years old I had read all the books in the Independence Public Library and our old Bible three times through." During the summers, Harry, his brother Vivian (1886-1965), and his sister Mary Jane (1889-1978) visited their grandparents' farm near Grandview. At the age of 18, Harry joined the Baptist Church.

First jobs. Truman wanted to go to the United States Military Academy at West Point, but his vision was not

War and its aftermath were major concerns. On Aug. 6, 1945, the United States dropped the first atomic bomb used in warfare on the Japanese city of Hiroshima, *left.* World War II ended soon afterward. In 1948 and 1949, the Allies staged a massive airlift, *below,* to deliver food and other necessities to Berlin, which had been blockaded by the Soviet Union.

The world of President Truman

The first fully electronic digital computer was built by engineers at the University of Pennsylvania in 1946.

"Iron Curtain" was a phrase first used by Winston Churchill in 1946 to describe the barriers against the West set up by Communist governments in Eastern Europe.

Fears of Communist infiltration in postwar America led to congressional hearings, "blacklists" of persons in the entertainment industry, and the controversial spy trials of Alger Hiss and Ethel and Julius Rosenberg.

British India was divided into two independent nations—India and Pakistan—in 1947.

The first supersonic flight took place in 1947. U.S. Air Force Captain Charles Yeager flew a Bell X-1 rocket plane to break the sound barrier.

Jackie Robinson became the first black baseball player in the major leagues when he joined the Brooklyn Dodgers in 1947.

Israel was founded on May 14, 1948. The first Arab-Israeli war began the next day, when Arab nations attacked Israel.

Civil war in Greece ended in 1949 with the defeat of Communist-led rebels.

The Communist People's Republic of China was founded in 1949.

The first nationwide telecast showed President Truman opening the Japanese Peace Treaty Conference in San Francisco in 1951.

Elizabeth II became queen of Great Britain in 1952.

Keystone; Walter Sanders, *Life* magazine. © Time Inc.

good enough to meet Army standards. After graduating from high school in 1901, Harry briefly attended business school in Kansas City. He also worked for a short time in the mailing room of the *Kansas City Star* and then took a job as a timekeeper for a construction crew of the Atchison, Topeka, and Santa Fe Railway Company. His next employment was as a clerk and later as a bookkeeper in two Kansas City banks. He moved to Grandview in 1906 and, with his father, operated the family farm. He worked on the farm until 1917.

Soldier. Truman was a member of the Missouri National Guard from 1905 to 1911. When the United States entered World War I in 1917, he helped organize a field artillery regiment that was attached to the 35th Division. Truman then became a lieutenant. Truman was sent to France early in 1918. There, as a captain, he commanded an artillery battery in the Vosges, Meuse-Argonne, and Sommedieu campaigns. Truman was honorably discharged in 1919. He soon joined the Army reserves as a major and later rose to colonel.

Truman's family. Six weeks after he returned home, on June 28, 1919, Truman married his childhood sweetheart, Elizabeth "Bess" Virginia Wallace (1885-1982). They had met at Sunday school when they were children. They had one child, Mary Margaret (1924-   ), whom they called Margaret. She had a brief career as a concert soprano and later became a writer.

Businessman. Before World War I, Truman had lost money in mining and oil investments. In 1919, he and his friend Eddie Jacobson invested their savings in a men's clothing store in Kansas City. They worked hard, keeping the store open from 8 a.m. to 9 p.m., but the business failed during the severe recession that began in 1921. Truman worked about 15 years to pay the store debts.

Political career

Discouraged by the failure of the store, Truman decided to seek a career in politics. He received help from

Important dates in Truman's life

1884 (May 8) Born in Lamar, Mo.
1917-1919 Served in the U.S. Army during World War I.
1919 (June 28) Married Elizabeth Virginia Wallace.
1922 Elected judge of Jackson County, Missouri.
1934 Elected to the United States Senate.
1944 Elected Vice President of the United States.
1945 (April 12) Became President of the United States.
1948 Elected President of the United States.
1972 (Dec. 26) Died in Kansas City, Mo.

Vincil Warren, Missouri Department of Natural Resources

Truman's birthplace was this frame house in Lamar, Mo. The family moved to Independence when Harry was 6 years old.

"Big Tom" Pendergast, the Democratic Party boss of Kansas City. Pendergast's nephew had known and admired Truman in the Army. Pendergast led one of the strongest political machines in the United States. He decided that Truman could win votes because of his farm background, his war record, and his friendly personality.

County judge. Pendergast supported Truman in his campaign for election as county judge of Jackson County. This post in Missouri resembled that of county commissioner in other states. Truman won the election, and served from 1922 to 1924. He lost the 1924 election because of a split in local Democratic forces. Truman attended the Kansas City School of Law during the mid-1920's, but did not obtain a degree. He served as presiding county judge from 1926 to 1934. The Pendergast machine was notoriously dishonest, but Truman won a reputation for honesty and efficiency. He supervised new projects financed by $14 million in tax funds and bond issues.

U.S. senator. In 1934, again with Pendergast's support, Truman was elected to the United States Senate. As a member of the Senate Interstate Commerce Committe, Truman directed an investigation of railroad finances. His staff found damaging evidence about many of Truman's friends in Missouri, but he ordered the investigation completed. A major result was the Transportation Act of 1940, which regulated railroad financing. Also during this time, a government study of the Pendergast political machine disclosed vote frauds and shady financial dealings. Pendergast pleaded guilty to income tax evasion, and he and many of his followers were sent to prison. The scandals did not touch Truman, but he refused to disclaim Pendergast. In 1940, Truman won reelection to the Senate.

The Truman Committee. In 1940, although the United States was not formally involved in World War II, the nation's defense spending rose to huge sums. Truman realized that the defense effort created many opportunities for waste and corruption. He remembered that many committees had investigated military spending after World War I—when they were powerless to recover wasted funds. Truman urged the Senate to set up a committee to investigate defense spending as it occurred. Early in 1941, the Senate established the Com-

Office of War Information courtesy Harry S. Truman Library

Truman took the oath of office as President on April 12, 1945, following the death of Franklin D. Roosevelt. Truman's wife, Bess, witnessed the event, which took place at the White House.

mittee to Investigate the National Defense Program. Truman was named chairman. The Truman Committee, as the group soon became known, uncovered waste and inefficiency. It saved the government about $15 billion and speeded war production.

Vice President. In 1944, many Democratic leaders believed that President Roosevelt would not live through a fourth term in the White House. They realized that the man they chose for Vice President would probably succeed to the presidency.

The contest for the vice presidential nomination almost split the party. Many liberals supported Vice President Henry A. Wallace for renomination. Others favored Supreme Court Justice William O. Douglas. Southern conservatives preferred James F. Byrnes, a former justice of the Court. Roosevelt refused to name a preference. But Robert E. Hannegan of St. Louis, Mo., a Truman supporter and chairman of the party's national committee, backed Truman as a compromise candidate. Truman had a national reputation as a result of his committee investigations. He also had a good voting record as a senator, and Roosevelt was willing to accept him. Byrnes withdrew, and the delegates nominated Truman on the second ballot.

Roosevelt and Truman easily defeated their Republican opponents, Governor Thomas E. Dewey of New York and Governor John W. Bricker of Ohio (see **Roosevelt, Franklin D.** [Election of 1944]). As Vice President, Truman presided over the Senate. During the 83 days he held this office, he worked hard to obtain Senate approval of Henry A. Wallace as secretary of commerce. He also broke a Senate tie by voting against an amendment prohibiting postwar delivery of goods through the Lend-Lease program (see **Lend-Lease**).

First Administration (1945-1949)

Late in the afternoon of April 12, 1945, Truman was suddenly summoned to the White House by telephone. He was taken to Eleanor Roosevelt's study, and she

Harry S. Truman Library

Truman headed a Senate committee that saved the government about $15 billion by finding waste in wartime spending.

stepped forward to meet him. "Harry," she said quietly, "the President is dead." Truman's first words were: "Is there anything I can do for you?" Mrs. Roosevelt replied: "Is there anything *we* can do for *you?* For you are the one in trouble now."

At 7:09 p.m., Truman took the oath of office as President. The next day, while talking to White House newsmen, he said: "Boys, if you ever pray, pray for me now. I don't know whether you fellows ever had a load of hay fall on you, but when they told me yesterday what had happened, I felt like the moon, the stars, and all the planets had fallen on me."

The end of World War II. When Truman became President, Allied armies were winning the war in Germany, and were preparing to invade Japan. Events moved swiftly. Thirteen days after Truman took office, the first United Nations conference met in San Francisco (see **San Francisco Conference**). Then, on May 7, Germany surrendered. Truman proclaimed May 8 as V-E Day (Victory in Europe Day). It was his 61st birthday.

In July, Truman traveled to Potsdam, Germany, to confer with Prime Minister Winston Churchill of Great Britain and Premier Joseph Stalin of the Soviet Union (see **Potsdam Conference**). While in Potsdam, the President received secret word that American scientists had successfully tested an atomic bomb for the first time. On his way home, Truman ordered American fliers to drop an atomic bomb on Japan. The first bomb fell on the city of Hiroshima on August 6. Three days later, a second atomic bomb was dropped on Nagasaki. Japan agreed to end the war on August 14, and formally surrendered on September 2. See **Nuclear weapon** (introduction; History); **World War II** (The atomic bomb).

Domestic program. Truman wanted to extend Roosevelt's "New Deal" policies. He drew up a program for reconstructing postwar America and presented it to Congress in September 1945. His requests included (1) extensive authority over the economy in the conversion from wartime to peacetime; (2) national health insurance; (3) a permanent Fair Employment Practices Commission (FEPC) to protect minority rights; (4) government aid for scientific research; and (5) public power projects on the Arkansas, Columbia, and Missouri rivers.

Vice President and Cabinet

Vice President	* Alben W. Barkley
Secretary of state	* Edward R. Stettinius, Jr.
	* James F. Byrnes (1945)
	* George C. Marshall (1947)
	* Dean G. Acheson (1949)
Secretary of the treasury	* Henry Morgenthau, Jr.
	* Frederick M. Vinson (1945)
	John W. Snyder (1946)
Secretary of war†	* Henry L. Stimson
	Robert P. Patterson (1945)
	Kenneth C. Royall (1947)
Secretary of defense	* James V. Forrestal (1947)
	Louis A. Johnson (1949)
	* George C. Marshall (1950)
	Robert A. Lovett (1951)
Attorney general	Francis Biddle
	* Tom C. Clark (1945)
	J. Howard McGrath (1949)
	James P. McGranery (1952)
Postmaster general	Frank C. Walker
	Robert E. Hannegan (1945)
	Jesse M. Donaldson (1947)
Secretary of the navy†	* James V. Forrestal
Secretary of the interior	* Harold L. Ickes
	Julius A. Krug (1946)
	Oscar L. Chapman (1950)
Secretary of agriculture	Claude R. Wickard
	Clinton P. Anderson (1945)
	Charles F. Brannan (1948)
Secretary of commerce	* Henry A. Wallace
	* Averell Harriman (1946)
	Charles Sawyer (1948)
Secretary of labor	* Frances Perkins
	Lewis B. Schwellenbach (1945)
	Maurice J. Tobin (1948)

*Has a separate biography in *World Book*.
†Reduced to non-Cabinet rank under secretary of defense, 1947.

Crippling labor disputes and shortages of consumer goods helped the Republicans gain control of Congress in the 1946 elections. The Republicans blocked most of Truman's domestic measures. Congress did approve Truman's plan to unify the armed forces under a single secretary of defense (see **Defense, Department of**). A

UPI/Bettmann Newsphotos

At the Potsdam Conference in Germany in July 1945, Truman conferred with Prime Minister Winston Churchill of Great Britain and Premier Joseph Stalin of the Soviet Union.

Harry S. Truman Library

The United Nations was established in 1945 at a conference in San Francisco. Truman, *second from left,* watched as U.S. Secretary of State Edward Stettinius signed the UN charter.

On his "whistle-stop" campaign for the presidency in 1948, Truman traveled by train and made more than 350 speeches.

Norristown *Times Herald*

UPI/Bettmann Newsphotos

Truman won an upset victory in 1948. He enjoyed a premature report of a win by Republican Thomas Dewey.

Quotations from Truman

The following quotations come from some of Harry Truman's speeches and writings.

The responsibility of great states is to serve and not to dominate the world.
Message to Congress, April 16, 1945

Sixteen hours ago an American airplane dropped one bomb on Hiroshima . . . The force from which the sun draws its power has been loosed upon those who brought war to the Far East.
Address to the nation, August 6, 1945

I believe that it must be the policy of the United States to support free peoples who are resisting attempted subjugation by armed minorities or by outside pressures. I believe that we must assist free peoples to work out their own destinies in their own way.
Speech before Congress, March 12, 1947

We shall not . . . achieve the ideals for which this nation was founded so long as any American suffers discrimination . . . If we wish to inspire the peoples of the world whose freedom is in jeopardy, if we wish to restore hope to those who have already lost their civil liberties, . . . we must correct the remaining imperfections in our practice of democracy.
Message to Congress, Feb. 2, 1948

We must embark on a bold new program for making the benefits of our scientific advances and industrial progress available for the improvement and growth of underdeveloped areas.
Inaugural Address, Jan. 20, 1949

Whenever you have an efficient government you have a dictatorship.
Lecture at Columbia University, April 28, 1959

commission was established to study ways of improving government efficiency, and Truman named former President Herbert Hoover to head it (see **Hoover Commission**). In 1947, after a long fight, Congress passed the Labor-Management Relations Act, or Taft-Hartley Act, over the President's veto (see **Taft-Hartley Act**). The act placed numerous restrictions on labor unions.

The Truman Doctrine. Soon after World War II, the Cold War developed between the Soviet Union and its former allies (see **Cold War**). The Communists gained control over one nation after another in Eastern Europe.

Truman realized that the United States would have to lead in the fight for freedom, spending as much as necessary to strengthen its war-torn allies. In 1946, Congress approved a $3,750,000,000 loan to Great Britain. Then, on March 12, 1947, Truman announced a doctrine of international resistance to Communist aggression. The Truman Doctrine guaranteed American aid to free nations resisting Communist propaganda or sabotage.

The Marshall Plan, outlined by Secretary of State George C. Marshall in 1947, extended the Truman Doctrine. It proposed that the war-damaged nations of Europe join in a program of mutual aid for economic recovery, assisted by grants from the United States. Communist nations rejected the plan, but 18 other countries eventually accepted it. See **Marshall Plan.**

Election of 1948 seemed certain to bring victory to the Republicans. United and confident, they faced a sharply divided Democratic Party. The Democratic National Convention nominated Truman on the first ballot, and picked Senator Alben W. Barkley of Kentucky for Vice President. A group of liberal Democrats had already left the party and formed the Progressive Party. The Progressives nominated former Vice President Wallace for President. Another group, made up of Southern Democrats who opposed a strong civil rights program, organized the Dixiecrat Party. They nominated Strom Thurmond, then governor of South Carolina. The Republicans again nominated Dewey for President, and chose Governor Earl Warren of California as his running mate. See **Dixiecrat Party; Progressive Party.**

Every public opinion poll predicted that Dewey would win a landslide victory. But, with an extraordinary show of fighting spirit, Truman made the experts look ridiculous. He traveled 31,000 miles (49,900 kilometers) by train in a "whistle-stop" campaign and made more than 350 speeches. He attacked what he termed the "do nothing" Republican Congress, calling it "the worst in my memory." Truman received a warm response with his simple language, earthy humor, and pluck. He also shrewdly appealed to the groups that had strongly supported Franklin D. Roosevelt—labor, farmers, liberals, minorities, and many middle-class consumers. In one of

Truman's election

Place of nominating convention	Philadelphia
Ballot on which nominated	1st
Republican opponent	Thomas E. Dewey
Dixiecrat opponent	Strom Thurmond
Progressive opponent	Henry A. Wallace
Electoral vote	303 (Truman) to:
	189 (Dewey)
	39 (Thurmond)
	0 (Wallace)
Popular vote	24,105,587 (Truman) to:
	21,970,017 (Dewey)
	1,169,134 (Thurmond)
	1,157,057 (Wallace)
Age at inauguration	64

the biggest upsets in political history, Truman won 28 states. Dewey won 16 and Thurmond, 4. Truman won with less than 50 per cent of the total popular vote.

Life in the White House. Early every day—often as early as 5:30 a.m.—Truman arose and went for a brisk walk, always accompanied by Secret Service agents and members of the media. At the White House, Truman often played the piano for visitors, and particularly enjoyed the music of Chopin and Mozart. The Trumans spent most evenings in a family living room upstairs.

The structural part of the White House had become dangerously weak, and engineers had to make extensive repairs. The rebuilding began late in 1948, and the Trumans moved to Blair House. They lived there until March 1952. See **Blair House; White House.**

On Nov. 1, 1950, two Puerto Rican nationalists tried to invade Blair House and assassinate the President. They killed one Secret Service guard and wounded another. One of the gunmen was killed and the other captured. Truman commented that "A President has to expect those things." He kept all his appointments that day, and took his usual walk the next morning.

Second Administration (1949-1953)

Foreign affairs. In the spring of 1949, the United States, Canada, Great Britain, France, and eight other na-

tions signed the North Atlantic Treaty, forming the North Atlantic Treaty Organization (NATO). They agreed that an attack on one member would be considered an attack on all. Other countries later joined NATO and helped group their armed forces to defend Western Europe. General Dwight D. Eisenhower served as the first supreme commander of NATO forces. See **North Atlantic Treaty Organization.**

In his inaugural address, Truman called for "a bold new program for making the benefits of our scientific advances and industrial progress available for the improvement and growth of underdeveloped areas." In 1950, Congress approved $35 million for the first part of this Point Four Program (see **Point Four Program**). Late in 1951, Truman asked Congress to set up a new foreign aid program for Communist-threatened countries in Southeast Asia. Congress established the Mutual Security Administration to strengthen military defenses in many countries. Western Europe had recovered economically from the war, so Truman changed the emphasis of foreign aid from economic help to mutual security. He believed that if the nation's allies were strong, America would be strengthened, too. See **Foreign aid.**

The Korean War began on June 25, 1950, when Communist forces from North Korea invaded South Korea. The United Nations demanded that North Korea withdraw. Truman decided to intervene to save South Korea's independence. On June 27, he announced that he had sent U.S. planes and ships to help South Korea. Congress cheered the announcement. That same day, the UN approved sending troops of other nations to join South Korean and American units. Truman ordered ground forces to South Korea on June 30. He later said that sending U.S. troops to South Korea—and thus taking the risk of starting World War III—was the hardest decision of his political career.

General Douglas MacArthur commanded all UN forces in Korea. His troops brought most of Korea under UN control by October 1950. But later that month, Chinese Communist troops joined the North Koreans. Truman recognized the urgency of the situation and put the

Truman's wife and daughter were known as "the bosses." The President playfully spoke of his wife Bess as "the boss" and of their daughter Margaret as "the one who bosses her." The family is shown above on Truman's 68th birthday.

Truman enjoyed playing the piano. The President often entertained visitors to the White House with a session at the keyboard.

Highlights of Truman's Administration

1945   (May 7) Germany surrendered to the Allies.
1945   (July 16) The first atomic bomb was tested.
1945   (Sept. 2) Japan's surrender ended World War II.
1945   (Oct. 24) The United Nations was founded.
1947   (May 15) Congress approved the Truman Doctrine.
1947   (June) Congress passed the Taft-Hartley Act over Truman's veto.
1947   (July) Congress unified the U.S. armed forces.
1948   (April 2) Congress approved the Marshall Plan.
1949   (April 4) The United States and 11 other nations set up the North Atlantic Treaty Organization (NATO).
1950   (June 27) The United States sent forces to defend South Korea against Communist aggression.

U.S. Army

General Douglas MacArthur received a medal from Truman in 1950, during the Korean War. In 1951, Truman dismissed MacArthur after MacArthur publicly disagreed with him on strategy.

United States on a semiwar basis. MacArthur wanted to attack Chinese Communist bases in Manchuria. But Truman believed that the fighting must be confined to Korea, and not be allowed to spread into a possible global war. MacArthur made several public statements criticizing this policy. In April 1951, Truman dismissed MacArthur, creating a nationwide furor. See **Korean War.**

Problems at home. The voters had elected a Democratic Congress in 1948. It soon proved almost as uncooperative in domestic affairs as the preceding Republican Congress had been. Truman waged an extensive reform program, which he called the "Fair Deal." "Every segment of our population and every individual has a right to expect from our government a fair deal," he declared. The program included (1) civil rights legislation; (2) repeal of the Taft-Hartley Act; (3) a new farm program stressing high farm income and low consumer prices; (4) federal aid to education; (5) a federal housing program; and (6) increases in the social security program. Southern Democrats joined conservative Republicans to defeat most of the President's domestic proposals. The Democrats lost strength in the 1950 congressional elections.

Charges of Communist infiltration into the federal government added to the President's concerns. Truman set up a federal board to investigate the loyalty of government employees, and the Department of Justice prosecuted leaders of the American Communist Party. A House committee investigated charges that Communists worked for the Department of State. The trials of Alger Hiss and Ethel and Julius Rosenberg revealed that spies had stolen secret information and given it to Soviet agents (see **Hiss, Alger; Rosenberg, Julius and Ethel**). Senator Joseph R. McCarthy of Wisconsin also accused the Department of State of employing Communists. Truman strongly rejected McCarthy's charges, and they were never proven.

Campaign of 1952. On March 29, 1952, Truman announced that he would not seek reelection. "I have served my country long, and I think efficiently and honestly," he said. "I do not feel that it is my duty to spend another four years in the White House." Instead, he campaigned for the Democratic candidate, Governor Adlai E. Stevenson of Illinois, who lost to Dwight D. Eisenhower.

Elder statesman

Truman left office on Jan. 20, 1953, and retired to his home in Independence. He published the two volumes of his memoirs, *Year of Decisions* in 1955 and *Years of Trial and Hope* in 1956. Truman also continued his active interest in politics and in the Democratic Party.

After Truman left the White House, his friends collected funds to build the Harry S. Truman Library in Independence. The library holds Truman's papers and souvenirs. It opened in 1957.

Truman became ill late in 1972 and entered the hospital on December 5 with severe lung congestion. He died on December 26. He was buried in Independence in the Truman Library courtyard.   Alonzo L. Hamby

Related articles in *World Book* include:

Cold War
Defense, Department of
Dewey, Thomas E.
Dixiecrat Party
Foreign aid
Hoover Commission
Marshall Plan
Nuclear weapon
Point Four Program
Potsdam Conference

President of the
    United States
Roosevelt, Franklin Delano
San Francisco Conference
United Nations
Vice President of the
    United States
Wallace, Henry Agard
World War II

Outline

I. **Early life**
    A. Childhood   C. Soldier   E. Businessman
    B. First jobs   D. Truman's family
II. **Political career**
    A. County judge   C. The Truman Committee
    B. U.S. senator   D. Vice President
III. **First Administration (1945-1949)**
    A. The end of World War II
    B. Domestic program
    C. The Truman Doctrine
    D. The Marshall Plan
    E. Election of 1948
    F. Life in the White House
IV. **Second Administration (1949-1953)**
    A. Foreign affairs   C. Problems at home
    B. The Korean War   D. Campaign of 1952
V. **Elder statesman**

Questions

What reforms did the "Fair Deal" call for?
Where did Truman meet his future wife?

What awesome decision did Truman make to end World War II?

What was the Truman Doctrine?

How did Truman win an upset victory in 1948?

Why did Truman dismiss General MacArthur in Korea?

What did the Truman Committee accomplish?

Why did some Democrats feel that Truman would make a good vice presidential nominee in 1944?

How did Truman fight Communism at home?

Why was the Democratic vice presidential nomination especially important in 1944?

Reading and Study Guide

See *Truman, Harry S.,* in the Research Guide/Index, Volume 22, for a *Reading and Study Guide.*

Additional resources

Donovan, Robert J. *Conflict and Crisis: The Presidency of Harry S. Truman, 1945-1948.* Norton, 1977. *Tumultuous Years: The Presidency of Harry S. Truman, 1949-1953.* 1982.

Ferrell, Robert H. *Truman: A Centenary Remembrance.* Viking, 1984.

Hamby, Alonzo L. *Beyond the New Deal: Harry S. Truman and American Liberalism.* Columbia Univ. Press, 1973.

Jenkins, Roy. *Truman.* Harper, 1986.

McCoy, Donald R. *The Presidency of Harry S. Truman.* Univ. Press of Kansas, 1984.

Ross, Irwin. *The Loneliest Campaign: The Truman Victory of 1948.* Greenwood,1977. First published in 1968.

Truman Doctrine. See Truman, Harry S.; Cold War (The Containment Policy).

Trumbull, John (1756-1843), an American artist, became known for his paintings of Revolutionary War scenes. Thomas Jefferson advised him about his historical subjects. From 1789 to 1794, Trumbull made portraits of the individuals he intended to include in the scenes. He later copied the portraits into his compositions.

Trumbull was born into a prominent family in Lebanon, Conn. After graduating from Harvard College in 1773, he enlisted in the Continental Army and served as an aide to George Washington. After the war, he resumed the study of painting in London under artist Benjamin West and planned his paintings of the American Revolution. In 1817, Trumbull received a commission to paint four large versions of war subjects in the Rotunda of the U.S. Capitol. The remaining years of his life were disappointing, partly because of his failing eyesight and quarrelsome disposition.   Elizabeth Garrity Ellis

For examples of Trumbull's work, see the pictures with the articles Adams, John; Burgoyne, John; Declaration of Independence; Hamilton, Alexander; Hessians; and Revolutionary War in America.

Trumbull, Jonathan (1710-1785), was governor of Connecticut in the Revolutionary period. He was the only prewar colonial governor who supported the patriots. Trumbull supplied the Continental Army with food, clothing, and munitions. This task kept him in close touch with General George Washington (see **Brother Jonathan**).

Trumbull was born in Lebanon, Conn. He built up a business with Britain, which failed just before war began. The experience helped him later in supplying the patriots. He served in the legislature and as deputy governor before holding office as governor from 1769 to 1784. In 1872, his statue was placed in the Capitol in Washington, D.C.   John W. Ifkovic

Trumbull, Lyman (1813-1896), was an American political leader. He strongly opposed slavery. As a United States senator, he supported President Abraham Lincoln

during the Civil War, and helped frame Amendment 13 to the U.S. Constitution, which abolished slavery. Trumbull guided Amendment 14, guaranteeing the rights of blacks, through Congress. He voted against conviction during President Andrew Johnson's impeachment in 1868.

Trumbull was born in Colchester, Conn., and moved to Illinois in 1837. He served in public office as a Democrat, a Republican, and a Liberal Republican. He served on the Illinois Supreme Court from 1849 to 1854 and in the U.S. Senate from 1855 to 1873. After leaving the Senate, Trumbull was active in Illinois politics as a Democrat and then as a Populist.   Frank L. Klement

Trumpet is a popular brass instrument in bands and orchestras. A player produces tones by blowing into a cup-shaped mouthpiece and vibrating the lips. The player changes notes by fingering the instrument's three

The trumpet is a popular brass instrument with a brilliant tone. A trumpet player can produce all notes of the scale by pressing the instrument's three piston valves in various combinations.

Northwestern University (WORLD BOOK photo by Ted Nielsen)

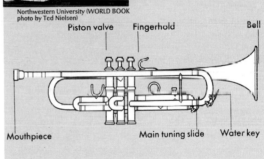

Piston valve   Fingerhold   Bell

Mouthpiece   Main tuning slide   Water key

WORLD BOOK illustration by Oxford Illustrators Limited

valves and changing lip tension. The largest part of the trumpet consists of a curved tube. Most trumpets used in bands are pitched in the key of B flat and have a tube $4\frac{1}{2}$ feet (1.4 meters) long. Orchestras use those kinds and ones with shorter tubes and pitched in other keys. The small diameter and cylindrical shape of its tube give the trumpet its brilliant, powerful sound.

Trumpets date back to about 1200 B.C. The valve trumpet was developed in 1813.   John Keil Richards

Trundle bed. See Bed (picture); **Colonial life in America** (Furnishings).

Trunk. See Tree (The parts of a tree).

Trust. See Antitrust laws.

Trust estate. See Trust fund.

Trust fund is money or other property managed by one person or group for the benefit of another person or group. Other terms for a trust fund include *corpus, principal,* and *trust estate.* The arrangement under which a trust fund is managed is called a *trust.*

In some cases, the property in a trust fund is taxed less heavily than property owned without such an arrangement. As a result, many people establish trust funds to reduce their taxes. Others create trust funds for the benefit of children or other people who cannot manage property themselves. Some people use trust funds to take advantage of an individual's or institution's special skill in managing property.

How a trust fund works. Most trust funds involve three parties: a *trustor,* a *trustee,* and a *beneficiary.* In some cases, the trustor is also the trustee or the beneficiary. The trustor, also called the *settlor* or *donor,* creates a trust fund by giving property to a trustee. The trustee holds or invests the fund for the good of the beneficiary. The trustee may have charge of the fund for a few years or for more than a lifetime, depending on the terms of the trust. After the trust has *terminated* (ended), the trustee distributes the property as directed in the terms of the trust.

Any sane adult may serve as a trustee. However, most trust funds are handled by *trust departments* of banks or by businesses called *trust companies.* In most cases, the fee for the trustee's services is set by an agreement between the trustor and trustee. Trustees must keep accounts of all trust funds they hold, invest, or distribute. In addition, they must follow the trustor's wishes concerning investment of the fund. If the trust does not indicate the trustor's wishes for investment, the trustee must follow guidelines set by state laws. A trustee must make good any losses that result from wrongful use of a trust fund.

Beneficiaries receive income from trust funds according to a variety of arrangements. For example, some beneficiaries periodically receive income earned by the trust fund. Other beneficiaries must wait and receive the accumulated income from the fund when they reach a certain age. Some beneficiaries receive payments from the trust fund until they reach a certain age, when they take possession of the fund themselves.

Kinds of trusts. A trust that operates during the trustor's life is called a *living* or *inter vivos trust.* A trust established by a will is called a *testamentary trust.* A *revocable trust* can be changed or abolished by the trustor. A trustor who gives up all rights to the trust fund creates an *irrevocable trust.* Trusts established for the benefit of churches, colleges, or other nonprofit organizations are *charitable trusts. Life insurance trusts* receive the proceeds of insurance policies on the life of the trustor.

Courts occasionally create *constructive trusts* to protect property. For example, a person who has property that belongs to another may be named *constructive trustee* of that property. Such an arrangement protects the property and ensures that it will be returned to the rightful owner.   T. Bryan Underwood, Jr.

See also **Receiver.**

Trust territory refers to an area administered by a country under the supervision of the United Nations (UN) Trusteeship Council. The administering country has complete authority over the government of a trust territory. It administers the territory under an agreement with the UN according to principles set down in the UN Charter.

A total of 11 trust territories were established after World War II ended in 1945. They included the former Italian colony of Somaliland and 10 of the 11 former mandates of the League of Nations (see **Mandated territory**). The 11th mandate, Namibia (South West Africa), remained under South Africa's control. However, its status has remained an issue of dispute between South Africa and the UN. Of the 11 trust territories, all but the U.S.-administered Trust Territory of the Pacific Islands became independent or voted to become a part of an independent nation between the mid-1950's and the mid-1970's. In 1986, all of the units of the Trust Territory of the Pacific Islands except the Palau Islands gained self-government (see **Pacific Islands, Trust Territory of the**). See also **United Nations** (The Trusteeship Council).

Robert J. Pranger

Trustee. See **Trust fund.**

Trusteeship Council. See **United Nations** (The Trusteeship Council).

Truth, Sojourner (1797?-1883), was the name used by Isabella Baumfree, one of the best-known American abolitionists of her day. She was the first black woman orator to speak out against slavery. She traveled widely through New England and the Midwest on speaking tours. Her deep voice, quick wit, and inspiring faith helped spread her fame.

Baumfree was born a slave in Ulster County, New York. She became free in 1828 under a New York law that banned slavery. In 1843, she experienced what she regarded as a command from God to preach. She took the name Sojourner Truth and began lecturing in New York. Her early speeches were based on the belief that people best show love for God by love and concern for others. She soon began directing her speeches toward the abolition of slavery.

Chicago Historical Society

Sojourner Truth

In 1864, she visited President Abraham Lincoln in the White House. She stayed in Washington, D.C., and worked to improve living conditions for blacks there. She also helped find jobs and homes for slaves who had escaped from the South to Washington. In the 1870's, she tried to persuade the federal government to set aside undeveloped lands in the West as farms for blacks. But her plan won no government support.

Otey M. Scruggs

Additional resources

Ortiz, Victoria. *Sojourner Truth, a Self-Made Woman.* Lippincott, 1974. For younger readers.
Pauli, Hertha. *Her Name Was Sojourner Truth.* Avon, 1976. First published in 1962.

Truth in Lending Act. See **Consumerism** (The right to information); **Usury.**

Truth serum. See **Thiopental.**

Truth table is a method of showing logical relationships. Truth tables are used by computer engineers, logicians, and others who reason by symbolic logic.

To understand truth tables, we must first understand some ideas of logic. A basic declarative sentence is a *proposition* if its meaning can be classified as true or false. For example, the sentences *"The door is open."* and *"The light bulb is not burned out."* are propositions.

A limited number of propositions when combined may form a *propositional function.* For example, the two propositions above may be combined into the propositional function *"The light in the refrigerator will be on if the door is open and the light bulb is not burned out."* The truth or falsity of a propositional function depends on the truth or falsity of each of the basic propositions and the way the function relates them.

The truth table corresponding to the above propositional function would look like this:

Basic propositions		Propositional function
Door open	Bulb not burned out	Light on
false	false	false
false	true	false
true	false	false
true	true	true

The table lists all combinations of true and false values that can be assigned to the basic propositions. The table is completed by indicating the truth or falsity of the propositional function for each entry.

Taylor L. Booth

Tryon, William. See North Carolina (Places to visit [Tryon Palace]; Revolution and independence).

Trypanosome, *TRIHP uh nuh sohm,* is a microscopic one-celled animal. It is a parasite in the blood and spinal fluid of human beings and other vertebrates. Some trypanosomes are parasites in plants. One kind causes African sleeping sickness. Others cause Chagas' disease and nagana, an African disease of animals. A trypanosome is

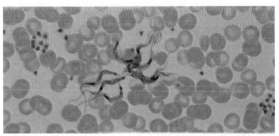

David M. Phillips, Taurus
Trypanosomes, *center,* **are shown among blood cells.**

long and thin, with a whiplike extension at one end called a *flagellum.* It also has a thin waving membrane down the length of its body. Many trypanosomes spend part of their lives inside certain insects.

Scientific classification. Trypanosomes are in the family Trypanosomidae. One trypanosome that causes sleeping sickness is *Trypanosoma gambiense.*   Ralph Buchsbaum

See also **Tsetse fly; Sleeping sickness.**

Tsar. See Czar.

Tschaikowsky, Peter Ilich. See Tchaikovsky, Peter Ilich.

Tserclaes, Johan. See Tilly, Count of.

Tsetse fly, *TSEHT see,* is a two-winged fly of Africa. It carries the animal parasites that cause African sleeping

sickness. These parasites are called *trypanosomes.*

There are about 20 kinds of tsetse flies. Most of them attack people. The flies look somewhat like ordinary houseflies, but they are larger and fold their wings flat over their backs in such a way that the wings do not stick out at an angle, as they do on houseflies. The tsetse fly has a long *proboscis* (beak) which it uses to pierce the skin of its victim. The fly sucks the blood of mammals. As it sucks the blood, it infects its victim.

The tsetse fly transmits a deadly disease called *nagana* to cattle and horses. Sleeping sickness and nagana are spread in much

WORLD BOOK illustration by Shirley Hooper, Oxford Illustrators Limited
Tsetse fly

the same way as malaria. The fly bites an animal or person already infected, picks up the germs, and infects the next person it bites.

The flies usually cannot infect people or animals until the germs have lived in their bodies for several days and have passed through the stomach to their salivary glands. But then, for at least 96 days, the flies can transmit the parasites to anyone they bite.

Tsetse flies breed slowly. The female fly produces only one egg at a time. The larva hatches from the egg and is nourished during the growing period inside the body of the parent. When the larva is full-grown, it is deposited on the ground, and it becomes a pupa.

Both male and female flies are active bloodsuckers. They are found chiefly along lake shores or river banks, making parts of Africa uninhabitable. In some regions, insecticide sprays control tsetse fly populations. Other successful control programs use radiation to sterilize male flies, making them unable to reproduce. Drugs that protect cattle from nagana are also used. However, political unrest has hampered tsetse fly control efforts in many parts of Africa.

Scientific classification. The tsetse fly belongs to the house fly and blow fly family, Muscidae. The most dangerous tsetse flies are *Glossina palpalis* and *G. morsitans.*   Sandra J. Glover

See also **Sleeping sickness; Trypanosome.**

Tsimshian Indians, *TSIHM shee uhn,* were a wealthy group of Pacific Coast Indians. They were also called Chimmesyan Indians. They lived in many small villages along the Nass and Skeena rivers in what is now British Columbia. They were the only Indians of the northern Northwest Coast to have tribal chiefs.

The Tsimshian lived by fishing, hunting, and gathering wild plants. Salmon was one of the most important foods in their diet. Their houses of large cedar beams and planks sometimes held seven to ten families, ruled by a house chief. Wealthy chiefs had slaves and servants. Each person had a place in a social class. Secret societies were also important. The Tsimshian made oceangoing canoes, totem poles, masks, rattles, boxes, and small objects of wood, bone, and ivory.

During the 1900's, the Tsimshian Indians rapidly adopted the customs of white people. But many people in British Columbia still speak the Tsimshian Indian language.   Melville Jacobs

TSS. See Toxic shock syndrome.

Tsunami. See Tidal wave.

Tsushima, Battle of. See Navy (Famous sea battles).

Tuamotu Islands, *TOO uh MOH too,* are an island group in the South Pacific (see **Pacific Islands** [map]). The Tuamotu group is made up of 75 reef islands and *atolls* (rings of coral islands). The islands stretch across almost 1,000 miles (1,600 kilometers) of water, and have dangerous sunken reefs. They cover about 300 square miles (775 square kilometers), and have a population of about 11,000. Polynesians live on the islands. Pearls and copra are the chief sources of income.

In 1606, Pedro Fernandes de Queirós, a Portuguese explorer in the service of Spain, became the first European to see the islands. A native king ruled the islands until 1881, when France annexed them. The islands are now part of French Polynesia, an overseas territory of France. France began using Mururoa atoll, in the Tuamotu group, as a nuclear bomb test area in 1965.
    Robert C. Kiste

Tuareg, *TWAH rehg,* are the largest group of nomads living in the Sahara. More than 300,000 Tuareg live in the desert, chiefly in Algeria, Mali, and Niger. The Tuareg are Muslims. They are related to the Berbers of northern Africa and speak a Berber language (see **Berbers**).

Most Tuareg herd camels, goats, sheep, and cattle and move about in areas of the Sahara where seasonal rainfall provides pasture for their livestock. Tuareg families live in tents made of either goatskins or mats woven from palm leaves. Men tend the herds, and women milk the livestock and grind grain to prepare meals. Milk is the most important food in the Tuareg diet.

The Tuareg are sometimes called the *Blue Men of the Desert.* They often wear indigo-dyed robes, which leave a blue color on their skin. The men wear turbans for protection against sandstorms and the sun. They wrap the turbans around their heads and across their faces to form a veil so that only their eyes can be seen.

Tuareg society has three main social classes—nobles, vassals, and slaves. The Tuareg are organized into confederations that consist of several noble and vassal tribes. A chief heads each confederation. The vassals in each confederation choose a noble as chief. Women and men are considered social equals. Husbands and wives separately own property, including livestock.

The Tuareg are believed to be descendants of people who originally lived in Libya over 2,000 years ago. The Tuareg fought against Turkish, Arab, and European rulers of North Africa through the years. They were fiercely independent until the French defeated them during the late 1800's and early 1900's. Droughts have always threatened their nomadic life. During a drought that lasted from 1968 to 1974, thousands of Tuareg and entire herds of their cattle died.   Candelario Sáenz and Barbara A. Worley

Tuatara, *too uh TAH ruh,* is a lizardlike reptile that lives only on a few small islands off the coast of New Zealand. Tuataras are the only living members of an ancient group of reptiles that appeared on earth more than 200 million years ago.

Tuataras have scaly, gray or greenish skin. They have a crest of enlarged scales down the back and tail. Male tuataras can grow more than 2 feet (60 centimeters) long. Females are shorter.

Tuataras sleep during the day, often in burrows dug by sea birds. They emerge from the burrows at night to hunt insects, amphibians, snails, birds, and small lizards. Tuataras have sharp teeth with which they easily tear up prey. A tuatara's tail breaks off easily. If an enemy seizes the tail, the tuatara sheds the tail and escapes. It then grows a new tail.

After mating with a male, the female tuatara carries from 8 to 15 eggs inside her body for nearly a year. She then deposits the eggs in a burrow, where they develop for more than a year before hatching. The eggs of no other reptile take as long to develop.

Tuataras grow slowly and do not mate until about 20 years of age. These animals live a long time. The longest a tuatara is known to have lived is 77 years.

Scientific classification. Tuataras make up the order Rhynchocephalia in the class Reptilia and the phylum Chordata. They are *Sphenodon punctatus.*   Raymond B. Huey

Tuareg shepherds gather in a marketplace in Niger, *above.* The Tuareg are the largest group of nomads in the Sahara.

The tuatara is a reptile found only on a few small islands off the New Zealand coast. Tuataras grow to about 2 feet (60 centimeters) in length.

Tuba is the general name for a number of musical instruments in the brass family. Tubas are the largest of the brass instruments and have the lowest pitch, serving as the bass voice in a brass section. A musician plays the tuba by vibrating the lips in a cup-shaped or funnel-shaped mouthpiece. The musician changes notes by changing lip tension and fingering the instrument's valves. Other brass instruments are held in a horizontal position, but the tuba is held vertically.

One popular type of tuba is the *baritone.* It is also called the *euphonium* or the *tenor tuba,* depending on

The upright tuba is used in the brass section of symphony orchestras. The instrument is played in a seated position with the bell pointed upward.

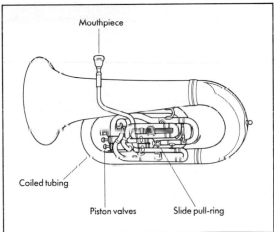

Mouthpiece

Coiled tubing

Piston valves   Slide pull-ring

WORLD BOOK illustration by Oxford Illustrators Limited

the manufacturer and the diameter of the instrument's tubing. The baritone has three or four valves and is widely used in concert bands and marching bands. The large *upright tuba* appears in symphony orchestras. It has from three to five valves. The three-valve *sousaphone* wraps around the musician's body and has a large flaring bell. It is the most common tuba in marching bands. The three-valve *marching bugle tuba* is a popular instrument in drum and bugle corps. The tuba is the newest member of the brass family.

John Keil Richards

Tube. See Electronics (Electron tubes); Television (Amplifiers and separators; The picture tube); Vacuum tube.

Tube. See London (Transportation); Subway.

Tuber, *TOO buhr,* is the thick, enlarged part of a stem that grows underground. The potato is the best example

of the tuber. The tuber stores the food, usually starch, for the plant. It has small scalelike leaves and tiny buds known as *eyes.* These eyes sprout new plants, which obtain their food from the tuber until their own roots and leaves are formed. The Jerusalem artichoke is another example of a tuber. See also **Jerusalem artichoke; Potato.**   William C. Beaver

Tuberculosis, *too BUR kyuh LOH sihs,* is an infectious disease that mainly affects the lungs but can also involve other organs. Tuberculosis is often called *TB* and was called *consumption* in the past. This disease once ranked among the most common causes of death in the world. Today, improved methods of prevention, detection, diagnosis, and treatment have greatly reduced both the number of people who get the disease and the number of people who die from it. However, tuberculosis remains a major concern in developing countries where these improvements are not widely available.

Tuberculosis strikes people of all ages but is more common among the elderly. The disease can also afflict animals, especially such livestock as cattle, hogs, and poultry. The disease is caused by rod-shaped bacteria called *tubercle bacilli.* The German physician Robert Koch discovered tubercle bacilli in 1882 (see **Koch, Robert**). Tubercle bacilli belong to a *genus* (group) of bacteria called *Mycobacterium.* They are *aerobes*—that is, they must have oxygen to live.

How tuberculosis affects the body

In most cases, a person becomes infected with tubercle bacilli by inhaling tiny droplets of moisture that contain *Mycobacterium tuberculosis* bacteria. These droplets form when a person with tuberculosis coughs or sneezes. Infection also can result from eating food contaminated with the bacteria or from drinking milk from cattle infected with *Mycobacterium bovis* bacteria. Such infection rarely occurs in developed countries where milk is pasteurized and animals are routinely tested for diseases.

The body expels many inhaled tubercle bacilli before they can do harm. Some bacilli settle into the layer of mucus that lines most of the respiratory system, including the nasal passages and the *tracheobronchial tree.* The tracheobronchial tree is the branching system of tubes that brings air to and from tiny air sacs called *alveoli* in the lungs. It consists of the *trachea* (windpipe), two *bronchi,* and hundreds of thousands of smaller airways called *bronchioles.* It is lined with cells that can move the layer of mucus covering them upward. Bacilli trapped in the mucus layer are moved up the airways toward the throat, mouth, and nose. The bacilli may then be sneezed, spat, coughed, or blown out. They also may be swallowed and pass harmlessly through the digestive tract.

Primary infection is likely to result from tubercle bacilli that penetrate beyond airways lined with mucus into the alveolar sacs deep in the lungs. Primary infection is a stage in the development of tuberculosis, but it does not always lead to the disease. Tubercle bacilli that enter an alveolar sac are usually engulfed by large, amebalike cells called *alveolar macrophages.* Normally, these cells are able to digest bacteria. However, tubercle bacilli resist digestion and most of them actually thrive and multiply inside the macrophages. Some of the macrophages carrying these bacteria may migrate to the mucus layer and be carried out of the body. Others may carry the bacteria to another part of the lungs, or into the lymph to a nearby lymph node, or even into the blood.

Within several weeks of the initial infection, a small, hard swelling called a *tubercle* forms in the alveolar sac. The tubercle begins to form as macrophages containing tubercle bacilli clump together. These macrophages are joined by *T cells* and possibly other white blood cells. In time, these clumps of cells grow larger and destroy surrounding lung tissue.

As cells inside the tubercle die, they form *caseous* (soft, cheeselike) areas that support the growth of tubercle bacilli. At the same time, tough scar tissue begins to surround the tubercles. This scar tissue prevents further spreading of the bacilli, and it may decrease the amount of oxygen they receive. The bacilli walled off by the scar tissue remain alive but inactive.

In an otherwise normal, healthy adult, primary infection by tubercle bacilli may produce no symptoms and may thus go undetected. In some cases, however, primary infection causes such symptoms as fever, rash, or nausea.

The disease known as tuberculosis develops if the tubercle bacilli again become active. It may occur immediately after the primary infection, especially in infants, children, and the elderly, and in people who have other illnesses. In most cases, however, tuberculosis develops long after the primary infection has occurred. What causes this reactivation of the bacilli is not entirely clear. It may occur when the body's defense mechanisms are impaired by another illness or by old age, or it may result from a second infection by tubercle bacilli. Reactivation of the bacteria causes the tubercles to rupture and the bacilli to reproduce rapidly. Cells may carry the bacteria to other parts of the lung or into the lymph vessels. The bacteria also may enter blood vessels and be transported to other organs, including the bones, brain, joints, kidneys, and skin.

In tuberculosis of the lungs, called *pulmonary tuberculosis,* alveolar macrophages and white blood cells accumulate at the sites of the reactivated bacteria and form caseous material. The caseous material eventually liquefies and moves up the respiratory tract with the mucus layer. The patient coughs this mucus and caseous material up as *sputum.*

Coughing and sputum production are the most common early symptoms of pulmonary tuberculosis. The cough is not usually severe and the symptoms are often mistaken for a lingering cold. If blood vessels in the lungs are damaged, there may be blood in the sputum. In advanced stages of the disease, the patient may cough up large quantities of blood. Other symptoms of advanced tuberculosis include chest pain, fever, sweating at night, fatigue, weight loss, and loss of appetite. Although tuberculosis may lead to a rapid death, it occurs

How tuberculosis develops — Most cases of tuberculosis begin with an infection deep in the lung, *left.* The top series of drawings below shows how invading bacteria called *tubercle bacilli* cause a primary infection. The bottom drawings illustrate how tuberculosis can later develop from the primary infection.

WORLD BOOK diagram by Robert Demarest

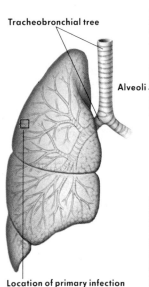
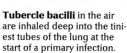
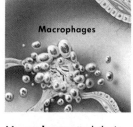
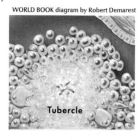

Tubercle bacilli in the air are inhaled deep into the tiniest tubes of the lung at the start of a primary infection.

Macrophages attack the invading bacilli. These cells may kill the bacteria or engulf them without killing them.

Other defending cells trap the remaining bacilli in hard lumps called *tubercles.* The trapped bacilli are harmless.

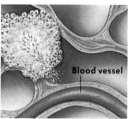
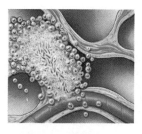

The bacilli break out of the tubercles if the body's defenses weaken. This marks the start of tuberculosis.

The bacilli multiply and invade surrounding tissue. Macrophages unsuccessfully attack the bacilli.

Multiplying bacilli break through the lung tube wall and invade a blood vessel. They may then spread.

more commonly as a long-term, progressively worsening disease.

Diagnosis of tuberculosis

Physicians use several methods to detect tuberculosis. The chief methods are skin tests, chest X rays, and laboratory tests.

Skin tests can determine if a person has been infected with tubercle bacilli in the past. However, such tests do not tell the physician whether the active disease is present. All types of skin tests are based on specific allergic reactions to the tubercle bacilli. The body develops the allergy to the bacilli within a few weeks after the primary infection.

Chest X rays may reveal tubercles or other signs of tuberculosis in the lungs. Chest X rays are usually done after a skin test has indicated a previous infection. However, chest X rays done for other reasons sometimes reveal the presence of tubercles.

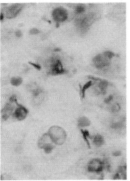

John R. Dalnauskas, M.D.

In diseased lung tissue, *above,* tubercle bacilli appear as short, red rods. This photograph magnifies the tissue 200 times.

Laboratory tests are normally the final step in the diagnosis of tuberculosis. A physician examines the patient's sputum to determine if bacilli are present. Sputum samples are treated with chemicals and stains to make the bacilli visible under the microscope. If bacilli are present, they are *cultured*—that is, grown in laboratory dishes or test tubes. Culturing determines whether they are *Mycobacterium tuberculosis* or other bacilli. It also helps find out which drugs will be most effective against the bacteria.

Treatment of tuberculosis

The first effective treatment for tuberculosis was provided by health resorts called *sanitariums.* Sanitariums were developed during the later 1800's by physicians in Europe and the United States. At a sanitarium, tuberculosis patients received bed rest, fresh air, and mild exercise. They also were isolated and thus kept from infecting other people. Sanitarium treatment helped many people overcome the disease. However, most of them had to spend months or even years in a sanitarium before they recovered.

Today almost all tuberculosis patients can be treated successfully with drugs. Isoniazid (INH) is one of the most effective antituberculosis drugs. Others include rifampin, ethambutol, para-amino salicylic acid (PAS), streptomycin, and pyrazinamide. These drugs stop the bacteria from multiplying and allow the body's natural defenses to work against the disease. Doctors normally prescribe two or more drugs at a time because tubercle bacilli may become resistant to only one medication.

Surgery was sometimes used in sanitariums to collapse a diseased lung, both to rest the lung and to decrease its oxygen level to discourage the growth of the tubercle bacilli. Doctors still perform surgery in some cases, but they remove the afflicted part of a tubercular lung rather than collapse the lung. The remaining part continues to function normally.

Prevention of tuberculosis

The drug isoniazid prevents most detected tuberculosis infections from developing into the disease. Doctors often prescribe isoniazid for people who have a positive skin test. They may also give the drug to children, elderly people, or others at special risk who live with someone who has tuberculosis.

A vaccine called BCG *(Bacillus Calmette-Guérin)* has been used in many parts of the world in an effort to prevent tuberculosis. However, the vaccine is not always effective, especially among certain populations. Physicians in the United States seldom prescribe BCG because tuberculosis occurs infrequently there.

Treatment and preventive action have greatly reduced the number of tuberculosis cases in developed countries, including the United States. The disease remains a major problem in a number of developing nations, especially those in Africa, where drugs for tuberculosis are not readily available.

During the mid-1980's, the United States had about 22,000 new cases of tuberculosis and about 1,700 deaths from the disease reported annually. Worldwide, the disease killed about 3 million people each year.

Michael G. Levitzky

See also **American Lung Association; Scrofula; Trudeau, Edward L.; Veterinary medicine.**

Additional resources

Dubos, René J., and Jean P. *White Plague: Tuberculosis, Man, and Society.* Little, Brown, 1952.
King, Lester S. *Medical Thinking: A Historical Preface.* Princeton, 1982. Uses tuberculosis to illustrate the evolution of medical thought.
Waksman, Selman A. *The Conquest of Tuberculosis.* Univ. of California Press, 1964.

Tuberose, *TOOB rohz,* is a plant of the agave family. It grows wild in tropical America and Asia. It is also raised

WORLD BOOK illustration by Lorraine Epstein

The tuberose is named for its tube-shaped rootstock, from which slender stems grow. Tuberose blossoms have a heavy, sweet fragrance. The flowers are used in making perfumes.

for use in perfumes and toilet preparations in central Europe, southern Africa, and in North Carolina and New Jersey. The tuberose has a heavy, almost sickening, odor. Its slender stem springs from a tubelike rootstock, and often grows 3 feet (91 centimeters) high. The stem of the tuberose bears waxy-white blossoms and has eight sword-shaped leaves. The tuberose is named for the shape of its rootstock, not for its resemblance to a tube-shaped rose. The tuberose is not a rose.

Scientific classification: The tuberose belongs to the agave family, Agavaceae. It is *Polianthes tuberosa.*   Donald Wyman

Tubman, Harriet (1820?-1913), was a black American whose daring rescues helped hundreds of slaves escape to freedom. She became the most famous leader of the *underground railroad,* which aided slaves fleeing to the free states or to Canada (see **Underground railroad**). Blacks called her Moses, after the Biblical figure who led the Jews from Egypt.

Tubman was born a slave in Bucktown, Md., near Cambridge. Her name was Araminta Ross, but as a child, she became known by her mother's name, Harriet. Her father taught her a knowledge of the woods that later helped her in her rescue missions. When Harriet was 13, she interfered with a supervisor to save another slave from punishment. The enraged supervisor fractured Harriet's skull with a 2-pound (0.9-kilogram) weight. She recovered but suffered blackouts for the rest of her life. She married John Tubman, a freed slave, in 1844.

Harriet Tubman escaped from slavery in 1849 and went to Philadelphia via the underground railroad, without her husband. She then vowed to return to Maryland and help other slaves escape. Tubman made her first trip back shortly after Congress passed the Fugitive Slave Act of 1850. This law made it a crime to help a runaway slave. Tubman returned 18 more times during the 1850's and helped about 300 slaves escape.

During one rescue mission, Tubman sensed that pursuers were following close behind, and so she and the fugitives boarded a southbound train to avoid suspicion. On another mission, Tubman had just bought some live chickens in Bucktown when she saw her former master walking towards her. She quickly let the chickens go and chased after them before he could recognize her. In 1857, Tubman led her parents to freedom in Auburn, N.Y.

Tubman never was caught and never lost a slave on any of her 19 rescue trips. She carried a gun and threatened to kill anyone who tried to turn back. Rewards for her capture once totaled about $40,000.

In the late 1850's, Tubman met with the radical abolitionist John Brown, who told her of his plan to free the slaves (see **Brown, John**). She considered Brown the true liberator of her race. Soon afterward, Tubman also became active in the women's rights movement in New England and New York.

In the Civil War (1861-1865), Tubman served as a nurse, scout, and spy for

Library of Congress
Harriet Tubman

the Union Army in South Carolina. During one military campaign, she helped free more than 750 slaves.

After the war, Tubman returned to Auburn, where she helped raise money for black schools. The author Sarah H. Bradford wrote *Scenes in the Life of Harriet Tubman* (1869), which described Tubman's work against slavery. In 1908, Tubman established a home in Auburn for elderly and needy blacks. It became known as the Harriet Tubman Home. The people of Auburn erected a plaque in her honor. A U.S. postage stamp bearing her portrait was issued in 1978.   Otey M. Scruggs

See also **Black Americans** (picture).

Additional resources

Conrad, Earl. *Harriet Tubman.* Eriksson, 1970. Reprint of 1943 edition.
Petry, Ann. *Harriet Tubman: Conductor on the Underground Railroad.* Harper, 1955.
Sterling, Dorothy. *Freedom Train: The Story of Harriet Tubman.* Doubleday, 1954. Suitable for younger readers.

Tubman, William V. S. (1895-1971), was president of Liberia from 1944 until his death in 1971. Educated in Liberia, he became a lawyer, and later a senator and associate justice of the Liberian Supreme Court. As president, he worked for progress in health, agriculture, and education. Tubman was born in Harper, Liberia.

T. Walter Wallbank

See also **Liberia** (History).

Tubular bells. See Chimes.

Tuchman, *TUHK muhn,* **Barbara Wertheim** (1912-   ), is an American historian who won two Pulitzer Prizes for general nonfiction. She received the first in 1963 for *The Guns of August* (1962), which deals with the early phase of World War I (1914-1918). She won the second in 1972 for *Stilwell and the American Experience in China, 1911-1945* (1971), which centers on the career of the U.S. general Joseph W. Stilwell.

Tuchman was born in New York City. During 1934 and 1935, she worked as a research assistant for the Institute of Pacific Relations. She then became a reporter for the *Nation* magazine and covered the Spanish Civil War (1936-1939). Her first book, *The Lost British Policy: Britain and Spain Since 1700,* was published in 1938. Since the mid-1950's, she has written a number of historical books. These works include *Bible and Sword: England and Palestine from the Bronze Age to Balfour* (1956), *The Zimmermann Telegram* (1958), *The Proud Tower: A Portrait of the World Before the War, 1890-1914* (1966), *Notes from China* (1972), *A Distant Mirror: The Calamitous Fourteenth Century* (1978), *Practicing History: Selected Essays* (1981), and *The March of Folly: From Troy to Vietnam* (1984).

Arthur Cyr

Wide World
Barbara Tuchman

Tucker, Richard (1914-1975), was generally considered the outstanding American operatic tenor of his day. The richness of his tone and the high-spirited characteristics of his singing earned him the nickname of the

"Jewish Caruso." A devout Orthodox Jew, Tucker was once a *cantor* (singer) in a synagogue.

Tucker was born in Brooklyn. His real name was Reuben Ticker. He made his debut at the Metropolitan Opera in 1945.   Max de Schauensee

Tucson, *TOO sahn* or *too SAHN,* Ariz. (pop. 330,537; met. area pop. 531,443), is a commercial and research center of the Southwest. It ranks second to Phoenix among Arizona's largest cities. Tucson's warm, dry, sunny climate makes it a popular health and winter resort area. Many retired men and women have settled there. Tucson lies in southern Arizona. For location, see **Arizona** (political map).

The Tucson Community Center, a convention and entertainment facility, stands in downtown Tucson. Downtown also includes United Bank Plaza, a group of office buildings, restaurants, and small shops in a plaza designed to look like a Mexican village.

Tucson is the home of the University of Arizona. Museums in the city include the Arizona State Museum and the Arizona Historical Society. The nearby Arizona-Sonora Desert Museum features animals and plants of the Sonora Desert in their natural surroundings. The Kitt Peak National Observatory, southwest of Tucson, is the site of the world's largest solar telescope. A noted landmark in the Tucson area is the San Xavier Mission, called the "White Dove of the Desert."

The University of Arizona and the federal, state, and local governments are the city's major employers. Tucson's industries include tourism, electronics manufacturing, and the production of copper.

Pima Indians and Papago Indians, who now call themselves *Tohono O'odham* (Desert People), lived in what is now the Tucson area before European explorers arrived there. In 1776, Juan Bautista de Anza established Tucson as a military outpost for the part of the Spanish territory in America that was called New Spain. In 1853, the city became part of the United States as a result of the Gadsden Purchase (see **Gadsden Purchase**). From 1867 to 1877, it was the capital of the Arizona Territory.

Tucson's population boomed from 1950 to 1965, in-

Thomas Kitchen, Tom Stack & Assoc.

Tucson is an important commercial, mining, and research center in southern Arizona. Because of its warm, dry, sunny climate, the city is also a popular resort.

creasing from 45,454 to 234,600. Many of the new residents had been stationed in the area with the armed services during World War II (1939-1945). Tucson has continued to grow rapidly since the mid-1960's. By 1980, the city's population had reached 330,537.

Tucson is the seat of Pima County. It has a council-manager government.   June Johnson Caldwell Martin

Tucumán, *TOO koo MAHN* (pop. 496,914), is a city in northwestern Argentina. Its full name is San Miguel de Tucumán. Tucumán lies at the foot of the Andes Mountains. It is the capital of the province of Tucumán. For location, see **Argentina** (political map).

Tucumán serves as the chief commercial center of northwestern Argentina. It is an important center of sugar production. Irrigated sugar cane fields lie outside the city. Other important industries in Tucumán include meat packing and milk and grain processing. The National University of Tucumán is in the city. Tucumán was founded by Spanish settlers in 1565. Parts of the city still have Spanish colonial architecture. Argentina's declaration of independence was signed in Tucumán in 1816.

Armin K. Ludwig and Richard W. Wilkie

Tudor, *TOO duhr,* **House of.** Tudor is the name of the family that ruled England from 1485 to 1603. The first Tudor ruler was Henry VII. He won his crown at the battle of Bosworth Field, defeating Richard III and ending the Wars of the Roses. Henry claimed the throne through his mother, Margaret Beaufort, a descendant of Edward III. Henry restored order to England after 30 years of civil war, and the nation took its first steps towards becoming a major world power.

His son, Henry VIII, continued his policies. Henry VIII broke all ties between England and the Roman Catholic Church. He was succeeded first by his son, Edward VI, and then in turn by his daughters, Mary I and Elizabeth I. The reigns of Edward and Mary were short and unhappy because of civil unrest, foreign wars, and religious disturbances. Under Elizabeth, however, England once again enjoyed the strong rule typical of the Tudors. At her death in 1603, the crown passed to King James VI of Scotland, the great-grandson of Henry VII's oldest daughter. He was the first Stuart king of England.

W. M. Southgate

See also **England** (History); **Henry (VII, VIII)**.

Tuesday is the name of the third day of the week. Its name comes from *Tiu,* or *Tiw,* the old Anglo-Saxon form of *Tyr,* name of the Norse god of war. Tyr was the son of Odin, or Woden, for whom Wednesday was named. The French call Tuesday *Mardi,* for Mars, the Roman war god. *Shrove Tuesday,* the day before Lent, was so-called because it was customary to confess and be *shriven* or *shrove* (receive absolution) by a priest. See also **Shrove Tuesday; Week.**   Grace Humphrey

Tufted titmouse. See Titmouse.

Tugboat, also called *tug* or *towboat,* is a small boat that is used to move large ships. Tugboats get their power from a steam or diesel engine. Tugboats used in harbors are powerful enough to tow large ocean liners or freighters. They can tow from the front or side, or push from the back. Most tugs are from 65 to 100 feet (20 to 30 meters) long, and are driven by engines with as much as 3,500 horsepower (2,610 kilowatts). Tugs used on inland lakes and rivers tow or push long lines of barges loaded with heavy cargoes. They have engines of

as much as 6,600 horsepower (4,920 kilowatts). See also
Barge (picture).   Robert H. Burgess

Tuileries, *TWEE luh reez* or *TWEEL REE,* a famous royal
palace, stood on the right bank of the river Seine in
Paris. During the French Revolution, mobs forced Louis
XVI and his family to live there instead of at Versailles. In
1792, the mobs killed Swiss guards who tried to defend
the royal family at the Tuileries. For a time, the Convention of the Revolution held its sessions in the Tuileries.
Napoleon made it his home, and it served as the royal
residence after the Restoration.

Catherine de Médicis began the building of the palace in 1564, but it was not completed until the 1600's. It
formed a long, narrow band of buildings with high
roofs and dormer windows. At one end it joined the
Louvre. The famous Tuileries Gardens covered 75 acres
(30 hectares) on the west side of the palace. Supporters
of the Commune destroyed most of the palace in 1871,
but the garden is still popular.   G. Holmes Perkins

Tulane University of Louisiana is a private university in New Orleans. It includes two liberal arts
schools—the College of Arts and Sciences for men and
H. Sophie Newcomb College for women. Tulane also
has coeducational schools of architecture, business administration, continuing education, engineering, graduate studies, law, medicine, public health and tropical
medicine, and social work. The university offers a junior-
year program of study abroad and special programs in
comparative law, Latin-American studies, and political
economy.

Tulane was founded in 1834 as the Medical College
of Louisiana. In 1884, it was renamed in honor of Paul
Tulane, a New Orleans merchant who gave the university its first endowment. For enrollment, see **Universities and colleges** (table).

Critically reviewed by Tulane University of Louisiana

Tularemia, *TOO luh REE mee uh,* also called rabbit
fever, is an infectious disease of many mammals, including human beings. Tularemia is caused by a bacterium,
Francisella tularensis. It was first reported in Tulare
County, California, in 1911. Tularemia is most often
transmitted by the bite of a tick or some other insect.
Human beings also can catch this disease by handling
infected animals, such as squirrels, rabbits, and rats. Tularemia causes a fever that comes and goes, and lasts
several weeks. The lymph glands become swollen
around the bite. If not treated by a physician, tularemia
often causes death.   Gary A. Heidt

Tulip is a lovely, graceful garden flower that came
from southern Europe and Asia. Although tulips grow in
many parts of the world, we generally associate them
with the Netherlands.

Tulips bloom in spring. They grow from bulbs, and
the leaves, stems, and flowers grow directly out of the
bulb. The stems range from 4 inches (10 centimeters) to
more than 30 inches (76 centimeters) tall. The tulip usually develops only one large, bell-shaped flower at the
tip of its stem. But there are types with more than one
stem or flower. The flowers usually grow erect on the
stem. They may be almost any solid color, and some tulips have flowers with two colors. In addition, the flowers of some tulips become streaked with other colors
because of virus diseases that affect the plant's color but
not its health.

Derek Fell

Tulips are colorful garden flowers that bloom in the spring.
Tulip leaves and the flower stem grow directly out of a bulb.

Gardeners plant tulip bulbs in autumn. They require a
well-drained, loamy soil of average richness. Usually
only professional tulip growers or plant breeders grow
the flowers from seed, because tulip seed does not produce a flowering bulb for four to seven years.

Thousands of varieties of tulips have developed from
a few *species* (kinds). Almost all the cultivated kinds of
tulips were developed from tulips of Asia Minor that
were brought to Vienna from Constantinople (now Istanbul) in the 1500's. The name *tulip* comes from a Turkish
word which means *turban.* The beautiful blossoms look
a little like turbans. Popular garden varieties of tulips include the Darwin hybrids and the Triumphs, Lily-flow-
ered, Fringed, and Parrot tulips.

After the tulip was brought to Europe, it became the
most fashionable flower in both England and Holland.
Interest in the flower developed into a craze in Holland,
called the *tulipomania,* between 1634 and 1637. Individual bulbs sold for huge prices. People invested their
money in tulips as American business people might invest in high-technology stocks. Many people lost fortunes in the tulip market, and finally the government
was forced to regulate the trade in bulbs.

Tulip cultivation is an important industry in the Netherlands today. It is also important in the northwestern
part of the United States. Billions of bulbs are produced
every year. Dutch growers produce nearly 2,000 varieties. About 400 of these are available in large quantities.

Scientific classification. Tulips belong to the lily family, Liliaceae. The tulip brought to Europe in the 1500's is *Tulipa ges-
neriana.*   August A. De Hertogh

See also **Flower** (picture: Garden perennials [Bulbs]);
Netherlands (picture: The Polders); **Ottawa** (Annual
events).

Tulip tree, also called *yellow poplar* and *tulip poplar,*
is the tallest broadleaf tree in the eastern United States.
In forests, it may grow 200 feet (61 meters) high, and its
trunk may be 5 to 10 feet (1.5 to 3 meters) thick at the
base. One of the most valuable of the North American
hardwoods, it grows from southern New England to
Florida and westward to southeast Missouri and Louisiana. It is the state tree of Indiana and Tennessee.

© Yeager and Kay, Photo Researchers

A tulip tree blossom resembles a tulip flower. The blossoms are an important source of nectar for bees.

The showy greenish-yellow blossoms of the tulip tree resemble tulips and are an important source of nectar for bees. Its distinctive leaves have a broad notch at the tip and two or four lobes. They are smooth, long-stalked, and graceful. The leaves turn butter-yellow in autumn. The *sapwood* (outer wood) is whitish. The *heartwood* (inner wood) is sunshine-yellow to pale-tan. The wood is easily worked and is used chiefly for furniture, veneer, boxes, and baskets.

Scientific classification. The tulip tree belongs to the magnolia family, Magnoliaceae. It is *Liriodendron tulipifera*.

Kenneth R. Robertson

See also **Tree** (Familiar broadleaf and needleleaf trees [picture]).

Tull, *tuhl,* **Jethro** (1674-1741), an English gentleman farmer, introduced many new farming methods. In his day, farmers sowed the seed by throwing it by hand. Tull regarded this practice as both wasteful and uncertain. So he invented a drill for boring straight rows of holes into which he dropped the seed. He also claimed that farmers could keep their soil fertile by frequent hoeing. His ideas were adopted slowly. He was born in Berkshire, and was educated at St. John's College, Oxford University. Tull traveled in France and Italy to observe farming methods. He wrote *Horse-hoeing Husbandry,* published in 1731.   C. B. Baker

See also **Agriculture** (The invention of new farm equipment).

Tulsa, *TUHL suh,* Okla. (pop. 360,919; met. area pop. 657,173), is a major center of the United States petroleum industry. Among the cities of Oklahoma, only Oklahoma City has more people than Tulsa has. Tulsa lies in northeastern Oklahoma along the Arkansas River. For location, see **Oklahoma** (political map). Tulsa serves as Oklahoma's busiest port and its chief manufacturing center.

During the 1830's, Creek Indians from Tallassee, Ala., settled in what is now the Tulsa area. The Creek named their new village after their former community, but this name in time was changed to Tulsa. Construction of the first railroad to Tulsa in 1882 brought white settlers to the area. But until 1901, Tulsa remained a small village. That year, the discovery of oil in nearby Red Fork attracted many people to the area. The petroleum industry helped make Tulsa one of the fastest-growing cities in the United States.

The city. Tulsa, the county seat of Tulsa County, covers about 177 square miles (458 square kilometers), including 5 square miles (13 square kilometers) of inland water. The Arkansas River divides the city into two parts, the larger of which lies east of the river. Tulsa's metropolitan area covers five entire counties—Creek, Osage, Rogers, Tulsa, and Wagoner.

A group of government buildings called the Civic Center forms the heart of downtown Tulsa. These buildings cover eight square blocks and include the city hall, the county courthouse, the main public library, and police headquarters. The Assembly Center, which has exhibit halls and an arena that seats 10,000 people, also stands in this area. A federal office building is located nearby.

More than 97 per cent of Tulsa's people were born in the United States. They are descendants of people of many nationalities. Blacks make up about 12 per cent of the population, and Tulsa has smaller groups of American Indians and Mexican Americans.

Economy. Tulsa has more than 1,000 manufacturing plants. The chief industries manufacture fabricated metal products and nonelectric machinery. The city leads the world in the manufacture of industrial heaters and *winches* (hoisting devices). Other Tulsa products include transportation equipment; metals; and clay, glass, and stone products. The city's largest employers include American Airlines, which has maintenance and engineering centers there, and McDonnell Douglas and Rockwell International corporations, two of the nation's biggest aerospace companies.

Oklahoma's largest oil refinery stands just outside the Tulsa business district. But the city has become more important as an administrative center of the U.S. petroleum industry than as an oil producer. Tulsa serves as a major control center of the industry, including distributors, manufacturers, producers, and research activities.

About 860 oil or oil-related companies maintain offices in the Tulsa area. More than 350 of these firms have headquarters in the city. Tulsa has large data-processing offices, including the credit card centers of several major oil companies. The city also is the national headquarters of the United States Jaycees.

Tulsa became a major port in 1970, after the McClellan-Kerr Arkansas River Navigation System was extended to Catoosa, 3 miles (5 kilometers) east of the city. This system links Tulsa's port, located near Catoosa on the Verdigris River, to the Mississippi River, the Gulf of Mexico, and the Atlantic Ocean. An industrial area is near the port. Many airlines use Tulsa International Airport. Freight trains also serve the city.

Education and cultural life. Tulsa's public school system includes about 95 elementary schools and 10 high schools, with a total of about 71,000 students. The city also has about 12 parochial and private schools, with about 3,700 students. Colleges in Tulsa include the University of Tulsa, Oral Roberts University, Oklahoma College of Osteopathic Medicine and Surgery, and Tulsa Junior College.

The Thomas Gilcrease Institute of American History and Art owns more than 5,000 works of art. This museum features one of the world's finest collections of Indian art and historical documents. It also exhibits the world's largest collections of works by the American

© Bill Barley, Shostal

Tulsa is Oklahoma's manufacturing center. Because of its location on the Arkansas River, it is a busy port. The city is also a center for the petroleum industry in the United States.

painters Thomas Moran, Frederic Remington, and Charles M. Russell. The Philbrook Art Center displays Italian Renaissance paintings and sculpture, Chinese jewelry, and American Indian baskets and pottery.

Two daily newspapers, the *World* and the *Tribune,* serve the city. Tulsa has 5 television stations and about 20 radio stations. Its public library has 21 branches in Tulsa County. The Tulsa Civic Ballet, the Tulsa Opera Company, and the Tulsa Philharmonic Orchestra perform at the Tulsa Performing Arts Center, which has four theaters.

Tulsa's largest park is Mohawk Park, which occupies 2,817 acres (1,140 hectares). It includes a golf course and a zoo with over 600 animals. The Tulsa Municipal Rose Garden, in Woodward Park, features about 12,000 rose plants. The annual Tulsa State Fair begins in late September at the Tulsa State Fairgrounds. The fairgrounds includes the world's largest livestock display barn and show ring and the Tulsa Exposition Center. The center has a $10\frac{1}{2}$-acre (4.2-hectare) continuous-area exhibition hall.

Government. Tulsa has a commission form of government. The voters elect a mayor and four commissioners to two-year terms. Each commissioner supervises a department of the city government. Tulsa gets most of its revenue from a sales tax.

History. Several Indian tribes once hunted in the area that is now Tulsa. During the 1830's, Creek Indians from Tallassee, Ala., settled in the Tulsa area. According to tradition, a Creek named Archie Yahola presided at tribal councils under a huge tree called the Council Oak in 1836. This tree still stands on Cheyenne Avenue in Tulsa.

In 1848, Lewis Perryman, a Creek, opened a village trading post on the Arkansas River. A post office called Tulsa was established at the ranch of his son, George Perryman, in 1879. The village had fewer than 1,000 people in 1882, when the Atlantic and Pacific Railroad—now part of the Burlington Northern system—was extended

from Vinita, Okla., to the Arkansas River near the present site of downtown Tulsa. Tulsa, or Tulsey Town, as it was sometimes called, became a cattle-shipping terminal. Tulsa was incorporated as a town in 1898. In 1900, it had a population of 1,390.

In 1901, the discovery of oil at nearby Red Fork attracted large numbers of people to the area. Tulsa became an oil center in 1905, when the large Glenn Pool oil field was opened 15 miles (24 kilometers) southwest. When Oklahoma gained statehood in 1907, Tulsa had a population of 7,298. Tulsa received a city charter in 1908. The oil boom increased the city's population to 72,075 by 1920 and to 141,258 by 1930, and Tulsa became known as the *Oil Capital of the World.*

The number of Tulsans increased to only 142,157 by 1940. But during World War II (1939-1945), workers flocked to Tulsa from rural areas to take factory jobs. The government built a huge bomber airplane factory in the city. By 1945, this plant employed almost 22,000 people and had become the largest factory in Oklahoma. The increased defense activities helped raise Tulsa's population to 182,740 by 1950. Today, the McDonnell Douglas Corporation and Rockwell International use the plant to make commercial and military aircraft.

During the 1960's, Tulsa completed its Civic Center. In 1970, the completion of the McClellan-Kerr Arkansas River Navigation System made Tulsa a major port. The navigation project, which included construction of many dams and locks, cost $1,200,000,000.

Tulsa's 41-story First National Bank & Trust Company Building was completed in 1973. In 1977, the 50-story Bank of Oklahoma Tower replaced it as Oklahoma's tallest structure. The Bank of Oklahoma Tower forms part of the Williams Center, a project covering 11 square blocks in downtown Tulsa. The project includes the Tulsa Performing Arts Center, completed in 1977.

Tulsa's growth continued. The city's population almost doubled between 1950 and 1980.   Gene Curtis

For the monthly weather in Tulsa, see **Oklahoma** (Climate). See also **Oklahoma** (pictures).

Tumbleweed is the popular name for several plants that grow in the prairie and plains regions of the United States. These plants develop rounded tops, and in autumn they wither and break off at the ground level. The dried plants are then carried or tumbled about by the wind, like great, light balls. As they move, they scatter their seeds about over the plains. These plants are considered great pests by farmers and ranchers. Tumbleweeds often pile up against barbed-wire fences or fill small gullies. The common tumbleweeds include the *Russian thistle* and an amaranth. All tumbleweeds are *annuals*—that is, they grow from seed to maturity and then die within one year.

Scientific classification. The Russian thistle is in the goosefoot family, Chenopodiaceae. It is *Salsola kali.*

Anton A. Reznicek

Tumboa. See Welwitschia.

Tumor is an abnormal growth of tissues in the body. Tumors are also called *neoplasms.* Some tumors are *benign.* They limit themselves to a certain region and do not spread elsewhere in the body. Once benign tumors are removed, they usually do not grow again. *Malignant tumors* (cancers) that are not completely removed can spread throughout the body, often destroying other tissues in the body (see **Cancer** [How cancer develops]). When cancer arises from the skin, tissues that line the body cavities, or nonblood-forming organs, it is called *carcinoma.* Cancer that affects bones, cartilages, and soft tissues is called *sarcoma. Leukemia* is cancer of the bone marrow or other blood-forming organs. Only a doctor can determine whether a tumor is benign or malignant.

Tumors may grow from any kind of tissue in the body. They may develop in the skin, in muscles, nerves, blood vessels, bones, or any organ. A well-known tumor is the mastoid tumor, which grows over the mastoid process just behind the ear (see **Mastoid**).

Tumors are often named after the tissue from which they grow. For example, a *lipoma* is a benign tumor made up of *lipid* (fat) tissue. *Gliomas* (nerve-tissue tumors) are made up of *glia,* the peculiar branched cells that support the nerves. *Lymphoma* is a malignant tumor of lymphoid tissue. It is one of the best-studied tumors, and it is highly treatable by chemotherapy and radiation therapy.   Martin D. Abeloff

Related articles in *World Book* include:

Biopsy	Leukemia	Neurofibro-
Cancer	Malignancy	matosis
Epithelioma	Mole	

Tumpline. See Indian, American (Family life [Transportation]).

Tuna, a fruit. See **Prickly pear.**

Tuna is any of 14 species of saltwater fish in the mackerel family. Tuna meat is a popular food in many countries and is sold canned, fresh, and frozen. The United States and Japan are the chief consumers of tuna. The tuna is also a leading game fish. The most important commercial types of tuna are the *albacore, bigeye, skipjack,* and *yellowfin.*

The largest tuna is the *bluefin,* which grows up to 10 feet (3 meters) long and weighs up to 1,500 pounds (680 kilograms). The smallest tuna is the *bullet mackerel,* which grows up to 20 inches (51 centimeters) long and weighs up to 5 pounds (2.3 kilograms).

Tuna rank among the swiftest fish. The bluefin can swim as fast as 45 miles (72 kilometers) per hour. Like other fish, the tuna has gills that take oxygen from the water passing over them. But unlike most fish, the tuna cannot pump water over its gills. Therefore, it must swim continuously in order to breathe.

Tuna live in temperate and tropical waters. In summer, they range as far north as Newfoundland and Norway in the Atlantic Ocean, and British Columbia and Northern Japan in the Pacific Ocean. Major tuna fisheries operate in the Atlantic, Pacific, and Indian oceans. Tuna sometimes migrate long distances and can cross

© Eric E. Peterson

Tuna are often caught by bait fishing. In this method, crews throw live bait overboard to attract the tuna. They then catch the fish by hook and line.

oceans or move from one ocean to another. One bluefin, tagged and released off Japan, was recaptured off the Pacific coast of northern Mexico. This fish had to swim at least 6,700 miles (10,800 kilometers) to reach its destination.

Tuna are caught in three main ways. In *bait fishing,* crews throw live bait overboard to attract the tuna and then catch them by hooks and lines attached to long poles. In *longlining,* tuna are caught with a line that is up to 81 miles (130 kilometers) long and has as many as 2,200 shorter lines with baited hooks. *Purse seining,* the chief method of catching skipjack and yellowfin tuna, encircles the fish in large nets called *purse seines.* In the eastern Pacific, crews locate yellowfin tuna by seeking schools of dolphins, which often swim above the fish. Some dolphins are trapped with the tuna and accidentally killed. The United States and other countries limit the killing of dolphins by requiring that the nets have escape chutes for dolphins.

Scientific classification. Tuna belong to the mackerel family, Scombridae. The albacore is *Thunnus alalunga;* the bigeye is *T. obesus;* the yellowfin is *T. albacares;* and the bluefin is *T. thynnus.* The skipjack is *Euthynnus pelamis,* and the bullet mackerel is *Auxis rochei.*   James Joseph

See also Fish (picture: Fish of coastal waters [Bluefin tuna]); **Fishing industry** (Where fish are caught).

Leading tuna-fishing countries

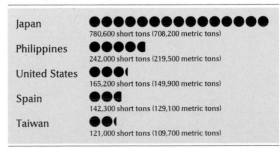

Japan	●●●●●●●●●●●●●●●
	780,600 short tons (708,200 metric tons)
Philippines	●●●●◖
	242,000 short tons (219,500 metric tons)
United States	●●●◖
	165,200 short tons (149,900 metric tons)
Spain	●●◖
	142,300 short tons (129,100 metric tons)
Taiwan	●●◖
	121,000 short tons (109,700 metric tons)

Figures are for 1983. Sources: *Fisheries Yearbook, Taiwan Area, 1983,* Taiwan Fisheries Bureau; *Yearbook of Fishery Statistics, 1983,* Food and Agriculture Organization of the United Nations.

WORLD BOOK illustration by John F. Eggert

The yellowfin tuna provides light meat for canning.

Tundra is a cold, dry region where trees cannot grow. Most tundras are covered by snow more than half the year. The long, cold winters and short, cool summers prevent the growth of trees in a tundra. But mosses, lichens, grasses, and grasslike plants called *sedges* grow in a tundra, and many kinds of animals live there. There are two kinds of tundras, *Arctic* and *Alpine.*

Arctic tundras lie near the Arctic Ocean. They include Greenland and the northern parts of Alaska, Canada, Europe, and Russia. Most are lowlands with many lakes, but some have mountains. Few people live in Arctic tundras, but some Eskimos live in areas where they can fish and hunt for food (see **Eskimo**).

Each spring, tundras come to life. Geese, terns, and other birds fly north to nest. The tundra plants grow rapidly and cover the ground with bright flowers. Caribou, reindeer, and musk oxen graze on these plants, and wolves prey on the grazing animals. Other tundra wildlife includes Arctic foxes and hares, grizzly bears, lemmings, polar bears, and ptarmigans. Seals and walruses live along the coastlines. Arctic char and a few other kinds of fishes live in the lakes and rivers. Mosquitoes, black flies, and other insects thrive.

Summer temperatures in an Arctic tundra range from about 37° to 54° F. (3° to 12° C). The soil remains permanently frozen from 1 to 5 feet (30 to 150 centimeters) below the surface of the ground. This soil, called *permafrost,* prevents water from draining away. As a result, most of the soil stays cold and wet throughout the summer.

Most of the precipitation in Arctic tundras comes from snow, which covers the ground from September to April or May. In the fall, caribou, reindeer, and most Arctic birds migrate south to winter feeding grounds. The other Arctic animals remain active in the tundra throughout the winter.

Arctic tundras have large deposits of coal, natural gas, oil, iron ore, lead, and zinc. The coal, oil, and natural gas can help meet the world's demands for fuel. Special pipelines were designed to transport the oil and gas with the least possible damage to the environment of the tundras.

Alpine tundras are on mountains throughout the world at altitudes where trees cannot grow. Permafrost rarely occurs in Alpine tundras, and most of these regions have well-drained soils. Deer, elk, and various species of mountain goats and sheep graze on Alpine tundras during the summer. Pikas, ptarmigans, woodchucks, and many kinds of insects also live in Alpine tundras. Lawrence C. Bliss

See also **Arctic; Biome** (map); **Permafrost.**

Additional resources

Barrett, Ian. *Tundra and People.* Silver Burdett, 1982. Suitable for younger readers.
George, Jean C. *One Day in the Alpine Tundra.* Harper, 1984. Suitable for younger readers.
Zwinger, Ann H., and Willard, Beatrice E. *Land Above the Trees: A Guide to American Alpine Tundra.* Harper, 1972.

Tundra wolf. See **Wolf.**

Tung oil is an oil that comes from the seed kernels of the tung tree. The tung tree originally grew in East Asia, chiefly in China. Tung oil is also called *China-wood oil, Japanese-wood oil,* or simply *wood oil.* The tree has also been successfully grown in the southern United States. Tung oil is one of the most powerful drying agents. The oil resists acids, alkalis, and alcohols.

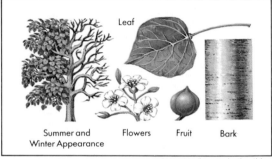

WORLD BOOK illustration by Chris Skilton

The tung tree is the source of tung oil.

Tung oil is widely used in paints, lacquers, varnishes, and printing inks. Paints containing tung oil help seal the underwater surfaces of swimming pools, dams, piers, and boats. Varnishes made with it help insulate wire and metallic surfaces. Tung oil helps some printing inks stick to metal surfaces such as bottle caps. Because of its relatively high cost, tung oil is sometimes replaced with epoxy resins and other synthetics.

Scientific classification. The tung tree belongs to the spurge family, Euphorbiaceae. It is classified as *Aleurites fordii.*
John R. Koch

WORLD BOOK illustration by Jean Helmer

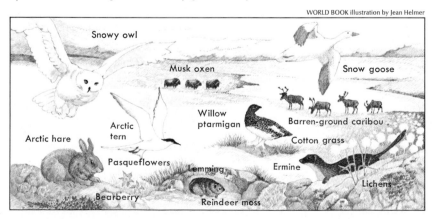

Many plants and animals live in the Arctic tundra. Lichens, mosses, and bright flowers cover the ground in summer. Each fall, Arctic hares, ermines, willow ptarmigans, and other tundra animals grow white winter coats. These white coats blend with the snow and help protect the animals from their enemies.

Tungsten, also called *wolfram,* is a moderately hard, silver-white metal, and one of the chemical elements. Tungsten has many uses. It has the highest melting point of all metals, and remains strong at very high temperatures. For these reasons, it is used in equipment that must withstand high temperatures. Tungsten is added to steel to make steel harder, stronger, and more elastic. Tungsten steel tools last longer than ordinary steel tools. Tungsten and carbon form tungsten carbide, an extremely hard substance used in the tips of high-speed cutting tools, and in mining and petroleum drills. *Carboloy* is the General Electric Company's trade name for a form of tungsten carbide.

Tungsten is widely used in the electronics industry. It is made into heating filaments for vacuum tubes used in radios, television sets, and other electronic equipment. It is also used to make filaments for electric lights and contact points for the ignition systems of automobiles. Compounds of tungsten with either calcium or magnesium are *phosphors* (chemicals that give off light). They are used in fluorescent lamps. Mixtures of alkali metals with different amounts of tungsten form *tungsten bronzes,* which are used in the paint industry.

Tungsten occurs in nature in the minerals scheelite (calcium tungstate, $CaWO_4$) and wolframite (ferrousmanganous tungstate, $[Fe,Mn] WO_4$). China and the Soviet Union are the leading tungsten-mining countries. In the United States, California and Colorado lead in mining tungsten. Tungsten is prepared from the minerals by first adding sodium hydroxide to convert the insoluble tungsten compounds into a solution of sodium tungstate (Na_2WO_4). Acid is then added to make tungstic trioxide (WO_3) come out of the solution. Tungstic trioxide is heated with hydrogen to form the pure metal.

Tungsten has the chemical symbol W. Its atomic number is 74 and its atomic weight is 183.85. Tungsten melts at about 3400° C and boils at about 5600° C. It was discovered in 1783 by two Spanish chemists, Fausto de Elhuyar and his brother Juan José.   S. C. Cummings

See also **Alloy** (Alloys of iron); **Element, Chemical** (tables); **Wolframite; Electric light** (The filament).

Tungsten carbide. See Tungsten.

Tunic, *TOO nihk,* is a loose, short garment, reaching from the neck to about the knee. It is usually fastened at the waist by a belt or girdle. The name comes from the

The Good Shepherd, a marble statue (late A.D. 200's) by an unknown Roman sculptor; Museo Pio Christiani, the Vatican (SCALA/Art Resource)

The tunic was a short, loose garment worn by the ancient Romans. The Greeks wore a similar garment called a *chiton.*

Latin word *tunica.* The tunica was a garment worn by people of ancient Rome. The men covered it with the *toga,* and the women with the *palla.* Greek men and women wore a similar garment called the *chiton.*

Tunic, or *tunicle,* also means a robe worn by a subdeacon of the Roman Catholic and some Episcopal churches during Mass.   Mary Evans

See also **Clothing** (Ancient times); **Toga.**

Tunicle. See Tunic.

Tuning. See Radio (The tuner; pictures: Building a radio transmitter); **Television** (Tuner).

Tuning fork is a device used for tuning musical instruments and for finding a standard pitch. It is made of metal and shaped like a U with a handle on the bottom.

A tuning fork produces a tone when struck. The tone is not affected by moisture and most other conditions that affect the pitch and tone of musical instruments. However, the tone is slightly affected by variations in temperature. The forks are made for any note of the scale, but those most often used are A, B flat, or the C above middle C. John Shore, an English trumpeter, is said to have invented the tuning fork in 1711. Today, various electronic devices are also used to tune musical instruments.   Reinhard G. Pauly

See also **Sound** (pictures).

Tunis, *TOO nihs* (pop. 596,654), is the capital and largest city of Tunisia. Tunis lies on the western shore of the Lake of Tunis, a shallow lagoon linked to the Mediterranean Sea by a narrow channel. For the city's location, see **Tunisia** (map). In addition to serving as the governmental center of Tunisia, Tunis is the headquarters for most of the country's banks and insurance companies. The Tunis area is Tunisia's chief industrial center. The main industries are food processing and textile manufacturing. Commerce and tourism also play important roles in the economy.

Tunis consists of an old and a modern section. The

Leading tungsten-mining countries

Annual tungsten production	
China	●●●●●●●●●●●●
	17,000 short tons (15,000 metric tons)
Soviet Union	●●●●●●●
	10,000 short tons (9,200 metric tons)
Canada	●●◖
	3,400 short tons (3,100 metric tons)
South Korea	●●
	2,900 short tons (2,600 metric tons)
Australia	●◖
	2,100 short tons (1,900 metric tons)
Portugal	●◖
	2,000 short tons (1,800 metric tons)

Figures are for 1985.
Source: *Minerals Yearbook, 1985,* U.S. Bureau of Mines.

old section, called the *medina,* is a crowded area with narrow, winding streets. The modern section has Western-style buildings and broad, tree-lined boulevards.

Thynes, a settlement on the site of present-day Tunis, was part of the ancient empire of Carthage. The settlement gradually developed into the city of Tunis. Arab Muslims captured Tunis in A.D. 698. From the early 1200's to the late 1500's, Tunis was a center for trade between Africa and Europe. Today several international organizations, including the Arab League, have their headquarters in Tunis.   Kenneth J. Perkins

Tunisia extends farther north than any other country in Africa. Its northern tip is only 85 miles (137 kilometers) from Sicily, a part of Europe. Both northern and eastern

Tunisia

▬▬▬	International boundary
———	Road
———	Railroad
———	Oil pipeline
✪	National capital
•	Other city or town
+	Elevation above sea level

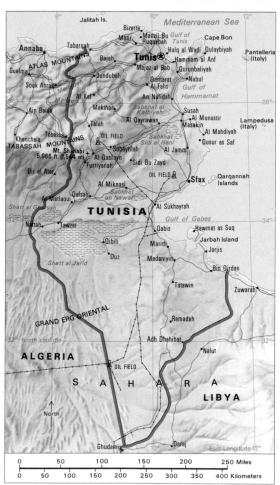

0   50   100   150   200   250 Miles
0   50 100 150 200 250 300 350 400 Kilometers

WORLD BOOK map

Facts in brief

Capital: Tunis.
Official language: Arabic.
Area: 63,170 sq. mi. (163,610 km²). *Greatest distances*—north-south, 485 mi. (781 km); east-west, 235 mi. (378 km). *Coastline*—639 mi. (1,028 km).
Population: *Estimated 1989 population*—7,729,000; density, 122 persons per sq. mi. (47 per km²); distribution, 57 per cent urban, 43 per cent rural. *1984 census*—6,966,173. *Estimated 1994 population*—8,511,000.
Chief products: *Agriculture*—barley, citrus fruit, olives, wheat, wine. *Mining*—iron, lead, lignite, phosphates, zinc. *Forestry*—oak, pine.
Flag: The flag has a large white circle on a red field. Inside the circle are a red crescent and star, emblems of the Muslim religion. See **Flag** (picture: Flags of Africa).
Money: *Basic unit*—dinar. See **Money** (table).

Tunisia border the Mediterranean Sea.

Tunisia is part of the Arab world, the Mediterranean area, and Africa. Almost all Tunisians speak Arabic and follow an Arab way of life. For hundreds of years, trade routes have connected Tunisia to Africa south of the Sahara. France controlled Tunisia from 1881 until Tunisia became independent in 1956. Tunisia shows many French influences. Tunis is its capital and largest city.

Government. Tunisia is a republic headed by a president. The people elect the president to a five-year term. The president appoints a Cabinet headed by a prime minister to assist him. Tunisia has a one-house legislature called the National Assembly. The people elect the 90 members of the National Assembly to five-year terms. All people who have been citizens for five years and who are 20 or older may vote. The president appoints a governor to head each of Tunisia's 13 provinces.

The Socialist Destour Party is Tunisia's chief political party. It has ruled the government since independence.

People. Life in Tunisia is more uniform than it is in most other African and Middle Eastern countries. This uniformity is chiefly due to the people's similarity in language and religion, and to the fact that political and cultural life is centered in one city, Tunis.

Small groups of Europeans, Jews, and Berbers live in Tunisia. But almost all Tunisians are Arabs and Muslims. French culture has influenced several features of Tunisian life, including architecture and food. Many Tunisians speak French as a second language.

Slightly more than half the people live in cities or towns. Most cities are divided into old and new sections. Narrow streets and covered markets characterize the old sections. Tree-lined avenues and European-style buildings are typical of the new sections. Many people in the cities wear Western-style clothes.

The rest of Tunisia's people live in villages or on farms. In the past, rural dwellings included many mud huts and tents. But today, most rural houses are made of stone or concrete. Many people in the rural areas continue to wear traditional Arab clothing—a turban or skullcap, and a long, loose gown, or a long coatlike garment with long sleeves.

Since the mid-1950's, the Tunisian government has devoted an average of one-fifth of its budget to education. Almost all primary school-age children and about one-third of secondary school-age children attend school. The country's higher education system includes the University of Tunis and professional schools.

Land. The uniformity of Tunisian life is also partly due to the country's geography. Two branches of the Atlas mountain range, which crosses northwestern Africa, extend into Tunisia. In Tunisia, the northern branch is called the Atlas Mountains, and the southern branch, the Tabassah Mountains. But the mountains are low. Few peaks reach more than 2,000 feet (610 meters), and the highest, Mount Shanabi, is just 5,066 feet (1,544 meters) above sea level. Unlike neighboring Algeria and Morocco, Tunisia has no hard-to-reach mountain regions which would cut the people off from the influences of the cities and plains.

Hills and grassland lie between the mountain ranges. Much of Tunisia's wheat is grown in the Majardah River valley in the north. The Majardah is the only river in Tunisia that does not dry up in summer.

From the Tabassah range, the land descends across a plateau to the Sahara in the south and to a coastal plain in the east. The plateau is covered with coarse grass. The people raise cattle, sheep, and goats. The southern desert contains great salt lakes and date palm oases.

The fertile coastal plain extends along the east coast from Sfax to Tunis. Cereals, citrus fruits, and olives are grown there. This region also has Tunisia's largest towns and cities.

Tunisia has hot, dry summers and warm, wet winters. The average temperatures are 79° F. (26° C) in summer and 52° F. (11° C) in winter. In the north, most rain falls in winter, but it is irregular and droughts occur every three or four years. There is little rain in the south.

Economy. Tunisia is a leading producer of phosphates. It also has petroleum resources that are used for its own needs and for export. Phosphates and petroleum account for about half the value of Tunisia's exports. Food processing and the manufacture of basic consumer goods account for most of the country's industrial production. Wheat, barley, grapes for wine, olives,

olive oil, and dates are Tunisia's chief farm products.

Most of Tunisia's major cities, industries, and fertile land are in the north and east. These regions are richer than the dry, less developed south. Although Tunisia is not rich in natural resources, it does have a more balanced economy than many of its neighbors.

The French left Tunisia with a good road and railroad system, and even more improvements have been achieved since independence in the mid-1950's. Tunisia's chief ports are Tunis, Halq al Wad, and Sfax.

History. People and ideas have entered northwest Africa through Tunisia for centuries. The Phoenicians began the Carthaginian Empire in Tunisia about 1100 B.C. According to tradition, the famous city of Carthage was founded near present-day Tunis about 814 B.C. The Romans defeated Carthage in 146 B.C., and ruled Tunisia for the next 600 years. In A.D. 439, the Vandals, a European tribe, invaded Tunisia, defeated the Romans, and captured Carthage. They ruled the region for almost 100 years. The Byzantines, from Constantinople (now Istanbul), ousted the Vandals in 534.

The Byzantines had loose control over Tunisia when Muslim Arabs from the Middle East invaded in the mid-600's. The Arab invasion was a turning point in Tunisia's history. Tunisia began to slowly become a part of Arab-Muslim civilization. The Ottoman Empire, which was centered in Asia Minor (now Turkey), won control of Tunisia in 1574. The Ottoman rulers appointed a *bey* (ruler) to govern Tunisia from Tunis. Tunisia was technically part of the Ottoman Empire until after World War I ended in 1918, but by the 1700's the beys in Tunis had achieved a large measure of independence.

In 1881, France imposed a protectorate over Tunisia. It controlled Tunisia's financial, foreign, and military affairs, leaving the bey only minor authority.

A Tunisian independence movement began before World War I began in 1914, but the most successful

Kurt Scholz, Shostal

Tunis, the capital and largest city of Tunisia, is the nation's political and cultural center. Tunisia's State Department Building stands in the foreground, overlooking a tree-shaded square.

B. Regent, Hutchison Library

At a Tunisian market place, people meet to buy and sell various commodities. In the picture above, merchants are weighing quantities of nuts and selling them to shoppers.

movement did not begin until 1934. Habib Bourguiba founded the Neo-Destour (New Constitution)—now Socialist Destour—Party that year. He led the independence struggle for more than 20 years. France finally granted Tunisia internal self-government in 1955, and full independence in 1956. France kept troops and military bases in Tunisia after independence. In the late 1950's and early 1960's, France, at Tunisia's demand, withdrew its troops and gave up its Tunisian bases.

Tunisia became a republic in 1957, and the people elected Bourguiba president. Bourguiba was reelected in 1959, 1964, and 1969. In 1975, he was named president for life. His government introduced many social and economic reforms. It gave voting rights to women and set up a national school system.

Tunisia has experienced enormous changes since gaining independence. But some of its successes have created new problems. The number of Tunisians who receive an education has increased greatly, but many of the educated people cannot find jobs that require their skills. The tourist industry has grown in Tunisia. Tourism provides income and jobs, but some people fear that influences caused by contact with tourists may cause the country to lose its Arab-Muslim heritage.

Many Tunisians admired the work of President Bourguiba and his Socialist Destour Party, but a growing number have rejected the single-party rule. In 1987, Prime Minister Zine el-Abidine Ben Ali removed Bourguiba from office. He claimed Bourguiba had become incapable of handling the presidency. Ben Ali, also of the Socialist Destour Party, then became president.

Leon Carl Brown

See also **Arab League; Bourguiba, Habib; Carthage; Olive; Tunis.**

Tunnel is an underground passageway. Tunnels are dug through hills and mountains, and under cities and waterways. They provide highways, subways, and railroads with convenient routes past natural and artificial obstacles. Tunnels are used in mining to reach valuable minerals deep within the earth. They also carry large volumes of water for hydroelectric power plants. Some tunnels provide fresh water for irrigation or drinking, and others transport wastes in sewer systems.

How tunnels are built

Tunnels are built through a variety of materials. Some are driven through the hard rocks of hills or mountains, or they are dug through soft earth. Others are buried in the ground under a body of water. Engineers study the material through which they intend a tunnel to pass in order to determine the kinds of methods and equipment to use in its construction.

Rock tunnels. Rock offers the greatest resistance to tunneling. The construction of most rock tunnels involves blasting. In order to blast rock, workers first move a large scaffold called a *jumbo* next to the tunnel *face* (front). Mounted on the jumbo are several drills, which are used to bore holes 6 to 12 feet (1.8 to 3.6 meters) into the rock. The holes, which measure only a few inches or centimeters in diameter, are packed with explosives. After these charges are exploded and the fumes sucked out, the pieces of rock, called *muck,* are carted away. If the tunnel is through strong, solid rock, it may not require extra support for its roof and walls. Most rock tunnels, however, are built through rock that is naturally broken by joints, or contains pockets of fractured rock. Workers prevent this weak rock from falling by erecting rings of steel beams, timbers, or other supports before blasting the next section. In most cases, a permanent lining of concrete is added later.

Some tunnels are built in soft, but firm rock such as limestone or shale. These tunnels are dug by tunnel-boring machines. A circular plate covered with *disk cutters* is attached to the front of these machines. As the plate slowly rotates, the disk cutters slice into the rock. Scoops on the machine carry the muck to a conveyor that removes it to the rear.

Artstreet

The Holland Tunnel passes under the Hudson River and connects New York City with Jersey City, N.J. The tunnel, opened to traffic in 1927, is more than 8,000 feet (2,400 meters) long.

Earth tunnels include tunnels that are dug through clay, silt, sand, or gravel, or in a muddy riverbed. Tunneling through such soft earth is especially dangerous because of the threat of cave-ins. In most cases, the roof and walls of a section of tunnel dug through these materials are held up by a steel cylinder called a *shield*. The shield is left in place while workers remove the earth inside it and install a permanent lining of cast iron or precast concrete. After this work is completed, jacks push the shield into the earth ahead of the tunnel, and the process is repeated. Some tunnel-boring machines have a shield attached to them and are able to position sections of concrete tunnel lining into place as they dig. Such a machine dug part of the London subway system.

Tunneling through the earth beneath bodies of water adds the danger of flooding to that of cave-ins. Engineers generally prevent water from entering a tunnel during construction by compressing the air in the end of the tunnel where the work is going on. When the air pressure inside the tunnel exceeds the pressure of the water outside, the water is kept out. This method was used to build the subway tunnels under the East River in New York City and the River Thames in London.

Immersed tunnels are built beneath bodies of water. They are generally less expensive to build than those dug by the shield or compressed-air methods. Construction of an immersed tunnel begins by dredging a trench across the bottom of a river, bay, or other body of water. Closed-ended steel or concrete tunnel sections are then floated over the trench and sunk into place. Next, divers connect the sections and remove the ends, and any water in the tunnel is pumped out. In most cases, the tunnels are then covered with earth. Immersed tunnels include the railroad tunnel under the Detroit River and the rapid transit tunnel under San Francisco Bay.

Kinds of tunnels

Tunnels are often classified according to their use. There are four main types: (1) railroad tunnels, (2) motor-traffic tunnels, (3) water tunnels, and (4) mining tunnels.

Railroad tunnels. Many great engineering feats were performed in building the railroads of Europe and the United States. The greatest of these involved the boring of long tunnels through the rocks of the Alps and the Rocky Mountains. Such tunnels reduce traveling time and increase the efficiency of trains. The steeper a locomotive must climb, the less weight it can pull. The steepest grade along a railway line determines the size of load a train can haul. Tunnels through mountains reduce steep grades and thus allow trains to haul more goods and people at less cost. For example, the Moffat Tunnel near Denver, Colo., reduced the altitude to which locomotives had to climb by 2,400 feet (730 meters) when it was completed in 1927.

Motor-traffic tunnels provide routes for automobiles, trucks, and other motor vehicles. Such tunnels are specially built to provide for the removal of exhaust fumes. For example, the Holland Tunnel, which is situated under the Hudson River and which links New York City and New Jersey, uses electric fans for ventilation. The giant fans are housed in four 10-story towers on the shore. These fans completely change the air in the tunnel every 90 seconds. They pump fresh air into the tunnel through ventilators in the road and suck exhaust fumes out through ventilators overhead. Many motor-traffic tunnels are also equipped with lights and special monitoring systems that help prevent traffic jams.

Water tunnels. Many tunnels provide water to city waterworks, to hydroelectric power plants, or to farms for irrigation. Others carry storm drainage or sewage. Most water tunnels measure 5 feet (1.5 meters) or more in diameter, and they have smooth linings that help the water flow. Tunnels carrying water to hydroelectric power plants must be strong enough to withstand extremely high water pressures.

Mine tunnels are made by blasting or by tunnelling machines. Mine shafts are not lined, but they may have

How a tunnel is constructed

A tunnel-boring machine digs into rock with attachments called *disk cutters*. The broken rock, called *muck*, then is removed by conveyor and rail car and brought to the surface in an elevator. Meanwhile, concrete sections of the tunnel lining are lowered through a shaft. A shield on the tunnel-boring machine holds up the roof until workers can erect a new section of tunnel lining.

WORLD BOOK illustration by Bill and Judie Anderson

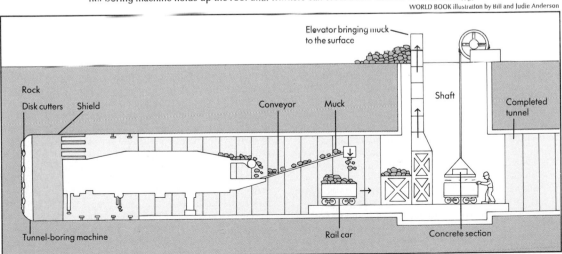

Elevator bringing muck to the surface

Rock
Disk cutters   Shield
Conveyor   Muck
Shaft
Completed tunnel
Tunnel-boring machine
Rail car
Concrete section

World's longest railroad tunnels

Tunnel	Location	Length In miles	Length In kilometers	Year opened
Seikan	Japan	33.5	53.9	1988
Channel	England-France	30.6	49.2	*
Ooshimizu	Japan	13.8	22.2	1982
Simplon I, II	Italy-Switzerland	12.3	19.8	1906, 1922
Shin Kanmon	Japan	11.6	18.7	1975
Apennine	Italy	11.5	18.5	1934
Rokko	Japan	10.1	16.3	1972
Furka	Switzerland	9.5	15.3	*
St. Gotthard	Switzerland	9.3	15.0	1882
Lötschberg	Switzerland	9.1	14.6	1913

*Under construction.

World's longest motor-traffic tunnels

Tunnel	Location	Length In miles	Length In kilometers	Year opened
St. Gotthard Road	Switzerland	10.1	16.3	1980
Arlberg	Austria	8.7	14.0	1978
Fréjus	France-Italy	8.1	13.0	1980
Mt. Blanc	France-Italy	7.3	11.7	1965
Gran Sasso	Italy	6.2	10.0	1976
Seelisberg	Switzerland	5.8	9.3	*
Ena	Japan	5.3	8.5	1976
Rokko II	Japan	4.3	6.9	1974
San Bernardino	Switzerland	4.1	6.6	1967
Tauern	Austria	4.0	6.4	1974

*Under construction.

supports. Most of the tunnels in mines are open only at one end.

History

About 15,000 years ago, prehistoric people in Europe used picks made of deer antlers and horse bones to dig tunnels for mining flint. By about 3500 B.C., people had learned to fracture rock at a tunnel face by building fires in front of it. Ancient Egyptians built tunnels for mining metals and storing water, and as approaches to tombs.

There were few developments in tunnel-building techniques until the A.D. 1600's, when gunpowder began to be used to blast through hard rock. The rise of railroads during the 1800's was accompanied by a great increase in tunnel building and the invention of several devices to aid in such construction. In 1825, a tunnel shield invented by Marc Isambard Brunel, a French-born engineer, was used for building a railroad tunnel under the River Thames in London. This tunnel, which was completed in 1843, was the first railroad tunnel to be built under a navigable river. The 9.3-mile (15-kilometer) St. Gotthard railroad tunnel, dug through the Swiss Alps between 1872 and 1882, was the first major tunnel to be built using dynamite and a jumbo. In the early 1900's, tunnel building was greatly speeded up through the invention of faster and lighter drills, harder drill bits, and mechanical muck loaders.

A tunnel-boring machine was first used in 1882, when the British began to drill a tunnel under the English Channel. This machine dug at a rate of about 40 feet (12 meters) in 24 hours. It cut about 8,000 feet (2,400 meters) before the British stopped the work. They feared that foreign armies could use the "chunnel" to invade Britain.

Today, many boring machines dig at rates of more than 400 feet (120 meters) in 24 hours. Some of the largest machines can cut round tunnels 35 feet (11 meters) in diameter. David A. Day

Related articles in *World Book* include:
Apennine Tunnel
Cascade Tunnel
Fréjus Tunnels
Hudson River Tunnels
Moffat Tunnel
Queens Midtown Tunnel
Saint Gotthard Tunnels
Simplon Pass and Tunnel
Subway

Tunney, Gene (1898-1978), an American boxer, defeated Jack Dempsey in 1926 to become world heavyweight champion. Tunney defended his title twice—against Dempsey in 1927 and Tom Heeney in 1928—and then retired. The second Tunney-Dempsey bout featured a controversial "long count." Dempsey knocked Tunney down in the seventh round, but refused to go immediately to a neutral corner. The referee delayed starting the count over Tunney for about five seconds. Tunney rose at the count of nine and went on to win the fight. See **Dempsey, Jack.**

Tunney was born in New York City. He was christened James Joseph but was called "Gene" because that was how his baby sister pronounced "Jim." Tunney began his professional boxing career in 1915. He enlisted in the U.S. Marine Corps in 1918 and won the American Expeditionary Forces light heavyweight title in Paris in 1919. He defeated Battling Levinsky for the U.S. light heavyweight title in 1922. Tunney lost his title to Harry Greb later in 1922, his only defeat in 77 professional bouts. He regained the title from Greb in 1923. Nigel Collins

Tunny. See Tuna.

Tupac Amaru. See Indian, American (After European contact); Peru (Spanish conquest and rule).

Tupelo, *TOO puh loh,* is the name of several large attractive trees native to North America and Southeast Asia. The *water tupelo* grows in swamps in the Southeastern United States. It has large leaves and grows up to 115 feet (35 meters) high. The trunk is swollen at the base. The tree bears tiny greenish-white flowers and dark purple fruit. The water tupelo is also called *sour gum* or *tupelo gum.* Its wood, known as gum, is widely used for cheap construction, such as paneling and crates. See also **Black tupelo; Tree** (Familiar broadleaf and needleleaf trees [picture]).

Scientific classification. Tupelo trees belong to the tupelo family, Nyssaceae. The water tupelo is *Nyssa aquatica.*

Kenneth R. Robertson

Tupí-Guaraní Indians, *too PEE GWAH rah NEE,* formed many tribes that spoke related languages. These forest Indians lived in eastern South America. Each tribe had a different name, such as Tupinamba or Omagua. Tupí-Guaraní languages served as the basis of the *lingua geral* (general language) of Brazil. One of them, Guaraní, is more widely spoken in rural Paraguay than Spanish, the country's official language.

The Tupí-Guaraní were farmers. Manioc, a root crop, provided their main food. They also planted yams, maize, peppers, and cotton. Their villages included from four to six big houses facing a square. Each family had its own partitioned section. Some tribes, especially along the Brazilian coast, were warriors and cannibals. They are now extinct. There are still a few peaceful Tupí-Guaraní tribes in Brazil. Charles Wagley

Tupper, Sir Charles   493

Sir Charles Tupper

**Prime Minister of Canada
1896**

Bowell	Tupper	Laurier
1894-1896	1896	1896-1911

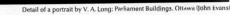
Detail of a portrait by V. A. Long; Parliament Buildings, Ottawa (John Evans)

Tupper, Sir Charles (1821-1915), served as prime minister of Canada for about 10 weeks in 1896. He was the oldest person to hold that office. Tupper, whose fellow Canadians called him the Grand Old Man of Canada, was almost 75 when he became prime minister.

Tupper accomplished little as his nation's leader, probably because he held office for such a short time. He worked hard, but with little success, to unite the Conservative Party, which had been badly divided since the death of Prime Minister John A. Macdonald in 1891.

Before Tupper became prime minister, he served in the Nova Scotia legislature and as premier of the province. Tupper helped establish the Dominion of Canada in 1867 and was one of the Fathers of Confederation. He also played an important part in bringing Nova Scotia into the Dominion. Tupper won election to the Canadian House of Commons in 1867. He held several Cabinet positions under Macdonald, who was prime minister from 1867 to 1873 and from 1878 to 1891.

Tupper, a master politician, became known for his ability to gain the cooperation of other public officials. He was a shrewd, unyielding debater and a skilled public speaker. Tupper lacked a sense of humor, but his dignified appearance made his attempts at wit seem funny.

Early life

Family background. Charles Tupper was born on July 2, 1821, in Amherst, N.S. He was the oldest of the three sons of Charles Tupper, a Baptist minister, and of Miriam Lockhart Lowe Tupper. Charles attended Horton Academy and Acadia College in Wolfville, N.S. He later studied medicine at the University of Edinburgh in Scotland and earned an M.D. degree in 1843. Tupper then returned to Amherst and entered the practice of medi-

cine. He helped found the Canadian Medical Association in 1867 and served as its first president.

Tupper's family. In 1846, Tupper married Frances Amelia Morse, the daughter of the chief clerk of the court in Amherst. The couple had three sons and three daughters. Their second son, Charles H. Tupper, served in the Canadian Parliament from 1882 to 1904 and held Cabinet positions from 1888 to 1896. Tupper's third son, William J. Tupper, served in the Manitoba Legislative Assembly from 1920 to 1922. He also held office as lieutenant governor of Manitoba from 1934 to 1940.

Early public career

Entry into politics. Tupper became well known in Nova Scotia through his successful medical practice. He entered politics in 1855, when he won election to the Nova Scotia legislature as a Conservative representative from Cumberland. He defeated Joseph Howe, the leader of the Liberal Party in Nova Scotia. Howe had been known for his role in persuading Great Britain to grant more control over local affairs to its North American colonies.

The leaders of the Nova Scotia Conservative Party quickly recognized Tupper's political and debating skills. In 1857, he became provincial secretary in the Cabinet of Premier J. W. Johnston of Nova Scotia, a Conservative. The Liberals gained a majority in the legislature and returned to power in 1860, but Tupper won re-election from Cumberland. In addition to serving as a member of the legislature in Halifax, he practiced medicine and served as the city's medical officer. He also was editor of the *British Colonist,* a Nova Scotia newspaper that supported the Conservative Party. Tupper campaigned to help the Nova Scotia Conservatives defeat the Liberals in 1863, and Johnston became premier again. In 1864, after Johnston left office to become a federal judge, the Conservatives named Tupper leader of the party and premier of Nova Scotia.

Premier. As premier, Tupper worked for government construction of railroads and for a system of nonreligious public schools. Tupper showed great courage when he introduced the School Act of 1864, which established public schools supported by tax funds. This act was unpopular in Nova Scotia.

Tupper also worked to promote a union of the three small maritime colonies—New Brunswick, Nova Scotia, and Prince Edward Island. He believed such a union would strengthen those colonies politically and economically. Talk of Canadian confederation began before Tupper's idea won public acceptance.

Confederation. Tupper represented Nova Scotia at the Charlottetown and Quebec conferences of 1864, which led to Confederation. The Quebec Resolutions, prepared at the Quebec Conference, proposed a union of the colonies of British North America. This union became known as the Dominion of Canada.

Led by Tupper, the Nova Scotia legislature approved the plan for the Canadian confederation. Nova Scotia became an original member of the Dominion when the British Parliament approved the resolutions in 1867. But many Nova Scotians opposed the union. They feared losing the increased independence they had gained in 1848, when Great Britain granted Nova Scotia more control over local affairs. In the 1867 election, the Liberals, led by Howe, opposed Confederation and won control of the Nova Scotia legislature.

Tupper was elected to the Canadian House of Commons in 1867. He was the only Nova Scotian in favor of Confederation whom the province elected to the House of Commons that year.

In 1868, the Nova Scotia legislature voted to repeal the Quebec Resolutions. Howe went to London and presented his anti-Confederation views to the colonial office. Tupper also went to the British capital, arguing that Nova Scotia should not leave the Dominion. The British government refused to let Nova Scotia drop out, and so the province remained in the Dominion.

Tupper persuaded Macdonald, the first prime minister of the Dominion, to offer a Cabinet position to Howe. Tupper then persuaded Howe to accept the post. By helping to bring Howe into the Dominion government, Tupper assisted in ending the anti-Confederation movement in Nova Scotia.

Rise to national prominence

Federal offices. After Tupper entered the House of Commons, Macdonald offered him a position in the Cabinet. Tupper refused the offer and advised Macdonald to appoint a Roman Catholic from Nova Scotia instead. Tupper, a Protestant, wanted to ensure the rights of the province's Catholic minority through representation in the national government. Macdonald followed his advice. In 1870, Tupper joined Macdonald's government as president of the Privy Council, a group formed to advise the representative of the British monarch in Canada.

Tupper held various Cabinet positions under Macdonald. He served as minister of inland revenue in 1872, as minister of finance in 1873 and 1874, and as minister

of public works in 1878. Queen Victoria of Great Britain knighted Tupper in 1879. From 1879 to 1884, he served as the first minister of railways and canals, one of the most important government positions. Tupper held that office during most of the construction of the Canadian Pacific Railway (now CP Rail), Canada's first transcontinental railroad.

Canadian high commissioner. In 1884, Tupper went to London as Canadian high commissioner to Great Britain. He returned to Canada in 1887 and became minister of finance. In 1888, he returned to London to serve again as high commissioner. In this position, Tupper worked to expand trade between Canada and Great Britain and to increase emigration from Britain to Canada. He also encouraged British investment in Canadian commerce and industry.

Prime minister

Macdonald died in 1891, three months after the Conservatives won the election that year. Tupper continued to serve as high commissioner in the Conservative governments of Sir John Abbott, Sir John Thompson, and Sir Mackenzie Bowell. Bowell became prime minister after Thompson died in 1894. In 1896, Bowell called Tupper home from London to serve as secretary of state in his Cabinet.

Bowell's poor handling of a government crisis over Manitoba schools led to the resignation of seven members of the Cabinet. Bowell resigned three months later, in April, 1896. The Conservatives called on Tupper to serve as prime minister and lead the party in the June election. Tupper succeeded Bowell as prime minister on April 27, 1896.

Tupper's many years in England had weakened his political strength at home. As prime minister, he faced a divided party and many political problems. The Manito-

© Albert Lee, Canapress

Sir Charles Tupper's home in Halifax, built in 1865, still stands at the corner of Tupper Grove and Armview Avenue.

© Alon Reininger, Contact from
Woodfin Camp, Inc.

© Marc & Evelyne Bernheim,
Woodfin Camp, Inc.

© George Holton,
Photo Researchers

© Craig Aurness,
Woodfin Camp, Inc.

© Robert Frerck, Woodfin Camp, Inc.

Turbans shown above are worn by a Bedouin of Israel, *top left;* a Hausa tribesman of Niger, *top right;* a Taureg of Algeria, *above left;* a man of northern Morocco, *above center;* and an Indian musician, *far right.* Turbans provide protection from the sun in hot countries of the Far East and the Middle East. Turbans may also indicate social rank.

ba school dispute continued to cause a crisis in the government. This problem had begun when the Manitoba legislature voted in 1890 to abolish the province's French-language Roman Catholic schools. While Tupper was in Bowell's Cabinet, he supported a bill in Parliament to restore the Catholic schools in Manitoba. But the Liberals did not allow a vote on the bill before the election. The Manitoba school dispute became the major issue of the 1896 campaign.

The Liberals won the June election, and Tupper left office on July 8. Wilfrid Laurier, the French-Canadian leader of the Liberal Party, became prime minister. Tupper took over as leader of the Opposition in the House of Commons.

Later years

Tupper served as Opposition leader until 1900, when he lost the election for his seat in the House. He then retired from public life and moved to Kent, England. Tupper visited Canada a number of times between 1900 and 1908. In 1908, he became a member of the United Kingdom Privy Council, composed of former prime ministers and Cabinet members who advised the British monarch.

Tupper spent much time writing his memoirs, and magazine articles on political issues. He died at his home in Kent on Oct. 30, 1915. Tupper was the last surviving Father of Confederation.   Alan Wilson

Tupungato, *TOO poong GAH toh,* is one of the five highest mountains in South America. It towers 22,310 feet (6,800 meters) in the Andes Mountains on the Chile-Argentina boundary. For the location of Tupungato, see Chile (terrain map).

Turaco. See Touraco.

Turban is a headdress. The name comes from the Persian word *dulband,* which means a scarf wound around the head. The first turbans were scarfs which men in the hot countries of the Orient and Middle East wrapped around their heads to provide protection against the sun. Gradually, turbans came to show differences in rank among the men of Oriental countries. A white muslin scarf wound around a small cap on the head was the headdress of the priests of India, and native princes of that country wore showy silk scarfs. At one time, the sultan of Turkey wore a turban that was decorated with three heron feathers and many precious stones. The country's grand vizier wore two heron feathers in his turban, and a turban with one heron feather marked less important officers of Turkey's government. Today, turbans are worn chiefly by the Hindus of India.

Turbinate bone, *TUR buh niht* or *TUR buh nayt.* There are three *turbinate* bones in the nose. These large, shelflike bones warm the air before it enters the lungs. They may be involved in sinus trouble and the common cold. See also **Nose** (with diagram).

An electric generator at a power plant, *left,* is driven by a steam turbine. High-pressure steam rushes past wheels in the turbine, causing them to spin rapidly. An axle transmits the mechanical energy of the rotating wheels to the generator. The steam turbine that powers this generator produces 119 million watts of power.

E. R. Degginger

Turbine, *TUR bihn* or *TUR byn,* is a device with a rotor that is turned by a moving fluid, such as water, steam, gas, or the wind. A turbine changes the *kinetic energy* (energy of movement) of a fluid into *mechanical energy* (energy in the form of mechanical power). Such energy can be used to run machinery. Mechanical energy is transmitted by a turbine through the spinning motion of the rotor's axle.

Turbines provide power for a variety of machines, including electric generators and water pumps. In fact, generators driven by turbines produce most of the electricity used to light homes and run factories. Turbines that power water pumps play an important role in irrigation projects throughout the world. Turbines are also used to turn the propellers of ships, and they are an essential part of jet-airplane engines.

The earliest known turbines date back to simple water wheels used by the ancient Greeks about 2,000 years ago. Today, turbines vary greatly in size and power, depending on their use. For example, a huge turbine that turns an electric generator can deliver nearly 750 million watts of power. But some turbines used to run shop machinery measure less than 1 inch (2.5 centimeters) in diameter and deliver under 750 watts.

How turbines work

The rotor is the rotating part of a turbine. In a simple turbine, it consists of a disk or wheel mounted on an axle. The axle sits either horizontally or vertically. The wheel has curved blades or buckets around the edges. Nozzles or movable gates called *guide vanes* aim the fluid at the blades or buckets and adjust its speed. In many turbines, a *casing* encloses the rotor. The casing holds the fluid against the rotor so that none of the fluid's energy is lost.

As a fluid passes through a turbine, it hits or pushes against the blades or buckets and causes the wheel to turn. When the wheel rotates, the axle turns with it. The axle is connected directly or through a series of gears to an electric generator, air compressor, or other machine. Thus, the circular motion of the spinning rotor drives a machine.

The rotors of some turbines have only one wheel. However, the rotors of others have as many as 50 or more. Multiple wheels increase the efficiency of the turbines, because each wheel extracts additional energy from the moving fluid. In a turbine with more than one wheel, the wheels are mounted on a common axle, one behind the other. A stationary ring of curved blades is attached to the inside of the casing in front of each wheel. These stationary blades direct the flow of the fluid toward the wheels. A wheel and a set of stationary blades is called a *stage. Multistage* turbines are those that have many stages.

Kinds of turbines

Turbines are sometimes classified according to their principle of operation. All turbines operate by *impulse* or *reaction,* or by a combination of these principles. In an impulse turbine, the force of a fast-moving fluid striking the blades makes the rotor spin. In a reaction turbine, the rotor turns primarily as a result of the weight or pressure of a fluid on the blades.

Turbines are more commonly classified by the type of

Principles of turbine operation

Impulse   Reaction

WORLD BOOK illustrations by Oxford Illustrators Limited

Turbine wheels turn by *impulse* or *reaction.* A pinwheel, *left,* is a simple impulse turbine that rotates when you blow air against the blades. A sprinkler, *right,* is a simple reaction turbine. Water squirting out of it under pressure causes the wheel to turn.

A water turbine is driven by water that "falls" from a great height through a pipe or other channel. The Pelton wheel turbine shown at the right in this photograph drives an electric generator in a paper mill.

L. S. Stepanowicz, Bruce Coleman Inc.

fluid that turns them. According to this method, there are four main kinds of turbines: (1) water turbines, (2) steam turbines, (3) gas turbines, and (4) wind turbines.

Water turbines are also called *hydraulic turbines.* Most water turbines are driven by water from waterfalls or by water that is stored behind dams. The turbines are used primarily to power electric generators at hydroelectric power plants. There are three main kinds of water turbines: (1) the Pelton wheel, (2) the Francis turbine, and (3) the Kaplan turbine. The type of water turbine used at a plant depends on the *head* available. A head is the distance the water falls before it strikes the turbine. Heads range from about 8 feet (2.4 meters) to more than 1,000 feet (300 meters).

The Pelton wheel is an impulse turbine. It is used with heads of more than 1,000 feet (300 meters). A Pelton's rotor consists of a single wheel mounted on a horizontal axle. The wheel has cup-shaped buckets around

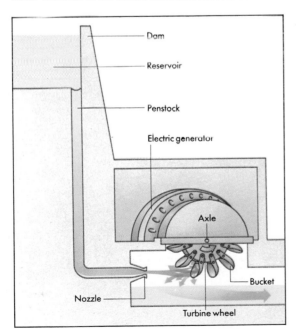

The Pelton wheel, *above,* is an impulse water turbine. The force of water striking the turbine wheel causes it to spin. Water falls toward the turbine through a pipe called the *penstock* and hits the buckets on the wheel in a high-speed jet.

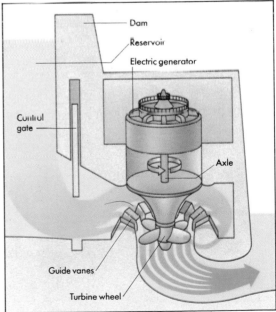

WORLD BOOK illustrations by Oxford Illustrators Limited

The Kaplan turbine is a reaction water turbine. The turbine wheel, which is completely underwater, is turned by the pressure of water against its blades. Guide vanes and a control gate regulate the amount of water reaching the wheel.

its perimeter. Water from a lake or reservoir drops toward the turbine through a long pipe called a *penstock.* One to six nozzles at the end of the penstock increase the water's velocity and aim the water toward the buckets. The force of these high-speed jets of water against the buckets turns the wheel.

The Francis turbine is used when the head is between about 100 feet (30 meters) and 1,000 feet (300 meters). A Francis turbine's rotor is enclosed in a casing. Its wheel has as many as 24 curved blades. Its axle is vertical. The wheel of a Francis turbine operates underwater. It is encircled by a ring of guide vanes, which can be opened or closed to control the amount of water flowing past the wheel. The spaces between the vanes act as nozzles to direct the water toward the center of the wheel. The rotor is turned chiefly by the weight or pressure of the flowing water.

The Kaplan turbine is used for heads of less than 100 feet (30 meters). The Kaplan rotor resembles a ship's propeller. It has from three to eight blades on a vertical axle. It works in a manner similar to that of a Francis turbine. Both the Kaplan turbine and the Francis turbine are reaction turbines.

Steam turbines drive the electric generators in most U.S. power plants. They also power ocean liners and large machinery. Multistage steam turbines are among the world's most powerful engines. Some steam turbines produce nearly 750 million watts of power.

Steam turbines are run by steam. In most cases, the steam is produced by water heated in a boiler by burning such fuels as coal, oil, or natural gas. In nuclear power plants, however, heat produced by splitting atoms in a nuclear reactor changes water to steam.

Steam enters a turbine at temperatures as high as 1200° F. (649°C) and pressures as high as 3,500 pounds per square inch (250 kilograms per square centimeter). The high-pressure steam rushes through the turbine, causing the turbine wheels to spin rapidly. Steam turbines are designed to use the impulse principle, the reaction principle, or a combination of both.

Many modern steam turbines have 50 or more stages set on a horizontal axle. Each stage of the turbine consists of a wheel and a ring of stationary blades. The curved blades of both the wheels and the stationary rings are shaped so that the spaces between them act as nozzles. The nozzles aim the steam and increase its speed before it goes on to the next stage. The steam follows a zigzag path between the wheel blades of one stage and the stationary blades of the next.

As steam passes through a multistage turbine, it expands to as much as 1,000 times its original volume. Each successive stage of the turbine is therefore larger than the previous one in order to make efficient use of the expanding steam. This arrangement of larger and larger stages gives steam turbines their characteristic conical shape.

Steam turbines may be either *condensing* or *noncondensing,* depending on how the steam leaving the turbine is used. Steam from a condensing turbine goes directly into a condenser. Cold water circulating in pipes in the condenser cools the steam into water. A vacuum is thus created, because the volume of water is much less than that of steam. The vacuum helps force steam through the turbine. The water is pumped back to the boiler to be made into steam again. The exhaust steam from noncondensing turbines is not cooled into water. Instead, it is used to provide heat for buildings and for a variety of industrial processes.

How a steam turbine works

Steam rushes through a steam turbine, turning a series of bladed wheels on a common axle. After the steam leaves the turbine, a condenser changes it into water, *left.* The cutaway view of a steam turbine, *right,* shows how a ring of stationary blades is positioned between each rotating wheel. Both the stationary blades and wheel blades aim the steam and increase its speed.

WORLD BOOK illustrations by Oxford Illustrators Limited

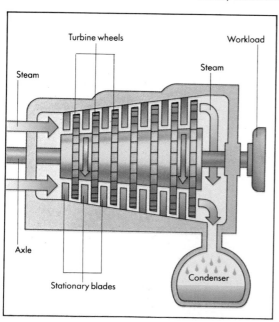

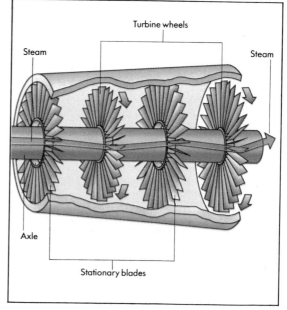

Gas turbines burn such fuels as oil and natural gas. Instead of using the heat to produce steam, as in steam turbines, gas turbines use the hot gases directly. Gas turbines are used to power electric generators, ships, and high-speed cars. They are also an important part of the engines in jet aircraft.

Most gas turbine systems have three main parts: (1) an air compressor, (2) a combustion chamber, and (3) a turbine. The combination of the air compressor and combustion chamber is commonly called a *gas generator.* In most gas turbine systems, the air compressor and turbine are mounted at either end of a common horizontal axle, with the combustion chamber between them. Part of the turbine's power runs the air compressor.

The air compressor sucks in air and compresses it, thereby increasing its pressure. In the combustion chamber, the compressed air combines with fuel and the resulting mixture is burned. The greater the pressure of the air, the better the fuel-air mixture burns. The burning gases expand rapidly and rush into the turbine, where they cause the turbine wheels to rotate. Hot gases move through a multistage gas turbine in much the same way that steam moves through a steam turbine. Stationary blades aim the moving gas at the rotor blades and adjust its velocity.

Most gas turbine systems make use of the hot exhaust gases from the turbine. In some systems, some of the exhaust gases are circulated to a device called a *regenerator.* There, the gases are used to warm up the high-pressure air from the compressor before it enters the combustion chamber. Such preheating of the air reduces the amount of fuel needed for combustion. In jet engines, much of the gas stream is used to develop thrust (see **Jet propulsion**).

Gas turbines run at even hotter temperatures than steam turbines. The hotter a gas turbine runs, the more efficiently it operates. The temperature in many gas turbines is 1600° F. (871° C) or higher.

Wind turbines, which are commonly called *windmills,* are driven by the wind. They were developed about 1,300 years ago, and through the centuries, they have been used chiefly to grind grain and pump water. In the late 1800's, thousands of communities in the United States used windmills to draw water from the ground. During the 1970's, shortages of oil led to increased interest in wind turbines as a potential source of energy for generating electricity.

There are two basic types of wind turbines: (1) horizontal axis wind turbines (HAWT's) and (2) vertical axis wind turbines (VAWT's).

Horizontal axis wind turbines. Traditional HAWT's have rotors with multiple blades or sails. They include *Dutch windmills* and *American windmills* (see **Windmill**). Most modern HAWT's that are used to generate electricity have two propellerlike blades. The rotor of these HAWT's is mounted on a tower or mast that holds the blades high enough off the ground to catch the wind stream. In order for the turbine to operate efficiently, the blades need to face into the wind, and the axle must lie parallel to the wind stream. As the wind blows, the rotor turns due to the impact of the air on the specially shaped blades. HAWT's are designed to adjust to changes in the speed and direction of the wind. The angle of the blades can be changed to keep the turbine operating at a constant rate, no matter what the wind speed is. In addition, these turbines can be rotated around a vertical axis to keep the rotor blades facing into the wind.

How a gas turbine system works

In a gas turbine system, compressed air is forced into a combustion chamber and mixed with fuel. A spark ignites the mixture and hot gases rush through the turbine, spinning the wheels. Wheel blades and stationary blades direct the gases through the turbine and increase their speed. Part of the turbine's power is used to run the air compressor.

WORLD BOOK illustration by Oxford Illustrators Limited

Air Compressor — Combustion Chamber — Turbine

Air intake · Fuel · Spark · Turbine wheels · Exhaust · Workload · Axle · Spark · Fuel · Stationary blades · Axle

© Lowell Georgia, Photo Researchers

The Darrieus wind turbine is a vertical axis wind turbine. Darrieus wind turbines are extremely efficient because they can catch the flow of wind from any direction.

Vertical axis wind turbines. The most efficient kind of vertical axis wind turbine was developed in the 1920's by a French inventor named Georges Darrieus. The Darrieus wind turbine looks like a giant eggbeater. It has two or three long curved blades attached at both ends to a vertical shaft. The Darrieus wind turbine can catch the flow of wind from any direction.

History

Water wheels are the oldest known turbines. They were used by the ancient Greeks as long ago as 100 B.C. for grinding grain and squeezing oil from olives. By the A.D. 300's, the Romans had introduced water wheels into many other parts of Europe.

The first windmills were probably built in the A.D. 600's in Iran. These early windmills were used for grinding grain and irrigating crops. By the 1100's they had spread to Europe. In the 1400's, people in the Netherlands began using windmills to drain marshes and lakes near the sea.

For many centuries, water wheels and windmills were the only useful turbines. The scientist Hero of Alexandria had built a small steam turbine about A.D. 60, but it had not been used to power anything (see **Steam engine** [History]). In 1629, Giovanni Branca, an Italian engineer, built an impulse steam turbine that was used in a stamping mill.

Early water wheels and windmills were less efficient than modern turbines, because much of the moving fluid escaped around the edges of the rotor blades. Dur-

ing the 1800's, engineers and inventors began developing more efficient, enclosed turbines. In 1824, Claude Burdin, a French engineer, introduced the word *turbine* in a scientific paper. It comes from the term *turbo,* the Latin word for a spinning object. Benoît Fourneyron, a French engineer, built the first successful enclosed water turbine in 1827. After Fourneyron's success, engineers soon overcame most of the problems that were involved in building efficient water turbines.

In 1849, an English-born inventor named James B. Francis built the first Francis turbine. The Pelton wheel, which had been invented by an American mining engineer named Lester A. Pelton, began to be produced during the 1880's. Victor Kaplan, an Austrian inventor, developed the design for the Kaplan turbine during the early 1900's.

In 1884, an English inventor, Charles A. Parsons, developed the first reaction steam turbine. In 1897, he used steam turbines to power his vessel, the *Turbinia.* In 1895, Charles G. Curtis, an American inventor, patented a multistage steam turbine that worked by both reaction and impulse. This turbine started a revolution in power production, because it was extremely efficient for its size and weight. During the early 1900's, steam turbines replaced steam engines in electrical generating stations.

John Barber, an English inventor, was issued a patent on a simple gas turbine system in 1791. In 1930, an English engineer named Frank Whittle received the first patent on the application of a gas turbine to propel aircraft. The first airplane to be powered by a turbojet engine was built by the Heinkel Company of Germany in 1939.

Marian Visich, Jr.

Related articles in *World Book* include:

Dam	Locomotive
Electric power	Ship (Increasing power and
Energy	speed)
Free-piston engine	Steam engine
Hydraulic engine	Water power
Hydraulics	Water wheel
Jet propulsion	Windmill

E. R. Degginger

A traditional windmill has blades radiating from a horizontal axis. Windmills have provided mechanical power for pumping water and performing other work for about 1,300 years.

Turbofan. See Jet propulsion (Turbofan).
Turbojet. See Jet propulsion (Turbojet).
Turboprop. See Jet propulsion (Turboprop); **Turbine** (Gas turbines).
Turbot, *TUR buht,* is a large flatfish that lives along the Atlantic Coast of Europe and in the Mediterranean Sea. From the side it looks almost as round as a plate. It seldom grows over 2 feet (61 centimeters) long and usually weighs from 18 to 30 pounds (8 to 14 kilograms). But fishing crews sometimes catch 55-pound (25-kilogram) turbot that measure more than 30 inches (76 centimeters) long. The turbot is flat and wide, with a long fin on its top and bottom ridges. Hard, round knobs cover its brown upper side. Both eyes are on the left side. The turbot lays as many as 10 million eggs, which float on

WORLD BOOK Illustration by Colin Newman, Linden Artists Ltd.
The flat-bodied turbot of Europe's North Atlantic coastal waters has eyes only on one side of its body. When it swims, the eyeless side is on the underside.

the surface of the ocean. The young fish that hatch settle to the bottom and live there.

Turbot are valuable commercially and are exported. Turbot became a favorite fish of the English. The *American spotted turbot* and the *hunnyhead turbot* also are flatfishes but belong to a different family.

Scientific classification. The European turbot belongs to the family Bothidae. It is *Scophthalmus maximus.*

David W. Greenfield

See also **Flatfish; Flounder.**

Turgenev, *tur GEN nyuhf,* **Ivan** (1818-1883), was one of the greatest Russian novelists. He was the first Russian writer to achieve substantial recognition in the West. Turgenev became noted for his realistic portrayals of the Russian nobility and intellectuals. He examined social and cultural interests in novels that read like a diary of that part of Russian society from the 1840's to the 1870's. These novels are *Rudin* (1856), *A Nest of Gentlefolk* (1859), *On the Eve* (1860), *Fathers and Sons* (1862), *Smoke* (1867), and *Virgin Soil* (1877).

In his novels and in the short story "The Diary of a

Brown Bros.
Ivan Turgenev

Superfluous Man" (1850), Turgenev described a type of educated, well-meaning, but disillusioned Russian nobleman. This type of character, known as the "superfluous man," is unable to find an outlet for his talents and energies. This passive and politically ineffective figure was the most common type of male character in Russian literature of Turgenev's time. In contrast, his female characters are more resourceful and strong-willed.

Turgenev's masterpiece, *Fathers and Sons,* is about the young Russian radicals of the 1860's. Bazarov, the main character of the book, is a *nihilist*—that is, a person who opposes all tradition and authority (see **Nihilism**). Bazarov is a powerful and convincing character, but he dies inactive and frustrated.

Ivan Sergeyevich Turgenev was born and raised on his family's estate in Orel. He first won recognition as a writer in 1852 with his "Hunter's Sketches." This collection contains sympathetic portrayals of the Russian peasants. Turgenev's best-known drama is *A Month in the Country* (1850). Turgenev spent several decades in the West, and he was part of a group who believed Russia's future depended on its adoption of the best elements of Western culture. Anna Lisa Crone

Turin, *TOO rihn* (pop. 1,103,520), is a city in northern Italy that lies on the Po River. Its Italian name is Torino (pronounced *toh REE noh*). Turin is the capital of Piedmont, one of Italy's 20 political regions. For location, see **Italy** (political map).

Turin is one of the loveliest places in northern Italy. Beautiful parks and botanical gardens stretch along the left bank of the Po. The great church of the Superga stands on a hill near the city. A cable railway runs to the top of the hill. From the hill, travelers enjoy a fine view of Turin. Many beautiful *piazzas* (public squares) provide open space in the city. The Shroud of Turin, a cloth thought to have been worn by Jesus Christ, is kept in a chapel in Turin (see **Shroud of Turin**).

Turin is an old city, with a long and interesting history. In 218 B.C. the Carthaginian general, Hannibal, crossed the Alps and captured the city. In A.D. 69 a great fire swept Turin and many buildings burned to the ground. From 1861 to 1865, Turin served as the capital of the Kingdom of Italy. The royal palace and park are still famous landmarks.

Educational institutions include several military schools, an observatory, museums, and a science academy. The University of Turin was founded in 1404. The city has a library with a collection of ancient writings.

During World War II, Turin served as an important munitions-manufacturing center for Italy and Germany. Many of the city's factories were destroyed by Allied air raids in 1942 and 1943. But the city recovered from the destruction of the war. Today, Turin has become one of Italy's leading industrial centers. Its chief products include fine silk materials and various kinds of Italian automobiles. Benjamin Webb Wheeler

Turing, Alan Mathison (1912-1954), an English mathematician, made important contributions to the development of electronic digital computers. In 1937, he described a hypothetical computing machine, now called the *Turing machine,* that could, in principle, perform any calculation. The device had a long tape divided into squares on which symbols could be written or read. The tape head of the machine could move to the left or to the right. The machine also had a table to tell it the order in which to carry out operations. The Turing machine became an important tool for determining what could be programmed on a computer.

Turing was born in London. He studied mathematics at Cambridge University and at Princeton University. During World War II (1939-1945), he helped crack German codes. After the war, he worked on a project to build the first British electronic digital computer. In 1950, he proposed a test for determining if machines might be said to "think." This test, now called the *Turing test,* is often mentioned in discussions of *artificial intelligence* (see **Artificial intelligence**). Arthur Gittleman

Turing machine. See Turing, Alan M.

Turk. See Turks.

Turkestan, *TUR kih STAN,* also spelled *Turkistan,* a vast geographical region in China, the Soviet Union, and Afghanistan, has no definite boundaries. It stretches from Siberia on the north to Iran, Pakistan, India, and Tibet on the south. The Mongolian Desert lies to the east, and the Caspian Sea to the west. The name *Turkestan* refers to the Turkic-speaking tribes that have lived in this region since as early as the A.D. 500's.

For hundreds of years, Turkestan has linked Europe with eastern Asia. Many ancient trade routes crossed the area, including Marco Polo's Golden Road. During World War II (1939-1945), Turkestan provided a route for transporting arms from the Soviet Union to China.

Soviet Turkestan, also called Western Turkestan, lies in the Soviet Union between the Caspian Sea and the Tian Shan range. The Kazakh, Kirghiz, Tajik, Turkmen, and Uzbek Soviet Socialist Republics make up Soviet Turkestan. Flat and sandy in the north and west, the land rises to form mountains in the southeast. Rivers

© Roland and Sabrina Michaud, Woodfin Camp, Inc.

A Soviet Turkestan woman weaves a rug on a loom. Turkestan rug weavers are world famous for their skill.

from the mountains flow inward, to disappear in the desert sands. Most of the people are Muslims, and make their living by farming and raising cattle. Irrigation ditches provide water for wheat, rice, millet, oats, and cotton. Chief cities include Tashkent, Alma-Ata, Karaganda, Frunze, Dushanbe, and Samarkand.

Chinese Turkestan, also called Eastern Turkestan, in the heart of Asia, extends east from Soviet Turkestan to the Gobi Desert and Tibet. The Tian Shan range on the north, and the Kunlun Mountains, rising over 20,000 feet (6,100 meters) on the south, border the region. Chinese Turkestan, which forms part of China's Xinjiang region, has a harsh, dry climate. The people are of Turkish origin, and are called *Uigurs.* They make their living by farming, raising domestic animals, and trading. Most of them are Muslims. Major cities include Urumqi, Hami, Karamay, Kashi, and Yining.

Afghan Turkestan is bounded on the north by the Amu Darya (Oxus River), and on the northwest by Soviet Turkestan. Uzbek chiefs ruled the country for a long time before Afghanistan gained possession of it. This part of southern Turkestan forms the Afghan province of Mazar-i-Sharif. Afghan Turkestan's many mountains have rich copper, iron, lead, and gold deposits. The people of this region are chiefly of Persian and Uzbek stock.

History. The known history of Turkestan began about the time of Christ, when much of it belonged to the Chinese Empire. In the 500's, Turkic-speaking tribes conquered the rich trading cities of Bukhara and Samarkand. In the 600's, Tibet gained control of Eastern Turkestan, but later the Chinese again took the region. Turkic-speaking nomads from central Asia invaded Turkestan in 1073. Followers of Genghis Khan swept through the land in the 1200's. Bukhara and Samarkand became centers of Muslim culture during the 1300's and 1400's.

Russia (the name for the Soviet Union before 1922) began to extend its rule to Western Turkestan soon after the Russian conquest of Siberia in the 1600's. During the 1700's, the Russian czars forced Kazakh tribes to recognize their authority. Most of Western Turkestan became Russian during the 1800's. The czar's government created the province of Turkestan and made Tashkent its capital. In 1887, an Anglo-Russian commission established the boundary between Afghanistan and Russian Turkestan.

In 1924, Soviet Turkestan was divided into five separate states. Each national group formed its own government under the Communist dictatorship of the Soviet Union. The Soviet government developed the region's resources. It also built schools, extended irrigation systems, and laid additional railroad lines.

Ancient Eastern Turkestan remained under Chinese rule. In the 900's, the Muslim religion began to spread over this entire area. The Muslims made repeated attempts to set up their own government, especially in the 1800's. Chinese Turkestan almost became an independent state from 1872 to 1876, under the kingship of Yakub Beg. But after he died, China regained control. Chinese Turkestan is now governed as a part of the province of Xinjiang. Zvi Gitelman

Related articles in *World Book* include:

Aral Sea	Kirghiz	Turkmenistan
Genghis Khan	Tajikistan	Uzbekistan
Kazakhstan	Tashkent	Xinjiang

Owen Franken, Stock, Boston

Remote mountain valleys are common in Asian Turkey. The Asian part of Turkey, called *Anatolia* or *Asia Minor,* is about 30 times as large as European Turkey, called *Thrace.*

Ian Berry, Magnum

Historic Istanbul, Turkey's largest city, is famous for its beautiful *mosques* (Islamic houses of worship). This mosque overlooks the Bosporus, part of a Turkish waterway called the *Straits.*

Turkey

Turkey is a Middle Eastern nation that lies both in Europe and in Asia. About 3 per cent of the country occupies the easternmost tip of southern Europe, a region called *Thrace.* Istanbul, Turkey's largest city, lies in this region of green, fertile hills and valleys. To the east, the rest of Turkey covers a large, mountainous peninsula called *Anatolia* or *Asia Minor.* Anatolia has several large cities, including the capital city of Ankara, and areas of rich farmland. But much of Anatolia is rocky, barren land.

Turkey borders Bulgaria on the northwest, Greece on the west, the Soviet Union and Iran on the east, and Iraq and Syria on the south. The Black Sea lies to the north, the Aegean Sea to the west, and the Mediterranean Sea to the south.

Three bodies of water—the Bosporus, the Sea of Marmara, and the Dardanelles—separate Anatolia from Thrace. These waters, often called the *Straits,* have had a major role in Turkish history. By its control of the Straits, Turkey can regulate the movement of ships between the Mediterranean Sea and the part of the Soviet Union on the Black Sea.

About 55 per cent of Turkey's people live in cities or towns. The rest live on farms or in small villages. Nearly all the people are *Muslims* (followers of Islam). Turkey is a developing country, and over half of its workers are

Andrew C. Hess, the contributor of this article, is Professor of Diplomacy at the Fletcher School of Law and Diplomacy, Tufts University.

farmers. However, Turkey's economy has become increasingly industrialized since the mid-1940's. As a result, manufacturing now contributes slightly more to the national income than does agriculture.

Various Asian and European peoples have ruled what is now Turkey since ancient times. During the A.D. 1300's, a group of Muslim Turks called the *Ottomans* began to build a powerful empire that eventually con

Facts in brief

Capital: Ankara.
Official language: Turkish.
Official name: Türkiye Cumhuriyeti (Republic of Turkey).
Head of state: President.
Political divisions: 67 provinces.
Area: 301,382 sq. mi. (780,576 km²). *Greatest distances—* north-south, 465 mi. (748 km); east-west, 1,015 mi. (1,633 km). *Coastline*—2,211 mi. (3,558 km).
Elevation: *Highest*—Mount Ararat, 17,011 ft. (5,185 m). *Lowest*— sea level along the coast.
Population: *Estimated 1989 population*—55,377,000; density, 184 persons per sq. mi. (71 per km²); distribution, 52 per cent rural, 48 per cent urban. *1985 census*—50,664,458. *Estimated 1994 population*—61,488,000.
Chief products: *Agriculture*—barley, corn, cotton, fruits, potatoes, sugar beets, wheat. *Manufacturing*—fertilizers, iron and steel, machinery, motor vehicles, processed foods and beverages, pulp and paper products, textiles and clothing.
National anthem: "İstiklâl Marşi" ("Independence March").
National emblem: Crescent and star.
National motto: *Yurtta sulh, Cihanda sulh* (Peace at home, peace in the world).
National holiday: National Day, October 29.
Money: *Basic unit*—lira. One hundred kurus equal one lira. For the lira's price in U.S. dollars, see **Money** (table: Exchange rates).

David Bellak, Jeroboam

Endless lines of traffic jam a wide, modern street in downtown Ankara, Turkey's capital. The city has grown into a center of commerce and industry since it became the capital in 1923.

Turkey's flag was adopted in 1936. The crescent and five-pointed star are traditional symbols of the Islamic faith.

The coat of arms, adopted in 1923, bears the nation's official name, Republic of Turkey, in Turkish.

WORLD BOOK map

Turkey is a country in the Middle East. It covers the peninsula of Asia Minor and a small section of southeastern Europe.

trolled much of the Middle East, southeastern Europe, and northern Africa. The Ottoman Empire ended in 1922. The next year, Turkey became a republic.

Islamic law had strongly influenced Turkish life for nearly 1,000 years. However, Turkey's new republican government introduced sweeping cultural and political reforms that discouraged or outlawed many traditional Islamic practices. Most Turkish people accepted the reforms. But many others, especially those living in rural areas, resisted the changes. This conflict over the role of Islam in Turkish life continues to divide the nation.

Government

Turkey is a republic. Its Constitution was adopted in 1982, following two years of military rule. It provides for a parliamentary form of government that includes a president, a prime minister and cabinet, and a legislature called the Grand National Assembly. The president, prime minister, and cabinet took office in 1982. The Grand National Assembly was first elected by the Turkish people in 1983. A second general election was held in 1987.

The president is Turkey's head of state, commander in chief of the armed forces, and the presiding officer at cabinet meetings. The 1982 Constitution provides that the chairman of Turkey's ruling military council should serve as president for seven years following the adoption of the Constitution. Succeeding presidents would be elected by the Grand National Assembly to seven-year terms.

The prime minister and cabinet. The prime minister is Turkey's head of government. The president selects the prime minister from among the most influential members of the legislature. The members of the cabinet, called the Council of Ministers, are nominated by the prime minister and appointed by the president. Cabinet ministers supervise the various government departments. The prime minister must submit a proposed government program and the names of all cabinet ministers to the legislature for a *vote of confidence*. The prime minister and cabinet must resign if the legislature refuses to grant a vote of confidence in their policies.

The Grand National Assembly was given the power by the Constitution to make Turkey's laws, ratify treaties, and declare war.

The Assembly consists of 400 deputies elected by the voters to five-year terms. If the president disapproves of any bill passed by the legislature, the bill is returned to the legislature. If the legislature then repasses the bill, it becomes law.

Court system. Courts throughout Turkey handle commercial disputes, criminal trials, and other cases. The Court of Cassation reviews the decisions of lower courts. The Constitutional Court determines the legality of laws passed by the legislature.

Local government. Turkey is divided into 67 provinces. Each province has a governor appointed by the president and a council elected by the province's people. Provinces are divided into counties, districts, *municipalities* (communities of 2,000 or more people), and villages.

Political parties. The Motherland Party is Turkey's largest political party. It favors an economic system free of government controls. Turkey's second largest party,

Turkey political map

——	International boundary
——	Road
——	Railroad
⚓	Dam and reservoir
✪	National capital
•	Other city or town
■	Ancient ruin

WORLD BOOK map

Cities, towns, and villages

Adana 574,515
*642,845..C 4
Adapazari 130,977
*195,069..B 2
Adiyaman ....53,719..C 5
Adrianople, see Edirne
Afyon ....74,562..B 2
Akhisar ....61,491..B 1
Aksaray ....62,927..C 3
Akşehir ....40,312..C 3
Alanya ....22,190..C 3
Alaşehir* ....25,611..C 2
Alexandretta, see
 Iskenderun
Aliboyköyü* ....43,532..B 2
Amasya ....48,066..B 4
Anamur ....23,025..D 3
Ankara 1,877,755
*2,238,967..B 3
Antakya, see Antioch
Antalya 173,501
*280,837..C 3
Antioch
 (Antakya) ...94,942..D 4
Artvin ....14,307..A 6
Aşkale ....12,171..B 6
Aydin ....74,021..C 1
Bafra ....50,213..A 4
Balikesir ......124,051..B 1
Bandirma ....53,497..B 1
Bartin ....20,786..A 3
Batman ....86,172..C 6
Bayburt ....22,578..B 6
Bayram-
 paşa* ....165,723..A 2
Bergama ....34,716..B 1
Bingöl ....28,146..B 6
Bitlis ....27,137..C 6
Bolu ....38,283..B 3

Bolvadin* ....30,333..B 2
Bornova ....60,397..B 1
Buca ....103,105..C 1
Burdur ....44,630..C 2
Bursa 445,113
*636,910..B 2
Camdibi* ....160,603..B 2
Çanakkale ....39,979..B 1
Çankiri ....34,933..B 3
Çarşamba ....28,422..A 4
Ceyhan ....57,307..C 4
Çorlu ....47,086..A 1
Çorum ....75,726..B 4
Denizli 135,373
*205,938..C 2
Diyarbakir 235,617
*374,264..C 6
Düzce ....37,858..B 3
Edirne (Adrian-
 ople) ....71,914..A 1
Edremit ....27,145..B 1
Elâzig 142,983
*187,025..C 5
Elbistan ....35,437..C 5
Erciş ....27,582..B 7
Ereğli ....50,105..A 3
Ereğli ....56,931..C 3
Erzincan ....70,982..B 5
Erzurum 190,241
*285,182..B 6
Esenler* ....68,509..A 2
Eskisehir 309,431
*343,923..B 2
Fethiye ....14,294..C 2
Gaziantep 374,290
*512,745..C 5
Gebze* ....58,318..B 2
Giresun ....45,690..B 5
Gölcük* ....45,950..B 2

Gültepe* ....48,240..C 1
Gümü-
 shane ....12,735..B 5
Güngören* ....74,761..A 2
Hakkâri ....18,009..C 7
Iğdir ....74,357..B 7
İnegöl ....45,237..B 2
İskenderun
 (Alexan-
 dretta) ....124,824..C 4
İsparta ....86,475..C 2
İstanbul 2,772,708
*2,909,455..A 2
İzmir
 (Smyrna) 757,854
*1,059,183..C 1
İzmit
 (Kocaeli) ...190,423
*318,026..B 2
Kadirli ....40,643..C 4
Kâğithane ......175,540..A 2
Karabük ....84,137..A 3
Karaköse ....40,532..B 7
Karaman ....51,208..C 3
Kars ....58,799..B 7
Kartal ....68,291..B 2
Kasta-
 monu ....35,464..A 3
Kayseri 281,320
*380,352..C 4
Keşan ....28,884..A 1
Kilimli* ....34,353..A 3
Kilis ....58,355..C 5
Kirikhan* ....49,891..C 4
Kirikkale ......178,401..B 3
Kirklareli ......36,296..A 1
Kirşehir ....49,913..B 4
Kocaeli,
 see İzmit

Kocasinan* ......96,312..A 2
Konya 329,139
*672,695..C 3
Kozan ....42,462..C 4
Kozlu ....32,121..A 3
Küçük-ek-
 mece* ....81,503..A 2
Küçükköy* ......100,406..A 2
Küçükyali* ......16,640..A 2
Kütahya ....99,436..B 2
Lülebur-
 gaz ....35,689..A 1
Malatya 179,074
*241,560..C 5
Maltepe ....90,439..A 2
Manisa ....94,167..B 1
Maraş 178,557
*281,382..C 5
Mardin ....39,137..C 6
Mersin ....216,308..C 4
Merzifon ....32,130..B 4
Muğla ....27,392..C 1
Muş ....40,977..B 6
Mustafa-
 kemalpaşa ...30,141..B 2
Nazilli ....60,003..C 1
Nevşehir ....37,161..C 4
Niğde ....39,835..C 4
Niksar ....23,655..B 5
Nizip ....38,967..C 5
Nusaybin ....30,981..C 6
Ödemiş ....40,736..C 1
Ordu ....52,785..B 5
Osmaniye ....84,212..C 4
Pendik* ....48,219..B 2
Polatli ....43,530..B 3
Reyhanli* ....31,003..D 4
Rize ....43,407..A 6
Salihli ....51,826..C 1

Samsun 198,749
*345,200..A 4
Selakoy* ....43,407..A 2
Seydişehir ......30,065..C 3
Siirt ....42,291..C 6
Silifke ....22,041..C 3
Silvan ....43,624..C 6
Sinop ....18,378..A 4
Sivas 172,864
*273,215..B 5
Siverek ....29,464..C 5
Smyrna, see İzmir
Soğanlik* ....34,769..A 2
Söke ....37,413..C 1
Soma ....30,420..B 1
Tarsus ....121,074..C 4
Tatvan ....34,769..C 6
Tekirdağ ....52,093..A 1
Tire ....32,291..C 1
Tokat ....60,855..B 4
Trabzon ....108,403..B 5
Tunceli ....12,859..B 5
Turgutlu ....55,396..B 1
Turhal ....46,864..B 4
Ümraniye* ....71,954..A 2
Ünye ....28,227..B 5
Urfa 147,488
*282,419..C 5
Uşak ....71,469..B 2
Uzunköprü* ......27,873..A 1
Van ....92,801..C 7
Viranşehir ......40,820..C 6
Yakacik* ....27,756..C 4
Yalova* ....41,823..B 2
Yarimca* ....35,407..B 2
Yenibosna* ......40,786..A 2
Yozgat ....36,349..B 4
Zile ....30,637..B 4
Zonguldak ......109,044..A 3

*Does not appear on map; key shows general location.
*Population of metropolitan area, including suburbs.

Source: 1980 census.

the Social Democracy Party, favors a mixture of free enterprise and government controls.

Armed forces. About 650,000 men serve in Turkey's army, navy, and air force. Men from 20 to 32 years old may be drafted for 18 months of service.

People

Population and ancestry. Turkey has a population of about 55,377,000. About 90 per cent of the people are descendants of an Asian people called *Turks.* Turks began to migrate to Anatolia from central Asia during the A.D. 900's. Kurds form Turkey's largest minority group, with more than 2 million members. Most of them live in the mountainous regions of the southeast.

Turkey also has several smaller minority groups. Nearly 300,000 Arabs, most of whom are farmers, live near the Syrian border. More than 100,000 Caucasians— people whose ancestors came from the Caucasus Mountains region just northeast of Turkey in what is now the Soviet Union—live in the provinces bordering the Black Sea. About 70,000 Greeks and 69,000 Armenians live in the Istanbul area.

About 48 per cent of Turkey's people live in cities and towns, and about 52 per cent live in rural areas. The number of urban dwellers has increased rapidly since the 1940's. Hundreds of thousands of people have left their farms and villages to seek work in the cities. But the cities do not have enough jobs for all the people. As a result, many Turkish people have gone abroad to work. Many Turkish citizens work in other parts of the Middle East and in such countries as Australia, Belgium, Canada, France, Switzerland, and especially West Germany.

Languages. More than 90 per cent of all Turks speak Turkish, the country's official language. About 6 per cent speak Kurdish. The rest speak Arabic, Greek, or one of the other languages of the minority groups.

The government began to develop the modern Turkish language in the late 1920's. For centuries, the written language was Ottoman Turkish, a complicated language

John Nicolais, Woodfin Camp, Inc.
A crowded street along the Istanbul waterfront reflects the rapid growth of Turkish cities since the 1940's. Slightly less than half of Turkey's people live in cities and towns.

Owen Franken, Stock, Boston
Education in Turkey has made rapid progress. But the nation still does not have enough schools or teachers. Many children, unlike these youngsters, do not receive a primary education.

written in Arabic characters. However, the Arabic alphabet had no letters to represent many sounds used in spoken Turkish. In addition, Ottoman Turkish included words and grammar from the Arabic and Persian languages. Ottoman Turkish was so difficult that only scholars and the ruling class learned to read it. In 1928, the government established a new alphabet and eliminated most foreign words from the language. It also ordered a language education program throughout the country and outlawed the use of Ottoman Turkish.

Ways of life have changed greatly in Turkey since the 1920's, when a new republican government was established. The government set out to make Turkey a modern state and so began a program to sweep away the customs and traditions of centuries.

Since the 1920's, one of the government's major goals has been to change the status of women in Turkish life. Men have dominated Turkish society for hundreds of years. Before the 1920's, women had almost no civil rights. Parents arranged the marriages of their daughters by means of a contract with the groom's family. The bride had little voice in the matter. Women could not vote and had difficulty getting a divorce. During the 1920's, the government outlawed the arrangement of marriages by contract and made it easier for women to get a divorce. It also gave women the right to vote and to receive alimony. Today, increased educational opportunities and exposure to Western ideas are gradually improving the position of Turkish women.

The government has also tried to bring the Kurds and other tribal people into the mainstream of modern Turkish life. Many Turks, as well as the Kurds, have lived in tribal groups as nomads or in isolated communities for centuries. During the 1920's, the government began to force these people to abandon their tribal way of life as a means of modernizing Turkish society. The Kurds revolted against these attempts several times in the 1920's and 1930's. Since then, some Kurds adopted modern Turkish culture while serving in the armed forces or attending school outside areas with large Kurdish popula-

David Bellak, Jeroboam

Islamic rituals, such as group prayer, *above,* play an important part in the daily life of most Turks. About 98 per cent of the people of Turkey are Muslims.

tions. However, tribes of Kurds and other Turkish people still travel across the countryside with their goats and sheep in search of pastures as their ancestors did.

Housing varies throughout Turkey. Turks who live near the Black Sea build thatch-roofed cottages with timber from nearby forests. In rural areas of Thrace and northeastern Anatolia, many people have replaced their old wooden homes with one-story houses of concrete blocks. Many villagers in central Anatolia live in flat-roofed houses of sun-dried brick. Stone houses are common in southern and western Anatolia.

Most wealthy Turks live in luxurious concrete block houses on the outskirts of cities or in suburban apartment complexes. Middle-class city dwellers live in old two- and three-story wooden houses or in concrete homes. The rapid growth of industry in the major cities has created a severe housing shortage among workers who moved to the cities from rural areas. As a result, large shantytowns have sprung up at the edges of Turkish cities.

Clothing worn by the people of Turkey changed dramatically during the 1920's. The government discouraged or forbade the wearing of certain garments required by Islamic custom. City dwellers and many rural people then adopted Western clothing styles. However, some Turks in rural areas still cling to Islamic tradition. Only a few men wear the traditional loose-fitting cloak and baggy trousers. But rural women still continue some of the old clothing customs. These women wear a simple blouse and pantaloons. They cover their head and often the lower part of the face with a scarf as a sign of modesty.

Food and drink. Cracked-wheat bread and yogurt are the chief foods of most Turks. Turks also eat much lamb, rice, and eggplant. Turkish cooks are especially famous for their tasty *shish kebab,* which consists of pieces of lamb, tomatoes, peppers, and onions cooked together on a skewer. They also combine rice with almonds, meat, pine nuts, and raisins in a dish called *pilaf.* For snacks, Turks enjoy *borek,* a flaky pastry stuffed with meat or cheese. A popular dessert is *baklava,* made of thin layers of pastry, honey, and chopped nuts. Another pastry, *kadayif,* is made with shredded wheat. Favorite beverages of the Turks include tea, thick coffee flavored with sugar, and a liquor called *raki,* which is made from raisins.

Recreation. Family outings and celebrations are the most common forms of recreation in Turkey. The people also enjoy drinking coffee or tea at a restaurant with a scenic view. Many men spend their leisure time in coffee houses playing the ancient dice game of backgammon. Archery, horseback riding, soccer, and wrestling are popular sports. A Turkish form of wrestling called

LeRoy Woodson

The Kurds of Turkey make up the nation's largest minority group. Most of them, like these women and children, live much as their ancestors did centuries ago. They roam the countryside with their livestock and live in caves and other temporary shelters.

greased wrestling is a favorite event at festivals and wrestling matches. Contestants wear tight leather trousers and cover their bodies with olive oil to make the holds more difficult. The Turkish people also enjoy concerts, movies, stage plays, and operas.

Religion. More than 98 per cent of the Turkish people are Muslims. However, Turkey has no state religion, and the Constitution guarantees religious freedom. The population thus includes members of the Armenian Apostolic and Greek Orthodox churches, Roman and Eastern Catholics, and Jews.

One of the most controversial issues in Turkey is whether Turkish society should be organized on a worldly or religious basis. Islamic law provides specific rules for all activities of life—economic, political, and social. In the 1920's, the government made religion a private matter, restricting it to personal morals and behavior. But many Turks strongly objected. Today, the dispute continues over what part Islam should have in Turkish life.

Education. About 69 per cent of Turkey's people 15 years old and older can read and write. The government's greatest challenge in education is in rural areas. The government spends about 10 per cent of its budget on public education, and much of this money is used for the education of rural people. But rising costs and a lack of qualified teachers prevent the nation from providing enough schools in rural areas.

Turkish law requires all children to attend a five-year primary school until they graduate or reach the age of 15. However, this law is difficult to enforce. After graduation, students may attend a middle school for three years. Some middle-school graduates enter a three-year

college-preparatory high school called a *lise*. Other middle-school graduates enroll in a vocational school or enter the work force. Many lise graduates go on to college. Turkey has about 25 universities. Istanbul University, the oldest and largest university in Turkey, was founded in 1453. The university has more than 30,000 students.

The arts. Turkey's most important contribution to the arts is in the field of architecture. In Istanbul stands the great-domed cathedral Hagia Sophia, a classic example of Byzantine architecture. It was built in the A.D. 500's, when Turkey was part of the Byzantine Empire. Turkish *mosques* (Islamic houses of worship) were built throughout Anatolia during the 1200's. These structures, with their thin *minarets* (towers), follow the Persian and Arabic style of architecture. Many of Turkey's finest buildings were constructed during the 1400's and the 1500's, when the Ottoman Empire was at its height. A large number were designed by Koca Sinan, who is considered Turkey's greatest architect. His majestic Mosque of Suleiman I in Istanbul is one of the world's most beautiful mosques.

For hundreds of years, Turkish craftworkers have made excellent dishes, bowls, and other objects of ceramics. Richly colored ceramic tiles decorate many mosques and palaces. Turkish weavers have long been famous for their elaborately designed rugs. They made many of the first Oriental rugs used in Europe.

Most of Turkey's traditional literature is written in the complicated Ottoman Turkish language and deals with religious themes and life during Ottoman rule. Modern Turkish literature centers largely on nationalism, social justice, and folk history. In some works, modern writers

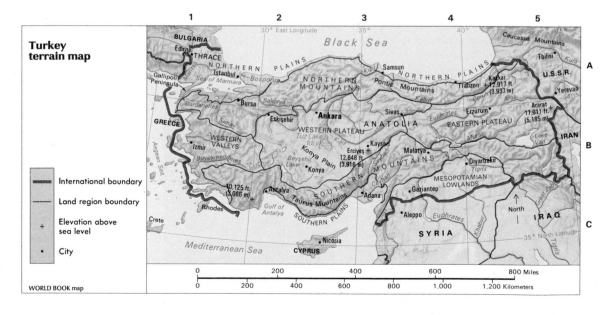

Turkey terrain map

International boundary

Land region boundary

+ Elevation above sea level

• City

WORLD BOOK map

Physical features

Aegean Sea ....B 1	Beyşehir Lake ....B 2	Dardanelles	Kaçkar (mountain) ....A 4	Sakarya River ....A 2
Anatolia	Black Sea ....A 3	(strait) ....A 1	Kelkit River ....A 4	Sea of Marmara ....A 1
(region) ....B 3	Bosporus	Erciyeş	Kizil River ....A 3	Seyhan River ....B 3
Ararat	(strait) ....A 2	(mountain) ....B 3	Konya Plain ....B 2	Simav River ....B 1
(mountain) ....B 5	Büyükmenderes	Euphrates River ....B 4	Lake Van ....B 5	Taurus Mountains ....C 2
Aras River ....A 5	River ....B 1	Gallipoli	Maritsa River ....A 1	Thrace (region) ....A 1
	Ceyhan River ....B 3	Peninsula ....A 1	Murat River ....B 4	Tigris River ....B 4
	Çoruh River ....A 4	Gulf of Antalya ....C 2	Pontic Mountains ....A 3	Tuz Lake ....B 2

include stories from ancient folk dramas about the legendary puppet character Karagöz (Black Eyes). In these folk dramas, the clever Karagöz produces much laughter as he outwits his enemies.

The land

Turkey covers 301,382 square miles (780,576 square kilometers) in the northwestern part of the Middle East. Much of Thrace and the coastal areas of Anatolia consist of lowlands and green, rolling plains. A broad expanse of dry highlands called the *Anatolian Plateau* stretches across central Anatolia. The plateau is bordered by the Pontic Mountains on the north and the Taurus Mountains on the south.

Turkey has several large saltwater lakes and numerous rivers. But most of the rivers dry up during the country's hot, dry summers. In the spring, many rivers become torrents as waters from the melting snows rush down from the mountains and overflow the riverbanks.

Turkey can be divided into eight land regions. They are (1) the Northern Plains, (2) the Western Valleys, (3) the Southern Plains, (4) the Western Plateau, (5) the Eastern Plateau, (6) the Northern Mountains, (7) the Southern Mountains, and (8) the Mesopotamian Lowlands.

The Northern Plains cover Thrace and extend along the Black Sea coast of Anatolia. Thrace's gently rolling grasslands make it an important farming and grazing region. Along the Black Sea coast, farmers raise corn, fruits, nuts, and tobacco.

The Western Valleys are broad, fertile river valleys along the Aegean Sea coast. The region produces barley, corn, olives, tobacco, and wheat. The value of its crop output exceeds that of any other region.

The Southern Plains are a narrow strip of land along the Mediterranean Sea. A great variety of crops, including cereal grains, citrus fruits, cotton, and olives, grow in the region's rich soil. Farmers must irrigate their fields during the hot, dry summer.

The Western Plateau, a region of highlands and scattered river valleys, extends across central Anatolia. The region receives very little rainfall. Farmers raise barley and wheat in the river valleys and wherever irrigation water is available. Goats, sheep, and other livestock graze on uncultivated land.

The Eastern Plateau is a rugged area of towering mountains and barren plains. It extends from the Western Plateau to Turkey's eastern border. The Taurus and Pontic mountains meet in this region. Mount Ararat, the country's highest point, rises 17,011 feet (5,185 meters) above sea level near the Iranian border. Most of the region's people are nomadic herders.

The Northern Mountains, or Pontic Mountains, rise between the Northern Plains and the Anatolian Plateau. Only a few roads and railroads connect the plateau with the Black Sea.

The Southern Mountains consist of the Taurus Mountains and several smaller ranges on the southern edge of the Anatolian Plateau. These mountains almost completely cut off the plateau from the Mediterranean Sea.

The Mesopotamian Lowlands are fertile plains and river valleys in southeastern Anatolia. Cereal grains and fruits grow well in the region's rich soil.

Climate

The climate differs greatly from one region of Turkey to another. Thrace and the south and west coasts of Anatolia have mild, rainy winters and hot, dry summers. Summer temperatures along the Aegean often rise above 90° F. (32° C). The Black Sea coast has cooler summers, with an average temperature of about 72° F. (22° C). Yearly rainfall in coastal areas averages from 20 to 30 inches (51 to 76 centimeters) along the Aegean and Mediterranean to more than 100 inches (254 centimeters) near the Black Sea.

Northeastern Turkey has mild summers but bitterly

Vast barren plains cover much of central Anatolia. The region receives little or no rain during the hot summer, and so few crops can be grown without extensive irrigation. Many of the region's people, like this herdsman, raise sheep or other livestock.

Turkey's gross national product

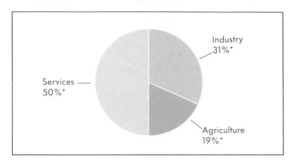

The gross national product (GNP) is the total value of goods and services produced by a country in a year. The GNP measures a nation's total economic performance and can also be used to compare the economic output and growth of countries. Turkey's GNP was $57,810,000,000 in 1984.

Production and workers by economic activities

Economic activities	Per cent of GDP* produced	Employed workers† Number of persons	Per cent of total
Manufacturing	25	2,036,843	11
Community, social, & personal services	20	2,558,098	14
Agriculture, forestry, & fishing	19	10,482,856	58
Trade	17	1,108,473	6
Transportation & communication	10	545,686	3
Construction	4	813,838	5
Utilities	3	41,923	‡
Mining	2	179,127	1
Finance, insurance, & real estate	§	299,130	2
Total	100	18,065,974	100

*Based on gross domestic product (GDP). GDP is the total value of goods and services produced within a country in a year.
†Figures are for 1980.
‡Less than 1 per cent.
§Included in Community, social, & personal services.
Sources: International Labor Organization; UN; World Bank.

cold winters. Temperatures sometimes fall to −40° F. (−40° C). Southeastern Turkey and the interior of Anatolia have cold winters with heavy snowstorms. Summers are hot, windy, and extremely dry.

Economy

Turkey has a developing economy. When the republican government came to power in the 1920's, Turkey was almost entirely an agricultural country. Under government direction, the number of factories increased from 118 in 1923 to more than 1,000 in 1941. Today, Turkey has over 30,000 factories. But agriculture remains an important economic activity. It provides jobs for about 58 per cent of the country's workers. However, farm output accounts for only about 20 per cent of the value of all goods and services produced in Turkey. Manufacturing employs only around 11 per cent of all workers, but the value of industrial production exceeds that of agricultural output.

The national government owns Turkey's communications systems, railroads, airports, and major utilities. The government also controls steel production, the mining

industry, the nation's forests, most of the banking system, and about 1 million acres (400,000 hectares) of farmland. However, most farms and small manufacturing and construction companies in Turkey are privately owned. Since 1963, the government has directed the nation's economic growth through a series of five-year plans. The government plans to increase the role of private industry in the economy.

Agriculture. Turkey's most productive farmlands are in the coastal regions, which have fertile soil and a mild climate. Farmers on the desertlike Anatolian Plateau raise wheat and barley. However, the plateau region often has long droughts that cause serious crop losses.

In most years, Turkey's farmers produce enough food for all the people plus a surplus to sell abroad. About 50 per cent of the cropland is used for grains. Wheat is the chief grain, followed by barley and corn. Large amounts of cotton are grown for both fiber and cottonseed oil. Tobacco, a major export, is grown along the Black and Aegean seas. Turkey is a major producer of fruits, nuts, and vegetables, including apples, eggplants, grapes and raisins, hazel nuts, melons, oranges, potatoes, sugar beets, and tomatoes. Turks also raise sheep, goats, and other livestock. Wool is Turkey's most valuable livestock product.

Manufacturing. Turkey's largest manufacturing industries are the processing of food and beverages and the production of textiles. Other leading manufactured products include fertilizers, iron and steel, machinery and metal products, motor vehicles, and pulp and paper products. Most factories and mills are in and around the large cities of northern and western Turkey.

Mining. Turkey is rich in mineral resources, but the mining industry is largely undeveloped. The country's most abundant mineral is coking coal, which is used in steelmaking. Turkey is one of the world's largest producers of chromite, the mineral from which chromium

Manufacturing is one of Turkey's chief industries. Most textile workers are employed in modern mills. Others, such as these women, work at home. The women are weaving an Oriental rug.

is obtained. The nation also produces and refines petroleum. Other minerals produced in Turkey include bauxite; boron; copper; iron ore; and *meerschaum,* a soft, white mineral that is used to make jewelry and tobacco pipes.

Foreign trade. The government's program to speed Turkey's industrial growth requires the nation to export as many products as possible and import large quantities of machinery and raw materials. The nation spends more money for these and other imports than it receives for its exports. As a result, Turkey has an *unfavorable balance of trade.* Turkey's chief imports include chemicals, machinery, iron and steel, motor vehicles, and petroleum. Major exports include clothing and textiles, cotton, fruits, nuts, and tobacco. Turkey's main trading partner is West Germany. Other leading partners include France, Great Britain, Iran, Iraq, Italy, and the United States.

Transportation and communication. Turkey's road network reaches almost all the nation's towns. But many roads are unpaved. Less than 2 per cent of the people own automobiles. Most Turks use buses, trains, or taxis. The railroad system links the country's chief cities. Government-owned Turkish Airlines serves many cities in Turkey, Europe, and the Middle East. Istanbul and Ankara have international airports. Turkey has many fine natural harbors. Istanbul and Izmir are the country's primary ports.

Turkey has more than 1,000 daily newspapers, representing many different political views. The government sometimes restricts what newspapers may print. Most Turkish families own a radio. Turkey has an average of about 1 television set for every 10 people.

History

Archaeologists have found evidence of an advanced society in what is now Turkey before 6000 B.C. The first

Ian Berry, Magnum

Hard-working Turkish farmers pick cotton in one of the country's cotton fields. Turkey is a world leader in cotton production, and cotton is one of the nation's most valuable exports.

inhabitants of the area to be recorded in history were a people called the Hittites. About 2000 B.C., they began to migrate to central Anatolia from Europe or central Asia. During the next several hundred years, they conquered much of Anatolia and parts of Mesopotamia and Syria. By 1500 B.C., the Hittites had created a powerful empire that made them the leading rulers of the Middle East. See **Hittites.**

From about 1200 to 500 B.C., large areas of Anatolia fell to the Phrygians, the Lydians, and other peoples. During the same period, the Greeks founded many city-states along Anatolia's Aegean coast. Between about 550 and 513 B.C., the Persian Empire seized control of Anatolia and Thrace. The Persians held control until Alexander the Great of Macedonia crushed their army in 331 B.C. After Alexander's death in 323 B.C., Anatolia became a battleground in the wars among his successors. Small kingdoms rose and fell until 63 B.C., when the Roman general Pompey conquered the region. Anatolia was at peace under Roman rule for nearly 400 years.

In A.D. 330, the Roman emperor Constantine the Great moved the capital from Rome to the ancient town of Byzantium in Thrace. Byzantium was renamed *Constantinople,* meaning *city of Constantine.* In 395, the Roman Empire split into two parts—the East Roman Empire, which included Anatolia and Thrace, and the West Roman Empire. Barbarians conquered the West Roman Empire in the mid-400's. But the East Roman Empire, also called the Byzantine Empire, thrived. Byzantine emperors thus came to rule all of what is now Turkey until the late 1000's. See **Byzantine Empire.**

The Seljuk Turks became one of the first Turkish peoples to rule in Turkey. The Seljuks were Muslims from central Asia east of the Caspian Sea. During the mid-1000's, they conquered Armenia; the Holy Land, or Palestine; and most of Iran. Then they invaded Anatolia. In 1071, the Seljuks destroyed most of the Byzantine power in Anatolia by defeating the Byzantine army in the Battle of Manzikert. They set up an empire with Iconium (now Konya) as the capital. From this point onward, the Christian religion and the Greek language of the Byzantine Empire were gradually replaced in Anatolia by Islam and the Turkish language.

In 1095, Christians in western Europe organized the first of a series of military expeditions called the *Crusades* to drive the Turks from the Holy Land (see **Crusades**). During the First Crusade (1096-1099), Christian troops defeated the Seljuk Turks in western Anatolia. As a result, the Byzantine Empire recovered about a third of Anatolia. But the crusaders then left the peninsula to fight in the Holy Land. The Seljuk Empire thus endured until 1243, when it was invaded by Asian nomads known as Mongols (see **Mongol Empire**).

The rise of the Ottoman Empire. The Mongol Empire was torn by internal struggles and soon fell apart. As a result, the Turks' influence in Anatolia continued to grow. During the 1300's, a group of Turks called the Ottomans began to build a mighty empire. In 1326, they seized the Anatolian city of Bursa, which became their capital. By the late 1300's, the Ottomans had conquered the western two-thirds of Anatolia; most of Thrace; and much of the Balkan Peninsula, including Greece. All that remained of the Byzantine Empire was the area around Constantinople.

Bettmann Archive

The conquest of Constantinople by the Turks in 1453 ended the Byzantine Empire, which had ruled in Turkey since the 300's.

In 1453, Ottoman forces led by Muhammad II captured Constantinople, ending the Byzantine Empire. The Turks called the city Istanbul and made it their capital. By 1481, their empire extended from the Danube River in Europe to southern Anatolia.

The Ottoman Empire reached its height in the 1500's. During the reign of Sultan Bayezid II, who ruled from 1481 to 1512, the empire became the leading naval power in the Mediterranean region. Ottoman forces conquered Syria in 1516 and Egypt in 1517. Suleiman I, whom Europeans called the *Magnificent,* ruled from 1520 to 1566. In 1526, his army conquered much of Hungary in the Battle of Mohács. Suleiman also expanded the empire's borders to Yemen on the south, Morocco on the west, and Persia on the east.

The start of the Ottoman decline. After the Battle of Mohács, European powers feared that the Turks would overrun Europe. However, European forces successfully defended Vienna, Austria, during a Turkish attack in 1529. In 1571, European fleets defeated the Turkish navy in the Battle of Lepanto, near Greece. The Turks again failed to capture Vienna in 1683.

During the 1700's, the Ottoman Empire continued to weaken. In 1774, the Turks lost a six-year war against Russia and were forced to allow Russian ships to pass through the Straits—the Turkish waters that link the Black Sea with the Mediterranean. The Ottoman Empire lost the Crimea, a peninsula in the Black Sea, to Russia in 1783.

"The Sick Man of Europe," as the Ottoman Empire came to be called, lost more territory during the 1800's. In 1821, Greek nationalists revolted against Ottoman rule. France, Great Britain, and Russia sided with the Greeks and sent forces to fight the Turks (see **Greece** [History]). The Treaty of Adrianople (Edirne) ended the fighting in 1829. It acknowledged the independence of Greece and gave Russia control of the mouth of the Danube River. The Turks also lost other Balkan territory in a series of wars with Russia (see **Russo-Turkish wars**). But European powers forced Russia to give up much of its gains at the Congress of Berlin in 1878. The Ottoman Empire continued to decline, however. The Turks had lost Algeria to France in 1830, and France seized Tunisia

in 1881. Great Britain gained Cyprus in 1878 and Egypt in 1882.

Ottoman leaders tried to halt the empire's decline through a reform program. They reorganized the military and improved the educational system. In 1876, the empire's first constitution was adopted. It provided for representative government and granted the people various freedoms. However, Sultan Abdul-Hamid II, who came to the throne the same year, set the constitution aside and ruled as a dictator. Government policies became increasingly violent, and Abdul-Hamid ruled by the use of fear. Religious persecution began to spread as members of various religious minorities became revolutionaries. Nationalist feelings were strong among the minorities. Ottoman officials, fearing further collapse of the already declining empire, reacted harshly. Violent attacks took place. Between 1894 and 1918, the Christian Armenians in the Ottoman Empire suffered an especially large loss of life (see **Armenia** [History]).

The Young Turks. During the late 1890's, small groups of Turkish students and military officers who opposed Abdul-Hamid's harsh policies banded together secretly. The most influential group was the Young Turks. In 1908, the Young Turks led an army revolt against Abdul-Hamid and forced him to restore constitutional government. But the sultan soon staged an unsuccessful counterrevolution, and the Young Turks made him give up the throne in 1909. They then ruled the empire through his brother Muhammad V.

The Young Turks wanted to restore the greatness of the Ottoman Empire. However, many Turkish people no longer cared about the idea of maintaining an empire. In addition, the empire's Christian minorities demanded freedom from Ottoman rule. And so the empire continued to crumble. Soon after the revolution in 1908, Bulgaria declared its independence, and Austria seized Bosnia. Italy took Libya in 1912. In 1913, the Ottoman Empire surrendered Crete, part of Macedonia, southern Epirus, and many Aegean islands to Greece. By 1914, the empire had lost all its European territory except eastern Thrace.

In 1914, the Ottoman Empire entered World War I on

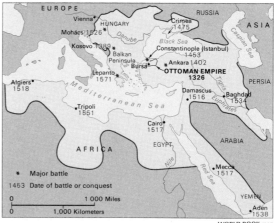

WORLD BOOK map

The Ottoman Empire began during the 1300's as a small state around the city of Bursa. It grew to include much of the Middle East and parts of northern Africa and southeastern Europe.

Important dates in Turkey

1500 B.C. The Hittites, the earliest known inhabitants of what is now Turkey, ruled in Anatolia.

63 B.C. The Roman general Pompey conquered Anatolia.

A.D. 330 Constantine the Great moved the capital of the Roman Empire to Byzantium and renamed the town Constantinople.

1071 The Seljuk Turks conquered most of Anatolia by defeating the Byzantine forces in the Battle of Manzikert.

1326 The Ottoman Turks captured Bursa, which marked the beginning of the Ottoman Empire.

1453 The Ottomans captured Constantinople, ending the Byzantine Empire.

1783-1914 The Ottoman Empire lost much of its territory in a series of military defeats.

1908 The Young Turks revolted against the government.

1914-1918 In World War I, the Ottoman Empire allied with Germany and lost much of its remaining territory.

1923 Mustafa Kemal (Atatürk) set up the Republic of Turkey and began a program to modernize the nation.

1947 Turkey received economic and military aid from the United States to resist Soviet expansion.

1960 Turkish army units overthrew the government and ruled until free elections were held in 1961.

1974 Turkish forces invaded Cyprus.

1980 Army units again took control of the government.

1983 The government was returned to civilian control.

---

the side of Germany and Austria-Hungary in an attempt to regain lost territory. In 1915, British, French, and other Allied troops tried to gain control of the Straits so that aid could be shipped to Russia. The Turks drove back the invaders, dealing the Allies a crushing defeat. However, the Allies won the war in 1918.

After World War I, the Allies set out to break up the Ottoman Empire. Allied troops occupied Istanbul and the Straits. In May 1919, Greek troops, protected by Allied fleets, landed at the Turkish port of Izmir. The Greeks then advanced into the country. The Turks deeply resented the Ottoman government's inability to defend their homeland.

Mustafa Kemal, a Turkish military hero, quickly organized a nationalist movement. Under the leadership of Kemal, a nationalist congress met in Sivas in September to form a new *provisional* (temporary) government. In April 1920, the congress organized the Turkish Grand National Assembly in Ankara and elected Kemal as Assembly president.

In August 1920, the sultan's government signed the harsh Treaty of Sèvres with the Allies (see **Sèvres, Treaty of**). The treaty granted independence to some parts of the empire and gave other parts to various Allied powers. The empire was reduced to Istanbul and a portion of Anatolia. As a result of the treaty, the sultan's popularity among the Turks declined further, while the power of Kemal and the nationalists grew. In September 1922, the nationalist forces finally drove the Greeks from the country. The Grand National Assembly then abolished the office of sultan, and the Allies agreed to draw up a new peace treaty with the nationalists. The Treaty of Lausanne, signed in 1923, set Turkey's borders about where they are today.

The republic of Turkey. The Grand National Assembly proclaimed Turkey to be a republic on Oct. 29, 1923,

and elected Kemal as president. Kemal and other nationalist leaders believed that the new nation could not survive without sweeping social changes.

During the 1920's and 1930's, the government did away with such Islamic traditions as the Arabic alphabet, Muslim schools, the Islamic legal system, and the wearing of the veil by women and the fez by men. It abolished the religious and civil office of the caliph. It also outlawed *polygyny,* the practice of having more than one wife at the same time. Women received the right to vote and to hold public office. All Turks were required to choose a family name. At the same time, the Grand National Assembly gave Kemal his surname—*Atatürk,* which means *father of the Turks.*

Atatürk held enormous political power. He controlled the Assembly and could appoint and dismiss the prime minister and cabinet without its approval. However, some Turks opposed Atatürk's anti-Islamic policies. The Kurds revolted against them in 1925, but the government put down the uprising.

Atatürk served as Turkey's president until he died in 1938. Ismet İnönü then became president. Under İnönü's leadership, Turkey avoided entering World War II (1939-1945) until February 1945, when Germany's defeat seemed certain. Turkey joined the United Nations (UN) the same year.

After World War II, the Soviet Union demanded control of territory in eastern Turkey and the right to build military bases along the Straits. Turkish leaders turned to the Western powers for help. In 1947, U.S. President Harry Truman announced the Truman doctrine, under which the United States would provide aid to any country threatened by Communism. The United States gave Turkey millions of dollars in economic and military aid. In return for this help, Turkey allowed the United States to build and operate military bases on Turkish soil.

The Republican People's Party, established by Atatürk, had governed Turkey since the establishment of the republic. However, in 1950, the Democrat Party won a majority in the Grand National Assembly. Celal Bayar became president, and Adnan Menderes became prime

United Press Int.

Kemal Atatürk founded the Republic of Turkey in 1923 and was its first president. In an attempt to modernize the nation, he introduced major cultural, political, and economic reforms.

minister. Unlike the Republicans, the Democrats encouraged foreign investments and wanted less government control of the economy. But by the late 1950's, a rise in the national debt and restrictions on freedom of speech had made the Democrat government unpopular.

The 1960's. Turkish military forces believed that the Democrat government had strayed too far from Atatürk's political principles. In 1960, army units led by General Cemal Gürsel seized control of the government and set up a provisional government. The military placed many former government leaders on trial. Prime Minister Menderes was hanged. President Bayar was sentenced to life imprisonment but was later released.

In 1961, Turkey adopted a new constitution. The provisional government then held free national elections. No party won a majority in the legislature. But two members of the Republican People's Party were chosen for the highest offices. Inönü became prime minister, and Gürsel became president. In 1965, the Justice Party won a majority in the legislature, and the party leader, Süleyman Demirel, became prime minister. Gürsel held office until 1966.

The Cyprus crisis. During the 1960's, Turkey and Greece nearly went to war over the issue of the Mediterranean island of Cyprus. In 1964 and 1967, fighting broke out on Cyprus between the island's Turkish minority and Greek majority. Both Turkey and Greece threatened to intervene before outside peacemakers arranged a settlement. But in 1974, Greek military officers overthrew the president of Cyprus. Turkish troops then invaded the island and captured much territory. The Turks on Cyprus later established a separate government. The Turks declared the captured territory an *autonomous* (self-governing) region in 1975, and an independent republic in 1983. However, the Greek Cypriots protested strongly against these measures. See **Cyprus** (History).

Recent developments. High taxes, inflation, and political unrest have troubled Turkey since the late 1960's. At that time, radical groups of Turks began staging such terrorist acts as bombings, kidnappings, and murders in an attempt to overthrow the government. In the 1970's, deep divisions developed between secular and religious groups. Since the mid-1970's, much fighting has taken place between the two sides. Terrorist acts have continued, and radicals of the two groups have accused each other of committing them.

Control of Turkey's government changed hands many times during the 1970's. In 1971, Prime Minister Demirel resigned under pressure from the military. A series of prime ministers then failed to form a stable government. In 1975, Demirel again became prime minister. In the late 1970's, the office passed back and forth between Demirel and Bülent Ecevit of the Republican People's Party several times. Demirel became prime minister in November 1979. In 1980, army leaders took control of the government and greatly reduced the civil disorder. A new Constitution was adopted in 1982. General Kenan Evren was named president until 1989 by a provision in the Constitution. Turkey returned to civilian rule in 1983 when parliamentary elections were held. Turgut Özal of the center-right Motherland Party became prime minister. Özal and his party won a second general election in 1987.   Andrew C. Hess

Related articles in *World Book* include:

Biographies

Atatürk, Kemal	Muhammad Ali
Barbarossa	Suleiman I
Muhammad II	

Cities and towns

Ankara	Istanbul
Antioch	Izmir
Edirne	Tarsus

History

Armenia	Ottoman Empire
Balkans	Russo-Turkish wars
Berlin, Congress of	Seljuks
Byzantine Empire	Sèvres, Treaty of
Crimean War	Sultan
Cyprus	Thrace
Janissaries	Turks
Kurdistan	World War I

Physical features

Ararat	Dardanelles	Marmara, Sea of
Bosporus	Euphrates River	

Other related articles

Asia Minor	Middle East
Bulgaria (History)	Romania (History)

Outline

I. Government
 A. The president
 B. The prime minister and cabinet
 C. The Grand National Assembly
 D. Court system
 E. Local government
 F. Political parties
 G. Armed forces

II. People
 A. Population and ancestry   F. Food and drink
 B. Languages   G. Recreation
 C. Ways of life   H. Religion
 D. Housing   I. Education
 E. Clothing   J. The arts

III. The land
 A. The Northern Plains
 B. The Western Valleys
 C. The Southern Plains
 D. The Western Plateau
 E. The Eastern Plateau
 F. The Northern Mountains
 G. The Southern Mountains
 H. The Mesopotamian Lowlands

IV. Climate

V. Economy
 A. Agriculture
 B. Manufacturing
 C. Mining
 D. Foreign trade
 E. Transportation and communication

VI. History

Questions

What is Turkey's chief economic activity?
Why was a new Turkish language developed?
What are the *Straits*?
How has the role of Turkish women changed since 1900?
Who are the Kurds?
Who was Kemal Atatürk?
How did Atatürk's modernization program revolutionize Turkish life during the 1920's?
Who were the Young Turks?
What are the chief foods of most Turks?
What was the Ottoman Empire?

Additional resources

American University. *Turkey: A Country Study.* 3rd ed. U.S. Government Printing Office, 1980.

Fodor's Turkey. McKay. Published annually.

Harris, George S. *Turkey: Coping with Crisis.* Westview, 1985. Introduction to modern Turkey.

Kinross, John P. D. B. *The Ottoman Centuries: The Rise and Fall of the Turkish Empire.* Morrow, 1979. First published in 1977.

Lewis, Bernard. *The Emergence of Modern Turkey.* 2nd ed. Oxford, 1968.

Spencer, William. *The Land and People of Turkey.* Rev. ed. Lippincott, 1972. Suitable for younger readers.

Turkey is a large North American bird related to chickens, peafowl, and pheasants. American Indians raised turkeys for food as early as A.D. 1000. Today, turkeys are a part of traditional Thanksgiving and Christmas dinners in many homes throughout the United States and Canada.

Male turkeys are called *toms,* and females are called *hens.* Baby turkeys are called *poults.* There are two species of turkeys: the *Yucatán turkey* and the *North American turkey.* The Yucatán turkey, which is also called the *ocellated* turkey, inhabits Guatemala and the Yucatán Peninsula of Mexico. It is a brilliantly colored bird that has eyelike spots on its tail. The North American turkey inhabits the United States and other areas in Mexico. This article discusses the North American turkey.

The body of a turkey. In general, wild turkeys have smaller heads and longer backs and legs than domestic turkeys do. Wild turkeys also have stronger wings and legs that enable them to fly and to run quickly. Domestic turkeys cannot fly.

Adult toms measure about 4 feet (1.2 meters) in length. Wild toms weigh from 10 to 16 pounds (4.5 to 7.3 kilograms). Some domestic toms weigh as much as 50 pounds (23 kilograms). The head and neck of toms are reddish and featherless. A long, loose piece of skin called a *wattle* extends from beneath the lower jaw

WORLD BOOK illustration by John Rignall, Linden Artists Ltd.

Common varieties of turkeys include the Bronze, *shown at the top;* the Bourbon Red, *middle;* and the wild turkey, *bottom.*

along the neck. At the base of the neck are small, wartlike structures called *caruncles.* A long, beardlike tuft of bristly feathers hangs from the center of the breast. Wild toms have plumage that is deep bronze in color. The color of domestic toms depends on variety.

Adult hens are dully colored and have no bristly beards. They are smaller than adult toms. Wild hens weigh from 6 to 10 pounds (2.7 to 4.5 kilograms). Some domestic hens weigh as much as 16 pounds (7.3 kilograms).

How wild turkeys live. Wild turkeys gather in small flocks in the forests. They eat small nuts, seeds, insects, berries, and other small fruits. At night, wild turkeys rest in trees. They build simple nests of dry leaves on the ground. Turkey eggs are about twice as large as ordinary chicken eggs. They have a pale creamy-tan color, speckled with brown.

Commercial turkey production. The United States turkey industry produces a gross income of about $905 million a year. On the average, people in the United States consume 12 pounds (5.4 kilograms) of turkey meat per person annually.

Most of the turkeys raised commercially in the United States are *White Hollands,* which have all-white plumage. However, the American Poultry Association also recognizes seven other varieties of domestic turkeys. They are the *Bronze,* the *Narragansett,* the *Bourbon Red,* the *Black,* the *Slate,* the *Royal Palm,* and the *Beltsville Small White.*

The Bronze turkey was the chief turkey raised in the United States until the 1960's. It has dull black feathers glossed with red and green on the front and bronze in

Leading turkey-producing states and provinces

Annual turkey production

North Carolina	31,850,000 turkeys
Minnesota	30,400,000 turkeys
California	20,500,000 turkeys
Arkansas	16,000,000 turkeys
Virginia	13,066,000 turkeys
Missouri	12,500,000 turkeys
Pennsylvania	7,100,000 turkeys
Indiana	6,941,000 turkeys
Ontario	6,731,000 turkeys
Iowa	6,300,000 turkeys

Figures are for 1985.
Sources: *Poultry,* April 1986, U.S. Department of Agriculture; *Production of Poultry and Eggs, 1985,* Statistics Canada.

the rear. The tail feathers of the Bronze turkey have white tips. The Narragansett resembles the Bronze turkey but does not have the red and green or bronze colors. The Bourbon Red is brownish-red with white wings. The Black turkey is all black, and the Slate turkey has slate-colored feathers. The Royal Palm is a small turkey colored black and white. The Beltsville Small White is all white.

Turkeys need much the same care as chickens, but they require more space to live in. They are more delicate, especially when young. They are particularly susceptible to cold rains. Young turkeys need more nutrients than young chickens because they grow faster. Toms reach market weight—approximately 24 pounds (11 kilograms)—about 19 to 20 weeks after hatching. Hens are marketed at about 14 to 16 weeks of age, when they weigh 10 to 12 pounds (4.5 to 5.4 kilograms).

Because of their size, turkeys provide a large yield of meat per bird. Large turkeys are particularly popular for use in restaurants, though they are too large for most families to eat at one meal. As a result, the turkey industry has developed boneless turkey roasts and turkey steaks for sale to consumers. Food companies also process turkey meat to make such products as cold cuts and hot dogs.

Scientific classification. The turkey belongs to the family, Phasianidae. The Yucatán turkey is *Agriocharis ocellata.* The North American turkey is *Meleagris gallopavo.*

Tommy L. Goodwin

See also **Farm and farming** (picture: Poultry farming); **Poultry** (Raising poultry).

Turkey carving. See **Meat** (pictures).

Turkey oak. See **Oak** (Red oaks).

Turkey red. See **Madder.**

Turkey red, a wheat variety. See **Wheat** (The spread of wheat farming).

Turkey vulture. See **Buzzard.**

Turkic peoples. See **Union of Soviet Socialist Republics** (People).

Turkish Angora cat. See **Cat** (Long-haired breeds; picture).

Turkish bath is one of the most thorough cleansing baths known. The Turks of medieval times believed in taking hot-air baths to preserve health, and their warriors spread this custom in most of the Middle East and parts of Europe. People in the Western World liked taking such hot-air baths, and they called them *Turkish baths.*

The process of taking such a bath is simple. Bathers wear only bathing clothes, or none at all. They first enter a sweating room which has dry heat in temperatures of about 160° F. (71° C). They then move to a room in which wet steam reaches a temperature of about 128° F. (53° C). The wet steam causes the bathers to perspire freely. The skin is then washed with warm water and soap or salve, and an attendant massages the body muscles. After being completely scrubbed and rubbed, the bathers dry off with a rough cloth or towel. Sometimes the hard skin of the feet is rubbed off with pumice stone. The bathers next take a cold shower or a swim, and then rest until their body temperature returns to normal.

The Turkish bath purifies the body of grease and dirt, and benefits many muscular ills. It is also sometimes used to relieve acute alcoholism. However, people who have heart trouble or a kidney disease should never take a Turkish bath. The *Russian bath* is similar to the Turkish bath, except that only steam is used. The Finns have a system of dry-heat bathing that is called a *sauna* (see **Sauna**).

Turkmenistan is a region that makes up the Turkmen Soviet Socialist Republic, one of the 15 republics of the Soviet Union. It lies north of Iran and Afghanistan, east of the Caspian Sea, and mostly west of the Amu Darya River. For location, see **Union of Soviet Socialist Republics** (political map). Turkmenistan has an area of 188,456 square miles (488,100 square kilometers), and a population of 3,118,000.

Most of the republic is a desert known as Kara Kum. Crops can be grown only by irrigation. Farming is the chief occupation. The leading products are cotton, wool, *astrakhan* (a fur taken from young lambs), a special breed of Turkoman horses, and Karakul sheep. The most thickly settled region of Turkmenistan is a strip of hilly country along the southeastern border. Most of the people are Muslims, and many belong to nomadic Turkic-speaking tribes. The capital is Ashkhabad. Turkmenistan became a republic of the Soviet Union in 1925.

Robert A. Lewis

See also **Merv.**

Turks are people who speak Turkic languages. There are about 10 Turkic languages. The main one is Turkish. Most of the approximately 90 million Turks in the world live in Turkey, the Soviet Union, the Balkan countries of southeastern Europe, Mongolia, China, and Iran. Turks form over 90 per cent of the people in Turkey. They rank second only behind the Slavs among the largest ethnic groups in the Soviet Union. The Soviet Turks include such groups as the Tartars and Kirghiz. Most Turks are *Muslims* (followers of Islam).

The Turks have had an important history. Their ancestors include the Huns and other nomadic people from Asia. The Huns conquered much of Europe during the A.D. 400's. During the 1000's, the Seljuk Turks seized Persia (now Iran) and then took over Asia Minor (now Turkey). The Ottoman Turks settled in Asia Minor during the late 1200's. By the 1500's, they had gained control of most of the Middle East, northern Africa, and southeastern Europe. The Ottomans were defeated in World War I (1914-1918). The modern nation of Turkey came into being in 1923.   Andrew C. Hess

See also **Kirghiz; Seljuks; Tartars; Turkey.**

Turks and Caicos Islands are barren, sandy islands that lie in the West Indies, about 90 miles (140 kilometers) north of the Dominican Republic. The two island groups form a British dependency in the Commonwealth of Nations. The main islands are Grand Turk and Salt Cay in the Turks Islands, and South Caicos, East Caicos, Grand or Middle Caicos, North Caicos, Providenciales, and West Caicos in the Caicos Islands. For the location of the Turks and Caicos Islands, see **West Indies** (map).

The islands cover a total land area of 166 square miles (430 square kilometers). Many of the 7,400 residents make their living by fishing. Lobster is the chief export. The capital and largest city is Grand Turk on the island of Grand Turk. In 1512, the Spanish explorer Juan Ponce de León sighted the Turks and Caicos Islands.

Gustavo A. Antonini

Turmeric, *TUR muhr ihk,* is a plant which grows in southern Asia. Its fleshy roots are the source of a substance, also called turmeric, which is used mainly for dyeing. These roots are hard and tough. On the outside, they are brownish- or yellowish-green. When they are broken, they show a resinous interior which varies from orange-brown to deep reddish-brown. The roots are ready for the market after being cleaned, boiled for some hours, and then dried in an oven. The yellowish powder which they yield when ground has a strong, aromatic odor and a strong, pungent taste.

Turmeric has been used for hundreds of years as a dyestuff and as a spice. It is an important ingredient of curry powder and is used to color mustard (see **Curry**). It does not yield a fast color, however, as a dyestuff. It has gone out of use as a medicine, but in India people mix it with milk to form a cooling lotion for the skin and eyes. Turmeric is useful in chemistry in making test papers for alkalies. With the addition of alkali, white paper soaked in a tincture of turmeric turns to reddish-brown and, on drying, to violet.

Scientific classification. Turmeric belongs to the ginger family, Zingiberaceae. It is classified as *Curcuma longa.*

Harold Norman Moldenke

Turner, Frederick Jackson (1861-1932), an American historian, became famous for a theory set forth in his paper, "The Significance of the Frontier in American History." Turner's theory emphasized the influence of an abundance of free land in strengthening democratic beliefs in the United States. He viewed the frontier, not as a line between east and west, but as a process that changed constantly, depending on the new area's natural resources and the backgrounds and beliefs of the people who moved into it. Turner founded a new school of thought in American history when he read this paper at the World's Columbian Exposition, which was held in Chicago in 1893.

Another work, *The Significance of Sections in American History* (1932), won the Pulitzer Prize for history in 1933. Turner also pioneered in using the materials and methods of the geographer, the economist, the sociologist, and the statistician in history. He was born in Portage, Wis., and taught at the University of Wisconsin and Harvard University.   Merle Curti

Turner, J. M. W. (1775-1851), was perhaps the greatest landscape painter in the history of English art. In many oil paintings and water colors, Turner departed from traditional ways of dealing with atmosphere, light, and color. Earlier artists had treated such elements realistically. In Turner's works, forms and outlines seem to dissolve into shimmering mist, steam, or smoke, or into the intense light of bright sky or water. By changing the way artists represented reality, Turner began a process continued by the impressionists and many other artists of the late 1800's and the 1900's.

Joseph Mallord William Turner was born in London. He began art training at the Royal Academy of Arts at the age of 14 and became an accomplished water-colorist. His early style shows the influence of the English artists J. R. Cozens and Thomas Girtin. The young painter was also influenced by the landscapes of the French painters Nicolas Poussin and Claude. Beginning in 1790, Turner exhibited at the Royal Academy. He was elected a member of the academy in 1802.

Turner's early paintings emphasize drama and romance. His oil painting *The Shipwreck* (1805) is an example. Later in his career, Turner stressed atmosphere in his pictures. He traveled widely, producing thousands of water-color sketches. In many of these sketches, he experimented with the brilliance of color. During the 1830's and 1840's, Turner painted a series of water-color views of Venice that rank among his masterpieces. Turner achieved a colorful, abstract quality in such oil paintings as *The Slave Ship* (1840) and *Rain, Steam, and Speed—The Great Western Railway* (1844). Many of his oil paintings reveal his fascination with the visual effects of fire and water. A famous example, *Burning of the Houses of Parliament* (about 1835), appears in **Painting** (Romanticism).   Douglas K. S. Hyland

See also **Ruskin, John.**

Procession of Boats with Distant Smoke, Venice (about 1840), an oil painting on canvas; The Tate Gallery, London

A painting by J. M. W. Turner, *left,* shows his fascination with the atmospheric effects of the sky, water, and intense light. This painting is one of many shimmering scenes of Venice that Turner painted late in his career.

John N. Turner

**Prime Minister of Canada
1984**

Trudeau
1980-1984

Turner
1984

Mulroney
1984-

Turner, John Napier (1929-   ), served as prime minister of Canada for $2\frac{1}{2}$ months in 1984. Turner, a Liberal, succeeded Prime Minister Pierre E. Trudeau, who had resigned. Turner called for a general election soon after he took office. But Brian Mulroney, the leader of the Progressive Conservatives, led his party to a landslide victory and replaced Turner as prime minister.

In 1988, Turner led the Liberal Party in another general election. But the Progressive Conservatives won the election, and Mulroney remained as prime minister.

Turner had been a corporation lawyer before he entered politics. He first held office in 1962, when voters from Montreal elected him to the Canadian House of Commons. Turner later served as registrar general and minister of consumer and corporate affairs in the Cabinet of Prime Minister Lester B. Pearson. Trudeau succeeded Pearson in 1968. Under Trudeau, Turner served as solicitor general and as minister of justice and attorney general before becoming minister of finance.

Turner's silver hair, blue eyes, and athletic build made him an impressive figure. Turner liked to ski, go canoeing, and play squash and tennis. He also enjoyed music, especially opera, and reading biographies.

Early life

Boyhood. John Napier Turner was born on June 7, 1929, in Richmond, England, near London. His father, Leonard Turner, was a British gunsmith. His mother, Phyllis Gregory Turner of Rossland, B.C., was an economist and a miner's daughter. She was studying at the London School of Economics and Political Science when she met her future husband. They were married in England. John had a sister, Brenda, born in 1931.

When John was 2 years old, his father died. The family then moved to Canada, and John's mother in time got a job as an economist with the federal tariff board in Ottawa. Later, during World War II (1939-1945), she became federal administrator of oils and fats. Various ministers in the Cabinet of W. L. Mackenzie King often discussed government activities in the family home. Partly as a result of these meetings, John developed an interest in public service at an early age.

John attended schools in Ottawa. He went to Normal Model Public School, Ashbury College, and St. Patrick's College. He was a bright, popular student, and he was active in sports. In 1945, John's mother married Frank Ross, a Vancouver industrialist.

College years. Turner graduated from St. Patrick's in 1945 and then entered the University of British Columbia. He was an outstanding student and won honors in political science. Turner also became a star sprinter on the track and field team. An injury ruined his chances to qualify for Canada's 1948 Olympic team. Turner received a Bachelor of Arts degree in 1949. He was named the most popular student in his class.

Turner won a Rhodes Scholarship to study at Oxford University in England. He studied law there and earned a bachelor's degree in jurisprudence in 1951 and a bachelor's degree in civil law in 1952. In 1952 and 1953, he took graduate courses in French civil law at the Sorbonne in Paris. He also became fluent in French. In 1954, he joined the Stikeman, Elliott law firm in Montreal.

Early political career

Entry into politics. Turner's government career began in June 1962, when he was elected to the Canadian House of Commons. Turner had run for office as a Liberal from the Montreal riding of St. Lawrence-St. George.

On May 11, 1963, Turner married Geills McCrae Kilgour of Winnipeg, one of his campaign workers. Turner and his wife had four children, Elizabeth (1964-), Michael (1965-), David (1968-), and James (1971-).

Early Cabinet posts. As a member of Parliament, Turner impressed Prime Minister Pearson. Pearson brought Turner into his Cabinet in 1965 as minister without portfolio. In April 1967, Pearson appointed Turner registrar general. In December 1967, Turner became minister of consumer and corporate affairs.

Pearson resigned as party leader and prime minister in April 1968. Turner campaigned hard to succeed him. But the party chose Pierre E. Trudeau, a Montreal professor. Turner ran third in the balloting.

In Trudeau's Cabinet. In April 1968, Trudeau gave Turner the additional office of solicitor general. Later in 1968, Trudeau made Turner minister of justice and attorney general. In this position, Turner introduced changes in criminal law that guaranteed legal services and eased bail requirements for the poor. He also established the Law Reform Commission of Canada. Many reforms proposed by this agency have become part of Canada's civil and criminal law.

In 1969, Turner helped push the Official Languages Act through the House of Commons. This act required federal facilities to provide service in both French and English if 10 per cent of the people in a particular area speak either language. In 1970, a crisis arose when the *Front de Libération du Québec* (FLQ), a terrorist group, kidnapped two officials. Turner worked to win parliamentary permission to put the War Measures Act into effect. This act allows the government to suspend civil liberties. Trudeau felt the act was necessary to help police deal with the crisis.

In January 1972, Trudeau appointed Turner minister of finance. In 1974, Turner introduced inflation-indexed personal tax exemptions. This system allowed individuals to make income tax deductions that reflected increases in the rate of inflation.

Return to private life. Rapid inflation continued to trouble the economy. Early in 1975, Turner began an effort to persuade labor and business leaders to accept voluntary limits on wage and price increases. But he failed to obtain an agreement. In September 1975, Turner surprised the nation by resigning from his powerful position in the Cabinet. In February 1976, he resigned

Important dates in Turner's life

1929	(June 7) Born in Richmond, England.
1949	Graduated from University of British Columbia.
1962	First elected to House of Commons.
1963	(May 11) Married Geills McCrae Kilgour.
1968	Appointed minister of justice and attorney general.
1972	Appointed minister of finance.
1975	Resigned as minister of finance.
1984	(June 30) Became prime minister.
1984	(Sept. 4) Liberals defeated in general election.
1988	(Nov. 21) Liberals lose another general election.

Canapress
John N. Turner was chosen to succeed Prime Minister Pierre E. Trudeau at the Liberal Party leadership convention in June 1984.

from the House of Commons. Turner's once promising political career appeared to be finished.

Political comeback

After ending his government service, Turner became a partner in the law firm of McMillan, Binch in Toronto. He greatly increased his personal wealth and was chosen to serve as a director by 10 large companies.

Return to politics. In February 1984, Trudeau announced his desire to resign as party leader and prime minister. Turner declared his candidacy for the leadership in March. During the leadership campaign, he promised programs to strengthen the then stalled Canadian economy. In June, the Liberal Party leadership convention chose Turner on the second ballot. Turner became prime minister on June 30.

The 1984 election. Early in July, Turner called a general election for Sept. 4, 1984. His rival party leaders were Brian Mulroney of the Progressive Conservative

Canada Wide from Canapress
The Turner family. From left to right are Turner; sons James, David, and Michael; daughter, Elizabeth; and wife, Geills.

Party and Edward Broadbent of the New Democratic Party. In the campaign, Turner said his first major goal as prime minister would be to lower the unemployment rate, which stood at 11 per cent. Mulroney and Broadbent charged that the Liberals did not know how to strengthen the economy.

In the election, the Liberals won only 40 of the 282 seats in the House of Commons—their worst defeat. The Conservatives won 211 seats. Mulroney succeeded Turner as prime minister on September 17.

The 1988 election. In 1988, Turner forced Mulroney to call another general election. He did so by asking Liberal Party members of the Canadian Senate to delay Parliament's ratification of a major U.S.-Canadian free-trade pact. Mulroney and U.S. President Ronald Reagan had signed the agreement in January 1988. The pact was to go into effect Jan. 1, 1989, but Turner declared that the Liberal senators would delay ratification until after that date. He promised that the senators would ratify the agreement before January 1 if the Progressive Conservatives won the election.

Mulroney called a general election for Nov. 21, 1988. The Progressive Conservatives won the election, and Mulroney remained as prime minister. After the election, the Canadian Senate approved the free-trade agreement, and the pact went into effect on schedule.

Christina McCall

Turner, Nat (1800-1831), a black slave and preacher, led the most famous slave revolt in United States history. In 1831, Turner and from 60 to 70 other slaves killed about 60 whites in Virginia. The victims included the family of Joseph Travis, Turner's owner.

More whites died during the rebellion led by Turner than in any other in the nation's history. The Virginia militia captured and hanged about 20 of the slaves, including Turner. In addition, angry whites killed about 100 innocent slaves. The rebellion caused the Southern States to pass strict laws for the control of slaves, especially those who were preachers.

Turner was born on a plantation in Southampton County, Virginia. His parents and grandmother encouraged him to become educated and to fight slavery. Through the years, Turner became the property of several other slaveowners. The son of one of his masters taught him to read and write. Turner became known as a forceful preacher who believed that God wanted him to free the slaves. This conviction led to his planning the rebellion.   Frank Otto Gatell

Additional resources

Nat Turner. Ed. by Eric Foner. Prentice-Hall, 1971.
Oates, Stephen B. *The Fires of Jubilee: Nat Turner's Fierce Rebellion.* New American Library, 1983. First published in 1975.

Turnip is a vegetable grown for its fleshy root and green leaves. Most turnip roots are globe-shaped. In most cases, they measure from 2 to 3 inches (5 to 8 centimeters) in diameter when harvested and weigh between $\frac{1}{2}$ and 1 pound (225 and 450 grams). Their smooth, firm flesh may be white or light yellow. The thin, hairy leaves of the turnip plant grow on stems that can reach a height of 18 inches (46 centimeters).

Turnips consist of about 90 per cent water. The roots are a good source of vitamin C and the leaves are rich in iron and vitamin A. Turnip roots are often boiled,

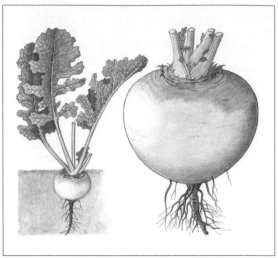

WORLD BOOK illustration by Jill Coombs

Turnips are grown for their edible leaves and roots. The leaves grow on stems, *above left.* The edible part of the root is globe-shaped and consists of smooth, firm flesh, *above right.*

mashed, and served with seasonings or sauce. The leaves are used in salads, soups, and stews. Cooked turnip leaves, called *turnip greens,* are a popular dish in the Southern United States.

There are several varieties of turnips. Those grown mainly for the root include Purple Top White Globe and Just Right. Shogoin is a popular variety grown primarily for its leaves.

Turnips are grown on farms and in home gardens throughout Europe and in Canada and the United States. In the United States, they are produced chiefly in the Southern States. Turnips thrive in cool weather, and they are able to withstand light frost. The plants grow quickly and are usually ready for harvest 45 to 55 days after planting. The seeds are planted in March for a spring harvest and in August or September for a fall harvest. Turnip seeds develop best in moderately dry, loose soil. The seeds are usually planted about $\frac{1}{2}$ inch (1.3 centimeters) deep and about 2 to 4 inches (5 to 10 centimeters) from one another in rows at least 12 inches (30 centimeters) apart. Turnips require large amounts of fertilizer, especially those turnips that are planted in the spring. Aphids, cabbage worms, and various beetle larvae are the chief pests that attack turnip roots and leaves.

Turnips probably originated in Asia or Europe. The ancient Greeks and Romans grew turnips and may have introduced them into northern Europe. Turnips have been popular in England since the 1500's and have been grown in the United States since colonial times.

Scientific classification. The turnip plant is in the mustard family, Cruciferae. It is *Brassica rapa.*   George R. Hughes

Turnpike is a road upon which a traveler must pay a fee, or toll, in order to use the highway. These roads were named *turnpikes* because in the early days travelers stopped at turnstiles, or turnpikes, to pay their fares before traveling farther. The first record of tolls being collected was on a Persian military road between Babylon and Syria about 2000 B.C.

Private investors brought the idea of building turnpikes to the United States from England. They formed turnpike companies to build the roads, and operated them for profit. The first turnpike in the United States was built in Virginia in 1785. From 1792 to 1810, investors organized 175 turnpike companies in New England. These companies spent over $5 million to build and improve nearly 3,000 miles (4,800 kilometers) of road.

Turnpike companies brought about many improvements in New England roads. They built bridges and surfaced the roads. Stage lines came into wide use as a result of the building of turnpikes. But in spite of the good they did, turnpikes proved to be poor business investments. By 1825 turnpike stocks in the United States had become nearly worthless, because the toll fees seldom paid for more than the cost of keeping up the roads.

State and local governments in the United States took over the task of building and maintaining roads. Interest in turnpikes revived during the depression of the 1930's. Several important toll roads were built after World War II, when taxes failed to provide enough money for new highways. Robert G. Hennes

See also **Pennsylvania Turnpike; Road**.

Turnsole. See Heliotrope.

Turnstone is the name given to two kinds of small shore birds. The name refers to their habit of turning over shells and pebbles with their bills as they look for food. The *ruddy turnstone* nests only in arctic regions. In winter it flies to far southern shores, reaching both coasts of the United States in its migrations. It is about 9 inches (23 centimeters) long, with black, white, and reddish-brown feathers. The *black turnstone* is slightly larger and lacks the reddish color. It nests along the shores of the Bering Sea to the Sitka district, and winters from southeastern Alaska to Lower California.

Scientific classification. Turnstones belong to the sandpiper family, Scolopacidae. The ruddy turnstone is *Arenaria interpres*. The black turnstone is *A. melanocephala*.

Alfred M. Bailey

Turntable. See Phonograph.

Turpentine is a colorless or yellowish liquid that has a strong odor and is highly flammable. It is used chiefly in making such chemical products as disinfectants, insecticides, medicines, and perfumes and in making synthetic rubber. It is also used as a thinner in paints and varnishes and for removing paint stains from clothing and the skin. Some turpentine is used in the processing and flavoring of certain foods.

Turpentine is made chiefly from longleaf pines and slash pines, which grow throughout the Southeastern United States. There are three types of turpentine. They are, in order of importance: (1) sulfate turpentine, (2) wood turpentine, and (3) gum turpentine.

Sulfate turpentine accounts for about 85 per cent of the turpentine produced in the United States. It is made from trees as they are converted into pulp. A vapor containing the turpentine forms during the pulping process. When the vapor cools, it becomes a liquid that contains sulfate turpentine.

Wood turpentine is produced from stumps and logs. The wood is gathered and taken to a steam distillation plant. There, it is shredded and mixed with a *solvent,* a chemical that dissolves other substances. The solution is then steamed to collect the turpentine. Wood turpentine makes up about 10 per cent of the turpentine made in the United States.

Gum turpentine is produced by *wounding* (cutting) the bark of living trees. A solution of sulfuric acid is applied to the wound, which measures about $\frac{1}{2}$ inch (1.3 centimeters) wide and $\frac{1}{2}$ inch deep. The acid causes gum to ooze out for as long as four weeks, until the wound closes. The wound is then reopened and a sulfuric acid solution is applied again. This procedure is repeated throughout the gathering period, which lasts from March to October. The gum is taken to a steam distillery where it is made into turpentine. Gum turpentine accounts for about 5 per cent of the turpentine produced in the United States. Harry E. Troxell

Turpin, Dick (1706-1739), was an English robber whose exploits have appeared in English legends and literature. As a youth, he joined a band of thieves who stole farm animals and deer. Later, he worked with Tom King as a highwayman, robbing travelers along the road from London to Oxford. He accidentally killed King while shooting at a constable. Finally, Turpin was arrested in York for stealing horses, was found guilty, and was hanged. William Ainsworth's novel *Rookwood* (1834) described Turpin's famous ride from London to Yorkshire on his horse, Black Bess. The story of this ride was originally told of an earlier highwayman named "Nicks." Richard Turpin was born in Hempstead, Essex, the son of an innkeeper. Knox Wilson

Turquoise, *TUR koyz* or *TUR kwoyz,* is a mineral widely used as a gemstone. It is prized for its color, which ranges from bright blue to blue-green. Turquoise is relatively soft, and so it is easy to shape and polish. It has a dull, waxy luster and is nearly *opaque* (nontransparent). Turquoise consists chiefly of a *hydrous aluminum phosphate,* a compound in which aluminum and phosphorus are chemically combined with water. Turquoise also contains copper, which gives the mineral its bluish color.

Turquoise occurs in arid regions. It is formed when surface rocks that are rich in aluminum undergo a chemical change. In most cases, turquoise results from the weathering of lava. Major deposits of turquoise are found in Iran and Tibet. Large amounts of the mineral also occur in the Southwestern United States, especially in Nevada and New Mexico.

People have used turquoise for jewelry and other decorative purposes since ancient times. It is one of the December *birthstones* (see **Birthstone**). The demand for turquoise remains so great that artificial varieties of the stone are produced. Maria Luisa Crawford

Turtle is the only reptile with a shell. Most kinds of turtles can pull their head, legs, and tail into their shell, which serves as a suit of armor. Few other backboned animals have such excellent natural protection.

Turtles, like all reptiles, are cold-blooded—that is, their body temperature stays about the same as the temperature of the surrounding air or water. Turtles cannot be warm and active in cold weather, and so they cannot live in regions that are cold throughout the year. They live almost everywhere else—in deserts, forests, grasslands, lakes, marshes, ponds, rivers, and the sea.

There are about 250 species of turtles, about 50 of which live in North America north of Mexico. Some tur-

E. R. Degginger

William M. Stephens, Tom Stack & Associates

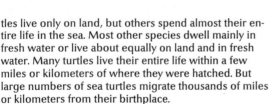

Clem Haagner, Bruce Coleman Inc.

Turtles live in a variety of habitats. The painted turtle, *upper left,* makes its home in fresh water. It uses its webbed feet for both swimming and walking. The green turtle, *lower left,* dwells in the sea. It has long, paddlelike flippers. The leopard tortoise, *above,* lives on land. Its stumpy legs and feet are well suited for walking on dry, rough ground.

tles live only on land, but others spend almost their entire life in the sea. Most other species dwell mainly in fresh water or live about equally on land and in fresh water. Many turtles live their entire life within a few miles or kilometers of where they were hatched. But large numbers of sea turtles migrate thousands of miles or kilometers from their birthplace.

Turtles vary greatly in size. The largest turtle species, the leatherback turtle, grows from 4 to 8 feet (1.2 to 2.4 meters) long. But the common bog turtle measures only about 4 inches (10 centimeters) in length.

Sea turtles, all of which swim rapidly, rank as the fastest turtles. One of these species, the green turtle, can swim for brief periods at a speed of nearly 20 miles (32 kilometers) per hour. On land, many kinds of turtles are slow, lumbering creatures. But some kinds of land turtles can move with surprising speed. For example, the smooth softshell turtle, a fresh-water species of North America, often can outrun a man on level ground.

The first turtles lived more than 185 million years ago. The *Archelon,* a sea turtle of about 25 million years ago, grew about 12 feet (3.7 meters) long. This creature died out, as did many other species. Today, many species of turtles face extinction because people hunt them for food and for their shells and gather their eggs. People also destroy their natural homes to make way for cities and farms.

At one time, pet shops throughout the United States sold thousands of painted turtles and red-eared turtles yearly. But medical researchers discovered that many of these turtles carried bacteria that cause *salmonella poisoning,* a serious illness in human beings. In 1975, the U.S. Food and Drug Administration banned the sale of most pet turtles.

The body of a turtle

Shell. Most species of turtles can pull their head, legs, and tail into their shell for protection. A few kinds of turtles, particularly sea turtles, cannot withdraw into their shell.

A turtle's shell consists of two layers. The inner layer is made up of bony plates and is actually part of the skeleton. Among most species, the outer layer consists of hard, horny structures called *scutes,* which are formed from skin tissue. Soft-shelled turtles and the leatherback turtle have an outer layer of tough skin rather than scutes. The part of the shell that covers the turtle's back is called the *carapace,* and the part that covers the belly is called the *plastron.* The carapace and the plastron are joined along each side of the body by a bony structure called the *bridge.*

Most turtles that live on land have a high, domed shell. Those that live in water have a flatter, more streamlined shell. Some species of turtles, including

Blanding's turtle, box turtles, and mud turtles, have a hinged plastron. They can close the plastron tightly against the carapace after withdrawing into their shell.

The shells of some kinds of turtles are plain black, brown, or dark green. But others have bright green, orange, red, or yellow markings.

Head. The head of most species of turtles is covered by hard scales. Turtles have no teeth, but they have a beak with a hard, sharp edge that they use to cut food. Many turtles have powerful jaws, with which they tear food and capture prey.

Legs and feet. A turtle's legs and feet vary according to the habitat of the species. Land turtles, particularly tortoises, have heavy, short, clublike legs and feet. Most fresh-water turtles have longer legs and webbed feet. Sea turtles have legs shaped like long paddles, with flippers instead of feet.

The hip bones and shoulder bones of the turtles, unlike those of any other animal, are inside the ribcage. This unusual feature enables most kinds of turtles to pull their legs inside their shell. The species that are unable to withdraw their legs cannot do so because the shell is too small.

Senses. Turtles have a well-developed sense of sight and of touch. Scientific experiments indicate that they also have a good sense of smell, at least for nearby objects. Turtles have a middle ear and inner ear, and a *tympanic membrane* (eardrum) forms their outer ear. A turtle can hear low-pitched sounds about as well as a human being can.

The life of a turtle

Young. Turtles hatch from eggs, which are fertilized within the female's body. One mating can result in the fertilization of all the eggs of a female for several years.

William M. Partington, NAS   Hladik, Jacana

Turtles have a hard beak. Among most species, such as the mud turtle, *left*, the beak is not covered. But a soft-shelled turtle, *right*, has fleshy lips that cover its beak.

Most kinds of turtles lay their eggs between late spring and late autumn, and some lay eggs more than once during this period. For example, a green turtle may lay as many as seven *clutches* (groups) of eggs during one breeding season.

All turtles, including sea and fresh-water species, lay their eggs on land. Among most species, the female digs a hole in the ground with her back feet when ready to lay her eggs. She lays the eggs in the hole and covers them with soil, sand, or rotting plant matter. The number of eggs laid varies. An African pancake tortoise lays only one egg per clutch, but a sea turtle may lay 200 eggs at a time.

The female turtle walks away after covering her eggs and does not return. The warmth of the sun hatches the eggs. The temperature at which the eggs are incubated also determines the sex of the hatchlings. Newly hatched turtles must dig their way to the surface of the

The skeleton of a land turtle
Bottom view

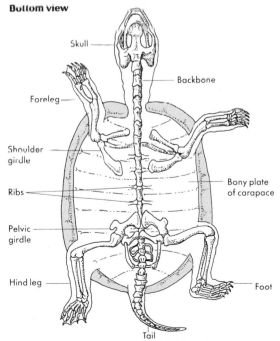

Skull

Backbone

Foreleg

Shoulder girdle

Ribs

Pelvic girdle

Hind leg

Foot

Bony plate of carapace

Tail

A turtle's shell provides excellent protection. Most turtles retract their head by pulling their long, flexible neck straight back in a U-curve. Scales protect the parts of the body exposed at the shell openings.

Backbone

Carapace

Rib

Plastron

WORLD BOOK illustrations by Marion Pahl

R. R. Pawlowski, Bruce Coleman Inc.

All turtles lay their eggs on land. Among most species, the female digs a hole in the ground, lays her eggs and covers them, and then leaves them. The sun's heat hatches the eggs. The female shown above is one of the side-necked species.

ground, obtain food, and protect themselves—all on their own.

Many animals prey on turtle eggs and newborn turtles. Various birds and mammals flock to beaches and eat baby sea turtles as they crawl toward the water. Fish attack many others as they enter the sea. Skunks, raccoons, and snakes dig up the nests of fresh-water turtles and devour the eggs.

Scientists believe turtles live longer than any other backboned animal. Some box turtles and tortoises have lived more than 100 years. Most of a turtle's growth occurs during the animal's first 5 to 10 years. The turtle continues to grow after reaching this age, but at a much slower rate.

Food. Most kinds of turtles eat both animals and plants. The organisms eaten by a turtle vary among the species. A few kinds of turtles, including green turtles and tortoises, feed almost entirely on plants. Certain fresh-water species, such as map turtles and soft-shelled turtles, eat chiefly animals.

Hibernation. Turtles, like other cold-blooded animals, cannot remain active in cold weather. Species that live in regions with harsh winters must hibernate. Most fresh-water turtles hibernate by burrowing into the

Alan Blank, Bruce Coleman Inc.

A baby desert tortoise hatches from its egg after about 100 days. Young turtles have a horny growth on the tip of their beak. This growth, called a *caruncle,* helps break open the shell.

warm, muddy bottom of a pond, stream, or other body of water. Land turtles bury themselves in soil or under rotting vegetation.

Some species of turtles survive hot, dry periods by going into a state of limited activity called *estivation.* Estivation somewhat resembles hibernation.

Kinds of turtles

There are seven main groups of turtles: (1) mud and musk turtles, (2) pond and marsh turtles, (3) sea turtles, (4) side-necked turtles, (5) snapping turtles, (6) soft-shelled turtles, and (7) tortoises.

Mud and musk turtles make up a family of 22 fresh-water species. They live in the Western Hemisphere, particularly in Central America. Mud and musk turtles of the United States include the common mud turtle, common musk turtle, razor-backed musk turtle, and yellow mud turtle.

Few mud and musk turtles grow more than 6 inches (15 centimeters) long. But these turtles have large heads and strong jaws, and they may bite. When disturbed, these turtles give off a foul-smelling substance called *musk* from glands on the bridge in front of their hind legs. The common musk turtle, whose musk has a particularly strong, unpleasant scent, is often called the "stinkpot."

Pond and marsh turtles form the largest family of turtles—about 90 species. Members of this family live in Asia, Europe, North and South America, and northern Africa. Pond and marsh turtles of North America include the box turtle, chicken turtle, diamondback terrapin, map turtle, painted turtle, red-eared turtle, spotted turtle, and wood turtle. Many of these species are brightly colored, with green, red, or yellow markings on their head, legs, and shell. Most pond and marsh turtles found in the United States are small, but some kinds may grow more than a foot (30 centimeters) long. The majority of pond and marsh turtles live in lakes, ponds, rivers, streams, and tidewater areas. A few species, including box turtles and wood turtles, dwell mainly on land.

Sea turtles. There are at least seven species of sea turtles. Six of them—the green turtle, the flatback, the hawksbill, the loggerhead, the Atlantic ridley, and the Pacific ridley—have bony, scute-covered shells. Most zoologists classify these species into one family. The seventh species, the leatherback, forms its own family. Its shell has far fewer bones than that of the other sea turtles and is covered with skin rather than scutes. Most sea turtles live in warm seas throughout the world. The leatherback often ventures into cold Canadian waters. All except the Australian flatback may be found in the coastal waters of the United States.

Sea turtles rank among the largest species. Even the smallest ones, the ridleys, grow up to 28 inches (70 centimeters) long and weigh nearly 100 pounds (45 kilograms). A leatherback may measure 8 feet (2.4 meters) long and weigh 1,500 pounds (680 kilograms). Sea turtles swim by beating their flippers much as a bird flaps its wings. Other turtles swim with a back-and-forth paddling motion. Sea turtles cannot withdraw into their shell, and so they depend on their size and swimming speed for defense.

Female sea turtles do not normally leave the water ex-

Giuseppe Mazza

Leonard Lee Rue, Bruce Coleman Inc.

Box turtles are well protected by their shell. The *carapace* (upper shell) forms a high dome, *left*. The *plastron* (lower shell) is hinged and can be pulled up against the carapace when the turtle is inside the shell, *above*. The box turtle shown above has its plastron only partly pulled up.

cept to lay their eggs. Most of the males never return to land after entering the sea as hatchlings. The females often migrate thousands of miles or kilometers to reach their breeding beaches. They drag themselves onto a sandy beach, bury their eggs, and then return to the sea. Female sea turtles are almost completely helpless while they are on land.

Side-necked turtles bend their neck sideways when withdrawing their head, instead of pulling straight back into their shell. There are about 55 species of these turtles, which are divided into two families. They live in Africa, Australia, and South America, mainly in areas south of the equator.

Snapping turtles make up a family of large, fresh-water turtles that live only in North America, Central America, and northern South America. There are two species of snappers. The common snapper, which may be found from Canada to Ecuador, grows as long as 19 inches (47 centimeters). The other species, the alligator snapper, lives in the Central and Southeastern United

States. Alligator snappers are the largest turtles of North America, except for sea turtles. An alligator snapper may measure more than 24 inches (60 centimeters) long and weigh over 200 pounds (91 kilograms).

Snapping turtles eat small water animals, such as fish, frogs, insects, snails, and young waterfowl. They also feed on plants, especially algae. Snappers have a large head and strong jaws. They may bite fiercely if disturbed. Snappers have a small shell that does not give much protection, and so they depend on their strong, sharp-edged jaws for defense.

Soft-shelled turtles make up a family of 21 species. These fresh-water turtles have a shell covered by smooth skin. They live in Africa, Asia, and North America. Three species of soft-shelled turtles—the smooth softshell, the spiny softshell, and the Florida softshell— live in the continental United States. Two species of Chinese softshells, both Asian species, are found in Hawaii.

Unlike other turtles, softshells have fleshy lips that cover their beak. Most kinds of softshells also have a

Jim Teason

The common snapping turtle has a small shell in relation to the rest of its body. The snapper cannot retreat into its shell for protection, and so it depends on its strong jaws for defense.

E. R. Degginger

A soft-shelled turtle has a round, flat shell covered by leathery skin. Most softshells also have paddlelike legs and a long, flexible nose that serves as an underwater breathing tube.

The **Galapagos tortoise** ranks as one of the largest land turtles. This huge reptile measures up to 4 feet (1.2 meters) long and may weigh more than 600 pounds (270 kilograms).

Udo Hirsch, Bruce Coleman Ltd.

long, tube-shaped nose that they push above the surface of the water in order to breathe. Most softshells do not grow much longer than a foot (30 centimeters), but some species measure up to 3 feet (91 centimeters) long. A soft-shelled turtle may bite when disturbed, and it can strike with lightning speed.

Tortoises form a family of about 50 species. These land turtles live in Africa, Asia, Europe, and North and South America, and on certain ocean islands. The tortoises of the Aldabra Islands and the Galapagos Islands are the world's largest land turtles. These huge reptiles may measure up to 4 feet (1.2 meters) long and may weigh up to 600 pounds (270 kilograms).

Three species of tortoises live in the United States. The desert tortoise makes its home in the dry areas of the Southwest. The gopher tortoise lives in sandy-soiled areas of the Southeastern United States. The Texas tortoise is found in scrub forests of southern Texas.

Tortoises live only on land. Most species are slow-moving creatures with a high, domed shell. But the African pancake tortoise has a flat, flexible shell. When in danger, this tortoise runs quickly into a crack in a nearby rock. It then takes a deep breath and inflates its body, wedging itself tightly in the crack.

Turtles and human beings

The activities of human beings are a serious threat to the survival of many turtles, and turtle conservation must improve to prevent certain species from becoming extinct. Wildlife experts classify more than 40 kinds of turtles as endangered. These rare turtles include many types of tortoises and most sea turtles.

People have long used turtle meat and eggs for food and turtle shells as ornaments. The most threatened species include the most economically valuable ones. For example, the green turtle is a popular food in many parts of the world. The use of its meat and eggs by humans has seriously endangered its survival. The hawksbill turtle also has almost been killed off because *tortoise shell,* a substance used in making ornamental objects, comes from its carapace. People further endanger turtles by poisoning their homes with pollution. They also continually replace forests, swamps, and other natural areas with cities and farms. This action almost ensures the extinction of certain kinds of turtles.

Some governments forbid the capture of rare species of turtles. Turtle preserves have been established in certain areas, and scientists are experimenting with raising valuable species on turtle farms. But zoologists must know more about how turtles live in the wild to save many of the endangered ones.

Scientific classification. Turtles make up the order Testudines (sometimes called Chelonia) in the class Reptilia and the phylum Chordata.   Carl H. Ernst

See also **Terrapin; Tortoise.**

Turtledove is a small European dove. The turtledove lives in woods and on farms, and migrates to warm climates in winter. It feeds mainly on small grains and seeds. The turtledove is shy and seldom seen. But its sad, cooing note is often heard in spring. The turtledove may raise two broods of young in a season. The female lays two eggs in a loose nest placed in a low tree, shrub,

WORLD BOOK illustration by Trevor Boyer, Linden Artists Ltd.

The **turtledove** is a slender, graceful bird that lives in woods and on farms in Europe. It is known for its soft cooing call.

or hedge. The mourning dove is sometimes wrongly called a turtledove.

Scientific classification. The turtledove belongs to the pigeon and dove family, Columbidae. It is classified as *Streptopelia turtur.*   Leonard W. Wing

Tuscany, *TUHS kuh nee,* is a political region, or state, in Italy. Its Italian name is Toscana (pronounced *toh SKAHN uh*). Tuscany lies on the western coast of Italy, and north of the city of Rome. It is made up of nine provinces. It covers an area of 8,877 square miles (22,991 square kilometers), and has a population of 3,570,926. Tuscany is an important agricultural and industrial center. Tuscan straw hats are known all over the world as *Leghorns.* Tuscany has the famous Italian cities of Florence, Pisa, Siena, and Leghorn (Livorno).

Tuscany has long been an important Italian center of art and learning. In early times, the territory was the home of an ancient people known as *Etruscans.* The Italian poets, Dante and Petrarch, used the language of Tuscany for their poems.   Benjamin Webb Wheeler

See also **Etruscans; Florence; Siena.**

Tuscarora Indians. See **Iroquois Indians.**

Tusk. See Elephant; Hog (Teeth); **Boar, Wild.**

Tuskegee University is a privately controlled, co-educational institution in Tuskegee, Ala. It has a college of arts and sciences and schools of agriculture and home economics, business, education, engineering and architecture, nursing and allied health, and veterinary medicine. The university offers bachelor's and master's degrees and a doctor's degree in veterinary medicine. It is the home of the George Washington Carver Research Foundation and the Tuskegee Archives.

The school was founded in 1881 by Booker T. Washington as the Tuskegee Normal and Industrial Institute, but it was more commonly known as the Tuskegee Institute. Washington was the most influential black leader and educator of his time in the United States. He served as Tuskegee's principal and instructor for 33 years. He stressed the importance of training in practical trade skills. The scientist George Washington Carver was one of the school's best-known instructors. In 1974, Congress established the Tuskegee Institute National Historic Site, which includes the George Washington Carver Museum. The school became Tuskegee University in 1985. For enrollment, see **Universities and Colleges** (table).   Critically reviewed by Tuskegee University

See also **Carver, George Washington; Washington, Booker T.**

Tussaud, *tuh SOH* or *too SOH,* **Marie Gresholtz,** *GREHS hohlts* (1760-1850), a Swiss modeler in wax, founded Madame Tussaud's Exhibition in London in 1802. Her descendants still maintain this famous museum of wax figures of prominent people. Some of the characters and scenes in the exhibition were modeled from life by Madame Tussaud and members of her family with remarkable accuracy. Additional figures for the museum are made each year.

Marie Gresholtz was born in Bern, Switzerland, and learned to model in her uncle's museum in Paris. In 1794 she married François Tussaud. During the French Revolution she was suspected of sympathy for the king. She was forced to model heads of the revolutionary leaders, and of victims of the guillotine. She was later imprisoned. When released, she moved to London with one of her two sons.   Helen E. Marshall

Tussock moth, *TUHS uhk,* makes up a family whose caterpillars have *tussocks* (tufts) of hair along the back. These hair tufts are often brightly colored. The caterpillars may also have distinct stripes on the back. The adult moths develop only dull colors.

About 20 kinds of tussock moths live in the United States. The *gypsy moth* and *brown-tail moth* were brought to the United States from Europe. Their caterpillars have done much damage to New England trees. The *white-marked moth* is another tussock moth, common in the eastern United States. The female has no wings.

The caterpillars, which are the moth larvae, damage trees by eating the leaves. The caterpillars often destroy whole orchards and forests. One method of control has been to import beetles that eat the caterpillars.

Scientific classification. Tussock moths make up the family Lymantriidae. The gypsy moth is *Lymantria dispar.* The brown-tail moth is *Euproctis chrysorrhea.*   Bernd Heinrich

See also **Brown-tail moth; Gypsy moth; Moth** (Tussock moths; illustrations).

Tutankhamen, *тоот ahngk AH muhn,* served as king of Egypt from about 1347 B.C. until his death in 1339 B.C. His name is also spelled *Tutankhamun* or *Tutankhamon.* His reign was unimportant. But interest in Tutankhamen began in 1922, when the British archaeologist Howard Carter discovered his tomb. The tomb had not been opened since ancient times and still contained most of its treasures. It is the only tomb of an ancient Egyptian king to be discovered almost completely undamaged. See **Carter, Howard.**

Tutankhamen became king at about the age of 9. He probably received much assistance from Ay, his *vizier* (minister of state). Scholars disagree on who Tutankhamen's relatives were. Some believe the king was a son-in-law of King Akhenaton. Others think Tutankhamen was the son of Akhenaton and the grandson of King Amenhotep III. Still others argue that Tutankhamen and Akhenaton were brothers. Tutankhamen's original name was *Tutankhaton,* meaning *the living image of Aton* or *the life of Aton is pleasing.*

Akhenaton had made Aton the sole god of Egypt. He wanted Egyptians to stop worshiping the chief sun god Amon and other traditional gods. However, many Egyptians, including the powerful priests devoted to Amon, rejected the worship of Aton. Thus, about four years after he became king, Tutankhaton took the name Tutankhamen and restored Egypt's old religion. See **Akhenaton.**

Historians believe Tutankhamen died at about the age of 18, but they are unsure about the cause of his death. Ay succeeded Tutankhamen as king and held his funeral in the Valley of the Kings, a burial center at Thebes. Horemheb, a leading general, later succeeded Ay as king. Horemheb and his successors destroyed or removed all monuments built by or in honor of Tutankhamen and others who had accepted Aton as Egypt's chief god. Partly because of these actions, little was known about Tutankhamen until Carter's discovery.

Carter searched for Tutankhamen's tomb for about 10 years. He finally discovered that its entrance had been hidden by debris from digging at the entrance of the nearby tomb of King Ramses VI. Tutankhamen's four-room tomb contained more than 5,000 objects, including many beautiful carved and gold-covered items. A

E. R. Degginger

The *larvae,* or caterpillars, of the tussock moth eat the leaves of trees and can destroy entire forests.

Robert Harding Associates

Ronald Sheridan

© Lee Boltin

© Lee Boltin

Beautiful treasures of Tutankhamen were found inside the young king's tomb in 1922. The most exquisite items included, *left to right,* a throne, a necklace honoring the sun, a gold death mask, and a small alabaster boat and pedestal.

magnificent lifelike gold mask of Tutankhamen covered the head and shoulders of the royal mummy.

Among the items discovered were luxurious chests, thrones, beds, linens, clothing, necklaces, bracelets, rings, and earrings. Carter also found chariots, bows and arrows, swords, daggers, shields, ostrich feather fans, trumpets, statues of Tutankhamen and many Egyptian gods, figures of animals, models of ships, toys, games, and storage jars containing precious oils. The ancient Egyptians believed in a life after death, called the *afterlife.* They had their favorite possessions and practical objects buried with them for later use in the afterlife. Most of the items found in Tutankhamen's tomb are now displayed in the Egyptian Museum in Cairo.

One of the most informative items in the tomb was a note on the handle of the king's fan. The note indicated that the young Tutankhamen hunted at Heliopolis, near modern Cairo. Wine-jar labels indicated the length of Tutankhamen's reign. Several objects included scenes that show Tutankhamen slaying foreign enemies in battle. But scholars doubt that these scenes pictured actual events.   Leonard H. Lesko

Additional resources

Brackman, Arnold. C. *The Search for the Gold of Tutankhamen.* Mason/Charter, 1976.
Carter, Howard, and Mace, A. C. *The Tomb of Tut-ankh-amen: Discovered by the Late Earl of Carnarvon and Howard Carter.* 3 vols. Cooper Square, 1963. Reprint of 1954 edition. First published in 1922-1933.
Hoving, Thomas. P. *Tutankhamun: The Untold Story.* Simon & Schuster, 1978.

Tutu, *TOO too,* **Desmond** (1931-   ), is a South African civil rights leader and Anglican archbishop. He has worked to end South Africa's strict racial segregation policy, known as *apartheid.* This policy prohibits blacks from mixing with whites in most activities, including education, housing, and politics. Tutu has asked foreign nations and businesses to limit trade and investment activities in South Africa until the government eliminates apartheid.

Tutu won the 1984 Nobel Peace Prize for his nonvio-

lent campaign against apartheid. In 1986, he became the first black to be elected archbishop of Cape Town. As archbishop, Tutu heads the Anglican Church in South Africa, Namibia, Mozambique, Swaziland, and Lesotho.

Tutu was born in Klerksdorp. In 1961, he was ordained an Anglican priest. In the mid-1960's, he received degrees in divinity and theology from King's

A. Tannenbaum, Sygma
Desmond Tutu

College in London. He worked as an educator in the early 1970's. Tutu became Anglican dean of Johannesburg, South Africa, in 1975, bishop of Lesotho in 1976, and bishop of Johannesburg in 1984.   Robert I. Rotberg

Tutuila. See American Samoa.

Tuva, *TOO vah,* is an autonomous republic in the Soviet Union. It lies in central Asia, between Siberia and Mongolia. Tuva has an area of 65,830 square miles (170,500 square kilometers) and a population of about 276,000. About 60 per cent of the people are Tuvinians, whose ancestors were Turkic-speaking people. Most of them raise cattle and other animals. Minerals produced in the republic include asbestos and cobalt. The chief exports of Tuva are wool and animal hides. Kyzyl is Tuva's capital.

The region was part of Outer Mongolia (now Mongolia) until 1911. It then became independent, but Russia and China had strong influence there. It became a Russian protectorate in 1914. In 1921, it became the independent nation of Tannu Tuva. The name was later changed to Tuva. The Soviet Union annexed Tuva in 1944.   Theodore Shabad

Tuvalu, *too VAH loo,* is a small island country in the South Pacific Ocean. It has a population of 7,000 and a land area of 10 square miles (26 square kilometers). Among the nations of the world, only Vatican City has fewer people, and only Vatican City, Monaco, and Nauru are smaller in area.

Tuvalu lies about 2,000 miles (3,200 kilometers) northeast of Australia. It consists of nine islands that are spread over about 360 miles (579 kilometers). People live on eight of the nine islands. The country's name means "eight together".

Tuvalu, formerly called the Ellice Islands, was ruled by Great Britain from the 1890's to 1978. It became independent in 1978.

Funafuti, a village of about 900 people, is the capital of Tuvalu. The country's national anthem is "Tuvalu mo te Atua" ("Tuvalu for God"). Its unit of money is the Australian dollar. For a picture of Tuvalu's flag, see **Flag** (Flags of Asia and the Pacific).

Government. Tuvalu is a constitutional monarchy and a member of the Commonwealth of Nations (see **Commonwealth of Nations**). A prime minister, chosen by a legislature of 12 members elected by the people, heads the government. Each island is administered by a council of 6 members. Island courts handle most trials. The High Court of Tuvalu hears appeals.

People. Most of the people of Tuvalu are Polynesians. They live in villages, most of which cluster around a church and a meeting house. Tuvaluan houses have raised foundations, open sides, and thatched roofs. The main foods of the people are bananas, coconuts, fish, and *taro,* a tropical plant with one or more edible rootlike stems. The islanders raise pigs and chickens to eat at feasts. Tuvaluans usually wear light, bright-colored cotton clothing.

The people speak the Tuvaluan language, and many also know English. Both languages are used in official government business. Each of the eight inhabited islands has an elementary school supported by the government. A few Tuvaluans attend a university in Fiji, an island country to the south.

Land and climate. The nine islands of Tuvalu are, from north to south, Nanumea, Niutao, Nanumanga, Nui, Vaitupu, Nukufetau, Funafuti, Nukulaelae, and Niulakita. Niulakita is uninhabited. Most of the islands are *atolls* (ring-shaped coral reefs) that surround lagoons. The

Tuvalu

- - - - International date line
(⌒) Barrier reef
⊛ National capital

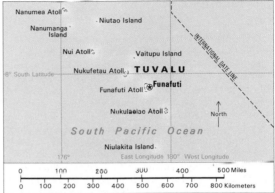

WORLD BOOK map

principal trees of Tuvalu are coconut palms and pandanus palms.

Tuvalu has a tropical climate, with daytime temperatures of about 80° F. (27° C). The southern islands receive about 140 inches (356 centimeters) of rain a year. The northern islands are drier.

Economy. Tuvalu has poor soil, few natural resources, almost no manufacturing, and no mining. Coconut palm trees cover much of the country, and the islanders use the coconuts to produce *copra* (dried coconut meat), their chief export (see **Copra**). The people grow such crops as bananas and taro for their own use. They also weave baskets and mats for export. Many young islanders work on ocean ships because of a lack of opportunities at home. Tuvalu receives aid from some other countries, including Australia and Great Britain.

History. The first inhabitants of Tuvalu probably came from Samoa hundreds of years ago. In 1568, Álvaro de Mendaña, a Spanish explorer, became the first European to see part of Tuvalu. But the islands remained largely unknown to Europeans until the early 1800's. Europeans called them the Ellice Islands. Great Britain took control of the islands in the 1890's. In 1916, Britain combined the islands with the Gilbert Islands to the north to form the Gilbert and Ellice Islands Colony. In 1975, the two island groups were separated. The Ellice Islands were renamed Tuvalu. Great Britain granted Tuvalu independence on Oct. 1, 1978.   Robert Langdon

See also **Funafuti**.

Tuzigoot National Monument stands near Clarkdale, in central Arizona. It contains the ruins of a large Indian pueblo that flourished between 1100 and 1450. Beads, pottery, and mosaics found there are now in the Tuzigoot Museum. The monument was established in 1939. For its area, see **National Park System** (table: National monuments).

Critically reviewed by the National Park Service

TV. See **Television**.

Cameramann International, Ltd. from Marilyn Gartman

The capital of Tuvalu is the village of Funafuti, *above.* The village is located on the island of Funafuti, which is one of the nine South Pacific islands that make up the country.

TVA. See Tennessee Valley Authority.

Twain, Mark (1835-1910), was the pen name of Samuel Langhorne Clemens, one of the major authors of American fiction. Twain is also considered the greatest humorist in American literature. Twain's varied works include novels, travel narratives, short stories, sketches, and essays. His writings about the Mississippi River, such as *The Adventures of Tom Sawyer, Life on the Mississippi,* and *Adventures of Huckleberry Finn,* have been especially popular among modern readers.

Early life

Boyhood. Mark Twain was born on Nov. 30, 1835, in Florida, Mo. In 1839, his family moved to Hannibal, Mo., a village on the Mississippi River. Here the young Twain experienced the excitement of the colorful steamboats that docked at the town wharf, bringing comedians, singers, gamblers, swindlers, slave dealers, and assorted other river travelers.

Twain also gained his first experience in a print shop in Hannibal. After his father died in debt in 1847, Twain went to work for a newspaper and printing firm. In 1851, he began assisting his older brother Orion in the production of a newspaper, the Hannibal *Journal.* Twain contributed reports, poems, and humorous sketches to the *Journal* for several years. Like many American authors of his day, Twain had little formal education. Instead of attending high school and college, he gained his education in print shops and newspaper offices.

Travels. In 1853, Twain left Hannibal, displaying the yearning for travel that he would experience throughout his life. He stayed briefly in cities such as St. Louis, New York City, Philadelphia, and Cincinnati, working for low wages in print shops. He then traveled to Keokuk, Iowa, to assist his brother with more printing business.

In 1857, Twain made plans to travel to South America, and in April of that year, he started down the Mississippi River toward New Orleans. At this point, he made a decision with important consequences for his life and

A poster advertises a lecture by Mark Twain. The frog was a character in the author's first important short story. Beginning in 1866, Twain traveled widely, delivering humorous lectures.

career. Instead of traveling to South America, he persuaded a riverboat pilot named Horace Bixby to teach him the skills of piloting. By April 1859, Twain had become a licensed riverboat pilot.

The profession of riverboat piloting paid well and brought Twain much attention, which he enjoyed. His piloting experiences also allowed him to observe the many kinds of people who traveled aboard the steamboats. He later reported that "in that brief, sharp schooling, I got personally and familiarly acquainted with about all the different types of human nature that are to be found in fiction, biography, or history."

Newspaper work in the West. The beginning of the American Civil War (1861-1865) abruptly closed commercial traffic on the Mississippi River. After serving for two weeks with a Confederate volunteer company, Twain chose not to become involved in the war. He traveled to Carson City, Nev., in 1861 with his brother Orion. Later, in *Roughing It* (1872), Twain humorously described his unsuccessful attempts at prospecting for gold and silver during this time and his eventual conclusion that he must support himself by newspaper journalism. He joined the staff of the Virginia City, Nev., *Territorial Enterprise* in the summer of 1862. He first began publishing under his pen name on Feb. 3, 1863, while working for the *Enterprise.* "Mark Twain" comes from a riverboat term meaning *two fathoms* (a depth of 12 feet, or 3.7 meters).

Twain next drifted westward to California, where he wrote for the San Francisco *Morning Call* and a literary journal, the *Californian.* On Nov. 18, 1865, his first popular story—about "The Celebrated Jumping Frog of Calaveras County"—appeared in the New York *Saturday*

Mark Twain was a great American humorist. A white linen suit and a cigar became his trademarks in public appearances.

Press. In 1866, Twain traveled to the Hawaiian Islands, where he acted as a correspondent for the Sacramento *Union.* Following his return to San Francisco, he began a profitable lecture tour. Twain soon began to sense that his talents were growing beyond the limitations of the West Coast newspapers and magazines of his day.

Success and fame

Return to the East. In 1867, Twain took a voyage to Europe and the Holy Land aboard the steamship *Quaker City.* His travel letters to the San Francisco *Alta California* and the New York *Tribune* were collected in a popular book, *The Innocents Abroad* (1869). In the book, Twain ridiculed the sights and manners of the countries he visited, and the American tourists traveling abroad.

Encouraged by the prospect of future wealth from a literary career, Twain courted a young woman from Elmira, N.Y., named Olivia L. Langdon, whose brother had sailed with him on the *Quaker City.* The couple were wed on Feb. 2, 1870. Following Twain's brief career as a newspaper editor and columnist in Buffalo, N.Y., he and his wife moved to Hartford, Conn., in 1871. Their infant son, Langdon, died in 1872, but three daughters, Susy, Clara, and Jean, were born between 1872 and 1880.

Productive years in Hartford. In 1874, Twain and his family moved into a luxurious new 19-room house in Hartford. There, Twain entertained many prominent authors. Literary periodicals in Boston and New York City published many of his writings. In his 20 years in Hartford, Twain wrote most of his best works either at home or in his study at Quarry Farm, near Elmira, N.Y.

The Gilded Age (1873), which followed *Roughing It,* was Twain's first novel. He wrote it with his friend and fellow Hartford writer, Charles Dudley Warner. The title refers to the decades following the Civil War. This book satirizes the selfishness and money-making schemes that were common during that time.

The Adventures of Tom Sawyer (1876) represents Twain's first major use of memories of his childhood. Twain modeled St. Petersburg—the home of an imaginative boy named Tom Sawyer, his friend Huck Finn, and the evil Injun Joe—after his home town of Hannibal.

A Tramp Abroad (1880) draws on a European tour that Twain took in 1878. The book's narrator describes a walking tour of Germany, Switzerland, and Italy. He

Mark Twain Memorial

Mark Twain's house in Hartford, Conn., was built with profits from his writings. The Twain family lived in the house from 1874 to 1891. The author wrote his best books during this time, despite a busy schedule of lecturing and traveling.

mixes stories, jokes, legends, and character sketches, while criticizing European guidebooks and culture.

The Prince and the Pauper (1882), set in England in the 1500's, describes the exchange of identities between the young Prince Edward and a poor boy named Tom Canty. This book pleased a refined circle of New England readers, but disappointed those who preferred the rugged energy of Twain's previous works.

Life on the Mississippi (1883) describes the history, sights, people, and legends of the steamboats and towns of the Mississippi River region. In the most vivid passages, chapters 4 through 17, Twain recalled his own piloting days. These chapters had originally been published in the *Atlantic Monthly* in 1875 as "Old Times on the Mississippi."

Adventures of Huckleberry Finn, generally considered Twain's greatest work, was published in Great Britain in 1884 and in the United States in 1885. Twain had begun the book in 1876 as a sequel to *Tom Sawyer.* It describes the adventures of two runaways—the boy Huck Finn and the black slave Jim—and is told from the point of view of Huck himself. Twain used realistic language in the novel, making Huck's speech sound like actual conversation and imitating a variety of dialects to bring the other characters to life. Tom Sawyer also reappears in certain chapters, and his antics provide the familiar humor for which Twain was known.

Twain's story about Huck Finn, the son of a town drunkard, became a controversial book. Huck's casual morals and careless grammar disturbed many readers in Twain's time, and the Concord, Mass., Free Public Library banned the novel in 1885. Some people have continued to dislike the novel because of Huck's unrefined manners and language. In addition, some modern readers object to Huck's simple acceptance of the principles of slavery and his use of racial stereotypes and the insulting term "nigger." However, for his time, Twain was liberal on racial issues. The deeper themes of *Huckleberry Finn* argue for the fundamental equality and universal aspirations of people of all races.

A Connecticut Yankee in King Arthur's Court (1889) introduces another colorful character, a machine shop foreman from Hartford, Conn., named Hank Morgan. Morgan finds himself magically transported back to England in the A.D. 500's. He decides to reform that society by introducing the economic, intellectual, and moral benefits of life in the 1800's. Through events in the book, Twain indirectly satirizes the reverent attitude of some British authors toward the legendary Knights of the Round Table. But at the same time, he raises questions about certain values in the American culture of his time.

Later years

Disappointments. In the 1880's, Mark Twain established and operated his own publishing firm. He also became interested in various investments, especially an elaborate typesetting machine. He lost almost $200,000 in investments in the machine between 1881 and 1894. Also, his publishing company declared bankruptcy in April 1894. Thus, in January 1895, Twain found himself publicly humiliated by his inability to pay his debts.

Twain eventually recovered from his financial difficulties, through his continued writing and a successful lecture tour in 1895 and 1896. During this much-publicized tour, Twain lectured in such places as India, South Africa, and Australia. By the time he returned, he had become an international hero. Twain enjoyed this attention, and his habits of smoking cigars or a pipe and wearing unconventional white suits contributed to his showy image. He also made use of his position as a public figure to cynically criticize U.S. foreign policy.

Although he was recovering from his financial problems by 1898, Twain had begun to experience tragedy in his personal life. Susy, his oldest daughter, died of meningitis in 1896, while her parents and sister Clara were abroad. In 1903, Twain sold the beloved house in Hartford, which had become too closely associated with Susy's death. His wife, Olivia, who had developed a heart condition, died on June 5, 1904. His youngest daughter, Jean, died on Dec. 24, 1909.

Later works. Despite his business and personal difficulties, Twain managed to continue writing. His works during his final years included *The American Claimant* (1892), about an impractical character named Colonel Mulberry Sellers. The novel was based on an unsuccessful play he wrote with author-critic William Dean Howells in 1883. *The Tragedy of Pudd'nhead Wilson* (1894) is a detective novel set in the village of Dawson's Landing, another name for Hannibal. In this story, Twain focused on racial prejudice as the most critical issue facing American society. He drew on actual historical sources in *Personal Recollections of Joan of Arc* (1896). In *Following the Equator* (1897), Twain recounted his experiences on his overseas lecture tour of 1895 and 1896. In his story "The Man That Corrupted Hadleyburg" (1899), he described a practical joke that exposed the greed of the smug leaders of a town.

As Twain's career progressed, he seemed to become increasingly removed from the humorous, cocky image of his younger days. More and more of his works came to express the gloomy view that all human motives are ultimately selfish. These works also reflect Twain's lifelong doubts about religion and his belief that all human acts are predetermined and free will is an illusion.

Twain died of heart disease on April 21, 1910. He left behind numerous unpublished manuscripts, including his large but incomplete autobiography. One pessimistic but fascinating tale, *The Mysterious Stranger,* was published in 1916, after Twain's death. This story, which exists in three versions, describes a visit by Satan to an Austrian village during the Middle Ages.

Modern reputation

Since the 1960's, some people have come to view Mark Twain's life and outlook as gloomy and even tragic. His later, more bitter works, such as *The Mysterious Stranger,* were neglected in the years immediately following his death. But they have recently received more attention, resulting in a broader understanding of Twain's personality and works. Most people now consider Twain more than just a colorful comic figure.

Although viewed as having a serious, sometimes pessimistic side, Twain remains best known as a humorist. He effectively used comic exaggeration to attack the false pride and self-satisfaction he saw in humanity. One of his greatest accomplishments was the development of a writing style that was distinctly American, rather than an imitation of the style of English writers. The loose rhythms of the language in his books give the impression of real speech. Twain's realistic prose style has influenced numerous American writers. Ernest Hemingway stated that "all modern American literature comes from . . . *Huckleberry Finn."*   Alan Gribben

See also **Connecticut** (Places to visit; picture); **Missouri** (Places to visit). For a *Reading and Study Guide,* see *Twain, Mark,* in the Research Guide/Index, Volume 22.

Additional resources

Budd, Louis J. *Our Mark Twain: The Making of His Public Personality.* Univ. of Pennsylvania Press, 1983.
Critical Essays on Mark Twain, 1867-1910. Ed. by Louis J. Budd. G. K. Hall, 1982. *Critical Essays on Mark Twain, 1910-1980.* 1983.
Kaplan, Justin. *Mr. Clemens and Mark Twain: A Biography.* Simon & Schuster, 1966. *Mark Twain and His World.* 1974.
Mark Twain Laughing: Humorous Anecdotes by and About Samuel Clemens. Ed. by Paul M. Zall. Univ. of Tennessee Press, 1985.

Tweed is a rough, heavy, hairy, woolen cloth that may contain synthetic fibers. Tweed is usually woven of fibers in two or more colors. Some tweed has a plain weave. Other tweed has a *twill* weave, with raised diagonal lines. A third way of weaving tweed is with the diagonal raised lines of yarn meeting each other to form "V's." This is called *herringbone twill.* In Scotland, where tweed was first woven, *twill* is often pronounced *tweel,* and *tweed* may have developed from this. Some people believe the cloth was named for the River Tweed. Genuine Harris Tweeds are made by hand. They are woven on the islands of the Outer Hebrides—chiefly on Lewis with Harris Island.

The yarns are dyed the colors of the heather in the Hebrides. The dyes are made from a type of vegetation called *lichens,* which grow on the rocks of the islands. The lichen has an odor, called *cretal smell,* which never leaves the cloth. Rainy weather brings out this smell in a Harris Tweed suit. After the yarn is dyed, the longwise, or *warp,* threads are put on the looms. When the cloth is woven, the weavers have a ceremony called *waulking,* which means *shrinking.* The cloth is soaked in soapy water. The weavers stand around a table and pass the cloth while singing *waulking songs.* Each weaver pounds and rubs the cloth. The cloth is then washed and dried and is ready to be made into clothing.

Tweed is a favorite cloth for sports clothing, and men's and women's coats and suits. Some tweeds are made in the United States, but they are usually lighter in weight and softer in texture than the cloth made in Scotland and England.   Kenneth R. Fox

Tweed, River, is a British waterway. The Tweed, which is 96 miles (154 kilometers) long, rises in Scotland's Southern Uplands. It flows eastward and forms the border between Scotland and England for about 17 miles (27 kilometers). It then flows through England for a short distance before emptying into the North Sea at Berwick-upon-Tweed (see **Great Britain** [political map]). The Tweed is navigable only near its mouth. Salmon and trout fishing are popular sports along the river.

Small towns, including Galashiels, Kelso, Peebles, and Melrose, lie along the banks of the River Tweed. During the 1800's, these towns built mills along the river to provide water power for their cloth and hosiery industries. Tweed cloth may have been named for the river. Abbotsford, the estate of the Scottish novelist Sir Walter Scott, is near Melrose.   Adrian Robinson

Tweed, William Marcy (1823-1878), was an American political boss who swindled New York City out of millions of dollars. He was born in New York City and received a grammar school education. He entered politics at an early age, and became boss of Tammany Hall. He organized his associates into the *Tweed Ring,* which sponsored schemes for city improvements. Millions of dollars went into the pockets of Tweed Ring members.

Thomas Nast exposed these corrupt practices in political cartoons, and many others fought Tweed. In 1871, the ring was broken up. Tweed was jailed, but escaped to Spain. In 1876, the Spanish government returned him to the U.S., and he died in prison.   W. B. Hesseltine

See also **Nast, Thomas; Tammany, Society of; Tilden, Samuel Jones.**

Additional resources

Callow, Alexander B., Jr. *The Tweed Ring.* Oxford, 1966.
Hershkowitz, Leo. *Tweed's New York: Another Look.* Doubleday, 1977.

Tweed Ring. See Tweed, William Marcy.
Tweedsmuir, Baron. See Buchan, John.
Twelfth Amendment. See Constitution of the United States (Amendment 12).
Twelfth Night is a Christian holiday celebrated 12 days after Christmas, on January 6. It marks the end of the Christmas season. Christians also observe the Feast of Epiphany on January 6 (see **Epiphany**). In Western Christian churches, this holiday commemorates the coming of the wise men to the Christ child. Among Eastern Christians, it celebrates the baptism of Jesus. In Italy and Spain, children still receive gifts on this day in remembrance of the gifts the wise men brought to Jesus. In the Greek Orthodox Church, the Blessing of the Waters takes place on January 6. In the ceremony, divers retrieve a cross thrown into a body of water by a priest.

Twelfth Night was originally celebrated in the Middle Ages at the end of the 12 days of Christmas. Much of the festivities were held at royal courts. William Shakespeare's comedy *Twelfth Night* was possibly first performed on January 6.   Robert J. Myers

Twelve Tables, Laws of the, were the first written laws of the Romans. The laws were inscribed on 12 tables, or tablets, that were fastened to the speaker's stand in the Roman Forum. They were the basis of private rights of Roman citizens. They dealt with legal procedures, property ownership, building codes, punishments for crime, and marriage customs.

The laws were drawn up in 451 and 450 B.C. by *decemvirs* (members of a council of ten men). The decemvirs based the laws on earlier Roman civil, criminal, and religious customs. The laws applied equally to all Roman citizens, and were written out so that the common people could know their legal rights. The original tables bearing the laws were destroyed about 390 B.C. But large parts of the laws are preserved in the works of Roman writers who, like all Roman boys, had learned them by heart.   Frank C. Bourne

12-tone music. See Music (Tone); Schönberg, Arnold; Berg, Alban.
Twelve Tribes. See Jacob; Jews (Early days); Palestine (Early history and Hebrew settlement; map).

Twentieth Amendment and later amendments to the Constitution. See **Constitution of the United States** (Amendments to the Constitution).

Twilight is the period just before sunrise and the period just after sunset when the light in the sky is soft and mellow. Although the sun is below the horizon, light can be seen because the rays are scattered by molecules of the earth's atmosphere. Morning twilight begins when the sun is about 18 degrees below the horizon and ends when the sun reaches the horizon. Evening twilight begins when the sun drops below the horizon and ends when it has sunk about 18 degrees below the horizon.

Twilight lasts the longest time at the North and South poles and the shortest time at the equator. During the six sunless months at the poles, dawn and dusk last a month each. But there is a period during Arctic and Antarctic summers when the sun never sinks below the horizon, and twilight does not occur. Just south of the Arctic, the summer sun never reaches 18 degrees below the horizon, and twilight lasts from sunset to sunrise. At the equator, twilight lasts about an hour, with some seasonal variations.   Sidney Rosen

Twill is a weave that is used in making many kinds of strong, durable cloth. In twill, the lengthwise threads, known as *warp*, meet the crosswise threads, called *weft* or *filling*, in such a way that diagonal lines form on the surface of the finished cloth in the areas where the yarns interlace. These diagonal lines may slant to the left or the right. They may be raised a little or a great deal. Many twill fabrics display an even number of warp and weft yarns on the surface, but some show more of one type than the other. Twill weaves can be varied to produce broken, entwining, figured, or reversing lines. Such materials as *serge, gabardine, denim,* and *cheviot* are twill-weave fabrics.   Phyllis Tortora

Twin Cities. See Minneapolis; Saint Paul.
Twine is tough cord made from the twisted strands of hard leaf fibers, usually those from the sisal or henequen plants. The strands are mixed with abacá to make manila hemp. Twine is made by drawing the fibers into slivers, which are combed and spun into twine. String is a type of twine, thinner than a cord and thicker than a thread. See also **Abacá; Sisal.**   Elizabeth Chesley Baity

Twinflower, also called Linnaea, *lih NEE uh,* is a favorite plant in rock gardens. The twinflower is an evergreen plant, which means that it does not shed its leaves in the winter. It has long, woody stems and roundish leaves. Its delicate flowers are shaped like bells, and are either pink or white. The flowers have a fragrant odor.

The twinflower grows best in soil that is loose and moist. The plant is reproduced by planting a cutting of the stem. The twinflower is native to Northern Europe, Asia, and North America. The Swedish botanist Carolus Linnaeus gave the plant the name Linnaea, a form of his own name, because it was his favorite among all the wild flowers of Sweden.

Scientific classification. The twinflower belongs to the honeysuckle family, Caprifoliaceae. It is *Linnaea borealis.*
    Paul C. Standley

Twins. See Multiple birth; Siamese twins.
Twister. See Tornado.
Two Sicilies, Kingdom of the. See Sicilies, Kingdom of the Two.
Tyche. See Fortuna.

Special Report
TWINS
1990 Year Book, p. 140

**10th President of
the United States 1841-1845**

**W. H.
Harrison**
9th President
1841
Whig

Tyler
10th President
1841-1845
Whig

Polk
11th President
1845-1849
Democrat

Oil painting on canvas (1842) by George Peter Alexander Healy; Corcoran Gallery of Art, Washington, D.C.

Tyler, John (1790-1862), was the first Vice President to become President upon the death of a chief executive. He succeeded William Henry Harrison, who died a month after taking office. Tyler, a Southern Democrat, had split with his party and had run with Harrison on the Whig Party ticket.

As President, Tyler soon became a man without a party. The Whig program clashed with many of Tyler's lifelong beliefs. He vetoed almost every important bill. Angry Whigs tried to impeach him, the first such move against a President. They failed, but the resulting friction destroyed the Whig program.

For more than 75 years after the courteous, soft-spoken Tyler left office, historians dealt harshly with him. President Theodore Roosevelt summed up this opinion when he said: "Tyler has been called a mediocre man, but this is unwarranted flattery. He was a politician of monumental littleness."

Many historians today take a different view. They regard Tyler as a President of exceptional courage and imagination who displayed great devotion to the principles of Thomas Jefferson. He inherited a political situation he had never expected and could not support. He could not have acted other than the way he did.

Historians also point to Tyler as the man who firmly established the right of the Vice President to succeed completely to the presidency. When Harrison died, many Whig leaders suggested that Tyler be called only "Acting President." Tyler, with a patience that irritated his enemies even further, took over the presidency in fact as well as in name.

During Tyler's Administration, many regions began to show signs of their future importance. Pittsburgh was becoming the home of busy ironworks. Cincinnati boasted of its well-paved streets and its schools that required children from 6 to 10 years old to learn algebra. Texas won its long fight to join the Union. Fighting with the Seminole Indians in Florida ended in 1842. Just two days after he signed the bill approving statehood for Texas, Tyler signed a bill making Florida a state.

Early life

John Tyler was born at Greenway estate in Charles City County, Virginia, on March 29, 1790. He was the second son of John and Mary Armistead Tyler. His father served at various times as governor, as speaker of the Virginia House of Delegates, and as a judge.

Young John had a mind of his own. When only 11 years old, he led a revolt against his tyrannical schoolmaster, William McMurdo. His father sent him to William and Mary College in 1802. The boy studied hard and became especially interested in political subjects. He relaxed from his studies by writing poetry and playing the violin. John graduated at the age of 17. He then studied law under his father and was admitted to the Virginia bar in 1809.

Public and political career

State legislator. At the age of 21, Tyler won election to the Virginia House of Delegates. He became a captain of volunteers when the War of 1812 began. But he resigned and returned to the legislature after a month because his company had seen no action.

Tyler's family. On March 29, 1813, Tyler married Letitia Christian (Nov. 12, 1790-Sept. 10, 1842), the daughter of a Virginia planter. They had five daughters and three sons. Mrs. Tyler died during her husband's presidency, and Tyler remarried 22 months later.

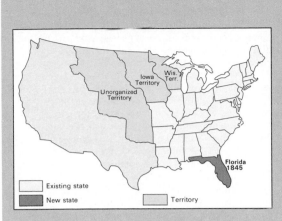

Florida became the 27th state on March 3, 1845, President Tyler's last full day in office. Tyler had brought an end to the Seminole War in Florida in 1842.

The world of President Tyler

Pioneers in covered wagons began to settle the West in the early 1840's. The first large group of settlers arrived in California in 1841. They had traveled in a train of 48 wagons along the Oregon Trail, the Humboldt River, and through the Sierra Nevada.

Newspaper editor Horace Greeley founded the *New York Tribune* in 1841 and remained its editor until his death in 1872. He became an influential spokesman against slavery.

James Fenimore Cooper published *The Deerslayer* in 1841. It was the last of five novels by Cooper, called *The Leatherstocking Tales,* that described life in the wilderness.

Experiments in communal living took root in Massachusetts, New York, and other states. One of the most famous communities was Brook Farm, near West Roxbury, Mass. It was founded in 1841 by social reformer George Ripley.

John C. Frémont and Kit Carson explored much of the territory between the Rocky Mountains and the Pacific Ocean in a series of expeditions in the early 1840's.

Ralph Waldo Emerson was a leading philosopher and literary figure of the 1840's. He published two volumes entitled *Essays* in 1841 and 1844. He served as editor of *The Dial,* a magazine of literature and philosophy, from 1842 to 1844.

The YMCA was founded in 1844 by a London clerk, George Williams.

The first public telegraph message was sent by inventor Samuel F. B. Morse in a demonstration for Congress in 1844. Morse tapped the message "What hath God wrought!" on a telegraph line from Washington, D.C., to Baltimore.

WORLD BOOK map

Congressman. Tyler ran for a vacant seat in the United States House of Representatives in 1816 and won an easy victory. He then was elected to a full term. In Congress, Tyler fought for a strict interpretation of the U.S. Constitution. He opposed any measure that extended the powers of the federal government. Tyler voted against John C. Calhoun's bill for internal improvements because he believed such projects increased federal control. He also denounced the Bank of the United States (see **Bank of the United States**).

Governor and senator. When Tyler was 31, he ran for the United States Senate but lost. He served briefly as chancellor of William and Mary College, then as governor of Virginia from 1825 to 1827. Tyler was elected to the Senate in 1827, and his convictions on strict interpretation of the Constitution soon put him in an awkward position. He denounced South Carolina's attempt to nullify acts of Congress, but he also believed that President Andrew Jackson's measures against nullification were illegal (see **Nullification**). When the Virginia legislature instructed him to support Jackson, Tyler resigned from the Senate and withdrew from the Democratic Party.

Tyler becomes a Whig. In 1840, the Whig Party was a loose coalition of groups with no agreed policies or political beliefs. In hope of luring Southern votes, the Whigs chose Tyler as the vice presidential running mate of William Henry Harrison. Tyler accepted, believing that the Whigs had dropped their fight for a national bank and protective tariffs. Tyler opposed these measures. The Whigs barnstormed to victory, shouting the

Important dates in Tyler's life

1790 (March 29) Born in Charles City County, Virginia.
1813 (March 29) Married Letitia Christian.
1816 Elected to the U.S. House of Representatives.
1825 Elected governor of Virginia.
1827 Elected to the United States Senate.
1840 Elected Vice President of the United States.
1841 (April 6) Sworn in as President.
1842 Mrs. Letitia Tyler died.
1844 (June 26) Married Julia Gardiner.
1861 Elected to Confederate House of Representatives.
1862 (Jan. 18) Died near Charles City, Va.

Virginia Division of Historic Landmarks

John Tyler's birthplace was this frame house on the family estate, called Greenway, in Charles City County, Va. Greenway lies on the James River between Richmond and Williamsburg.

© White House Historical Association, photograph by the National Geographic Society

Letitia Christian Tyler, John Tyler's first wife, suffered a stroke in 1839. She remained an invalid in the White House until her death in 1842. The President remarried 22 months later.

slogan "Tippecanoe and Tyler too." Harrison and Tyler defeated President Martin Van Buren by a huge majority. See **Harrison, William Henry.**

Tyler's Administration (1841-1845)

Opposition to the Whigs. President Harrison died one month after his inauguration, and Tyler was sworn in as President on April 6, 1841. He kept all the members of Harrison's Cabinet. Senator Henry Clay, the Whig leader in Congress, quickly submitted a legislative program. It called for a new Bank of the United States and for higher tariffs. Congress passed these bills, and Tyler replied with a sharply worded veto. That night, an

Tyler's Cabinet

Secretary of state	* Daniel Webster
	Abel P. Upshur (1843)
	* John C. Calhoun (1844)
Secretary of the treasury	Thomas Ewing
	Walter Forward (1841)
	John C. Spencer (1843)
	George M. Bibb (1844)
Secretary of war	* John Bell
	John C. Spencer (1841)
	James M. Porter (1843)
	William Wilkins (1844)
Attorney general	John J. Crittenden
	Hugh S. Legaré (1841)
	John Nelson (1843)
Postmaster general	Francis Granger
	Charles A. Wickliffe (1841)
Secretary of the navy	George Edmund Badger
	Abel P. Upshur (1841)
	David Henshaw (1843)
	Thomas W. Gilmer (1844)
	John Y. Mason (1844)

*Has a separate biography in *World Book.*

armed mob marched to the White House. Hoodlums shouted insults at Tyler and hurled rocks through the windows. Tyler calmly issued guns to the White House servants and stood firm against the mob. The rioters melted away. When Congress passed a second bank bill, Tyler vetoed it again. He said it included all the abuses of a private banking monopoly.

The Whigs disown Tyler. Tyler's second veto set off more Whig demonstrations against the President. Mobs burned him in effigy. The entire Cabinet resigned, except for Secretary of State Daniel Webster. Clay resigned from the Senate. Soon afterward, the Whigs rushed through a bill to give the states money from public-land sales. Tyler vetoed it. The Whigs came back with another measure linking distribution of this money with a higher tariff. Tyler vetoed that bill, too.

Attempt at impeachment. The fight between Tyler and his own party became increasingly bitter. On Jan. 10, 1843, Whigs introduced impeachment resolutions in the House of Representatives. But the charges were so farfetched that even some Whigs sided with the Democrats to defeat the impeachment attempt by a vote of 127 to 83.

Tyler's accomplishments. In 1841, Tyler approved the Pre-Emption Act, which allowed a settler to claim 160 acres of land by building a cabin on the property. This law sped settlement of Illinois, Wisconsin, Minnesota, and Iowa. Tyler brought an end to the Seminole War in Florida in 1842. That same year, a dispute with Great Britain over the boundary between Maine and Canada was settled on terms set up by Webster, who had remained in the Cabinet for this purpose (see **Webster-Ashburton Treaty**). The United States signed a treaty with China in 1844 that opened the Orient to American traders for the first time.

The annexation of Texas provided the chief issue during the last half of Tyler's term. The Texans had declared their independence from Mexico in 1836 and had petitioned to join the Union. Tyler favored annexation, but Northern congressmen opposed him because Texas would have been a slave state. Congress did not act until after the election in 1844 of James K. Polk, who supported annexation. With annexation then a certainty, the House and Senate passed a joint resolution admitting Texas. Tyler signed it on March 1, 1845. Two days later, on Tyler's last full day in office, he signed a bill admitting Florida to the Union. Texas formally joined the Union on Dec. 29, 1845, after Tyler had left office.

Life in the White House. Letitia Tyler was suffering from the effects of a paralytic stroke when her husband became President. Her only public appearance in the White House was at the wedding of her daughter, Elizabeth, on Jan. 31, 1842. Mrs. Tyler died on Sept. 10, 1842. Tyler's daughter-in-law, Priscilla Cooper Tyler, served as White House hostess until the spring of 1844. Tyler's daughter, Letitia Tyler Semple, then served as hostess until June of that year.

In 1844, Tyler was cruising on the U.S.S. *Princeton* to watch the firing of a new naval gun. The gun exploded, killing eight people, including David Gardiner, a former New York state senator. Tyler had been courting Gardiner's daughter Julia (1820-1889), who was also among the guests on the ship. The death of Gardiner brought Tyler and Julia closer together. They were married in

Detail of an oil painting on canvas (1849) by Francisco Anelli; Copyrighted by the White House Historical Association (photograph by the National Geographic Society)

Julia Gardiner Tyler was 24 years old when she married the widowed President in New York City. Their marriage in 1844 made Tyler the first President to marry while in office.

New York City on June 26, 1844. Tyler was the first President to be married while in office. Julia Tyler served as first lady for eight months and delighted the capital with her brilliant entertaining. President Tyler and his second wife had seven children.

Later years

Spurned by both Whigs and Democrats, Tyler retired to Sherwood Forest, his estate near Charles City, Va. He lived quietly until just before the Civil War. Then, in February 1861, he headed a Southern peace mission to Washington seeking a compromise on the issues that threatened the Union. Congress rejected the Southerners' proposals. In April, at a Virginia secession convention, Tyler voted in favor of Virginia leaving the Union. He won election to the Confederate House of Representatives in November 1861, but died on Jan. 18, 1862, before taking his seat. In 1915, Congress dedicated a monument to Tyler's memory in Hollywood Cemetery, at Richmond, Va., where he is buried beside his second wife.   Hugh Russell Fraser

Outline

Questions

Why did Tyler resign from the Army?
Why and how did the Whigs desert Tyler?
How did Tyler show independence as a U.S. senator?
Why did Tyler's second marriage arouse interest?
Why did Daniel Webster remain in Tyler's Cabinet after the other members had resigned?
Why did Tyler oppose the Bank of the United States?

Additional resources

Chitwood, Oliver P. *John Tyler: Champion of the Old South.* Russell & Russell, 1964. First published in 1939.
Morgan, Robert J. *A Whig Embattled: The Presidency Under John Tyler.* Shoe String, 1974. First published in 1954.

Tyler, Moses Coit (1835-1900), became the first great authority on early American literature. His chief books were *A History of American Literature During the Colonial Time, 1607-1765* (1878); and *The Literary History of the American Revolution, 1763-1783* (1897). In 1881, at Cornell University, he became the first professor of American history in the United States. He was born in Griswold, Conn.   Merle Curti

Tyler, Royall (1757-1826), was an American playwright and lawyer. His satire *The Contrast* (1787) was the second American play and the first American comedy performed by professional actors. The play was inspired by a New York City performance of Richard Brinsley Sheridan's English comedy *The School for Scandal* (1777). The "contrast" in Tyler's comedy of manners is between British-inspired vanity and homespun American ingenuity. The latter is represented by Jonathan, the first in a long line of "stage Yankees" in American theater.

Tyler's writing is patriotic and humorous. He wrote five other plays, but only one was performed. Tyler also wrote a novel, *The Algerine Captive* (1797); and a series of satirical letters, *The Yankey in London* (1809).

Tyler was born in Boston, and graduated from Harvard College in 1776. He was an officer in the Revolutionary War and served as chief justice of the Vermont Supreme Court from 1807 to 1813.   Frederick C. Wilkins

Tyler, Wat. See Wat Tyler's Rebellion.

Tylor, Sir Edward Burnett (1832-1917), a British anthropologist, is often regarded as the father of anthropology in the English-speaking world. His books stimulated the development of this science. Tylor was born in London. He traveled widely. Although he never studied formally at a university, he was professor of anthropology at Oxford from 1896 to 1909. He wrote *Researches into the Early History of Mankind* (1865) and *Primitive Culture* (1871). See also **Culture** (Characteristics of culture); **Mythology** (How myths began); **Religion** (The origin of religion).   David B. Stout

Tyndale, *TIHN duhl,* **William** (1494-1536), was an early English leader of the Reformation. He is best known for translating the Bible from Greek and Hebrew into English. His work later became important as a basis for the King James Version of the Bible.

Tyndale first translated the New Testament in an effort to make the Scriptures more widely available, but he could not get it published in England. After leaving England permanently in 1524, he finally had his translation published in Germany and had copies smuggled into England. See **Bible** (Early English translations).

Tyndale was born in Gloucestershire. He studied at Oxford and Cambridge universities from 1510 to about

1521 and was ordained a priest. He was strongly influenced by the ideas of his friend, the German Reformation leader Martin Luther. Tyndale was executed by Roman Catholic authorities as a Protestant heretic in Belgium.   Peter W. Williams

Tyndall, *TIHN duhl,* **John** (1820-1893), was a British physicist and natural philosopher. He is best known for his experiments on the scattering of light of different colors by small particles. The bluish appearance of a light beam passing through something like a soap solution is called the *Tyndall effect.* Tyndall was also interested in the biological sciences. In 1876, he described the action of a *Penicillium* mold in slowing the growth of bacteria. This was more than 50 years before Sir Alexander Fleming's chemical work on penicillin. Tyndall was born in Leighlin Bridge, Ireland. He became director of the Royal Institution in 1867.   G. Gamow

Type is a letter, number, or other character used in printing. The words and numbers in all printed materials, including books, magazines, and newspapers, are made from type. There are two chief kinds of type, *metal type* and *photographic type.*

Metal type, or *hot type,* consists of small pieces of metal that have raised letters on top. It is made by machines that force a mixture of molten lead and other metals into *matrices* (molds) of each character.

Photographic type, also called *cold type,* consists of photographic images of letters. It may be produced by several methods, all of which are called *photocomposition.* In one method, printers make a film negative that contains a *font,* a set of all the characters of one style and size. A beam of light is projected through a character on the negative, producing a photographic positive of that character. *Cathode-ray tube photocomposition* is another method of producing type. Detailed instructions for the shape of each character in a font are stored in a computer. Using these instructions, a device called a cathode-ray tube projects beams of electrons that reproduce the character images on a screen. The images are then focused through a lens onto photosensitive paper or film. See **Photocomposition.**

Another kind of type, called *dry transfer* or *rub-down type,* is often used to compose only a few words. Each character consists of a thin layer of hardened ink at-

David R. Frazier

Type is used in producing books, magazines, newspapers, and other printed materials. The two chief kinds of type are metal type and photographic type, both of which are shown above.

tached to a piece of waxed paper. The ink is simply rubbed onto another piece of paper.

Type is made in many sizes and thousands of styles. Each style of type, or *type face,* has its own characteristics. Some styles of type have bold, heavy lines, and other type faces have a thin, graceful appearance.

Classes of type. There are four general classes of type styles: (1) roman, (2) sans-serif, (3) script, and (4) italic.

Roman types have small finishing strokes called *serifs* that extend from the main strokes of the letters. These types include the most commonly used styles. Printers use roman types for books, magazines, and newspapers. Popular roman styles include Baskerville, Bodoni, Garamond, and Times Roman.

Roman types include a few designs called *black letter* and a few called *uncial.* Black letter designs have highly decorative letters with thick, heavy lines. The first European printing types were black letter. Uncial designs are based on a letter style that was popular from the A.D. 300's to 700's. They were first produced in type in the 1900's. Most uncial letters look like rounded capitals. The first roman-style type similar to the ones used today

---

Classes of type   Type is made in thousands of styles. These type styles are grouped into four general classes: roman, sans-serif, script, and italic. A few styles of each class are shown below.

WORLD BOOK diagram

Roman

Give me liberty or give me death.
14-point Baskerville

Give me liberty or give me death.
14-point Garamond

Sans-Serif

Give me liberty or give me death.
14-point Helvetica Medium

Give me liberty or give me death.
14-point Univers Medium

Script

Give me liberty or give me death.
14-point Bank Script

Give me liberty or give me death.
14-point Kaufmann Bold

Italic

Give me liberty or give me death.
14-point Garamond Italic

Give me liberty or give me death.
14-point Futura Medium Italic

Parts of letters

This diagram shows the main parts of lower-case letters. Printers measure the distance from the top of an *ascender* to the bottom of a *descender* to determine the point size of type.

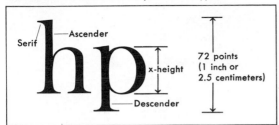

WORLD BOOK diagram

was perfected about 1470 by a French printer named Nicolas Jenson.

Sans-serif types have no serifs. *Sans* is a French word that means *without.* Sans-serif styles are often used for advertisements, headings, and texts. Popular styles of this class include Futura, Helvetica, and Univers. William Caslon IV, an English printer, made the first sans-serif type about 1816.

Script types resemble handwriting. The *lower-case* (small) letters of many script styles are joined together. This class of types is widely used in advertising. Script styles include Bank Script, Brush, and Kaufmann. The first script types were produced in the mid-1500's.

Italic types have slanted letters that *look like this.* Italics are often used to emphasize a word or a group of words. Most italic types are designed to accompany a roman or sans-serif type. The titles of many books, magazines, and newspapers are printed in italics. This class includes such styles as Baskerville Italic and Futura Italic. Aldus Manutius, an Italian printer, developed the first italic type in 1490.

Sizes of type. Printers in some countries, including the United States, Canada, England, and Mexico, use a special scale to measure the size of type and the length of lines of type. This scale is called the *American Point System.* One *point* on the scale equals 0.013837 inch

Some type sizes

The most common sizes of type range from 6-point to 72-point. A few of the sizes within this range are shown below.

WORLD BOOK diagram

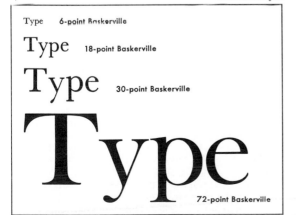

Type 6-point Baskerville

Type 18-point Baskerville

Type 30-point Baskerville

Type 72-point Baskerville

(0.3514598 millimeter). One inch (2.5 centimeters) equals about 72 points. Printers measure the length of a line of type in *picas.* One pica equals 12 points.

The point size of type refers to the height of the characters. The height of the main part of a small letter is called the *x-height.* Such letters as *a, c, e,* and *x* have only an x-height, but others have strokes that extend above or below the x-height. Letters with *ascenders* include *b, d,* and *f.* Letters with *descenders* include *g, j,* and *p.* The point size of any type is the distance from the top of the ascenders to the bottom of the descenders. It may include a slight space above the ascenders or below the descenders.

Metal type ranges in size from 4-point to 120-point. However, most styles are not made in all sizes. The most common sizes include those from 6-point to 72-point. You are now reading 9-point type.

Most photographic type is made in only a few small sizes. A font can be enlarged or reduced to other type sizes by lenses in the photographic equipment. In cathode-ray tube photocomposition, instructions for enlarging or reducing type size are stored in the computer.

In some European countries, including France, Germany, and Italy, type is measured by the *Didot point.* This point is slightly larger than the American point.

History. Until the 1400's, most books were produced by people who copied them by hand. About 1440, a German printer named Johannes Gutenberg made the first practical use of *movable type.* Movable type consists of an individual piece of type for each character. It had been invented about 1045 by Bi Sheng, a Chinese printer, but did not become widely used.

For about 400 years, printers *set* (assembled) all type by hand. In the 1880's, Ottmar Mergenthaler, a German instrument maker, invented the *Linotype.* This machine assembled matrices from which whole lines of type were *cast* (molded) as solid slugs. In 1887, an American inventor named Tolbert Lanston developed a machine called the *Monotype,* which cast individual pieces of type and set them into lines. Printers still use the Linotype and Monotype. See **Linotype; Monotype.**

One of the first commercially practical machines to produce and set photographic type was invented in the 1940's. During the 1950's and 1960's, engineers developed new phototypesetting machines that set type much faster than the earlier kinds. These machines can be linked to computers that handle many tasks formerly performed by people. For example, the computers "tell" the machine how to *justify* (align) lines of type and hyphenate words. Other developments in typesetting included machines that reproduced type characters from computer instructions onto the screen of a cathode-ray tube. J. C. McCracken

Related articles in *World Book.* See the article on **Printing** for an explanation of how type is used in the printing process. See also the following articles:

Type metal. See Alloy (Other alloys).
Typesetting. See Printing (Typesetting).

WORLD BOOK photo by Steven Spicer

Ted Nielsen

A typewriter prints when a typist strikes a key, forcing a character against an inked ribbon onto paper, *above.* The characters on some typewriters are attached to levers, *lower left.* Many have the characters on a rotating ball, *lower right.*

Ted Nielsen

A word processor is a machine that allows the typist to revise material quickly and easily without retyping the entire document. Most word processors have televisionlike *display screens,* which show the text as it is typed or edited.

Typewriter is a machine that produces printed letters and figures on paper. People in homes and offices throughout the world use typewriters to write rapidly and neatly. The typewriter ranks as the most widely used kind of business machine.

Kinds of typewriters. There are four basic kinds of typewriters: (1) manual, (2) electric, (3) electronic, and (4) text-editing, usually called *word-processing typewriters* or *word processors.* A manual typewriter operates entirely by the power supplied by the typist's hands. An electric typewriter has an electric motor to provide power, and so the typist only needs to touch the keys lightly. Such a typewriter costs more to buy and operate than a manual typewriter, but it is easier to use. It also enables a person to type faster and more neatly.

Some electric typewriters, called *self-correcting typewriters,* erase typing errors. Chemically treated correcting ribbons cause any incorrect figure to peel off when the typist presses a certain key. The typist then types the correct character in the space left blank.

Manufacturers make portable models of manual, electric, and electronic typewriters. The greater compactness and lighter weight of portable typewriters make them popular among students and travelers.

Electronic typewriters resemble electric typewriters but include a tiny computer called a *microprocessor.* The microprocessor enables the typewriter to automatically perform such functions as setting margins and underlining. Most microprocessors in electronic typewriters also have a *memory,* which can store names, dates,

addresses, and other material that a typist frequently repeats. When the typist presses the appropriate key, the machine "recalls" the stored material and types it automatically. On some electronic typewriters, a *display screen* shows material as it is typed.

With word processors, the material the operator types is stored on a magnetic card, tape, or disk. The typist can make corrections by simply typing over an error. The typist can also add, delete, or move individual letters, words, lines, and paragraphs without retyping the entire document. After a document is typed and stored, the machine prints it out at the touch of a button. Some word-processing units print as many as eight pages per minute.

Most word processors have an electronic display screen. A microprocessor enables the machine to handle a variety of tasks. For example, most word processors can sort and merge lists, perform mathematical equations, and transfer information to other word processors and to computers over telephone lines.

Parts of a typewriter. Most manual, electric, and electronic typewriters have similar basic features. The machine has a keyboard that consists of buttons called *keys.* Each key carries two characters—letters, numbers, punctuation marks, or other symbols. A key forms one end of a lever that has a bar of metal type at the other end. When the typist strikes a key, the type bar rises and hits an inked ribbon or a thin strip of carbon tape. The ribbon or tape is in front of the paper, on which the type bar prints a letter or other character. A hard rubber roll

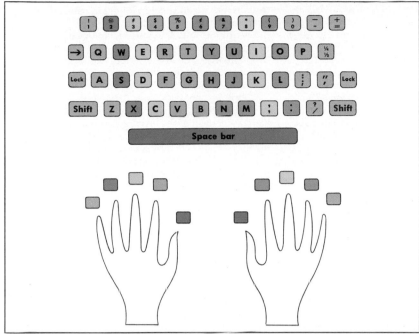

A typewriter keyboard has a standard arrangement of keys. The colors shown in this diagram indicate which finger is used to strike each key. Either thumb is used for the space bar.

called a *platen* holds the paper in the typewriter. The platen and paper automatically move one space to the left after the typist strikes a key.

Some typewriters do not have type bars. Instead, they have a ball-shaped *font* or *typing element,* which contains a complete set of all the characters. When the typist strikes a key, the ball turns so that the correct character hits the paper. The ball moves along the line being typed, but the platen does not move. The type style or size can easily be changed by replacing the ball.

Many electronic typewriters have a printing element called a *daisy wheel.* When the typist strikes a key, the daisy wheel spins until the appropriate character is in position.

A warning bell rings when the typist nears the end of a line. A lock prevents any typing past a particular point unless the typist presses the margin-release key. Most

typewriters also have an automatic ribbon reverse, a backspace lever, and a *tabulator,* which enables the machine to line up numbers or words in columns.

Typewriter manufacturers produce more than 5,000 kinds of keyboards and over 100 type styles. Some keyboards have the letters and symbols of various languages, and others feature special symbols, such as those used in music.

Some typewriters have large type for the partially sighted. Some typewriters for the blind are equipped with special devices that "speak" the characters as they are typed. Others type in braille.

On many typewriters, each letter or other character fills the same amount of space on the paper. But some typewriters feature *proportional spacing,* in which the space taken by each character varies according to its size. Proportional spacing gives letters the appearance

Early typewriters included a Lambert, *left,* made by the Gramophone and Typewriter Company about 1900; a Columbia, *center,* produced in 1886; and a Blickensderfer, *right,* first made in 1893. The earliest successful portable typewriter appeared in the early 1900's.

of having been printed. Some machines have a *justifier,* a device that provides right-hand margins that are even.

History. During the 1700's and 1800's, many inventors in Europe and the United States tried to develop a practical typewriter. It had to be accurate, easy to use, fast, and inexpensive. In 1867, Christopher Latham Sholes, an inventor from Milwaukee, designed the first one with the help of Carlos Glidden and Samuel W. Soulé. They patented it in 1868. Sholes continued to improve the invention. In 1873, E. Remington and Sons, a gun manufacturer, became interested in Sholes's typewriter. The company marketed the machine in 1874, and other firms soon began to produce typewriters. The first successful portable typewriter appeared in the early 1900's. Electric typewriters came into use in the 1920's.

Through the years, many improvements have been made in the design and operation of typewriters. Today, many word processors perform many of the same functions as personal computers.   Eileen Feretic

See also **Edison, Thomas A.** (The Wizard of Menlo Park); **Glidden, Carlos; Sholes, Christopher L.; Teletypewriter.**

Typhoid fever is a serious bacterial disease that results in fever, weakness, and, in severe cases, death. It was once common in all heavily populated regions. However, as methods of good hygiene and sanitation were developed, typhoid fever occurred less often. It is now relatively rare in areas that have modern standards of sanitation.

Cause and spread. Typhoid fever is caused by a bacterium called *Salmonella typhi* (abbreviated *S. typhi*). This organism passes indirectly from one person to another, chiefly through contaminated water or food. Victims of typhoid fever shed *S. typhi* in their *feces* (solid body wastes) and urine. Apparently healthy persons, called *carriers,* also spread the bacteria. Carriers do not have symptoms of typhoid fever, but they harbor the bacteria in their body and release it in their feces.

Human body wastes that contain *S. typhi* can contaminate food or water in several ways. For example, flies can carry the bacteria from feces to food. Food that has been handled by carriers is another common source of infection. In regions with poor sanitation, the bacteria often spread after water supplies are contaminated by human wastes.

Symptoms of typhoid fever usually develop one to three weeks after a person has consumed contaminated food or water. Most cases last about four weeks after the symptoms begin. During the first week, the person has a rising fever, with headaches and abdominal pain. The fever peaks and remains high during the second week. In many cases, rose-colored spots appear on the chest and abdomen. The person becomes weak and, in severe cases, delirious. By the start of the third week, a greenish, soupy diarrhea develops in most cases. The disease reaches its height at this point. Unless complications occur, the person gradually improves during the end of the third week and during the fourth week.

Serious, sometimes fatal, complications can develop. The bacteria may produce *ulcers* (open sores) in the intestine. If the ulcers become severe, they can make holes in the intestinal wall. In such cases, the contents of the intestines spill into the abdomen, and serious abdominal infections can follow. In other instances, the intestines may bleed severely. Blood transfusions may be necessary to prevent death.

Treatment and prevention. Physicians use antibiotic drugs to treat typhoid fever (see **Antibiotic**). These drugs check the growth of *S. typhi* and speed recovery. The use of antibiotics greatly reduces the risk of dying from typhoid fever.

Good personal hygiene and public sanitation are the best methods of preventing the spread of typhoid fever. Effective control of the disease also requires the identification and treatment of carriers. Such measures have made typhoid fever rare in developed countries.

A vaccine made from killed typhoid fever bacteria provides partial protection for several years. This vaccine is given to people who live in or travel to countries where the disease is widespread.

Paratyphoid fever is a disease that resembles typhoid fever in terms of symptoms, spread, and treatment. It results from infections of *Salmonella* organisms other than *S. typhi.*   James L. Franklin

See also **Typhoid Mary.**

Typhoid Mary was a name sometimes used in referring to Mary Mallon (1868?-1938), the first known carrier of typhoid fever in the United States. She had recovered from the disease but, as a carrier, continued to spread typhoid fever germs to others. She infected at least 53 persons with typhoid fever between 1900 and 1915. Three of these people died of the disease.

Little is known about Mary Mallon's early life. She was born in Ireland and went to New York, where she worked as a cook. George Soper, a sanitation engineer, connected her to at least six typhoid fever outbreaks in that state. Mallon refused to quit working as a cook, and so she was confined to a hospital. She remained there for over 20 years until she died.   Peter C. English

Typhoon is a violent, low-pressure tropical storm that occurs in the western Pacific Ocean. Typhoons are similar to hurricanes (see **Hurricane**). Typhoons begin near the equator and move westward, gathering intensity and size. They advance slowly, usually at about 10 to 15 miles (16 to 24 kilometers) per hour. But the circular winds around the center are very strong, often reaching speeds of 150 miles (240 kilometers) per hour. The diameter of a typhoon can be as large as 300 miles (480 kilometers).

The heavy rains and powerful winds of a typhoon can cause severe land and property damage and loss of life. A violent and destructive rush of seawater, called a *storm surge,* also often accompanies a typhoon as it moves onto land.   Wayne M. Wendland

See also **Cyclone.**

Typhus, *TY fuhs,* is any one of a group of important diseases caused by *rickettsias.* These are tiny organisms that look like small bacteria but often behave like viruses (see **Rickettsia**). In human beings, they damage the lining and walls of blood vessels, causing bleeding and skin rashes. Some types of these germs infect animals as well as people. Scientists often call the infected animals "reservoirs" of the disease. Typhus diseases may be transmitted from person to person or from animals to people by lice, fleas, ticks, or mites. The diseases are named for the way they affect the human population (*epidemic typhus*), for the type of reservoir host (*murine,* or *rat, typhus*), or for the *vector,* or carrier (*tick typhus*). In the United States, tick typhus is called Rocky Mountain spotted fever (see **Rocky Mountain spotted fever**).

Epidemic typhus is a serious type of typhus spread by the human body louse. This typhus has been associated with wars throughout history. Crowding, uncleanliness, and human misery during wartime favor the transfer of infected lice from one person to another. Often, more soldiers die of typhus than in combat. Observers estimated that typhus killed more than 3 million people in Russia during the revolutionary period after World War I (1914-1918). Typhus epidemics occurred in North Africa, Yugoslavia, Japan, and Korea during World War II (1939-1945). Typhus also was common in many Nazi concentration camps. Scientists estimate that about 25 of every 100 people infected during a typhus epidemic die.

Primary symptoms of all typhus diseases are headache, skin rash, and stupor or delirium. The patient's temperature may rise to more than 104° F. (40° C), remain high for three or four days, and then drop rapidly. Some people who recover from typhus harbor the live germs in their bodies. Years later these organisms may cause another attack. This makes it possible for immigrants to the United States to have typhus years after their arrival. When typhus recurs in this way it is called *Brill-Zinsser disease.* The disease was named for two American physicians who studied it extensively.

Murine typhus, also called *endemic typhus,* is a mild form of the disease. It is transmitted to people by the rat flea. Like epidemic typhus, this disease occurs throughout the world, but does not spread as easily or rapidly. It was once a common disease in the southeastern United States. During the 15-year period that ended in 1946, scientists reported about 40,000 cases. Since then, better control of rat populations and rat fleas in urban areas has resulted in a sharp decline in the occurrence of murine typhus. Today, about 50 to 100 cases are reported annually in the United States.

Treatment. Doctors use antibiotics, particularly the tetracyclines and chloramphenicol, to treat typhus diseases. They also use specially prepared vaccines to prevent the diseases. To control the spread of typhus, particularly during an epidemic, medical personnel often use insecticides. They dust people and their clothing with these substances, which kill the insects that carry the disease.   Thomas P. Monath

See also **DDT; Virus.**

Tyrannosaurus rex. See **Dinosaur** (Saurischians; picture: When dinosaurs lived); **Prehistoric animal** (picture: Animals of the Mesozoic Era).

Tyranny, *TIHR uh nee,* is a term used throughout history to describe various forms of government by rulers who have unrestricted power. In ancient Greece, for example, *tyranny* simply meant absolute rule by one person. Many Greek tyrants were kind, capable rulers.

The term *tyranny* can also refer to government by an absolute ruler who gained power through military force or political trickery. Such tyrants are not supported by a majority of the people and must use force to maintain their rule.

Another definition of *tyranny* is a government in which a person or a group of persons rules in cruel, oppressive, or unjust ways. In many cases, tyrants use their power primarily for their own benefit. Absolute rulers who intend to promote the welfare of society also may be called tyrants if they suppress the freedom of the people. Today, the word *tyranny* is frequently used to describe a dictatorship.   Alexander J. Groth

See also **Absolutism; Dictatorship.**

Tyre is the British spelling for *tire.* See **Tire.**

Tyre, *tyr,* was an ancient Phoenician seaport. It stood on the Mediterranean Sea in what is now southern Lebanon. Part of the city stood on the mainland and part on an island across a narrow channel. Tyre was an important shipping port, handling goods from Mesopotamia

Typhoon clouds and winds whirl around the *eye,* a calm area in the center of the storm. This photograph was taken in 1984 from the space shuttle *Discovery, lower right.*

Huge waves pound a coastline as a typhoon moves onto land. This violent onrush of seawater, called a *storm surge,* can demolish buildings and cause floods, sometimes taking many lives.

and Arabia. The city was also noted for the purple dye and fine glass that were manufactured there. The people of Tyre were noted as sailors as well as for their cultural and intellectual activities.

Egypt controlled Tyre before about 1100 B.C. Tyrians carried on trade for the Egyptians with the peoples of Asia Minor and the Aegean Sea. The city enjoyed its greatest prosperity between 1100 and 573 B.C. Part of that time, Tyre was ruled by Assyria, then by Babylonia, and the city was also briefly allied with Israel. Because of its island location, Tyre resisted capture for centuries. Tyrian merchants competed for trade with Greek merchants on the Mediterranean Sea. Tyre founded several trading colonies, including Carthage and Utica on the Mediterranean coast of North Africa and Gades (now Cádiz, Spain), on the Atlantic Ocean.

In 573 B.C., King Nebuchadnezzar II of Babylonia crushed a 13-year Tyrian revolt. Alexander the Great conquered the city in 332 B.C. and built a road from the mainland to the island, creating a peninsula upon which the present town of Tyre stands (see **Lebanon** [map]). Tyre later became a part of the Roman and then Byzantine (East Roman) empire. Christian crusaders occupied the city from A.D. 1124 until Muslims captured it in 1291.

Louis L. Orlin

See also **Phoenicia.**

Tyrol, *TY rohl,* or *tuh ROHL,* also spelled *Tirol.* The Tyrol is a beautiful mountainous region in western Austria and northern Italy. Before World War I, it was a crownland of Austria. The Treaty of St.-Germain, signed in 1919, divided the region into two parts. Northern Tyrol was given to Austria and Southern Tyrol was given to Italy.

Austrian Tyrol. The Northern Tyrol has an area of 4,883 square miles (12,647 square kilometers) and a population of about 586,000. It is a scenic country, with beautiful mountains and many rivers. Important rivers include the Inn, the Ziller, the Lech, and the Isar. The Tyrol is a province of Austria. Its capital is Innsbruck, a city in the Inn Valley. See **Innsbruck.**

Italian Tyrol. The part of the Tyrol in Italy is known as *Trentino-Alto Adige.* It extends southward from the southern boundary of Austria to the Italian provinces of Brescia, Verona, and Vicenza. It is about 100 miles (160

Bruce Coleman Ltd.

The Tyrol has many picturesque towns, such as this village in the valley of the Inn River. The Alps, which tower in the background, make the Tyrol a popular skiing area.

kilometers) wide. The Italian Tyrol is divided into the provinces of Bolzano and Trento, which cover 5,256 square miles (13,613 square kilometers). About 870,000 people live in the area. Some 250,000 of them are German-speaking. Between World Wars I and II, the region was called *Venezia Tridentina.*

The land and its resources. The Alps cover most of the Tyrol. The region is much like Switzerland except that it has no large lakes. The Ötztal Alps rise about 12,500 feet (3,810 meters) above sea level. Along the Tyrol's northeastern boundary, the Hohe Tauern mountain chain rises over 12,400 feet (3,780 meters) at Grossglockner peak. The Kitzbühel Alps form the eastern border, and the Ortler Mountains stretch along the southwestern frontier. Brenner Pass cuts through the Tyrol at the Austro-Italian border. Adolf Hitler and Benito Mussolini held many meetings at Brenner Pass during World War II.

The Tyrol is a winter playground for the people of many countries. Skiing and tobogganing are favorite sports. The warm summers in the Tyrol attract vacationists and mountain climbers. Mineral springs in the south make the Italian Tyrol a popular health resort. Many people also visit Trento, a famous art center.

Forests cover more than half of the Tyrol region, but there are a few scattered farming districts. The Southern Tyrol is famous for its vineyards and fruit orchards. The mountains of Tyrol have some mineral deposits, including zinc, sulfur, coal, iron, and copper.

History. The Romans conquered the Tyrol in 15 B.C. Later, the region fell into the hands of various warring German tribes. In 1363, it became part of Austria. In 1919, the northern part of the Tyrol became a province of the Austrian republic. The Southern Tyrol was given to Italy. The Italians promised political and cultural autonomy to the large German-speaking minority in the Italian Tyrol, but the Fascist government of Italy suppressed all German clubs and newspapers, and forbade the teaching of the German language in the area. During

WORLD BOOK map

The Tyrol is a region in Europe that includes part of western Austria and northern Italy. The map at the left shows its location. A map of the region itself appears at the right.

World War II, thousands of German citizens in the Italian Tyrol were moved to Germany. In 1946, in spite of Austrian objections, the Southern Tyrol was again given back to Italy. By an agreement signed with Austria, Italy promised autonomy for German-speaking South Tyroleans. In the late 1950's, these people claimed they had not received autonomy and began fighting for it. A number of border skirmishes occurred between Italians and German-speaking South Tyroleans. Italy and Austria tried to reach an agreement but failed. In 1971, the Southern Tyrol conflict was finally settled after Italy granted the region a large amount of autonomy.

William J. McGrath

See also **Alps; Austria** (picture: A centuries-old festival).

Tyrothricin. See Dubos, René J.

Tyrrell, *TIHR ehl,* **Joseph Burr** (1858-1957), was a Canadian geologist, historian, and mining engineer. He conducted studies during several expeditions in northwestern Canada that aided the development of the Canadian mining industry.

Tyrrell was born in Weston, Ont., near Toronto. He graduated from the University of Toronto in 1880 and joined the Geological Survey of Canada in 1881. In 1884, near Drumheller, Alta., Tyrrell discovered the first dinosaur bones ever found in Canada. Shortly afterward, he discovered one of the nation's largest coal deposits nearby.

During 1893 and 1894, Tyrrell traveled from Lake Athabasca across the barren lands of the Northwest Territories to Hudson Bay. These lands then formed the largest unexplored area in North America. During one eight-month period, he covered about 3,200 miles (5,150 kilometers), mostly through wilderness. This expedition included about 900 miles (1,448 kilometers) traveled largely on snowshoes. Tyrrell mapped the region and predicted correctly that the minerals there would greatly increase Canada's wealth.

Tyrrell left the Geological Survey of Canada in 1898 and became a mining engineer and manager. He joined the Kirkland Lake Gold Mining Company in 1924 and served as president of the firm from 1931 until his death. Tyrrell wrote many articles about geology and exploration in Canada and edited the journals of fur trader Samuel Hearne, surveyor Philip Turnor, and geographer David Thompson.   Barry M. Gough

Tyrrhenian Sea, *tih REE nee uhn,* an arm of the Mediterranean Sea, lies between Italy, Sicily, Sardinia, and Corsica. It has an area of 60,000 square miles (155,399 square kilometers). It is sometimes called the Tuscan Sea, and its Italian name is *Mare Tirreno.* For location, see **Italy** (physical map). The Tyrrhenian Sea connects with the Ligurian Sea to the north. The Strait of Messina links it with the Ionian Sea to the south. Principal ports on its shores include Naples and Palermo.

Tyson, Mike (1966-   ), became the youngest person to win a heavyweight boxing championship. In 1986, Tyson defeated Trevor Berbick to win the World Boxing Council (WBC) version of the title. Tyson was 20 years old when he won the fight.

Tyson became the undisputed and undefeated world champion in 1987 by defeating James Smith for the World Boxing Association (WBA) title and Tony Tucker for the International Boxing Federation (IBF) version of the title. By the late 1980's, Tyson had become the dominant boxer in the sport, known especially for his powerful punches and his aggressive pursuit of his opponents.

Michael Tyson was born in Brooklyn, N.Y. He began boxing at the age of 13 and became a professional fighter in 1985. Tyson stands 5 feet 11½ inches (182 centimeters) tall and weighs about 220 pounds (100 kilograms).   Dave Nightingale